THE NEW CORPORATE FINANCE

Where Theory Meets Practice

W9-AZT-976

EDITED BY

Donald H. Chew, Jr.
Stern Stewart & Co.

McGraw-Hill, Inc.
New York   St. Louis   San Francisco   Auckland
Bogotá   Caracas   Lisbon   London   Madrid   Mexico
Milan   Montreal   New Delhi   Paris   San Juan
Singapore   Sydney   Tokyo   Toronto

McGraw-Hill Series in Advanced Topics in Finance and Accounting

CONSULTING EDITORS
Ray Ball
Clifford W. Smith, Jr.

Ball and Smith: The Economics of Accounting Policy Choice
Chew: The New Corporate Finance: Where Theory Meets Practice
Schwert and Smith: Empirical Research in Capital Markets
Smith: The Modern Theory of Corporate Finance

THE NEW CORPORATE FINANCE
Where Theory Meets Practice

1 2 3 4 5 6 7 8 9 0 DOH DOH 9 0 9 8 7 6 5 4 3 2

ISBN 0-07-011046-8

This book was assembled by Concepts Unlimited.
The editor was Kenneth A. MacLeod;
the production supervisor was Al Rihner.
The cover was designed by Karen K. Quigley.
R.R. Donnelley & Sons Company was printer and binder.

To my parents Elsie and Don, wife Sue, brothers Rick and Ken, and all the rest of the family near and far. And to all the financial economists I've had the good fortune to work with during the past ten years.

TABLE OF CONTENTS

INTRODUCTION: FINANCIAL INNOVATION IN THE 1980s

by Donald H. Chew, Jr., Stern Stewart & Co.

The past 30 years have witnessed remarkable changes in the theory and practice of corporate finance. Beginning with the work of Franco Modigliani and Merton Miller in the late 1950s, the evolution of the "modern" theory of corporate finance into its present shape has both anticipated and responded to a wave of innovations in corporate practice. The late '50s saw the first tender offers by corporations for other public companies—a development that, with the aid of "contingent" bank financing, contributed to the building of leveraged conglomerates in the 1960s. The 1970s gave rise not only to original-issue "junk bonds," but to stock options and a host of other exchange-traded "derivatives" such as futures on foreign exchange, interest rates, and commodity prices.

It was during the 1980s, however, that the rate of financial innovation accelerated most dramatically. Building on the success of the futures markets established in the '70s, the '80s spawned an astonishing variety of new "risk management" tools: (1) currency, interest rate, and commodity swaps; (2) exchange-traded options on foreign currencies, interest rates, and commodity prices; (3) futures on stock market indexes, as well as other new futures contracts on an expanding range of currencies, interest rates, and commodity prices; and (4) "hybrid" debt securities combining standard debt issues with forward- or option-like features. At the same time, a burgeoning junk bond market, besides furnishing capital for promising growth companies too small to obtain investment-grade credit ratings, was also making possible an unprecedented wave of leveraged acquisitions, large stock buybacks, divestitures, spin-offs, and multi-billion dollar LBOs—all of which have been yoked together under the name of "corporate restructuring."

As the pace of innovation quickened, moreover, the relationship between theory and practice became more dynamic. On the one hand, theoretical advances helped stimulate the process of inno-

vation. Indeed, the 1980s can be viewed as a decade in which Wall Street first adopted and then pushed to their limits principles of financial economics that most practicing businessmen once dismissed as hopelessly arcane. But if theory has affected practice, the flood of new corporate securities, risk management approaches, and organizational structures has provided financial economists with a vast laboratory in which to observe and test the workings of our capital markets. And, as should become clear from the articles in this book, such experimentation is helping finance scholars extend and, in some cases, revise their thinking—which in turn promises to influence corporate practice in the 1990s.

THE CONSEQUENCES OF CORPORATE RESTRUCTURING

Before tracing the progression of academic thought that contributed to the new developments in corporate finance, let's briefly examine the economic consequences of financial innovation. What has really been accomplished by all this change? And to begin with the most controversial, let's consider the case of corporate restructuring.

In the popular mind the verdict on leveraged restructuring has already been pronounced. As a result of the cluster of bankruptcies starting in 1989, the popular outrage over the S&L debacle, and the depressed economic climate of the 1990s, Wall Street is now being subjected to a backlash of public opinion, political scrutiny, and "reregulation" reminiscent of the 1930s. On the one hand, corporate restructuring brought about a pronounced trend toward smaller, less diversified, more efficient—and in some cases private—corporations. But, in the process of streamlining corporate America, the leveraged restructuring movement also enriched a breed of capitalists known as "corporate raiders" while imposing painful changes upon some corporate managers, employees, and local communities. It is, predictably, these latter effects the mass media and politicians have seized upon. Those few media accounts of LBOs and leveraged takeovers that manage to expand their focus beyond the "morality play" of private greed and misery almost invariably reach the same conclusion: Leveraged restructurings and other forms of "financial engineering" are destroying the competitive future of American industry by forcing shortsighted cutbacks in employment, R&D, capital investment.

From financial economists, however, we are hearing a very different assessment of the *public* consequences of corporate restructuring. A large and growing body of academic research suggests the leveraged restructuring movement created enormous increases in stockholder value—and thus, presumably, major improvements in corporate efficiency. On the basis of this research, Harvard professor Michael Jensen has offered $650 billion as a conservative estimate of the stockholder gains arising from mergers, takeovers, divestitures, spin-offs, and LBOs over the period 1976 to 1990. These numbers represent only the gains to the "sellers" in such transactions, not to the "buyers" (a group which includes those raiders whose allegedly vast profits became a favorite media target during the 80s). Nor does this estimate include the value of efficiency improvements by companies pressured by the *threat* of takeover into reforming without a visible transaction.

As Jensen also reports, a growing body of work on LBOs and other leveraged recapitalizations has documented significant improvements in corporate operating efficiency—improvements that would appear to justify much of the stock price increases accompanying these transactions. Moreover, there is no evidence in such companies of major cutbacks, on average, in employment, maintenance expenditures, or R&D. Indeed, at the height of leveraged restructuring activity, the U.S. economy was near the midpoint of a 92-month expansion that saw record-high percentages of people employed, as well as steady increases in corporate capital spending and R&D.

Of course, many of the highly leveraged transactions (HLTs) executed in 1986 and thereafter have gotten into trouble—in large part, as Jensen argues, because of a gross misalignment of incentives between dealmakers and investors that led to systematic overpayments. And thus part of the stockholders gains from HLTs have come at the expense of the bondholders and lenders that financed the deals. But Jensen places a likely upper bound of $50 billion on total losses to bondholders, banks, and other creditors from leveraged transactions. The current recovery of the junk bond market, together with the recent relaxation by bank regulators of the HLT constraints, suggests that eventual losses may well turn out to be far less than this estimate.

Such losses, it's also important to recognize, are dwarfed not only by the stockholder gains from restructuring, but also by losses on commercial real estate loans. Such loans are by far the largest troubled asset category for S&Ls (junk bonds hardly show up in the statistical analysis!), not to mention many commercial banks. And if pushed to speculate, I would argue that such real estate losses, along with the regulatory reaction and "credit crunch" they have provoked, are the primary contributors to the current weakness of the economy.

Some macro data recently released by the Commerce Department are also sharply inconsistent with the popular claim that the restructuring of the '80s weakened the international competitiveness of the U.S. manufacturing sector. According to the U.S. Bureau of Labor Statistics, the productivity of U.S. manufacturing increased dramatically between 1982 and 1990, while the real unit costs of labor declined sharply. Partly reflecting such productivity gains as well as the depreciation of the dollar, the export of U.S. goods and services increased by 75% in real terms during the six-year period 1985-1991. Such continuing export growth is all the more encouraging, given the depressed condition of most of the world's developed economies since the beginning of 1989.

THE 1990s: INNOVATION AND THE CREDIT CRUNCH

Today, of course, leveraged restructuring is down (though not altogether out), and there are few signs of a well-functioning corporate control market. The only "hostile" deal of note in the '90s to date has been AT&T's acquisition of NCR, a transaction that suggests a return to the diversifying acquisitions of the '60s and '70s—the very activity that provided many opportunities for corporate raiders in the first place. And, as if to reinforce that lesson of the '80s, AT&T's market value predictably dropped by some 15% during the month after the deal was first announced. (For corporate finance theorists, it was also edifying to watch AT&T's

management volunteer to raise the purchase price when granted the ability to use "pooling" rather than "purchase" accounting.)

But if the scale of leveraged restructuring is now greatly diminished, financial innovation is continuing on the other major front established in the '80s: corporate risk management. The corporate use of futures, swaps, and options, while rising steadily throughout the '80s, has if anything accelerated in the 1990s. Rather ironically, the regulatory crackdown on one form of financial innovation—LBOs and other HLTs—has provided the impetus for another by contributing greatly to the credit crunch. As I argue below, the '90s have seen a flurry of new securities—notably derivatives and "hybrid" debt instruments incorporating derivatives—designed to help smaller, riskier companies raise capital in the face of restrictive credit conditions.

The primary reason for the strength of corporate interest in risk management is thus somewhat different today from what it was 10 years ago. The rise and expansion of new kinds of futures, swaps, and options during the late '70s and early '80s was primarily a capital market response to the sharp increases in the volatility of exchange rates, interest rates, and commodity prices. Besides offering investors and corporations a low-cost means of hedging against such price volatility, these new markets also provided financially sophisticated corporations with opportunities for financing "arbitrages." For example, combining zero-coupon, yen-denominated debt issues with yen-dollar currency swaps reportedly enabled some large, well-known corporations to reduce their all-in funding costs below that of the U.S. Treasury. And creating "synthetic" fixed-rate debt by coupling floating-rate issues with interest rate swaps reportedly reduced the cost to riskier borrowers of conventional fixed-rate funding (although the extent of the cost savings from this strategy has surely been exaggerated).

When coupled with increased price volatility, the high *level* of interest rates in the early 1980s also contributed to another innovation in corporate risk management: the proliferation of new kinds of corporate hybrid debt issues. Hybrids are so called because they effectively combine a conventional straight fixed-rate debt issue with a forward- or option-like feature. One familiar example is convertible debt, which amounts to lower-coupon debt combined with an option (technically, a warrant) on the firm's equity.

What is distinctive about the hybrid debt instruments of the '80s is that their payoffs, instead of being tied to the issuing company's stock price, were linked to a growing variety of *general* economic variables. In 1980, for example, Sunshine Mining issued bonds whose principal repayment was tied to future silver prices. Subsequent corporate hybrids introduced in the '80s indexed principal or interest payments to exchange rates, interest rates, stock market indices, and the prices of commodities such as oil, gold, copper, and natural gas. Such securities were designed to enable somewhat riskier companies—typically those with significant exposures to commodity prices—to reduce their interest payments to manageable levels by giving bondholders, in effect, an equity-like participation in corporate profits.

The 1990s are also proving, as a recent *New York Times* article put it, "Hot Times for Hybrids." Unlike the '80s, however, the current stimulant to hybrids is not the level of interest rates (which are quite low by recent standards), but rather the pronounced widening of credit *spreads* that now exists for all but blue-chip borrowers. Such spreads reflect not only a natural market "correction" in response to recent bank and bondholder losses, but also the effect of the severe regulatory constraints imposed on all non-investment-grade debt beginning in 1989.

As Charles Smithson and I have argued (see *"The Uses of Hybrid Debt in Managing Corporate Risk"*), many companies today are using hybrid debt to lower their risk profiles, and thus their current interest payments. By lowering interest payments and stabilizing the expected level of (after-interest) operating cash flow, such innovative instruments are enabling issuers to avoid the disproportionately higher funding costs now imposed on corporate borrowers. In this sense, financial innovation in the form of new hybrid debt securities is playing a role much like that of junk bonds in the early '80s: They are allowing riskier companies to raise capital on economic terms, thus helping them weather the restrictive financing climate of the '90s.

Such securities innovation also provides yet another illustration of Merton Miller's conception of regulatory change as "the grain of sand in the oyster" that irritates the financial system into invention. The continuing proliferation of new forms of hybrid debt into the '90s demonstrates once again the ingenuity of our capital markets in circumventing regulatory obstacles to economic growth.

THE BEGINNINGS OF MODERN THEORY

With this allusion to Professor Miller, let's turn from this survey of more recent changes in corporate financial practices to a brief account of the development of the theory.

The modern theory of *corporate* finance begins with the well-known "irrelevance" propositions formulated by Franco Modigliani and Merton Miller in the late 1950s and early 1960s. Given the dramatic recapitalizations of the '80s, typically accompanied by large increases in stockholder value, it may seem odd to begin with the notion that corporate financial policies "do not matter." The M&M propositions are the natural starting point because they represent the first attempt to apply rigorous economic logic to corporate financial decision-making in aggregate.

In so doing, Miller and Modigliani began the transformation of the study of corporate finance from what then amounted to an apprenticeship system transmitting folklore between generations—in effect, the traditional Harvard Business School case-study approach—into a more systematic and scientific discipline. (The Nobel Prizes awarded first to Modigliani in 1985 and then to Miller in 1990 are only the most visible acknowledgments of the aspirations of corporate finance to the internal consistency and predictive power of a "hard" science.)

But what do the M&M "irrelevance" propositions really say about financial decision-making? Paradoxically, the M&M capital structure propositions appear to say that a company's financial policy—whether it chooses to fund its operations with debt or equity, and what kinds of securities it chooses to issue—have no material effect on the value of its shares. And the twin companion to this capital structure proposition seems to say that the firm's dividend policy—the fraction of earnings it chooses to pay out to stockholders rather than retain—also has no effect on market value. That value, according to M&M, is determined solely by corporate investment and operating decisions, by those "real" decisions that produce the firm's operating cash flows. (More precisely, the value of the firm was formulated by M&M as the discounted present value of "future cash flows from the firm's present assets and future growth opportunities," net of "the additional investment necessary to initiate and sustain those flows.")

Corporate capital structure and dividend decisions were accordingly viewed as nothing more than ways of dividing up the operating cash flows produced by the business and repackaging them for distribution to investors. And, as long as such "merely financial" decisions are assumed not to affect the "real" decisions in any systematic way—for example, provided management behaves the same whether its debt-to-equity ratio is 30 percent or 300 percent—then such financial decisions "do not matter."

But, as Miller himself said in his 1989 reassessment of *"The Modigliani-Miller Propositions After Thirty Years"* (in this book),

the view that capital structure is literally irrelevant or that "nothing matters" in corporate finance, though still sometimes attributed to us, is far from what we ever actually said about the real-world applications of our theoretical propositions.

The M&M propositions were intended to hold only under a deliberately restrictive set of conditions, the most important of which are as follows: (1) there are no significant differences in the tax treatment accorded different securities; (2) reliable information about the firm's earnings prospects is freely available to investors (and, by implication, what management knows about the future is not significantly different from what investors know); and (3) corporate investment decisions, as mentioned above, are not influenced by financing (or dividend) choices.

What, then, do the M&M propositions have to say to corporate practitioners, to those financial executives who get paid a lot of money to make decisions that purportedly do not matter? There are really two distinct messages: a negative one and a positive one.

The negative one is captured in Stewart Myers's formulation that "there is no magic in leverage." Investment bankers who market debt instruments to their clients are fond of showing them the wonderful effect of increasing leverage on pro forma earnings per share. The message of Miller and Modigliani is that this effect is an illusion. It is true that if companies issue debt and use the proceeds to retire their shares, then EPS will go up as long as the return on invested capital simply exceeds the after-tax corporate borrowing rate—which, of course, is hardly an acceptable standard of profitability. What such analysis fails to mention is that, as companies take on more financial leverage, the risk of the equity rises commensurately.

And as the risk of the equity increases, stockholders increase their required rate of return, the P/E of the firm goes down, and the net effect is a wash.

One of the accomplishments of LBOs and other leveraged recaps was to reveal the fundamental futility of "managing earnings" by manipulating accounting techniques. The leveraged restructuring movement thus held out another important lesson for corporate managers: Until the hostile takeover movement came to an abrupt halt around the middle of 1989, public companies that continued to make uneconomic investment and financing decisions guided by the old accounting yardsticks were creating opportunities for aggressive investors piercing the veil of accounting statements to focus on underlying cash flow. To corporate raiders and other investors in private (or highly leveraged) companies, EPS was clearly irrelevant! All that mattered to them was the expected ability of the business to generate adequate cash flow to service the debt and leave themselves with a large enough return on their equity investment to justify the large financial risk.

In short, the discounted cash flow valuation framework stemming from the Chicago school principle of market efficiency—and tirelessly advocated by my colleague Joel Stern over the past 20 years—was being put to use daily during the restructurings of the '80s. Unfortunately, it was not the majority of professional corporate executives who came to understand that "earnings per share don't count," but rather the corporate raiders who were supplanting them. (In fact, a Lou Harris poll conducted as recently as 1989 showed that 55% of corporate managers continue to believe that earnings are a more important determinant of corporate stock prices than cash flow.)

Now let's turn to the positive side of the argument. The positive import of the M&M propositions, and thus their main message to corporate practitioners, can be seen by turning the propositions "upside down"—as Clifford Smith likes to say—"and standing them on their heads." That is, if changes in corporate financial or dividend policy cause significant changes in stock values, they are likely to do so only for the following reasons: (1) they affect taxes paid by issuers or investors; (2) they provide a credible "signal" to investors of management's confidence (or lack thereof) in the firm's future earnings; or (3) they affect the probability that management will operate as efficiently as possible, undertaking only profitable investments and returning "excess" capital to investors.

BEYOND THE IRRELEVANCE PROPOSITIONS: TAX AND SIGNALLING EFFECTS

The academic process of relaxing each of these conditions was begun by Miller and Modigliani themselves almost 30 years ago. In the so-called "tax-adjusted" M&M proposition presented in a 1963 paper, they argued that the benefits of substituting tax-deductible interest payments for non-deductible (and thus potentially twice-taxed) dividend payments could push the optimal capital structure toward 100% debt—provided, of course, the offsetting costs of high leverage were not too great.

In the early 1960s, of course, the world did not conform to this vision, and M&M were inclined to dismiss their model, in Miller's words, as "simply another inconsequential paradox arising from an economist's frictionless dreamworld." Facing the reality of corporate debt-equity ratios in the early 1960s that were not much higher than they were in the low-tax 1920s, Miller recalls,

we seemed to face an unhappy dilemma: either corporate managers did not know (or perhaps care) that they were paying too much in taxes; or something major was being left out of the model. Either they were wrong or we were....[Our thinking] suggested that the high bond ratings in which the management took so much pride may actually have been a sign of their incompetence; that the managers were leaving too much of their stockholders' money on the table in the form of unnecessary corporate income tax payments.

In sum, many finance specialists, myself included, remained unconvinced that the high-leverage route to corporate tax savings was either technically unfeasible or prohibitively expensive in terms of expected bankruptcy or agency costs.

In the 1980s, this kind of tax "arbitrage" between debt and equity likely played some role in every leveraged acquisition or recapitalization accomplished by Wall Street. Debt-equity ratios in LBOs, and in some public recaps, achieved levels that Miller described as "far beyond anything we ever dared use in our classroom illustrations of the tax advantage." Of the rise of junk bonds, Miller says simply, "The only puzzle is why it took so long."

But tax savings alone, as Miller noted in his Nobel Prize speech, could not account for the "size of the observed LBO premiums." And Miller himself qualified the tax-adjusted M&M proposition in his 1976 Presidential Address to the American Finance Association. Entitled "Debt and Taxes," the paper argued that the tax savings of corporate debt financing were exaggerated by the failure to account for any *increase* in taxes paid by the holders of corporate debt. To the extent such holders are taxable (although many clearly are not), some of the savings from converting equity into debt will be offset by the increase in taxes paid by the new debtholders.

Some financial economists have attempted to take finance theory beyond capital structure irrelevance by exploring the possibility that corporate financial decisions provide "signals" to investors about the firm's earnings prospects. To the extent management knows more about the firm's prospects than outside investors, corporate choices among financing alternatives—indeed, the very attempt to raise outside capital—could communicate "insider" information about the company's future. To take the most obvious case, large block sales of stock by insiders are almost always accompanied by significant decreases in share values.

But while signalling theories help explain why the market typically reacts negatively to announcements of equity offerings, and positively to major exchange offers to retire equity with new debt, they have not furnished a convincing explanation of how (value-maximizing) corporations in the aggregate choose their capital structures. As Miller himself concluded in his 1986 paper on "The Informational Content of Dividends," none of the signalling models has provided—nor is one likely to provide—a signalling "equilibrium" in which one dividend or financial policy is clearly superior to another. That is, even though signalling theories offer a plausible explanation of how investors interpret *changes* in corporate leverage and payout ratios, they nevertheless fail to address the questions of optimal capital structure and dividend policy.

FURTHER BEYOND THE IRRELEVANCE PROPOSITION: THE RISE OF AGENCY COST THEORY

Perhaps the most significant departure from the M&M irrelevance propositions—one with more definite import for financial policy—can be traced to a 1976 paper written by Michael Jensen and William Meckling called "Theory of the Firm: Managerial Behavior, Agency Costs, and Capital Struc-

ture." What the theory of "agency costs" accomplished was to call attention to the potential loss in value of public corporations caused by the divergence of interest between management and shareholders. Most finance scholars, including Jensen and Meckling, began by arguing that the agency costs of separating ownership from control could not be too great for several reasons: product market competition (including challenges from foreign competitors) as well as a market for executive labor should both serve to limit the natural tendency of management to pursue its own interest at the expense of shareholders; and management incentive plans are presumably designed to reduce this conflict of interest. If all of these fail to join managerial and stockholder interests, then a vigorously operating takeover market—in academic parlance, the "market for corporate control"—should prevent self-serving managers from entrenching themselves. But the size and consistency of the stockholders gains from the leveraged restructurings of the '80s suggest otherwise.

The relevance of "agency cost" theory to developments in the 1980s was set forth in Jensen's 1986 paper, "The Agency Costs of Free Cash Flow: Corporate Finance and Takeovers," published in the *American Economic Review*. Jensen's "Free Cash Flow" theory said, in short, that leveraged acquisitions, stock repurchases, and management buyouts of public companies were adding value to corporations by squeezing capital out of organizations that had few profitable growth opportunities. Subjecting companies in mature industries to the "discipline" of high leverage was also intensifying the search for operating efficiencies.

Before the wave of hostile takeovers and LBOs in the 1980s, corporate managements in mature industries could continue their customary practice of reinvesting excess capital ("free cash flow") in their core businesses even while the expected returns to capital at the margin were falling lower and lower. Or, if things got bad enough, they would choose to diversify into unrelated businesses through acquisition. (For example, oil companies facing a massive "free cash flow" problem in the early '80s responded initially by choosing both strategies, thus inviting the attention of Boone Pickens.) The massive substitution of debt for equity in the '80s provided a systematic solution to this "free cash flow" problem by converting discretionary dividend payments into contractual, and considerably more demanding, payments of interest and principal. As Miller himself rephrased Jensen's argument, "By accepting such heavy debt-service burdens, the managers made a binding commitment to themselves and to the other residual equity holders against yielding to the temptations to pour the firm's good money down investment ratholes."

The Re-Emergence of Active Investors. Besides returning excess capital to investors and curbing uneconomic reinvestment, the replacement of equity by debt also allowed for the concentration of equity ownership among large investors. In *"Corporate Control and the Politics of Finance"* (in this book), Jensen argues that such concentration facilitated the rise—or, more precisely, the re-emergence of "active investors" in the U.S., a group that includes "Warren Buffet, Carl Icahn, Sir James Goldsmith, and the principals of KKR and Forstmann Little." Active investors, as Jensen defines them, are those holding large blocks of a company's stock (sometimes its debt as well) who "actually monitor management, sit on boards, are sometimes involved in dismissing management, are often intimately involved in the strategic direction of the company." On occasion (witness Warren Buffet's recent assumption of the chairmanship of Salomon Brothers), they even manage.

Active investors are by no means a new phenomenon. In the Japanese and German economies, Jensen maintains, large-block stockholders, notably commercial banks, have long been the most effective force binding management's interests to those of its stockholders. And, prior to the enactment of Glass Steagall and other legislative acts of the 1930s and '40s, investment and commercial bankers like J.P. Morgan played a similar role in the U.S., sitting on boards of directors, monitoring management, and sometimes enforcing changes in management.

But, over the 50-year period between 1930 and the beginning of the '80s, the rift between corporate ownership and control continued to grow. Between 1937 and 1990, according to Jensen and Kevin Murphy, the percentage equity ownership of the CEOs of the largest U.S. companies fell 10-fold, from roughly 3 percent to less than .03 percent today. Corporations also became much larger over this period, but only by a factor of 3 or 4 times (in real dollars), thus implying a 60-70% reduction in the real dollar investment of corporate CEOs in their own companies' stocks.

As for the sharp growth in the size of U.S. companies since the '30s, part of it was undoubtedly justified by scale economies in some businesses. But perhaps the largest contributor to such corporate growth was the trend toward corporate conglomeration initiated during the late 1960s—a development that, although initially welcomed by stockholders, ended up contributing significantly to the negative real returns to stockholders over the decade of the 1970s.

For Jensen, the rise of the LBO held out an economic solution to "massive inefficiencies" arising from the corporate conglomerate movement—which in turn was a predictable consequence of the growing separation of ownership and control. Indeed, Jensen views "LBO associations" such as KKR and Forstmann Little as "new organizational forms" that compete directly with the headquarters of large public conglomerates. They are said to accomplish with professional staffs that number in the 30s or 40s what many hundreds of headquarters employees are supposed to do in public conglomerates.

"In effect," Jensen argues, "the LBO association substitutes incentives provided by compensation and ownership for the direct monitoring and centralized decision-making in the typical corporate bureaucracy." In the average Fortune 1000 firm, Jensen reports, the CEO's total compensation changes by $3 for every $1000 change in shareholder value. By comparison, the average CEO in an LBO firm experiences a change of $64 per $1000. And the partners of the LBO firm itself (the KKRs of this world), which is the proper equivalent of a conglomerate CEO, earn close to $200 per $1000 change in value. Given such dramatic concentrations of ownership and improvements in the pay-to-performance correlation, it is not surprising that researchers are now finding major operating improvements in firms that have gone private.

The Privatization of Bankruptcy? In equally provocative fashion, Jensen also argued that the highly leveraged transactions of the 80s, though clearly more likely to get into financial trouble, created far stronger incentives to reorganize troubled companies outside of court. Such a shift in incentives was leading, at least in the first part of the '80s, to a Japanese-like "privatization of bankruptcy" in which active investors (like the main banks in Japanese *keiretsu*) were using low-cost means (typically involving exchange offers) to avoid our costly and chronically inefficient Chapter 11 process.

This "privatization" movement, however, came to an abrupt halt in 1989 as a result of regulatory interference with the junk bond and credit markets, a change in the tax code, and a misguided bankruptcy court ruling. As Jensen also acknowledges, however, our private capital markets were by no means blameless in provoking this regulatory overreaction. A gross misalignment of incentives (which Jensen calls a "contracting failure") between dealmakers and suppliers of capital in LBOs and other HLTs led to a concentration of overpriced deals in the latter years of the 1980s. But capital market adjustments to this problem—including larger equity commitments, lower upfront fees, and more conservative deal prices—were already well underway when the set of regulatory initiatives launched in 1989 overrode them, thereby adding significantly to HLT defaults and bankruptcies.

Workout veteran David Schulte (adviser to Revco and partner with Sam Zell in putting together the billion dollar Zell-Chilmark Fund), confirms Jensen's argument in the following assessment of current trends in reorganization:

I've always hated bankruptcy. The problem I have with Chapter 11 is that it takes a business problem and turns it...into a legal case. I don't know what a guy who wears a black robe has to offer that the parties in interest can't do privately themselves...If we could devise a simple way for exchange offers to work outside of Chapter 11... investors would be well served and we'd all be a lot better off. In short, I'd like to have a non-bankruptcy bankruptcy. It's virtually impossible to do an out-of-court deal right now. All in all, 1990 was a very bad year for exchange offers.

Part of the current difficulties in reorganizing troubled companies outside of court can be traced to the dispersion of claims among creditors. In the last half of the '80s, the problem of systematic overpayments was greatly compounded by the sale of the debt to public junk bondholders (whom, it now appears, could only be induced to reorganize their claims through the agency of Milken and Drexel) and commercial banks' practice of "participating" or "assigning" rather than holding their loans. All this ensured that if companies did get into trouble, then private reorganizations would be very difficult.

And when troubled companies, unable to reach an out-of-court consensus, then filed for protection under Chapter 11, some of the problems would only be exacerbated. As described by articles in the closing section of this book, the unanimity provisions of the Trust Indenture Act, the grant of "exclusivity" to management (and routine extensions thereof), and failures to enforce strict priority of claims all serve only to intensify fighting among creditors. In so doing, they also remove any incentive for interested parties to provide unbiased information about the underlying

value of the firm, thus making creditor consensus all the more difficult to reach.

Noted bankruptcy lawyer Leonard Rosen sums up the current situation as follows:

I always thought that the purpose of a workout was first to create the biggest possible pot, and then to fight about the division of the pot afterwards. That was the spirit in which workouts used to be done in the old days....

What worries me [today]...is that, if creditor fights about the division of the pot start at the beginning of the process, then nobody's probably paying attention to more fundamental questions like: Have we got the right management running the business? And are they making the right strategic and operating decisions?...We're starting the fights so early, spending so much energy on the intercreditor struggle, and creating such divisiveness in the process that we're making it much less likely that companies will be restructured quickly and economically.

Jensen and other economists argue that much of the intensity of intercreditor conflicts built into our current Chapter 11 process could be eliminated simply by auctioning the control of bankrupt companies to the highest bidder. Such a process, which is already well-developed in countries like Germany, would effectively separate the valuation of the assets from destructive squabbles over how that value is to be divided among claimholders. Such an auction process would also help preserve operating value by shielding the day-to-day management of Chapter 11 companies from such potentially destructive conflicts.

Insulating operations from claimholder conflicts is, of course, what Chapter 11 is supposed to accomplish. And the process actually appears to have worked quite well in some cases. For example, Allied and Federated Stores have re-emerged from bankruptcy after incurring legal and administrative costs of only about 3% of total asset value; and operations remain fundamentally profitable (indeed, stores like Bloomingdale's were reporting record operating earnings throughout their stay in Chapter 11). Such well-managed reorganizations, however, should not be allowed to obscure the sheer waste of investor value in cases like Eastern Airlines and Revco (see Karen Wruck's *"What Really Went Wrong With Revco?"*). It is the latter cases that expose the fundamental flaws in the current system.

In sum, the movement toward a "privatization of bankruptcy" described by Jensen has been derailed (although the new movement toward "pre-packaged" bankruptcy represents a promising hybrid between a private workout and formal bankruptcy). And thus the "costs of financial distress" today appear considerably higher than economists like Jensen once predicted. But the verdict is not yet in. Financial economists are now mining a rich new lode of data to determine if bankruptcy costs are indeed as large as critics of restructuring have made them out to be. Findings from this research, besides contributing to the ongoing debate about optimal capital structure, will also likely affect future developments in corporate practice.

BACK TO THE FREE CASH FLOW PROBLEM (WITH A DIGRESSION ON THE MEDIA)

We are told almost daily by the financial press that corporate America suffers from an underinvestment problem—from a failure to invest in new technologies, modern plant and equipment, and the education of its workforce. All this may well be true (especially in cases where management bonuses are determined largely by near-term EPS). Moreover, as Michael Jacobs argues convincingly in his book *Short-Term America*, shareholders of U.S. companies may rationally demand higher and quicker payoffs because they have virtually no power to influence corporate policy.

What we are almost never told by the press, however, is that much of corporate America has also long had a chronic "overinvestment" problem. The case of RJR-Nabisco documented in "*Barbarians at the Gate*" is undoubtedly one of the most flagrant cases (remember Ross Johnson's insisting to John Greeniaus that he find a way to spend the "excess" profits of his tobacco division rather than raise stockholder expectations by revealing its true profit potential). But the fact that Johnson was held up by *Fortune* as a model corporate leader only a month before the LBO suggests that major inefficiencies in cash-rich companies may be not only widespread, but very difficult to detect by outsiders. And the large stockholder gains from the corporate control transactions of the '80s are suggestive evidence of the systematic waste of shareholder capital by companies dedicated to growth at all cost.

Why is it important that such growth be checked? At the end of the 1970s, when the Dow was trading around 900 and the outlook for corporate America was far from bright, Lester Thurow complained in his apocalyptic bestseller *The Zero-Sum Society* that "mixed" economies like ours—those in which government was always intervening to "correct" free-market solutions that were politically unacceptable—had one very serious (and to Thurow irremediable) problem. Such economies could not bring about the large-scale "disinvestment" in declining industries, with the resulting cuts in employment and real wages, necessary to release growth capital for emerging industry.

When I heard Thurow repeat this point in a speech at MIT in the mid-80s, I raised my hand and objected that the then burgeoning leveraged restructuring movement was a free-market solution to precisely that "disinvestment" problem. The widespread substitution of temporary debt capital for more permanent equity—in leveraged takeovers, leveraged buyouts, and leveraged buybacks—was forcing excess capital out of companies in mature industries like oil and gas, tobacco, forest products, publishing, broadcasting, tires, food processing, and commodity chemicals.

It is no coincidence, moreover, that while billions of dollars of capital were being squeezed out of our largest companies and returned to stockholders, the venture capital industry was booming. Funding for the U.S. venture capital industry achieved its peak in 1987, close to the time when the volume of leveraged restructurings was reaching its own high point. At the same time, the small and medium-sized U.S. companies that prospered throughout the '80s were contributing to record employment and capital spending.

Today, of course, the economy is in recession. Widespread failures in the S&L industry, combined with a number of highly-publicized cases of troubled leveraged transactions, have led to a significant re-regulation of our financial markets. With the eclipse of the new issue market for junk bonds, the application of HLT rules to commercial bank lending, and new restrictions on insurance companies, funding for large highly-leveraged transactions has all but disappeared and there are few signs of a well-functioning corporate control market.

In one sense, the financial press is right in attributing part of the current conditions in our debt and takeover markets to too many unsound transactions. Such transactions, as Jensen argued, have been overpriced by their promoters and, as a consequence, overleveraged. What seems equally clear, however, is that intense political pressures to curb the corporate control market have greatly compounded the existing problems, creating a capital shortage for non-investment-grade companies, and thereby contributing significantly to the recession.

The media, as suggested earlier, have played no small role in inflaming popular opinion and bringing political forces to bear on private economic activity. Populist attacks on Wall Street financiers and concentrations of financial power continue to be the order of the day for most mass-market publications. Even business publications such as the *Wall Street Journal* (at least the front-page stories) and *Forbes* resort increasingly to the techniques of muckraking sensationalism while avoiding all but the most simplistic economic analysis.

Perhaps the nadir of this kind of journalism was a piece by Susan Faludi on KKR's LBO of Safeway Stores that, ironically, won a Pulitzer prize for "explanatory" journalism. The irony stems from the fact that, from an economist's perspective, the Safeway LBO is one of the most unambiguously successful of the leveraged transactions of the '80s. Although now considerably smaller, the company has become extraordinarily profitable, capital spending (largely on store renovation) has increased significantly, and employee morale has improved in large part because the increased profitability has restored the basis for future growth. And while journalists are doubtless continuing their obsession with a handful of unfortunate individuals displaced by such changes, financial economists from the Harvard Business School are now at work anatomizing the transformation of Safeway into a remarkably efficient competitor.

There are a number of reasons why the quality of business journalism in this country continues to be poor. Although the business establishment undoubtedly furnishes the media with a major portion of its advertising revenues, it is probably unnecessary to go much beyond the incentives of the press to appeal to the mass markets, to the "man on the street," to arrive at the heart of the problem. As American movie producers and popular novelists have long understood, the American public is most responsive to stories that pit simple goodness against unmistakable evil. In this modern-day "morality play," the principal requirement is that heroes and villains be clearly distinguished from one another, and that all ambiguity be suppressed. The more heinous the villain, the greater the pleasure taken in his defeat (another essential requirement of popular American film) by the forces of good.

In economic life, however, all successful actions come at a cost, all change that increases social wealth comes at the expense of some groups and individuals. In this world where choices are rarely between good and evil, but only between the lesser of two evils (for all change causes pain to some), it is often the most callous-seeming actions that produce the greatest benefits for the economy at large. Those benefits, and their beneficiaries, cannot be detected—much less subjected to measurement— by the unaided eye of the journalist.

To return to our earlier argument, the primary accomplishment of the leveraged restructuring movement has been to stimulate general economic growth by forcing resources (people and capital) out of mature or shrinking industries and into vital ones. In the typical newspaper account, we learn much about the personal plights of employees who lose their jobs. But what the average journalist fails to acknowledge is that not all employment and corporate investment are "good for the economy," and that overall growth depends importantly on the ability to transfer people and capital from where they are not needed to where they are. Such mobility of resources, in the long run, is likely not only to add to stockholder wealth, but to increase total employment and corporate spending. And by each of these indicators of general economic performance, the 1980s were very productive indeed. (The fact that wage rates have fallen in some industries, so often deplored by market critics, is in fact a sign that the control market was doing its job in making our industry more competitive internationally.)

In the typical journalistic account of a leveraged takeover, we also generally learn very little about why the acquirer (or "raider") can afford to pay large premiums over current value to buy out the existing stockholders. Such premiums are invariably attributed to market undervaluation, which in turn is ascribed to the shortsightedness of investors. Rarely is there an account of the corporate inefficiencies and expected operating changes that typically make the payment of such premiums possible (though *Barbarians at the Gate* surely provides the first). And never have I seen a story that attempts to trace the subsequent path of stockholder capital liberated by restructurings and then describe the productive activities and new employment that capital eventually makes possible.

Private distress makes good copy, as always, but social benefits are difficult to detect with the journalist's tools. Here the statistical methods and abstract "truths" of the economist must serve.

A WORD ABOUT THIS BOOK

This book consists of 57 articles written, for the most part, by financial economists. The articles are divided into seven sections. The first presents more recent evidence attesting to the efficiency of our capital markets, and the remaining six examine the implications of market efficiency for the following aspects of corporate management: (1) evaluating capital investment opportunities; (2) setting capital structure and dividend policies; (3) raising capital and choosing among the continually broadening spectrum of financing vehicles; (4) managing corporate risks (including the corporate uses of derivatives such as futures, swaps, and options); (5) corporate restructuring designed to increase stockholder value; and (6) reorganization of financially troubled companies.

Each of these 57 articles was published previously in one of three publications for which I served as founding editor: the Continental Bank's *Journal of Applied Corporate Finance* and its two predecessors, the *Midland Corporate Finance Journal* (1983-1987) and the *Chase Financial Quarterly* (1981-1982). The fundamental aim of each of these publications has been the same: To "translate" outstanding research in corporate finance—conducted primarily by academics at our business schools and published in academic journals—into reasonably plain English for corporate executives, and to provide a meeting ground for theorist and practitioner by stressing the practical import of the research.

In closing, I would like to thank my colleagues Joel Stern and Bennett Stewart for their help in launching this now ten-year publishing effort. My largest debt, however, is to all the financial economists that have contributed to these publications, making them—and thus this book—possible.

PART I

MARKET EFFICIENCY

To the extent management aims to serve its stockholders, all operating as well as financing decisions are grounded in some theory of market pricing. How management decides to use the assets at its disposal, which yardsticks it uses to evaluate performance, and what it chooses to tell investors all depend fundamentally on its understanding of how the stock market works.

This section begins with Bennett Stewart's debunking of "*Market Myths.*" Much of the behavior of corporate America, Stewart argues, is dictated by unthinking adherence to what he calls the "Accounting Model of Value"—at its most simplistic, the notion that the market establishes a company's value by capitalizing its current earnings at a "standard" industry-wide multiple. In place of the Accounting Model, Stewart proposes adoption of the "Economic Model of Value" as the basis for corporate decision-making. The Economic Model estimates a company's worth as the sum of all future expected operating cash flows, net of required new investment and discounted at a cost of capital that reflects risk and investors' alternative investment opportunities. It is essentially this model, Stewart claims, that the most sophisticated, influential investors (the "lead steers") use in pricing corporate securities.

After a long exposition of the follies of accounting-based as opposed to value-based management, Stewart goes on to challenge a number of other popular beliefs about the market—namely, (1) that dividends are an important fundamental variable in the pricing of stocks; (2) that the prevalence of short-sighted institutional investors prevents the market from taking the long view of corporate performance; and (3) that efforts to increase investors' demand for a company's shares by appealing to small investors also increase the value of those shares. ("It is unfortunate," says Stewart, "that most of what passes for investor relations is "retail" as opposed to "wholesale" in orientation, aims to inform the herd and not the lead steers, and stimulates volume instead of price.")

Since the stock market crash of October 1987, charges of investor irrationality and "excess volatility" have been more widely sounded than ever. And adding fuel to the unfailingly populist clamor of the press, a number of recent academic studies have purported to demonstrate that the market overreacts both to general economic news and to changes in the fortunes of individual companies. In "*How Rational Investors Deal with Uncertainty,*" Seha Tinic, Keith Brown, and Van Harlow argue that reports of the death of efficient markets theory are greatly exaggerated. Their own recent studies suggest that what appear to be predictable price "corrections" following overreactions by the investing public are better understood as rational responses to abrupt changes in investment risk.

In "*How Investors Interpret Changes in Corporate Financial Policy,*" Paul Healy and Krishna Palepu attempt to explain why investors react in fairly consistent ways to announcements of three kinds of corporate policy changes: (1) dividend initiations, (2) common stock offerings, and (3) stock splits. As the authors found in their own recent studies, both dividend initiations and stock splits are followed by several years of sustained increases in earnings, thus vindicating the market's initially positive reaction. Announcements of stock offerings, by contrast, presage a period of significantly higher operating risk and share price volatility, thus justifying the generally negative market response.

Critics of takeovers and restructurings argue that the market is short-sighted, putting excessive weight on current earnings and penalizing long-term investment. Most financial economists reason, however, that while management may focus on the short term (in part because its bonuses are so often tied to reported accounting earnings), investors have strong incentives to take the long view.

In "*Competitive Decline and Corporate Restructuring,*" Randall Woolridge explores the market's ability to capture long-term expectations in current prices. Woolridge reviews the existing controversy, and presents the results of his recently completed study. Consistent with earlier work performed by SEC economists and others, Woolridge's study finds that the market responds positively, on average, to corporate announcements of long-term capital commitments such as (1) participations in joint ventures, (2) increases in R&D spending, (3) new product introductions, and (4) capital expansions and improvements. The paper also purports to demonstrate that more than half of the present value of the Dow Jones 30 Industrials is reflecting the market's expectations of earnings beyond a five-year horizon.

But if the market seems to reward promising long-term corporate investment, it also began, in the late 1970s and early '80s, to react with strong skepticism to a once popular form of corporate investment: diversifying acquisitions. Indeed, many of the acquisitions consummated during these years were divested within the next five years.

In "*Do Bad Bidders Become Good Targets?*," Ken Lehn, former Chief Economist of the SEC, and his colleague Mark Mitchell report finding that the market's "short-run" response to announcements of acquisitions provides a remarkably accurate forecast of whether the acquisition will later be reversed through divestiture. As the title of the article suggests, the market response was also systematically negative to announcements of acquisitions by companies that soon after became takeover candidates themselves (within the next five years). The findings of this study thus provide not only powerful testimony to the stock market's ability to anticipate the eventual value added (or lost) by corporate acquisitions, but also persuasive evidence for the role of "bust-up" takeovers in dismantling inefficient conglomerates (a theme we return to later in the "corporate restructuring" section of this book).

In "*The Motives and Consequences of Debt-Equity Swaps and Defeasances*," Professors John Hand and Patricia Hughes add to the bulk of academic research attesting to the stock market's ability to distinguish artificial from real increases in earnings. The evidence on the timing of swaps and defeasances strongly suggests they were used by corporate treasuries in the 1980s to disguise temporary downturns in operating earnings. But investors, far from being fooled by the accounting treatment, actually responded in systematically negative fashion to announcements of both swaps and defeasances. In the case of swaps, moreover, the larger the reported accounting gain from the swap, the more negative the stock market reaction.

One last interesting testimony to market efficiency is furnished by "*An Analysis of Trading Profits: How Trading Rooms Really Make Money.*" In this article, Alberic Braas and Charles Bralver of Oliver, Wyman & Co. (a bank strategy consulting group) attempt to correct some popular misconceptions about the profitability of bank trading operations. Based on their work with more than 40 large trading operations, the authors conclude that, for most trading rooms, speculative "positioning" is not a reliable source of profits. The primary source of profit is dealings with customers. Stable profits can also be expected from interdealer trade, but only from traders who work for large institutions with heavy order flows and who adopt a "jobber" style of trading.

DHC

MARKET MYTHS

*by G. Bennett Stewart, III
Stern Stewart & Co.**

I t is easy to forget why senior management's most important job is to create value. Of course, a higher value increases the wealth of the company's shareholders who, after all, are the owners of the enterprise. But, of greater import, society at large benefits. The quest for value drives scarce resources to their most productive uses and their most efficient users. The more effectively resources are deployed, the more robust will be economic growth and the rate of improvement in our standard of living. Adam Smith's invisible hand is at work when investors' private gain is a public virtue. And, although there are exceptions to this rule, most of the time there is a happy harmony between creating market value and enhancing the quality of life.

The pursuit of value often is made more difficult by a failure to understand how share prices are really set in the stock market. I regularly encounter senior executives and board members who believe stock prices are determined by some vague combination of earnings, growth, return, book value, cash flow, dividends, and the demand for their shares. (In one particularly memorable meeting, I was harangued for several hours by an elderly gentleman who claimed that mysterious forces—the so-called "gnomes" of Wall Street—controlled the market. His "voodoo valuation" framework will not be formally rebutted in this book.)

Confusion over what it is that investors really want can make it difficult for management to reach sensible decisions regarding business strategy, acquisitions and divestitures, accounting methods, financial structure, dividend policy, investor relations, and, most important of all (let's be honest), bonus plans. With the competition for capital growing ever more hostile and global, the cost of ignorance is escalating. It is high time management learns the answer to the question: What is the engine that drives share prices?

*This article is a slightly abbreviated version of Chapter 2 of the author's forthcoming book, *The Quest for Value: A Guide for Senior Management* (Harper & Row, 1990).

IN SEARCH OF VALUE: THE ACCOUNTING MODEL VERSUS THE ECONOMIC MODEL

Right away there are two competing answers. The traditional "accounting model" of valuation contends that Wall Street sets share prices by capitalizing a company's earnings-per-share (EPS) at an appropriate price/earnings multiple (P/E). If, for example, a company typically sells at ten times earnings, and EPS is now $1.00, the accounting model would predict a $10 share price. But, should earnings fall to $0.80 per share, then—however temporary the downturn—the company's shares are expected to fall to $8.

The appeal of this accounting model is its simplicity and apparent precision. Its shortcoming is an utter lack of realism; the accounting model assumes, in effect, that P/E multiples never change. But P/E multiples change all the time—in the wake of acquisitions and divestitures, changes in financial structure and accounting policies, and new investment opportunities. P/E multiples, in short, adjust to changes in the "quality" of a company's earnings. And this makes EPS a very unreliable measure of value.

A competing explanation—the "economic model" of value to which I subscribe—holds that share prices are determined by smart investors who care about just two things: the cash to be generated over the life of a business, and the risk of the cash receipts. More precisely, the economic model states that a company's intrinsic market value is determined by discounting its expected future "Free Cash Flow" (FCF) back to a present value at a rate that reflects its "cost of capital."

The cost of capital is the rate of return required to compensate investors for bearing risk. It is a rate determined in practice by adding a premium for risk to the yield prevailing on relatively risk-free government bonds.

FCF is the cash flow generated by a company's operations that is free, or net, of the new capital invested for growth. To compute it, imagine that all of a company's cash operating receipts are deposited in a cigar-box, and that all of its cash operating outlays are taken out, regardless of whether the outlays are recorded by the accountants as expenses on the income statement or as expenditures on the balance sheet. What's left over in the cigar box is FCF.

Which is the more desirable, then, positive or negative FCF? While you may be tempted to say a positive FCF will maximize a company's value, the correct answer actually is: It depends. It depends on the expected rate of return on the new investments a company is making. A profitable company investing lots of capital to expand (such as Federal Express) has a negative FCF, while an unprofitable company shrinking its assets to pay creditors (like Western Union) generates positive FCF. Which company is worth more? In this case (and many others like it), the company with the negative FCF creates greater value.

People say to me, "Bennett, you are a great believer in cash flow. Why is it that your incentive compensation plans do not reward management for generating more Free Cash Flow, if that is what determines value?"

"Ah," I say, "because it is Free Cash Flow over the entire life of the business that matters. FCF in any one year is a nearly meaningless measure of performance and value. A positive or negative FCF cannot be judged to be good or bad without examining the quality of FCF—that is, the rate of return earned on the investments."

But now I am getting ahead of myself. There will be plenty of time later to expound on the finer points of the economic model. For now, let's return to the fundamental debate: Is it earnings or cash flow that truly drives stock prices?

Because most companies' earnings and cash flow move together most of the time, it can be difficult to say for sure whether stock prices truly result from capitalizing earnings or discounting cash flow. To sort out this potentially misleading correlation, academic researchers have studied how share prices react to events that cause a company's earnings and its cash flow to depart from one another.

The Accounting Model Versus the Economic Model—Some Evidence

The accounting model relies upon two distinct financial statements—an income statement and balance sheet—whereas the economic model uses only one: sources and uses of cash. Because earnings are emphasized in the accounting model, whether a cash outlay is expensed on the income statement or is capitalized on the balance sheet makes a great deal of difference. In the economic model, where cash outlays are recorded makes no difference at all—unless it affects taxes. This conflict is highlighted when a company is permitted to choose between alternative accounting methods.

LIFO vs. FIFO. Switching from FIFO (First In, First Out) to LIFO (Last In, First Out) inventory cost-

Purchase vs. Pooling

ing in times of rising prices decreases a company's reported earnings because the most recently acquired and, hence, most costly inventory is expensed first. But, in so doing, it saves taxes, leaving more cash to accumulate in the cigar box.

Now we have an important question: Does the market focus on the decline in earnings or the increase in cash? Following the empirical tradition of the "Chicago School," let's find out what investors actually do to stock prices instead of asking them what they might do.

Professor Shyam Sunder demonstrated that companies switching to LIFO experienced on average a 5 percent increase in share price on the date the intended change was first announced. An analysis performed by a second group of researchers revealed that the share price gain was in direct proportion to the present value of the taxes to be saved by making the switch. Taken together, these studies provide powerful evidence that share prices are dictated by cash generation, not book earnings.

These findings also prove that a company adopting LIFO will sell for a higher multiple of its earnings than if it used FIFO. The higher multiple is consistent with the higher quality of LIFO earnings; inventory holding gains are purged from income, and there are the tax savings besides.

And if, as this research suggests, a company's share price depends upon the "quality" as well as the quantity of its earnings, then the accounting model of value collapses. It collapses because a company's P/E multiple is not a primary *cause* of its stock price, as the model seems to suggest, but a consequence of it. The accounting model cannot answer the question: What determines a company's stock price in the first place?

In the LIFO-FIFO example, earnings go down while cash goes up. Let us now examine a second accounting choice, one where earnings go down but there is no change in cash.

The Amortization of Goodwill. When the purchase method is used to account for an acquisition, any premium paid over the estimated fair value of the seller's assets is assigned to goodwill and amortized against earnings over a period not to exceed forty years. Because it is a non-cash, non-tax-deductible expense, the amortization of goodwill per se is of no consequence in the economic model of valuation. In the accounting framework, by contrast, it matters because it reduces reported earnings.

With pooling-of-interests accounting, by contrast, buyers merely add the book value of the sellers'

assets to their own book value. No goodwill is recorded or amortized, and this usually makes the acquiror's subsequent reported earnings and return on equity look much better than if purchase accounting had been employed.

Now, if the amortization of goodwill were the only difference between pooling and purchase, I might consider a preference for pooling accounting to be harmless. But, many times sellers will take only cash, or buyers are unwilling to issue equity, thereby ruling out pooling transactions. Avoiding a sensible transaction merely because it must be recorded under purchase rules is the height of folly.

Sad to say, it was apparently just this foolish thinking that prevented the disposition of some of Beatrice's last remaining properties. The press has reported on more than one occasion that interested suitors balked at purchasing Beatrice units because of a concern over how the market would react to the enormous goodwill they would be forced to record. H. J. Heinz, for one, canned a bid in part over just such a concern with goodwill.

Now, if Don Kelly, Beatrice's CEO at that time, was asking too high a price—one that the potential buyers could not justify by the likely future generation of cash—then that would have been a good reason for them to step back. But if, as the press suggested, the potential buyers walked away from value-adding acquisitions merely because it would have required the recognition and amortization of goodwill, then they let the accounting tail wag their business dog (and I can only shake my head in wonder).

As these cases suggest, it is important to know whether investors are fooled by the cosmetic differences between purchase and pooling, or if instead they penetrate accounting fictions to focus on real economic value. To find out which answer is correct, let us once again trust our eyes and not our ears. Let's look over the shoulders of researchers who have carefully studied the shares prices of acquiring companies.

Hai Hong, Gershon Mandelker and Robert Kaplan, while associated with Carnegie-Mellon's business school, examined the share prices of a large sample of American companies making acquisitions during the 1960s. They divided all the acquirors into two camps: those electing purchase and those using pooling. Over the interval covered by their study, it was much easier to qualify an acquisition for pooling than it is now. Most acquisitions could be recorded using either purchase or pooling, with the choice largely up to management.

Thus, if it were true that investors were concerned with the recognition and amortization of goodwill, the stock prices of purchase acquirors should have underperformed the pooling acquirors. And yet, no significant difference in stock returns could be detected.

This evidence supports the view that accounting entries that do not affect cash do not affect value. It also proves that what matters in an acquisition is only how much cash (and cash-equivalent value) is paid out to consummate the transaction relative to how much cash is likely to flow in afterwards, and not how the transaction is recorded by accountants.

The studies I have cited (along with many other tests of share price behavior too numerous to review here) offer persuasive evidence that share prices are determined by expected cash generation and not by reported earnings. A company's earnings explain its share price only to the extent that earnings reflect cash. Otherwise, earnings are misleading and should be abandoned as the basis for making decisions (and, as I shall argue later, for determining bonuses).

Just Say No

Just how damaging an addiction to earnings can be is illustrated by the case of RJR, the tobacco giant. As reported in a recent *Wall Street Journal* article, RJR puffed up its sales and earnings for several years prior to its LBO by "loading" cigarette inventories on its distributors. Dealers were encouraged to purchase billions of surplus cigarettes just before semi-annual price increases were put into effect. (Company officials estimated that there were a staggering 18 billion exess cigarettes on dealers' shelves as of January 1, 1989.) As a result, RJR was able to report higher sales and earnings. But, in so doing, management forfeited future sales at higher prices, accelerated the payment of excise taxes and turned off smokers with cigarettes that had turned stale.

Within months of the LBO, RJR announced it would discontinue this harmful practice cold turkey, slashing cigarette shipments 29% in the third quarter and 17% in the fourth quarter of 1989 compared to year earlier levels. Though the accounting symptoms look bad (reported profits will be reduced by about $170 million in each quarter), the vital signs of corporate health are restored right away."

"This is a very positive development for the company as far as cash flow is concerned," noted Kurt von der Hayden, RJR's CFO. "I view it as a very positive contribution to our debt service.

Because RJR offered extended payment terms to induce its dealers to load inventories, cash flow would not be hurt by the shipment drop. But excise taxes will be postponed, production and distribution can become more efficient and fresher cigarettes may help to stem a further loss of market share to Phillip Morris.

A former senior RJR officer said that management had been aware of the problem, but couldn't withdraw from the practice because they feared the impact on earnings would have outraged Wall Street, James W. Johnston, the head of the RJR Tobacco Company, stated, "Here is probably the clearest, most positive statement of what we can accomplish by being private for a while."

For shame! What about the evidence that the stock market really responds to the generation of cash and not to illusory accounting profits? As my colleague Joel Stern puts it, "Run your public company as if it were privately-held, and you will be making the right decision for your public stockholders." And maybe you won't be vulnerable to its being taken private at twice the current stock price (RJR traded for $55 a share before being taken private for $110 a share.)

Kick the earnings habit. Join the Cash Flow generation.

MORE TROUBLES WITH EARNINGS

Is R&D an Expenditure or Expense?

Another problem with earnings as a measure of value is the improper accounting for research and development. Accountants are required to expense R&D outlays as if their potential contribution to value is always exhausted in the period incurred. But common sense says otherwise.

Why would Merck, the spectacularly successful pharmaceutical company, spend more than 10 percent of its sales each year on R&D if it did not expect a substantial return to follow? In fact Merck is looking for a long-term payoff from such spending, and so are its investors. The company's shares sell for a multiple of over 20 times reported earnings and nearly 10 times accounting book value. Merck's earnings and book value apparently understate the company's value by a wide margin. Expensing R&D is one of the reasons why.

While the payoff from any one of its projects is unpredictable, Merck's overall R&D spending is almost certain to bear fruit. Like any capital expenditure that is expected to create an enduring value, Merck's R&D should be capitalized onto the balance sheet and then amortized against earnings over the period of projected payoff from its successful R&D efforts. Such accounting would lead Merck to report both a higher book value and higher current earnings, thereby making the company's actual P/E and price-to-book multiples more understandable.

The accountants' cavalier dismissal of R&D is what accounts in part for the sky-high share price multiples enjoyed by the many small, rapidly growing high-tech Silicon Valley and Route 128 firms. As in Merck's case, their stock prices capitalize an expected future payoff from their R&D while their earnings are charged with an immediate expense. It is especially ironic to note that, following the acquisitions of R&D-intensive companies, the accountants will agree to record as goodwill for the buyer the R&D they had previously expensed for the seller. Thus, according to the accountants, R&D can be an asset if acquired but not if it is home-grown. (Again, I shake my head in wonder.)

What possible justification could there be for writing off R&D as an immediate expense when it is so obviously capitalized in stock market values? My answer is that the accountants are in bed with the bankers.

Accountants Take Downers, Too

To protect their loans, bankers prefer to lend against assets that retain value even if the borrower must be liquidated. Such "tangible" assets include receivables, inventories, and property, plant and equipment—assets that have a use to others. But because an insolvent company is unlikely to recover much value from its prior R&D investments (if it did, why is it going bankrupt?), lenders are reluctant to lend against it. Their accounting pals accommodate their desire for concreteness by expensing "intangibles" like R&D.

Accountants, to be sure, do not accept my contention that they are the unwitting slaves of the bankers. They explain their overzealous pen strokes as an adherence to the "principle of conservatism," a slogan that in practice means, "when in doubt, debit." You may have more appreciation for the poor accountants' cynical bent if I told you they are much more likely to be sued for overstating earnings than for understating them. So perhaps their conservatism is more pragmatic than principled.

The key question remains: Are the investors who set share prices knee-jerk conservatives or hard-headed realists when it comes to R&D? Do they consider R&D a cost to be expensed or an expenditure to be capitalized?

Stock prices provide the answer that economic realism prevails (the academic evidence to support this is reviewed later in this article). R&D outlays should be capitalized and amortized over their projected lives—not because they always do create value, but because they are expected to.

Full Cost Vs. Successful Efforts

One objection that might be raised to capitalizing R&D is that it may leave assets on a company's books that no longer have any value. What if the R&D fails to pay off? Should not at least the unsuccessful R&D outlays be expensed? I say no. Full-cost accounting is the only proper way to assess a company's rate of return.

The issue of successful efforts versus full cost accounting is best illustrated by oil companies. With successful efforts accounting, an oil company capitalizes only the costs associated with actually finding oil; all drilling expenditures that fail to discover economic quantities of oil are immediately expensed against earnings. While such a policy reduces earnings early on, it causes a permanent reduction in assets that eventually leads to the overstatement of future rates of return.

With full-cost accounting, by contrast, an oil company capitalizes all drilling outlays onto its balance sheet and then amortizes them over the lives of the successful wells. If you believe (as I do) that part of the cost associated with finding oil is that unsuccessful wells have to be drilled (if not, why are they drilled in the first place?), then full-cost accounting must be employed to properly measure an oil company's capital investment and thus its true rate of return.

The misuse of successful efforts accounting is not limited just to oil companies, though. Any company that writes off an unsuccessful investment will subsequently overstate the rate of return its investors have realized. Such an overstatement may tempt management to overinvest in businesses that really are not as profitable as they seem to be on paper.

Citibank illustrates the point. In 1987, Citibank took a $3 billion charge to earnings to establish a reserve for the eventual charge-off of LDC loans. Now Citibank sleeps better, for in the years after the charge-off, loan losses are charged against the reserve, never to touch earnings. And, with $3 billion of equity erased with an accounting stroke of the pen, Citibank's accounting return on equity has rebounded quite smartly. Management may wonder why, though, with such an improved return, the bank still sells for such a lowly multiple. One reason is that while Citibank has employed successful efforts accounting, the market uses full cost to judge rates of return.

To overcome such distortions, the economic model of accounting for value would reverse unusual write-offs by taking the charges off the income statement and adding them back to the balance sheet. This way a company's rate of return will rise only if there is a genuine improvement in the generation of cash from operations after the write-off.

Abraham Briloff, an accounting professor at NYU, is one who has fallen into the trap of advocating successful efforts accounting. For example, in a book entitled "Unaccountable Accounting," he chastised United Technologies for not writing down the goodwill associated with its acquisition of Mostek, a semiconductor company. He argued that, in light of the severe operating problems that materialized at Mostek in the years after the acquisition, the goodwill on UT's books clearly overstated Mostek's value to UT's stockholders, and should be written off just as if it were an unsuccessful drilling expenditure.

I am afraid that Briloff labors under the mistaken belief that a company's balance sheet somehow attempts to represent its market value. He and, it seems, the entire accounting profession apparently have forgotten one of the first principles of economics: sunk costs are irrelevant.

Burn the Books

As any first year economics student knows, the cash already invested in a project is an irrecoverable sunk cost that is irrelevant to computing value. Market values are determined not by the cash that has gone into the acquisition of assets, but by the cash flow that can subsequently be gotten out of them. Therefore, a company's book value simply cannot be a measure of its market value (as Briloff seems to assume).

Rather, a company's balance sheet can at best be a measure of "capital"—that is, the amount of cash deposited by (debt as well as equity) investors in the company. Whether such "capital" translates into "value" depends upon management's success in earning a high enough discounted cash flow rate of return on that capital. This is the question that, although critical to the economic model of value, no balance sheet can answer. This judgment is best left to the stock market.

The Deferred Tax Chameleon

The inadequacy of conventional accounting statements is further exposed by the question: Is the deferred tax reserve appearing on a company's balance sheet debt or equity? Clearly the accountants cannot decide; that's why they stick it in the no man's land between debt and equity. My answer to the question is uncomfortably close to the accountants' hedged position. I too say, "It depends."

Pity the pessimistic lenders, for they must consider the deferred tax reserve to be a debt-like liability. Bankers realize that if a company's condition deteriorates, it probably will not be able to replace the assets that give rise to the deferral of taxes. Moreover, should the assets be sold to secure debt repayment, the company may be obligated to pay a recapture of the past deferred tax benefit. In either event, the deferred tax reserve is quite rightly considered by creditors to be a quasi-liability that uses up a company's capacity to borrow money.

But if you divorce yourself from the downright depressing company of lenders and take up with the more genial society of shareholders, you will discover that the entire character of the deferred tax reserve changes right before your eyes. For as long as a company remains a viable going concern—an assumption taken for granted in the stock market valuation of most companies—the assets that give rise to the deferral of taxes will continue to be replenished. Because the shareholders in a going concern do not expect the company's deferred tax reserve ever to be repaid, it is properly considered to be the equivalent of common equity and thus a meaningless accounting segregation from net worth.

Furthermore, if the deferred tax reserve is properly considered to be a part of shareholders' equity, then to be consistent the year-to-year change in the reserve ought to be added back to reported profits. That way taxes are taken as an expense only when paid, not when provided for by the accountants.

An analogy can be drawn to the Individual Retirement Accounts (IRAs) many people opened some years back. If you are accounting for yours properly, you must consider only part of the funds in your account to be true equity. An accountant would insist that you set aside a deferred tax reserve because eventually you will have to pay taxes when you withdraw the funds from the account. Do you expect to earn a return from that part of your account that is the deferred tax reserve, or do you consider that to be a free loan from the government?

Of course, you expect to earn a return on the entire balance in your account. Nonetheless, I have heard otherwise level-headed corporate executives suggest that their corporate deferred tax reserve ought to be considered a free advance from the government. But, just as you do, corporations should expect to earn a return on all cash invested, no matter what the accountants may call it.

Steal This Book

Permit me one final accounting irony. No doubt the cash you parted with to buy this book has been expensed by your company's accountants. I wish they had had the charity (if not the wisdom) to capitalize it. They insult me by assuming that, when you put this book down for the last time, you will forget everything you've read.

Where They Ought To Be

The accountants, then, are stuck between a rock and a hard place. They can prepare financial statements either for creditors or for stockholders—that is, either for judging a company's debt capacity or its stock market value. But they simply cannot do both at once. It should be clear by now that the lenders won this debate: The accountants take the position that a company is more dead than alive.

Managers must stop making business decisions with financial statements that assume their company is one day away from bankruptcy. To make realistic judgements of performance and value, accounting statements must be recast from the liquidating perspective of a lender to the going concern perspective of shareholders. The balance sheet must be reinterpreted as the cash invested in a "capital" account, and not as the value of "assets". To do this, all of the investments a company makes in R&D along with bookkeeping provisions that squirrel away cash from operations (for deferred tax reserve, warranty reserve, bad debt reserve, inventory obsolescence reserve, deferred income reserve, etc.) must be taken out of earnings and put back into equity capital (a topic discussed in numbing detail in a later chapter).

EARNINGS PER SHARE DO NOT COUNT

Although EPS suffers from the same shortcomings as earnings, it is such a popular measure of corporate performance that it warrants further attention.

Consider an acquisition in which a company selling for a high P/E multiple buys a firm selling for a low P/E ratio by exchanging shares. Because fewer of the high P/E shares are needed to retire all the outstanding low P/E shares, the buyer's EPS will always increase. Many think that is good news for the buyer's shareholders. And, yet, it will happen even if the combination produces no synergies.

To see how really silly is a preoccupation with EPS, reverse the transaction so that now the low P/E firm buys the high-multiple company through a share exchange. This time the buyer's EPS must always decrease; a greater number of low-multiple shares will have to be issued to retire all the high-multiple ones. Many think such EPS dilution signals bad news for the buying company's shareholders, and advise that it be avoided at all cost.

But regardless of which company buys or which sells, the merged company will be the same, with the same assets, prospects, risks, earnings and value. Can the transaction really be desirable if consummated in one direction but not in the other? Of course not. Yet, that is what accounting EPS suggests.

Let's take an example. Assuming that two companies each currently earn $1.00 a share and have 1,000 shares outstanding, and that one firm sells for 20 times earnings while the other sells at 10 times its earnings, the facts are as shown in Exhibit 1.

EXHIBIT 1

	Hi	Lo	Hi Buys Lo	Lo Buys Hi
No. Shares	1,000	1,000	1,500*	3,000**
Total Earnings	$1,000	$1,000	$2,000	$2,000
Total Value	$20,000	$10,000	$30,000	$30,000
Price p/Share	$20.00	$10.00	$20.00	$10.00
EPS	$1.00	$1.00	$1.33	$0.66
P-E Ratio	20	10	15	15

* Hi must issue 500 shares at $20 to retire all 1,000 of Lo's $10 shares.
** Lo must issue 2000 shares at $10 to retire all 1,000 of Hi's $20 shares.

To make it simple, assume that there are no synergies and that the buyers pay precisely market price for the seller's shares. With fair value paid for value acquired, these transactions have all the excitement of kissing your sister. A proponent of the economic model would expect the acquiror's stock price to sit still.

Yet, when Hi buys Lo, EPS increases to $1.33 and when Lo buys Hi, EPS falls to $0.66. Preoc-

MANAGERS MUST STOP MAKING BUSINESS DECISIONS WITH FINANCIAL
STATEMENTS THAT ASSUME THEIR COMPANY IS ONE DAY AWAY FROM
BANKRUPTCY. TO MAKE REALISTIC JUDGEMENTS OF PERFORMANCE AND
VALUE, ACCOUNTING STATEMENTS MUST BE RECAST FROM THE LIQUIDATING
PERSPECTIVE OF A LENDER TO THE GOING CONCERN PERSPECTIVE OF
SHAREHOLDERS.

cupied with EPS, accounting enthusiasts may see a good deal and a bad deal when in fact the two transactions are both the same: Lo-Hi is just Hi-Lo with a two-for-one stock split.

EPS does not matter because, in the wake of an acquisition, a company's P/E multiple will change to reflect a deterioration or improvement in the overall quality of its earnings. In our example, observe that no matter which firm buys and which sells, the combined company will have a P/E multiple of 15 (the consolidated value of $30,000 divided by the consolidated earnings of $2,000). Hi's 20 P/E must fall, and Lo's 10 P/E must rise.

Hi must give up part of its P/E multiple to acquire relatively more current earnings from Lo, and Lo must surrender part of its current earnings to purchase Hi's more promising future growth prospects and a higher multiple. P/E counters EPS, rendering it a meaningless measure of an acquisition's merits.

In the economic model, what does matter is the exchange of value, and not the exchange of earnings so popular with accounting enthusiasts. If a buyer receives from a seller a value greater than it gives, this difference (which I call *Net Value Added*) will accrue to the benefit of the buyer's shareholders (in many cases the benefit will show up as an increase in the value of the buyer's shares immediately after the deal is announced).

Now if this seems a simple and sensible way to judge an acquisition's merits, please note that it has nothing to do with EPS. If a prospective acquisition promises to generate a positive Net Value Added for the buyer, but the accountants inform us that EPS will be diluted, then I conclude that the acquiror will sell for a higher P/E multiple, that's all. Once again, a company's P/E multiple is not the cause of its stock price, but a consequence of it. Let's take an example.

I once advised a large telecommunications company on an acquisition in which EPS dilution was a potential stumbling block. Our client was thinking about buying a company engaged in a rapidly growing and potentially highly-profitable business—one that appeared to have an excellent strategic fit with its own capabilities and business plan. I was enthusiastic about the transaction because I saw a prospect for the value created through the combination to be shared by both the buyer and the seller (the candidate was a unit of another company).

The chairman, too, was enthusiastic until he saw how much the deal would dilute EPS. He pointed out that the P/E multiple they would have to pay was much higher than their own, so that the acquisition would lead to a substantial dilution in EPS.

I remarked that the target had far brighter growth prospects than they did so that, when the new business was added to their more mature operations, he could expect his company to command a higher P/E multiple. He said: "You mean it's like adding high-octane gas to low-octane gas; our octane rating will increase."

"Right," I said. "The candidate has supercharged earnings, and when you add them to your under-powered earnings, your pro forma earnings power will take off. Your multiple will climb, and that will counter the dilution in EPS."

"Then we are in big trouble," he said. "My compensation plan is tied to EPS. We are rewarding just the quantity of earnings. But you're telling me that the quality of our earnings matters, too. So what should we do?"

"Well, you could change your incentive compensation plan," I said, "and then make the acquisition."

Which is what they did. And on the date of the announcement of the transaction, the seller's stock price increased, our client's price increased, and a key competitor's stock price plunged. Now that is what I call a successful acquisition. The seller wins. The buyer wins. And the competition gets clobbered.

I warn you, however, that my definition of a successful acquisition is different from that of many investment bankers. For them, successful acquisitions are all those that happen.

That's No Reason to Spin Off

A spin-off is a pro rata distribution of the shares of a subsidiary unit to the shareholders of the parent. It is simply the reverse of a stock-for-stock acquisition, and is subject to the same accounting quirks. This time, though, instead of acquiring a lower-multiple company to boost EPS, the accounting enthusiast will recommend spinning one off to boost the parent company's P-E multiple.

Referring again to the example presented above, suppose Hi did acquire Lo to form Hi-Lo, a company that sells for a P/E multiple of 15, an even blend of Hi's 20 multiple and Lo's 10 multiple. Now why not spin off Lo to leave behind a company that sells for Hi's P/E of 20? Is this really advisable? I don't think so, but for a definitive answer you will have to ask an investment banker whose finger is on the pulse of the market.

Seriously, though, the increase in P/E cannot by itself benefit Hi-Lo's shareholders. They are still stuck with their pro rata share of the low-multiple business after it is spun off. The spin-off merely takes Lo's earnings from Hi-Lo into a separate company where they are capitalized at Lo's multiple of 10. Thus, the increase in multiple that attaches to Hi's earnings is offset by the diminished multiple the market places on Lo's share of the consolidated profits. No matter how the accounting pie is sliced, it's still the same pie.

Just such a spinoff was used to "undo" R.J. Reynolds' acquisition of Sea Land, a containerized shipping operation whose P/E multiple was even lower than that of Reynolds. Several years after acquiring it, Reynolds' management decided to spin off Sea Land to its shareholders and was quite pleased to note that as a result Reynold's P/E multiple jumped from 7.5 to 9.5. But that increase in multiple just reversed the decline suffered when Reynolds first acquired Sea Land, no doubt to increase EPS.

So what we have described here is an investment banker's fantasy—an infinite deal generator: Have Hi multiple acquire Lo multiple in an exchange of shares to improve Hi's EPS (never mind, please, the collapse in P/E), and then, after a respectable period lapses, spin off shares in Lo to improve the multiple (never mind what happens to EPS); and then have Hi reacquire Lo to improve Hi's EPS . . . and, well, you get the idea (and the investment bankers get the fees).

Now please don't get the idea that I oppose spin-offs. As a matter of fact, I believe that spin-offs have been one of the most neglected tools of corporate finance. But the merits of a spin-off and other financial restructurings simply cannot be judged by the accounting model of value.

THE PROBLEM WITH EARNINGS GROWTH

Earnings growth also is a misleading indicator of performance. While it is true that companies that sell for the highest stock price multiples are rapidly growing, rapid growth is no guarantee of a high multiple.

To see why, consider a situation in which two companies, X and Y, have the same earnings, and are expected to grow at the same rate. At this point, we would be forced to conclude that both companies would sell for the same share price and P/E multiple because, as far as we can tell, they are identical.

Suppose now that X must invest more capital than Y to sustain its growth. In this case Y will command a higher share price and P/E multiple because it earns a higher rate of return on the new capital it invests. X merely spends its way to the growth that Y achieves through a more efficient use of capital.

This example illustrates that earnings growth for any company is determined by multiplying a measure of the *quality* of its investments—the rate of return—by a measure of the *quantity* of investment—the investment rate:

Growth = Rate of Return × Investment Rate

The rate of return is measured in relevant cash flow terms before financing costs. The investment rate equals new capital investment (both for working capital and for fixed assets) divided by earnings. The investment rate is the ratio of a company's uses-of-funds for operations to its sources-of-funds from operations—one which indicates the fraction or multiple of current earnings that are plowed back into the business.

To make the example more concrete, suppose X and Y are growing earnings at 10 percent, but X must invest all of its earnings to grow at that rate whereas Y needs to invest only 80 percent of its earnings to keep pace. Y would warrant a higher value because it earns a 12.5 percent rate of return on capital, while X returns just 10 percent.

From this information, you may be tempted to conclude that X is worth less than Y simply because it would not be able to pay a dividend while Y could. However, even though X reinvests all of its earnings it still could pay a dividend simply by raising new debt or equity. In fact, X could grow at the same rate as Y, pay the same dividends as Y, and even have the same capital structure as Y (if it periodically raises equity), but still be worth significantly less.

Financial cosmetics are widely available to gloss over a company's true performance. Rate of return is the only measure that allows Y to be reliably distinguished from X.

Growth Gone Haywire: The Case of W.T. Grant

I had an opportunity, while completing the Chase Manhattan Bank's credit training program in 1976, to analyze W.T. Grant's financial performance over the period leading up to the eventual liquidation of the company in 1975. Grant's management decided in the late 1960s to embark on an aggressive growth strategy to shift their stores from depressed inner-city locations to more attractive suburban ones.

Besides the brick and mortar investment, this strategy also entailed a large initial outlay for the new stores' inventory. To build volume, store managers were compensated to generate more sales.

Not surprisingly, credit approval became quite lax. This plan led to impressive sales and reported earnings gains for a time; but, with the pile-up of receivables and inventories, it also resulted in a cash flow problem. In fact, with poor and declining rates of return on capital, Grant's Free Cash Flow was negative for each year from 1968 to 1975. And, despite this need for new capital, dividends were maintained at 30 percent of earnings and not a penny of new equity was raised. Growth was financed with new debt, commercial paper, and leases. By 1974 the grim reaper was at the company's door.

W. T. Grant's management apparently forgot one important principle: growth without a commitment to careful capital management—earning an acceptable rate of return—is a sure formula for disaster. Their bankers forgot something, too. Risky expansions should be financed with equity, not with debt.

In sum, rapid growth can be a misleading indicator of added value because it can be generated simply by pouring capital into a business. Earning an acceptable rate of return is essential to creating value. Growth adds to value only when it is accompanied by an adequate rate of return. If returns are low, growth actually reduces value. (Just ask Saatchi and Saatchi.)

THE ROLE OF LEAD STEERS

How can it be true, as I claim, that the cash generated over the life of a business (adjusted for risk) is what determines share prices when most investors seem to be preoccupied with such traditional accounting measures as earnings, EPS, and earnings growth? The answer is that prices in the stock market, like all other prices, are set "at the margin" by the smartest money in the game, leaving the majority of investors as mere price-takers. The concept of marginal pricing—one of the most difficult in all economics to grasp—can be illustrated by the metaphor of the "Lead Steers" made popular by Joel Stern. He says, "If you want to know where a herd of cattle is heading, you need not interview every steer in the herd, just the lead steer."

The stock market works in very much the same way. While millions of people invest in the stock market, a relative handful of prominent investors account for the great majority of trades. For example, about 55 percent of the volume on the NYSE consists of block trades of 10,000 shares or more, and over two-thirds of all volume is attributable to trades of 5,000 shares or more. The importance of small, unsophisticated investors has been exaggerated in the press and, I am afraid, in the minds of many senior executives.

The price of oil is set in just this way, too. When I pull my car into a gas station, I may feel in some way responsible for determining the price of oil. But, no, I am just a price-taker. Be it cash or credit, the price is posted, and I can take or leave it. I realize now that the price of oil is set by professional oil traders who compete with each other to get the price right before the other traders do.

But even this characterization is not really accurate. For the astute traders I just tipped my hat to must in turn bow to the economic forces of supply and demand. They cannot make oil depart from the price that will clear the market—the one that will leave no excess supply or unsatisfied demand. You see, even the lead steers do not really lead. They too must follow the will of economic forces.

My point is this: Let's not confuse the process by which prices are set in the market with the economic forces that truly set market prices.

A Lead Steer Up Close

Getting a "lead steer" to reveal his true investment strategy is about as easy as getting a magician to disclose the secret to his tricks. Both prefer that you enjoy their performance without figuring out how it is done. As one particularly astute investor (who wishes to remain anonymous) put it to me: "Why should I popularize my approach—that's my edge."

But there are some who will draw the curtain back for a tantalizing peek at their magic. What they reveal goes far beyond a myopic preoccupation with next quarter's EPS. Consider, as but one example, O. Mason Hawkins, president of Southeastern Asset Management, Inc. (SAM), an investment management firm located in Memphis, Tennessee. Since hanging out a shingle in 1975, Hawkins has never had a down year, and only once has he underperformed the S&P 500—and this with a billion dollars under active management. According to CDA Investment Technologies (a firm which evaluates portfolio management), SAM was the fifth best money manager for the five years ending June 30, 1988, with an annualized return of 19.7 percent versus 14.4 percent for the market.

"WE'D RATHER GET WITH A GUY WHO PAYS HIMSELF $100,000 A YEAR AND
CAN MAKE MILLIONS ON HIS STOCK THAN SOMEONE... WHO'S MAKING A
MILLION DOLLARS A YEAR AND HAS A COUPLE HUNDRED SHARES OF HIS
STOCK... WE ARE LOOKING FOR A PARTNER RATHER THAN AN ADVERSARY
IN THE EXECUTIVE OFFICE."
—O. MASON HAWKINS—

Here is some straight bull from Mr. Hawkins:

Our investment philosophy is based on the approach of trying to buy stocks at a significant discount from what we appraise their private market value to be. There are several ways to do that.

The first method is to determine what the free cash flow is and can be in the coming business cycle under normalized conditions. Then we buy the company at a very reasonable multiple of that free cash flow.

Another way is liquidating value; we simply add up all the assets on the balance sheet, subtracting all the liabilities, and adjust for things like understated inventories or real estate, overfunded or underfunded pensions, overdepreciated plant and equipment, and trademarks, franchises and brandnames. We come up with a net value for what the company could be liquidated for on the courthouse steps, if it came to that, and buy the company at a significant discount.

We also take sales in the marketplace, arm's-length transactions between competent businessmen, and compare what they will pay for businesses versus the market value of the company we are looking at.

We talk with management, we talk with suppliers, we talk with competitors. However, we reach most of our conclusions by looking at the numbers and analyzing them.

Next comes the qualitative things, because we don't want to own stocks just because they are cheap . . . We are interested in companies whose insiders, management members and board members, have a vested interest in the company and who are adding to that position. We are looking for a partner rather than an adversary in the executive office.
—The Daily News, *April 29, 1986*

We're trying to avoid a situation like Phillips Petroleum, where management was virtually willing to destroy the company in order to maintain their positions.
—Pensions and Investment Age, *February 17, 1986*

We'd rather get with a guy who pays himself $100,000 a year and can make millions on his stock than someone . . . who's making a million dollars a year and has a couple hundred shares of his stock.
—Investor's Daily, *November 1, 1985*

Mason practices what he preaches. He sold sixty percent of his firm to employees and then invested the proceeds in a mutual fund that they manage. Hawkins admits, though, that having his own mother-in-law's money in the fund is his greatest motivation to perform well.

Mason Hawkins' record and philosophy is typical of the "lead steer" investors who truly set stock prices: they think like businessmen, not like accountants. Perhaps surprisingly, many of the lead steers have no formal association or identity with Wall Street, preferring the anonymity and perspective that is gained by distancing themselves from "the Street." You can't find them. They find you.

DIVIDENDS DO NOT MATTER

At this point I will make a bold statement. Not only do earnings and earnings growth not matter; dividends do not matter either.

In the economic model, paying dividends is an admission of failure—management's failure—to find enough attractive investment opportunities to use all available cash. Companies are valued for what they do, not for what they do not do. By paying dividends, management has less money available to fund growth. The value of profitable investment opportunities forgone is subtracted from share price.

If management chooses to raise debt or equity to replace the dividend, then current shareholders' interests are diluted by introducing new claims on future cash flow. Such a policy makes a company incur transactions costs for unnecessary financings, and forces investors to pay taxes on dividends that might otherwise be deferred as capital gains. So why pay dividends?

What if a company has exhausted its investment opportunities? Then it certainly would be better to pay dividends rather than to make unrewarding investments. In most cases, however, it would be even better to use the funds to buy back stock. Then only the investors who choose to sell will be taxed; and they will be taxed only on the gain realized after the basis in their shares is applied against the proceeds from the sale. Although the tax rate on capital gains is now the same as it is for dividends, so long as the tax basis in the shares is not zero investors will pay a lower tax on a capital gain. The Tax Reform Act of 1986 did not make dividends attractive, only less unattractive than before.

Moreover, if paying any dividends at all is thought to be advisable, then borrowing to pay them all at once is probably even better. One benefit is the corporate income taxes saved when debt replaces equity, and yet no additional tax burden is placed on investors. Shareholders will just pay in advance the discounted present value of the taxes they otherwise would have paid over time. Moreover, it will probably reassure investors to know that the tendency of cash-rich companies to overinvest in their undeserving basic businesses and to make overpriced acquisitions will be reined in by the obligation to service debt first. And, it may also bring about the transfer of a more significant equity stake into the hands of key managers and employees, thereby heightening their incentives to add value.

But I am getting ahead of the story at hand. I will discuss the benefits of such financial restructurings in greater detail later on in this book. For now, let me summarize the discussion thus far by saying that, depending upon where a company's cash flow is in relation to its investment needs, it makes sense either to pay no dividends at all or to pay them all at once. The middle of the road is the most reckless place to drive a company's dividend policy.

But the corporate perspective certainly is not all that matters on this question. What about investors? Do they want dividends?

Granted some may need cash for consumption, and thus may require a dividend. But they can create their own dividend by selling or borrowing against some of their shares or, better yet, by adding income-yielding bonds and preferred stocks to a non-dividend paying common stock portfolio. Investors who need cash do not need to get it from every component of their portfolio.

Even so, the payment of dividends actually taking place is out of all proportion to the consumption needs of investors. Most get reinvested back into the market, but only after the brokers' turnstile has been ticked. Besides, if a cash yield is so desirable, why have deep-discount bonds, which pay no cash return at all, become so popular? Much like a non-dividend paying common stock, the return on such bonds is entirely in the form of expected price appreciation.

Does paying a dividend make a stock less risky to own? Some argue that a bird in the hand (a dividend) is worth two in the bush (capital gains). But the retort is not that dividends not paid will show up as capital gains for sure, but that dividends that are paid are capital gains lost for sure. Stock prices fall by the amount of any dividends paid, never to be recouped. Paying certain dividends out of uncertain

earnings cannot make earnings, or common shares, any less risky. It only makes the residual capital gain that much riskier.

It is true that some investors will not buy the shares of companies that do not pay at least a nominal dividend. Will the share prices of companies that pay no dividends be penalized by not appealing to this group? Absolutely not. Once again, share prices are not set by a polling technique in which all investors have a vote on value. Prices in the stock market are set at the margin. So long as there are a sufficient number of investors with sufficient wealth who are not seeking dividends, companies that pay few or no dividends have no cause for concern. They will sell for their fair value.

How can the view that I am articulating for investors—namely, that "dividends do not matter"—be reconciled with the fact that dividend announcements often have a pronounced effect on stock prices? Managements and boards of directors apparently have conditioned investors to associate dividend increases with a healthy outlook and dividend cuts with impending catastrophe. For example, in 1983, Bethlehem Steel halved the dividend and the stock price collapsed. At the same time, management disclosed their intention to close basic steelmaking at the Lackawanna mill, a decision that would trigger the payment of one billion dollars in unfunded vested pension benefits.

Bethlehem's stock price would have collapsed no matter what had happened to the dividend. But, in light of the company's need for cash, cutting the dividend made sense. And thus, there is just a correlation, but not a true causal relationship, between dividend announcements and share prices. Radical changes in dividend policy simply tend to coincide with the release of other important news to the market.

The Evidence on Dividends

Finally, and most decisively, let us once again turn to definitive academic research to answer the question.

The most important empirical study on dividends appeared in the prestigious *Journal of Financial Economics* in 1974. Although it has been updated and retested on several occasions, the fundamental findings have withstood the test of time. The study, performed by Professors Fischer Black and Myron Scholes, tested whether the total returns achieved during the period 1936 to 1966 from 25 carefully-constructed portfolios depended upon the dividend yield or dividend payout ratios of the underlying stocks. Their analysis revealed that the return to investstors was explained by the level of risk, and was not at all affected by how the return was divided between dividends and capital gains. They found that within a given risk category, some stocks paid no dividends, some paid modest dividends, and some paid a lot of dividends, but all experienced the same overall rate of return over time.

Black and Scholes concluded that investors will do best by assuming that dividends do not matter and by ignoring both payout and yield in choosing their stocks (that is, they should worry about risk, diversification, taxes and value, but not dividends per se). Their advice to corporate managers is no less important than it is to investors: Do not formulate dividend policy in an attempt to influence shareholders' returns. Instead, set dividend policy in the context of the company's own investment needs and financing options, and then carefully explain it to investors.

THE MYTH OF MARKET MYOPIA

It is easy to imagine that the pressure put on money managers to perform each quarter will force them to ignore the long-term payoffs from farsighted business decisions and instead focus only on near-term results. Here is the popular view of a myopic stock market, as articulated by Donald N. Frey, the former CEO of Bell & Howell:

When the typical institutional portfolio in the U.S. has an annual turnover rate of 50% and some smaller ones have turnover rates of more than 200%, it is no surprise that American business is hobbled compared with foreign rivals ... Playing the market the way our money managers do ignores two critical factors: the time required to bring a product from development to market and the time required to redirect resources from a maturing business to a new one ... The pressure for short-term results puts unnecessary hurdles in the way of sound management. Investors' expectations for simultaneously high dividends on stocks, high interest rates on bonds, and rapid growth in the price of securities force managers to forgo many of their most promising ventures. Ultimately, these pressures rob consumers of future products, workers of future jobs, and investors of future profits.

Frey is joined in this view by Andrew C. Sigler, chairman and CEO of Champion International Corporation, a large paper products company:

The only pressure I have on me is short-term pressure. I announce that we're going to spend half a billion dollars at Courtland, Alabama, with a hell of a payout from redoing a mill and my stock goes down two points. So I finally caved in and announced I'm going to buy back some stock, which makes no sense. If the economy is supposedly run by corporations and corporations are supposed to invest and be competitive, buying back your own stock, if you have alternatives, makes no sense. But you can't fight it. The share price today is refined constantly by that proverbial young man looking at a CRT screen. There's an assigned P-E ratio based on what I did last quarter and what I'll do next quarter.

Now, in one sense, Frey and Sigler are right. Because rates of interest have been quite high this past decade, especially in real terms, distant payoffs are more heavily discounted by investors. Projects must pay off more quickly and handsomely in order to pass muster. That is just a fact of life with which all projects must contend.

After all, the amount of capital available for companies to invest is limited. It is constrained in the aggregate to an amount equal to just what individuals throughout the world choose to save. High real interest rates are the result of too many promising projects chasing too little savings. A high rate of interest is the market's way of attracting more savings with the one hand and discouraging less rewarding capital projects with the other in order to strike a balance between the available supply of and demand for capital.

For management to ignore this obvious market signal is to misallocate capital, to destroy wealth and welfare, and to attract raiders like bees to honey. Frey and Sigler seem not to understand that capital budgeting is the process of deciding which projects ought not to be funded so that other, even more promising ones can be.

But their allegations go farther still. They claim our economic system is fundamentally flawed because of the tendency of investors—mainly professional money managers—to be unduly shortsighted. If it were true that stock prices failed to reflect the true value of insightful investment decisions, then regulations preventing hostile corporate takeovers (a fate, I might add, that eventually befell Bell & Howell) might be in order.

Unfortunately—at least for those who believe in greater market regulation—their claims are refuted by both logic and observations of share prices. Economic logic says that a company's stock price should depend upon the cash expected to be generated over the entire life of the business—otherwise there are large profit opportunities for long-term investors. The simple fact that stocks trade at multiples of current earnings is *prima facie* evidence of the stock market's extended time horizon. For, with a stock selling at a multiple of, say, just 10 times earnings, it would have to be held for ten years for the earnings to recoup just the principal paid, and held indefinitely for an appropriate return on investment to be earned.

Moreover, differences in P/E ratios indicate that the market responds to the relative prospects for profitable growth. If all the market cared about was near-term earnings, wouldn't all companies sell for the same P/E ratio? But it is precisely those companies whose prospects for long-run growth and profitability are brightest that sell for the highest P/E multiples; and this is a strong sign of market sophistication.

The CEOs also go astray when they accuse institutional investors of impatience. The long-term nature of pension and life insurance liabilities suggests that most of the large institutional investors accused of a short-term mentality actually would be better off investing in risky stocks that promise a higher long-term payoff than more conservative investments are apt to provide.

And, apparently, the institutions do just that. A study undertaken by the SEC's economics staff shows that institutional investors own a far larger percentage of the shares of R&D-intensive companies than of more mature, blue-chip stocks. Far from indicating shortsightedness, this ownership pattern reveals patience and, indeed, a positive appetite for long-run payoffs.

But even if it is true that money managers are evaluated each quarter—and no doubt many are—it still does not logically follow that share price movements each quarter are dictated by that quarter's results. In fact, because share prices are forward looking, share price movements quarter-to-quarter must be determined by the change in outlook extending beyond that quarter into the indefinite future. For, if share price movements did respond myopically to quarterly results, a simple trading rule would exist: just buy "depressed" stocks (those where the most recent earnings understate the long-term outlook) and sell short overpriced ones (where current earnings overstate long-term value), and you will outperform the market over time. But such a simple investment rule does not work.

Most fundamentally, does the frenetic trading activity that Frey in particular disparages arise from a short-term horizon on the part of American investors? And does trading activity motivated by a quick payoff depress the value of companies investing for the long term? Not at all.

For every buyer there must be a seller, and for every seller a buyer. If both buyers and sellers are equally shortsighted, trading per se would have no effect on value. For if the seller is selling because of an unwarranted concern over a near-term earnings problem, is the buyer buying because of an unjustified enthusiasm about near-term earnings prospects? Trading volume simply does not affect the level of stock prices (a theme to which I will return shortly).

The real reason why the market rises or falls is simply that the lead steers decide that intrinsic value has changed. When this happens, trading volume may surge as investors adjust their portfolios to accommodate a new market value. It may seem as if the trading volume is what causes a change in value when, in fact, it is the trading volume that results from a change in value. Beware of correlation masquerading as a cause.

I believe that the increase in trading volume this past decade is best explained as a consequence of the deregulation of brokerage commissions in May 1976 and the automation of the brokerage industry, both of which have made the U.S. the low-cost producer of trades worldwide. Lower trading costs mean more trades, and more trades mean that even more information is being digested by market participants and actively impounded into stock market values. In my view, the growing demands placed on management to invest capital wisely actually are the result of an increasingly efficient and sophisticated capital market. They are not, as the CEOs assert, some new-found institutional focus on the short term at the expense of the long term. But, again, do not take my word for it. Nor the words of Frey or Sigler, for that matter. Let's consult the academic experts who have no axe to grind.

The Evidence on Market Myopia

Definitive evidence proving the market's far-sightedness comes from research performed by John McConnell of Purdue University and Chris Muscarella of Southern Methodist University. They examined share price reactions to announcements of capital spending plans (like Mr. Sigler's Courtland new machines), including research and development outlays. Because of the lag between making an investment and realizing its payoff, the immediate effect of an increase in a company's capital spending would be to reduce both its earnings and cash flow—a result Mr. Sigler is convinced leads inevitably to a markdown in a company's stock price.

Indeed, if the market were dominated by the callow, computer-driven automatons familiar to Mr. Sigler, then share prices would be expected to decline with almost any planned capital spending increase, no matter how significant might be the long-term payoff. If, however, the projects to be undertaken are generally sound—ones in which discounted cash flows over the lives of the investments offer promising returns—and if the market is dominated by astute, forward-looking lead steers, then share prices should rise despite any negative near-term accounting consequences. The converse would be true for an announced decrease in capital spending.

McConnell and Muscarella's evaluation of 547 capital spending announcements made by 285 different companies over the period 1975 to 1981 reveals a statistically significant share price appreciation for companies announcing an increase in capital spending, and a decrease in share price for firms announcing reductions.

Their findings do not imply that every single capital spending increase was greeted favorably (Sigler's Courtland project, for example, was not), only that most were. When in early 1984 Federal Express announced Zapmail, a service designed to preempt fax machines, the company's stock fell in price nearly $10 a share, from the mid-$40s to the mid-$30s. Several years later, the project was called off in the wake of a widespread proliferation of fax machines, and Federal's stock price rose by nearly $8 a share. Investors heaved a sigh of relief to learn that no more money would be poured into a black hole. The point, though, is that Federal Express's share price fell initially not because the market was unable to visualize the long-run payoff from the Zapmail project, but because it saw the consequences so clearly.

Will Sigler's Courtland project suffer a similar fate? Only time will tell. For now, he is free to rail against the stock market and to protest that spending half a billion dollars to redo a paper mill is the world's best use for that scarce capital (despite the fact that his stock price fell when the project was first announced and rose when, by repurchasing shares, he freed up funds for other companies to invest). Essen-

tially, then, we have one man's opinion arrayed against the collective wisdom of market investors who, in moving stock prices, are putting their money where their mouth is.

The R & D Issue. Returning to the research of McConnell and Muscarella, let me mention that they also discovered that share prices reacted no differently to announcements of stepped-up research and development that was to be immediately expensed against earnings than they did in cases of new capital expenditures to be added to the balance sheet. Here is the proof that R&D is a capital expenditure, not an expense, and should be capitalized onto a company's books just like any other capital expenditure that is intended to create an enduring value.

They also found that 111 capital spending announcements made by 72 public utilities over the same time period had, as expected, no discernible impact on share price. The explanation here is that regulators constrain public utilities to charging prices intended to provide only a zero net present value for new capital projects.

The McConnell/Muscarella study provides impressive evidence that, far from being myopic, the market:
- factors into stock prices a realistic estimate of the long-run payoff from management's current investment decisions;
- is able to distinguish value-adding from value-neutral opportunities; and
- does not care whether the accountants expense or capitalize value-building outlays.

The burden of proof lies on those who think otherwise.

SUPPLY AND DEMAND

Mr. Frey's aforementioned concern about excessive trading volume is particularly confusing to me because I have met with many CEOs who are concerned that their stock price is depressed because of insufficient trading activity, a view to which I also cannot subscribe.

Both misconceptions hinge on the belief that share prices are set by a relationship between supply and demand, and that management accordingly can (and should) market its common stock in much the same fashion as any other consumer product. After all, if the number of common shares outstanding is fixed, would not advertising in concert with frequent analysts' presentations spark demand for the shares and thereby raise their price through a surge in volume?

Don Carter, Chairman and Chief Executive Officer of The Carter Organization, the world's largest proxy solicitation and corporate governance firm, is (quite predictably) a proponent of the supply/demand model of stock price behavior. "Every company," he asserts,

has a shareholder family and that family consists of many components: mom and pop shareholders, institutional shareholders, management holdings, and speculative holdings. We identify those holders and generate two-way communication by mail or visit, to learn why they own their stock. Their answer will help us in our search for new investors with similar motives. Our job is to make sure that those who are in the stock stay in it, and those who are not—come in and join the party. When you have more buyers than sellers, the stock price will rise—period. It's still supply and demand that determines stock price.

Bell South has in the past adopted this "Madison Avenue" approach to Wall Street. For some time, hardly a week would pass without a full-page advertisement appearing in the *Wall Street Journal* touting the company's investment appeal. After the reader was informed of a little-known fact—namely, that rapid growth in population in the southeastern part of the United States is expected to continue—Bell South would let us know that they were preeminently positioned to benefit from this trend. We were then advised to call our broker and purchase their shares.

To repeat our opening question: Will such a campaign increase share price? It will not, because it simply is not true that the supply of a company's shares is fixed. Instead, supply is perfectly flexible by virtue of options and short-selling. The lead steers can combine call options on Bell South stock with less risky T-bills to create a position equivalent to owning Bell South stock, but without owning Bell South stock directly. Or, they could sell Bell South shares short—that is, sell shares they do not own. When this happens, the total number of shares owned by all investors will exceed the number of shares that have been issued by the company, with the difference being accounted for by the short sales. Would you be surprised to learn that Bell South has one of the largest short positions of any stock on the Big Board?

Another, though admittedly less precise, approach to recreating the unique investment opportunity that Bell South claims it represents would be for investors to purchase certain proportions of the shares of other regional telephone companies, such as Bell Atlantic, along with, say, Walmart, or Food Lion—retailers who, like Bell South, are benefiting from the burgeoning growth of the Southeast.

Through these and other actions, sophisticated investors can create an artificial supply of a company's shares or close proxies for those shares in order to offset any surge in demand a PR campaign might generate. And the evidence on this issue reveals that efforts to promote a company's appeal to investors lead to an increase in trading volume, but not in stock price, thereby benefiting brokers (and maybe Don Carter), but not shareholders.

An elegant indictment of trading volume comes from Warren Buffet, the highly-regarded Chairman of Berkshire Hathaway:

One of the ironies of the stock market is the emphasis on activity. Brokers, using terms such as "marketability" and "liquidity," sing the praises of companies with high share turnover . . . But investors should understand that what is good for the croupier is not good for the customer. A hyperactive market is the pickpocket of enterprise.

Flexibility in the demand for a company's shares also makes trading volume an unimportant determinant of value. Investors for the most part are not interested in buying shares of stock in only a single company. To diversify risk, investors hold a portfolio of stocks. The attributes that an investor wants a portfolio to exhibit—in terms of income, risk, potential for capital appreciation, exposure to the business cycle, etc.—can be obtained by selecting shares from among a wide variety of easily substitutable companies. When shares are purchased to play a role in a portfolio, the shares of stocks in individual companies will be priced much like undifferentiated commodities; advertising will serve to raise only volume, not price.

The Evidence on Supply and Demand

Fortunately, this important issue has also been the subject of expert academic research. A test conducted by Professor Myron Scholes as part of his doctoral dissertation at the University of Chicago provides strong evidence that share prices are determined by intrinsic values and not by an interaction between supply and demand.

His ingenious study examined secondary offerings where already-issued shares of a company's common stock are sold by investors who own them. Because no new shares are sold, a secondary offering by itself should not affect the intrinsic cash-flow value of a company. And yet, a supply-demand enthusiast would predict that, given a downward sloping demand schedule, additional shares could be sold only at a discount from market price. The greater the number of shares unleashed on the market, presumably the greater would be the discount required to induce investors to take up the shares. Another implication of the supply-demand view is that the price decline would likely be temporary. After the surplus supply of shares is absorbed into the market, a more normal share value should return.

Secondary offerings thus provide a very clear test of whether intrinsic value or supply and demand best explains how individual company's share prices are set.

Professor Scholes did find that secondary offerings reduced share price (an average of two percent measured against the market), but the price decline was unrelated to the size of the offering. It is reasonable to assume that secondary issues are timed by sellers to occur when they believe the shares are overvalued. Scholes concluded, therefore, that the price decline was caused by the adverse connotation associated with the decision to sell, and not the temporary "overhang" of supply.

He obtained further support for this interpretation by dividing the sellers into various groups. The largest price decline was associated with sales by management (as when Charles Schwab sold large blocks of Bank of America stock shortly before a more devastating decline in share price), the next largest by venture capitalists and by others close to the company, and little, if any, price decline was detected following large block sales by third-party institutions. Scholes study showed that the quality of information rather than the quantity of shares traded is what determines the depth of the price discount.

Scholes traced the price decline several months after the offering and found that it persisted, though not in every case, as some shares recovered in value and others fell further. But, as a statistical statement, the price decline apparently was in response to some likely fundamental decline in the company's prospective economic performance.

Scholes' research offers convincing and reassuring evidence that stock prices are set by the lead steers' appraisal of intrinsic values (that is, the prospect for cash generation and risk), not supply and demand.

Lest the case be overstated, I add that that supply and demand do play a role in determining share values, but only in the aggregate. The intersection of the aggregate demand for capital relative to its worldwide supply determines the underlying level of real interest rates and hence, indirectly, the value of all stock markets. But it is only in setting the value of the market as a whole, and not for any single company, that supply and demand operate.

There are two important implications of Scholes' research. First, the objective of investor relations should be to revise expectations, rather than to stimulate demand. To increase share price, management must convince the right investors—the "lead steers"—to pay more, not simply convince more investors in the herd to buy. It is unfortunate that most of what passes for investor relations is "retail" as opposed to "wholesale" in orientation, aims to inform the herd and not the lead steers, and stimulates volume instead of price.

Second, the price decline associated with raising new equity capital can be mitigated through a clear program of financial communication and by raising equity through a pre-announced sequence of small issues (ideally a 415 shelf registration). Investment bankers' protestations about the "market overhang" from a shelf registration should be discounted as an obvious attempt to use the discredited supply-demand argument to their own benefit.

IN CONCLUSION

Earnings, earnings per share, and earnings growth are misleading measures of corporate performance. Earnings are diminished by bookkeeping entries having nothing to do with recurring cash flow, and are charged with such value-building capital outlays as research and development, all in an attempt to placate lenders' desire to assess liquidation value. EPS at best measures only the quantity of earnings, but the quality of earnings reflected in the P/E multiple matters, too. Rapid earnings growth can be manufactured by pouring capital into substandard projects; earning an adequate rate of return is far more important than growing rapidly.

While many investors are fooled by accounting shenanigans, the investors who matter are not. Stock prices are not set through a polling technique where all investors have an equal vote. They are set rather by a select group of "lead steers" who look through misleading accounting results to arrive at true values. The rest of the herd, though blissfully ignorant of why the price is right, is well protected by the informed judgments of the "lead steers."

While it is fashionable to think so, the market is not myopic. The investors who set stock prices take into account the likely payoff from a capital project, no matter how distant, but discount it for the additional investment, risk, and time involved in getting there. On those occasions when a company's stock price responds unfavorably to a new capital project, it probably is not because the market is unable to visualize the eventual payoff. The real reason is that the market predicts that the long-run return will be inadequate; and its judgment will prove to be right more often than not. The record shows conclusively that betting against the market is simply not rewarding.

The best research on the subject shows that paying dividends does not enhance the total return received by investors over time. But paying dividends may deprive worthwhile projects of capital, or may force the company and investors to incur unnecessary transactions costs. And because boards of directors usually are loathe to cut the dividend except in the most dire circumstances, dividends become an additional and unnecessary fixed cost of running the business. Returning excess cash through periodic share repurchases, or a large, one-time, special dividend (with future dividends suspended to support the repayment of debt) is likely to be more rewarding than paying out a stream of dividends over time.

Stimulating investors' demand for shares will increase share volume, but not share price, benefiting brokers, but not shareholders. Lead steers head off a stampeding herd of investors by selling shares short or buying puts, providing an artificial supply of shares to siphon off any temporary surge in demand. To increase share price through more effective financial communication, management needs to convince the right investors that the company is worth more, not just persuade more investors to buy the stock.

The sophisticated investors, or "lead steers," who set stock prices, care about the generation of cash and the risks taken over the entire life of the business. This is the economic model of corporate value creation.

Despite the impressive evidence assembled in the academic community in support of an economic model of value, many companies still forsake truly economic decisions in deference to an earnings totem. How many senior managers of publicly-traded companies, for example, relish the thought of switching to LIFO to save taxes, gladly ignore goodwill amortization when an acquisition is contemplated, and care not a whit about the hit to earnings suffered when capital spending is increased? Not many, I suspect. They have been hypnotized by the cant of the popular press, sell-side security analysts, and many investment bankers and accountants into believing the myth that the market wants earnings, and wants it now. To make matters much worse, their incentive compensation often is tied to near-term earnings and earnings-related measures, so that they cannot afford to let their common sense be their guide.

What is the answer? Senior managers and boards of directors must be educated about how the stock market really works, and their compensation schemes must change accordingly.

HOW RATIONAL INVESTORS DEAL WITH UNCERTAINTY

(OR, REPORTS OF THE DEATH OF EFFICIENT MARKETS THEORY ARE GREATLY EXAGGERATED)

*by Keith C. Brown,
University of Texas at Austin,
W. V. Harlow, Salomon Brothers Inc.
and Seha M. Tinic,
University of Texas at Austin*

M uch academic research in finance in the past quarter century has been devoted to examining the proposition that corporate securities are priced by "rational" investors in an "efficient market." Stated most simply, the proposition says that the intensive pursuit of large returns by stock market investors ensures that, for the vast majority, only modest ones will be had. This argument, which has been refined and tested as the "efficient markets hypothesis" (EMH), could well be described as the foundation of modern financial theory.

* This article is based on our paper, "Risk Aversion, Uncertain Information, and Market Efficiency," *Journal of Financial Economics* 22 (1988), 355-385. The opinions and analyses presented herein are those of the authors and do not necessarily represent the views of Salomon Brothers Inc.

In the 1960s and 1970s, finance scholars amassed a large body of empirical evidence attesting to the efficiency of capital markets. So extensive was this research, and so consistently supportive in its findings, that Professor Michael Jensen of the Harvard Business School has called the EMH the best-documented proposition in all of the social sciences.[1] And, besides dominating academic research for two decades, the EMH and valuation models like the Capital Asset Pricing Model have made significant inroads into Wall Street thinking and practice. Currently, for example, over $150 billion is invested in "index" funds—those which deliberately refrain from active investment strategies and instead attempt simply to mimic the broad market.

Professional money managers, needless to say, have never looked kindly on the EMH. Among many top corporate executives, too—especially those who would like to attribute the bulk of corporate raiders' profits to systematic market undervaluation—the idea of investor rationality arouses skepticism. And when you add to these more or less predictable sources of resistance the heightened political concern about stock market volatility, especially in the wake of the October '87 Crash, proponents of the EMH seem to find themselves in an increasingly defensive position these days.

Much of the criticism, however, stems from a faulty understanding of what the theory really claims for itself. We will begin here by trying to dispel some of the misconception by explaining what economists mean when they speak of an "efficient market."

Efficient markets theory is, at bottom, simply an extension to capital markets of the "zero profits theorem" that economists have long applied to competitive goods markets. Briefly stated, the EMH holds that competition among investors for information ensures that the current prices of widely traded financial assets are "unbiased" predictors of the future values of those securities. The EMH thus does *not* say that today's price is the "right" price, but only that it is an "unbiased" indicator of future value—that is, neither too high nor too low on average. And, therefore, a company's future stock price (adjusted for risk and for general market movements which affect all stocks) is equally likely to be higher or lower than today's price.

For corporate management, then, today's stock price can be understood as the market's collective estimate—although a "noisy" estimate, to be sure—of the present value of the company's future risky cash flows (or, more precisely, the "certainty equivalents" of those flows). And unless one has significant inside information (or can confidently predict the the future direction of the market as a whole), the current price may well be the most reliable estimate of the value of the company *as it is currently being run*.

For investors contemplating purchase of a company's stock, the theory implies that they should expect to earn a "normal" rate of return—nothing more, nothing less—*at any given time* they choose to invest. And, in fact, the well-documented failure of the vast majority of professional fund managers to outperform market-wide averages consistently is one of the strongest pieces of testimony to the efficiency of our financial markets.

RECENT ACADEMIC CHALLENGES: THE OVERREACTION HYPOTHESIS

Over the last few years, however, in addition to the natural skepticism of practitioners, the EMH has begun to face stronger challenges from within the academic community. In the late 1970s, to be sure, a number of "anomalies" were detected that appeared to provide investors with "trading rules" that would allow them to earn consistently above-average returns. For example, one could buy a portfolio of stocks with low P/E ratios or buy a portfolio of small capitalization stocks in December to take advantage of the "January effect." But most of these anomalies may have little bearing on the validity of the EMH. They may instead be the result of flawed models of the relationship between risk and expected returns.

More serious charges against the EMH, however, have arisen from fairly recent studies claiming to have discovered two distinct, but related forms of investor irrationality: (1) "excessive" long-run stock price volatility and (2) short-term investor "overreaction" to the news of dramatic financial events. Because our own research concerns the second of these two issues, we concentrate our attention largely on the question of investor overreaction. (The research on long-run market volatility is summarized very briefly in footnote 6 below.)

Recent studies by Werner DeBondt and Richard Thaler purport to demonstrate that both the market-wide responses to general economic news and the

---

1. Michael Jensen, "Some Anomalous Evidence Regarding Market Efficiency," *Journal of Financial Economics* 6 (1978), 95-101.

stock price reactions to individual company "events" tend to overshoot their "equilibrium" levels—and then only gradually find their way back to those levels. That is, the market as a whole (and the price of individual stocks as well) systematically exaggerates the economic consequences of major events by raising prices too high when the news is good and cutting prices too sharply when the news is bad. In so doing, the studies argue, capital markets are providing investors with consistently exploitable opportunities for abnormal profits.[2]

In an efficient market, by contrast, prices are expected to respond to major events by moving quickly (if not "instantly") to their new equilibrium levels. How do we know that prices have moved to their proper levels? The answer is that future price movements from these new levels should turn out to be "randomly distributed" around these new levels. In such a market, although investors will certainly overreact in some cases, they learn from their mistakes —because such mistakes, after all, are costly to them. And thus the cases in which investors overreact should be balanced by others in which they "underreact," such that subsequent adjustments, on average, should be roughly equal to zero. This, in effect, was what Eugene Fama found in his classic 1965 study, "The Behavior of Stock Market Prices."[3]

The recent findings of DeBondt and Thaler seem to imply, however, that investors do not learn from their past mistakes and that they consistently misread new information. Formulated as the "Overreaction Hypothesis" (OH), their argument suggests that large movements in stock prices are followed, on average, by large adjustments in the opposite direction. The hypothesis also predicts that the larger the initial price change (that is, the bigger the "surprise" to the market), the larger will be the amount of the initial overreaction, and hence the greater the subsequent price adjustment.

Our Findings

Over the past several years, we have studied this issue of market overreaction and come to a different

conclusion. We too observed one of the findings that DeBondt and Thaler reported—the tendency of large stock price declines to be followed by a series of small upward adjustments. But we also made a discovery that contradicts their Overreaction Hypothesis: namely, that large stock price *increases* are also accompanied by small positive (or at least non-negative) adjustments, and not by the negative adjustments predicted by DeBondt and Thaler.[4]

In this article, we present a modified version of the EMH that we call the Uncertain Information Hypothesis (UIH). As noted above, the EMH, at least in its traditional form, starts with the assumption that investors have "complete" information and are thus able to move stock prices quickly to their new proper levels. Our UIH model attempts to extend efficient markets theory by showing how investors would respond "rationally" in situations of major uncertainty—those in which the assumption of complete information clearly does not hold.

As we will argue in the pages that follow, great uncertainty among investors leads, at least initially, to heightened price volatility and thus greater risk for investors. Because investors require higher returns for bearing greater risks, they respond to favorable as well as unfavorable surprise events by setting stock prices, on average, below their expected values. As the uncertainty over the eventual outcome is gradually clarified, subsequent price changes will tend to be positive, on average, regardless whether the initial event was good or bad. In this sense, positive price adjustments following major shocks are better understood as rational responses to increased risk than as chronic overreactions by the investing public.[5]

THE UNCERTAIN INFORMATION HYPOTHESIS

The standard version of the EMH is based on the clearly unrealistic assumption that investors have immediate access to all of the information they need to revise security prices in a definitive, once-and-for-all manner. In the real world, of course, some events are so little anticipated and of such consequence that

2. For the original specification of this proposition, see W. DeBondt and R. Thaler, "Does the Stock Market Overreact?", *Journal of Finance* 40 (1985), 793-805. Subsequent investigations were also performed in J. Howe, "Evidence on Stock Market Overreaction," *Financial Analysts Journal* 42 (1986), 74-77 and W. DeBondt and R. Thaler, "Further Evidence on Investor Overreaction and Stock Market Seasonality," *Journal of Finance* 42 (1987), 557-581.

3. E. Fama, "The Behavior of Stock Market Prices", *Journal of Business* 38 (1965), 34-105.

4. See K. Brown and V. Harlow, "Market Overreaction: Magnitude and Intensity", *Journal of Portfolio Management* 14 (1988), 6-13.

5. The notion that a short-run pattern of stock price increases following major price declines is consistent with a market comprised of rational, risk-averse investors has some precedent in the finance literature. See R. Merton, "On Estimating the Expected Return on the Market: An Exploratory Investigation," *Journal of Financial Economics* 2 (1980), 225-243.

their ultimate effect on stock prices cannot be immediately determined. In the face of such uncertainty, our theory says, investors effectively form what economists refer to as "conditional probability distributions." Such distributions can be visualized as decision-tree-like diagrams that lay out a number of possible outcomes and assign probabilities to each. By multiplying the value of each possible outcome by its probability, one arrives at an "expected value" for the company's shares. (In the Appendix, we provide a detailed illustration of this process.)

But, as our version of the EMH goes on to say, because of the increased uncertainty and thus greater risk attending such events, investors also *immediately* discount the value of the firm *below* the expected value of this probability distribution. This discount on the shares then disappears gradually, along with the uncertainty that gave rise to it.

For example, upon the unexpected death of a company's talented CEO, the stockholders will quickly mark down the value of the company's shares. But a more precise assessment of the consequences will not be possible until the market learns more about the company's plans for a successor. So, in the immediate aftermath of the announcement, the best that investors will be able to do is to reset stock prices based on a subjective "guess" (or, more precisely, a probability distribution of guesses) about the longer-range effect. And, given investors' aversion to risk, this first guess is more likely to fall below than above the eventual value.

The point of this example is that the unanticipated information affects investors in two ways. First, as the bad news is initially received, projections of the fortunes of the firm in question are immediately revised downward. Second, the level of uncertainty facing investors in this company increases, causing a *further reduction* in the value of the firm's shares. Thus, even if this increase in uncertainty is not permanent, it nevertheless represents a potential source of risk for which investors will demand to be compensated (at least until the source of the risk is removed).

A similar market reaction can be envisioned in the case of unexpectedly good news. Suppose that a company announces it has developed a new technology that promises to reduce its production costs significantly. As in the previous example, to the extent that this information takes investors by surprise, any immediate adjustments to the firm's stock price will be based on a crude forecast of the ultimate consequences of the event. While such an announcement should cause an overall increase in the value of the firm, it might also raise the level of uncertainty about its future performance—which would cause the stock price increase to be less than otherwise.

Of course, we could also have constructed other examples where an event might actually reduce uncertainty. In fact, it is entirely reasonable to suggest that certain news releases—such as the announcement of the jury's verdict in a closely contested trial—might have the effect of decreasing the riskiness of holding corporate shares. Our UIH model simply assumes that major surprises will typically increase the variability and risk of stock returns.

Contrast with the Overreaction Hypothesis

In cases of bad news, then, the pattern of investors' responses predicted by our Uncertain Information Hypothesis will be indistinguishable from that predicted by the Overreaction Hypothesis. That is, the initial decline in stock prices will be followed, on average, by a price increase. The difference between the two theories becomes apparent only in the case of good news. In contrast to the Overreaction Hypothesis, our model predicts what would appear to be an underreaction; that is, an initial price increase followed, on average, by a further increase.

These propositions are demonstrated graphically in Figure 1. For purposes of comparison, Panel A shows the adjustment of stock prices to bad news under the traditional EMH. The arrival of bad news drives the value of the security down from its previous level, P, to P_B; and there is no further adjustment after the initial response. In this case, the stock price moves immediately to its new "intrinsic" value.

In contrast, Panel B shows the pattern of price changes that would accompany unfavorable surprises under the Uncertain Information Hypothesis (and under the Overreaction Hypothesis as well). According to our UIH model, the arrival of bad news would not only decrease the expected cash flows of the security but also increase their systematic risk. With this additional uncertainty, the present value of the "certainty equivalents" of the risky cash flows is P^*_B, which could be significantly less than P_B in a stock market dominated by risk-averse investors. But, as the uncertainty is resolved, the price increases to P_B from P^*_B to reflect the associated reduction of investor risk.

THE UIH ALSO SUGGESTS THAT, TO THE EXTENT INVESTORS' RISK AVERSION
DECREASES WITH HIGHER LEVELS OF STOCK PRICES, THE SUBSEQUENT
UPWARD PRICE ADJUSTMENTS AFTER MAJOR UNFAVORABLE SURPRISES ARE
EXPECTED TO BE GREATER THAN THE ADJUSTMENTS
FOLLOWING FAVORABLE EVENTS.

FIGURE 1
STOCK PRICE CHANGES IN RESPONSE TO UNFAVORABLE AND FAVORABLE UNCERTAIN INFORMATION

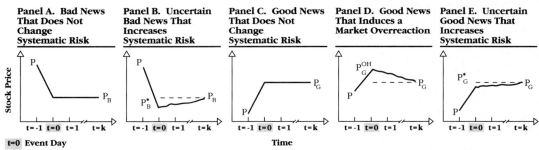

The effect of favorable surprises on stock prices is shown in Panels C, D, and E. In the standard EMH, in which the consequences of the news are immediately and clearly known, the price of the stock increases quickly from P to P_G; and there is no adjustment thereafter. The Overreaction Hypothesis (illustrated in Panel D) predicts that the price will overshoot the mark, rising to P_G^{OH} and then falling back to P_G.

Our UIH model, in contrast to both the standard EMH and the OH, suggests that if the good news also increases the uncertainty about the stock's future cash flows, then the price will initially rise only to P^*_G, and then gradually adjust further up to P_G as the uncertainty is dispelled. As in the case of bad news, this delayed price adjustment is caused by investors' rational demand for higher expected returns to compensate them for the heightened uncertainty.

Although the preceding discussion is couched in terms of favorable and unfavorable surprises affecting the systematic risks of individual stocks, our UIH model is equally relevant to market-wide surprises that affect the values of broad-based stock indexes. The UIH claims that major favorable and unfavorable surprises about the economy will typically increase the risk of holding common stocks in general. Thus, the returns on market portfolios following major shocks would also

be expected to exhibit the same "asymmetric" pattern (i.e., apparent overreaction to bad news, underreaction to good) shown in Panels B and E in Figure 1. Moreover, the UIH also suggests that, to the extent investors' risk aversion decreases with higher levels of stock prices, the subsequent upward price adjustments after major unfavorable surprises are expected to be greater than the adjustments following favorable events.

The heart of our UIH theory, then, can be summarized by the following propositions: (1) on average, stock return variability will increase following the announcements of major unanticipated events; (2) the average price adjustments following the initial market reactions to both "negative" and "positive" events will be positive (or, in the case of the latter, at least non-negative); and (3) to the extent the market's risk-aversion decreases as the level of stock prices increase, post-event price increases will be larger for negative events than for positive ones. The important point here is that the portfolios are priced rationally in both situations, and there are no *ex ante* opportunities for investors to earn riskless profits by "arbitraging" price overreactions or underreactions. Under this scenario, one only has the *illusion* that investors consistently overreact to bad new and underreact to good.[6]

---

6. It should be noted that the debate between the OH and the UIH is related to another class of market efficiency tests that focus on what is known as "mean reversion" in security prices. The mean reversion hypothesis can be visualized by showing a path of stock prices that swing wildly ("excessively") back and forth across some "trend line" measure of "intrinsic" value. In effect, it suggests a long-run pattern of overreactions followed regularly by "corrections."

Several recent studies have examined this proposition. (See, in particular, E. Fama and K. French, "Dividend Yields and Expected Stock Returns", Journal of Financial Economics 22 (1988), 3-25; J. Poterba and L. Summers, "Mean Reversion in Stock Prices: Evidence and Implications", *Journal of Financial Economics* 22 (1988), 27-60; and E. Fama and K. French, "Permanent and Temporary Components of Stock Prices", Journal of Political Economy 96 (1988), 246-273.)

The general conclusion that has been drawn from the evidence amassed to date is that there appear to be "predictable" return components in security prices. More precisely, it has been shown that from 25 to 45 percent of the variability of stock returns over a three- to five-year time horizon can be predicted from returns in previous periods.

As intriguing as these results are, they can still be "explained" in two different ways: (1) investors are irrational and thus prices often depart from fundamental values in a way that should provide the opportunity for abnormal profits; or (2) both the risks borne and the risk premiums demanded by rational investors change significantly over time in ways as not yet fully understood. Of course, the OH is consistent with the former explanation while the UIH is consistent with the latter.

TABLE 1
DESCRIPTIVE STATISTICS
FOR THE TWO SAMPLES
OF UNANTICIPATED
EVENTS USED TO TEST
THE UIH

Sample	Sample Size	Mean	Standard Deviation	MAX	MIN
Market Index:					
Positive Events	36	1.34%	0.40%	2.67%	1.03%
Negative Events	39	− 1.27	0.42	− 1.00	− 3.47
Individual Firms:					
Positive Events	4,788	4.26%	1.77%	22.09%	2.50%
Negative Events	4,317	− 4.06	1.79	− 2.50	− 30.63

TESTING THE UIH

Defining Unexpected Events

As we have outlined the theory, the UIH attempts to explain investor reactions to major unanticipated events. In devising a test of our theory, the first question that arises is, how do we know when a "major" event has occurred? To avoid introducing any subjective bias on the part of the researcher, we defined "events" using strictly quantitative criteria.

In the case of general market reactions, all daily price movements greater than one percent of a broad market index were considered as events.[7] Over the 24-year period from 1962 through 1985, we found 75 such events: 36 positive and 39 negative.

In the case of individual companies, we deemed as events all daily percentage returns (adjusted for risk and expected return) greater than 2.5 percent by the 200 largest companies in the S&P 500.[8] As expected, there were far more company-specific than market-wide events, even with the difference in the sample criterion. Over the same 24-year period, we found 9,105 events, of which 4,788 were positive and 4,317 were negative. (Table 1 summarizes the statistical characteristics of both samples of events.)

The Effect of Surprises on Volatility

Because the primary prediction of the UIH is that major surprises will tend to increase investor uncertainty, our first task was to compare the level of price volatility before and after the events. To allow for direct comparison of events that took place over a 24-year period, we defined the date of the event to be "Day 0" for all cases in both samples regardless of where it fell in calendar time. Then, a subsequent period running from Day +1 to Day +60 was examined in order to estimate the appropriate measure of "post-event" volatility.

In measuring pre-event (or "normal") volatility, we used different measures for the two different samples. For the sample of market-wide surprises, risk was measured as the variance of the observed stock price returns. We compared the level of post-event variance to the same measure calculated by using all "non-event" days; that is, all days during the 1962-1985 sample period that did not fall in one of the 60-day periods that followed the 75 surprises.

For the sample of individual companies, we measured the stock price "betas" (or covariances) over the period two hundred days prior to the event (Day −200 to Day −1), and then compared those to the betas calculated over the sixty-day period following the event (Day +1 to Day +60).

General Market Volatility. In Panel A of Table 2, we report the results of the return variance analysis on our market-wide sample in the form of three different sets of data: (1) all non-event days; (2) all post-event days following favorable surprises; and (3) all post-event days following unfavorable surprises. As shown there, major surprises appear to affect investor risk precisely as the UIH predicts. The "F-statistics" are measures of the statistical significance of the difference

---

7. More precisely, we determined that an "event" had occurred if the market return on any given day departed from its "expected value" by more than one percent. The expected return to the market index was estimated by the average daily return of an equally-weighted index of all NYSE and ASE companies over the 60 days immediately preceding the event. We chose such a seemingly small number as one percent on the assumption that, because of the natural diversification within the market portfolio, deviations from the expected daily return would not have to be extremely large to be considered a bona fide surprise.

8. Expected returns were estimated differently for the individual firm events than for the market index events. Remember that investors' expected (or, alternatively, "required") returns are a function of risk. And because major surprises change the level of risk, they can be expected to change expected returns as well. Consequently, before calculating the set of abnormal post-event price changes, we first re-estimated expected returns for both the general market index and the individual companies using data from a time period *not affected by* the event.

TABLE 2
CHANGES IN RISK INDUCED BY UNANTICIPATED EVENTS

Panel A. Marketwide Events

Sample	Number of Observations	Variance	F-Statistic for Difference with (i)
(i) Nonevent Days	1,936	0.00004862	—
(ii) Postevent Days: Positive Events	2,160	0.0006342	1.30***
(ii) Postevent Days: Negative Events	2,340	0.00006515	1.34***

*** denotes significance at the 1% critical level

Panel B. Individual Firm Events

Period	Positive Events	Negative Events
Avg. Beta Coefficient:		
Preevent (Day-200 to-1)	1.00441	1.00875
Postevent (Day +1 to +60)	1.05615	1.07257
Subsequent Days (Day +61 to +260)	1.02472	1.03285
F-Statistics:		
Preevent-Postevent	22.74**	31.87**
Preevent-Subsequent	4.56*	6.09**
Postevent-Subsequent	8.42**	12.34**

** and * denote significance at the 5% and 10% critical levels, respectively

between the non-event risk level and the two post-event risk levels; and they suggest that we can be quite confident in concluding that the events in question are consistently followed by a measurable increase in general market volatility. Our analysis also suggests that, although negative events had a somewhat larger impact on risk than positive ones, the difference was not statistically significant.

Company-Specific Volatility. For the sample of individual company events, the results listed in Panel B of Table 2 are equally striking. As mentioned above, for each of 9,105 events we compared the firm's beta before and after the event. Also, in order to get a better sense of whether these company-specific volatility changes were permanent, we computed a third beta for each event over a time period judged to be well beyond the event itself (from Day +61 to Day +260).

Two conclusions can be drawn from these findings. First, as with the market-wide sample, unanticipated events result in a sharp increase in the systematic risk of individual firms. The increases averaged 5.2 percent (1.056/1.004) for favorable surprises and 6.3 percent (1.073/1.009) for negative ones. Second, it is also clear that much of this risk increase is temporary. As shown in the column labeled "Subsequent Days," the average betas for both positive and negative events trend back toward

their pre-event levels.[9] Nevertheless, they continue to remain somewhat above their values prior to the surprise. Thus, it appears that unanticipated events have both a permanent and a temporary effect on investors' perception of company risk.

Figure 2 provides a graphic illustration of the increases in total risk (that is, variance as distinguished from covariance (or beta)) that accompany unexpected changes in the stock prices of individual companies.[10] The graph shows the changes in the "cross-sectional" variances computed separately for each of the positive and negative individual companies over the period Day –60 to Day +60. Like the data summarized in Table 2, Figure 2 also demonstrates that much of the increase in risk is only temporary.[11]

These findings about volatility are consistent, then, with the primary prediction of the UIH: namely, a large increase in uncertainty (as reflected in price volatility) followed by a gradual resolution of that uncertainty. Whether investors receive additional compensation for bearing this additional risk, as the UIH also predicts, is the question to which we now turn.

The Effect of Surprises on Prices

Having established that major surprises increase price volatility, we then calculated the daily "abnor-

9. Specifically, the level of risk in the Day +61 to Day +260 interval retains only 39% (=[1.02472 – 1.00441]/[1.05615 – 1.00441]) of the buildup accumulated during the postevent period for positive events and 38% (=[1.03285 – 1.00875]/[1.07257 – 1.00875]) for negative surprises.

10. This method of calculating the volatility for individual securities has the advantage of not being tied to any explicit return-generating relationship, such as

the single index market model. It is apparent from this display, however, that our earlier conclusions are still valid.

11. To be exact, allowing the –60 to Day –5) and (Day +5 to Day +60) intervals to proxy for the portion of the pre-event and post-event periods outside the immediate vicinity of the event, the average cross-sectional variance increased from 0.000339 to 0.000390 for positive surprises and from 0.000357 to 0.000399 for negative ones.

TABLE 3
CUMULATIVE AVERAGE RESIDUALS FOLLOWING UNANTICIPATED EVENTS

Panel A: Marketwide Events

Event Day	Positive Events (N = 36)		Negative Events (N = 39)	
	CAR (%)	T-Stat	CAR (%)	T-Stat
+ 1	0.014	0.10	0.145	0.96
+ 2	−0.084	−0.48	0.454	2.20**
+ 3	0.007	0.03	0.669	2.67**
+ 4	0.194	0.81	0.685	2.33**
+ 5	0.403	1.54	0.630	1.85*
+10	0.493	1.31	1.047	2.23**
+20	1.346	2.53**	1.360	2.07**
+30	1.360	2.06**	1.550	1.99*
+40	1.183	1.53	1.227	1.47
+50	1.527	1.67	1.349	1.41
+60	0.542	0.54	1.499	1.43

Panel B: Individual Firm Events

Event Day	Positive Events (N = 4,788)		Negative Events (N = 4,317)	
	CAR (%)	T-Stat	CAR (%)	T-Stat
+ 1	0.118	3.69**	0.045	1.28
+ 2	0.153	3.27**	0.112	2.22**
+ 3	0.095	1.65*	0.139	2.29**
+ 4	0.075	1.13	0.210	3.01**
+ 5	0.080	1.09	0.278	3.59**
+10	0.030	0.29	0.397	3.71**
+20	−0.032	−0.22	0.346	2.33**
+30	−0.048	−0.27	0.281	1.56
+40	0.058	0.29	0.377	1.81*
+50	−0.086	−0.39	0.474	2.05**
+60	−0.134	−0.54	0.542	2.15**

** and * denote significance at the 5% and 10% critical levels, respectively

mal" stock price returns for both sets of surprises (again, market-wide as well as company-specific), and then averaged them "cross-sectionally" over a 60-day period trailing the events. As in the earlier study of volatility, separate averages were calculated for the "good news" and "bad news" subsets of both the market-wide and the company-specific samples. And, finally, these 60 daily average returns were added together to produce "cumulative average returns" (CARs) for each of these four different categories of events.

Table 3 displays a representative portion of the post-event CARs along with their associated significance tests. The complete set of CARs over the 60-day post-event period for each subsample is illustrated in Figure 3. What both exhibits make clear is that, on average, investors did indeed receive additional compensation in the wake of major surprises both favorable and unfavorable. And this point is reinforced by the statistical observation that only the positive CARs in Table 3 (as well as those not listed there) were statistically significant.

What is also clear, however, is that the positive price adjustments were considerably higher after bad news than good. In the cases of good news about individual companies, the CARs pictured in Figure 3 seem to suggest that the uncertainty is resolved very quickly (in as short a period as 5 days), and that stock returns fluctuate randomly around

zero thereafter (in a pattern much like the one predicted by the standard EMH).

The Relationship Between Risk and Return

Having established that major surprises increase both risk and return in the stock market, the final goal of our study was to investigate the strength of the relationship between the two. All models of rational investor behavior assume that investors require greater returns for bearing risk. Consequently, in evaluating the initial price shocks and subsequent adjustments in our samples of events, we would expect to find that the level of increase in the CARs is positively related to the level of increase in volatility.

To test the relationship between risk and return in this case with any degree of precision would have required the use of a formal model of the risk-return relationship—a source of controversy that we wanted to steer clear of. So, we chose instead to run two relatively informal tests that examine certain aspects of this risk-return relationship.

The first of these tests focused on the market-wide surprises. In constructing this experiment, we reasoned that if investors exhibit what is known as "constant relative risk aversion"—that is, if the amount of additional return needed to compensate an added unit of risk remains roughly the same

FIGURE 2
STOCK RETURN VOLATILITY BEFORE AND AFTER MAJOR UNANTICIPATED EVENTS

Panel A. Positive Events   **Panel B. Negative Events**

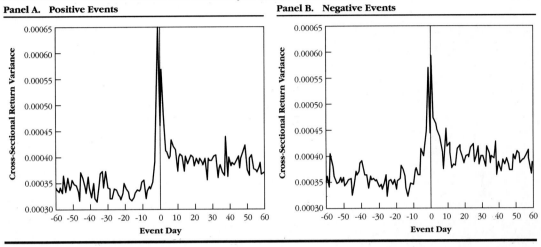

FIGURE 3
CUMULATIVE ABNORMAL RETURNS FOLLOWING UNEXPECTED PRICE-CHANGE EVENTS

Panel A. Marketwide Events   **Panel B. Individual Firm Events**

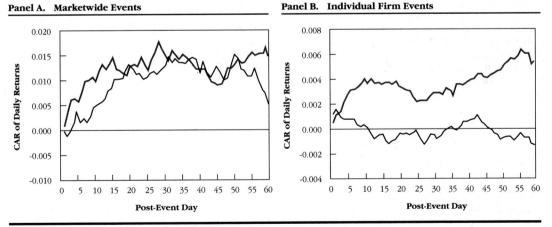

regardless of the relative level of stock prices—then the expected risk premium on the market index should be directly proportional to the variance of market returns.[12] This, in turn, implies that the percentage increase in post-event expected returns should be roughly equal to the percentage increase in post-event risk.

In fact, as reported in Panel A of Table 4, the increases in post-event returns tended to be somewhat larger than the increases in risk (the "elasticity coefficient" for the whole sample was 1.58). Without a more precisely formulated model of risk and return, however, it is difficult to say whether this represents "excessive" compensation for increased

---

12. See R. Merton, cited in note 5.

OUR FINDINGS DEMONSTRATE RATHER CONVINCINGLY THAT, REGARDLESS
OF THE RISK MEASURE USED, POST-EVENT UNCERTAINTY IS AN INCREASING
FUNCTION OF THE SIZE OF THE INITIAL PRICE CHANGE. THE LARGER
THE INITIAL MARKET REACTION TO A SURPRISE, THE GREATER
THE SUBSEQUENT LEVEL OF INVESTOR UNCERTAINTY AND THUS
THE HIGHER THE MEASURE OF RISK.

TABLE 4
THE RELATIONSHIP BETWEEN POSTEVENT RISK AND RETURN

Panel A. Risk and Expected Return Changes for Marketwide Events

Sample	% Change In Expected Return	% Change Risk	Ratio
All Events	41.838%	26.523%	1.577
Positive Events Only	49.393	30.440	1.623
Negative Events Only	46.538	33.998	1.369

Panel B. Event Magnitudes and Risk Changes for Individual Firm Events

Sample	Dependent Variable	Estimated Coefficient $\alpha 0$	$\alpha 1$	F-Stat
Positive Events	β	0.8912	3.8733	65.58***
(N = 4,788)	σ_j^2	0.0002	0.0050	299.35***
Negative Events	β	0.9250	−3.6352	53.20***
(N = 4,317)	σ_j^2	0.0002	−0.0054	351.77***

*** indicates significance at the 1% critical level

risk. What is important for our purposes is that the findings in Panel A are consistent with the direction of the relationship that would be expected in an efficient market.

In the case of company-specific surprises, we used regression analysis to determine whether the size of the initial price change was highly correlated with the subsequent increase in risk. Two measures of risk were tested, systematic risk (as measured by a company's beta) and total risk (as measured by total variance).

As reported in Panel B of Table 4, our findings demonstrate rather convincingly that, regardless of the risk measure used, post-event uncertainty is an increasing function of the size of the initial price change. The larger the initial market reaction to a surprise, the greater the subsequent level of investor uncertainty and thus the higher the measure of risk.

In sum, the findings of these two tests, together with the earlier results, provide strong support for our claim that investors "rationally" increase their expected returns to compensate for the increased risk attending major unanticipated events. Now, we attempt to apply our model of investor behavior to the biggest "surprise" in recent stock market history, the October '87 Crash, to see how the claim of investor rationality stands up under extreme uncertainty.

THE UIH AND THE MARKET CRASH OF 1987

On Monday, October 19, 1987, the stock market suffered its largest one-day loss in history, with the S&P 500 losing more than 20 percent of its value.

Explanations for this stunning decline have been many and varied, with blame being cast on everything from order execution procedures on the exchanges and NASDAQ to program trading and portfolio insurance. While we don't presume to be able to shed light on the underlying causes of "Black Monday," we can attempt to use the Uncertain Information Hypothesis to deduce what should have been expected to happen on the days following the crash.[13]

Given the magnitude of the price shock of October 19, the UIH would have predicted the following: (1) volatility in the stock market should increase dramatically; and (2) overall market values should trend upward as the volatility gradually falls toward more normal levels and the general uncertainty disappears. And this is indeed what happened in the wake of the Crash. As shown in Figure 4, the volatility of the S&P 500 market index increased dramatically after October 19, reflecting the substantial increase in the level of investor uncertainty about the market.

The measures of market volatility presented in Figure 4 are not based on direct observations. Traditional estimates of volatility (such as the standard deviations of stock returns) could not be directly calculated in this case because there is only one observation surrounding the event. For this reason we were forced to derive a substitute measure of volatility from changes in other variables. Our surrogate measure of general market volatility was the daily *implied* standard deviation (ISD) of stock price movements using the closest-to-the-money call option on the actual index (that is, the SPX option).[14]

---

13. Because the Crash occurred after the sample period of our original study, an alternative set of data must be considered. Additionally, inasmuch as Black Monday represents a single unanticipated event, the depth of the statistical analysis is obviously quite limited.

14. For a description of this method of volatility estimation, see J. Cox and M. Rubinstein, *Options Markets*, Englewood Cliffs: Prentice-Hall, 1985.

THE STOCK MARKET RATIONALLY RESPONDS TO ANY EVENT WHICH
INCREASES STOCK RISK BY LOWERING THE CURRENT PRICE, AND THEREBY
INCREASING THE LEVEL OF EXPECTED RETURN FOR NEW INVESTORS.
CONVERSELY, WHEN THE PERCEIVED RISK AND VOLATILITY FALL, THEN
INVESTORS LOWER THEIR REQUIRED RATES OF RETURN
AND STOCK PRICES RISE.

FIGURE 4
IMPLIED VOLATILITY OF
THE S&P 500 INDEX
BEFORE AND AFTER THE
STOCK MARKET CRASH
OF OCTOBER, 1987

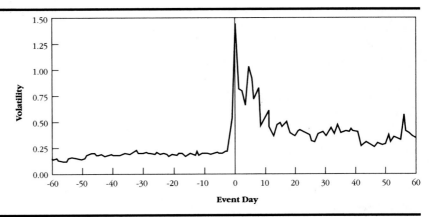

To provide some idea of how much volatility changed with the Crash, the average ISD for the period Day −60 to Day −5 was 18.9% while the comparable figure for the period Day +5 to Day +60 was 43.3%. On the day of the Crash itself, moreover, the ISD went to 145%, more than seven and a half times its pre-Crash value!

In Figure 5, we show the cumulative return as well as the volatility of the S&P 500 index during the 60 days after Black Monday. Once again, the consistently positive sign (excepting a single negative value) on the illustrated pattern of price changes confirms the prediction of the UIH. More important, however, it also appears that the daily returns and risk measures are inversely related; that is, on the days that the volatility measure increases, the S&P tends to fall. (In fact, when the daily realized return is compared to the daily change in the ISD, the estimated correlation coefficient is both negative (−0.544) and significant at the 1% critical level.) And this is exactly the relationship that should exist between these variables in an efficient market. The stock market rationally responds to any event which increases stock risk by lowering the current price, and thereby increasing the level of *expected* return for new investors. Conversely, when the perceived risk and volatility fall, then investors lower their required rates of return and stock prices rise.[15]

CONCLUDING COMMENTS

The efficient markets hypothesis (EMH) is based, in part, on the assumption that reliable information is instantly and costlessly available to investors. In this artificial world of relative certainty, prices are expected to adjust to major events quickly and accurately (or, at least, in an unbiased way, neither systematically overshooting nor undershooting the mark).

In a modification of the EMH called the Uncertain Information Hypothesis (UIH), we discard this assumption of "complete information" and attempt to show how the introduction of uncertainty changes rational investors' responses to new information. In contrast to the EMH, the UIH suggests that in response to surprise events that add greatly to uncertainty (about either the market as a whole or an individual company), both the risk and the required return to stockholders are expected to increase. And thus, whether the news is good or bad, stock prices will immediately trade at a level below their expected value equivalents to reflect the temporary increase in risk. But, as much of the uncertainty disappears over time, required returns should progressively fall back toward normal levels and stock prices should rise to reflect the decrease in risk.

The evidence of our recent study of the market's response to surprises—which examines all 75

---

15. A far more detailed development of these arguments is given in K. French, W. Schwert, and R. Stambaugh, "Expected Stock Returns and Volatility", *Journal of Financial Economics* 19 (1987), 3-29.

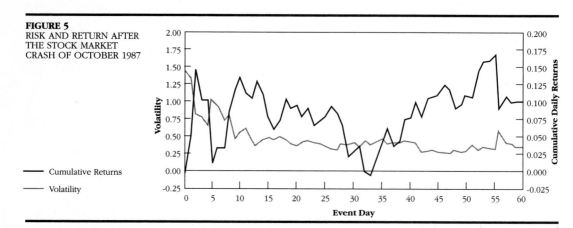

FIGURE 5
RISK AND RETURN AFTER
THE STOCK MARKET
CRASH OF OCTOBER 1987

—— Cumulative Returns

—— Volatility

market-wide daily (unexpected) price swings greater than 1 percent and over 9,000 company-specific price movements greater than 2.5 percent over the period 1962-1985—provides strong support for our argument. Our findings demonstrate that regardless of whether the news was good or bad, the average pattern of price adjustments after the initial reaction was significantly positive. Because the volatility of prices was also shown to rise significantly after both good and bad surprises—and then to fall gradually back toward normal levels—these incremental returns to stockholders are interpreted by us as compensating investors for bearing the added risk associated with uncertainty.

While we did find results that could be construed as evidence of market overreaction to large negative shocks, we argue that such apparent overreaction could equally well be viewed as reflecting a large increase in investors' required returns and, thus arguably, in the market-wide risk premium. In fact, we showed that the level of volatility after major surprises is composed of a small permanent as well as a larger transitory component.

What is the import of our findings for efficient markets theory? The main prediction of market efficiency is that the stock market should provide no

consistent opportunities for investors to earn more than normal rates of returns (again, adjusted for risk). For this principle to hold, any apparently predictable trend in stock prices—that is, any "trading rule" based on a systematic market "overreaction" to bad news or "underreaction" to good—must turn out, on closer inspection, to be an illusion.

In this case, the illusion is created by the process of averaging the responses by investors (many of which overshoot, while others undershoot their expected stock values) to a large number of events. It is true that if you bought all the individual stocks on the day following a daily price movement of more than 2.5 percent, you would earn what *appears* to be an "excess" rate of return over a very few days. But, if you then adjusted that rate of return for the increased risk of this investment strategy by taking account of the increased price volatility, you would likely discover that you had earned what finally amounts to nothing more than a normal rate of return.

Thus, while we have little doubt that the debate over market efficiency will continue for some time, our research suggests that abandoning the assumptions of investor rationality and market efficiency in favor of loosely formulated alternatives may be premature.

FIGURE 6
PROBABILITY
DISTRIBUTION OF
POSSIBLE STOCK MARKET
OUTCOMES (INCLUDING
UNANTICIPATED EVENTS)

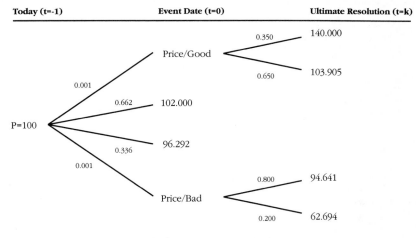

Where: Price/Good = $[(.350)(1/140.000) + (.650)(1/103.905)]^{-1} = 114.211$
and: Price/Bad = $[(.200)(1/62.694) + (.800)(1/94.641)]^{-1} = 85.888$

APPENDIX ■ THE UNCERTAIN INFORMATION HYPOTHESIS: AN EXAMPLE

We begin by assuming that the stock market is comprised of risk-averse investors whose preferences can be characterized by logarithmic utility function over the terminal value of their wealth.[16] We also assume, for simplicity, that the stock market represents the entire source for investor wealth and that prior to the arrival of any new information (t = −1) the level of a broadly based index of stock is 100. Now, supposing that investors make rational judgements about new information, Figure 6 gives a probability distribution summarizing investors' beliefs about future payoffs to their investments.

The first thing to notice in this display is that investors have allowed for the possible occurrence of four distinct outcomes. Two of these events can be regarded as "normal" in the sense that their impact will be immediately assimilated into market prices (i.e., 102.000 or 96.292). The other two potential outcomes represent "uncertain" surprises. Both of these unexpected events have been structured so that investors can immediately establish: (i) whether they represent good or bad news, and (ii) what the possible eventual effect of the event will be. While these latter two events are treated as being quite unlikely (as evidenced by their assigned probabilities of 0.001), they nonetheless present a practical difficulty for investors trying to evaluate the market at time t = −1 since their resolution, if they do occur, will not be immediate.

To see this, observe from Figure 6 that in the wake of the unexpected good news announcement, investors know only that the ultimate payoff will either be 140.000 (with a 35% probability) or 103.905 (with a 65% probability). Similarly, the unfavorable surprise offers eventual payoffs of 62.694 or 94.641 with 20% and 80% likelihoods, respectively. The challenge that investors face is to establish an economically justifiable value for the market in the face of an uncertain information event.

Stated differently, what will be the prices set immediately after the announcement of a favorable (i.e., Price/Good) and an unfavorable (i.e., Price/Bad) news? The Uncertain Information Hypothesis predicts that rational investors will initially react to the occurrence of these unlikely events

---

16. Specifically, a logarithmic utility function expresses an investor's level of satisfaction in terms of the value of his or her wealth as follows: U = log (P). This functional form is commonly employed to represent the investor preferences because it exhibits two attributes that are consistent with observed behavior: (i) decreasing absolute risk aversion, and (ii) constant relative risk aversion. For a more detailed explanation, see K. Arrow, *Essays in the Theory of Risk Bearing*, Chicago: Markham Publishing, 1971.

by setting prices so as to maximize the expected utility of their terminal wealth.[17] As indicated at the bottom of the display, these values are equal to 114.211 and 85.888, respectively. Establishing this result has two important consequences. First, since all of the probabilities and potential outcomes (regardless of when they are resolved) are known at time t = −1, investors are able to make the following *unconditional* forecast of the expected return of their stock investment before any event occurs:

$$E(R) = [(.662)(102.000/100) + (.336)(96.292/100)$$
$$+ (.001)(114.211/100) + (.001)(85.888/100)] −1$$
$$= 0.078\%$$

Using this value, it is also easily confirmed that an unconditional forecast of the standard deviation (i.e., risk) of the stock market is:

$$\sigma = 2.768\%$$

The second consequence of our assumption about investor reaction to uncertain information is apparent upon calculation of revised estimates of E(R) and σ when an unexpected event actually occurs. Specifically, the arrival of the unexpected good news event will prompt investors to initially revalue the index to 114.211 and then compute the following *conditional* forecasts of expected return and risk in the stock market:

$$E(R/Good) = [(.650)(103.905/114.211)$$
$$+ (.350)(140.000/114.211)] −1 = 2.038\%$$
$$\text{and } \sigma_{Good} = 15.074\%.$$

In the same fashion, following an unfavorable surprise which initially pushes the value of the market index down to 85.888, forecasts of the subsequent return characteristics conditioned on the attendant uncertainty are:

$$E(R/Bad) = [(.800)(94.641/85.888)$$
$$= (.200)(62.694/85.888)] −1 = 2.752\%$$
$$\text{and } \sigma_{Bad} = 14.878\%$$

The critical aspect of this example—indeed, the main point of the UIH—is that the arrival of unanticipated information has caused the riskiness and, hence, the expected return of the stock investment to increase. This was seen to be true whether the uncertain informational event had a negative (i.e., bad news) or positive (i.e., good news) initial impact. Thus, in the aftermath of such surprises one should expect that market will increase in value. On average, then, the observed pattern of stock prices following unanticipated bad news will superficially resemble the corrections necessitated by the actions of overreactive, irrational investors.

From the above example, however, this interpretation—which is the central prediction of the OH—is clearly incorrect since the initial level of [Price/Bad] was set in rational anticipation of a subsequent stock price movement either up to 94.641 (with 80% probability) or *down* to 62.694 (with 20% probability). Thus, the illusion of overreaction is solely a mathematical artifact caused by averaging realized returns over a large number of negative events. Further, after a favorable surprise, the UIH would predict that the observed pattern of stock returns should, on average, resemble an *underreaction* to the initial event. In any case, the principal point of the example is that seemingly predictable postevent price adjustments need not imply irrationality on the part of investors, particularly if the events increase uncertainty. Thus, empirical results that confirm an increase in risk following substantive unanticipated news events would be consistent with the predictions of the UIH.

---

17. Given the specification of the logarithmic utility function U = log (P), marginal utility can be expressed as U′ = (1/P). The UIH predicts that investors will set P_0 equal to $E[(U′(P_1)/E[(U′(P_1)])xP_1]$, or $P_0 = E[1/P_1]^{−1}$. For simplicity, we assume here that the risk-free rate of return is 0.00%.

HOW INVESTORS INTERPRET CHANGES IN CORPORATE FINANCIAL POLICY

by Paul M. Healy, Massachusetts Institute of Technology and Krishna G. Palepu, Harvard University

In May 1987, Apple Computer announced that it would pay $5 million in cash dividends on its common stock (four cents per share) for the first time in its history. On the day of the announcement, the market value of Apple's equity rose by $219 million.

In May 1986, Embart announced that it intended to issue 2.75 million shares to raise $102 million in new equity. Following the announcement, the market value of its existing equity fell by $23 million.

In February 1989, General Motors declared a 2-for-1 stock split for the first time since 1955, and increased its dividends. The announcement led the market value of GM's equity to increase by $1.3 billion.

Academic research has confirmed what practicing businessmen have long suspected—namely, that changes in corporate financial policies affect stock prices in systematic and thus fairly predictable ways. Announcements of equity offerings are generally accompanied by large decreases in the stock prices of the issuing firms. Dividend increases and stock splits typically lead to significant price increases.

What is relatively new is the explanation for why the market responds in this way. Finance scholars now argue that corporate policy changes affect stock prices because such changes convey information to investors about future performance.[1] Corporate managements, they reason, often have better information than investors about their companies' future profitability, investment opportunities, and business risks. And managers can be expected to use this information when making decisions about the appropriate level of dividends or financial leverage. For this reason, investors may look to such policy changes to reveal management's expectations about future earnings and investment opportunities. Hence, the effect on stock prices.

Wall Street analysts and corporate executives, however, tend to tell a different story. The conventional wisdom on common stock offerings, for example, is that they decrease stock prices by increasing the supply of a given company's shares. The popular account of stock price reactions to dividend increases is that investors value current income in the form of cash dividends more highly than capital gains. And stock splits are often said to increase stock prices by expanding the number of potential investors.

What each of these popular explanations have in common is their reliance on some form of market malfunction (economists call them "inefficiencies"). For example, it is true that if each company's stock were really unique, an increase in that stock's supply would cause the price to fall. But, as finance theorists have long argued, there are many close substitutes in our capital markets for any individual stock; and thus an increase in the supply of a single company's stock should have no important effect on price. Conversely, given this implied horizontal demand curve for securities, the attempt to increase potential investor "demand" through a stock split should be equally ineffective.

On the dividend question, financial economists have long argued that, apart from tax effects, investors should be indifferent between receiving income in the form of dividends and capital gains. In fact, when dividend tax rates exceeded those on capital

*We are grateful for the helpful comments of Paul Asquith, Gordon Donaldson, Bob Kaplan, and Richard Leftwich.

1. For examples of information-based models see Stewart Myers and Nicholas Majluf, "Corporate Financing and Investment Decisions When Firms Have Information That Investors Do Not Have," *Journal of Financial Economics*, Vol. 13 No. 2 (1984), Merton Miller and Kevin Rock, "Dividend Policy Under Asymmetric Information," *Journal of Finance*, (1985), and Michael Brennan and Thomas Copeland, "Stock Splits, Stock Prices, and Transaction Costs", *Journal of Financial Economics*, Vol. 22 No. 1 (1988).

gains (before the Tax Reform Act of 1986), taxable investors should actually have preferred capital gains to dividends.

In three recent studies, we attempted to discover which version of the story is correct. Do financial decisions influence stock prices because they provide new information to investors, or because capital markets do not work well? In one study, we looked at companies that decided to pay dividends for the first time. In a second study, we investigated publicly traded companies' decisions to issue additional common stock after a long period of financing by debt and retained earnings. The third examined the performance of companies that split their stock.[2]

HOW DO INVESTORS VIEW FIRST-TIME DIVIDEND PAYMENTS?

The vast majority of public companies pay cash dividends.[3] Moreover, they appear to try to maintain a stable, predictable dividend policy. As early as 1956, John Linter's classic study of corporate dividend policy showed that managers consider expected future earnings as well as current earnings in setting dividend policy—presumably because they are very reluctant to cut dividends in the future.[4]

To the extent this model of dividend policy-making reflects actual behavior, we would expect managers to increase dividends only when earnings increases are expected to be sustained in the future. And, if management turns out to be right more often than not, then reasonably astute investors will come to recognize that dividend increases represent managers' forecast of higher earnings.[5] Such implicit forecasts, moreover, will carry considerably more weight than straightforward earnings forecasts because, unlike mere statements, dividend increases are backed up by a commitment to pay out cash.

One of our recent studies attempted to determine whether a special subset of dividend increases—namely, dividend initiations—provided reliable signals of future earnings increases. (We defined dividend initiations as either payments for the first time in a firm's history, or after a hiatus of at least ten years.) We tested this proposition by comparing the earnings growth pattern of 131 NYSE and ASE companies that started (or resumed) dividend payments over the period 1970 to 1979.

As shown in Table 1 and Figure 1, this group of companies report relatively flat earnings until the year before the announcement of the first dividend payment. Then, earnings increase markedly and continue to grow at impressive rates for the next three years.

To give some indication of the size of such changes, the average earnings increases are 43 percent in year 1 (the year before the initiation), 55 percent in year 1, 22 percent in year 2 and 35 percent in year 3.[6] When most companies experience a pattern of large earnings increases like this, the increases typically turn out to be temporary and are reversed in later years.[7] For companies initiating dividends, however, the earnings are sustained through year 4 and thus appear to be relatively permanent.[8]

In short, the actual earnings increases following first-time dividend payments suggest that managers' implicit forecasts of unusual earnings growth are indeed realized. It is not surprising, then, that recent research has also shown that the stock market responds very positively to announcements of dividend initiations. In fact, the average market-adjusted increase in stock price in the two days surrounding the dividend announcement is roughly 4 percent.

Furthermore, it turns out that the larger the *yield* of the initial dividend, the more positive is the immediate stock price reaction to a given company's announcement of a dividend initiation. And, perhaps even more telling, the larger the market's positive reaction to the announcement, the larger are the future earnings increases actually realized by companies initiating the dividend.

This, needless to say, is persuasive evidence that dividend changes provide useful "signals" to investors.

2. Our original research on these issues is presented in the following papers: (1) Paul Healy and Krishna Palepu, "Earnings Information Conveyed by Dividend Initiations and Omissions" *Journal of Financial Economics*, Vol. 21 No. 2 (1988); (2) Paul Healy and Krishna Palepu, "Earnings and Risk Changes Surrounding Primary Stock Offers," *Journal of Accounting Research*, (1990); and (3) Paul Asquith, Paul Healy, and Krishna Palepu, "Earnings and Stock Splits," *The Accounting Review*, (July 1989).

3. In 1987, 76% of NYSE and ASE firms listed on Standard and Poor's Compustat files paid cash dividends.

4. John Linter, "Distribution of Incomes of Corporations Among Dividends, Retained Earnings and Taxes," *American Economic Review*, Vol. 46 (1956). See also Eugene Fama and H. Babiak, "Dividend Policy: An Empirical Analysis," *Journal of the American Statistical Association*, Vol. 63 (1968).

5. Managers could also initiate dividend payments when they forecast that their firms' earnings will be more stable relative to past earnings. In this case, investors will view dividend initiations as a signal of a decrease in the riskiness of the initiating firms.

6. In our original research, we compute earnings performance as earning changes divided by stock prices. Here we convert these values to earnings growth rates by assuming that the average P/E ratio is 10 times.

7. For further evidence on this see L. Brooks and D. Buckmaster, "First-Difference Signals and Accounting Time-Series Properties," *Journal of Business Finance and Accounting* (1980).

8. These findings do not change when we control for industry earnings patterns in years surrounding the dividend initiations.

TABLE 1 EARNINGS GROWTH RATES IN YEARS SURROUNDING FIRST-TIME DIVIDEND PAYMENTS BY 131 FIRMS IN THE PERIOD 1970 TO 1979*	Year Relative to Dividend Initiation	Number of Firms	Mean Earnings Growth Rate	Median Earnings Growth Rate
	−4	130	14.9%	17.4%
	−3	129	−7.1	7.6
	−2	128	12.9	10.5
	−1	131	42.7**	28.0
	1	130	55.0**	40.2
	2	130	22.0**	35.9
	3	130	35.0**	28.2
	4	128	3.5	19.5

* In our original research we compute earnings performance as earnings changes standardized by stock prices. Here we convert these values to earnings growth rates by assuming that the average price earnings ratio for the sample firms is ten.
** Significantly different from zero at the 10% level or lower.

FIGURE 1
MEDIAN EARNINGS
GROWTH RATES IN YEARS
SURROUNDING FIRST TIME
DIDIDEND PAYMENTS*

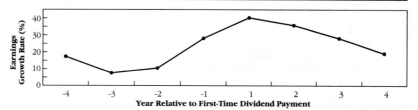

*In our original research we compare earnings performance as earnings changes standardized by stock prices. Here we convert these values to earnings growth ratios by assuming that the average price-earnings ratio for the sample firms is ten.

HOW DO INVESTORS VIEW STOCK OFFERINGS?

Finance theory suggests that corporate management should (if they do not already) determine the mix of debt and equity in their companies' capital structures by balancing the tax benefits of debt financing with the associated costs of financial distress.[9] Companies with high and stable profits are likely to borrow more because they can use interest tax shields without fear of financial distress. Companies with low or volatile profits are likely to borrow less because of the increased threat of financial difficulty.

Studies of actual corporate capital structures tell a somewhat different story about the management decision-making process. These provide strong evidence that, rather than adhering to a stable target ratio that reflects the trade-off between tax benefits and financial distress, managements instead typically fund new investments using retained earnings and,

if necessary, external debt financing. Only rarely do they resort to external equity financing; and when they do, it is usually only when they believe that the firm's current debt ratio is too high (or that its debt capacity has been used up) given their expectations about the level or riskiness of future earnings.[10]

Given this reasoning, we might expect managers to make equity offerings when they expect the company's business risk to be higher than previously anticipated, or the level of future earnings to be lower. And, to the extent that managers have better information than investors about the company's future earnings and risk, investors will interpret announcements of equity offerings as "signals" of management's expectations.

Using a sample of 93 seasoned stock offerings over the period 1966 to 1981, we attempted to test whether equity issues convey information about companies' business risk, future earnings, and target

9. See Gordon Donaldson, *Corporate Debt Capacity*, Division of Research, Harvard Business School: Boston (1961), and Harry DeAngelo and Ron Masulis, "Optimal Capital Structure under Corporate and Personal Taxation," *Journal of Financial Economics*, (1980).

10. Publicly listed corporations raise additional capital through equity offerings very infrequently. For a discussion of corporate financing practices see Gordon Donaldson, *Managing Corporate Wealth*, Praeger: New York (1984), and Richard Brealey and Stewart Myers, *Principles of Corporate Finance*, McGraw-Hill: New York (1988).

debt-equity ratios. If a company made multiple offerings less than five years apart, we used only the first offering. The sample therefore comprised firms for which equity offers were relatively rare events. All 93 firms were listed on the NYSE or ASE.

We estimated both the mean and median changes in business risk and leverage for the two years before and the two years after the equity offer. We used two measures of a firm's business risk: (1) asset beta and (2) an index of the firm's earnings volatility.[11]

As shown in Table 2, the average asset betas of the companies issuing equity are stable before the offer, but increase markedly after the offer. On average, asset betas increase by 23 percent (from 0.66 to 0.80) in the year after the equity offer. (This increase is, in a statistical sense, quite reliable.) The asset betas remain at the higher level in year 2, indicating that the beta increase in year 1 is not a temporary phenomenon.

We also found that earnings volatility, an alternative measure of business risk, increases sharply after the equity offer. The earnings volatility index is virtually unchanged in years before the offer, but later more than doubles (from 0.9 to 2.5). These patterns in beta and earnings volatility indicate that the offering firms experience a substantial increase in their business risk after the equity offer announcement.

To examine whether equity offerings signal future earnings declines, we analyzed the post-offer earnings performance as well as revisions in *Value Line* analysts' forecasts. We found no evidence, however, that the offering companies have lower earnings after the equity offer relative to either their pre-offer levels or the earnings of other firms in their industries. Further, analysts do not reduce their earnings forecasts after the announcements of equity issues.

It therefore appears that the managers of the offering firms anticipate future increases in business risk and respond by issuing additional equity to reduce financial leverage. The stated uses of equity-offer proceeds reported in the *Wall Street Journal* and in offer prospectuses indicate that a majority of firms intended to use these proceeds to retire debt and thus reduce leverage

ratios. And subsequent changes in corporate debt ratios suggest that results match intentions. After the equity offering, the average debt-equity ratio decreases by 20% (from 0.95 to 0.76), and remains at the lower level.

The net effect of the increase in business risk combined with the decrease in financial leverage is to increase equity betas. On average, equity betas increase by 8 percent in the offer year (from 1.23 to 1.33). (This increase, moreover, is statistically reliable; and there is no significant change in equity betas in other years.)

The economic significance of this average increase in equity betas of the offering firms can be quantified using a simple valuation model. Start by making the following assumptions: cash flows are constant in perpetuity, the discount rate is determined by the Capital Asset Pricing Model, the market's risk premium is 8%, and the risk-free rate is 10%. Given these assumptions, an expected increase in the equity beta from 1.23 to 1.33 will lead to a stock price decline of 4 percent.[12]

And, in fact, we find that the actual stock price reaction to the announcement of equity offers in our sample is consistent with this prediction. The average, risk-adjusted return is − 3.1 percent in the two days surrounding the offer announcement.[13]

Apparently, then, managers of companies issuing new equity forecast an increase in their companies' business risk, and therefore an increase in the probability of financial distress. They respond by issuing common stock and use the proceeds to retire existing debt, thereby reducing their firms' financial leverage. Investors recognize that managers have superior information and interpret offer announcements accordingly: they revise the offering firms' equity betas upward. And increases in earnings volatility of the offering firms in the years following the offer confirm that managers' forecasts of increased business risk are on average correct.

HOW DO INVESTORS VIEW STOCK SPLITS?

Surveys of managers' views on stock splits show that a vast majority regard splits as a means to keep

---

11. Asset betas measure the sensitivity of a firm's stock returns to market fluctuations after controlling for financial leverage. The asset beta B_a for a firm is estimated as follows:

$$B_a = B_e (1+D/E)$$

where, B_e is the equity beta estimated using the market model, and D/E is the ratio of the book value of debt to the market value equity (financial leverage). See Robert Hamada, "The Effect of Firm's Capital Structure on the Systematic Risk of Common Stocks," *Journal of Business*, Vol. 27 (1972) for a discussion of the relation between asset betas, equity betas, and leverage.

The earnings volatility index is constructed using the variance of changes in EPS as a percentage of stock price across the sample firms. The index for each year is the ratio of the variance in that year to the variance in year −3.

We computed asset betas, earnings volatility indices, and debt-equity ratios also for the offering firms' industries. The industry values are not reported in this paper for brevity, but are used in our tests to confirm that the results for the sample firms are not driven solely by industry-related factors.

12. For Further details on this calculation, see Paul Healy and Krishna Palepu, "Earnings and Risk Changes Surrounding Primary Stock Offers," *Journal of Accounting Research*, (1990).

13. In our sample the average ratio of the offer proceeds to the pre-offer equity value of the firm is 12.5%. Thus, the 3% decline in the stock price of the offer firms translates into a loss of about 25% of the proceeds of the proposed offer.

TABLE 2
CHANGES IN BUSINESS RISK
AND LEVERAGE IN YEARS
SURROUNDING SEASONED
EQUITY OFFERS FOR 93
FIRMS IN THE PERIOD
1966 TO 1981[a]

Variables	Year Relative to Equity Offer				
	−3	−2	−1	1	2
Business Risk:					
Asset Beta					
Mean	0.71	0.67	0.66	0.80	0.83
Median	0.64	0.61	0.62	0.78	0.79
Change in Asset Beta					
Mean		−5.6%	−3.0%	22.7%*	3.8%
Median		−3.1%	−1.6%	24.2%*	1.3%
Earnings Volatility Index	1.0	1.0	0.9	2.5	2.3
Leverage:					
Debt-Equity Ratio					
Mean	1.01	1.05	0.95	0.76	0.80
Median	0.68	0.74	0.72	0.56	0.59
Change in D-E Ratio					
Mean		4.0%	−9.5%	−20.0%*	5.3%
Median		7.4%	−6.8%	−20.8%	1.8%

[a] Two measures of business risk are used: asset betas and an earnings volatility index. Asset betas are unlevered equity betas; the earnings volatility index is the variance of the annual change in earnings as a percent of the stock price before the equity offer in each year relative to the value in year −3. Leverage is the book debt-equity ratio.
* Significant different from zero at the 10% level or lower.

their firm's price within an optimal trading range.[14] Companies typically split their stocks after permanent increases in earnings, since the news of favorable earnings is likely to push their stock prices above the target trading range. By contrast, companies with only temporary increases in earnings are unlikely to split their stock, since their stock prices will not appreciate beyond the target range.

Given this reasoning, we suggest that a company's decision to split its stock could well be determined by its managers' forecasts of whether past or current earnings growth is permanent. If managers have better information than investors about the permanence of earnings growth, investors may infer that past earnings increases are permanent from the announcement of a split.

Using a sample of 121 stock distributions of at least 25 percent over the period 1970 to 1980, we tested whether stock-splitting firms have permanent increases in their earnings. (Since stock splits are often accompanied by explicit or implicit increases in cash dividends and since dividend increases sig-

nal earnings increases, we restricted the sample to firms that did not pay cash dividends at the split date.)[15] None of these firms had made a stock distribution in the prior five years. The sample therefore comprised relatively large and infrequent stock distributions. All the sample firms were listed on the NYSE or ASE.

As shown in Figure 2 and Table 3, companies that split their stocks have large earnings increases for several years before the stock split,[16] as well in the year of the split. In effect, earnings increase by 12 percent two years before the split (year −2), 26 percent in year −1, and 20 percent in year 1.[17] The implied confidence of management about future earnings thus appears to be substantiated; and the earnings of the splitting firms do not decline over the next five years.

While the splitting firms' share prices increase before the split, we find that stock prices do not fully reflect the unusually large earnings increases in these years. Perhaps, without the split, investors would expect such increases to be temporary and reverse

14. H.K. Baker and P.L. Gallagher, "Management's View of Stock Splits," *Financial Management* (1980) report that 94% of the managers surveyed viewed stock splits as a means to keep their firm's price within an optimal trading range. Current finance theories do not address why firms have a preferred trading range. Optimal trading ranges may arise to reduce costs of trading, and to attract a broad and heterogeneous base of stockholders. For further discussion see Josef Lakonishok and Baruch Lev, "Stock Splits and Stock Dividends: Why, Who, and When," *Journal of Finance* (1987).

15. Many firms that split their stock do not decrease their dividend per share proportionally. For these firms the split announcement is accompanied by an increase in the total dividends paid. We have excluded these firms from our sample to isolate earnings changes around stock splits, since we have documented that firms that increase their dividend have large earnings increases.

16. See footnote 6.

17. Pre-split earnings increases are due to both industry- and firm-specific factors. When we controlled for industry earnings patterns in years surrounding the stock splits, we found that the sample firms were in industries that performed well but out-performed their industries in the year before the split.

COMPANIES THAT SPLIT THEIR STOCKS HAVE LARGE EARNINGS INCREASES
FOR SEVERAL YEARS BEFORE THE STOCK SPLIT, AS WELL IN THE YEAR OF THE
SPLIT... THE IMPLIED CONFIDENCE OF MANAGEMENT ABOUT FUTURE
EARNINGS THUS APPEARS TO BE SUBSTANTIATED; AND THE EARNINGS OF
THE SPLITTING FIRMS DO NOT DECLINE OVER THE NEXT FIVE YEARS.

FIGURE 2
MEDIAN PERCENT
CHANGES IN EPS
SURROUNDING
STOCK SPLITS

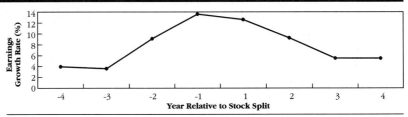

*In our original research we compare earnings performance as earnings changes standardized by stock prices. Here we convert these values to earnings growth ratios by assuming that the average price-earnings ratio for the sample firms is ten.

TABLE 3
EARNINGS GROWTH RATES
IN YEARS SURROUNDING
STOCK SPLITS BY
NON-DIVIDEND PAYING
FIRMS IN THE PERIOD
1970 TO 1980*

Year Relative to Stock Split	Number of Firms	Mean earnings Growth Rate	Median earnings Growth Rate
−4	44	10.5%**	4.1%
−3	61	6.6	3.7
−2	84	12.4**	9.2
−1	100	2.55**	13.7
1	118	20.3**	12.8
2	117	9.1	9.3
3	110	− 6.5	5.6
4	101	21.0	5.5

* In our original research we compute earnings performance as earnings changes standardized by stock prices. Here we convert these values to earnings growth rates by assuming that the average price earnings are for the sample time of ten.
** Significantly different from zero at the 10% level or lower.

themselves in later years—because large earnings increases, as mentioned earlier, are typically followed by declines. A stock split thus may help investors recognize that pre-split earnings increases are permanent.

How does the market respond to announcements of splits? The average market-adjusted stock price increase in the two days surrounding the split announcement is 3.7 percent. Further, the stock price reaction to the split announcement is proportional to earnings increases in *prior* years. That is, firms with higher earnings growth in the two years before the split experience higher stock price reactions to the split announcement.

In short, investors appear to view stock splits as signals that previous earnings increases will be sustained.

CLOSING REMARKS

There are no obvious reasons why corporate policy changes such as stock splits, dividends, and equity offerings should affect stock prices in any consistent or systematic way.

The evidence from our recent research suggests that managers make capital structure, dividend policy, and stock split decisions when they foresee changes in their companies' business risk or earnings levels. Subsequent changes in the actual values of these business fundamentals tend to bear out the implied management forecasts. Sophisticated investors appear to pay attention to such forecasts, and to incorporate them accurately into their own forecasts of future corporate performance.

COMPETITIVE DECLINE AND CORPORATE RESTRUCTURING: IS A MYOPIC STOCK MARKET TO BLAME?

by J. Randall Woolridge,
Pennsylvania State University

MYOPIC MARKETS OR MYOPIC MANAGERS?

In recent years many observers have attributed the competitive decline of U.S. industry in world markets to corporate management's preoccupation with short-term performance. In a classic *Harvard Business Review* article, for example, Robert Hayes and William Abernathy accused management of being short-sighted and not keeping their companies technologically competitive over the long run.[1] The emphasis on short-term profitability is predicted by some to have disastrous long-term implications, leading ultimately to the "de-industrialization of America."[2]

Corporate managers, however, respond to this charge by putting the blame on capital markets. Investors, they argue, are short-sighted, compelling management to sacrifice long-term investment and maximize current earnings—or else face the threat of takeover. Andrew Sigler, CEO of Champion International, has become one of the most prominent spokesmen for this view. "There is intense pressure for current earnings," Sigler says, "So the message is: Don't get caught with long-term investments. And leverage the hell out of yourself. Do all the things we used to consider bad management."[3] And Sigler's statement appears to have struck a sympathetic chord in many of America's top executives. In a survey of 100 CEOs of major corporations, 89 agreed that America's competitive edge has been "dulled" by its failure to emphasize long-term investment, and 92

percent of this group felt that Wall Street's preoccupation with quarterly earnings was the cause.[4]

In the meantime, academic theory suggests that investors have strong incentives to take the long view of corporate performance; and what evidence we have supports this theory. Michael Jensen, in fact, has turned the popular "short-term" argument on its head by asserting that "managers may behave myopically but markets do not." As Jensen argues,

There is little formal evidence on the myopic managers issue, but I think this phenomenon occurs. Sometimes it occurs when managers hold little stock in their companies and are compensated in ways that motivate them to take actions to increase accounting earnings rather than the value of the firm. It also occurs when managers make mistakes because they do not understand the forces that determine stock values...There is much evidence inconsistent with the myopic markets view, and none that supports it.[5]

The purpose of this article, then, is to evaluate current claims about the allegedly destructive role of the capital markets in corporate restructuring and the competitive decline of U.S. industry. My approach is to review the existing theory and evidence, and then introduce two further pieces of evidence. The first examines the market response to announcements of corporate long-term investments of several kinds (joint ventures, major capital expenditures, product strategies, and largescale R & D projects) to

1. Robert H. Hayes and William J. Abernathy, "Managing Our Way to Economic Decline," *Harvard Business Review*, (July-August 1980), pp. 67-77.
2. "Will Money Managers Wreck the Economy," *Business Week*, (August 13, 1984), pp. 86-93.
3. See Judith H. Dobrznyski, "More Than Ever, It's Management for the Short Term," *Business Week*, (November 24, 1986), pp. 92-3.

4. Business Bulletin, *Wall Street Journal*, (June 12, 1986), p.1.
5. Michael Jensen, "The Takeover Controversy: Theory and Evidence," *Midland Corporate Finance Journal*, Volume 4 Number 2 (Summer 1986), p. 11.

see if the markets actually penalize companies for committing capital to undertakings with distant, uncertain payoffs. The second is a less formal attempt to estimate the fraction of current stock prices that reflect corporate cash flows expected beyond a five-year horizon. Taken together, these two experiments provide suggestive evidence about the time horizon used by investors in valuing securities.

SOME BACKGROUND

The capital markets in this country have become dominated by large financial institutions. Recent statistics indicate that pension and mutual fund managers now control some 60 percent of all common shares and, on average, account for 80 to 90 percent of all daily trades.[6] According to the popular "short-term argument," the quarter-to-quarter performance figures of institutional investment managers, which are often reported in the financial press, are very important in retaining old accounts and in attracting new investors. Presumably, in pursuit of competitive quarterly performance figures, money managers follow investment strategies that place a premium on short-term corporate performance, which forces corporate managers to focus constantly on quarter-to-quarter earnings per share at the expense of long-term competitive growth. As Peter Drucker writes (in a *Wall Street Journal* editorial entitled "A Crisis of Capitalism"):

Everyone who has worked with American managements can testify that the need to satisfy the pension fund manager's quest for higher earnings next quarter, together with the panicky fear of the raider, constantly pushes top managements toward decisions they know to be costly, if not suicidal, mistakes. The damage is greatest where we can least afford it: in the fast-growing middle-sized high-tech or high-engineering firm that needs to put every available penny into tomorrow—research, product development, market development, people development, service—lest it lose leadership for itself and for the U.S. economy.[7]

The short-term orientation of managers is said to manifest itself in several ways. Managers are accused of being risk averse, forsaking investments with longer-run payoffs such as research and devel-opment expenditures. They are blamed for boosting short-term earnings, potentially at the expense of long-term growth, through financial innovations such as sale/lease backs and common stock repurchases. In addition, managers are said to concentrate their efforts in merger and acquisition activity and other "financial games," instead of devoting their attention to strategic product market issues. Other common charges against management are these: strategic decisions in product development are purely market-driven, showing little imagination; managers are biased towards buying productive resources and processes from others and against developing new productive resources and processes to gain competitive advantage; and, finally, innovation is discouraged by the short-term orientation of managers, which instead fosters imitation and backward integration because of their more predictable results.

The debate over the investment time horizon of the market, and its alleged role in the competitive decline of U.S. industry, is only one strand of a much larger contemporary issue in corporate America: namely, corporate governance. Managerial performance in creating value for shareholders has come under close scrutiny in the markets, and those firms which fall short risk being taken over. Indeed, the market for corporate control has heated up with growing numbers of hostile tender offers and proxy fights.

Managers have responded in essentially two different ways. One response has been to restructure their companies themselves through various actions aimed at increasing shareholder value. These restructurings have included redeploying or selling assets (and thereby allowing these resources to be employed in higher-valued uses), divesting or selling off poorly performing divisions (again, to some other corporate user who anticipates improving performance), decreasing uneconomic overhead, strategically repositioning primary business units, and making efficient use of cash and leverage (which often includes some form of settlement with shareholders).

The second class of managerial reactions to the increase in takeover activity has been to seek protection from the corporate control market through contracting agreements with corporate boards, and

6. For statistics and a discussion of the dominance of institutional investors in the markets, see Michael Blumstein, "How the Institutions Rule the Market," *The New York Times*, (November 25, 1984), Section 3, p.1.

7. Peter Drucker, "A Crisis of Capitalism," *The Wall Street Journal*, (September 30, 1986), p.31.

through regulatory proposals that alter the regulation of tender offers and change shareholder voting procedures and other corporate governance rules. Overall, as managers have come under greater pressure to perform on behalf of shareholders, the relationship between management and shareholders has become increasingly strained.[8]

Many observers have debated the merits of the current restructuring of corporate America. Managers argue that they must balance the interests of stockholders with those of other corporate stakeholders, such as employees, suppliers, customers, and communities. Hicks B. Waldron, chairman of Avon Products, makes the point this way: *We have 40,000 employees and 1.3 million representatives around the world. We have a number of suppliers, institutions, customers, communities. None of them have the democratic freedom as shareholders do to buy or sell their shares. They have much deeper and more important stakes in our company than our shareholders.*[9]

As such, management claims it must be protected from "overzealous" institutional stockholders who demand immediate results—and from corporate raiders and their allies, Wall Street arbitrageurs, who stand willing to pounce on firms whose short-term performance and stock price falters.

Managers contend that they need patient investors who are willing to accept the risks of long-term equity investment.[10] To illustrate this point, they cite such statistics as the relatively high turnover rates on institutional stock portfolios (over 60 percent, on average, in recent years) and stock returns in Japan, where stocks have grown over sixfold since 1970 (and turnover rates are one-third those of U.S. institutions).[11] Andrew Sigler, cited earlier, is somewhat more succinct in his evaluation of the short-term perspective of institutional investors: "What right does someone who owns the stock for an hour have to de-

cide a company's fate. That's the law, and it's wrong."[12]

According to T. Boone Pickens, however, management's short-term theory is "pure hokum." "Increasing acceptance of the short-term theory," Pickens argues,

has freed executives to scorn any shareholders they choose to identify as short-termers. Executives aim their contempt not only at the initiators of takeover attempts but at the arbitrageurs and the institutional investors who frequently trade in and out of stocks.[13]

Institutional investors themselves vigorously object to the notion that they are "only short-term" investors and insist that they are only interested in portfolio value gains which, given the forward-looking nature of the market, result from enhanced future prospects.[14] At the same time, however, they profess to be "fed up" with corporate managers who mismanage assets and then hide behind the "cloak" of social responsibility. It goes without saying that institutional investors oppose management entrenchment procedures—the proxy process, poison pills, greenmail, golden parachutes, staggered boards, and dual classes of common stock—all of which serve to reduce the discipline imposed on management through the market for corporate control. In articulating what is probably the position of most institutional investors, Richard M. Schlefer of the College Retirement Equities Fund says, "We view tender offers as a kind of free, competitive market for management. The best managers will end up running a company."[15]

THE MARKET RESPONSE TO STRATEGIC INVESTMENT DECISIONS

With few exceptions, the short-term theory of managerial and capital market behavior is inconsistent with the contemporary literature in finance and

8. For example, see C. Power and V. Cahan, "Shareholders Aren't Just Rolling Over Anymore." *Business Week*, (April 27, 1987), pp. 32-33.

9. See Bruce Nussbaum and Judith Dobrznyski, "The Battle for Corporate Control," *Business Week*, (May 18, 1987), pp. 102-109.

10. John G. Smale, chairman and CEO of Proctor & Gamble Co., recently wrote on the responsibilities of shareholders. Whereas he does not specify what shareholders' responsibilities actually are, he makes the distinction between 'traditional shareholders' and 'temporary owners', who " . . . play a role that can lead to the acquisition of corporate assets through creative financing for the purpose of reaping a quick profit." See John G. Smale, "What About Shareholders' Responsibility?," *The Wall Street Journal*, (October 16, 1987), p.20.

11. For an extended version of the "patient investor" argument, see Donald Frey, "The U.S. Needs Patient Investors," *Fortune*, (July 7, 1986), 125-126; and Karen Pennar, "Is the Financial System Shortsighted?," *Business Week*, (March 3, 1986), pp. 82-3.

12. B. Nussbaum and J. Dobrznyski, "The Battle for Corporate Control," *Business Week*, (May 18, 1987), pp. 102-109.

13. T. Boone Pickens, "Professions of A Short-Termer," *Harvard Business Review*, (May-June 1986), pp. 75-79. A rebuttal to Pickens arguments is provided in W. Law, "A Corporation is More Than Its Common Stock," *Harvard Business Review*, (May-June 1986), pp. 80-83.

14. Seely argues that corporations should actually court institutional investors. He claims that higher levels of institutional common stock ownership leads to higher stock liquidity and lower market-related volatility. Furthermore, he maintains that "overowned" stocks have outperformed "underowned" stocks, and that "underowned" stocks are more vulnerable to takeovers since these companies tend to have a low profile on Wall Street and therefore have been neglected by institutions. See Michael Seely, "In Praise of Institutional Investors," *Fortune*, (April 15, 1985), p. 167.

15. See Bruce Nussbaum and Judith H. Dobrznyski, "The Battle for Corporate Control," *Business Week*, (May 18, 1987), pp. 102-109.

economics. Economic theory suggests that an active market for managerial labor and corporate control compels managers to maximize shareholder wealth over the long-run which, among other things, entails making strategic investment decisions today which ensure growth tomorrow. In addition, many empirical studies have demonstrated that the capital markets, full of institutional as well as individual investors looking to take advantage of arbitrage opportunities, do not systematically misprice securities.

Therefore, security prices are presumed to provide an unbiased estimate (that is, neither too high nor too low, on average) of long-term investment value. Consequently, whereas managers continue to make their case in the financial press that long-term investments are "hazardous" in today's capital markets, most economists would be reluctant to blame the capital markets for inducing myopic behavior by managers.

Economic Theory and Real Corporate Investment

According to traditional valuational theory, the market value of a firm is equal to the sum of (a) the net present value of cash flows generated from assets in place and (b) the net present value of expected cash flows from investment opportunities that are expected to be available to and undertaken by the firm in the future. The market value of a firm changes as the market receives either general market or firm-specific information which changes the market's expectations about either (a) or (b) above.

As such, upon announcement of corporate strategic investment decisions, the market provides its immediate "best guess" about the effect of these strategic investment decisions on the present value of all future cash flows. In a competitive and efficient market, arbitrageurs should prevent any systematic mispricing of securities.

In economists' model of a perfectly competitive industry, entry and exit are assumed to be costless, products are undifferentiated, and there are increasing marginal costs of production. In such an environment, products are sold strictly on the basis of price, each firm produces up to the point where price equals marginal cost, and the long-run industry equi-

librium is reached in which price equals average cost (including a charge for capital, or "normal" level of profit). In equilibrium, total revenues equal total costs for the industry and individual firms alike; and because costs include the required return on the capital employed by each firm, in the long-run actual and required returns on capital are equal.

In perfectly competitive factor and product markets, then, strategic investment decisions with positive net present values do not exist; that is, the factors associated with strategic investment decisions are priced in factor and product markets void of imperfections such that the net present value of these decisions is zero. If a strategic investment decision is perceived to have a positive net present value, it instantaneously attracts new entrants to the industry, which in turn increases factor prices and capacity and drives product prices down. Higher factor prices and lower product prices reduce returns to all the firms, which forces weaker firms to leave the industry. With fewer competitors, factor prices decline and product prices rebound, increasing returns for the surviving firms until once again actual and required returns are equal. As such, in this perfectly competitive environment, the search by corporate planners for strategic investments with positive net present values is doomed to failure.

The ability of strategic investment decisions to generate positive net present values rests, then, on "imperfections" in product and factor markets. It is these "imperfections" that permit one firm to gain competitive advantage over others in its industry. Firms can gain competitive advantage through strategic decisions which allow the firm to become the low-cost producer or to differentiate its product on the basis of service or quality such that customers are willing to pay a premium for the product. These competitive advantages form "barriers to entry" to potential entrants and result in an imperfectly competitive market in which strategic investment decisions with positive net present values are possible.[16]

The Hypotheses

In this study, I am defining strategic investment decisions as those corporate resource allocations that involve a substantial commitment of capital with

---

16. Alan Shapiro, for example, has identified five major areas where strategic investment decisions can create, preserve, or enhance barriers to entry and generate positive net present values. These areas are (1) economies of scale; (2) product differentiation: (3) cost advantages; (4) access to distribution channels; and (5) government policy. (See Alan Shapiro, "Corporate Strategy and the Capital Budgeting Decision," *Midland Corporate Finance Journal*, (Spring 1985), pp. 22-36.)

the expectation of an uncertain payoff in the future.[17] By definition, therefore, these decisions are made in anticipation of increasing long-term growth at the expense of lower short-term earnings.

The stock market reaction to announcements of strategic investment decisions can be thought of as having two components: (1) a price reaction which reflects general, overall factors influencing managerial strategic decisions and firm valuation; and (2) price reactions to individual situations in which the market reacts positively or negatively to a strategic announcement based on (a) the information available to investors at the time of the announcement (for example, to what extent was the strategy announcement expected?) and (b) the perception of the market regarding the soundness of the strategic investment decision.

How, then, should the market be expected to respond to such announcements? I have laid out the alternative hypotheses as follows:[18]

Positive Stock Price Reaction

Shareholder Value Maximization (SVM) - Traditional finance theory posits that managers seek to maximize the market value of the firm. According to this hypothesis, managers are compelled by market forces to make strategic investment decisions aimed at maximizing shareholder value. Therefore, strategic investment announcements are interpreted by investors as managerial decisions with expected positive net present values and therefore are accompanied by significantly positive abnormal stock returns;

Neutral Stock Price Reaction

Highly Competitive Markets (HCM) - The ability of strategic decisions to generate positive net present values and to increase stock prices rests on imperfections in factor and product markets which permit a firm to gain competitive advantage over others in the industry. However, equilibrium in a perfectly competitive market requires that the level of factor and product prices be set such that strategic decisions cannot generate positive net present values. Whereas the assumptions of a perfectly competitive world are unduly restrictive, it is possible that, in a highly competitive market, products and factors are priced so as to virtually eliminate excess returns. In such a market, strategic investment decisions with positive net present values would be rare, and thus strategic announcements would be accompanied by no change in stock prices; and

Rational Expectations Market (REM) - In a rational expectations market environment, security prices reflect investors' expectations that managers will undertake strategic investments to provide for future growth and increases in shareholder value. As such, according to this hypothesis, security prices do not react to announcements of strategic investment decisions, even though investors' may believe that these investments have positive net present values; and

Negative Stock Price Reaction

Myopic Stock Market (MSM) - Many observers have argued that investors in the U.S., especially the large and powerful financial institutions, are too short-sighted, focusing on quarter-to-quarter earnings and thereby preventing managers from pursuing strategies aimed at long-term competitive advantage and growth. According to MSM hypothesis, strategic investment announcements which involve decisions

17. Research into the valuation impact of strategic investment decisions is concentrated in the area of intercorporate acquisitions. For a review of the evidence on intercorporate mergers and tender offers and shareholder returns, see Michael Jensen and Richard Ruback, "The Market for Corporate Control: The Scientific Evidence," *Journal of Financial Economics*, (April 1983), pp. 323-329.

Several recent studies, however, have evaluated the market's response to the kinds of strategic investment decisions that I am considering in this paper. For example, John McConnell and Chris Muscarella examined the reaction of stock prices to 658 announcements of increases and decreases in the dollar amount of planned capital expenditures and discovered that announcements of increases (decreases) in capital budgets are associated with significantly positive (negative) abnormal stock returns for industrial firms. (See John McConnell and Chris Muscarella, "Corporate Capital Expenditures Decisions the Market Value of the Firm," *Journal of Financial Economics*, (July 1985), pp. 399-422.) John McConnell and Tim Nantell investigated the relationship between joint venture formation and announcement day stock returns. Their sample included 210 firms involved in 136 joint ventures over the 1972-79 time period. They discovered joint venture formations to be associated with significantly positive announcement day returns. (See John McConnell and Timothy Nantell, "Corporate Combinations and Common Stock Returns: The Case of Joint Ventures," *Journal of Finance*, (June 19850 pp. 519-536.) Greg Jarrell, Ken Lehn, and Wayne Marr analyzed the relationship between research and development (R&D) expenditures and stock prices as part of a larger study of institutional stock ownership, long-term investments, and tender offers. Using a sample of 62 R&D announcements taken from the *Wall Street*

Journal, over the 1973-83 period, they found these announcements to be associated with significantly positive stock returns. (See Greg Jarrell, Ken Luhn, and Wayne Marr, "Institutional Ownership, Tender Offers, and Long-Term Investments," The Office of the Chief Economist, Securities and Exchange Commission (April 19, 1985).)

18. Several comments on these hypotheses and tests are in order: (1) in the tests which follow, the stock price reaction to strategic investment announcements may reflect some or all of the specific and general considerations discussed here. However, only the dominant general factor influencing stock prices can be determined. Specific factors are presumed to average out over the sample; (2) While the lack of any statistically significant stock price movement is consistent with both the HCM and the REM hypotheses, it is also consistent with other joint and confounding hypotheses. As such, strict inferences in this case are not possible; and (3) it is arguable that a negative strategic announcement/stock return relationship is also consistent with some theories of managerial behavior which conflict with the SVM hypothesis. An alternative interpretation of negative stock returns is that managers may be engaging in activities with negative net present values. These may result from traditional agency problems in which managers' interests conflict with those of stock holders. For capital expenditures, this argument is similar to Malatesta's size-maximization hypothesis for stock returns of acquiring firms in mergers. As such, this hypothesis would be supported in this study if stock prices are discovered to react negatively to capital expenditures announcements. See Paul Malatesta, "The Wealth Effect of Merger Activity and the Objective Functions of Merging Firms," *Journal of Financial Economics*, (April 1983), pp. 155-181.

TABLE 1	Category		Number of Announcements
STRATEGIC INVESTMENT ANNOUNCEMENTS:	**Joint Venture Formation**		161
	Research and Development	39	
	Shared Assets/Resources	35	
	Asset Construction	87	
	Research and Development		45
	Advances	27	
	Initial Expenditures	18	
	Product Strategies		168
	New Product/Old Business Line	105	
	New Product/New Business Line	39	
	Old Product/New Geographic Market	24	
	Capital Expenditures		260
	General Capacity Expansion Construction	194	
	Plant Modernization Construction	31	
	Capital Budgets Increases	35	

with long-term payoffs (such as research and development and capital expenditures) at the risk of reducing short-term earnings result in a significant decrease in stock prices.

The Data

To examine the relationship between strategic investment decision announcements and stock prices, I gathered a large sample of strategic investment announcements from articles appearing in the *Wall Street Journal*. With the aid of a computer, I searched the "What's News" column (over the period June 1972 to December of 1984) for announcements that appeared to indicate a major corporate strategic investment. When a likely candidate was located, I then read the article to determine the strategic nature of the announcement and whether or not other significant information was also published. In cases where the announcements included other information concerning a firm's sales or earnings, or if other announcements concerning sales or earnings appeared in the *Wall Street Journal* within one day of the strategic investment decision announcement, they were excluded from the sample.

After this winnowing process, I was left with 634 strategic announcements made by 347 different companies operating in 81 different industries.[19] These announcements were then classified into one of four

general areas based on their strategic orientation: (1) joint ventures, (2) research and development expenditures, (3) product strategies, and (4) capital expenditures for expansion or modernization. These four general categories were refined further into more specific subcategories (all of which are listed in Table I).

The four general categories may be summarized as follows:

Joint ventures: Joint ventures are typically employed when two or more firms lack a necessary component to compete in a particular market. The purposes behind joint venture formation take many forms, which range from joint research projects aimed at developing new technology, to joint production projects to take advantage of the engineering strengths of more than one firm, to joint marketing efforts to gain access to new markets. Management and development costs are usually shared by the firms, as are the profits from the venture. Joint ventures reduce the risk and potential financial losses inherent in new projects, but at the expense of reduced rewards if the project proves to be successful.[20]

The sample of joint venture formations was further broken down according to the purpose behind formation, e.g., research and development, shared resources, and asset construction.

Research and development expenditures: A number of studies report that R&D expenditures exert a

19. By year, the sample breaks down as follows:

Year	No.	Year	No.	Year	No.	Year	No.	Year	No.
1972	40	1975	35	1978	56	1981	32	1984	44
1973	93	1976	28	1979	25	1982	49		
1974	33	1977	84	1980	40	1983	75		

As may be expected, the annual number of the strategic investment decision announcements is closely related to the level of overall economic activity.

20. Strategists like the joint venture concept. According to one theorist, joint ventures are one of twelve "grand strategies" which "serve to provide the basis for achieving long-term objectives" (see J. Pearce, "Selecting Among Alternative Grand Strategies," *California Management Review* (Spring 1982), pp. 23-31). Michael Porter describes joint ventures as a type of "long-term alliance which broadens the effective scope of the firm's value chain" (Michael Porter, *Competitive Advantage* (NY: The Free Press, 1985).

TABLE 2
COMMON STOCK
RETURNS AROUND
STRATEGIC
INVESTMENT
ANNOUNCEMENTS

Day	Mean Raw Return	Percent Greater Than 0	Market-Adjusted Return	T-Stat	Cumulative Market-Adjusted Return
N = 634					
− 1	+0.360	46.53	+0.295	+2.95	+0.360
0	+0.350	51.42	+0.355	+4.27	+0.710
+30	—	—	—	—	+0.984
Panel A: Joint Venture Formations N = 161					
− 1	+0.526	48.45	+0.384	+1.92	+0.384
0	+0.447	51.55	+0.399	+2.02	+0.783
+30	—	—	—	—	+1.412
Panel B: Research and Development Expenditures N = 45					
− 1	+1.042	57.78	+0.944	+2.47	+0.944
0	+0.400	48.89	+0.251	+0.93	+1.195
+30	—	—	—	—	+1.456
Panel C: Product Strategies N = 168					
− 1	+0.421	50.60	+0.402	+2.29	+0.402
0	+0.487	54.76	+0.440	+2.84	+0.842
+30	—	—	—	—	−0.350
Panel D: Capital Expenditures N = 260					
− 1	+0.099	40.77	+0.058	+0.36	+0.058
0	+0.194	49.62	+0.290	+2.45	+0.348
+30					+1.499

strong positive impact on profitability.[21] But, a significant time gap exists between when the expenditures are made and when they affect profitability. One study found that peak profits accrued four to six years after R&D spending occurred.[22] However, the returns from R&D expenditures are uncertain and can fluctuate considerably from year to year.

The sample of R&D announcements were further classified according to information contained in the announcement: some announcements involved expenditures to new R&D projects, while others provided details on commitments to ongoing R&D projects and programs.

Product strategies: The Development and launching of new products, as well as entrance into new markets with existing products, are strategic decisions which are essential for long-run growth. However, they both involve a commitment of resources and, as such, are risky and costly in the short run.

The product strategy announcements fall into three categories: new product introductions into old business lines, the introduction of new products into new business lines, and the introduction of old products into new geographic markets.

Capital expenditures: Like other strategic investment decisions, the commitment of funds for capital projects is necessary to ensure the long-term vitality of a business firm. Capital expenditures are provided for projects such as capacity expansions, plant modernization, as well as general expenditures to update equipment. Like R&D expenditures, the returns on capital expenditures are uncertain and may not come until some time in the future. In addition, after a capital project is undertaken, short-term earnings will be depressed until the project is completed and begins to generate revenues or reduce operating costs.

Capital expenditures are further categorized as follows: general capacity expansion construction (including mining and exploration), plant modernization projects, and general increases in capital budgets.

The Results

With the aid of a computer, I calculated stock price changes in response to the entire sample of stra-

21. See H. Grabowski and D. Mueller, "Industrial Research and Development, Intangible Capital Stocks, and Firm Profit Rates," *Bell Journal of Economics*, (Fall 1978), pp. 328-342; Z. Griliches, "Productivity, R&D, and Basic Research at the Productivity Rates," *American Economic Review*, (May 1983), pp. 215-218; and Edwin Mansfield, "How Economists See R&D," *Harvard Business Review*, (November-December 1981), pp. 98-106.

22. Sherer, cited in note 21.

SOME EXAMPLES OF THE MARKET'S RESPONSE TO STRATEGIC ANNOUNCEMENTS	Company	Date	Nature of Announcement	2-Day Return
	Imperial Chemical	3/9/77	Plan to build two plants in Britain at total cost of $181 million	5.51%
	Union Camp	8/31/77	Plan to spend $250 million to double output of linerboard mill	4.13%
	Reynolds Metals	9/15/78	Plan to spend $70 million to expand sheet-and-plate plant	2.01%
	Washington Post	5/22/78	Joint venture to build and operate news-print mill costing $100 million	2.50%
	Motorola	8/12/81	Plan to spend $120 million to expand semiconductor plant in Scotland	2.42%
	Westinghouse	4/2/82	Increased capital spending by 33%, to $800 million, to enter cable TV market	1.56%
	J.C. Penney	2/1/83	Plan to spend $1 billion over next 5 years to modernize 450 stores	7.15%
	DuPont	8/12/83	Plan to spend $100 million on R&D to improve automotive/industrial coatings	2.54%
	PSA	11/17/83	Purchase of 20 British Aerospace 100-seat jets for $300 million	2.23%
	Wang Labs	4/18/84	Plan to acquire 15% interest in InteCom to pursue joint marketing & product dev.	6.41%
	Federal Express	7/30/84	Plan to spend $1.2 billion over next 10 years to expand new ZapMail service	2.27%

tegic announcements both in the two-day period surrounding the public announcement and over a period of 30 trading days following the announcement. These returns were adjusted for the overall market return (as measured by the return for the S&P 500), and then averaged across the entire sample. Average, market-adjusted returns were also calculated for each of the four categories of investment described above.[23] The results are summarized in Table 2.

All Strategic Investment Announcements: For the entire sample of 634 strategic investment announcements, the market-adjusted returns (MMARs) over the two-day period surrounding the announcement averaged a positive 0.7 percent. (The MMARs for days −1 and 0 were .295% (t = 2.95) and .355% (t = 4.27), respectively, which are the two largest MMARs over the 32 day period (day −1 to day +30).) Over this 32-day period these stocks outperformed the S&P 500 by about 1 percent.

Joint Venture Formations: As shown in Table 2, the average, two-day, market-adjusted return to 161 announcements of joint ventures was a positive 0.8 percent, roughly the same as the market response to the broad sample. Over the thirty-two day period following (and including) the announcement days, the cumulative excess market return to joint venture formations was 1.4 percent. (The largest positive response to subcategories of joint ventures (not shown in the Table) were those in which assets or resources were to be shared.)

Research and Development Expenditures: The two-day market returns to 45 announcements of R&D expenditures averaged a positive 1.2 percent (reflecting MMARs for day −1 and day 0 of .944% and .251%). As in the case of joint ventures and the overall sample, there is no evidence of stock price declines in the subsequent 30 days.

The subsample statistics indicate that the announcements of expenditures on ongoing R&D programs, as opposed to new projects, were received

23. In all cases, the announcements appeared in the *Wall Street Journal* on day 0. However, in some instances, the announcements were actually made on day −1.

Therefore, returns on these two days should provide an indication of the market's evaluation of the announced strategic investment decision.

more positively by the market.

Product Strategies: For 168 announcements of product strategy announcements, the market's two-day response averaged 0.8 percent, again mirroring the market reaction to the broad sample. (In addition, the returns for the two-day event period represent the largest average price movements over the entire 32-day period.) Most of these gains, however, are lost over the following 30-day period, and the cumulative average return becomes slightly negative.

The subsample results indicate that the market responds positively to the announcements of new product introductions, be they in old or new business lines. The most positive market response is associated with the introduction of new products in old business lines.

Capital Expenditure Announcements: For 260 announcements of large capital spending programs, the average two-day, market-adjusted return was 0.35 percent. (The return of .29 percent on day 0 is the largest over the 32-day period.) In addition, these stocks outperformed the S&P 500 by almost 1.5 percent over the 32-day period. As such, there is no evidence of a subsequent price decline following capital expenditure announcements.

Within the subcategories, expenditures for general capacity expansion and for capital budget increases were received most positively by investors.[24]

Summary of Findings

The consistently positive stock market reaction to announcements of various types of corporate strategic investment decisions provides significant support for the proposition that these announcements are interpreted by investors as managerial decisions with expected positive net present values. Thus, the results support the hypothesis that management is encouraged by market forces to make strategic investment decisions aimed at maximizing shareholder value.

The results offer no support for the propositions that (1) product and factor markets are so highly competitive that investment returns approximate the

cost of capital and that (2) security prices reflect investors' expectations that managers will undertake profitable strategic investments aimed at providing for future growth and increases in shareholder value. In addition, and more important, these results contradict the popular notion that the markets are myopic, focusing on quarter-to-quarter earnings to the exclusion of considerations of long-term competitive growth.

THE FUNDAMENTAL VALUATION OF COMMON STOCKS

The positive reaction of stock prices to corporate strategic investment decisions suggests that the market looks well beyond the next quarter in setting security prices. Nonetheless, critics of the market claim that day-to-day security price fluctuations, generated to a large extent by the buying and selling of institutional investment managers pursuing short-term trading profits, do not reflect long-term corporate prospects. As noted by Alfred Rapport, however, "it's important to distinguish between the daily scurrying of investors and the forces that determine market prices."[25]

According to the fundamental valuation theory presented earlier, the current price of a security is equal to the present value of all future cash flows to investors. The discount rate, which reflects the risk of the security and the time value of money, represents investors' required rate of return. Using this model, and using both current dividends and accounting earnings as proxies for expected net cash flows (which should be reasonable, at least over a broad sample of firms), we can perform a little experiment to assess the investment time horizon of the stock market.

Table 3 provides recent and projected data for the Dow Jones Industrials. For each security, the data given include the stock price, the P/E ratio, current dividends and earnings, and Value Line Investment Survey's estimated beta and 5-year projected dividends' and earnings' growth rates. Using the Capital Asset Pricing Model (CAPM) to estimate investors' re-

24. The positive returns associated with capital expenditure announcements, and especially the results for the capacity expansion subsample, provide evidence against the size-maximization hypothesis, as discussed in Malatesta (1983) and footnote number 18.

25. See Alfred Rappaport, "Don't Sell Stock Market Horizons Short," *The Wall Street Journal*, (June 27, 1983), p. 22. In this article Rappaport discusses the results of a study which is similar in form to the analysis that follows.

TABLE 3
LONG-TERM VALUE INDEXES DOW JONES INDUSTRIALS MARCH 1988

| Company | Stock Price | Beta | P/E | Earnings Per Share | | | |
				Current Earnings	Earnings Yield	Projected Earnings Growth	Pres Val Next 5 Yr Earnings
Allied-Signal	$32.75	0.95	13	$2.60	7.9%	5.5%	$11.38
Alcoa	**$45.38**	**1.25**	**11**	**$4.14**	**9.1%**	**17.5%**	**$24.55**
American Express	$26.00	1.45	21	$1.25	4.8%	16.5%	$7.12
AT&T	**$29.38**	**0.80**	**16**	**$1.85**	**6.3%**	**16.5%**	**$11.02**
Bethlehem Steel	$19.88	1.45	80	$0.25	1.3%	NMF	
Boeing Company	**$47.88**	**0.95**	**16**	**$3.00**	**6.3%**	**10.5%**	**$15.05**
Chevron Corp.	$43.75	0.95	18	$2.50	5.7%	6.5%	$11.24
Coca-Cola	**$38.00**	**0.95**	**16**	**$2.45**	**6.4%**	**11.0%**	**$12.46**
DuPont	$86.75	1.15	12	$7.39	8.5%	12.0%	$38.09
Eastman Kodak	**$41.38**	**0.85**	**12**	**$3.55**	**8.6%**	**23.5%**	**$25.36**
Exxon Corp.	$42.25	0.75	13	$3.20	7.6%	4.5%	$13.80
General Electric	**$43.88**	**1.05**	**18**	**$2.43**	**5.5%**	**11.0%**	**$12.27**
General Motors	$70.00	1.00	7	$10.00	14.3%	3.0%	$40.69
Goodyear Tire	**$58.13**	**1.20**	**8**	**$7.70**	**13.2%**	**23.0%**	**$52.94**
IBM	$116.13	0.95	13	$8.72	7.5%	12.5%	$46.18
International Paper	**$43.25**	**1.25**	**12**	**$3.60**	**8.3%**	**22.5%**	**$24.34**
McDonald's Corp.	$47.38	1.00	17	$2.85	6.0%	15.5%	$16.31
Merck & Co.	**$163.25**	**0.90**	**24**	**$6.68**	**4.1%**	**22.0%**	**$45.72**
Minnesota Mng.	$59.00	1.05	15	$3.95	6.7%	13.5%	$21.34
Navistar Int'l.	**$5.50**	**1.25**	**25**	**$0.22**	**4.0%**	**NMF**	
Phillip Morris	$93.00	1.05	12	$7.80	8.4%	21.0%	$51.45
Primerica	**$29.13**	**1.00**	**9**	**$3.30**	**11.3%**	**17.5%**	**$19.91**
Procter & Gamble	$82.63	0.85	18	$4.59	5.6%	11.0%	$23.50
Sears & Roebuck	**$36.25**	**1.30**	**8**	**$4.50**	**12.4%**	**12.0%**	**$22.96**
Texaco	$42.25	0.75	26	$1.65	NMF	2.0%	
USX Corp.	**$32.88**	**0.95**	**26**	**$1.25**	**3.8%**	**NMF**	
Union Carbide	$23.88	NMF	11	$2.17	9.1%	NMF	
United Technologies	**$40.63**	**1.10**	**9**	**$4.35**	**10.7%**	**9.5%**	**$21.02**
Westinghouse	$53.25	1.30	10	$5.12	9.6%	12.5%	$26.48
Woolworth (F.W.)	**$45.13**	**1.10**	**12**	**$3.80**	**8.4%**	**14.0%**	**$20.74**
Mean*	$55.67	1.04	14	$4.45	8.1%	13.8%	$24.64

*All Mean figures exclude companies with incomplete data.
**Key assumptions—Risk-free interest rate equals   8.00%
                    —Market risk premium equals   2.50%

quired rate of return, the present value of the next five years of dividends and earnings is computed.[26] Comparing each of these figures to the current stock price provides an estimate of the proportion of the current price which may be attributed to short-term (next five years) versus long-term (beyond five years) dividends and earnings. Those proportions of the current stock price attributable to dividends and earnings beyond 5 years I am calling the "Long-term Value Indices" ("LVI"s—"LVID" for dividends and "LVIE" for earnings).

With the Dow Jones Industrials valued at a P/E of 14, which approximates the historic range, the average LVID is about 80 percent and the average LVIE is 55 percent. As might be expected, companies with poorer growth prospects tend to have lower LVIs, and vice-versa.[27] Rappaport reported similar LVI results, which he summed up in the following manner:

26. In applying the CAPM, the interest rate on five-year Treasury securities was employed as the risk-free rate of interest, and a market risk premium of 2.5% was assumed. The latter estimate was provided by a major investment banking firm.

27. In his broader-based study, Rappaport reports the lowest LVIs for public utilities and the highest LVIs for companies in the electronic components, medical instruments, retail drugs, radio-TV transmitting equipment, and electronic computers industries.

Long-Term Value Index** (LVI)	Dividends Per Share				
	Current Dividend	Dividend Yield	Projected Dividend Growth	Pres Val Next 5 Yr Dividends	Long-Term Value Index** (LVI)
65.3%	$1.80	5.5%	6.0%	$7.98	75.6%
45.9%	**$1.20**	**2.6%**	**7.0%**	**$5.36**	**88.2%**
72.6%	$0.76	2.9%	11.0%	$3.74	85.6%
62.5%	**$1.20**	**4.1%**	**5.0%**	**$5.23**	**82.2%**
	NIL	NIL	NIL		
68.6%	**$1.40**	**2.9%**	**9.5%**	**$6.84**	**85.7%**
74.3%	$2.40	5.5%	2.5%	$9.66	77.9%
67.2%	**$1.20**	**3.2%**	**5.5%**	**$5.25**	**86.2%**
56.1%	$3.40	3.9%	7.0%	$15.30	82.4%
38.7%	**$1.80**	**4.4%**	**7.0%**	**$8.26**	**80.0%**
67.3%	$2.00	4.7%	6.5%	$9.12	78.4%
72.0%	**$1.40**	**3.2%**	**11.0%**	**$7.07**	**83.9%**
41.9%	$5.00	7.1%	9.0%	$24.00	65.7%
8.9%	**$1.60**	**2.8%**	**4.0%**	**$6.61**	**88.6%**
60.2%	$4.40	3.8%	11.0%	$22.38	80.7%
43.7%	**$1.20**	**2.8%**	**9.0%**	**$5.66**	**86.9%**
65.6%	$0.50	1.1%	13.0%	$2.67	94.4%
72.0%	**$3.84**	**2.4%**	**20.0%**	**$24.94**	**84.7%**
63.8%	$2.12	3.6	11.0%	$10.71	81.9%
	NIL	**NIL**	**NIL**		
44.7%	$3.60	3.9%	18.5%	$22.23	76.1%
31.6%	**$1.60**	**5.5%**	**5.5%**	**$6.98**	**76.0%**
71.6%	$2.80	3.4%	6.0%	$12.50	84.9%
36.7%	**$2.00**	**5.5%**	**5.5%**	**$8.55**	**76.4%**
	NIL	NIL	NIL		
	$1.20	3.7%	10.0%	$5.94	81.9%
	$1.50	6.3%	3.0%		
48.2%	**$1.40**	**3.4%**	**8.5%**	**$6.58**	**83.8%**
50.3%	$1.72	3.2%	13.0%	$9.01	83.1%
54.0%	**$1.32**	**2.9%**	**14.0%**	**$7.20**	**84.0%**
55.3%	$2.30	3.8%	9.1%	$9.99	82.1%

In short, prices behave as if the market cares most about companies' long-term prospects, even though the financial community appears to emphasize short-term financial results. The most plausible explanation of this seeming paradox is that investors often see long-term implications in current information, including reported earnings, and use the latest results to reassess a company's prospects.

Overall, these results suggest that the market places considerable emphasis on a company's long-term prospects in valuing securities. As noted by Rappaport, high LVIs are an indication of the market's confidence in the ability of well-managed companies to gain and sustain a competitive advantage in the future.

CONCLUDING COMMENT

This study provides evidence that (1) common stock prices react positively to announcements of corporate strategic investment decisions and (2) the market appears to place considerable emphasis on prospective long-term developments in valuing securities. These results contradict the popular press accounts|which blame |the competitive|decline and corporate restructuring of U.S. industry on a myopic stock market. They are in fact strong evidence for the opposing claim (widely held by financial economists) that the popular "short-term theory" is, as Boone Pickens says, "pure hokum."

DO BAD BIDDERS BECOME GOOD TARGETS?

by Mark L. Mitchell and Kenneth Lehn,
U.S. Securities and Exchange Commission*

S ince the publication of Adolph Berle and Gardiner Means's *The Modern Corporation and Private Property* in 1932, it has been widely recognized that the interests of management and stockholders can diverge in public corporations with diffuse equity ownership. More recent developments in the theory of corporate finance—most notably, Michael Jensen and William Meckling's formulation of "agency cost" theory in the late 1970s—have called attention to the potential loss in value of public companies caused by the separation of ownership and control.[1]

Until the 1980s, however, most finance scholars, including Jensen and Meckling, continued to assume that the agency costs of separating ownership from control in our public companies could not be very great. Even if corporate boards of directors were not very effective in performing their prescribed role as overseers of stockholder interests, most financial economists reasoned that competition from international product markets and the existence of a market for executive labor should serve to limit the natural tendency of corporate management to put its own interests ahead of stockholders'. Executive compensation plans were also assumed to reduce this potential conflict of interest. And if all of these forces failed to join managerial with stockholder interests, then a vigorous takeover market (in academic parlance, the "market for corporate control") was thought to provide the ultimate deterrent to stockholder neglect.[2]

---

* This article is a shorter, less technical version of an article by the same title published in the *Journal of Political Economy* (1990). The views expressed herein are those of the authors and do not necessarily reflect the views of the SEC or of the authors' colleagues on the staff of the SEC.

1. See Michael C. Jensen and William H. Meckling, "Theory of the Firm: Managerial Behavior, Agency Cost and Ownership Structure," *Journal of Financial Economics* 3 (October 1976), pp. 305-60.

2. The seminal work on the market for corporate control (and indeed the origin of the phrase) is Henry Manne's article, "Mergers and the Market for Corporate Control," *Journal of Political Economy* 73 (April 1965), pp. 110-20. Another important early study is Robin Marris, "A Model of the Managerial Enterprise." *Quarterly Journal of Economics* 77 (May 1963), pp. 185-209. For more recent surveys of scholarship on the control market, see Michael C. Jensen and Richard S. Ruback, "The Market for Corporate Control: The Scientific Evidence," *Journal of Financial Economics* (April 1983), pp. 5-50; and Gregg A. Jarrell, James A. Brickley, and Jeffry M. Netter, "The Market for Corporate Control: The Empirical Evidence Since 1980," *Journal of Economic Perspectives* 2 (Winter 1988), pp. 49-68.

But the events of the 1980s have suggested otherwise. For most finance scholars, the proliferation of management buyouts and leveraged acquisitions by private investors has strengthened, if not indeed confirmed, the belief that the agency costs associated with outside equity ownership are far greater than once believed. In quite recent work, moreover, Jensen has argued that corporate takeovers, besides providing the ultimate "solution," may also have been an important part of the "problem." As Jensen suggests, the potential conflict between management and stockholders is most likely to surface in mature companies that generate substantial "free cash flow"—that is, more cash than management can profitably reinvest. In such cases, stockholders are best served by managements who pay out the excess capital to investors, say, in the form of large stock repurchases. But, to the extent corporate managements are more intent on maintaining growth than increasing profitability—and, as Jensen argues, there is a natural bias toward growth in large organizations with dispersed owners—they will choose to reinvest "free cash flow" at rates well below the corporate cost of capital rather than returning it to shareholders. And this practice can cause corporate stock prices to fall well below so-called "break-up" values.

One of the most prominent ways of reinvesting cash flow, and thus perpetuating unprofitable corporate growth, is by making value-reducing acquisitions—particularly, diversifying acquisitions. In this sense, as mentioned above, corporate takeovers operate not only as a disciplining force, but may also be one of the principal managerial practices that other takeovers are designed to stop. Given this potential for destroying stockholder value through corporate acquisitions, Jensen goes on to suggest that many takeovers in the 1980s—especially hostile takeovers followed by divestitures—have been motivated by the opportunity to create value simply by reversing prior mistaken acquisitions by target companies. In short, Jensen offers a plausible rationale for what have become known as "bust-up" takeovers.[3]

In this article, we report the findings of a series of statistical tests we designed to explore the following issues: Can takeover targets be distinguished from companies that do not become targets solely by the profitability of their past acquisitions? Specifically, do target companies systematically make acquisitions that the stock market judges more harshly than the acquisitions of companies that are not later taken over? And, more generally, does the market response to announcements of acquisitions provide a useful prediction of how such acquisitions will turn out?

An Illustrative Case. There is, of course, considerable anecdotal evidence to support the proposition that one of the primary motives for takeovers in the 1980s was simply to reverse mistaken acquisitions. In 1986, for example, Sir James Goldsmith made an unsuccessful takeover bid for Goodyear Tire & Rubber Co. For the right to assume control, Goldsmith offered a premium of approximately $1.13 billion over (and roughly 30 percent of) the current (pre-offer) equity value of the company. His declared intent was to sell Goodyear's petroleum and aerospace divisions, and to concentrate the company's focus on its tire and rubber operations.

What evidence do we have that Goodyear's past acquisitions were reducing the value of the company? When Goodyear announced its first major petroleum acquisition—its 1983 purchase of Celeron Oil for approximately $800 million—its stock price fell by over 10% on the day of announcement, amounting to a loss of almost $250 million for Goodyear stockholders. And, if we consider the market reaction over a longer period—one extending from five trading days before through 40 trading days after the announcement—the decline in Goodyear's stock price was almost 24%, representing shareholder losses of close to $600 million. Viewed in this light, the 30 percent premium over current market value offered by Goldsmith in 1986 could be interpreted largely as a recouping of the losses sustained by Goodyear's shareholders three years earlier when Goodyear began its diversification into the oil industry.[4]

---

3. See Michael C. Jensen, "Agency Costs of Free Cash Flow, Corporate Finance, and Takeovers," *American Economic Review* (May 1986), pp. 323-29. For a more extensive treatment of the argument that one of the primary causes of hostile takeovers may be "friendly" takeovers, see Amar Bhide, "The Causes and Consequences of Hostile Takeovers," *Journal of Applied Corporate Finance* (Summer 1989).

4. The S & P 500 index increased by about 60 percent from shortly before the first announcement of the Celeron acquisition in February 1983 through 20 days before the first announcement of Goldsmith's bid in October 1986. If the shareholder losses ($249 million [announcement day] and $573 million [-5,40 window]) associated with Goodyear's energy acquisition had instead been invested in the S & P 500 during this period, they would have increased to $401 million and $923 million, respectively. In this sense, the premium offered by Goldsmith can be seen as restoring much of the equity value in Goodyear that had been lost through acquisition.

Although Goodyear eventually defeated Goldsmith's takeover attempt, it was forced to adopt a major restructuring program similar to the one proposed by Goldsmith. Not surprisingly, the restructuring program included the sale of a substantial part of Celeron Oil. As a consequence, even after the offer was removed, Goodyear's stock price continued to reflect at least part of the 30% premium offered by Goldsmith.

The important question for economists, then, is as follows: Is this Goodyear case representative of a broadly recurring phenomenon, or is it just an isolated instance? To answer this question, we examined the stock market's reactions to announcements of 345 major acquisitions made by two sets of companies during the period 1982-1986: 113 acquisitions by 77 acquiring companies that later themselves became targets of other takeover attempts (henceforth referred to as "targets"); and a control group of 232 acquisitions by 133 acquiring companies that were not subjected to takeover bids ("nontargets"). We also attempted to distinguish between those acquiring companies that eventually became targets of hostile bids ("hostile targets") and those that received "friendly" bids ("friendly targets").

Here is a brief overview of our findings:

■ For the entire sample of acquisitions over the period 1982-1986, the average stock price effect associated with the acquisition announcements was not significantly different from zero.

■ In the cases of the 113 acquisitions by companies that later became targets themselves, the stock prices of the acquiring companies *declined* significantly (by over 3 percent, on average) during a 45-day period surrounding the announcements of the transactions.

■ In the case of the 232 acquisitions by companies that did *not* become targets of bids (at least through June 1988), the stock prices of the acquiring companies *increased* significantly upon announcement—in fact, by roughly the same 3 percent over the 45-day period.

■ Of the entire sample of acquisitions made between 1982-1986, 81 (or roughly 20%) were divested by the end of 1988. Over 40% of the acquisitions by companies that eventually became targets were later divested, as compared to only 9 percent for nontargets. In the case of the targets, moreover, the announcements

of acquisitions later divested were associated with an average 7 percent stock price decline during the 45-day period surrounding the announcements.

■ In the 81 cases of acquisitions later divested by both target and nontarget companies, the stock prices of the acquiring companies fell significantly (by 4 percent, on average) during the 45-day period surrounding the announcements. In the case of the acquisitions not divested, the average market response was a positive 1.9 percent.

■ Holding size (equity value) and the percentage of equity held by management constant, the probability of a company's becoming a target—especially a hostile target—during the period 1982-1988 was inversely and significantly related to the stock price effects associated with announcements of the firm's acquisitions. That is, the more negative the market's response to an acquisition, the greater the likelihood of a subsequent takeover attempt.

In short, our results suggest that one major source of value in many corporate takeovers—especially hostile takeovers—during the 1980s was the restoration of stockholder value that had been destroyed by the targets' prior acquisition strategies. Moreover, our finding of sharply negative market responses to acquisitions later divested provides strong support for the "efficiency"of the stock market. That is, when companies announce acquisitions, the stock market provides a useful forecast of the probability that the acquisitions will either succeed or eventually be reversed through divestiture.

THE DATA

The complete sample for our study consisted of 1158 public corporations in 51 industries covered by *Value Line* at the end of 1981.[5] The sample excluded two highly regulated industries (financial services and electric utility) covered by *Value Line*, as well as all companies in industries with fewer than ten listed firms. This modified sample of *Value Line* companies ended up including 64.4% of the companies in the 1981 S&P 500 Index and 75.2% of the companies in the 1981 Fortune 500.

Each of the 1158 companies was then classified into one of four groups based upon whether the firm was a takeover target during the period January 1980

---

5. Every quarter *Value Line* examines the financial prospects of about 1,500 firms in more than 65 industries.

TABLE 1
FREQUENCY OF
DIFFERENT TYPES OF
CONTROL TRANSACTIONS
DURING 1980-88

Nontargets (N=600)	Numbers	Percentage
No Control Transaction	600	(51.8%)
Hostile Targets (N=228)		
Successful HTO	58	(5.0%)
Unsuccessful HTO	69	(6.0%)
Unsuccessful HTO, Followed by Merger	51	(4.4%)
Unsuccessful HTO, Followed by LBO	21	(1.8%)
Unsuccessful HTO, Ending in Greenmail	7	(0.6%)
Proxy Fight	21	(1.8%)
Unsolicited Large Open Market Purchase	1	(0.1%)
Friendly Targets (N=240)		
Merger or Friendly Tender Offer	163	(14.1%)
LBO	53	(4.6%)
Unsuccessful LBO	10	(0.9%)
Unsuccessful LBO, Followed by Merger	14	(1.2%)
Miscellaneous (N=90)		
Greenmail, Absent a Tender Offer	11	(0.9%)
Large Targeted Repurchase (Possible Greenmail)	10	(0.9%)
Large Open Market Purchases	16	(1.4%)
Bankruptcy Filings or NYSE Suspensions	26	(2.2%)
Significant Corporate Restructuring	27	(2.3%)
Total Sample	**1158**	*(100.0%)*

HTO = Hostile Tender Offer
LBO = Leveraged Buyout

through July 1988. The four categories were as follows: (1) nontargets; (2) hostile targets; (3) friendly targets; and (4) miscellaneous companies.

As shown in Table 1, 600 (or 51.8%) of the 1158 companies were "nontargets." Such companies neither received takeover bids, paid greenmail, filed for bankruptcy, significantly restructured, nor were subjected to large unsolicited open market purchases. The "hostile" target group consisted of 228 firms (19.7% of the total) that were targets of either successful or unsuccessful hostile tender offers, proxy contests (in which the dissenting shareholder sought control), and large unsolicited open market purchases (in which the purchaser attempted to secure control). The "friendly" target group contained 240 firms (20.7% of the sample) that were targets of both successful and unsuccessful friendly tender offers, mergers, and leveraged buyouts. The miscellaneous category contained 90 companies (7.8%) that, in the absence of a tender offer, either paid greenmail, filed for bankruptcy, were subjected to large open market purchases in which the purchaser expressed no interest in securing control, or made large targeted stock repurchases or otherwise significantly restructured.

Our next step was to examine The Dow Jones *Broadtape* for the announcements of *major* acquisitions by the 1158 firms during 1982-1986. By major we meant only those acquisitions in which the disclosed purchase price was at least five percent of the market value of the acquiring company's common equity 20 trading days prior to the first announcement of the acquisition. Such acquisitions included acquisitions of other public companies, acquisitions of private companies, and purchases of assets, divisions, subsidiaries and stock of other companies.[6]

As shown in Table 2, 280 (or 24%) of the 1158 sample companies made a total of 401 acquisitions that amounted to at least five percent of their equity value during the period. Of these 401 acquisitions, 232 were made by 166 companies that did not become takeover targets; 113 were made by 77 companies that did

---

6. Both the NYSE and the ASE require member firms to disclose to Dow Jones any information, such as news of an acquisition, that might be expected to significantly affect their stock prices. Dow Jones transmits the disclosed information across the *Broadtape* to subscribers across the country. Subsequent editions of the Wall Street Journal carry most of the Broadtape stories.

TABLE 2
SUMMARY STATISTICS
FOR ACQUISITIONS
DURING 1982-86

No. of Firms[a]	No. of Acqr. Firms[b]	No. of Acquis.[c]	Avg. and Median Rel. Size of Acquis.[d]	Form of Financing					
				All Cash[e]	All Stock	Cash and Stock	Cash and Notes	Cash and Target Debt	Other
Total sample									
1158	280	401	.37	254	45	49	21	18	14
	(.24)	(.35)	(.18)	(.63)	(.11)	(.12)	(.05)	(.04)	(.03)
Nontargets									
600	166	232	.36	144	27	27	12	13	9
	(.28)	(.39)	(.18)	(.62)	(.12)	(.12)	(.05)	(.06)	(.04)
All Targets									
467	77	113	.35	79	13	11	5	3	2
	(.17)	(.24)	(.17)	(.70)	(.12)	(.10)	(.04)	(.03)	(.02)
Hostile Targets									
228	48	70	.30	50	9	6	1	3	1
	(.21)	(.31)	(.18)	(.71)	(.13)	(.09)	(.01)	(.04)	(.01)
Friendly Targets									
240	29	43	.42	29	4	5	4	0	1
	(.12)	(.18)	(.15)	(.67)	(.09)	(.12)	(.09)	(.00)	(.02)
Miscellaneous									
170	38	56	.44	31	5	11	4	2	3
	(.22)	(.33)	(.22)	(.55)	(.09)	(.20)	(.07)	(.04)	(.05)

a. The number of firms in the entire sample (1158) is less than the number of firms (1238) obtained by adding the firms in the four categories. This discrepancy occurs because of the inclusion of some of the firms in the target categories and the miscellaneous category (see footnote 9). Similarly, the number of acquiring firms in the entire sample (280) is less than the number of acquiring firms (281) obtained by adding the acquiring firms in the four categories.
b. Numbers in parentheses indicate the proportion of firms in each category that made acquisitions.
c. Numbers in parentheses indicate the number of acquisitions as a proportion of the number of firms in each category.
d. Median relative sizes of acquisitions are shown in parentheses below average relative sizes.
e. Numbers in parentheses indicate the proportion of acquisitions that made up the various forms of financing for each category.

become targets; and the remaining 56 were made by 38 companies classified as miscellaneous. Of the 113 acquisitions by companies that later received bids themselves, 70 were made by 48 companies that later received hostile bids; and 43 were made by 29 companies that received friendly bids.[7]

Several modes of payment can be used in making acquisitions. For each acquisition, we collected the form of payment from *Mergers and Acquisitions* and *The Wall Street Journal.* The data indicate that purely cash offers were the predominant form of payment, accounting for 254 (63%) of the acquisitions. At least some cash was used in 354 (88%) of the acquisitions. In contrast, purely stock transactions accounted for only 45 (11%) of the acquisitions, and at least some stock was used in 103 (26%) of the acquisitions. Although one study has found that the form of payment is correlated with the market's reaction to an acquisition announcement,[8] we found that the form of payment did not differ substantially

7. It is tempting, but probably wrong, to infer from Table 2 that nontarget firms make acquisitions more often than targets. This inference is unwarranted because the sample period is effectively longer for nontargets than for targets. For the target companies, we recorded only acquisitions made from January 1982 through three months prior to the first announcement of their suitor's interest in acquiring control. For example, if the first announcement of a bid for a target firm occurred in March 1984, we recorded acquisitions for only the two years 1982 and 1983.

One conclusion that does emerge unambiguously from Table 2 is this: Because 79% of the hostile targets did not make a large acquisition during the sample period preceding the reception of their bids, our "bad bidder" explanation of hostile takeovers is at best a partial explanation for these transactions. As also

shown in Table 2, the relative size of the acquisitions relative to the acquiring firms do not vary much between the target and nontarget subsamples, thus allowing for comparison of the empirical results below.

8. See Paul Asquith, Robert F. Bruner, and David W. Mullins, Jr., "Merger Returns and the Form of Financing," (Manuscript. Cambridge: Harvard University, 1987). This study finds that, for a sample of 343 mergers and tender offers that occurred during 1973-83, there were significant positive stock price reactions to acquiring firms for cash offers and negative reactions for stock offers. We find a higher proportion of cash offers in our study than do Asquith et al. They focus on mergers and tender offers, whereas our study examines all acquisitions, including purchases of assets and divisions, which are generally cash offers.

TABLE 3
ABNORMAL STOCK MARKET PERFORMANCE ASSOCIATED WITH FIRMS ANNOUNCING ACQUISITIONS DURING 1982-86

[handwritten: CAR's - ot Average Daily AR's]

[handwritten right margin: stock increased this much in a 60 day period]

Category	Event Window				
	[0]	[-1,1]	[-5,1]	[-5,40]	[-20,40]
Entire Sample	-0.21**	-0.08	0.14	0.70	0.57
(n=401)	(2.18)	(-0.45)	(0.53)	(1.05)	(0.75)
	42.39	46.63	50.37	54.11	53.12
Nontargets	0.09	0.49**	0.82**	3.32***	3.48***
(n=232)	(0.66)	(2.19)	(2.42)	(3.80)	(3.46)
	44.83	48.71	56.03	62.93	62.07
All Targets	-0.78***	-0.93***	-1.27***	-3.38***	-3.46***
(n=113)	(-4.59)	(-3.16)	(-2.82)	(-2.93)	(-2.60)
	39.82	39.82	38.05	38.05	38.94
Hostile Targets	-0.95***	-1.50***	-1.34**	-3.37**	-3.19**
(n=70)	(-4.64)	(-4.22)	(-2.46)	(-2.42)	(-2.00)
	38.57	37.14	35.71	38.57	40.00
Friendly Targets	-0.50*	-0.01	-1.17	-3.39*	-3.91*
(n=43)	(-1.68)	(-0.02)	(-1.47)	(-1.67)	(-1.67)
	41.86	44.19	41.86	37.21	37.21
Miscellaneous	-0.31	-0.69	0.14	-1.93	-3.33
(n=56)	(-1.01)	(-1.32)	(0.17)	(-0.94)	(-1.42)
	37.50	51.79	51.79	50.00	44.64

Note.—z-statistics are in parentheses and percent abnormal returns that are positive are listed below z-statistics.
* Significant at the 10 percent level. ** Significant at the 5 percent level. *** Significant at the 1 percent level.

among the samples of nontargets, hostile targets, and friendly targets.

THE STOCK MARKET RESPONSE

For each of the 401 acquisitions in our sample, we calculated shareholder rates of return based on stock price reactions to the announcements of the transactions. We measured the market response over five different "event windows," ranging in length from just the day of the announcement itself to the 60-day period extending from 20 days before the announcement until 40 days after. We also adjusted all such calculations to eliminate the effect of general market movements and differences in risk among individual stocks.

The Market Reaction to Acquiring Companies

As shown in the first row of Table 3, the average announcement-day market response to the entire sample of 401 acquisitions was -0.21%. The market-adjusted returns over the other four windows ranged from -0.08% [day -1, day +1] to 0.70% [-5,+40]; and none of these returns was significantly different from zero. Like most prior "event" studies of mergers and

acquisitions, these results suggest that, on average, acquiring companies earn normal rates of return on their investments—a finding consistent with a competitive market for corporate control.

But, as shown in the second and third rows of Table 3, the market response to announcements of acquisitions made by companies that later became targets differed significantly from the response to acquisition announcements by nontarget companies. The average announcement-day return associated with 113 acquisitions made by all target companies was -0.78%; and, as the event window widened, the negative response became progressively more pronounced, reaching a -3.46% over the 60-day event window. (All of these estimates, moreover, were highly statistically significant.) The fact that the returns become significantly more negative as the event window extends beyond the acquisition announcements suggests that, as the market learned more about these acquisitions during the succeeding weeks (about such things as the purchase price, definitiveness of the acquisition, and expected synergies), it took an increasingly dim view of the prospects for the acquisition and the acquiring company.

By contrast, the average stock price reaction to announcements of 232 acquisitions by companies

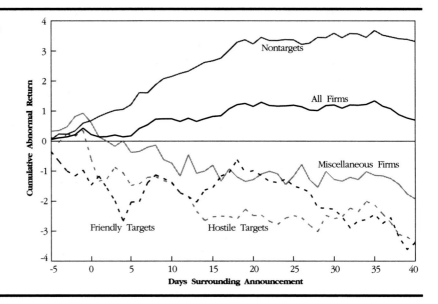

FIGURE 1
STOCK PRICE REACTIONS
TO ACQUISITION
ANNOUNCEMENTS
(1982-86)

that did not later become targets ranged from neutral to sharply positive—depending, again, on the event window chosen. The average announcement-day return for these nontarget companies was 0.09%, and became progressively larger with each extension of the window, reaching a high of 3.48% over the 60-day window. (With the exception of the announcement-day return, all of these estimates were significant at the 0.05 level or higher.) In sharp contrast to acquisitions by target companies, as more information became available to investors about acquisitions by nontarget companies, their reaction to the new business combination became more positive.

Finally, our results showed no statistically significant market reaction—regardless of the window chosen—to the 56 acquisitions made by the group of companies classified as "miscellaneous."

As summarized in Figure 1, then, our findings demonstrate that the stock market assigned a negative value to acquisitions by companies that later became takeover targets, especially targets of hostile offers. At the same time, it positively valued acquisi-

tions by companies that were not subjected to takeover bids during the sample period.[9]

A COMPARISON OF DIVESTITURE RATES (Along With Some Striking Evidence On Market Efficiency)

The results presented so far show that, on average, acquisitions by targets—especially hostile targets—reduce their stock prices, whereas nontarget companies make acquisitions that increase their stock prices. Broadly speaking, there are two plausible explanations for the market's negative reaction to the acquisitions made by targets: (1) target companies tend to make acquisitions that the market expects to reduce the combined operating profitability of acquirer and acquired (what might be called "negative synergies"); and (2) targets tend to overpay for acquisitions the market believes will otherwise increase the combined profitability of the combined companies (so much so that the overpayment exceeds the expected synergies from the combination).[10]

9. Though the difference in the market's response to acquisitions by nontargets and the other groups is obvious from the exhibit, there is little apparent difference between the market reaction to the hostile target, friendly target and miscellaneous groups. As shown in Table 3, however, the estimates are statistically significant in all event windows for the hostile target category, but not significant in two of the windows for the friendly target category or any of the windows for the miscellaneous category.

10. For theories of bidder overpayment, see Richard Roll, "The Hubris Hypothesis of Corporate Takeover," *Journal of Business* (April 1986), pp. 197-216; and Bernard Black, "Bidder Overpayment in Takeovers," *Stanford Law Review* 41 (February 1989), pp. 597-660.

These two explanations are by no means mutually exclusive since acquirers can both overpay and make otherwise poor acquisition choices. (In fact, many of the diversifying acquisitions of the 1970s and early 80s probably fit both categories.) And, technically, of course, any mistaken acquisition represents a form of overpayment—one in which the returns do not justify the investment. Both explanations, moreover, are consistent with the argument that takeovers function (ultimately) as a means of disciplining managers who fail to maximize stockholders' wealth.

But there is nonetheless an important difference between these two explanations—one that could lend itself to testing. Those acquisitions that prove to have "negative synergies"—or, alternatively, those that prove to have greater value to other potential acquirers—are much more likely to be divested than otherwise synergistic acquisitions for which the acquirer overpaid. In the case of "negative synergies," the motive behind many takeovers is to "undo" inefficient acquisitions previously made by the targets. In the case of overpayments for otherwise sound investments, takeovers can serve to restrain managers in target firms from further waste of stockholder capital through future overpayments; but, in such cases, there will be little opportunity to create value simply by divesting past acquisitions.

Although unable to devise a way of testing the overpayment explanation, we attempted to measure the extent of the "negative synergy" hypothesis by comparing the rate at which acquisitions made by targets were subsequently divested with the corresponding divestiture rate for nontargets during the sample period. Target divestitures were defined to be all acquisitions by targets that were divested during a period ranging from three months prior to the reception of their bid through the end of the sample period (June 1988). Such transactions thus included the following: (1) divestitures by targets to defend against a takeover; (2) divestitures as part of a restructuring program after defeating a takeover attempt; and (3) divestitures by acquiring firms following successful takeovers of the targets.

Nontarget divestitures, by definition, consisted of acquisitions that were divested voluntarily by the end of the sample period.

To the extent that "negative synergies," then, and not "overpayment," was motivating the takeovers of "bad bidders," we expected the divestiture rate to be significantly higher for targets than for nontargets. We also expected the stock market reaction to announcements of acquisitions later divested to be significantly more negative than the price reactions to acquisitions that were retained. This relationship was expected to hold, moreover, not only for the sample of targets, but for the nontargets and miscellaneous companies as well.

The Data. We were able to track subsequent divestitures of acquisitions from three sources: annual issues of *Mergers and Acquisitions*, *The Wall Street Journal Index* and Standard & Poor's *Directory of Corporate Affiliations* for each of the years 1982-1988. We also relied on telephone conversations with representatives of the acquiring companies to confirm our findings.

The data revealed that 81 (or 20.2%) of our entire sample of 401 acquisitions over the period 1982-1986 were subsequently divested during the period 1982-1988. Moreover, there was a significant difference in the rate of divestiture by targets and nontargets. Whereas only 9.1% (21/232) of the acquisitions made by nontargets were later divested, over 40% (46/113) of the acquisitions made by targets were divested, either in response to or following successful or unsuccessful takeover attempts. (The z-statistic for this difference in divestiture rates was a highly significant 6.34.) There was, however, no significant difference in divestiture rates between hostile targets and friendly targets (the rates were 41.9% (18/43) for acquisitions made by friendly targets, and 40% (28/70) for acquisitions made by hostile targets). It is also noteworthy that *only two* of the friendly targets and none of the hostile targets divested previously acquired units *without the threat of takeover*.

The Market Response to Acquisitions as a Predictor of Future Divestiture

As shown in Table 4, the stock price reaction to announcements of acquisitions later divested was significantly more negative than the market response to acquisitions not so divested. For the entire sample of 81 divested acquisitions, the average announcement-day return was −1.26% (significant at the 0.01 level). Using the longer 60-day window, the acquiring companies underperformed the market by 5.59%, on average (and, again, all of these estimates were significant at the 0.01 level for all windows).

By contrast, the announcement-day return for the acquiring companies of the 320 acquisitions that were not later divested was 0.05% (not statistically significant). As we used longer event windows, the returns

TABLE 4
ABNORMAL STOCK MARKET PERFORMANCE ASSOCIATED WITH FIRMS ANNOUNCING ACQUSITIONS DURING 1982-86 THAT ARE SUBSEQUENTLY DIVESTED VERSUS ACQUISITIONS DURING 1982-86 THAT ARE NOT SUBSEQUENTLY DIVESTED

PANEL A: ACQUISITIONS THAT ARE SUBSEQUENTLY DIVESTED

PANEL B: ACQUISITIONS THAT ARE NOT SUBSEQUENTLY DIVESTED

Category	Event Window				
	[0]	[−1,1]	[−5,1]	[−5,40]	[−20,40]
Entire Sample	−1.26***	−1.75***	−1.53***	−4.01***	−5.59***
(n=81)	(−6.15)	(−4.93)	(−2.81)	(−2.88)	(−3.48)
	35.80	30.86	38.27	35.80	32.10
Nontargets	−1.16***	−1.66**	−0.57	2.55	2.48
(n=21)	(−2.86)	(−2.30)	(−0.53)	(0.92)	(0.78)
	42.86	28.57	47.62	61.90	57.14
All Targets	−1.45***	−1.56***	−2.07***	−7.04***	−8.91***
(n=46)	(−5.58)	(−3.46)	(−3.01)	(−3.99)	(−4.38)
	30.44	30.44	34.78	23.91	21.74
Hostile Targets	−2.01***	−2.59***	−1.84**	−4.96***	−6.35***
(n=28)	(−7.13)	(−5.30)	(−2.46)	(−2.59)	(−2.88)
	28.57	21.43	32.14	28.57	28.57
Friendly Targets	−0.58	0.04	−2.44*	−10.27***	−12.90***
(n=18)	(−1.19)	(0.05)	(−1.89)	(−3.09)	(−3.37)
	33.33	44.44	38.89	16.67	11.11
Miscellaneous	−0.75	−2.38**	−0.45	−3.21	−5.91
(n=12)	(−1.16)	(−2.11)	(0.26)	(−0.73)	(−1.16)
	50.00	41.67	41.67	33.33	25.00
Entire Sample	0.05	0.35*	0.56**	1.89***	2.13**
(n=320)	(0.50)	(1.90)	(1.99)	(2.63)	(2.57)
	44.06	50.63	53.44	58.75	58.44
Nontargets	0.21	0.70***	0.96***	3.40***	3.58***
(n=211)	(1.59)	(3.07)	(2.78)	(3.80)	(3.47)
	45.02	50.71	56.87	63.03	62.56
All Targets	−0.32	−0.50	−0.72	−0.87	0.28
(n=67)	(−1.47)	(−1.33)	(−1.26)	(−0.59)	(0.17)
	46.27	46.27	40.30	47.78	50.75
Hostile Targets	−0.25	−0.77*	−1.00	−2.31	−1.08
(n=42)	(−0.94)	(−1.70)	(−1.45)	(−1.31)	(−0.53)
	45.24	47.62	38.10	45.24	47.62
Friendly Targets	−0.45	−0.05	−0.25	1.56	2.56
(n=25)	(−1.24)	(−0.08)	(−0.27)	(0.64)	(0.91)
	48.00	44.00	44.00	52.00	56.00
Miscellaneous	−0.18	−0.23	0.30	−1.58	−2.63
(n=44)	(−0.56)	(−0.40)	(0.34)	(−0.71)	(−1.02)
	34.09	54.55	54.55	54.55	50.00

Note.—z-statistics are in parentheses and percent abnormal returns thatare positive are listed below z-statistics.
* Significant at the 10 percent level. ** Significant at the 5 percent level. *** Significant at the 1 percent level.

became progressively more positive, reaching 2.13% for the 60-day window (significant at the 0.01 level).

This finding of a statistically significant negative market response to announcements of acquisitions that are later divested, together with a positive and significant price reaction to acquisitions that are retained, delivers a strong message of market efficiency. In essence, the market reaction to announcements of acquisitions amounts to an immediate unbiased forecast—that is, one that turns out to be right on average—of the likelihood that the assets now being acquired will ultimately be divested.

In the case of the 46 acquisitions later divested by just the target companies, our findings strongly support the argument that many takeovers in the 1980s were designed primarily to reverse past acquisition mistakes. The average announcement-day return associated with these acquisitions was −1.45% (significant at the 0.01 level); and the average return fell to −8.91% when using a 60-day window. By contrast, the average announcement-day return associated with 67 acquisitions by targets that were not later divested was −0.32%; and estimates using longer event windows were also not reliably different from zero.

In short, the average negative stock price effect associated with acquisitions made by targets was largely the result of the subset of acquisitions later divested, whether in "bust-up" takeovers, or during or following an unsuccessful takeover attempt. Such evidence provides support for the "negative synergies" as opposed to the "overpayment" explanation for the market's negative reaction to acquisitions (although, as suggested earlier, it is impossible to distinguish completely between the effects of the two).

The results on divested acquisitions by the nontarget categories were also of interest. The average announcement-day return associated with 21 acquisitions made by nontargets that were later voluntarily divested was −1.16% (significant at the 0.01 level). In contrast, the announcement-day return associated with 211 nontarget acquisitions not so divested was 0.21% (not significant). Over the 60-day period, however, the return was a positive (and highly significant) 3.58%. On average, these results indicate that the nontarget companies eventually chose voluntarily to divest those acquisitions whose prospects the market pronounced from the outset to be poor.

The rate of divestiture by acquiring companies, as noted earlier, was significantly higher for targets (40.7%, 46/113) than for nontargets (9.1%, 21/232). And, perhaps equally telling, there were only two divestitures by target companies *prior* to a takeover threat. In this sense, the *voluntary* divestiture rate for targets (1.8%, 2/113) was actually considerably lower than the divestiture rate for nontargets (z-statistic = 3.23). The clear suggestion here is that many of the nontargets that sold off past acquisitions

may have avoided takeover attempts precisely by voluntarily divesting less profitable acquisitions. Had the target companies done the same, or refrained from such acquisitions in the first place, they too may have avoided bids.

CONCLUSION

The evidence presented in this article supports economists' concept of the "market for corporate control" (specifically, takeovers) as a mechanism for disciplining managers who operate their companies in ways that do not maximize profits. It also provides support for Michael Jensen's more recent "free cash flow" theory, which views takeovers as a means of disciplining managers who "waste" excess corporate capital on value-reducing acquisitions instead of paying it out to stockholders.

The evidence also bears directly on popular objections to hostile takeovers.

First, although critics lament the rise of so-called "bust-up" takeovers during the 1980s—those that led to large divestitures—our findings are consistent with the argument that such bust-up takeovers promote economic efficiency by reallocating the targets' assets to higher-valued uses or more efficient users.

Second, our results cast new light on existing research into the effect of takeovers on the equity value of acquiring companies. Critics of hostile takeovers often argue that although target shareholders fare well in takeovers, such transactions frequently reduce the equity value of the acquirers. Our evidence illuminates this controversy by suggesting that takeovers can be at once a source of the problem of stockholder neglect and a solution to that problem. Although we find that the returns to acquiring companies are approximately zero *in the aggregate*, use of the aggregate data obscures the fact that the market discriminates very clearly between "good" bidders and "bad" bidders. Bad bidders, the evidence demonstrates, are far more likely to become the next takeover candidates.

THE MOTIVES AND CONSEQUENCES OF DEBT-EQUITY SWAPS AND DEFEASANCES:

MORE EVIDENCE THAT IT DOES NOT PAY TO MANIPULATE EARNINGS

by John R. M. Hand,
University of Chicago, and
Patricia J. Hughes,
University of Southern California

■

On February 9, 1982, Hammermill Paper registered with the Securities and Exchange Commission to swap as many as 400,000 common shares for $13.4 million of the company's 8.07% promissory notes due February 1, 1997. The resulting swap increased Hammermill's 1st quarter earnings by $3.7 million, accounting for more than a third of its earnings for that period. Between February 9 and 10, the market value of Hammermill's equity fell by 4.5%.

On January 28, 1985, United Airlines announced that its preceding 4th quarter earnings included a $3 million extraordinary gain from the defeasance of $38 million of outstanding notes, and that earnings for all of 1984 included a defeasance gain of $21.5 million, representing 7.6% of UAL's 1984 net income. Between January 28 and 29, the market value of UAL's equity declined by 4.6%.

■

During the period of high interest rates in the early 1980s, many companies availed themselves of two new techniques for retiring discounted debt: debt-equity swaps and insubstance defeasances. These transactions were touted by investment bankers as a means of increasing reported earnings without increasing taxes. They were also held up as a way of achieving reductions of balance sheet leverage. Using debt-equity swaps, for example, companies could retire an amount of (book value) debt significantly greater than the amount of equity issued in exchange.

Skeptics, however, pointed out that such transactions had no economic substance. The increase in earnings did not represent any increase in corporate operating cash flow; and the value to stock-holders of reductions in the market price of the debt below par should already have been reflected in corporate stock prices. In a reasonably sophisticated market, they reasoned, transactions designed primarily to project accounting illusions should confer no benefits on stockholders. And, to the extent swaps and defeasances actually impose costs on stockholders or provide "signals" of bad news ahead, they may well end up reducing corporate stock prices.

In this article, we present the findings of our own recent research on swaps and defeasances. This research was designed to answer the following two questions: What were the principal corporate motives for these transactions? And what were the consequences for stockholders?

SOME BACKGROUND

What is a Debt-Equity Swap? In a debt-equity swap, an investment banker purchases a company's bonds in the open market, exchanges those bonds for a new issue of the company's common stock, and then sells the stock to investors. A swap thus combines a new equity issue with a retirement of debt. Because the difference between the book and market values of retired bonds is included in reported earnings, debt-equity swaps increase earnings during periods of high interest rates.

As mentioned above, however, there is no corresponding increase in corporate cash flow. And in fact the reduction in interest tax shields that accompanies debt-equity swaps may actually reduce after-tax operating cash flow. In addition to higher corporate taxes, an additional cost of debt-equity swaps are investment banker fees that average close to 4% of the market value of the newly issued stock.

What Is a Defeasance? In an insubstance defeasance, a company buys U.S. government securities with cash payouts identical in amount and timing to those promised by some of its own outstanding bonds. The government securities are then placed with a trustee who services the company's bonds using the cash flows from the government securities. While the defeased bonds remain outstanding and continue to trade, they are removed from the firm's balance sheet, and the difference between the book value of the defeased bonds and the cost of the government securities is included in earnings.

As in the case of debt-equity swaps, the accounting income from a defeasance does not correspond to an increase in cash flow. Unlike a swap, the interest tax shield from a defeased debt issue remains intact; but because the company also incurs additional taxes on the interest earned on the portfolio of Treasury bonds, the net effect is also likely to be an increase in the total amount of corporate taxes.

Why Did They Come About When They Did? The rise of debt-equity swaps and insubstance defeasances in the 1980s can be seen as the fairly direct consequence of changes in the tax code.

Prior to the 1980s, companies simply bought back their discounted debt in the open market. Such direct repurchases first became popular in the early 1970s, presumably because the rise in interest rates allowed companies to realize large accounting gains by buying back their debt well below par. The practice became so common that, in 1975, the Financial Accounting Standards Board issued FAS #4, which prescribed that gains and losses from early debt retirement be classified as "extraordinary." Until 1981, moreover, the gains arising from the repurchase of discounted debt were essentially tax-free.

The practice of directly repurchasing discounted debt came to an end with the the Bankruptcy Tax Act of 1980, which eliminated this favorable tax treatment. Then, in 1981, with interest rates again on a sharp rise, Salomon Brothers created the debt-equity swap in order to facilitate tax-free retirements of discounted debt. Between August 1981 and June 1984, approximately 290 swaps were performed by 170 different companies.

This movement in turn came to an abrupt halt when a provision in the Deficit Reduction Act of 1984 made the gains from swaps taxable. As a consequence, insubstance defeasances, aided by a ruling from the FASB (#76) that permitted the defeased debt to be removed from the balance sheet, then became the preferred vehicle for retiring debt. The popularity of defeasances, however, was ended by the decline in interest rates that began at the end of 1984. (See Figure 1, which clearly demonstrates that the frequency of these transactions depends critically on the level of interest rates.)

SOME NEW EVIDENCE

Two recently published studies have examined both the corporate motives for and the stockholder consequences of swaps and defeasances. In the first, one of the present writers looked at a sample of 245 debt-equity swaps completed during the three-year period August 1981 to June 1984.[1] In the second, we (along with a third researcher, Steve Sefcik) analyzed data on 80 defeasances executed during the period April 1981-February 1987.[2]

---

1. John Hand, "Did Firms Undertake Debt-Equity Swaps for an Accounting Paper Profit or True Financial Gain?," *The Accounting Review*, Vol. 64 No. 4 (1989).

2. John Hand, Patricia J. Hughes, and Stephan E. Sefcik, "Insubstance Defeasances: Security Price Reactions and Motivations," *Journal of Accounting and Economics*, Vol. 13 No. 1 (1990).

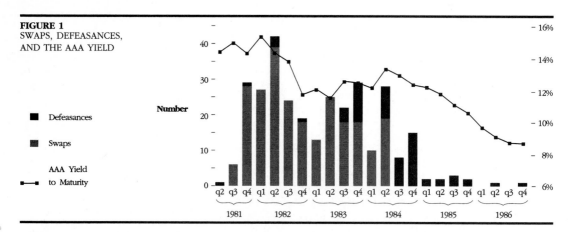

FIGURE 1
SWAPS, DEFEASANCES,
AND THE AAA YIELD

Defeasances

Swaps

AAA Yield
to Maturity

TABLE 1
SWAPS AND DEFEASANCES

Sample Statistics
($ in millions)

Item	Minimum	Median	Maximum
SWAPS			
Face Value of Debt Swapped	1.1	21.1	197.5
Market Value of Equity Issued	0.9	15.1	164.4
Reported Swap Gain	-2.2	4.8	87.3
Coupon on Bonds Swapped	3.75%	8.1%	14.25%
Numbers of Years to Maturity for Bonds Swapped	0.25	15.1	28.2
DEFEASANCES			
Book Value of Debt Defeased	1.8	21.4	550.0
Cost of Riskless Securities	2.2	19.6	550.0
Reported Defeasance Gain	-12.4	0.7	132.0
Coupon on Bonds Defeased	3.0%	7.9%	14.4%
Number of Years to Maturity for Bonds Defeased	0.04	6.2	90.0

Corporate Motives

In the case of both swaps and defeasances, the coupons on the retired debt were in most cases significantly lower than market rates (see Table 1). As suggested earlier, the larger this difference, the greater the opportunity for cosmetic improvements of income statements and balance sheets.

'Managing' the Income Statement. The research produced strong evidence that managers used debt-equity swaps to smooth quarterly earnings. In the average swap, quarterly EPS in the quarter the swap was transacted was lower than reported EPS in any of the twelve quarters preceding and twelve quarters following the swap. And, as shown in Figure 2, swaps appear to have been very effective in disguising a temporary downturn in operating earnings.

In the case of defeasances, we chose to focus on trends in annual EPS for only those defeasing companies that reported defeasance gains greater than the median. Our assumption in so doing was that such firms were most likely to be smoothing earnings. The results of this analysis, as shown graphically in Figure 3, provide strong support for our contention that income "management" was a primary motive for defeasances. Further confirming our suspicions, the research also showed that both swaps and defeasances were concentrated near the ends of the quarters in which they were executed.

'Managing' the Balance Sheet. Unlike a debt-equity swap, in which the investment bankers use the proceeds of an equity offering to repurchase the debt, a defeasance requires cash to purchase the portfolio of government securities. How were such defeasances financed? And were they designed to make a permanent change in corporate capital structures?

To answer these questions, we examined the financial statements of 64 defeasing companies and

FIGURE 2
THE ROLE OF SWAPS
IN MANAGING EARNINGS

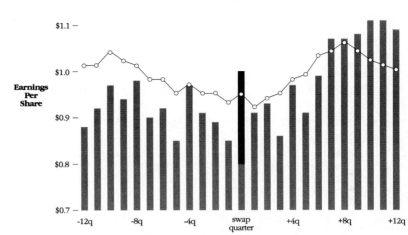

o—o Median Quarterly EPS
for the S&P 500

▨ Median Quarterly EPS
for the Swapping Firms

■ Median EPS Swap Gain
for the Swapping Firms

Event Quarter Relative to the Swap Quarter

FIGURE 3
DEFEASANCES AND
EARNINGS MANAGEMENT

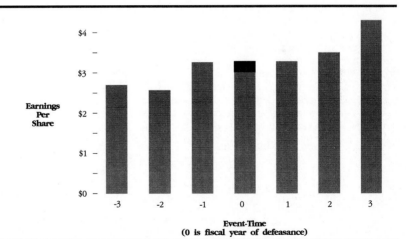

▨ EPS Excluding
Defeasance Gain

■ Defeasance Gain

Event-Time
(0 is fiscal year of defeasance)

Note: 64 of the 80 defeasances in our sample had both annual EPS data and information on the amount of the defeasance
gain. This figure represents the median of those 32 cases in which the defeasance gain was the largest.

a control group of other companies matched by industry, size, and fiscal year-end. Our results, as summarized in Table 2, show that defeasances were financed, on average, by some combination of excess cash and new stock issues. Also not surprising, they were undertaken by companies with

higher debt-equity ratios, possibly either to improve the look of the balance sheet or to avoid running up against restrictions in bond covenants.

What was surprising, however, was that one year after the defeasance, the leverage ratios of defeasing companies actually *increased* significantly

TABLE 2
DEFEASANCE FINANCING
($ in millions)

	Year Before Defeasance	Year of Defeasance	Year After Defeasance
Cash and Marketable Securities			
Defeasing Firms	610.4	593.4	643.3
Matched Firms	324.0	325.3	347.1
Long-term Debt Issued			
Defeasing Firms	141.4	107.8	164.2
Matched Firms	156.4	280.9	656.4
Common and Preferred Stock Issued			
Defeasing Firms	30.5	47.3	22.1
Matched Firms	32.0	14.7	31.2
Debt/Equity Ratio			
Defeasing Firms	0.74	0.78	1.14
Matched Firms	0.64	0.59	0.46

relative to the control group. The fact that many companies followed defeasances with new debt issues suggests that there was no underlying intent to reduce the amount of leverage in the target capital structure. And this reinforces our suspicion that the primary corporate motive for defeasances was simply to boost reported earnings.

The Consequences (Or Did the Stock Market Buy It?)

To determine whether investors capitalized such earnings into stock prices, the research examined the stock market reactions to the initial public release of information about the transactions. In the case of the 245 debt-equity swaps, the price movements were measured over the two trading days surrounding the registration of the transactions with the SEC. In the case of defeasances, we looked at two-day price reactions to announcements of 35 defeasances that appeared in the *Wall Street Journal*.

The Market Response

	Swaps	Defeasances
Mean abnormal return	-1.3%	-0.86%
(t-statistic)	(-7.9)	(-2.4)
% of negative returns	69%	66%

The average stock price reaction to debt-equity swaps was -1.3%. In the case of defeasances, the price movement was -0.86%. In the case of swaps, moreover, the larger the accounting gain from the swap, the more negative the market's response.

Stock market investors, then, do not appear to have been misled by such artificial increases in earnings. In fact, the evidence suggests that investors may have understood the underlying corporate motive for such transactions all too clearly. Anticipating a decline in operating cash flow, they correctly marked down the value of the shares before the lower earnings actually materialized.[3]

Wealth Transfer to Bondholders? Another tenable explanation for the negative market reaction to defeasances concerns its effect on the prices of outstanding bonds. Because the defeasance portfolio is irrevocably dedicated to servicing the defeased bonds, some speculated that a wealth transfer from stockholders to bondholders would result from the reduction in bond default risk. And, in fact, for our 35 public announcements of defeasances, we found the average price response of 24 bond issues to be a positive 1 percent (with a **t** statistic of 3.1). If the total operating value of the firm (debt plus equity) remains unchanged, such increases in bond values represent reductions in the value of the equity.

CONCLUDING COMMENTS

The evidence from our recent research suggests that managers undertake costly debt-equity swaps and defeasances in "bad times" in order to disguise downturns in reported earnings. Stock market investors, far from being fooled by such accounting illusions, respond negatively to these transactions. While reductions in corporate leverage and the associated tax shields partly explain the negative reaction, it also seems likely that investors correctly interpret such attempts to manipulate earnings as a sign of poor operating results ahead.

---

3. The somewhat more negative investor response to debt-equity swaps than to defeasances may have much to do with the fact that swaps involve the issue of new equity. It is now well-documented that announcements of corporate equity offerings reduce stock prices—by 2 or 3 percent, on average.

AN ANALYSIS OF TRADING PROFITS: HOW MOST TRADING ROOMS REALLY MAKE MONEY

*by Albéric Braas
and Charles N. Bralver,
Oliver, Wyman & Company*

Our observation of more than 40 large trading operations has led us to conclude that most trading rooms should be managed to generate stable profits by taking little positioning risk. This prescription is founded on three basic observations, each of which is developed in one of the three main parts of this article:

1. The Myth of Speculative Positioning as the Best Source of Profit. In this section we argue that, for most trading rooms, positioning is not a reliable source of revenues and profits.

2. The Value of the Turn. Here we take the view that more money is made trading interdealer volume than is customarily believed—but that it only happens if traders adopt a "jobber" style of trading.

3. The Power of Customer Business. Here we show the value of trading with customers and conclude that, for most trading rooms, it should be viewed as the primary source of revenue and profit.

THE MYTH OF SPECULATIVE POSITIONING AS BEST SOURCE OF PROFIT

Traders are naturally inclined to believe that the primary source of earnings in trading fixed income securities, equities, or foreign exchange is positioning. The underlying premise is that quality traders are able to predict the movements of interest rates, foreign exchange rates, and stock prices with sufficient accuracy to "beat the market"—if not consistently, then at least more often than not.

Having analyzed trading rooms around the world, for smaller operations in regional centers as well as major players, our experience suggests the above premise is ill-founded. For most trading rooms and traders, the financial markets are in fact very efficient, and betting on price movements is not a sound business proposition. Just as economists cannot consistently predict interest rates and mutual fund managers do not outperform the market year after year, traders cannot be expected to "outguess" movements in the value of trading instruments with any degree of reliability.

It is instructive to track the pattern of traders' positions relative to subsequent market movements. Exhibit 1, which reflects our analysis of a large foreign exchange trading desk in New York, shows the relationship (or the conspicuous absence thereof) between one group of successful traders' positions in Swiss francs and Deutsche marks and subsequent changes in the spot market prices of those currencies. If these traders were consistently making money by taking positions, long positions would be strongly correlated with up movements and short positions with down movements; the dots would lie along an upward-sloping diagonal running from lower left to upper right. In this case, they do not—and it is our experience as an adviser that they seldom do.

There are, however, a few significant exceptions. We know of three situations in which traders can make money by positioning. First, positioning-taking tends to be profitable when the market experiences a lift or slide of significant duration. One example is the decline of the dollar in 1987, when most foreign exchange traders went short and made money. The slide may not have been foreseeable; but once it was underway, it seemed easy to call. Unfortunately, such situations are rare, and hence cannot be relied upon to generate sustained profits over time. Second, traders can make money by positioning when they have some proprietary

EXHIBIT 1
PRICE CHANGE VS.
POSITION SIZE

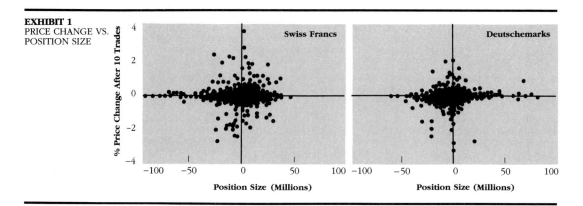

source of information. And, third, consistent profits from positioning can also be expected if the firm has sufficient market power to influence prices. Most markets have a handful of dealers large enough to be "trend-setters"—dealers whose quotations get everybody's attention. Besides being able to influence price by their actions, these influential players also benefit from a kind of proprietary information. Because they trade in larger volume with the largest institutional investors (some of which are large enough to move the market themselves), they may be better able to anticipate market movements as they see the order flow from such dominant customers. Being a lead dealer to those customers and receiving those orders before the rest of the market constitutes a significant advantage.

Furthermore, in some cases, the use of increasingly sophisticated computer models to track and analyze data appears to have become another source of proprietary information and competitive advantage. For example, some investment banks seem to owe their success in the mortgage-backed securities market to their computer-driven fixed-income research and to the sheer volume of their trading—both of which allow them to structure, hedge, and price the instruments with more confidence and accuracy than their competitors.

In sum, position-taking is not for everybody. Only market leaders can leverage the competitive advantage acquired in the interdealer markets or in working with their customer base into their house positions; others are best advised to minimize speculative positions most of the time. This prescription also applies to institutions that hire successful traders from other trading houses; such traders often

"lose their touch" when they find themselves in a disadvantaged environment. All too often, we find trading rooms that have no competitive advantage taking positions as if they did. Almost invariably, revenues and profits are disappointing and unreliable. Even in cases where there are initial or periodic bursts of profit and enthusiasm, such profits are typically dissipated in subsequent years or quarters. In these cases, the present value of the revenue stream is not likely to justify investment in state-of-the-art infrastructure and multi-desk trading floors. Our experience, in short, is that few trading rooms earn an acceptable return on the capital put at risk through positioning; and many even fail to cover expenses.

This is not to say, however, that trading must be a losing game for those institutions that do not have the competitive leverage to position effectively against market movements. There are other, more reliable, sources of profits from a trading room.

THE VALUE IN THE TURN (OR, WHO KEEPS THE BID-OFFER SPREAD?)

Any trading market, at any point in time, consists of all the parties prepared to buy or sell at specified prices. Where the buying and selling pressure meets is within the "bid-ask" (or "bid-offer") spread—the spread in the interdealer market between the best posted bid and the best posted offer at a point in time. The bid-ask spread is relatively high on illiquid securities like municipal bonds and junk bonds but very thin on liquid assets like foreign exchange.

Some traders argue that there is no such thing as a bid-offer spread in a transaction, that each trade is

A GIVEN TRADER'S AVERAGE, LONG-RUN TENDENCY TO RETAIN THE
BID-ASK SPREAD IS A FUNCTION OF THE "MARKET POWER" OF
HIS OR HER INSTITUTION. MARKET POWER TRANSLATES INTO CONTROL OF
"BARGAINS," WHICH IN TURN TRANSLATE INTO REVENUES.

EXHIBIT 2
MARKET SHARE VERSUS
INTERDEALER STRENGTH

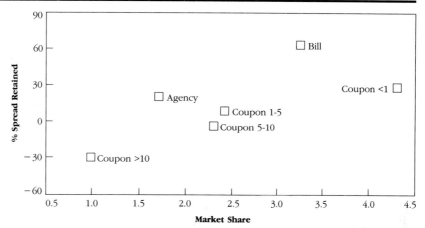

a bargain struck, and that the range between the bid and the offered prices is simply a negotiating framework within (or outside of) which the bargain is concluded. Our view, however, is that the price at which an interdealer bargain is struck is a function of the relative power of the two parties in the instrument traded. One party's offered price often becomes the counterparty's bid price. In repeated transactions between these two parties, this counterparty will consistently find itself on the wrong side of the market bid-offer in the bargain.

The advantaged parties in such situations generally turn out to be those players with stronger market-making capacity; and the other dealers with whom they trade are essentially forced to trade at the prices quoted by those market-makers. The possession of such an advantage in turn seems to be a function of market share. This phenomenon is especially clear in our analysis of thousands of trades for a primary dealer in U.S. Government securities. As illustrated in Exhibit 2, the percentage of the spread retained interdealer in each of six different trading instruments appears to be a direct function of the dealer's share of the interdealer volume in a given instrument.

Our experience has convinced us, then, that a bid-ask spread materializes when dealers with larger market share transact with smaller dealers. And, as our analysis has consistently demonstrated, a given trader's average, long-run tendency to retain that spread is a function of the "market power" of his or her institution. Market power translates into control of "bargains," which in turn translate into revenues.

A head fixed-income trader for a New York powerhouse put it best when he told us, "Any trader I put in the 5- to 7-year note chair makes a lot of money for us. Each of them thinks he is making the money with his smart calls. But it's really the chair that makes the money." Although there is some exaggeration in this statement, the message here is that the predictability and sustainability of trading profits is the result of the market-maker's ability to retain a disproportionate share of the bid-offer spread in a large volume of trades. Like the "golden crumbs" in Tom Wolfe's *Bonfire of the Vanities*, 70% spread retention on billions of dollars of daily volume represents a sizeable and consistent stream of revenue.

There are two keys to spread retention. First, the firm must have considerable financial muscle and trade flows. Second, traders must adopt a "jobbing" attitude, striving continuously to buy at or close to the bid side and to resell quickly at the offer side. This implies a lot of volume, but relatively small positions of short duration (and hence low risk).

THE POWER OF CUSTOMER BUSINESS

A good predictor of long-term success in a trading room is the status of salespeople relative to traders. The most successful Wall Street firms have long recognized that distributing and selling securities (or other financial instruments) to smaller dealers and to institutional customers not only keeps them better-informed than their competitors, but also is a stable source of earnings. Too often salespeople are viewed as second-class

TOO OFTEN SALESPEOPLE ARE VIEWED AS SECOND-CLASS CITIZENS IN
TRADING ROOMS—BECAUSE, ONCE AGAIN, THE MYTH OF POSITION-TAKING
AS THE BEST SOURCE OF PROFIT OVERSHADOWS THE ADDED VALUE IN
THE DISTRIBUTION SIDE OF THE BUSINESS.

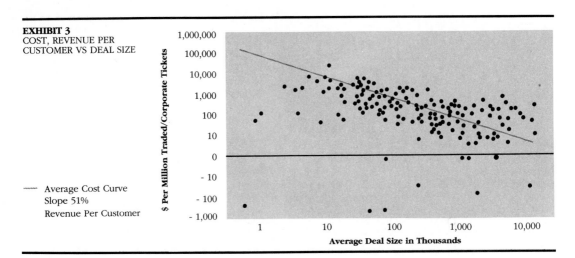

EXHIBIT 3
COST, REVENUE PER
CUSTOMER VS DEAL SIZE

— Average Cost Curve
Slope 51%
Revenue Per Customer

citizens in trading rooms—because, once again, the myth of position-taking as the best source of profit overshadows the added value in the customer side of the business. One typical result of this misconception is an undervalued, undermotivated salesforce that is required to sell an irregular flow of products based on traders' house positions and "views." The ultimate effect is a dissatisfied customer base and highly volatile earnings.

It is often argued that the interdealer business and the customer business are so closely interrelated that it is not possible to separate the revenue and the profits generated by each. We believe, however, that by marking large numbers of transactions to market (that is, determining where the actual price of each stood relative to the market prices at the time of sale), senior management can set transfer prices between trading and sales that provide a reasonably reliable split of revenues between the two.

Our examinations of over forty trading desks around the world have shown that, contrary to popular belief, customer business represents a significant portion of trading revenues—generally between 60 percent and 150 percent (in which case positioning loses money) of total revenues.

One of our clients, for example, reported about $10 million of pre-tax profit for a given time period in trading U.S. government securities. During the period, the client had conducted almost $400 billion of customer business and over $500 billion of interdealer business.

Upon closer examination, by marking individual trades to market, we decomposed the firm's

"gross trading profit" of $30 million into the following categories:

Customer Revenue	$26 million
Spread Retention (Interdealer)	8 million
Trading Profit (Positioning)	(4) million
■ Gross Trading Profit	$30 million
Expenses	(20) million
■ Net Profit (pre-tax)	$10 million

In this case, which is far more representative than one might think, customer revenues were actually covering up positioning *losses*—losses that amounted to 40 percent of net profit.

Not all dealings with customers are profitable, however. As shown in Exhibit 3, many (particularly small) trades are in fact priced below cost. This tends to happen either because too few trading rooms really understand their fully loaded costs or because their business has become too competitive.

In general, though, a large portion of customer business yields mark-ups relative to true interdealer prices; and the value of the mark-ups is often greater than the cost of a well-organized salesforce. Dealing with customers allows you to price sales not only at the offer but often above it, while purchasing at or below the bid. Even when customers are powerful enough to avoid any mark-up relative to dealers' prices, they typically buy at or close to the major dealers' offer prices and sell at or close to the bid prices. For those dealers who can source most of their trades at the market bid prices and resell at the

EXHIBIT 4
PERCENTAGE OF
BID-OFFER SPREAD
RETAINED

Products	Customer Trades Over $1 MM	Products	Customer Trades Over $1 MM
Bills		**Off-the-Run Coupons**	
On the run	94	Less than 1 year	59
Off the run	100	1-5 years	73
		Over 5 years	100
Active Coupons		**Agencies**	
2, 3, 4 years	56	Less than 5 years	91
5, 7, 10 years	92	Over 5 years	88
20, 30 years	94		

market offer, customer business generates a consistently profitable revenue stream.

As shown in Exhibit 4, one of our clients (also a primary government securities dealer) was able to retain a consistently large percentage of the bid-offer spread in dealing with its larger customers. As in the case illustrated in Exhibit 2, the percentage retained in each instrument was shown to vary directly with the institution's relative position in that instrument.

Of course, the largest institutional customers sometimes hold market power comparable to that of the major dealers. Those customers, while providing essential information flows, often "play the markets" themselves and know how to take advantage of the dealers' willingness to provide market liquidity. With such customers, dealers can rarely price to gain full compensation for that service.

The key to a profitable customer business, then, is to concentrate on those customer segments in which one holds (or can build) some type of comparative advantage. For this reason, the appropriate market focus will differ for every salesforce. The largest dealers typically do well with the large institutional investors who use them selectively as first-tier suppliers of securities, and whose main concerns are product depth and a knowledgeable salesforce. Regional dealers or banks generally have a competitive advantage with smaller institutional investors in their region—and that business, we have observed, can be very profitable.

It is also often argued that by making markets (by standing ready to quote prices continuously to customers), dealers often end up with unwanted positions that must be unwound at a net loss over time. The resulting losses, it is further argued, tend to offset much if not all of the other revenue from customer business.

By tracking traders' positions, however, we have demonstrated over and over again that, except

in rare periods of large price movements, this argument is fundamentally groundless. Inventories, to be sure, must often be maintained in illiquid markets to allow efficient sale of securities to customers. And although such inventories are subject to the ups and downs of the markets, the resulting exposure from taking such long positions should be viewed as simply one of the costs of functioning as a market-maker—a cost that when properly managed, as our own work repeatedly bears out, is far outweighed by the value of a strong customer franchise.

Even in liquid markets, moreover, it is clear that customer flows determine the ability to generate consistent trading profits. The more continuous the flow of customer orders, the less positioning risk any given trader is forced to bear, thus allowing him or her to function strictly as a broker. For example, in an analysis of a client that deals in the UK equity market, we found that its trading in stocks with high customer-volume ratios produced consistently higher profits than stocks with smaller customer order flows. Further supporting evidence comes from our observation (illustrated in Exhibit 5) that the overall foreign exchange trading profits of some of the major banks around the world are strongly correlated with the degree of their penetration of the *customer* side of their markets.

For most trading rooms, then, sales is and will remain the principal source of consistent and stable revenue and profits. For many operations, "trading" and "trading and sales" are misnomers. The business should really be called "sales and trading," because much of what are called "trading" profits are really the result of a good customer base and the resulting flow of orders and information.

With advances in technology and increasing customer sophistication, margins in the business have narrowed; and today there are more salespeople than the industry can profitably employ. But,

EXHIBIT 5
FOREX TRADING PROFITS
LARGE US AND EUROPEAN
FX BANKS 1988

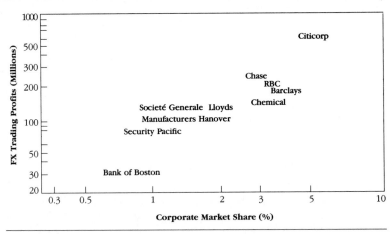

Sources: Annual Reports, Bernstein Research, Euromoney, OWC Analysis

in our view, the current problem of oversupply (and hence excess costs) will not reduce the value of sales in the trading environment. Customer business will simply have to be executed in a cheaper and more efficient fashion in the future.

CONCLUSION

The above insights have major implications for managing the vast majority of trading desks, including those who erroneously believe they can trade head to head with the Salomons of this world.

First, sales (and not speculative trading) is the only reliable source of stable revenues for most trading rooms. The "trading" strategy should be subordinated to the "sales" strategy and speculative positioning should be kept to the strict minimum necessary to be credible and to operate. This, of course, implies a low-risk profile that should suit many senior managements.

Second, sales and trading is much more than an opportunistic business driven by individual traders' skills at outguessing the market. It is a business in which profits are largely driven by fundamental competitive advantage. The business lends itself to strategic management by:
■ Understanding and monitoring the real sources of revenue—in essence opening the "black box" and creating a meaningful MIS for senior management;
■ Recognizing one's existing limitations and not letting them become weaknesses;
■ Identifying one's existing or potential strengths (particularly with specific customer segments) and focusing one's energy on them.

The third major implication is that positioning (and market arbitrage) should be pursued as a goal in itself only by the very few competitors that, through market power or sophisticated, proprietary computer systems, can price, evaluate risk, or set trends in a manner that most others cannot.

PART II
CAPITAL BUDGETING

One of the major tasks of corporate financial management is to evaluate investment opportunities. In many companies, this investment function is separated from the financing decisions typically performed by the corporate treasury, and is instead entrusted to a corporate planning or strategy group. Perhaps partly as a result of this separation of the investment and financing functions within the corporation, corporate strategy has developed for the most part independently of the discipline of financial economics. Fairly recently, however, some financial economists have begun to making an attempt to bring principles of corporate finance to bear directly on matters of corporate strategy.

For example, in "*Corporate Strategy and the Capital Budgeting Decison,*" Alan Shapiro presents a corporate-finance based approach to corporate strategy—one that attempts to account for the performance of those companies that managed to prosper even in the troubled climate of the 1970s. Shapiro's method, which combines a survey of the relevant academic research with a series of illustrations culled from a journal he has been keeping over the past 15 years, is an interesting use of | anecdotal evidence" to give concrete substance to the empirical data.

Another source of contention between financial analysts and strategists is the heavy reliance of the former on quantitative methods. In the early 1980s, the *Harvard Business Review* ran a series of articles assailing the shortsightedness of American corporate investment practices. The blame for this alleged myopia was placed, in large part, on the widespread use of the analytical technique known as discounted cash flow analysis, or "DCF." And because DCF has long been advocated by financial economists as the most reliable method for assessing economic value, the whole of finance theory seems to have been implicated.

In "*Finance Theory and Financial Strategy,*" Stewart Myers sheds welcome light on this controversy by separating what may be valid in such claims from what is not. As Myers points out, much of the criticism of DCF involves a misreading of the underlying theory, and is indeed aimed not at "finance theory, but at habits of financial analysts that financial economists are attempting to reform" (and the article offers a list of the most prominent abuses of the DCF method).

Nevertheless, as Myers acknowledges, part of the "gap" that has long divided the disciplines of finance and corporate strategy can be attributed to the real (as opposed to imagined) limitations of the DCF method. When properly applied, DCF remains the best available technique for evaluating certain kinds of investments: namely, those companies or investments producing fairly predictable cash flow streams. Where the DCF method falls down, however, are in those kinds of investments that offer significant operating or strategic options—that is, the right, but not the obligation, to, say, build on a vacant property, develop an oil reserve, expand or contract a mining operation, or to shift the use of existing capabilities among a variety of different markets. It is impossible to capture the value of such "real options" using the simple DCF technique; and options pricing theory, as Myers suggests, now seems to hold the best solution to this problem.

In "*A New Approach to Evaluating Natural Resource Investments,*" Michael Brennan and Eduardo Schwartz extend Myers' article by showing how corporate planners may benefit from the use of commody futures prices and option pricing models to evaluate commodity-type investments (such as copper mines, oil wells, and timberlands). Presenting the outlines of an approach they used in an actual Canadian resource project, Brennan and Schwartz demonstrate that the Black-Scholes option pricing model, with subsequent modifications by Robert Merton, can be adapted to evaluating such operating options.

In "*Valuing Offshore Oil Properties with Option Pricing Models,*" Daniel Siegel, James Smith, and James Paddock apply such an option pricing method to the specific task of valuing undeveloped oil reserves. What makes this article especially interesting is that the authors had the opportunity to test the effectiveness of their pricing model against the one used by an actual oil company (using that firm's financial and geological data) in bidding on properties in the Gulf of Mexico in the early 1980s. In each of the six bids studied, the option pricing approach came up with a higher value for the tract than did the firm, which was using a conventional DCF analysis (and, it turns out that two of the six bids produced by the authors' method would have won the bidding).

Skeptics, of course, will correctly point out that outbidding all competitors all the time is hardly the aim of a useful, cost-effective pricing method. The authors accordingly devised a test of such cost-effectiveness by calculating a percentage measure of "money left on the table" by the winning bids; and by this measure, the bids generated by the authors' pricing model outperformed those of the industry bidders.

In the final article, "Liquidity and the Cost of Capital," Yakov Amihud and Haim Mendelson discuss the implications for corporate management of a fairly recent research discovery: namely, that liquidity is a major determinant (as important in fact as systematic risk or "beta") of the level of expected stock returns. Less liquid stocks earn proportionately higher rates of return (before transaction costs) over long periods of time, thus representing a higher cost of capital for corporate management. The authors also explore a number of corporate responses designed to reduce the cost of capital by increasing the liquidity of stocks and bonds.

DHC

CORPORATE STRATEGY AND THE CAPITAL BUDGETING DECISION

by Alan Shapiro,
University of Southern California

The decade 1974 through 1983 was a dismal one for American business in general. It began with the deepest economic decline since the Depression and ended with national recoveries from back-to-back recessions in the early 1980s. Yet throughout these dark years, 13 companies on the Fortune 500 list of the largest U.S. industrial companies were money-making stars, earning consistently high returns. These firms averaged at least a 20 percent return on shareholders' equity (ROE) over this ten-year span. (To gain some perspective, a dollar invested in 1974 at a compound annual rate of 20 percent would have grown to $6.19 by the end of 1983, a healthy return even after allowing for the effects of inflation.) Moreover, none of these firms' ROE ever dipped below 15 percent during this difficult period.

The 13 were led by a profit superstar, American Home Products, whose ROE not only averaged 29.5 percent during the 1974-83 decade, but also has held above 20 percent for 30 straight years. To appreciate the significance of such a feat, one dollar invested at 20 percent compounded annually would be worth over $237 at the end of 30 years.

What type of firm can achieve such a remarkable record? Far from being the prototypical high-tech firm or a lucky oil company, American Home Products is the low-profile producer of Anacin, Chef Boy-Ar-Dee pasta products, Brach's candy, and Gulden's mustard, in addition to prescription drugs and non-drug products such as cardiovascular drugs, oral contraceptives, and infant formula.

In general, high technology firms were not well represented among the 13, which included just IBM and two pharmaceutical companies, SmithKline Beckman and Merck. IBM, moreover, with an average ROE of 20.5 percent, ranked only 11th out of the 13, far behind such low-tech firms as Dow Jones (26.3%), Kellogg (24.8%), Deluxe Check Printers (24.1%),

and Maytag (23.1%). It was even less profitable than a steel company (Worthington Industries—23.9%) and a chemical firm (Nalco Chemical—21.5%)).

The demonstrated ability of a firm such as Deluxe Check Printers—a firm on the trailing edge of technology, described as a "buggy whip company threatened with extinction by the 'checkless society'"—consistently to earn such extraordinary returns on invested capital must be due to something more than luck or proficiency at applying sophisticated techniques of investment analysis. That something is the knack for creating positive net present value (NPV) projects, projects with rates of return in excess of the required return. The scarcity of this skill is attested to by the fact that aggregate profits of $68.8 billion for the Fortune 500 in 1983 were, in real terms, 22 percent below the $43.6 billion earned in 1974, a recession year. Keep in mind also that the Fortune 500 have been disciplined savers, re-investing over $300 billion of retained earnings in their businesses over the ten-year period. This massive reinvestment alone should have produced considerably higher real earnings than 1974's.

This evidence notwithstanding, it is usually taken for granted that positive NPV projects do exist and can be identified using fairly straightforward techniques. Consequently, the emphasis in most capital budgeting analyses is on estimating and discounting future project cash flows. Projects with positive net present values are accepted; those that fail this test are rejected.

It is important to recognize, however, that selecting positive NPV projects in this way is equivalent to picking under-valued securities on the basis of fundamental analysis. The latter can be done with confidence only if there are financial market imperfections that do not allow asset prices to reflect their equilibrium values. Similarly, the existence of economic rents—excess returns that lead to positive net present values—is the result of monopolistic control over product or factor supplies (i.e., "real market imperfections").

It is the thesis of this article that generating projects likely to yield positive excess returns is at least as important as the conventional quantitative investment analysis. This is the essence of corporate strategy: creating and then taking advantage of imperfections in product and factor markets. Thus, an understanding of the strategies followed by successful firms in exploiting and defending those barriers to

13 Stars of The Decade 1974–1983			
	Company	Average ROE 1974–1983	Total return to investors 1974–1983*
	American Home Products	**29.5%**	**6.6%**
	Dow Jones	26.3%	29.8%
	Mitchell Energy	**26.0%**	**26.4%**
	SmithKline Beckman	25.4%	19.7%
	Kellogg	**24.8%**	**13.3%**
	Deluxe Check Printers	24.1%	13.4%
	Worthington Industries	**23.9%**	**41.7%**
	Maytag	23.1%	14.5%
	Merck	**21.9%**	**3.8%**
	Nalco Chemical	21.5%	11.4%
	IBM	**20.5%**	**11.3%**
	Dover	20.3%	26.6%
	Coca-Cola	**20.3%**	**2.9%**
	Median total return to investors for the 13:	13.4%	
	Median total return to investors for the Fortune 500:	13.6%	

*Total return to investors as calculated by *Fortune,* April 30, 1984. It includes both price appreciation and dividend yield to an investor and assumes that any proceeds from cash dividends, the sale or rights and warrant offerings, and stock received in spinoffs were reinvested at the end of the year in which they were received. The return reported is the average annual return compounded over the ten-year period.

Although the 13 have earned extraordinary returns on shareholders' equity capital, Exhibit 1 shows that returns to the shareholders themselves have been less than earthshaking. This is consistent with the efficient market hypothesis, the idea that prices of traded securities rapidly reflect all currently available information. Since the high return on equity capital earned by the 13 is not news to investors—these firms have consistently been outstanding performers—investors back in 1974 had already incorporated these expectations in their estimations of firm values. This means that a firm's expected high ROE is already "priced out" or capitalized by the market at a rate that reflects the anticipated riskiness of investing in the company's stock. As a result, investors will earn exceptional returns only if the firm turns out to do even better than expected, something that by definition is not possible to predict in advance. The fact that the 13's median annual total return to investors (stock price appreciation plus reinvested dividends) of 13.4 percent is almost identical to the Fortune 500's median return of 13.6 percent indicates that investor expectations about the relative performances of both groups of firms were subsequently borne out.

This illustrates the key distinction between operating in an efficient financial market and operating in product and factor markets that are less than perfectly competitive. One can expect to consistently earn excess returns only in the latter markets; competition will ensure that excess returns in an efficient market are short-lived. However, it is evident from the generally dismal performance of the Fortune 500 that it is no mean trick to take advantage of those product and factor market imperfections that do exist.

Only firms that can bring to bear on new projects competitive advantages that are difficult to replicate have any assurance of earning excess returns in the long run.

entry created by product and factor market imperfections is crucial to any systematic evaluation of investment opportunities. For one thing, it provides a qualitative means of identifying, or ranking, ex ante those projects most likely to have positive net present values. This ranking is useful because constraints of time and money limit the number and range of investment opportunities a given firm is likely to consider.

More important, a good understanding of corporate strategy should help uncover new and potentially profitable projects. Only in theory is a firm fortunate enough to be presented, at no effort or expense on its part, with every available investment opportunity. Perhaps the best way to gain this understanding is to study a medley of firms, spanning a number of industries and nations, that have managed to develop and implement a variety of value-creating investment strategies. This is the basic approach taken here.

The first section discusses what happens to economic rents over time, and thus to opportunities for positive NPV projects, in a competitive industry. The second section considers in more detail the nature of market imperfections that give rise to economic rents and how one can design investments to exploit those imperfections. The third section presents the available evidence on the relationship between various competitive advantages and rates of return on invested capital. The fourth introduces a normative approach to strategic planning and investment analysis. The fifth and final section deals with the rationale and means for domestic firms to evolve into multinational corporations.

Competitive Markets and Excess Returns

A perfectly competitive industry is one characterized by costless entry and exit, undifferentiated products, and increasing marginal costs of production. These undifferentiated products, also known as commodities, are sold exclusively on the basis of price. In such an industry, as every student of microeconomics knows, each firm produces at the point at which price equals marginal cost. Long-run equilibrium exists when price also equals average cost. At this point, total revenue equals total cost for each firm taken individually and for the industry as a whole. This cost includes the required return on the capital used by each firm. Thus, in the long run, the actual return on capital in a competitive industry must equal the required return.

Any excess return quickly attracts new entrants to the market. Their additional capacity and attempts to gain market share lead to a reduction in the industry price and a lowering of returns for all market participants. In the early 1980s, for example, the high returns available in the video-game market, combined with the ease of entry into the business, attracted a host of competitors. This led to a red-ink bath for the industry in 1983, followed by the exit of a number of firms from the industry. Conversely, should the actual return for the industry be below the required return, the opposite happens. The weakest competitors exit the industry, resulting in an increase in the industry price and a boost in the overall return on capital for the remaining firms. This process, which is now taking place in the oil refining business, continues until the actual return once again equals the required return.

The message from this analysis is clear: the run-of-the-mill firm operating in a highly competitive, commodity-type industry is doomed from the start in its search for positive net present value projects. Only firms that can bring to bear on new projects competitive advantages that are difficult to replicate have any assurance of earning excess returns in the long run. These advantages take the form of either being the low-cost producer in the industry or being able to add value to the product—value for which customers are willing to pay a high (relative to cost) price. The latter type of advantage involves the ability to convert a commodity business into one characterized by products differentiated on the basis of service and/or quality. By creating such advantages, a firm can impose barriers to entry by potential competitors, resulting in a less-than-perfectly competitive market and the possibility of positive NPV projects.

Barriers to Entry and Positive Net Present Value Projects

As we have just seen, the ability to discourage new entrants to the market by erecting barriers to entry is the key to earning rates of return that consistently exceed capital costs. If these barriers did not exist, new competitors would enter the market and drive down the rate of return to the the required return. High barriers to entry and the threat of a strong reaction from entrenched competitors will reduce the risk of entry and so prolong the opportunity to earn excess returns.

This analysis suggests that successful investments (those with positive NPVs) share a common characteristic: they are investments that involve creating, preserving, and even enhancing competitive advantages that serve as barriers to entry. In line with this conclusion, the successful companies described by Thomas Peters and Robert Waterman in their bestseller, *In Search of Excellence,* were able to define their strengths—marketing, customer contact, new product innovation, low-cost manufacturing, etc.—and then build on them. They have resisted the temptation to move into new businesses that look attractive but require corporate skills they do not have.

A clearer understanding of the potential barriers to competitive entry can help to identify potential value-creating investment opportunities. This section now takes a closer look at the five major sources of barriers to entry—economies of scale, product differentiation, cost disadvantages, access to distribution channels, and government policy—and suggests some lessons for successful investing.[1]

Economies of Scale

Economies of scale exist whenever a given increase in the scale of production, marketing, or distribution results in a less-than-proportional increase in cost. The existence of scale economies means that there are *inherent cost advantages in being large.* The more significant these scale economies, therefore, the greater the cost disadvantage faced by a new entrant to the market. Scale economies in marketing, service, research, and production are probably the principal barriers to entry in the mainframe computer industry, as GE, RCA, and Xerox discovered to their sorrow. It is estimated, for example, that IBM spent over $5 billion to develop its innovative System 360, which it brought out in 1963. In natural resource industries, firms such as Alcan, the Canadian aluminum company, and Exxon are able to fend off new market entrants by exploiting economies of scale in production and transportation.

High capital requirements go hand-in-hand with economies of scale. In order to take advantage of scale economies in production, marketing, or new product development, firms must often make enormous up-front investments in plant and equipment, research and development, and advertising. These capital requirements themselves serve as a barrier to entry; the more capital required, the higher the barrier to entry. This is particularly true in industries such as petroleum refining, mineral extraction, and mainframe computers.

A potential entrant to a market characterized by scale economies in production will be reluctant to enter unless the market has grown sufficiently to permit the construction and profitable utilization of an economically-sized plant. Otherwise, the new entrant will have to cut price to gain market share, destroying in the process the possibility of abnormal profits. By expanding in line with growth in the market, therefore, entrenched competitors can preempt profitable market entry by new competitors.

Consider, for example, the economics of the cement industry. The low value-to-weight ratio of cement makes the cement business a very regional one; beyond a radius of about 150 to 200 miles from the cement plant, the costs of transport become prohibitive unless cheap water or rail transportation is available. At the same time, the significant economies of scale available in cement production limit the number of plants a given region can support. For instance, suppose that demand in a land-locked region is sufficient to support only one or two modern cement plants. By expanding production and adding substantial new capacity to that already available, a firm can significantly raise the price of market entry by new firms and make plant expansion or replacement by existing competitors look much less attractive. This type of move obviously requires a longer timeframe and the willingness to incur potential losses until the market grows larger.

Scale economies are all-important in the grocery retailing business, on the level of the individual store as well as the city-wide market. Whether a store has $100,000 or $10,000,000 in annual sales, it still needs a manager. In addition, the cost of constructing and outfitting a supermarket doesn't increase in proportion to the number of square feet of selling space. Thus, the ratio of expenses to sales exhibits a significant decline as the volume of sales rises.

1. See, for example, Michael E. Porter, "How Competitive Forces Shape Strategy," *Harvard Business Review,* March-April 1979, pp. 137-145 for a good summary and discussion of these barriers to entry and their implications for corporate strategy.

Firms that make technology pay off are those that closely link their R&D activities with market realities.

Similarly, whether it has 10 percent or 25 percent of a given market, a supermarket chain has to advertise and supply its stores from a warehouse. The higher the share of market, the lower the advertising cost per customer, the faster the warehouse will turn over its inventory, and the more likely its delivery trucks will be used to capacity. These cost efficiencies translate directly into a higher return on capital.

The relationship between the market dominance of a supermarket chain in a given market and its profitability is evident in the relative returns for firms following contrasting expansion strategies. Chains such as Kroger and Winn-Dixie, which have opted for deep market penetration in a limited geographic area (ranking number 1 or 2 in almost all their major markets), have realized returns on equity that far exceed their equity costs. On the other hand, chains such as A&P and National Tea, which expanded nationally by gaining toe-hold positions in numerous, though scattered markets, have consistently earned less than their required returns.

Computer store chains, to take another example, also enjoy significant economies of scale. These show up in the form of lower average costs for advertising, distribution, and training. Even more important, they receive larger discounts on their products from the manufacturers.

LESSON #1: Investments that are structured to fully exploit economies of scale are more likely to be successful than those that are not.

Product Differentiation

Some companies, such as Coca-Cola and Procter & Gamble, take advantage *of enormous advertising expenditures* and *highly-developed marketing skills* to differentiate their products and keep out potential competitors wary of the high marketing costs and risks of new product introduction. Others sell expertise and high-quality products and service. For example, Nalco Chemical, a specialty chemical firm, is a problem-solver and counselor to its customers while Worthington Industries, which turns semifinished steel into finished steel, has a reputation for quality workmanship that allows it to charge premium prices. As indicated in the introduction to this article, both have been handsomely rewarded for their efforts, with average equity returns exceeding 20 percent annually from 1974 to 1983.

Pharmaceutical companies have traditionally earned high returns by developing unique products that are protected from competition by patents, trademarks, and brand names. Three outstanding examples are SmithKline Beckman's Tagamet, for treating stomach ulcers, and Hoffman-La Roche's tranquilizers, Librium and Valium. American Home Products also owes a great deal of its profitability to several patented drugs.

Similarly, the development of technologically-innovative products has led to high profits for firms such as Xerox and Philips (Netherlands). A fat R&D budget, however, is only part of the activity leading to commercially successful innovations. To a great extent, the risks in R&D are commercial, not technical. Firms that make technology pay off are those that closely link their R&D activities with market realities. They always ask what the customer needs. Even if they have strong technology, they do their marketing homework. This requires close contact with customers, as well as careful monitoring of the competition. Studies also indicate that top management involvement is extremely important in those firms that rely heavily and effectively on technology as a competitive weapon. This requires close coordination and communication between technical and business managers.

Failure to heed that message has led to Xerox's inability to replicate its earlier success in the photocopy business. In addition to its revolutionary copier technology, Xerox developed some of the computer industry's most important breakthroughs, including the first personal computer and the first network connecting office machines. But, through a lack of market support, it has consistently failed to convert its research prowess into successful high-tech products.

Service is clearly the key to extraordinary profitability for many firms. The ability to differentiate its computers from others through exceptional service has enabled IBM to dominate the worldwide mainframe computer business with a market share of over 75 percent. Similarly, Caterpillar Tractor has combined dedication to quality with outstanding distribution and after-market support to differentiate its line of construction equipment and so gain a commanding 35 percent share of the world market for earthmoving machinery. American firms, such as the auto companies, that have been somewhat lax in the area of product quality have fallen prey to those Japanese firms for which quality has become a religion.

What may not be obvious from these examples is that it is possible to differentiate anything, even

What may not be obvious from these examples is that it is possible to differentiate anything, even commodity businesses.

commodity businesses such as fast food, potato chips, theme parks, candy bars, and printing. The answer seems to be quality and service as companies like McDonald's, Disney, Frito-Lay, Mars, and Deluxe Check Printers have demonstrated. Cleanliness and consistency of service are the hallmarks of Disney and McDonald's, with both rating at the top of almost everyone's list as the best mass service providers in the world. Similarly, it is said that at Mars plants are kept so clean one can "eat off the factory floor."

High quality work and dependability have helped Deluxe Check Printers flourish in a world supposedly on the verge of doing without checks. It fills better than 95 percent of orders in two days, and ships 99 percent error free.

Frito-Lay's special edge is a highly-motivated 10,000 person sales force dedicated to selling its chips. They guarantee urban supermarkets and rural mom and pop stores alike a 99.5 percent chance of a daily call. Although they get only a small weekly salary, the sales people receive a 10 percent commission on all the Lay's, Doritos, and Tostitos they sell. So they hustle, setting up displays, helping the manager in any way possible, all the while angling for that extra foot of shelf space or preferred position that can mean additional sales income. There are also tremendous side benefits to close contact with the market. Frito can get a market test rolling in ten days and respond to a new competitive intrusion in 48 hours.

A similar level of service is provided by Sysco, a $2 billion firm in the business of wholesaling food to restaurants and other institutional business. It is a very mundane, low-margin business—one where low cost is seemingly all that matters. Yet, behind its slogan, "Don't sell food, sell peace of mind," Sysco earns margins and a return on capital that is the envy of the industry. Even in that business, a large number of customers will pay a little more for personalized service. And in a low-margin business, a little more goes a long way.

Sysco's secret was to put together a force of over 2,000 "marketing associates" who assure customers that "98 percent of items will be delivered on time." They also provide much more, going to extraordinary lengths to produce a needed item for a restauranteur at a moment's notice. Chairman John Baugh summed it up as follows:

The typical food service company picks a case of frozen french fries out of the warehouse and drops it on the restaurant's back porch. Where is the skill in that? Where is the creativity? Service isn't a free lunch. The price tag (and cost) is higher; but even at the lower end of the market, most customers (not all, to be sure) will pay some additional freight for useful service.[2]

Other firms have made their owners wealthy by understanding that they too are *selling solutions to their customers' problems,* not hardware or consumables. John Patterson, the founder of National Cash Register, used to tell salesmen: "Don't talk machines, talk the prospect's business." Thomas Watson, the founder of IBM, patterned his sales strategy on that admonition. Thus, while other companies were talking technical specifications, his salesmen were marketing solutions to understood problems, such as making sure the payroll checks came out on time.

These days, Rolm Corp., a leader in the crowded market for office communications systems, is taking a page out of IBM's book. It has built up a service force of over 3,400 employees whose main job is to reassure customers mystified by the complexities of modern technology, while selling them more equipment. The common strategic vision and approaches of the two firms may help explain why IBM, when it decided to enter the telecommunications business, did so by acquiring Rolm (in 1984) rather than another firm.

The contrast between the approaches followed by IBM and DEC is particularly revealing. DEC has developed excellent narrow-purpose minicomputers, trusting that application solutions can be developed by others to justify advanced technology. That simple strategy—selling machines on their merits to scientists and engineers—worked spectacularly for two decades, turning DEC into the world's second-largest computer company. One consequence of that strategy, however, is that DEC never needed to and never did develop the kind of marketing orientation IBM is noted for.

The advent of the personal computer, which can perform many of the functions of a minicomputer at a fraction of the cost, has underscored the shortcomings inherent in DEC's product- rather than market-oriented strategy. As its traditional business has stagnated, DEC has attempted to reposition itself to

---

2. Quoted in *Forbes,* October 11, 1982, p. 58.

compete in the nimble new world of personal computers. But it has failed thus far to adapt marketing and sales strategies to the new, less technically-sophisticated customers it has tried to attract.

The results are painfully obvious. On October 18, 1983, DEC's stock nose-dived 21 points after it announced that quarterly earnings would be 75 percent lower than the year before. Thus far at least, IBM, and its strategy of utilizing proven technology to market solutions to known problems, has prevailed in the marketplace.

LESSON #2: Investments designed to create a position at the high end of anything, including the high end of the low end, differentiated by a quality or service edge, will generally be profitable.

Cost Disadvantages

Entrenched companies often have cost advantages that are unavailable to potential entrants, independent of economies of scale. Sony and Texas Instruments, for example, take advantage of the *learning curve* to reduce costs and drive out actual and potential competitors. This concept is based on the old adage that you improve with practice. With greater production experience, costs can be expected to decrease because of more efficient use of labor and capital, improved plant layout and production methods, product redesign and standardization, and the substitution of less expensive materials and practices. This cost decline creates a barrier to entry because new competitors, lacking experience, face higher unit costs than established companies. By achieving market leadership, usually by price cutting, and thereby accumulating experience faster, this entry barrier can be most effectively exploited.

Proprietary technology, protected by legally-enforceable patents, provides another cost advantage to established companies. This is the avenue taken by many of the premiere companies in the world, including 3M, West Germany's Siemens, Japan's Hitachi, and Sweden's L. M. Ericsson.

Monopoly control of low-cost raw materials is another cost advantage open to entrenched firms. This was the advantage held for so many years by Aramco (Arabian-American Oil Company), the consortium of oil companies that until the early 1980s had exclusive access to low-cost Saudi Arabian oil.

McDonald's has developed yet another advantage vis-a-vis potential competitors: it has already acquired, at a relatively low cost, many of the best fast-food restaurant locations. Favorable locations are also important to supermarkets and department stores.

A major cost advantage enjoyed by IBM's personal computer is the fact that software programs are produced first for it since it has a commanding share of the market. Only later—if at all—are these programs, which now number in the thousands, rewritten for other brands. Companies that don't develop IBM look-alikes must either write their own software, pay to have existing software modified for their machines, or wait until the software houses get around to rewriting their programs.

Sometimes, however, new entrants enjoy a cost advantage over existing competitors. This is especially true in industries undergoing deregulation, such as the airlines and trucking. In both of these industries, regulation long insulated firms from the rigors of competition and fare wars. Protected as they were, carriers had little incentive to clamp down on costs. And still they were quite profitable. The excess returns provided by the regulatory barrier to entry were divided in effect between the firms's stockholders and their unionized employees.

Deregulation has exposed these firms to new competitors not saddled with outmoded work rules and high-cost employees. For example, new low-cost competitors in the airline industry, such as People's Express and Southwest Airlines, have much lower wages (about half of what big airlines pay) and more flexible work rules (which, for example, permit pilots to load baggage and flight attendants to man reservations phones).

One firm that managed to stay ahead of the game is Northwest Airlines. For years, Northwest has been run as if competition were fierce, while still making the most of the protections of regulations. It gained a reputation for fighting labor-union demands and hammered away to increase productivity. As a result, Northwest's overhead costs are only about 2 percent of total costs, compared with about 5 percent for major competitors. Similarly, its labor costs are about two-thirds the industry average. Consequently, it is the most efficient of the major airlines, which has greatly enhanced its competitive position.

LESSON #3: Investments aimed at achieving the lowest delivered cost position in the industry, coupled with a pricing policy to expand market share, are likely to succeed, especially if the cost reductions are proprietary.

A change in government regulations can greatly affect the value of current and prospective investments in an industry.

Access to Distribution Channels

Gaining distribution and shelf space for their products is a major hurdle that newcomers to an industry must overcome. Most retailers of personal computers, for example, limit their inventory to around five lines. Currently, over 200 manufacturers are competing for this very limited amount of shelf space. Moreover, the concentration of retail outlets among chains means that new computer makers have even fewer avenues to the consumer. This presents new manufacturers with a Catch-22: you don't get shelf space until you are a proven winner, but you can't sell until you get shelf space.

Conversely, well-developed, better yet unique, distribution channels are a major source of competitive advantage for firms such as Avon, Tupperware, Procter & Gamble, and IBM. Avon, for example, markets its products directly to the consumer on a house-to-house basis through an international network of 900,000 independent sales representatives. Using direct sales has enabled Avon to reduce both its advertising expenditures and the amount of money it has tied up in the business. Potential competitors face the daunting task of organizing, financing, and motivating an equivalent sales force. Thus, its independent representatives are the entry barrier that allows Avon consistently to earn exceptional profit margins in a highly competitive industry. Similarly, the sales forces of Frito-Lay, Sysco, and IBM help those firms distribute their products and raise the entry barrier in three very diverse businesses.

Conversely, the lack of a significant marketing presence in the U.S. is perhaps the greatest hindrance to Japanese drug makers attempting to expand their presence in the U.S. Marketing drugs in the U.S. requires considerable political skill in maneuvering through the U.S. regulatory process, as well as rapport with American researchers and doctors. This latter requirement means that pharmaceutical firms must develop extensive sales forces to maintain close contact with their customers. There are economies of scale here: the cost of developing such a sales force is the same, whether it sells one product or one hundred. Thus, only firms with extensive product lines can afford a large sales force, raising a major entry barrier to Japanese drug firms trying to go it alone in the U.S.

One way the Japanese drug firms have found to get around this entry barrier is to form joint ventures with American drug firms, in which the Japanese supply the patents and the American firms provide the distribution network. Such licensing arrangements are a common means of entering markets requiring strong distribution capabilities. Union Carbide, for example, follows a strategy of using high R&D expenditures to generate a diversified and innovative line of new products. Since each new product line requires a different marketing strategy and distribution network, firms like Union Carbide are more willing to trade their technology for royalty payments and equity in a joint venture with companies already in the industry.

LESSON #4: Investments devoted to gaining better product distribution often lead to higher profitability.

Government Policy

We have already seen in the case of the airline, trucking, and pharmaceutical industries that government regulations can limit, or even foreclose, entry to potential competitors. Other government polices that raise partial or absolute barriers to entry include import restrictions, environmental controls, and licensing requirements. For example, American quotas on Japanese cars have limited the ability of companies such as Mitsubishi and Mazda to expand their sales in the U.S., leading to a higher return on investment for American car companies. Similarly, environmental regulations that restrict the development of new quarries have greatly benefited those firms, such as Vulcan Materials, that already had operating quarries. The effects of licensing restrictions on the taxi business in New York City are reflected in the high price of a medallion (giving one the right to operate a cab there), which in turn reflects the higher fares that the absence of competition has resulted in.

A change in government regulations can greatly affect the value of current and prospective investments in an industry. For example, the Motor Carrier Act of 1935 set up a large barrier to entry into the business as it allowed the Interstate Commerce Commission to reject applicants to the industry. The Act also allowed the truckers themselves to determine their rates collectively, typically on the basis of average operating efficiency. Thus carriers with below-average operating costs were able to sustain above-average levels of profitability. It is scarcely surprising, then, that the major trucking companies pulled out all the stops in lobbying against deregulation. As expected, the onset of trucking deregulation, which greatly reduced the entry barrier, has led to lower profits for trucking companies and a significant drop in their stock prices.

LESSON #5: Investments in projects protected from competition by government regulation can lead to extraordinary profitability. However, what the government gives, the government can take away.

Investment Strategies and Financial Returns: Some Evidence

Ultimately, the viability of a value-creating strategy can only be assessed by examining the empirical evidence. Theory and intuition tell us that companies which follow strategies geared towards creating and preserving competitive advantages should earn higher returns on their investments than those which do not. And so they do.

William K. Hall studied eight major domestic U.S. industries and the diverse strategies followed by member firms.[3] The period selected for this study was 1975-1979, a time of slow economic growth and high inflation. These were especially hard times for the eight basic industries in Hall's study. They all faced significant cost increases that they were unable to offset fully through price increases. In addition, companies in each of these industries were forced by regulatory agencies to make major investments to comply with a variety of health, environmental, safety, and product performance standards. To compound their problems, competition from abroad grew stronger during this period. Foreign competitors achieved high market shares in three of the industries (steel, tire and rubber, and automotive); moderate shares in two others (heavy-duty trucks and construction and materials handling equipment); and entry positions in the other three (major home appliances, beer, and cigarettes).

The net result of these adverse trends is that profitability in the eight basic industries has generally fallen to or below the average for manufacturers in the United States. According to Table 1, the average return on equity for these eight industries was 12.9 percent, substantially below the 15.1 percent median return for the Fortune 1000. A number of firms in

these industries have gone bankrupt, are in financial distress, or have exited their industry.

Yet this tells only part of the story. As Table 1 also shows, some companies survived, indeed prospered, in this same hostile environment. They did this by developing business strategies geared towards achieving one or both of the following competitive positions within their respective industries and then single-mindedly tailoring their investments to attain these positions:

1. Become the lowest total delivered cost producer in the industry, while maintaining an acceptable service/quality combination relative to competition.
2. Develop the highest product/service/quality differentiated position within the industry, while maintaining an acceptable delivered cost structure.

Table 2 provides a rough categorization of the strategies employed by the two top-performing companies in each of the eight industries studied. In most cases, the industry profit leaders chose to occupy only one of the two competitive positions. Perhaps this is because the resources and skills necessary to achieve a low-cost position are incompatible with those needed to attain a strongly differentiated position.

At least three of the 16 leaders, however, combined elements of both strategies with spectacular success. Caterpillar has combined lowest-cost manufacturing with outstanding distribution and after-sales service to move well ahead of its domestic and foreign competitors in profitability. Similarly, the U.S. cigarette division of Philip Morris has become the industry profit leader by combining the lowest-cost manufacturing facilities in the world with high-visibility brands, supported by high-cost promotion. Finally, Daimler Benz employs elements of both strategies, but in different business segments. It has the lowest cost position in heavy-duty trucks in Western Europe, along with its exceptionally high-quality, feature-differentiated line of Mercedes Benz cars.

Other examples of the benefits of attaining the low-cost position in an industry or picking and exploiting specialized niches in the market abound. For example, the low-cost route to creating positive NPV investments has been successfully pursued in, of all places, the American steel industry. The strategy has involved building up-to-date mini-mills employing non-union workers who earn substantially less than

---

3. William K. Hall, "Survival Strategies in a Hostile Environment," *Harvard Business Review,* September-October 1980, pp. 75-85.

TABLE 1
Return on Equity in Eight Basic Industries: 1975–1979*

Industry	Return on Equity	Leading Firm	Return on Equity
Steel	7.1%	Inland Steel	10.9%
Tire and rubber	**7.4**	**Goodyear**	**9.2**
Heavy-duty trucks	15.4	Paccar	22.8
Construction and materials handling eq.	**15.4**	**Caterpillar**	**23.5**
Automotive	15.4	General Motors	19.8
Major home appliances	**10.1**	**Maytag**	**27.2**
Beer	14.1	G. Heilman Brewing	25.8
Cigarettes	**18.2**	**Philip Morris**	**22.7**
Average—eight industries	*12.9*	*Average—leading companies*	*20.2*
Median—Fortune 1000	*15.1*		

TABLE 2
Competitive Strategies Employed by Leaders in Eight Basic Industries*

Industry	Low Cost Leader	Meaningful Differentiation	Both Employed Simultaneously
Steel	Inland Steel	National	——
Tire and rubber	**Goodyear**	**Michelin (French)**	
Heavy-duty trucks	Ford, Daimler Benz (German)	——	——
Construction and materials handling equipment	——	**John Deere**	**Caterpillar**
Automotive	General Motors	Daimler Benz	——
Major home appliances	**Whirlpool**	**Maytag**	——
Beer	Miller	G. Heilman Brewing	
Cigarettes	**R. J. Reynolds**	——	**Philip Morris**

*From William K. Hall, "Survival Strategies in a Hostile Environment"

members of the United Steelworkers Union. Mini-mills melt scrap, which is cheaper in the U.S. than anywhere else, and their modern plant and equipment and simplified work practices greatly reduce their need for labor. Chapparal Steel of Midlothian, Texas, a big—and profitable—mini-mill, has pared its labor costs to a mere $29 on a ton of structural steel. This compares with average labor costs of $75 a ton at big integrated U.S. plants.

The chief disadvantage is that their steelmaking capabilities are limited. They can't, for example, make the industry's bread-and-butter item: flat-rolled steel. But in the product areas where mini-mills do compete—rod, bar, and small beams and shapes—big producers have all but surrendered. So,

too, have foreign mills. In just two years, Nucor Corp's mini-mill in Plymouth, Utah cut the Japanese share of California's rod and bar market from 50 to 10 percent.

Taking a different tack, Armstrong Rubber Co. has specialized in grabbing small market segments overlooked by its rivals. Today, Armstrong ranks second in industrial tires and second or third in both the replacement market for all-season radials and in tires for farm equipment and off-road recreational vehicles. Its niche-picking strategy relies heavily on the design and production innovations arising from its large investments in research and development.

A number of chemical firms, including Hercules, Monsanto, Dow, and Belgium's Solvay, have

It is unclear how Xerox, for whom high technology has been the chief competitive advantage, can earn excess returns in a business in which it has no experience.

attempted to lessen their dependence on the production of commodity chemicals and plastics by investing heavily in highly profitable specialty products for such industries as electronics and defense. These specialty chemicals are typically sold in smaller quantities but at higher prices than traditional bulk commodity chemicals. Perhaps the most successful chemical "niche-picker" is Denmark's Novo Industri—one of the world's largest producers of enzymes and insulin, and a pioneer in genetic engineering techniques. Novo's continued success is largely due to its ability to find and exploit small but profitable market niches. For instance, industry analysts credit Novo's success at selling enzymes in Japan to the company's ability to outdo even Japanese purity standards and to concentrate on small specialty markets that Japan's chemical giants can't be bothered with. In fact, most of Novo's markets appear too small for giant chemical firms such as Germany's Hoechst or Du Pont to pursue.

James River Corp. has combined cost cutting with product differentiation to achieve spectacular growth and profits in the paper-goods industry, an industry where many companies are struggling to hold their own. Typically, James River buys other companies' cast-off paper mills and remakes them in its own image. It abandons all or most of the commodity-grade paper operations. It refurbishes old equipment, and supplements it with new machinery to produce specialty products (automobile and coffee filters, airline ticket paper, peel-off strips for Band-Aids, and cereal-box liners) that are aimed at specific markets and provide higher profits with less competition. At the same time, James River cuts costs by extracting wage concessions from workers and dismissing most executives. It also raises the productivity of those employees who stay by allowing many of them to join the company's lucrative *profit-sharing* programs. James River's success in following this two-pronged strategy is reflected in its 1983 net income of $55.1 million, 332 times larger than its 1970 earnings of $166,000.

Designing an Investment Strategy

Although a strong competitive edge in technology or marketing skills may enable a firm to earn excess returns, these barriers to entry will eventually erode, leaving the firm susceptible to increased com-

petition. Existing firms are entering new industries and there are growing numbers of firms from a greater variety of countries, leading to new, well-financed competitors able to meet the high marketing costs and enormous capital outlays necessary for entry. Caterpillar Tractor, for example, faces a continuing threat from low-cost foreign competitors, especially Japan's Komatsu, which is second in world-wide sales. To stay on top, therefore, a firm's strategy must be constantly evolving, seeking out new opportunities and fending off new competitors.

Xerox clearly illustrates the problems associated with losing a competitive ege. For many years, Xerox was the king of the copier market, protected by its patents on xerography, with sales and earnings growing over 20 percent annually. The loss of its patent protection has brought forth numerous well-heeled competitors, including IBM, 3M, Kodak, and the Japanese, resulting in eroding profits and diminished growth prospects. Xerox has tried to transfer its original competitive advantage in technology to new products designed for the so-called office of the future. However, its difficulties in closely coordinating its R&D and marketing efforts have led to a series of serious, self-confessed blunders in acquisitions, market planning, and product development. For example, as mentioned earlier, the basic technology for the personal computer was developed by Xerox's Palo Alto Research Center in the early 1970s, but it remained for Apple Computer and IBM to capitalize on this revolutionary product.

More recently, Xerox's 1982 acquisition of Crum & Forster, a property and casualty insurance company, has called into question the company's strategy. It is unclear how Xerox, for whom high technology has been the chief competitive advantage, can earn excess returns in a business in which it has no experience. As we have already seen, firms that stick to their knitting are more likely to succeed than those that don't.

Common sense tells us that, in order to achieve excess returns over time, the distinctive competitive advantage held by the firm must be difficult or costly to replicate. If it is easily replicated, it will not take long for actual or potential competitors to apply the same concept, process, or organizational structure to their operations. The competitive advantage of experience, for example, will evaporate unless a firm can keep the tangible benefits of its experience proprietary and force its competitors to go through the same learning process. Once a firm loses its competitive advantage, its profits will erode to a point where it can no longer earn excess returns. For this reason, the firm's competitive advantage has to be constantly monitored and maintained so as to ensure the existence of an effective barrier to entry into the market. Should these barriers to entry break down, the firm must react quickly either to reconstruct them or build new ones.

Caterpillar has reacted to Komatsu's challenge by attempting to slash its costs, closing plants, shifting productions overseas, forcing union and nonunion workers alike to take pay cuts, eliminating many positions, and pressuring its suppliers to cut prices and speed deliveries. To get lower prices, the company is shopping around for hungrier suppliers, including foreign companies. This is reflected in its philosophy of worldwide sourcing, as described by its director of purchasing: "We're trying to become international in buying as well as selling. We expect our plants, regardless of where they're located, to look on a worldwide basis for sources of supply."[4] For example, German and Japanese companies now supply crankshafts once made exclusively in the U.S.

One important source of extra profit is the quickness of management to recognize and use information about new, lower-cost production opportunities. The excess profits, however, are temporary, lasting only until competitors discover these opportunities for themselves. For example, purchasing the latest equipment will provide a temporary cost advantage, but this advantage will disappear as soon as competitors buy the equipment for their own plants. Only if the equipment is proprietary will the firm be able to maintain its cost advantage. Along the same line, many American electronics and textile firms shifted production facilities to Taiwan, Hong Kong, and other Asian locations to take advantage of lower labor costs there. However, as more firms took advantage of this cost reduction opportunity, competition in the consumer electronics and textiles markets in the U.S. intensified, causing domestic prices to drop and excess profits to dissipate. In fact, firms in competitive industries must continually seize new non-proprietary cost reduction opportunities, not to earn excess returns but simply to make normal profits, or just survive.

Similarly, marketing-oriented firms can earn excess returns by being among the first to recognize and exploit new marketing opportunities. For exam-

ple, Crown Cork & Seal, the Philadelphia-based bottle-top maker and can maker, reacted to slowing growth in its U.S. business by expanding overseas. It set up subsidiaries in such countries as Thailand, Malaysia, Ethiopia, Zambia, Peru, Ecuador, Brazil, and Argentina. In so doing, as it turns out, they guessed correctly that in those developing, urbanizing societies, people would eventually switch from home-grown produce to food in cans and drinks in bottles.

Profitable markets, however, have a habit of eventually attracting competition. Thus, to be assured of having a continued supply of value-creating investments on hand, the firm must institutionalize its strategy of cost reduction and/or product differentiation. Successful companies seem to do this by creating a corporate culture—a set of shared values, norms, and beliefs—that has as one of its elements an obsession with some facet of their performance in the marketplace. McDonald's has an obsessive concern for quality control, IBM for customer service, and 3M for innovation. Forrest Mars set the tone for his company by going into a rage if he found an improperly wrapped candy bar leaving the plant. In order to maintain its low-cost position in the structural steel market, Chaparral Steel has teams of workers and foremen scour the world in search of the latest production machinery and methods.

Conversely, AT&T's manufacturing orientation, which focused on producing durable products with few options, was well-suited to the regulated environment in which it operated throughout most of its existence. But such an inward-looking orientation is likely to be a significant barrier to the company's ability to compete against the likes of IBM and other market-oriented, high-tech companies that react quickly to consumer demand. Prior to the breakup of AT&T, the manufacturers at Western Electric, AT&T's manufacturing arm, freely decided which products to make and when. They controlled the factories, supplying telephones to a captive market of Bell companies. AT&T was essentially an order taker, no more needing a sales force than any other utility does. There were no competitors forcing quicker market reaction nor any marketers challenging manufacturers' decisions.

Although AT&T claims that it is now "market-driven," evidence abounds that the company's older, entrenched manufacturing mentality is still dominant. Unless AT&T can change its corporate cul-

4. As quoted in the *Wall Street Journal* (August 10, 1971), p.1.

ture—a difficult and demanding task for any company, much less for a giant set in its ways—and marry manufacturing and marketing, it will have a difficult time competing with firms such as IBM in the office automation and computer businesses it has set its sights on.

The basic insight here is that sustained success in investing is not so much a matter of building new plants as of seeking out lower-cost production processes embodied in these plants, coming up with the right products for these plants to produce, and adding the service and quality features that differentiate these products in the marketplace. In other words, it comes down to people and how they are organized and motivated. The cost and difficulty of creating a corporate culture that adds value to capital investments is the ultimate barrier to entry; unlike the latest equipment, money alone can't buy it.

In the words of Maurice R. (Hank) Greenberg, president of American Insurance Group (A.I.G.), a worldwide network of insurance companies that has enjoyed spectacular sucess by pioneering in territory relatively unpopulated by competitors, "You can't imitate our global operation. It's just incapable of being reproduced. Domestically, we have some imitators for pieces of our business, but not the entire business. And in any event, you can only imitate what we've done. You can't imitate what we're thinking. You can't copy what we're going to do tomorrow."[5]

Corporate Strategy and Foreign Investment

Most of the firms we have discussed are multinational corporations (MNCs) with worldwide operations. For many of these MNCs, becoming multinational was the end result of an apparently haphazard process of overseas expansion. But, as international operations become a more important source of profit and as domestic and foreign competitors become more aggressive, it is apparent that domestic survival for many firms is increasingly dependent on their success overseas. To ensure this success, multinationals must develop global strategies that will enable them to maintain their competitive edge both at home and abroad.

Overseas Expansion and Survival

It is evident that if one's competitors gain access to lower-cost sources of production abroad, following them overseas may be a prerequisite for domestic survival. One strategy often followed by firms for whom cost is the key consideration, such as Chapparal Steel, is to develop a global scanning capability to seek out lower-cost production sites or production technologies worldwide.

Economies of Scale. A somewhat less obvious factor motivating foreign investment is the effect of economies of scale. We have already seen that in a competitive market, prices will be forced close to marginal costs of production. Hence, firms in industries characterized by high fixed costs relative to variable costs must engage in volume selling just to break even.

A new term has arisen to describe the size necessary in certain industries to compete effectively in the global marketplace: *world scale*. These large volumes may be forthcoming only if firms expand overseas. For example, companies manufacturing products such as mainframe computers that require huge R&D expenditures often need a larger customer base than that provided by even a market as large as the United States in order to recapture their investment in knowledge. Similarly, firms in capital-intensive industries with significant economies of scale in production may also be forced to sell overseas in order to spread their overhead over a higher volume of sales.

To take an extreme case, L. M. Ericsson, the highly successful Swedish manufacturer of telecommunications equipment, is forced to think internationally when designing new products since its domestic market is too small to absorb the enormous R&D expenditures involved and to reap the full benefit of production scale economies. Thus, when Ericsson developed its revolutionary AXE digital switching system, it geared its design to achieve global market penetration.

Many firms have found that a local market presence is necessary in order to continue selling overseas. For example, a local presence has helped Data General adapt the design of its U.S. computers and software to the Japanese market, giving the company

5. Wyndham Robertson, "Nobody Tops A.I.G. in Intricacy—or Daring," *Fortune,* May 22, 1978, p. 99.

a competitive edge over other U.S. companies selling computers in Japan. Data General has also adopted some Japanese manufacturing techniques and quality-control procedures that will improve its competitive position worldwide.

More firms are preparing for global competition. For example, although Black & Decker has a 50 percent market share worldwide in power tools, new competitors like the Japanese are forcing the company to change its manufacturing and marketing operations. Black & Decker's new strategy is based on a marketing concept known as "globalization," which holds that the world is becoming more homogenized and that distinctions between markets are disappearing. By selling standardized products worldwide, a firm can take advantage of economies of scale, thereby lowering costs and taking business from MNCs that customize products for individual markets. Until recently, the latter strategy of customization was the one that Black & Decker followed; the Italian subsidiary made tools for Italians, the British subsidiary tools for Britons.

By contrast, Japanese power-tool makers such as Makita Electric Works don't care that Germans prefer high-powered, heavy-duty drills and that Americans want everything lighter. Instead, Makita's strategy, which has been quite successful, is based on the notion that if you make a good drill at a low price, it will sell from Brooklyn to Baden-Baden. In response, Black & Decker recently unveiled 50 new power tools, each standardized for world production. It plans to standardize future products as well, making only minimal concessions, which require only minor modifications, to cultural differences.

Knowledge Seeking. Some firms enter foreign markets for the purpose of gaining information and experience that is expected to prove useful elsewhere. For instance, Beecham, an English firm, deliberately set out to learn from its U.S. operations how to be more competitive, first in the area of consumer products and later in pharmaceuticals. This knowledge proved highly valuable in competing with American and other firms in its European markets. Unilever, the Anglo-Dutch corporation, learned to adapt to world markets, with impressive results, the marketing skills it acquired in the U.S. through its American affiliate Lever Bros.

In industries characterized by rapid product innovation and technical breakthroughs by foreign competitors, it pays constantly to track overseas developments. The Japanese excel in this. Japanese firms systematically and effectively collect information on foreign innovation and disseminate it within their own research and development, marketing, and production groups. The analysis of new foreign products as soon as they reach the market is an especially long-lived Japanese technique. One of the jobs of Japanese researchers is to tear down a new foreign computer and analyze how it works as a base on which to develop a product of their own that will outperform the original. In a bit of a switch, as pointed out above, Data General's Japanese operation is giving the company a close look at Japanese technology, enabling it quickly to pick up and transfer back to the United States new information on Japanese innovations in the areas of computer design and manufacturing. Similarly, Ford Motor Co. has used its European operations as an important source of design and engineering ideas and management talent.

Designing a Global Expansion Strategy

The ability to pursue systematically policies and investments congruent with worldwide survival and growth depends on four interrelated elements.
1. The first, and the key to the development of a successful global strategy, is to understand and then capitalize on those factors that have led to success in the past. In order for domestic firms to become global competitors, therefore, the sources of their domestic advantage must be transferable abroad. A competitive advantage predicated on government regulation, such as import restrictions, clearly doesn't fit in this category.
2. Second, this global approach to investment planning necessitates a systematic evaluation of individual entry strategies in foreign markets, a comparison of the alternatives, and selection of the optimal mode of entry.
3. The third important element is a continual audit of the effectiveness of current entry modes. As knowledge about a foreign market increases, for example, or sales potential grows, the optimal market penetration strategy will likely change.
4. Fourth, top management must be committed to becoming and/or staying a multinational corporation. Westinghouse demonstrated its commitment to international business by creating the new position of President-international and endowing its occupant with a seat on the company's powerful manage-

ment committee. A truly globally-oriented firm—one that asks, "Where in the *world* should we develop, produce, and sell our products and services?"—also requires an intelligence system capable of systematically scanning the world and understanding it, along with people who are experienced in international business and know how to use the information generated by the system.

Summary and Conclusions

We have seen that rates of return in competitive industries are driven down to their required returns. Excess profits quickly attract new entrants to the market, lowering returns until actual and required returns are again equal. Thus, the run-of-the-mill firm operating in a highly competitive market will be unable consistently to find positive net present value investments—ones which earn excess returns relative to their required returns. The key to generating a continual flow of positive NPV projects, therefore, is to erect and maintain barriers to entry against competitors. This involves either building defenses against potential competitors or finding positions in the industry where competition is the weakest.

The firm basically has two strategic options in its quest for competitive advantage: it can seek lower costs than its competitors or it can differentiate its product in a number of ways, including high advertising expenditures, product innovation, high product quality, and first-rate service.

Each of these options involves a number of specific investment decisions: construction of efficient-scale facilities and vigorous pursuit of cost reduction through accumulated experience, in the case of cost leadership; if product differentiation is the main goal, the focus is on advertising, R&D, quality control, customer-service facilities, distribution networks and the like. The more an investment widens a firm's competitive advantage and reduces the chances of successful replication by competitors, the greater the likelihood that investment will be successful.

Despite our understanding of the subject matter, it is difficult to give a set of rules to follow in developing profitable investment strategies. If it were possible to do so, competitors would follow them and dissipate any excess returns. One must be creative and quick to recognize new opportunities. Nevertheless, without dictating what should be done in every specific circumstance, there are some basic lessons we have learned from economic theory and the experiences of successful firms. The basic lessons are these:

1. Invest in projects that take advantage of your competitive edge. The corollary is, stick to doing one or two things and doing them well; don't get involved in businesses you are unfamiliar with.

2. Invest in developing, maintaining, and enhancing your competitive advantages.

3. Develop a global scanning capability. Don't be blindsided by new competitors or lower-cost production techniques or locations.

4. Pick market niches where there is little competition. Be prepared to abandon markets where competitors are catching up and apply your competitive advantages to new products or markets.

Assuming that a firm does have the necessary resources to be successful internationally, it must carefully plan for the transfer of these resources overseas. For example, it must consider how it can best utilize its marketing expertise, innovative technology, or production skills to penetrate a specific foreign market. Where a particular strategy calls for resources the firm lacks, such as an overseas distribution network, corporate management must first decide how and at what cost these resources can be acquired. It must then decide whether (and how) to acquire the resources or change its strategy.

FINANCE THEORY AND FINANCIAL STRATEGY

by Stewart Myers,
*Massachusetts Institute of Technology**

Strategic planning is many things, but it surely includes the process of deciding how to commit the firm's resources across lines of business. The financial side of strategic planning allocates a particular resource, capital.

Finance theory has made major advances in understanding how capital markets work and how risky real and financial assets are valued. Tools derived from finance theory, particularly discounted cash-flow analysis, are widely used. Yet finance theory has had scant impact on strategic planning.

I attempt here to explain the gap between finance theory and strategic planning. Three explanations are offered:

1. Finance theory and traditional approaches to strategic planning may be kept apart by differences in language and "culture."

2. Discounted cash flow analysis may have been misused, and consequently not accepted, in strategic applications.

3. Discounted cash flow analysis may fail in strategic applications even if it is properly applied.

Each of these explanations is partly true. I do not claim that the three, taken together, add up to the whole truth. Nevertheless, I will describe both the problems encountered in applying finance theory to strategic planning, and the potential payoffs if the theory can be extended and properly applied.

The first task is to explain what is meant by "finance theory" and the gap between it and strategic planning.

The Relevant Theory

The financial concepts most relevant to strategic planning are those dealing with firms' capital investment decisions, and they are sketched here at the minimum level of detail necessary to define "finance theory."

Think of each investment project as a "mini-firm," all-equity financed. Suppose its stock could be actively traded. If we know what the mini-firm's stock would sell for, we know its present value. We calculate net present value (NPV) by subtracting the required investment.

In other words, we calculate each project's present value to investors who have free access to capital markets. We should therefore use the valuation model which best explains the prices of similar securities. However, the theory is usually boiled down to a single model, discounted cash flow (DCF):

$$PV = \sum_{t=1}^{T} \frac{C_t}{(1 + r)^t},$$

where PV = present (market) value;

C_t = forecasted incremental cash flow after corporate taxes—strictly speaking the mean of the distribution of possible $\tilde{C}_t$'s;

T = project life (C_T includes any salvage value);

r = the opportunity cost of capital, defined as the equilibrium expected rate of return on securities equivalent in risk to the project being valued.

NPV equals PV less the cash outlay required at t=0.

*This article was first published in *Interfaces* 14: 1 January-February 1984 (pp. 126-137). It is reprinted with permission of The Institute of Management Science.

Since present values add, the value of the firm should equal the sum of the values of all its mini-firms. If the DCF formula works for each project separately, it should work for any collection of projects, a line of business, or the firm as a whole. A firm or line of business consists of intangible as well as tangible assets, and growth opportunities as well as assets-in-place. Intangible assets and growth opportunities are clearly reflected in stock prices, and in principle can also be valued in capital budgeting. Projects bringing intangible assets or growth opportunities to the firm have correspondingly higher NPVs. I will discuss whether DCF formulas can capture this extra value later.

The opportunity cost of capital varies from project to project, depending on risk. In principle, each project has its own cost of capital. In practice, firms simplify by grouping similar projects in risk classes, and use the same cost of capital for all projects in a class.

The opportunity cost of capital for a line of business, or for the firm, is a value-weighted average of the opportunity costs of capital for the projects it comprises.

The opportunity cost of capital depends on the use of funds, not on the source. In most cases, financing has a second-order impact on value: you can make much more money through smart investment decisions than smart financing decisions. The advantage, if any, of departing from all-equity financing is typically adjusted for through a somewhat lowered discount rate.

Finance theory stresses cash flow and the expected return on competing assets. The firm's investment opportunities compete with securities stockholders can buy. Investors willingly invest or reinvest cash in the firm only if it can do better, risk considered, than the investors can do on their own.

Finance theory thus stresses fundamentals. It should not be deflected by accounting allocations, except as they affect cash taxes. For example, suppose a positive-NPV project sharply reduces book earnings in its early stages. Finance theory would recommend forging ahead, trusting investors to see through the accounting bias to the project's true value. Empirical evidence indicates that in-vestors do see through accounting biases; they do not just look naively at last quarter's or last year's EPS. (If they did, all stocks would sell at the same price-earnings ratio.)

All these concepts are generally accepted by financial economists. The concepts are broadly consistent with an up-to-date understanding of how capital markets work. Moreover, they seem to be accepted by firms, at least in part: any time a firm sets a hurdle rate based on capital market evidence and uses a DCF formula, it must implicitly rely on the logic I have sketched. So the issue here is not whether managers accept finance theory for capital budgeting (and for other financial purposes). It is why they do not use the theory in strategic planning.

The Gap Between Finance Theory and Strategic Planning

I have resisted referring to strategic planning as "capital budgeting on a grand scale" because capital budgeting in practice is a bottom-up process. The aim is to find and undertake specific assets or projects that are worth more than they cost.

Picking valuable pieces does not ensure maximum value for the whole. Piecemeal, bottom-up capital budgeting is not strategic planning.

Capital budgeting techniques, however, ought to work for the whole as well as the parts. A strategic commitment of capital to a line of business is an investment project. If management does invest, they must believe the value of the firm increases by more than the amount of capital committed—otherwise they are throwing money away. In other words, there is an implicit estimate of net present value.

This would seem to invite application of finance theory, which explains how real and financial assets are valued. The theory should have direct application not only to capital budgeting, but also to the financial side of strategic planning.

Of course it has been applied to some extent. Moreover, strategic planning seems to be becoming more financially sophisticated. Financial concepts are stressed in several recent books on corporate strategy.[1] Consulting firms have developed the con-

1. See, for example, W. E. Fruhan, Jr., *Financial Strategy: Studies in the Creation, Transfer and Destruction of Shareholder Value*, (Homewood, Illinois: Richard D. Irwin, Inc., 1979); M. S. Salter and W. A. Weinhold, *Diversification Through Acquisition* (New York: The Free Press, 1979); and H. Bierman, *Strategic Financial Planning*, (New York: The Free Press, 1980).

If the market were willing to pay extra for diversification, closed-end funds would sell at premiums over net asset value, and conglomerate firms would be worth more to investors than their components separately traded.

cepts' strategic implications.[2]

Nevertheless, I believe it is fair to say that most strategic planners are not guided by the tools of modern finance. Strategic and financial analyses are not reconciled, even when the analyses are of the same major project. When low net present value projects are nurtured "for strategic reasons," the strategic analysis overrides measures of financial value. Conversely, projects with apparently high net present values are passed by if they don't fit in with the firm's strategic objectives. When financial and strategic analyses give conflicting answers, the conflict is treated as a fact of life, not as an anomaly demanding reconciliation.

In many firms, strategic analysis is partly or largely directed to variables finance theory says are irrelevant. This is another symptom of the gap, for example:

• Many managers worry about a strategic decision's impact on book rate of return or earnings per share. If they are convinced the plan adds to the firm's value, its impact on accounting figures should be irrelevant.

• Some managers pursue diversification to reduce risk—risk as they see it. Investors see a firm's risk differently. In capital markets, diversification is cheap and easy. Investors who want to diversify do so on their own. Corporate diversification is redundant; the market will not pay extra for it.

If the market were willing to pay extra for diversification, closed-end funds would sell at premiums over net asset value, and conglomerate firms would be worth more to investors than their components separately traded. Closed-end funds actually sell at discounts, not premiums. Conglomerates appear to sell at discounts, too, although it is hard to prove it since the firm's components are not traded separately.

Much of the literature of strategic planning seems extremely naive from a financial point of view. Sometimes capital markets are ignored. Sometimes firms are essentially viewed as having a stock of capital, so that "cash cows" are needed to finance investment in rapidly growing lines of business. (The firms that pioneered in strategic planning actually had easy access to capital markets, as do almost all public companies.) Firms may not like the price they pay for capi-

tal, but that price is the opportunity cost of capital, the proper standard for new investment by the firm.

The practical conflicts between finance and strategy are part of what lies behind the recent criticism of U.S. firms for allegedly concentrating on quick payoffs at the expense of value. U.S. executives, especially MBAs, are said to rely too much on purely financial analysis, and too little on building technology, products, markets, and production efficiency. The financial world is not the real world, the argument goes; managers succumb to the glamour of high finance. They give time and talent to mergers, spinoffs, unusual securities, and complex financing packages when they should be out on the factory floor. They pump up current earnings per share at the expense of long-run values.

Much of this criticism is not directed against finance theory, but at habits of financial analysis that financial economists are attempting to reform. Finance theory of course concentrates on the financial world—that is, capital markets. However, it fundamentally disagrees with the implicit assumption of the critics who say that the financial world is not the real world and that financial analysis diverts attention from, and sometimes actively undermines, real long-run values. The professors and textbooks actually say that financial values rest on real values and that most value is created on the left-hand side of the balance sheet, not on the right.

Finance theory, however, is under attack, too. Some feel that any quantitative approach is inevitably short-sighted. Hayes and Garvin, for example, have blamed discounted cash flow for a significant part of this country's industrial difficulties. Much of their criticism seems directed to misapplications of discounted cash flow, some of which I discuss later. But they also believe the underlying theory is wanting; they say that "beyond all else, capital investment represents an act of faith."[3] This statement offends most card-carrying financial economists.

I do not know whether "gap" fully describes all of the problems noted, or hinted at, in the discussion so far. In some quarters, finance theory is effectively ignored in strategic planning. In others, it is seen as being in conflict, or working at cross-purposes, with other forms of strategic analysis. The problem is to explain why.

2. See Alberts, W. A. and McTaggart, James M. 1984, "Value-based Strategic Investment Planning," *Interfaces*, Vol. 14, No. 1 (January-February), pp. 138-151.

3. R. H. Hayes and D. A. Garvin, "Managing as If Tomorrow Mattered," *Harvard Business Review*, Vol. 60, No. 3 (May-June), 1982, pp. 70-79.

Two Cultures and One Problem

Finance theory and strategic planning could be viewed as two cultures looking at the same problem. Perhaps only differences in language and approach make the two appear incompatible. If so, the gap between them might be bridged by better communication and a determined effort to reconcile them.

Think of what can go wrong with standard discounted cash flow analyses of a series of major projects:

• Even careful analyses are subject to random error. There is a 50 percent probability of a positive NPV for a truly borderline project. Firms have to guard against these errors dominating project choice.

• Smart managers apply the following check. They know that all projects have zero NPV in long-run competitive equilibrium. Therefore, a positive NPV must be explained by a short-run deviation from equilibrium or by some permanent competitive advantage. If neither explanation applies, the positive NPV is suspect. Conversely, a negative NPV is suspect if a competitive advantage or short-run deviation from equilibrium favors the project.

In other words, smart managers do not accept positive (or negative) NPVs unless they can explain them.

Strategic planning may serve to implement this check. Strategic analyses look for market opportunities—that is, deviations from equilibrium—and try to identify the firm's competitive advantages.

Turn the logic of the example around. We can regard strategic analysis which does not explicitly compute NPVs as showing absolute faith in Adam Smith's invisible hand. If a firm, looking at a line of business, finds a favorable deviation from long-run equilibrium, or if it identifies a competitive advantage, then (efficient) investment in that line must offer profits exceeding the opportunity cost of capital. No need to calculate the investment's NPV: the manager knows in advance that NPV is positive.

The trouble is that strategic analyses are also subject to random error. Mistakes are also made in identifying areas of competitive advantage or out-of-equilibrium markets. We would expect strategic analysts to calculate NPVs explicitly, at least as a check; strategic analysis and financial analysis ought to be explicitly reconciled. Few firms attempt this. This suggests the gap between strategic planning and finance theory is more than just "two cultures and one problem."

The next step is to ask why reconciliation is so difficult.

Misuse of Finance Theory

The gap between strategic and financial analysis may reflect misapplication of finance theory. Some firms do not try to use theory to analyze strategic investments. Some firms try but make mistakes.

I have already noted that in many firms capital investment analysis is partly or largely directed to variables finance theory says are irrelevant. Managers worry about projects' book rates of return or impacts on book earnings per share. They worry about payback, even for projects that clearly have positive NPVs. They try to reduce risk through diversification.

Departing from theoretically correct valuation procedures often sacrifices the long-run health of the firm for the short, and makes capital investment choices arbitrary or unpredictable. Over time, these sacrifices appear as disappointing growth, eroding market share, loss of technological leadership, and so forth.

The non-financial approach taken in many strategic analyses may be an attempt to overcome the short horizons and arbitrariness of financial analysis as it is often misapplied. It may be an attempt to get back to fundamentals. Remember, however: finance theory never left the fundamentals. Discounted cash flow should not in principle bias the firm against long-lived projects, or be swayed by arbitrary allocations.

However, the typical mistakes made in applying DCF do create a bias against long-lived projects. I will note a few common mistakes.

Ranking on Internal Rate of Return

Competing projects are often ranked on internal rate of return rather than NPV. It is easier to earn a high rate of return if project life is short and investment is small. Long-lived, capital-intensive projects tend to be put down the list even if their net present value is substantial.

The internal rate of return does measure bang per buck on a DCF basis. Firms may favor it because they think they have only a limited number of bucks. However, most firms big enough to do formal strategic planning have free access to capital markets. They may not like the price, but they can get the money. The limits on capital expenditures are

The non-financial approach taken in many strategic analyses may be an attempt to overcome the short horizons and arbitrariness of financial analysis as it is often misapplied.

more often set inside the firm, in order to control an organization too eager to spend money. Even when a firm does have a strictly limited pool of capital, it should not use the internal rate of return to rank projects. It should use NPV per dollar invested, or linear programming techniques when capital is rationed in more than one period.[4]

Inconsistent Treatment of Inflation

A surprising number of firms treat inflation inconsistently in DCF calculations. High nominal discount rates are used but cash flows are not fully adjusted for future inflation. Thus accelerating inflation makes projects—especially long-lived ones—look less attractive even if their real value is unaffected.

Unrealistically High Rates

Some firms use unrealistically high discount rates, even after proper adjustment for inflation. This may reflect ignorance of what normal returns in capital markets really are. In addition:

• Premiums are tacked on for risks that can easily be diversified away in stockholders' portfolios.

• Rates are raised to offset the optimistic biases of managers sponsoring projects. This adjustment works only if the bias increases geometrically with the forecast period. If it does not, long-lived projects are penalized.

• Some projects are unusually risky at inception, but only of normal risk once the start-up is successfully passed. It is easy to classify this type of project as "high-risk," and to add a start-up risk premium to the discount rate for all future cash flows. The risk premium should be applied to the start-up period only. If it is applied after the start-up period, safe, short-lived projects are artificially favored.

Discounted cash flow analysis is also subject to a difficult organizational problem. Capital budgeting is usually a bottom-up process. Proposals originate in the organization's midriff, and have to survive the trip to the top, getting approval at every stage. In the process political alliances form, and cash flow forecasts are bent to meet known standards. Answers—not necessarily the right ones—are

worked out for anticipated challenges. Most projects that get to the top seem to meet profitability standards set by management.

According to Brealey and Myers's Second Law, "The proportion of proposed projects having positive NPV is independent of top management's estimate of the opportunity cost of capital."[5]

Suppose the errors and biases of the capital budgeting process make it extremely difficult for top management to verify the true cash flows, risks, and present value of capital investment proposals. That would explain why firms do not try to reconcile the results of capital budgeting and strategic analyses. However, it does not explain why strategic planners do not calculate their own NPVs.

We must ask whether those in top management—the managers who make strategic decisions—understand finance theory well enough to use DCF analysis effectively. Although they certainly understand the arithmetic of the calculation, they may not understand the logic of the method deeply enough to trust it or to use it without mistakes.

They may also not be familiar enough with how capital markets work to use capital market data effectively. The widespread use of unrealistically high discount rates is probably a symptom of this.

Finally, many managers distrust the stock market. Its volatility makes them nervous, despite the fact that the volatility is the natural result of a rational market. It may be easier to underestimate the sophistication of the stock market than to accept its verdict on how well the firm is doing.

Finance Theory May Have Missed the Boat

Now consider the firm that understands finance theory, applies DCF analysis correctly, and has overcome the human and organizational problems that bias cash flows and discount rates. Carefully estimated net present values for strategic investments should help significantly. However, would they fully grasp and describe the firm's strategic choices? Perhaps not.

There are gaps in finance theory as it is usually applied. These gaps are not necessarily intrinsic to finance theory generally. They may be filled by new

---

4. See R. A. Brealey and S. C. Myers, *Principles of Corporate Finance* (New York: McGraw-Hill Book Company, 1981), pp. 101-107.

5. Brealey and Myers, *Principles of Corporate Finance*, cited in note 4, p. 238.

Many managers distrust the stock market. Its volatility makes them nervous, despite the fact that the volatility is the natural result of a rational market. It may be easier to underestimate the sophistication of the stock market than to accept its verdict on how the firm is doing.

approaches to valuation. However, if they are the firm will have to use something more than a straight-forward discounted cash flow method.

An intelligent application of discounted cash flow will encounter four chief problems:
• Estimating the discount rate,
• Estimating the project's future cash flows,
• Estimating the project's impact on the firm's other assets' cash flows—that is, through the cross-sectional links between projects, and
• Estimating the project's impact on the firm's future investment opportunities. These are the time-series links between projects.

The first three problems, difficult as they are, are not as serious for financial strategy as the fourth. However, I will review all four.

Estimating the Opportunity Cost of Capital

The opportunity cost of capital will always be difficult to measure, since it is an expected rate of return. We cannot commission the Gallup Poll to extract probability distributions from the minds of investors. However, we have extensive evidence on past average rates of return in capital markets and the corporate sector.[6] No long-run trends in "normal" rates of return are evident. Reasonable, ballpark cost of capital estimates can be obtained if obvious traps (for example, improper adjustments for risk or inflation) are avoided. In my opinion, estimating cash flows properly is more important than fine-tuning the discount rate.

Forecasting Cash Flow

It's impossible to forecast most projects' actual cash flows accurately. DCF calculations do not call for accurate forecasts, however, but for accurate assessments of the mean of possible outcomes.

Operating managers can often make reasonable subjective forecasts of the operating variables they are responsible for—operating costs, market growth, market share, and so forth—at least for the future that they are actually worrying about. It is difficult for them to translate this knowledge into a cash

flow forecast for, say, year seven. There are several reasons for this difficulty. First, the operating manager is asked to look into a far future he is not used to thinking about. Second, he is asked to express his forecast in accounting rather than operating variables. Third, incorporating forecasts of macroeconomic variables is difficult. As a result, long-run forecasts often end up as mechanical extrapolations of short-run trends. It is easy to overlook the long-run pressures of competition, inflation, and technical change.

It should be possible to provide a better framework for forecasting operating variables and translating them into cash flows and present value—a framework that makes it easier for the operating manager to apply his practical knowledge and that explicitly incorporates information about macroeconomic trends. There is, however, no way around it: forecasting is intrinsically difficult, especially when your boss is watching you do it.

Estimating Cross-Sectional Relationships Between Cash Flows

Tracing "cross-sectional" relationships between project cash flows is also intrinsically difficult. The problem may be made more difficult by inappropriate project definitions or boundaries for lines of businesses. Defining business units properly is one of the tricks of successful strategic planning.

However, these inescapable problems in estimating profitability standards, future cash returns, and cross-sectional interactions are faced by strategic planners even if they use no financial theory. They do not reveal a flaw in existing theory. Any theory or approach encounters them. Therefore, they do not explain the gap between finance theory and strategic planning.

The Links Between Today's Investments and Tomorrow's Opportunities

The fourth problem—the link between today's investments and tomorrow's opportunities—is much more difficult.

---

6. For estimates of capital market returns over the period 1926 to the present, see R. G. Ibbotson and R. A. Sinquefield, *Stocks, Bonds, Bills and Inflation: The Past and the Future*, Financial Analysts Research Foundation, Charlottesville, Virginia, 1982. For estimates of historical returns on capital from a corporate perspective, see D. M. Holland and S. C. Myers, "Trends in Corporate Profitability and Capital Costs," in R. Lindsay, ed., *The Nation's Capital Needs: Three Studies*, Committee on Economic Development, Washington, DC, 1979.

DCF is less helpful in valuing businesses with substantial growth opportunities or intangible assets. In other words, it is not the whole answer when options account for a large fraction of a business's value.

Suppose a firm invests in a negative-NPV project in order to establish a foothold in an attractive market. Thus a valuable second-stage investment is used to justify the immediate project. The second stage must depend on the first: if the firm could take the second project without having taken the first, then the future opportunity should have no impact on the immediate decision. However, if tomorrow's opportunities depend on today's decisions, there is a time-series link between projects.

At first glance, this may appear to be just another forecasting problem. Why not estimate cash flows for both stages, and use discounted cash flow to calculate the NPV for the two stages taken together?

You would not get the right answer. The second stage is an option, and conventional discounted cash flow does not value options properly. The second stage is an option because the firm is not committed to undertake it. It will go ahead if the first stage works and the market is still attractive. If the first stage fails, or if the market sours, the firm can stop after Stage 1 and cut its losses. Investing in Stage 1 purchases an intangible asset: a call option on Stage 2. If the option's present value offsets the first stage's negative NPV, the first stage is justified.

The Limits of Discounted Cash Flow

The limits of DCF need further explanation. Think first of its application to four types of securities:

1. DCF is standard for valuing bonds, preferred stocks and other fixed-income securities.
2. DCF is sensible, and widely used, for valuing relatively safe stocks paying regular dividends.
3. DCF is not as helpful in valuing companies with significant growth opportunities. The DCF model can be stretched to say that Apple Computer's stock price equals the present value of the dividends the firm may eventually pay. It is more helpful to think of Apple's price, P_0, as:

$$P_0 = \frac{EPS}{r} + PVGO, \text{ where}$$

EPS = normalized current earnings
    r = the opportunity cost of capital

PVGO = the net present value of future growth opportunities.

Note that PVGO is the present value of a portfolio of options—the firm's options to invest in second-stage, third-stage, or even later projects.

4. DCF is never used for traded calls or puts. Finance theory supplies option valuation formulas that work, but the option formulas look nothing like DCF.

Think of the corporate analogues to these securities:

• There are few problems in using DCF to value safe flows, for example, flows from financial leases.

• DCF is readily applied to "cash cows"—relatively safe businesses held for the cash they generate rather than for strategic value. It also works for "engineering investments," such as machine replacements, where the main benefit is reduced cost in a clearly-defined activity.

• DCF is less helpful in valuing businesses with substantial growth opportunities or intangible assets. In other words, it is not the whole answer when options account for a large fraction of a business's value.

• DCF is no help at all for pure research and development. The value of R&D is almost all option value. Intangible assets' value is usually option value.

The theory of option valuation has been worked out in detail for securities—not only puts and calls, but warrants, convertibles, bond call options, and so forth. The solution techniques should be applicable to the real options held by firms. Several preliminary applications have already been worked out, for example:

• Calculations of the value of a Federal lease for off-shore exploration for oil or gas. Here the option value comes from the lessee's right to delay the decisions to drill and develop, and to make these decisions after observing the extent of reserves and the future level of oil prices.[7]

• Calculating an asset's abandonment or salvage value: an active second-hand market increases an asset's value, other things equal. The second-hand market gives the asset owner a put option which increases the value of the option to bail out of a poorly performing project.[8]

The option "contract" in each of these cases is

---

7. See the article in this issue by James Paddock, Daniel Siegel, and James Smith, which deals with the use of option pricing models in valuing offshore petroleum leases.

8. See S. C. Myers and S. Majd, "Applying Option Pricing Theory to the Abandonment Value Problem," Sloan School of Management, MIT, Working Paper, 1983.

fairly clear: a series of calls in the first case and a put in the second. However, these real options last longer and are more complex than traded calls and puts. The terms of real options have to be extracted from the economics of the problem at hand. Realistic descriptions usually lead to a complex implied "contract," requiring numerical methods of valuation.

Nevertheless, option pricing methods hold great promise for strategic analysis. The time-series links between projects are the most important part of financial strategy. A mixture of DCF and option valuation models can, in principle, describe these links and give a better understanding of how they work. It may also be possible to estimate the value of particular strategic options, thus eliminating one reason for the gap between finance theory and strategic planning.

Lessons for Corporate Strategy

The task of strategic analysis is more than laying out a plan or plans. When time-series links between projects are important, it's better to think of strategy as managing the firm's portfolio of real options.[9] The process of financial planning may be thought of as:
• Acquiring options, either by investing directly in R&D, product design, cost or quality improvements, and so forth, or as a by-product of direct capital investment (for example, investing in a Stage 1 project with negative NPV in order to open the door for stage 2).
• Abandoning options that are too far "out of the money" to pay to keep.
• Exercising valuable options at the right time—that is, buying the cash-producing assets that ultimately produce positive net present value.

There is also a lesson for current applications of finance theory to strategic issues. Several new approaches to financial strategy use a simple, traditional DCF model of the firm.[10] These approaches are likely to be more useful for cash cows than for growth businesses with substantial risk and intangible assets.

The option value of growth and intangibles is not ignored by good managers even when conventional financial techniques miss them. These values may be brought in as "strategic factors," dressed in non-financial clothes. Dealing with the time-series links between capital investments, and with the option value these links create, is often left to strategic planners. But new developments in finance theory promise to help.

Bridging the Gap

We can summarize by asking how the present gap between finance theory and strategic planning might be bridged.

Strategic planning needs finance. Present value calculations are needed as a check on strategic analysis and vice versa. However, the standard discounted cash flow techniques will tend to understate the option value attached to growing, profitable lines of business. Corporate finance theory requires extension to deal with real options. Therefore, to bridge the gap we on the financial side need to:
• Apply existing finance theory correctly.
• Extend the theory. I believe the most promising line of research is to try to use option pricing theory to model the time-series interactions between investments.

Both sides could make a conscious effort to reconcile financial and strategic analysis. Although complete reconciliation will rarely be possible, the attempt should uncover hidden assumptions and bring a generally deeper understanding of strategic choices. The gap may remain, but with better analysis on either side of it.

---

9. See W. C. Kester, "Today's Options for Tomorrow's Growth," *Harvard Business Review* (March-April 1984).

10. See, for example, Chapter 2 of W. E. Fruhan, Jr., *Financial Strategy: Studies in the Creation, Transfer and Destruction of Shareholder Value*, (Homewood, Illinois: Richard D. Irwin, Inc., 1979).

A NEW APPROACH TO EVALUATING NATURAL RESOURCE INVESTMENTS

by Michael Brennan and Eduardo Schwartz, University of California at Los Angeles

The plight of the contemporary capital budgeting analyst may be compared to that of the 19th-century physician. Long on learning, he is short on technique, and such technique as he does possess can be acquired in a matter of weeks by the intelligent layman. For, while understanding of the operation of capital markets has progressed rapidly during the past two decades, significant innovations in corporate capital budgeting techniques have been markedly absent. Such innovations as have been proposed—linear programming, simulation and decision-tree analysis—have failed to win widespread acceptance; and the implementation of corporate capital budgeting rules remains largely a matter of reaching for the discount tables or the pocket calculator.

The object of capital budgeting is to find investment projects whose value exceeds their cost. Setting aside difficulties associated with determination of the cost of projects,[1] the essential problem is that of appraising or valuing the asset which will be created by an investment, be it an oil refinery, a ship or a computer assembly plant. In this sense the task of the financial analyst is not unlike that of the appraiser or realtor who ventures opinions on the value of real properties. It is instructive to note that real estate appraisals typically start from the known prices at which similar properties have changed hands in the recent past and then make marginal adjustments to reflect differences in location, size and so on.

At first blush this approach bears no relation to the procedures followed by financial analysts in appraising investment projects. As is often the case, however, first impressions are misleading. In fact the financial analyst also proceeds by adjustment from the known values of some assets to an estimate of the value of the hypothetical asset—that is, the outcome of the investment project under consideration. The difference is simply that while the realtor makes modest interpolations from the prices of neighbouring properties, the financial analyst typically makes enormous extrapolations from the known values of completely unrelated assets: in fact, from the value of a portfolio of riskless bonds whose time pattern of cash flows corresponds to that of the investment project.

We shall argue that the whole apparatus of the classical discounted cash flow approach to capital budgeting is predicated upon an analogy between a real investment project and a portfolio of riskless bonds. Such an analogy may be appropriate in some contexts—one thinks naturally of public utilities—but it is obviously inappropriate in many other cases (and nowhere perhaps more so than in the realm of natural resource investments, our primary concern in this paper). The challenge to the financial analyst is to choose an asset of known value which is closest in characteristics to the asset whose value is to be determined. Since this choice must contain an element of judgment, capital budgeting is as much a matter of art as of technique. Unfortunately, many text books leave the mistaken impression that capital budgeting is simply a question of mechanical application of the rules of discounting.

In the case of natural resource investments, the relevant asset whose value is known will often be a portfolio consisting of riskless bonds and either the commodity which is to be produced by the investment project—be it gold, oil or lead—or a futures contract on that commodity. This is most easily seen in the case of a gold mine which will produce a known output at a known cost. If the costs are known,

---

1. These may be far from trivial as recent experience with nuclear power plants reveal.

While the realtor makes modest interpolations from the prices of neighbouring properties, the financial analyst typically makes enormous extrapolations from the known values of completely unrelated assets.

they can be discounted, like the payments on a Treasury bond, at the riskless interest rate, leaving only the problem of valuing the output. This latter task is simple if there exists a market for forward delivery, or a futures market for the commodity. The present value of an ounce of future production is equal simply to the appropriate current futures price discounted at the riskless interest rate (to reflect the fact that payment is deferred). Indeed it turns out that this discounted futures price for gold is almost exactly equal to the current spot price because of arbitrage considerations which we shall elucidate below. This means that for any commodity which, like gold, is held for investment or speculative purposes, future output can be evaluated at the current spot price without any discounting.

For commodities which are held in inventory for commercial rather than investment purposes, the situation is somewhat more complex, since it is necessary to take account of the net benefits yielded by an inventory of the commodity. The principal benefits of the inventory are, first, production cost savings made possible by avoidance of the interruptions in production which would be inevitable in the absence of an inventory and, second, the ability to take advantage of unforeseen local increases in the demand for the commodity. Collectively these benefits, net of the costs of storage of the inventory, are known as the "convenience yield" of an inventory of the commodity. It is the *marginal* convenience yield, then, or the extra services yielded by an additional unit of inventory, which must be taken into account in valuing future units of production.

It turns out that the present value of a unit of future production of the commodity is equal to the current spot price discounted by the marginal convenience yield. Moreover this marginal convenience yield may be inferred from the relation between the spot and futures prices of the commodity.

Note that this convenience yield approach avoids simultaneously the twin problems of assessing the expected future spot price at which the commodity will be sold, and of assigning a discount rate appropriate to the risk of these revenues. On the other hand it is necessary to estimate the convenience yield, which may itself be a function of the spot price of the commodity. The scope for error in estimating the convenience yield, however, is much less than in estimating future spot prices and discount rates.

Thus far we have assumed that the future output

of the project is known; however, this assumption is unlikely to be the case in most situations. Future output will depend upon a number of factors which are unknown at the time the project is evaluated: most notably, on geological features which will be revealed only as production takes place, and on future market conditions. Depending on actual future prices, production may be changed, or a project shut down or even abandoned with resulting costs of closure, redundancy and so on.

These operating options are extremely difficult to evaluate under the classical present value approach. They may be valued in a quite straightforward manner, however, and the optimal operating policies determined, by treating the project as an *option* on the commodity, and adapting the option pricing paradigm originally developed by Fischer Black and Myron Scholes (1973) and elaborated by Robert Merton (1973). Indeed so flexible is this approach that it is possible to value individual components of the cash flows from a project—for example, to calculate the present value of a royalty, an income tax or redundancy payments—and, even more important, to determine the effect of alternative fiscal arrangements on the optimal operating policies of the projects. However, before we present this new approach to capital budgeting for natural resource investments, it will prove useful to consider in more detail the limitations of the classical discounted cash flow model.

The Classical Discounted Cash Flow Model

The classical Discounted Cash Flow or Present Value procedure for capital budgeting has now almost everywhere replaced cruder payback or accounting rate of return methods. It involves a comparison between the cost of an investment project and the present value of the cash flows the project will generate, which is calculated according to the well-known formula:

$$(1) \quad PV = \frac{C_1}{1+K} + \frac{C_2}{(1+K)^2} + \ldots \frac{C_n}{(1+K)^n}$$

where C_t is the cash flow expected in period t and k is the appropriate discount rate. Formula (1) is also the one used to arrive at the value of a bond, where C_t is the coupon payment, C_n is the final repayment of principal and k is the interest rate. This is not fortui-

This approach avoids simultaneously the twin problems of assessing the expected future spot price and of assigning a discount rate appropriate to the risk of these revenues.

tous, since the origin of the formula and its only rigorous justification is precisely in its application to bonds or known cash flows.

The application of the formula to the valuation of real risky assets is made possible by two more or less tacit assumptions or conventions. The first is that uncertain future cash flows can be replaced by their expected values and that these expected cash flows can be treated as given at the outset. The second is that the discount rate is known and constant, and that it depends solely upon the risk of the project. Let us consider the limitations of an approach based on these assumptions and see why the underlying bond analogy may be a poor one for some investment projects, especially in the field of natural resources.

First, the classical approach, by assuming that the cash flows to be discounted are given at the outset, presupposes a static approach to investment decision-making—one which ignores the possibility of future management decisions that will be made in response to the market conditions encountered. Over the life of a project, decisions can be made to change the output rate, to expand or close the facility, or even to abandon it. The flexibility afforded by these decision possibilities may contribute significantly to the value of the project.

To introduce an analogy which we shall develop further below, the classical approach may be likened to valuing a stock option contract while ignoring the right of the holder not to exercise when it is unprofitable. To some extent this drawback of the classical approach may be overcome by employing a scenario or simulation approach in which alternative scenarios—involving for example different price outcomes and management responses—are generated and the resulting cash flows estimated. These cash flows are then averaged across scenarios and discounted to arrive at the present value.

Unfortunately this scenario or simulation approach gives rise to two further problems. First, it requires that the appropriate policy for each scenario be determined in advance. Sometimes this will be possible. For example, if the output rate can be adjusted costlessly, the simple rule of setting marginal cost equal to price may sometimes be optimal.[2] But more generally this will not be possible. If it is costly to close or abandon a project, then the decision to close is itself an investment decision with uncertain

future cash flows depending on commodity prices. The optimal closure policy must therefore be determined simultaneously with the original capital budgeting decision.

Even more fundamentally, the degree of managerial discretion in making future operating decisions will tend to affect the risk of the project under consideration. A project which can be abandoned under adverse circumstances will be less risky than one that cannot; it will be even less risky if part of the initial capital investment can be recovered in the event of abandonment. The classical approach offers no way of allowing for this risk effect except through some *ad hoc* adjustment of the discount rate.

In fact the tacit assumption concerning the discount rate is the second Achilles' heel of the classical approach. Given any set of expected cash flows, there almost always exists some discount rate which will yield the correct present value. But the determination of this discount rate presents an almost insurmountable task, and current procedures cannot be regarded as any more than highly imperfect rules of thumb. Thus these procedures all assume that the discount rate is constant, which is tantamount to assuming that the risk of the project is constant over its life. And this is, of course, highly unlikely. Not only will the risk depend in general upon the remaining life of the project, it will almost certainly depend upon the current profitability of the project through an operating leverage effect. Hence, not only will the discount rate vary with time, it will also be uncertain.

Even if the appropriate discount rate were deterministic and constant, the problems of estimation would still be formidable. In principle the discount rate should depend upon the risk of the project, but how is this risk to be assessed? The generally approved procedure is to use the Capital Asset Pricing Model and to base the discount rate on the beta of the project as estimated from other firms with similar projects. In practice these other firms consist in effect of portfolios of projects, sometimes in unrelated industries, and this makes the assignment of betas to individual projects a hazardous undertaking.[3] Transferring these betas to the project under consideration creates further problems, for a new project is likely to have a cost structure which differs in a systematic fashion from existing, mature projects. The problem is compounded by the consideration, mentioned

---

2. For an extractive industry even this may not be the case, for it may be better to leave the resource in the ground in the expectation of more favourable prices in the future.

3. Fuller and Kerr (1981) describe well the difficulties of arriving at a beta estimate even for a division of a corporation.

The classical approach presupposes a static approach to investment decision-making—one which ignores the possibility of future management decisions.

above, that the latitude of future operating decisions inherent in a project will affect its risk, and is unlikely to be duplicated in existing projects.

Of course these problems are often ignored in practice and a single corporate discount rate based on the weighted average cost of capital is employed for all projects, regardless of risk. As is well known, however, the price of this simplification is a capital budgeting decision system which contains systematic biases as between projects with different risks and different lives. And, as we have argued, such a decision system will lead to the systematic undervaluation of projects with significant operating options.

A final practical difficulty with the classical approach is the necessity to forecast expected output prices for many years into the future. This problem is particularly acute for natural resource industries, where annual price fluctuations of 25 to 50 percent are not uncommon. Under these conditions a wide range of possibilities for the path of expected future spot prices will appear plausible, and the calculated present value of the project will depend upon some arbitrary selection among them.

The foregoing appears to constitute a fairly strong indictment of the classical discounted cash flow approach to capital budgeting. It would be premature, however, to conclude that the approach is without merit, or that it should be discarded in favour of some even worse approach, such as the old payback rule. The limitations of the classical approach arise because it is based fundamentally on an analogy between a portfolio of riskless bonds and a real investment project. In many cases this analogy may be useful; for example, in situations in which the scope for future managerial discretion is limited, and the fiction of other similar risk projects can be maintained. Moreover, even if these conditions are not satisfied, the bond analogy underlying the classical approach may still be the best method available.

In general the appropriate analogy will depend upon the type of project under consideration. For natural resource projects, as we shall show, a better analogy than the classical model is provided by the option pricing or contingent claims paradigm. This approach treats a natural resource extraction project or mine as an option on the underlying commodity. It will prove helpful first, however, to consider the principles involved in valuing a simple gold mine assuming no scope for future managerial discretion.

A Simple Gold Mine

Consider a gold mine which will produce a known output of 1000 ounces at a cost of $200,000 over each of the next two years. The present value of the mine is simply the difference between the present value of the reserves, which will depend upon the future spot price of gold, and the present value of the costs. Since the costs are certain, the bond analogy applies precisely to them, and they may be discounted at the current bond rate, R, say 10 percent, to yield as follows:

$$(2)\ PV(Costs) = \frac{200,000}{1.1} + \frac{200,000}{1.1^2} = \$347,107.$$

To value the output or revenues of the mine, let us suppose initially there exist futures markets for gold deliverable in one and two years, and that the current futures prices are F_1 and F_2. Now an individual who goes long in a one-year futures contract agrees to take delivery of one ounce of gold in one year in return for a payment of F_1, which will also take place in one year.[4] He is effectively buying gold for future delivery at a *current,* or present value, price of $F_1/(1+R)$, where the discounting reflects the fact that payment is deferred for one year. Similarly, an individual who goes short in a futures contract agrees to make delivery of the gold in one year in return for receiving F_1 at that time. He is effectively selling gold for future delivery at a current or present value price of $F_1/(1+R)$. Thus the futures market reveals to us directly the present value of an ounce of gold deliverable in t years as $F_t/(1+R)^t$.

Now the owner of the gold mine owns nothing but the right to deliver 1000 ounces of gold in one and two years after incurring the necessary extraction costs dealt with above. It follows that the present value of this gold for future delivery is given by the equation:

$$(3)\ PV\ (Revenues) = \frac{1000\ F_1}{1.1} + \frac{1000\ F_2}{1.21}$$

where the interest rate, R, is 10 percent. It follows that the present value of the mine is simply the difference between expressions (3) and (2), and the gold mine is equivalent to a portfolio consisting of gold futures and bonds.

Note that this approach obviates any need either

---

4. We are ignoring the technical distinctions between futures markets and forward markets.

The classical approach may be likened to valuing a stock option contract while ignoring the right of the holder not to exercise when it is unprofitable.

to forecast the future spot price of gold, an exceedingly difficult task, or to determine an appropriate discount rate for revenues from sales of gold, which is also a difficult task. Instead, the present value of the mine is expressed solely in terms of observables, the futures prices and the interest rate.

It may be objected that the value of the mine yielded by this approach does not correspond to that obtained by an analyst using his own forecasts of future gold prices. This is quite possible. The value does correspond, however, to the price at which the gold mine could be sold today—a price which depends solely on current market expectations about future gold prices, which in turn are reflected in futures prices. Thus it is important to distinguish between the current market value of the mine, which is what the present value analysis is intended to yield, and deviations between the market's and the analyst's expectations about the future spot price of gold. If the analyst believes that gold is undervalued by the market, then it is quite possible for him to speculate on his hunches in the futures market; but he should not confuse his hunches with his estimate of the current market of the mine.

A second objection that may be made to the foregoing analysis is that there do not exist futures markets for delivery beyond a couple of years, and yet the mine may have a production life of many more years. As we shall see, however, the existence of a futures market is not critical to our analysis. For a commodity which is held for investment purposes, such as gold, the futures price is always equal to the current spot price compounded forward at the interest rate. Thus the futures price for delivery in t years, F_t, may be written as

(4) $F_t = S_o(1+R)^t$

where S_o is the current spot price of gold. Relation (4) permits us to infer what the futures would be, from the current spot price and the interest rate, even if no futures contract of the relevant maturity is actually traded.

To see why relation (4) must hold, consider an individual who is holding gold for investment purposes as part of his portfolio. If the futures price is less than the value given by expression (4), it will pay him to sell his gold at the current spot price, S_o, and enter into a future's contract to repurchase the gold in t years at F_t. The proceeds of the gold sale invested in bonds will yield $S_o(1+R)^t$ at a time t and he will require only F_t to make good on the futures contract,

leaving him with a certain profit $S_o(1+R)^t - F_t$. So long as F_t is below the value implied by (4), it will pay all holders of gold to sell spot and repurchase in the futures market. But since the world stocks of gold must be held by someone, it cannot be profitable for them all to sell gold and repurchase it via a futures market transaction. Thus the futures price cannot be less than the value given by expression (4). Moreover, the futures price cannot exceed this value either, for then unlimited riskless profits would follow from a strategy of purchasing gold to hold in inventory and simultaneously selling futures contracts.

Therefore, the only equilibrium price for gold for future delivery is the compounded value of the current spot price as given by (4). Substituting this value for the futures price in expression (3) for the present value of the mine revenues, we find

(5) PV (Revenues)

$$= \frac{1000 \times S_o(1.1)}{1.1} + \frac{1000 \times S_o(1.1)}{1.1^2}$$

$$= 1000 \times S + 1000 \times S$$

$$= 2000 \times S_o.$$

To express this in words, the present value of the mine revenues is obtained by valuing the future output at the *current spot price* of gold without discounting. Thus, careful reasoning reveals that it is possible to value a gold mine without making any of the hazardous assumptions about future prices of gold which would be required under the classical present value approach. Instead of treating the gold mine as analogous to a portfolio of bonds, as the classical approach does, we recognize that it is more akin to a portfolio of gold and of bonds sold short—with the latter corresponding to the production costs.

Now gold is something of a special case since its high value and imperishability make the costs of storing it in inventory negligible, and since individuals do in fact store it in safety deposit boxes for investment purposes. The situation is somewhat different for most other metals. No one, as far as we know, holds ingots of lead, zinc or aluminum in their safety deposit boxes. Instead these metals are held in commercial inventories by refiners and fabricators who use the metals in their production processes. We consider next how the foregoing analysis must be modified to account for the holding of commercial inventories.

The limitations of the classical approach arise because it is based fundamentally on an analogy between a portfolio of riskless bonds and a real investment project.

A Simple Copper Mine

Let us consider next the example of copper held in inventory not by individual investors, but by manufacturers of copper wire and piping and others who have a commercial interest in the metal. These inventories are held, like inventories of any raw material, because they permit production to proceed smoothly without interruptions caused by shortages of raw materials. Some inventories will continue to be held even if the spot price is expected to decline; the decline in the value of the inventory is offset by the convenience of having the inventory on hand. This benefit of having an inventory on hand is referred to as the *convenience yield* of the inventory. The marginal convenience yield is the benefit yielded by the marginal unit of inventory net of any costs of physical storage, deterioration, etc.

Commercial holders will add to their inventories until the marginal convenience yield, C, is equal to the financial costs of carrying inventory. These costs consist of the interest on the funds tied up in inventory, $S_o \times R$, less the capital gain, $(F_1 - S_o)$, which is realized if a futures contract is entered into to eliminate the inventory price risk:

$$(6) \quad C = S_o \times R + (S_o - F_1)$$

Solving for the one period futures price,

$$(7) \quad F_1 = S_o(1 + R) - C.$$

Comparing expression (7) with the corresponding expression (4) for gold futures, we see that the only difference lies in the convenience yield, C, which tends to reduce the futures relative to the spot price.

The *marginal* convenience yield will depend on the size of the total inventories in the economy. When commercial inventories are large, the benefit of an additional unit of inventory will be correspondingly small. At the same time spot prices will also be low because of the excess supply of the commodity. Therefore it is reasonable to take the convenience yield as proportional to the current spot price, $C = cS$.[5] Substituting into (7) we find that the futures price for delivery in t periods is

$$(8) \quad F_t = S_o(1 + R - c)^t.$$

We are able to use expression (8) to evaluate the revenues from a copper mine in just the same way we could evaluate the revenues from the gold mine. The only difference is that we must value the future output at the current spot price discounted at the convenience yield.[6] For example, if our copper mine will produce 100 pounds of copper in each of the following two years and the convenience yield is 2 percent we find that

$$PV(\text{Reserves}) = \frac{100 \times S_o}{1.02} + \frac{100 \times S_o}{1.02^2} = 194 \times S_o.$$

There is only one remaining problem, and that is the appropriate convenience yield. Fortunately this can be computed from the current spot and futures prices and the interest rate using expression (8).

The Mine as an Option

To this point we have seen how to value a mine whose output rate is predetermined, regardless of the price at which the output can be sold. In practice the owner of a mine generally has the right to choose the optimal output rate, to close the mine, to re-open it, or even to abandon it as circumstances dictate. Because of these decision possibilities, a mine is most appropriately regarded as a complex option on the resources contained in the mine. Just as a stock option gives the holder the right to acquire shares at a fixed exercise price, ownership of a mine confers the right to acquire the output of the mine at a fixed exercise price equal to the variable cost of production. Consequently, a mine may be valued by combining the valuation principles already presented with the option pricing approach pioneered by Black-Scholes (1973) and Merton (1973). The option pricing approach implies that the value of the mine satisfies a certain differential equation subject to a set of boundary conditions which we shall now consider.

The value of the mine will depend upon whether it is currently open and producing or closed and incurring maintenance costs. It will also depend upon the unexploited inventory remaining in the mine. And just as in the case of the fixed output mines already discussed, it will depend upon the current spot price of the commodity. Finally, the mine value will also depend upon an index of operating costs.

To be more specific, we will begin by defining the following symbols:

---

5. More complex relations between the convenience yield and the spot price can also be taken into account.

6. A technical note: this approach is exact only for continuous compounding. In practice discrete compounding makes a negligible difference.

For natural resources projects, a better analogy than the classical model is provided by the option pricing or contingent claims paradigm.

Q	the remaining mine inventory
S	the current spot price of the commodity
OC	an index of mine operating costs
V(Q,S,OC)	the current value of an operating mine
N(Q,S,OC)	the current value of a non-operating mine.

Then we have the following boundary conditions:

Mine Exhaustion: When the inventory in the mine is exhausted, the mine can no longer operate. In this case its value depends solely on the salvage value, which may be negative.

N(Q,S,OC) = Salvage Value

Premature Abandonment: If output prices are sufficiently low, and the cost of maintaining a non-operating mine are sufficiently high, it may pay to abandon a mine even though there is a positive remaining inventory. The abandonment possibility places a floor under the value of the mine so that

N(Q,S,OC) ≥ Salvage Value

Operating Decisions: If the variable costs of operation are constant, and the mine has no influence on the price at which output can be sold, it will always be optimal either to operate the mine at its full capacity rate, q, or to shut it down temporarily. There will generally be costs involved with shutting the mine—redundancy payments and so on. However, the ability to shut down means that the value of an operating mine can never be less than the value of the mine shut less the costs of shutting:

O(Q,S,OC) ≥ N(Q,S,OC) - shutting costs.

Similarly, since a shut mine can always be re-opened at a cost, the value of a non-operating mine cannot be less than the value of an operating mine minus the costs of re-opening, so that

N(Q,S,OC) ≥ O(Q,S,OC) - re-opening costs.

Cash Flows: When the mine is operating it generates a cash flow which is given by

$$q(S(1 - r) - A(OC)) (1 - t_c) - t_r O$$

where q is the capacity output rate, r is a royalty rate which is charged on the value of output, $A(OC)$ is the average cash cost of production at the capacity output, t_c is the corporate tax rate, and t_r is the real estate tax rate, which is assumed to be charged on the value of the mine, O. When the mine is shut the cash flow is given by the negative of the maintenance costs and real estate taxes.

Given these conditions the equation for the mine value may be solved simply on a personal computer. The nature of the solution is illustrated in Figure 1, which plots the mine value as a function of the spot price for a given level of mine inventory, Q, and level of operating costs, OC. To understand this figure suppose that the mine is initially shut and that the spot price is between S_1 and S_2. As the spot price rises, the value of the operating mine begins to exceed the value of the mine shut, but not be enough to justify incurring the costs of opening the mine. It is not optimal to open the mine until the spot price reaches S_2, at which point the value of the mine in operation exceeds its value shut by just the amount of the opening costs. Once opened, the mine will remain in operation even if the spot price drops. It will not be optimal to shut the mine unless the price drops to S_1, at which point the value of the shut mine exceeds the value of the operating mine by the amount of the shutting cost. If the salvage value of the mine is zero, it will not be optimal to actually cease maintenance and abandon the mine until the spot price falls to S_o.

Valuing a Gold Mine

To gain some further insight into our valuation procedure and the data inputs required to implement it, we shall consider a specific numerical example. The data for our hypothetical gold mine are presented in Table 1. It is instructive to compare the data required here with those required for a classical discounting analysis. First, we do not require any projections for the price of gold or specification of a "cost of capital" for the mine. We require instead that the convenience yield of gold be specified.[7] Additional data required by this approach, but not by the classical discounting approach, are the standard deviation

---

7. The futures/spot price relation for gold reveals a zero convenience yield.

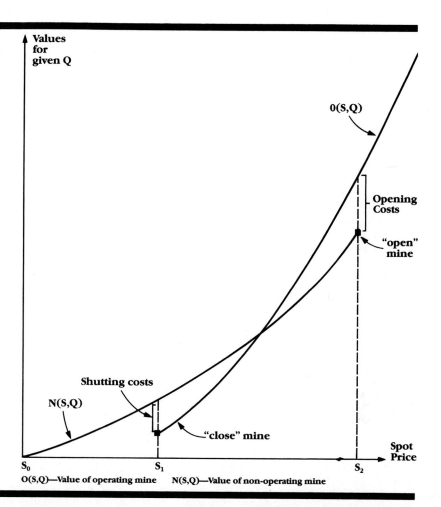

FIGURE 1
The Value of a Mine in Terms of the Current Spot Price of the Commodity

Values for given Q

O(S,Q)

Opening Costs

"open" mine

Shutting costs

N(S,Q)

"close" mine

Spot Price

S_0 S_1 S_2

O(S,Q)—Value of operating mine   N(S,Q)—Value of non-operating mine

Table 1
Data for a Hypothetical Gold Mine

Mine
Capacity Output Rate: 50 thousand ounces per year
Current Mine Inventory: 1 million ounces
Average Production Costs (Current Prices): $250 per ounce
Opening Cost (Current Prices): $1 m
Shutting Cost (Current Prices): $1 m
Annual Maintenance Cost (Current Prices): $1 m per year
Salvage Value: –0–
Cost Inflation Rate: 9% per year

Gold
Convenience Yield: 0% per year
Price Risk: 20% per year

Taxes
Real Estate: 2% per year
Income: 48%
Royalty: 2%

Interest Rate: 9% per year

This approach obviates any need either to forecast the future spot price of gold or to determine an appropriate discount rate.

Table 2
Value of Gold Mine for Different Gold Prices

Gold Price $/ounce	Mine Value ($m)		Value of [1] Options ($m)	Risk [2] % per year
	Open	Shut		
100	–0–	–0–	–	–
150	**1.08** –	**2.08**	–	**154**
200	8.65 –	9.65	–	82
250	**20.02**	**20.85**	**24.36**	**68**
300	34.86	34.78	17.22	57
350	**51.82**	**50.96**	**9.75**	**49**
400	70.04	69.04	9.29	43
450	**89.05** –	**88.05**	**7.73**	**40**
500	108.58 –	107.58	6.51	37
550	**128.47** –	**127.47**	**5.57**	**35**
600	148.60 –	147.60	4.81	33

– Indicates it is optimal to open mine if currently shut.
– Indicates it is optimal to shut mine if currently open.
[1] Options to open/shut and to abandon.
[2] Standard deviation of rate of return.

or risk of the gold price per unit time,[8] the maintenance costs for a shut mine, the costs of opening and shutting the mine and the salvage value. The reason these data are not required for a classical discounting is that the options of shutdown or abandonment are never explicitly included in this type of analysis.

Table 2 shows the value of the mine when it has a 20-year inventory of production for different gold prices.[9] Note that the value of the mine depends upon whether it is currently open and operating or shutdown. If the mine is currently operating it is optimal to shut it down if the gold price falls below $230. Since the variable cost of production is $250, this implies that it is optimal to maintain production even when the mine is operating at a loss in order to avoid the costs of shutdown and possible subsequent reopening. On the other hand, if the mine is currently closed, it is not optimal to open it until the gold price has risen to $380, which is substantially above the variable costs of production.

The column "Value of Options" represents the difference between the value of our hypothetical mine when it is open and in production, and the value of an otherwise identical mine which must be operated at full capacity until it is exhausted in 20 years. This comparison is of interest because the assumption of continuous production is implicit in the classical discounting approach. It is clear that the value of the options to shut the mine and subsequently re-open it, or even to abandon it, is a very substantial fraction of the total value of the mine, particularly when the gold price is in the neighborhood of the variable cost of production. Valuation approaches which ignore these operating options are likely to underestimate substantially the value of the mine.

The final column of the table shows how the risk of the mine varies with the price of gold: when the price is low, the operating leverage is high. As the price rises the operating leverage declines and the risk of the mine falls until for very high gold prices it approaches the price risk of gold itself, 20 percent.

While Table 2 shows the value of the complete mine for a range of gold prices, Table 3 shows how, given a particular current gold price of $350, the present values of the different elements of the cash flow combine to yield the value of the mine. This type of analysis is likely to be particularly useful in evaluating cost-saving investments for a given mine. We can see immediately, for example, that a 10 percent saving in operating cost will have a pre-tax present value of $15.9m and an after-tax present value of $15.9m × (1 − .48) = $8.27m.

8. In general the standard deviation of the rate of return on the commodity can be obtained from an historical time series of commodity prices. For those commodities, like gold, on which traded options exist, an implied standard deviation can also be obtained using an appropriate option pricing model [Black and Scholes (1973)].

9. Note that we have neglected the effects of depreciation allowances associated with the investment in the mine. The present value of tax savings due to these allowances should be added to the figures in the table.

TABLE 3 Valuing the Components of Mine Revenue	Gross Revenue	$m. 322.5
	Royalty	6.5
	Net Revenue	316.0
	Operating Cost	159.0
	Taxable Income	157.0
	Corporate Tax	75.4
	After Tax Cash Flow	81.6
	Opening Costs	.3
	Shutdown Costs	.7
	Maintenance Costs	6.9
	Salvage Value	–
	Real Estate Tax	21.9
	Net Cash Flow	51.8
	Current gold price: $350 per ounce	

The model also makes possible an analysis of the effects of alternative tax and royalty arrangements, taking into account the fact that these not only affect the shares of risk borne by the government and the owner of the mine, but also change the mine owner's optimal policy for operating the mine.

Conclusion

We have argued in this paper that traditional approaches to capital budgeting suffer from some severe limitations. These are particularly acute in the natural resource sector, where output prices are especially volatile. The problems include the forecasting of future output prices, the determination of an appropriate discount rate, and the inability to allow for management flexibility in future operating decisions. The alternative approach we have de-

largely overcomes these problems by using the hitherto neglected information contained in futures prices—the convenience yield—and by recognizing that a mine can be treated as a type of option on the underlying commodity.[10] The approach has already been applied with some success to the analysis of a large resource project in Canada.

While our focus here has been on natural resource projects where futures markets for the underlying commodity exist, the basic principles underlying the analysis lend themselves with appropriate modification to applications in other context in which the role of management in influencing future operations and cash flows is significant. This is the typical case, we believe, and while the traditonal analysis views capital investments, like children, as hostages to fortune, our approach recognizes that, like children also, they are often amenable to their progenitors' guidance.

---

10. For a more detailed description of this approach see Brennan and Schwartz (1985).

VALUING OFFSHORE OIL PROPERTIES WITH OPTION PRICING MODELS

by Daniel Siegel, Northwestern University, James Smith, University of Houston, and James Paddock, Tufts University

Introduction

For the past several decades, the most prominent technique for performing valuations for the purposes of capital budgeting has been the discounted cash flow (DCF) approach. Using this approach, analysts compute expected cash flows and discount them at a risk-adjusted rate of interest. The appropriate discount rate typically comes out of an asset pricing model such as the Capital Asset Pricing Model (CAPM). Recently, however, both practitioners and academics have pointed out that the actual application of the DCF approach is very difficult when a project involves one or more significant operating options. Operating options arise when management can defer its choice of action until a future date when some important uncertainty is resolved. These operating options make it difficult to calculate expected cash flows and even more difficult to calculate risk-adjusted discount rates because of the complicated risk structures introduced by the operating options. A final problem arises because the optimal exercise of operating options is not independent of the project valuation. Because important operating options are so often present in real investment opportunities, these problems amount to a serious criticism of the DCF approach.

Several recent papers have suggested that a new type of capital budgeting approach should be formulated incorporating the now well-developed theory of the pricing of options in financial markets.[1] By drawing an analogy between financial options and operating options, one might hope to be able to deal explicitly with the valuation problems described above. The purpose of this article is to demonstrate how insights from financial option pricing theory can be applied to a particular problem involving operating options: the valuation of undeveloped oil reserves. This is a particularly interesting problem for a number of reasons. There are several operating options involved in extracting oil, including the option to explore, develop, and extract. Further, both the United States Geological Survey (USGS) and oil firms have expressed considerable displeasure with the performance of their DCF valuation models. Finally, the problem provides a case study of the adjustments that one needs to make to financial option pricing theory in order to apply the theory to capital budgeting for real projects with important operating options.

The article will proceed as follows: First, we develop the analogy between undeveloped oil reserves and stock call options that justifies use of option pricing models. Second, we discuss ways of estimating the various "parameters," or inputs, that are necessary to generate a solution. Third, we consider the special problems caused by development lags and the development timing decision. Fourth, we consider the sensitivity of values to changes in the critical inputs. Last, we show how our valuation tech-

---

* Much of this paper is based upon our paper "Option Valuation of Claims on Real Assets: The Case of Offshore Petroleum Leases," Northwestern University Department of Finance Working Paper No. 4, 1985.

1. For an excellent review of this literature see S.P. Mason and R.C. Merton, "The Role of Contingent Claims Analysis in Corporate Finance," in *Recent Advances in Corporate Finance*, E.I. Altman and M.G. Subrahmanyam, eds. (Homewood, IL: Richard D. Irwin, 1985).

TABLE 1 Comparison of Variables for Pricing Models of Stock Call Options and Undeveloped Petroleum Reserves	**Stock Call Option**	**Undeveloped Reserve**
	*Current Stock Price	*Current Value of Developed Reserve
	*Variance of Rate of Return on the Stock	*Variance of Rate of Change of the Value of a Developed Reserve
	*Exercise Price	*Development Cost
	*Time to Expiration	*Relinquishment Requirement
	*Riskless Rate of Interest	*Riskless Rate of Interest
	*Dividend	*Net Production Revenue less Depletion

nique performs relative to the DCF approach using data from several actual offshore petroleum properties.

The Option Embedded in Undeveloped Oil Reserves

The basic analogy underlying our pricing proposal is as follows: Much as a call option on a stock gives its holder the right to buy a share of stock by paying the exercise price, an undeveloped oil reserve gives its owner the right to "acquire" a developed reserve by paying the development cost. Further, much as a stock pays dividends to its owner, the holder of developed reserves receives production revenues (net of depletion). Table 1 lists the important features of a call option on a stock (or, at least, all those necessary to enable one to price it) and the corresponding aspects of the managerial option implicit in holding an undeveloped reserve.

To price a stock option using standard option pricing models (such as the Black-Scholes model and its variants), it is necessary (and sufficient) to have reasonably accurate estimates of the following variables: (1) the current stock price; (2) the expected variance of the rate of change of the stock price (typically expressed as a percentage standard deviation per annum); (3) the exercise price; (4) the time to expiration of the contract; (5) the current risk-free rate of interest; and (6) the dividend yield on the stock. By analogy, we show that to price an undeveloped oil reserve, we need estimates of only the following: (1) the current value of developed reserves; (2) the variance of the rate of change in the value of developed reserves; (3) the present value of the after-tax cost of developing the reserves; (4) the time to relinquishment; (5) the riskless rate of interest; and (6) the net production revenue rate (less depletion). Because an undeveloped reserve can be

developed at any time before the relinquishment date, the analogy here is with an American option (as distinguished from a European option, which can only be exercised at maturity) on a dividend-paying stock. As with an option on a dividend-paying stock, we will need to account for the possibility of early exercise (that is, development before the relinquishment date).

This analogy between a stock option and an undeveloped reserve does break down at one point, however, thus requiring some modification in the standard option pricing models. In the case of a stock call option, receipt of the stock occurs at the same time as the outlay of the exercise price. In the case of an undeveloped oil reserve, it takes time to develop the reserve and thus there is a lag between the decision to develop the reserve (that is, exercise the development option) and the actual payoff. This lag must be accounted for in the pricing model. We show later how this can be done in a straightforward manner.

Estimating the Inputs

We now consider each of the parameter inputs in turn (while deferring discussion of the special problems of accounting for development lags and early exercise). For purposes of this article, we will use values that prevailed in the United States during late 1980 for the Gulf of Mexico. We use this period because our empirical results, presented later, are based on prices and conditions representative of this time period and at this location. Nevertheless, the technique we demonstrate should be applicable to any period or region.

Developed Reserve Value

Like stocks, developed reserves are assets traded in reasonably liquid markets. Thus, we can ob-

It is precisely because this market value already captures the market's discounting of expected production profits to their present value that the proposed option valuation approach requires so few parameter inputs.

serve transaction prices that represent the market value of the developed reserve. While the market value of a developed reserve is not quoted in the *Wall Street Journal* as such, industry participants provide estimates of this value that fall within a fairly narrow range. In fact, it is precisely because this market value already captures the market's discounting of expected production profits to their present value that the proposed option valuation approach requires so few parameter inputs. Notice that this market value implicitly includes deductions for expected taxes and royalties, as well as allowances for depreciation of tangible development costs associated with the producing reserve. Thus, there is no need for the projection of future operating cash flows and estimation of risk-adjusted discount rates that makes the use of DCF analysis such an imprecise tool, especially in the hands of inexperienced users.

Needless to say, the appropriate value is that of a developed reserve of the type that the development expenditure will produce. In our own calculations, we relied on the analysis presented in a study by Gruy, Garb, and Wood (1982).[2] Their analysis, which focused on a number of private sales of developed oil reserves in the period 1981-1982, indicates that a value of approximately $12 per barrel of developed oil reserves is a reliable estimate of the average price at this time. In arriving at a useful estimate of gas prices, we relied on private correspondence with an investment banker, who indicated that a figure of $3 per mcf was appropriate.

Standard Deviation of the Rate of Change of the Value of a Developed Reserve

Like the standard deviation of stock prices, the standard deviation of the market price of developed reserves cannot be directly observed and thus must be estimated. One technique is to estimate this standard deviation directly from past data on market values of developed reserves. Unfortunately, while developed reserves are traded in competitive markets, market value data is not publicly available at regular enough intervals to estimate this standard

deviation directly. We can, however, use the standard deviation of the rate of change of crude oil prices as a proxy for the standard deviation of the rate of change of developed reserve values (which of course assumes that the ratio of the value of crude oil prices to developed reserves is relatively constant).[3] Using monthly data for the period 1974-1980, we found that the annualized real (i.e., CPI-deflated) standard deviation (σ) of the refiner cost of imported crude oil was 14.2 percent.

There is always some risk, of course, in predicting the future on the basis of the past. But the period of 1974-1980 is probably representative of the type of period that market participants might have expected to occur from 1980 on. It includes periods of crisis, as well as periods of relative tranquility. Furthermore, to provide a check on the plausibility of this standard deviation estimate, we also constructed 95 percent confidence intervals for real future crude prices that are implied in our standard deviation estimates. These confidence intervals give an estimate of the range in which real crude oil prices are expected to fall 95 percent of the time.

Of course, there is always the possibility that the price volatility could change in the future. To capture a possible increase in perceived uncertainty, we also examine a standard deviation of 25 percent. The ranges of future prices shown in Table 2 are 95 percent confidence intervals for year one through ten.[4] The implied prices shown in Table 2 suggest that 14.2 percent was probably the more reasonable estimate of the market's expectations about the future volatility of oil prices. In late 1980, for example, it should have seemed plausible that within five years OPEC might have weakened, causing a drop in the real price of oil to $20.04 per barrel. It might also have been plausible to imagine a recurrence of oil shortages and prices rising as high as $71.36 per barrel. Based on this reasoning, we adopt 14.2 percent as our "base case" estimate of expected price volatility, though we also continue to report results based on the assumption that the standard deviation might be as high as 25 percent. (Of course, given the fact that crude prices recently fell as low as $12 per barrel, the higher measure of volatility also seems quite plausible. But this is based on hindsight; the perti-

---

2. See H.J. Gruy, F.A. Garb, and J.W. Wood, "Determining the Value of Oil and Gas in the Ground," *World Oil*, Volume 194, 1982, pp. 105-108.

3. We can get a reasonable estimate using a result from the Gruy et al study, cited earlier (which, incidentally, is commonly used by industry participants), that the value of developed reserves tends to be about one third of crude oil prices. This

approximate relationship has in fact held for a number of years.

4. We assume that the expected rate of increase in real value is 3 percent for $\sigma=0.142$ and 5 percent for $\sigma=0.250$, in order to calculate these numbers. The confidence intervals are in fact not very sensitive to these assumptions.

Thus, there is no need for the projection of future operating cash flows and estimation of risk-adjusted discount rates that makes the use of DCF analysis such an imprecise tool, especially in the hands of inexperienced users.

TABLE 2
Per Barrel Crude Oil
Wellhead Price
Ranges Implicit in
Standard Deviations

Year	$\sigma = 14.2\%$		$\sigma = 25\%$	
	lower	upper	lower	upper
1	27.37	48.30	21.56	58.62
2	24.57	54.86	17.31	71.21
3	22.67	60.63	14.58	82.44
5	20.04	71.36	11.05	103.45
10	16.18	97.51	6.54	154.42

Year 0 is 1980 with a price of $36 per barrel.
Note: The ranges of future prices are 95 percent confidence intervals for years one through ten assuming that oil prices are distributed log-normally: $\ln(S_t/S_0) \sim N[(\text{exrate} - .5\sigma^2)t,(\sigma^2)t]$

exrate = expected rate of price increase and S_t = crude oil price at t.

nent question here is which is the better estimate of the market's *then current* (i.e. in 1980) expectation of future price volatility.)

Development Costs

Since development typically takes a number of years, the appropriate measure of development costs is the present value of real after-tax development expenditures. The discount rate should be fairly low because the development expenditures themselves are not extremely risky. The riskless rate is not quite appropriate, however, because there is some risk in the cost of labor and materials. As mentioned above, depreciation allowances for tangible development expenditures are associated with the developed reserve and are included in that value. Approximately 50 percent of development expenditures in the Gulf of Mexico are intangible and can be expensed for tax purposes. Therefore, after-tax development costs will be about 77 percent $(.50+(1-.46).50)$ of the actual present value of development expenditures.

Relinquishment Requirements

The expiration of the lease depends upon the tract. Typically, such contracts range from 5 to 10 years. For the sample we examine later (USGS Sale A62), the time to expiration is 5 years.

Riskless Rate

Because investors are interested in after-tax rates of return, the appropriate riskless rate is the after-tax real return on treasury securities for an investor who is indifferent between taxable and tax-free riskless debt. A study by Skelton shows that, in the case of long-term treasury bonds, the marginal tax rate (implied in the pricing of such bonds for the period under study) appears to be around 25 percent.[5] For bonds with shorter maturities, however, the marginal tax rate appears to be as high as 50 percent. Until very recently, a common estimate of the average real riskless rate was about two percent. By choosing an intermediate marginal tax rate of 37.5 percent, we thus arrived at a real riskless rate of 1.25 percent.[6]

Net Production Revenue Less Depletion

Like ownership of a dividend-paying stock, ownership of a developed and producing oil reserve provides cash income to its owners. In calculating the value of a call option on a dividend-paying stock, one must know the dividend "yield" (that is, the percentage of total price represented by the annual dividend payout) because dividends paid out reduce the value of the option. Correspondingly, in using option pricing models to value an undeveloped re-

5. See J. Skelton, "Banks, Firms and the Relative Pricing of Tax-Exempt and Taxable Bonds," *Journal of Financial Economics*, Volume 12, 1983, pp. 343-356.
6. See L. Trigeorgis, "Valuing Real Investment Opportunities: An Options Approach to Strategic Capital Budgeting," Unpublished doctoral dissertation, Harvard University (1986).

serve, one must estimate the production "payout ratio"—that is, net production revenue (less depletion) as a percentage of the market value of the reserve.

We can estimate this production "payout ratio" by making a few reasonable assumptions: (1) the per barrel value of a developed reserve is equal to one third of the market price of crude oil (the so-called "one third" rule); (2) per barrel operating costs average 30 percent of the market price per barrel of crude oil; (3) depreciation represents 20 percent of the market price of crude oil; and (4) the production rate—that is, the percentage of the total remaining reserve which is developed each year—is assumed to be 10 percent.

On the basis of the above assumptions, it can be shown that the payout ratio is 4.1 percent (see Appendix A for this calculation). In effect, this means that holding a developed reserve is like holding a stock with a dividend "yield" of 4.1 percent. And while this rate will differ across different types of reserves, the method of calculating the payout ratio will be the same.

Development Lags, Development Timing, and Reserve Valuation
Development Lags

In the case of a call option on a stock, the owner receives the stock immediately upon paying the exercise price. In the case of an undeveloped reserve, by contrast, the holder must wait until development is complete. We have modelled the exercise price as one payment equal to the present value of development expenditures. Because of the time it takes to develop, we can think of paying the development expenditure now and receiving the developed reserve only after the development period. Because of this lag, we can also think of receiving the present value of the developed reserve upon payment of the present value of development expenditures.

This present value is easy to compute. It can be calculated simply by discounting the *current developed reserve* value by the payout ratio. (For a technical explanation, see Appendix B.) If, for example, the development lag is about one year as in the Gulf of Mexico, then the present value of a $12 per barrel developed reserve equals $11.52. Expressed in mathematical terms,

$V' = e^{-.041 \times 1.0} \times \$12.0 = \$11.52$

As this formulation makes clear, and as one would expect, the value of the developed reserve diminishes as the development lag increases.

Development Timing

As in the case of an American call option on a dividend-paying stock, the owner of an undeveloped reserve may choose to exercise the option early—that is, before the period of relinquishment ends. Figure 1 shows on what basis the decision to develop is made. The way to use this graph is as follows: Calculate the ratio $C = V'/D$, where V' is the present value of the developed reserve received after the expected development lag, and D is the development cost. If, for the current time to expiration, this ratio is below the line, the rule is do not exercise. If this ratio is above the line, exercise immediately. Thus, as part of the solution to this problem, we also provide an optimal development-timing rule. This rule is analogous to the rule which determines when to exercise a similar stock call option which pays a continuous dividend at a given rate (such as in an approximation to an index option) and the computer programs which solve these two problems are identical.

Reserve Valuation

We can now use these parameter inputs to place a value on an undeveloped reserve. Table 3, which presents the reserve value per dollar of development cost, is derived using these parameters. It represents the solution to a reasonably complicated partial differential equation; and although this equation may not have a great deal of direct, intuitive appeal, the solution can be gotten fairly quickly using a personal computer. As is clear from the table, this value will depend upon the ratio of per barrel reserve value to per barrel development cost.

Example of Undeveloped Reserve Valuation

To provide an example of how Table 3 and the supporting model might be used, suppose that you own an undeveloped reserve with the following characteristics:
• the developed reserve is expected to yield 100 million barrels of oil;

Even though this reserve could not be profitably developed under current conditions, the right to develop such reserves in the future nevertheless presently has a positive value of over $60 million.

**FIGURE 1
Optimal Timing
of Exercise**

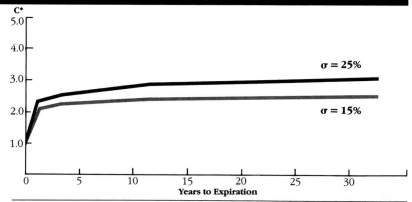

For a given number of years to expiration, if C = V/D is less than C*, the firm defers development (exploration and development). If C exceeds C*, investment should proceed immediately. σ represents the standard deviation of the rate of change of V. To account for investment lags, replace V by V′.

**TABLE 3
Option Values per $1
of Development Cost**

V′/D	σ = 14.2 percent			σ = 25 percent	
	T = 5	T = 10	T = 15	T = 5	T = 10
Out-of-the-Money					
0.70	.00655	.01322	.01704	.04481	.07079
0.75	.01125	.01966	.02410	.05831	.08650
0.80	.01810	.02812	.03309	.07394	.10392
0.85	.02761	.03894	.04430	.09174	.12305
0.90	.04024	.05245	.05803	.11169	.14390
0.95	.05643	.06899	.07458	.13380	.16646
In-the-Money					
1.00	.07661	.08890	.09431	.15804	.19071
1.05	.10116	.11253	.11754	.18438	.21664
1.10	.13042	.14025	.14464	.21278	.24424
1.15	.16472	.17242	.17599	.24321	.27349

1. This table uses a payout ratio of 4.1 percent.
2. Because option values are homogeneous in the development cost, total option value is the entry in this table times the total development cost.

• the present value of the development cost is $11.79 per barrel;
• the development lag is 3 years;
• relinquishment is after a period of 10 years;
• the expected standard deviation of the value of developed reserves is 14.2 percent;
• the payout ratio (net production revenues/value of reserves) is 4.1 percent; and
• the value of the developed reserve today is $12 per barrel.
Given this information, we would proceed toward a solution as follows:

Step 1: Calculate the present value of a developed reserve (V′): V′=e^{-(.041)×3}×$12=$10.61 per barrel
Step 2: Calculate the ratio of reserve value to development cost, C.
C=V′/D=$10.61/$11.79=.90
Step 3: Calculate the value of undeveloped reserves:
Value=(Option Value per $1 Development Cost (from Table 3))×(Total Development Cost)
=(0.05245)×($1179.0 Million)=$61.84 Million
The meaning of this exercise, then, is that even though this reserve could not be profitably developed under current conditions, the *right* to

The big advantages of the option valuation technique over the conventional DCF method appear to be in valuing those properties that are marginal or sub-marginal.

TABLE 4 Undeveloped Reserve Values(In $ Millions)	σ = 14.2 percent			σ = 25 percent	
V'/D	T = 5	T = 10	T = 15	T = 5	T = 10
0.70	7.72	15.59	20.09	52.83	83.46
0.80	21.34	33.15	39.01	87.18	122.52
0.90	47.44	61.84	68.42	131.68	169.66
1.00	90.32	104.81	111.19	186.33	224.85
1.10	153.77	165.35	170.53	250.87	287.96

Note: This table uses a payout ratio of 4.1 percent and 100 Million Bbls of Oil.

develop such reserves in the future nevertheless presently has a positive value of over $60 million.

Sensitivity of Values to Parameter Changes

We now look at how sensitive these undeveloped reserve values are to changes in some of the inputs. Table 4 uses the same inputs as the above example as a base case to demonstrate how the value of undeveloped reserves changes in response to changes in the standard deviation (σ) of the value of developed reserves, the relinquishment period (T), and the ratio (C) of the discounted value of developed reserves (V') to the per barrel costs of development (D).

There are several things to note in Table 4. First, increases in time to relinquishment lead to increases in option value. Second, increases in the standard deviation, or volatility, of oil prices lead to increases in option value. And third, the more out-of-the-money is the property, the more pronounced are the first two effects. Notice, for example, that when C=0.70 and σ = 14.2 percent, lengthening the time to relinquishment from T=5 to T=10 more than doubles the value of the property (15.59/7.72). For C=1.10, by contrast, the percentage increase is less than 10 percent (165.35/153.77). Thus, longer relinquishment requirements on sub-marginal tracts can have a large impact on value (and thus bonus bids). Notice also that when C=0.70 and T=5, increasing the standard deviation from 14.2 percent to 25 percent increases the value of the property by almost 700 percent. For C=1.10, the increase is only about 150 percent.

Thus, increases in oil price variability are also most likely to affect the value of sub-marginal properties. As a general rule, then, the big advantages of the option valuation technique over the conventional DCF method appear to be in valuing those properties that are marginal or sub-marginal. For those projects where development is clearly profitable, the clear choice (as shown earlier in Figure 1) is to develop the property immediately.

An Application: The Valuation of Offshore Oil Leases

An important application of the above technique is that of determining the appropriate bid for a lease on an offshore oil property. As mentioned earlier, industry participants and government representatives have expressed dissatisfaction with the performance of discounted cash flow valuations. We suspect that much of this can be attributed to the failure of the DCF approach to take account of real operating options.

In order to value a *lease*, as distinguished from an outright sale of an undeveloped reserve, we need to modify the analysis presented above. In particular, we have valued an undeveloped reserve assuming that we know the number of barrels of reserves and the cost of developing them. When evaluating a lease, we must come up with probability distributions for both the expected quantity of reserves and for the associated exploration costs. The end result of this process, and thus the estimated value of a lease, is the average value of the undeveloped reserve calculated on the basis of the above probability distributions.[7]

---

7. We can simply take the expected value because the quantity and cost risk is unsystematic, in the sense that it is uncorrelated with general economy-wide movements.

114

TABLE 5
Option Value Analysis of Sale A62 Tracts (In $ Million)

Tract	Option Value	Company X Bid	Average Bid	High Bid
1	19.550	9.135	19.500	49.190
2	59.100	38.625	42.670	120.730
3	20.650	6.130	14.080	33.390
4*	71.310	20.674	28.230	51.030
5*	60.350	28.555	21.480	41.790
6	22.140	4.296	20.010	55.120
Average	42.183	17.903	24.328	58.542

Note: * refers to tracts that would have been won by Company X using option value bidding.

In this section we report some empirical results based on a group of six tracts awarded in Federal Lease Sale A62, which was held on September 30, 1980. We were able to obtain necessary geological and economic data from a U.S. oil company (henceforth "Company X"). In fact, we took our input data directly from the worksheets Company X used to prepare its own internal valuations of the six tracts. While Company X processed the data using a conventional DCF approach, we processed the same data using the option valuation approach and came up with significantly different results.

Company X provided estimates of recoverable reserves for each tract that took the form of a triangular distribution—that is, estimates of the "minimum," "maximum," and "expected" volume of recoverable reserves for each tract. In addition to this "triangular" distribution, Company X also reported estimates of the "dry hole risk" associated with each tract—that is, the probability that no recoverable reserves would be found.

We used these company estimates to form a "lognormal" distribution, which is more representative of actual distributions of recoverable reserves.[8] We also used Company X's estimated schedule of exploration and development expenditures to calculate the present value of investment per barrel of recoverable reserves.[9] These input data, together with the parameter values discussed above, allowed us to calculate the option values for each tract that are reported in Table 5.[10]

Relative to the industry, Company X was a low bidder in sale A62. It bid below the industry average on all six of the tracts it pursued and won none of them. In contrast, the option values we computed were 136 percent larger than Company X's bids on average, and 73 percent larger than the average industry bids. And, because we used the same tract-specific reserve and cost data as Company X, the dramatic difference between the Company's and our estimates of value is not due to different underlying views of the geologic potential of the tracts.

Bidding performance can be evaluated in several ways. One important aspect is the percentage of tracts that are actually won. As noted above, Company X won none of the tracts it pursued. In contrast, simply bidding the computed option values would have won two of the six tracts; i.e., our option value twice exceeds the reported high bid. Of course, anyone can win tracts by bidding aggressively. It is fair to ask whether simply bidding the computed option values is too aggressive. The answer seems pretty clearly to be "no." On average, the computed option value is only 72 percent of the high bid, so there is no systematic tendency to outbid the industry across the board.

How aggressive should the bids be? One common measure of aggressive bidding is the amount of money "left on the table"—that is, the difference between the highest and second highest bids. The amount of money left on the table shows how much a company could have saved and still won the tract.

The figures in Table 6 show that option value

---

8. We converted the triangular distributions to a lognormal distribution by assuming that the minimum and maximum estimates correspond to 5% and 95% percentile points of a lognormal distribution. We also tried several other techniques which used the 50% point. Our reported results are the most conservative of the approaches we tried.

9. Company X reported investment expenditures only for the "expected"

scenario; i.e., investments needed to develop the expected volume of recoverable reserves. As in our previous paper, we assumed that capital costs vary directly with recoverable reserves raised to the 2/3 power. This is consistent with the notion that there are significant economies of scale in development.

10. For a complete description of how we used the data to value the reserve, see our previous paper.

Because we used the same tract-specific reserve and cost data as Company X, the dramatic difference between the Company's and our estimates of value is not due to different underlying views of the geologic potential of the tracts.

TABLE 6 Performance of Option Value Bidding (In $ Million) Tract	Tracts Won By Co X	Tracts Won By Option	L.O.T. By Option	% L.O.T. By Option	L.O.T. By Industry	% L.O.T. By Industry
1	0	0			5.42	11%
2	0	0			53.83	45%
3	0	0			16.56	50%
4	0	1	20.28	28%	38.92	76%
5	0	1	18.56	31%	6.24	15%
6	0	0			27.32	50%
Total	0	2	(Wtd Avg)	30%	(Wtd Avg)	58%

Notes:
1. Wtd Avg refers to the weighted average percentage, weighted by the size of the bid.
2. L.O.T. refers to "Left on the Table."

bids are less aggressive by this measure than the industry norm. Overall, the six winning industry bids left 58 percent on the table. The two winning option value bids would have left only 30 percent on the table. In other words, the option value bids are more cost effective in this case study than were the actual bids of the industry.

Conclusion

In this paper we have shown how one can adapt financial option pricing theory in order to value the operating options available to the owner of undeveloped petroleum properties. It is worthwhile to note that we have performed a very complicated valuation problem in a very straightforward way. We have not needed to forecast oil prices. We have not had to use any risk-adjusted discount rates (except for that used in calculating the present value of development expenditures). Finally, we have provided an easy solution to the problem of optimal development timing. That we have used so few parameter inputs comes from our use of market information about developed reserve prices. This is similar to the intuition for stock options. The technique makes efficient use of market information. Our results suggest that this technique has a great deal of promise in practical application.

LIQUIDITY AND COST OF CAPITAL: IMPLICATIONS FOR CORPORATE MANAGEMENT

by Yakov Amihud,
New York University and Tel Aviv University;
*and Haim Mendelson, Stanford University**

For the past 20 years, finance theory has been dominated by the view that a stock's expected rate of return is determined largely by the level of its risk. There has been much controversy, to be sure, about whether risk is better measured by the single factor "beta," as proposed by the Capital Asset Pricing Model, or by the multiple factors set forth in Arbitrage Pricing Theory. But there has been little serious disagreement with the proposition that risk, however measured, is the primary determinant of investors' required returns on stocks.

In 1986, we published a study demonstrating that portfolios of less-liquid stocks provide investors with significantly higher returns, on average, than highly liquid stock portfolios, even after adjusting for risk.[1] In fact, the liquidity factor appears as important as the risk measures in determining stock returns.

Why does liquidity affect stock returns? The most straightforward answer is that investors price securities according to their returns *net* of trading costs; and they thus require higher returns for holding less liquid stocks to compensate them for the higher cost of trading. Put differently, given two assets with the same cash flows but with different liquidity, investors will pay less for the asset with the lower liquidity.

Some economists have reasoned that, because trading costs represent only a small fraction of the price of a security, the increase in value resulting from increased liquidity cannot amount to more than a "second-order" effect. It is important to realize, however, that the overall effect of trading costs of, say, 4 percent of an asset's value is substantially higher than 4 percent, because these costs will be incurred *repeatedly*—whenever the asset is traded.

*This article is based closely on our paper, "Liquidity and Asset Prices: Financial Management Implications," *Financial Management*, Spring 1988. We thank Don Chew, the editor of this journal, for his comments and suggestions.
1. Amihud, Yakov and Haim Mendelson, "Asset Pricing and the Bid-Ask Spread," *Journal of Financial Economics*, Vol. 17, 1986: pp. 223-249. See also "The Effects of Beta, Bid-Ask Spread, Residual Risk and Size on Stock Returns," *Journal of Finance*, June 1989, pp. 479-486.

Consider a security whose holding period is two years, which is the historical average holding period of NYSE stocks. A trading cost of $0.04 on a $1 stock represents a cost stream of $0.04 every two years. The present value of this cost stream, assuming an 8% discount rate, is equal to

$$.04 + .04/1.08^2 + .04/1.08^4 + .04/1.08^6 + \ldots = .28.$$

Thus, the 4 percent cost per transaction represents a total reduction of 28 percent in the potential market value of the asset (that is, assuming it could be traded costlessly).

We thus suggest that investors require a considerable liquidity "premium" for holding illiquid securities. This finding has important implications for corporate management as well as investors. For corporate management, such liquidity premia on the company's financial claims (stocks and bonds) represent a significantly higher cost of capital, which means that the company must earn a higher return on its capital in order to increase shareholder value. For this reason, providing greater liquidity for the company's claims will reduce investors' required rates of return and increase the value of the claims. To illustrate, in the above example, cutting trading costs from 4 percent to 2 percent would increase the market value of the security by about 20 percent.

Increasing liquidity, however, is also likely to be costly. Thus, management must weigh the benefits of increased liquidity against the costs.

In the pages that follow, we briefly review our evidence on liquidity and stock returns. After pointing out the implications of this research for investors, we examine the costs and benefits of liquidity from corporate management's perspective. In the process, we examine the role of a number of corporate policies and institutional arrangements in increasing the liquidity of corporate shares.

THE EVIDENCE

Our research examined the effect of liquidity on stock prices by looking at the relationship between stock returns and their bid-ask spreads. The bid-ask spread is the difference between the buying and selling prices offered by traders and market makers

in the stock. For example, suppose that the buying price for IBM is 124 7/8 and the selling price is 124 3/4. The bid-ask spread is then 1/8 of a point, or 0.1 percent of the stock price. The bid and ask prices on another actively traded stock, Time Inc., were 127 5/8 and 128 at the opening of trade on June 2, 1989. The bid-ask spread here was thus 3/8 of a point, three times higher than that of IBM.

We estimated the relationship between stock returns and bid-ask spreads using a large sample of New York Stock Exchange stocks during the period 1961-1980. We divided all NYSE stocks into seven groups according to quoted bid-ask spreads. The average spread of the group with the lowest spread was 0.5% compared to 3.2% for the group with the highest spread—a considerable difference. Stocks with high bid-ask spreads are relatively illiquid. Their trading volume is low, they are held by fewer investors, their prices are more volatile and there are fewer dealers making a market in them. Thus, the bid-ask spread (which represents the cost of immediate execution) is a natural measure of a stock's illiquidity.

We found that, on average, an increase of 1 percentage point in the bid-ask spread was compensated by an additional stock yield of 0.21 percent per month (or about 2.5 percent per annum), after adjusting for differences in risk. (The results of our analysis are illustrated in Figure 1.)

How important is this liquidity effect in dollars and cents? Consider a security that generates a perpetual cash flow of $1.00 per month with a bid-ask spread of 2 percent and a required net return of 1.5 percent per month. According to our estimates, the required compensation for a 2 percent spread is about 1.92 percent per month, and the market value of the security will be $1.00/0.0192 = $52.08. If the liquidity of this security can be increased so that its spread is reduced from 2 percent to 1 percent, the required monthly return will decline to about 1.71 percent and its market value will increase to $1.00/.0171 = $58.45, a 12 percent increase in value. Thus, liquidity changes can have a major effect on price.

More recently, we have studied the effect of illiquidity on short-term fixed-income securities.[2] There, too, we found a significant liquidity effect: bonds with higher bid-ask spreads have significantly higher yields to maturity.

---

2. Amihud, Yakov and Haim Mendelson, "Liquidity, Maturity and the Yields on U. S. Treasury Securities," Working Paper, 1989.

EXHIBIT 1
THE ESTIMATED
RELATIONSHIP BETWEEN
EXCESS RETURNS AND
BID-ASK SPREADS FOR
NYSE STOCKS

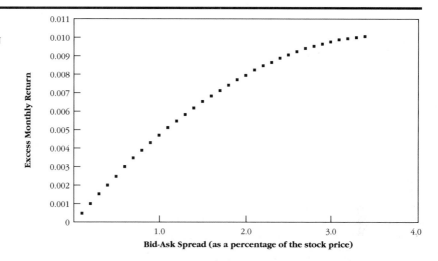

Finally, there is strong evidence on the value of liquidity from the prices of "letter" stocks. Some companies whose stocks are publicly traded also issue "letter" stocks that are not registered with the Securities and Exchange Commission, and thus the trading of these securities is restricted. Restricted stocks are identical in every other respect to their publicly traded counterparts (in terms of dividends, rights in liquidation, voting, etc.), but they can become publicly traded only following a lengthy procedure—all of which renders them quite illiquid. Evidence suggests that letter stocks sell at a discount of about 25% relative to their publicly-traded counterparts. This discount is another demonstration of the value the market assigns to liquidity.

These results have a number of important implications for the individual or institutional investor. First, low-liquidity investments should produce higher average returns to their holders over a long period of time (and perhaps this is the reason for the unusually high long-run returns on illiquid assets such as real estate, artwork, coins, and the like). Privately placed securities, stocks of thinly-traded small firms (especially OTC) and equity in LBO investments also yield relatively higher returns than heavily traded stocks, even after adjusting for risk. These higher returns are not, as some scholars have suggested, an "anomaly" in an otherwise efficient market. Rather, as proposed earlier, they represent the additional compensation required by investors for the higher costs of transacting.

The observed higher returns on low-liquidity assets are *gross* returns. An investor who is a frequent trader may see these higher returns offset by the higher transaction costs on illiquid assets, and the *net* return may then be lower than on liquid assets whose gross returns are lower. Thus, an investment in a low-liquidity asset will yield a higher net return only for the long-term investor. On the basis of our research, investors can determine, for any given investment horizon, which liquidity-group of securities to hold.

Our research also highlights the importance of developing liquidity-increasing investment vehicles such as mutual funds. Further, our results provide guidance to fund managers by relating the investment horizon, the fund's "load," and the variability and size of its cash flows to its investment policy.

Finally, improvements in trading mechanisms in the capital markets, such as further automation of trading, have also created substantial economic benefits by increasing the liquidity of traded securities.[3] According to our research, continued improvements in securities markets, along with their globalization, should lead to lower required returns and thus to higher stock prices.

---

3. Amihud, Yakov and Haim Mendelson, "Liquidity, Volatility and Exchange Automation," *Journal of Accounting, Auditing and Finance*, 1989, pp. 369-395.

IMPLICATIONS FOR FINANCIAL MANAGEMENT

The value of liquidity implies that corporate management can increase the firm's value by increasing the liquidity of its stocks and bonds.[4] As we have seen, investors require a higher expected return from an asset with lower liquidity to compensate for its higher trading costs. By increasing the liquidity of the firm's financial claims, management can effectively reduce its cost of capital for any level of corporate risk.

Benefits and Costs of Increased Liquidity

Increasing liquidity is clearly not costless. For example, the most obvious method of increasing liquidity—an initial public offering of stock—entails large up-front underwriter fees as well as recurring shareholder servicing and disclosure costs. In addition, there are the "agency costs" that result from the separation of ownership from control, and from the consequent weakening of management incentives to maximize efficiency. Having publicly traded shares also imposes regulations and constraints on management and exposes the information generated inside the firm to competitors.

We have analyzed the trade-off between the benefits and costs of increased liquidity elsewhere. But we will take a moment here to summarize the four major implications that arise from our analysis:

1. The benefits of increasing liquidity are likely to be greater for corporations whose stocks and bonds already enjoy a relatively high level of liquidity. This is because liquid assets are typically held by frequent traders who are more sensitive to changes in liquidity. Low-liquidity assets, by contrast, tend to be held by investors with long planning horizons, who can depreciate the illiquidity costs over longer periods and thus are less sensitive to improvements in asset liquidity.

2. On the other hand, the costs of increasing liquidity are also likely to be an increasing function of the initial level of liquidity. That is, the costs of improving liquidity are likely to be greater when liquidity is already relatively high.

3. Because the benefits of increased liquidity are proportional to the value of the firm, the dollar value of a reduction in cost of capital resulting from greater liquidity will be more beneficial to larger firms, thus reinforcing point 1.

4. In many cases, especially among small, relatively illiquid firms, the costs of increased liquidity are likely to be greater than the benefits.

Investors—especially those with greater need for liquidity—attempt on their own to minimize the costs of illiquidity. While this dampens the illiquidity effect, the empirical evidence demonstrates that this effect is still substantial. Even for highly liquid short-term fixed-income instruments, we found a substantial liquidity effect on the yield to maturity. In letter stocks, the illiquidity discount amounts to about 1/4 of the value of the stock; and, in publicly traded stocks, the liquidity effect is as significant as the risk effect.

CORPORATE METHODS OF INCREASING LIQUIDITY

Now we consider some of the various institutional and contractual arrangements that serve to increase the liquidity of corporate securities.

Going Public

"Going public" through an initial public offering of shares is the most fundamental way of increasing liquidity. By means of this transaction, the firm changes its form of organization from what is legally recognized as a "close" corporation (one in which the claims on its equity value are restricted to a relatively small group of manager-owners) to that of a public corporation (whose equity claims can be transferred without restriction). Holders of the publicly traded common stock of public corporations are not required to have an active role in the corporation and can sell their shares on an exchange. By contrast, the residual claims of the close corporation are illiquid by their very nature. The lower liquidity results from restrictions which increase the costs of finding a qualified buyer, negotiating a price and transferring ownership of the claims.

The costs of going public, as mentioned earlier, include the underwriting costs (which can amount to as much as 10 percent of the gross proceeds of the offering), as well as the cost of registering with the

---

4. Our notion of liquidity should not be confused with corporate liquidity, which relates to its working capital position.

SEC and reorganizing to comply with regulations on public corporations. In addition to these "one-time" costs, there are also recurring costs of public ownership such as shareholder-servicing costs, as well as the legal and accounting costs of satisfying the various reporting requirements, exchange fees, mailings etc. Studies have estimated these recurring costs to run from $100,000 or $200,000 per year, not including management time.[5]

Another important cost of the public corporation is making some information freely available to competitors, which can use it to the corporation's detriment. The publicly available information also enables various parties (such as interest groups) to probe into the corporation's affairs.

Finally, the public corporation bears "agency costs" that arise from the conflict of interest between shareholders and professional managers in the widely held public corporation.[6] For example, LBOs and other forms of the close corporation are reportedly able to establish far more effective managerial compensation schemes (providing extraordinary rewards for extraordinary performance) with less fear of popular and political reaction than can public companies.

The choice of organizational form (private vs. public) thus demonstrates the general trade-off involved in any corporate liquidity-increasing policy. On the one hand, the profitability of the close corporation is expected to exceed that of its public counterpart simply by virtue of stronger incentives for efficiency. On the other hand, the cost of capital of the public corporation is expected to be lower because of its greater liquidity, thus increasing the value to investors of a given level of operating profits.

In considering the decision to be a public corporation or to be privately held, the firm must balance the benefits of lower cost of capital against the costs of dispersed ownership. In some cases, especially for smaller firms without large requirements for new investment, the advantages of private ownership are more likely to outweigh the costs of illiquidity.

The Liquidity of Debt

The bond markets also provide evidence that liquid debt instruments have a lower yield to maturity, thus lowering the corporate cost of capital. Even for highly liquid short-term fixed-income instruments, we found that a reduction in the bid-ask spread from 3 to 0.8 basis points (from 0.03% to 0.008% of total value) is associated with a 40 basis point (0.4%) reduction in the annual yield to maturity on these instruments.[7]

It is well known, moreover, that "on the run" government bonds are more liquid and have lower yields than those that become "off the run." The same applies to corporate bonds. A highly liquid, heavily traded bond, such as an AT&T issue, has a quoted bid-ask spread of about 3/8 of 1 percent. By contrast, bond issues with low liquidity are quoted with spreads as high as 2 or 3 percent.[8] "Junk" bonds, for example, usually have wide bid-ask spreads, suggesting that their high yields are not all due to risk (and therefore do not necessarily imply superior performance). Also important, the returns on privately-placed bonds, which are highly illiquid, exceeded those on publicly-issued corporate bonds by about 50 basis points, on average, during the period 1961-1977.[9]

These results demonstrate the importance of liquidity considerations in corporate debt policy. When issuing corporate debt, it is therefore important to consider not only the design of the debt features and conditions, but also the liquidity of the instrument: Where and how will it be traded? What will be its trading volume? And will any of its features reduce its liquidity?

Public policy decisions can also affect the liquidity, and hence the value, of debt claims. For example, the recent adoption of Rule 144A by the Securities and Exchange Commission, which loosens the restraints on reselling unregistered securities, is expected to bring about an increase in private placement of debt issues that would substitute for publicly-placed bonds.[10]

5. See Schneider, Carl W., Joseph M. Manko and Robert S. Kant, "Going Public: Practice, Procedure and Consequences," *Villanova Law Review*, Vol. 27; November 1981: pp. 1-48; and Borden, Arthur M., "Going Private—Old Tort, New Tort or No Tort," *New York University Law Review*, Vol. 49; 1974: pp. 987-1042.

6. See Jensen, Michael C. and William H. Meckling, "Theory of the Firm: Managerial Behavior, Agency Costs and Ownership Structure," *Journal of Financial Economics*, Vol. 3; October 1976: pp. 306-360.

7. See Amihud and Mendelson cited in Note 2.

8. P. Fabozzi, H. Sauvin, R. Wilson and J. Ritchie, "Corporate Bonds," in R. Fabozzi and I. Pollack, *The Handbook of Fixed Income Securities*, Dow Jones-Irwin, Homewood, Ill, 1989.

9. Holding constant quality, duration and tax treatment. See Zwick, Burton, "Yields on Privately Placed Corporate Bonds," *Journal of Finance*, Vol. 35; 1980: pp. 23-29.

10. See Philip Maher, *Investment Dealers' Digest*, September 4, 1989, pp. 13-20.

The Design of Securities and Standardization of Claims

The design of securities has a large effect on their liquidity and thus on the return required by investors. What may be attractive to some investors may be unattractive to others, resulting in a negative effect on the marketability of the security. Therefore, the advantages of innovative designs of new securities should be weighed against the disadvantages of the lower liquidity that may result.

Sophisticated securities design is particularly apparent in direct investment agreements and in restricted claims in privately placed issues. As one observer has commented, "The list of private deals in 1989 for the most part has been a shopping list of financial engineering... anything that required more explanation to investors than the average investment-grade issue."[11]

By contrast, the rules governing the sharing of the firm's value among investors are remarkably uniform and simple in publicly-issued securities. The capital structure of a typical public corporation contains a variety of short- and long-term debt with fairly familiar features, and one type of equity that provides for the proportional division of the residual value—that which remains after the debt claim is satisfied—among the stockholders.

The preference of issuers of privately placed securities to have customized claims suggests that there may be considerable costs in using standardized claims due to the loss of flexibility. However, securities with unusual contractual provisions are typically far more difficult to trade than securities with a standard contractual form. Non-standard claims require more information and more resources to assess their value, and the very features which make them suitable for the original investors could make them unsuitable for other investors, thus reducing their liquidity. On the other hand, standard claims enjoy greater liquidity in the marketplace. Thus, what offsets the inferiority (and higher costs) of standardization is the higher liquidity of standardized claims.

A case of securities design where liquidity may have played an important role was that of the Unbundled Stock Units (USUs) introduced in 1988. The USUs split the stock into three components—a straight bond, an incremental dividend preferred share, and a warrant or an equity appreciation certificate. The USUs had some tax advantages and also had an appeal to specific clienteles. However, they suffered from a lower liquidity than the underlying shares of stock. There were higher costs in trading the USUs because the trading costs—which are not proportionate to value but include a considerable fixed cost —had to be paid on trades in each of the three components. And due to the relatively thin trading in each component relative to the trading volume in the underlying stock, the market-impact costs of trading in these securities would have been quite high. These illiquidity costs of the USUs may well have contributed to their failure.[12]

Another case in point is the substitution in recent years of publicly traded high-yield bonds for private placements and negotiated bank debt. Privately placed debt allows the custom-tailoring of restrictive covenants and provisions, which in turn allows potentially better control over agency problems and other risks. Also, it removes the need to disclose information which could be used by competitors. These advantages, however, are often outweighed by the marketability of tradable bonds with standard covenants.

In sum, while "financial engineering" and the design of special securities might look beneficial to the issuer, the associated illiquidity costs should also be taken into account because the reduction in liquidity of special securities may increase the return required by investors.

Asset Securitization

Increasing the uniformity of financial claims in order to increase their liquidity is an important motive behind the widespread securitization movement. Securitization involves the pooling and repackaging of individual loans into standard debt securities which are then sold to the public. For example, investment bankers have effectively standardized mortgage investments by pooling them and using them as collateral for liquid debt securities. Commercial banks, investments banks, and finance subsidiaries like GMAC have done much the same with auto loans and

---

11. Philip Maher, cited in note 10.

12. In addition to other factors. See R. Sah and N. Vasavada, "Unbundled Stock Units: What Went Wrong?," *Investment Management Review*, May-June 1989.

credit card receivables. And, in a fairly recent development, commercial banks are issuing debt securities backed by portfolios of corporate and LBO loans. Because of competition between financial intermediaries, at least part of the benefits of increased liquidity are being passed on to the original borrowers in the form of lower interest rates.

Disclosure of Inside Information

A corporation can affect the liquidity of its claims—and consequently its cost of capital—by the amount and quality of the information it releases to investors. The liquidity of a security is reduced when investors suspect that insiders are trading on the basis of privileged information. In that case, market-makers widen the bid-ask spread in order to protect themselves against better-informed traders, and to be compensated for bearing greater risk.[13] Therefore, a commitment by management to make internal information promptly available to the public—say, in the form of accounting reports and special announcements—will reduce the risk of trading against "insiders." This policy should bring about a narrower bid-ask spread, greater liquidity, and thus a lower cost of capital.

By law, publicly traded companies are required to publish periodic accounting reports, and to promptly inform the public of any event which may affect their valuation. But even without these formal requirements, it may well be in the best interest of public companies voluntarily to provide more and better inside information in order to increase the liquidity of their claims. Indeed, consistent with our analysis, most NYSE-listed firms published financial statements long before they were required to do so by the Securities Exchange Act of 1934.

Here, too, there are trade-offs to consider. Making inside information publicly available may not be in the interests of insiders; and, if such information can be used against the firm by competitors, it may not be in the interest of investors either. But, against these potential costs of releasing more information, the corporation should consider the beneficial effect on the liquidity of the corporate claims.

Our argument that liquidity considerations give rise to voluntary corporate disclosure, even at a cost,

is also supported by the existence of the bond-rating system. Although companies issuing public debt are under no formal obligation to have their bonds rated, almost all firms voluntarily pay the rating agencies to rate their publicly issued bonds. In the case of private placements, however, companies do not pay to have their debt rated. When such debt is not intended to be traded, the firm derives little benefit from increasing the liquidity of these bonds.

An issuer of debt claims can find an alternative to a full disclosure of information by buying insurance or a guarantee from a financial institution. In this case, the liquidity of the debt claims depends on the financial strength of the insurer, and the issuer has to disclose the information mainly to the insurer rather than to the public. This can be useful for LBO firms whose equity is privately held but have publicly issued debt claims.

Limited Liability

By limiting stockholders' losses to the amount of their investment, the limited liability provision increases the liquidity of stocks. Without limited liability, investors would trade stocks very cautiously, the market would become thin and the bid-ask spreads would be considerably higher since buyers and sellers would set prices to protect themselves.

But there are also costs associated with limiting shareholders' liability. For one thing, like all forms of insurance, the limited liability provision gives rise to the well-known "moral hazard" problem—briefly stated, the tendency for most activities to experience higher losses when the burden of such losses has been transferred from an agent to a third-party insurer. And besides moral hazard, limited liability also spawns a related "agency" or incentive problem. When levered public companies approach insolvency, the insurance policy effectively bestowed upon stockholders gives management (as a representative of stockholders) an incentive to take on ever larger risks because they have claims that resemble call options (that is, an upside without a commensurate downside). This problem, like that of moral hazard, can be illustrated by the extreme case of insolvent S&Ls. In such cases, the existence of deposit insurance (like limited liability) provides

13. See Bagehot, Walter, "The Only Game in Town," *Financial Analysts Journal*, Vol. 27; March/April 1971: pp. 12-14. There is also evidence that an unexpected release of information by the firm causes a widening of its bid-ask spread; see Morse, Dale and Neal Ushman, "The Effect of Information Announcements on the Market Microstructure," *The Accounting Review*, Vol. 58; 1983: 247-258.

the management of failing S&Ls with the incentive to take ever larger risks with depositors' funds to bail themselves out.

Alternative arrangements involving extended stockholder liability could help reduce the moral hazard and agency costs described above. But, in imposing much larger risks on stockholders, extended liability would greatly reduce the liquidity of corporate equities. The fact that public corporations dominate private partnerships and other extended liability vehicles as the major form of American business suggests that the liquidity benefits of limited liability outweigh the costs arising from incentive problems.

Underwriting New Public Issues

A corporation considering the use of an underwriter to issue its securities should take into account (among other things) the liquidity-increasing functions it provides that the corporation cannot perform on its own. First, the underwriter provides "stabilization" of the price of the new issue during the offering period. Then, for some time thereafter, it serves as a market-maker, prepared to step in and provide liquidity as necessary by buying or selling the security.

Another liquidity-increasing service provided by underwriters is the "certification" of the new issue. The underwriting investment bank is an independent agency that takes on the responsibility of providing the public with accurate information about the new issue. It carries out a search process through the firm's records ("due diligence") for any information deemed relevant and publishes a prospectus which details the state of the firm and the expected use of the funds. In effect, the underwriter is a credible outsider that puts its reputation on the line when offering a new issue to its network of investors. At the same time, issuers can protect sensitive information that might compromise their competitive position. This process of certification effectively reduces the bid-ask spread of the new issue and thus increases its liquidity.

Stock Denominations

Liquidity considerations may also explain why companies split their stocks and why stocks are typically issued in relatively small denominations to begin with. For example, instead of having 10 million shares worth $20 each, a company could choose to have only a thousand shares worth $200,000 each. (A somewhat less dramatic version of the latter approach is Warren Buffet's Berkshire Hathaway, whose shares are currently trading at around $8,500.) And the cost savings in servicing the smaller group of shareholders would be considerable.

Lower per share trading ranges may increase liquidity by reducing dealer spreads.[14] This may be related to the fact that block trades incur unusually high liquidity costs. Not only are such blocks difficult to sell at the prevailing market price, but they also incur direct costs that include the underwriter's spread (averaging 5 percent), which is an increasing function of the number of shares sold relative to the issue size, as well as other expenses (averaging 1.7 percent) for offerings registered with the SEC.[15] By issuing shares with smaller denominations, the firm increases the divisibility of its securities, makes small transactions possible, and thus facilitates greater dispersion of ownership. All of these factors may increase the liquidity of the shares.

Listing on Organized Exchanges

Securities markets differ in their method of trading and depth, and this affects the liquidity of the assets traded in them.[16] A company can thus affect the liquidity of its shares of stock by choosing where they will be traded.

Evidence suggests that the desire to increase liquidity may motivate companies to "list" on the large and organized securities exchanges. In particular, firms that listed on the NYSE have experienced significant declines in the spread of their stocks after listing. One study found, for example, that while the pre-listing average OTC median bid-ask spread for their sampled stocks was 3.45 percent

---

14. Wood, John H. and Norma L. Wood (*Financial Markets* Harcourt Brace, 1985), p. 170) discuss divisibility as a liquidity attribute and suggest that "there is some evidence that divisibility may exert an indirect influence on security returns by affecting dealer spreads." See also W. Baker and P. Gallagher, "Management View of Stock Splits," *Financial Management* 9, 1980, pp. 73-77. They found that the majority of managers questioned cited liquidity as motivating stock splits; but Copeland (see "The Evidence Against Stocks Splits," *Chase Financial Quarterly,* Vol. 1, No. 1) found that stock splits have negative liquidity effects.

15. See Mikkelson, Wayne H. and M. Megan Partch, "Stock Price Effects and Costs of Secondary Distributions," *Journal of Financial Economics,* Vol. 14; 1985: pp. 165-194.

16. See Amihud, Yakov and Haim Mendelson, "Trading Mechanisms and Stock Returns: An Empirical Investigation," *Journal of Finance,* Vol. 42; July 1987: pp. 533-553.

and the average inside (narrowest) spread was 1.73 percent, the post-listing average NYSE spread for the same stocks was 1.24 percent.[17]

This liquidity effect may explain the findings of a number of studies that report increases in the stock prices of firms that apply for listing.[18] In fact, high-spread stocks enjoyed a greater price increase around the time they applied for listing than did stocks with a low spread. This suggests that the increased liquidity due to listing on the NYSE lowered the required return on stocks which had suffered from low marketability.

The link between listing and liquidity is also apparent from the findings of yet another study that the value increases associated with exchange listing were higher in the pre-NASDAQ than in the post-NASDAQ period.[19] This result suggests a narrowing of the differences between the liquidity services provided by the NYSE and the OTC since the implementation of the NASDAQ system.

CONCLUSION

Our recent research has demonstrated that less-liquid securities (stocks and bonds) provide investors with significantly net higher returns than more liquid securities, even after adjusting for risk. These higher returns reflect the "liquidity premium" required by investors for bearing the added trading costs of illiquid securities. For investors who expect to hold their stocks for a long period of time, investing in a portfolio of low-liquidity stocks is likely to provide significantly higher risk-adjusted returns.

For corporate management, such liquidity premia represent significantly higher costs of capital. Thus, increasing the liquidity of corporate stocks and bonds, which reduces investors' required rates of return, can increase the value of the firm *for any given cash flow it generates*.

There are a number of corporate policies designed to increase liquidity. Besides the obvious measures of going public and listing on organized exchanges, management can increase liquidity by properly designing the features of the corporate stocks and bonds, and by providing better information to investors.

As we pointed out, corporate measures to increase liquidity impose significant costs. Among such costs are large underwriters' fees for initial public offerings, recurring shareholder-servicing costs, the release of information which could be used by the firm's competitors, and the costs arising from increased regulation and public scrutiny. In addition, to the extent that increased liquidity means a greater diffusion of ownership, it imposes a most important cost resulting from the further distancing of ownership from control. In the current environment of corporate restructuring, the strengthening of management incentives in private (or recapitalized) companies has clearly proved to be a powerful force for greater efficiency.

This last point is particularly applicable to the recent wave of "going private" transactions, since such moves are the ultimate in reducing the liquidity of the firm's claims.[20] In choosing between the public and private forms of ownership, corporate management has to choose between the value of making the firm's capital claims more liquid—thus reducing its cost of capital—and the benefits of private ownership.[21]

17. See Klemkosky, Robert C. and Robert M. Conroy, "Competition and the Cost of Liquidity to Investors," *Journal of Economics and Business*, Vol. 37; 1985; pp. 183-195.

18. See Ying, Louis K. W., Wilbur L. Lewellen, Larry B. Schlarbaum and Ronald C. Lease, "Stock Exchange Listings and Securities Returns," *Journal of Financial and Quantitative Analysis*, Vol. 10; 1977: pp. 415-435.; Grammatikos, Theoharry and George J. Papaioannou, "Market Reaction to NYSE Listings: Tests of Marketability Gains Hypothesis." *Journal of Financial Research*, 10, Fall 1980, pp. 215-227.

19. See Sanger, Gary C. and John J. McConnell, "Stock Exchange Listing, Firm Value and Security Market Efficiency: The Impact of NASDAQ," *Journal of Financial and Quantitative Analysis*, Vol. 21; March 1986; pp. 1-25.]

20. See Yakov Amihud, "*Leveraged Management Buyouts* and Shareholders' Wealth," In Leveraged Management Buyouts, Dow Jones-Irwin, 1989.

21. Measures undertaken by investors to reduce the cost of illiquidity may have contributed to the recent increase in "going private" transactions. See Jay Light, "The Privatization of Equity," and Michael Jensen, "Eclipse of the Public Corporation," *Harvard Business Review*, September-October 1989.

Errata

Editor's Note: In the Spring 1987 issue of this journal we neglected to print the following Appendices to the article, "Valuing Offshore Oil Properties with Option Pricing Models," by Daniel R. Siegel, James L. Smith, and James L. Paddock.

Appendix A: Calculating the Production Payout Ratio

In using option pricing models to value an undeveloped reserve, one must estimate the production "payout ratio"—that is, net production revenue (less depletion) as a percentage of the market value of the reserve. Begin by calculating the net production revenue less depletion as follows:

Total payout = [(production rate)×(per bbl profit)] − [(production rate) × (reserve value)]

The first term on the right hand side represents profits and the second term depletion.

Dividing the per barrel payout by the per barrel value of a developed reserve yields the payout ratio:

payout ratio = (payout)/(developed reserve value)

To get a numerical value for this payout ratio, we make the following assumptions: (1) the per barrel value of a developed reserve is equal to one third of the market price of crude oil; (2) per barrel operating costs average 30 percent of the market price per barrel of crude oil; (3) depreciation represents 20 percent of the market price of crude oil; and (4) the production rate is assumed to be 10 percent.

If we let

P = net production revenue, per barrel
V = market price of a developed reserve, per barrel
S = market price of crude oil, per barrel
OC = operating cost, per barrel (including royalty)
D = depreciation allowance, per barrel
x = OC/S, assumed constant over time
y = D/S, assumed constant over time
t = corporate tax rate, and
g = production rate, then after-tax per barrel profit from production is as follows:

$P = S - OC - (S - OC - D) = S(1-x) - .46S(1-x-y)$

Using the "one-third rule", $S/V = 3$,

$P = 3V(1-x) - (.46)(3)V(1-x-y)$

Finally, this implies

payout ratio = g[.62 − 1.62x + 1.377y]

Assuming, as explained above, that x = 0.30, y = 0.20, and g = 0.10, we get a payout ratio equal to 4.1%. Thus, in effect, holding a developed reserve is analogous to holding a stock with a dividend rate of 4.1%.

APPENDIX B: Accounting for the Development Lag

Because of the time it takes to develop an oil reserve, we can think of paying the development expenditure now and receiving the developed reserve only after the development period. Because of this lag, we can also think of receiving the present value of the developed reserve upon payment of the present value of development expenditures.

This present value can be calculated simply by discounting the *current developed reserve* value by the payout ratio. The reason we discount by value of the current developed reserve value by the payout ratio is this: Just as a stockholder expects a normal rate of return in the form of a combination of dividends and capital gains, so stockholder with a fair or "normal" rate of return. Similarly, the net production revenue less depletion, plus the expected capital gain on the developed (and producing) reserve must offer the holder of a developed reserve the prospect of a fair rate of return. Thus, the payout ratio of a producing reserve plus the capital gain must be expected to yield a fair rate of return.

Now, suppose that the total rate of return on holding producing developed reserves is r^*. Then, the expected rate of capital gain on the developed reserve must be equal to the total return, r^*, minus the payout ratio (p).

Suppose, then, that the development lag is t' years. Then let V' be the present value of the developed reserve received in t' years.

$$V' = V \times e^{(r^*-p)t'} \times e^{-r^*t'} = V \times e^{-(p)t'}$$

= expected value in t years discount factor.

Thus, the appropriate present value comes from discounting the *current developed reserve value* by the payout ratio. If, for example, the development lag is about one year as in the Gulf of Mexico, then the present value of a $12 per barrel developed reserve equals $11.52. Expressed in mathematical terms,

$$V' = e^{-.041 \times 1.0} \times \$12.0 = \$11.52$$

PART III

CAPITAL STRUCTURE AND DIVIDEND POLICY

The articles in this section are devoted largely to questions of corporate capital structure: Is there such a thing as "optimal" capital structure? What are the real benefits and costs of leverage? Does the relative scarcity of triple A-rated companies suggest that corporate America is acquiring a greater appreciation of the value of debt financing? Or are U.S. companies mortgaging the futures of their organizations by taking on too much debt?

In the 1980s, these questions attained a prominence, and indeed an urgency, unprecedented in our corporate history. For, along with the wave of corporate restructuring activities—acquisitions, divestitures, leveraged buyouts, spin-offs, and major stock repurchases—many companies underwent dramatic changes in capital structure. In the LBO movement, for example, newly private companies were launched with debt-to-asset ratios upwards of 90%. Large public companies, traditionally leveraged at 20% to 30%, resorted to the junk bond market to make large acquisitions and, in so doing, raised their debt ratios well above 50%. At the same time, many corporate restructurings have included major stock repurchase programs that seem to reflect a more explicit, permanent decision to leverage the capital structure.

As I said in my "Introduction," after the dramatic recapitalizations of the 1980s, often accompanied by large increases in stock prices, it may seem odd to begin this section with Merton Miller's reassessment of the "*The Modigliani-Miller Propositions After Thirty Years.*" For it was Miller who, with Franco Modigliani, formulated in 1958 the now classic "M&M" capital structure "irrelevance" proposition—stated baldly, the argument that a corporation's debt-equity ratio should not affect the value of its shares. A few years after came its equally venerated companion, the M&M dividend irrelevance proposition—the notion that share values are influenced primarily by a corporation's expected earnings power, and not by the percentage of those earnings paid out as dividends.

The empirical import of the M&M propositions— and thus their central message to corporate practitioners—can be seen by turning the propositions "on their heads." That is, if changes in corporate capital structure or dividends do increase stock values, they are likely to do so only for the following reasons: (1) they reduce taxes or transaction costs: (2) they provide a reliable "signal" to investors of management's confidence in the firm's earnings prospects; or (3) they increase the probability that management will undertake only profitable investments.

In this article, after recounting the thinking behind the propositions, Professor Miller goes on to consider the contribution of each of these three factors to an explanation of the leveraged restructuring movement of the '80s. Part of the discussion focuses on the beneficial effect of debt finance on managerial efficiency and corporate reinvestment decisions—especially in companies in mature industries with too much "free cash flow" (for more on this, see the articles by Michael Jensen in later sections). But the greatest stress falls on the tax advantage of debt over equity, an argument put forth by Miller and Modigliani in 1963. In brief, the "tax-adjusted" M&M proposition says that the benefits of substituting tax-deductible interest payments for non-deductible (and thus twice-taxed) dividend payments could push the optimal capital structure toward 100% debt (provided, of course, the offsetting costs of high leverage are not too great).

In "*The Search for Optimal Capital Structure*," Stewart Myers reviews the corporate capital structure decision in similarly broad terms, presenting academic insights accumulated throughout the 1960s and 1970s. He begins by dispelling the fallacy that there is "magic" in leverage. When marketing debt or preferred instruments, investment bankers begin as a matter of course by demonstrating the positive effects of such instruments on EPS and ROE. The catch is that using greater leverage will always cause EPS to rise, as long as the additional earnings generated from the new capital merely exceed the firm's after-tax borrowing rate (hardly, of course, an acceptable standard of profitability). Because increased leverage means not only higher expected returns but also higher risks for equity investors, it is doubtful that such leveraging of EPS and ROE has any positive effect on stock prices. Thus, in reasonably sophisticated markets, the capital structure decision reduces mainly to consideration of market distortions or imperfections: taxes, the costs of bankruptcy (or, more inclusive, "financial distress"), imperfect information, and conflicts of interest between lenders and management as representative of the shareholder interests.

In "*Behavioral Rationality in Finance: The Case of Dividends,*" Merton Miller addresses the "puzzle" of corporate dividend behavior that has vexed the academic community for the last 25 years. The "puzzle" is this: Given the strongly preferential treatment given capital gains relative to ordinary (dividend) income from 1945 until the Tax Reform Act of 1986, why have American companies persisted in paying, and why do investors seem to want, ever more dividends? Miller defends the ærationality" of U.S. corporate dividend policy by noting that dividend payouts in the post-World War II era have been significantly lower (in response, it appears, to the increasing personal income tax burden) than in the 1920s and early 1930s. And, lest you think this has little application to the current tax environment in which there is no capital gains differential, Miller also cites an impressive body of evidence documenting the responsiveness of stock prices and corporate dividend-paying behavior to major changes in tax regimes (in Canada and the U.K., as well as a short-lived tax on retained earnings levied on U.S. corporations in the 1930s).

In "*The Bond Refunding Decisio*n," Alan Kraus begins by dismissing the popular rationale for including the call provision in standard bond agreements: namely, the expected interest savings they provide if rates decline. In a sophisticated market, the corporation pays in advance for such savings in the form of a higher interest rate on callable bonds. The explanation for the standard use of the call provision rests on other factors such as taxes, operating flexibility, and gains from shifting interest rate risk to investors.

Kraus's analysis of when to call and refund a bond issue reflects recent developments in option pricing theory. Consistent with the other financing prescriptions of modern finance, the refunding rule offered here is not influenced at all by management's intuition about future interest rates.

DHC

THE MODIGLIANI-MILLER PROPOSITIONS AFTER THIRTY YEARS

by Merton H. Miller,
University of Chicago*

I t has now been 30 years since the Modigliani-Miller Propositions were first presented in "The Cost of Capital, Corporation Finance and the Theory of Investment," which appeared in the *American Economic Review* in June 1958. I have been invited, if not to celebrate, at least to mark, the event with a retrospective look at what we set out to do on that occasion and an appraisal of where the Propositions stand today after three decades of intense scrutiny and often bitter controversy.

*This article is a shortened version of an article that appeared in the *Journal of Economic Perspectives* (Fall 1988) and is reprinted here with permission of the American Economic Association, the journal's publisher. The author would like to acknowledge helpful comments on an earlier draft made by George Constantinides, Melvin Reder, Lester Telser, Hal Varian, Robert Vishny, and by the editors of the *Journal of Economic Perspectives*, Carl Shapiro, Joseph Stiglitz, and Timothy Taylor.

THE VIEW THAT CAPITAL STRUCTURE IS LITERALLY IRRELEVANT OR THAT
"NOTHING MATTERS" IN CORPORATE FINANCE, THOUGH STILL SOMETIMES
ATTRIBUTED TO US,...IS FAR FROM WHAT WE EVER ACTUALLY SAID ABOUT
THE REAL-WORLD APPLICATIONS OF OUR THEORETICAL PROPOSITIONS.

Some of these controversies can by now be regarded as settled. Our Proposition I, which holds the value of a firm to be independent of its capital structure (its debt/equity ratio), is accepted as an implication of equilibrium in perfect capital markets. The validity of our then novel arbitrage proof of that proposition is also no longer disputed, and essentially similar arbitrage proofs are now common throughout finance.[1] Propositions analogous to, and often even called, M and M propositions have spread beyond corporation finance to the fields of money and banking, fiscal policy, and international finance.[2]

Clearly Proposition I, and its proof, have been accepted into economic theory. Less clear, however, is the empirical significance of the MM value-invariance Proposition I in its original sphere of corporation finance.

Skepticism about the practical force of our invariance proposition was understandable given the almost daily reports in the financial press, then as now, of spectacular increases in the values of firms after changes in capital structure. But the view that capital structure is literally irrelevant or that "nothing matters" in corporate finance, though still sometimes attributed to us (and tracing perhaps to the very provocative way we made our point), is far from what we ever actually said about the real-world applications of our theoretical propositions. Looking back now, perhaps we should have put more emphasis on the other, upbeat side of the "nothing matters" coin: showing what *doesn't* matter can also show, by implication, what *does.*

This more constructive approach to our invariance proposition and its central assumption of perfect capital markets has now become the standard one in teaching corporate finance. We could not have taken that approach in 1958, however, because the analysis departed too greatly from the then accepted way of thinking about capital structure choices. We first had to convince people (including ourselves!) that there could be *any* conditions, even in a "frictionless" world, where a firm would be indifferent between issuing securities as different in legal status, investor risk, and apparent cost as debt and equity. Remember that interest rates on corporate debts were then in the 3 to 5 percent range, with equity earnings/price ratios—then the conventional measure of the "cost" of equity capital—running from 15 to 20 percent.

The paradox of indifference in the face of such huge spreads in the apparent cost of financing was resolved by our Proposition II, which showed that when Proposition I held, the cost of equity capital was a linear increasing function of the debt/equity ratio. Any gains from using more of what might seem to be cheaper debt capital would thus be offset by the correspondingly higher cost of the now riskier equity capital. Our propositions implied that the *weighted average* of these costs of capital to a firm would remain the same no matter what combination of financing sources the firm actually chose.

Though departing substantially from the then conventional views about capital structure, our propositions were certainly not without links to what had gone before. Our distinction between the real value of the firm and its financial packaging raised many issues long familiar to economists in discussions of "money illusion" and money neutrality. . .

In the field of corporate finance, however, the only prior treatment similar in spirit to our own was by David Durand in 1952 (who, as it turned out, also became our first formal critic).[3] Durand had proposed, as one of what he saw as two polar approaches to valuing shares, that investors might ignore the firm's then-existing capital structure and first price the whole firm by capitalizing its operating earnings *before* interest and taxes. The value of the shares would then be found by subtracting out the value of the bonds. But he rejected this possibility in favor of his other extreme, which he believed closer to the ordinary real-world way of valuing corporate shares. According to this conventional view, investors capitalized the firm's net income *after* interest and taxes with only a loose, qualitative adjustment for the degree of leverage in the capital structure.

That we too did not dismiss the seemingly unrealistic approach of looking through the momentary capital structure to the underlying real flows may

1. Examples include Cornell and French (1983) on the pricing of stock index futures, Black and Scholes (1973) on the pricing of options, and Ross (1976) on the structure of capital asset prices generally. For other, and in some respects, more general proofs of our capital structure proposition, see among others, Stiglitz (1974) for a general equilibrium proof showing that individual wealth and consumption opportunities are unaffected by capital structures; Hirshleifer (1965) and (1966) for a state preference, complete-markets proof; Duffie and Shafer (1986) for extensions to some cases of incomplete markets; and Merton (forth-

coming) for a spanning proof.

Full citations for all articles mentioned are listed in the References section at the end of this article.

2. See, for example, Wallace (1981) on domestic open-market operations; Sargent and Smith (1986) on central bank foreign-exchange interventions; Chamley and Polemarchakis (1984) on government tax and borrowing policies; and Fama (1980),(1983) on money, banking, and the quantity theory.

3. Durand (1959).

well trace to the macroeconomic perspective from which we had approached the problem of capital structure in the first instance. Our main concern, initially, was with the determinants of *aggregate* economic investment by the business sector. The resources for capital formation by firms came ultimately from the savings of the household sector, a connection that economists had long found convenient to illustrate with schematic national income and wealth T-accounts, including, of course, simplified sectoral balance sheets such as:

BUSINESS FIRMS		HOUSEHOLDS	
Assets	Liabilities	Assets	Liabilities
Productive Capital	Debts owed to households	Debts of firms	Household net worth
	Equity in firms owned by households	Equity in firms	

Consolidating the accounts of the two sectors leads to the familiar national balance sheet in which the debt and equity securities no longer appear:

Assets	Liabilities
Productive Capital	Household Net worth

The value of the business sector to its ultimate owners in the household sector is thus seen clearly to lie in the value of the underlying capital. And by the same token, the debt and equity securities owned by households can be seen not as final, but only as intermediate, assets serving to partition the earnings (and their attendant risks) among the many separate individual households within the sector.

Our value-invariance Proposition I was in a sense only the application of this macroeconomic intuition to the microeconomics of corporate finance; and the arbitrage proof we gave for our Proposition I was just the counterpart, at the individual investor level, of the consolidation of accounts and the washing out of the debt/equity ratios at the sectoral level. In fact, one blade of our arbitrage proof had the arbitrager doing exactly that washing out. If levered firms were undervalued relative to unlevered firms, our arbitrager was called on to "undo

the leverage" by buying an appropriate portion of both the levered firm's debt and its shares. On a consolidated basis, the interest paid by the firm cancels against the interest received and the arbitrager thus owned a pure equity stream. Unlevered corporate equity streams could in turn be relevered by borrowing on individual account if unlevered streams ever sold at a discount relative to levered corporate equity. That possibility of "homemade leverage" by individual investors provided the second and completing blade of our arbitrage proof of value invariance.

Our arbitrage proof drew little flak from those who saw it essentially as a metaphor—an expository device for highlighting hidden implications of the "law of one price" in perfect capital markets. But whether the operations we called arbitrage could *in fact* substitute for consolidation when dealing with real-world corporations was disputed. Could investors, acting on their own, really replicate and, where required, wash out corporate capital structures—if not completely, as in the formal proof, then by enough, and quickly enough, to make the invariance proposition useful as a description of the central tendency in the real-world capital market? These long-standing and still not completely resolved issues of the empirical relevance of the MM propositions will be the primary focus of what follows here.

Three separate reasons (over and above the standard complaint that we attributed too much rationality to the stock market) were quickly offered by our critics for believing that individual investors could not enforce the corporate valuations implied by Propositions I and II. These lines of objection, relating to dividends, debt defaults, and taxes, each emphasized a different, distinctive feature of the corporate form of business organization. And each in turn will be reexamined here, taking full advantage this time, however, of the hindsight of thirty years of subsequent research and events. . .

■ ARBITRAGE, DIVIDENDS, AND THE CORPORATE VEIL

The law of one price is easily visualized in commodity settings where market institutions deliberately provide the necessary standardization and interchangeability of units. But to which of the many features of an entity as complex as an operating business firm would our financial equilibration extend?

We opted for a Fisherian rather than the

standard Marshallian representation of the firm. Irving Fisher's view of the firm—now the standard one in finance, but then just becoming known—impounds the details of technology, production, and sales in a black box and focuses on the underlying net cash flow. The firm for Fisher was just an abstract engine transforming current consumable resources, obtained by issuing securities, into future consumable resources payable to the owners of the securities. Even so, what did it mean to speak of firms or cash flow streams being different, but still "similar" enough to allow for arbitrage or anything close to it?

Some of the answers would be provided, we hoped, by our concept of a "risk class," which was offered with several objectives in mind. At the level of the theory, it defined what today would be called a "spanning" set; the uncertain underlying future cash flow streams of the individual firms within each class could be assumed perfectly correlated, and hence perfect substitutes. But the characteristics of those correlated streams could be allowed to differ from class to class. Hence, at the more practical level, the risk class could be identified with Marshallian industries— groupings around which so much academic and Wall Street research had always been organized.[4] We hoped that the earnings of firms in some large industries such as oil or electricity generation might vary together closely enough not just for real-world arbitragers to carry on their work of equilibration efficiently, but also to offer us as outside observers a chance of judging how well they were succeeding. Indeed, we devoted more than a third of our original paper (plus a couple of follow-up studies) to empirical estimates of how closely real-world market values approached those predicted by our model. Our hopes of settling the empirical issues by that route, however, have largely been disappointed.[5]

INVESTOR ARBITRAGE WHEN DIVIDENDS DIFFER: THE DIVIDEND-INVARIANCE PROPOSITION

Although the risk class, with its perfect correlation of the underlying real cash streams may have provided a basis for the arbitrage in our formal proof, there remained the sticking point of how real-world market equilibrators could gain access to a firm's operating cash flows, let alone to two or more correlated ones. As a matter of law, what the individual equity investor actually gets on buying a share is not a right to the firm's underlying cash flow but only to such cash dividends as the corporation's directors choose to declare. Must these man-made payout policies also be assumed perfectly correlated along with the underlying cash flows to make the equilibration effective? If so, the likely empirical range of the value-invariance proposition would seem to be narrow indeed.

A second MM-invariance proposition—that the value of the firm was independent of its dividend policy—was developed in part precisely to meet this class of objections. The essential content of the dividend-"irrelevance" argument was already in hand at the time of the original leverage paper and led us there to dismiss the whole dividend question as a "mere detail" (not the last time, alas, that we may have overworked that innocent word "mere"). We stated the dividend-invariance proposition explicitly, and noted its relation to the leverage proof in the very first round of replies to our critics.[6] But because dividend decisions were controversial in their own right, and because considering them raised so many side issues of valuation theory and of practical policy, both private and public, we put off the fuller treatment of dividends to a separate paper that appeared three years after the first one.[7]

That the close connection in origin of the two invariance propositions has not been more widely appreciated traces not only to their separation in time, but probably also to our making no reference to arbitrage (or even to debt or equity) in the proof of the dividend-invariance proposition. Why bring in arbitrage, we felt, when an even simpler line of proof would serve? The dividend invariance proposition stated only that, *given* the firm's investment decision, its dividend decision would have no effect on the value of the shares. The added cash to fund the higher dividend payout must come from somewhere, after all; and with investment fixed, that somewhere could only be from selling off part of the firm. As long as

---

4. Remember, in this connection, that the capital asset pricing models of Sharpe (1964) and Lintner (1965) and their later extensions that now dominate empirical research in finance had yet to come on the scene. For some glimpses of how more recent asset pricing frameworks can accommodate the MM propositions without reference to MM risk classes or MM arbitrage, see Ross (1988).

5. Direct statistical calibration of the goodness of fit of the MM value-invariance propositions has not so far been achieved by us or others for a variety of reasons, some of which will be noted further in due course below.

6. See Modigliani and Miller (1959), especially pages 662-668.

7. See Miller and Modigliani (1961).

the securities sold off could be presumed sold at their market-determined values, then, whether the analysis was carried out under conditions of certainty or uncertainty, the whole operation of paying dividends, again holding investment constant, could be seen as just a wash—a swap of equal values not much different in principle from withdrawing money from a pass-book savings account.

The Informational Content of Dividends

Managerial decisions on dividends thus might affect the cash component of an investor's return; but they would not affect the *total* return of cash plus appreciation, and the total is what mattered. In practice, of course, even changing the cash-dividend component often seemed to matter a great deal, at least to judge by the conspicuous price jumps typically accompanying announcements of major boosts or cuts in dividends. These highly visible price reactions to dividend announcements were among the first (and are still the most frequently mentioned) of the supposed empirical refutations of the MM value-invariance principle. By invoking the dividend-invariance proposition to support the leverage-invariance proposition, we seemed to have succeeded only in substituting one set of objections for another.

But, as we suggested in our 1961 dividend paper, these price reactions to dividend announcements were not really refutations. They were better seen as failures of one of the key assumptions of both the leverage and dividend models, *viz.* that all capital market participants, inside managers and outside investors alike, have the same information about the firm's cash flows. Over long enough time horizons, this all-cards-on-the-table assumption might, we noted, be an entirely acceptable approximation, particularly in a market subject to S.E.C. disclosure rules. But new information is always coming in; and over shorter runs, the firm's inside managers were likely to have information about the firm's prospects not yet known to or fully appreciated by the investing public at large. Management-initiated actions on dividends or other financial transactions might then serve, by implication, to convey to the outside mar-

ket information not yet incorporated in the price of the firm's securities.

Although our concern in the 1961 dividend paper was with the observed announcement effects of dividend decisions, informational asymmetry also raised the possibility of strategic behavior on the part of the existing stockholders and/or their management agents. Might not much of the price response to dividend (and/or other capital structure) announcements simply be attempts by the insiders to mislead the outsiders; and if so, what point was there to our notion of a capital market equilibrium rooted solely in the fundamentals? Our instincts as economists led us to discount the possibility that firms could hope to fool the investing public systematically. But, at the time, we could offer little more support than a declaration of faith in Lincoln's Law—that you can't fool all of the people all of the time.

By the 1970s, however, the concept of an information equilibrium had entered economics, and came soon after to the field of corporate finance as well.[8] In 1978, for example, Stephen Ross showed how debt/equity ratios might serve to signal, in the technical sense, managements' special information about the firm's future prospects.[9] But the extent to which these and subsequent asymmetric information models can account for observed departures from the "invariance" propositions has not so far been convincingly established.[10]

The Interaction of Investment Policy and Dividend Policy

The dividend-invariance proposition, as we initially stated it, highlights still another way in which the corporate form of organization, and especially the separation it permits between ownership and management, can have effects that at first sight at least seem to contradict the MM value-invariance predictions. Recall that the dividend-invariance proposition takes the firm's investment decision as given—which is just a strong way of saying that the level of investment, whatever it might be, is set by management *independently* of the dividend. Without imposing such an "other-things-equal" condition, there would, of course, be no way of separating

---

8. Bhattacharya (1979) noted the formal similarity between Spence's (1973) job-market signalling model and the MM dividend model with asymmetric information.

9. Ross (1977).

10. For a recent survey of results on dividend signalling, see Miller (1987). For a more general survey of asymmetric information models in finance, see Stiglitz (1982).

the market's reaction to real investment events from reactions to the dividend and any associated, purely financial events.

In the real world, of course, the financial press reports single-company stories, not cross-sectional partial regression coefficients. In these single-company tales, the investment decision and the dividend/financing decisions are typically thoroughly intertwined. But if the tale is actually one of cutting back unprofitable investments and paying out the proceeds as dividends, followed by a big run-up in price, then the MM invariance proposition may seem to be failing, but is really not being put to the test. Nor is this scenario only hypothetical. Something very much like it appears in a number of the most notorious of recent takeover battles, particularly in the oil industry where some target firms had conspicuously failed to cut back their long-standing polices of investment in exploration despite the drastic fall in petroleum prices.

In a sense, as noted earlier, these gains to shareholders from ending a management-caused undervaluation of the firm's true earning power can also be viewed as a form of capital-market arbitrage, but not one that atomistic MM investors or arbitragers can supply on their own. Once again, the special properties of the corporate form intrude, this time the voting rights that attach to corporate shares and the majority-like rules (and sometimes supermajority rules) in the corporate charters that determine the control over the firm's decisions. Much of the early skepticism, still not entirely dispelled, about the real empirical force of inter-firm arbitrage (MM-arbitrage included) traces to these properties of corporate shares beyond their purely cash-flow consequences. A particular example of the obstacle they offered to effective capital market equilibrium was that of closed-end investment funds. In 1958, as still today, closed-end funds often sold at a substantial discount to net asset value—a discount that could be recaptured only by the shareholders merely (that word again) by getting enough of them to vote to convert to open-end fund status . . .

[Omitted here from the original is a section entitled "MM Invariance with Limited Liability and Risky Debt."]

■ THE MM PROPOSITIONS IN A WORLD WITH TAXES

We have no shortage of potential candidates for forces that might well lead the market to depart systematically and persistently from the predictions of the original MM value-invariance propositions. One such likely candidate, the third of the original lines of objection, has loomed so large in fact as to have dominated academic discussions of the MM propositions, at least until the recent wave of corporate takeovers and restructurings became the new focus of attention. That candidate is the corporate income tax, the one respect in which everyone agreed that the corporate form really did matter.

The U.S. Internal Revenue Code has long been the classic, and by now is virtually the world's only, completely unintegrated tax system imposing "double taxation" of corporate net income. A separate income tax is first levied directly on the corporation; and, except for certain small and closely held corporations, who may elect to be taxed as partnerships under Subchapter S of the Code, a second tax is then levied at the personal level on any income flows such as dividends or interest generated at the corporate level. Double taxation of the interest payments is avoided because interest on indebtedness is considered a cost of doing business and hence may be deducted from corporate gross income in computing net taxable corporate earnings. But no such allowance has been made for any costs of equity capital.[11]

If the separate corporate income tax were merely a modest franchise tax for the privilege of doing business in corporate form, as was essentially the case when it was introduced in the early years of this century, the extra burden on equity capital might be treated as just one more on the long list of second-order differences in the costs of alternative sources of capital for the firm. But, at the time of our 1958 article, the marginal tax rate under the corporate income tax had been close to and sometimes over 50 percent for nearly 20 years, and it remained there for almost another 30 years until dropped to 34 percent by the recent Tax Reform Act of 1986. The cost differentials of this size were just too big to be set aside in any normative or empirical treatments of real-world capital structure choices.

---

11. Two exceptions should be noted for the record. An undistributed profits tax from which dividends were deductible was in force for two years in the late 1930s. The excess-profits tax during World War II also allowed a deduction not for dividends, but for the "normal profits" of the firm.

THE TAX-ADJUSTED MM PROPOSITION...SUGGESTED THAT THE HIGH
BOND RATINGS, IN WHICH THE MANAGEMENT TOOK SO MUCH PRIDE,
MAY ACTUALLY HAVE BEEN A SIGN OF THEIR INCOMPETENCE; THAT THE
MANAGERS WERE LEAVING TOO MUCH OF THEIR STOCKHOLDERS' MONEY
ON THE TABLE IN THE FORM OF UNNECESSARY CORPORATE INCOME TAX.

Strictly speaking, of course, there is one sense, albeit a somewhat strained one, in which the basic value-invariance does go through even with corporate taxes. The Internal Revenue Service can be considered as just another security holder, whose claim is essentially an equity one in the normal course of events (but which can also take on some of the characteristics of secured debt when things go badly and back taxes are owed). Securities, after all, are just ways of partitioning the firm's earnings: the MM propositions assert only that the sum of the values of all the claims is independent of the number and the shapes of the separate partitions.

However satisfying this government-as-a-shareholder view may be as a generalization of the original model, the fact remains that the government, though it sometimes gives negative taxes or subsidies for some kinds of investment, does not normally buy its share with an initial input of funds that can serve to compensate the other stockholders for the claims on income they transfer to the Treasury. Nor are we talking here of taxation-according-to-the-benefits or of the rights of eminent domain, or even of whether the corporate tax might ultimately be better for the shareholders, or for the general public, than alternative ways of raising the same revenue. For the nongovernment equity claimholders, the government's claim to the firm's earnings is a net subtraction from their own.

THE MM TAX-ADJUSTED LEVERAGE PROPOSITION

Allowing for that subtraction can lead to a very different kind of MM Proposition, though one, as we showed in our Tax Correction article (1963), that can still be derived from an arbitrage proof along lines very similar to the original.[12] This time, however, the value of the firm (in the sense of the sum of the values of the private, nongovernmental claims) is *not* independent of the debt/equity division in the capital structure. In general, thanks to the deductibility of interest, the purely private claims will increase in value as the debt ratio increases. In fact, under conditions which can by no means be dismissed out of hand as implausible, we showed that the value of the private claims might well have no well-defined interior maximum. The optimal capital

structure might be all debt!

In many ways this tax-adjusted MM proposition provoked even more controversy than the original invariance one—which could be, and often was, shrugged off as merely another inconsequential paradox from some economists' frictionless dream-world. But this one carried direct and not very flattering implications for the top managements of companies with low levels of debt. It suggested that the high bond ratings of such companies, in which the management took so much pride, may actually have been a sign of their incompetence; that the managers were leaving too much of their stockholders' money on the table in the form of unnecessary corporate income tax payments—payments which in the aggregate over the sector of large, publicly-held corporations clearly came to many billions of dollars.

We must admit that we too were somewhat taken aback when we first saw this conclusion emerging from our analysis. The earlier modeling of the tax effect in our 1958 paper, which the 1963 paper corrected, had also suggested tax advantages in debt financing, but of a smaller and more credible size. By 1963, however, with corporate debt ratios in the late 50s not much higher than in the low tax 1920s,[13] we seemed to face an unhappy dilemma: either corporate managers did not know (or perhaps care) that they were paying too much in taxes; or something major was being left out of the model. Either they were wrong or we were.

The Offsetting Costs of Debt Finance

Much of the research effort in finance over the next 25 years has been spent, in effect, in settling which it was. Since economists, ourselves included, were somewhat leerier then than some might now in offering mass ineptitude by U.S. corporate management as an explanation for any important and long-persisting anomalies, attention was naturally directed first to the possibly offsetting costs of leveraging out from under the corporate income tax. Clearly, leveraging increased the riskiness of the shares, as we ourselves had stressed in our original Proposition II and its tax-adjusted counterpart. A sequence of bad years, moreover, might wipe out the firm's taxable income and, given the very ungenerous treatment of losses in our tax law, that

---

12. Modigliani and Miller (1963).
13. See Miller (1963).

could reduce, possibly quite substantially, any benefits from the interest tax shields. A run of very bad years might actually find a highly-levered firm unable (or, as the option theorists might prefer, unwilling) to meet its debt-service requirements, precipitating thereby any of the several processes of recontracting that go under the general name of bankruptcy. These renegotiations can be costly indeed to the debtor's estate, particularly when many separate classes of creditors are involved.[14]

The terminal events of bankruptcy are not the only hazards in a high-debt strategy. Because the interests of the creditors and the stockholders in the way the assets are managed need not always be congruent, the creditors may seek the additional protection of restrictive covenants in their loan agreement. These covenants may not only be costly to monitor but may foreclose, if only by the time delay in renegotiating the original terms, the implementation of valuable initiatives that might have been seized by a firm less constrained. Nor should the transaction and flotation costs of outside equity financing be neglected, particularly in the face of information asymmetries. Prudence alone might thus have seemed to dictate the maintenance of a substantial reserve of untapped, quick borrowing power, especially in an era when those managing U.S. corporations (and the financial institutions buying their debt securities) still had personal memories of the debt refinancing problems in the 1930s.

We dutifully acknowledged these well-known costs of debt finance, but we were hard put at the time to see how they could overweigh the tax savings of up to 50 cents per dollar of debt that our model implied. Not only did there seem to be potentially large amounts of corporate taxes to be saved by converting equity capital to tax-deductible interest debt capital, but there appeared to be ways of doing so that avoided, or at least drastically reduced, the secondary costs of high-debt capital structures. The bankruptcy risk exposure of junior debt could have been blunted with existing hybrid securities such as income bonds, to take just one example, under which deductible interest payments could be made in the good years, but passed or deferred in the bad years without precipitating a technical default. For reducing the moral hazards and agency costs

in the bondholder-stockholder relation, the undoing-of-leverage blade in the original MM proof offered a clue: let the capital suppliers hold some of each—equity as well as debt—either directly or through convertible or exchangeable securities of any of a number of kinds. In sum, many finance specialists, myself included, remained unconvinced that the high-leverage route to corporate tax savings was either technically unfeasible or prohibitively expensive in terms of expected bankruptcy or agency costs.

JUNK BONDS, LEVERAGED BUY-OUTS AND THE FEASIBILITY OF HIGH-LEVERAGE STRATEGIES

A number of recent developments in finance can be seen as confirming the suspicions of many of us academics in the early 1960s that high-leverage strategies to reduce taxes were indeed entirely feasible. Among these, of course, is the now large outstanding volume of what are popularly known as "junk bonds." The very term is a relic of an earlier era in which the distinguishing characteristic of bonds as investments was supposedly their presence at the low-risk end of the spectrum. High-risk, high-yield bonds did exist, of course, but were typically bonds issued initially with high ratings by companies that had subsequently fallen on hard times. The significant innovation in recent years—and it is still a puzzle as to why it took so long—has been in the showing that, contrary to the conventional wisdom, junk bonds could in fact be issued and marketed successfully by design, and not just as "fallen angels."

The designs utilizing new risky-debt securities have often taken the very conspicuous form of "leveraged buyouts" of the outside shareholders by a control group typically led by the existing top management. The device itself is an old one, but had been confined mainly to small firms seeking both to assure their continuity after the death or retirement of the dominant owner-founder, and to provide more liquidity for the entrepreneur's estate. The new development of recent years has been the ability, thanks in part to the market for junk bonds, to apply the technique to a much wider range of publicly-held, big businesses with capitalizations now routinely in the billions, and with new size records

---

14. The perceived complexity of the present bankruptcy code (and perhaps even the very reason for having such a code) reflect mainly the need for resolving conflicts within and between the various classes of creditors. The difficulties parallel those encountered elsewhere in "common pool" problems. (See Jackson (1987)).

being set almost every year.

The debt/equity ratios in some recent LBOs have reached as high as 9 to 1 or 10 to 1 or even more—far beyond anything we had ever dared use in our numerical illustrations of how leverage could be used to reduce taxes. The debtor/creditor incentive and agency problems that might be expected under such high leverage ratios have been kept manageable partly by immediate asset sales, but over the longer term by "strip financing"—trendy investment banker argot for the old device of giving the control and most of the ownership of the equity (except for the management incentive shares) to those providing the risky debt (or to the investment bankers they have designated as monitors). The same hold-both-securities approach, as in our arbitrage proof, has long been the standard one in Japan where corporate debt ratios are, or are at least widely believed to be, substantially higher than for their U.S. counterparts.

Some Possible Non-tax Gains from Leveraging

The recent surge of leveraged buyouts not only shows the feasibility of high-leverage capital structures for reducing corporate income taxes, but also suggests at least two other possible sources for the gains to the shareholder that may accompany a major recapitalization with newly-issued debt. The firm may, for example, already have had some long-term debt outstanding when the additional debt needed to accomplish the buyout was arranged. Even in a world without taxes, the no-gain-from-leverage implication of the original MM invariance proposition might fail if the new debt was not made junior in status to the old, if the old bond covenant was "open ended," as many still are, and if the new bonds were issued under it. Assuming no change in the underlying earning power from the recapitalization, the original creditors would then find the value of their claim diluted. The benefits of this dilution of the old bondholders accrue, of course, to the stockholders, which is why it has often been labeled "theft," particularly by the adversely affected bondholders. (Finance specialists prefer the less emotionally charged term "uncompensated wealth transfer.")

The high debt ratios in LBOs also redirect attention to the assumption, shown earlier to be crucial to the MM dividend-invariance proposition, that the firm's financial decisions can be taken as independent of its real operating and investment decisions. That assumption never sits well and certainly the notion that heavy debt burdens might indeed lead to overcautious business behavior has long been part of the folk wisdom on the dangers of debt. The new wrinkle to the interdependence argument brought in recently by the defenders of LBOs has been to stress the positive *virtues* of having managers face large debt obligations. Managements in such firms must work hard and diligently indeed to achieve any earnings above interest to enhance the value of the residual equity they hold in the firm. By accepting such heavy debt-service burdens, moreover, the managers are making a binding commitment to themselves and to the other residual equity holders against yielding to the temptations, noted earlier, to pour the firm's good money down investment ratholes.[15]

Voluntary Recapitalizations and the MM Dividend Proposition

High debt ratios have been installed in some U.S. firms in recent years, not just by outside-initiated LBOs but through voluntary recapitalizations—sometimes, it is true, merely for fending off an imminent hostile takeover, but sometimes also with the tax benefits very clearly emphasized. Even apart from the tax angles, nothing in the practice of finance these days could be more quintessentially MM than these often highly visible "self takeovers," as some wag has dubbed them. Leverage-increasing recapitalizations of this kind do indeed raise the firm's debt/equity ratio, but because the proceeds of the new bonds floated are turned over to the shareholders, the self takeovers also reunite in a single operation the two Siamese-twin MM propositions, the leverage proposition and the dividend proposition (joined together originally at birth, but soon parted and living separate lives thereafter).

The dividend proposition, as noted earlier, was put forward initially to overcome a line of objection to the leverage proof. But how dividends might actually affect real-world prices raises other issues which in turn have led to as much controversy, and to an

---

15. This view of debt service as a device for reining in managerial discretion is a major strand in what has come to be called the "free cash flow" theory of corporate finance. For an account of that theory, see Jensen (1988).

even larger number of discordant empirical findings, than for the leverage propositions. Once again, moreover, major tax differentials intruded, this time the gap between rates on dividends and capital gains under the personal income tax, with again what seemed in the late 50s and early 60s to be strikingly unorthodox policy implications. Some high-income stockholders clearly would have been better off if the firm paid no dividends and simply reinvested its earnings or bought shares in other corporations. That much every real-world conglomerator and every public finance specialist surely knew.

But the value-for-value presumption of the MM dividend proposition carried within it some further advice. There were better ways to avoid taxes on dividends than pouring the firm's money down ratholes: use the money to buy back the firm's shares! For the taxable shareholders, buybacks at market-determined prices could transform heavily-taxed dividends into less-heavily taxed capital gains and, better yet, into unrealized capital gains for shareholders who choose not to sell or trade their shares. Unlike a declared regular dividend, moreover, an announced share repurchase, whether by tender or by open market purchases, carried no implied commitments about future payouts.

PERSONAL-CORPORATE TAX INTERACTIONS AND CAPITAL MARKET EQUILIBRIUM

These tax-advantaged dividend-substitution properties of share repurchase may also offer a clue as to why the leveraging of corporate America out from under the corporate income tax may have been so long delayed. The point is not so much that share repurchase by itself has been a major vehicle deliberately invoked by corporations to reduce the personal income taxes of their shareholders, though its potential for that purpose certainly has not been lost on corporate treasurers and directors.[16] But the very presence of such a possibility at the corporate level serves as a reminder that the U.S. tax system has not one but two distinct taxes that bear on capital structure choices. Any model of capital market equilibrium must allow for both, and for their interactions.

In particular, under reasonable assumptions, the joint corporate-personal tax gains from corporate leverage, G_L, can be expressed in the following relatively transparent formula:

$$G_L = [1 - \frac{(1-t_c)(1-t_{PS})}{(1-t_{PB})}] B_L$$

where B_L is the value of the levered firm's interest-deductible debts, t_c is the marginal corporate tax rate, and t_{PS} and t_{PB} are the marginal investor's personal marginal tax rates on, respectively, income from corporate shares and income from interest-bearing corporate debts.[17] In the special case in which the personal income tax makes no distinction between income from debt or from equity (i.e., $t_{PS} = t_{PB}$), the gain from leverage reduces to $t_c B_L$, which is precisely the expression in the MM tax model.[18] But in the contrasting extreme special case in which (a) the capital gains provisions or other special reliefs have effectively eliminated the personal tax on equity income, (b) full loss offsets are available at the corporate level, and (c) the marginal personal tax rate on interest income just equals the marginal corporate rate ($t_{PB} = t_c$), the purely tax gains from corporate leverage would vanish entirely. The gains from interest deductibility at the corporate level would be exactly offset by the added burden of interest includability under the personal tax—an added burden that, in equilibrium, would be approximated by risk-adjusted interest rate premiums on corporate and Treasury bonds over those on tax-exempt municipal securities.

This somewhat surprising special case of zero net gain from corporate leverage has inevitably received the most attention, but it remains, of course, only one of the many potentially interesting configurations for market equilibrium. Stable intermediate cases are entirely possible in which some gains to corporate leverage still remain, but thanks to the capital gains or other special provisions driving t_{PS} below t_{PB}, or to limitations on loss offsets, those gains at the corporate level are substantially below those in the original MM tax model. The tax gains from lev-

---

16. Most economists, upon first hearing about share repurchase as an alternative to dividend payments, assume that the Internal Revenue Service must surely have some kind of magic bullet for deterring so obvious a method of tax avoidance. It doesn't, or at least not one that will work in the presence of even minimally-competent tax lawyers.

17. See Miller (1977).

18. That special case assumes, among other things, that debt, once in place, is maintained or rolled over indefinitely. For valuing the tax savings when debts are not perpetuities, see the comment on this paper by Franco Modigliani that appears in the same issue of *Journal of Economic Perspectives* (Fall 1988) as this article originally appeared in.

erage might, in fact, even be small enough, when joined with reasonable presumed costs of leverage, to resolve the seeming MM anomaly of gross under-leveraging by U.S. corporations.[19]

THE MM PROPOSITIONS AND THE RECENT TAX REFORM ACT

Any such "Debt and Taxes" equilibrium, however, that the corporate sector might have reached in the early 1980s by balancing costs of debt finance against MM tax gains from leverage must surely have been shattered by the Tax Reform Act of 1986. That act sought, among other things, to reverse the long steady slide, accelerating in the early 1980s, in the contribution of corporate income taxes to total federal tax revenues. But, in attempting to increase the load on corporations, Congress seemed to have overlooked some of the interactions between corporations and individual investors that lie at the heart of the MM propositions and their later derivatives. For shareholders taxable at high marginal rates on interest or dividends under the personal income tax, for example, maintaining assets in corporate solution and suffering the corporate tax hit might make sense, provided enough of the after-corporate tax earnings could be transmuted into long-deferred, low-taxed capital gains by profitable reinvestment in real assets. In fact, over much of the life of the income tax, when shares were held largely by wealthy individuals and hardly at all by pension funds or other tax-exempt holders, the corporate form of organization for businesses with great growth potential may well have been the single most important tax shelter of all.

But the pattern of tax advantages that encouraged the accumulation of wealth in corporate form appears to have been altered fundamentally by the Tax Reform Act of 1986. The Investment Tax Credit and related tax subsidies to fixed investment have been phased out. The marginal rate on the highest incomes under the personal income tax has now been driven to 28 percent and, hence, below the top corporate rate of 34 percent. The long-standing personal income tax differential in favor of long-term realized capital gains has been eliminated, though

income in that form still benefits from a variety of timing options and from the tax-free write-up of any accumulated gains when the property passes to heirs. The analogous tax free write-up privileges for corporate deaths or liquidations, however, formerly allowed under the so-called *General Utilities* doctrine, have now been cut back by the TRA and some of its recent predecessors, reducing still further the tax benefits of the corporate form.

To finance specialists familiar with the MM propositions, these combined changes suggest that Congressional hopes of substantially increasing the yield of the corporate income-tax—that is to say, their hopes of reinstating the double taxation of corporate profits—may well be disappointed.[20] Our capital markets and legal institutions offer too many ways for averting the double hit. Corporations can split off their cash-cow properties into any of a variety of non-corporate "flow-through" entities such as master limited partnerships or royalty trusts. And, as has been the running theme of this entire section, firms retaining corporate form can always gut the corporate tax with high-leverage capital structures. In fact, under not entirely implausible conditions (notably that the marginal bondholder is actually a tax-exempt pension fund rather than a taxable individual investor, implying that the t_{PB} is zero) the incentive to leverage out from under the corporate tax may now actually be as high or higher than it was back in 1963. The statutory top corporate tax rate has indeed been cut; but with the Investment Tax Credit and Accelerated Depreciation also blown away by the Tax Reform Act of 1986, many capital-intensive corporations may now, for the first time in a very long while, be facing the unpleasant prospect of actually paying substantial corporate taxes.

And perhaps that observation can serve as a fitting note of uncertainty, or at least of unfinished business, on which to close this look back at the MM propositions. The open questions about those propositions have long been the empirical ones, as noted here at many points. Are the equilibria the propositions imply really strong enough attractors to demand the attention of those active in the capital markets either as practitioners or as outside observers? In the physical or biological sciences, one

19. For some recent empirical tests of such an intermediate equilibrium using the premium over municipals, see Buser and Hess (1986). Kim (1987) offers a wide-ranging survey of recent theoretical and empirical research on capital market equilibrium in the presence of corporate-personal income tax interactions.

20. For some recent signs of Congressional concerns on this score, see Brooks (1987) and Canellos (1987).

can often hope to answer such questions by deliberately shocking the system and studying its response. In economics, of course, direct intervention of that kind is rarely possible, but nature, or at least Congress, can sometimes provide a substitute. The U.S. tax system is a pervasive force on business decisions of many kinds, but especially so on the class of financial decisions treated in the MM propositions. Tax considerations have for that reason always figured prominently in the field of finance. Occasionally, the profession may even see changes in the tax regime drastic enough for the path of return to a new equilibrium to stand out sharply against the background of market noise. Whether the Tax Reform Act of 1986 is indeed one of those rare super shocks that can validate a theory remains to be seen.

REFERENCES

Bhattacharya, Sudipto, "Imperfect Information, Dividend Policy and the 'Bird in the Hand' Fallacy." *Bell Journal of Economics* 10.1 (Spring 1979): 259-70.

Black, Fischer, and Cox, John, "Valuing Corporate Securities: Some Effects of Bond Indenture Provisions." *Journal of Finance* 31.2 (May 1976): 351-67.

Black, Fischer, and Scholes, Myron, "The Pricing of Options and Corporate Liabilities." *Journal of Political Economy* 81.3 (May-June 1973): 637-54.

Brooks, Jennifer J. S., "A Proposal to Avert the Revenue Loss from 'Disincorporation.'" *Tax Notes* 36.4 (July 27 1987): 425-428.

Buser, Stephen A., and Hess, Patrick J., "Empirical Determinants of the Relative Yields on Taxable and Tax-exempt Securities." *Journal of Financial Economics* 17 (May 1986): 335-56.

Canellos, Peter C., "Corporate Tax Integration: By Design or by Default?" *Tax Notes* 35.8 (June 8 1987): 999-1008.

Chamley, Christopher, and Polemarchakis, Heraklis, "Assets, General Equilibrium and the Neutrality of Money." *Review of Economic Studies* 51.1 (January 1984): 129-38.

Cornell, Bradford, and French, Kenneth, " Taxes and the Priclng of Stock Index Futures." *Journal of Finance* 38.3 (June 1983): 675-94.

Duffie, Darrell, and Shafer, Wayne, "Equilibrium and the Role of the Firm in Incomplete Markets." Manuscript, (August 1986).

Durand, David, "Costs of Debt and Equity Funds for Business: Trends and Problems of Measurement." In Conference on Research in Business Finance. National Bureau of Economic Research. New York. (1952): 215-47.

Durand, David, "The Cost of Capital. Corporation Finance and the Theory of Investment: Comment." *American Economic Review* 49.4 (September 1959): 639-55.

Fama, Eugene, "Banking in the Theory of Finance." *Journal of Monetary Economics* 6.1 (January 1980): 39-57.

Fama, Eugene, "Financial Intermediation and Price Level Control." *Journal of Monetary Economics* 12.1 (January 1983): 7-28.

Hirshleifer, Jack, "Investment Decision under Uncertainty: Choice Theoretic Approaches." *Quarterly Journal of Economics* 79 (November 1965): 509-36.

Hirshleifer, Jack, "Investment Decision under Uncertainty: Applications of the State Preference Approach." *Quarterly Journal of Economics* 80 (May 1966): 611-17.

Jackson, Thomas H., *The Logic and Limits of Bankruptcy Law.* Cambridge. Mass.: Harvard University Press. 1986.

Jensen, Michael C., "Takeovers: Their Causes and Consequences." *Journal of Economic Perspectives* 2 (Winter 1988): 21-48.

Kim, E. Han, "Optimal Capital Structure in Miller's Equilibrium." in *Frontiers of Financial Theory.* Edited by Sudipto Bhattacharya and George Constantinides [Totowa. N.J.: Renan and Littlefleld. 1987]. forthcoming.

Lintner, John. "The Valuation of Risk Assets and the Selection of Risky Investments in Stock Portfolios and Capital Budgets." *Review of Economics and Statistics* 47 (February 1965): 13-37.

Merton, Robert C., "Capital Market Theory and the Pricing of Financial Securities." in *Handbook of Monetary Economics* edited by Benjamin Friedman and Frank Hahn. Amsterdam: North Holland. forthcoming.

Merton, Robert C., "On the Pricing of Corporate Debt: The Risk of Interest Rates." *Journal of Finance* 29.3 (May 1974): 449-70.

Miller, Merton H., "The Corporate Income Tax and Corporate Financial Policies." In *Stabilization Policies*, The Commission on Money and Credit, Prentice-Hall. Inc., New Jersey. (1963): 381-470.

Miller, Merton H., "Debt and Taxes." *Journal of Finance* 32.2 (May 1977): 261-75.

Miller, Merton H., "The Informational Content of Dividends." In *Macroeconomics and Finance: Essays in Honor of Franco Modigliani.* Editors Rudiger Dornbusch. Stanley Fischer and John Bossons. MIT Press. Cambridge. MA. (1987): 37-58.

Miller, Merton H., and Modigliani, Franco, "Dividend Policy. Growth and the Valuation of Shares." *Journal of Business* 34.4 (October 1961): 411-33.

Miller, Merton H., and Modigliani, Franco, "Some Estimates of the Cost of Capital to the Utility Industry, 1954-7." *American Economic Review* 56. 3 (June 1966): 333-91.

Miller, Merton H., and Scholes, Myron S, "Dividends and Taxes." *Journal of Financial Economics* 6.4 (December 1978): 333-64.

Modigliani, Franco, "Debt, Dividend Policy, Taxes, Inflation and Market Valuation." *Journal of Finance* 37.2 (May 1982): 255-73.

Modigliani, Franco, and Miller, Merton H., "The Cost of Capital. Corporation Finance and the Theory of Investment." *American Economic Review* 48.3 (June 1958): 261-97.

Modigliani, Franco, and Miller, Merton H., "The Cost of Capital, Corporation Finance and the Theory of Investment: Reply." *American Economic Review* 49.4 (September 1959): 655-69.

Modigliani, Franco, and Miller, Merton H., "Corporate Income Taxes and the Cost of Capital: A Correction." *American Economic Review* 53.3 (June 1963).

Ross, Stephen, "The Determination of Financial Structure: The Incentive Signalling Approach." *Bell Journal of Economics* 8.1 (Spring 1977): 23-40.

Ross, Stephen, "Return, Risk and Arbitrage." In *Risk and Return in Finance.* Editors Irwin Friend and James Bicksler. Vol. 1. Ballinger. Cambridge MA.(1976): 189-219.

Rubinstein, Mark, "Derivative Assets Analysis." *Journal of Economic Perspectives* 1 (Fall 1987): 73-93.

Sargent, Thomas J., and Smith, Bruce D., "The Irrelevance of Government Foreign Exchange Operations." Manuscript, 1986.

Sharpe, William F., "Capital Asset Prices: A Theory of Market Equilibrium under Conditions of Risk." *Journal of Finance* 19 (September 1964): 425-42.

Spence, Michael, "Job-Market Signalling." *Quarterly Journal of Economics* 87.3 (August 1973): 355-79.

Stiglitz, Joseph, "A Re-Examination of the Modigliani-Miller Theorem." *American Economic Review* 59, 5 (December 1969): 784-93.

Stiglitz, Joseph, "On the Irrelevance of Corporate Financial Policy." *American Economic Review* 64.6 (December 1974): 851-66.

Stiglitz, Joseph, "Information and Capital Markets." In *Financial Economics: Essays in Honor of Paul Cootner.* Editors William F. Sharpe and Cathryn Gootner, Prentice Hall, New Jersey (1982): 118-58.

Stoll, Hans R. "The Relationship Between Put and Call Option Prices," *Journal of Finance* 24 (December 1969): 801-24.

Wallace, Neil, "A Modigliani-Miller Theorem for Open Market Operations." *American Economic Review* 71.5 (June 1981): 267-74.

THE SEARCH FOR OPTIMAL CAPITAL STRUCTURE

by Stewart Myers,
Massachusetts Institute of Technology

The search for optimal capital structure is like the search for Truth or Wisdom: you will never completely attain either goal. However, there has been progress.

No one has found the formula for optimal capital structure, but we have learned where *not* to look for it. We have accumulated several useful facts and insights. We can identify some of the costs and benefits of debt vs. equity financing. We can say, with reasonable confidence, what kinds of firms ought to borrow relatively more, and what kinds less.

In this paper, I will sketch some of what we know and don't know about firms' choice of capital structure.

First, I will argue that there is no magic in leverage—nothing supporting a *presumption* that more debt is better. Debt may be better than equity in some cases, worse in others. Or it may be no better and no worse. Sometimes all financing choices are equally good.

The case for or against debt financing must therefore be built up from a more detailed look at the firm and capital markets. The smart financial manager ends up asking not general, but specific questions, such as:

1. Is there a net tax advantage to borrowing for my firm?
2. What are the odds that a given capital structure will bring financial embarrassment or distress? What would be the cost of such financial trouble?
3. Is subsidized financing available? If so, are strings attached?
4. Should my firm's existing dividend policy constrain its financing choices? (For example, sticking to a generous dividend payout might force use of debt or new common stock issues.)
5. What are the costs of issuing securities under alternative financing plans?

In this paper, I address the first two questions only—which leaves out lots of fascinating practical and conceptual questions. However, it's worth taking the time to review the main ideas on taxes and financial distress with some care. I conclude below that there is a moderate tax advantage to corporate borrowing, at least for companies that are reasonably sure they can use the interest tax shields. Of course the costs of possible financial distress should limit borrowing. These costs are most important for risky firms—no surprise there—*and* for firms whose value depends on intangible assets. Growth firms should borrow less, other things equal.

I end up proposing a three-dimensional checklist for financial managers. The dimensions are taxes, risk, and asset type. This checklist, and the reasoning underlying it, should help financial managers think more clearly about the problem of optimal capital structure.

Assumptions and Objectives

A warning is necessary before plunging in. The warning is implicit in Brealey and Myers's Fourth Law:[1]

You can make a lot more money by smart investment decisions than by smart financing decisions. The Law does not say financing is irrelevant, only that investment has priority. Financing decisions should be shaped to support the firm's investment strategy, not vice versa.

I will therefore assume the firm's *investment* decision has already been set. I will fix the left hand side of the balance sheet and consider changes only on the right.

Another important preliminary point is to ask what the firm is trying to achieve by its financing decision. The standard objective is this: given the firm's assets and investment plan, find the capital structure that maximizes firm value. Thus, if the only choices are "debt" and "equity," we set up a market value balance sheet,

If capital markets are doing their job, all efforts to increase value by tinkering with capital structure are fruitless.

Market Value Balance Sheet

Assets, tangible and intangible, including growth opportunities	Debt (D)
	Equity (E)
	Market Value of Firm (V=D+E)

and try to find the debt *proportion* that makes the market value of the firm as large as possible.

No Magic in Financial Leverage

The entries on the right hand side of the balance sheet are financial assets—paper claims that have value only because of the real assets (including intangibles and growth opportunities) on the left. Think of the balance sheet this way:

Market Value Balance Sheet

Real assets	Paper assets

The idea is to create value by shuffling the paper assets—by dividing, recasting or recombining the *paper* claims on the firm's *real* assets.

Yet creating true value out of paper sounds like alchemy. Since firm value rests on real asset value, we would not expect purely financial (paper) transactions to change the overall value of the firm.

Of course there could be an effect if the financial transactions were costly, if they affected the firm's tax liability, or if they weakened the firm's incentives to pursue valuable investment opportunities. But set these possible imperfections aside for just a moment. If we ignore the imperfections and reject alchemy, then we must conclude that firm value should not depend on the debt ratio.

Proposition I

In general, if capital markets are doing their job, all efforts to increase value by tinkering with capital structure are fruitless. This is Modigliani and Miller's (MM's) famous Proposition I.

When a firm chooses its capital structure, it sells its real assets to investors as a package of financial claims. Think of the design of the package as a marketing problem. Then you will see plenty of everyday analogies to MM's Proposition. Imagine going to the supermarket with their proposition in mind. You would predict that "The price of a pie does not depend on how it is sliced," or "It costs no more to assemble a chicken—from wings, drumsticks, breasts, etc.—than to buy one whole."

MM's theorem does *not* hold in the supermarket. The slices cost more than the whole pie. An assembled chicken costs more than a chicken bought whole. Whole milk mixed at home from skim milk and cream costs more than whole milk bought at the store.

There are two reasons why the parts cost more than the whole. In the case of chickens, these are:
1. *Costs on the Demand Side.* Consumers are willing to pay extra to pick and choose the pieces they like. It's costly for them to buy whole chickens, cut them up and sell the pieces they don't want.
2. *Costs on the Supply Side.* It's costly for supermarkets to cut up the chickens and sell the pieces separately.

Note that *both* conditions are necessary to explain why the pieces sell for more than the whole. Suppose supermarkets found a way to cut and package the pieces at trivial cost. Then competition would drive out any extra charge for the pieces. Consumers would still be *willing* to pay extra, but they would not have to. On the other hand, suppose there are costs on the supply side, but not on the demand side. (That is, suppose consumers could cut up the chickens and trade in the pieces, costlessly.) Then, consumers would not pay any extra for the pieces offered by supermarkets. Supermarkets would sell only whole chickens.

I apologize for bringing poultry into the world of high finance, but the analogy is almost exact. The firm that uses only common equity financing sells its assets whole. The firm that issues a more complex package of securities sells the assets in pieces. Let's assume investors want the complex package. It will sell at a higher price *only* if there are costs on *both* the supply side and the demand side. It must be costly for the firm to create the complex package, and it must be costly for investors to replicate it.

However, in capital markets, the costs are

1. The Fourth Law will appear in the second edition of R.A. Brealey and S.C. Myers, *Principles of Corporate Finance*, New York: McGraw-Hill Book Co.

much lower, relative to the sums involved, than in the grocery store. Suppose a whole chicken costs $2.50 and the corresponding pieces $3.00. The valuation error is $.50—small change. The same percentage valuation error on, say, $250 million of real assets is $50 million, which surely is enough to get managers' and investors' attention.

It's not clear why investors would be willing to pay 20 percent more for levered firms than for unlevered ones. However, if some market imperfection created a clientele willing to pay that much extra for levered firms, then there would be a big profit opportunity for corporate treasurers. Since it costs relatively little to turn an unlevered firm into a levered one, the *supply* of levered firms would expand until the valuation error was wiped out.

The firm is creating and selling paper assets, not real ones. So long as investors value these paper assets by the real assets underlying them, then changes in capital structure won't affect value. To repeat: there is no magic in financial leverage.

Opportunities to Issue Specialized Securities

Under what conditions is this "no magic" result violated? When the firm, by imaginative design of its capital structure, can offer some *financial service* to investors—a service investors find costly or impossible to provide for themselves. The service must be unique, or the firm must be able to provide it more cheaply than competing firms or financial intermediaries.

Thus, you look for an unsatisfied clientele—a group of investors willing to pay a premium for a particular financial instrument. The trouble is that the needs of the obvious clienteles have already been met.

For example, most investors would have difficulty borrowing with limited liability on personal account. There is a *demand-side* cost facing investors who want to borrow with limited liability. Some investors would like to borrow indirectly, with limited liability, through the corporation. This creates a clientele of investors who would be willing to pay a premium for the shares of a levered firm.

These investors would be willing to pay a premium for levered firms' stock, but they don't have to. The costs on the *supply side* are trivial. Firms can create levered equity just by borrowing. The supply

of levered equity will therefore expand until the clientele seeking limited liability is satiated. Competition among firms will eliminate any premium.

It's hard to believe that investors would pay a premium for one more garden variety bond, or for the stock of the firm issuing the bond. The only "magic" in capital structure comes as a reward to financial innovation, when firms find ways to create *new* portfolio opportunities for investors, or new ways to provide old opportunities at lower cost.

Financial innovation does occur, of course. It has been going on for generations. We see the result in today's capital markets, which offer an elaborate infrastructure of financial institutions and a remarkably rich menu of traded securities.

Innovation proves that *some* financing decisions matter. If financing were always totally irrelevant, there would be no incentive to innovate, and the menu of securities would not change.

The rewards for financial innovation go mostly to innovators, however, not to followers. The recent introduction of zero-coupon bonds provides a good example. The first corporations who issued zero-coupon bonds obtained very attractive yields. They uncovered a clientele of domestic investors who wanted to "lock-in" long-term interest rates and who could hold the bonds in tax-sheltered accounts. There was also a clientele of foreign investors who could avoid income tax on these bonds' price appreciation. However, the *supply* of zero-coupon bonds expanded rapidly as soon as these instruments' attractiveness was clear. Competition also came from zero-coupon bonds issued by brokerage houses and backed up by Treasury bonds, e.g., Merrill Lynch's TIGRs (Treasury Income Guarantee Receipts). Some of the tax loopholes that contributed to the bonds' initial attractiveness were subsequently closed.[2]

All these changes have eroded the attractiveness of zero-coupon bonds. Issues will no doubt continue, but at yields much less attractive to the firm.

When a firm tries to create value through financial innovation, it competes *in capital markets* with thousands of other firms and financial institutions. This competition implies that investors do not have to pay a premium for standard securities.

Thus, the choice of capital structure should not matter, except for temporary windows of opportu-

---

2. See David Pyle, "Is Deep Discount Debt Financing a Bargain?," *Chase Financial Quarterly*, Vol. I, Issue 1, 1981.

Stockholders do receive more earnings per dollar invested, but they also bear more risk.

nity, in which the alert firm may gain by issuing a specialized security. Finding a window does not necessarily call for a move to a higher debt ratio, however. The opportunity might be for a new type of equity, or for a hybrid or convertible instrument.

Leverage and Earnings

Here is one immediate payoff from thinking through MM's "no magic in leverage" proposition: it teaches us *not* to worry about the impact of leverage on earnings per share (EPS).

EPS is the most widely used yardstick of management performance. Normally an increase in EPS is good news, because it signals better operating results. However, sometimes management is tempted to manufacture EPS increases through paper transactions—e.g., by borrowing.

Borrowing increases the book rate of return on equity if the after-tax book rate of return on the firm's assets exceeds the after-tax interest rate. Normally a higher book rate of return on equity means higher EPS. However, this does not make stockholders better off and does not increase the real value of the firm.

Suppose a firm issues debt and retires equity, holding its assets and operating income constant. Suppose it is sufficiently profitable that EPS increases. Are investors really better off?

Increased leverage diverts a larger fraction of the firm's operating income to lenders, and a smaller fraction to stockholders. However, the total going to all investors in the firm must be exactly the same. Lenders and stockholders *considered jointly* receive no more and no less than before.

Stockholders do receive more earnings per dollar invested, but they also bear more risk, because they have given lenders first claim on the firm's assets and operating income. Stockholders bear more risk per dollar invested, and the more the firm borrows the more risk they bear. Lenders accept a lower dollar return per dollar invested because they have a safer claim. If they don't *give up* value by accepting a relatively low rate of return, how can stockholders gain on their side of the transaction? Higher return for higher risk, lower return for relative safety—it ought to be a fair trade. In fact MM *prove* it is a fair trade, provided that investors and financial intermediaries are alert and rational.

Managers who borrow *just* to boost EPS can increase firm value only by systematically fooling investors. Perhaps it's possible to fool some inves-

tors some of the time. It's more likely that these managers are fooling themselves.

Taxes

If there are any useful generalizations about capital structure, they must rest on issues not yet discussed. The first of these is taxes.

Unfortunately, "debt and taxes" is an exceedingly messy subject, one which tends to drive out other equally interesting issues. I will just list the few things we can say with confidence, and then move on.

First, interest is tax deductible. The tax saving from debt financing is greatest for firms facing a high marginal tax rate.

Second, few firms can be *sure* they will show a taxable profit in the future. If a firm shows a loss, and cannot carry the loss back against past taxes, its interest tax shield must be carried forward with the hope of using it later. The firm loses at least the time value of money while it waits. If its difficulties are deep enough, the wait may be permanent, and the interest tax shield is lost forever.

Therefore interest tax shields are worth more to some firms than others. They ought to be worth a great deal to IBM, whose taxable income is relatively high and stable. They ought to be worth very little to Wheeling-Pittsburgh Steel, which has large accumulated tax loss carryforwards and uncertain prospects.

Think of the *expected realizable* value of the tax shield on an extra dollar of promised future interest payments. This amount depends on (1) the probability that the firm will have taxable income to shield and (2) its marginal tax rate if it does have taxable income.

This brings us to the third point: the more the firm borrows, the less the expected realizable value of future interest tax shields. I have plotted this relationship as the top line in Figure 1.

Fourth, there are other ways to shield income. Firms have accelerated writeoffs for plant and equipment. They have the investment tax credit. Investments in research and many other intangible assets can be expensed immediately. So can contributions to the firm's pension fund.

How soon the top line in Figure 1 turns down depends on how profitable it is—i.e., how much income it has to shield—and on how many dollars of *non-interest* tax shields it has. The line *always* turns down if debt is high enough; however, there is

FIGURE 1. The Tax Benefit of Debt Financing

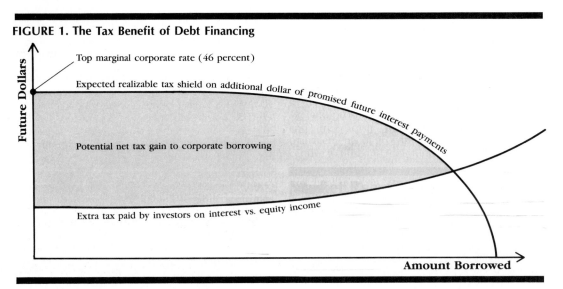

some debt burden which would drive even IBM into the bankruptcy courts.

Fifth, and finally, equity investors get a tax break relative to lenders. This partially, perhaps wholly, offsets the corporate interest tax shield.

In the United States, a corporation's income is taxed twice, first at the firm level and again when the income is passed through to lenders and stockholders. The interest lenders receive is all ordinary income. Stockholders, on the other hand, receive part of their income as capital gains. When a firm borrows in place of equity financing, the Internal Revenue Service loses at the corporate level but usually gains at the investor level (because interest is taxed more heavily than equity income). I have shown the net loss at the investor level as the bottom line in Figure 1. The shaded area between the lines is the potential tax gain to corporate borrowing when both levels are considered.

Here is where we hit trouble. We do not know whether the shaded area in Figure 1 is big, small, or possibly nonexistent. We cannot know until we can fix the position of the two lines that form the upper and lower boundaries of the shaded area.

The upper boundary is not too much of a problem. Most firms, if they had no debt at all, would pay the full 46 percent marginal rate. That gives the starting point on the vertical axis. We also know the general shape of the declining curve. The only question is when the line starts to bend down sharply, but that could be judged case by case.

The bottom boundary's position is a deep mystery, however. Some believe there is not much difference between the effective tax rates faced by debt and equity investors. That would imply a low bottom line and a correspondingly large tax gain to corporate borrowing, perhaps as much as 46 cents per dollar of interest paid. At the other extreme, Merton Miller has presented an ingenious, appealing, but probably oversimplified model,[3] in which the tax rate faced by the *marginal* investor in bonds is about 46 percent higher than the rate that investor would pay on stocks. If that's the way the world works, the tax gain to the firm from corporate borrowing just balances the tax loss to investors. The firm would have to pay such a high interest rate to bribe investors to hold its bonds that it might as well issue equity. There would be no net tax gain to corporate borrowing.

Each of these positions has extreme implications for debt policy. If the net tax gain is very large, firms that pay taxes at the full 46 percent corporate rate ought to borrow very large amounts—a triple-A debt rating would be an extremely expensive luxury. Yet, such firms as IBM and Eastman Kodak do not seem to suffer from their conservative financing.

---

3. "Debt and Taxes," *Journal of Finance*, May 1977.

*If the net tax gain is very large, a triple-A debt rating
would be an extremely expensive luxury.*

On the other hand, if the net tax gain is zero for IBM, as Merton Miller's model implies, then it must be strongly *negative* for Wheeling-Pittsburgh. In other words, Wheeling-Pittsburgh should see Big Money in negative debt: it could set up a money machine by issuing equity to buy the debt of other corporations. If you find these recommendations unacceptable, you are more or less forced into an intermediate view, in which there is a modest net tax advantage for IBM, and a modest disadvantage for Wheeling-Pittsburgh, but not so large as to dominate other factors.

I am not brave enough to take either of these extreme positions. Pending further evidence I conclude that there is a moderate tax advantage to corporate borrowing, at least for companies that are reasonably sure they can use the interest tax shields. For companies that cannot use the interest tax shields there is a moderate tax *disadvantage*.

Trouble

Every corporate treasurer knows that too much borrowing can lead to financial trouble. That one fact is all many care to know. When they start losing sleep over the firm's bond rating, they stop borrowing.

However, there's a lot going on behind the label "trouble." We need to distinguish among the different *kinds* of trouble and to look carefully at the *costs* of trouble.

Financial trouble has its own extensive literature, usually under a more imposing title such as "Costs of Financial Distress." I will offer just a few examples and observations chosen to show the literature's practical implications.

Heartbreak Hotel

Suppose your firm's only asset is a large downtown hotel, mortgaged to the hilt. The recession hits. Occupancy rates fall, and the mortgage payments cannot be met. The lender takes over and sells the hotel to a new owner and operator. You use your firm's stock certificates for wallpaper.

What are the costs of bankruptcy? In this example, probably very little. The value of the hotel is, of course, much less than you had hoped, but that is due to the lack of guests, not to default on the loan. The costs of bankruptcy are only the costs of the default itself. As Richard Brealey and I wrote elsewhere,[4]

Bankruptcies are thought of as corporate funerals. The mourners (creditors and especially shareholders) look at their firm's present sad state. They think of how valuable their securities used to be and how little is left. Moreover, they think of the lost value as a cost of bankruptcy. That is the mistake. The decline in the value of assets is what the mourning is really about. That has no necessary connection with financing. The bankruptcy is merely a legal mechanism for allowing creditors to take over when the decline in the value of assets triggers a default. Bankruptcy is not the cause of the decline in value. It is the result.

The direct bankruptcy costs of Heartbreak Hotel are restricted to items such as legal and court fees, real estate commissions, and the time and talent spent by the lender in sorting things out. The costs are proportionally larger for small firms (there are economies of scale in going bankrupt) and larger for firms with complex capital structures.[5]

Who pays the costs? At first glance it seems that the lender does, because the costs diminish the net value of the assets the lender recoups. Lenders of course realize this and charge an insurance premium every time a new loan is made. The size of the premium depends on the probability of trouble and the costs likely in the event of trouble. Your firm paid this premium when it mortgaged the hotel; these premiums cover bankruptcy costs on average. Thus, *shareholders* end up paying for *expected* bankruptcy costs every time they issue risky debt.

Fledgling Electronics Goes Under

Suppose we repeat the story of Heartbreak Hotel for Fledgling Electronics. Everything is the same, except for the underlying real assets—not real estate, but a high-tech going concern, a growth

---

4. *Principles of Corporate Finance*, New York, McGraw-Hill Book Co., p. 385.

5. Direct bankruptcy costs would virtually disappear if someone could design a "no fault" system of bankruptcy, in which the assets of the defaulting firm could be transmitted to the creditors by executing a few standard documents. But it is difficult to imagine this working for large firms, which typically have many classes of creditors with conflicting interests. No fault bankruptcy would also undercut another purpose of the law, which is to protect the firm as a going concern for time enough to give reorganization, instead of liquidation, a fair try.

company whose most valuable assets are technology, investment opportunities, and its employees' human capital.

Fledgling is of course more likely to get into trouble for a given degree of financial leverage than a hotel is, but the point here is to contrast what happens *if* a default occurs.

First, you would have a much more difficult time cashing in Fledgling's assets by just selling them off. Many of its assets are intangibles which have value only as part of a going concern.

Could the value of Fledgling, as a going concern, be preserved through default and reorganization? That would require a complete insulation of Fledgling's operating and investment plans from the bankruptcy process. Unfortunately, this is costly and probably infeasible.

Default creates a variety of operating and investment problems. The odds of defections by key employees are higher than if the firm had started out with less debt and had never gotten into financial trouble. Aggressive investment in new products and technology will be more difficult; each class of creditors will have to be convinced that it is in their interest for the firm to raise more money and put the money into risky assets.[6] Special guarantees may have to be given to customers who doubt whether the firm will be around to service its products. Finally, the time that management spends solving these and other problems has its own opportunity cost.

I have taken the extreme cases of the hotel and the electronics firm to make a crucial distinction: some asset values can pass through bankruptcy and reorganization largely unscathed. Other asset values are likely to be considerably diminished. The losses are greatest for the intangible assets that are linked to the health of the firm as a going concern, for example, technology, growth opportunities, and human capital.

The moral is: *think not only of the probability that borrowing will bring trouble. Think also of the value that may be lost if trouble comes.*

The Costs of Avoiding Bankruptcy

Since "You can make a lot more money by smart investment decisions than by smart financing decisions," financing decisions ought to be ar-

ranged to support investment decisions. However, when default or bankruptcy threatens, things can get turned around; the financing side can gain the upper hand. Managers may pass up good investment opportunities in an attempt to conserve cash and keep the firm "alive."

Suppose your hotel, under threat of default, reduces customer services, defers painting guest rooms and cuts corners in the restaurant kitchens. Assume these were sensible outlays—that is, they would have been undertaken if the firm had no debt, other things equal. Then we can say that the threat of default reduces the value of your firm's *real assets*, because it thwarts expenditures that would increase that value.[7] Even if default is avoided, there is still a cost of financial distress, equal to the value lost because of foregone investments.

Fledgling Electronics is liable to the same underinvestment problem, but the value loss could be much greater. A year's delay in painting a room may not permanently undercut that hotel's competitive position, but falling a year behind in technology or product design could wipe out a substantial fraction of Fledgling Electronics' value.

People say "You have to spend money to make money." The threat of default often leads managers *not* to spend as much as they should. The loss in value from good investments passed by is a cost of financial distress even if the firm finally regains its financial health. The extent of loss depends on how valuable the foregone investments are, and on how costly it would be for the firm to catch up. The loss is likely to be greatest for firms whose market value rests primarily on technology, human capital and growth opportunities—another reason why Fledgling Electronics should have a more conservative debt policy than a firm holding tangible assets such as real estate.

Why Should a Firm Ever Pass Up Good Investments?

Some financial economists find it hard to believe that a firm—even firms in financial distress—would ever pass up a positive net present value (NPV) investment. It's clearly in the *joint* interests of all debt and equity securityholders to raise the money to take such investments. There must be

---

6. The funds would probably be raised by giving a new class of creditors a prior claim in the firm's assets.

7. That is, expenditures with positive *net* present value.

The problem is that stockholders will have to share the extra value created by their additional investments with creditors.

some hidden cost.

The costs do exist. They are fundamentally costs of producing and transmitting information. Because information is costly, it is difficult for creditors—or any outside investor—to know what the firm's true risks and prospects are. It becomes difficult for creditors to know when managers are "doing the right thing" for the firm, and when they are acting in their own narrower interests, or in the interests of stockholders. Debt contracts become costly to write and cumbersome for the firm.[8] It becomes costly for creditors to monitor the firm's performance. Finally, it becomes costly to renegotiate the firm's financing.

Consider the following questions with these information costs in mind.[9]

Q: Why don't stockholders and creditors of a firm in financial distress get together and *jointly* advance the funds necessary to undertake all positive-NPV investments?

A Sometimes they do.[10] However, it's costly for outside investors to find out what the positive-NPV investments really are. (They may suspect managers of trying to raise money to keep the firm alive even if its prospects are not all that great.)

It is also costly and time-consuming to negotiate an agreement in which each class of security-holder makes its share of the sacrifices necessary to allow the firm to take the right investments. Such an agreement may end up being almost as costly and time-consuming as a complete reorganization of the firm's capital structure.

Despite these costs, creditors will make considerable sacrifices for firms they consider worth keeping afloat as going concerns. Think of Chrysler and International Harvester.[11]

However, it's costly to negotiate these sacrifices, sometimes so costly that the sacrifice is not made and good investments are passed by. With either outcome the *overall* value of the firm (i.e., its joint value to all creditors and stockholders) is diminished. This value loss could be avoided by not borrowing so much in the first place.

Q: If joint action by creditors and stockholders is costly, why doesn't the firm just issue stock to

finance its positive-NPV investments? For that matter, why doesn't it eliminate the whole problem by issuing stock to pay off the debt?

A: Let's take the second question first. If the firm is in serious financial trouble, its debt is no longer a safe security. The debt's market value has fallen substantially below its par or face value. If the firm issues stock and repays the *face* value of debt, stockholders are buying back the debt for considerably more than it is worth. In other words, paying off the creditors at par is always a negative-NPV investment for stockholders of a firm in financial distress.[12]

Suppose equity is issued not to pay off creditors, but to finance additional *real* investment by the firm. The problem here is that stockholders will have to share the extra value created by these investments with the creditors. Every time the value of the firm increases by one dollar, creditors are better off. Shareholders do not capture the full reward their additional investment creates. When the firm is sound and the debt is safe anyway, the proportion of the extra value captured by creditors is small. However, when the firm is in trouble, the proportion can be substantial. Thus it is often not in the stockholder's interest for firms in financial distress to raise and invest new equity capital, except through a *negotiated* reorganization of the firm's financing—and that, as I have argued before, is costly and time-consuming.

Back to the Underinvestment Problem

All this boils down to a few simple points. First, a firm that falls into financial distress may pass up good investment opportunities, or it (and its security holders) may have to renegotiate its financing in order to avoid passing up the good opportunities. Both possibilities are costly.

Second, firms can reduce the probability of these costs by not borrowing so much in the first place.

Third, if the firm lands in financial trouble, the magnitude of loss from underinvestment depends on how good its investment opportunities are. Who

8. Clifford Smith and Jerrold Warner give an excellent description of how debt contracts are written and why they are written as they are. See "On Financial Contracting: An Analysis of Bond Covenants," *Journal of Financial Economics,* June 1979.

9. I discuss these questions more carefully and extensively in "The Determinants of Corporate Borrowing," *Journal of Financial Economics,* November 1977.

10. For example, lenders often allow troubled firms to break covenants and defer debt service. When this is done, stockholders, and often employees, are expected to make sacrifices too: for example, no dividends to stockholders and no bonuses to managers.

11. They may still be forced to decide to let International Harvester sink.

12. Of course, shareholders can always try to buy the debt back at *market* value. Getting creditors to accept this offer is another matter, except as part of a negotiated reorganization.

cares if a firm passes up investment opportunities if the opportunities are worth no more than they cost?

This gives one more reason for Fledgling Electronics, or any firm whose value depends on growth opportunities or intangible assets, to borrow less than a hotel chain. The "underinvestment problem" may explain the low debt ratios in the pharmaceutical industry, where value depends on continued success in research and development, and in consumer-products companies, where sustained, massive investment in advertising is necessary to maintain product recognition and market share. We can also understand why highly profitable growth companies, such as Hewlett-Packard, Digital Equipment Corporation and IBM, tend to use mostly equity financing. Recent empirical research by Michael Long and Ileen Malitz, and by Scott Williamson, confirms that firms whose assets are weighted towards intangible assets and growth opportunities borrow significantly less, on average, than firms holding mostly tangible assets-in-place.[13]

Conclusion

Let me try to sum up this paper's main ideas. The first, most fundamental one is Modigliani and Miller's "no magic in leverage" proposition. The firm markets its *real* assets and *operating* income to investors by issuing a package of financial assets. However, if capital markets are doing their job, one package is as good as another. In particular, there is no presumption that borrowing is a good thing, even if debt is kept to "moderate" levels.

However, there does seem to be some tax advantage to borrowing for firms which make full use of interest tax shields. On the other hand, costs of financial trouble threaten firms that borrow too much. The financial manager should consider not just the probability of trouble, but also the value lost from trouble if it does occur. This value loss is greatest for firms with valuable intangible assets and growth opportunities.

Thus the choice of capital structure, when discussed with the broad brush required by this short paper, boils down to taxes, risk and asset type. For example, a safe, consistently profitable company, with few intangible assets or growth opportunities, ought to find a relatively high debt ratio attractive. A risky growth company ought to avoid debt financing, especially if it has other ways of shielding its income from taxes.

I will cheerfully admit that this three-item checklist of taxes, risk and asset type does not tell the financial manager how much debt to issue. For example, a firm with average risk, lots of unsheltered taxable income, *but* few tangible assets, could use this paper's qualitative arguments to support either a high or low debt ratio. Such a firm would probably decide that any middle-of-the-road debt ratio is OK, and base its financing choices on more down-to-earth considerations, such as issue costs, opportunities for subsidized financing, and so on.

Nevertheless, the checklist does tell the financial manager what's important and what isn't. It gives him or her a *framework* for thinking about optimal capital structure. As always, the financing *decision* finally rests on the manager's shoulders.

13. Both studies hold risk constant. See M. Long and I. Malitz, "Investment Patterns and Financial Leverage," National Bureau of Economic Research, January 1983, and S. Williamson, "The Moral Hazard Theory of Corporate Capital Structure: Empirical Tests," Unpublished Ph.D. Dissertation, MIT, November 1981.

BEHAVIORAL RATIONALITY IN FINANCE: THE CASE OF DIVIDENDS

Merton H. Miller,
*University of Chicago**

Introduction

As the title suggests, this paper attempts to get to the specifics of the behavorial rationality theme of this conference by focusing on an area in the main core of finance—namely, the demand for and supply of dividends—where, by common consent, the essentially "rationalist" paradigm of the field seems to be limping most noticeably. Important and pervasive behavior patterns on both the paying and the receiving ends have despairingly been written off as "puzzles" even by theorists as redoubtable as Fischer Black.[1] Behaviorists have homed in on precisely these same dividend-related soft spots in the current body of theory.[2] We seem to have, in sum, an ideal place to look for signs of an imminent "paradigm shift" in the behavorial direction of precisely the kind envisioned by some of the other contributors to this conference.

The dividend-related difficulties and supposed anomalies at issue here are more than just the parochial concern of finance specialists. The finance model of the firm, after all, *is* the standard economists' model of the firm, but with some of the components grouped differently[3]...The two models of the firm, the finance model and the price theory model, are variations on a single theme; moreover, the anomalies burdening any one class of users must be of some concern to the other classes as well.

How much concern should we show at this point about our dividend anomalies? Less, I will argue here, after a fresh look at the evidence, than I and others in finance may once have thought.[4] This is not to say that we do not have our share and more of still-unsolved problems. Finance, after all, is one of the newer specialty areas in economics. But I do not see us in such disarray, even on the much-mooted dividend issues, that we must think of abandoning or even drastically modifying the basic economics/ finance paradigm on which the field has been built.

The first task of the paper will be to sketch out briefly what the supposed dividend anomalies are all about. Their perception as anomalies will then be shown to a considerable extent to be traceable to a misinterpretation of the basic model, to a misreading of the empirical record, and perhaps also to exaggerated expectations of what our models can hope to accomplish.

EDITOR'S NOTE: This paper was written in 1985, on the occasion of a University of Chicago conference on "The Behavioral Foundations of Economic Theory," and thus well before the recent tax changes were enacted into U.S. law. Its focus, accordingly, is on past dividend policies and their interpretation rather than on likely future policies. Nevertheless, the economic logic and supporting evidence remain undisturbed and, indeed, bear directly on unexpected changes in U.S. corporate dividend policy over the next few years.

*This article is a slightly condensed version of a paper of the same title published in the *Journal of Business* Vol. 59 No. 2 (October 1986), pp. S451-468; and it is reprinted here with permission of the University of Chicago Press.

The author wishes to acknowledge helpful comments on an earlier version of this paper that have been received from Nai-fu Chen, Jean-Marie Gagnon, Gur Huberman, Kose John, James Poterba, and especially Melvin Reder.

1. See especially his much-cited 1976 article, "The Dividend Puzzle," *Journal of Portfolio Management* 2 (Winter): 72-77.

2. See especially H. Shefrin and M. Statman, "Explaining Investor Preference for Cash Dividends," *Journal of Financial Economics* 13, no. 2 (June, 1984): 253-82.

3. Deleted from original at this point: "The finance version, focusing on the interaction between the firm and the capital markets, subsumes the details of optimizing output, product pricing, and factor-input combinations into a single intertemporal 'transformation function' of current resource inflows to future resource outflows. The firm in finance becomes, as it were, simply an abstract engine that 'uses money today to make money tomorrow,' as Alfred P. Sloan, that most quintessential of finance-oriented business executives once (almost) described his General Motors Corporation. The firm's objective function, reflecting the specifically intertemporal statement of the firm's problem, must go beyond the familiar rubric of maximizing 'profits' to maximizing the net present value of future cash flows." The relation between the finance and economics model of the firm is discussed at length by Eugene Fama and Merton H. Miller in *The Theory of Finance* (New York: Holt, Rinehart & Winston, 1972), Chapter 3.

4. See, for example, the introduction to Merton Miller and Myron Scholes, "Dividends and Taxes," *Journal of Financial Economics* 6, no. 2 (December, 1978): 333-64.

The Dividend Anomalies

The dividend anomalies at issue here are mainly tax-related. They are instances in which a substantial body of corporate managers, presumably acting on behalf of their shareholders, appears to have been responding (or, more precisely, failing to respond) over long periods to large and persistent incentives in the tax system.

Recall the essential tax facts [see Editor's Note]. Under U.S. law, the net income of the large, publicly held corporations that are our main concern is first subject to tax at progressive rates that quickly reach 46 percent. Marginal rates at these levels (and higher) were first reached during World War II and have been maintained with only minor changes over the entire period since then. Any dividends paid by the corporation out of its current or accumulated past after-tax earnings are subject to tax (with the inevitable minor exceptions) at the regular progressive rates under the personal income tax.[5] These rates currently peak at 50 percent, their low point for the postwar era; but the maximum has reached as high as 92 percent in the years during and immediately following World War II. The dividends received would also be taxable under state income taxes as well.

By contrast, the portion of the after-corporate tax profits not paid out in dividends, but retained in the firm, is not directly subject to personal income tax.[6] The earnings retained by the corporation may still be reached by the tax system, but by a somewhat more indirect route. The retained earnings increase the value of the shares—or at least that is the presumption in the model whose anomalies are being probed. Should the share subsequently be sold at a price greater than its original cost, the price appreciation will constitute a taxable capital gain. The rates applied to such gains are hard to describe briefly; but, for individual holders, the rates on realized capital gains are never higher than those on ordinary income and are typically lower. For securities owned for more than a minimum holding period—which has varied from six months to one year in the post-World War II era—the statutory rate on gains has rarely been more than half the regular rates and then only for taxpayers who have triggered one of the minimum-tax provisions that Congress tends to enact in its periods of loophole-closing frenzy. The maximum rate on capital gains was capped for much of the postwar era at 25 percent, so the maximum gap between the top rate on ordinary income and on capital gains could have been as much as 67 percentage points! Remember, that is for *realized* gains only. Shares not sold during one's lifetime but held for one's estate escape the capital gains tax altogether.

Our tax law, in sum, thus places a substantial penalty on dividends as opposed to retained earnings/capital gains. Why, then, in the face of these penalties, do firms continue to pay them? Before the modern finance model was developed, economists and public finance specialists may have presumed that firms had no better alternative. Investment in projects at declining rates of profitability could proceed until the marginal return on internally financed investments had been driven to equality with the stockholders' after-tax dividend return. But thereafter, paying out the funds and taking the dividend tax hit would dominate further pouring of funds into low-return rat holes.

In the finance model, however, there are better alternatives to dividend payouts than wasteful real investments[7]....In such a setting, the firm is pictured as taking any internally generated funds remaining after profitable real investment opportunities have been exhausted and using them not for paying tax-disadvantaged dividends but for the purchase of securities, either its own or those of other firms (or governments). On these financial investments the firm will presumably earn not a rat-hole return but the same market, risk-adjusted return that serves as its own capital budgeting cutoff. The firm's share-

5. For tax years after 1981, the first $100 of dividends ($200 on a joint return) could be excluded from income. Special provisions, which expired at the end of 1985, were also made for the dividend reinvestment plans of utilities. Prior to 1936, dividends were exempt from the low, flat-rate normal tax but fully subject to the progressive surtaxes.

6. Small, closely held corporations, but only such, may elect to be taxed as partnerships under subchap. S of the Internal Revenue Code. In this case, no corporate income tax is levied and the entire net profit of the corporation, whether distributed or not, is taxed as ordinary personal income to the shareholders.

7. Deleted from original at this point: "The technological concavity in the opportunity set imposed by the law of diminishing returns on real investment can be bypassed, as it were, for any one firm by adjoining the essentially linear technology of transactions in securities in well-functioning capital markets. The production function in the finance model of the firm is only weakly concave, not strictly concave."

The critical role of external securities in the dividend supply function was first noted explicitly in my 1961 paper with Franco Modigliani, "Dividend Policy, Growth, and the Valuation of Shares," *Journal of Business* 34, no. 4 (October): 411-33. That was indeed a major thrust of our paper, though somewhat obscured perhaps by the more controversial and provocative material on the valuation of shares. Our point, however, is also a fairly direct implication of the standard Fisherian model of the finance firm, as can clearly be seen from our discussion in ch. 2 of Eugene Fama and Merton Miller, *The Theory of Finance* (New York: Holt, Rinehart & Winston, 1972).

The anomaly plaguing the current finance model...rests essentially on the belief that firms are systematically failing to benefit their shareholders by converting high-taxed dividends to low-taxed capital gains.

holders, moreover, whatever their tax status, would, if they are behaving rationally, also seem to be unanimous in favoring such a strategy.[8] Some of the shareholders, like pension funds and university endowments, are themselves tax-exempt and hence have no incentive to shun dividends. But, by the same token, they would seem to have no tax incentive to oppose the efforts of their taxable brethren to improve their lot by transforming the firm's return from fully taxable dividends to untaxed or at least lower-taxed capital gains. (It may be a weak-inequality form of unanimity, but it is still unanimity.)[9]

Such, then, is the anomaly plaguing the current finance model of the dividend-paying firm. It rests essentially on the belief that firms are systematically failing to benefit their shareholders by converting high-taxed dividends to low-taxed capital gains. Most nonspecialists will suspect that the most likely route for resolving the anomaly is on the cost-of-conversion side. Surely, they will presume, there can be no free lunches in conversions. They will certainly be correct with respect to one of the main financial strategies for conversion suggested by the underlying model—namely, buying the securities of other firms and (and governments). It may be instructive, therefore, to get at least that class of distractions out of the way before turning to the more serious issues raised by the other conversion strategy of buying back the firm's own securities.[10]

The Costs of Avoiding Cash Payouts by Buying Outside Securities

A first look at the finance model can all too easily lead one to the belief that even investing in government bonds normally would be better (and never worse) for the shareholders than paying out cash dividends. Not so, however. In fact, holding significant amounts of government bonds or other purely financial instruments is not even a feasible alternative for corporations under U.S. tax laws.

The infeasibility is more than just a matter of Internal Revenue Code section 532, which imposes a penalty tax for "improper accumulation of surplus." That provision has indeed been part of the code almost from its inception, and its purpose has been precisely to keep shareholders from avoiding the personal income tax on dividends by piling up cash in the corporation. But few firms have ever been caught in its meshes.[11]

The moral to be drawn from this lack of bite, however, is precisely the opposite of that usually drawn, which is that the section is a toothless tiger, not even worth mentioning as a deterrent to cutting back on dividends. Clearly, from the section's existence and history we know that both Congress and the Internal Revenue Service are aware of the potential for dividend tax avoidance via corporate hoarding as well as of the steps that would have to be taken to close off that route. That they have not troubled to do so suggests that the route is not being sufficiently traveled to make an effort via section 532 worthwhile.

Section 532 has been rendered largely superfluous for publicly held corporations by another and much more fundamental tax provision, the corporation income tax itself. Under that tax, the interest earned on any government bonds in the corporate hoards would be taxable in principle at the full marginal corporate rate of 46 percent.[12] Hence any pension fund or other institutional holder offered a choice between receiving an immediate cash dividend or having the corporation invest the cash in government bonds would not be indifferent, or anywhere close to it, even though the institution itself

---

8. Not quite. Nothing in our tax law ever seems that clear-cut. Corporations holding shares in other corporations are permitted to exclude 85% of intercorporate dividends received. The effective minimum tax on intercorporate dividends is about 7%, which is substantially below the corporate capital gains tax. Corporate holdings of shares for investment purposes, however, are predominantly in the form of preferred stocks. Corporate shareholding is worth a mention but is not a major part of the story to be developed here.

9. Another qualification should be entered for the record. Where a firm has adopted a dividend reinvestment plan (DRIP) with a significant price discount (frequently as high as 5%) on the shares acquired, its institutional investors would no longer be neutral between dividends and capital gains but would strongly prefer dividends. By reinvesting the dividends and then immediately selling off the shares so acquired, they pick up a substantial quasi-arbitrage profit. Relative to the issues of concern here, however, DRIPs are of too recent an origin and too limited a scope to play any major explanatory role.

10. Although the emphasis in this paper will be on the conversion opportunities available to firms, individuals too have methods for converting dividends to capital gains. In principle, as shown in a paper I co-authored with Myron Scholes

("Dividends and Taxes," *Journal of Financial Economics* 6, no. 2 (December): 333-64), these tactics could make the corporate conversion possibilities redundant; but, in practice, these techniques are likely to be availed of only by the small (but possibly important) minority of stockholders who regularly buy stocks on margin.

11. The penalty will not be invoked if the firm can show that its accumulations have a "valid business purpose," and proving that presents little challenge to even a moderately competent tax lawyer. In the past few years, the Internal Revenue Service has begun to put some additional muscle behind its enforcement efforts and to reach firms substantially larger than had earlier been the case. But the firms affected have all been closely held or at least clearly controlled by a dominant shareholder. No publicly traded firm with widely dispersed ownership (of the kind that the finance model is concerned with) has even been hit by sec. 532. The similarly motivated personal holding company penalties are also confined to closely held corporations.

12. The inevitable qualification: the IRS will tolerate a limited amount of stashing away of tax-free investments by "overfunding" the firm's pension fund.

No shortage exists of...drawbacks to a policy of holding securities beyond the liquidity needs of the business. Too much of the benefits would accrue to the firm's creditors and the treasures might attract raiders, as the story of the Rhine Maidens and their ring reminds us.

was tax-exempt and subject to no tax on either dividends or capital gains. Nor are institutional investors the only body of shareholders disadvantaged when a taxable corporation uses otherwise available funds to purchase securities that those investors could acquire directly. Taxable shareholders can also be hurt if the numbers are such that the front-end bite of the dividend tax on the dollars paid out turns out to be less than the present value of the stream of additional corporate tax payments incurred on the funds invested. Precisely where that boundary lies need not be spelled out in detail. The present concern is simply whether observed corporate dividend behavior can be regarded as anomalous relative to the standard finance model because investment in securities by the firm would be a uniformly or even weakly superior alternative to paying dividends. Merely establishing that a cutoff exists means that the answer is no.[13]

To dispose of a dividend-related anomaly by invoking a tax argument is never entirely satisfactory even when, as here, the anomaly itself is tax-induced. The dividend policies of firms and individuals today are similar, at least in broad outline, to those found before the present tax system and in countries with tax regimes very different from our own. It is worth emphasizing, therefore, that the tax case against corporate hoarding is offered here in the sense of sufficiency, not necessity. No shortage exists of other costs and drawbacks to a policy of holding securities at the corporate level beyond the liquidity needs of

the business. Too much of the benefits would accrue to the firm's creditors and, more to the point, the treasures might attract raiders, as the story of the Rhine Maidens and their ring reminds us. Indeed, much of the presumed motivation of the acquirers, and certainly much of their rhetoric, in recent highly publicized takeover struggles, has focused precisely on getting unproductive assets out of corporate solution and into the hands of the shareholders.[14] Hoarding, in sum, is not a feasible alternative to dividends. With that established, we can turn now to some dividend-conversion strategies available to the firm that make the tax anomaly less easy to shrug off.

Share Repurchase and the Supply of and Demand for Dividends

Rather than buy government securities or securities of other firms, a firm, in this country at least, always has the option of purchasing its own securities.[15] This route can get excess funds out of corporate solution, thus avoiding the class of difficulties just seen but without creating dividends, which are taxable as ordinary income under the personal income tax.

At first sight, the policy of share repurchase may seem to benefit only those shareholders who choose to take the other side of the firm's offer to buy. But that is not so. The policy of share repurchase, like the quality of mercy, is twice blessed. It blesses not only

---

13. The argument in this section about the purely tax disadvantages of financial investment relative to dividends was first made in the finance literature, as far as I am aware, by David Emanuel ("Debt and Taxes, Dividends and Taxes, and Taxes," Mimeographed. Dallas: University of Texas (1983)). Essentially the same point could have been made, though in a less transparent way, in terms of standard finance "capital structure" models. In a so-called before-tax equilibrium world (as in Modigliani and Miller (1963), for example), any investment in taxable, interest-bearing securities would be "negative leverage" and hence would, ceteris paribus, lower the value of the shares. In an "after-tax equilibrium" world (as in Miller (1977)), holding of taxable securities by the firm would deprive the tax-exempt and low-bracket shareholders of the "bondholders' surplus" that they could earn with the funds on their own. Investments by corporations in preferred stock of other taxable corporations are less tax disadvantageous to institutional and low-bracket holders than investments in interest-bearing securities, thanks to the 85% exclusion on intercorporate dividends received. Hence the great popularity in recent years of new instruments such as ARPs (adjustable rate preferreds) or MARs (multiple adjustable rate preferreds) as temporary abodes for cash. To the extent, however, that yields adjust and issues recapture some of the tax benefits, as appears to be the case, the corporate buyers are paying what Scholes, Mazur, and Wolfson (see "A Model of Implicit Taxes and their Effect on Empirical Estimates of Income Tax Progressivity," Mimeographed. Stanford, Calif.: Stanford University (1984)) have dubbed an "implicit tax" over and above the nominal 7% (i.e., .46 x .85). For holdings of common stock by corporations, the implicit tax on the dividends is smaller. Some would argue, as we shall see, that it is substantially negative because dividends sell at such a substantial discount. Even if true, however, it would clearly be a self-referencing paradox to imagine every cash-rich dividend-paying corporation to be avoiding payment of dividends by investing in the dividend-

paying shares of other cash-rich corporations. Of course, cash-rich firms could purchase the shares of cash-poor corporations. Indeed, some, but only some, of the seeming merger wave of recent years has been so motivated. But merger activity that eliminates one firm's securities from the capital markets is perhaps more appropriately treated as real investment than as financial investment. (I have benefited from discussions of these issues with my colleague Gur Huberman but absolve him from responsibility for any errors.)

14. Interestingly enough, the raiders have been zeroing in on hoards of passive investment funds even when held in tax-exempt form in overfunded pension plans (see, for example, L. Asinof, "Excess Pension Assets Lure Corporate Raiders," *Wall Street Journal* (September 22, 1985). For a discussion of some moral hazard problems in overfunding pension plans, see also R. A. Ippolito, "The Economic Function of Underfunded Pension Plans," *Journal of Law and Economics* 28, no. 3 (October, 1985): 611-51.) Recent spin-offs of developed oil field properties into limited partnerships (not subject to corporate income tax) offer additional examples of efforts to get what amounts to passive "investment income" out of corporate form and attendant tax burdens.

15. The qualification is made because the frequently heard, conventional wisdom is that corporate law in Great Britain and in most European countries rules out share repurchase. Perhaps so, if taken literally; but one suspects that there must be other, equivalent tactics that permit a business to reduce in size. In Belgium, the explicit restrictions appear to apply only to self-tenders, not to open-market purchases. In Canada, Jean-Marie Gagnon of Laval University in Quebec, commenting on an earlier version of this paper, notes that share repurchase very definitely is permitted under Canadian law, subject, however, to the standard restrictions on actions damaging to the firm or its creditors. He suspects that a misinterpretation of those restrictions may be the source of the folk belief that share repurchase is somehow illegal.

154

The feeling that empirical research has established that dividends have, in fact, long been selling at a substantial discount appears to be the major contributor to the sense of unease within the profession about the status of the model.

those who sell but also those who do not. In fact, the nonsellers are thrice blessed because their benefit takes the form not of realized, but of unrealized capital gains.[16] Note also that when allowance is made for the taxes, stayers under the buy-back plan might be better off than under a dividend plan, even if the firm had to pay the sellers a premium over the market price, as is often the case when the firm tenders for the shares. The gain from nontaxability more than offsets the loss from dilution.[17]

Share repurchase is thus clearly superior to corporate hoarding as a method of transforming current dividends into current capital gains. But it is not a costless alternative to paying dividends. Brokerage fees must be incurred, and, in the case of tenders, often underwriting expenses must be paid as well. Still, transaction costs of this kind seem small when compared with the statutory tax differentials between dividends and capital gains. So much so, in fact, that it might be daunting to a behavioral theorist of the firm to venture even a boundedly rational explanation of why dividends continue to be paid (at least by firms other than public utilities).[17a]

Remember, however, that in the finance model of the supply of dividends, whose possibly anomalous status is our concern, the tax differentials under the personal income tax do not enter the firm's objective function directly. The managers of large, widely held corporations are not pictured there as solving dividend decision problems by performing "thought experiments," as we here have been doing, about what might or might not be in the best interests of this or that group of the shareholders (though they may well tend to couch their explanations in those terms). Rather, as with constructing any other supply function in the theory of the firm, the managers are assumed to be responding to the

signals conveyed to them by market prices. The process is a bit harder to visualize for dividends, perhaps, because the price of dividends relative to capital gains is not quoted directly, as such, in the columns of the *Wall Street Journal*. But that price can be *inferred*, at least within tolerable limits, from the stock prices and dividend yields reported there and from the analyses, formal and informal, performed on that and other relevant data by financial analysts within and outside the firm.

For the finance model of dividend supply to be held anomalous, therefore, or at least as requiring important structural modifications (including, quite possibly, the grafting on of major elements from the behavioral theory of the firm), it would be sufficient (and, in my view, also necessary) to show that the observed market price of dividend return can confidently be placed too far below the observed market price of capital gain return to be plausibly attributed to the likely cost of converting current dividends to current capital gains. The feeling that empirical research has established that dividends have, in fact, long been selling at a substantial discount appears to be the major contributor to the sense of unease within the profession about the status of the model. It is important, therefore, to be clear about what has and what has not been shown about the market price of dividends relative to capital gains.

The Empirical Record

The conventional impression that academic empirical research has shown a large and long-standing price penalty on dividends is perhaps nowhere so neatly capsulized as in a "box score" table added to the last edition of Brealey and Myers's excellent textbook

---

16. For nonspecialists, perhaps the following numerical example may help sort things out. Suppose, to keep things simple, there were no taxes to complicate calculations, and suppose a firm with 1 million shares outstanding had set aside $4 million for return to the shareholders. Suppose further that, after it announced the setting aside of $4.00 per share, the *cum-dividend* price of each share at this time were to be $44. After the dividend was paid, each shareholder would have $4.00 in cash plus an *ex-dividend* share worth $40, ceteris paribus. Imagine now that, instead of paying the dividend, the firm had used the same $4 million to buy 90,909 shares at the predistribution price of $44. The nonselling shareholders receive no cash, of course, but each of their shares now represents a larger fraction of the firm. In fact, each will be worth $44 ($40,000,000/909,091). Thus every stockholder winds up with the same net worth of $44 per share no matter which policy the firm follows in disposing of the cash. The only difference is in how the net worth is divided between cash and shares (a uniform $4.00 in cash and $40 in shares for every holder under the dividend route vs. $44 in cash for the sellers and $44 in stock for the stayers under the buy-back route).

17. But the premium cannot be set too high or the procedure becomes self-defeating. If everyone tenders and is prorated, the cash distribution is

"proportional" and will be treated as a dividend for tax purposes. Under present rules, a reduction in fractional interest in the corporation of 20% or more is required to assure any stockholder that payments received in a share self-tender offer are not deemed to be merely disguised dividends. These restrictions do not apply to open-market repurchases and are moot, of course, even under self-tenders for nontaxable institutional shareholders. But that does not mean that such investors will be indifferent between dividends and self-tenders. A tender offer at a premium above market (but not so far above to get even the taxable holders to tender) may well be better for them than a dividend after all costs have been taken into account.

17a. Public utility managements have found a policy of high dividends combined with frequent external equity financing to be a useful strategy for forcing their regulators to keep utility rates high enough to continue attracting new funds from investors. Investors realize this, of course, and hence utility stocks historically have tended to attract a clientele that strongly prefers cash dividends to plow-back induced capital gains.

18. Richard Brealey and Stewart Myers, *Principles of Corporate Finance*. 2d ed. New York: McGraw-Hill, 1984, p. 348.

[According to a study by Marshall Blume,] the relation between risk-adjusted returns and dividend yields was U-shaped. The market appeared to demand a return premium both from those firms paying the most in dividends and from those paying the least.

on corporate finance.[18] Ten separate statistical studies of the average cross-sectional relation between risk-adjusted stock returns and dividend yields are summarized therein. In eight of the ten studies, the regression coefficient representing the return premium for dividends—or, equivalently, the price discount for dividends—was substantial both in absolute size (equivalent, say, to an effective "tax differential" on dividends over capital gains of from 25 percent to as high as 56 percent) and relative to its reported standard error. There were only two exceptions to the modal result.[19] One was the classic study by Black and Scholes.[20] If the results of the Black-Scholes study had to be expressed as a single point estimate, then it too would have been a dividend discount on the order of 20 percent. But the essential message of the paper, stressed repeatedly by the authors themselves, was that with the data and techniques then available, the differential in the weight on dividends relative to capital gains could not be pinned down in size or even in sign.

The other study departing from the general trend was one by Miller and Scholes.[21] In that study, however, our concern was not to provide the best estimate of the dividend coefficient but to show that the dividend coefficient reported in another and very influential study (Litzenberger and Ramaswamy (1978))[22] was sensitive to seemingly small adjustments in the definition of dividend yield used. In addition, and more to the present point, we showed that what Scholes and I called the "short-run measure" of dividend yield used by Litzenberger and Ramaswamy was, for a variety of reasons, inappropriate for measuring the market price obtainable for dividends supplied. On that score, at least, some-

thing approaching a consensus has emerged, and virtually all recent cross-sectional empirical work on the dividend issue has relied on so-called long-run measures of dividend yield, in the same spirit as the original Black-Scholes study, though with some improvements in detail.[23]

One of the most provocative of these post-Black-Scholes studies is that of Marshall Blume.[24] Blume showed that, looking solely at firms that were actually paying dividends, there did indeed appear to be a substantial average cross-sectional dividend yield premium—an excess return so large, in fact (as Blume noted), as to be beyond plausibility as a compensation solely for tax differentials. But the cross-sectional scatters showed that the relation between risk-adjusted returns and dividend yields (which, when properly scaled, is the sought-for measure of the market price for dividends) was U-shaped. The market appeared to demand a return premium both from those firms paying the most in dividends and from those paying the least (i.e., zero).

Attempting to account for puzzling extreme observations can sometimes turn up important neglected aspects of the problem under study, and such indeed proved to be the case with Blume's "U." Donald Keim noticed that the firms at the two ends of the U—the zero-dividend firms and the highest-dividend firms—were primarily small companies.[25] What made that observation so interesting was the rapidly building mountain of research on the so-called small-firm effect.

The small-firm effect is the finding—by now amply documented both here and abroad—that small firms, even after adjustment for the standard CAPM-based measures of risk, appear to earn signifi-

---

19. There is even one very small piece of evidence often cited in support of the position that the relative price of dividends may actually be *higher* rather than lower than that of capital gains. This is the case of Citizens' Utility as reported by John Long ("The Market Valuation of Cash Dividends: A Case to Consider," *Journal of Financial Economics* 6, no. 3 (June/September, 1978): 235-64). The company was allowed by the Treasury to issue two class of shares, one paying cash dividends and the other dividends in stock, with the stock dividend shares convertible to the cash dividend shares. The ratio of the stock dividend to the cash dividend was subject to change (and hence to some uncertainty at the time of purchase). But after making reasonable adjustments, Long concludes that the cash dividend shares were selling at a premium relative to the stock dividend shares. It is difficult, however, to know how much weight to place on observations on a stock so thinly traded. For an updated look at Citizens' Utility that comes to somewhat different conclusions, see J. Poterba, "The Citizens' Utility Case: A Further Dividend Puzzle," Working Paper no. 339. Cambridge: Massachusetts Institute of Technology, 1985.

20. F. Black and M. Scholes, "The Effects of Dividend Yield and Dividend Policy on Common Stock Prices and Returns," *Journal of Financial Economics* 1, no. 1 (May, 1974): 1-22.

21. M. Miller and M. Scholes, "Dividends and Taxes: Some Empirical Evidence," *Journal of Political Economy* 90, no. 6 (December, 1982): 1118-41.

22. R. Litzenberger and K. Ramaswamy, "The Effect of Personal Taxes and

Dividends on Capital Asset Prices," *Journal of Financial Economics* 7, no. 2 (June, 1979): 163-95.

23. The use of short-run measures of dividend yield makes a test essentially one of the size of the momentary cum-dividend/ex-dividend (cum-ex) differential. The substantial body of literature attempting to use the direct, cum-ex route to establish the discount for dividends has established that the differential is certainly affected by taxes but that transactions costs, dividend "arbitrage" games, and the distortion of the normal patterns of transactions around ex days make it impossible to draw any reliable inferences about the price of dividends over the longer intervals that are relevant for the supply curve of dividends. For an account of the current state of the cum-ex experiments, see B. Grundy, "Trading Volume and Stock Returns around Ex-dividend Days," Mimeographed. Chicago: University of Chicago, Graduate School of Business, 1985.

24. Marshall Blume, "Stock Returns and Dividend Yields: Some More Evidence," *Review of Economics and Statistics* 62 (November, 1980): 567-77.

25. Donald Keim, "Further Evidence on Size Effects and Yield Effects: The Implications of Stock Return Seasonality," Mimeographed. Chicago: University of Chicago, Graduate School of Business, 1982. Many of these high-yield firms, of course, are likely to be once-large firms that have recently become smaller because of adverse business conditions, but have not yet adjusted their dividends to their new, lower level of earnings.

We may not be able to say as much as we would like about the long-run equilibrium price of dividends; but...evidence is accumulating that the quantity of dividends does vary appropriately in response to significant exogenous shocks to demand or supply.

cantly higher rates of return than do large firms.[26] These higher returns, moreover, appeared to have a marked seasonal pattern: they occurred mostly in January.[27] The same was true of the dividend-yield return premiums on each arm of Blume's U. What, therefore, were all the dividend studies measuring? Dividend effects? Small-firm effects? January effects? All of the above? None of the above?

Since Keim's work, the focus of empirical research has shifted to seeking more powerful econometric methods for isolating the separate contributions of these effects. The search, however, has yet to produce much in the way of results[28]...

Until recently, at least, we could hope that these difficulties would someday be overcome and that eventually we would get a sharp enough fix on the market price of dividends to determine whether the aggregate corporate supply of dividends has really been in the long-standing disequilibrium relative to the predictions of the standard, value-maximizing model of the firm. My colleagues Nai-Fu Chen, Bruce Grundy, and Robert Stambaugh, however, have been devoting their not inconsiderable econometric prowess to this task and have reluctantly concluded that the estimating equations are too sensitive even to small variations in the risk measure to establish confidently whether dividends sell at a discount relative to capital gains.[29] We are back to Black and Scholes!

This inconclusiveness is certainly not the best that one could have hoped for; but it is also not the worst. At least, it puts to rest the charge that the corporate sector has systematically failed to respond to the price signals being sent by the market. No clear and steady signal to management to reduce dividends is coming through the noise.[30]

But we can actually do somewhat better than this. We may not be able to say as much as we would like about the long-run equilibrium *price* of dividends; but, as will be shown in the next section, evidence is accumulating that the *quantity* of dividends brought to market does vary appropriately in response to significant exogenous shocks to demand or supply.[31] After all, comparative statics—explaining and predicting the economy's adjustment to change—is why we build maximizing models in the first place.

The Response to Shocks

The most promising place to look for experiments testing the dividend supply and demand model is along the fault line between the corporate and personal income taxes. While a method of integrating the two taxes that is not open to serious attack on economic or political grounds has yet to be found (and, indeed, may not exist), the possibility is always on the tax policy agenda. When such switches in tax regime are implemented, drastic, order-of-magnitude changes can occur in the relative demand price of dividends, the supply price of dividends, or both.

In the United States, such changes in regime have unfortunately (or perhaps fortunately) been rare. A deduction at the corporate level for part of dividends paid was a feature of the recent Treasury tax reform bill, but it remains unlikely that academic researchers will ever have the benefit of observing that particular comet. Aside from these periodically proposed and usually aborted integration schemes (which would not leave even a trace for an event study) and some trivial relief under the personal income tax such as the flat $100 dividend exclusion

26. For a recent survey, see G. W. Schwert, "Size and Stock Returns and Other Empirical Regularities," *Journal of Financial Economics* 12, no. 1 (June, 1983): 3-12.

27. Donald Keim, "Size-related Anomalies and Stock Return Seasonality: Further Empirical Evidence," *Journal of Financial Economics* 12, no. 1 (June, 1983): 13-32.

28. Deleted from original at this point: "This should not be entirely surprising in view of the higher degree of collinearity between each of the intertwined effects and between each of them and the CAPM-based risk measure. There is the further complication that the true functional form of the relation between returns and the variables may not be the linear one to which we are effectively restricted. If, then, we happen to turn up a significant coefficient for one or more of our variables, how can we be confident that we are seeing genuine economic contributions and not mere correlations of the variable with residuals induced by the misrepresentation of the functional form?"

29. N.-F. Chen, B. Grundy, and R. Stambaugh, "Changing Risk, Changing Expectations, and the Relation between Expected Return and Dividend Yield," Mimeographed. Chicago: University of Chicago, Graduate School of Business, 1985.

30. If the tax penalty on dividends does not show up in the price of

dividends, where can it have gone? The answer to be offered in this paper (and proposed earlier by Black and Scholes, though in somewhat different terms) is that the quantity of dividends supplied has adjusted. The current equilibrium price of dividends, at the intersection of demand and supply, is now not easily distinguished from the price of capital gains, suggesting that the fabled "marginal shareholder" is a tax-exempt institution, or at least someone with a low cost of switching between dividends and capital gains.

31. Soon we may also have at least some indirect evidence as to whether the market for dividends is so far out of equilibrium as to generate substantial arbitraging side flows between "clienteles," i.e., between those who might have high relative demand prices for dividends and those who might have low cost demand prices. Recent Treasury rulings have permitted one firm, the Americus Trust, to purchase shares of ordinary corporations and reissue them in two pieces, one giving rights (essentially) to the dividends and the other (essentially) to the capital appreciation. The two pieces can be recombined at any time and turned in to the trust for a single underlying share. At present, only two stocks are involved, AT&T and Exxon, but more are promised. A separation of dividends and capital gains has long been available, though less efficiently, via so-called dual funds. The aggregate holdings of all such funds, however, represent only a tiny fraction of corporate shares outstanding.

During the two years of 1936 and 1937, when the cost of not paying dividends was increased so sharply, the flow of cash dividends paid surged dramatically.

(which, of course, affects no decisions at the margin), I am aware of only one major, detectable change of regime in the United States since the income tax took its modern form during World War I. I refer to the Undistributed Profits Tax of 1936. This now-all-but-forgotten piece of New Deal legislation levied a tax on corporate profits remaining after corporate income taxes (then at a rate of 11 percent in the top bracket), interest on U.S. government securities, and payment of taxable cash dividends. The rates of the undistributed profits tax were progressive, starting at 7 percent of undistributed profits and reaching a maximum rate of 27 percent when 100 percent of after-tax income was retained.

The tax was in force for only two years, 1936 and 1937. It was still technically on the books in 1938, but by then it had been virtually emasculated.[32] During the two years of 1936 and 1937, when the cost of not paying dividends was increased so sharply, the flow of cash dividends paid surged dramatically. A study undertaken shortly after the incident, while memories were still fresh, puts the extra flow of dividends (beyond what might normally have been expected at that stage of the business cycle) at about 33 1/3 percent.[33] A collapse of equivalent magnitude occurred in 1938, when the tax was, mercifully, put to death.

Although the episode of the Undistributed Profits Tax exhausts the list of major regime changes in the United States, the set of instructive experiments can be expanded substantially by drawing on experience from abroad. In 1973, for example, Canada abandoned its long-standing policy, common to all tax systems adapted from the old British model, of exempting from tax all capital gains and losses (except for brokers and others in the business of dealing in securities). The same Canadian statute also reduced effective tax rates on dividends so that the combined effect (though not uniform across all income levels) amounted on balance to a substantial tipping of the scales in favor of dividend income.

For the period immediately after the shift, Khoury and Smith report a significant increase in the rate of growth of dividends on the part of a representative sample of Canadian firms.[34] They also find significant differences, in the predicted direction, between the dividend payout policies before and after the tax change of their Canadian sample relative to a matched sample of comparable U.S. firms.

In Great Britain, as many as five distinct changes in tax regime can be discerned in the post-World War II era as Labour and Conservative governments alternated their tenure in office. The direction of change in the relative burdens on dividends and capital gains was not always uniform across all income levels; also, dividend responses by firms were inhibited over part of the period by direct controls on dividends.[35] Still, a study by Poterba and Summers was able to document reasonably clear signals of the appropriate kind being sent to management by changes in stock prices in the period following the changes and of an appropriate adaptation of dividend flow to those signals when firms had the freedom to do so.[36]

Although changes in tax regime provide the most dramatic and hence informative experiments, changes in the rate structure, if sudden enough and drastic enough, can be almost as effective. In the United States, for example, the transition of the income tax from a minor nuisance to a major engine of income redistribution was a matter of only a few years. Surtax rates on ordinary income, which would include dividends, surged upward in the mid-1930s and were ratcheted up again during the the rearmament period of the late 1930s and the war years of the early 1940s. The adustments of corporate payout policies (and of individual portfolio strategies) to the new environment was masked for a while by concern with other, even more massive tax effects on corporate profits--notably, those coming from the excess-profits tax and the carryback of postwar losses and unused credits against wartime taxes. But by the early 1950s, the increased reliance on retained earnings by U.S. corporations, compared with their payout practices in the 1920s and early 1930s, was widely noted among economists. In fact, it is worth remembering that the classic dividend

32. See D. L. Rolbein, "Noncash Dividends and Stock Rights as Methods for Avoidance of the Undistributed Profits Tax," *Journal of Business* 12, no. 3 (July, 1939): especially pp. 221-22, n.3.

33. See G. E. Lent, *The Impact of the Undistributed Profits Tax, 1936-37.* New York: Columbia University Press, 1948.

34. N. T. Khoury and K. V. Smith, "Dividend Policy and the Capital Gains Tax in Canada," *Journal of Business Administration* 8, no. 2 (Spring, 1977): 19-37.

35. The United Stated too has long been known to institute dividend controls. Under the Nixon price controls of 1973-74, dividend growth was to be

"voluntarily" restricted by firms to 5%. A noticeable bulge in share repurchases occurred during this period. In fact, some cynics regarded the spectacle of leading corporate officials standing at the side of Arthur Burns and calling for voluntary dividend restrictions as a classic example of the Brer Rabbit tactic of pleading not to be thrown into the briar patch.

36. J. M. Poterba and L. H. Summers, "The Economic Effects of Dividend Taxation," in E. Altman and M. Subrahmanyam (eds.), *Recent Advances in Corporate Finance.* Homewood, Ill.: Irwin, 1985.

study of John Lintner (1956) was undertaken precisely in response to the then-controversial issue of whether there had indeed been a fundamental shift in the corporate propensity to save.[37] Lintner concluded that there had not been a shift. But a subsequent, much more detailed study by John Brittain (1966) showed quite convincingly that a downward shift in corporate dividend payout policies had occurred and that it could not be attributed to any of the proposed explanatory factors other than the change in the tax environment.[38] Poterba and Summers, moreover, report that the shift first noted by Brittain appears to have been a permanent one. They find no signs in the period after Brittain's study of any return to prewar payout patterns.[39]

Although major tax changes of the kind discussed above are likely to provide the most direct demonstrations of the comparative statics of the finance/dividend model, they are certainly not the only detectable shocks to which the underlying demand curves and supply curves are subject. We seem, in fact, to be undergoing just such a major shock at the moment in the form of a dramatic reduction in the cost of going back and forth between cash and securities.

These costs of getting in and out of cash are important to the model if only because they are presumed to be a major part of what justifies our speaking of a demand curve for dividends. The direct and indirect costs of converting shares to cash, if high enough, create a demand for cash dividends, even on the part of taxable investors, that would support a nonzero equilibrium supply of dividends by the corporate sector. With the coming of discount brokers, however, and with new financial instruments such as Cash Management Accounts that can make a portfolio of stocks the virtual equivalent of a checking account, the liquidity benefits of dividend-paying shares are fast eroding. The demand curve for cash dividends would thus appear to be shifting to the left.[40] Furthermore, casual observation of corporate share repurchase activity (especially, but not only, in connection with well-publicized take-overs and recapitalizations) suggests that supply too is adjusting--but slowly. In the last

analysis, it may well be this slowness to adjust, as well the seemingly endless persistence on both sides of the market of long-outmoded habits of thought about dividends, that is at least partly responsible for the concern within the profession about the predictive power of the underlying model.

Some of what appears to be sluggishness in corporate dividend policies relative to model predictions can be traced to the failure, in the short run, of the model's strong information assumptions. The equilibrium conditions in the model are worked out under essentially "double dummy" rules in which all the players are presumed to know each other's cards. Over the long pull, disclosure policies, both mandatory and voluntary, may make this a reasonable enough approximation. But in the shorter run-- and certainly at the time that any single particular dividend in the temporal sequence is under active consideration--management can be presumed to know more than outside investors about the current and immediate prospects of the firm. Under these conditions of asymmetric information, dividend decisions can take on an additional strategic dimension that, on balance, tends to inhibit changes in policy. That inhibition is likely to be particularly strong where, as at present, the objective conditions seem to be suggesting a fall in the demand for dividends. Passing or cutting the dividend has often been taken by the market as a bad-news signal despite the most elaborate educational preparation by the management and its public relations support teams. Many, indeed, are the corporate treasurers who have wished to be the *second* major firm in their industry to slash dividends.

Taking these strategic and information-related elements more formally into the basic model is clearly desirable and is, in fact, currently the focus of much research.[41] But developments of the underlying apparatus in these directions should not be taken as implying any systematic drawing away from the rationality postulate. If anything, signaling models and other models in information economics tend, in some ways, to place even greater demands on the rationality assumption than the valuation models from which they are taken.[42]

37. J. Lintner, "The Distribution of Incomes of Corporations among Dividends, Retained Earnings and Taxes," *American Economic Review* 46 (May, 1956): 97-113.

38. J. Brittain, *Corporate Dividend Policy*, (Washington, D.C.: Brookings, 1966).

39. Poterba and Summers (1985, p. 270), cited in note 36.

40. It was thus somewhat ironic that dividend relief was included among the administration's and Ways and Means Committee tax reform proposals. The technological improvements and regulatory changes that have lowered the cost of security transactions by individuals have also done so for corporations. Reductions at that level have reduced the cost of both increasing dividends (by outside finance) and decreasing dividends (by share repurchase) so that the net effect remains unclear.

In the shorter run...management can be presumed to know more than outside investors about the current prospects of the firm. Under these conditions, dividend decisions can take on an additional strategic dimension that, on balance, tends to inhibit changes in policy.

Conclusion: What Role for Behavorial Models of Dividends?

The purpose of this paper has been to show that the rationality-based market equilibrium models in finance in general and of dividends in particular are alive and well—or at least in no worse shape than other comparable models in economics at their level of aggregation. The framework is not so weighed down with anomalies that a complete reconstruction (on behavioral/cognitive or other lines) is either needed or likely to occur in the near future.

Having tried to establish that, let me conclude on a more conciliatory note by freely conceding again that, at the most micro-decision level, behavioral/cognitive elements are very much a part of the picture.[43] If the concern is primarily with the fine details of specific cases (as it may well often tend to be in many business school finance classes), they cannot be ignored. It was not a lack of command over standard theoretical tools that led John Lintner to encapsulize his months of observation of actual dividend decisions in the neat little behavioral model we have all come to call the Lintner model.[44] (I assume it to be a behavioral model, not only from its form, but because no one has yet been able to derive it as the solution to a maximization problem, despite 30 year of trying!) Nor should we be surprised to find evidence of "satisficing," "organizational slack," "rules of thumb," or "bounded rationality" in the making of individual dividend decisions. Corporate treasurers have many

other, and often vastly more important, problems to contend with on a day-to-day basis, particularly in the volatile and takeover-jittery capital markets of recent years. The amounts of money involved in a quarterly dividend are typically not large in relation to corporate cash and financing flows (though crises do occasionally arise), and many corporate officers find it convenient under normal conditions to defer (or to pretend to defer) to the judgment of the firm's directors, who have the technical responsibility for declaring the dividend. Policy reviews and changes do occur, but only fitfully and at a pace that all recently hired M.B.A.'s are bound to regard as maddeningly slow.

The behavioral/cognitive elements in decisions involving dividends (including, perhaps, even some of the cognitive, cash-preference illusions imagined by Shefrin and Statman[45]) are also likely to loom larger for individual investors who hold modest amounts of stock directly and who, unlike institutional and other large investors, do not rely heavily on professional portfolio advisers. For these investors, stocks are usually more than just the abstract "bundles of returns" of our economic models. Behind each holding may be a story of family business, family quarrels, legacies received, divorce settlements, and a host of other considerations almost totally irrelevant to our theories of portfolio selection. That we abstract from all these stories in building our models is not because the stories are uninteresting, but because they may be too interesting and thereby distract us from the pervasive market forces that should be our principal concern.

Author's Note:

How the new tax law will affect corporate dividend policies is difficult to say at this point because so many changes were made at once and because they don't all push in the same direction. Certainly, lowering the top rate of taxation on dividends and raising the top rate on capital gains tilts against retaining cash earnings for investment in the corporation. But it doesn't follow that paying the cash out as dividends will be the best alternative. For many companies it may pay to recapitalize with debt, pay the cash out as

interest, and so at least avoid paying the still-heavy corporate income tax. For others, given the diminution of the traditional capital-gains offset to the heavy penalty of double taxation of corporate earnings, it may even pay to abandon the corporate form of organization altogether. About all we can confidently predict as of now is that capital structure, dividend policy, and organizational form will continue to be major issues in finance in both academia and in practice.

—Merton Miller

41. For a survey of some recent efforts, see my paper, "The Informational Content of Dividends," in J. Bossons, R. Dornbusch, and S. Fischer (eds.), *Macroeconomics: Essays in Honor of Franco Modigliani,* (Cambridge, Mass.: MIT Press, forthcoming 1987).

42. The same strong thread of rationality also runs through another and even larger current stream of research in finance, i.e., the literature on agency theory and optimal contracting.

43. See my article, "Debt and Taxes," *Journal of Finance* 32, no. (May, 1977): especially pages 272-273.

44. Lintner, 1956, cited earlier in note 37.

45. Sheffrin and Statman, cited earlier in note 2.

AN ANALYSIS OF CALL PROVISIONS AND THE CORPORATE REFUNDING DECISION

by Alan Kraus,
University of California at Los Angeles

Introduction

Almost all publicly-traded corporate bonds, and most preferred stock issues, have call provisions written into their indenture agreements. Such provisions allow the issuer to repurchase the bonds or preferreds at a specified price (generally expressed as a percentage above par value). As a rule, the call privilege cannot be exercised until the "deferred call" period—usually five to ten years from the date of issue—has elapsed. When interest rates fall, corporate treasurers servicing long-term bonds issued at higher rates thus have the option of calling those bonds, and replacing them with a new issue. The purpose of a bond refunding, in such cases, seems to be to reduce current interest costs.

The callability of bond and preferred stock issues raises two questions that corporate treasurers must address. The first is whether to issue callable bonds in the first place, rather than an equivalent but noncallable issue. The second, and more often asked, is: Given that a callable bond or preferred has been issued, when does it make sense to call and refund it?

Why corporations routinely attach call provisions to their bond issues remains an unresolved question in academic finance literature. In the first part of this article, I focus primarily on the "classic" motive: reduction of interest costs. If management, or its financial advisors, has superior ability to forecast interest rates, then it is quite easy to explain why, and under what circumstances, management would choose to attach a call provision to a new issue. But if corporate management has no special foreknowledge of future interest rates, as capital market theory would suggest, then the incentives to make a new bond issue callable are less clear. Tax considerations, restrictive bond covenants, and the reduction of corporate risk are the other possibilities I explore. All in all, though, it appears that no single factor has yet been identified that adequately explains the call provisions observed on virtually all corporate bonds and preferred stock.

In the second part of the article, I offer a relatively simple and straightforward refunding strategy. The conventional wisdom on the bond refunding issue, which reflects most of the available finance literature, has made the refunding decision depend heavily on management's interest rate forecasts. My prescription, grounded in principles of options pricing, finally has nothing to do with management's expertise in forecasting interest rates.

The call provisions on corporate bonds, I will argue, are much like the call options on stocks traded on the Chicago Board Options Exchange. The corporate refunding strategy should be designed to maximize the value of the company's call option on its bond, thus minimizing the value of the outstanding bonds. Ignoring the costs of a new issue, the prescription that comes out of this analysis is very simple: call the bond as soon as its price reaches the call price. When new issue expenses are included in the analysis, the optimal refunding strategy is a little more complicated. The basic principles are the same, however, and a refunding rule can still be stated in fairly simple terms.

The Call Provision

How Much Does It Cost?

As suggested, the most obvious reason for management to include call provisions in indenture agreements is to preserve the option, should inter-

Calling bonds to refinance at a lower interest rate is a "zero sum game" between shareholders and bondholders.

est rates fall, of refinancing high-interest debt at lower rates. The stronger management's conviction that rates will fall, and the steeper the expected fall, the stronger is this motive for including the call provision. It should be recognized, however, that the bond markets are not likely to have significantly different expectations about future rates. To the extent that investors share management's conviction that long-term rates will fall from current levels (which, in most cases, will already be reflected in an inverted yield curve), this motive for including the call provision loses its justification.

As was pointed out a decade ago,[1] calling bonds to refinance them at a lower interest rate is a "zero sum game" between shareholders and bondholders. Any expected gains to the issuer from being allowed to refund a bond at a lower rate are expected losses to (or, more precisely, capital gains foreited by) the bondholders from having to accept a lower rate on their funds. Exercise of the call privilege is the issuer's prerogative and thus will occur only when it benefits shareholders at the expense (in almost all cases) of bondholders. Bondholders, however, are well aware of this possibility and price bond issues accordingly. For this reason, they demand higher rates of interest on callable than on otherwise equivalent noncallable bonds.

Stated most simply, the coupon rate on a *callable* bond issue must be set high enough to make the present value of expected payments to bondholders (based on the probability that the bonds are actually called) the same as if the issue were non-callable.[2] This means that if management and investors hold identical expectations about interest rates, the higher coupon rate that just allows a callable bond to sell at par would make management indifferent between the alternatives of (1) including the call provision and paying a higher rate and (2) issuing a non-callable issue, also at par, but paying a lower rate.

A simple numerical example will illustrate the point. Assume that management plans to issue perpetual bonds of $100 face value with annual coupons, and that a coupon rate of 15 percent would allow a *noncallable* issue to be sold at par. Suppose further that all market participants agree there is a 50 percent chance that, a year from now, the going yield on perpetual, noncallable bonds will have

fallen to 12 percent. If the rate does fall to 12 percent, the noncallable bond with a 15 percent coupon rate will be trading at $125 (=$15/0.12). There is also an equal chance that the going yield will rise to 20 percent, thus causing the same bond to trade at $75 ($15/0.20). Finally, assuming that the current one-year interest rate is also 15 percent, equal to the long-term rate, we can see (below) that the noncallable issue would sell at par:

$$V_{Noncallable} = \frac{\text{First year's coupon} + \text{Expected price at year end}}{1.0 + \text{One-year rate}}$$

$$= \frac{\$15 + (.5)(\$125) + (.5)(\$75)}{1.15} = \$100$$

Suppose instead that management proposes to make the bond callable one year hence, *and only then*, at a call premium of $15 over par. If the noncallable yield next year falls to 12 percent, then all market participants agree the company will exercise its call privilege. In this case, the call provision allows management to retire for $115 ($100 par value plus the $15 premium) a security that would otherwise, in the absence of a call provision, be worth $125 to the bondholders. To put it a little differently, the call privilege enables the company to retire for $115 a security paying $15 per annum, which could then be immediately reissued, in the form of a noncallable bond paying the same $15, for proceeds of $125 (excluding new issue costs). Thus, if rates fall to 12 percent, exercise of the call has the effect of transferring $10 of bondholders' capital gains to shareholders.

Because of this possibility of forfeiting part of their expected gains to shareholders, investors will not pay $100 for the *callable* bond carrying only a 15 percent coupon rate. In fact, under the conditions described above, the market would require a coupon rate of 16.43 percent for the callable bond to be issued at par:

$$V_{Callable} = \frac{\$16.43 + (.5)(\$115) + (.5)(\frac{\$16.43}{0.20})}{1.15} = \$100$$

The issuer's choice here is thus between issuing a noncallable bond with a 15 percent coupon rate and a callable bond requiring payments of 16.43 percent. In this case, the cost of including the call privi-

1. This observation was first made by Stewart Myers in a "Discussion" appearing in the *Journal of Finance*, Vol. 26, No. 2 (1971). Its implications were discussed in my own article, "The Bond Refunding Decision in an Efficient Market," *Journal of Financial and Quantitative Analysis*, Vol. 8, No. 5 (1973).

2. This ignores the effect of differences in default risk among companies, and the risk aversion of investors.

lege is 143 basis points.

Just how large an increment to the coupon rate would be required in an actual issue will obviously depend on a great many factors. There is little evidence on the size of this increment, partly because it is hard to measure directly when virtually all corporate issues are callable. One study of the debt of A.T.&T. and subsidiaries estimated a coupon rate increment of 30 basis points required by tax-exempt investors for callable bonds with yields in the 8 percent range.[3] Given today's higher interest rates, and the much larger variation over time in rates, the required coupon rate increment might well be several times this amount. The greater the possibility and magnitude of a fall in rates, the larger the cost of including the call provision. For example, the more downward sloping the yield curve, the greater the required premium in coupon rate for issuing a callable.

Let's now estimate the value of the call provision from the standpoint of the corporate issuer. To calculate the present value of expected payments on the callable bond, start by assuming that a coupon of $16.43 is made the first year. If rates rise to 20 percent, then the call is not exercised and annual payments of $16.43 continue in perpetuity. If rates fall to 12 percent, the bond will be called for $115. It can then be replaced with a noncallable promising $16.43 per year in perpetuity, which can be sold for $136.92 ($16.43/0.12).

Thus, in the case of a callable bond, the stream of expected payments can be viewed as a series of certain annual payments of $16.43 reduced by a 50 percent chance of a $21.92 ($136.92 − $115) gain to shareholders one year hence. The present value of the stream of expected payments is:

$$V = \frac{\$16.43}{0.15} - \frac{(.5)(\$21.92)}{1.15} = \$109.53 - \$9.53 = \$100$$

This is identical to the present value of payments under the noncallable alternative. Under the conditions described above, management should have no preference between issuing a 15 percent noncallable bond and a 16.43 percent callable bond.

In practice, of course, call provisions extend over many years, so that the comparison facing the

financial manager rests on much more complicated interest rate scenarios than the one in our example. Still, the basic principles are the same.

Valuing the Call Privilege

The call privilege is very similar to the call options on stocks traded by individual investors. In fact, a callable bond can be viewed as a noncallable bond on which the purchaser (the bondholder) has written a call option held by the issuer (the borrowing company).[4] There are two major differences, however, between the corporate issuer's option to call its bonds, and the call options on securities available to individual investors. First, in buying a callable bond issue, all purchasers automatically assume liability for the call option; the option cannot be detached from the underlying security. Second, the company's call option cannot be sold—it can only be exercised or allowed to expire. With these qualifications, then, the value of a callable bond can be expressed as follows:

Callable Bond = Noncallable Bond − Call Option

Continuing with the example from the previous section, recall that the value of the callable, perpetual bond carrying a $16.43 coupon is $100. At the same time, a noncallable, perpetual bond offering a coupon payment of $16.43 per year would have a value of $109.53 ($16.43/0.15) when the yield on such bonds is 15 percent. In this case, then, the value of the call option is $9.53, which is exactly the present value of the expected gain from exercise of the call privilege as calculated in the previous section.

Using the formulation above as a framework for examining the decision to issue a callable bond, I now want to consider reasons why the corporate issuer might place a higher value on the call option than investors who buy the bonds.

1. Call Provisions & Interest Rate Forecasting

As with any option, paying for the call privilege represents a gamble on future events that the buyer of the option takes against the writer of the option. In the case of the call privilege on a bond, the gam-

3. See W.M. Boyce and A.J. Kalay, "Tax Differentials and Callable Bonds," *Journal of Finance*, Volume 34, Number 4 (1979).

4. This view of the call provision is implicit in the analysis by Michael Brennan and Eduardo Schwartz in "Convertible Bonds: Valuation and Optimal Strategies for Call and Conversion," *Journal of Finance*, Volume 32, Number 5 (1977). It has also been discussed by J.B. Yawitz and J.A. Anderson in "The Effect of Bond Refunding on Shareholder Wealth," *Journal of Finance*, Volume 32, Number 5 (1977).

ble is on the future course of interest rates. If bond issuers believe they are more astute than the bond market in general, and if they feel rates are likely to fall significantly before the bond matures, they might be convinced the gamble is loaded in their favor. In this case, they might have good reason to attach a call provision to the issue.

Returning to our earlier illustration, assume once more that investors believe the odds of interest rates going to 12 percent or 20 percent are each one-half. Suppose, however, that management does not share this belief. Instead they assign a 60 percent probability to a rate of 12 percent, and only 40 percent to the chance of its rising to 20 percent. For our perpetual bond paying $16.43 annually and callable at $115, when the rate drops to 12 percent, the value of the bond (without the call provision) rises to $136.92 ($16.43/0.12), and management exercises the call privilege. The shareholders realize a gain, and the bondholders a loss, of $21.92 ($136.92 − $115). In this case, the call option will be valued at $11.44 (.6 × $21.92/1.15) by the issuer and at $9.53 (.5 × $21.92/1.15) by investors.

Thus, if the callable bond is issued at a price between $98.09 ($109.53 − $11.44) and $100, it will be preferred to the noncallable alternative by *both* the corporate issuer and investors. Management will have purchased a call option for less than its perceived value of $11.44, while bondholders receive more than the $9.53 of capital gains they expect to give up through exercise of the call.

Management may also prefer the callable alternative if it believes there is a chance of a greater drop in interest rates than investors foresee—even if management assigns a smaller probability to rates falling than investors. For example, assume investors still believe the chance of rates going to 12 percent is one-half. Suppose management foresees only a 30 percent probability that rates will fall, but believes that if a decline does occur, it will result in a rate of 10 percent. An interest rate at this level would raise the value of the bond (without the call provision) to $164.30 ($16.43/.10), producing a gain to shareholders of $49.30 from exercising the call privilege. The call option will then be valued by the issuer at $12.86 (.3 × $49.30/1.15).

Because investors will still value the call option at $9.53, the callable bond can be issued at any price between $96.67 ($109.53 − $12.86) and $100; and it will again be preferred to the noncallable by both issuer and investors. The point is that the value of the call option depends on both the chance of interest rates falling and on the magnitude of the fall.

There are several compelling reasons, however, for doubting that callable bonds are issued primarily because of management's confidence in its ability to forecast interest rates. First, although managers possess inside information about their companies' prospects, it is difficult to see why they should have any comparative advantage over the general market in forecasting an economy-wide variable such as the level of interest rates. Indeed, given the structure of incentives, we would expect market investors to be, if anything, better informed than corporate treasurers on interest rate developments.

Second, assuming that corporate management could consistently outperform bondholders in predicting interest rates, this fact would become known over time by bond investors as they watched how, on average, they (the bondholders) lost money on the call provision. In pricing future callable issues, investors would interpret the call provision as a signal of management's expectation that rates were likely to fall below current levels. Having recognized managers' forecasting superiority, investors would insist on further increases in the coupon rate until management would finally see the benefits of including the call provision nullified by the increased cost of the call. Under these circumstances, one would expect new bond issues to be divided fairly evenly between callables and noncallables.

Third, even if issuers proved consistently right in forecasting interest rates and bondholders remained unaware of their own relative forecasting deficiency, we would still expect new issues to be split between callables and noncallables. For, management will place more value than investors on the call privilege only when they are more confident that rates will *fall*. If management were convinced rates could only go higher, there would be no reason to incorporate the call provision. A consistent preference for issuing callables thus rests not only on management's superior forecasting, but also on the belief that, during the period the call is in effect, rates are always likely to fall well below current levels. Neither of these conditions is consistently reliable. That both should hold simultaneously seems highly improbable, to say the least.

2. The Call Provision and Taxes

In our earlier examples, no consideration was given to the effect of taxes paid by either the investor or the issuing company. When taxes are introduced, and provided the bondholder is taxed at a lower marginal rate than the corporation, a callable bond will be preferred to its noncallable equivalent by both the investor and the company.

To illustrate the tax argument, let us assume the investor is a tax-exempt institution, such as a pension fund, while the issuer pays a 50 percent corporate income tax. Coupon and call premium payments are, of course, taxable income to the bondholder and deductible by the issuing company.

Because the investor pays no tax, our example shows that he will be indifferent between the 15 percent noncallable bond and the 16.43 percent callable bond. From the issuer's viewpoint, however, the alternatives must be evaluated using after-tax discount rates applied to after-tax cash flows.

The introduction of taxes does not affect the value of the noncallable bond:

$$V = \frac{\text{After-tax coupon}}{\text{After-tax discount rate}} = \frac{(.50)(\$15)}{(.50)(.15)} = \$100$$

For the callable bond, however, an after-tax calculation from the issuer's standpoint produces a different result. The after-tax value of the $16.43 coupon is $8.21. Because the call premium is tax-deductible to the company, the after-tax value of the $115 call price is $107.50 ($100 + (.50 × $15)). Similarly, if bond yields rise to 20 percent, the after-tax rate is 10 percent; and given that the current one-year interest rate is 15 percent, the one-year after-tax discount rate becomes 7.5 percent. Thus, the after-tax cost of the callable bond to the issuer is calculated as follows:

$$\frac{\$8.21 + (.5)(\$107.50) + (.5)(\$8.21/0.10)}{1.075} = \$95.82$$

The corporate issuer will thus prefer the callable at any price above $95.82 to the noncallable equivalent issued at par. Tax-exempt investors will prefer the callable bond at any price below $100. Thus, at any price within this range, both the issuer and the investor gain from the inclusion of the call provision.

The simplest explanation for this tax advantage is that the call provision, with the associated higher coupon rate, transfers tax-deductible interest costs from later to earlier periods. This increases the present value of the interest tax shield to the company. Whenever the lender has a lower tax rate than the borrower, it is to their mutual advantage to arrange a loan having higher taxable payments at the start and lower taxable payments later.[5]

This tax argument is correct as far as it goes. But as a complete explanation for the almost universal inclusion of call provisions, it has some shortcomings. For one thing, there are certainly bond investors whose marginal tax rates are not lower than those of corporations issuing callable bonds. If callable bonds are priced so that investors with tax rates no lower than the corporate rate are willing to hold them, then the potential tax benefits from debt financing fall entirely to those investors with lower tax rates. Under these circumstances, there is no corporate tax incentive to issue callable instead of noncallable bonds.

What evidence we have,[7] however, suggests that the implied tax rate on corporate bonds is roughly 20 to 30 percent, which, while significantly greater than zero, is still a good deal lower than the statutory corporate rate of 46 percent. Thus, there is probably yet some tax advantage to callable over noncallable bonds.

In the case of preferred stock, however, the tax incentives would appear to favor noncallable over callable issues. Preferred stock dividends are not deductible for corporate taxes; and to the extent that the marginal tax rate of investors pricing preferred issues is positive,[8] companies should benefit by deferring payments to investors through the noncallable alternative. Because the inclusion of call provisions on preferred issues is virtually as automatic as on bond issues, the tax explanation does not fully account for the prevalence of callable bonds.

3. The Call Provision, Bond Covenants, and Operating Flexibility

Because bondholders are not represented on the corporation's board of directors, bond indenture agreements contain various covenants and re-

---

5. This explanation is at the heart of the tax advantage of zero coupon bonds, in which the investor effectively receives all interest payments, and the corporation a large part of its tax shield, in the early years.

6. Indeed, in an address to the American Finance Association in 1976, Merton Miller went so far as to suggest that corporations would continue to issue debt until the tax rate of the marginal bond investor equaled the marginal corporate rate, thus nullifying the tax advantage of debt relative to equity financing.

7. See, for example, David Pyle, "Is Deep Discount Debt Financing a Bargain?" in Chase Financial Quarterly, Vol. 1, Issue 1 (1981).

8. Because preferreds are sold largely to institutional or corporate investors, which are usually either tax-exempt or have an 85 percent exclusion, preferred issues carry rates far below bond issues. Thus, in the case of preferred issues, there is probably no tax-based reason to prefer either option: noncallable or callable.

Call provisions seem unnecessarily inefficient if management's main purpose is to preserve options to invest or disinvest.

strictions to persuade bond market investors to hold corporate debt. Such covenants often restrict a company's investment decisions, forbidding mergers or the sale of certain assets. Corporate issuers agree to these restrictions because they reduce investor uncertainty and the negative effects of bondholders' perceived lack of control over management decisions. Imposing such restrictions effectively reduces the interest costs of a new issue.

In certain cases, however, such covenants may prove so restrictive that the cost to the company in foregone opportunities may exceed their savings in capital-raising costs. One plausible motive for including call provisions in the company's debt is to provide a way of getting around such restrictions. Suppose, for example, that a merger opportunity comes along that represents a positive net present value investment. At the same time, however, undertaking such a merger would increase the risk of the bonds, thus reducing their value. If the indenture agreement contains a restriction on mergers, bondholders will invoke the restrictions to prevent the merger. If the bonds are noncallable, the only recourse of the shareholders would be to repurchase all the bonds. This move could be doomed, however, because the bondholders could demand to receive all of the net gain from the merger (say, in the form of convertible bonds) in return for renegotiating the covenants.

If the bonds are callable, however, the call price places an upper limit on what the issuer must pay to redeem the bonds. This flexibility to undertake otherwise restricted investments may partly explain the customary inclusion of call provisions in corporate bond issues.[9] Many deferred call provisions explicitly distinguish between a call for the purpose of refunding the debt at lower interest rates (which cannot be done during the deferment period) and a call for redemption without refunding (which can be done any time). The latter kind of provision seems more clearly intended to preserve management's investment and operating flexibility.

This rationale for the call provision, however, is also far from complete. The call provisions actually included in indenture agreements seem unnecessarily inefficient if management's main purpose is to preserve options to invest or disinvest. Because call prices are generally fixed at a percentage above

face value, calling a bond issue rarely makes sense unless the bonds are trading near or above par. When issues are selling at deep discounts from par, the size of the premium over market necessary to redeem the bonds will offset, in most cases, the gains expected from pursuing the restricted investment opportunity.

Indeed, as interest rates rise above the coupon rate on a callable bond, the value of the call option (in terms both of preserved operating flexibility and expected interest savings) to the company is effectively driven to zero. If call provisions were designed expressly to preserve management's flexibility (regardless of the course of market interest rates), the call price should be specified as a premium *not* over par, but over the discounted value of the coupons and principal on the bond, using as a discount rate the current long-term Government bond rate, or a well-defined long-term yield index. Defined and indexed in this manner, a call provision (solely for the purpose of redemption, not refunding) would make exercise of the call privilege equally attractive regardless of the current level of interest rates. Because call provisions are not written this way, we can conclude that management's desire to preserve investment options, although no doubt important in some cases, does not explain the near universal use of the call provision.

4. The Call Provision and Reduction of Interest Rate Risk

There is still one other potential advantage provided by the call feature on corporate bonds or preferred stock. Although this explanation has received little, if any, attention in the finance literature, it offers another clue to the puzzle—one that gets closest to management's concern about the need to protect the company against exposure to changes in interest rates. Whether such concern is legitimate, however, and whether most large, well-diversified public corporations should actively manage interest rate risk are open questions.[10]

The essence of the argument is that the call provision reduces the sensitivity of the bond's (or preferred's) value to movements in interest rates. Interest rate volatility means greater variability in bond prices, and thus greater risk for bondholders.

---

9. See Z. Bodie and R. A. Taggart, "Future Investment Opportunities and the Value of the Call Provision on a Bond," *Journal of Finance*, Volume 33, No. 4 (1978).

10. See Bluford Putnam's "Managing Interest Rate Risk: An Introduction to Financial Futures and Options," *Chase Financial Quarterly*, Vol. 1, Issue No. 3.

Changes in interest rates, especially in real interest rates, also have a major impact on the economy. Increases in real interest rates, such as those experienced during the first year and a half of the Reagan administration, raise all investors' expected returns, thus depressing the value of not only bonds, but corporate assets and stock prices as well. In this sense, stockholders, like bondholders, may be subject to interest rate risk.

My argument is that, by reducing the sensitivity of a bond's value to the systematic risk of interest rate movements, the call provision may reduce the systematic risk of shareholders as well as bondholders.

To see how the call provision reduces the sensitivity of the bond's value to changes in interest rates, recall the earlier formulation:

$$\frac{\text{Callable}}{\text{Bond}} = \text{Noncallable Bond} - \text{Call Option}$$

As market interest rates rise, the market values of the noncallable bond and the call option held by the company both decline. Thus, the difference between their values—that is, the value of the callable bond—changes less than the value of the noncallable bond.

To return once more to our example, if interest rates one year hence are either 20 percent or 12 percent, the value of the noncallable bond will be either $75 ($15/0.20) or $125 ($15/0.12). Given the same interest rate forecast, however, the value of the callable bond will be either $82.15 ($16.43/0.20) or $115. (Remember the $115 assumes the bond is called when rates fall to 12 percent.) Thus, with the same expectations for interest rates, the value of the noncallable bond will fall or rise by $25; the callable bond's value will fall $17.85 or rise $15.

Assuming that the values of enough companies are sensitive to interest movements such that changes in rates systematically affect the value of the market portfolio, interest rate changes are a component of market-wide, systematic risk. If so, the question becomes: How does a reduction in the systematic risk of a company's bonds affect the risk of its stockholders' investment? The answer depends largely on how the company's operating cash flows (and thus the value of the company's assets) are affected by changes in interest rates and inflation.

If the company's earnings keep pace with interest rates, and thus its real, inflation-adjusted cash flows remain relatively constant over time, then a reduction in the systematic risk of the company's debt represents a reduction in the risk of its equity as well. (In fact, such a company is really not exposed to any systematic interest rate risk.[11]) To see why this is so, recall that the market value of the firm (i.e., the discounted value of expected future cash flows) can be viewed as the sum of the market values of its debt and equity. Formulated in an equation,

$$V_F = \frac{\text{Normalized Annual Cashflow}}{\text{Cost of Capital}} = V_D + V_E$$

Solving for the value of the equity,

$$V_E = V_F - V_D$$

Holding real operating cash flows constant (and this of course is the crucial assumption), it is clear that the use of a call provision to reduce the sensitivity of the bonds' value to interest changes benefits shareholders by reducing the risk of the equity. Lower risk, other things equal, means higher stock prices.

Conversely, for those companies whose assets contain real, systematic risk due to interest rate movements (that is, their real operating cash flows and hence the value of their assets fall when inflation and interest rates rise), the systematic risk of the equity will actually be increased by making the bonds callable.

The values of companies in industries with high asset turnover (retailing, for example) are generally less sensitive to interest rate movements. Therefore, such companies might have more reason to include call provisions in their bonds. At the other extreme are industries, like mining and heavy manufacturing, with very long-lived assets and a resulting greater sensitivity of total real value to interest rate movements. Companies in these industries would have less reason for including—and indeed perhaps a positive reason for not having—a call provision in their bond agreements.

The Refunding Decision

Most of the voluminous literature dealing with callable bonds has been concerned with the refund-

---

11. In the case of near perfect correlation between interest rates and operating cash flows, floating rate debt is actually the best prescription. Floating-rate debt is an extreme form of the call provision, in the sense that it comes closest to stabilizing the value of the debt at par.

ing question: When does it make sense to call an outstanding bond issue and replace it with another? Even if the decision to include or exclude a call provision in a bond issue is largely irrelevant, once management has chosen to pay the higher cost to make the bonds callable, the refunding decision definitely "matters."[12]

How to Measure the Value of Calling a Bond Issue

In measuring the benefits of a refunding to shareholders, the traditional literature assumes that the refunding will result in debt carrying lower coupon payments, but the same principal. Comparing new debt with lower coupon obligations to an outstanding issue with the same face value assumes, in effect, that management has changed its leverage target—not as measured in book terms, but in terms of the market value of future obligations. As such, the traditional comparison actually reflects the value of interest savings not only from exercise of the call provision, but also from a decrease in the company's market leverage ratio.

Recall that a callable bond is equivalent to a noncallable bond promising the same stream of promised coupons and principal plus a call option on the noncallable bond held by the corporate issuer. The stream of promised coupons and principal is, of course, a liability of the firm. The call option, however, should be viewed as an asset. Therefore, to isolate the value of a refunding from the effect of a change in leverage, it is necessary to assume that when the call option is exercised, the retired debt is replaced with the same stream of promised payments. This effectively fixes the liability leverage ratio, measured in terms of the market value of promised payments.[13]

Furthermore, as suggested earlier, the value of the call provision comes from management's ability to repurchase (at below its market value) a noncallable bond having coupons and principal equal to those of the callable bond. This tells us that the benefit of a refunding should be calculated assuming the retired debt will be replaced with *noncallable* bonds, even when the intended new issue is callable. The value of exercising the call provision,

therefore, is the market value of the promised payments of the callable bond (without the call provision) less the call price (and all incremental costs associated with a refunding).

This method for quantifying the benefits of a refunding, as the reader may recall, was illustrated in our earlier numerical example. Remember that if the going yield on (noncallable) bonds falls to 12 percent, the noncallable equivalent value of a callable paying 15 percent rises to $125 ($15/.12). If the call price is $115, the current exercise value of the company's call option on its bonds is $10. To determine the net benefit of a refunding, the value of this call option would then be reduced by the after-tax present value of the expenses of issuing replacement bonds.

Even if the net benefit is positive, however, it does not necessarily follow that the optimal decision is to call the bonds immediately. The reason is simple: the optimal time to "cash in" the call privilege by exercising it is when the value of doing so is *greatest*, not merely when it has become positive.

The Refunding Rule Without New Issue Expenses

In the pages that follow, I am going to concentrate on the question of refunding policy for *publicly-traded* bonds. This will allow us to state a refunding rule which relies on bond prices alone. In the case of private placements, the refunding principle is fundamentally the same. In the absence of directly observable prices, however, management must rely on estimates of yields on equivalent *noncallable* corporate bonds (see previous paragraph) to make the refunding decision.

The guiding principle for the optimal call policy can best be illustrated by returning to the earlier formulation of a callable bond as a noncallable bond combined with a short position (from the bondholder's perspective) in a call option:

Callable Bond = **Noncallable Bond** − **Call Option**

Because the callable bond represents a liability of shareholders, maximizing shareholders' value

---

12. See Myers and Kraus, both articles cited earlier and in References.

13. Effectively, the call option has been converted into cash by being exercised. While it is true that the shift in assets from converting the call option into cash may itself represent a change in leverage, this is of secondary significance compared to the change in the present value of promised debt payments.

means minimizing the value of the callable bond. The value of the noncallable is determined largely by market interest rates. Consequently, minimizing the value of the callable bond means adopting that refunding policy which maximizes the value of the company's call option.[14]

This prescription admittedly ignores the costs of issuing replacement bonds. But, it is helpful to begin the analysis by setting aside such costs. In many cases, management may feel that the extra issue expenses associated with a refunding are trivial. For a large bond issue, direct flotation costs may be on the order of 1 percent or less of face value—less than one month's interest cost. Only direct flotation costs are really incremental to a refunding, since duplicate interest payments can be offset by holding the funds in interest-bearing securities.

The optimal refunding policy depends, to a large extent, on how the prices of callable bonds behave as interest rates fall and the bonds trade near the call price. The value of a *noncallable* bond, assuming no risk of default, would depend largely on the current level of interest rates. The value of a *callable* bond also depends primarily on the level of interest rates—at least over a certain range of (higher) interest rates. But, as interest rates fall lower and lower, the price begins to be influenced progressively more by investors' expectations about when the bonds will be called.

Investors' expectations, however, are conditioned by management's past behavior in calling bonds, thus creating a circular chain of causality. The refunding rule I propose relies completely on observable bond prices. Accordingly, it must be based on what refunding policy the bond market is expecting management to follow. To make the truly optimal refunding decision (on the basis of foresight, not hindsight), managers must *know* exactly what investors expect management to do, given the opportunity to refund at a given interest rate. Although far from self-evident at this point, all this will become much clearer as we proceed.

It does not make sense to base a refunding policy on the assumption that bondholders are naive. Bondholders would certainly prefer that corporate treasurers never exercise the call privilege. If such behavior became the rule, then bond prices would continue to rise ever higher above their call price as interest rates fell ever lower. The bond market, however, recognizes that corporate managements are paid to act in the interests of shareholders, not bondholders. Therefore, we should begin by assuming that, in pricing callable bonds, the market expects management to make refunding decisions designed to increase shareholder wealth—by limiting the value of outstanding bonds.

For those companies whose new issue expenses are relatively trivial, the optimal refunding rule is very simple: call the bonds *as soon as* their price reaches the call price. Such a policy maximizes the value of the corporate option, minimizing the value of outstanding bonds. Furthermore, refunding should be undertaken at the same time the bonds are called under this rule, provided management accepts the market's expectations about future interest rates. If management has different expectations than the market, and is willing to act on them, then this may lead management to modify its *refunding* strategy. Nevertheless, management should still *call* the bonds as soon as their price reaches the call price.

If the bonds are trading below the call price, it is clear that an immediate call is not optimal. In this case, exercising the call privilege would give the bondholders an amount greater than the bonds market value. But if the callable bonds are trading at the call price, it is not optimal to delay exercising the call privilege as interest rates fall by even a slight amount. As soon as the market realized that management was delaying the call, the bonds would move a bit higher in price. Since the aim should be to minimize the value of the callable bonds, management should prevent this price move by calling the bonds as soon as they trade at the call price.

Suppose interest rates have dropped enough that the bonds are trading at their call price, but management is convinced that rates will soon fall much lower. Wouldn't it be justified in delaying a refunding to obtain a lower interest rate? Ignoring issue expenses, the answer is no: the bonds should be called now and refunded with a new issue. But, at the same time, management should insist that the replacement bonds be callable at any time after issue. This new call option could be purchased at a much lower premium in coupon rate than it is worth *if* management is correct that rates are about

---

14. This argument was put forth by Brennan and Schwartz, cited earlier, and and by Jonathan Ingersoll in "A Contingent-Claims Valuation of Convertible Securities," *Journal of Financial Economics*, Volume, Number 3 (1977).

to fall. The corporate treasurer who takes this action is essentially speculating *against the market* on interest rates. I doubt that this is a wise course to follow but, in any case, it does not change the rule I have given for the optimal time to call the bonds.

The Refunding Rule With New Issue Costs

As demonstrated earlier, the value of a callable bond to investors includes the present value of the call premium bondholders receive if the bonds are called. This value does not, of course, include the amount of issue expenses connected with the replacement bonds (although, as we shall see, bond prices are definitely affected by the existence of these costs). If such expenses are relatively important, the principle of maximizing the value of the corporate call option should be modified to accommodate these additional costs. With this in mind, maximizing the value of the call privilege to shareholders means minimizing the value of the callable bond plus new issue expenses associated with the refunding.

As a first step, assume management formulates its refunding policy in terms of a critical level of a specific market interest rate. That is, assume management has decided to call and refund outstanding bonds carrying a, say, 14 percent coupon when the yield on 30-year government bonds falls to 8 percent. If the yields on corporate bonds trading *without* the call privilege could be directly observed, then the refunding policy could be formulated in terms of corporate yields: i.e., "Call when the single-A (noncallable) yield falls to 10 percent." But, because virtually all corporate bonds are callable, the yields on noncallable corporate bonds are usually not observable. For this reason, we must use the yields on long-term government bonds as a proxy for "the interest rate."

When bonds are trading well below par, a fall in interest rates generally causes an increase in bond prices roughly equal to the increase in present value of the promised coupons and principal. But, when bonds are trading above par value, and "the interest rate" approaches the critical level at which the market anticipates a call, bond prices will begin to move in a very different pattern. This pattern of interest rate changes and callable bond prices is shown in Figure 1.

The solid curve in the diagram represents the value of the callable bond as the interest rate varies. The dashed curve represents what the market value of the bonds would be, were they not callable.

At all interest rates lower than (to the left of) R_1, the gross benefits of refunding (before new issue costs) are positive. However, the path of callable bond prices above assumes that the market does not expect management to call the bonds until the interest rate falls to R^*.

The first question that arises, then, is: If refunding appears beneficial at interest rates higher than R^*, why would the market expect management to wait for a rate decline to R^* before calling the bonds?

As I emphasized in the previous section, the benefit to shareholders of a refunding comes from repurchasing the stream of promised coupons and principal at less than its market value. In terms of Figure 1, this means that management would surely not want to call the bonds when the interest rate is above (to the right of) R_1. In this range of interest rates, the market value of the stream of coupons and principal is less than the call price. Refunding in this range would mean a loss to shareholders, even before considering the costs of a new issue.

When the interest rate is between R_1 and R_2, though the gross benefit to refunding is positive, the market value of the callable bonds is less than their call price. Exercising the call privilege in this situation would give bondholders an amount greater than the bonds' market value, thus penalizing shareholders. If corporations regularly followed such a policy, the bond market would anticipate such action by bidding up the price of the bonds to their call price as they reached that interest rate (between R_1 and R_2) which triggers their call.

Indeed, it is a fundamental rule of bond market behavior that the price of callable bonds must be bid right to the call price as the interest rate falls to the level the market expects to trigger a call. Notice, though, that the price of the callable bond reaches the call price when the interest rate falls to R_2. Does this mean, then, that the market expects the bonds to be called when the interest rate reaches R_2?

The answer is no. If the market expected the bonds to be called when the interest rate reached R_2, then no one would be willing to pay more than the call price for the bonds. Investors, however, are aware that consideration of issue expenses leads management to delay refunding until the interest rate reaches R^*. Recognizing this, they are willing to

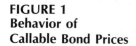

**FIGURE 1
Behavior of
Callable Bond Prices**

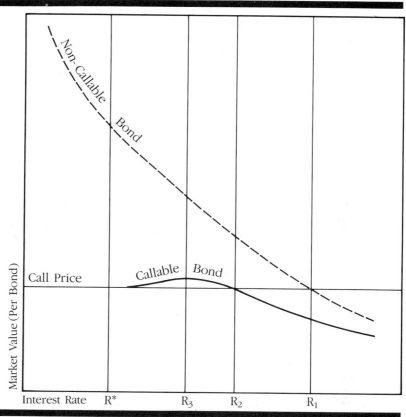

buy the bonds at a price higher than the call price, but lower of course than the present value of the stream of coupons and principal (the dashed curve in Figure 1), when the interest rate falls below R_2. (This pattern is exaggerated in Figure 1 for the sake of clarity.)

If the interest rate then falls far enough to approach R^*, the price of the callable bonds must be bid toward the call price, because that is the amount bondholders will receive when the bonds are called. At first glance, this might cause the reader to wonder why a rational investor would be willing to pay the market price shown in Figure 1 at interest rate level R_3, especially since it appears the bond's price will fall whether the interest rate moves down or back up from R_3. This paradox is easily resolved, however. Though an investor buying the bond at R_3 will sustain a capital loss if interest rates move sharply either way, this possible loss is offset by the

expected gain from receiving a coupon yield (on his purchase price) that exceeds the going interest rate.

As I have argued, then, the effect of extra issue expenses on management's *expected* refunding policy allows callable bonds to trade above their call price. In the absence of such costs, management's refunding objective would simply be to minimize the value of outstanding bonds. This aim would be served, as stated earlier, by calling the bonds when, and only when, their value reaches the call price.

Clearly, this is an easy strategy to implement. A refunding rule modified to take account of new issue costs is not quite as simple. But it, too, can be based largely, if not entirely, on the behavior of market prices. Such a refunding policy would require the same amount of analysis: virtually none.

If management does not wish to rely solely on market pricing, then the correct approach to the refunding decision would be to estimate the critical interest rate, R*, and then simply establish an auto-matic mechanism for calling the bonds when the rate falls to that pre-specified level. The calculation of this rate, however, is a formidable mathematical task. Not only does it go far beyond the scope of this article, but I know of no work in the finance litera-ture that points to such a calculation having been done in a fully satisfactory way.

Rather than pursuing this path, though, man-agement should seriously consider adopting the re-funding policy which relies completely on the mar-ket prices of outstanding callable bonds. How would such a policy work? The answer comes di-rectly from the behavior of bond prices suggested by Figure 1. The crucial assumption underlying Fig-ure 1, once again, is that the market expects man-agement to initiate a refunding when the interest rate falls to R*. This expectation will be based, as suggested, on the market's own assessment of when refunding is most advantageous to shareholders, which in turn will be based largely on the compa-ny's—and indeed all companies'—past refunding behavior. Given this assumption, then, as interest rates approach R*, the bond price will be bid down toward the call price.

If corporate treasurers have instituted refund-ing policies that, on average, benefit shareholders, *and* if the market is doing its job in interpreting past corporate policy as a predictor of future policy, then management should take its cue for refunding di-rectly from the market. As Figure 1 illustrates, the bonds' price will rise to and above the call price as interest rates fall below R_2. When further interest rate declines cause the price to converge back on the call price, then that is the bond market's signal that the optimal time for a refunding is now at hand.

Such a refunding policy has the great virtue of simplicity, requiring only the monitoring of the bonds' price behavior. Unlike most of the tradi-tional finance literature, my refunding rule substi-tutes the collective judgment of the market for man-agement's forecasts of interest rates. When management's view is significantly different from the market's, basing the call decision on intuition about future rates is simply a gamble which the cor-porate treasurer should not expect to win with reg-

ularity. If managers are convinced they have supe-rior predictions about future interest rates, they can act on these beliefs by taking positions in interest rate futures or options on government bonds. The success of these speculative endeavors would be much easier to evaluate.[15]

The market price behavior of callable bonds reflects not only the collective assessment of the di-rection and probability of future changes in interest rates. In addition, as we have seen, it contains an implicit estimate of the size of corporate refunding costs, and their consequences for the timing of a refunding. As such, bond prices provide manage-ment with an unbiased signal when, and when not, to call its bonds. It is doubtful that a corporate staff of analysts can reliably improve on the mathematics of the market.

At the extreme, of course, if *all* bond issuers followed this refunding policy, the policy would be a failure. Investors would catch on to the game, real-izing that bonds would never be called as long as they traded above the call price. In this highly im-probable case, investors would be willing to bid higher and higher prices for a callable bond as in-terest rates fell, and the bond would never be called.

In fact, though, corporations do call their bonds. And they can be expected to continue to do so, regardless of the market price of the bonds, if interest rates fall far enough. Investors therefore can never afford to assume bonds will not be called when trading above the call price.

This condition is really all that is necessary to support my recommendation for refunding policy. It is enough simply to ensure that the individual investor will not venture to pay more for the call-able bond than he reckons it would be worth, as-suming that managers are acting in the shareholder interest. To the extent that investors themselves see bond prices as reflecting the optimal refunding pol-icy, their own pricing behavior actually tends to keep subsequent pricing of bonds consistent with management policy. The more consistent are corpo-rate refundings with investor expectations (e.g., the more often companies call bonds when their price returns to the call price), the stronger and more

---

15. Although these markets involve transactions with much shorter maturi-ties than that of the typical call provision on a corporate bond, the maturities available are certainly sufficient to cover the horizon of any realistic interest rate forecast. Furthermore, such clearly speculative action would have the advantage in accountability of being a clear reflection of management's willingness to act on its own forecasts of interest rates.

When a bond's price converges back on the call price,
then that is the bond market's signal to call.

confident are investor expectations. And this strengthening of market expectations increases the probability that this proposed refunding rule, based entirely on market pricing, is indeed the optimal one.

Conclusion

The call provision provides management with a form of insurance against the risk of interest rate changes, and, more specifically, against the risk of being locked into a fixed-interest rate contract. By paying investors a higher coupon rate, management limits the upside potential for bondholders, thus placing a ceiling on a shareholders' liability. As with other forms of insurance, the expected value of the call provision to shareholders (excluding risk preferences) is zero. That is, in a market where investors and management have roughly the same expectations about interest rates, there is no benefit to shareholders (in advance, that is, when all decisions are made, and on an expected value basis) from gambling on the possibility of interest rate declines by including call provisions.

In attempting to solve the mystery of why companies routinely include call provisions in their bond issues, I came to the following conclusions:

1. Paying the price of the call provision in the form of a higher coupon rate may be justified if management, or its financial advisors, knows more about the course of future interest rates than the bond market. But if prescience about interest rates is the only reason for including the call privilege, there will certainly be circumstances when issuers will have compelling reasons *not* to include a call provision on new debt: namely, whenever, the probability of interest rates rising above current levels seems far greater than a decline. For this reason, it is difficult to attribute the almost universal use of the call provision solely to management's faith in its interest forecasts.

2. The call provision may add value by reducing the chances of bondholders blocking desirable investments by the company. If this is a main purpose of the call provision, however, the call price should not be specified as a percentage above par value, but defined with respect to some observable interest rate level, such as long-term government bond yields.

3. The call provision may have a tax advantage to the corporation, especially when the bonds are privately placed with a tax-exempt lender. To the extent that the investor tax rate built into corporate bond yields is not significantly lower than the company's marginal tax rate, this tax advantage disappears. There is no tax advantage, and perhaps a slight tax disadvantage, to including a call provision on a preferred stock issue.

4. The call provision reduces the sensitivity of a bond's value to changes in interest rates, thus reducing the variability of the debt. For companies whose assets are relatively insensitive to interest rate movements, reductions in the risk of the debt directly reduce the risk of the equity. To the degree that all companies are systematically affected by interest rate risk, the call provision thus may lower the company's required return on equity capital.

The optimal refunding strategy can be stated in fairly simple terms, especially when new issue costs are ignored. When modified to take account of the additional costs of refunding, the rule is still simple if based on the collective judgment of the market, as reflected in the movement of bond prices:

1. If issue expenses are ignored, the bond should be called as soon as it trades at the call price.

2. When issue expenses are significant, the bond should be called when interest rates decline sufficiently such that the bond has traded above the call price and then, with a further decline in rates, returned to the call price.

3. If management does not wish to rely solely on market pricing, then it can attempt the very complex mathematical task of estimating the critical interest rate (expressed as a level of, say, 30-year government bonds) at which call is optimal. Or, less ambitiously, for any given rate of interest, it can estimate and then weigh the benefits of a refunding against new issue costs. The latter, of course, is not an optimizing policy.

4. Management's expectations about future interest rates should not influence the refunding strategy. When the price of the callable bond reaches the call price (either on the way up, if refunding costs are minimal, or on the way down, if they are significant), management should not defer the call because they expect a further decline in rates. If the company wishes to serve its shareholder interests by speculating on interest rates, management should take the more direct and accountable step of taking positions in the interest rate futures or government bond options markets.

PART IV

RAISING CAPITAL

In "*Raising Capital: Theory and Evidence*," Clifford Smith provides a concise review of academic research bearing on (1) the stock market's response to announcements by public companies of different kinds of securities offerings and (2) the relative efficiency of different methods of marketing corporate securities—that is, rights vs. underwritten offerings, negotiated vs. competitive bid contracts, and traditional vs. shelf registration. Somewhat surprisingly, at least to academics, the research confirms that the average market reaction to security offerings of all kindsòdebt and equity, straight and convertible, and issued by utilities as well as industrials—is "consistently either negative or not significantly different from zero... Furthermore, the market's response to common stock issues is more strongly negative than its response to preferred stock or debt offerings. It is also more negative to announcements of convertible than non-convertible securities, and to offerings by utilities than industrials."

In the first half of the article, Smith evaluates a number of explanations that have been offered to account for these findings. For example, the expected dilutive effect of new equity and convertibles on EPS is dismissed as an "accounting illusion" that should have no effect on economic values. Skepticism is also expressed about the time-honored "price-pressure" argument that maintains that large issues of new securities must be offered at a discount from market prices, even in heavily traded markets like the New York Stock Exchange. In place of these traditional arguments, Smith suggests that the most plausible explanation of the market's systematically negative response to equity and convertibles is a relatively new "information asymmetry" hypothesis. In brief, the argument holds that because of the possibility of inside information and given the incentives of management as insiders to exploit outside investors by issuing overvalued securities, the mere act of announcing new equity or convertibles often releases a negative signal to the market about the firm's cash flow prospects (at least, relative to those reflected in its current stock price), thus causing stock prices to fall on average.

In the second part of the article, Smith uses this "information asymmetry" argument to explain why firm commitment underwritten offerings predominate over rights offerings, negotiated over competitive bids, and traditional registration over the new shelf registration procedure (although the latter is gaining ground, especially in debt issues). The mere possibility of insider information creates a demand by potential investors for the issuing firm to hire reputable underwriters to "certify" the value of the new securities. The guarantee of quality, as well as the commitment to maintain an after-market, provided to investors is much stronger in the case of firm underwritten offerings, especially those which are negotiated with a single investment banker rather than auctioned through a competitive bid and registered using the traditional rather than the new shelf procedure. In cases where such certification services are unnecessary, however, shelf registration can provide significant savings in transaction costs.

In "*Financing Corporate Growth*," Professors Alan Shapiro and Brad Shapiro provide a broad survey of financing issues faced by all public corporations—tax consequences, concerns about financial and operating flexibility, potential conflicts among bondholders and stockholders, effects on management incentives, and establishing credibility with investors. They then go on to narrow their focus to the financing problems confronting so-called "growth" companies. Growth companies, especially those whose value resides largely in intangible assets, are likely to need lots of equity and perhaps large cash balances to provide the flexibility necessary to execute their investment plans in the most timely way. Because of the uncertainty and risks they represent for investors, such companies are likely to find the use of public capital markets expensive, and the discounts on their securities steep.

For this reason, the authors argue, bank loans or other forms of "inside" debt such as private placements may provide a special financing opportunity for such companies because of the flexibility offered by the close relationship between borrower and investor. For those growth companies large enough to tap public credit markets, convertible bonds may also be especially useful because of their stock-option-like conversion feature, which helps overcome bondholders' normal reluctance to bear large and ill-defined risks.

In "*An Overview of Corporate Securities Innovation*," John Finnerty argues that some new securities succeed by addressing a fundamental need of issuers and investors, while others are designed merely to exploit a passing tax or regulatory quirk. The former become part of the mainstream of corporate finance vehicles, while the latter predictably disappear along with the 5artificial" impulses that gave rise to them. Finnerty attempts to separate the wheat from the chaff both by furnishing new issue data on over 60 securities introduced in the last 20 years and by commenting on probable sources of "valued added" in each case.

In the articles that follow in this section, we attempt to trace the rising curve of the corporate lifecycle.

In "*Aspects of Financial Contracting in Venture Capital*," William Sahlman shows that the common venture capital practices of using convertible preferred stock and providing for the commitment of capital in well-thought-out stages are both important means by which users of venture capital are able to "signal" their confidence to investors and thus overcome the "credibility gap" that confronts all companies in raising capital.

In "*An Introduction to Mezzanine Finance and Private Equity*," John Willis and David Clark of the Continental Bank's Equity Capital Corporation describe a financing technique commonly used to fund buyouts of private companies by operating management and private investment groups. The economy-wide movement in the 1980s to concentrate equity in mature businesses in as few hands as possible led to a widening of the financing "gap" between the senior debt and the available conventional equity. In the larger LBOs, this gap was closed by the evolution of the junk bond market. The private mezzanine market arose to meet the requirements of transactions in the small to middle market—those up to, say, $200 million.

From the subjects of venture capital and small management buy-outs, we move to a review of academic research on "*Initial Public Offerings.*" Authors Roger Ibbotson, Jay Ritter, and Jody Sindelar attempt to explain a well-documented research finding that has puzzled finance scholars for years. IPOs are significantly "underpriced"—by as much as 18 percent on average, on the authority of Ritter's exhaustive study of the period 1960-1987. The research also shows that IPOs tend to run in cycles of "hot" and "cold" markets. That is, markets characterized by large average underpricing (large initial run-ups in the aftermarket) lead to a heavier volume

of initial offerings, which in turn are associated with progressively lower underpricing over time. Lower underpricing in turn appears to lead to lower volume and thus the onset of "cold" markets. The authors review the explanations that have recently been offered to account for this peculiar pattern while also reporting some interesting new evidence on the pricing of venture-capital-backed and mutual fund IPOs, as well as "reverse" LBOs.

In "*Raising Equity in an Efficient Market*," Bruce Jurin discusses alternative methods for raising equity. Although much of this ground is covered by Smith in the first article in this section, Jurin presents an interesting, if somewhat idiosyncratic account of why firm underwritten offerings dominate the four other methods of raising equity. It also sheds some light on the rights vs. underwriting controversy cited by Smith.

From IPOs and other equity offerings, we move to the subject of bank loan financing, which, as mentioned above, may be the best debt financing alternative for those companies unable to tap the public debt markets. In a fairly recent theoretical study entitled <What's Different About Banks?," the University of Chicago's Eugene Fama argues that banks have a comparative advantage over public investors and other financial institutions in making short-term loans because of their access to deposit histories and continuous customer relationships. In the article "*Are Banks Different?*," Christopher James and Peggy Wier report some evidence from the stock market suggesting that bank loans may indeed possess some unique advantages over other forms of financing.

Nevertheless, in the 1980s, the astonishing growth of the junk bond market provided many smaller companies with an economic alternative to bank loans and private placements. In "*The Growing Role of Junk Bonds in Corporate Finance*," Robert Taggart and Kevin Perry state the case for junk bonds, showing significant benefits to issuers and investors alike. For investors, they offer in effect a hybrid instrument (part debt, part equity) with an accordingly intermediate risk profile; they also, somewhat surprisingly, have a lower sensitivity to interest rate changes than investment-grade corporates and Treasury bonds. For issuers, they have provided not only a means of amassing large pools of capital for takeovers by "raiders" (which accounts for the regulatory assault on that market), but also what amounts to a tax-deductible, equity-like form of fixed-rate medium-term financing for the normal business operations of "middle market" (and thus the vast majority of American) corporations.

Many junk bond issues—especially for emerging growth companies—included conversion features. In "*The Case for Convertibles*," Michael Brennan and Eduardo Schwartz explain the appeal of convertible financing for small, rapidly growing companies: it overcomes the financing problem caused by investor uncertainty about the underlying risks of companies' operations. Besides offering a useful discussion of when to call convertibles, the authors also make short work of the popular notions that convertibles represent "cheap debt" and are equivalent to "selling equity at a premium."

In "*The Origin of LYONs: A Case Study in Financial Innovation*," John McConnell of Purdue University and Eduardo Schwartz of UCLA provide an account—admittedly second-hand—of the thinking that went into the design of the highly successful Liquid Yield Option Notes pioneered by Merrill Lynch in 1985. (The LYON and its imitations accounted for roughly half the convertible debt issued in 1991, which was a boom year for convertibles generally.) Such an account is "second-hand" because Professors McConnell and Schwartz were not present at the creation of the security (Merrill's then Options Marketing Manager, Lee Cole, is credited with the original insight). Their role was rather to design a model to "price" the security—one that not only turned out to be remarkably accurate (it overestimated the first-trading-day closing price of the first LYON issue by only 1.5%), but also enabled Merrill to answer charges that it was grossly underpricing the security.

LYONs are part of a broader class of debt securities known as hybrids—those that combine conventional, fixed-rate debt with an embedded forward, swap, or option. In "*The Uses of Hybrid Debt in Managing Corporate Risk*," Charles Smithson and I attempt to explain why the 1990s are proving "Hot Times for Hybrids" (to borrow a recent New York Times title). In the early 1980s, when interest rates were much higher than they are today, hybrids like Sunshine Mining's silver-linked bond issue were used by riskier companies to help reduce their interest costs to manageable levels. But though rates are much lower today, credit spreads have widened considerably for all but blue-chip borrowers. In many cases, companies are using hybrid debt to lower their risk profile and thus avoid the higher funding costs now associated with being a riskier corporate borrower.

In "*The Persistent Borrowing Advantage of Eurodollar Bonds*," Wayne Marr and John Trimble report the results of their own recent studies documenting large cost savings by U.S. corporate borrowers in the Eurodollar market. The existence of such a large and persistent borrowing advantage," the authors point out, "runs counter to the conventional wisdom of financial economists that international capital markets are becoming ever more "integrated." And the article goes on to provide an "educated guess" about the real source of these interest savings—one which centers on the value to investors of the "anonymity" conferred by the bearer form of these bonds.

In "*Project Finance: Raising Money in the Old-Fashioned Way*," John Kensinger and John Martin describe a new wave of project financings to fund ventures such as oil and gas exploration, independent electric power construction, factory construction and operation, and corporate R&D. Like structured securitized credit, project finance shifts well-defined risks from the issuer's balance sheet to investors more willing to bear them. Further like securitized credit, it shields investors from the "reinvestment risk" they would otherwise face by lending on a general obligation basis—the risk that management will waste excess cash on low-return projects. This is also an important reason why project financings are now being used to fund growth in LDCs.

DHC

■

RAISING CAPITAL: THEORY AND EVIDENCE

by Clifford Smith,
University of Rochester

Corporations raise capital by selling a variety of different securities. The *Dealers' Digest* (1985) reports that over $350 billion of public securities sales were underwritten between 1980 and 1984. Of that total, 63 percent was straight debt, 24 percent was common stock, 6 percent was convertible debt, 5 percent was preferred stock, and the remaining 2 percent was convertible preferred stock. Besides choosing among these types of securities, corporate management must also choose among different methods of marketing the securities. In issues that accounted for 95 percent of the total dollars raised between 1980 and 1984, the contracts were negotiated between the issuing firm and its underwriter; in only 5 percent of the offers was the underwriter selected through a competitive bid. Shelf registration, a relatively new procedure for registering securities, was employed in issues accounting for 27 percent of the total dollars raised; the remaining 73 percent was raised through offerings using traditional registration procedures.

Despite the critical role that capital markets play in both financial theory and practice, financial economists have only recently begun to explore the alternative contractual arrangements in the capital raising process and the effect of these choices on a company's cost of issuing securities. This article has two basic aims: (1) to examine the theory and evidence concerning the market's response to security offer announcements by public corporations; and (2) to evaluate the different methods of marketing corporate securities (rights versus underwritten offers, negotiated versus competitive bid contracts, traditional vs. shelf registration, etc.), with attention given to the special case of initial public equity offers.

Market Reactions to Security Offer Announcements

A public company seeking external capital must first decide what type of claim to sell. In making that decision, it is important to understand the market's typical reaction to these announcements.

Presented in Table 1 is a summary of the findings of recent academic research on the market's response to announcements of public issues (grouped by industrial firms and utilities) of common stock, preferred stock, convertible preferred stock, straight debt and convertible debt. Perhaps surprisingly, the average abnormal returns (that is, the price movements adjusted for general market price changes) are consistently either negative or not significantly different from zero; in no case is there evidence of a significant positive reaction. Furthermore, the market's response to common stock issues is more strongly negative than its response to preferred stock or debt offerings. It is also more negative to announcements of convertible than non-convertible securities, and more negative to announcements of offerings by industrials than utilities.

I would first like to examine potential explanations of these findings. Let me start by briefly noting a number of arguments that have been proposed to account for at least parts of this overall pattern of market responses, and then go on to consider each in more detail.

EPS Dilution: The increase in the number of shares outstanding resulting from an equity (or convertible) offering is expected to reduce (fully diluted) reported earnings per share, at least in the

*This article is based on "Investment Banking and the Capital Acquisition Process," *Journal of Financial Economics* (1986). This research was supported by the Managerial Economics Research Center, Graduate School of Management, University of Rochester.

Management may possess important information about the company that the market doesn't share. Investors recognize this information disparity and revise their estimate of a company's value in response to management's announced decisions.

**TABLE 1
The Stock Market Response to Announcements of Security Offerings**

In the columns below are the average two-day abnormal common stock returns and average sample size (in parentheses) from studies of announcements of security offerings. Returns are weighted averages by sample size of the returns reported by the respective studies listed below. (Unless noted otherwise, returns are significantly different from zero.) Most of these studies appear in the forthcoming issue of the University of Rochester's *Journal of Financial Economics* 15 (1986), but full citations for all can be found in the reference section at the end of this issue.

| | Types of Issuer | |
Type of Security Offering	Industrial	Utility
Common Stock	−3.14%[a]	−0.75%[b]
	(155)	(403)
Preferred Stock	−0.19%[c,*]	+0.08%[d,*]
	(28)	(249)
Convertible Preferred Stock	−1.44%[d]	−1.38%[d]
	(53)	(8)
Straight Bonds	−0.26%[e,*]	−0.13%[f,*]
	(248)	(140)
Convertible Bonds	−2.07%[e]	n.a.[g]
	(73)	

[a] Source: Asquith/Mullins (1986), Kolodny/Suhler (1985), Masulis/Korwar (1986), Mikkelson/Partch (1986), Schipper/Smith (1986)
[b] Source: Asquith/Mullins (1986), Masulis/Korwar (1986), Pettway/Radcliffe (1985)
[c] Source: Linn/Pinegar (1986), Mikkelson/Partch (1986)
[d] Source: Linn/Pinegar (1986)
[e] Source: Dann/Mikkelson (1984), Eckbo (1986), Mikkelson/Partch (1986)
[f] Source: Eckbo (1986)
[g] Not available (virtually none are issued by utilities)
* Interpreted by the authors as not statistically significantly different from zero

near term. New equity is also expected to reduce reported ROE. It has been suggested that such anticipated reductions in accounting measures of performance reduce stock prices.

Price Pressure: The demand curve for securities slopes downward. A new offering increases the supply of that security relative to the demand for it, thus causing its price to fall.

Optimal Capital Structure: A new security issue changes a company's capital structure, thus altering its relationship to its optimal capital structure (as perceived by the market).

Insider Information: Management may possess important information about the company that the market doesn't share. Investors recognize this information disparity and revise their estimate of a company's value in response to management's announced decisions. This effect works through two channels:

Implied Cash Flow Change: Security offers reveal inside information about operating profitability; that is, the requirement for external funding may reflect a shortfall in recent or expected future cash flows.

Leverage Change: Increases in corporate leverage are interpreted by the market as reflecting management's confidence about the company's prospects. Conversely, decreases in leverage, such as those brought about by equity offers, reflect management's lack of confidence about future profitability.

Unanticipated Announcements: To the extent an offer is anticipated, its economic impact is already reflected in security prices. Thus, market reactions to less predictable issues should be greater, other things equal, than to more predictable issues.

Ownership Changes: Some security offerings accompany actual or expected changes in the ownership or organization of the company, which in turn can influence market reaction to the announcement.

Before considering each of these possibilities at greater length, let me emphasize that some of the above arguments have more explanatory power than others. But no single explanation accounts, to the exclusion of all others, for the complete pattern of market responses documented by the research.

Studies of stock price reactions to accounting changes have provided convincing testimony to the sophistication of the market, which contradicts the claims of the EPS dilution argument.

EPS Dilution

Many analysts argue that announcements of new equity issues depress stock prices because the increase in the number of shares outstanding is expected to result in a reduction, at least in the near term, of reported earnings per share. The expected fall in (near-term) EPS causes stock prices to fall.

Underlying this argument is the assumption that investors respond uncritically to financial statements, mechanically capitalizing EPS figures at standard, industry-wide P/E multiples. Such a view is, of course, completely at odds with the theory of modern finance. In an efficient market, the value of a company's equity—like the value of a bond or any other investment—should reflect the present value of all of its expected future after-tax *cash flows* (discounted at rates which reflect investors' required returns on securities of comparable risk). This view thus implies that even if near-term EPS is expected to fall as the result of a new equity offering, the issuing company's stock price should not fall as long as the market expects management to earn an adequate rate of return on the new funds. In fact, if the equity sale is perceived by the market as providing management with the means of undertaking an exceptionally profitable capital spending program, then the announcement of an equity offering (combined perhaps with an announcement of the capital expenditure plan) should, if anything, cause a company's price to rise.

There remains a strong temptation, of course, to link the negative stock price effects of new equity announcements to the expected earnings reduction. But to accept this argument is to mistake correlation for causality. We must look to other events to assess whether it is the expected earnings dilution that *causes* the market reaction, or whether there are other, more important factors at work. I believe that studies of stock price reactions to accounting changes have provided convincing testimony to the sophistication of the market, which contradicts the claims of the EPS dilution argument.[1] Such studies provide remarkably consistent evidence that markets see through cosmetic accounting changes, and that market price reactions generally reflect changes in the expected underlying cash flows—that is, in the long-run prospects for the business. In short, there is no plausible theoretical explanation—nor is there

credible supporting evidence— that suggests that the reductions in expected EPS accompanying announcements of stock offerings should systematically cause the market to lower companies' stock prices.

Price Pressure

In a somewhat related explanation, some argue that the price reduction associated with the announcement of a new equity or convertible issue is the result of an increase in the supply of a company's equity. This price pressure argument is based on the premise that the demand schedule for the shares of any given company is downward sloping, and that new shares can thus be sold only by offering investors a discount from the market price. The greater the proportional amount of new shares, the larger the discount necessary to effect the sale.

Modern portfolio theory, however, attaches little credibility to the price pressure argument—not, at least, in the case of widely-traded securities in well-established secondary markets. The theory says that investors pricing securities are concerned primarily with risk and expected return. Because the risk and return characteristics of any given stock can be duplicated in many ways through various combinations of other stocks, there are a great many close substitutes for that stock. Given this abundance of close substitutes, economic theory says that the demand curve for corporate securities should more closely approximate a horizontal line than a sharply downward sloping one. A horizontal demand curve in turn implies that an issuing company should be able to sell large quantities of new stock without any discount from the current market price (provided the market does not interpret the stock sale itself as releasing negative insider information about the company's prospects relative to its current value).

What does the available research tell us about the price pressure hypothesis? I will simply mention a few studies bearing on this question.

The first serious study of price pressure was Myron Scholes's doctoral dissertation at the University of Chicago. Scholes examined the effect on share prices of large blocks offered through secondary offerings. According to the price pressure hypothesis, the larger the block of shares to be sold, the larger the price decline would have to be to induce increasing

---

1. For an excellent review of this research, see Ross Watts, "Does It Pay to Manipulate EPS?," *Chase Financial Quarterly* (Spring 1982). Reprinted in *Issues in Corporate Finance* (New York: Stern Stewart & Co., 1983).

The largest price declines were recorded when the secondary sale was made by corporate officers in the company itself—that is, by insiders with possibly privileged information about the company's future.

numbers of investors to purchase the shares. By contrast, the intrinsic value view suggests that the stock price would be unaffected by the size of the block to be sold. It says that at the right price, the market would readily absorb additional shares.

Scholes found that while stock prices do decline upon the distribution of a large block of shares, the price decline appears to be unrelated to the size of the distribution. This finding suggests that the price discount necessary to distribute the block is better interpreted as a result of the adverse information communicated by a large block sale than as a result of selling pressure. This interpretation was reinforced by the additional finding that the largest price declines were recorded when the secondary sale was made by corporate officers in the company itself—that is, by insiders with possibly privileged information about the company's future.[2]

In another study on price pressure, Avner Kalay and Adam Shimrat recently examined bond price reactions to new equity offers. They reason that if price pressure (and not adverse information) causes the negative stock price reaction, there should be no reduction in the value of the company's outstanding bonds upon the announcement of the stock issue—if anything, the new layer of equity should provide added protection for the bonds and cause their prices to rise. The study, however, documented a significant drop in bond prices, suggesting that the market views an equity offering as bad news, reducing the value of the firm as a whole.[3]

Another recent study of price pressure was conducted by Scott Linn and Mike Pinegar. They examined the price reaction of outstanding preferred stock issues to announcements of new preferred stock issues by the same company. They found that the price of an outstanding preferred stock did not fall with the announcement of an additional new preferred issue, thus providing no support for the operation of price pressure in the market for preferred stock.[4]

In short, there is little empirical evidence in support of price pressure in the market for widely-traded stocks. The observed stock price declines, as I shall suggest later, are more plausibly attributed to negative "information" effects.

Optimal Capital Structure

Financial economists generally agree that firms have an optimal capital structure and a number of researchers have suggested that the price reactions documented in Table 1 reflect companies' attempts to move toward that optimum. This explanation might be useful if we found broad samples of firms experiencing positive market responses to their new security issues. But because the market reaction to most security offerings appears systematically negative (or at best neutral), it is clear that any attempt by firms to move toward a target capital structure is not the dominating factor in the market's response. If we were to use the market's reaction to new security offerings as the basis for any useful generalization about companies' relationship to their optimal structure, we would be put in the embarrassing position of arguing that new security offerings routinely move companies away from, not toward, such an optimum. Thus, I raise this possibility largely to dismiss it.

Information Disparity Between Management and Potential Investors

The documented reductions in firm value associated with security sales—which, after all, are voluntary management decisions—thus present financial economists with a puzzle. One possible explanation is that new security sales are optimal responses by management to changes for the worse in a company's prospects. Alternatively, a company's current market valuation may seem to management to reflect excessive confidence about the future, and it may attempt to exploit such a difference in outlook by "timing" its equity offerings. Investors habituated to stock offerings under such conditions will discount, as a matter of course, the stock prices of companies announcing security offerings. In such circumstances, even if a security sale increases the value of the firm by allowing it to fund profitable projects, it could lead potential investors to suspect that management has a dimmer view of the company's future than that reflected in its current market value.

2. For the published version of Scholes's dissertation, see "Market for Securities: Substitution versus Price Pressure and the Effects of Information on Share Prices," *Journal of Business* 45 (1972), 179-211.

3. Avner Kalay and Adam Shimrat, "Firm Value and Seasoned Equity Issue: Price Pressure, Wealth Redistribution, or Negative Information," New York University working paper, 1986.

4. See Scott Linn and J. Michael Pinegar, "The Effect of Issuing Preferred Stock on Common Stockholder Wealth," Unpublished manuscript, University of Iowa, 1985.

The market responds negatively, as a rule, to announcements of security sales, dividend reductions, and decreases in new investment.

It is now well documented that managers have better information about the firm's prospects than do outside investors.[5] There is also little doubt that outsiders pay attention to insider trading in making their own investment decisions. Given these observations, I believe that the findings in Table 1 are driven in large part by this potential disparity of information between management and the market, and the incentives it offers management in timing the issue of new securities.

Furthermore, I would argue that, as a result of this potential information disparity, new security offerings affect investors' outlook about a company through two primary channels: (a) the implied change in expected net operating cash flow and (b) the leverage change.

Implied Changes in Net Operating Cash Flow. Investors, of course, are ultimately interested in a company's capacity to generate cash flow. Although a new security offering might imply that the company has discovered new investment opportunities, it might also imply a shortfall in cash caused by poor current or expected future operating performance. As accounting students learn in their first year of business school, "sources" must equal "uses" of funds. Consequently, an announcement of a new security issue must imply one of the following to investors: (1) an expected increase in new investment expenditure, (2) a reduction in some liability (such as debt retirement or share repurchase) and hence a change in capital structure, (3) an increase in future dividends, or (4) a reduction in expected net operating cash flow. If new security sales were generally used only in anticipation of profitable new investment or to move capital structure closer to an optimal target ratio, then we should expect positive stock price reactions to announcements of new offerings. But if unanticipated security issues come to be associated with reductions in future cash flows from operations, then investors would systematically interpret announcements of security sales as bad news.

This argument can be generalized to consider other announcements which do not explicitly link sources and uses of funds. Using the above line of reasoning, we would interpret announcements of stock repurchases, increases in investment expenditures, and higher dividend payments as signaling increases in expected operating cash flow and, thus, as good news for investors. Conversely, security offerings, reductions in investment expenditures, and reductions in dividend payments all would imply reductions in expected operating cash flow.

The academic evidence on market responses to announcements of new securities sales, stock repurchases, dividend changes, and changes in capital spending (summarized in Table 2) is broadly consistent with this hypothesis. As shown in the upper panel of Table 2, announcements of security repurchases, dividend increases, and increases in capital spending are greeted systematically by increases in stock prices. The market responds negatively, as a rule, to announcements of security sales, dividend reductions, and decreases in new investment (an exception has been the oil industry in recent years, in which case the market's response to increases in capital spending has been negative, and positive to announced cutbacks in investment). On the basis of this evidence, the market appears to make inferences about changes in operating cash flow from announcements that do not explicitly associate sources with uses of funds.

I should point out, however, that although this explanation helps to explain non-positive price reactions to announcements of all security sales, it provides no insight into the questions of why investors respond more negatively to equity than debt sales, to convertible than non-convertible issues, and to sales by industrials rather than utilities.

Information Disparity and Leverage Changes. Suppose that a potential purchaser of securities has less information about the prospects of the firm than management. Assume, furthermore, that management is more likely to issue securities when the market price of the firm's traded securities is higher than management's assessment of their value. In such a case, sophisticated investors will revise their estimate of the value of the firm if and when management announces a new security issue. Furthermore, the larger the potential disparity in information between insiders and investors, the greater the revision in expectations and the larger the negative price reaction to the announcement of a new issue.

Because debt and preferred stock are more senior claims on corporate cash flows, the values of these securities are generally less sensitive to changes in a company's prospects than is the value of common stock. Thus, this problem of potential insider information that management faces whenever it issues a

5. See Jeffrey Jaffe's seminal study of insider trading, "Special Information and Insider Trading," *Journal of Business* 47 (1974), 410-420.

Because debt and preferred stock are more senior claims on corporate cash flows, the values of these securities are generally less sensitive to changes in a company's prospects than is the value of common stock.

TABLE 2
The Stock Market Response to Announcements of Changes in Financing, Dividend, and Investment Policy

In the columns below are the average two-day common stock abnormal returns and average sample size from studies of changes in financing, dividend, and investment policy grouped by implied changes in corporate cash flows. Returns are weighted averages by sample size of the returns reported by the respective studies. (Unless otherwise noted, returns are significantly different from zero.) Full citations for all studies mentioned can be found in the reference section at the end of this issue.

Type of Announcement	Average Sample Size	Two-Day Announcement Period Return
Implied Increase in Corporate Cash Flow		
Common Stock Repurchases:		
Intra-firm tender offer[a]	148	16.2%
Open market repurchase[b]	182	3.6
Targeted small holding[c]	15	1.6
Calls of Non-Convertible Bonds[d]	133	−0.1*
Dividend Increases:		
Dividend initiation[e]	160	3.7
Dividend increase[f]	280	0.9
Specially designated dividend[g]	164	2.1
Investment Increases[h]	510	1.0
Implied Decrease in Corporate Cash Flow		
Security Sales:		
Common stock[i]	262	−1.6
Preferred stock[j]	102	0.1*
Convertible preferred[k]	30	−1.4
Straight debt[l]	221	−0.2*
Convertible debt[l]	80	−2.1
Dividend Decreases[f]	48	−3.6
Investment Decreases[h]	111	−1.1

[a] Source: Dann (1981), Masulis (1980), Vermalen (1981), Rosenfeld (1982)
[b] Source: Dann (1980), Vermalen (1981)
[c] Source: Bradley/Wakeman (1983)
[d] Source: Vu (1986)
[e] Source: Asquith/Mullins (1983)
[f] Source: Charest (1978), Aharony/Swary (1980)
[g] Source: Brickley (1983)
[h] Source: McConnell/Muscarella (1985)
[i] Source: Asquith/Mullins (1986), Masulis/Korwar (1986), Mikkelson/Partch (1986), Schipper/Smith (1986), Pettway/Radcliff (1985)
[j] Source: Linn/Pinegar (1986), Mikkelson/Partch (1986)
[k] Source: Linn/Pinegar (1986)
[l] Source: Dann/Mikkelson (1984), Eckbo (1986), Mikkelson/Partch (1986)
* Interpreted by the authors as not significantly different from zero.

new security is most acute in the case of equity offerings. Similarly, the values of convertible debt and convertible preferred stock are also generally more sensitive to changes in firm value than non-convertible debt and preferred because of their equity component—but less sensitive, of course, than common stock; hence the information disparity should be more problematic for convertible than for straight securities.

The case of utility offerings is somewhat different. In the rate regulation process, managers of utilities generally petition their respective regulatory

The market responds positively to leverage-increasing transactions and negatively to leverage-decreasing transactions; the larger the change in leverage, the greater the price reaction.

authorities for permission to proceed with a new security issue. This petitioning process should reduce the price reaction of utilities announcements relative to industrials for three reasons: (1) it could reduce the differential information between manager and outsiders; (2) it could limit managers' discretion as to what security to sell; (3) it could reduce managers' ability to "time" security offerings to take advantage of inside information. Because of this regulatory process, utilies do not face as great a problem in persuading the market to accept its securities at current prices.

Thus, while this information disparity hypothesis does not predict whether the response to announcements of debt and preferred issues will be negative or positive, it does predict that the reaction to common stock sales will be more negative than the response to preferred or debt, more negative to convertible than non-convertible issues, and to industrial than utility offerings.[6]

This second, leverage-related channel through which the information disparity problem operates can be distinguished from the implied cash flow explanation by examining evidence from events that *explicitly* associate sources and uses of funds: namely, exchange offers, conversion-forcing calls of convertible securities, and security sales in which the proceeds are explicitly intended for debt retirement. Research on announcements of these transactions (summarized in Table 3) documents the following: (1) the market responds positively to leverage-increasing transactions and negatively to leverage-decreasing transactions; (2) the larger the change in leverage, the greater the price reaction. Accordingly, debt-for-common offers have larger positive stock price reactions than preferred-for-common offers, and common-for-debt offers have larger negative price reactions than common-for-preferred offers.

In Table 4 the analysis of the two channels is combined to provide additional insight into the information disparity explanation. The events to the upper left of the table tend to have positive stock price reactions, those in the lower right tend to have negative reactions while those along the diagonal tend to be insignificant. Hence, a common stock offering, which implies both a reduction in future operating cash flow and a reduction in leverage, prompts the largest negative market response of all the security offers. A stock

repurchase, by contrast, suggests increases both in operating cash and leverage, and accordingly receives strong endorsement by the market. It seems to provide a credible expression to investors of management's confidence about the company's future performance (at least relative to its current value).

Unanticipated Announcements

Because stock price changes reflect only the unanticipated component of announcements of corporate events, the stock price change at the announcement of a security offering will be larger, all else equal, the more unpredictable is the announcement. For example, debt repayment (either from maturing issues or sinking-fund provisions) requires the firm to issue additional debt to maintain its capital structure. Given a target capital structure and stable cash flows, debt repayment must be matched with a new debt issue; hence the more predictable are principal repayments, the more predictable will be new debt issues. Similarly, the predictability of earnings (and thus internally generated equity) will determine the predictability of a new equity issue. Therefore, one should expect a new debt issue to be more predictable than a new equity issue because principal repayments are more predictable than earnings.

Another reason for the greater predictability of public debt offerings is related to the cost structures of public versus private debt. Flotation costs for publicly-placed debt appear to have a larger fixed component and more pronounced economies of scale than bank debt. Thus, a firm tends to use bank lines of credit until an efficient public issue size is reached; then the firm issues public debt and retires the bank debt. If investors can observe the amount of bank borrowing and the pattern of public debt issues, then more predictable announcements of public bond issues should have smaller price reactions.

Utilities use external capital markets with far greater frequency than industrials, thus making utility issues more predictable. For this reason alone, we would expect utilities' stock prices to exhibit a smaller reaction to announcements of new security sales. In short, the relative predictability of announcements of security offerings helps explain both the observed differences in market reactions to

6. But if the evidence across classes of securities is consistent with the information asymmetry hypothesis, some data within security classes is apparently inconsistent. When Eckbo (1986) and Mikkelson/Partch (1986) disaggregate their bond data by rating class, neither study finds higher rated, less risky (and thus less sensitive to firm value) bonds to be associated with smaller abnormal returns. Eckbo also finds more negative abnormal returns to mortgage bonds than non-mortgage bonds. (References for studies are cited in full at the end of this issue.)

A stock repurchase, by contrast, suggests increases both in operating cash and leverage, and accordingly receives strong endorsement by the market.

TABLE 3
The Stock Market Response to Announcements of Pure Financial Structure Changes:
Exchange Offers, Security Sales with Designated Uses of Funds, and Calls of Convertible Securities

Below is a summary of two-day announcement effects associated with the events listed above. Because each of these transactions explicitly associate sources with uses of funds, they represent virtually pure financial structure changes. (Unless otherwise noted, returns are significantly different from zero.) Full citations for all studies mentioned can be found in the reference section at the end of the article.

Type of Transaction	Security Issued	Security Retired	Average Sample Size	Two-Day Announcement Period Return
Leverage-Increasing Transactions				
Stock Repurchase[a]	Debt	Common	45	21.9%
Exchange Offer[b]	Debt	Common	52	14.0
Exchange Offer[b]	Preferred	Common	9	8.3
Exchange Offer[b]	Debt	Preferred	24	2.2
Exchange Offer[c]	Income Bonds	Preferred	24	2.2
Transactions with No Change in Leverage				
Exchange Offer[d]	Debt	Debt	36	0.6*
Security Sale[e]	Debt	Debt	83	0.2*
Leverage-Reducing Transactions				
Conversion-forcing Call[e]	Common	Convertible	57	−0.4*
Conversion-forcing Call[e]	Common	Preferred	113	−2.1
Security Sale[f]	Convertible Debt	Convertible Bond	15	−2.4
Exchange Offer[b]	Common	Debt	30	−2.6
Exchange Offer[b]	Preferred	Preferred	9	−7.7
Security Sale[f]	Common	Debt	12	−4.2
Exchange Offer[b]	Common	Debt Debt	20	−9.9

[a] Source: Masulis (1980)
[b] Source: Masulis (1983) (Note: These returns include announcement days of both the original offer and, for about 40 percent of the sample, a second announcement of specific terms of the exchange.)
[c] Source: McConnell/Schlarbaum (1981)
[d] Source: Dietrich (1984)
[e] Source: Mikkelson (1981)
[f] Source: Eckbo (1986) and Mikkelson/Partch (1986)
* Not statistically different from zero.

common stock versus debt issues and to the offerings of industrials versus those of utilities.

Changes in Ownership and Control

Some security sales involve potentially important changes in ownership or organizational structure. In such transactions, part of the observed price reaction may reflect important changes in the ownership and control of the firm. For example, equity carve-outs (also known as partial public offerings) are transactions in which firms sell a minority interest in the common stock of a previously wholly-owned subsidiary. In contrast to the negative returns from the sale of corporate common stock reported earlier, equity carve-outs are associated with significant *positive* returns of 1.8 percent for the five days around the announcement.

In this case, the problem of the potential information disparity which appears to plague equity offerings seems to be offset by positive signals to investors. What are these signals? As Katherine Schipper and Abbie Smith argue in the article following this one, equity carve-outs may suggest to the market that management feels the consolidated firm is not receiving full credit in its current stock price for the value of one of its subsidiaries. If such is the information management communicates by offering separate equity claims on an "undervalued" subsidiary, then carve-outs could provide a means of raising new equity capital that neutralizes the negative signal released by announcements of seasoned equity offerings. Also worth noting, the public sale of a minority interest in a subsidiary carries potentially important control implications. For example, the sale of subsidiary stock allows management of the subsidiary to have a

In contrast to the negative returns from the sale of corporate common stock, equity carve-outs are associated with significant positive returns.

TABLE 4

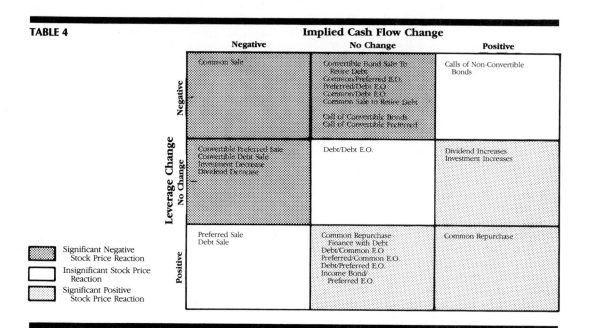

| | | **Implied Cash Flow Change** | | |
		Negative	No Change	Positive
Leverage Change	Negative	Common Sale	Convertible Bond Sale To Retire Debt Common/Preferred E.O. Preferred/Debt E.O. Common/Debt E.O. Common Sale to Retire Debt Call of Convertible Bonds Call of Convertible Preferred	Calls of Non-Convertible Bonds
	No Change	Convertible Preferred Sale Convertible Debt Sale Investment Decrease Dividend Decrease	Debt/Debt E.O.	Dividend Increases Investment Increases
	Positive	Preferred Sale Debt Sale	Common Repurchase Finance with Debt Debt/Common E.O. Preferred/Common E.O. Debt/Preferred E.O. Income Bond/Preferred E.O.	Common Repurchase

Significant Negative Stock Price Reaction

Insignificant Stock Price Reaction

Significant Positive Stock Price Reaction

market-based compensation package that more accurately reflects the subsidiary's operating performance. In fact, 94 percent of the carve-outs studied adopted incentive compensation plans based on the subsidiary's stock.[7]

Academic research in general suggests that changes in ownership and organization affect stock prices (see Table 5). The evidence summarized in the upper panel suggests that voluntary organizational restructuring on average benefits stockholders. The research findings summarized in the lower panel suggests that announcements of transactions that increase ownership concentration raise share prices while those that reduce concentration lower share prices. For example, in equity offers where a registered secondary offering by the firm's management accompanied the primary equity, the average stock price reaction was -4.5 percent, almost 1.5 percent more negative than the average response to industrial equity offerings. This is the case, incidentally, in which the information problem becomes most acute: not only is the firm issuing new stock, but man-

agement is using the offering to further reduce its ownership stake—the reverse of a leveraged buyout.

Summing Up The Market's Reaction to Securities Offerings

Table 6 offers a pictorial summary of the various hypotheses and how each contributes to our understanding of the research findings on new security issues. Those arguments focusing on the information gap between management and investors appear to have the most explanatory power. The extent to which announcements are unanticipated helps explain differences in the market's response to debt vs. equity offerings, and to industrial vs. utility issues. And in the special cases when the offer accompanies ownership or organizational changes, there are important additional insights available. The price pressure hypothesis may have some validity, but for widely-traded securities I remain skeptical. The dilutive effects on EPS and ROE of new equity and convertible offerings are

7. See the article immediately following in this journal: Katherine Schipper and Abbie Smith, "Equity Carve-outs." See also the academic piece on which the above article is based, "A Comparison of Equity Carve-outs and Seasoned Equity Offerings: Share Price Effects and Corporate Restructuring," *Journal of Financial Economics* 15 (1986), pp. 153-186.

Carve-outs could provide a means of raising new equity capital that neutralizes the negative signal released by announcements of seasoned equity offerings.

TABLE 5
The Market Response to Announcements of Organizational and Ownership Changes

In the columns below are summaries of the cumulative average abnormal common stock returns and average sample size from studies of announcements of transactions which change corporate control or ownership stucture. Returns are weighted averages by sample size of the returns reported by the respective studies. (Unless otherwise noted, returns are significantly different from zero.) Full citations for all studies mentioned can be found in the reference section at the end of this issue.

Type of Announcement	Average Sample Size	Cumulative Abnormal Returns
Organizational Restructuring		
Merger: Target[a]	113	20.0%
Bidder[a]	119	0.7*
Spin-Off[b]	76	3.4
Sell-Off: Seller[c]	279	0.7
Buyer[d]	118	0.7
Equity Carve Out[e]	76	0.7*
Joint Venture[f]	136	0.7
Going Private[g]	81	30.0
Voluntary Liquidation[h]	75	33.4
Life Insurance Company Mutualization[i]	30	56.0
Savings & Loan Association Charter Conversion[j]	78	5.6
Proxy Fight[k]	56	1.1
Ownership Restructuring		
Tender Offer: Target[l]	183	30.0
Bidder[l]	183	0.8*
Large Block Acquisition[m]	165	2.6
Secondary Distribution: Registered[n]	146	−2.9
Non-Registered[n]	321	−0.8
Targeted Share Repurchase[o]	68	−4.8

[a] Source: Dann (1980), Asquith (1983), Eckbo (1983), Jensen/Ruback (1983)
[b] Source: Hite/Owers (1983), Miles/Rosenfeld (1983), Schipper/Smith (1983), Rosenfeld (1984)
[c] Source: Alexander/Benson/Kampmeyer (1984), Rosenfeld (1984), Hite/Owers (1985), Jain (1985), Klein (1985), Vetsuypens (1985)
[d] Source: Rosenfeld (1984), Hite/Owers (1985), Jain (1985), Klein (1985)
[e] Source: Schipper/Smith (1986)
[f] Source: McConnell/Nantell (1985)
[g] Source: DeAngelo/DeAngelo/Rice (1984)
[h] Source: Kim/Schatzberg (1985)
[i] Source: Mayers/Smith (1986)
[j] Source: Masulis (1986)
[k] Source: Dodd/Warner (1983)
[l] Source: Bradley/Desai/Kim (1985), Jensen/Ruback (1983)
[m] Source: Holderness/Sheehan (1985), Mikkelson/Ruback (1985)
[n] Source: Mikkelson/Partch (1985)
[o] Source: Dann/DeAngelo (1983), Bradley/Wakeman (1983)
* Interpreted by the authors as not significantly different from zero.

nothing more than accounting illusions; *given* that the security is fairly priced at issue, and that management expects to earn its cost of capital on the funds newly raised, there is no real economic dilution of value caused by a new equity offering. Finally, optimal capital structure theories, at this stage of development, seem to offer little insight into the general pattern of price reactions to new security sales.

Alternative Methods of Marketing Security Offerings

Once having decided on the terms of a security to sell, management then must choose among a number of methods to market the issue. It can offer the securities on a pro rata basis to its own stock-

Despite evidence that the out-of-pocket expenses of an equity issue underwritten by an investment banker are from three to 30 times higher than the costs of a non-underwritten rights offering, over 80 percent of equity offerings employ underwriters.

TABLE 6

| | | Research Finding | | |
	Returns ≤ 0	Common ≤ Debt or Preferred	Convertibles ≤ Non-Convertibles	Industrials ≤ Utilities
Optimal Capital Structure	No	No	No	No
Implied Cash Flow Change	Yes	No	No	No
Leverage Change	No	Yes +	Yes	Yes
Unanticipated Announcements	No	Yes	No	Yes
Ownership Changes	Yes*	Yes*	Yes*	No
Price Pressure	No	No	No	No

Potential Explanations

+ But only for Debt, not Preferred
* In Special Cases

holders through a rights offering, it can hire an underwriter to offer the securities for sale to the public, or it can place the securities privately. If management chooses to use an underwriter, it can negotiate the offer terms with the underwriter, or it can structure the offering internally and then put it out for competitive bid. The underwriting contract can be a firm commitment or a best efforts offering. Finally, the issue can be registered with the Securities and Exchange Commission under its traditional registration procedures; or, if the firm qualifies, it can file a shelf registration in which it registers all securities it intends to sell over the next two years.

Let's look at the major alternatives for marketing securities to provide a better understanding of why certain methods predominate.

Rights versus Underwritten Offerings

The two most frequently used methods by which public corporations sell new equity are firm-commitment underwritten offerings and rights offerings. In an underwritten offering, the firm in effect sells the issue to an investment bank, which resells the issue to public investors (or forms a syndicate with other investment banks to do so). The initial phases of negotiation between the issuing company and the investment banker focus on the amount of capital, the type of security, and the terms of the offering. If the firm and its chosen underwriter agree to proceed, the underwriter begins to assess the prospects, puts together an underwriting syndicate, prepares a registration statement, and performs what is known as a "due diligence" investigation into the financial condition of the company.

In a rights offering, each stockholder receives options (or, more precisely, warrants) to buy the newly issued securities. One right is issued for each share held. Rights offerings also must be registered with the SEC.

Despite evidence that the out-of-pocket expenses of an equity issue underwritten by an investment banker are from three to 30 times higher than the costs of a non-underwritten rights offering,[8] over 80 percent of equity offerings employ underwriters. Perhaps the most plausible rationale for using underwriters is that they are effective in monitoring the firm's activities and thus provide implicit guarantees to investors when they sell the securities. This monitoring function would be especially valuable in

---

8. See my paper, "Alternative Methods for Raising Capital: Rights versus Underwritten Offerings," *Journal of Financial Economics* 5 (1977), 273-307.

The less the potential disparity between management's and the market's estimation of the value of the company, the greater are the likely savings to a company from using the competitive bidding process.

light of the information disparity between managers and outside stockholders discussed in the first part of this article.

Thus, in addition to providing distribution channels between issuing corporations and investors, the investment banker performs a monitoring function analogous to that which bond rating agencies perform for bondholders and auditing firms perform for investors and other corporate claimholders. While such activities are expensive, such monitoring of management increases the value of the firm by raising the price investors are willing to pay for the company's securities.

Negotiated versus Competitive Bid Contracts

The evidence also suggests that competitive bid offerings involve lower total flotation costs than negotiated offers.[9] In fact, it has been estimated that companies which use negotiated contracts can expect their total issue costs to be higher, on average, by 1.2 percent of the proceeds. Nevertheless, the primary users of competitive bids are regulated firms which are required to do so. Companies not facing this regulatory constraint (Rule 50 of the Public Utilities Holding Company Act) appear overwhelmingly to choose negotiated offers.

This behavior may be attributed partly to the fact that the variance of issuing costs has been found to be higher for competitive bid than for negotiated offers. Executives whose compensation is tied to accounting earnings might prefer a more stable, if somewhat lower, bottom line resulting from the use of negotiated offerings. Another potentially important problem with competitive bids is the difficulty in restricting the use of information received by investment bankers not awarded the contract. Hence, companies with valuable proprietary information are likely to find the confidentiality afforded by negotiated bids more attractive.

Probably most important, though, is that the monitoring, and thus the guarantee provided investors, is much more effective in the case of negotiated offerings than in competitive bids. With a negotiated offer, the issuing firm has less control over the terms and timing of the offer; hence, investors have

fewer worries that the issue will be structured to exploit their information disadvantage.

This leads me to generalize about the kinds of companies which are likely to benefit from using competitive bids. The less the potential disparity between management's and the market's estimation of the value of the company, the greater are the likely savings to a company from using the competitive bidding process. For this reason, regulated utilities (those not already subject to Rule 50) stand to benefit more from the use of competitive bids than unregulated firms. Also, in the case of more senior claims such as debt and preferred stock, the informational asymmetry problem is less pronounced, as I have suggested, because the value of the claim is less sensitive to firm value. Thus straight debt, secured debt and non-convertible preferred stock should all be sold through competitive bids more frequently than common stock, convertible preferred stock or convertible bonds. And this is apparently the case.[10]

Shelf versus Traditional Registration

Prior to any public security offering, the issue must be registered with the SEC. Using traditional registration procedures, the issuing firm, its investment banker, its auditing firm, and its law firm all typically participate in filing the required registration statements with the SEC (as well as with the appropriate state securities commissions). The offering can only proceed when the registration statement becomes effective.

In March of 1982, however, the SEC authorized Rule 415 on an experimental basis, and it was made permanent in November 1983. It permits companies with more than $150 million of stock held by investors unaffiliated with the company to specify and register the total dollar amount of securities they expect to offer publicly over the next two years. The procedure is called shelf registration because it allows companies to register their securities, "put them on the shelf," and then issue the securities whenever they choose.

After the securities are registered, management can then offer and sell them for up to two years on a continuous basis. Rule 415 also allows the company to modify a debt instrument and sell it without first

---

9. See Sanjai Bhagat and Peter Frost, "Issuing Costs to Existing Shareholders in Competitive and Negotiated Underwritten Public Utility Equity Offerings," *Journal of Financial Economics* 15 (1986).

10. See the article which appears later in this issue, James R. Booth and Richard L. Smith, "The Certification Role of the Investment Banker in the Pricing of New Issues." The article is based on their study, "Capital Raising, Underwriting and the Certification Hypothesis," *Journal of Financial Economics* 15 (1986).

Because of the additional flexibility afforded management by the shelf procedure, there is greater opportunity for management to exploit its inside information and issue (temporarily) overvalued securities.

filing an amendment to the registration statement. Thus, shelf registration allows qualifying firms additional flexibility both in structuring debt issues and in timing all security issues.

Because of the additional flexibility afforded management by the shelf procedure, there is greater opportunity for management to exploit its inside information and issue (temporarily) overvalued securities. Thus, the information disparity problem attending new issues should be especially great in cases of shelf registration. Potential investors anticipating this problem will exact an even larger discount in the case of shelf offerings than in offerings registered through traditional procedures. Hence, stock price reactions to announcements of new offerings registered under Rule 415 could be more negative, other things equal, than those under traditional registration procedures.

It is largely for this reason, I would argue, that shelf registration has been used far more frequently with debt than with equity offerings.

A Special Case: Initial Public Offerings

Private firms that choose to go public typically obtain the services of an underwriter with which to negotiate an initial public equity offering (IPO). IPOs are an interesting special case of security offers. They differ from offerings previously discussed in two important ways: (1) the uncertainty about the market clearing price of the offering is significantly greater than for public corporations with claims currently trading; (2) because the firm has no traded shares, examination of stock price reactions to initial announcements is impossible. The first difference affects the way these securities are marketed; the second limits the ways researchers can study the offerings.

Underpricing

The stock price behavior of IPOs from the time the initial offer price is set until the security first trades in the aftermarket demonstrates unmistakably that the average issue is offered at a significant dis-

count from the price expected in the aftermarket. In fact the average underpricing appears to exceed 15 percent. (For a summary of the results of studies of offer prices for initial public equity offerings as well as new issues of seasoned equity and bonds, see Table 7.) Once the issue has begun trading in the aftermarket, however, the returns to stockholders appear to be normal.

In an IPO, as suggested, there is a large amount of uncertainty about the market-clearing price. Furthermore, as some observers have argued, this uncertainty creates a special problem if some investors are considerably more knowledgable than others—for example, institutions relative to, say, individuals (especially since the Rules of Fair Practice of the NASD prohibit raising the price if the issue is oversubscribed). Assume, for the sake of simplicity, that we can divide all potential investors into two distinct groups: "informed" and "uninformed." Under these conditions, if the initial offer price were set at its expected market-clearing price, it is not difficult to demonstrate that uninformed investors would earn systematically below normal returns. If an issue is believed by informed investors to be underpriced, then those investors will submit bids and the issue will be rationed among informed and uninformed investors alike. If the issue is overpriced, however, informed investors are less likely to submit bids and the issue is more likely to be undersubscribed. In this process, uninformed investors systematically receive more of overpriced issues and less of underpriced issues.[11]

Recognizing their disadvantaged position in this bidding process, uninformed investors will respond by bidding for IPOs only if the offer price is systematically below their estimate of the aftermarket price in order to compensate them for their expected losses on overpriced issues. Such a bidding process would also account for the well-documented observation that underpricing is greater for issues with greater price uncertainty.

The above explanation has been tested using data from IPOs in the following way. Given that there is an equilibrium amount of underpricing (i.e., one which has proved to be acceptable to issuers in order to sell the issue), we can hypothesize that an investment banker that repeatedly prices issues below

11. For a systematic formulation of this "informed-uninformed" investor dichotomy and its effects on IPO pricing, see Kevin Rock, "Why New Issues Are Underpriced," *Journal of Financial Economics* 15 (1986).

*Recognizing their disadvantaged position in this bidding process,
uninformed investors will respond by bidding for IPOs only if the offer
price is systematically below their estimate of the after-market price
to compensate them for their expected losses on overpriced issues.*

**TABLE 7
The Underpricing of
New Security Issues**

Presented below is a summary of estimates of the underpricing of new securities at issuance by type of offering. Underpricing is measured by the average percentage change from offer prices to aftermarket price. Full citations for all studies mentioned can be found in the reference section at the end of this issue.

Type of Offering	Study	Sample Period	Sample Size	Estimated Underpricing
Initial Public Equity Offering	Ibottson (1974)	1960–1969	120	11.4%
Initial Public Equity Offering	Ibbotson/Jaffe (1975)	1960–1970	2650	16.8
Initial Public Equity Offering	Ritter (1984)	1960–1982	5162	18.8
		1977–1982	1028	26.5
		1980–1981	325	48.4
Initial Public Equity Offering	Ritter (1985)	1977–1982		
Firm Commitment			664	14.8
Best Efforts			364	47.8
Initial Public Equity Offering:	Chalk/Peavy (1985)	1974–1982	440	13.8
Firm Commitment			415	10.6
Best Efforts			82	52.0
Equity Carve-Outs	Schipper/Smith (1986)	1965–1983	36	0.19
Seasoned New Equity Offering	Smith (1977)	1971–1975	328	0.6
Seasoned New Utility Equity Offering:	Bhagat/Frost (1986)	1973–1980	552	−0.30
Negotiated			479	−0.25
Competitive Bid			73	−0.65
Primary Debt Issue	Weinstein (1978)	1962–1974	412	0.05
	Sorensen (1982)	1974–1980	900	0.50
	Smith (1986)	1977–1982	132	1.6

this equilibrium level will lose the opportunity for further business. If the investment banker repeatedly overprices (or does not underprice by enough), however, he loses investors.

A recent study by Randy Beatty and Jay Ritter estimated an underpricing equilibrium and then examined the average deviation from that level of underpricing by 49 investment bankers who handled four or more initial public offerings during the period 1977-1981. When they compared the subsequent performance of the 24 underwriters whose average deviation from their estimated normal underpricing was greatest with that of the remaining 25 underwriters, the market share of those 24 firms fell from 46.6 to 24.5 percent during 1981-1982; and five of the 24 actually closed down. For those 25 with the smallest deviation from the estimated underpricing equilibrium, market share goes from 27.2 to 21.0 percent, and only one of the 25 ceases operation. (The remaining 54.5 percent of the business in 1981-

1982 was underwritten by firms which did fewer than four IPOs from 1977-1981.)[12]

As Table 7 shows, security issues by public corporations are also typically underpriced, but much less so than in the case of IPOs. Seasoned new equity issues have been found to be underpriced by 0.6 percent. There is some disagreement about the degree of underpricing of seasoned bonds, with estimates ranging from 0.05 percent to as high as 1.2 percent of the offer price. Seasoned equity issues by utilities, however, appear to be *overpriced* by 0.3 percent.

Best Efforts versus Firm Commitment Contracts

There are two alternative forms of underwriting contracts that are typically used in IPOs. The first is a firm commitment underwriting agreement, in which the underwriter agrees to purchase the whole

---

12. See Randolph P. Beatty and Jay R. Ritter, "Investment Banking, Reputation, and the Underpricing of Initial Public Offerings," *Journal of Financial Economics* 15 (1986).

In a best efforts contract, the firm provides potential investors not only with an implicit call option (because of the rule against raising the price), but also gives them the option to put the shares back to the firm if the issue is undersubscribed.

issue from the firm at a specified price for resale to the public. The second is a "best efforts" agreement. In such an arrangement, the underwriter acts only as a marketing agent for the firm. The underwriter does not agree to purchase the issue at a predetermined price, but simply sells as much of the security as it can and takes a predetermined spread. The issuing company gets the net proceeds, but without any guarantee of the final amount from the investment banker. This agreement generally specifies a minimum amount that must be sold within a given period of time; if this amount is not reached, the offering is cancelled. From 1977-1982, 35 percent of all IPOs were sold with best efforts contracts. Those issues, however, raised only 13 percent of the gross proceeds from IPOs over that period, implying that larger IPOs tend to use the firm commitment method.

The choice between firm commitment and best efforts comes down, once again I think, to resolving the problems created by the information disparity between informed and uninformed investors. The preceding argument for underpricing firm commitments can be contrasted with the incentives in a best efforts contract. Consider that in the case of a best efforts IPO, if the issue is overpriced and the issue sales fall short of the minimum specified in the underwriting contract, the offer is cancelled and the losses to uninformed investors are reduced. Structuring the contract in this manner reduces the problem faced by uninformed potential security holders, and thus reduces the discount necessary to induce them to bid.

Thus, the relative attractiveness of the two types of contracts will be determined, in part, by the amount of uncertainty associated with the price of the issue. The prohibition against raising prices for an oversubscribed issue (imposed by the NASD's Rules of Fair Practice) means that the company has effectively given a free call option to potential stockholders. Thus, relative to a best efforts contract, the expected proceeds to the issuer in a firm commitment IPO are reduced as the amount of uncertainty about after-market prices increases. In a best efforts contract, the firm provides potential investors not only with an implicit call option (because of the rule against raising the price), but also gives them the option to put the shares back to the firm if the issue is undersubscribed. Because of these implicit options

provided investors in best efforts contracts, the greater the uncertainty about the after-market price of an IPO, the more attractive are best efforts contracts to investors; hence, the more likely are issuers to choose that form over a firm commitment.

To summarize, firm commitment offerings are more likely the less the uncertainty about the market-clearing security price. Consistent with this hypothesis, one study found that the average standard deviation of the aftermarket rates of returns for 285 best efforts offerings was 7.6 percent in contrast to a 4.2 percent standard deviation for 641 firm commitment offerings.[13]

Stabilization Activity and the Green Shoe Option

Underwriters typically attempt to stabilize prices around the offer date of a security. In the case of primary equity offers by listed firms, this stabilization is accomplished by placing a limit order to purchase shares with the specialist on the exchange. I believe this activity represents a bonding mechanism by the investment banker—one that promises investors that if the issue is overpriced, they can sell their shares into the stabilizing bid, thereby cancelling the transaction.

The Green Shoe option (so named because it was originally used in an offering by the Green Shoe Company) is frequently employed in underwritten equity offers. It gives the underwriter the right to buy additional shares from the firm at the offer price. This is equivalent to granting the investment banker a warrant with an exercise price equal to the offer price in the issue. The total quantity of shares exercisable under this option typically ranges between 10 and 20 percent of the offer. Obviously, the option is more valuable if the offer price is below the market value of the shares; thus, the Green Shoe option is another potentially effective bonding mechanism by which the investment banker reassures investors that the issue will not be overpriced. That is, if a new offering prospectus contains a Green Shoe provision, potential investors (especially the less-informed) will reduce their forecast of the probability that the issue will be overpriced because the returns to the underwriter from the Green Shoe are lower if the warrant cannot be exercised.

---

13. See Jay Ritter, "The 'Hot Issue' Market of 1980," *Journal of Business* 57 (1984).

The Green Shoe option is equivalent to granting the investment banker a warrant with an exercise price equal to the offer price in the issue.

Implications for Corporate Policy

Recent research on the stock market response to new security offers consistently documents a significant negative reaction (on the order of 3 to 4 percent on average) to announcements of new equity issues by industrial companies. Convertible issues, both debt and preferred, also typically are greeted by a negative, though smaller, price change (of roughly 1 to 2 percent). By contrast, the market reaction to straight debt and preferred issues appears to be neutral.

The critical question, of course, is—Why does the market systematically lower the stock prices of companies announcing new stock and convertible offers? Such financing decisions, after all, are voluntary choices by management intended, presumably, to increase the long-run value of the firm by providing necessary funding.

After consideration of several possible explanations, I argue that the primary cause of this negative response is the potential for management to exploit its inside information by issuing overvalued equity (or convertibles, which of course have an equity component). Investors recognize their vulnerability in this process and accordingly reduce their estimate of the firm's value. The result, in the average case, is that the new equity is purchased by investors at a discount from the pre-announcement price.

This theory and evidence has a number of managerial implications. Perhaps the most important is that management should be sensitive to the way the market is likely to interpret its announcement of a new issue. For example, if the company is contemplating a primary equity offering and an executive asks to include a registered secondary in the offer, the board of directors should recognize that this can be a very expensive perk; in such cases the market price typically falls by almost 5 percent upon the announcement. This is probably the surest means of arousing the market's suspicion that insiders have a different view of the company's future than that reflected in the current stock price.

Perhaps the best way for management to overcome this information problem is to state, as clearly as possible, the intended uses for the funds. For example, if management intends to use the proceeds for plant expansion, management should say so—emphatically. We know that the market responds positively, on average, to announcements of increases in capital spending plans (with the exception of the case of oil companies in recent years, where the reverse has been true).[14] Consequently, short of revealing proprietary information which could compromise the firm's competitive position,[15] management should benefit from the attempt to be as forthright as possible in sharing with the investment community its investment opportunities, corporate objectives, capital structure targets, and so forth.

This strategy is not meant to contradict the obvious: namely, that current stockholders benefit when management issues stock or convertibles when the market price proves to have been high; and that debt or preferred stock is better if the company proves to be undervalued (though, in the absence of significant inside information, I would suggest that this can only be determined with hindsight). The problem, however, is that this kind of managerial opportunism may prove an expensive strategy for a firm that wants to maintain its access to capital markets. If management develops a reputation for exploiting inside information, the price discount the market exacts for accepting subsequent new issues could be even larger.

In the second part of the article, I attempt to show how the use of investment bankers as underwriters also helps to solve this financing problem arising from the possibility of insider information. The fact that management may have an incentive to issue overvalued securities causes a demand for "bonding" the firm's actions—that is, investors will offer more for the securities if they are provided a credible promise that they will not be exploited.

In those cases where the information disparity between management and investors is likely to be greatest, and to have the worst potential consequences for new investors (i.e., for equity holders, and especially in the case of smaller firms in less heavily traded markets), the demand for the bonding or certification provided by the banker is also likely to be the greatest. For this reason I have argued that underwritten issues provide stronger guarantees to in-

14. A study by John McConnell and Chris Muscarella ("Corporate Capital Expenditure Decisions and the Market Value of the Firm," *Journal of Financial Economics* 14 (1985)) found that announcements of increases of corporate capital spending were accompanied by a 1 percent increase, on average, of the announcing company's stock price.

15. For example, when Texas Gulf Sulphur discovered substantial mineral deposits in Canada, immediate release of that information would have substantially increased the cost of adjacent mineral rights then under negotiation.

vestors than rights offers; issues with negotiated underwriting contracts are more strongly bonded than competitive bid issues; issues registered using traditional procedures are more strongly bonded than those employing the new shelf registration procedures; and issues containing a Green Shoe option are more strongly bonded than those without. Therefore, for example, an industrial equity issue should more frequently be registered using traditional rather than shelf registration procedures, and sold under a negotiated, firm commitment rather than a competitive bid contract; it is also more likely to include a Green Shoe option. By contrast, a nonconvertible debt issue by a utility is more likely to be sold under a competitive bid contract and registered using the new shelf registration procedures.

The above argument is not to deny that shelf registration procedures have significantly lowered the fixed costs of public issues for some industrial companies. In fact it should be especially cost-effective for large, well-established companies, especially in the case of public debt offers.

To take greatest advantage of the potential savings from shelf registration, I believe that management must change some of its practices with respect to debt offerings. Instead of using a line of credit at a bank until a large public issue can be made, qualifying companies could use the shelf registration process to place several smaller issues. In order to retain the additional liquidity in secondary markets associated with larger issues, I expect companies to begin offering multiple issues with the same coupon rate, coupon dates, maturity dates, and covenants—instead of designing all new issues to sell at par.

FINANCING CORPORATE GROWTH

by Bradford Cornell,
University of California, Los Angeles, and
Alan C. Shapiro,
University of Southern California

R apid growth poses special problems for finan- cial managers. They must raise large amounts of cash to fund this growth, often for risky and rela- tively young firms. Nonetheless, it is misleading to speak of "financial management for growing compa- nies" as if it were a special subject unrelated to finan- cial management in general. The ultimate goal of fi- nancial policy, whether a company is growing or not, is to maximize the value of shareholders' equity. In addition, the set of financial instruments and policies available to a financial manager does not change just because a company is growing rapidly. It makes sense, therefore, to examine the financial tools avail- able to all firms to boost market value before talking about the appropriate financial strategies for grow- ing firms.

Broadly speaking, there are two basic approach- es for using finance to increase the value of the firm. Both these approaches can be illustrated by thinking of the firm as producing a cash flow "pie"—that is, total operating cash flow distributable to all investors (debtholders, stockholders, and others). The first approach takes the size of the cash flow pie to be in- dependent of financial policy, so that the principal role of finance is to divide the pie into slices by issu- ing varying types of securities. The object of this divi- sion is to match the securities' characteristics with the desires of investors so as to maximize the total proceeds from the sale of the securities.

The second approach focuses on ways in which financial policy can increase the size of the value pie by affecting operating and investment decisions. Un- derlying this approach is the view that a company is a complex web of "contracts" tying together disparate corporate stakeholders such as investors, manage- ment, employees, customers, suppliers, and distri- butors. This approach assumes that the firm's future operating cash flow may depend significantly upon the perceptions and incentives of the firm's non- investor stakeholders. Financial policy can be used to increase the size of the cash flow pie by strength- ening stakeholder relationships—for example, by improving management incentives or increasing the confidence of suppliers and customers.

The next two sections of the paper examine each of these approaches in greater detail. Once the basic tools of financial management have been laid out, we turn in Section 3 to the issue of what con- stitutes a growth company. Sections 4 and 5 address the main questions of the paper: How are growth companies unique, and given these special characteristics, what financial management tech- niques are best suited for such companies?

SLICING THE PIE

Even if corporate operating cash flow is unaf- fected by financial policy, it may be possible to sell claims to a given cash flow pie at a higher aggregate price by cleverly packaging these claims. In this sense, corporate finance is analogous to marketing. The firm needs money to finance future investment projects. Instead of selling some of its existing assets to raise the required funds, it will sell the rights to the future cash flows generated by its current and prospective projects. It can sell these rights directly and become an all-equity financed firm. But the firm may get a better price for the rights to its future cash flows by repackaging these rights before selling them to the investing public.

There are two basic situations in which such repackaging may add to firm value. First, since different securities are taxed in different ways, repackaging can potentially reduce the government's share of the pie and thereby increase the cash flow available for eventual distribution to investors. Second, total revenue from the sale of rights to the pie may be increased if securities can be devised for which specific investors are willing to pay a higher price. There are four circumstances in which investors may pay more in the aggregate for claims to the cash flow pie: (1) the securities are better designed to meet the special needs and desires of a particular class of investors; (2) the securities are more liquid; (3) the securities reduce transaction costs; or (4) the security structure reduces the "credibility gap" between management and potential investors that exists whenever companies raise capital from outside sources.

Tax Factors in Financing

The uneven tax treatment of various components of financial cost introduces the possibility of reducing after-tax financing costs by reducing the government's share of the cash flow pie. Most notably, many firms consider debt financing to be less expensive than equity financing because interest payments are tax deductible whereas dividends are paid out of after-tax income.

As Merton Miller has noted, however, this comparison is misleading for two reasons.[1] First, it ignores personal taxes. Second, it ignores the supply response of corporations to potential tax arbitrage. In the absence of any restrictions, the supply of corporate debt can be expected to rise as long as corporate debt is less expensive than equity. As the supply of debt rises, the yield on this debt must increase in order to attract investors in progressively higher tax brackets. This process continues until the tax rate for the marginal debtholder equals the marginal corporate tax rate. At that point, there is no longer a corporate tax incentive for issuing more debt.

This process illustrates a key insight that underlies Miller's argument: The supply of securities in the capital markets is almost infinitely elastic. As soon as there is a small advantage to issuing one type of security rather than another, alert financial managers and investment bankers quickly alter their behavior to profit from this discrepancy. They will continue to issue the cheaper security until the discrepancy disappears. For this reason, opportunities to create value through the issuance of new securities are small and unlikely to persist.

Only in rare instances will a tax advantage persist "at the margin." The example of zero coupon bonds illustrates one such case. In 1982, PepsiCo issued the first long-term, zero-coupon bond. Although they have since become a staple of corporate finance, zero-coupon bonds initially were a startling innovation. Zeros don't pay interest, but are sold at a deep discount from par. For example, the price on PepsiCo's 30-year bonds was around $60 for each $1,000 face amount of the bonds. Investors' gains come from the difference between the discounted price and the face value they receive at maturity.

These securities appeal to those investors who like to be certain of their long-term return. The locked-in return means that investors know the maturity value of their investment, an important consideration for pension funds and other buyers who have fixed future commitments to meet. Normal bonds don't provide that certainty, because the rate at which coupons can be reinvested is unknown at the time of issue. But despite the potential market for such bonds, they did not exist until PepsiCo's 1982 issue.

The pent-up demand for its $850 million face value offering gave PepsiCo an extraordinarily low cost of funds. The net borrowing cost to the company was under 10 percent, almost four percentage points lower than the yield at that time on U.S. Treasury securities of the same maturity. But zero-coupon bonds did not remain such a low-cost source of funds for long. Once firms saw these low yields, the supply of zero-coupon debt expanded rapidly. In addition, clever Wall Street firms discovered how to manufacture zeros from existing bonds. They bought Treasury bonds, stripped the coupons from the bonds, repackaged the coupons, and sold the

---

1. Merton H. Miller, "Debt and Taxes," *Journal of Finance*, May 1977, pp. 261-276.

coupons and the principal separately as a series of annuities and zero-coupon bonds.

The increase in the supply relative to the demand for zeros resulted in a jump in their required yields, negating their previous cost advantage. But the tax advantage—one which is associated with any original issue discount debt (OID)—remained. The tax advantage to a firm from issuing zeros rather than current coupon debt stems from the tax provision that allows companies to amortize as interest the amount of the original discount from par over the life of the bond. The firm benefits by receiving a current tax write-off for a future expense. By contrast, if it issues current coupon debt, the firm's tax write-off and expense occur simultaneously. The tax advantage from OIDs, which is maximized by issuing zero-coupon bonds, translates into a reduction in the company's cost of debt capital.

But these tax savings don't tell the whole story. Investors must pay tax on the amortized portion of the discount each year even though they receive no cash until the bond matures. Thus the tax advantage to the firm from issuing zeros has been offset by the higher pre-tax yields required by investors to provide them with the same after-tax yields they could earn on comparable-risk current coupon debt. As a result, corporations issuing zeros will only realize a tax benefit to the extent that the marginal corporate tax rate exceeds the marginal investor tax rate. At the extreme, if these marginal tax rates are equal, the tax advantage to an issuing corporation will be completely eliminated by the tax disadvantage to the investor.

The initial purchasers of zero-coupon bonds were primarily of two groups: (1) tax-exempt institutional investors such as pension plans and individual investors (for their tax-exempt IRAs) who sought to lock in higher yields; and (2) Japanese investors, for whom the discount was treated as a non-taxable capital gain if the bonds were sold prior to maturity. Selling to the tax-exempt segment of the market yielded maximum benefits to the issuers of zeros since the disparity in marginal tax rates was at its greatest.

The supply of tax-exempt institutional money, however, is limited. Furthermore, the Japanese government has ended the tax exemption for zero-coupon bond gains; Japanese investors have accordingly demanded higher yields to compensate for their tax liability. The reaction by the Japanese government illustrates another important point concerning financial strategy: If one devises a legal way to engage in unlimited tax arbitrage through the financial markets, the government will eventually change the law.

More limited tax arbitrage, however, may persist for some time. For example, companies with tax losses or excess tax credits can sell preferred stock to other corporations and thereby reduce investor taxes without a corresponding increase in their taxes. The reason is that corporate investors can exclude from taxable income 70 percent of the preferred (or common) dividends they receive. This means that a corporate investor in the 34 percent tax bracket faces an effective tax rate of only 10.2 percent (.3 × 34%) on preferred dividends. As a result, corporate investors are willing to accept a lower yield on preferred stock than on comparable debt securities. Hence, companies in low tax brackets (who are unable to make full use of the interest tax write-off) should be able to raise funds at a lower after-tax cost with preferred stock instead of debt. Similarly, leasing (rather than buying) assets enables low tax bracket companies to raise funds at a lower cost by passing along the depreciation tax deduction to investors in higher tax brackets in return for a lower effective interest rate.

Financial Innovation

To the extent that the firm can design a security that appeals to a special niche in the capital market, it can attract funds at a cost that is less than the required return on securities of comparable risk. But as we noted in the case of zeros, such a rewarding situation is likely to be temporary because the demand for a security that fits a particular niche in the market is not unlimited, and because the supply of securities designed to tap such niches is likely to increase dramatically once a niche is recognized.

As one further example of this process, major investment banks are currently trying to create value by exploiting what they perceive as profitable niches in the mortgage market. Investment banks such as First Boston, Salomon Brothers, and Goldman Sachs have been purchasing mortgages and repackaging them into complex derivative securities which offer unique risk-return combinations. To the extent that such unique securities are desirable to investors, the investment banks can sell them for more than the cost of the mortgages. Once a particular security structure proves to be profitable, however, other firms aggressively enter the business and drive profits down.

In general, the high elasticity of supply means that repackaging a security's payment stream so that it reallocates risk from one class of investors to another is unlikely to be a sustainable way of creating value. The only niche that is likely to persist as a profitable opportunity in the face of competitive pressure is a niche that involves the government. For instance, by substituting its credit for the credit of a ship buyer, the U.S. government, under the Merchant Marine Act of 1936, subsidizes the financing of U.S.-built vessels. Other subsidized loan programs include those administered by the Synfuels Corporation, Economic Development Administration, the Farmers Home Administration, the Export-Import Bank, and the ubiquitous Small Business Administration.

However, even these governmental niches are not free from competition. For instance, when the government makes subsidized loans available to "small business," it produces an incentive for firms to restructure to satisfy the criteria for being "small." Furthermore, the government severely restricts the supply of securities that can take advantage of these loan subsidy programs.

Increasing Liquidity

Liquidity or marketability is an important attribute of a financial security. One measure of a security's marketability is the spread between the bid and ask prices at which dealers are willing to satisfy buyers' or sellers' demands for immediate execution of their trades. There is substantial empirical evidence that investors are willing to accept lower returns on more liquid assets.[2] Other things being equal, therefore, a firm can increase its market value by increasing the liquidity of the claims it issues.

There are a number of ways in which firms can increase the liquidity of their claims. The most important include going public, standardizing their claims (which includes the securitization of bank loans), underwriting new public issues, buying insurance for a bond issue, and listing on organized exchanges.

Because most liquidity-enhancing measures entail significant costs (for example, legal and underwriting fees and reporting costs), however, the firm must trade off the benefits of increased liquidity against the costs. This cost-benefit calculation can best be formulated by expressing the value of increased liquidity as the market value of the firm's equity multiplied by the percentage reduction in its required return.

This expression implies that the advantages of liquidity enhancement tend to be greatest for large firms (which have higher market values) and for firms whose securities are already highly liquid. The latter implication also follows from the observation that low-liquidity assets tend to be held by investors who are willing to hold assets for longer periods of time. Thus, liquidity is less valuable to them than to investors in more liquid assets.[3]

Reducing Transaction Costs

By reducing transaction costs associated with raising money, the firm can increase its net proceeds. The use of investment bankers to underwrite new security issues, shelf registration under Rule 415, and extendible notes are ways in which the costs of raising money can be reduced. Similarly, the use of secured debt and leasing can reduce enforcement costs by giving a lender or lessor clear title to the pledged or leased assets. Because the costs associated with repossessing assets are more likely to be incurred the higher the probability of bankruptcy, companies in shakier financial positions will find this particular benefit of leasing or secured borrowing more valuable than those in better financial shape.

Bridging The Credibility Gap

One of the key costs associated with issuing new securities arises from the financing problem caused by so-called informational "asymmetries." In plainer terms, corporate management may have inside information about the company's prospects that it can use to exploit potential investors by issuing overpriced securities.[4] Recognizing management's ability and incentives to exploit them by issuing overvalued securities, rational investors will revise downward their estimates of a company's value as soon as management announces its intent to issue

2. See, for example, Yakov Amihud and Haim Mendelson, "Asset Pricing and the Bid-Ask Spread," *Journal of Financial Economics*, 17, 1986, pp. 223-249.

3. Liquidity may also have disadvantages in some circumstances. In situations where management commitment is critical and uncertainty is high, such as leveraged buyouts and venture capital, management arguably should be "locked in" to the firm, at least for a while.

4. The problem of informational asymmetry is discussed in Stewart C. Myers and Nicholas Majluf, "Corporate Financing and Investment Decisions When Firms Have Information Investors Do Not," *Journal of Financial Economics*, 1984, pp. 187-221.

new securities. For example, on February 28, 1983, AT&T announced its plan to issue about $1 billion of new common stock. Investors took the equity issue as a bad sign and responded by reducing AT&T's market value by $2 billion.[5]

For companies trying not to misrepresent the value of their assets, the credibility problem imposes a potentially large cost on the use of securities to raise funds. This cost should not be confused with the cost of capital—the return required by investors to hold the company's securities. Rather the cost of issuing securities referred to here is an added discount at which these securities must be sold because of the potential for important inside information.

The riskier the security being issued, the more important this credibility gap becomes, and the larger the discount applied by investors fearful of buying lemons. Conversely, if the firm can issue essentially riskless debt the discount will be zero because the return to the new debt does not depend on management's information advantage.

These observations imply that companies can overcome the credibility problem by raising funds in accordance with what Stewart Myers calls the financing "pecking order."[6] The most common corporate practice, as Myers observes, is to use the least risky source first—that is, retained earnings—and then use progressively riskier sources such as debt and convertibles; common stock offerings are typically used only as a last resort. Myers's explanation for this pattern of financing preferences is that it reduces the security price discount imposed by investors when companies raise new capital. By using internal funds, companies avoid the credibility problem altogether. If companies must go to the capital markets, they face smaller discounts by issuing securities in ascending order of risk: first debt, then hybrids such as convertible bonds, and finally equity.

This set of financing practices has two results: (1) it minimizes the amount of new equity that must be raised and (2) it forces companies to issue equity only when necessary. By limiting management's discretion over when to issue new equity, adherence to the financing pecking order reduces investors' suspicion that management is simply trying to "time" the market and "unload" overpriced stock.

By reducing this credibility gap, then, companies get better prices for their securities. And when they are forced to issue new equity, where the credibility problem is most acute, all but the largest companies tend to use firm commitment offerings (rather than, say, shelf registration or best efforts). Besides providing distribution channels for new issues, underwriters also perform an implicit role of "certifying" to outside investors that the securities are fairly valued. They do this by putting their reputation on the line with investors when pricing new issues.[7]

USING FINANCE TO INCREASE THE CASH FLOW PIE

The modern corporation, as we said before, is an interrelated set of contracts among a variety of stakeholders: shareholders, lenders, employees, managers, suppliers, distributors, and customers. Although these stakeholders have a common interest in the firm's success, there are potentially costly conflicts of interests. To the extent that financial policy can reduce these conflicts, it can enlarge the cash flow pie and thereby increase the value of the firm.

In this respect, recent research has identified three sources of conflict related to financial policy. The first problem stems from the separation of ownership and control. Professional managers who do not own a significant fraction of equity in the firm are likely to be more directly interested in maximizing their own "utility" than the value of the firm. This creates a conflict between managers and outside shareholders.

A second area of conflict involves stockholders and bondholders. Because the value of common stock equals the market value of the firm (that is, total assets) minus the value of its liabilities, managers can increase shareholder wealth by reducing the value of the bonds. This possibility is at the root of stockholder-bondholder conflicts.

Third, under certain circumstances, firms may have incentives to act in ways that conflict with the best interests of the individuals that do business with them. For example, an airline in financial distress may choose to reduce maintenance expense in order to improve short-run cash flow.

---

5. For information on the events surrounding this issue, see "American Telephone and Telegraph Company (1983)" in Butters, Fruhan, Mullins, and Piper, *Case Problems in Finance* 9th edition (Homewood, Ill.: Richard D. Irwin, 1987).

6. Stewart C. Myers, "The Capital Structure Puzzle," *Journal of Finance*, July 1984, pp. 575-592.

7. The certification role of investment bankers is discussed in Clifford W. Smith, Jr., "Investment Banking and the Capital Acquisition Process," *Journal of Financial Economics*, 1986 and James R. Booth and Richard Smith, "Capital Raising, Underwriting and the Certification Hypothesis," *Journal of Financial Economics*, 1986.

Stockholder-Manager Conflicts

Managers, like all other economic agents, are ultimately concerned with maximizing their own utility, subject to the constraints they face. Although management is legally mandated to act as the agent of shareholders, the laws are sufficiently vague that management has a good deal of latitude to act in its own behalf. This problem, together with the separation of ownership and control in the modern corporation, results in potential conflicts between the two parties. The agency conflict between managers and outside shareholders derives from three principal sources.[8]

The first conflict arises from management's tendency to consume some of the firm's resources in the form of various perquisites. But the problem of overconsumption of "perks" is not limited to corporate jets, fancy offices, and chauffeur-driven limousines. It also extends, with far greater consequences for shareholders, into corporate strategic decision-making. As Michael Jensen points out, managers have an incentive to expand the size of their firms beyond the point at which shareholder wealth is maximized.[9] Growth increases managers' power and perquisites by increasing the resources at their command. Because changes in compensation are positively related to sales growth, growth also tends to increase managerial compensation.[10]

As Jensen has argued persuasively, the problem of overexpansion is particularly severe in companies that generate substantial amounts of "free cash flow"—that is, cash flow in excess of that required to undertake all economically sound investments (those with positive net present values). Maximizing shareholder wealth dictates that free cash flow be paid out to shareholders. The problem is how to get managers to return excess cash to the shareholders instead of investing it in projects with negative net present values or wasting it through organizational inefficiencies.

A second conflict arises from the fact that managers have a greater incentive to shirk their responsibilities as their equity interest falls. They will trade off the costs of putting in additional effort against the marginal benefits. With a fixed salary and a small equity claim, professional managers are unlikely to devote energy to the company equivalent to that put forth by an entrepreneur.

Finally, their own risk aversion can cause managers to forgo profitable investment opportunities. Although the risk of potential loss from an investment may be diversified in the capital markets, it is more difficult for managers to diversify the risks associated with losing one's salary and reputation. Forgoing profitable, but risky, projects amounts to the purchase by management of career insurance at shareholder expense.

Stockholder-Bondholder Conflicts

An important feature of corporate debt is that bondholders have prior but fixed claims on a firm's assets, while stockholders have limited liability for the firm's debt and unlimited claims on its remaining assets. In other words, stockholders have the option to "put" the firm to the bondholders if things go bad, but to keep the profits if the firm is successful. This option becomes more valuable as company cash flows increase in variability because the value of equity rises, and the value of debt declines, with increases in the volatility of corporate cash flows. If there is a significant amount of risky debt outstanding, the option-like character of equity gives shareholders an incentive to engage in risk-increasing activities—e.g., highly risky projects—that have the potential for big returns. (Witness the behavior of many of the troubled Texas S & Ls.) Similarly, management can also reduce the value of pre-existing bonds and transfer wealth from current bondholders to stockholders by issuing a substantial amount of new debt, thereby raising the firm's financial risk.

Alternatively, if the firm is in financial distress, shareholders may pass up projects with positive net present values that involve added equity investment because most of the payoffs go to bondholders. The failure to invest in such projects reduces the value of bondholder claims on the firm as well as the total value of the firm.

Non-Investor Stakeholder Conflicts

The potential conflict between a company and its non-investor stakeholders can best be understood by viewing stakeholders as buying a set of im-

8. The agency conflict is discussed in Michael C. Jensen and William H. Meckling, "Theory of the Firm: Managerial Behavior, Agency Costs and Ownership Structure," *Journal of Financial Economics*, October 1976, pp. 305-360.

9. Michael C. Jensen, "Agency Costs of Free Cash Flow, Corporate Finance, and Takeovers," *American Economic Review*, May 1986, pp. 323-329.

10. Evidence on this point is supplied by Kevin J. Murphy, "Corporate Performance and Managerial Remuneration: An Empirical Analysis," *Journal of Accounting and Economics*, April 1985, pp. 11-42.

plicit claims from the company.[11] For example, the manufacturer of a car, a pump, or a refrigerator is implicitly committed to supplying parts and service as long as the article lasts. Similarly, although managers typically have no formal employment contract, they often perceive an implicit contract that guarantees lifetime jobs in exchange for competence, loyalty, and hard work. Before deciding to carry a new product line, a retailer frequently receives promises from the manufacturer about delivery schedules, advertising, and future products and enhancements. Implicit claims are also sold to other stakeholders, such as suppliers and independent firms that provide repair services and manufacture supporting products.

EXAMPLES OF IMPLICIT CLAIMS BOUGHT BY STAKEHOLDERS

CUSTOMERS:
○ continuing stream of service and parts
○ durability
○ performance/timeliness of delivery
○ availability of complementary products and services

EMPLOYEES AND MANAGERS:
○ safe work environment
○ fair evaluation process
○ opportunity for advancement
○ lifetime employment in return for competence and loyalty

SUPPLIERS AND DISTRIBUTORS:
○ advertising
○ future products and enhancements

These examples illustrate two key characteristics of implicit claims. First, they are too nebulous and depend too heavily upon external circumstances to be reduced to written contracts at reasonable cost. Second, because implicit claims cannot be reduced to writing, they cannot be unbundled from and traded independently of the goods and services the firm buys and sells.

In general terms, the firm is promising its stakeholders that it will make a "best efforts" attempt to satisfy them whatever happens in the future. This implicit claim clearly cannot be reduced to a legal agreement, but stakeholders' assessments of what such claims are worth are likely to be a key determinant of, for example, how much customers will pay for the company's products and the effort that employees, suppliers, and other stakeholders will make on behalf of the company.

The price stakeholders will pay for implicit claims depends on their expectations of future payoffs. In forming these expectations, stakeholders understand that it may turn out to be in the company's interest to renege on such claims after the fact; that is, absent other information about a firm, they will expect the firm to promise the maximum payout *ex ante*, but only to deliver the amount that maximizes the value of the firm *ex post*.[12] Firms can engage in this type of behavior because implicit claims have little legal standing. Typically, the firm can default on its implicit claims without going bankrupt. This means that corporate stakeholders such as customers, suppliers, and employees must look to the firm, not the courts, for assurance that their implicit claims will be honored.

Under these circumstances, stakeholders are frequently willing to pay a substantial premium for the claims of firms they trust. For example, IBM computers are purchased not because they offer the latest technology, longest warranties, or lowest prices, but because customers value the wide variety of implicit claims that IBM sells with its machines more highly than the implicit claims of smaller, competing manufacturers.

Because the payoffs on implicit claims are uncertain, even when the possibility of bankruptcy is remote, stakeholders who purchase implicit claims from the firm will seek to determine whether the firm has the organizational structure, management skills, and financial strength to make good on its implicit claims. Thus the value of these claims will be sensitive to information about the firm's financial condition.

Financially healthy firms typically have a strong incentive to honor their implicit claims. Myopic behavior on the part of the firm—for example, improving cash flow today by defaulting on implicit claims sold in the past—will damage the firm's reputation for quality products and reliable service, and thereby

---

11. This section is based on Bradford Cornell and Alan C. Shapiro, "Corporate Stakeholders and Corporate Finance," *Financial Management*, April 1987, pp. 5-14.

12. Rational economic behavior implies that the firm will do whatever is in its self-interest to do after the fact. If all goes well, it will generally be in the firm's best interest to honor its commitments.

lower the price at which it can sell future implicit claims. Nevertheless, a firm having difficulty scraping up enough cash to pay its creditors may be tempted to cut corners in service and products. For such a firm, the long-run value of a strong reputation may be less important than generating enough cash to make it through the next day.

Recognizing these possibilities, stakeholders will pay less for the implicit claims of financially troubled firms. In practical terms, this means that a company in financial distress, or even one that may wind up in financial distress, will have to discount its product prices, pay more to its employees, and receive worse terms from its suppliers and distributors.[13] The net result is that companies that have difficulty convincing stakeholders of their ability or willingness to honor their implicit claims may be placed at a competitive disadvantage relative to their more financially secure rivals.

Thus, firms have clear-cut incentives to find ways of assuring the market that they will not engage in opportunistic behavior. Such mechanisms include things like the following: providing managers with incentives, such as stock options, to act in accordance with shareholder interests; bearing monitoring costs in the form of audits, specific reporting procedures and other surveillance methods; and including various restrictive covenants in bond and bank loan agreements.

The firm can also use its capital structure as a conflict management tool. Unfortunately, a financial policy designed to reduce one source of conflict often opens the door to other conflicts. For instance, one way to lessen the opportunity of management to waste the firm's free cash flow is to reduce the scope of management discretion by issuing additional debt. Issuing more debt, however, increases potential stockholder-bondholder conflicts and also raises the probability of financial distress. On the other hand, adding equity to the capital structure will reduce conflicts between stockholders and bondholders but increase the likelihood of conflicts between management and stockholders over the disposition of free cash flow. It may also increase the government's share of the pie.

In short, any change in capital structure is likely to mitigate some problems and aggravate others.

Managers must attempt to balance these effects in light of the firm's special characteristics. It is in this sense that it is meaningful to speak of financial policy for a growth company. The special characteristics of rapidly growing companies mean that some costs and conflicts are greater and others smaller than in the case of mature companies. Therefore, it makes sense first to discuss the distinctive features of a growth company and then to suggest how those features affect the choice of financial policy.

THE SPECIAL FEATURES OF GROWING COMPANIES

The most obvious sign of a rapidly growing company is its large appetite for cash. Even though income rises along with sales, cash flow is generally negative because the investment required to finance the growth in sales typically exceeds the current net operating cash flow. A company, or its division, usually begins to generate substantial free cash flow only after the business matures and sales growth slows. Therefore, the ability to locate potential sources of external funds and to arrange them in an attractive financial package are major factors affecting corporate growth. The absence of free cash flow also reduces the likelihood that this will be a source of conflict between management and shareholders.

The second prominent feature of growing companies is less obvious, but critical nonetheless in devising a financial plan. For a company to grow in value, not just in size, it must have access to investment opportunities with positive net present values. These opportunities may be thought of as growth options.[14] Such options include the possibility of increasing the profitability of existing product lines as well as expanding into profitable new products or markets.

Growth options are typically the primary source of value in rapidly expanding firms. Such firms often have few tangible assets in place; their assets instead consist primarily of specialized knowledge and management skill. For example, Genentech, a gene-splicing company, had a stock market value of over $3 billion in late 1986 even though earnings for the year were only $11 million, giving it a P/E ratio of over 270 to 1. Clearly, the market was valuing Genentech's future ability to capitalize on its re-

13. The costs of financial distress are elaborated on in Alan C. Shapiro and Sheridan Titman, "An Integrated Approach to Corporate Risk Management," *Midland Corporate Finance Journal*, Summer 1985, pp. 41-56.

14. The idea of growth options was introduced by Stewart C. Myers,

"Determinants of Corporate Borrowing," *Journal of Financial Economics*, November 1977, pp. 138-147. For discussion of new techniques for valuing such options, see Volume 5 Number 1 of the *Midland Corporate Finance Journal*, which is devoted entirely to that subject.

search in areas such as anti-cancer therapy and blood clot dissolvers for heart attack victims.

A third key aspect of growth companies is that the market is likely to have a particularly difficult time in establishing their values. Unlike companies whose value depends primarily on familiar, straightforward projects, the value of a growth company depends on the value of growth options, for which there are no obvious comparables. Instead, such valuations must be based on expectations about future profits from yet-to-be-developed products (as in the case of Genentech) or novel market niches (as in the case of Federal Express). This difficulty in valuing growth options both exacerbates the credibility problem and increases the potential for conflicts among managers, investors, and non-investor stakeholders.

The credibility gap between management and investors is likely to be most pronounced in the case of growth companies because management in such cases will often have far better information about the future profitability of undeveloped products and untapped market niches. This greater possibility for important inside information increases the amount by which investors will discount the price of new corporate securities to compensate for their informational disadvantage. The natural management response to this problem, which is to provide investors with additional information, is often not credible because such statements are likely to be self-serving. Nor is the provision of such information to outsiders a possible alternative in many cases, because going public with the information necessary to evaluate its investments could jeopardize the company's competitive position.

Investors must also cope with the problem of uncertainty about management's abilities and commitment. The problems of managerial shirking and misrepresentation, which are liable to exist in all firms, are especially critical in growth companies because the value of growth options is especially dependent on the performance of management. The higher the percentage of value accounted for by growth options, the worse these problems are likely to be (unless management has a sizeable equity stake in the company).

Bondholders' fears of being exploited are also magnified in the case of growth companies. Growth options often involve the possibility of future projects whose actual undertaking depends on how events unfold over time. Also, other things being equal, the riskier an investment the more valuable is an option on it. Taken together, these factors increase the risk to bondholders of opportunistic behavior on the part of shareholders of companies with substantial amounts of growth options.

Another problem for bondholders is that growth options typically have little value apart from the firm. The absence of a secondary market for such options limits their use as security for debt claims.

Stockholders and bondholders are not the only parties for whom the wider information gap besetting growth companies is an important problem. Non-investor stakeholders such as customers and suppliers must make "firm-specific investments" whose returns depend on management's ability to exploit growth options effectively. If the firm fails to expand and develop new products, those parties that chose to do business with the firm will suffer. To reassure these stakeholders, management must do more than simply promise to honor their implicit claims; it must find some means to "bond" those promises. These bonding mechanisms are particularly important for growth companies because, in most instances, management has not had the time to develop its reputation or the reputation for the firm's products.

FINANCING GROWTH COMPANIES

In the first two sections of this article, we presented a checklist of issues to guide the financial manager in his or her attempt to make financial choices that maximize the value of the firm. Some of these issues are more important for growth companies than others.

Taxes, for example, are primarily of concern to companies in the highest effective tax bracket. Companies with fairly stable or predictable incomes, and with little other means of shielding their income from taxes, know that they will be in the highest corporate tax bracket each year. Examples include consumer goods firms, utilities, some computer manufacturers, and packaged foods companies. Growth companies, by contrast, are typically unsure of their tax bracket because it is unclear whether they will have net taxable income in any given year. On average, therefore, the effective tax rate for these companies is significantly below the maximum corporate rate. Moreover, since the variability of profit is likely to be higher for a growth company, there is a lower probability that they will be able to make full use of the interest tax shield, particularly at high levels of debt. This means that the tax advantages of debt are less valuable for growth companies than for mature companies.[15]

Although growth companies are unlikely to be able to benefit from the tax advantages of debt, taxes may still play a role in their financing strategy. Specifically, low tax bracket growth companies may be able to use financing to transfer certain tax benefits to other companies that can more fully utilize them in return for a lower effective cost of funds. For example, we saw earlier that low-tax-bracket companies may be able to raise funds at a lower after-tax cost with preferred stock than with debt. Similarly, leasing (rather than buying) assets allows a growth company that isn't sufficiently profitable to make current use of all its depreciation deductions to transfer these deductions to investors in higher tax brackets; in return it gets financing with a lower effective interest rate.

As discussed earlier, there are two reasons for designing innovative securities: (1) to satisfy unmet market demand for a particular security with a unique risk/return trade-off; and (2) to solve specific incentive problems and resolve potential conflicts. Only the second reason is likely to be a reliable source of value for growth companies. As also noted earlier, unmet demands for new securities are unlikely to persist for long in a competitive financial marketplace. Furthermore, a growth company may be at a disadvantage in introducing innovative securities. Because of the relatively large credibility gap that faces growth companies, investors are likely to be especially wary of new securities from such companies that promise unique risk/return trade-offs. Fearing that these securities may be designed to exploit their ignorance, investors are likely to discount them more heavily, thereby negating the benefits of innovation.

Increasing liquidity and reducing transaction costs are potentially useful ways to increase the value of a firm. However, the benefits of these actions are apt to be smaller for growth companies. Growth companies are likely to attract investors who are more interested in long-run capital appreciation. Such investors typically follow a buy-and-hold strategy, so that the benefits of increasing liquidity or

reducing transaction costs are likely to be minimal. When weighed against the costs of increasing liquidity or lowering transaction costs, therefore, such measures appear to be less beneficial for growth companies than for more mature companies.

The Credibility Gap and the Problem of Financing Growth Companies

Growth companies, then, are not likely to have a comparative advantage in creating value by dividing up the cash flow pie. By contrast, measures designed to bridge the credibility gap are likely to be particularly valuable for growth companies. Both investor and non-investor stakeholders will be more uncertain about the future prospects of a growth company than about the prospects of a more mature firm. Measures the firm can take to resolve this uncertainty will both raise the price that investors are willing to pay for its securities and reduce potential conflicts among the various corporate stakeholders.

The problem of credibility for growth companies is so pervasive that it affects all aspects of their financing. Perhaps the best way to introduce the problem is to consider a growing firm that needs new funds to exercise a growth option. Assume the firm is making a straightforward choice of debt or equity. To make the example concrete, suppose the option is the chance to invest in the development of a new software package for word processing.

If the firm goes to the equity market today to finance development of the product, credibility will be a serious issue. How are investors to know exactly what the product will look like, and whether management will be capable of producing the product on schedule, effectively marketing it, and enhancing and supporting it? Because of this uncertainty, the firm has an incentive to delay exercising its growth option until investors become better informed.

Competitive conditions, however, provide an incentive for early exercise. Because these options are often shared with other competitors and cannot generally be traded, a company that waits to exercise a shared growth option—such as the chance to enter a new market or to invest in a new technology—may find that competitors have already seized the oppor-

---

15. There is another reason why the tax advantage of debt is unlikely to be significant for a growth company. Recall that Merton Miller has argued that debt will be issued in aggregate until the tax advantage at the corporate level of issuing more debt is fully offset by the higher returns demanded by investors who must pay tax on their interest receipts. Even if some tax advantage to debt remains, Miller's argument implies that only those firms that face the highest effective tax rates are likely to benefit from issuing more debt. Growth companies are unlikely to fall into this category.

tunity. For instance, a software firm that delays developing its new word processing program may find that, by the time the program ships, customers are committed to a competing product. (The problem is analogous to deciding whether to exercise an option on a dividend-paying stock before maturity; you preserve the option by waiting but forgo the dividend.)

The message here is that companies must structure their financing to remain flexible enough to exercise growth options at the opportune moment. In this regard, future flexibility may be as important as current flexibility. Many strategically important investments—such as investments in R&D, factory automation, a brand name, or a distribution network—are often but the first link in a chain of subsequent investment decisions. The company must be prepared to exercise each of these related growth options in order to fully exploit the value of the initial investment. Moreover, stakeholders will condition the price they are willing to pay for the company's implicit claims today on the company's financial capacity to exercise these growth options in the future and provide them with the services and products they expect.

For example, if our software firm decides it must have the funds today to retain its flexibility, then it must issue equity at a big discount or go to the debt market. As noted earlier, the discount on debt will be much smaller because the cash flows received by creditors are less sensitive to the performance of the firm. However, there is a cost to issuing debt which is likely to be particularly great for growing firms.

First, the cost of financial distress is apt to be particularly large for growing firms. As we have seen, much of the value of a growing company comes from growth options which, as also noted, are highly intangible assets. Such intangible assets will rapidly depreciate in value if the firm experiences—or even seems likely to experience—financial trouble. Because the probability of financial distress increases with financial leverage, the expected cost of financial distress increases with the amount of debt issued.

Recognizing the costs of financial distress, creditors of growing firms require detailed covenants to protect themselves against potential managerial opportunism and incompetence. These covenants are likely to be especially restrictive for highly-leveraged growth companies because these companies, by their nature, are engaged in high-risk activities. Although restrictive loan covenants avoid many of the potential conflicts associated with debt financing—by limiting management actions that are potentially harmful to bondholders—they also may turn out to be costly to shareholders because they constrain management's choice of operating, financial, and investment policies and reduce its capacity to respond to changes in the business environment. For example, lenders may veto certain high-risk projects with positive net present values because of the added risk they would have to bear without a corresponding increase in their own expected returns.

The opportunity cost associated with the loss of operating and investment flexibility will be especially high for firms with substantial growth options because such firms must be able to respond quickly to continually changing product and factor markets. All else being equal, therefore, the high costs of financial distress, together with the costs associated with resolving the conflicts of interest between shareholders and bondholders, reduce the optimal amount of debt in a growth firm's capital structure. For example, in explaining why his company shunned debt, the chief financial officer of Tandem Computer commented, "We were a young company competing with the likes of IBM. Not taking on debt was a marketing decision because we might not get customers if we seemed financially shaky."[16] By contrast, established firms operating in stable markets can afford more debt since their competitive stance will be less compromised by the restrictions and delays associated with high financial leverage.

Faced with this unsatisfactory trade-off between the steep discount on new equity and the restrictive covenants associated with issuing straight public debt, growth companies are well advised to look elsewhere for funds. One place to start is with a commercial bank.

The Role of Bank Loans in Financing Growth Companies

A banking relationship may solve many of the problems associated with public debt. The potential advantages of a bank credit are twofold: First, the firm can more readily custom-tailor a set of terms

---

16. This statement appeared in Kate Ballen, "Has the Debt Binge Gone Too Far?" *Fortune*, April 25, 1988, pp. 87-94.

and conditions in face-to-face negotiations with its bankers than by trying to deal with a large number of smaller investors. Second, renegotiating certain covenants in response to changing circumstances is less cumbersome with a bank loan. The flexibility, discretion, and durability of these arrangements is what is termed a "banking relationship."

Richard K. Goeltz, Vice President-Finance of Seagram & Sons, Inc., makes this point as follows: *There is an important advantage in dealing with individual bankers rather than an amorphous capital market. One can explain a problem or need to account officers at a few institutions. Direct communications with the purchasers of [bonds] are almost impossible. These investors, as is the case for most public issues, have little feeling of commitment to the borrower or sense of continuity ... If the borrower can modify the terms and conditions of the former more easily and inexpensively than the latter, then the bank loan will be less costly, even if the effective interest rates are identical.[17]*
The advantages of a banking relationship to a growing company stem from the personal nature of the relationship between borrower and lender. Presumably, bankers, who deal directly with the borrower, have lower costs of monitoring client activities than do bondholders, who are anonymous (in the case of bearer bonds) or are not interested, as are banks, in a long-term relationship with the borrower.

Some recent research supports this assumption. The basic argument of this work is that banks play the part of delegated monitors who check on the behavior of the firm's managers.[18] Specifically, it is claimed that banks have a comparative cost advantage in information gathering and monitoring relative not only to investors in public capital markets, but relative to other financial institutions as well. This comparative advantage arises in large part from banks' ongoing deposit history with the borrower and from the short-term repeat lending activity in which banks specialize.[19]

When a firm is unable to make interest payments on time or when its financial statements indicate problems, the banker's first response is to examine the firm's condition more closely. Such examination is particularly valuable for growth companies because much of their value arises from options that will be lost if the firm cannot get financing on sufficiently flexible terms. If the banker finds that the firm's prospects are promising, he can reschedule the firm's payments, waive a covenant, or even increase the amount of the bank's loan.

The relationship with a bank can also reduce a growth company's information problem with other investors. The view that bankers, as insiders, have better information about the firm's prospects than outsiders and are better able to supervise its behavior implies that the loan approval process should convey two pieces of positive information about the borrowing firm to outside investors: (1) the bank believes the firm is sound, and (2) the bank will supervise corporate management to ensure that it behaves properly. In support of this argument, a recently published study by Christopher James (presented in a later article in this issue) documents a consistently positive stock market response to companies announcing the arrangement of loan commitments from commercial banks.[20]

Another important aspect of a banking relationship is the provision of continuous access to funds. In the typical commercial banking relationship, the bank can be viewed as writing options for its loan customer. Through such devices as credit lines or lending commitments, the borrower can choose the timing and the amount of the loan; the borrower can often prepay or refinance the loan at a nominal fee. Most important, the bank makes an implicit, and sometimes explicit, commitment to provide funds in times when the borrower finds them difficult to obtain from other sources. This flexibility is critical for growth companies because the timing of their investment program is so difficult to forecast.

Despite the advantages of bank debt, banks cannot supply all the financing required by growth companies. The difficulties are three: First, bank debt is still debt, which retains many restrictive features. Second, like any form of debt, bank loans increase

17. Richard Karl Goeltz, "The Corporate Borrower and the International Capital Markets", manuscript dated March 6, 1984, p.5.

18. The information production and monitoring services of banks are discussed, respectively, by Tim Campbell and William Kracaw, "Information Production, Market Signalling, and the Theory of Financial Intermediation," *Journal of Finance*, September 1980, pp. 863-882 and Douglas W. Diamond, "Financial Intermediation and Delegated Monitoring," *Review of Economic Studies*, August 1984, pp. 393-414.

19. For a good review of this literature, see Mitchell Berlin, "Bank Loans and Marketable Securities: How Do Financial Contracts Control Borrowing Firms?" *Business Review*, Federal Reserve Bank of Philadelphia, July/August 1987, pp. 9-18.

20. See Christopher James and Peggy Wier, "Are Bank Loans Different?," *Journal of Applied Corporate Finance* Vol. 1 No. 2, which is based in turn on Christopher James, "Some Evidence on the Uniqueness of Bank Loans," *Journal of Financial Economics*, 19 (1987).

the probability of financial distress, with all its adverse consequences for firms trying to sell implicit claims. Third, from the standpoint of the creditor, financing high-risk investments such as growth options is not attractive. The creditor bears all the downside risk without sharing in the upside benefits. Growth options also make poor collateral; their value in liquidation is usually nil.

The Role of Venture Capital in Financing Growth Companies

In the case of start-ups, whose assets are comprised primarily if not exclusively of growth options, bank loans are virtually unobtainable. Venture capital has evolved as a solution to these problems. In effect, venture capitalists provide private equity. But, in return, they demand a much closer relationship, more control, and a significantly higher expected rate of return.

Venture capitalists also typically demand a financial structure that shifts a great deal of risk onto company management. In order to ensure that the founders remain committed to the business, venture capital firms try to structure the deal so that management benefits only if the firm succeeds. This usually involves modest salaries for managers, with most compensation tied to profits and the appreciation in the value of their stock.

Moreover, the venture capitalist usually buys preferred stock convertible into common shares when and if the company goes public. Besides giving the venture capitalist a prior claim on the assets of the firm in liquidation, one obvious effect of using preferred stock instead of straight equity is to transfer risk from the venture capitalist to the entrepreneur. But, this is probably not the primary reason for using convertible preferred because there are no clear net gains to the venture capitalist from simply transferring risk; if the founders have to bear more risk, they will raise the price to the venture capitalist of acquiring a given stake in the firm.

As William Sahlman argues (in the article following this one), two more likely reasons for using a financial structure that shifts a major share of the risk to the founders are as follows: (1) to force the founders to signal how strongly they believe in the forecasts contained in their business plan; and (2) to strengthen the founders' incentive to make the company succeed by ensuring that they benefit greatly only if they meet their projections. By their willingness to accept these terms, the founders increase investors' confidence in the numbers contained in the business plan. The venture capitalist, therefore, is willing to pay a higher price for his equity stake. The financial structure also motivates management to work harder and thereby increases the probability that a favorable outcome will occur.

To further limit their downside risk, venture capitalists also rarely give a start-up company all the money it needs at once. Typically, there are several stages of financing. At each stage, the venture capitalists will give the firm enough money to get it to the next product or market development milestone. By staging the commitment of capital, the venture capitalist gains the option of abandoning the project or renegotiating a lower price for future purchases of equity in line with new information.

In return for this option, the venture capitalist is willing to accept a smaller ownership share for a given investment. The founders benefit from this financing structure because it means giving up a smaller share of ownership for the needed funding. If the venture progresses according to plan, the founders will be able to bring in future capital with less dilution of their ownership share. Staged financing thus provides the founders with the option to raise capital in the future at a higher valuation.

Both of these venture capital practices, the use of convertible preferred stock and staged capital commitment, can be seen as means of overcoming the "credibility gap" that confronts all growth companies in raising capital.

The Role of Private Placements in Financing Growth Companies

Although bank loans and venture capital offer the benefit of flexibility that comes with a close relationship, they are both expensive. The interest rates on bank loans are generally higher than the rates on straight debt, and venture capitalists demand a high rate of return for the risks they bear and the time they invest. For this reason, growth companies have an incentive to issue securities despite the problems discussed earlier. The key is to design such securities so as to minimize the credibility gap that leads to a large discount on equity and to restrictive covenants on debt.

A growing firm that needs flexible debt financing may be able to secure such funds by way of a private placement. As in the case of bank debt, dealing directly with the ultimate investor opens the possibility for negotiation and renegotiation of the lending terms. In addition, the firm may be able to provide a few creditors with sensitive strategic information that it would not want to make publicly available.

Unfortunately, there is one major complication that arises when growing firms attempt private placements. Because privately placed securities are difficult to sell prior to maturity, investors will want to be assured at the outset that payments will be made over the life of the security. It is just such assurances that are difficult for growth companies to provide. This produces an incentive for the creditors to protect themselves with restrictive covenants and thereby leads to the same problem that exists with publicly issued debt.

The Role of Convertible Securities in Financing Growth Companies

Another alternative to straight debt is to issue bonds or preferred stock that are convertible into common stock at the bondholder's option. If the conversion features are set properly, convertible securities can overcome some of the problems that cause investors to demand strict covenants on straight debt. Convertibles offer investors participation in the high payoffs to equity when the firm does better than expected while simultaneously offering them the downside protection of a fixed-income security when the firm's value falls. If a firm with convertibles is expected to undertake high-risk projects, the value of the conversion option will increase (because stock price volatility increases an option's value), offsetting to some extent a decline in the value of the fixed income portion.

As Michael Brennan and Eduardo Schwartz have argued, this offset means that the value of an appropriately designed convertible should be relatively insensitive to the risk of the issuing company.[21] This feature of convertibles is particularly valuable when investors and management disagree about the risk of a company, as is likely to be the case with rapidly growing firms. Consider the case of company which investors believe to be very risky, but which management, with privileged information, believes is only moderately risky. Assume further that management is confronted with the choice of paying a coupon rate of 12 percent on straight debt when companies that management deems of comparable risk are paying only 10 percent. In such a case, as Brennan and Schwartz illustrate, management is likely to be able to sell a convertible bond issue with the same conversion premium but only a slightly higher coupon rate (say, 8 percent relative to 7.75 percent) than the moderately risky company.

The reason, again, that the effect of the divergence in risk assessment is much less for the convertible than for straight debt is that the value of convertibles is much less sensitive to changes in risk; or, to put it a little differently, the implicit warrant in a convertible protects bondholders from large changes in risk. Thus, if the market overestimates the risk of a small growth company (and thereby undervalues the company's straight debt), it will overvalue the convertible's call option feature. In this sense, convertible securities are well suited for coping with differing assessments of a company's risk.[22]

The problem with convertibles for growth firms, however, is that the very flexibility they afford investors may actually reduce management's financing flexibility. Once issued, a convertible bond is a hybrid security which effectively becomes an equity claim when times are good (and the value of the firm appreciates) but a straight debt claim when the value of the firm falls. It is, of course, precisely when times are bad that debt can cause problems for growth companies short of tangible assets. At the same time, however, the coupon reduction on convertibles relative to straight debt may significantly reduce the debt service burden and, with it, the likelihood of financial distress. Also, the less restrictive covenants associated with convertibles provide management with more flexibility in responding to unforeseen events than does straight debt.

---

21. Michael Brennan and Eduardo Schwartz, "The Case for Convertibles," *Chase Financial Quarterly*, Spring 1982, pp. 27-46: reprinted in this issue.

22. A convertible issue may also provide more advantageous financing terms if management believes the market is undervaluing the company's stock. Convertible securities can be seen as an alternative to equity which allows the firm to issue common stock at a higher price, albeit on a deferred basis, thereby avoiding current market fears that management has chosen to sell equity because it is overpriced. Even if the call option embedded in the convertible security is under-

priced due to the credibility gap, when the true information is ultimately revealed, and the issue is converted into common stock, the firm will receive a higher price than it would have received had it sold equity directly.

Of course, if management truly believes that the stock market is undervaluing the company's shares, the least expensive financing option would be to issue straight debt. Thus, convertibles are the best choice in this situation only if straight debt is inappropriate under the circumstances, for example, because of the added restrictive covenants that would come along with it.

Corporate Stakeholders and the Financial Policy of Growth Companies

Capitalizing on growth options involves more than developing a new product or exploiting a new market niche. The company must develop relationships with customers, suppliers, and distributors, all of whom make "firm-specific investments" when they do business with the company. In making these commitments, as we argued before, customers and other stakeholders are in effect purchasing implicit claims for timely delivery, product support, future enhancements, and the like. The prices they pay for these claims depends on how confident they are that the company will be able to honor them.

Established firms can use reputation to "bond" their implicit claims. Customers realize that if IBM were to fail to stand behind one of its machines, the resulting damage to IBM's reputation would be very costly. They understand, therefore, that it is not in IBM's best interest to default on its implicit claims.

Unfortunately, this bonding mechanism is not available to growth companies, which by definition have not had time to develop a reputation. Therefore, growing firms must turn to alternative mechanisms for bonding implicit claims. One possibility is to use financial policy.

In a capital market with information freely available to all and without material transaction costs, financial policy would not play an important role in the firm's effort to convince stakeholders that it will honor its implicit claims. Because a company can always go to the capital markets whenever it needs to finance its growth options, all the company has to do is to convince stakeholders that it has a profitable sequence of growth options. Stakeholders will then take it for granted that the firm will go to the capital market whenever it comes time to exercise a growth option.

However, this "perfect markets" view overlooks the credibility gap problem that we have stressed throughout this paper. A growth company always faces a significant problem whenever it goes to the capital market. This problem is exacerbated if the company even *appears* likely to face financial distress. Under these circumstances, financial policy can play an important role in bonding implicit claims.

The problem from a stakeholder standpoint is as follows: If a growing firm develops a cash shortage or faces financial distress, it may be in the company's interest to default on implicit claims rather than go to the capital market. Even if the company intends to honor its implicit claims, the disruption to its operations caused by financial difficulty may not allow the company to provide stakeholders with their expected payoffs. For this reason, the firm must convince stakeholders up-front that it has the financial resources to see projects through to completion; otherwise they will not make commitments to the firm.

To reassure stakeholders, growth companies generally should maintain substantial financial resources in the form of unused debt capacity, large quantities of liquid assets, excess lines of credit, and access to a broad range of fund sources. This financial flexibility helps preserve operating flexibility. A firm that has left itself with financial reserves for contingencies can respond to an adverse turn of events by allowing long-term considerations to prevail. By contrast, a firm with a high debt-to-equity ratio, minimal liquidity, and few other financial resources might have to sacrifice its long-term competitive position to generate cash for creditors.

The Critical Importance of Financial Flexibility for Growth Companies

The ability to marshall substantial financial resources also signals competitors, actual and potential, that the firm will not be an easy target. Consider the alternative, a firm that is highly leveraged, with no excess lines of credit or cash reserves. In such a case, a competitor can move into the firm's market and gain market share with less fear of retaliation. In order to retaliate—by cutting price, say, or by increasing advertising expenditures—the firm will need more money. Because it has no spare cash and can't issue additional debt at a reasonable price, it will have to go to the equity market. But we have already seen that firms issuing new equity face a credibility gap. The credibility problem will be particularly acute when the firm is trying to fend off a competitive attack. Thus, a firm that lacks financial reserves faces a Hobson's choice: Acquiesce in the competitive attack or raise funds on unattractive terms.

Similarly, when opportunity knocks, a firm with substantial financial resources will be better positioned to take advantage of it than a firm with few financial resources and bound by tightly drawn debt covenants. Thus, firms with valuable growth options should place a high priority on financial flexibility.

In the attempt to preserve financing flexibility,

however, management must perform what amounts to a balancing act. Recall that corporate managers historically have demonstrated a strong preference to fund new investment with the least risky sources available: first, retained earnings, next, straight debt, and, last (and only if necessary), common stock. This financial "pecking order," as Stewart Myers argues, reflects the attempt to avoid the greater information costs (in the form of larger price discounts) of riskier offerings. By adhering to the pecking order and overcoming one problem, however, management may well be creating another. The reason: a firm that issues debt today thereby increases the probability that it "must" raise equity tomorrow—perhaps on very unfavorable terms.

In short, a firm that needs to raise funds today faces a trade-off. If sources low on the pecking order (internal funds and debt) are used in the current period, then current financing costs appear to be low. But, as a result, the firm faces the hidden opportunity cost of being pushed up the pecking order in the uncertain future and thus being forced to issue more costly equity.[23] Conversely, if the firm reverses the pecking order and instead issues equity in the current period (and the funds are held as cash), then current costs may be higher, but the option to move "down" the pecking order in the future may actually provide the firm with a cheaper source of funds overall.

For growth companies, then, beginning with a substantial equity endowment and thus preserving the option to move "down" the pecking order is likely to be the favored strategy. A balance sheet heavily weighted toward equity, and perhaps including large cash balances at various times, should provide growth firms with the kind of financing flexibility necessary to exercise their "growth options."

As we saw earlier, however, too much financial flexibility may also create its own problems. For one thing, there is a tax penalty associated with investing corporate funds in marketable securities because the interest on these securities is taxed twice, once at the corporate level and again at the investor level. But potentially more important, companies with excess financial resources are more insulated from the discipline exerted by the financial marketplace.

On the other hand, the weakening of management incentives that tends to come with financial "slack" is most likely to be a problem for mature companies where managers have much smaller equity stakes than those typically held by managers of growth companies. Thus, although new equity for growth companies may be expensive to raise, providing the management of such firms with an "equity cushion" is much less likely to introduce some of the incentive problems that come with corporate age and prosperity. With growth options to finance and free cash flow generally negative, the managements of growth companies have a clear incentive to husband their funds wisely. Moreover, the knowledge that such managements typically have major equity stakes in their firms provides comfort to outside equity investors that they often do not have with large established companies.

FINANCING GROWTH COMPANIES: SUMMING UP

Despite all the complexities involved in financing a growth company, our suggestions for policy are relatively simple and straightforward. First, complicated strategies designed to divide the cash flow pie in unusual ways are unlikely to be profitable exercises for growth companies. Younger and rapidly growing firms whose credibility is not yet established are at a comparative disadvantage in this arena relative to mature firms such as General Electric or General Motors.

Second, for a rapidly expanding company, the primary role of finance should be to preserve the growth options that are its principal source of value. Growth options, which are opportunities to undertake future investments, are different from on-going projects in that their cash requirements and their future payoffs are generally more uncertain. This uncertainty compounds the credibility problem that any company faces whenever it issues new securities (Is management selling securities now, investors will ask, because it knows they are overvalued?). In addition, the potential conflicts between managers and investors, between managers and non-investor stakeholders (such as customers and suppliers), and different groups of investors (such as stockholders and bondholders) are aggravated when the company's future is hazy. These credibility problems and potential conflicts have the effect of increasing the

---

23. As mentioned earlier, the financing costs referred to here are added discounts due to the credibility gap. These are costs the company must pay in addition to the normal cost of capital associated with the securities being issued.

discount at which the company can sell its securities or, alternatively, reducing the flexibility of the terms on which securities can be sold. The task confronting the financing manager is to minimize the discount while still providing the financial flexibility to allow the company to exercise its growth options at the opportune time.

One way to improve the terms of this trade-off is to develop a close working relationship with the providers of funds. This means that a banking relationship, or some other source of "private" debt, may be particularly important for those growth companies with enough tangible assets to support moderate amounts of debt. In the case of start-ups, venture capital—probably structured in the form of convertible preferred—most likely will be the principal source. In both of these cases, the credibility problem is partly resolved by the close relationship between management and the provider of funds that allows for the exchange of information on a confidential basis. Moreover, these funding sources can negotiate financing terms which offer management considerable financial and operating flexibility while at the same applying strong pressure for performance. And by their willingness to accept such terms, management can in turn signal its confidence to the providers of capital.

If a growth firm is able to tap the public capital markets in an economical manner, the security should be carefully designed to minimize the credibility and conflict problems. For instance, convertible securities, by giving bondholders an option to convert to equity, reduce the incentive for managers to exploit bondholders by undertaking riskier-than-expected projects. They also reduce the valuation consequences of differences of opinion between management and investors about the riskiness of the company. These considerations increase the flexibility of the terms at which debt will be provided and reduce the discount demanded by investors.

Finally, a growing company cannot make financial policy without considering its non-investor stakeholders. If customers, suppliers, and distributors feel that the firm is so financially weak that its longevity is in question, they will not make the investment required to develop a relationship with the firm. Without such commitment from non-investor stakeholders, the firm is likely to fail before it can fully develop its growth options. For this reason, a growing firm must demonstrate that it has financial strength and flexibility. Thus, the analysis in this article points to one unavoidable conclusion: A growth company needs a good deal of equity up-front (despite the steep discount at which it might be forced to issue its securities); debt is to be used with care and moderation.

AN OVERVIEW OF CORPORATE SECURITIES INNOVATION

*by John D. Finnerty,
Fordham University and
McFarland Dewey & Co.**

T he rapid pace of securities innovation over the past two decades has brought about revolutionary changes in the array of financial instruments available to corporate treasurers and investors. A variety of factors have stimulated the process of securities innovation. Among the most important are increased interest rate volatility and the frequency of tax and regulatory changes. Also, the deregulation of the financial services industry and increased competition within investment banking worldwide have placed greater emphasis on being able to "engineer" new securities.

The purpose of securities innovation is to develop new financial instruments that increase investor wealth—and, ultimately, of course, general economic growth. To achieve this end, the new security must enable issuers and investors to accomplish something they could not achieve with existing securities. For investors, this means higher (after-tax) returns for bearing a given level of risk, greater liquidity, or perhaps just a more desirable *pattern* of payoffs. For issuers, securities innovation holds out the possibility of reducing the corporate cost of capital, thus expanding the range of investments companies should be willing to undertake. The challenge facing corporate treasurers is to determine whether issuing a new type of security will benefit the company and its shareholders—or just enrich the investment bankers who designed and sold it.

When Is an Innovative Security "Significant"?

Some securities innovations are designed primarily to circumvent provisions of the tax or regulatory code. Indeed, Merton Miller has likened the role of regulation in stimulating innovation to that of the grain of sand in the oyster.[1] And since few things in this world are as mutable as the current tax code or set of regulations, securities intended to overcome such obstacles are likely to disappear along with the tax or regulatory quirk that gave rise to them.

Significant securities innovations, by contrast, are those that endure because they provide a new way of meeting *fundamental* economic demands of issuers or investors. For example, financial futures have enjoyed an ever-expanding role in corporate finance since their start in the early 1970s.[2] But some securities innovations developed within the past two decades, such as zero coupon bonds, were issued in large volume for a time but have since been issued only infrequently—because changes in tax law eliminated their advantages or more recent innovations superseded them. Other innovations, such as extendible notes, medium-term notes, and collateralized mortgage obligations, have had a more lasting impact. Still others, such as indexed currency option notes, variable duration notes, and certain commodity-linked bonds, disappeared quickly—in some cases after just a single issue. And many others, such as unbundled stock units, failed to catch on at all.

---

*This article is a revised and updated version of my earlier article, "Financial Engineering in Corporate Finance: An Overview," *Financial Management* (Winter 1988), pp. 14-33. New issue data were provided by Securities Data Company, Inc.
1. "Financial Innovation: The Last Twenty Years and the Next," *Journal of Financial and Quantitative Analysis* (December 1986), pp. 459-471.

2. Cited by Merton Miller as perhaps the most significant financial innovation in the past 25 years. See Miller, 1986, cited above.

In this article, I describe a variety of innovative corporate securities and attempt to identify the sources of value added by each of them. In some cases, my assessments of value added can be interpreted as carrying my forecast of the security's "staying-power." Although many of the new securities defy categorization, I have organized the following discussion by assigning them all into one of the following four categories: (1) new debt instruments; (2) new types of preferred stock; (3) new forms of convertible securities; and (4) new types of common equity instruments. Besides discussing innovations in each of four categories, the article also provides four tables listing some 60 distinct new securities I have been able to identify. For each security, the tables provide a brief description of its distinctive features, probable sources of value added, the date of first issue, and an estimate of the number of issues and total new issue volume for each security through year-end 1991.[3]

DEBT INNOVATIONS

Innovative debt securities, and the process of securities innovation generally, can add value in the following ways:
- by reallocating some form of risk from issuers or investors to other market participants more willing to bear them;
- by increasing liquidity—that is, the ability of investors to sell without lowering the price or incurring high transactions costs;
- by reducing the "agency costs" that arise from conflicts of interest among management, shareholders, and creditors;
- by reducing issuers' underwriting fees and other transaction costs;
- by reducing the combined taxes of issuer and investors; and
- by circumventing regulatory restrictions or other constraints on investors or issuers.

Risk Reallocation

Most of the debt innovations (see Table 1) involve some form of risk reallocation as compared to conventional debt instruments. Risk reallocation,

as mentioned, adds value by transferring risks away from issuers or investors to others better able to bear them. Risk reallocation may also be beneficial if a company can design a security that better suits the risk-return preferences of a particular class of investors. Investors with a comparative advantage in bearing certain risks will pay more—or, alternatively, require a lower yield premium—for innovative securities that allow them to specialize in bearing such risks.

For example, an oil producer could design an "oil-indexed" debt issue with interest payments that rise and fall with the level of oil prices, and investors might be willing to charge significantly lower yields for two reasons: (1) the company's after-interest cash flows will be more stable than in the case of a straight, fixed-rate debt issue, thereby reducing default risk; and (2) some investors may be seeking a "play" on oil prices not otherwise available in the commodity futures or options market. In this latter sense, many securities innovations that reallocate risk also add value by "completing the market."

That investors are willing to pay more for such "scarce securities" is clear from a different process of securities innovation. Financial intermediaries have made considerable profits by simply buying outstanding securities, repackaging the cash flows from those securities into two or more new securities, and then selling the new securities.[4] The success of stripped U.S. Treasury securities (created by "stripping" the coupon payments from bearer U.S. Treasury bonds) and stripped municipal securities illustrates that the sum of the parts can exceed the whole when a particular debt service stream is subdivided and its constituent parts sold separately. As another example, investment banks purchased portfolios of mortgages from originating institutions, placed them in trusts or special purpose corporations, and then used those new entities to issue new securities called *mortgage pass-through certificates*. The debt payments to the mortgage certificate holders are serviced with the cash flows from the purchased mortgage portfolios; and the investment banker pockets the difference (with an important exception to be noted later) between the payments it receives from the individual mortgages and the coupon it pays on the pass-through securities.

3. The year the security was first issued, and the number of issues and aggregate proceeds raised through year-end 1991, were provided by Securities Data Company, Inc.

4. This aspect of financial innovation is emphasized by Stephen Ross in "Institutional Markets, Financial Marketing, and Financial Innovation," *Journal of Finance* (July 1989), pp. 541-556.

Investors with a comparative advantage in bearing certain risks will pay more—or, alternatively, require a lower yield premium—for innovative securities offering risk-return patterns that allow them to specialize in bearing such risks.

Like mortgage pass-through certificates, *credit card receivable-backed securities* and *loan-backed certificates* also represent undivided ownership interests in portfolios of credit card receivables and other consumer loans, respectively. Such securities enable the financial institutions that originated the individual loans to transfer the interest rate risk as well as the default risk (or at least a portion of it)[5] of those loans to other investors. Investors, in turn, are willing to accept lower yields on the securitized assets because of the diversification provided by the pooling process.

Managing Reinvestment Risk. Pension funds are concerned about the "reinvestment risk" they face when attempting to reinvest interest payments received on standard debt securities. *Zero coupon bonds* were designed in part to appeal to such investors by eliminating the need to reinvest interest payments. With zeros, interest is effectively reinvested and compounded over the life of the debt issue at the yield to maturity at which the investor purchased the bond. When PepsiCo sold the first issue of zero coupon bonds in 1982, the yield to maturity was almost four percentage points lower than the yield on U.S. Treasury securities of the same maturity!

Managing Prepayment Risk. Both *collateralized mortgage obligations* (CMOs) and *stripped mortgage-backed securities* address a somewhat different kind of "reinvestment risk"—one that investors in mortgage pass-through certificates found troublesome.[6] Most mortgages are prepayable at par at the option of the mortgagor after some brief period. The fact that many mortgages will be paid off if interest rates decline creates a significant prepayment risk for lenders; that is, if their principal is returned prematurely, they will be forced to reinvest at lower rates.

To address this "prepayment" risk, CMOs repackage the mortgage payment stream from a portfolio of mortgages into several series of debt instruments—sometimes more than two dozen—that are prioritized in terms of their right to receive principal payments. In the simplest form of CMO, each series must be repaid in full before any principal payments can be made to the holders of the next series. By so doing, such a CMO effectively shifts most of the mortgage prepayment risk to the lower priority class(es), and away from the higher priority class(es), which benefit from a significant reduction in the uncertainty as to when the debt obligation will be fully repaid.

With the same motive, *stripped mortgage-backed securities* divide the mortgage payment stream into two separate streams of claims. In their most extreme form, such securities offer one set of claims on interest payments exclusively (IOs) and another on just principal repayments (POs).[7]

Other New Vehicles for Managing Interest Rate Risk. *Adjustable rate notes* and *floating rate notes* are among the many other innovative securities developed in response to rising and increasingly volatile interest rates. By adjusting interest payments to correspond to changes in market interest rates, such floating-rate securities reduce the lender's principal risk by transferring interest rate risk to the borrower. Of course, such a transfer exposes the *issuer* to floating interest rate risk. But such a reallocation of interest rate risk can be of mutual benefit to issuers with assets whose values are directly correlated with interest rate changes. For this reason, banks and credit card companies are prominent among issuers of these securities.

Inverse Floaters. A recently introduced mechanism for transferring interest rate risk goes by two different names because it has two different sponsoring securities firms. *Yield curve notes* and *maximum rate notes*, known collectively as "inverse floaters," carry an interest rate that decreases as interest rates rise (and vice versa).[8] Investors with long horizons find inverse floaters useful for immunization purposes because of their very long duration.

---

5. The securities are often issued in a senior-subordinated structure. The senior class of securities, which is sold to investors, has a prior claim to the cash flows from the underlying collateral pool. The issuer typically retains the subordinated interest in the collateral pool, although in many cases in recent years the subordinated class has also been sold to investors. The relative sizes of the senior and subordinated classes determine how the default risk is allocated between the two classes.

6. See Frank J. Fabozzi (ed.), *The Handbook of Mortgage-Backed Securities*, Chicago, Probus, 1985; also F. J. Fabozzi (ed.), *Advances & Innovations in the Bond and Mortgage Markets*, Chicago, Probus, 1989.

7. The introduction of these securities also enhanced market completeness because of their duration and convexity characteristics. The apparent failure to understand fully the riskiness of these securities led to a substantial and highly publicized financial loss in 1987 by a major brokerage house. For an account, see J. Sterngold, "Anatomy of a Staggering Loss," *New York Times* (May 11, 1987), pp. D1ff.

8. Typically, the incentive in issuing an inverse floater is to fix the coupon by entering into an interest rate swap agreement. The two transactions together benefit the issuer when they result in a lower cost of funds than a conventional fixed-rate issue. For a discussion of inverse floaters, see L.S. Goodman and J.B. Yawitz, "Innovation in the U.S. Bond Market," *Institutional Investor Money Management Forum* (December 1987), pp. 102-104.

Managing Price and Exchange Rate Risks.[9] Commodity-linked bonds were developed in response to rising and increasingly volatile prices. The principal repayment and, in some cases, the coupon payments of a commodity-indexed bond are tied to the price of a particular commodity, such as the price of oil, or the price of silver, or a specified commodity price index. As mentioned earlier, such bonds are often structured to enable the producer of a commodity to hedge its exposure to a sharp decline in commodity prices and thus in its revenues. And, to the extent interest or principal payments rise and fall with the company's revenues, the new security will reduce the volatility of the company's (after-interest) cash flow. Such securities effectively increase a company's debt capacity by shifting the debt service burden from times when the commodity producer is least able to pay to periods when it is most able to do so.

Dual currency bonds, indexed currency option notes, principal exchange rate linked securities (PERLs), and *reverse principal exchange rate linked securities* (Reverse PERLs) illustrate different forms of currency risk reallocation. They are attractive to institutions that would like to speculate in foreign currencies but cannot, for regulatory or other reasons, purchase currency options directly.

Enhanced Liquidity

If a company can securitize a loan so it becomes publicly traded, lenders will require a lower yield to reflect their ability to sell the security without lowering the price or incurring high transactions costs. Examples of such securitization are CMOs, credit card receivable-backed securities, stripped mortgage-backed securities, and loan-backed certificates. They are all publicly registered securities that, because of their liquidity, have yields significantly lower than those on the underlying assets.[10]

For example, when General Motors Acceptance Corporation began issuing automobile loan-backed securities, it noted that its cost of funds was significantly lower than the cost of factoring receivables. Interestingly, the Resolution Trust Corporation recently announced that it intends to issue securities backed by commercial mortgages and that its issues will increase the amount of such securities outstanding by about 25%.

Reductions in Agency Costs

A new security can increase shareholder value by reducing the agency costs that arise out of inherent conflicts of interest among professional corporate managers, stockholders, and bondholders. For example, managers in some cases may increase shareholder value at the expense of bondholders by leveraging up the firm. *Interest rate reset notes* address this problem by adjusting the coupon to a current market rate on a future date, providing bondholders with protection against a drop in the issuer's credit standing prior to that date.[11] Similarly, *credit sensitive notes* and *floating rate, rating sensitive notes* bear a coupon rate that varies inversely with the issuer's credit standing.[12]

Puttable bonds provide a series of put options that also protect bondholders against deterioration in the issuer's credit standing. Certain puttable bonds reduce agency costs by giving investors the right to put the bonds back to the issuer if there is a change in control of the corporation or if the corporation increases its leverage above some stated threshold through a recapitalization. Such "poison put" options protect bondholders against "event risk."[13]

Increasing rate notes, when used in connection with a bridge financing, provide an incentive for the issuer to redeem the notes (using the proceeds of a "more permanent" financing) on schedule. Unfortunately, as many issuers have discovered, if the

---

9. For a more detailed consideration of hybrid debt securities designed to manage commodity and exchange rate risks, see the article by Charles Smithson, "The Uses of Hybrid Debt in Managing Corporate Risk," later in this issue.

10. The issuer often retains a subordinated interest in the underlying collateral pool so that a large portion of the actual yield reduction results from the investors' senior position with respect to mortgage or receivable pool cash flows. Such lower yields, moreover, do not necessarily imply a lower overall cost of capital for the issuing firm. Asset securitization, in a sense, involves carving out a company's highest-quality assets and selling them on a stand-alone basis. To be certain that there is an overall reduction in the issuer's cost of capital, one has to examine the effect on the firm's other liabilities, including the risk of the firm's equity.

11. A variant of reset notes, known as "remarketed" reset notes, includes a put option that protects investors against the possibility of the issuer and the

remarketing agent conspiring to set a below-market coupon rate. It also provides a flexible interest rate formula (in the event the issuer and the remarketing agent cannot agree on a rate) that provides for a higher interest rate should the issuer's credit standing decline.

12. These securities, however, have a potentially serious flaw: The interest rate adjustment mechanism will tend to increase the issuer's debt service burden just when it can least afford it—when its credit rating has fallen, presumably as a result of diminished operating cash flow.

13. Bondholders began to demand such protection in high-grade debt issues in the wake of the LBO of RJR Nabisco. The announcement of that transaction triggered decreases of between 15% and 20% in the market value of publicly traded RJR Nabisco debt.

increasing rate notes cannot be refinanced as quickly as originally planned, the increasing coupon rate acts like a ticking time bomb that threatens to damage the issuer's credit standing by continually eroding the issuer's interest coverage.

Reductions in Transaction Costs

A number of innovative debt securities increase stockholder value by reducing the underwriting commissions and other transaction costs associated with raising capital. *Extendible notes, variable coupon renewable notes, puttable bonds, remarketed reset notes*, and *euronotes* and *euro-commercial paper* are all designed to reduce issuance expenses and other forms of transaction costs by giving the issuer or investor the option to extend the security's maturity. For example, extendible notes typically provide for an interest rate adjustment every two or three years, and thus represent an alternative to rolling over two- or three-year note issues that does not incur additional issuance expenses. Refinements of the extendible note concept, such as certain puttable bonds and remarketed reset notes, give the issuer greater flexibility in resetting the terms of the security.

Euronotes and euro-commercial paper represent the extension of commercial paper to the Euromarket.[14] Transaction cost savings result from the use of commercial paper because corporations invest directly in one another's securities rather than through a financial intermediary.

Reducing Investor Transaction Costs. By issuing securities backed by a diversified portfolio of assets, some companies may benefit by providing investors with a degree of diversification that could be significantly more expensive to accomplish on their own—which, in turn, could also lead to a reduction in investors' required yields. As mentioned earlier, mortgage pass-through certificates, credit card receivable-backed securities, and loan-backed certificates may all lead to a reduction in issuers' overall cost of capital for this reason.[15]

Reductions in Taxes

Corporate issuers can increase stockholder value by designing securities that reduce the total amount of taxes payable by the company and its investors. Such "tax arbitrage" takes place whenever a corporation issues debt to investors with a marginal tax rate on interest income that is lower than the corporation's marginal income tax rate.

Zero coupon bonds, which do not make interim interest payments but instead pay all debt service in a single lump sum at maturity, represent a good example of such arbitrage activity. Prior to passage of the Tax Equity and Fiscal Responsibility Act of 1982 (TEFRA), the U.S. tax code allowed an issuer of zero coupon bonds to amortize the original issue discount—the difference between the face amount of the bonds and their issue price—on a straight-line basis for tax purposes. Being able to deduct interest expense for tax purposes faster than interest on the bonds implicitly compounded produced significant tax savings for corporate issuers. The size of such tax savings, moreover, was a direct function of the level of interest rates: the higher the yield on the issue, and thus the greater the discount to be amortized, the larger the savings. When interest rates rose sharply in 1981 and 1982, there was a flood of low coupon bonds and zero coupon bonds, sold primarily to tax-exempt pension funds, to exploit this tax loophole. Since that period of high interest rates (and a change in the tax law), however, they have all but disappeared (except in convertible form).

Circumvention of Regulatory Restrictions or Other Constraints

Bank regulations specifying the requirements for debt instruments to qualify as "primary capital" have changed several times in recent years. Banks and their financial advisers have responded predictably with new debt securities designed primarily to meet such requirements. Examples include *equity contract notes*, which obligate holders contractually to convert the notes into common stock of the bank (or its holding company); *equity commitment notes*, which the issuer (or its parent) commits to refinance by issuing securities that qualify as capital; and sinking fund debentures that pay sinking fund amounts in common stock rather than cash.

Variable coupon renewable notes represent a refinement of the extendible note concept. The maturity of the notes automatically extends 91 days

---

14. See *Recent Innovations in International Banking*, Bank for International Settlements, April 1986.

15. See the important qualification noted in footnote 10.

at the end of each quarter—unless the holder elects to terminate the automatic extension, in which case the interest rate spread decreases. A holder wishing to terminate the investment would avoid the reduction in spread by selling the notes in the marketplace. These features were designed to meet regulatory investment restrictions then faced by money market mutual funds.[16]

Commodity-linked bonds are attractive to institutions that would like to speculate in commodity options, or invest in them as an inflation hedge, but that cannot for regulatory or other reasons purchase commodity options directly. Similarly, bonds with interest or principal payments tied to a specified foreign exchange rate or denominated in a foreign currency are attractive to institutions that would like to speculate in foreign currencies but cannot make such investments directly. Many of the securities developed in the 1980s and since then contain embedded commodity options or currency options of various forms and were motivated by a desire to circumvent regulatory investment restrictions.

PREFERRED STOCK INNOVATIONS

Preferred stock offers a tax advantage over debt to corporate investors in the U.S. Because U.S. corporations are permitted to deduct from their taxable income 70% of the dividends they receive from unaffiliated corporations, corporate cash managers have a tax incentive to purchase preferred stock rather than commercial paper or other short-term debt instruments, the interest on which is fully taxable. Nontaxable corporate issuers find preferred stock cheaper than debt because corporate investors are willing to pass back part of the value of the tax arbitrage by accepting a lower dividend rate.

Managing Interest Rate Risk with Preferreds

Purchasing long-term, fixed-dividend-rate preferred stock, however, exposes the purchaser to the risk that rising interest rates could lead to a fall in the price of the preferred stock that would more than offset the tax saving. A variety of preferred stock instruments (see Table 2) have been designed to deal with this problem.

Adjustable rate preferred stock was designed to lessen the investor's principal risk by having the dividend rate adjust as interest rates change. The dividend rate adjusts according to a formula specifying a fixed spread over Treasuries. But, at times the spread investors have required to value the securities at par has differed significantly from the fixed spread specified in the formula, causing the value of the security to deviate significantly from its face amount.[17]

Convertible adjustable preferred stock (CAPS) was designed to eliminate this deficiency by making the security convertible on each dividend payment date into enough shares to make the security worth its par value. But, although CAPS have traded closer to their respective face amounts than adjustable rate preferred stocks, there have only been 13 CAPS issues. Issuer reluctance may have stemmed from the security's conversion feature, which could force the issuer to issue common stock or raise a large amount of cash on short notice.

Auction rate preferred stock carried the evolutionary process a step further. The dividend rate is reset by Dutch auction every 49 days, which represents just enough weeks to meet the 46-day holding period required to qualify for the 70% dividends received deduction. There are various versions of auction rate preferred stock that are sold under different acronyms (MMP, Money Market Preferred; AMPS, Auction Market Preferred Stock; DARTS, Dutch Auction Rate Transferable Securities; STAR, Short-Term Auction Rate; etc.) coined by the different securities firms that offer the product. Although the names may differ the securities are the same.[18]

In an effort to refine the adjustable rate preferred stock concept further, there have been at least two attempts to design a superior security, but only one was successful. *Single point adjustable rate stock* (SPARS) has a dividend rate that adjusts automatically every 49 days to a specified percentage of the 60-day high-grade commercial paper rate. The security is designed so as to afford the same degree of

---

16. Variable coupon renewable notes were given a nominal maturity of one year, which was the maximum maturity permitted money market mutual fund investments. Also, because of the weekly rate reset, variable coupon renewable notes were permitted to count as 7-day assets in meeting the 120-day upper limit on a money market mutual fund's dollar-weighted average portfolio maturity.

17. This result increases the volatility of the security's rate of return. One study documents the high volatility of adjustable rate preferred stock holding-period

returns relative to those of alternative money market instruments. See B.J. Winger, C.R. Chen, J.D. Martin, J.W. Petty, and S.C. Hayden, "Adjustable Rate Preferred Stock," *Financial Management* (Spring 1986), pp. 48-57.

18. At least one study has documented the tax arbitrage that auction rate preferred stock affords under current tax law. See M.J. Alderson, K.C. Brown, and S.L. Lummer, "Dutch Auction Rate Preferred Stock," *Financial Management* (Summer 1987), pp. 68-73.

TABLE 1 ■ SELECTED DEBT INNOVATIONS

■ Security	■ Year Issued	■ No. of Issues	■ Aggregate Proceeds ($B)
□ Distinguishing Characteristics	□ Risk Reallocation		
● Enhanced Liquidity	● Reduction in Agency Costs		
○ Reduction in Transaction Costs	○ Tax and Other Benefits		
■ Adjustable Rate Notes and Floating Rate Notes	■ 01/21/75	■ 2,372	■ 385.0
□ Coupon rate floats with some index, such as the 91-day Treasury bill rate.	□ Issuer exposed to floating interest rate risk but initial rate is lower than for fixed-rate issue.		
● Price remains closer to par than price of fixed-rate note of same maturity.			
■ Bonds Linked to Commodity Price or Commodity Price Index	■ 04/10/80	■ 34	■ 1.9
□ Interest and/or principal linked to a specified commodity price or commodity price index.	□ Issuer assumes commodity price risk in return for lower (minimum) coupon. Serves as a hedge if the issuer produces the commodity.		
	○ Attractive to investors who would like to speculate in commodity options but cannot, for regulatory reasons, purchase them directly.		
■ Collateralized Mortgage Obligations (CMOs) and Real Estate Mortgage Investment Conduits (REMICs)	■ 04/23/81	■ 3,548	■ 701.0
□ Mortgage payment stream is divided into several classes which are prioritized in terms of their right to receive principal payments.	□ Reduction in prepayment risk to classes with prepayment priority. Appeals to different classes of investors; sum of parts can exceed whole.		
● More liquid than individual mortgages.			
■ Commercial Real Estate-Backed Bonds	■ 03/14/84	■ 53	■ 8.4
□ Nonrecourse bonds backed by specified piece (or portfolio) of real estate.	□ Reduced yield due to greater liquidity.		
● More liquid than individual mortgages.	○ Appeals to investors who like to lend against real estate properties.		
■ Credit Card Receivable-Backed Securities	■ 01/16/87	■ 151	■ 66.9
□ Investor buys an undivided interest in a pool of credit card receivables.	□ Supplemental credit support in the form of a letter of credit, surety bond, limited guarantee, over-collateralization, or senior/subordinated structure.		
● More liquid than individual receivables.			
○ Investors could not achieve the same diversification as cheaply on own.			
■ Credit Sensitive Notes	■ 12/6/89	■ 4	■ 1.0
□ Coupon rate increases (decreases) if the issuer's credit rating deteriorates (improves).	□ Protects the investor against deterioration in the issuer's credit quality because coupon increases when rating declines.		
■ Deferred Interest Debentures	■ 09/17/82	■ 6	■ 0.5
□ Debentures that accrue—and do not pay in cash—interest for a period.	□ Reduces bankruptcy risk during the interest deferral period.		
■ Dollar BILS	■ 08/22/88	■ 1	■ 0.1
□ Floating rate zero coupon note with effective interest rate determined retrospectively based on value of a specified corporate bond index.	□ Issuer assumes reinvestment risk. Useful for hedging and immunization purposes because Dollar BILS have a zero duration when duration is measured with respect to the specified index.		
■ Dual Coupon Bonds/Fixed-Floating Rate Bonds	■ 11/25/85	■ 12	■ 1.4
□ Interest is calculated on a fixed-rate basis during the early life of the bond and on an inverse-floating-rate basis for the bond's remaining life.	□ Issuer exposed to the risk that interest rates may decrease during the inverse-floating-rate period because the coupon will increase if the specified market benchmark interest rate decreases.		
	○ Useful for hedging and immunization purposes because of very long duration.		
■ Dual Currency Bonds	■ 01/21/83	■ 291	■ 22.7
□ Interest payable in US dollars but principal payable in a currency other than US dollars.	□ Issuer has foreign currency risk with respect to principal repayment obligation. Currency swap can hedge this risk and lead, in some cases, to yield reduction.		
	○ Euroyen-dollar dual currency bonds popular with Japanese investors subject to regulatory restrictions and desiring income in dollars without principal risk.		

TABLE 1 ■ SELECTED DEBT INNOVATIONS (Continued)

	■	■	■
■ **Euronotes and Euro-commercial Paper**	N/A	N/A	N/A

□ Euro-commercial paper is similar to US commercial paper. □ Elimination of intermediary brings savings lender and borrower can share.

○ Corporations invest in each other's paper directly rather than through an intermediary.

	■	■	■
■ **Extendible Notes**	03/09/82	332	42.8

□ Interest rate adjusts every 2-3 years to a new interest rate the issuer establishes, at which time note holder also has option to put notes back. □ Coupon based on 2-3 year put date, not on final maturity.

○ Lower transaction costs than issuing 2 or 3-year notes and rolling them over. ● Investor has a put option, which provides protection against deterioration in credit quality or below-market coupon rate.

	■	■	■
■ **Floating Rate, Rating Sensitive Notes**	06/28/88	9	1.6

□ Coupon rate resets quarterly based on a spread over LIBOR. Spread increases if the issuer's debt rating declines. □ Issuer exposed to floating interest rate risk but initial rate is lower than for fixed-rate issue.

● Price remains closer to par than the price of a fixed-rate note of the same maturity. ● Investor protected against deterioration in the issuer's credit quality because of increase in coupon rate when rating declines.

	■	■	■
■ **Global Bonds**	06/14/89	60	31.1

□ Debt issue structured so as to qualify for simultaneous issuance and subsequent trading in U.S., European, and Japanese bond markets.

● Structure facilitates a relatively large issue. Simultaneous trading in U.S., Europe and Japan coupled with large size enhance liquidity.

	■	■	■
■ **Increasing Rate Notes**	04/12/88	8	1.3

□ Coupon rate increases by specified amounts at specified intervals. □ Defers portion of interest expense to later years, which increases duration.

● When issued with bridge financing, step-up in coupon rate compensates investors for the issuer's failure to redeem the notes on schedule.

	■	■	■
■ **Indexed Currency Option Notes**	10/24/85	1	0.2

□ Issuer pays reduced principal at maturity if specified foreign currency appreciates sufficiently relative to the US dollar. □ Investor assumes foreign currency risk by effectively selling the issuer a call option denominated in the foreign currency.

○ For investors who would like to speculate in foreign currencies but cannot purchase currency options directly.

	■	■	■
■ **Indexed Sinking Fund Debentures**	07/12/88	6	3.7

□ The amount of each sinking fund payment is indexed to a specified interest rate index (typically the 10-year constant maturity Treasury yield). □ The security's duration and convexity are closer to those of a fixed-rate mortgage than a conventional fixed-rate bond ; so it is useful to financial institutions that invest in mortgages for duration-matching purposes.

	■	■	■
■ **Interest Rate Reset Notes**	12/06/84	41	6.0

□ Interest rate is reset 3 years after issuance to the greater of (i) the initial rate and (ii) a rate sufficient to give the notes a market value equal to 101% of their face amount. ● Reduced (initial) yield due to the reduction in agency costs.

○ Investor is compensated for a deterioration in the issuer's credit standing within 3 years of issuance.

	■	■	■
■ **Loan-Backed Certificates**	03/07/85	456	103.2

□ Investor buys an undivided interest in a pool of automobile, manufactured housing, residential second-lien, or other consumer loans. □ Supplemental credit support in the form of letter of credit, limited guarantee, surety bond, over-collateralization, or senior/subordinated structure. Provider of credit support bears residual default risk. Reduced yield due to the benefit to the investor of credit support, diversification, and greater liquidity.

● More liquid than individual loans.

○ Investors could not achieve same diversification as cheaply on their own. ○ Can be structured as sale of assets to remove loans from balance sheet.

	■	■	■
■ **Medium-Term Notes**	04/17/73	1,426	690.2

□ Notes are sold in varying amounts and in varying maturities on an agency basis. □ Issuer bears market price risk during the marketing process.

○ Agents' commissions are lower than underwriting spreads.

TABLE 1 ■ SELECTED DEBT INNOVATIONS (Continued)

■ Mortgage-Backed Bonds	■ 11/14/73	■ 38	■ 7.1

☐ Bonds issued by financial institutions (or other borrowers) that are collateralized by a specified pool of mortgages.

☐ Collateral provides added security to the investors making possible a lower interest rate than an unsecured issue of like maturity.

■ Mortgage Pass-Through Certificates	■ 09/21/77	■ 1,400	■ 336.4

☐ Investor buys an undivided interest in a pool of mortgages.

☐ Supplemental credit support in the form of a letter of credit, surety bond, limited guarantee, senior/subordinated structure, insurance or a reserve fund. Provider of credit support bears residual default risk. Reduced yield due to the benefit to the investor of credit support, diversification, and greater liquidity.

● More liquid than individual mortgages.

○ Investors could not achieve same diversification as cheaply on their own.

○ Can be structured as sale of assets to remove loans from balance sheet.

■ Negotiable Certificates of Deposit	■ 07/10/79	■ 118	■ 5.2

☐ Certificates of deposit are registered and sold to public on an agency basis.

☐ Issuer bears market price risk during the marketing process.

● More liquid than non-negotiable CDs.

○ Agents' commissions are lower than underwriting spreads.

■ Pay-in-Kind Debentures/Variable Duration Notes	■ 09/18/87	■ 4	■ 1.4

☐ Debentures on which the interest payments can be made in cash or additional debentures, at the option of the issuer. Variable duration notes give the issuer this option throughout the life of the security.

☐ Defers the risk that the issuer will not be able to make timely debt service payments. Reduces bankruptcy risk during the pay-in-kind period.

■ Principal Exchange Rate Linked Securities	■ 03/12/87	■ 20	■ 1.4

☐ Principal repayment is linked to a specified foreign exchange rate. Amount of repayment in U.S. dollars increases (decreases) as the specified foreign currency appreciates (depreciates) relative to the dollar.

☐ Investor has effectively purchased a call option on the specified foreign currency and sold a put option on the same currency.

○ Attractive to investors who would like to speculate in foreign currencies but cannot purchase currency options directly.

■ Puttable Bonds	■ 08/16/73	■ 822	■ 107.5

☐ Bond redeemable at holder's option, or in case of "poison put" bonds, if a certain specified "event" occurs.

☐ Option to redeem benefits holders if interest rates rise.

● Put option provides protection against deterioration in issuer's credit standing.

■ Real Yield Securities	■ 1/20/88	■ 3	■ 0.4

☐ Coupon rate resets quarterly to the greater of (i) change in consumer price index plus the "Real Yield Spread" (3.0% in the first such issue) and (ii) the Real Yield Spread, in each case on a semi-annual-equivalent basis.

☐ Issuer exposed to inflation risk, which may be hedged in the CPI futures market. Real yield securities have a longer duration than alternative inflation hedging instruments.

● Real yield securities could become more liquid than CPI futures, which tend to trade in significant volume only around the monthly CPI announcement date.

○ Investors obtain a long-dated inflation hedging instrument that they could not create as cheaply on their own.

■ Remarketed Reset Notes	■ 12/15/87	■ 3	■ 1.4

☐ Interest rate reset at end of each interest period to a rate remarketing agent determines will make notes worth par. If issuer and remarketing agent can not agree on rate, then the coupon rate is determined by formula which dictates a higher rate the lower the issuer's credit standing.

☐ Coupon based on length of interest period, not on final maturity.

● Designed to trade closer to par value than a floating-rate note with a fixed interest rate formula.

● Investors have a put option, which protects against issuer and remarketing agent agreeing to set a below-market coupon rate; flexible interest rate formula protects investors against deterioration in issuer's credit standing.

○ Intended to have lower transaction costs than auction rate notes and debentures, which require periodic Dutch auctions.

■ Reverse Principal Exchange Rate Linked Securities	■ 10/03/88	■ 6	■ 0.5

☐ Principal repayment is linked to a specified foreign exchange rate. Amount of repayment in U.S. dollars increases (decreases) as the dollar appreciates (depreciates) relative to the specified foreign currency.

☐ Issuer has effectively purchased a call option on the specified foreign currency and sold a put option on the same currency.

○ For investors who would like to speculate in foreign currencies but cannot purchase currency options directly.

220

TABLE 1 ■ SELECTED DEBT INNOVATIONS (Continued)

■ **Spread-Adjusted Notes**	■ 05/08/91	■ 1	■ 0.2
□ The interest rate spread off a specified Treasury benchmark yield is reset on each interest payment date through a Dutch auction.	□ Investor protected against credit risk but, unlike conventional auction rate debt, is still exposed to interest rate risk.		
	● Interest rate spread off Treasury benchmark yield will increase if issuer's credit standing deteriorates—whether or not issuer's credit rating changes.		
■ **Spread Protected Debt Securities**	■ 01/15/87	■ 1	■ 0.1
□ The notes can be redeemed on a specified date (in one case, 2 years after issuance) prior to maturity, at the option of the holders, at a price equal to the present value of the remaining debt service stream calculated on the exercise date by discounting the future debt service payments at a rate equal to a specified Treasury benchmark yield plus a fixed spread.	□ Investor protected against credit risk up until the put date but is not protected against interest rate risk.		
	● Investor has a put option, which provides protection against deterioration in the issuer's credit standing prior to the put date.		
■ **Standard & Poor's 500 Index Notes (SPINs)/Stock Index Growth Notes (SIGNs)/Equity-Indexed Notes**	■ 11/30/89	■ 304	■ 12.0
□ Zero coupon note, principal payment on which is linked to appreciation in value of specified share price index above a specified threshold.	□ Equivalent to a package consisting of a zero coupon bond and a long-dated call option on a specified share price index.		
○ Cheaper than buying a combination of a zero coupon note and rolling over a series of shorter-term options.			
■ **Step-Down Floating Rate Notes**	■ 07/11/88	■ 14	■ 3.1
□ Floating rate notes on which the interest margin over the specified benchmark (e.g., 30-day high-grade commercial paper rate) steps down to a smaller margin on a specified date during the life of the instrument.	□ Designed to reduce interest rate margin to reflect direct dependence of required margin on remaining maturity of notes.		
■ **Stripped Mortgage-Backed Securities**	■ 01/14/88	■ 136	■ 38.3
□ Mortgage payment stream subdivided into two classes: one with below-market coupon and the other with above-market coupon, or one receiving interest only and the other receiving principal only from mortgage pools.	□ Securities have unique option characteristics that make them useful for hedging purposes. Designed to appeal to different classes of investors; sum of the parts can exceed the whole.		
■ **Super Premium Notes**	■ 11/18/88	■ 5	■ 0.9
□ Intermediate-term U.S. agency debt instrument (typically maturing in between 1 and 3 years) that carries a coupon rate well above current market rates (and therefore sells at significant premium to its face amount).	□ Attractive to government bond funds that would like to report very high-coupon debt in their portfolios and do not have to amortize the premium over the life of the instrument (or in some cases, money market mutual funds that do not have to show a capital loss even at redemption). As a result, Super Premium Notes provide a lower cost of funds than conventional U.S. agency notes of like maturity.		
■ **Variable Coupon Renewable Notes**	■ 03/16/88	■ 4	■ 1.2
□ Coupon rate varies weekly and equals a fixed spread over the 91-day T-bill rate. Each 91 days the maturity extends another 91 days. If put option exercised, spread is reduced.	□ Coupon based on 1-year termination date, not on final maturity.		
○ Lower transaction costs than issuing 1-year note and rolling it over.	○ Designed to appeal to money market mutual funds, which face tight investment restrictions, and to discourage put to issuer.		
■ **Variable Rate Renewable Notes**	■ 02/02/88	■ 24	■ 5.0
□ Coupon rate varies monthly and equals a fixed spread over the 1-month commercial paper rate. Each quarter the maturity automatically extends an additional quarter unless the investor elects to terminate the extension.	□ Coupon based on 1-year termination date, not on final maturity.		
○ Lower transaction costs than issuing 1-year note and rolling it over.	○ Designed to appeal to money market mutual funds, which face tight investment restrictions.		
■ **Yield Curve Notes/Maximum Rate Notes/Inverse Floating Rate Notes**	■ 11/18/85	■ 48	■ 4.3
□ Interest rate equals a specified rate minus LIBOR.	□ Issuer exposed to the risk that interest rates may decrease, which would raise the coupon. Can reduce yield relative to conventional debt when coupled with an interest rate swap against LIBOR.		
	○ Useful for hedging and immunization purposes because of long duration.		
■ **Zero Coupon Bonds (sometimes issued in series)**	■ 04/22/81	■ 452	■ 38.0
□ Non-interest-bearing. Payment in one lump sum at maturity.	□ Issuer assumes reinvestment risk. Issues sold in Japan carried below-taxable-market yields reflecting tax advantage over conventional debt.		
	○ Straight-line amortization of original issue discount pre-TEFRA. Japanese investors realize significant tax savings.		

> **When a highly leveraged company approaches insolvency, managers have an incentive to take on riskier projects. Convertible bonds control this incentive, and thus reduce this potential conflict between bondholders and shareholders, by allowing the bondholders to share in the higher returns the riskier projects might provide.**

liquidity as auction rate preferred stock, but with lower transaction costs since no auction need be held. The problem with SPARS, however, is that the fixed dividend rate formula involves a potential agency cost that auction rate preferred stock does not. Because the dividend formula is fixed, investors will suffer a loss if the issuer's credit standing falls. Primarily for this reason, there have been only two SPARS issues.

Remarketed preferred stock, by contrast, pays a dividend that is reset at the end of each dividend period to a dividend rate that a specified remarketing agent determines will make the preferred stock worth par. Such issues permit the issuer considerable flexibility in selecting the length of the dividend period (it can be as short as one day). Remarketed preferred also offers greater flexibility in selecting the other terms of the issue. In fact, each share of an issue could have a different maturity, dividend rate, or other terms, provided the issuer and holders so agree. Remarketed preferred has not proven as popular with issuers as auction rate preferred stock, but that could change due to the greater flexibility remarketed preferred affords.

Variable cumulative preferred stock was born out of the controversy over whether auction rate preferred stock or remarketed preferred stock results in more equitable pricing. This variation effectively allows the issuer to decide at the beginning of each dividend period which of the two reset methods will determine the dividend rate at the beginning of the next dividend period.

CONVERTIBLE DEBT/PREFERRED STOCK INNOVATIONS

Convertible bonds (see Table 3) reduce agency costs arising from possible conflicts of interest between bondholders and stockholders. The conflict is this: Once a company issues significant amounts of debt, its managers can take actions, subject only to the restrictions imposed by the bond indenture, that increase shareholder value at the expense of bondholders. For example, when a highly leveraged company approaches insolvency, managers have an incentive to take on riskier projects—even those

with negative expected net present values—as long as they offer the possibility of extraordinarily high returns. Financial economists refer to this as the "asset substitution problem." Convertible bonds control this incentive, and thus reduce the potential conflict, by allowing the bondholders to share in the higher returns that riskier projects might provide.[19]

Convertible reset debentures provide for a coupon adjustment to a current market rate on a specified future date, which protects bondholders against deterioration in the issuer's credit standing prior to the reset date. Such deterioration could result from actions managers take to increase stockholder value. Certain *puttable convertible bonds* reduce agency costs by giving bondholders the right to put the bonds back to the issuer if there is a change in control of the corporation, or if the corporation increases its leverage above some stated threshold through a recapitalization.

Convertibles and Taxes. Many of the convertible debt innovations involve a form of tax arbitrage because 80-90% of convertible bond investors are tax-exempt.[20] The tax motive is especially clear in the case of *convertible exchangeable preferred stock.* This security starts out as convertible perpetual preferred stock, but the issuer has the option to exchange the preferred for an issue of convertible subordinated debt with the same conversion terms and with an interest rate that equals the dividend rate on the convertible preferred. The exchange feature enables the issuer to reissue the convertible preferred as convertible debt should it become taxable in the future, but without having to pay additional underwriting commissions. Not surprisingly, a large volume of such securities have been issued by companies that were not currently taxpayers for federal income tax purposes. Similarly, *exchangeable auction rate preferred stock* permits the issuer to exchange auction rate notes for auction rate preferred stock on any dividend payment date.

Adjustable rate convertible debt was a very thinly disguised attempt to package equity as debt. The coupon rate varied directly with the dividend rate on the underlying common stock, and there was no conversion premium (at the time the debt was issued). After just three issues, the IRS ruled that the

---

19. For a more detailed examination of these sources of shareholder-debtholder conflict, see Clifford W. Smith and Jerold B. Warner, "On Financial Contracting: An Analysis of Bond Covenants," *Journal of Financial Economics,* 7 (1979), pp. 117-161. See also Chapter 9 of Douglas Emery's and my recently

published book, *Principles of Finance with Corporate Applications,* (West, St. Paul, 1991).
20. See J.D. Finnerty, "The Case for Issuing Synthetic Convertible Bonds," *Midland Corporate Finance Journal* (Fall 1986), pp. 73-82.

TABLE 2 ■ SELECTED PREFERRED STOCK INNOVATIONS			
■ **Security**	■ **Year Issued**	■ **No. of Issues**	■ **Aggregate Proceeds ($B)**
□ **Distinguishing Characteristics**	□ **Risk Reallocation**		
● **Enhanced Liquidity**	● **Reduction in Agency Costs**		
○ **Reduction in Transaction Costs**	○ **Tax and Other Benefits:** SEE NOTE		
■ **Adjustable Rate Preferred Stock**	■ 05/11/82	■ 140	■ 11.0
□ Dividend rate reset each quarter based on maximum of 3-month T-bill, 10-year, or 20-year Treasury rates plus or minus a specified spread.	□ Issuer bears more interest rate risk than a fixed-rate preferred would involve. Lower yield than commercial paper.		
● Security is designed to trade near its par value.			
■ **Auction Rate Preferred Stock (MMP/DARTS/ AMPS/STAR)**	■ 08/27/84	■ 381	■ 25.2
□ Dividend rate reset by Dutch auction every 49 days. Dividend is paid at the end of each dividend period.	□ Issuer bears more interest rate risk than a fixed-rate preferred would involve. Lower yield than commercial paper.		
● Security is designed to provide greater liquidity than convertible adjustable preferred stock.	● Dividend rate each period is determined in the marketplace, which provides protection against deterioration in issuer's credit standing .		
■ **Convertible Adjustable Preferred Stock**	■ 09/15/83	■ 13	■ 0.5
□ Issue convertible on dividend payment dates into number of issuer's common shares, subject to cap, equal in value to par value of preferred.	□ Issuer bears more interest rate risk than a fixed-rate preferred would involve. Lower yield than commercial paper.		
● Security is designed to provide greater liquidity than adjustable rate preferred stock (due to the conversion feature).			
■ **Fixed Rate/Adjustable Rate or Auction Rate Preferred**	■ 11/16/84	■ 6	■ 0.4
□ Fixed-dividend-rate preferred stock that automatically becomes adjustable rate or auction rate preferred after a specified length of time.	□ Once the adjustment or auction period begins, issuer bears more interest rate risk than a fixed-rate preferred would involve.		
● Security is designed to trade near its par value once the adjustment or auction period begins.			
■ **Indexed Floating Rate Preferred Stock**	■ 10/01/85	■ 3	■ 0.2
□ Dividend rate resets quarterly as a specified percentage of 3-month LIBOR.	□ Issuer bears more interest rate risk than a fixed-rate preferred would involve. Lower yield than commercial paper.		
● Security is designed to trade closer to its par value than a fixed-dividend-rate preferred.			
■ **Remarketed Preferred Stock (SABRES)**	■ 06/27/85	■ 77	■ 4.5
□ Perpetual preferred stock with a dividend rate that resets at the end of each dividend period to a rate the remarketing agent determines will make the preferred stock worth par. Dividend periods may be of any length, even 1 day. Different shares of a single issue may have different periods and different dividend rates.	□ Issuer bears more interest rate risk than a fixed-rate preferred would involve. Lower yield than commercial paper.		
● Security is designed to trade near its par value.	○ Remarketed preferred stock offers greater flexibility in setting the terms of the issue than auction rate preferred stock, which requires a Dutch auction for potentially the entire issue once every 49 days.		
■ **Single Point Adjustable Rate Stock**	■ 12/13/85	■ 2	■ 0.2
□ Dividend rate reset every 49 days as a specified percentage of the high-grade commercial paper rate.	□ Issuer bears more interest rate risk than a fixed-rate preferred would involve. Lower yield than commercial paper.		
● Security is designed to trade near its par value.			
○ Security is designed to save on recurring transaction costs associated with auction rate preferred stock.			
■ **Variable Cumulative Preferred Stock**	■ 07/07/88	■ 8	■ 0.5
□ At start of dividend period issuer can select between auction method and remarketing method to reset dividend rate at beginning of next period.	□ Issuer bears more interest rate risk than a fixed-rate preferred would involve. Lower yield than commercial paper.		
● Security is designed to trade near its par value.	● The maximum permitted dividend rate increases according to a specified schedule if the preferred stock's credit rating falls.		
○ Saves on transaction costs the issuer would otherwise incur if it wanted to change from auction reset to remarketing reset or vice versa.	○ Security is designed to give the issuer the flexibility to alter the method of rate reset.		

NOTE: All preferred stock innovations are designed to enable short-term corporate investors to take advantage of the 70% dividends received deduction.

The assurance provided investors by the put option [in puttable stock] may be
especially valuable in the case of initial public offerings, where investor uncertainty
is particularly great and investment bankers are accordingly forced to underprice
IPOs.

security is equity for tax purposes, thereby denying the interest deductions. And the security, not surprisingly, has not been issued since that ruling.

Zero coupon convertible debt, which includes *Liquid Yield Option Notes* (LYONs)[21] and *ABC Securities*, represents a variation on the same theme. If the issue is converted, both interest and principal are converted to common equity, in which case the issuer will have effectively sold common equity with a tax deductibility feature.

Debt and warrants exercisable into the issuer's common stock can be combined into a unit to create synthetic convertible debt, the features of which mirror the features of conventional convertible debt.[22] Synthetic convertible bonds enjoy a tax advantage relative to a comparable convertible debt issue because, in effect, the warrant proceeds are deductible for tax purposes over the life of the debt issue.

Meeting Regulatory Restrictions. Banks have issued *capital notes* because they can be substituted for equity (subject to certain restrictions) for regulatory purposes while still generating the normal interest tax shields provided by debt. For example, prior to the passage of FIRREA, banks issued interest-deductible *debt with mandatory common stock purchase contracts* (which qualified as primary capital for regulatory purposes because conversion was mandatory).[23]

COMMON EQUITY INNOVATIONS

Five of the common equity innovations listed in Table 4 serve to reallocate risk: the Americus Trust, callable common stock, puttable common stock, SuperShares, and unbundled stock units.

The first *Americus Trust* was offered to owners of AT&T common stock on October 25, 1983. Since then, more than two dozen other Americus Trusts have been formed. An Americus Trust offers the common stockholders of a company the opportunity to strip each of their common shares into a PRIME component, which carries full dividend and voting rights and limited capital appreciation rights, and a SCORE component, which carries full capital appreciation rights above a threshold price. PRIMES and SCORES appear to expand the range of securities available for inclusion in investment portfolios, thus helping make the capital markets more complete.[24] Unfortunately, a recent change in tax law made the separation of a share of common stock into a PRIME and a SCORE a taxable event, and no new Americus Trusts have been formed since that change in law took effect.

Callable common stock consists of common stock, typically issued by a subsidiary company, that is sold by the parent company subject to a stock purchase option agreement. The option agreement provides for periodic step-ups in the call price and may require the parent company to exercise all the outstanding purchase options if any are exercised. The option agreement gives the parent company the right to reacquire the subsidiary's shares at a pre-specified price, which limits the shareholder's capital appreciation potential.

Puttable common stock involves the sale of put options along with a new issue of common stock.[25] By giving investors the right to put their shares back to the firm at a price no less than the price they paid, the put option reduces the information "asymmetry" associated with a new share issue.[26] The assurance provided investors by this put option may be especially valuable in the case of initial public offerings, where investor uncertainty is particularly great and investment bankers are accordingly forced to underprice IPOs.

SuperShares are intended to divide the stream of annual total returns on the S&P 500 portfolio of common stocks into two components that are similar to the two components created by the Americus Trust: (1) Priority SuperShares that pay the dividends on the S&P 500 stocks and provide limited capital appreciation and (2) Appreciation SuperShares that

21. See John McConnell and Eduardo Schwartz's account of "The Origin and Evolution of the LYON" in this issue of the *JACF.* For a more technical analysis, see also McConnell and Schwartz, "LYON Taming," *Journal of Finance* (July 1986), pp. 561- 576.

22. See Finnerty (1986), cited above, and E.P. Jones and S.P. Mason, "Equity-Linked Debt," *Midland Corporate Finance Journal* (Winter 1986), pp. 47-58.

23. The Financial Institutions Reform, Recovery and Enforcement Act of 1989 (FIRREA) established new minimum capital standards for financial institutions. Prior to the passage of FIRREA, banks could include mandatory convertible debt in primary capital up to 20% of the sum of the other elements of primary capital. FIRREA excludes mandatory convertible debt from "core capital," which is the new definition of what was formerly called primary capital.

24. The AT&T Americus Trust was formed prior to the breakup of AT&T. The trust therefore provided an opportunity for investors to acquire units representing shares in pre-reorganization AT&T (i.e., proportionate interests in post-reorganization AT&T and in the seven regional holding companies AT&T spun off) perhaps more cheaply than they could by accumulating the shares of the different entities on their own.

25. As discussed by Chen and Kensinger, such a package of securities is comparable to a convertible bond. A.H. Chen and J.W. Kensinger, "Puttable Stock: A New Innovation in Equity Financing," *Financial Management* (Spring 1988), pp. 27-37.

26. Puttable common stock issues often provide a schedule of increasing put prices in order to ensure a minimum positive holding period rate of return.

TABLE 3 ■ SELECTED CONVERTIBLE DEBT/PREFERRED STOCK INNOVATIONS

■ Security	■ Year Issued	■ No. of Issues	■ Aggregate Proceeds ($B)
□ Distinguishing Characteristics	□ Risk Reallocation		
● Enhanced Liquidity	● Reduction in Agency Costs		
○ Reduction in Transaction Costs	○ Tax and Other Benefits		

■ **ABC Securities**	■ 02/06/91	■ 2	■ 0.4

□ Non-interest-bearing convertible debt issue on which the dividends on the underlying common stock are passed through to bondholders if the common stock price rises by more than a specified percentage (typically around 30%) from the date of issuance.

○ If issue converts, the issuer will have sold, in effect, tax deductible common equity. If holders convert, entire debt service stream is converted to common equity.

■ **Adjustable Rate Convertible Debt**	■ 04/18/84	■ 3	■ 0.4

□ Debt the interest rate on which varies directly with the dividend rate on the underlying common stock. No conversion premium at issuance.

○ Effectively, tax deductible common equity. Security has since been ruled equity by the IRS. Portion of each bond recorded as equity on the issuer's balance sheet.

■ **Cash Redeemable LYONs**	■ 06/20/90	■ 1	■ 0.9

□ Non-interest-bearing convertible debt issue that is redeemable in cash for the value of the underlying common stock, at issuer's option.

○ If issue converts, the issuer will have sold, in effect, tax deductible common equity. Issuer does not have to have its equity ownership interest diluted through conversion.

■ **Convertible Exchangeable Preferred Stock**	■ 12/15/82	■ 129	■ 10.1

□ Convertible preferred stock that is exchangeable, at the issuer's option, for convertible debt with identical rate and identical conversion terms.

○ Issuer can exchange debt for the preferred when it becomes taxable with interest rate the same as the dividend rate and without any change in conversion features. Appears as equity on the issuer's balance sheet until it is exchanged for convertible debt.

○ No need to reissue convertible security as debt—just exchange it—when the issuer becomes a taxpayer.

■ **Convertible Reset Debentures**	■ 10/13/83	■ 8	■ 0.6

□ Convertible bond the interest rate on which must be adjusted upward, if necessary, 2 years after issuance by an amount sufficient to give the debentures a market value equal to their face amount.

● Investor is protected against a deterioration in the issuer's credit quality or financial prospects within 2 years of issuance.

■ **Debt with Mandatory Common Stock Purchase Contracts**	■ N/A	■ N/A	■ N/A

□ Notes with contracts that obligate note purchasers to buy sufficient common stock from the issuer to retire the issue in full by its scheduled maturity date.

○ Notes provide a stream of interest tax shields, which (true) equity does not. Commercial bank holding companies have issued it because it counted as "primary capital" for regulatory purposes.

■ **Exchangeable Auction Rate Preferred Stock/Remarketed Preferred Stock**	■ 11/20/86	■ 5	■ 0.1

□ Auction rate preferred stock or remarketed preferred stock that is exchangeable on any dividend payment date, at the option of the issuer, for auction rate notes, the interest rate on which is reset by Dutch auction every 35 days.

□ Issuer bears more interest rate risk than a fixed-rate instrument would involve.

● Security is designed to trade near its par value.

○ Issuance of auction rate notes involves no underwriting commissions.

○ Issuer can exchange notes for the preferred when it becomes taxable. Appears as equity on the issuer's balance sheet until it is exchanged for auction rate notes.

■ **Liquid Yield Option Notes (LYONs)/Zero Coupon Convertible Debt**	■ 12/18/70	■ 124	■ 17.0

□ Non-interest-bearing convertible debt issue.

○ If issue converts, the issuer will have sold, in effect, tax deductible equity. If holders convert, entire debt service stream converts to common equity.

■ **Preferred Equity Redemption Cumulative Stock (PERCS)/ Mandatory Conversion Premium Dividend Preferred Stock**	■ 08/16/91	■ 7	■ 4.7

□ Preferred stock that pays a cash dividend significantly above that on the underlying common stock in exchange for a conversion option that has a capped share value.

□ Investor trades off a portion of the underlying common stock's capital appreciation potential in return for an enhanced dividend rate.

■ **Puttable Convertible Bonds**	■ 07/21/82	■ 667	■ 44.8

□ Convertible bond that can be redeemed prior to maturity, at the option of the holder, on certain specified dates at specified prices.

● Issuer is exposed to risk that the bonds will be redeemed early if interest rates rise sufficiently or common stock price falls sufficiently. Investor has one or more put options, which provide protection against deterioration in credit quality.

Like the Americus Trust and SuperShares, USUs were designed to give shareholders
more flexibility in choosing among the different components of the total returns
from common stock; each of these new forms would effectively allow shareholders
to tailor the corporation's dividend policy to suit their own preferences.

provide capital appreciation above the Priority SuperShares' capital appreciation ceiling. The new securities are issued by a trust that contains a portfolio of common stocks that mirrors the performance of the S&P 500 Index and a portfolio of Treasury bills. The trust also issues two other classes of securities, one of which (Protection SuperShares) functions like portfolio insurance.

Unbundled stock units (USUs) were intended to divide the stream of annual total returns on a share of common stock into three components: (1) a 30-year "base yield" bond that would pay interest at a rate equal to the dividend rate on the issuer's common stock (thereby recharacterizing the "base" dividend stream into an interest stream), (2) a preferred share that would pay dividends equal to the excess, if any, of the dividend rate on the issuer's common stock above the "base" dividend rate, and (3) a 30-year warrant that would pay the excess, if any, of the issuer's share price 30 years hence above the redemption value of the base yield bond. Despite extensive marketing efforts, the USU concept failed to gain wide investor support and encountered regulatory obstacles that led to its withdrawal from the marketplace before a single issue could be completed.[27] Like the Americus Trust and Super-Shares, USUs were designed to give shareholders more flexibility in choosing among the different components of the total returns from common stock; each of these new forms would effectively allow shareholders to tailor the corporation's dividend policy to suit their own preferences.

HOW TO MAKE SECURITIES INNOVATION WORK TO YOUR COMPANY'S ADVANTAGE

Prospective issuers of securities are often bombarded with new securities ideas. How can a company decide whether a new security is more advantageous than existing alternatives? A new security may be different, but is it really better for the issuer's shareholders?

Here is a checklist of important considerations for corporate treasurers in evaluating the issuance of new securities:

■ How do the new security's features differ from the features of the most closely comparable conventional securities?

■ How will interest (or dividend) payments and principal payments vary under different interest rate conditions? If the interest (or dividend) or principal payments depend on exchange rates, commodity prices, or some other general economic variable, how do the debt service requirements vary under different scenarios?

■ Under what circumstances might the holders be able to force redemption to their advantage and to the issuer's disadvantage? Will the issuer be adequately compensated for bearing this early redemption risk?

■ Under what circumstances might the issuer be able to force redemption to its advantage and to investors' disadvantage? Is such a call option worth more to the issuer than the "call premium" investors will build into the interest rate? Alternatively, will the new security limit the issuer's optional redemption flexibility more than conventional securities—and if so, will the issuer receive compensation for reduced flexibility in the form of a lower interest rate?

■ Are there any unusual covenant or other restrictions on the issuer's operating or financial flexibility relative to conventional securities? If so, will the issuer be fully compensated through a reduced interest rate?

■ Does the new security entail any sort of risk-shifting when compared to conventional securities? If so, does this risk-shifting work to the issuer's advantage? For example, does it appreciably reduce the risk of financial distress, and if so, are investors charging a lower interest rate to reflect this reduced risk?

■ Does the new security enhance investors' liquidity by making it publicly marketable or by broadening the base of investors? And, if so, does the reduction in interest costs resulting from greater liquidity outweigh the expected cost of the resulting reduction in the company's ability to reorganize its more dispersed claims in the event of financial distress?

■ How do the underwriting spread and other issuance costs compare to the cost of issuing conventional securities?

■ Does the new security confer tax benefits or impose tax liabilities on either the issuer or investors as compared to conventional securities of the same type? If there is a significant net tax advantage, does

---

27. Victor Borun and I analyze USUs and explain how negative tax attributes and investors' liquidity concerns apparently outweighed the benefits of USUs. J.D. Finnerty and V.M. Borun, "An Analysis of Unbundled Stock Units," *Global Finance Journal* (Fall 1989), pp. 47-69.

TABLE 4 ■ SELECTED COMMON EQUITY INNOVATIONS

■ **Security**	■ **Year Issued**	■ **No. of Issues**	■ **Aggregate Proceeds ($B)**
□ **Distinguishing Characteristics**	□ **Risk Reallocation**		
● **Enhanced Liquidity**	● **Reduction in Agency Costs**		
○ **Reduction in Transaction Costs**	○ **Tax and Other Benefits**		
■ **Americus Trust**	■ N/A	■ N/A	■ N/A
□ Outstanding shares of a particular company's common stock are contributed to five-year unit investment trust. Units may be separated into PRIME component, which embodies full dividend and voting rights in the underlying share and permits limited capital appreciation, and SCORE component, which provides full capital appreciation above stated price.	□ Stream of annual total returns on a share of stock is separated into a dividend stream (with limited capital appreciation) and a residual capital appreciation stream.		
	○ PRIME component would appeal to corporate investors who can take advantage of the 70% dividends received deduction. SCORE component would appeal to capital-gain-oriented individual investors.		
	○ PRIME component resembles participating preferred stock if the issuer's common stock dividend rate is stable. SCORE component is a longer-dated call option than the ones customarily traded in the options market.		
■ **Callable Common Stock**	■ 05/23/91	■ 2	■ 0.1
□ Common stock of a subsidiary sold by the parent subject to a stock purchase option agreement. Exercise prices step up overtime. Callable common stock often issued with warrants to purchase common stock of the parent company.	□ Call option causes holders of the callable common stock to forgo capital appreciation in excess of the strike price (unless the callable common stock was sold in units that include warrants to buy the parent company's common stock).		
	● Warrant to purchase parent company's shares enables holders of callable common stock to share in the upside if the common stock is called away.		
	○ Issuer retains the right to regain 100% ownership of the subsidiary's common stock.		
■ **Master Limited Partnership**	■ 11/29/82	■ 114	■ 9.1
□ A business is given the legal form of a partnership but is otherwise structured, and is traded publicly, like a corporation.	○ Eliminates a layer of taxation because partnerships are not taxable entities.		
■ **Paired Common Stock**	■ 08/20/86	■ 4	■ 0.3
□ Common shares of two related companies are paired and trade as a unit. Can be used when a company has a real estate-related business that can be organized as a real estate investment trust (REIT) but wishes to conduct other operations that a REIT is not permitted to engage in.	○ A REIT is not subject to federal income taxation on the income it distributes to its shareholders (except for certain specified classes of income).		
■ **Puttable Common Stock**	■ 11/84	■ 3	■ 0.1
□ Issuer sells a new issue of common stock along with rights to put the stock back to the issuer on a specified date at a specified price.	□ Issuer sells investors a put option, which investors will exercise if the company's share price decreases.		
	● The put option reduces agency costs associated with a new share issue that are brought on by informational asymmetries.		
	○ Equivalent under certain conditions to convertible bonds but can be recorded as equity on the balance sheet so long as the company's payment obligation under the put option can be settled in common stock.		
■ **SuperShares**	■ None Issued	■ N/A	■ N/A
□ A trust is formed to hold a portfolio of common stocks that comprise the S&P 500 and a portfolio of Treasury bills. The trust sells four hybrid securities: (1) Priority SuperShares paying dividends on the S&P 500 and providing limited capital appreciation, (2) Appreciation SuperShares providing appreciation above the Priority SuperShares' appreciation ceiling, (3) Protection SuperShares providing the value of any decline in the S&P 500 below some specified level, and (4) Money Market Income SuperShares paying proceeds from the Treasury bill portfolio after Protection SuperShares have been paid.	□ Shareholders can hold the components of total return in any proportions they choose, and Protection SuperShares function like portfolio insurance.		
■ **Unbundled Stock Units**	■ None Issued	■ N/A	■ N/A
□ The total return stream from a share of common stock would be divided into three components: (1) a 30-year base yield bond (BYB) paying an interest rate equal to the dividend rate on the underlying common stock at the time the trust was formed plus limited capital appreciation, (2) a 30-year preferred stock instrument paying a dividend rate equal to the excess, if any, of the common dividend rate above the base rate, and (3) a 30-year warrant providing capital appreciation above the BYB's redemption value.	□ Shareholders could hold the components of a common share's total return in any proportions they choose.		

Does the new security enhance investors' liquidity by broadening the base of investors? If so, does the reduction in interest costs resulting from greater liquidity outweigh the expected cost of the resulting reduction in the company's ability to reorganize in the event of financial distress?

it involve significant risk the IRS will disallow the intended tax treatment?
■ Are there significant regulatory benefits?
■ Are there accounting benefits? Will these benefits enhance shareholder value?
■ On balance, will issuing the new security add sufficiently more to shareholder value than the available alternatives to justify the risk inherent in issuing an unfamiliar security? Or, can comparable benefits be obtained just by using a simpler, more conventional securities structure?

CLOSING REMARKS

Securities innovation increases the efficiency with which capital markets perform their central role of channeling savings into corporate investment. Innovative securities that offer more cost-effective means of transferring risks, increase liquidity, and reduce transaction and agency costs all act to reduce market frictions that otherwise reduce efficiency.

Securities innovations are a profit-driven response to changes in the economic, tax, and regulatory environment. One of the more important questions concerning the process of securities innovation is whether that process has reached the point

of diminishing returns. If the tax regime remains static, interest rates stabilize, and the regulatory landscape solidifies, diminishing returns to securities innovation are bound to set in eventually. But, to the extent that securities innovation occurs in response to unexpected economic, tax, and regulatory "shocks," a steady stream of such abrupt shifts can keep the process of securities innovation going indefinitely. And, together with a continuously changing economic and regulatory climate, further consolidation within the financial services industry will continue to intensify competition, driving market participants to seek better securities designs and more efficient ways of conducting securities transactions.

For a corporate treasurer or chief financial officer, the opportunity to issue a new security, and to become part of the process of securities innovation, is a tempting prospect. Those companies that innovate successfully can increase shareholder value (along with "reputational capital"). But the process is not costless (or riskless), as the failed experiment with unbundled stock units so clearly demonstrates. A company should decide to issue a new security only after it has determined that the new security is truly innovative and that issuing it will increase shareholder value.

ASPECTS OF FINANCIAL CONTRACTING IN VENTURE CAPITAL

by William A. Sahlman,
Harvard Business School

INTRODUCTION

During much of the 1960s and 1970s, academic discussions of corporate capital structure routinely began with the assumption that a firm's financing decisions had no material effect on its intrinsic economic value. Setting aside tax consequences and the possibility of a costly bankruptcy, the value of the firm was assumed to depend solely on the level and risk of a firm's operating cash flows. And operating profitability in turn was assumed to depend entirely on corporate investment decisions that are made prior to, and completely independently of, financing choices.[1] In the last ten years or so, however, finance scholarship has progressively reversed this assumption while entertaining the possibility that the way a transaction is financed can influence operating outcomes in predictable, systematic ways.[2] And the results of this new thinking—especially the contribution of the "agency cost" literature to our understanding of the current wave of financial restructurings—have been interesting.[3]

Further support for this relatively new direction in finance may also come from an area of study beyond the usual academic focus on public corporations: namely, the venture capital markets. For, the interaction of entrepreneur and venture capitalist has resulted in the evolution of a unique set of financial contracts. And in no other kind of transaction does the implied link between value and financial structure appear so strong and direct as in the typical venture capital deal. As I hope to show in this article, an effective financial design may well be the difference between a flourishing and a failed (if not a still-born) enterprise.

---

1. The original formulation of the capital structure "irrelevance" argument was by Franco Modigliani and Merton Miller, "The Cost of Capital, Corporation Finance and the Theory of Investment," *American Economic Review* 53 (June 1958).

2. The first major theoretical departure from the capital structure "irrelevance" argument came with the formulation of the "agency cost theory" by Michael C. Jensen and William Meckling, "Theory of the Firm: Mangerial Behavior, Agency Costs and Capital Structure," *Journal of Financial Economics,* 3 (October 1976).

3. I am thinking, especially, of Michael Jensen's article, "Agency Cost of Free Cash Flow, Corporate Finance and Takeovers," *American Economic Review* (May 1986). For an extended elaboration of Jensen's arguments, see also Vol. 1 No. 1 of this journal.

FIRST PRINCIPLES

As is true of all financial transactions, structuring a venture capital deal involves the allocation of economic value. Value, in turn, is determined by the interaction of three major ingredients: cash, risk, and time.

My colleague Bill Fruhan argues that all financial transactions can be classified into three categories: those that create value, those that destroy value, and those that transfer value between two or more parties.[4] This taxonomy can be readily transferred to venture capital because almost all venture capital deals either create, destroy, or transfer value. For example, a sound deal that provides appropriate incentives for an entrepreneur is likely to result in significantly higher value to be shared by entrepreneur and venture capitalist alike. The same deal, while increasing total value, may also have opposite effects on the value of two different claims on total value (for example, debt and equity), thus providing an example of a value transfer. Finally, a promising deal that is not well-designed can result in a failed venture, the extreme case of value destruction.

A Simple Example

Before turning to the case of venture capital, let's begin by considering a very simple project with the following characteristics:

Investment Required at Time 0..............................$1000

Annual Cash Flow...$500

Total Number of Cash Payments...................................$5

Terminal Value (end of year 5)..............................$1000

The resulting cash flows are put in Table 1. Suppose also that the payment of these cash flows is guaranteed by the government and that the current appropriate (risk-free) discount rate is 10%.

In this case, the present value of the future cash flows is $2,516, and the net present value of the project is $1,516. If you owned the rights to this investment project, you would be indifferent between selling the rights to another person (with the same information) for $1,516 or keeping the project for yourself. Any offer above that value would induce you to sell. In this simple deal, the cash flows are known with certainty by both the buyer and the seller. Moreover, each agrees, or is likely to agree, on the appropriate discount rate to apply to convert future cash flows to the present. And, finally, the expected cash flows are not affected by any action by the buyer or the seller. Given these conditions, it is easy to describe the terms on which a deal such as this one will trade.

Dealmaking in the Real World

If the world consisted principally of investment projects like this one, then the study of deals would not be very important, or very interesting. In the real world, however, the following conditions are far more likely to apply:
- the future cash flows are unknown (both in amount and timing);
- the appropriate discount rate is unknown;
- any two parties analyzing the same deal will disagree about the future cash flows, the appropriate discount rate to apply, or both;
- the sources of potential disagreement are many, and range from simple disagreement based on

TABLE 1	Period	0	1	2	3	4	5
	Investment	(1,000)					
	Cash Inflow		500	500	500	500	500
	Terminal Value						1,000
	Net Cash Flow	(1,000)	500	500	500	500	1,500

4. William E. Fruhan, Jr., *Financial Strategy: Studies in the Creation, Transfer, and Destruction of Shareholder Value* (Homewood, IL: Richard D. Irwin, Inc. 1979).

common knowledge to the fact that the parties may be governed by different rules (for example, tax treatment) to the possibility that one party knows more than the other;

● there will be conflicts of interest: one or more of the dealmakers may be in a position to influence the outcome of the project so as to benefit at the expense of the other participants; and

● the terms that govern the allocation of the cash flows will themselves affect the nature (amount, timing, and risk) of the cash flow stream.

Now, take the same basic expected cash inflows and outflows from the example above, but introduce uncertainty. That is, the annual cash flow is *expected* to be $500 per year, but the actual number will only be known over time. In this case, it may be appropriate to apply a higher discount rate than before (especially if the new risk includes a systematic, or market-related, component).

Suppose the appropriate discount rate were 20% instead of 10%. In this case, the present value of the cash flows would be $1,897 (instead of $2,516), and thus the net present value would be $897 (instead of $1,516). If someone offered you $1,000 today for the right to exercise the option to invest in this project, then you would gladly sign it over. If you were to offer to sell for $800, then any investor would gladly buy.

In the preceding paragraph, I assumed that buyers and sellers could agree on the expected cash flows and on the discount rate. Obviously, Pandora's box could be opened further, and the introduction of differences and disagreements between dealmakers will reveal many other grounds on which to trade.

If, for example, the parties to the deal disagree about the magnitude or the nature of the risk inherent in the cash flow, then they will apply different discount rates in their analysis. This sort of disagreement may render impossible an agreement on an appropriate price. Or, it may expand the set of possible deal terms. For example, if the potential seller used a discount rate of 20% and the buyer thought 10% to be the correct figure, then there would be a wide range of prices (in this case, between $897 and $1,516) at which the seller would gladly sell and the buyer willingly buy the right to make the investment. Or, if the buyer thought the cash flows would rise at an annual rate of 5%, then even if the buyer and seller used the same discount rate (of 20%), they would both be willing to accept a price between $897 (the seller's minimum) and $1,026 (the buyer's maximum).

Allocating Cash Flow

Now the fun starts. Suppose this generic deal is now called a start-up venture, and the two parties negotiating are identified as the entrepreneur and the venture capitalist. The venture capitalist uses a discount rate of 40% for projects like the one under consideration. The question is, what proportion of the equity will the venture capitalist demand in order to justify investing the $1,000 capital required to get the project off the ground?

To answer this question, you must determine what proportion of each future cash flow figure would provide a 40% annual rate of return to the venture capitalist, given an initial investment of $1,000. One way to attack this problem is to calculate the present value of the gross future cash flows, using the venture capitalist's 40% required return. In so doing we find that the present value is equal to $1,204.

This is the total "value pie" to be split between entrepreneur and venture capitalist. If the venture capitalist only needs to invest $1,000 to receive all of these cash flows, then he would increase his net present value by $204. If the venture capitalist owned only 83% ($1,000/$1,204) of the deal, however, then the present value of his share of the future cash flows would be $1,000, exactly equal to the cost of the investment. Therefore, the venture capitalist would willingly pay $1,000 to buy 83% of the equity in this hypothetical venture because the anticipated return would be 40% per year. The entrepreneur would be left with the remaining 17% of the equity, corresponding to $204 divided by $1,204.

Allocating Risks

The analytics described above are straightforward, and are based on some simplifying assumptions. Suppose, however, that the venture capitalist and the entrepreneur are in the process of negotiating a deal and that the forecasts are those included in the company's business plan. The venture capitalist, having seen hundreds of unfulfilled "conservative" projections in the past, is skeptical about the numbers. Partly, his skepticism is already reflected in the high discount rate applied to the estimates, a discount rate that is higher than the true expected return on the venture capital portfolio. Other than buying simple common equity, and thus implicitly agreeing to a proportional risk-reward sharing scheme, how else could the venture capitalist structure a deal with the

TABLE 2	Common Stock (Proportional Sharing)	Venture Capitalist		Entrepreneur		Total	
	Share of Total Stock		83%		17%		100%
	Annual Cash Rec'd: Bad Scenario	$373	83%	$77	17%	$450	100%
	Annual Cash Rec'd: Good Scenario	$456	83%	94	17%	550	100%
	Expected Annual Cash Received	$415	83%	85	17%	500	100%
	PV of Cash Received (incl. TV)	$1,000	83%	204	17%	1,204	100%
	Net PV (incl. investment)	$0		204		204	
	Std. Dev'n of PV (and of NPV)	$85	83%	18	17%	102	100%

	Preferred Stock	Venture Capitalist		Entrepreneur		Total	
	Share of Total Stock		83%		17%		100%
	Annual cash Rec'd: Bad Scenario	$415	93%	$35	7%	$450	100%
	Annual Cash Rec'd: Good Scenario	$415	73%	135	27%	550	100%
	Expected Annual Cash Received	$415	83%	85	17%	500	100%
	PV of Cash Received (incl. TV)	$1,000	83%	204	17%	1,204	100%
	Net PV (incl. investment)	$0		204		204	
	Std. Dev'n of PV (and of NPV)	$0	0%	102	100%	102	100%

entrepreneur to assuage his skepticism?

One possibility would be to invest in the form of preferred (or, more commonly, convertible preferred) stock.[5] In this alternative, the venture capitalist would have a prior claim on the earnings of the company, and may also have a prior claim on the liquidation value of the company. Suppose, for example, that the venture capitalist asks for a preferred stock that entitles him to receive up to $415 in the form of dividends from the company each year before the entrepreneur receives anything. (Note that $415 is equal to 83% of the expected cash flow of $500.) Also assume that the two parties split the $1,000 return of capital in the final year according to the original 83%/17% rule. What has changed?

In this new situation, a great deal has changed; there has been a major shift in risk from the venture capitalist to the entrepreneur. This shift in risk occurs even though the expected return to each party remains the same. To explore this risk-shifting process, suppose there were really two different, but equally likely scenarios for future cash flows. In the first, the actual cash flows turn out to be $450 per year. In the other, the cash flows are $550 per year. The terminal value is the same under either scenario.

Obviously, under both the proportional sharing rule and the new preferred stock arrangement, the expected total annual cash flow is $500, the expected total present value is $1,204, and the expected total net present value is $204. The standard deviation of the total expected present value is $102.

Under the straight equity deal, the venture capitalist and entrepreneur share proportionately (83%/17%) both the risk and the reward. That is, the venture capitalist has an expected present value of $1,000, and expected net present value of $0, and a standard deviation of expected present value of $85; the entrepreneur has an expected present value of $204, an expected net present value of $204, and a standard deviation of expected present value of $18. Note that the total risk in the project, as measured by the standard deviation, is split according to the 83%/17% rule.

Under the new preferred stock deal, however, the venture capitalist has managed to shift all of the risk to the entrepreneur. That is, given the narrow range of possible cash flow outcomes, the venture capitalist will always receive his $415 per annum cash flow. The entrepreneur, however, will no longer receive 17% of the cash flows regardless of the actual cash flow; instead, he will receive $35 per

5. Convertible preferred is the convention; we use straight preferred for purposes of simplicity in exposition.

year in the bad scenario (7% of the expected value) and $135 in the favorable scenario (27%). The standard deviation of the venture capitalist's return is now zero, while the standard deviation of the entrepreneur's present value is $102.

The reader should ignore the fact that the example is contrived and slightly silly. No investor would demand a 40% return for a riskless project. Also, the lower and upper bound of possible annual cash flows are purely arbitrary and meant only to simplify the example to show how risk is shifted from one party to the other. In the real world, the lower bound would almost always be significantly lower than the expected value of the venture capitalist's share, thus forcing the venture capitalist to bear enough risk to justify use of a 40% return requirement. And if the lower bound were below the expected value of the venture capitalist's share, then the expected present value would be lower than in the previous scenarios unless the entrepreneur were required to meet the shortfall in preferred stock dividends out of his own pocket, or the venture capitalist were entitled to receive a bonus payment during the favorable scenario.

Why would the venture capitalist suggest using preferred stock rather than straight equity? The obvious reason would be to try to improve his reward-to-risk ratio. But simply transferring risk to the entrepreneur by gaining liquidation preferences is probably not the primary motive for structuring venture capital deals this way. Two other possibilities come to mind: (1) by increasing the entrepreneur's risk, the venture capitalist is trying to "smoke out" the entrepreneur, and get the entrepreneur to signal whether she really does believe the forecasts in the business plan; and (2) the venture capitalist is trying to provide the strongest possible incentives for the entrepreneur to do at least as well as projected. If the business exceeds plan, then the entrepreneur will share disproportionately in the benefits of doing so. Given the entrepreneur's strong incentives to beat the plan, structuring the deal this way may actually increase the probability that a more favorable outcome will occur.

Summing Up

Let's stop here for a moment and briefly and review our progress to this point.

The process of financial contracting in venture capital focuses on a few very simple questions:

- how is cash allocated?
- how is risk allocated?
- what are the incentives for both parties in the deal? In the examples above, we looked at two simple versions of common arrangements for sharing risk and reward. In the first example, a proportional sharing scheme was employed. In the second, a non-proportional scheme was introduced in which the venture capitalist demanded a fixed dollar return, regardless of the actual outcomes.

There are of course a myriad of possible variations on this theme. It is possible to combine proportional sharing schemes with fixed hurdles. Or, the timing of the hurdles can be altered. There are also many other mechanisms for affecting the allocation of value and the implicit incentives in a given deal. What is important to note, at this point, is that investors can infer information about the abilities and convictions of entrepreneurs by offering different deal terms and gauging the response. The ability to signal intentions credibly may enable some entrepreneurs to obtain funding that would not have been available were there no means for communicating true abilities or convictions.

Staged Capital Commitment

Suppose you present an investment proposal to a venture capitalist that calls for an expenditure of $20 million to build a semiconductor fabrication facility. The $20 million will be required over a three-year period. How will the venture capitalist respond to your offer to sell him 75 percent ownership of the venture for $20 million?

After picking himself up off the floor, the venture capitalist will begin a process of trying to educate you about the real world. And, if he has not been too offended by your proposal, he will make a counter-proposal. The terms of the counter-offer will likely call for staged infusions of capital over time. In the first round, for example, the venture capitalist might offer to invest $1 million for the purpose of assembling the managerial team, writing a business plan, completing engineering specifications, conducting market research, and testing the feasibility of the process.

The $1 million capital would be expected to last about nine months. At that point, the venture would be expected to raise additional capital for the purpose of building a prototype manufacturing plant. That process might require $4 million in capital. Finally, there would be plans for a third round of fi-

TABLE 3

Round of Financing	Amount Invested This Round	% Rec'd This Round	Cumulative		Implied Valuation (Post Money)
			VC's Share	Founder's Share	
First Round	$1,000,000	50.0%	50.0%	50.0%	$2,000,000
Second Round	$4,000,000	33.3%	66.7%[6]	33.3%	$12,000,000
Third Round	$15,000,000	25.0%	75.0%	25.0%	$60,000,000

nancing for the purpose of building a full-scale manufacturing facility and beginning to market. The investment required at that point might be $15 million.

With respect to valuation at each stage of the process, it is entirely possible that the entrepreneur will end up owning the 25% share that he demanded in the initial negotiation. But the process by which that ownership is attained will be very different. One plausible scenario is described in Table 3.

In this plan, the company raises the total of $20 million over three rounds. At each point new capital is infused into the company, the valuation increases. In the first round, for example, the venture capitalist demands 50% of the company for only $1 million. In the last round, however, the venture capitalist is content to receive only 25% of the company in return for $15 million, thus implying a post-money valuation of $60 million.[6]

Why does the venture capitalist demand that capital be staged over time rather than committed up-front? Why would any self-respecting entrepreneur accept such a process? Remember that the venture is scheduled to run out of capital periodically; if it cannot raise capital at the second or third rounds, then it goes out of business and the entrepreneur is out of a job.

To begin to understand the reasons underlying this seemingly peculiar process, it is important to think about how the venture under consideration will evolve over time. In particular, what new information will the venture capitalist and the entrepreneur have at each point that the company goes back to raise capital?

Consider the point at which the company needs to raise $4 million. At this point, the venture capitalist

and entrepreneur will know how the company has performed relative to its initial business plan. What is the management team like? How do they work together? Does the new business plan make sense? Has the company developed complete engineering specs? How has the perceived opportunity changed? Does the market research reveal adequate demand? What new competition exists? How have valuations in the capital market changed since the previous financing round? These are the types of questions that can be answered at the end of the first nine months of operation. If all goes well, the major risks outstanding at the time of the first round of financing—the "people risk" due to the lack of a complete management team, the technical risk from the lack of produce specification, and the market risk due to the lack of market research—will have been greatly reduced. If so, the venture capitalist will be willing to buy shares at a much higher price, thus in effect accepting a lower expected rate of return.

If the company continues to proceed as hoped while approaching the third round of financing, there should be a similar reduction in perceived risk to the investor. Whereas, at the second round, consulting engineers could evaluate the product specifications for the venture capitalist, now there will be an actual product. Market research and initial marketing should by now have produced verifiable interest in the product, if not a backlog of orders. At this stage, then, the venture capitalist is evaluating an investment in a real product, within a known competitive context, on the eve of full-scale production and marketing. The increase in valuation at the third round reflects the further reduction in risk of investing at this point.

---

6. Note that, although the venture capitalist purchases a third of the company in this round, he only increases his cumulative share by a sixth (to 66.7%). When a company issues new shares of stock to raise capital, the resulting dilution is essentially charged proportionately to each existing shareholder. Thus, the venture capitalist's share increases only by that portion of the new equity he does not already hold. To compute the cumulative shares:
Second Round: $50.0\% + (33.3\% \times (1 - 50.0\%)) = 66.7\%$
Third Round: $66.7\% + (25.0\% \times (1 - 66.7\%)) = 75.0\%$

Suppose, however, that all does not go according to plan. At the time the $4 million is required, the company has not done well, and there are new competitors not previously anticipated. At this point, the venture capitalist can either abandon ship and allow the company to fail, or can strike a new price with the entrepreneur that reflects the less sanguine outlook. For example, the venture capitalist might demand as much as 50% of the company for his $4 million, implying a total valuation of only $8 million.

The point here is simple: by staging the commitment of capital the venture capitalist gains the options to abandon and to revalue the project as new information arrives. These are extremely valuable options, as will be demonstrated later.

But does this process make sense from the standpoint of the entrepreneur? Go back to the original proposal. Remember that the entrepreneur asked for $20 million in return for 75% of the shares. It seems likely that, even if the venture capitalist had been willing to consider the offer, he would have demanded a much higher share of the company than 75%, given the enormous risk as of the first round. This would likely have created a situation in which neither side would have found it sensible to proceed. The entrepreneur would have had too little incentive to risk his career, and the venture capitalist would have been worried about this loss of motivation. (As a general rule, if there does not appear to be enough room to provide sufficient incentives to management, then the deal probably won't get done.)

The Value of the Option to Abandon

Why do the venture capitalist and the entrepreneur seem to end up better off under the alternative of staged capital commitment? To explore this issue, it will make sense to return to our simple example at the beginning. For a $1,000 initial investment, the projected cash flows were $500 per year for each of five years, followed by a $1,000 return of capital at the end of the fifth year. Suppose that instead of a simple $1,000 investment up-front, the investment can be made in two stages of $500 each. Suppose also that there is great uncertainty about the future annual cash flows to be received. There is a 50% chance they will be $50 per year and a 50% chance they will turn out to be $950 per year; and the expected value thus remains $500 per year.

We will now explore two different sets of rules governing this investment project. In the first, the ven-

ture capitalist has no choice but to invest the second $500 in the second year; that is, even if the actual annual cash flows turn out to be $50, the $500 will be spent. Under the second set of rules, the venture capitalist has the right, or option, to decide whether or not to invest the second $500. He can make this decision at the end of the first year, just after he has learned what the actual annual cash flows will be. If he decides not to invest (that is, to abandon the project) then he forfeits the right to receive any of the annual cash flows, and receives a reduced share, $750, of the terminal payment of $1,000. The different possible sets of cash flows are provided in Table 4.

What is the present value of the investment project under the different sets of rules? Evaluating the first is easy; the expected present value of the cash inflows and outflows is $846 and the expected net present value is $346. Note that the latter figure is higher than the $204 determined in the previous section because the venture capitalist is now allowed to defer investing $500 for one year.

Under the second set of rules, the venture capitalist must evaluate whether or not it makes sense to invest in the second year, after the actual cash flows are revealed. If the cash flows turn out to be $950 per year, then the venture capitalist would be crazy not to spend the $500 necessary to receive the annual cash flows. (An investment that required investing $500 to receive $950 immediately, not to mention $950 for four years and an additional $250 of terminal value, has an infinite internal rate of return.)

If, however, the cash flows turn out to be only $50 per year, then the venture capitalist has a tougher analysis. If he invests $500, he will receive $50 immediately and $50 a year for 4 years, as well as an additional $250 in terminal value. If he chooses not to invest, he will forfeit the $50 payment stream and the additional terminal value.

Given a discount rate of 40%, it turns out that he is much better off deciding not to invest. The net present value of the incremental investment from that point forward is −$292. By not investing, the venture capitalist raises the net present value of the project as a whole, as of year 1, from −$97 to $195, thus "creating" $292 in value.

After determining the optimal decision, conditional on the arrival of new information, the venture capitalist can then evaluate the entire project looking forward. Because he can cut off the investment process if the cash flows turn out to be low, the ven-

TABLE 4

	0	1	2	3	4	5	PV @ 40%
RULE I: VC MUST INVEST IN BOTH YEARS							
Good Scenario		$950	$950	$950	$950	$ 950	$1,933
Bad Scenario		50	50	50	50	50	$ 102
Expected Ann's Cash		500	500	500	500	500	$1,018
Terminal Value						1,000	$ 186
Expected Cash In.		500	500	500	500	1,500	$1,204
Investment	($500)	(500)					($ 857)
Expected Net Cash	($500)	$0	$500	$500	$500	$1,500	$ 346

	0	1	2	3	4	5	PV @ 40%
RULE II: VC HAS OPTION TO ABANDON IN YEAR ONE							
Good Scenario							
Annual Cash Flow		$950	$950	$950	$950	$ 950	$1,933
Terminal Value						$1,000	$ 186
Investment	($500)	(500)					($ 857)
Net Cash Flow	($500)	$450	$950	$950	$950	$1,950	$1,262
Bad Scenario							
Annual Cash Flow		$ 0				$ 0	
Terminal Value						$ 750	$ 139
Investment	($500)						$ 500
Net Cash Flow	($500)	$ 0	$ 0	$ 0	$ 0	$ 750	($ 361)
Expected (or Average) Value of Scenarios							
Expected Net Cash	($500)	$225	$475	$475	$475	$1,225	$ 451

EXPECTED VALUE OF OPTION TO ABANDON (RULE I − RULE II): $104

ture capitalist has an expected present value of $951 and an expected net present value of $451.

The new expected net present value of $451 can be compared to the $346 determined when the venture capitalist had no choice. Somehow, an extra $104 of value has been created simply by changing the rules a little bit. This difference is the value of the option to abandon. To gain this option, the venture capitalist would be willing to invest up to an additional $104 at the outset for a given level of ownership.

In this regard, the process of estimating the value of the option to abandon is usually far more complex than that described above. This is so because the number of possible scenarios is effectively infinite, as is the number of points in time at which the value of continuing the project must be evaluated. Despite the obvious complexity of the real world, financial economists have devised promising techniques for valuing such operating options by using an offshoot of option pricing theory called "contingent claims analysis."[7]

This analysis reveals, among other things, that the value of the option to abandon is higher under the following conditions:
- the greater the uncertainty about the future value of the venture;

7. See Volume 5 Number 1 of the *Midland Corporate Finance Journal*, which is devoted almost entirely to the applications of contingent claims analysis in capital budgeting.

- the greater the amount of time before the actual decision to abandon must be made; and
- the higher the ratio of the value of the abandoned project (the liquidation value) to the value of the project if pursued (present value of additional free cash flow less additional investment).

It is important to note that the traditional process of calculating expected net present values does not give the same answer as the process described above, in which each decision is evaluated at each point in time and the decision tree folded back to the present assuming optimal decisions are made at each intermediate point in time. In our example, to be sure, the difference in approaches does not change the basic fact that the project looks good. But it is very easy to imagine situations in which the value of the option to abandon might be sufficiently high to change the net present value from negative to positive. Such might be the case when there is great uncertainty and the investor has the option to stage the capital investment over time. But, this is exactly the case in most venture capital investments; and this is why one almost always sees staged capital commitment in these investments.

Application to Dealmaking

From the above analysis, it seems clear that a driving force behind staged capital commitment is the preservation of the option to abandon. This option has great value to the venture capitalist. And, indeed, the option is exercised relatively frequently in the real world.

But let's return once more to the view of the entrepreneur. Because the option to abandon is valuable to the venture capitalist doesn't necessarily mean, after all, that it adds value for the entrepreneur. Wouldn't the entrepreneur almost always be better off if the venture capitalist committed all the required capital up-front?

While generalizations are dangerous, staged capital commitment probably makes as much sense for the entrepreneur as for the venture capitalist. The reason, as I suggested earlier, is that the entrepreneur has a chance to minimize the dilution he suffers by bringing in outside capital. Because there is more value initially (precisely because of the option to abandon), the share of value awarded to the venture

capitalist is lower, holding all other things constant.

In addition, staged capital commitment not only provides the venture capitalist with the option to abandon, but also gives the entrepreneur the option to raise capital at a higher valuation. The entrepreneur is betting that there will be positive results on which to base higher and higher valuations as the company grows, thus necessitating less dilution at each stage that new capital is required. And the willingness of the entrepreneur to bet on himself, as we have seen, sends a positive signal to the venture capitalist.

The entrepreneur, then, faces a conflict of motives in raising capital. On the one hand, he is tempted to raise only the minimum necessary amount of capital to avoid selling too much stock in early rounds at low prices, thus suffering great dilution. At the same time, however, he is also tempted to raise excessive amounts of capital early to preserve the option to continue operations through tough times. Some have described this problem confronting the entrepreneur as "the horse race between fear and greed"—that is, between the fear of running out of capital and the desire to retain maximum possible ownership (and I will return to this later).

Finally, there is an additional and powerful reason why the deal should be structured in stages. There is no more powerful motivator than the knowledge that the enterprise is scheduled to run out of cash in the relatively near future. In the parlance of entrepreneurial finance, the rate at which a company consumes cash is called the "burn rate." Given any level of initial cash and a burn rate, it is possible to calculate the "fume date"—the date on which the company will have exhausted its cash and will be operating solely on fumes. The existence of periodic "fume dates" focuses the energies of management on creating value from limited resources; and this process can accrue to the benefit of both entrepreneur and venture capitalist.

To summarize, then, a common technique used in financing new ventures is to infuse capital over time, retaining the option to abandon the venture at any point that the net present value looking forward is negative. This technique appeals to venture capitalist and entrepreneur alike. The venture capitalist preserves a valuable option and also creates the strongest possible incentives for management to create value

---

8. The reader should also keep in mind the tension that exists in such situations between the entrepreneur and the venture capitalist. For the venture capitalist, a single venture is but one of many. For the entrepreneur, the venture is all they have. Abstract discussions of the option to abandon should be tempered with knowledge that people's careers and egos are at stake.

and meet goals. The entrepreneur minimizes dilution and also benefits to the extent that his energies are appropriately focused on value creation.

But while the above example tends to suggest that the preservation of such financing options is an unequivocal boon, the reader should also always keep in mind the fact that the real world is more complicated and that providing such options to the venture capitalist may create its own problems. For example, having a periodic "fume date" will work in many situations as a motivating factor. In others, though, it may create incentives to aim for short-term success rather than long-term value creation. This may or may not be in the best interests of both parties. Also, the future cash flows will never be known with any degree of certainty. Because of the great uncertainty remaining at any stage of development, some ventures will be abandoned even though they actually have excellent prospects; and some will be funded when they should not be.

It is worth noting in passing, however, that many successful companies have gone through periods when they came very close to their "fume date." Many have also had to change their business plans dramatically as new information was revealed. These realities often make the staged capital commitment process not only valuable to entrepreneur and venture capitalist alike, but also a very trying experience for anyone involved.

The Option to Re-Value a Project

In the preceding section, the focus was on achieving some understanding of the option to abandon a given project. There are also steps short of abandonment that warrant consideration. The process of staged capital commitment involves periodically evaluating whether to continue funding and investment and, if so, on what terms. The right to revalue a given project has value when compared to an alternative situation in which the future financing terms are decided irrevocably at the start of the venture.

Suppose a venture starts with a 50/50 split in equity ownership between the entrepreneur and the venture capitalist. One year after the venture starts, the company needs more capital. The question is: At what price will the new capital come in? If the original deal awarded the venture capitalist the right to invest in future rounds at a price to be negotiated later, the answer will depend on the progress the company has made since its last funding as well as

the state of the economy and capital markets at the time. If the prospects are good, then the value will be relatively high; if not, value will be low. In the former case, the entrepreneur will suffer minor dilution; in the event of poor performance, the dilution factor will be much larger.

Now, suppose that instead of flexible pricing on the second round of financing, the venture capitalist was granted a fixed price option at the beginning to buy one million shares at a price of $10.00 per share at any point within two years. If the justifiable per share price at the end of two years is above $10.00, then the venture capitalist will exercise the option. If the price is below $10.00, the venture capitalist will walk away from the option, thereby truncating the lower side of the return distribution.

But if the company really needs the $10 million, and the justifiable price is below $10.00 per share, then the money will not necessarily be forthcoming. Moreover, another outside investor might find the existence of the call option (actually warrants in this case) problematic in terms of investing because of the potential for future dilution if the company does succeed in increasing value above $10.00 per share. If the money cannot be raised, then the venture will suffer and may even fail.

Flexibility in future pricing can make the difference between a venture succeeding and failing when performance is not as favorable as expected. The reader might argue that no venture capitalist will walk away from a venture with value simply because of some inflexible deal provisions. But the situation described above has occurred many times and a complex game of "chicken" develops between the entrepreneurial team and the venture capitalists, in which each tries to obtain the best deal. The result of such a game can be very detrimental to the economic vitality of the enterprise. Moreover, it should also be remembered that the venture capital fund has many companies in its portfolio, and the venture capitalist may well decide to walk away from one investment that is not performing up to expectations even if doing so seems not to make sense.

The Option to Increase Capital Committed

Another option to be considered is the right to increase funding to a company, particularly if the company is doing well. Consider a start-up venture in the specialty retailing area. The company's business plan calls for having 20 stores in the Northeast by the end of two years. Suppose after the first year, the company has 6 stores, each of which is performing well above expectations. It might make sense for the entrepreneur and venture capitalist to accelerate the rate at which new stores are introduced. To do so will entail raising additional capital. The venture capitalist will welcome the opportunity to invest more heavily in such a successful venture, and would like to lock in the right to do so. The entrepreneur, however, would want to ensure that the price at which additional capital is raised reflects the superior past performance and prospects of the company.

In this example, the right to increase capital invested at some intermediate point is very valuable. One unresolved issue, however, is who should "own" the right to invest more money. To whom does the benefit of superior performance belong?

One way in which venture capitalists gain the right to invest more, while still allowing the entrepreneur to benefit from success, is by asking for rights of first refusal on all subsequent financings. By doing so, they buy the option to invest later, but only on whatever terms are deemed appropriate by the capital market.

In sum, there are a variety of financing options—options to abandon, to re-value, and to increase capital committed—built into the financing contracts fashioned by the professional venture capital community. Over the life of any venture capital portfolio, there are likely to be some losers, some winners, and some intermediate performers. Successful funds generate high rates of return by cutting their losses early, not investing great amounts in early rounds, and letting their winners run by investing larger amounts of money in multiple rounds of financing. Phrased differently, they frequently exercise their options to abandon and their options to participate in later rounds of financing. You will also discover that some of the most successful companies in their portfolios had a distress round of financing in which the ability to re-value the investment was the difference between continued financing and bankruptcy. Prominent examples are Federal Express and MCI Communications.

ANTICIPATING THE CONSEQUENCES OF FINANCING DECISIONS

Managers and capital suppliers are making extraordinarily complex decisions in environments characterized by great uncertainty. More important, they must live with the consequences of those decisions. One way to approach the task of decision-making is to ask three questions before making a decision:

- What can go wrong?
- What can go right?
- What decisions can be made today and in the future that will maximize the reward-to-risk ratio?

These simple questions are designed to force the decision-maker to confront uncertainty directly and to manage the uncertainty.

One of the most critical issues in venture capital financing, as we have seen, is the decision whether to raise capital in excess of expected requirements. A risk common to virtually every venture ever started is that all will not go as planned and that the introduction of a product or the sales response will fail to meet expectations. It is also often the case that the company will have to change the focus of its efforts dramatically as it gathers more information about the opportunity.

To raise capital in excess of anticipated needs is equivalent to buying an option to change strategy as required, or to keep the company on sound financial footing until results do match expectations. Of course, in gaining that option, the venture capitalist is denied valuable options to revalue or to abandon. One compromise is not to raise excess capital, but nevertheless to retain the option to call on the investors for additional capital if needed, in return for which the current equity round would have to be sold at a lower price.

Maximizing the reward-to-risk ratio also requires examining the other side of the spectrum—what can go right—and ensuring that in the event of the venture's success, the value created can be fruitfully harvested. One means of harvest is for the venture to be acquired after a period of years. The question is: what decisions can management make that will increase the likelihood that such a rewarding end to the venture will take place? In this regard, management must carefully avoid introducing any form of "poison pill" into its capital structure that will preclude a buyout offer.

To illustrate, some start-up companies raise capital from a major participant in the industry. Although doing so may provide necessary capital and some expertise or marketing, it may also mean that no other large competitor of the original funder will even consider an offer later on. A start-up can thus lose the option to market the company to the highest bidder in the industry. In this situation, as when any option is being given up, this route should be pursued only if there are sufficient offsetting benefits.

Venture capitalists often ensure that they will profit in the event of success by gaining the right to force the company to go public, or the right to sell stock jointly with the company's public offering. By structuring an investment in the form of preferred stock, a venture capitalist can also profit from a success that is too modest to permit a public offering—that is, by recovering capital through the redemption of preferred stock and the payout of accumulated dividends. Such a structure also permits the venture capitalist to receive some payout in the form of dividends in the event of a "sideways" scenario.

The process of anticipating good or bad news and making decisions that maximize the chance that the good will outweigh the bad is a critical element of good decision-making. Moreover, it is not all that difficult to decide what events, good or bad, are likely to occur in any venture over time. These events will occur with respect to:

- the people (e.g., death, motivation);
- the individual company (e.g., production or marketing issues);
- the industry in question (e.g., competition, substitutes);
- the sociological environment (social rules/legal system); and,
- the state of the economy and capital markets (e.g., boom, recession, lower or higher stock prices).

Sensible deals will preserve options to react to and receive maximum benefit from good news, and will also protect the company from going under when bad news arises. Sensible deals will also provide strong incentives to all parties to skew the outcome towards the good news side of the ledger.

An Example of a Bad Deal

Anyone familiar with start-up companies recognizes that a common problem is that the company consumes more cash than was projected when it raised capital. Frequently, the primary cause is a shortfall in revenues which may occur for many different reasons. And because running out of cash is not an uncommon occurrence, any deal terms that govern the relationship between the company and the suppliers of capital must reflect the likelihood that the company will require more capital.

Unfortunately, deals are very often designed that make it extremely difficult to raise capital when

the company needs to. For example, in one case, the original capital suppliers to a start-up demanded the option to acquire up to 51% of the common stock that would be outstanding at any time in the following three years. The option could be exercised at a fixed price equal to the price paid in the first round of financing. The same group also got the right of first refusal on all subsequent financings, for a period lasting 60 days.

There were several problems that arose as time passed. First, the company's progress was disappointing when compared against the business plan projections. The result was that the company needed a significant infusion of capital long before anticipated. The logical supplier of the new capital was the group owning the option. But, there was a problem: the financing group had very little incentive to exercise their option early. Doing so would sacrifice the value of being able to wait to learn more about the company. And that value was considerable because of the length of time left on the option and the high risk involved in the venture.

On the other hand, potential new capital suppliers were confronted with the problem that they might be diluted immediately after they invested because the original financing group could then acquire up to 51% of the *then outstanding* shares at a fixed price. Moreover, because the group had a 60 day right of first refusal, the new potential investors also faced the possibility that the investment of time and energy required to evaluate the deal might go for naught if the original investors exercised their right of first refusal. This was entirely possible because the very fact that the new investors were interested would signal that the company's prospects were attractive to a third party. A final problem was that the original financing group did not really have sufficient resources to exercise their options when the money was needed.

This example demonstrates precisely where the thought process described above is critical in designing deals. Neither management *nor* the investors should have signed this deal. Doing so was essentially a bet that everything would transpire exactly as outlined in the business plan, an outcome that probably has only a 10 percent chance of happening. The financial structure almost drove this company into bankruptcy and only very intense negotiations to modify the deal saved the company.

Having stated boldly that this deal should never have been signed, we now ask if a different deal could have been structured to accomplish the same basic objectives. First, the investors were clearly interested in preserving three options: (1) the right to control the company (the "51%" option); (2) the right to invest more money at a fixed price for an extended period of time; and (3) the right to maintain their ownership position in the event a subsequent financing round was about to take place at an unfairly low valuation. Management was interested in raising enough capital to get the company off the ground. At the same time, however, it wanted to minimize the dilution from selling shares at a low valuation relative to that possible on future rounds if the company did well.

If both parties had anticipated the future by asking questions detailed at the beginning of this section, the deal they struck could have been quite different while still satisfying the implicit objectives of each party. To illustrate, both the investors and the management would probably have been far better off to raise additional capital in the first place. The company was already far behind the plan when this deal was made, and there was not sufficient new (positive) information on which to base a new capital infusion. The investors and management had raised too little capital for the company to get to the point where a new, better informed decision about whether or not to proceed could be made.

Second, the investor group could have structured a deal in which they simply paid a lower initial price per share for the company, rather than acquiring the right to invest more money at a fixed price later. The investors purchased a package consisting of some common stock and some rights. On the surface, it would appear that they paid a relatively high price per share of stock. But when a portion of the original investment capital is attributed appropriately to these "ancillary" rights, then the actual economic price paid for the common stock turns out to be far lower. If the investor group had structured a simpler deal in which they paid the lower price, they would have been confronted with far less trouble later.

With respect to the right to invest more money later, this goal could have been accomplished by gaining proportional rights of first refusal, which would allow the investor to participate in later rounds of financing in proportion to the equity already held. Such rights, however, should not be structured so as to discourage another outside group from investing the time and resources required to decide whether or not to invest.

Also, the deal could have been structured with a "ratchet," enabling the original investors to be protected against subsequent financing rounds at lower prices. With a ratchet in place, the shares owned by the original investor would be retroactively adjusted so that the effective price per share paid would be no higher than the price paid by the subsequent round.

Finally, with respect to the control issue, the investor group was deluded into believing that 51% was a magical figure, and the only way to retain control in the situation. In reality, control vests in the hands of those who have capital when capital is needed. Control can also be attained by having a majority representation on the board of directors, or through employment contracts with rigid performance specifications. The particular mechanisms by which this investor group sought to retain control — the rolling 51% option — almost brought the company to its knees.

CONCLUSION

We began this note on venture capital by introducing a relatively simple example of a deal, one in which the entrepreneur sought capital from a venture capitalist. We saw that the terms negotiated affected the split of cash and the split of risk, and hence the split of value between the supplier and the user of capital. We then pointed out that alternative structures would affect the incentives of the entrepreneur such that the total amount of value at stake was affected by the terms negotiated.

We then took the relatively simple single-investment type deal and expanded the terms to include the more realistic possibility that the investment would be made in several distinct stages over time. In so doing, we discovered that certain options provided venture capitalists, both explicit and implicit, are valuable to venture capitalist and entrepreneur alike, and thus improve the terms on which the entrepreneur is able to raise capital. Staging capital infusions into ventures, for example, enables the venture capitalist to retain the option to abandon a project if that makes sense. We also observed that the entrepreneur enters into such contracts willingly, though there are obvious possible scenarios in which having structured the deal that way will not have been in the best interests of the entrepreneur.

Similarly, both parties can gain from providing the other party the option to re-value a project, or from the venture capitalist's option to increase capital committed if the project proves unexpectedly successful. Building such options into venture capital contracts also helps overcome initial differences of opinion between venture capitalist and entrepreneur as to, say, the probability of different outcomes. Such options also provide a signaling mechanism, if you will, by which entrepreneurs can credibly communicate to investors their confidence in the project and in their own abilities.

These options not only add to the total project value as of a first financing round, but also provide a structure for avoiding a financing impasse should things not work out as planned. The terms of financing must allow the company to obtain the capital necessary for survival in (temporary) bad-news scenarios, as well as providing for the exploitation of good-news scenarios. If the deal is structured such that it is almost impossible to raise additional capital (for example, there is an implicit "poison pill" built into the contract), then the financial structure of the deal will reduce instead of adding to the value of the project.

The message that seems to emerge most clearly, then, from this look at venture capital is this: The total value of an investment opportunity may depend critically on the financing terms governing the deal. By restructuring terms, the size of the total economic "pie" can be dramatically changed—for better or worse. The extent to which these insights into venture capital markets have a bearing on the financial practices of public corporations remains an open question, but one that surely merits further attention.

AN INTRODUCTION TO MEZZANINE FINANCE AND PRIVATE EQUITY

by John R. Willis and David A. Clark, Continental Bank

The rapid growth of the mezzanine finance market in recent years is part of the restructuring movement that has swept across Corporate America in the 1980s. Although much corporate restructuring is taking place inside companies, the most visible signs of change are the leveraged transactions—the management buyouts, recapitalizations, and leveraged takeovers—that seem to receive daily attention from the press. Leveraged transactions, as their name suggests, involve the financing of a business operation with a relatively small amount of equity capital and a relatively large amount of debt. Mezzanine finance has become one of the two major financing tools for executing such highly leveraged transactions; the other, of course, is its better-known close cousin, high-yield ("junk") bonds.

Like junk bonds, mezzanine finance occupies a position in the middle level (hence the name "mezzanine") of the capital structure—that is, somewhere between the senior debt at the top and the common equity layer at the bottom. Also like many junk bond investments, a mezzanine investment often involves holdings in more than one position; it can take the form of subordinated debt, junior subordinated debt, or preferred stock (or some combination of the three), together with an equity-like claim such as a warrant.

Further like the junk bond market, the mezzanine market is flourishing because more operators and principals are seeking operating companies in which to invest, more institutions are willing to make large capital commitments for untraditional but highly promising investments, and more intermediaries have emerged to match operators with investors.

One clear result of this process is that operating companies seem to be commanding higher prices than ever before. Such acquisition premiums, combined with the desire to concentrate equity ownership in as few hands as possible, have led to a widening of the financing "gap" between the senior debt and the available conventional equity. In the larger deals, this gap has been closed by the evolution of the large, efficient public market for junk bonds. The private mezzanine market has arisen to meet the requirements of transactions in the small to middle market—those up to, say, $200 million.

In this article, we begin by providing a brief look at the history of leveraged transactions (also known as "structured financings"), compare the conventions and practices in the mezzanine finance market with those of the junk bond market, and then illustrate the mezzanine financing technique with two examples.

SOME BACKGROUND

The most direct line of descent from modern structured financings traces back to the old practice of new owner-managers' buying out the founder's interest in a business. Although certainly prevalent in the 1960s and before, such transactions were then primarily restricted to small firms seeking to ensure their continuity after the founder's departure, or at least to provide liquidity for the founder or his estate.

Up until the late 1960s, the financing for such old-fashioned management buyouts typically took the form of the "asset-based" bank loan. In such cases, the lending bank was typically fully secured by all of the firm's assets—most notably, receivables, inventory, and plant and equipment. But, as the size of these buyouts became progressively larger, asset-based loans became insufficient to fund the entire purchase price. And the market responded by creating, in effect, a new financing vehicle to overcome this obstacle. Some very aggressive insurance companies, in search of a higher risk-reward profile than the one provided by their customary secured investments, agreed to provide a portion of acquisition financing in the form of an unsecured subordinated loan in return for equity participation. Thus were the beginnings of mezzanine finance.

In the early 1970s, we also saw the beginnings of a practice that has reached full development in the 1980s: the sales by conglomerates of divisions or smaller operations to their line managers together with financial principals. As these deals got progressively larger, and as a parallel movement arose to take public companies private through leveraged buyouts, the demand for "intermediate" financing greatly expanded. A milestone was reached in 1979, when Kohlberg, Kravis & Roberts ("KKR") acquired Houdaille Industries for $343 million. This was the first such deal to exceed $100 million in financing. After the Houdaille transaction, market activity accelerated. Other major players such as Forstmann Little entered the field and buyouts in the range of $200-400 million became more and more common.

The development of the so-called "jumbo" deals did not occur until the 1983-1984 period, when corporate raiders began to emerge. The $1.5 billion recapitalization of Metromedia, although a slight variation on the theme of the LBO, was the largest transaction at the time. Since then, structured financings have become ever larger and more commonplace, culminating in KKR's recent acquisition of RJR-Nabisco for $24.8 billion.

What has brought about the growth of such leveraged transactions? There have been a number of factors at work, but some are clearly more fundamental to the process than others.

First, there was the emergence of firms like KKR and Forstmann Little that specialize in arranging such buyouts. In addition to these two premier firms, there are now scores more. The better-known names include Wesray and Clayton & Dubilier. Also, most of the major Wall Street firms such as First Boston, Morgan Stanley, Lazard Frères, Merrill Lynch, and Shearson Lehman Hutton have put together their own equity deal funds. To provide an indication of the current size of this market, KKR's fund exceeds $5.5 billion, Forstmann Little's has reached $2.5 billion and Lazard Frères' has surpassed $1.5 billion. The total amount of capital available for LBOs is now estimated at $30 billion.

A second major market force that has fueled the growth in structured financings has been the development of the "junk bond" market. This market has grown from around $8 billion in 1976 to well over $180 billion today. It seems clear that many of the large hostile transactions we have witnessed in recent years have been made possible only by the development of this market for publicly traded, subordinated, below-investment grade debt. Mezzanine finance, as we shall discuss later, has provided a means to finance relatively smaller transactions, and is typically used only in "friendly" transactions.

A third major element in the rise of structured financings was the tremendous amount of liquidity available within the international banking system. LBOs and other structured financings became a more attractive investment for banks than conventional alternatives such as loans to major U.S. corporations, to sovereign borrowers in developing countries, and to the real estate and oil and gas sector. Such untraditional bank investments in leveraged transactions have taken the forms of mezzanine finance and private equity, as well as the more familiar senior loans.

A fourth major element in the growth of leveraged transactions has been foreign investment in the U.S. The long decline in the dollar's value since its peak in early 1985 has led to a tremendous surge in the purchase of American companies by foreign corporations.

The factors we have described thus far all relate to the capital or "supply" side of the equation. What is really driving this large-scale mobilization of capital for leveraged transactions, however, are the perceived opportunities to earn large profits by

IN PRACTICE, A MEZZANINE ISSUE IS DESIGNED TO FILL THE FINANCING "GAP"
BETWEEN THE AMOUNT THE SENIOR SECURED LENDER WILL PROVIDE AND THE
AMOUNT OF EQUITY CAPITAL THE PRINCIPAL (AND HIS BACKERS) ARE ABLE AND
WILLING TO COMMIT.

recapitalizing and restructuring corporations. The presence of these opportunities, combined with the financial innovations that have allowed such transactions to take place, has put increasing pressure on corporate management to increase returns to shareholders. In some cases, this has meant corporate acquisitions of competitors with the aim of achieving consolidation within a shrinking industry, such as we have witnessed in the oil, tobacco, automotive, and food industries. It has also led, however, to the breaking up of large conglomerates into smaller pieces, most of which have been sold to single-industry firms if not to their own operating management.

An important result of this pressure from shareholder activists is an increasing trend for companies to recapitalize themselves to forestall the threat of takeover. For companies in mature businesses with lots of operating cash flow and more capital than they can profitably invest, recapitalizations that retire large amounts of stock with debt are an efficient means of returning capital to investors while increasing management's ownership of the equity. LBOs similarly provide incumbent management with a means of deflecting shareholder unrest while concentrating equity ownership.

Having offered this brief survey of leveraged transactions, let's now take a look at the role of the mezzanine market in financing corporate recapitalizations.

WHAT IS MEZZANINE FINANCE?...

A mezzanine issue, as stated earlier, occupies one or more intermediate positions in the corporate capital structure between the senior debt and the common equity. A mezzanine investment typically takes the form of subordinated debt, junior subordinated debt, or preferred stock (or some combination of each). It also virtually always includes equity participation in some form, whether as warrants, stock appreciation rights, or common stock.

It is almost always placed privately, and carries an intermediate term that ranges from 5 to 12 years. If it is entirely debt, a mezzanine issue generally carries a coupon of 400 to 700 basis points over treasuries, depending on the risk of the transaction, the degree of subordination, and market conditions. Mezzanine issues also have taken the form of securities that don't pay current cash interest—such as zero coupons and PIKs (payment in kind). And

because mezzanine finance also typically includes an equity component, the decision to invest in a mezzanine issue generally combines aspects of both a conventional credit decision and an investment decision.

In practice, a mezzanine issue is designed to fill the financing "gap" between the amount the senior lender will provide and the amount of equity capital the principal (and his backers) are able and willing to commit. From the issuer's standpoint, mezzanine finance may appear to be very expensive borrowing. But, because the decision to use mezzanine financing typically follows an understanding that the senior debt capacity has been exhausted, the issuer may choose to view it as inexpensive equity—since his only alternative may be to raise additional equity from outside sources and thus further dilute his ownership.

Neither of these perspectives on the "cost" of mezzanine finance tells the real, or at least the complete, story. In truth mezzanine finance is neither "expensive debt" nor "cheap equity." But, like the convertible bond issues they resemble, mezzanine issues occupy a middle ground between debt and common equity on the risk-reward spectrum; and, as such, their real "cost of capital" is considerably higher than that of senior debt, but considerably lower than that of straight equity.

In practice, mezzanine investors say they expect returns in the range of 20-30 percent. And, given that private investors in the equity alone typically look for annual returns around 35-50 percent, this 20-30 percent range can be taken as a reasonable estimate of the "cost" of mezzanine capital. Where investors' expectations fall within this range will likely depend on the risk of the transaction. The higher the proportion of equity promised, of course, the higher the expected return; and thus the higher the cost of the mezzanine capital.

...AND HOW DOES IT DIFFER FROM JUNK BONDS?

To provide a more detailed picture of the mezzanine finance market, let's set it against its "public" counterpart, the high-yield or junk bond market.

Junk bonds are typically public securities. The size of junk bond issues often exceeds $100 million and they trade in relatively liquid secondary markets. Investors in junk bonds include mutual funds, savings and loans, insurance companies, and pension funds.

Mezzanine issues, by contrast, are much smaller, and typically fall in the range of $3 to $40 million. They are privately placed or directly negotiated by the issuer with a private purchaser. And although the equity component will sometimes have registration rights, mezzanine investments are generally highly illiquid and bought with the expectation of being held until maturity. Because of this lack of liquidity, mezzanine issues are likely to have much tighter covenants limiting the issuer's flexibility to sell assets, take on additional debt, or distribute cash to investors. There are also typically stricter requirements for reporting and corporate maintenance than in the case of junk bond issues.

The junk bond market is, of course, far larger than the mezzanine market. Estimates by Drexel Burnham put the volume of outstanding junk bonds at the end of 1988 at roughly $180 billion. Although there are no reliable estimates of the size of the mezzanine market (because it is private), our best guess would fall in the range of $10-30 billion.

But if the sizes of the two markets are quite different, changes in the availability and cost of funding in the mezzanine market closely parallel those in the junk bond market. The correlation between conditions in these markets has been so strong that we can reasonably use the high-yield market as a surrogate for the mezzanine market.

As shown in Exhibit 1, the volume and cost (measured as a spread over treasuries) of junk bonds has proven to be sensitive to major "events," such as the stock market scandals and the stock market crash of 1987. It is also sensitive to sharp rises in interest rates as can been seen, for example, in April 1987. At such times, junk bond yields have risen dramatically and new issues have all but disappeared. But the market has also proved to be highly resilient, with yields and volume returning to normal levels in fairly short order. These developments, as suggested, have been mirrored by those in the mezzanine market.

Equity Participation

Unlike most junk bonds, mezzanine issues, as mentioned earlier, almost always include an equity component. Warrants are typically the preferred form of equity participation, by investors and issuers alike.

Let's take a moment to look at some of the major features of these warrants. Perhaps most important, the exercise price of these warrants is generally nominal. And thus the value of the warrant is at least equal in value to that of the common equity.

Although such warrants typically have a 10-year life, the targeted "exit horizon" is much shorter, generally in the range of 3 to 6 years. There are also generally put provisions that allow the investor to sell the warrants back to the issuer—as well as call provisions that allow the issuer to redeem them—well before maturity. A common arrangement gives the mezzanine investor a put option allowing it to "put" the warrants back to the issuer at an agreed-upon exit value beginning at the end of year 4. The exit value is usually based on the appraised value using a discounted cash flow formula or an agreed-upon multiple of operating income. In return for granting this put option, the issuer typically seeks to negotiate a call option—one that generally begins a year after the put option can first be exercised—to redeem the warrants for a price in the range of 100-110 percent of assessed fair market value. The mezzanine investor may also negotiate registration rights on its shares, as well as so-called "piggy back" registration rights allowing it to sell its shares along with an equity offering by the issuer.

THE CRITERIA

What kinds of companies are good candidates for mezzanine financing? Below is a list of criteria that we at the Continental Bank use in evaluating investment opportunities.

■ Companies with strong, proven operating management at key levels (either already in place or, if the key manager is selling, identified elsewhere).

■ Companies manufacturing and selling products which are not subject to rapid technological change.

■ Companies which manufacture a proprietary product and enjoy a strong market position either locally or nationally.

■ Companies whose manufacturing efficiencies establish them—or have the potential to establish them—among the "low-cost" producers within an industry.

■ Distribution concerns or companies that manufacture and sell products used in industrial markets. Some consumer products companies with widely accepted consumer use could also be considered, provided that an inordinate amount of advertising dollars are not required to keep the product visible.

■ Companies with cash flow predictability that are normally not subject to wide or prolonged cyclical swings in profitability.

■ Companies whose current balance sheet provides room for additional leverage in the new capital structure.

EXHIBIT 1

HIGH YIELD DEBT NON-
CONVERTIBLE BOND
OFFERINGS BY MONTH

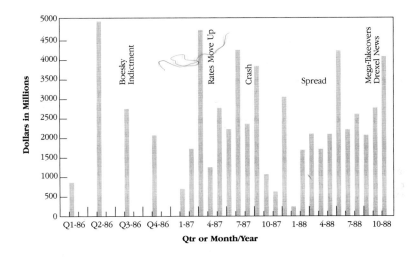

HIGH YIELD MARKET
(AVERAGE YIELD COMPARED TO
TEN YEAR TREASURY)

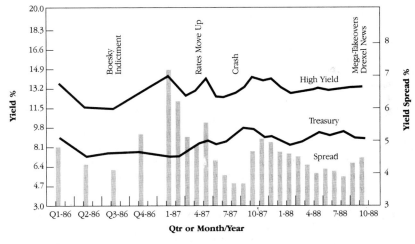

■ A purchase price, including existing debt, of not more than 8 times operating cash flow. Exceptions to this rule are made for turnaround opportunities or if a strong break-up program is an integral part of the logic of the acquisition.
■ Operations not subject to significant import threats or other unmanageable economic risks.

■ Companies which have demonstrated the ability to maintain acceptable margins even in economic downturns.
■ Companies with good asset quality and, preferably, a weighted balance in favor of current assets rather than large investment in fixed assets.
■ Companies that possess quantifiable liabilities.

EXHIBIT 2

EBIT (Operating) Model	Capital Structure (Balance Sheet) Model
4.0 X Senior Debt	60% Senior Debt
2.0 X Mezzanine	30% Mezzanine
.5 X Equity	10% Equity

THE PROTOTYPE

Let's now turn to an illustration of a typical transaction involving mezzanine debt.

As shown in Exhibit 2, there are essentially two ways of viewing the standard capital structure that arises from a buyout. One is referred to as the "EBIT" or "Operating" Model and the other as the "Balance Sheet" Model.

In the "Operating" Model, we have assumed that the price paid for the buyout is fixed at 6.5X earnings before interest and taxes. (This pricing formula simply reflects the use of a "rule of thumb" —one that is modified, in practice, by considering a number of factors such as the stability of operating cash flows, the prospects for growth, and the current level of interest rates.) The amount of the senior debt is equal to 4X EBIT, the amount of mezzanine finance is half the amount of senior debt, or 2X EBIT, and the equity corresponds to the remaining fraction of the purchase price.

Expressed in terms of percentages, the senior capital thus represents slightly more than 60 percent of total capital, mezzanine finance accounts for just over 30 percent, and the remaining 8 percent or so is the equity layer. In this sense, the "Operating

Model" shown in Exhibit 2 has roughly the same financing proportions as the "Balance Sheet" model (also known in the industry as the standard "60-30-10") shown next to it.

Some of the other rules of thumb that fall out of the "60-30-10" prototype include the following:
- Senior interest coverage of 1.75X EBIT
- Total cash interest at 1.25 EBIT (which would apply to the mezzanine debt at the margin)
- Senior bank debt amortization in 7-8 years
- Senior debt paid out before junior debt begins to amortize
- Mezzanine debt amortized in 10-12 years.

To show how these conventions might be applied, consider the simple case of XYZ company with revenues of $200 million and an EBIT of $20.5 million. Assuming the company is valued at about 6.5X EBIT, let's say the purchase price turns out to be $133 million. In this case, the "60-30-10" standard would produce a capital structure consisting of about $80 million in senior debt, $40 million in mezzanine finance, and $13 million in equity.

To make the example slightly more realistic, let's also assume that $20 million of the mezzanine debt is senior subordinated coupon debt, and that the other $20 million is junior subordinated PIK'd debt—

that is, it doesn't pay interest in cash, but instead increases the principal amount of the debt on which interest will eventually be paid.

Who would be the providers of capital in such a deal and what would be their expectations and requirements?

The most likely source of the senior debt are commercial banks. The interest rate would typically float (say, at LIBOR plus 2½ %) and closing fees would run about 2 percent. The debt would be amortized over a period no longer than 8 years, and the lenders would seek to reduce their exposure by taking security in the assets, requiring covenants subordinating other capital, and distributing part of the loan to other investors.

Sources of the mezzanine finance, whether the senior or the junior subordinated debt, would include the sellers themselves, both public and private "high yield" or "mezzanine" funds, LBO or other private equity funds, as well as most of the institutions providing senior debt. The senior subordinated debt would pay a fixed coupon 400-500 basis points over comparable treasuries as well as an equity participation (usually in the form of warrants). The debt would be unsecured, have limited covenant protection, and have a 10-12 year term (with some provision for exit after 3-7 years). Underwriting fees would run 2-4 percent.

The junior debt, in this case, pays no coupon (but instead makes payments in kind). The implied yield on the debt ranges from 600-800 basis points over treasuries; and the debt is likely to have warrants or be convertible into common stock. There is even less covenant protection, and fees run on the order of 2-5 percent.

Providers of the equity include, besides management, other private investors, public and private equity funds, insurance companies, pension funds, investment banks, and commercial banks. Such investors often seek board representation, have return expectations of 40-50 percent per annum, and look for a 3- to 7-year exit horizon.

In the above example, let's assume the negotiation process ends up producing the following capital structure (in millions):

Senior debt	$80	LIBOR + 2.5%
Mezzanine	$40	22-25% return expectations
Sub. Coupon Debt	$20	14.50% interest plus warrants
Sub. PIK Debt	$20	16.00% implied interest plus warrants
Outside equity	$12	40% return, 70% of company
Management	$1	50% return, 10% of company

Now, having outlined this hypothetical deal, the expectations of different investors, and the capital structure that has resulted from the negotiation process, let's see how such a deal might turn out. Assume that, after five years, the company is sold for the same 6.5X EBIT multiple for which it was originally purchased. If we also assume that EBIT has grown at a compounded rate of 10 percent per year, and thus increased from $20 to $33 million at the end of year 5, then the sale price turns out to be roughly $215 million.

Under this scenario, which could be characterized as a successful transaction, the returns to the various investors would be as follows. The senior debt of course earns its 2.5% over LIBOR (11.5 in this example) for five years. The subordinated coupon debtholders end up owning 6.6 percent of the company, and earn an annual IRR of 21 percent. The subordinated PIK debtholders end up owning 15% of the company, and earn an IRR of 27 percent. The outside equity, which ends up owning 67% of the company, earns an annual IRR of 49 percent. And management, on an original investment of $1 million, ends up owning 11% of the company, and earns an annual IRR of 69 percent.

A CASE STUDY IN MEZZANINE FINANCING

Having set forth some rules of thumb in the above illustration, let's now look at an actual example of a mezzanine financing—one that the Continental Bank recently had a hand in.

By way of background, our client is the manager of a West Coast radio broadcasting company owning four pairs (AM/FM) of stations. Two years earlier, the manager bought the stations together with an investor group. And, as a result of a limited initial investment and earn-out provisions, he had increased his ownership to 12 percent of the company.

Having achieved this level, the manager then became interested in buying out the investor group and acquiring a much larger stake in the company. We were asked to play a role both as adviser and as placement agent for both the senior and the junior debt in the transaction that eventually took place.

The equity investors were willing to be cashed out for a "fair" return. The manager and the investor group agreed on a purchase price of $45 million ($18 million for the equity, $26 million for debt repayment, and about $1 million in fees), thus providing the equity investors a 45 percent rate of return over a period less than two years. Investors in the mezzanine debt would earn a return of 27 percent with the value of the coupon (PIK'd) plus warrants for 10 percent of the company.

An interesting aspect of this case was the fact that the subordinated PIK'd debt had a "window" in its no-call provision that allowed refinancing at the two-year point—and only then. Because this expensive debt could not later be refinanced, the principal had a strong incentive to "turn" the deal at the two-year mark; and this consideration in fact determined the timing of the buyout.

Working with financial institutions that arranged the senior financing, we devised a structure for the $45 million buyout that was as follows (in millions):

SOURCES		USES	
Cash	$ .75	Stock Purchase	$ 18.00
Bank Revolver	1.50	Debt Refinancing	25.80
Bank Term	28.50	Closing Costs	1.20
Mezz, PIK	14.25		
TOTAL	$ 45.00		$ 45.00

Note that this transaction was designed to be accomplished without the infusion of any additional outside equity (although the equity component associated with the mezzanine debt would amount to 30% of the company). The manager intended simply to roll his entire 12 percent stake into the deal. Based on the buyout price of $18 million for the 88 percent of the company owned by the investor group, the implied value of the manager's 12 percent was $2.2 million. But the manager felt that his equity was worth considerably more, and his reasoning was as follows: The trailing EBIT of the company was $4.5 million, and thus the purchase price of $47.2 million represented a multiple of 10.5X operating cash. Because the comparable multiple in sales of similar companies was in the 11-12X range, he wanted to capitalize the $4.5 million EBIT at 11.5 times to yield a value of $51.75 million for the entire firm. This $51.75 million value compares to a $47.2 million value for the entire firm. Therefore the implied value is an additional $4.5 million above the $2.2 million rolled into the deal, producing an implied equity value of almost $7 million.

Our job was to help the manager convince an equity-oriented mezzanine investor that this $7 million of implied equity was indeed real—and that the company's operations could support a capital structure with $45 million in debt. If we were unsuccessful, the principal would have had to attract additional equity capital—perhaps as much as $3 million, in which case the principal would have ended up owning about 33 percent of the company instead of the 100 percent (again, minus the implied 30 percent equity portion of the mezzanine) he wanted.

The deal modelled out as follows:

CAPITAL STRUCTURE (AS MULTIPLE OF OPERATING PROFIT).

	Actual		Implied	
	Amount	Multiple	Amount	Multiple
Senior Debt	$ 30.0	6.7X	$ 30.0	6.7X
Mezzanine	14.2	3.2X	14.2	3.2X
Equity	2.2	.5X	6.7	1.5X
		10.4X		11.4X

Using either the "implied" or the "actual" case, the debt-to-EBIT multiples are more aggressive than the 4/2/.5 prototype presented earlier (as they would have to be, given a purchase price of over 10X). And the coverage ratios, with senior interest coverage at 1.36 and total interest coverage, at .90, are also considerably lower than the standard 1.75 and 1.25.

Having structured the deal in this manner, we decided that while we would need to find both aggressive senior lenders and mezzanine investors, the real key to the deal would be in finding the right mezzanine player. We agreed to approach three insurance companies and three private mezzanine funds, all of which we identified as equity-oriented investors interested in the communications business. For the senior financing, we approached three regional banks and two industrial commercial finance companies.

After much negotiation and due diligence, we closed the deal largely on the terms outlined above. The senior financing was provided by a regional bank at 2½ percent over LIBOR, with some principal amortization and a balloon at 8 years. There was substantial covenant protection, security in all assets, and subordination (through both inter-creditor agreements and sub-debt documents) of all other claims. The mezzanine layer was provided by an insurance company, and involved an unsecured, subordinated PIK'd issue carrying a coupon of 15 percent and having a 10-year maturity. It also included warrants for 30 percent of the company.

As a result of the use of mezzanine financing, the manager acquired his company without giving up direct outside equity (although he will end up having the mezzanine investor as a 30 percent partner). His expectation is that he will earn over 100 percent per annum on his investment of 2.2 million, and that he will either sell or restructure the company in the next five years.

A CASE INVOLVING PRIVATE EQUITY

Our client in this case was a mid-western manufacturing company in a mature, slow-growth industry. The opportunity was brought to us by an operating professional with many years of experience in the industry. He had worked with the Continental Bank in his prior role as CEO of a much larger concern, and he now approached our equity group as a potential financial partner.

After reviewing the history and prospects of the company and its industry, we both structured and participated in the financing of the transaction. Also, because of the fragmented nature of the industry, we agreed to use the company as a vehicle to pursue strategic add-on acquisitions within the industry.

In valuing the company, we relied on their historical performance, industry and competitive analysis, extensive due diligence, and the input of our partner. Given the mature nature of the business, we believed that the target company's revenues would grow at a rate slightly in excess of inflation, with a reasonable increase in gross margins brought about by improvements in production and changes in the product mix. Operating margins were also expected to benefit from moderate reductions in G&A and better use of distribution channels.

In arriving at a purchase price we typically try to pay less than 7X trailing EBITA (earnings before interest, taxes, and amortization) for companies that are underperforming in their industry. In this case, we paid $63.6 million or 5.9X trailing EBIT (which also amounted to 7.5X the average EBIT of the preceding two years). We believed this to be a fair price for the business because of its predictable growth prospects, product reputation, and identifiable production enhancements and product mix changes.

Working with the senior and subordinated lenders, we devised a structure for the $63.6 million as follows:

SOURCES

	Amount	%
Senior Debt	$39.6	62.3%
Sen. Sub. Debt 14.25%	16.0	25.2%
Pref. Stock (10% PIK)	7.2	11.3%
Common Equity	0.8	1.2%
	63.6	100%

USES

	Amount	%
Purchase Price	30.8	48.4%
Existing Debt	26.2	41.1%
Fees	1.4	2.3%
Noncompete	5.2	8.2%
	63.6	100%

The senior debt carried a current interest rate of LIBOR plus 2.5%, with approximately 50 percent in the form of a revolving line of credit and the remainder in the form of a six-year term loan at LIBOR plus 3%. The EBITA senior interest coverage was 1.97X in year one, increasing to 5.53X by year five.

The subordinated debt had an eight-year life with a current interest rate of 14.25%. Total interest coverage was 1.36X in year one, rising to 3.02X by year five. The subordinated debt was scheduled to be repaid in three equal annual payments beginning in year six.

The subordinated debt also carried warrants for 15% of the company. To allow mezzanine investors to realize the value of those warrants, the investors were given the right to put them back to the issuer at the end of year 4 at their appraised market value. In return for this put option, the issuer was given a call option giving it the right to redeem the warrants at the end of year 5, again at appraised market value.

Based on an EBIT exit multiple of 6.5X, the mezzanine investors expected an internal rate of return on their investment of 22.4%. The table on the next page outlines the equity investment in the transaction together with the different investors' expectations.

The equity invested in the transaction was contributed in the following proportions: 10% by management, 30% by the investor, and 60% by an affiliate of Continental. In addition, management was given options to purchase an additional 5% of the company as a further incentive. Both the direct investment and the options granted management will vest according to a tenure- and performance-based formula over 5 years.

EQUITY OWNERSHIP

Contributed	Prfrd	Common	Fully Diluted Equity Ownership (1)	IRR (1)
Mezzanine	0.0	0.0	15.0% (2)	22.4%
Investor Group	2.1	0.3	30.0% (3)	54.0%
Continental	4.4	0.4	42.8% (3)	43.1%
Management	0.7	0.1	11.4% (4)	57.1%
	7.2	0.8	100.0%	

(1) Based on an exit multiple of 6.5X 5th-year EBIT.
(2) In the form of warrants
(3) As diluted by the mezzanine ownership and management options.
(4) Includes 5% management options exercised in year 5.

The deal was structured with preferred as well as common equity to provide our operating partners with a "capital appreciation carried interest," both for originating the deal and as partial compensation for their active management of the company on an ongoing basis. This is accomplished through the 9-to-1 preferred/common structure, which has the added virtue of ensuring that all parties are returned their invested capital before any carried interest is received.

The use of mezzine finance and private equity gave the operator the ability to leverage his own equity capital and to acquire control of this attractive company.

IN CLOSING

The mezzanine finance market is an important financing innovation that has arisen to fill the financing "gap" between the senior debt financing and the available equity financing in relatively small leveraged transactions—generally with purchase prices in the range of $25-250 million. By combining more conventional subordinated debt with PIK securities that pay no interest and with equity-like features such as warrants, mezzanine financing appears to have significantly enlarged the debt capacity of companies in mature businesses with stable cash flows. In so doing, it has also furthered an economy-wide movement toward greater concentration of ownership among operating managers and investor groups, which in turn is increasing corporate profits and efficiency.

INITIAL PUBLIC OFFERINGS

by Roger G. Ibbotson and
Jody L. Sindelar, Yale University, and
Jay R. Ritter, University of Michigan*

A privately held firm or successful venture capital project raises capital and achieves greater liquidity by going public. These initial public offerings are almost always quite risky. Risks are faced by each of the three major parties involved: issuer, investment banker, and investors. The pricing of initial public offerings (IPOs) is difficult, both because there is no observable market price prior to the offering and because many of the issuing firms have little or no operating history. If the price is set too low, the issuer does not get the full advantage of its ability to raise capital. If it is priced too high, then the investor would get an inferior return and consequently might reject the offering. Investors, moreover, would be unwilling to purchase offerings from an investment banker with a record of overpriced offerings. Without accurate pricing, the market could wither as one side or the other is unsatisfied. Without a healthy market for IPOs, young growth companies would have only limited access to the public in raising capital.

The empirical evidence on the pricing of IPOs provides a puzzle to those who otherwise believe in efficient financial markets. Numerous empirical studies have shown that unseasoned new issues are significantly underpriced, on average.[1] For example, a study by one of the present authors found positive initial stock price performance of 11.4 percent, while a more recent study by another of us found an average initial return of 18.8 percent.[2] Given the level of competition in financial markets, this is a surprising result. A number of hypotheses have been offered to explain the underpricing, but to date there is still no persuasive, widely accepted, and test-supported explanation of IPO underpricing.

To add to this surprising underpricing phenomenon, there is also strong evidence of a recurring pattern of alternating "hot" and "cold" new issue markets.[3] Hot issue markets have average initial returns that sometimes reach unbelievable levels; for example, new issues were underpriced, on average, by 48 percent during the 15-month period starting in January 1980. These markets also tend to be associated with increasing volume. Following these hot periods, there tend to be periods of "heavy" volume accompanied by relatively low initial returns (and thus less underpricing).

These heavy issue markets then frequently give way to periods of poor initial performance and "light" volume. For example, in 1971 there were 391 offerings with relatively high average initial returns, followed by 562 offerings in 1972 with moderate returns, which in turn were followed by 105 offerings in 1973 with negative returns. In the mid-1970s, there were very few offerings, but by 1980 life returned to the new issues market with a spate of oil and gas offerings.

This paper updates previous research on IPOs using data through the end of 1987 and then reviews the related literature that attempts to explain these puzzling results. We try to explain why new issues have been underpriced and how to interpret hot and cold, and heavy and light markets. We conclude with some words of advice to issuers and investors, who may be able to gain from knowledge of these market phenomena.

---

*The authors gratefully acknowledge the financial support of the J. Ira Harris Center for the Study of Corporate Finance at the Michigan Business School.

1. These studies are summarized in Table 7 of Clifford W. Smith, Jr., "Raising Capital: Theory and Evidence," *Midland Corporate Finance Journal*, 4 (Spring 1986), pp. 6-22.

2. The two studies cited are, respectively, Roger G. Ibbotson, "Price Performance of Common Stock New Issues," *Journal of Financial Economics* 2. (September 1975), pp. 235-272; and Jay. R. Ritter, "The 'Hot Issue' Market of 1980," *Journal of Business* 57 (April 1984), pp. 215-240. The difference between Ibbotson's 11.4 percent and Ritter's 18.8 percent can be attributed to differing sample selection criteria. Ibbotson excludes issues with an offering price of less than $3.00 per share, whereas Ritter includes them. These low-priced issues (penny stocks) tend to be the riskiest, and have the highest initial performance.

3. These hot and cold issue markets were first documented by Roger G. Ibbotson and Jeffrey F. Jaffe in "'Hot Issue' Markets," *Journal of Finance* 30 (September 1975), pp. 1027-42, which analyzes the 1960-70 period. The continued existence of this phenomenon is documented in Ritter (1984), cited in footnote 2, for the 1960-82 period.

INSTITUTIONAL ASPECTS

The Process

Going public provides the firm with more capital while at the same time allowing the original owners to diversify their holdings. The publicly traded price also provides management and shareholders with important outside information about the firm's value.

The issuer of the stock decides to sell a portion of his firm and presumably wants to receive as much as possible in return. The price at which the company can trade ownership for cash depends upon overall market conditions, the specifics of the firm, and the policies of investment bankers.

The firm that wants to go public will generally seek an underwriter, or syndicate of underwriters. The issuer prefers a more prestigious underwriter because this prestige provides a favorable signal to the market. However, prestigious investment banking firms remain that way only by using discretion in choosing the firms that they will bring public. They may refuse more speculative issues. Thus, new issuers search for the best underwriter and the most favorable conditions possible.

The initial public offerings can be made by either of two methods: "best efforts" or "firm commitment."[4] In best efforts contracts the issuer and underwriter negotiate an offering price. The underwriter uses its "best efforts" to raise all of the desired capital at the negotiated price, usually receiving a percentage of the capital raised as its fee. If there is not enough demand at this price, the offer is withdrawn from the market and the issuer does not raise any capital. It is unlikely that a second offering will be made at a lower price. The best efforts offering reduces the risk faced by the underwriter and leaves much of the risk to be borne by the issuer.

By contrast, in the case of the firm commitment offering, the underwriter guarantees that the agreed-upon amount of capital will be raised. In effect, the underwriter buys all of the stock issued at an agreed-upon price (with a price spread to compensate the underwriter) and is then responsible for selling it all.

The underwriter may later reduce the public offering price, but nonetheless delivers to the issuer the entire sum that was previously specified. Thus, it is crucial to the underwriter that the price is set appropriately.

When the issuer and underwriter agree to an initial public offering, the parties must comply with the Securities Act of 1933. The Act was designed to disclose information to potential investors, giving investors the right to sue if there is misleading information or material omission of fact. The restrictions are stricter for S-1 offerings (greater than $7.5 million in gross proceeds) than they are for S-18 offerings (less than $7.5 million). The smallest offerings (less than $1.5 million in gross proceeds) are eligible for a Regulation A offering, which involves even fewer requirements. In this paper, we confine our attention to the two larger classes of IPOs.[5]

According to SEC regulations the underwriter, after investigating the issuing firm, files the necessary information (e.g., type of business, nature of security, financial statements) in the preliminary prospectus. Then there is a period of at least twenty days in which the SEC reviews the submitted material. During this "cooling off" period the underwriter surveys the market. Information is sent to prospective investors and, in a firm commitment offering, the investors are asked to indicate their willingness to purchase shares at some price (to "circle" their demand). This information is used by the underwriter to set the offering price. The final price is usually set at a pricing meeting the afternoon before the formal initial public offering.

Setting the Price

Setting the price of an initial public offering is crucial to a successful offering. But even after the underwriters' surveys of the market and investigation of the issuer, considerable uncertainty remains about how the broader market will receive the issue. The difficulty in pricing arises from the fact that IPO firms, by definition, have no price history (although "reverse LBOs," as will be seen later, provide an interesting exception). Yet the underwriter has to set

4. On an institutional basis, it happens that firm commitment offerings are typically conducted by the more prestigious underwriters and the size of the offering is on average more than four times as large as best efforts offerings. See Jay R. Ritter, "The Costs of Going Public," *Journal of Financial Economics* 19 (December 1987), pp. 269-81. Both Ritter and Gershon Mandelker and Artur Raviv, "Investment Banking: An Economic Analysis of Optimal Underwriting Contracts," *Journal of Finance* 32 (June 1977), pp. 683-694, suggest that the best efforts method is used when there is greater uncertainty about the issuing firm. Various studies have

found that the degree of underpricing declines as the prestige of the underwriter increases. See, for example, Richard Carter and Steven Manaster, "Initial Public Offerings and Underwriter Reputation," unpublished Iowa State and University of Utah working paper (1988).

5. For an analysis of Regulation A Offerings, see Hans R. Stoll and Anthony J. Curley, "Small Business and the New Issues Market for Equities," *Journal of Financial and Quantitative Analysis* 5 (1970), pp. 309-322.

the price to satisfy both his clienteles, the issuer and the investors.

If the price is set too low, the issuer does not realize his full potential to raise capital. Although initial public offerings are one-time-only events for specific firms, the reputation of the underwriter is important in helping other new issuers choose their underwriters. Consequently, the underwriter has the incentive to keep the initial price relatively high.

On the other hand, if the price is set too high, the firm commitment underwriter has a financial loss because he has to lower the price (break the syndicate) to sell the entire issue. In the best efforts case, if the price is too high, the issue is withdrawn, and the issuer raises no capital and the investment banker receives no commissions. On the other hand, if the price is set too low, the issuer suffers excessive dilution of ownership.

EMPIRICAL FINDINGS

The results of our collective research on IPOs are summarized in two figures and a table. In Figures 1 and 2, we present the monthly average initial returns (or percentage underpricing) and the monthly volume of IPOs over the period 1960-1987. The extent of the underpricing and the hot-and-cold, heavy-and-light cycles are clearly demonstrated.

The monthly average initial returns are calculated by taking an equally-weighted average of the initial returns on all the offerings in a given calendar month. Because daily stock prices of OTC stocks (where almost all IPOs begin trading) are more readily available in recent years than in periods prior to NASDAQ, we chose to use two different methods of calculating the initial returns for the periods 1960-76 and 1977-87. For the 1960-76 period, the initial returns are computed as the percentage return from the offering price to the bid price at the end of the month following the offering, net of the market return (as measured by the dividend-inclusive S&P 500 return). For the 1977-87 period, the initial returns are measured as the percentage return from the offering price to the first closing bid price, a period that is normally one day; these returns are not adjusted for market movements.[6]

Table 1 presents the contents of the two figures

on a year-by-year basis. The first column presents the number of IPOs, the second column the average initial return, and the third column the gross proceeds raised, with the vast majority of the funds going to the firms, and only a small part going to selling shareholders. During this 28-year period, 8668 companies have gone public. (Actually, this understates the number by several thousand, since we exclude small Regulation A offerings from our count, and our data sources undoubtedly have omitted some smaller offerings.) This number gives an indication of the dynamic nature of the U. S. economy. It is far in excess of the number of publicly traded firms that have disappeared through bankruptcy, mergers, or takeovers during this period.

Several aspects of these exhibits are striking, especially the pronounced cycles in volume and underpricing. The cycles in underpricing allow one to predict next month's average intial return based upon the current month's average with a high degree of accuracy. (In technical terms, the first-order autocorrelation of monthly average initial returns displayed in Figure 1 is 0.62 for the full 28-year period.) Furthermore, the persistence of underpricing shows no signs of abating: the average initial return for the decade of the 1960s was 21.25 percent, for the 1970s it was 8.95 percent, and for the 1980s (through 1987), it has been 16.09 percent. In the 1970s, it should be pointed out, there was a sustained period of light volume in which average initial returns were negative.

The persistence of volume from month to month is even stronger (the first-order autocorrelation of monthly volume is 0.88). High-volume months are almost always followed by high-volume months, with the exceptions being associated with sharp market drops, such as the October 1987 crash.

Using the data in Table 1, we also measured the correlation between the average initial return and the number of new offerings. The correlation using contemporaneous yearly data is 0.12, while the correlation of the average initial return with the following year's number of new offerings is 0.49. We interpret these numbers as evidence that initial returns lead volume. Further, inspection of the monthly data shows that average initial returns lead volume by roughly 6 to 12 months.[7] Because it takes at least sev-

---

6. The conclusions regarding underpricing seem to be fairly insensitive to the length of the initial return interval, and whether (or how) market risk adjustments are made. For evidence on this, see, for example, R. E. Miller and F. K. Reilly, "An Examination of Mispricing, Returns, and Uncertainty for Initial Public Offerings,"

Financial Management (Summer 1987), pp. 33-38.

7. The correlation coefficient between monthly volume and lagged average initial returns is maximized for a lag of 8 months, although there is also a strong relation for other lags in the 5 to 16 month range.

FIGURE 1
AVERAGE INITIAL RETURNS BY MONTH FOR S.E.C.-REGISTERED INITIAL PUBLIC OFFERINGS.[1]

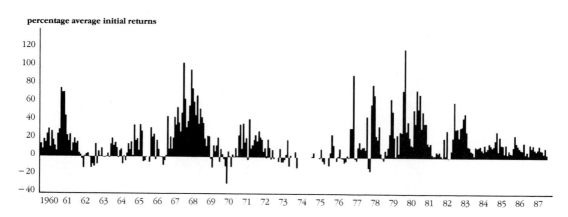

FIGURE 2
NUMBER OF OFFERINGS BY MONTH FOR S.E.C.-REGISTERED INITIAL PUBLIC OFFERINGS.[2]

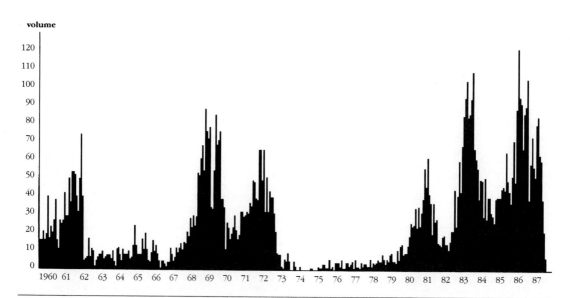

1. Returns for January 1960–October 1970 are from Ibbotson and Jaffe (1975). Returns for November 1970–December 1987 constructed by authors. See text for definitions.
2. Volume for January 1960–October 1970 taken from Ibbotson and Jaffe (1975). Volume for November 1970–December 1974 from the "New Market Names" section of *Investment Dealer's Digest*. Volume for January 1975—December 1987 from *Going Public—The IPO Reporter*.

TABLE 1
NUMBER OF OFFERINGS, AVERAGE INITIAL RETURN AND GROSS PROCEEDS OF INITIAL PUBLIC OFFERINGS IN 1960-87

Year	Number of Offerings [1]	Average Initial Return,% [2]	Gross Proceeds $ Million [3]
1960	269	17.83	553
1961	**435**	**34.11**	**1,243**
1962	298	-1.61	431
1963	**83**	**3.93**	**246**
1964	97	5.32	380
1965	**146**	**12.75**	**409**
1966	85	7.06	275
1967	**100**	**37.67**	**641**
1968	368	55.86	1,205
1969	**780**	**12.53**	**2,605**
1970	358	-0.67	780
1971	**391**	**21.16**	**1,655**
1972	562	7.51	2,724
1973	**105**	**-17.82**	**330**
1974	9	-6.98	51
1975	**14**	**-1.86**	**264**
1976	34	2.90	237
1977	**40**	**21.02**	**151**
1978	42	25.66	247
1979	**103**	**24.61**	**429**
1980	259	49.36	1,404
1981	**438**	**16.76**	**3,200**
1982	198	20.31	1,334
1983	**848**	**20.79**	**13,168**
1984	516	11.52	3,932
1985	**507**	**12.36**	**10,450**
1986	953	9.99	19,260
1987	**630**	**10.39**	**16,380**
TOTAL	8,668	16.37	83,984

1. The number of offerings excludes Regulation A offerings (small issues, raising less than $1.5 million currently). Data are from Ibbotson and Jaffe (1975) for 1960-70, Ritter (1984) for 1971-82, *Going Public: The IPO Reporter* for 1983-85, and *Venture* magazine for 1986-87. The authors have excluded real estate investment trusts (REIT's) and closed-end mutual funds.
2. Initial returns are computed as the percentage return from the offering price to the end-of-the-calendar-month bid price, less the market return, for offerings in 1960-76. For 1977-87, initial returns are calculated as the percentage return from the offering price to the end-of-the-first-day bid price, without adjusting for market movements. Data are from Ibbotson and Jaffe (1975) for 1960, Ritter (1984) for 1971-82, and prepared by the authors for 1983-87. The latter numbers have been prepared with the assistance of Choo-Huang Teoh, using data supplied by Robert E. Miller.
3. Gross proceeds data comes from various issues of the *SEC Monthly Statistical Bulletin* and *Going Public: The IPO Reporter.* The gross proceeds numbers reported here have been adjusted to remove REIT and closed-end mutual fund offerings.

eral months from the decision to go public until the offering is consummated, it appears that many firms initiate the process when they observe a very receptive market to the offerings of other firms, especially for firms in their own industry.

The Effects of Investor Uncertainty on Underpricing

Table 2 presents average initial returns for 2439 IPOs in 1975-84 that were listed in *Going Public: The IPO Reporter.* (These 2439 firms exclude closed-end mutual funds, REITs, and offerings not using an investment banker.) Here the IPO firms are categorized according to their annual sales, with the idea that sales may serve as a proxy for the degree of investor uncertainty about a firm's value. As shown in the table, larger firms are underpriced less. This pattern has been noted in many recent studies, using a variety of measures of investor uncertainty (for example, age of the firm, gross proceeds, assets, and the number of uses for the proceeds specified by the offering).

TABLE 2
AVERAGE INITIAL RETURNS CATEGORIZED BY ANNUAL SALES OF ISSUING FIRM

Annual sales of issuing firm, $[1]	Number of firms[2]	Average initial return, %[3]
0	386	42.9
1 – 999,999	678	31.4
1,000,000 – 4,999,000	353	14.3
5,000,000 – 14,999,999	347	10.7
15,000,000 – 24,999,999	182	6.5
25,000,000 and larger	493	5.3
All	2439	20.7

1. Annual sales are measured as the 12-month revenue for the year prior to going public. No adjustments for the effects of inflation have been made.
2. Firms included are those using S-1 or S-18 registration forms, or with Federal Home Loan Bank Board approval, and listed in *Going Public: The IPO Reporter* for 1975-84. Issues not using an investment banker are excluded.
3. Initial returns are calculated as the percentage return from the offering price to the first recorded closing bid price. No adjustments for market movements have been made.

More speculative issues also tend to have offering prices below $3.00 per share. Whether or not these "penny stocks" are included in the sample has a large effect on the equally-weighted average initial return calculations. For example, of the 2439 issues used in constructing Table 2, the average initial return on those firms priced at less than $3.00 per share is 42.8 percent, while the average initial return on the higher-priced issues is only 8.6 percent.

Another piece of evidence suggesting the effect of investor uncertainty on IPO underpricing is the recent experience of "reverse LBOs." In the 1980s, dozens of firms, or divisions of firms, have gone private in leveraged buyouts, only to go public again within a few years. These reverse LBOs present a unique opportunity to examine IPOs with a more established track record. A study by Chris Muscarella and Michael Vetsuypens finds that for 76 firms converting first from public to private and then back to public ownership during the period 1976-87, the average initial return to IPO investors was only 2.1 percent.[8]

In summary, these results suggest that (1) initial public offerings are significantly underpriced, on average; (2) the more established an issuer and hence the less investor uncertainty about the firm's real value, the lower the amount of underpricing; (3) hot and cold performances come in waves, the persistence of which is predictable; (4) cold issue markets have average initial returns that are not necessarily positive; (5) the number of new offerings also comes in waves of heavy and light activity which are highly serially correlated; and (6) underpricing appears to lead the number of new offerings by roughly six to twelve months.

SOME IDEAS ON NEW ISSUES: UNDERPRICING, HOT, COLD, HEAVY, AND LIGHT MARKETS

Most of the theories put forward to explain IPO underpricing rest on assumptions about differences of information between parties (or "information asymmetries") about the value of the new issue. One such theory is built on the premise that the underwriter has significantly better information than the issuer.[9] In firm commitment offerings, the underwriter has the incentive to set a relatively low price to ensure that the entire issue sells at the predetermined price. Because of its information advantage, the underwriter may be able to convince the issuer that a relatively low price is appropriate if the issuer is unable to ascertain its own underlying val-

8. See Chris J. Muscarella and Michael R. Vetsuypens, "The Underpricing of 'Secondary' Initial Public Offerings," unpublished Southern Methodist University working paper (1988). A study of closed-end mutual fund IPOs sheds additional light on the hypothesis. Since these offerings have very little uncertainty about the underlying value, the hypothesis predicts little underpricing. A study by J. W. Peavy ("Closed-end Fund New Issues: Pricing and Aftermarket Trading Considerations," 1987 Southern Methodist University working paper) finds that, for 45 closed-end mutual fund IPOs in 1986 and 1987, the average initial return was only 1.0 percent.

9. Baron and Holmstrom analyze how to devise a contract such that the relatively less informed issuer can delegate the pricing and marketing of the new issue without being taken advantage of by the underwriter. See David P. Baron and Bengt Holmstrom, "The Investment Banking Contract for New Issues Under Asymmetric Information: Delegation and the Incentive Problem," *Journal of Finance* 35 (1980), pp. 1115-1138.

THE EXTENT TO WHICH THE UNDERWRITER CAN TAKE ADVANTAGE OF
ISSUERS IS LIMITED BY THE UNDERWRITER'S DESIRE TO PROTECT ITS
REPUTATION AND AND THUS ITS FUTURE BUSINESS WITH OTHER
POTENTIAL ISSUERS.

ue. This view is based on the reasoning that, although issuers know more about the specifics of their businesses, the underwriters may be more informed about the market-clearing prices—because the underwriter surveys the markets, conducts "due diligence" investigations of the issuing company, receives proprietary information from the issuer, and has substantial experience in new issues.

To be sure, the extent to which the underwriter can take advantage of issuers is limited by the underwriter's desire to protect its reputation and thus its future business with other potential issuers. Competition among underwriters should also limit the ability of one underwriter to take advantage of an issuer.

One recent study casts doubt on this notion of systematic exploitation of issuers by underwriters. In this study, Muscarella and Vetsuypens, mentioned earlier, examined the underpricing of IPOs of another special group of issuers: investment banks going public.[10] They find that, for the 38 investment banks that went public during 1970-87, the average initial return was 7.1 percent—an amount of underpricing comparable to that of other similar size IPOs. The fact that presumably well-informed investment bankers also appear to underprice their own IPOs suggests that there may indeed be an "equilibrium" level of underpricing—a level which issuers, underwriters, and investors thus appear to accept as necessary to the process.

An alternative explanation of underpricing, developed by Kevin Rock, emphasizes the asymmetry of information among potential investors.[11] According to this view, some investors become informed about the true value of a new issue, while others remain uninformed because it is more difficult or costly for them to become informed. The underwriter is assumed not to know for certain how much the market would be willing to pay for the issue. Thus the underwriter (and the issuer) generally err in setting the price: some stocks are overvalued and others are undervalued. The informed investors line up to buy the undervalued stock and avoid the overvalued issues. As a consequence, the uninformed investors will, on average, end up buying less of the undervalued and more of the overvalued

issues, thereby earning a less than average return. Because issuers must continue to attract uninformed as well as informed investors, new issues must be underpriced on average to provide uninformed investors with acceptable rates of return.

One of the present authors extends this reasoning to try to explain the hot and cold periods of new issues. Hot markets, this argument goes, occur when issues are characterized by great uncertainty and issues have to be discounted even more than usual to attract uninformed investors.[12] Cold markets occur when there is comparatively less uncertainty and therefore less discounting. Empirical support for this hypothesis, however, is relatively weak, as variations in the riskiness of new issues appear to explain only a small portion of the cycles in average initial returns. Even if this hypothesis had been supported, moreover, it does not provide any explanation of the cycles in volume.

These theories of IPO underpricing based on information asymmetries are all fairly recent, and have met with partial acceptance by financial economists. Some of the more traditional explanations—all of which are viewed with skepticism—are as follows:[13]

1. Regulations require underwriters to set the offering price below the expected value. (But note that while regulatory constraints may be important in explaining underpricing in countries such as Korea and Japan, there is no explicit regulation that seems to require underpricing in the U.S.)

2. Underwriters collude to exploit inexperienced issuers and to favor investors. The large number of underwriters makes collusion seem unlikely at best. However, a single prestigious underwriter might conceivably be able to achieve a somewhat monopsonistic position with respect to a single issuer if there were high fixed costs of search on the part of the issuer.

3. Underpriced new issues "leave a good taste" with investors so that future underwritings from the same issuer can be sold at attractive prices. While it is unusual for established companies to issue equity with any regularity (with the possible exception of utilities), one study has found that approximately

10. See Chris J. Muscarella and Michael R. Vetsuypens, "A Simple Test of Baron's Model of IPO Underpricing," unpublished Southern Methodist University working paper (1988).

11. See Kevin F. Rock, "Why New Issues Are Underpriced," *Journal of Financial Economics* 15 (1986), pp. 187-212.

12. See Ritter (1984), cited in note 2. Beatty and Ritter also investigate the idea that the greater is the uncertainty about the value of the firm on the part of the

investors, the more discounting is necessary to attract uninformed investors. Their empirical analysis suggests that greater disclosure by the issuer will reduce the underpricing necessary to attract investors. See Randolph P. Beatty and Jay R. Ritter, "Investment Banking, Reputation, and the Underpricing of Initial Public Offerings," *Journal of Financial Economics* 15 (1986), pp. 213-232.

13. Roger Ibbotson [1975], cited in note 2.

one-third of the companies that went public in the late 1970s and early 1980s have issued additional equity to the public at least once since then.[14]

One way of testing this hypothesis is to look at issues financed with venture capital money. Venture capital firms invest in many companies that they expect to go public in the future; and they may accordingly wish to underprice current new issues if it makes it easier to sell other new issues that they have financed in the future. However, a recent study has found that venture capital-backed IPOs are underpriced by approximately the same amount as other IPOs of comparable size.[15] This finding is inconsistent with the argument that IPOs are deliberately underpriced to maintain continued investor participation in IPO markets, which would predict steeper discounting of venture capital-backed issues. Because venture capitalists are sophisticated financial advisors, the study results also contradict the earlier argument that underpricing reflects the systematic exploitation of disadvantaged issuers by underwriters, which would predict *lower* underpricing of venture capital-backed issues.

4. "Firm commitment" underwriting spreads do not cover all of the risks, so that the underwriter underprices new issues to compensate. In this case, investors would benefit and would be expected to have to pay for this benefit. And it seems, in fact, they did pay for it before "May Day" (the May 1975 decontrol of brokerage commissions), when large or active investors were overpaying for brokerage. In that environment, brokers might be expected to rebate excessive commissions, perhaps by providing access to underpriced new issues.

5. Through tradition or some other arrangement, the underwriting process consists of underpricing offerings with full (or partial) compensation via side payments from investors to underwriters to issuers.

6. The issuing corporation and underwriter perceive that underpricing constitutes a form of insurance against legal suits. The SEC Act of 1933 allows civil liability suits in the case of misinformation. If there is misinformation, but a cushion of safety in the underpricing, then the probability of losses followed by a law suit is diminished.

While this explanation is logically sound, it does not account for the size of the initial discounts that are sometimes observed in the new issue market. Furthermore, it appears that the more prestigious underwriters typically compensate their preferred customers for losses prior to a lawsuit. Just the implicit threat of a suit and a tarnished reputation seem incentive enough to elicit compensation.

As shown above, then, there are several possible explanations of the underpricing of initial public offerings. None taken alone, however, is entirely satisfactory. The question remains why, in a competitive market where it is reasonable to believe that most stocks are fairly priced, is there persistent and systematic underpricing of IPOs? Furthermore, why are there hot and heavy cycles of underpricing and volume followed by cold spells having zero or negative initial performance and light volume? A completely convincing theory would be able to explain both the underpricing on average and the cycles in both volume and underpricing.

POLICY IMPLICATIONS

The unseasoned new issue market is unusual in a variety of ways, demonstrating apparent deviations from the otherwise efficient market. Although we have not been able to offer completely satisfying explanations of our findings, we can offer tentative advice to investors and issuers.

What should investors do? They should buy new issues during a hot issue market when they are generally underpriced. They ought to suspect, however, that the more underpriced an issue, the harder it is to get. Not all issues are underpriced, even during "hot" markets. In cold markets, conversely, significantly underpriced issues are much less likely, but they do exist.

According to one view, "outsiders" that regularly participate in the IPO process will only get enough of the underpriced issues to compensate for any overpriced issues they might get. Thus, only "insiders" should buy new issues since they are the only ones who should expect to come out ahead. According to another view, though, no investor receives abnormal gains after all accounts are settled; even informed investors and preferred clients must rebate their apparent gains.

14. See Ivo Welch, "Seasoned Offerings, Imitation Costs, and the Underpricing of Initial Public Offerings," unpublished University of Chicago working paper.
15. See Christopher Barry, Chris Muscarella, John Peavy, and Michael Vetsuypens, "Venture Capital and Initial Public Offerings," unpublished Southern Methodist University working paper.

Neither of these arguments comes to terms, however, with the puzzling, but well-established fact that there have been high-volume, high-performance markets in which it was both hard to lose and relatively easy to find something to buy. It appears to be extremely unlikely that one had to be an insider to gain or had to rebate all the profits. Thus, if another hot issue market emerges, we recommend that investors buy, and buy most in the early part of the cycle when stocks are the most underpriced. On average, the more speculative offerings have the greatest initial run-ups.

One other observation: It also seems possible to predict which issues are most likely to appreciate by comparing the final offering price with the offering price range listed on the front page of the preliminary prospectus of a firm commitment offering. The preliminary prospectus is generally issued about three weeks prior to the offering date, and during this interval the underwriters conduct pre-selling activities, achieving better knowledge about the demand for an issue in the process. As an example, in the March 1986 offering of Microsoft, the preliminary prospectus indicated an offering price range of $16-$19 per share. The actual offering price was $21 per share. The stock closed at $27.75 on its first day of trading.[16]

While this is an extreme example, when investment bankers find unanticipatedly strong or weak demand, they adjust the offering price, but only partially. If they adjust the offering price up, it is because they have found exceptionally strong demand. But since they only adjust partially, there seems to be an extremely high probability of a positive initial return when the offering price is increased from the range indicated in the preliminary prospectus. Similarly, if the offering price is lowered, it is very likely that there will be a low or even negative initial return. Thus, we recommend that investors pay attention to the direction of the price change in deciding whether or not to submit a purchase order.

What should issuers do? They should issue in the heavy markets that typically follow hot issue markets. In these periods, issuers get the highest price for their securities relative to the efficient (after-market) publicly traded price at a time when the market is still willing to pay high multiples for unseasoned new issues. The low number of offerings during cold issue markets may be due to a perceived lack of buyers and to the lower multiples received by issuers. The issuer should try to make its initial public offering during a heavy spell when issues are less severely underpriced.

If possible, issuers should use a firm commitment offering with a prestigious underwriter. To some degree, the quality of the underwriter "certifies" the quality of the issuer, thus increasing the price that investors are willing to pay. A best efforts transaction may expose the firm to too great a risk that the offering is undersubscribed and then withdrawn, thus denying capital to the would-be issuer. Furthermore, best efforts issues tend to be more severely underpriced.

Finally, issuers should disclose as much information as possible about their firm—short of divulging valuable competitive secrets—at the time of issue. As the recent case of the "reverse LBOs" suggests, the less uncertainty investors have about the value of the issuing firm, the lower the amount of underpricing necessary to attract them.

---

16. For an informative account of the Microsoft offering, see Bro Uttal, "Inside the Deal that Made Bill Gates $350,000,000," *Fortune* 114 (July 21, 1986), pp. 23-33.

RAISING EQUITY IN AN EFFICIENT MARKET

by Bruce Jurin, Chase Manhattan Bank

In an efficient market, all securities issued by corporations should command a "fair" price—one which offers investors the expectation of earning an adequate return for the risk accepted. But even if all securities are fairly priced, a particular form may be more beneficial to a given issuer because of the individual circumstances facing that issuer. In raising equity, for example, corporations can choose from among several methods. And though the firm's shares will command a fair price regardless of the method chosen, the issuer can gain by choosing the method which best fits its own circumstances.

There are four important considerations that determine which method of issuing equity is best. The first is the direct costs of execution, the transaction costs. The second is taxes. Both the tax effect to the corporation and to the equityholders can be significant and must be taken into account. The third is the risk associated with obtaining the desired amount of funds; some methods guarantee a level of proceeds and some do not. The final consideration, and the most complicated, is the "information" effect of a method of issue. All equity-raising techniques suffer from the market's perception that management may raise equity only if it thinks the equity is overvalued.

The direct costs of an issue are pretty much self-explanatory. These costs include filing, legal registration, and underwriting spreads. Tax effects are also self-explanatory. Guarantee of the level of proceeds is more subtle, but also potentially important. Suppose a company has a venture which is expected to be very profitable, but needs considerable financing to get it off the ground. In such a case, the cost of raising insufficient funds may be very great if the company is forced to cancel or delay the venture. But if the company is raising equity simply to cover its expenses over the next three years, management may not be as concerned about the exact amount of funds raised. The information effects of raising equity are also subtle; management may unwittingly send negative signals to the market just by announcing its intention to issue new equity. The importance of the information effect of the equity offering depends on the amount and quality of information that the market currently has about the issuer.

In the pages that follow, we will take each of these considerations in discussing five methods of raising equity capital.

Specific Methods of Raising Equity

The Common Underwriting

The most often used method for raising equity in the United States is a common "underwriting." In fact, the common underwriting is so prevalent that all other forms are deemed "alternative" methods of raising equity.

In a firm underwritten offering, the issuing corporation hires an underwriter, usually an investment bank, which essentially agrees to buy the shares and resell them. The underwriter also handles most of the paperwork that the SEC requires. Since the investment banker is buying the stock and reselling it, marketing of the new issue falls on its shoulders.

The entire process for a common underwriting generally takes several weeks. A group of underwriters typically form a syndicate, with the lead underwriter handling most of the transaction details; the syndicate partners sell their shares and thus share the lead underwriter's risk in underwriting securities. After the syndicate is formed, it publishes a "tombstone" advertisement, letting the public know who is issuing shares, how many are being issued, and when the issue can be bought. At that point, the company cum underwriter submits the necessary documents to the SEC, which reviews it for at least two weeks (which, incidentally, is a law). In the meantime, the syndicate starts lining up buyers, and sends out a detailed prospectus on the offering. The prospectus has data on the offering and the company, but does not disclose the actual price at which the offering will eventually take place. Potential buyers submit to the underwriters non-binding bids on how many shares they expect to buy. Then, a day or two before issue, the underwriter and company agree to the offer price.

What are the relevant factors in assessing the desirability of a common underwriting? First of all, the underwriter of course receives a fee for performing the underwriting, usually on the order of 6 percent of the proceeds. Most of the underwriter's fee is compensation for marketing the issue to buyers and for bearing the risk in holding unsold securities in the after-market. The issuer itself bears almost all of the risk that its price will fall between the time the offering is announced and when the price of the issue is set by the underwriter. And because the number of shares is usually set well ahead of time, while the price is set at the last minute, it is very difficult for the issuer to know how many shares to raise if a specific dollar amount is needed. Therefore, unless it attempts to raise far more shares than it needs (based on the current price), the issuer inevitably faces some risk that insufficient funds are raised.

At first glance, then, the issuing company seems to bear the lion's share of the risk. Moreover, it seems to put itself at the mercy of the underwriter in the actual pricing of the issue. Because the price is not set until the day before the shares hit the market, the underwriter could set the price so low that it bears no risk in selling all of the shares. In such an event, the company could respond by cancelling the issue; but having paid much of the out-of-pocket expenses already, it may find itself in a bind and thus accept the lower price.[1]

Fortunately, this does not appear to happen. The principal reason it does not happen, ethical considerations aside, is the value of maintaining a good reputation. To an underwriter, reputation is everything. Once an underwriter is registered with the SEC for an issue, it can indeed virtually eliminate its risk by setting a price very low. But such an action would be observed by the entire financial community. As a result, other issuing firms would be much less likely to place their trust in an underwriter that so abused its pricing prerogative.

Thus, the actual contracting and monitoring of the price-setting mechanism is a complicated one. The judge of whether the investment banker has unfairly used its contracting advantage is the outside financial community. What is striking about this price-setting arrangement, which implies a risk-sharing arrangement, is that no price-setting formula is set ahead of time. The major risk involved in the offering is that the company's share price will drop before the issue date, which is why the underwriter does not want to commit to a price ahead of time. The two parties could formally set (in writing) the offer price as a function of the actual share price on the issue date. But the very fact that this is not done implies that the common informal practice is more efficient. And, the common practice is that the price is almost always set by the underwriter at a fraction below the market price at the time of issue.

This arrangement would appear to suggest that the company bears most of the risk of the price decline up to the time of the issue. But the underwriter also takes on a considerable amount of price risk; it bears all of the risk that the shares may drop in value immediately after issue. If the price falls after issue, the underwriter will be out the difference between the agreed upon-price and the market price. The total risk to underwriters is in fact great enough that they form syndicates. The syndicate both spreads the risk and increases the marketing channels through which the shares are introduced. Underwriters also almost always hedge themselves in options markets, when possible. But even if its position is perfectly hedged, the underwriter suffers damage to its reputation if the stock in question turns out to be a lemon.[2]

The fact the underwriter continues to bear some risk is critical to the dominance of the common

---

1. Such a contracting scheme is the classic case of expropriation of "quasi-rents" by one of the contractors. No amount of competition per se can avoid this problem. Once the company names its main underwriter to the SEC nothing can keep the underwriter from expropriating from the issuer...except its desire to maintain its reputation as an underwriter. Therefore, expropriating quasi-rents is optimal only if the immediate gain is greater than the expected loss from a damage in its reputation. Since any given issue is usually a small matter for an underwriter, expropriation of quasi-rents does not occur regularly.

2. What statistical evidence we have strongly supports the hypothesis that underwriters bear risk, since underwriter compensation is strongly positively correlated with the variance of the stock price.

Because the price is not set until the day before the shares hit the market, the underwriter could set the price so low that it bears no risk in selling all of the shares.

underwriting over the alternatives. If the underwriter did not accept the risk, the common underwriting would probably be an unsuccessful technique for raising equity.

Why is this risk-bearing function important? The answer comes down to something economists call "asymmetry of information." In plainer language, management is in a position to know more about the prospects of the company than investors. And if management believes the firm's prospects are favorable, and the equity is undervalued, then it has an incentive to raise the firm's debt-to-equity ratio by issuing debt rather than equity. Conversely, if management believes that the future is unfavorable, or less favorable than the view that is reflected in the current stock price, then it best serves current stockholders by selling equity at overvalued prices, before the market comes to share management's less sanguine view of the future.

For this reason, when a company announces its intention to raise equity, investors will have some grounds for assuming that management believes the stock is overvalued—possibly on the basis of information that is not available to the market—and such investors will drop the price at which they are willing to buy.

Thus, when issuing new equity, management is often faced with the task of reassuring investors that the new issue does not portend bad times ahead. Investors will be most likely to believe management when they see somebody else's financial fate hanging on the success of the stock, especially when the other party is reputable and has access to inside information about the issuing firm. That is where the underwriter comes into the picture. If investors see that the underwriter suffers financial loss when the share price falls, they are more likely to believe management; at least they are convinced that the underwriter believes that the share price will not fall. Indeed, this is probably the crucial role that investment bankers play in a common underwriting—certifying the current value of the shares by bearing price risk in the after-market.

The underwriter, then, performs many roles in a common underwriting. The underwriter handles most of the paperwork details of the issue. It handles all aspects of the marketing. It takes on a considerable amount of risk to both its capital and its reputation; and, most important of all, the very fact that it does so certifies to investors the value of the shares. Investment bankers also claim to give other related financial advice. They are even given the ability to grossly underprice the issue at the last moment, but the value of their reputation prevents them from doing so to a great degree. For all these services, the investment banker earns a fairly hefty compensation.

Two more comments about underwriters bear scrutiny. The first relates to underwriter compensation. Many have expressed an inability to comprehend the size of underwriter compensation. The fee charged, so runs the claim, is disproportionate to the risk the underwriter is forced to bear; since they set the price so late in the process, they need bear little risk. This argument ignores the fact that underwriters bear considerable risk to their reputations. Indeed, common underwritings would be less successful if they did not, since investor confidence would be much lower.

The second relates to the structure of the investment banking industry as a whole. Because of the apparent absence of barriers to entry, it would at first appear that the industry would be very competitive with low profits. Although evidence suggests that the industry is indeed competitive, the importance of reputation appears to keep profits from falling. Companies with excellent reputations have a distinct competitive advantage over upstarts. Issuers know that established underwriters have more to lose if their reputation is damaged, and so will tend to rely on those firms. For this reason, the established investment banking firms appear to have a competitive advantage that is not easily disturbed by the entry of new firms.

This brings us at last to the tax considerations in contemplating a common underwriting. Fortunately, the tax aspects of an underwriting are not very complex. The entire fee is taxable income to the underwriter. The costs are subtracted from the basis of the shares received for the issuer, so they are not deductible. Because financial advisory is typically tax deductible, one obvious tax-reducing strategy would be to somehow separate and reclassify part of the underwriting fee as costs of general financial consulting. This way, although the total fees would still be taxable to the underwriter, the issuing company would be able to deduct the financial advisory part of the fee that is typically bundled into the overall charge. Because underwriters perform a thorough examination of the company prior to the offering, such a tax strategy would seem to be justifiable to the tax authorities. However, I do not know of any companies which have attempted this tax strategy to date.

[Even] if its position is perfectly hedged, the underwriter suffers damage to its reputation if the stock in question turns out to be a lemon....The fact the underwriter continues to bear some risk is critical to the dominance of the common underwriting over the alternatives.

The Best Efforts Agreement

A best efforts underwriting is usually considered as very similar to a common underwriting. Structurally, they look alike. Their economics, however, are vastly different. Best efforts agreements are mentioned often in textbooks on finance as a workable equity-raising scheme. Below, it will be shown why they are rarely used.

In a best efforts agreement, the issuing firm hires an investment bank to sell as many shares as it can, getting a commitment fee for each share sold. The investment bank is under no compulsion to sell them; it simply gives its "best effort" to sell what it can, but does not guarantee sales. Best efforts agreements usually have very low fees and, for that reason, many have expressed suprise that the technique is not used more often.

The most commonly offered explanation for the lack of popularity of best efforts agreements is the notion that underwriters have less incentive to work hard to sell them; their fees are lower and the underwriter is at little risk if the shares are not sold. But in a competitive industry like investment banking, sellers for best efforts agreements will be found unless underwriters are at full capacity. The reason investment bankers' fees are lower is that the risk they bear is significantly smaller. This is not to say there is no merit to the argument; clearly, an investment banker will be most concerned with selling shares they are committed to in a firm underwriting. But it is hard to believe that an investment banker would avoid selling best efforts shares, since there are still nice fees to be obtained.

If you look at the four factors we introduced earlier, it becomes clear why best efforts are rare. Their advantage is that they have lower fees. But the risk borne by the issuing company is enormous! How can any company plan investments that require cash when the cash flow is so uncertain?

In the face of this uncertainty, there are only a few cases in which such an offering makes sense. First of all, the issuing company could ensure that sufficient shares would be sold by agreeing to a low enough price, thereby satisfying its cash flow needs. Generally, however, the company would be better off just doing a common underwriting, paying a higher fee, and getting a higher price.

Another case in which best efforts may seem to be a viable financing method occurs when the issuing company is not greatly concerned about the amount of the proceeds. Such indifference implies that its investment program does not strongly depend on the company's cash position. And this indifference will cause investors to ask: Why is this firm raising equity in the first place? If the company has a strong demand for cash to undertake profitable investments, it will not use best efforts. Therefore, a best efforts occurs when a company is raising equity but does not need the cash for investment. There is only one plausible motive for such an action: management thinks the stock is overvalued.

A best efforts agreement, then, is a flag to investors that the stock is overvalued. Making matters worse, no underwriter has put itself in a position of risk if the shares do not sell. Thus, the negative information released by announcement of a best efforts offering is likely to cause a considerable fall in the issuing firm's stock price. I suspect that is principally for this reason that best efforts arrangements are so rarely used, even though the out-of-pocket fees are very low.

Auctions

Auctions can be of two kinds. The first is that whereby the issuing company directly auctions its securities to the public. The second, known as a "competitive bid," is an auction among investment bankers to become the lead underwriter. Both are quite rare outside the electric utility industry, in which utilities are required by law to auction the right to sell issues among investment bankers. Most French companies also are required to auction their securities issues among investment bankers. The direct public auction has some useful features for some debt issues but, for reasons presented below, is rarely used in equity offerings.[3]

A direct public auction will work only for very large, visible companies. The clear advantage of such an auction are the savings on underwriter fees. One disadvantage, however, is that because there is no underwriter, the issuing company bears all of the price risk. Perhaps most important, no third party is certifying for investors the value of the shares by plac-

---

3. The auction between investment bankers is very logical under some equilibria conditions, which apparently are not evident in current domestic markets.

Investors will be most likely to believe management when they see somebody else's financial fate hanging on the success of the stock, especially when the other party is reputable and has access to inside information about the issuing firm.

ing their reputation and financial well-being behind the stock. In this sense, direct public auctions suffer from the same "information" problems that beset best efforts agreements. Unlike a best efforts agreement, in which the investment banker uses its marketing channels to find immediate buyers, in the case of a public auction the issuer simply gives general notice that it is selling the shares; and the buyers must then step forward. To make such direct auctions worthwhile, then, the savings in underwriting fees have to be great enough to offset all these disadvantages.

It may seem that the disadvantages to direct offerings are so great that they would never occur. But the biggest borrower in the world, the United States government, auctions off billions of dollars of debt each week. The reasons are clear: there is no difficulty in finding buyers for treasury bills; the risk in raising sufficient funds is practically non-existent; asymmetric information is not an issue; and thus the government can raise the debt through an auction with very low costs. These same considerations also pertain to the debt issues of many companies. The reason debt is more likely to be issued in this manner is that the information and risk factors are so much less important. Some very large companies may find direct offerings useful for new equity issues, but this group would be very limited. (These same factors, incidentally, that favor a direct auction would also tend to favor a rule 415 "shelf registration" issue.)

Now let's consider the "competitive bid," the auction among underwriters to become the lead underwriter. The distinctive feature of this scheme is that the lowest bidding underwriter must commit to a price in advance, so that the underwriter assumes all the price risk. Since the underwriter has decided to bear such a risk, the bids will all tend to be substantially lower than they would have been otherwise.

But perhaps the important problem with auctions is that investment bankers must make the bid *before* they investigate the company. No investment banker will take on the fixed costs of investigating the company and lining up buyers unless it is reasonably assured of getting the contract. Therefore, the investment banker is bidding blindly. The banker not only takes on all the risk that is shared in a common underwriting, but it must take it on without knowledge. Therefore, the bids for the underwriting will be low indeed if there is perceived risk in the stock. In addition, even though the issue is underwritten, it will not increase investor confidence; it may actually undermine it. Recognizing that the underwriter made the bid without investigating the value of the issue, investors will wonder why the company is forcing the investment banker to make a bid ahead of time, instead of letting them examine the firm's condition. They will suspect the issuer of trying to hide something.

This problem of asymmetric information problem is not nearly as great if the auction is required by law. In this case, investors do not automatically infer that the auction is a means of concealment. One can also argue, although with somewhat less validity today, that the law forcing auctions is not so burdensome to utilities because the volatility of the value of utility stocks is considerably smaller than that of unregulated firms.[4]

Rights Offerings

A rights offering is probably the most complex of all equity-raising techniques; and the confusion is heightened by the fact that there are several kinds of rights issues, each having different characteristics. In a rights offering, the company issues rights to its current stockholders; each right gives them the option of buying a share of stock at a given ("striking") price. Warrants offer a similar option. The difference between rights and warrants is that rights are always issued to current shareholders in an amount proportional to their holdings. The shareholders do not have to pay for the rights; they simply receive them in the mail. The rightholders now have the option of exercising their rights, which allows them to maintain their percentage of ownership, or of selling some or all of the rights. Whether or not the rights are sold by the original shareholders, the rights will be exercised by their eventual owners if and only if the stock price is above the exercise price on the ex-rights day.

---

4. A number of observers have expressed surprise that auctions are not more prevalent, given the possibility of lower flotation costs; they also have the apparent advantage of taking the last-minute pricing prerogative out of the hands of the investment banker. This argument should be discounted under current domestic laws since expropriation of quasi-rents does not appear to be a problem. It could be an issue if a particularly large placement was being underwritten, and the stock price suddenly dropped; the immediate gain to forcing a very low price could then be greater than the loss in reputation. And it is possible that an equilibrium could be reached where quasi-rent expropriation did become a major issue. But even if this were so, it is more likely that firms and underwriters would agree to a formula ahead of time, which means risk sharing, instead of resorting to the drastic (boundary) condition where the underwriter assumes all risk.

A best efforts agreement, then, is a flag to investors that the stock is overvalued. Making matters worse, no underwriter has put itself in a position of risk if the shares do not sell.

Rights issues became a hot topic in the academic world when published data suggested that rights offerings were by far the cheapest way to carry out an equity offering. When the data were examined closely, however, it became apparent that the rights offering were so cheap because their use was largely confined to corporate transfers of funds among parent companies and their own subsidiaries. A good number of the issues, in fact, were done by subsidiaries of AT&T.

Why are subsidiaries likely to use rights offerings? Rights offerings are the ideal way to get equity into a subsidiary. The subsidiary issues rights to the "existing" shareholder(s), which is mostly the parent firm. The parent then "exercises" the rights, putting cash into the subsidiary. There is no question that rights offer the cheapest way for companies to go through the motions of money transfers in consolidated entities.

The question that is more interesting is whether rights provide a useful mechanism for raising equity for corporations in a normal context. But before entering a discussion of rights issues, it is important to distinguish between the two main forms. The rights issue can be standard, whereby the company simply issues the rights to the shareholders. The rights issue can also be underwritten, whereby an underwriter guarantees execution of any and all unexercised rights.

The transaction costs involved in a rights issue are of a very different form than they are for a firm commitment common issue. Both kinds of offerings incur many legal and filing charges. In a firm commitment, the costs include preparing a prospectus and lining up buyers for the new issue. The members of the syndicate attempt to sell the issue to a selective group of their best buyers. In a rights offering, by contrast, the company is required to contact every one of its shareholders. In addition, they must set up a mechanism for the selling of the rights. From these observations, it should be clear that the transactions costs of executing a rights offering depend critically on the number of shareholders. The high transaction costs for companies with many shareholders tends to make rights offerings favored only for companies with a high concentration of ownership; and these, with some exceptions, tend to be smaller companies.

But, there is also a problem with rights offerings for small companies. Small public companies typically do not have long histories as public companies. Small companies go public because they cannot raise enough capital on their own. And if a small public company is raising more equity, it needs even more capital—capital that the concentrated block of owners presumably do not have the means or inclination to contribute themselves. If they did, why even bother with a rights issue? Why not just do a private placement, or better yet, why not just take the company private again?

The upshot of this reasoning is that in most companies with concentrated ownership that need capital and are doing a rights offering, the major stockholders are not expected to exercise their rights. One of the advantages of a rights offering is supposed to be that it allows current owners to maintain their position, but if insiders holding a very large proportion of a company's stock are not expected to contribute to the offering, then outside investors will be skeptical about the insiders' assessment of the value of the firm. Announcements of a rights offerings under these circumstances should result in falling stock prices.

To make matters worse, tax laws strongly discourage rights for the stockholders of those very corporations that are most likely to have cost savings in issuing rights. In a rights offer, provided the offer does not give off any negative signal to the market, the value of a share before the rights offering should equal the value after the rights offering plus the value of the rights. The IRS splits up the basis of the share in a similar way. Therefore, if an investor sells his rights, the IRS considers it a partial sale of equity, and the investor must pay taxes. He also has a lower basis for his remaining shares. For this reason, rights offerings have negative tax consequences for firms that have had large capital gains.

This, then, leaves little fertile ground for rights offerings. Rights, as suggested, make the most sense for public firms that have concentrated shareholders; and these, again as suggested, tend to be smaller companies that went public after discovering a need for more more capital. Small firms that went public tend to be the successful ones—those which have had appreciable gains above the basis of their original investment. As stated above, most of these companies also went public because their owners were unable to contribute more of the capital. So a rights offering is probably a poor choice for the shareholders of these firms; they are forced to sell and pay taxes or contribute capital that they do not have. Thus, it seems clear why rights offerings, aside from the intra-company paper transactions mentioned above, are rare.

Rights offerings are the ideal way to get equity into a subsidiary....[they] offer the cheapest way for companies to go through the motions of money transfers in consolidated entities.

But the story does not end here; there are further complications. Rights have a risk advantage over other equity-raising mechanisms. Recall that a right will be exercised on the expiration date if and only if the exercise price is above the stock price. Thus, either all or none of the rights are likely to be exercised. Because a company can control the number of rights and the striking price of the rights, it can control the amount of cash it receives from the offering *provided* the share price is above the striking price at expiration. Therefore, in a rights offering, the company either gets *exactly* what it wanted, or it gets nothing. As it stands, this may seem like a risky ploy, since the company may indeed get nothing. But companies do have two options to mitigate this risk.

One method is to keep the striking price at a very low level, reducing the probability of the stock price falling below the exercise price. Indeed, many observers have suggested that a rights offerings with a low exercise price is the best way to raise equity largely for this reason.

The second method is to have the issue underwritten, so that the underwriter agrees to exercise any unexercised shares. This scheme, however, places a great risk on underwriters. In practice, the underwriter usually gets paid a fee for each unexercised right it assumes, so that the company effectively shares some of this risk even in an underwritten rights offering.

The biggest problem with rights, however, as we have already suggested, is the negative information that is likely to be released by the mere announcement of a rights offering. First, let's consider a standard (non-underwritten) rights agreement. In such an offering, nobody certifies the value of the stock, because nobody is hurt if the company's stock price falls. In most standard rights issues, the striking price is kept comfortably below the current share price, so that the prospects for the offering are not affected by poor performance. If the inside shareholders sell their rights, investors will be even more convinced of the poor opportunities that the company faces. An investor will see the company as a closely held organization (or presumably it would not bother with rights) that is using a low-risk technique to raise new equity. Furthermore, the investor reasons, this closely held company's key investors cannot contribute more capital; they will probably be "forced" to sell their rights, and even suffer tax consequences.

The inference an investor is likely to make is that these major shareholders are trying to sell their interest in a "sneaky" way. Note that it is easier to sell a part of the total ownership interest when the striking price is well below the current share price, which it must be to ensure the rights will be exercised. This very strong negative information can be avoided if the market sees that the rights are exercised, or if concentration is not so great, but these cases will probably be the exception rather than the rule.

Underwritten rights offerings have the opposite effect. The underwriter agrees to cover the difference between the market price and the striking price. Unlike a common underwriting, the underwriter in a rights issue does agree to a price ahead of time. Therefore, the position the underwriter has is even riskier than that in a common underwriting. And the higher the striking price relative to the current price, the greater the underwriter's risk. So an underwritten rights offer with a high striking price is an excellent technique for raising equity while maintaining investor confidence. But, of course, the underwriter must be paid and compensated for its risk.

An underwritten rights offer, then, is likely to be a good alternative to a common underwriting in cases where the company wants a guaranteed level of new funds and is very confident about its prospects. The major difference between the techniques is, once again, the risk-sharing arrangement. In a common underwriting, the underwriter bears little of the price risk before the issue hits the market; in an underwritten rights issue, the underwriter bears all of the risk.

Rule 415: "Shelf" Registration

We began this article by examining the major equity-raising technique, the common underwriting, which has been the dominant form of equity offerings. We will end with the upstart, the shelf registration technique, which is the only serious threat to the firm commitment. It is also the simplest technique.

A 415 offering allows certain companies meeting a minimum size and traded life requirement to register shares to be sold with the SEC. These shares can then be sold any time within the next three years. They are held "on the shelf" and then sold at any time the company deems appropriate.

The 415 offering therefore has two appealing features relative to the common underwriting. First of all, filing fees are relatively small. No prospectus is needed. Companies can also play underwriters off against one another; they can give small amounts to

In most companies with concentrated ownership that need capital and are doing a rights offering, the major stockholders are not expected to exercise their rights.

different investment bankers at different times to determine who does the best job. The other major advantage has to do with the risk issue. Unlike a common underwriting, in which the company is usually forced to raise more funds than it needs to ensure that sufficient funds are available, in a shelf registration the company can register many shares and then sell as many as they need at any given time. Once the right to use a 415 is granted by the SEC, the registered shares can then be sold immediately. There is therefore practically no risk that the shares will drop between announcement and issue. Unwanted shares are merely "left on the shelf."

The information effects are more difficult to assess. Clearly, there will be less confidence in a "shelf" registration than in a common underwriting, because nobody has researched the company and taken a risky position in the shares. But the effects may not be as strong as with other non-certified offers if the cash is raised in small amounts.

So shelf registration has an advantage over a firm underwriting in the form of lower issue costs and greater flexibility in "timing" the issue and tailoring the amount of funds raised; it has a relative disadvantage in terms of the potential information effect. Thus, large, well-known companies with frequent security issues are likely to find shelf registration a very cost-effective alternative to the common underwriting. Smaller, obscure companies, by contrast, will probably be better off using common underwritings.

ARE BANK LOANS DIFFERENT?: SOME EVIDENCE FROM THE STOCK MARKET

by Christopher James and Peggy Wier, University of Oregon

raditionally, economists have focused on the role of commercial banks in the payment system. Banks are unique, the argument goes, because unlike other financial institutions, they provide transaction services by taking demand deposits. This involvement in the money supply process has been the basis for regulations, such as reserve requirements, designed to facilitate monetary control and for regulations intended to preserve the soundness of banks and the payment system.

But banks, of course, do more than gather deposits. And they are more than passive investors—as the older research tends to suggest—which simply channel their deposits into a pool of assets earning slightly higher rates of return than those paid out to depositors. In fact, commercial banks constitute a major source of capital for U.S. public corporations. Indeed, as shown in Table 1, in any given year over the ten-year period from 1977 to 1986, at least a third—and in several years more than half—of the new debt raised by all American industrial corporations was provided by financial institutions, chiefly banks.

In somewhat belated recognition of this role, the attention of academic economists has recently shifted away from the payment system and toward the distinctive contribution by banks and other financial institutions to the process of providing capi-

SECURITIES SALES, AFTER ALL, ARE VOLUNTARY MANAGEMENT
DECISIONS. AND PROVIDED THE PROCEEDS ARE USED TO FINANCE
PROFITABLE NEW INVESTMENT OPPORTUNITIES, THE CHANGE IN THE
MARKET VALUE OF THE FIRM SHOULD BE POSITIVE, IF ANYTHING, IN
RESPONSE TO SUCH ANNOUNCEMENTS.

TABLE 1
LOANS FROM FINANCIAL INSTITUTIONS TO
NON-FINANCIAL CORPORATIONS AS A
PERCENTAGE OF NEW DEBT FINANCING,
1977 THROUGH 1986

Year	Percentage
1977	50.73
1978	**52.64**
1979	54.60
1980	**37.32**
1981	49.51
1982	**52.24**
1983	43.68
1984	**46.81**
1985	34.44
1986	**38.38**
Average	46.02

Source: Federal Reserve Statistical Release Z.7, various years.

tal for corporate investment. For example, in 1985 the University of Chicago's Eugene Fama published a paper in the *Journal of Monetary Economics* entitled "What's Different About Banks?" In that paper Professor Fama argued that banks have a comparative advantage in gathering information about and in monitoring corporate borrowers.[1] In another paper published two years later, Christopher James (one of the present authors) described an intriguing empirical "regularity" uncovered by his work: namely, announcements by public firms of new bank lending agreements elicit, on average (and in a very strong majority of cases) a significantly positive reaction from the stock market.[2] This finding offers a pointed contrast to the neutral to negative responses that have recently been found to accompany almost all other kinds of securities offerings: private placements of debt, straight public debt, preferred stock, convertible debt, convertible preferred, and common stock.[3]

This pronounced difference between the mar-

ket reaction to announcements of bank loans and public securities raises the question of whether there is indeed anything "different" about bank loans. In this paper we present the findings of recent studies in more detail and explore the possibility that banks have some unique advantages in their role as providers of capital.

THE MARKET REACTION TO SECURITIES OFFERINGS

Table 2 provides a summary of recent academic research on the market's reaction to announcements of public securities offerings. The major findings of this research are as follows: (1) the market response to companies issuing common stock is significantly negative (on the order of 3 percent, on average); (2) the response to convertible offerings, both debt and preferred, is also significantly negative (although less so than in the case of common); and (3) the response to straight debt and preferred offerings, although slightly negative on average, is not significantly different from zero.[4]

These results came as something of a surprise, at least to the academic finance profession. Securities sales, after all, are voluntary management decisions. And provided the proceeds are used to finance profitable new investment opportunities, the change in the market value of the firm should be positive, if anything, in response to such announcements. Thus, we were confronted with a puzzle in need of an explanation.

The explanation now most widely accepted, at least by financial economists, originates in a paper by Stewart Myers and Nicholas Majluf entitled, "Corporate Financing and Investment Decisions When Firms Have Information That Outsiders Do Not Have."[5] The paper begins by observing that new securities offerings are not the primary method which firms use to finance new investment projects. Most corporate capital requirements are instead financed with internally generated funds—that is, retained earnings. And this has been especially true of the

1. Eugene Fama, "What's Different About Banks?," *Journal Of Monetary Economics* 15, 1985.

2. Christopher James, "Some Evidence on the Uniqueness of Bank Loans," *Journal of Financial Economics* 19 (1987).

3. The lone exception is "equity carve-outs," or partial public offerings by the subsidiaries of U.S. public companies. As documented by Katherine Schipper and Abbie Smith ("A Comparison of Equity Carve-Outs and Seasoned Equity Offerings: Share Price Effects and Corporate Restructurings," *Journal of Financial Economics* 15 (1986), announcements of these offerings are accompanied by a

roughly 3 percent increase in the value of the parent corporation's stock price.

4. For an excellent review of this literature see Clifford Smith "Investment Banking and the Capital Acquisition Process," *Journal of Financial Economics* 15 1986. For a less technical version of the same paper, see Clifford Smith, "Raising Capital: Theory and Evidence," *Midland Corporate Finance Journal* Spring 1986.

5. See Stewart Myers and Nicolas Majulf "Corporate Financing and Investment Decisions When Firms have Information that Outsiders Do Not Have" *Journal of Financial Economics* 13, 1985. See also Clifford Smith (1986), cited in note 4.

TABLE 2
STOCK PRICE RESPONSE TO ANNOUNCEMENTS OF
PUBLIC SECURITIES OFFERING[a]
(SAMPLE SIZE IS IN PARENTHESES)

Type of Security Offering	Two Day Abnormal Returns
Common Stock	−3.14%
	(155)
Preferred Stock	−.19%
	(28)
Convertible Preferred Stock	−1.44%*
	(53)
Straight Bonds	−.26%
	(248)
Convertible Bonds	−2.07%*
	(73)

a. The information contained in this table is from Clifford Smith's article entitled, "Raising Capital: Theory and Evidence," *Midland Corporate Finance Journal*, Spring 1986. The returns reported are for industrial corporations. The studies reporting these results are cited in Smith, 1986.
* Significantly different from zero.

1980s. Since 1980, for example, the proportion of capital raised internally has exceeded 60 percent. During the same period net new equity has been negative; that is, in the aggregate, firms have repurchased more equity than they have issued. Public and private borrowing account for the rest of the capital raised.[6]

This set of financing preferences—starting with internal funds, moving next to debt, and then finally to the riskiest security, common stock—is now known as the financial "pecking order." To account for this pattern, Myers and Majluf point to the well-known (and now well-documented) observation that a corporation's managers often have better information about the firm's prospects, and hence about its actual current value, than do outside investors. Thus, while a new security offering might mean that the firm has profitable new investment opportunities, it also might suggest that management thinks that the firm's earnings will be lower than previously expected; that is, management's expectation of a shortfall in cash profits may be the real reason for the new offering.

Potential investors cannot confidently distinguish between these two possible signals from management. Investors do know, however, that if management's aim is to maximize the wealth of their current stockholders, it will try to issue new securities when it believes the firm is *overvalued* relative to its prospects. Put a little differently, managers are more likely to offer securities when they expect a fall in firm profits after the offering (and thus think the firm is "overvalued") than when they anticipate a subsequent rise in profits (and think the firm is "undervalued").

For this reason, a new issue is likely to signal management's belief that the firms' outstanding securities are currently overvalued. Recognizing management's incentives to issue overvalued securities, the market systematically discounts the value of firms announcing new offerings. And this discount is largest in the cases of common stock and convertible offerings because the value of these securities is most sensitive to changes in the expected profitability of the firm.

Given this rational market "bias" against new offerings (which in turn explains management's preference for internal funds over, especially, new equity issues), some companies with genuinely profitable investment opportunities may have a financing problem. If it is costly for management to convey information about these opportunities in a detailed and reliable fashion (since investors know that all firms have an incentive to exaggerate the promise of new projects), such firms are likely to find themselves undervalued in the market (again, at least relative to insiders' expectations). Unless investors can be convinced of the profitability of these opportunities, firms that possess them are in the uncomfortable position of penalizing their existing stockholders by selling underpriced securities or seeking other, private sources of funds. As noted earlier, the most commonly used source is internally generated cash. But what of the firm whose retained earnings are insufficient to fund its projects?

THE ROLE OF BANKS AND OTHER FINANCIAL INSTITUTIONS

In the paper cited earlier, "What's Different About Banks?," Eugene Fama makes the distinction between "inside" and "outside" debt. Inside debt is defined as a loan for which the lender has access to information about the borrower that is not other-

---

6. These data are reported by Richard Brealey and Stewart Myers in *Principles of Corporate Finance*, 3rd ed. (McGraw-Hill, 1988), pp. 312-313.

wise publicly available. For example, the lender may participate in the firm's decision-making as a member of executive committees or as a member of the board of directors. Outside debt, by contrast, is a publicly-traded claim, for which the debtholder relies on publicly available information generated by bond rating agencies, independent audits, or analyst reports. Bank loans and privately placed loans are inside debt, and publicly-traded bonds and commercial paper are examples of outside debt.

Inside debt, moreover, appears to be a major source of financing for smaller public corporations as well as privately held firms. As presented in Table 1 earlier, bank loans represented some 46 percent of all debt financing by U.S. (non-financial) corporations between 1977 and 1986. Private placements of bonds, which are essentially loan sales to a limited number of investors (typically insurance companies and pension funds), accounted for about 30 percent of all bond issues over the same period.

There are several possible advantages to using inside debt. First, inside debt may provide a possible solution to the problem of "information asymmetry" that attends all public securities offerings. For example, to the extent banks have better information about, and thus greater confidence in, a given firm's future than outsiders, they would price their loans to reflect this information advantage. For firms with strong relationships with local bankers, but no chance of gaining an investment grade bond rating (perhaps for reasons of size alone), the cost of a bank loan or private placement can be substantially lower than the cost of borrowing through a public securities offering.

Second, inside debtholders are in a better position to monitor the firm after the debt is issued. Private placements and bank loans typically contain detailed restrictive covenants, often custom-tailored to the specific problems and opportunities of the borrower. Renegotiating the credit in response to unexpected developments is much easier when there is only one or several lenders than when there are several hundred or even thousands of anonymous investors. Also, in the case of bank loans, firms may be able to lower their debt costs by borrowing from banks with which they maintain a deposit relationships, because these banks already have information useful for evaluating and monitoring credit quality.

Third, there may be an advantage to maintaining confidentiality about the firm's investment op-

portunities. Companies may not wish to reveal to the public the information that lenders require. For example, suppose a firm is raising capital for an investment that involves a new marketing strategy, the value of which would be reduced if competitors learn of it prior to its introduction. Borrowing from insiders permits the firm to keep its strategy secret.

Finally, the use of inside debt allows borrowers to avoid the costly and time-consuming process of registering issues with the Securities and Exchange Commission. It should be noted, however, that there are also costs to negotiating inside debt, and while the fixed costs of public issues are relatively large, variable costs are small. For this reason, inside debt is more likely to be used for smaller borrowings—that is, when the size of the issues are not large enough to benefit from the considerable economies of scale in floating new public issues.

A testable implication of the hypothesis that bank loans and other types of private debt avoid the negative signal associated with public offerings is that announcements of such inside debt transactions will have a positive effect on the stock prices of the borrowing firms. The loan approval process itself may convey positive information to market participants about the financial strength of the firm, especially in the case of smaller firms without access to public capital markets. Loan renewals and new extensions may provide a credible "seal of approval" to equity investors and other claimants of the firm, who therefore need not undertake similar costly evaluations of the firm's financial condition.

Bank Loans versus Private Placements

Thus far we have looked at some possible advantages of inside over outside debt. But is there any reason to believe that bank loans differ in important ways from "inside" debt provided by other financial institutions? One possibility is the difference in the quality and timeliness of information that results from an ongoing deposit and customer relationship. The history of a borrower as a depositor (and, more generally, as a customer for a variety of the bank's services) may provide banks with a significant cost advantage in evaluating and monitoring the risks of loans. This special information, although not especially privileged in the case of Fortune 500 companies, is likely to be particularly valuable in making short-term loans to smaller firms without established credit histories.

If the access to a deposit history and a continuous customer relationship does indeed provide banks with a comparative advantage over other inside lenders, one would expect banks to dominate the market for short-term lending. Moreover, one would expect the stock market reaction to announcements of bank loans to be more favorable than price reactions to announcements of private placements of debt. In announcing a loan agreement, a company declares its willingness to subject itself to periodic evaluations by a reputable bank; and this willingness is likely to provide a positive signal to the market about management's view of the firm's prospects.

Two observations tend to support the argument that a deposit history gives banks a comparative advantage. First, banks often require that borrowers maintain compensating balance requirements (i.e. have a deposit account at the lending institution), which suggests that both borrowers and lenders view the deposit account as an integral part of the lending relationship. Second, commercial banks are the dominant suppliers of short-term debt, particularly to smaller corporate borrowers. At the end of 1986, commercial banks held $541 billion in commercial and industrial loans, most of which had a maturity of less than one year. The next largest source of short-term financing is the commercial paper market with $79 billion in paper issued by industrial firms outstanding. The commercial paper market is limited, however, to relatively large well-known borrowers.

THE MARKET REACTION TO BORROWING ANNOUNCEMENTS

As mentioned at the beginning, a recently published study by one of the present authors examines the stock price reactions to announcements of new bank loans, private placements of debt, and straight public debt offerings.[7] The test sample consists, more specifically, of all public straight debt offerings, private placements of debt with nonbanking institutions (primarily insurance companies), and new commercial loans announced (in the *Wall Street Journal*) by 300 randomly selected non-financial companies over the period 1973-1983. All 300 firms are traded either on the New York or American Stock Exchanges.

The bank loan agreements in the sample consist of new credit agreements as well as the expansion of existing agreements. They also include both term loans and extensions of lines of credit (that is, commitments to lend). The most common agreement, however, involves a line of credit whereby the borrowing can be converted, at the firm's option, into a term loan. The private placements consist of debt sold for cash to a restricted number of institutional investors. Approximately 70 percent of the agreements involved an insurance company as the principal lender.

For the random sample of 300 companies, the study produced 207 financing announcements, which can be broken down as follows: 80 bank loan agreements, 37 private debt placements, and 90 public straight debt offerings. As shown in Table 3, the amount of capital raised by public debt offerings is considerably larger than private borrowing agreements. And, not surprisingly, the firms using private placements and bank loans are significantly smaller than companies issuing public straight debt. In fact, the average size of both the private placement and bank loan sample is about 25 percent of the average size in the straight debt sample. These findings merely confirm the widely-held view that private placements and bank loans typically involve small- and medium-size firms.

As also presented in Table 3, bank loans have considerably shorter maturities than either privately placed debt or straight debt. Indeed, the longest term bank loan is twelve years, which is less than the median maturity of either privately placed or public debt.

The Results

For each of 207 financing announcements, the percentage change in the firm's stock price was calculated over the two days surrounding the announcement date. The price changes were then adjusted for the firm's risk and for general market movements in order to provide an estimate of the return attributable to the financing announcement.

As summarized in Table 4, the market responded to 80 announcements of bank loan arrangements by raising the stock prices of the borrowing companies by 2 percent on average; positive responses

---

7. See Christopher James, "Some Evidence on the Uniqueness of Bank Loans," cited before in note 2.

TABLE 3
DESCRIPTIVE STATISTICS
FOR COMMERCIAL BANK
LOANS, PRIVATELY
PLACED DEBT, AND
PUBLICLY PLACED
STRAIGHT DEBT FOR A
RANDOM SAMPLE OF 300
NYSE- AND AMEX-TRADED
NON-FINANCIAL FIRMS
(1974-1983).[a]

	Type of borrowing					
	Commercial bank loans (sample size = 80)		Privately placed debt (sample size = 37)		Public straight debt (sample size = 90)	
Descriptive measure	Mean (Range)	Median	Mean (Range)	Median	Mean (Range)	Median
Debt amount (millions of dollars)	72.0 (4-800)	35.0	32.3 (5-120)	25.0	106.2 (10-10,000)	75.0
Firm size (millions of dollars)[b]	675 (28.6-10,311)	212	630 (20.2-6,365)	147	2,506 (47-59,540)	1,310
Debt amount/market value of common stock	0.72 (0.04-2.6)	0.46	0.52 (0.04-2.6)	0.25	0.26 (0.02-1.5)	0.15
Maturity of debt (years)[c]	5.6 (0.6-12)	6.0	15.34 (3-25)	15.0	17.96 (1-40)	20.0
Number of firms	52		34		43	
Number of firms with publicly traded debt outstanding[d]	25		16		30	

a. Statistics given in the first row are the mean followed by the median. The range is provided in the second row.
b. Firm size is for December 31 of the year immediately preceding the security offering or borrowing. Firm size equals the book value of all liabilities and preferred stock plus the market value of common stock oustanding. The market value of common stock is the product of the number of shares oustanding and the closing price per share at year-end preceding the announcement. Closing prices are from the *Security Owners Stock Guide*. The book value of liabilities and the number of shares outstanding are from *Moody's* manuals.
c. Maturity of the loan or debt offering is from the *Wall Street Journal* article. No information on maturity was provided for twenty-four bank loans, two private placements, and nine straight debt offerings. For bank loans that are convertible to term loans, the maturity of the term loan is used.
d. Firms are classified as having publicly traded if the *Moody's* manual report the firm had rated debt outstanding at year-end preceding the financing announcements.

were recorded in 66 percent of the announcements. Moreover, the market responded more strongly to the nine cases in which no actual borrowing was announced (3.7%) than to the 71 cases in which borrowing was announced (1.7%).

By contrast, the market response to the 37 private placements averaged −0.9 percent (significantly different from zero at the 10% level), with 56 percent of the announcements eliciting a negative response. Consistent with the findings of other studies reported in Table 2, the average market reaction to the 90 announcements of public straight debt offerings was −0.1 percent and thus indistinguishable from zero; 56 percent of these issues were also associated with a negative reaction.

If the positive price response to bank loan announcements reflected some benefit associated with borrowing through a financial intermediary, we

TABLE 4
STOCK PRICE RESPONSE TO ANNOUNCEMENTS OF CORPORATE BORROWING[a]
(SAMPLE SIZE IS IN PARENTHESES)

Type of Borrowing Arrangement	Two Day Abnormal Returns
Bank Loan Agreement	1.93%* (80)
Private Placement of Debt	−91% (37)
Public Straight Debt	−11% (90)

a. The information contained in this table is from Christopher Jame's article entitled "Some Evidence on the Uniqueness of Bank Loans," *Journal of Financial Economics*, 19, 1987.
*Significantly different from zero.

THE FACT THAT THE PRICE REACTION TO THE ANNOUNCEMENTS OF PRIVATE PLACEMENTS IS NEGATIVE SUGGESTS THAT COMMERCIAL BANKS MAY INDEED HAVE A LENDING ADVANTAGE OVER INSURANCE COMPANIES AND PENSION FUNDS, AND THAT BANK LOANS MAY WELL BE A SPECIAL FORM OF "INSIDE" DEBT.

TABLE 5
PERCENTAGE STOCK PRICE REACTION TO CORPORATE BORROWING, GROUPED BY THE STATED PURPOSE OF THE BORROWING[a] (SAMPLE SIZE IS IN PARENTHESES)

| | | Type of Borrowing | | | | | |
| | | Bank Loans | | Private Placements | | Public Straight Debt | |
Purpose		Avg. % Ret.	Avg. % Mat.	Avg. % Ret.	Avg. Mat.	Avg. % Ret.	Avg. Mat.
Repay Debt		1.14 (17)	6.5	.51 (5)	14.2	-.35 (32)	17.4
Capital Expenditures		1.20* (24)	5.9	.23 (5)	16.6	.55 (34)	18.9
General Purposes		4.67* (8)	4.6	.26 (9)	17.1	.07 (9)	17.1
Repay Bank Loans		3.10 (11)	5.8	-2.07* (18)	14.4	-1.63* (12)	18.4
No Purpose Given		1.74 (20)	4.7	na	na	.69 (3)	14.0

a. The information contained in this table is from Christopher James' article entitled, "Some Evidence on the Uniqueness of Bank Loans," *Journal of Financial Economics, 19, 1987.*
* Significantly different from zero.

would expect to see a similar price reaction for the announcement of private placements. But the fact that the price reaction to the announcements of private placements is negative suggests that commercial banks may indeed have a lending advantage over insurance companies and pension funds, and that bank loans may well be a special form of "inside" debt.

INTERPRETING THE STOCK PRICE REACTION

This pronounced difference in price reactions to bank loans and private placements may also arise, however, from diffences in important aspects of the borrowing arrangement—such as maturity of the issue, purpose of the borrowing, or the risk of the borrower—that may have nothing to do with the identity of the lender. To examine this possibility, the study also tested whether the market reaction varied systematically with the stated purpose of the borrowing, the maturity of the offering, the default risk of the borrower, and the size of the borrower.

With regard to the stated purpose of the borrowing, we classified all 207 financing announcements (based on Wall Street Journal articles) into five categories: (1) debt refinancing, (2) capital ex-

penditures, (3) "general corporate" purposes, (4) repayment of bank loans, and (5) no purpose given. As presented in Table 5, the average response to bank loan announcements was positive for all of the purpose categories. By contrast, the average reaction to both private placements and public debt offerings was not significantly different from zero for all categories except one. Somewhat surprisingly, in the 18 cases of private placements and 12 cases of public debt where the funds were to be used expressly to repay bank loans, the average market responses were −2.1 percent and −1.6 percent respectively. Given this adverse reaction, why do managements choose to replace bank debt with private placements and public debt?

The most obvious explanation for the use of private placements and straight debt to repay bank loans is that management wants to lengthen the maturity of its debt. As shown in Table 3, the average maturity of the 80 bank loans in the sample was 6 years, as compared to 15 years for the 37 private placements and 20 years for the 80 public debt offerings. But why, then, would longer maturities have a more negative effect on the market reaction?

A company's choice of maturity may send a signal to the market about management's view of the firm's earnings prospects. When a company seeks financing, whether it involves the renewal of a loan or the issuance of new securities, the process of raising capital triggers a review of the borrowing company's current condition (and presumably its prospects) by reputable financial intermediaries (whether an investment bank, insurance company, or commercial bank). Corporate managements, by virtue of their their willingness to submit themselves to the more frequent, periodic reviews required by loan arrangements, effectively signal their confidence in the firm's future. That is, when management expects the firm's credit condition to improve tomorrow (and feels that the firm is undervalued today), then it has an incentive use shorter maturities today and to refinance after the improvement takes place. By contrast, the management of a company that expects its credit position to deteriorate (and whose equity may thus be overvalued) is more likely to attempt to extend the maturity of its debt.[8]

This raises a different, but nonetheless interesting issue: Why do banks specialize to such a degree in shorter maturities?[9] If a continuing relation between a bank and its customer results in lower costs of refinancing, commercial banks should also have a comparative advantage in making long-term loans to their existing customers. In particular, while a change in a firm's earnings prospects may result in a shift in its maturity preference, it is not clear why this action should result in a change in the intermediary used (for example, from banks to insurance companies). We have no good answers to this puzzle. Perhaps banks are reluctant to make long-term loans because of regulatory pressures, or perhaps they want to avoid a mismatch with liabilities that are principally short-term.

A second factor that may explain the difference in the stock price reactions to the various borrowing arrangements are differences in the risk of the debt issued. The financing problem caused by the potential for inside information is expected to be most acute for smaller, riskier firms.[10] For, in cases where the perceived default risk of the new issue is appreciably higher, the price of the debt is expected to be more sensitive to changes in the firm's expected cash flows.

To examine the possible effect of default risk on the market reaction, the study used bond ratings as a proxy for risk. As shown in the top half of Table 6, companies issuing straight debt are far more likely to have rated debt outstanding—no surprise here—than the companies using bank loans and private placements. More than half of the firms announcing bank loans and private placements did not have a bond rating. Thus, to the extent we can rely on the rating agencies, firms announcing bank loans and private placements have considerably higher default risk.

In the lower half of Table 6, we present results showing that for each type of borrowing agreement, the market response is more positive the higher the debt rating. This result both confirms and contradicts the arguments we have made in this paper. On the one hand the fact that the riskiest private placements and public debt offerings elicit significant negative responses supports the "information asymmetry" hypothesis presented earlier. On the other hand, the fact that the largest positive market response attends announcements of bank loans by the highest-rated companies (and thus presumably those firms least in need of a bank's implicit "seal of approval") remains something of a puzzle.

In considering this puzzle, though, it is important to keep in mind two things. First, the sample of bank loans rated A or better contains only nine companies, and is thus hardly sufficient to provide a basis for generalization. Second, unlike the cases of private placements and public debt offerings, where the market reaction becomes markedly more negative with increases in default risk, the positive reaction to bank loans remains consistently and significantly positive over all risk categories.

Viewed in this light, the results seem to suggest that the use of bank financing is an effective means for management to overcome the "information problem"—one that is especially troublesome for small companies trying to raise capital for new investment.

SUMMARY

One explanation for the neutral to negative reaction associated with the announcement of public securities offerings is the potential for management

---

8. See Mark Flannery, "Asymmetric Information and the Risky Debt Maturity Choice," *Journal of Finance* 41 1986.
9. The Federal Reserve Board's Survey of the Terms of Bank Lending confirms this specialization by banks in short-term lending. The May 1987 survey reports that only 13 percent of commercial loans have a maturity of more than one year;

and these loans had an average maturity of four years.
10. It is well-known, for example, that smaller companies tend to rely on bank loans and private placements; and, as shown in Table 3, the median market value of the bank loan sample was $212 million, compared to $147 million for the private placement firms and $1.31 billion for companies issuing public debt.

TABLE 6
STOCK PRICE REACTION TO CORPORATE BORROWING GROUPED BY THE RATING OF OUTSTANDING DEBT[a]

PANEL A: DEBT RATING*

Type of event	Proportion of firms rated AA[b] or better	Proportion of firms rated A	Proportion of firms rated BAA or below	Proportion of firms with rated debt
Bank loan agreements	0.12 (5)	0.10 (4)	0.78 (25)	0.48 (34)
Private placements	0.12 (2)	0.20 (3)	0.68 (11)	0.47 (16)
Public straight debt offerings	0.31 (20)	0.41 (27)	0.28 (18)	0.69 (65)

PANEL B: AVERAGE TWO-DAY PREDICTION ERRORS BY DEBT RATING[c]

	Rated A or better	Rated BAA or below	Not rated
Bank loan agreements	3.89% (2.82)	1.77% (1.92)	1.76% (2.18)
Private placements	1.18% (1.68)	0.30% (0.21)	-2.03% (-2.90)
Public straight debt offerings	0.40% (1.72)	-0.32% (-1.42)	-1.08% (-1.45)

a. Rating refers to the bond rating of the most recently issued debt prior to announcement. Ratings were obtained from *Moody's* manuals.
b. Sample size is in parentheses.
c. Z-value in parentheses: the null hypothesis is that the average standardized prediction error equals zero. $Z = N(\overline{ASPE}^t)$, where $\overline{ASPE}$ is the average standardized prediction error and N is the number of firms in the sample.

to exploit inside information by issuing securities when they believe that the firm is overvalued. Investors recognize this incentive and interpret announcements of public offerings accordingly.

One way for managers to acquire new financing without sending this message to the market is to issue "inside debt." By arranging a bank loan or, alternatively, a private placement, management may be able to mitigate the problem of "information asymmetry" that attends all financing by substituting commercial bankers or a small group of institutional investors for a large, diffuse body of investors.

In this article, we present evidence from the stock market that bank loans are the most effective form of inside debt. We also suggest that banks have an advantage over other inside lenders in evaluating and in monitoring the borrowing firm—in large part because of an ongoing deposit and customer relationship. The evidence suggests that, in some respects, bank loans are indeed unique.

THE GROWING ROLE OF JUNK BONDS IN CORPORATE FINANCE

Kevin J. Perry, Baring America Asset Management Company and Robert A. Taggart, Jr., Boston University

T he growing volume of newly-issued "junk" bonds has been among the most controversial of recent developments in corporate finance. Preferring to call them "high yield" bonds, their promoters extol them as an essential cog in the revitalization of American industry.[1] Their critics, by contrast, denounce them as "securities swill" and have called for restrictions on investment in junk bonds by financial institutions and on the the issuance of junk bonds in hostile takeover attempts.[2]

What are junk bonds, and why have they aroused such heated and conflicting emotions? What are the capital market conditions that have fueled the growth in junk bonds? What factors should a corporate treasurer consider in deciding whether to issue junk bonds? The present article seeks to shed light on these questions.

---

1. Because of its more widespread popular usage, the term "junk bonds" is used throughout this article.

2. See Felix G. Rohatyn, "Junk Bonds and Other Securities Swill," *The Wall Street Journal*, April 18, 1985.

THE TOTAL AMOUNT OF JUNK BONDS OUTSTANDING HAS BEEN
ESTIMATED AT ABOUT $125 BILLION BY THE END OF 1986, AND AT
ABOUT $137 BILLION BY THE MIDDLE OF 1987. THIS REPRESENTS MORE
THAN 20 PERCENT OF THE ENTIRE CORPORATE BOND MARKET.

TABLE 1
NEW ISSUES OF
JUNK BONDS
($ BILLIONS)

Year	(1) Newly-Issued Public Straight Junk Bonds[1]	(2) Exchange Offers and Private Issues Going Public[2]	(3) Total Junk Bond Issuance n(1) + (2)m	(4) Total Public Bond Issues by U.S. Corporations[2]	(5) (1) as % of (4)	(6) (3) as % of (4)
1987	28.9	n.a.	n.a.	219.1	13.2	n.a.
1986	34.3	11.3	45.6	232.5	14.8	19.6
1985	15.4	4.4	19.8	119.6	12.9	16.6
1984	14.8	0.9	15.8	73.6	20.1	21.5
1983	8.0	0.5	8.5	47.6	16.8	17.9
1982	2.7	0.5	3.2	44.3	6.1	7.2
1981	1.4	0.3	1.7	38.1	3.7	4.5
1980	1.4	0.7	2.1	41.6	3.4	5.0
1979	1.4	0.3	1.7	25.8	5.4	6.6
1978	1.5	0.7	2.1	19.8	7.6	10.6
1977	0.6	0.5	1.1	24.1	2.5	4.6

1. From Drexel, Burnham Lambert (1987). 1987 figure from *Investment Dealer's Digest*.
2. From *Federal Reserve Bulletin*. 1987 figure from *Investment Dealer's Digest*.

RECENT GROWTH OF THE JUNK BOND MARKET

Junk bonds are those rated below Ba by Moody's or below BBB— by Standard and Poor's. That is, they are bonds with below investment grade ratings. Unrated corporate bonds are usually included in the junk bond category as well.

Under their broadest definition, junk bonds include private placements and public issues, convertible and straight debt, low-rated municipal bonds and even low-rated preferred stock. For the most part, however, this article focuses on the largest segment of the market: public, straight debt issued by U.S. corporations.

Junk bonds have existed ever since the first bond ratings were published by John Moody in 1909. In fact, junk bonds were a significant source of corporate funds throughout the pre-war period, accounting for 17 percent of total rated, publicly issued straight corporate debt during the years 1909-43. Downgradings during the Depression swelled the supply of junk bonds so that they grew from 13 percent of total corporate debt outstanding in 1928 to 42 percent in 1940.[3]

Junk bonds were less widely used as a source of corporate funds in the early postwar years. Between 1944 and 1965, for example, they accounted for only 6.5 percent of total corporate bond issues,[4] and from the mid-sixties to the mid-seventies they were used even less frequently. By 1977, junk bonds accounted for only 3.7 percent of total corporate bonds outstanding and most of these were "fallen angels" or bonds initially issued with investment grade ratings and subsequently downgraded.[5]

In 1977, however, the market began to change, as newly-issued junk bonds started to appear in larger volume. Although this has been widely heralded as the birth of the new-issue junk bond market, it is perhaps more accurately viewed as a resurgence of the flourishing market of the prewar years. In either case, the growth of new issues, as documented in Table 1, has been impressive, particularly since 1983.[6]

Between cumulative new issues and additional fallen angels, the total amount of junk bonds outstanding has been estimated at about $125 billion by the end of 1986, and at about $137 billion by the middle of 1987.[7] This represents more than 20 percent of

3. As reported by Thomas R. Atkinson, *Trends in Corporate Bond Quality* (New York: National Bureau of Economic Research, 1967).
4. Ibid.
5. As reported by Edward I. Altman and Scott A. Nammacher, *Investing in Junk Bonds* (New York: John Wiley & Sons, 1987).
6. It is true that new issues of junk bonds were much reduced in the wake of the stock market crash of October 1987. After running slightly ahead of the 1986 pace for the first three quarters of 1987, new issues of junk bonds totaled only $4.4 billion in the fourth quarter, compared with $8.7 billion for the comparable period

in 1986. Often overlooked, however, is the fact that corporate debt issues in general were much reduced in the fourth quarter of 1987. Thus junk bond issues still represented 11.7 percent of total corporate debt issues for the fourth quarter of 1987, not much different from their share for 1985 and 1986.

7. The 1986 estimate was provided by Drexel Burnham Lambert ("The Case for High Yield Securities," April 1987) and the 1987 estimate by Edward I. Altman, in "Analyzing Risks and Returns in the High Yield Bond Market," forthcoming in *Financial Markets and Portfolio Management*, Zurich, Switzerland.

TABLE 2
ESTIMATED OWNERSHIP
OF JUNK BONDS
DECEMBER, 1986

Type of Investor	Estimated Holdings ($ Billions)	% of Total
Mutual Funds	40	32
Insurance Companies	40	32
Pension Funds	15	12
Individuals	15	12
Thrift Institutions	10	8
Other (Foreign Investors, Securities Dealers, etc.)	5	4
Total	125	100

Source: Rasky (1986)

the entire corporate bond market. Approximately one-third of all junk bonds outstanding consisted of fallen angels as of year-end 1986.[8]

On the investor side, the junk bond market is primarily institutional. More than 50 mutual funds now specialize in holding junk bonds and these, together with other nonspecialized mutual funds, hold nearly one-third of junk bonds outstanding. The estimated ownership distribution of junk bonds as of December, 1986, is shown in Table 2.

INVESTMENT CHARACTERISTICS OF JUNK BONDS

Presumably, the attraction that junk bonds hold for investors is a high expected return. Expected returns are impossible to measure, and realized returns are an imperfect proxy because of their substantial variation from year to year. Over longer periods, however, junk bonds to seem to offer higher average realized rates of return. For the period 1977 to 1986, for example, a study by Marshall Blume and Donald Keim calculated an annualized compound monthly rate of return of 11.04 percent for an index of junk bonds, compared with 9.6 percent for an index of AAA-and AA-rated corporate bonds and 9.36 percent for an index of long-term Treasury bonds.[9]

In exchange for these higher returns, investors in junk bonds can expect to bear higher levels of risk. Their lower ratings, of course, suggest a higher risk

of default.[10] In addition, junk bonds tend to have fewer restrictive covenants than other bonds, and they are frequently subordinated. Thus junk bondholders have less flexibility to accelerate the bankruptcy process in the event that the borrower's condition deteriorates, and they stand lower in the line of creditors if bankruptcy does occur.

Measured default rates are, in fact, higher for junk bonds than for corporate bonds generally. For the period 1970 through 1986, a recent study by Ed Altman calculates the junk bond default rate (that is, par value of defaulting junk bonds divided by total junk bonds outstanding) as 2.22 percent, compared with 0.20 percent for all straight, public corporate debt. Influenced by the LTV and Texaco bankruptcies, the junk bond default rate was 3.39 percent for 1986 and 4.69 percent for 1987 (through August 31).[11]

The default rate, however, is probably not the best measure of the risk of holding junk bonds. Losses on defaulting bonds are rarely equal to their entire par value. For the period 1974 to 1986, for example, the weighted average default loss was 1.10 percent, compared with a default rate of 1.67 percent for the same period. In addition, junk bonds and investment grade bonds have different sensitivities to interest rate changes and to fluctuations in the value of the issuing firm's assets.

The importance of these additional factors is illustrated by Blume and Keim's finding that, for the period 1977 to 1986, their junk bond index had a lower standard deviation of monthly returns than did

---

8. See Susan F. Rasky, "Tracking Junk Bond Owners," *The New York Times*, December 7, 1986.

9. Marshall E. Blume and Donald B. Keim, "Lower Grade Bonds: Their Risks and Returns," *Financial Analysts Journal* 43 (July/August, 1987), pp. 26-33. A similar return relationship prevailed during 1987, even though junk bonds were hurt by the October stock market crash. The return on the Drexel Burnham Lambert Composite Index of high yield bonds was 5.41 percent for all of 1987, as

opposed to − 0.35 percent for comparable-duration treasury bonds (for the fourth quarter alone, analogous return figures were 2.73 percent for junk bonds versus 6.73 percent for treasuries).

10. In the Blume and Keim return calculations, default losses are already recognized to the extent that bonds in default are retained in the index as long as they have quoted market prices.

11. See Altman (1988), as cited in note 7.

their indices of either high-grade corporates or long-term Treasuries (2.86 percent versus 3.73 percent and 4.02 percent respectively).[12] Thus, after the fact, junk bonds actually had lower total risk than did their investment-grade counterparts. This seemingly paradoxical result may be attributed to two factors.

First, since junk bonds have higher coupon rates, they have shorter "durations" than investment grade bonds. That is, the weighted average of the times at which cash is received over the life of the bond is shorter for a junk bond.[13] This in turn implies that junk bond values are less sensitive to interest rate fluctuations than the values of investment grade bonds. Since the 1977-86 period was one of substantial interest rate fluctuations, this factor may have dominated the relative variability of realized bond returns.

Second, junk bonds are typically protected by smaller equity cushions than investment grade bonds, and thus are more sensitive to fluctuations in the value of the issuing firm's assets. The value of the assets in turn reflects the present value of the operating cash flows they generate. As a result, the variability of junk bond returns is more heavily influenced by sector, industry, and firm-specific factors than is that of investment grade bonds. However, much of the risk stemming from these fluctuations may be diversifiable. Thus the risk of a large portfolio or index may be substantially less than the average risk of the individual bonds.

Taken as whole, the investment characteristics of junk bonds are unlike those of either high grade bonds or common stocks. Their lower sensitivity to interest rate changes and the diversifiability of a substantial portion of their risk make them unlike high-grade bonds. Like common stocks, junk bond values move up and down with the value of the issuing firms' assets. Unlike common stocks, however, this upward movement is truncated for junk bonds beyond a certain point. This is because most junk bonds are callable; and if the issuing firm's creditworthiness improves dramatically, it will find it advantageous to call the bonds and refinance at a lower rate.

In the final analysis, investing in junk bonds may be most akin to a covered call option strategy, whereby a portfolio manager buys common stocks but also writes call options on those stocks. If the stocks fail to appreciate, the portfolio manager still receives the premium income from having written the call options. If the stocks do appreciate, however, the portfolio's upside potential is limited, because the stocks will be called away.

In a similar fashion, junk bonds' high current yield affords the investor some protection against the possibility that the firm's assets will decline in value. If, on the other hand, the firm's fortunes improve substantially, the junk bondholders participate to some degree, but that participation is limited by the fact the firm will ultimately call the bonds away.

CAPITAL MARKET CONDITIONS AND THE RISE OF THE JUNK BOND MARKET

Capital Markets in the 1970s and '80s

It is natural to wonder why junk bonds suddenly regained a significant share of the total corporate debt market after having been relatively dormant for a number of years. Several key factors emerged in the 1970s and '80s that brought about fundamental changes in the overall capital market environment. These same factors were conducive to the growth in junk bonds.

The first factor has been increasing competition on an international scale. Industry boundaries and firms' market shares have become more fluid; and the financial services, transportation, communication and energy industries, as well as major segments of U.S. manufacturing, have all undergone extensive restructuring. Deregulation has been a factor in several of these industries. In banking, for example, the erosion of interest rate ceilings has forced banks to compete on a broader scale in financial markets. It could be argued that these and other moves toward deregulation have often been a response to, rather than a cause of, increased competitive pressure. Whatever their source, these pressures have generated substantial capital market activity in the form of mergers and divestitures, issues and repurchases of securities, and the start-ups of new firms and liquidation of old ones. Regulatory changes that have given financial institutions greater flexibility should also be mentioned. For example,

---

12. Blume and Keim (1987), cited in note 9.

13. Over the period 1978-83, for example, Altman and Nammacher (1987), cited in note 5, calculated an average duration of 8.53 years for bonds in the Shearson-Lehman Long-Term Government Bond Index versus 6.64 years for their junk bond index. For further discussion and applications of the duration concept, see Stephen Schaefer, "Immunization and Duration. A Review of Theory, Performance and Applications." *Midland Corporate Finance Journal* 2 (Fall, 1984), pp. 41-58).

TABLE 3

COMPOSITION OF
CREDIT MARKET
DEBT RAISED BY
U.S. NONFINANCIAL
CORPORATIONS

Period	1977-83	1984-86
Total Credit Market Debt Raised ($ Billion)	$565.4	$535.1
Proportion of Credit Market Debt Accounted for by (%):		
Bank Loans	40.6%	32.7%
Commercial Paper	4.4	5.0
Finance Co. Loans	11.0	11.6
Tax-Exempt Bonds	12.9	6.5
Corporate Bonds	25.9	43.7
Mortgages	2.1	0.5
Other	3.0	0.0
Total	100.0	100.0
Note: Credit Market Debt as % of Total Sources of Funds	23.3	36.3

Source: Federal Reserve Flow of Fund Accounts

the ERISA standards of 1973 for pension fund investments essentially replaced the "Prudent Man" rule with a rule of reasonable compensation for risks incurred. This allowed pension fund to compete more broadly for investment opportunities.

A second important factor has been uncertain inflation and interest rate volatility. As exemplified by the response to the Federal Reserve's switch from interest rate to money supply targets in October 1979, the prices of fixed income securities have become more variable. This has spurred investors to seek protection against sudden changes in rates and has induced them to increase their portfolio turnover. For corporations, changing inflation rates have contributed to sharp fluctuations in the availability of internal funds relative to total financing needs. Thus many firms have found themselves moving in and out of the capital markets more frequently, and facing highly variable conditions when doing so.

The third important factor in changing capital market conditions is at least partially motivated by the first two. Securities issuers have greatly expanded the range of their potential sources of funds. In part, the increasingly global nature of competition in many industries has led to raising funds on an international scale as well. This is exemplified by the growth of the Eurobond markets, in which U.S. corporations raised an average of $28.4 billion in both 1986 and 1987, up from just $300 million in 1975. In addition, the need to move in and out of markets more frequently has led to an emphasis on reducing the costs of external financing. Since 1982, corpo-

rations have taken advantage of the shelf registration rule (Rule 415) to cut their underwriting costs. They have also sought to raise funds in public markets, where possible, circumventing more costly borrowing through financial intermediaries.

This disintermediation has been especially apparent in recent years, as indicated in Table 3. As the corporate bond market has expanded, the share of corporate debt financing accounted for by bank loans has declined. Although it is less apparent in the table, use of the commercial paper market by the most creditworthy corporations has also eroded banks' traditional lending relationships with their prime customers. These developments, combined with competition from foreign banks and other financial institutions, have turned prime lending into more of a low-margin commodity business. The banks have thus been forced to turn to lower grade credits in an attempt to maintain their profitability.

The Influence of Capital Market Conditions on the Junk Bond Market

The same factors that have molded capital market developments more generally have been important contributors to the recent growth of the junk bond market. Let us consider in turn the impact of these factors on investors, underwriters, and issuers of junk bonds.

Hurt by unexpected inflation during the 1970s, investors have sought higher returns and greater flexibility. Thus junk bonds, with their premium yields and shorter durations, grew more attractive by the late 1970s. This attractiveness was enhanced by the widely-noticed performance of Keystone's B4 Fund, a pioneer junk bond fund that inspired the start-up of other such funds.

Investors also found that traditional loss-protection measures were inadequate in a rapidly changing environment. High credit quality, for example, offered little protection against volatile interest rates. Similarly, restrictive covenants in bond indentures proved insufficient to guard against the losses imposed by massive corporate restructurings.[14] As a result, investors have increasingly emphasized liquidity relative to credit quality or contractual provisions. Despite their higher default risk and fewer restrictive covenants than other corporate bonds, junk bonds' attractiveness to investors has thus been greatly enhanced by the development of a liquid secondary market.

In this sense, the rise of the junk bond market has paralleled the "securitization" phenomenon more generally. Because little or no secondary market existed, mortgages, auto loans, and other receivables were formerly held to maturity by their originators or by specialized intermediaries. Increasingly, however, they have been packaged as asset-backed securities, and a more active secondary market has developed. In a similar vein, junk bonds are akin to medium or long-term loans that might formerly have been originated and held by commercial banks and insurance companies. With the development of a secondary market, however, they are now more widely traded.

Changing capital market conditions have also rapidly eroded the stigma that was formerly attached to junk bond underwriting and trading. As in commercial banking, prime-quality underwriting has become more of a low margin business as worldwide competition, shelf registration and issuer pressure have all combined to squeeze profits. This has in turn sparked a search for new opportunities. Merger and acquisition advising is one such opportunity that has been pursued by many securities firms. Providing investment banking services to below-investment grade companies, which comprise about 95 percent of all U.S. corporations, is another natural target.

The latter opportunity was especially attractive

to Drexel Burnham Lambert in the late 1970s, since it did not have a strong investment grade client base. It did, however, have a well established junk bond trading operation under the direction of Michael Milken. Thus it had already developed a network of investors and an expertise in secondary market-making.

When Drexel Burnham began underwriting junk bonds in 1977, it was therefore able to provide investors with the liquidity they needed to make these securities attractive. Drexel quickly became, and remains today, the leading underwriter of junk bonds; but other firms have recognized the potential profitability of the business and have entered the market as well.

Junk bonds also afforded Drexel Burnham a way to enter the lucrative merger and acquisition business and thus to participate in the restructuring boom. The firm began financing leveraged buyouts with junk bonds in 1981 and hostile takeover bids in late 1983. Drexel was able to capitalize on its established investor network to mobilize large amounts of funds within very short periods. Again, competitors have followed suit or have come up with alternative means of raising cash quickly, such as committing their own capital in the form of "bridge loans."

Finally, capital market conditions of recent years have also enhanced the appeal of junk bonds for issuers. Junk bond underwriting spreads are high, typically falling in the three to four percent range, compared with less than one percent for investment grade issues.[15] Still, there are reasons to believe that junk bond financing can offer cost advantages to issuers.

Investors, for example, appear to be willing to accept lower expected returns in exchange for greater liquidity.[16] Hence, investors' ability to trade their bonds in a secondary market can lower the cost of junk bond financing relative to negotiated debt, for which secondary trading is thin or nonexistent. This should be particularly the case in recent years, as volatile market conditions have dictated increased investor emphasis on liquidity.

In addition, rapidly changing financing needs and competitive situations have necessitated flexibility for issuing corporations. In this respect, the implicit cost of junk bond financing may have been less than that of other sources in recent year. For exam-

14. See S. Prokesch, "Merger Wave: How Stock and Bonds Fare," *The New York Times,* January 7, 1986.

15. As reported by Henny Sender, "Don't Junk the High-Yield Market Yet," Institutional Investor 21 (March, 1987).), pp. 163-66.

16. See Yakov Amihud and Haim Mendelson, "Asset Pricing and the Bid-Ask Spread," *Journal of Financial Economics* 17 (December, 1986), pp. 223-49.

ple, junk bonds have allowed lower-grade firms to raise larger amounts of money in a shorter period than would be possible from negotiated sources. Junk bonds also tend to have fewer restrictive covenants and more liberal call provisions than many types of negotiated debt. Recent market conditions have apparently created a willingness on the part of some investors to make these concessions in exchange for greater liquidity. In fact, it could be argued that investors' demand for liquidity has greatly facilitated the placement of junk bonds from the largest leveraged buyouts.

THE ROLE OF JUNK BONDS IN CORPORATE FINANCIAL POLICY

Given that junk bonds have established a solid position in the corporate debt market, we now examine their role in corporate financial policy. When should a corporation consider issuing junk bonds?

Stewart Myers' "pecking order" theory provides a useful starting point.[17] Myers notes that a firm's managers typically know more about its true value than other capital market participants. If the managers act in the interests of their existing shareholders, they will thus try to issue securities at times when they know them to be overvalued. Recognizing this incentive, however, market participants will then interpret securities issues as a sign that they are overvalued. That in turn reduces the amounts they are willing to pay for the securities.

This problem of unequal information gives rise to a pecking order of sources of funds. Internally generated funds are unaffected by the problem, since their use entails no new securities issues. The closer a company's debt securities are to being riskless, the less severe is this problem as well. This is because the value of riskless securities will be unaffected by revisions in the estimated value of the company's assets. Riskier securities such as equity, however, will clearly be affected by investors' perceptions of firm value. Since the mere fact of their issuance is likely to lead to downward revisions in their value, managers will be reluctant to issue these securities.

The pecking order, then, implies the following rules for financial policy: (1) Use internal funds first,

until these have been exhausted; (2) to the extent that external funds must be relied upon, issue debt first, the less risky the better; (3) issue common stock only as a last resort, after all debt capacity has been exhausted.

Junk bonds occupy an intermediate position in this pecking order. They are more susceptible to the investor information problem than investment grade debt, but less so than common stock. For a firm that needs large amounts of external financing for its current investment plan, junk bonds can allow the firm to fully use its available debt capacity and thus avoid an equity issue.

At what point is debt capacity used up? While it is difficult to identify a given firm's optimal debt ratio with any precision, finance theory does suggest certain characteristics that will lead some firms to have higher debt capacities then others.[18]

The first of these is the firm's tax-paying status. The tax-deductibility of interest is one of the potential advantages of debt. Firms pay for this advantage, however, because the more debt they issue in the aggregate, the more they bid up the returns on debt securities relative to equity. Thus firms that already have large tax shields (for example, from depreciation and loss carry forwards) relative to their cash flow would find little tax benefit from additional debt, even though they would be implicitly paying for this benefit. For such firms, debt capacity is likely to be relatively low.[19]

A second important determinant of debt capacity is the riskiness of the firm's assets. The costs of bankruptcy and of resolving conflicts of interest among security holders are closely related to the perceived probability of default. The fact that a company's bonds are rated below investment grade is, of course, itself an indication that perceived default risk is relatively high. Hence, issuers of junk bonds should carefully weigh the potential costs of bankruptcy and claimholder conflicts against the dilution that might be entailed by an equity issue. In particular, a firm that plans to return to the debt markets on a regular basis in the future should be wary of increasing its debt ratio suddenly and sharply through the issuance of junk bonds today. To the extent that this undermines the value of its already outstanding

17. See "The Capital Structure Puzzle," *Journal of Finance* 39 (June, 1984), pp. 575-92. Reprinted in *Midland Corporate Finance Journal* 3, Fall 1985, pp. 6-18).

18. For a discussion of these characteristics, see Stewart C. Myers, "The Search for an Optimal Capital Structure," *Midland Corporate Finance Journal* 1 (Spring, 1983), pp. 6-16.

19. Since the new tax law reduces nondebt tax shields by eliminating the Investment Tax Credit and lengthening allowable depreciation schedules, it may tend to increase debt capacity for many firms.

bonds, the firm can expect investors to extract a penalty yield or more stringent covenants the next time it returns to the market.

A third factor affecting a firm's debt capacity is the composition of its assets. A firm whose value stems largely from assets already in place is likely to have a greater debt capacity than one for which future investment opportunities comprise a substantial portion of current market value. This is because debt that is issued now can weaken the firm's incentive to undertake those future investments. The riskier is the firm's currently outstanding debt, the more the future projects will tend to bolster the bondholders' position. Because they must share the value of these projects, however, equityholders' willingness to undertake them will be less than if they captured the entire value themselves. In the face of this potential problem, firms with significant future growth opportunities will tend to rely less heavily on debt financing today.

The foregoing analysis suggests that the ideal junk bond issuer is a firm that can take full advantage of the interest tax shields, that does not have a potential for severe bankruptcy costs or conflicts among security holders, and that has a total market value that is largely attributable to assets in place. One such firm would be the prototypical leveraged buyout candidate: a firm with a mature business that generates a high but relatively steady level of cash flows. Another might be a younger firm that has already cleared the hurdles of developing its product and establishing a market position but that now needs capital to finance its major expansion phase.

One other factor should also be considered by the potential junk bond issuer. The arguments advanced above concerning debt capacity and the pecking order of funds sources do not distinguish between public and private debt. Hence the issuer must decide whether it is better to rely on the public market or to negotiate a private agreement with a financial institution. The more highly the issuer values the flexibility entailed by call provisions and less restrictive covenants, the more the choice will tend toward public debt. The public market will also be favored the more investors are willing to make yield concessions in exchange for the possibility of secondary trading.

PUBLIC POLICY ISSUES

If junk bonds are simply one possible choice in an entire spectrum of funds sources, why have they aroused such controversy in pubic policy circles? The general economic conditions described earlier--especially worldwide competitive upheaval and uncertain inflation combined with interest rate volatility--have been accompanied by many painful dislocations. Although total employment has expanded, the wave of restructurings has brought plant closings and loss of jobs in a number of industries and localities. Changes in control have extended the threat to job security to the most senior executive ranks. Competition and volatile market conditions have also aroused fears over the safety of the financial system. These developments have in turn generated heated debate over such issues as industrial policy and the regulation of financial institutions. And because they are a highly visible product of the same economic forces that have caused these dislocations, junk bonds have become enmeshed in the same policy debates.

However, the true contribution of junk bonds to these perceived policy problems may be more symbolic than real. Their very label tends to surround junk bonds with the unsavory aura that makes them a convenient target. Their real influence is less easy to detect.

Consider, for example, the role of junk bonds in financing mergers and acquisitions. This has been the subject of several congressional hearings and various restrictions on junk bond financing of hostile takeover bids have been proposed.[20] Sometimes lost amidst the furor, though, is the fact that junk bonds account for only a small fraction of all merger and acquisition financing. The peak occurred in 1986, when junk bond issues were related to 7.8 percent of the $190 billion in total merger financing (*Mergers and Acquisitions*, 1987). This was up from 4.3 percent in 1985 and 2.6 percent in 1984. Merger and tender offer transactions have accounted for at most 41 percent of public junk bond issue proceeds in any given year, this occurring in 1986.

It cannot be denied that the availability of the junk bond market has strengthened the credibility of takeover threats, allowing larger amounts of funds to

---

20. To date, the only restriction actually imposed has been the Federal Reserve Board's 1986 determination that a shell corporation, set up for the purpose of making a takeover bid, is subject to margin requirements under Regulation G. The impact of this ruling is limited, however, by numerous stated exceptions. See M. Langley and J.D. Williams, "Fed Board Votes 3-2 to Restrict the Use of 'Junk' Bonds in Takeovers," *The Wall Street Journal* (January 9, 1986).

be raised in a shorter time period than was previously thought possible. Nevertheless, merger-related activity does not absorb a majority of the proceeds from junk bond issues, and bank loans are a far bigger source of merger financing than junk bonds.

The junk bond market has also been discussed frequently in conjunction with the recent insider trading charges, and revelations connected with the Boesky scandal have apparently triggered some decreases in junk bond prices, at least temporarily.[21] While the SEC has recommended that charges be brought against Drexel Burnham and several of its employees, however, no systematic involvement of junk bond market participants in insider trading has been established as yet. Furthermore, as with mergers and acquisitions generally, the issue is broader than junk bonds. Tender offers can create opportunities for insider trading, but it is not clear why offers that will be financed with junk bonds are more susceptible to such opportunities than others.

Consider finally the connection between junk bonds and the safety of the financial system. Some have argued that junk bonds represent part of a general weakening of corporate financial strength in recent years. However, it is at least debatable whether such weakening has in fact occurred.[22] When measured in market value terms, the ratio of debt to total capital for U.S. nonfinancial corporations has actually declined by more than 20 percent since 1974. Even if it were conceded that U.S. corporations have relied too heavily on debt financing, it should be noted that junk bond issues account for only six percent of the total credit market debt that companies have raised during the period 1977-1986.

It has also been argued that junk bond invest-ments can weaken the safety of financial institutions. Acting on these arguments the state of New York has recently moved to limit unapproved junk bond investments by insurance companies.[23] Given their default risk, it is of course true that an ill-conceived junk bond investment program can lead to trouble. But the number of ways to make risky investments is almost unlimited. They include, for example, issuing short-term debt and investing in long-term Treasury securities that are free of default risk. Limiting junk bond investments, but not other investments, is unlikely to significantly enhance the safety of financial institutions.

CONCLUSION

The rapid growth of the junk bond market has been impressive, but controversial. Most of the controversy stems from the fact that the market's development has coincided with the rise of such emotional policy issues as industrial restructuring and corporate control. It has been argued here, however, that the junk bond market is a product of the same forces — international competition, volatile capital market conditions, and the search for new funds sources — that have given rise to these policy issues. It is a symptom rather than a cause of those forces.

For the corporate treasurer, the development of this market represents a significant financial innovation. It allows companies that do not qualify for investment grade bond ratings to tap the public market and thus to take advantage of investors' willingness to pay for liquidity. For such firms, access to the junk bond market can be an important alternative to privately negotiated debt.

21. Estimates of these price decreases range from one to four percentage points (see Randall Smith, "Junk Bonds Lag Market Since Boesky Case, But Exact Gap Proves Difficult to Measure," *The Wall Street Journal*, December 4, 1986). Much of these losses, however, appear to have been recouped within about two months (see Randall Smith, "Junk Bonds Retain Strength and Discount Latest Fallout From Insider Trading Scandal," *The Wall Street Journal*, February 18, 1987).

22. See, for example, Robert A. Taggart, Jr.. "Corporate Financing: Too Much Debt?," *Financial Analysts Journal* 42 (May/June, 1986), pp. 35-42.
23. See Johnnie L. Roberts, "New York Limits Assets Insurers Put in Junk Bonds," *The Wall Street Journal*, June 1

THE CASE FOR CONVERTIBLES*

by Michael J. Brennan and
Eduardo S. Schwartz
University of California, Los Angeles

THE CONVERTIBLE SECURITY

Until fairly recently, the popularity of convertible securities was something of a mystery to financial economists. To those well-versed in the literature of "efficient markets," there seemed no convincing reason why convertible bonds—which, after all, represent nothing more than straight debt securities combined with options on the company's stock—should provide issuing companies with financing benefits. Why, the question was asked, should sophisticated investors be willing to pay more (thus costing the corporate issuer less) for these securities in combination than for separate offerings of straight debt and straight equity?

The characteristic response from the business schools was to attribute the use of convertibles to a widespread, but relatively harmless delusion entertained by corporate treasurers and fostered (unwittingly or otherwise) by their financial advisors. This popular misconception, which continues to captivate a good number of investment bankers and their corporate clients, is that convertible bonds (or preferreds) are a cheap source of capital because (1) they carry coupon rates below the market rates of interest on straight debt (or preferred) and (2) they allow companies to sell stock at a premium over the current price.

The astute corporate treasurer has probably long suspected that such an apparent "free lunch" is tainted. And if he has had any exposure to theoretical finance and the modern conception of "cost of capital," his suspicions will have been confirmed. For there is general agreement—among academics, at least—that the real economic cost of convertibles to the issuing corporation is not reflected by the explicit interest rate (just as the dividend yield on common fails to represent the corporate "cost of equity"). The real cost of a convertible bond is considerably higher than the coupon rate; and, because of the conversion rights, it is also higher than the company's borrowing rate on straight and, for that matter, on

* This article was originally published in the *Chase Financial Quarterly* (Vol. 1 No. 3) and is reprinted with the permission of the Chase Manhattan Bank.

subordinated debt. In fact, because of its hybrid nature—part debt, part equity—the cost of convertible debt is best thought of as a weighted average of the explicit interest charges, and the implicit opportunity costs associated with the conversion or equity option.

A New Explanation

It is probably true to say that the slow spread of the "gospel" of modern finance has had a modest success in dispelling the popular illusions surrounding convertibles. And that many corporate managers now perceive convertibles to be more expensive than they look. To the perplexity of academics, however, the popularity of convertibles has shown little sign of abating. Consequently, as "positive" financial economists, we have been faced with the task of finding a *convincing* explanation—one that is consistent with rational investors and sophisticated financial markets.

In this article, after first examining the conventional arguments more closely, we offer a relatively new rationale for the use of convertibles. Instead of relying on the naivete of corporate financial officers or the marketing facility of investment bankers, our explanation centers largely on an important feature of convertibles: *the relative insensitivity of their value to the risk of the issuing company*. This insensitivity makes it easier for the bond issuer and purchaser to agree on the value of the bond—even when they disagree on the risk of the company—and, thus, to come to terms. It also protects the bondholder against the adverse consequences of management policies which would increase the risk of the company.

The market, as a general rule, exacts a premium for bearing additional uncertainty. Companies unable to provide investors with assurance about the level and stability of their risks may be forced to bear interest costs on straight debt that are considerably higher than management's expectations would warrant. The advantage of a well-designed convertible, as we will argue, is that its value is not much affected by changes in company risk; and that investors are willing to provide funds on better terms when their uncertainties about risk are allayed.

The available evidence, moreover, supports our theory by suggesting that the companies issuing convertibles tend to be those for which uncertainty about risk is likely to be greatest; that is, the companies for which the costs of straight debt appear prohibitively (and needlessly) expensive. For large, mature corporations with strong credit ratings, however, there still appears to be no good reason for issuing convertibles.

The Call Question

In the third section of this article, we explore the issue of when companies should call their convertibles. The call provision, which is a feature of most corporate bonds, takes on added significance in the case of convertibles because of the holder's rights to convert into common stock.

But, if our theory is now better able to account for the corporate decision to issue convertibles, some mystery still surrounds the call decision—both the conventional corporate practice and the market's response to the announcement of calls. Our theory provides a fairly simple rule for the corporation to follow in exercising its call option: namely, to call a convertible as soon as the conversion price exceeds the call price, while providing enough of a margin to ensure conversion.

The actual call policies of corporations, however, depart significantly from this apparently optimal policy. Convertible securities, whether bonds or preferreds, are not generally called until their premium over the call price is significantly larger. Moreover, when corporations actually do call their convertibles, their stock prices tend to decline, which seems to suggest that the decision to call convertibles is in general a mistake.

We provide answers to both of the questions: Why do companies delay so long in forcing conversion? Why does the market respond negatively when they finally do? But neither are completely satisfying. We can account for companies' actual call behavior only as the result of a common, but misguided concern with the effects of conversion on reported (undiluted) earnings per share. In response to the second of these puzzles, our best guess is that the market has come to associate forced conversions with companies anticipating hard times. As a result, announcements of convertible calls may be conveying negative information about management's outlook for the company.

In the final part of the article, we present the outlines of a model we have recently devised for the pricing and valuation of convertible securities. Our model, which incorporates the insights of the Black-Scholes Options Pricing Model (now widely used by professional option traders on the Chicago Exchange), permits analysis of the contributions of various features to the value of convertibles.

In designing a convertible bond contract, the corporate treasurer (and/or his investment banker) faces the complex problem of juggling conversion and call price schedules, coupon rates, maturity and other bond characteristics. The potential application of our model is to assess the value of a convertible with a given set of features or, alternatively, to estimate the effect of a change in one or more provisions on the value of the bond. It is also useful in arriving at decisions to force conversion.

THE COMMON MISCONCEPTION

The idea that the convertible offers a cheap source of finance stems from arguments of the following kind. Suppose, as might reasonably be the case, that if a company can float senior debt at 14 percent, it can also issue a convertible debenture with a conversion premium of 15 percent carrying a coupon rate of only 11 percent. The 15 percent conversion premium means that if the current stock price is $40, the bondholder has the right to convert into common at $46, or 15 percent above the current stock price.

Now if, as the conventional argument runs, the company performs poorly and the stock price does not rise, the bondholders will not find it advantageous to exercise their conversion option. The issuing company will then have obtained debt financing at a cost of 11 percent, or 300 basis points below the going rate for senior debt. On the other hand, if the firm prospers and the share price rises, bondholders will convert. For each $1000 raised, the company will have to issue 21.74 ($1000/$46) shares. In this case, management will in effect have sold common stock at the conversion price of $46, or 15 percent above the stock price at the time the funds were raised.

Thus, whether the bond is converted or not, the company will have done better with convertibles than with the alternative source of funds. Or so it seems.

The argument is beguiling because it involves sleight of hand. Notice that it compares the convertible to straight debt only when the company performs poorly, but compares the convertible to common stock when the firm performs well. This is similar to the argument that it is best to buy fire insurance on only 50 percent of the value of your house. If the house burns down, 50 percent insurance is better than none; and if the house does not burn down, 50 percent insurance is cheaper than full insurance.

This argument is clearly fallacious since it neglects to point out that 50 percent insurance is worse than full insurance if the house burns down, and more expensive than no insurance if the house does not burn down. Similarly, the convertible will turn out to be more expensive than common stock if the company does poorly, because the debt will still have be serviced. If the company does very well, the convertible will have been more expensive than straight debt, for then the convertible bond purchasers will participate in the stockholders' profits.

It is clear that the case for the convertible cannot be made on the basis of this "heads you win, tails you also win" kind of argument. The convertible bondholder is perhaps best thought of as a kind of fair-weather stockholder and foul-weather bondholder. To compensate for the fact that he is not the ideal type of business partner, the convertible purchaser accepts less advantageous terms for the debt or stock with which he will finally end up: thus is the convertible coupon below the straight debt coupon, and the conversion price above the current stock price.

A somewhat stronger case can be made for the cost advantage of the convertible if it is assumed that the company's stock is significantly overpriced or underpriced. Suppose, for example, that the stock at $40 is so overpriced that management can be *sure* that the bond will not be converted. By issuing the convertible, the company would then be selling 14 percent debt at a cost of only 11 percent.

This is certainly an attractive proposition. But how often can management be sure that the conversion option is worthless, unless they are fraudulently concealing information about the company? Moreover, in such circumstances, it would almost certainly be better to sell the overpriced stock itself.

Suppose, on the other hand, that the stock is so underpriced that management can be sure that the bondholders will convert. Then, by issuing the convertible, the company is in effect selling stock at the higher conversion price. In these circumstances, however, it would be even better to issue straight debt, retiring it with proceeds of a stock issue after the stock price has risen.

In general, arguments for convertibles based on the assumed mispricing of the common stock come down to nothing more than the observation that the convertible is a hybrid security—part stock, part bond. Therefore, if the stock is undervalued and so a costly source of funds, the convertible will be less undervalued. But straight debt, in this case, will be even less undervalued. If the stock is overvalued, the convertible will also be overvalued, and therefore a less costly source of funds than straight debt. Common stock, however, will be even less costly. In short, the argument that the company's stock is improperly valued does not provide a sensible justification for issuing convertibles.

WHY, THEN, CONVERTIBLES?

If the traditional argument for convertibles does not deserve serious attention, is there another explanation for their popularity? And, furthermore, is this explanation consistent with the financing behavior of companies in American capital markets?

The institutional explanation of convertibles is that certain financial institutions are restricted as to the amount of common stock they can hold, and that convertibles provide a means by which such institutions can increase their equity position. There may be an element of truth in this. But the further suggestion that such institutions bid up the price of convertibles so that companies can reduce their financing costs by appealing to this restricted segment of the market is unlikely to be true.

A more reasonable account of capital market behavior would show that firms in aggregate supply enough convertibles to satisfy the demand of this segment of the market, so that there are no "scarcity rents"—or, in this case, major cost reductions—to be had. After all, chocolate manufacturers do not expect to make more money on sugarless chocolate because diabetics are prohibited from consuming the regular kind. By the same logic, this preference for convertibles by some institutions should not provide any significant cost reduction to companies issuing them.

A more convincing rationale for convertibles—one that has received a good deal of support in the academic finance community—centers on the effect of changes in risk on the value of securities. Recall that, as a general rule, the higher the risk associated with a company's operations (and the greater the market's uncertainty about that risk), the higher the interest cost that a company will be forced to pay. At least, on its straight debt. In the case of convertibles, however, higher risk may not mean a correspondingly greater burden of financing costs for the issuing company. That is, the use of convertibles may

effectively shelter companies of high and indeterminate risk from prohibitively high costs of straight debt capital.

To see why this is true, note that a convertible is roughly equivalent to a package of straight debt and warrants. Instead of issuing a $1,000 bond which is convertible into 21.74 shares at a conversion price of $46, a corporation could issue a package of one $1,000 straight bond and 21.74 warrants with an exercise price of $46; and the consequences would be almost identical. Such bond-warrant combinations are indeed a quite popular alternative to convertible bonds.

How, then, would warrants in combination with a debt offering affect investors' perception of the risks involved in holding such securities? Although there are exceptions to this rule, companies with higher operating and financial risk tend to have more volatile stock prices. As noted earlier, companies with higher risk and, hence, greater price volatility pay higher rates for straight debt. And increases in the market's perception of a company's risk will cause a reduction in the value of its straight bonds.

The effect of increased risk and volatility on a warrant, however, is the opposite. Remember that the holder of a warrant profits from increases in the stock price above the exercise price, but is protected against declines below the exercise price. That is, there is an "asymmetry" in the return to the warrant which *increases* as the spread of possible future stock prices widens. In other words, as the risk and price volatility of the company increases, the value of the warrant increases. For instance, a warrant on the shares of an electronics company will be worth considerably more than a warrant (with the same conditions) on a utility's shares.

In the case of a convertible security, then, the effect of an increase in risk on the cost of a straight debt offering is offset, to an extent, by its effect on the value of the warrant. As a result, the value of an appropriately designed convertible security (or its equivalent package of straight debt and warrants) will be largely unaffected by the risk of the issuing firm.

Practically, this means that two companies at different points along the risk spectrum, facing very different costs of straight debt, could issue convertibles with nearly identical maturities, conversion premiums and coupon rates. Such a case is illustrated in Table 1. Note that while the terms of the convertible debt sold by the medium- and high-risk companies are almost identical, the proportions of the convertible's value which are accounted for by

TABLE 1

COUPON RATES REQUIRED ON NEW ISSUES OF
STRAIGHT AND CONVERTIBLE DEBT

	Company Risk	
	Medium	**High**
Convertible Debt	11%	11.25%
Straight Debt	14%	16%

the straight debt element and by the conversion feature will be quite different. For the higher-risk company, less of the convertible's value will be accounted for by the straight debt component, and correspondingly more by the conversion or warrant element.

We are not suggesting, in this example, that convertibles offer higher-risk companies a "free lunch."[1] We are arguing, however, that the inclusion of warrants in a debt package provides a kind of financing "synergy" which allows companies with high and uncertain risk to raise capital on more advantageous terms.

Consider the further case of a company whose managers believe it to be one of medium risk, but which is perceived by the market to be high risk. Facing a 16 percent coupon rate, when companies of what it deems comparable risk are paying only 14 percent, the management of such a company may find straight debt prohibitively expensive. Although convertible debt will also appear expensive, because the company must pay 11 1/4 percent coupon instead of the 11 percent it considers reasonable, the effect of the divergence in risk assessment between management and the market is much less for the convertible than for the straight debt.

In such a situation, management will undoubtedly prefer to issue the convertible. Notice that the role of the convertible in this situation is independent of any mispricing of the stock. Even if the market and management agree that the stock is correctly priced, the convertible is still useful in resolving their disagreement over the risk of the company's operations.

The relevant risk is not only the risk of the company's existing operations, but also the risk of any future operations in which the firm may become involved over the life of the bond. It has been pointed out that the management of a company with straight debt outstanding will have an incentive to increase the risk of the firm, since the downside risk is borne by the bondholders while the upside returns accrue solely to the stockholders. In reasonably sophisticated capital markets, purchasers of straight debt issued by companies for which this behavior is a real possibility will demand a correspondingly higher coupon rate to compensate for this anticipated future risk. In this case also, the cost of straight debt will look high relative to the risk of the company's existing operations.

Because of their option on the firm's equity, however, purchasers of a convertible issue are likely to be much less concerned by the prospect of increases in the future risk of the company. For although an increase in risk would reduce the straight debt value of their bonds, it would also increase the value of the warrant element. Consequently, when there is doubt about the future policies of the company, the convertible is likely to be the preferred instrument. It should also be noted that because the convertible holders are protected against this type of expropriation, managements issuing convertible, rather than straight debt reduce their own incentive to increase the risk of the firm simply to transfer wealth from the bondholders to the existing stockholders.[2]

For the reasons offered above, convertibles are most likely to be used by companies which the market perceives as risky, whose risk is hard to assess, and whose investment policy is hard to predict.

The Evidence

The data on the corporate use of convertibles seem to be consistent with our theory. In a study

---

1. This example is not meant to suggest that because the terms of the two convertible issues are nearly identical, the cost of the convertible is identical for the two companies. Remember that convertible debt is a hybrid security, partly straight debt and partly (a call option on the company's) equity. The opportunity cost of a convertible debt issue should thus be thought of as a weighted average of the company's cost of debt and equity capital. For the higher-risk company in this example, the fact that it has both a higher cost of straight debt and a higher implicit cost of equity suggests that its convertible will have a higher implicit cost. But,

more important, the fact that a much greater portion of the value of its convertible rests in the warrant or equity component means that the convertible holder has been promised a more substantial equity stake in the the higher-risk company: this, of course, translates into a higher opportunity cost of capital.

2. This argument was first presented formally by Michael C. Jensen and William H. Meckling in "Theory of the Firm: Managerial Behavior, Agency Costs, and Capital Structure," *Journal of Financial Economics*, Volume 3, pp. 305-360. (1976).

published in 1980, Wayne Mikkelson found that highly-levered and high-growth companies were more likely to issue convertibles.[3] High leverage is certainly related to risk, and it is high-growth firms whose future investment is hardest to predict. Mikkelson also found that the longer the term of the issue, the more likely it was to contain a conversion feature. This is also consistent with the theory because longer maturities involve greater risks of a shift in companies' investment policies.

Interestingly enough, Mikkelson also found that convertibles are much more frequently offered publicly than placed privately. This is evidence against the institutional explanation of convertibles, which would have the demand for them coming primarily from institutions. It is also consistent with the stress our theory lays on uncertainty in risk assessment, since it is undoubtedly easier for the financial institutions involved in private placements to assess the risks of individual companies than for the public at large.

A more recent study by Donald Chew provides further confirmation of Mikkelson's findings. In an attempt to identify some of the financial characteristics which distinguish companies issuing convertibles from those issuing straight debt only, this study reported that over the period 1977-1980, convertible issuers tended to have higher market and earnings variability. They were also, on average, considerably smaller, younger, and growing more rapidly. All of these characteristics translate fairly directly into greater investor uncertainty about risk, and higher potential rewards associated with the conversion privilege.

CONVERSION AND CALL POLICIES

Having offered a corporate motivation for issuing convertibles, we now want to consider the question of conversion—first from the perspective of investors, and then from the standpoint of management formulating call policies for convertible issues.

A rational bondholder will not convert his bond as long as the coupon on the bond exceeds the dividends on the shares into which the bond is convertible—not unless the conversion privilege is about to expire or change adversely. By postponing conversion the bondholder continues to enjoy a greater income, and literally keeps his options open. Indeed,

even if the dividend forgone exceeds the bond coupon, the investor may yet decide to postpone conversion because of the greater flexibility he retains.

The issuing company can, of course, induce bondholders to convert simply by raising the dividend on the common stock sufficiently high. At some point the opportunity cost of forgoing the higher dividend will ensure that bondholders voluntarily choose to convert.

If the bond is callable, and if the conversion value of the bond exceeds the call price, the bondholders can also be induced to convert by calling the bond for redemption. For example, if each $1000 bond is convertible into 25 shares of stock, and the share price is $50, the conversion value of the bond is $25 \times \$50 = \$1250$. Suppose that each bond is callable at $1100. If the company calls the bond, the bondholder may either redeem the bond at the call price of $1100 or convert the bond into common stock with market value of $1250. Faced with these alternatives, the bondholders will have no difficulty in deciding to convert the bond; and the company would be said to have "forced conversion" by calling the convertible.

When should a company call its convertibles? Assuming that management's objective is to maximize the value of the common stock, the appropriate policy—at least, in theory—is to call as soon as the value of the convertible reaches the call price. This will typically occur when the conversion value of the bonds is equal to the call price. Such a call policy minimizes the value of the convertible by putting the lowest possible lid on its value. That is, by forcing conversion or redeeming the issue, management effectively limits the value of the convertible by eliminating the warrant component—and the flexibility it provides the investor. Because the convertible represents a liability of the existing stockholders, acting to minimize its value increases the value of the common stock.

There are a couple of considerations which would make the proposed call policy somewhat impractical. First, bondholders typically must be given 30 days notice of call. Secondly, management may wish to avoid the costs associated with issuing new securities if the bonds are redeemed rather than converted into stock. The effect of these considerations on the optimal policy is to delay the call until the con-

3. Mikkelson, W.H. "Convertible Security Calls and Securityholder Returns: Evidence on Agency Costs, Effects of Capital Structure Change, and Supply Effects," *Journal of Financial Economics* (1980).

version value is sufficiently above the call price—high enough such that management can be reasonably assured that fluctuations in the stock price during the call notice period will not cause the investors to redeem rather than to convert the bonds.

A study by Jonathan Ingersoll has shown that using this modification of the original rule, the optimal timing for calling a convertible would be when the conversion values were, at most, 6-8 percent above the call price.[4]

The actual call policies of corporations, however, do not even approximate this proposed optimal policy. In a 1965 survey of corporations with convertibles outstanding, Eugene Brigham found that only 23 percent planned to force conversion as soon as conversion could be assured (the optimal policy); another 23 percent planned to encourage conversion by raising dividends; and the remaining 54 percent had no clear plans to force conversion. Ingersoll confirmed Brigham's results, finding that the median company among all firms calling convertibles between 1968 and 1975 waited until the conversion values of its bonds was 43.9 percent higher than the call price.[5]

It is difficult to explain such behavior on a rational basis. It has been suggested that, by forcing conversion, the company loses the advantage of the tax deductibility of interest payments on the bonds. While, in principle, this tax advantage could be regained by making a new issue of bonds and retiring stock, this kind of recapitalization involves additional underwriting costs. (Mikkelson found that only 23 of his 113 corporations forcing conversion replaced the debt.)

This tax-based rationalization of corporate call policies is further weakened by Ingersoll's finding that companies calling their convertible preferreds behaved in roughly the same way: the median corporation delayed call until the conversion value exceeded the call price by 38.5 percent. There is no corporate tax advantage associated with preferred shares.

Alternative explanations rely on notions of fair play and management concern with (undiluted) earnings per share. It is argued that it is unfair to deprive the bondholders of the full benefit of their conversion privilege; and that if the company enforces its call rights, it may experience difficulty in selling convertibles in the future. The idea, however, that corporate treasurers are constrained by these misdirected scruples (which, after all, will reward convertible holders only at the expense of the existing stockholders) seems far-fetched. Furthermore, the supposedly adverse consequences for future issues can be avoided by placing appropriate restrictions on the call privilege for those issues. Some convertibles, for example, restrict the corporation's right to call to periods during which the conversion value of the bonds exceeds the call price by a stated percentage. In the absence of such provisions, though, self-imposed restrictions on the use of the call privilege seem just silly.

Another motive for deferring conversion is management's concern with the effect on reported (undiluted) earnings per share. Conversion of outstanding bonds or preferreds will typically reduce this figure, spreading the company's earnings over a larger number of shares. To the extent that management believes the market value of its shares responds to announcements of accounting transactions without any economic consequences, it may wish to postpone this formal declaration that all future cash flows are now to be divided among a larger group of stockholders. In a reasonably sophisticated market, however, investors will have already anticipated the conversion, recognizing that fully diluted EPS provides a better guide to the value of the company's stock. Consequently, we remain a bit skeptical of the idea that excessive concern with the effect of reduced EPS on stock prices accounts for the widespread tendency to put off conversion.

There is, however, another reason for managers' heeding reported earnings per share—one consistent with rational behavior: namely, their compensation may be tied to this figure. If such is the case, then tying the bonus to undiluted EPS is creating the wrong incentive for financial managers, rewarding actions which detract from instead of contribute to stockholder value.

It is interesting to note, however, that management's alleged concern with the stock price implications of forcing conversion seems to find justification in Mikkelson's puzzling discovery that announcements of convertible bond calls are accompanied, on average, by a 2 percent *drop* in stock prices. In the case of forced conversions on preferred issues, the average market response is a negative 1/3 percent. It

---

4. Jonathan Ingersoll, "A Contingent-Claims Valuation of Convertible Securities," *Journal of Financial Economics*, Volume 4, Number 3 (May, 1977).

5. Jonathan Ingersoll, "An Examination of Corporate Call Policies on Convertible Securities," *Journal of Finance*, Volume 32, pp. 463-478. (1977).

is unlikely that these negative reactions are attributable to a systematic error by the market in interpreting the reported earnings figures.

Mikkelson tentatively attributes this market response to the tax effect discussed earlier; that is, the negative response reflects the market's recognition of the loss of the interest tax shield associated with the bonds. Some indirect support for this position is provided by a study demonstrating a positive stock price response to companies that issue debt to retire stock, which is essentially the reverse of converting outstanding bonds.[6] The problem with this explanation is that it implies that managements systematically make financial decisions which are contrary to the interest of their shareholders; and we are reluctant to rest with such a conclusion.

A more palatable explanation, and the one that we favor, would attribute Mikkelson's findings to an "information effect." That is, the market may have become conditioned to associate convertible calls with unfavorable events having nothing to do with the conversion. For example, if managements, in anticipation of difficult times, have a tendency to clear the decks of fixed and semi-fixed obligations by forcing conversion, the market would then come to recognize forced conversions as unfavorable auguries, and mark down the stock prices accordingly.

In summary, corporate call policies and their effects remain obscure. Managers seem to delay too long in exercising their call privileges. Yet the stock price tends to decline when they do exercise it. We have suggested that the delay may be due to management's concern with the negative effect on reported EPS. The negative stock price reaction to the announcement of a call may be attributable to tax effects or to information effects. We favor the information hypothesis because, unlike the tax hypothesis, it does not imply that managers are acting against the shareholder interest. At this point, however, we do not have the evidence to make a confident choice among these alternatives.

PRICING A CONVERTIBLE ISSUE

At the outset, we stated that most of the existing models for valuing convertibles (and thus for pricing new convertible issues) are inadequate. Such models have been based on simplistic analyses which assume the future is known with certainty. The price of the company's stock is assumed to grow at a given rate; and on the basis of this assumption, conversion is assumed to take place a pre-determined number of years after the security is issued.

The problem with such models is their failure to reflect the essential feature of the convertible: the conversion *option* gives the bondholder the right to wait until current uncertainties are at least partially resolved before deciding to be treated as a fixed claim holder or as an equity investor. By assuming that the future evolution of the bond is known with certainty, conventional valuation techniques assume away the *raison d'etre* of the security. Recent advances in the theory of option pricing have enabled us to construct a richer model, one which takes account of future uncertainties.

Our own research, in combination with the work on options by Fischer Black and Myron Scholes, has led to the development of a more realistic means of valuing and analyzing convertible securities.[7] Our model relies on a fundamental principle underlying the Black-Scholes Options Pricing Model: namely, that the expected rate of return on a convertible security should be equal to the expected rate of return on an equivalent risk portfolio consisting of bonds and the company's common stock. Unlike the older certainty models, which are essentially static in nature, our model is a dynamic, continually-adjusting formula which enables the user to determine the effect of changes in several key variables on the value of the convertible.

Our valuation model takes the form of a fairly complicated differential equation, which yields the value of convertible securities only with the aid of a computer. But though the equation itself would probably have little meaning for readers unfamiliar with quantitative methods, a simplified account of what the model says about how convertibles are valued by investors can be compressed into a sentence or two.

The major determinants of a convertible's value are: the coupon rate on the bond (or the preferred dividend); the current level of interest rates

6. Ronald Masulis, 1980, "The Effects of Capital Structure Change on Security Prices: A Study of Exchange Offers," *Journal of Financial Economics*, Vol. 8, pp. 139-178.

7. See Fischer Black and Myron Scholes, "The Pricing of Options and Corporate Liabilities," *Journal of Political Economy*, Volume 81, Number 3 (May-June, 1973); Robert Merton, "The Theory of Rational Option Pricing," *Bell Journal of Economics and Management Science*, Volume 4, Number 1 (Spring 1973); and Michael Brennan and Eduardo Schwartz, "Convertible Bonds: Valuation and Optimal Strategies of Call and Conversion," *Journal of Finance*, Column 32, Number 5 (December, 1977).

(including the company's current yields on straight debt and preferred); the conversion price; the level *and* the volatility of the company's stock price; the dividend yield on the stock; the call provisions; and the maturity of the issue. The general relationships betweeen a convertible's value and the major variables are these: The lower the coupon rate relative to the company's borrowing rates on straight securities, the lower the price of the convertible. The higher the stock price relative to the conversion price, and the greater the volatility of the underlying stock price, the higher the value of the convertible. Also, the lower the call price, and the sooner the call can be exercised, the lower the value. And, finally, the higher the common dividend, the lower the value of the convertible (since higher dividends mean less price appreciation).

There is nothing exceptional about the identification of these determinants, and the direction in which they affect convertible prices. The virtue of our model lies rather in its improved ability to analyze and quantify the effects of changes in these crucial variables on the price of a given security.

For the sake of illustration, consider the example described in Table 2. Given the bond characteristics summarized in this table and the measure of the risk (and volatility) of the company's common stock—and further assuming that both the investor

TABLE 2
BASIC CHARACTERISTICS OF A CONVERTIBLE ISSUE

Financial Markets

Treasury Bill Rate	15%
10 year Government Rate	14.46%

The Issuing Firm

Capitalization	1 million shares of common stock
	No Senior Debt
Stock Price	$44.02
Dividend/Share	$ 2.08

The Convertible Issue

Issue Size	$6 million
Coupon Rate	8%
Conversion Price	$54
Maturity	10 years
Callable after 5 years	
Recovery in Bankruptcy	$2/3$ of par value

TABLE 3
BOND VALUE SENSITIVITY ANALYSIS

	Bond Value	Effect of Change on Bond Value
Basic Characteristics	$ 997	
Non-callable	1032	3.5%
Non-callable, non-convertible	787	−21.1
Stock Price: 10% increase	1045	4.9
Firm Risk: 10% increase	1007	1.0
Coupon Rate: 10% increase	1028	3.2
Conversion Price: 10% decrease	1047	8.0
Call Period Deferred: 1 year increase	1005	0.8
Call Price: 10% increase	1005	0.8

and management follow the optimal conversion and call policies outlined earlier—our model estimates the values of the bond at $997 per $1000 of par value.

In Table 3, the results of a sensitivity analysis show the effect of changes in various parameters and bond characteristics on the value of the bond. For example, removal of the company's right to call the bond should increase its value by 3.5 percent, or $35 per $1000. On the other hand, also removing the conversion privilege, which would make the bond a straight non-callable bond, would reduce its value by 21.1 percent.

Note the relative insensitivity of the bond's value to the risk of the firm. In this case, a 10 percent increase in risk actually results in a 1 percent increase in the value of the convertible. This supports the rationale for convertibles we offered above: they are likely to be especially attractive to an issuing company which is perceived as more risky by the market than by management. Such a company would be burdened by a penalty coupon rate on a straight bond issue, whereas it may actually benefit from the higher risk perceived by the market if it issues a convertible.

Table 3 also contains the kind of information which would be most valuable to an issuer in designing a convertible, because it enables management to determine the relative costs and benefits of various improvements and concessions in the basic terms of the issue. For example, a 6.4 percent reduction in the conversion price from $54 to $50.54 could be granted in return for a 10 percent reduction (6.4% × 5.0/3.2) in the coupon rate. As the variety of possible bond contracts continues to increase, effective analysis of the alternative possibilities demands a valuation model of this type.

CONCLUSION

1. We have shown the fallacy in the conventional argument that convertibles are a cheap source of funds. That convertibles allow companies to borrow at below market rates and to sell stock at premiums over the present price does not mean that they provide cost advantages to the issuer. The real opportunity cost of convertible debt, reflecting its hybrid character, should be thought of as a weighted average of the company's cost of straight debt and the considerably higher cost associated with the conversion or equity option.

2. The most plausible rationale for the continuing popularity of convertbles lies in their insensitivity to company risk. This allows them to be issued on terms that look fair to management, even when the market rates the risk of the issuer higher than does management of the issuing company.

This rationale receives strong support from the available evidence. Companies issuing convertible bonds tend to be characterized by higher market and earnings variability, higher business and/or financial risk, stronger growth-orientations, and shorter corporate histories than their straight debt counterparts. Such companies stand to benefit most from convertible financing.

3. Although our theory suggests that management should force conversion of convertibles soon after the value of the security rises above the call price, companies tend to delay calling their convertibles well beyond this point. We surmise that this may be due to management's misguided preoccupation with reported earnings-per-share.

4. When a convertible call is announced, the company's stock price tends to drop. Although a tax-based explanation of this market response has been offered, we favor the "information" hypothesis suggesting that convertible calls are interpreted by the market as management's effort to clean up the balance sheet in the face of impending difficulties.

5. We offer a brief introduction to the Brennan-Schwartz valuation model for pricing convertible securities. By incorporating some of the insights of the Black-Scholes Option Pricing Model, the model represents a significant advance over the older static models of convertible pricing.

THE ORIGIN OF LYONs: A CASE STUDY IN FINANCIAL INNOVATION

by John J. McConnell,
Purdue University, and
Eduardo S. Schwartz,
University of California at Los Angeles

Viewed at a distance and with scholarly detachment, financial innovation is a simple process. Some kind of "shock"—say, a sudden increase in interest rate volatility or a significant regulatory change—is introduced into the economic system. The shock alters the preferences of either investors or issuers in such a way that there then exists no financial instrument capable of satisfying a newly-created demand. Observing the unsatisfied demand, an entrepreneur moves quickly to seize the opportunity by creating a new financial instrument. In the process, the entrepreneur reaps an economic reward for his efforts, investors and issuers are better served, and the entire economic system is improved.

On closer inspection, however, the actual process of financial innovation turns out, like most other human endeavors, to be a lot less tidy than economists' models would have it. In this article, we provide an "up-close" view of the origin and evolution of one financial instrument—the Liquid Yield Option Note (LYON).

The LYON is a highly successful financial product introduced by Merrill Lynch in 1985. Between April 1985 and December 1991, Merrill Lynch served as the underwriter for 43 separate LYON issues, which together raised a total of $11.7 billion for corporate clients. LYON issuers include such well-known firms as American Airlines, Eastman Kodak, Marriott Corporation, and Motorola. In 1989, other underwriters entered the market and have since brought an additional 13 LYON-like issues to market. In the words of a recent *Wall Street Journal* article, the LYON is "one of Wall Street's hottest and most lucrative corporate finance products."[1]

As academics examining a new security, we begin by posing the questions: What does the LYON provide that was not available previously? Does the LYON really increase the welfare of investors and issuers, or is it simply a "neutral mutation"—that is, a now accepted practice that serves no enduring economic purpose, but is sufficiently harmless to avoid being extinguished by competitive forces?[2]

In the spirit of full disclosure, however, we must admit that we are not entirely disinterested observers. Our association with the LYON is longstanding. When the early LYON issues were being brought to market in April 1985, questions arose about LYON pricing. We were hired by Merrill Lynch to develop a model for analyzing and pricing this new financial instrument. A by-product of this assignment was the opportunity to learn about the train of events that led to the creation of the LYON, and we have since followed the evolution of this market with interest. In the pages that follow, we relate what we have observed, thought, and contributed during the development of this new security.

WHAT IS A LYON?

The LYON is a complex security. It is a *zero coupon, convertible, callable, and puttable* bond. None of these four features is new, it is only their combination that makes the LYON an innovation. These general features of the instrument are perhaps best illustrated by considering a specific issue. Because it was the first one, we consider the LYON issued by Waste Management, Inc. on April 12, 1985.

According to the indenture agreement, each Waste Management LYON has a face value of $1,000

---

1. Randall Smith, "Tax Status of LYONs, One of Street's Hottest Products, Gets IRS Challenge," Dec. 17, 1991, p. C1.

2. Merton H. Miller introduced this Darwinian metaphor in "Debt and Taxes," *Journal of Finance* (May 1977), p. 273.

and matures on January 21, 2001. There are, by definition, no coupon interest payments. If the security is not called, converted, or redeemed (i.e., put to the issuer) prior to that date, and if the issuer does not default, the investor will receive $1,000 per bond. If this turns out to be the case, moreover, and based on an initial offering price of $250 per bond, the investor will receive an effective yield-to-maturity of 9%.

The Investor's Conversion Option. At any time prior to maturity (or on the maturity date), the investor may convert the bond into 4.36 shares of Waste Management common stock. Given a stock price of about $52 at the time of issue, this conversion ratio would appear to indicate an initial conversion "premium" of about 10% ($250/4.36 = $57.34). But, because the LYON is a *zero coupon* convertible and thus issued at a large discount from par value, the conversion "premium" is not fixed. That is, as we discuss in more detail later, the minimum share price at which holders would willingly exchange their bonds for 4.36 shares effectively increases throughout most of the life of the bond.

The Investor's Put Option. Although not entirely new, the most unfamiliar feature of the LYON is the right it gives investors to put the bond to Waste Management beginning on June 30, 1988, and on each subsequent anniversary date, at pre-determined exercise prices that increase through time, as shown below:

Date	Put Price	Implied Yield	Date	Put Price	Implied Yield
6/30/88	$301.87	6 %	6/30/95	$613.04	9 %
6/30/89	333.51	7	6/30/96	669.45	9
6/30/90	375.58	8	6/30/97	731.06	9
6/30/91	431.08	9	6/30/98	798.34	9
6/30/92	470.75	9	6/30/99	871.80	9
6/30/93	514.07	9	6/30/00	952.03	9
6/30/94	561.38	9			

Based on the issue price of $250.00 per bond, this schedule of put exercise prices provides investors with a minimum 6% rate of return at the date of first exercise, rising in three 1% increments to a level of 9% over the next three years.

The Issuer's Call Option. Finally, Waste Management has the right to call the LYON at fixed exercise prices that also increase through time. Although the issuer may call the LYON immediately after issuance, the investor does receive some call protection because Waste Management may not call the bond prior to June 30, 1987 unless the price of the Waste Management common stock rises above $86.01. The schedule of call prices is as shown below:[3]

Date	Call Price	Date	Call Price
Issuance	$272.50	6/30/94	$563.63
6/30/86	297.83	6/30/95	613.04
6/30/87	321.13	6/30/96	669.45
6/30/88	346.77	6/30/97	731.06
6/30/89	374.99	6/30/98	798.34
6/30/90	406.00	6/30/99	871.80
6/30/91	440.08	6/30/00	952.03
6/30/92	477.50	Maturity	1,000.00
6/30/93	518.57		

As in the case of convertibles generally, investors may respond to the call by choosing either to accept redemption payment from the issuer or convert their bonds into stock.

As mentioned earlier, although the LYON is a complex security, it is not entirely new. Callable convertible bonds certainly existed prior to the LYON, as did zero coupon bonds. And so did put and call options on a wide array of common stocks. What demand, then, did the LYON fulfill that was not being adequately met by an already existing financial instrument?

THE SEEDS OF THE IDEA

To address that question, it is useful to trace the history of the LYON. This history begins with Merrill Lynch and Mr. Lee Cole. During the mid-1980s, Merrill Lynch was the largest broker of equity options for retail (that is, non-institutional) investors. During that period, owing to the success of its Cash Management Accounts (CMAs), Merrill Lynch was also the largest manager of individual money market accounts. Individuals had over $200 billion invested in CMAs. CMAs are funds invested essentially in short-term government securities and, for this reason, are subject to little interest rate risk and virtually no default risk.

---

3. The imputed interest is computed by increasing the call prices at a rate of 9.0% per year compounded semiannually. If the LYON is called between the dates shown above, the call price is adjusted to reflect the "interest" accrued since the immediately preceding call date shown in the schedule.

During 1983, Lee Cole was Options Marketing Manager at Merrill Lynch. Cole discerned (or, more aptly, divined) a pattern in the transactions of individual retail customers. As Options Marketing Manager, Cole observed that individuals' primary activity in the options market was to buy calls on common stocks. The most active calls had a maximum term to maturity of 90 days and often expired unexercised. Viewed in isolation, this strategy appeared to be very risky.

In reviewing customers consolidated accounts, however, Cole observed that many options customers also maintained large balances in their CMA accounts while making few direct equity investments. From these observations, Cole deduced a portfolio strategy: Individuals (or at least some individuals) were willing to risk a fraction of their funds in highly volatile options as long as the bulk of their funds were largely safe from risk in their CMA accounts. They also avoided direct equity investment. He leaped to the further inference that funds used to buy options came largely from the interest earned on CMA accounts. In short, individuals were willing to risk all or a fraction of the interest income from their CMAs in the options market so long as their principal remained intact in their CMA account.

With these observations and deductions in hand, Cole drafted a memorandum describing in general terms a corporate security that would appeal to this segment of the retail customer market. In drafting his memo, Cole's intent was to design a security that would allow corporations to tap a sector of the retail market whose funds were currently invested in government securities and options. The security described therein eventually turned into the LYON. Because it is convertible into the stock of the issuer, the LYON effectively incorporates the call option component of the portfolio strategy perceived by Cole. Because of the put option, the investor is assured his principal can be recovered by putting the bond back to the issuer at pre-specified exercise prices. The LYON thus approximates the features of the trading strategy as perceived by Cole.

If Cole's theory were correct, the LYON would be a desirable security for individual investors and would give corporation issuers access to an untapped sector of the retail market. As with most theories, however, Cole's rested upon a number of unproven assumptions. The ultimate question, of course, was whether the security would pass the market test.

THE SEARCH FOR THE IDEAL ISSUER

It takes two sides to make a market. And while Cole had identified what he perceived to be a demand by investors, that demand could not be satisfied by every issuer. The ideal issuer would have to satisfy at least two, and perhaps three, criteria: First, because of the put feature and the downside protection desired by investors, issuers would have to have an investment-grade bond rating—and the higher the rating the better. At the same time, however, the issuer's equity would have to exhibit substantial volatility, otherwise the security would not provide the "play" desired by option investors. These two features were critical. Because the initial target market for the security was to be individuals, a third highly desirable characteristic of the issuer would be broad name recognition.

Beginning in mid-1984, the investment banking department of Merrill Lynch began the search for the first LYON issuer. That task turned out not to be a simple one. First, the population of candidates was obviously limited to those firms that needed to raise funds. Second, every issuer, even those issuing already tried and true securities, is anxious about the possibility that an issue might "fail." That anxiety is compounded when a new instrument is proposed—especially one as complex as the LYON. Third, because investment-grade credit ratings tend to be assigned firms with less volatile earnings (and thus, presumably, less volatile stock prices), the subset of companies with investment-grade ratings and volatile stock prices is a fairly small one.

After repeated presentations to a variety of potential issuers and after repeated rejections, Waste Management, Inc. expressed an interest in the security and authorized Chuck Lewis and Thomas Patrick, the Merrill Lynch representatives, to move forward with a proposal. Furthermore, Waste Management exhibited most (perhaps all) of the requisite characteristics of the ideal issuer. Its debt was rated Aa. In terms of volatility, the annual variance of its common stock of 30% placed it in the top half of all NYSE stocks. The only question was whether Waste Management had sufficient name recognition to attract Merrill Lynch's retail customers.

Its stock was traded on the NYSE and it operated in communities throughout the country. It specialized in the disposal of industrial and household waste; but it was not necessarily a well-known consumer product. The Waste Management name

Over time, the fraction of LYONs purchased by retail customers has averaged roughly
50%. Furthermore, the zero coupon, puttable, convertible bond apparently has
staying power. Of the total proceeds raised through convertible bonds during 1991,
roughly half were zero coupon, puttable convertibles.

was by then a familiar one, however, to the extensive Merrill Lynch brokerage network. Over the period 1972 through 1985, Merrill Lynch had managed four separate new equity issues for Waste Management, a number of secondary equity issues, and nine issues of industrial revenue bonds. All of these raised the broker and customer awareness of the company.

Over the same 1972-1985 time period, Merrill Lynch had also arranged a private placement of $50 million in debt for Waste Management and had represented the company in two hostile takeovers. This working relationship may have been the key factor necessary to overcome "first-issuer anxiety."

In any event, Merrill Lynch finally brought the first LYON to market in April 1985, roughly two years after Lee Cole drafted his outline memorandum. The issue sold out quickly and Cole turned out to be at least partly right. In the case of a traditional convertible bond issue, roughly 90% of the issue is typically purchased by institutional investors with only a tiny fraction taken by retail customers. In the case of the first LYON, approximately 40% was purchased by individual investors. Apparently Merrill Lynch had designed a corporate convertible that appealed to an otherwise untapped sector of the market.

And the appeal of the LYON to the retail sector of the market has persisted. For example, Euro Disney raised $965 million with a LYON issue in June 1990. Of that issue, 60% was purchased by individual investors and 40% by institutions. Individuals accounted for over 45,000 separate orders. Over time, the fraction of LYONs purchased by retail customers has varied from issue to issue, but has averaged roughly 50% of the total. Furthermore, the zero coupon, puttable, convertible bond apparently has staying power. Of the total proceeds raised through convertible bonds during 1991, roughly half were zero coupon, puttable convertibles.

Merrill Lynch, moreover, as the entrepreneurial source of this successful innovation, has profited handsomely from the LYON. In the case of the typical convertible bond, the underwriter's spread is about 1.7% of the dollar amount of funds raised. For the earliest LYONs, the spread was 3% and, at the present time, continues to be about 2.5% of the amount of funds raised. Additionally, Merrill Lynch

was able to "corner" the market for almost five years before other investment bankers brought LYON-like securities to market. According to the *Wall Street Journal* article cited earlier, since 1985 Merrill Lynch has earned some $248 million from sale of LYONs.

THE CASE FOR CONVERTIBLES
(Or, Financing Synergies From
Combining Debt with Call Options)

But this brings us to the obvious question: What was the source of the gains to issuers and investors from the LYON that would allow Merrill Lynch to earn such large rewards?

Because the LYON is a variant of the convertible, let's begin by revisiting the "case for convertibles" made by Michael Brennan and Eduardo Schwartz in an article published in 1981.[4] The popular argument for convertible bonds is that they provide "cheap debt" (that is, they carry coupon rates below those on straight debt) and allow companies to sell stock "at a premium" relative to the current market price. But, as Brennan and Schwartz demonstrate, this reasoning conceals a logical sleight of hand: It effectively compares convertibles with a debt issue under one set of circumstances (when the firm's stock price doesn't rise and there is no conversion) and with a stock issue under another (the stock price rises and the issue converts). What it fails to point out is that the convertible issuer would have been better off issuing stock in the first set of circumstances and straight debt in the second. In short, convertibles do not provide the average issuer with a financing "bargain."

After exposing this popular fallacy, Brennan and Schwartz go on to argue that the real source of convertibles' effectiveness is that *their value is relatively insensitive to the risk of the issuing company.* Increases in company risk reduce the value of the bond portion of a convertible, but at the same time increase the value of the built-in option (by increasing the volatility of the stock price). Because of this risk-neutralizing effect, convertibles are useful in resolving disagreements (arising from what academics refer to as "information asymmetries") between management and would-be investors about the risk

4. Michael Brennan and Eduardo Schwartz, "The Case for Convertibles," *Chase Financial Quarterly*, Vol. 1 No. 3 (Fall 1981). Reprinted in *Journal of Applied Corporate Finance*, Vol. 1 No. 2 (Summer 1988). This article extends insights about the role of convertibles formulated earlier by Michael C. Jensen and William H.

Meckling, "Theory of the Firm: Managerial Behavior, Agency Costs, and Capital Structure," *Journal of Financial Economics* (1976), pp. 305-360. See also Clifford W. Smith and Jerold B. Warner, "On Financial Contracting: An Analysis of Bond Covenants," *Journal of Financial Economics*, 7 (1979), pp. 117-161.

of a company's operations. And it is largely for this reason that the use of convertibles tends to be concentrated among relatively smaller, high-growth companies with volatile earnings—the kind of companies, in short, that ordinary fixed-income investors shy away from. Convertibles are also well-suited to such issuers because the lower current interest payments reduce the risk of financial distress, which is likely to be especially disruptive for companies on a high-growth track.

Convertibles are also effective in cases where management has significant opportunity to increase the risk of the firm's activities. When such risk-shifting is a real possibility, the firm will be required to pay an especially high premium to issue straight debt, far more than management believes is warranted given its true intentions for the company. Convertible debt, because it can be exchanged for common stock, provides the bondholder with built-in insurance against such risk-shifting behavior.

But what has all this to do with the LYON—which, after all, is intended for investment-grade companies? To the extent the equity values of LYON issuers are more volatile than those of other investment-grade issuers, LYON issuers also presumably benefit from this risk-neutralizing effect that comes from combining debt with options.

To have succeeded in the manner it has, the LYON must also provide benefits that go well beyond those of conventional convertibles. The success of the LYON, as suggested earlier, has much to do with Merrill Lynch's ability to design a convertible that would appeal to individual investors.

RETAILING CONVERTIBLES
(Or, the Value of the Put Option)

Lee Cole was apparently correct in his assessment that there was a latent demand among retail investors for a convertible-like payoff structure—one combining, in the case of the LYON, a *zero-coupon*, fixed-income component with an equity call option. By offering what amounts to a continuous option position, such a convertible would have the added appeal to investors of potentially large transactions costs savings. Recall that, under the call-option-cum-CMA strategy perceived by Cole, investors were purchasing a series of calls that expire at

90-day (or shorter) intervals, thereby incurring commission costs at least four times a year.[5] By buying and holding a newly issued LYON, the retail investor could maintain continuous ownership of an option position over the life of the bond without paying any brokerage fees.

But, to allow retail investors to take advantage of these long-dated, low-transaction-cost options, Cole realized the new security would have to be designed to overcome retail investors' normal resistance to convertibles. This could be accomplished, in part, by choosing only issuers with investment-grade bond ratings and with "name-recognition." But, to reduce the principal risk to levels acceptable to retail investors, the new security would also have to include a stronger, contractual assurance.

Hence the put option. By giving investors the right to put the notes back to the company after three years (and at one-year intervals thereafter), the Waste Management LYON greatly reduced the exposure of investors' principal to a sharp increase in interest rates as well a drop in the issuer's credit standing. In so doing, it dramatically increased the value of the security. (As we show later, the put option accounted for almost 20% of the value of the Waste Management LYON at the time of issue.)

Of course, granting investors such an option could turn out to be costly to the LYON issuer. A jump in rates or fall in operating cash flows could force the company to retire the bonds at the worst possible time. For this reason, LYONs issuers are likely to "self-select" in the following sense: Among companies with sufficient market volatility to provide LYONs investors with the desired option "play," LYONs issuers will also tend to be those with greatest confidence in the ability of their operations to weather a sharp rate increase, and the need to raise new capital under those conditions.

In short, ideal LYONs issuers are companies for which the benefit of granting the put option (and thereby gaining a retail following) most outweighs the expected cost of having to deliver on that option.

A Retail Clientele Effect?

But this brings us back to the alleged benefits of appealing to a retail clientele. Generally speaking, the "modern theory" of finance has offered little

---

5. Traded equity options are available with maturities as long as 270 days, but such options are much less liquid than their 90-day counterparts.

> The popular argument for convertible bonds conceals a logical sleight of hand: It compares convertibles with a debt issue when the stock price fails to go up and with a stock issue when the price goes up. What it fails to point out is that the convertible issuer would have been better off issuing stock in the first set of circumstances and straight debt in the second.

encouragement to explanations of securities designed for specific kinds of investors. But there are notable exceptions. Robert Merton, in his 1987 Presidential Address to the American Finance Association, developed a model of asset pricing in which the size of the firm's investor base is an important determinant of the price of the firm's securities.[6] Starting from the assumption that investors invest only in a limited set of securities about which they have information, Merton's proposed model suggests that securities markets may effectively be "segmented"—that is, companies lacking retail investors may be selling at a sharp "information discount" relative to their retail-owned counterparts. To the extent such segmentation exists—and this is still a matter of sharp contention—management actions that expand the firm's investor base would increase the firm's value.

Moreover, a recent study by Greg Kadlec and John McConnell provides empirical support for the predictions of Merton's model.[7] Their study reports that the prices of stocks newly listed on the NYSE during the 1980s increased in value by 5% to 6% at the time of listing. Also suggestive, this increase in value is significantly correlated with the increase in the *number of investors* in the firm's stock from the year before to the year after listing. In sum, if we extend Merton's argument and this supporting evidence to the case of the LYON, it is plausible that the LYON's extension of convertibles to a previously untapped sector of the market could be providing significant value for issuers.

The Appeal to Institutional Investors

But what about institutional investors? Why would they "pay up" for a convertible with a put option relative to an otherwise identical convertible bond without one? To this question, our answer is again tentative and follows from the form of potential payoffs under the LYON.

During the mid-1980s, portfolio insurance began to flourish as a popular tool for portfolio managers.

The general objective of portfolio insurance is to provide upside potential while limiting downside risk. And that is essentially the payoff pattern presented by the LYON. If the underlying stock price increases, the value of the LYON increases accordingly. If the stock price falls or interest rates increase, the LYON holder is protected by the floor provided by the put exercise price.

To the extent some institutional investors are willing to "pay" for portfolio insurance, then those investors might also be willing to pay a slight premium for the "insurance" provided by the LYON. Over time, however, as more LYON-like securities are brought to market, and as more investment bankers produce competing products, the spread commanded by underwriters should decline. In the meantime, Merrill would have earned its "reward."

ENTER THE MODEL BUILDERS

It was only after the Waste Management LYON had been brought to market successfully that Merrill Lynch asked us to build a model to value the security. Why the need for a model? The answer has as much to do with marketing as with the need of traders and issuers to analyze and price the security. The answer is also reassuring to those like us who view modern finance theory as a powerful, but practical, scientific discipline with important implications for corporate managers and investors.[8]

Following the issuance of the Waste Management LYON, Merrill Lynch intensified its effort to bring additional issues to market, both to increase the liquidity of the market for the security and to demonstrate that the security was not just a passing curiosity.[9] Following the success of the first LYON, other potential issuers showed more interest, but also asked more questions.

Three questions typically came up: First, what was a "fair" price for a specific LYON given the characteristics of the company and security in question?[10] Second, how would the security react under different market conditions? Third, under what

6. See Robert Merton, "A Simple Model of Capital Market Equilibrium with Incomplete Information," *Journal of Finance*, Vol. 42 (July 1987).

7. Greg Kadlec and John J. McConnell, "The Effect of Market Segmentation and Illiquidity on Asset Prices: Evidence from Exchange Listings," unpublished manuscript, Krannert School of Management, Purdue University (1992).

8. The model can also be used to determine the appropriate LYON hedge ratio.

9. It goes without saying that generating a fee for bringing the security to market was also an important consideration, but to continue generating fees from LYON issues it was necessary to demonstrate the continued viability of the security.

10. Interest in this question was motivated, at least in part, by critics who used a crude option pricing model to argue (to potential issuers) that the Waste Management LYON was underpriced by roughly 30%. The likely cause of such underpricing, as this article goes on to explain, was its failure to take account of the interaction of the values of the various components of the LYON.

conditions would investors elect to convert the security to common stock? This last question was asked by managers concerned about the dilutive effect of conversion on the company's EPS.

Pricing the LYON

The model we developed to answer those questions is based on the Brennan-Schwartz (1977) model for analyzing convertible bonds—which is based in turn upon the classic Black-Scholes (1973) option pricing model.[11] Interestingly, with some minor modifications, this model is still used by Merrill Lynch to analyze LYONs today.

Given the similarity between a LYON and an call-option-cum-CMA strategy, the great temptation in developing a model to analyze this security is simply to sum the value of the components: to add the values of the put and call options to that of a zero-coupon (callable) bond issued by the same firm. The problem with such an approach, however, is that it ignores the *interactions* between these values. For example, both the issuer's call option and the investor's conversion rights reduce the value of the put option (by reducing the expected maturity of the put). The value of the conversion option is similarly reduced by the issuer's call option and the put option, both of which reduce the probability of eventual conversion. Because of these interactions, the value of the LYON depends both on the conversion and redemption strategies followed by the investor and the call strategy followed by the issuer.

Our model makes the by-now standard assumptions of the option pricing literature that the investor follows conversion and redemption strategies that maximize the value of the security, while the issuer adheres to a call strategy that minimizes the security's value.[12] These assumptions, coupled with the assumptions that the value of the LYON depends upon the issuer's stock price and that securities are all priced to eliminate arbitrage profits, yield a fairly complicated differential equation for valuing and analyzing the LYON. Despite its complicated appearance, the equation can be solved numerically on a personal computer in a few minutes.

The "intuition" underlying the model is this: The higher the general level of interest rates, the lower the value of the LYON; the higher the volatility and the level of the issuer's stock price, the greater the value of the LYON; the lower the LYON call price and the sooner the call can be exercised, the lower the value of the LYON; the higher the dividend on the issuer's stock, the lower the value of the LYON (since higher dividends imply less stock price appreciation and less chance of conversion); and, of course, the higher the put exercise prices, the higher the value of the LYON.

For purposes of illustration, consider the Waste Management LYON described earlier. The table below presents the basic market characteristics, the characteristics of the firm, and the features of the bond as of the issue date. Given these characteristics, our model predicted that the market value of the bond as of the issue date should be $262.70. In fact, at the close of the first day of trading, the bond's price was $258.75. We tracked the bond over the next 30 days and determined that the model's predicted prices closely tracked the actual closing prices, but were typically slightly above the closing price. Apparently, the model has a slight upward bias in valuing the LYON.

Interest rate of intermediate term bond	11.21%
Stock price	$52.25
Stock price volatility	30.0%
Dividend yield	1.6%
LYON maturity	15 years
Face value	$1,000/bond
Conversion ratio	4.36 shares/bond
Call prices	In text
Put prices	In text

Sensitivity Analysis

In the following table, we show the effects of changes in market conditions, the issuing company, and feaures of the security on the value of Waste Management's LYON. There are a number of interesting insights from this "sensitivity analysis." The value of the Waste Management LYON is highly

11. For the formulation of the Black-Scholes option pricing model, see Fischer Black and Myron Scholes, "The Pricing Options and Corporate Liabilities," *Journal of Political Economy*, Vol. 81, No. 3 (May-June 1973). For the extension of that model to the valuation of convertible bonds, see Michael Brennan and Eduardo Schwartz, "Convertible Bonds: Valuation and Optimal Strategies for Call and Conversion," *Journal of Finance*, Vol. 32, No. 5 (December 1977).

12. This discussion draws heavily on our article "LYON Taming," *Journal of Finance* (July 1986). Whether investors and issuers follow these strategies is an issue of some contention. For a discussion of this controversy see Michael Brennan and Eduardo Schwartz, "Convertible Securities," *Palgrave Dictionary of Accounting and Finance* (MacMillan, 1992).

Given the features of the bond, the characteristics of the firm, and market conditions as of the issue date, our model predicted that the market value of the bond as of the issue date should be $262.70. In fact, at the close of the first day of trading, the bond's price was $258.75.

insensitive to interest rate changes (a 200 basis point increase in yields would cause less than a 4% decline in the value of the LYON). But this insensitivity to rates is caused by the put option, which our analysis indicates accounts for almost 20% of the security's value. That is, *without* the put option, the LYON's value would be reduced from roughly $260 to under $215 per bond. At the same time, however, the *issuer's* call option reduces the value of the LYON by roughly $20 per bond (or 8% of its total value). It does so, as mentioned, by reducing both the probability of the investor exercising his conversion rights and the likely length of time that option is allowed to remain outstanding.

	Bond Value	Effect of Change on Bond Value
Basic features	$262.70	
Stock price to $56.00	271.68	+8.98
Stock price volatility to 40.00%	271.89	+9.19
Dividend yield to 3.0%	260.78	-1.92
Interest rate to 13.21%	252.38	-10.32
Without call	283.29	20.59
Without put	215.04	-47.66

The Question of Conversion

As noted, one question of frequent concern to LYON issuers is the stock price at which investors will choose to convert the bond to stock. In deciding whether to convert, the investor weighs the value of dividends forgone by holding the LYON against the downside protection provided by the put. Thus, if the dividend yield is relatively low, the benefits of conversion (to obtain the dividend) are also relatively low. But, even for low-dividend paying stocks, if the stock price rises high enough, it will be so far above the put price that the protection provided by the investor's put option becomes negligible.

Our model assumes the critical conversion stock price is the price at which the investor becomes indifferent between holding the LYON and converting to common stock. As illustrated in the next table, the critical conversion stock price for the Waste

Management LYON changes throughout its life, increasing steadily throughout the first 13 years, and declining sharply thereafter. There are two opposite effects driving these changes—one that is present in all convertibles and one that is unique for the LYON. As in the case of a conventional, current-coupon convertible, the optimal conversion price of the LYON is reduced because the value of the conversion option is shrinking along with the remaining time to maturity. But, unlike conventional convertibles, the conversion price in the case of the LYON is also *increased* through time by the fact that the redemption price increases while the conversion ratio remains constant (4.36 shares per bond)—which, of course, reduces the value of the conversion option. In all but the last two years, the latter effect dominates the former.

Date	Conversion Stock Price	Date	Conversion Stock Price
Issue	$129.50	6/30/93	$273.00
6/30/85	132.00	6/30/94	287.00
6/30/86	145.50	6/30/95	301.50
6/30/87	158.50	6/30/96	316.00
6/30/88	173.50	6/30/97	329.50
6/30/89	194.50	6/30/98	339.00
6/30/90	217.00	6/30/99	340.00
6/30/91	238.50	6/30/00	317.50
6/30/92	257.00	1/21/01	229.36

IN CLOSING

It is difficult to generalize from a single observation—and the Liquid Yield Option Note is just one of many successful financial innovations of the 1980s. The case history of the LYON does illustrate, however, that successful financial innovation requires ingenuity, perseverance, and, perhaps, a measure of good fortune. It also illustrates the potential practical power of modern financial theory in assisting in the development of new financial products and strategies. As practitioners of the science of modern finance, we were fortunate enough to be present at the creation of what now appears to be a successful financial innovation.

THE USES OF HYBRID DEBT IN MANAGING CORPORATE RISK

by Charles W. Smithson,
Chase Manhattan Bank, and
Donald H. Chew, Jr.,
Stern Stewart & Co.

T he corporate use of hybrid debt securities—those that combine a conventional debt issue with a "derivative" such as a forward, swap, or option—increased significantly during the 1980s. And, while many of the more esoteric or tax-driven securities introduced in the last decade have disappeared, corporate hybrids now seem to be flourishing. In so doing, they are helping U.S. companies raise capital despite the restrictive financing climate of the '90s.

Hybrid debt, to be sure, is not a new concept. Convertible bonds, first issued by the Erie Railroad in the 1850s, are hybrid securities that combine straight debt and options on the value of the issuer's equity.[1] What is distinctive about the hybrid debt instruments of the 1980s is that their payoffs, instead of being tied to the issuing company's stock price, are linked to a growing variety of *general* economic variables. As illustrated in Figure 1, corporate hybrids have appeared that index investor returns to exchange rates, interest rates, stock market indices, and the prices of commodities such as oil, copper, and natural gas.

The recent wave of corporate hybrids began in 1973, when PEMEX, the state-owned Mexican oil producer, issued bonds that incorporated a *forward contract* on a commodity (in this case, oil). In 1980, Sunshine Mining Co. went a step further by issuing bonds incorporating a commodity *option* (on silver). In 1988, Magma Copper made yet another advance by issuing a bond giving investors a *series of commodity options* (on copper)—in effect, one for every coupon payment.

Other new hybrids, as mentioned, have had their payoffs tied to interest rates, foreign exchange rates, and the behavior of the stock market. In 1981, Oppenheimer & Co., a securities brokerage firm, issued a security whose principal repayment is indexed to the volume of trading on the New York Stock Exchange. Notes indexed to the value of equity indexes appeared in 1986, and inflation-indexed notes (tied to the CPI) were introduced in 1988.

---

1. The date for the introduction of convertible bonds is reported by Peter Tufano in "Financial Innovation and First-Mover Advantages," *Journal of Financial Economics*, 25, pp. 213-240.

FIGURE 1 ■ DEVELOPMENT OF HYBRID SECURITIES: 1973-1991

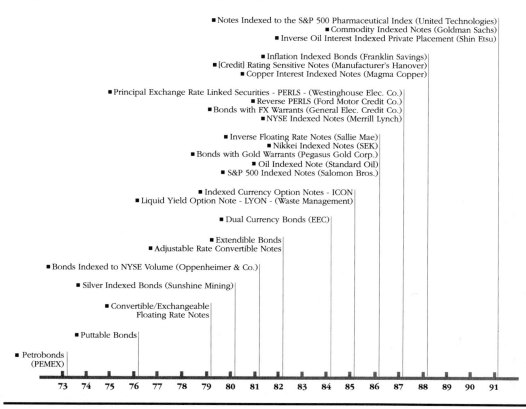

The 1980s also saw new hybrids with payoffs that, like those of convertibles, are tied to company-specific performance. For example, the Rating Sensitive Notes issued by Manufacturer's Hanover in 1988 provide for increased payments to investors if Manny Hanny's creditworthiness declines. And the LYON™ pioneered and underwritten by Merrill Lynch in 1985 grants investors not only the option to convert the debt into equity, but also the right to "put" the security back to the firm.

The pace of hybrid innovation peaked around 1987. But hybrids are now staging a comeback. As the title of a recent *Wall Street Journal* article put it, 1991 was "A Boom Year for Newfangled Trading Vehicles."[2] The past year witnessed the introduction of notes indexed to a subset of a general equity index, Goldman Sachs' notes indexed to a commodity index, private placements incorporating options on commodities, and a boom in convertible debt.

Why do companies issue, and investors buy, such complex securities? Before the development of derivative products in the 1970s, investors may have been attracted by the prospect of purchasing a "bundle" of securities—say, debt plus warrants—that they could not duplicate themselves by purchasing both of the components separately. And this "scarce security" or "market completion" argument also holds for some of today's debt hybrids (especially those that provide longer-dated forwards and options than those available on organized exchanges).

---

2. December 26, 1991, p. C1. The *Journal* article dealt more with exchange-traded products than with hybrids.

LYON™ is a trademark of Merrill Lynch & Co.

But, because active exchanges now provide low-cost futures and options with payoffs tied to all variety of interest rates, exchange rates, and commodity prices, markets are becoming increasingly "complete," if you will. Given the existence of well-functioning, low-cost markets for many of the components making up the hybrid debt instruments, we have to ask the following question: Is there any reason investors should be willing to pay more for these securities sold *in combination* rather than separately?

In this article, we argue that hybrid debt offers corporate treasurers an efficient means of managing a variety of financial and operating risks—risks that, in many cases, cannot be managed if the firm issues straight debt and then purchases derivatives. By hedging such risks and thereby increasing the expected stability of corporate cash flows, hybrids may lower the issuer's overall funding costs.[3] At the same time, though, part of the present corporate preference for managing price risks with hybrids rather than derivative products stems from current restrictions on the use of hedge accounting for derivatives, as well as tax and regulatory arbitrage opportunities afforded by hybrids.

PRICE VOLATILITY: THE NECESSARY CONDITION FOR HYBRIDS

The stability of the economic and financial environment is a key determinant of the kinds of debt instruments that dominate the marketplace. When prices are stable and predictable, investors will demand—and the capital markets will produce—relatively simple instruments.

In the late 1800s, for example, the dominant financial instrument in Great Britain was the *consol*: a bond with a fixed interest rate and no maturity— it lasted forever. Investors were content to hold infinite-lived British government bonds because British sovereign credit was good and because inflation was virtually unknown. General confidence in price level stability led to stable interest rates, which in turn dictated the use of long-lived, fixed-rate bonds.

But consider what happens to financing practices when confidence is replaced by turbulence and uncertainty. As one of us pointed out in an earlier issue of this journal, in 1863 the Confederate States of America issued a 20-year bond denominated not in Confederate dollars, but in French Francs and Pounds Sterling. To allay the concern of its overseas investors that the Confederacy would not be around to service its debt with hard currency, the issue was also convertible at the option of the holder into cotton at the rate of six pence per pound. In the parlance of today's investment banker, the Confederate States issued a *dual-currency, cotton-indexed* bond.[4]

The Breakdown of Bretton Woods and the New Era of Volatility

Throughout the 1950s and most of the 1960s, economic and price stability prevailed in the U.S., and in the developed nations generally. Investment-grade U.S. corporations responded predictably by raising capital in the form of 30-year, fixed-rate bonds (yielding around 3-4%). But, toward the end of the '60s, rates of inflation in the U.S. and U.K. began to increase. There was also considerable divergence among developed countries in monetary and fiscal policy, and thus in rates of inflation. Such pressures led inevitably to the abandonment, in 1973, of the Bretton Woods agreement to maintain relatively fixed exchanged rates. And, during the early 1970s and thereafter, the general economic environment saw higher and more volatile rates of inflation along with unprecedented volatility in exchange rates, interest rates, and commodity prices. (For evidence of such general price volatility, see Figure 2.)

In response to this heightened price volatility, capital markets created new financial instruments to help investors and issuers manage their exposures. Indeed, the last 20 years has seen the introduction of (1) futures on foreign exchange, interest rates, metals, and oil; (2) currency, interest rate, and commodity swaps; (3) options on exchange rates, interest rates, and oil; and (4) options on the above futures and options. Flourishing markets for these products in turn helped give rise to corporate hybrid debt securities that effectively incorporate these derivative products.

---

3. For preliminary evidence of the impact of issuing hybrid debt on the firm's cost of capital, see Charles Smithson and Leah Schraudenbach, "Reflection of Financial Price Risk in the Firm's Share Price," Chase Manhattan Bank, 1992.

4. Waite Rawls and Charles Smithson, "The Evolution of Risk Management Products," *Journal of Applied Corporate Finance*, Vol. 1 No. 4 (1989).

In return for being granted this upside participation, bondholders will reduce the risk premium they charge. Indeed, the greater the expected volatility of the commodity price in question, the more valuable is that embedded option to the bondholders.

FIGURE 2 ▪ GENERAL PRICE VOLATILITY

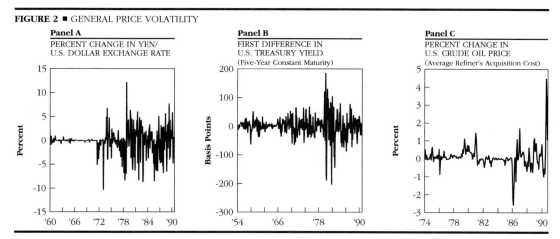

Panel A
PERCENT CHANGE IN YEN/
U.S. DOLLAR EXCHANGE RATE

Panel B
FIRST DIFFERENCE IN
U.S. TREASURY YIELD
(Five-Year Constant Maturity)

Panel C
PERCENT CHANGE IN
U.S. CRUDE OIL PRICE
(Average Refiner's Acquisition Cost)

USING HYBRIDS TO MANAGE COMMODITY RISK

Unlike foreign exchange and interest rates, which were relatively stable until the 1970s, commodity prices have a long history of volatility. Thus, it is no surprise that hybrid securities designed to hedge commodity price risks came well before hybrids with embedded currency and interest rate derivatives.

As mentioned earlier, the Confederacy issued a debt instrument convertible into cotton in 1863. By the 1920s, commodity-linked hybrids were available in U.S. capital markets. A case in point is the gold-indexed bond issued by Irving Fisher's Rand Kardex Corporation in 1925. Similar to the PEMEX issue described earlier, the principal repayment of this gold-indexed bond was tied directly to gold prices.[5] Fisher realized that he could significantly lower his firm's funding costs by furnishing a scarce security desired by investors—in this case, a long-dated forward on gold prices. And Fisher's successful innovation was imitated by a number of other U.S. companies during the '20s.

Like so many of the financial innovations of the 1920s, however, that wave of hybrid debt financings was ended by the regulatory reaction that set in during the 1930s.[6] Specifically, the "Gold Clause"

Joint Congressional Resolution of June 5, 1933 virtually eliminated indexed debt by prohibiting "a lender to require of a borrower a different quantity or number of dollars from that loaned." And it was not until October 1977, when Congress passed the Helms Amendment, that the legal basis for commodity-indexed debt was restored.

Hybrids with Option Features

The hybrids issued by Rand Kardex and PEMEX represent combinations of debt securities with forward contracts; that is, the promised principal repayments were designed to rise or fall directly with changes in the prices, respectively, of gold and oil. In the case of PEMEX, moreover, this forward-like feature reduced the risk to investors that the issuer wouldn't be able to repay principal; it did so by making the *amount* of the principal vary as directly as possible with the company's oil revenues.

Unlike the PEMEX and Rand Kardex issues, Sunshine Mining's 15-year silver-linked bond issued in 1980 combined a debt issue with a *European option*[7] on silver prices. In this case, the promised principal repayment could not fall below a certain level (the face value), but would increase proportionally with increases in the price of silver price above $20 per ounce at maturity.[8] Because most of

---

5. See J. Huston McCulloch, "The Ban on Indexed Bonds," *American Economic Review* 70 (December 1980), pp. 1018-21.

6. See Merton Miller's account of financial innovation in the 1920s and 1930s in the first article of this issue.

7. European options can be exercised only at maturity, as distinguished from American options, which can be exercised any time before expiration.

the commodity-linked hybrids that followed the Sunshine Mining issue in the '80s contain embedded options rather than forwards, let's consider briefly how the embedding of options within debt issues manages risk and lowers the issuer's cost of capital.

How Hybrids with Options Manage Risk. Corporate bondholders bear "downside" risk while typically being limited to a fixed interest rate as their reward. (In the jargon of options, the bondholder is "short a put" on the value of the firm's assets.) Because of this limited upside, they charge a higher "risk premium" when asked to fund companies with more volatile earnings streams. Like the forward contract embedded in the PEMEX issue, options also provide bondholders with an equity-like, "upside" participation. In return for this upside participation, bondholders will reduce the risk premium they charge. Indeed, the greater the expected volatility of the commodity price in question, the more valuable is that embedded option to the bondholders.[9]

Unlike hybrids with forwards, hybrids with embedded options provide investors with a "floor"— that is, a minimum principal repayment or set of coupons. And, though options therefore effect a less complete transfer of risk than in the case of forwards (in the sense that the firm's financing costs don't fall below the floor in the event of an extreme decline in commodity prices), investors should be willing to pay for the floor in the form of a reduced base rate of interest. To the extent they lower the rate of interest, option-like hybrids reduce the probability of default, thus reassuring bondholders and the rating agencies.

A good example of corporate risk management with options was a 1986 issue of Eurobonds with detachable gold warrants by Pegasus Gold Corporation, a Canadian gold mining firm. In effect, this issue gave investors two separable claims: (1) a straight debt issue with a series of fixed interest payments and a fixed principal repayment; and (2) European options on the price of gold. By giving bondholders a participation in the firm's gold revenues, the inclusion of such warrants reduced the coupon rate on the bond—which in turn lowered the issuer's financial risk.

Probably the most newsworthy hybrid in 1986, however, was Standard Oil's *Oil-Indexed Note*. This hybrid combines a zero-coupon bond with a European option on oil with the same maturity. The issue not only aroused the interest of the IRS, but also succeeded in rekindling regulatory concerns about the potential for "speculative abuse" built into hybrid securities.[10]

Commodity Interest-Indexed Bonds. The commodity hybrids mentioned thus far are all combinations of debt with forwards or options with a single maturity. In effect, they link only the principal repayment to commodity prices, but not the interim interest payments. But, in recent years, hybrids have also emerged that combine debt with a *series of options* of different maturities—maturities that are typically designed to correspond to the coupon dates of the underlying bond.

In 1988, for example, Magma Copper Company issued *Copper Interest-Indexed Senior Subordinated Notes.* This 10-year debenture has embedded within it 40 option positions on the price of copper—one maturing in 3 months, one in 6 months, ..., and one in 10 years. The effect of this series of embedded option positions is to make the company's quarterly interest payments vary with the prevailing price of copper, as shown below:

Average Copper Price	Indexed Interest Rate
$2.00 or above	21 %
1.80	20
1.60	19
1.40	18
1.30	17
1.20	16
1.10	15
1.00	14
0.90	13
0.80 or below	12

In 1989, Presidio Oil Company issued an oil-indexed note with a similar structure, but with the coupons linked to the price of natural gas. And, in 1991, Shin Etsu, a Japanese chemical manufacturer,

---

8. From the perspective of 1991, during which the silver price has averaged $4.00 per ounce, this exercise price of $20 per ounce may seem bizarre. But keep in mind that this bond was issued in early 1980. During the period October 1979-January 1980, the price of silver averaged $23 per ounce.

9. For a discussion of how the equity option embedded in convertibles could make convertible bondholders indifferent to increases in the volatility of corporate cash flow, see Michael Brennan and Eduardo Schwartz, "The Case for Convertibles," *Chase Financial Quarterly* (Fall 1981). Reprinted in *Journal of Applied Corporate Finance* (Summer 1988).

10. See James Jordan, Robert Mackay, and Eugene Moriarty, "The New Regulation of Hybrid Debt Instruments," *Journal of Applied Corporate Finance*, Vol. 2 No. 4 (Winter 1990).

issued a hybrid with a similar structure; however, the issue was a private placement and the coupon payment floated *inversely* with the price of oil.

The Case of Forest Oil:
The Consequences of Not Managing Risk

It was Forest Oil, however, and not Presidio, that first considered issuing natural gas-linked debt. But Forest's management was confident that natural gas prices would go higher in the near future and thus decided that the price of the natural gas-linked debt would turn out to be too high. Unfortunately, the company's bet on natural gas prices ended up going against them. Natural gas prices since the issue was contemplated have fallen dramatically, and the company has been squeezed between high current interest costs and reduced revenues. Indeed, the squeeze has been so tight that Forest has been forced to restructure its debt.

USING HYBRIDS TO MANAGE FOREIGN EXCHANGE RISK

As Figure 2 suggests, exchange rates became more volatile following the abandonment of the Bretton Woods agreement in 1973. As a result, many companies have experienced foreign exchange risk arising from transaction, translation, and economic exposures.

The simplest way to manage an exposure to foreign exchange risk is by using a forward foreign exchange contract. If the firm is long foreign currency, it can cover this exposure by selling forward contracts. Or if it has a short position, it can buy forwards.

Dual Currency Bonds. Similar to PEMEX's oil-indexed issue, the simplest FX hybrid debt structure is a *Dual Currency Bond*. Such a bond combines a fixed-rate, "bullet" (that is, single) repayment bond and a long-dated forward contract on foreign exchange. For example, in 1985, Philip Morris Credit issued a dual-currency bond in which coupon payments are made in Swiss Francs while principal will be repaid US Dollars.

PERLs. A variant of the dual currency structure is the *Principal Exchange Rate Linked Security*. In 1987, Westinghouse Electric Company issued *PERLs*

wherein the bondholder received at maturity the principal the USD value of 70.13 million New Zealand dollars. The issuer's motive in this case was likely to reduce its funding costs by taking advantage of an unusual investor demand for long-dated currency forwards. Earlier in the same year, and presumably with similar motive, Ford Motor Credit Company issued *Reverse PERLs*. In this case, the principal repayment varied inversely with the value of the yen.[11]

Creating a Hybrid By Adding Options

As in the case of commodity-linked hybrids, forward-like FX hybrids seemed to have given way to structures containing warrants or other option-like features. In 1987, for example, General Electric Credit Corporation made a public offering made up of debt and yen-USD currency exchange warrants.

Bonds with Principal Indexed (Convertible) to FX. Like bonds with warrants, convertible bonds are made up of bonds and equity options. But there is one important difference: In the case of bonds with warrants, the bondholder can exercise the option embodied in a warrant and still keep the underlying bond. With convertibles, the holder must surrender the bond to exercise the option. Sunshine Mining's Silver-Indexed Bonds and Standard Oil's Oil Indexed Notes are similar constructions. The bondholder can receive either the value of the bond or the value of the option, but not both.

When this debt structure appeared with an embedded foreign currency option, the hybrid was called an *Indexed Currency Option Note* (or *ICON*). This security, which was first underwritten by First Boston in 1985, combines a fixed rate, bullet repayment bond and a European option on foreign exchange.[12]

USING HYBRIDS TO MANAGE INTEREST RATE RISK

Some companies have significant exposures to interest rates. Take the case of firms that supply inputs to the housing market. When interest rates rise, the revenues of such firms tend to fall. The use of standard, floating-rate bank debt in such cases would likely increase the probability of default.

---

11. See Michael G. Capatides, *A Guide to the Capital Markets Activities of Banks and Bank Holding Companies*, (Browne & Co.), 1988, p. 132.

12. In his article in this issue, "Securities Innovation: An Overview," John Finnerty notes that ICONs "were introduced and disappeared quickly."

Creating a Hybrid with Embedded Swaps

To manage interest rate risk, such companies may be best served by a debt instrument wherein the coupon payment actually declines when interest rates rise. Such an *Inverse Floating Rate Note*—or a *Yield-Curve Note*, as it was called when first issued by the Student Loan Marketing Association (Sallie Mae) in the public debt market in 1986—can be decomposed into a floating-rate, bullet repayment note and a plain vanilla interest rate swap for twice the principal of the loan.

Creating a Hybrid By Adding Options

Just as bondholders can be provided options to exchange their bonds for a specified amount of a commodity or foreign currency, hybrid securities have been issued that give bondholders the option to exchange a bond (typically at maturity) for another bond (typically with the same coupon and maturity).

Convertible/Exchangeable Floating Rate Notes. These hybrids, which give the holder the right to convert to (or exchange for) a fixed-rate bond at a pre-specified interest rate, first appeared in 1979. Such notes contain embedded "put" options on interest rates; that is, investors are likely to exercise their conversion or exchange rights only if interest rates fall below a certain level.

Extendible Notes. The same, moreover, is true of extendible notes, which give the holder the right to exchange the underlying bond for a bond of longer maturity. Such bonds first appeared in 1982.

USING HYBRIDS TO REDUCE CONFLICTS BETWEEN BONDHOLDERS AND SHAREHOLDERS

In "normal" circumstances—that is, when operations are profitable and the firm can comfortably meet its debt service payments and investment schedule—the interests of bondholders and shareholders are united. Both groups of investors benefit

from managerial decisions that increase the total value of the firm.

In certain cases, however, corporate managements find themselves in the position of being able to increase shareholder value *at the expense of bondholders*.[13] For example, as happened in a number of leveraged recapitalizations, management could reduce the value of outstanding bonds by increasing debt or adding debt senior to that in question. (In professional circles, this is known as *event risk*; in academic parlance it is the *claims dilution problem*.) Or, if the firm were in danger of insolvency, management could choose—as did some S&L executives—to invest in ever riskier projects in desperate attempts to save the firm (the *asset substitution problem*). Finally, a management squeezed between falling revenues and high interest payments could choose to pass up value-adding projects such as R&D or, if things are bad enough, basic maintenance and safety procedures (the *underinvestment problem*).[14]

Corporate debtholders are well aware that such problems can arise, and they accordingly protect themselves by lowering the price they are willing to pay for the debt. For corporate management, such lower prices translate into higher interest payments, which in turn further raise the probability of financial trouble.

Hybrids reduce these shareholder-bondholder conflicts by reducing current interest rates, shifting debt service payments to periods when firms are better able to pay, stabilizing cash flow, and thereby reducing the likelihood of financial distress. In so doing, they also raise the price of the corporate debt to investors and lower the overall corporate cost of capital.

Using Hybrids to Reduce the Claims Dilution Problem (or Protect Against "Event Risk")

Puttable Bonds. Introduced in 1976, these bonds give their holders the option to "put" the bond back to the issuer. Such an option would be exercised only if interest rates rise or the issuer's credit

13. For the seminal discussion of the effect of conflicts between shareholders and debtholders (and between management and shareholders as well) on the behavior of the firm, see Michael C. Jensen and William H. Meckling, "Theory of the Firm: Managerial Behavior, Agency Costs, and Capital Structure," *Journal of Financial Economics* (1976), pp. 305-360.

14. For an account of the underinvestment problem, see Stewart Myers, "The Determinants of Corporate Borrowing," *Journal of Financial Economics* (1977).

For a more detailed examination of these sources of shareholder/debtholder conflict, see Clifford W. Smith and Jerold B. Warner, "On Financial Contracting: An Analysis of Bond Covenants," *Journal of Financial Economics*, 7 (1979), pp. 117-161.

FIGURE 3
OIL-LINKED CREDIT-
SENSITIVE SYNDICATE

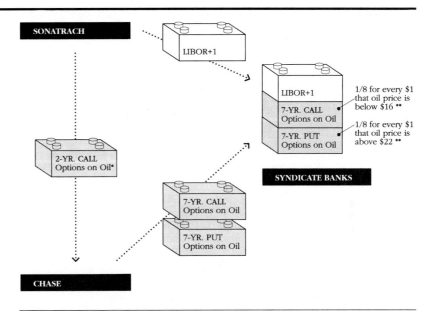

*During the first two years, if the price of oil exceeds $23, Sonatrach will pay a supplemental coupon to Chase.
**In the first year, the syndicate receives additional interest if the price of oil falls outside the range of $16-$22. In year 2, the range widens to $15-$23, then to $14-$24 in year 3, and to $13-$25 in years 4 through 7.

standing falls. In this sense, puttable bonds give bondholders both a call option on interest rates and an option on the credit spread of the issuer.[15] Such put options thus protect bondholders not only against increases in interest rates, but also against the possibility of losses from deteriorating operating performance or leveraged recapitalizations. In the wake of the widely publicized bondholder losses accompanying the KKR buyout of RJR Nabisco in 1989, the use of put options to protect against such "event risk" enjoyed a new vogue.

Floating Rate, Rating Sensitive Notes. These notes, issued by Manufacturer Hanover in 1988, contain explicit options on the issuer's credit standing. In this security, Manufacturer's Hanover agreed to pay investors a spread above LIBOR that increased with each incremental decline in the bank's senior debt rating.

From the standpoint of risk management, however, there is an obvious flaw in the design of this security. Although it may partially compensate investors for increases in risk, it actually increases the probability of default instead of reducing it. The security increases the corporate debt service burden precisely when the issuing firm can least afford it— when its credit rating has fallen and, presumably, its operating cash flow declined.

A hybrid structure designed to overcome this problem was a syndication of oil-indexed bonds created by Chase Manhattan for Sonatrach (the state hydrocarbons company of Algeria) in 1990. As illustrated in Figure 3, the transaction was structured so that Chase accepted two-year call options on oil from Sonatrach and then transformed those two-year calls into seven-year calls and puts that were passed on to the syndicate members. Investors were compensated for a below-market interest by a payoff structure that would provide them with higher payoffs in the event of significantly *higher or lower* oil prices.

---

15. Extendible notes also provide bondholders with an option on the firm's credit standing. But, unlike puttable debt, it represents the opportunity to benefit from increases in the firm's credit standing, or decreases in the spread. In the case of extendible notes, if the credit spread of the issuer decreases, the right to extend the maturity of the note (at the old credit spread) has value.

For the issuer, however, the security requires higher payments to Chase *only in the event of higher oil prices*. If the price of oil declines, although the syndicate members receive a higher yield, the increase comes from Chase, not Sonatrach.

Using Hybrids to Reduce the Asset Substitution and Underinvestment Problems

Convertibles. At the outset, we noted that convertible bonds contain embedded options on the company's equity. By providing bondholders with the right to convert their claims into equity, management provides bondholders with the assurance that they will participate in any increase in shareholder value that results from increasing the risk of the company's activities—whether by leveraging up or undertaking riskier investments. By lowering current interest rates and thus reducing the likelihood of financial trouble, convertibles also reduce the probability that financially strapped companies will be forced to forgo valuable investment opportunities.[16]

Convertibles (and debt with warrants, their close substitutes) are also potentially useful in resolving disagreements between bondholders and shareholders about just how risky the firm's activities are. The value of convertibles are risk-neutral in the following sense: Unexpected increases in company risk reduce the value of the bond portion of a convertible, but at the same time increase the value of the embedded option (by increasing volatility). It is largely because of this risk-neutralizing effect—and for their role in reducing the "underinvestment problem" mentioned below—that convertible issuers tend to be smaller, newer, riskier firms characterized by high growth and earnings volatility.[17]

The Case of LYONs

While a number of bonds are puttable or convertible, the Liquid Yield Option Note (LYON) introduced by Merrill Lynch in 1985 is both puttable and convertible. The combination of the put and conversion features are especially useful in controlling the asset substitution, or risk-shifting, problem just described.[18] For this reason, the LYONs structure should be particularly attractive to issu-

ers with substantial capital investment opportunities and a wide range of alternative investment projects (with varying degrees of risk).

It is thus interesting to note that the LYON structure was first used to fund companies where the asset substitution problem was acute. Take the case of Waste Management, the first issuer of LYONs. Although Waste Management is today a household name among even small investors, in 1985 the company could best be viewed as a collection of "growth options." As such it posed considerable uncertainty for investors.

THE ECONOMIC RATIONALE FOR ISSUING A HYBRID SECURITY

We are still left with a fundamental question: Given the well-functioning, low-cost markets for derivative products available today, why should a corporate issuer ever prefer the "bundled" hybrid to simply issuing standard debt and buying or selling the derivatives. We now discuss the following three reasons why corporate management might choose hybrids:

(1) If the firm issuing the hybrid can provide investors with a "play" not available otherwise—that is, a derivative instrument not available in the traded derivatives markets—the issuing firm will consequently be paid a premium for "completing the market."

(2) The hybrid may enable the issuer to take advantage of tax or regulatory arbitrages that would lower the cost of borrowing.

(3) By embedding a risk management product into a hybrid, the issuer may be able to obtain hedge accounting treatment, which may not be allowed if the derivative was bought or sold separately.

Using Hybrids to Provide Investors with a "Play"

The most straightforward reason for issuing a hybrid is to provide investors with a means of taking a position on a financial price. If the issuer provides a "play" not otherwise available, the investor will be willing to pay a premium, thereby reducing the issuer's cost of funding. (And, if the hybrid provides

---

16. More technically, the underinvestment problem arises from the fact that, in financially troubled firms, an outsized portion of the returns from new investments must go to help restore the value of the bondholders' claims before the shareholders receive any payoff at all. This has also been dubbed the "debt overhang" problem.

17. For an exposition of this argument, see Michael Brennan and Eduardo Schwartz, "The Case for Convertibles," *Chase Financial Quarterly* (Fall 1981). Reprinted in *Journal of Applied Corporate Finance* (Summer 1988).

18. As described at length in the next article in this issue, the put feature also enabled Merrill Lynch to tailor the security for its network of retail investors.

investors with a "scarce security" not otherwise obtainable, it may also provide corporate issuers with a hedge they can't duplicate with derivative products.)

The "play" can be in the form of a forward contract. Perhaps the best example of such is dual currency bonds, which provided investors with foreign exchange forward contracts with longer maturities than those available in the standard market. The forward contracts embedded in dual currency bonds have maturities running to 10 years, whereas liquidity in the standard foreign exchange forward market declines for maturities greater than one year, and falls very significantly beyond five years.

The "play," however, has more commonly been in the form of an option embedded in the bond—generally an option of longer maturity than those available in the standard option market. Sunshine Mining's Silver Indexed Bond fits this category, as do Standard Oil's Oil Indexed Note and the gold warrants issued by Pegasus Gold Corporation. In 1986 long-dated options on stock market indices were introduced with the development of hybrid debt in which the principal was indexed to an equity index. While the first such debt issues were indexed to the Nikkei, Salomon Brothers' "S&P 500 Index Subordinated Notes (SPINs)" have probably received more public attention. A SPIN is convertible into the value of the S&P 500 Index, rather than into an individual equity. Since then, debt has been issued that is indexed to other equity indices (for example, the NYSE index) or subsets of indices. For example, in 1991, United Technologies issued a zero-coupon bond indexed to the S&P Pharmaceutical Index.

Using Hybrids to "Arbitrage" Tax and/or Regulatory Authorities

Hybrid debt has also been used to take advantage of asymmetries in tax treatment or regulations in different countries or markets. One classic example is a case of "arbitrage" reported in *Business Week* under the provocative title, "A Way for US Firms to Make 'Free Money'." The "free money" came from two sources:

(1) A difference in tax treatment between the U.S. and Japan—the Japanese tax authorities ruled

that income earned from holding a zero-coupon bond would be treated as a capital gain, thereby making interest income on the zero non-taxable for Japanese investors. In contrast, U.S. tax authorities permitted any U.S. firm issuing a zero coupon bond to deduct from current income the imputed interest payments.

(2) A regulatory arbitrage—The Ministry of Finance limited Japanese pension funds' investments in non-yen-dominated bonds issued by foreign corporations to at most 10% of their portfolios. The Ministry of Finance also ruled that dual currency bonds qualified as a yen issue, thus allowing dual currency bonds to command a premium from Japanese investors.

Consequently, U.S. firms issued zero-coupon yen bonds (to realize the interest rate savings from the tax arbitrage), and then issued a dual currency bond to hedge the residual yen exposure from the yen zero, while realizing a further interest savings from the regulatory arbitrage.

Tax-Deductible Equity. Perhaps the most thinly disguised attempt to issue tax-deductible equity was the *Adjustable Rate Convertible Debt* introduced in 1982.[19] Such convertibles paid a coupon determined by the dividend rate on the firm's common stock; moreover, the debt could be converted to common stock at the current price at any time (i.e., there was no conversion premium). Not surprisingly, once the IRS ruled that this was equity for tax purposes, this structure disappeared.

On a less aggressive level, hybrid structures like Merrill Lynch's LYON take advantage of the treatment of zero coupon instruments by U.S. tax authorities—that is, zero coupon bonds allow the issuer to deduct deferred interest payments from current income (although the holder of the bond must declare them as income). Given the impact of the IRS ruling on adjustable rate convertible debt, it is not surprising that a great deal of attention has been given to the tax status of the LYON.

Using Hybrids to Obtain Accrual Accounting Treatment for Risk Management

If a U.S. company uses a forward, futures, swap, or option to hedge a specific transaction (for example, a loan or a purchase or a receipt), it is

---

19. This point is made by John Finnerty in his article in this issue.

Except for the highest-rated companies, most firms today face *non-price* credit restrictions that have greatly enlarged credit spreads. Many such companies are using hybrid debt to lower their risk profile and thus avoid the higher funding costs now associated with being a riskier borrower.

relatively simple to obtain accrual accounting treatment for the hedge. (Changes in the market value of the hedging instrument offset changes in the value of the asset being hedged, so there is no need to mark the hedging instrument to market.)

If, however, the firm wishes to use one of the risk management instruments to hedge expected net income or an even longer-term economic exposure, the current position of the accounting profession is that the hedge position must be marked to market. Some companies have been reluctant to use derivatives to manage such risks because this accounting treatment would increase the volatility of their reported income—*even while such a risk management strategy would stabilize their longer-run operating cash flow.*

With the use of hybrids, by contrast, which contain embedded derivatives, the firm may be able to obtain accrual accounting treatment for the entire package. Accountants are accustomed to valuing convertible debt at historical cost; and, given this precedent, they can extend the same treatment to hybrids.[20]

CONCLUDING REMARKS

Beginning in 1980 with Sunshine Mining's issue of silver-linked bonds, U.S. corporations have increasingly chosen to raise debt capital by embedding derivatives such as forwards or options into their notes and bonds. In the early '80's, such hybrids typically provided investors with payoffs (at first only principal, but later interest payments as well) indexed to commodity prices, interest rates, and exchange rates. But, in recent years, companies have begun to issue debt indexed to general stock market indices and even subsets of such indices.

Critics of such newfangled securities view them as the offspring of "supply-driven" fads. According to this view, profit-hungry investment banks set their highly-paid "rocket scientists" to designing new securities that can then be foisted on unsuspecting corporate treasurers and investors.

As economists, however, we begin with the assumption that capital market innovations succeed only to the extent they do a better job than existing products in meeting the demands of issuers and investors. The evidence presented in these pages, albeit anecdotal, suggests that hybrid debt is a capital market response to corporate treasurers' desire to manage pricing risks and otherwise tailor their securities to investor demands. In some cases, especially those in which hybrids feature long-dated forwards or options, hybrids are furnishing investors with securities they cannot obtain elsewhere.

Like the remarkable growth of futures, swaps, and options markets beginning in the late '70s, the proliferation of corporate hybrids during the '80s is fundamentally an attempt to cope with increased price volatility. The sharp increase in the volatility of exchange rates, interest rates, and oil prices—to name just the most important—during the 1970s provided the "necessary condition" for the rise of hybrids.

But another important stimulant to hybrids has come from other constraints on companies' ability to raise debt. In the early '80s, for example, when interest rates were high, hybrid debt was used by riskier firms to reduce their interest costs to manageable levels. Given the current level of interest rates today, most companies would likely choose to borrow as much straight debt as possible. But except for the highest-rated companies, many firms also now face *non-price* credit restrictions that have greatly enlarged credit spreads. In some such cases, companies are using hybrid debt to lower their risk profile and thus avoid the higher funding costs now associated with being a riskier corporate borrower. In other cases, hybrids are providing access to debt capital that would otherwise be denied on any terms.

---

20. See J. Matthew Singleton, "Hedge Accounting: A State-of-the-Art Review," *Journal of Banking and Finance*, 5 (Fall 1991), pp. 26-32.

THE PERSISTENT BORROWING ADVANTAGE IN EURODOLLAR BONDS: A PLAUSIBLE EXPLANATION

by Wayne Marr, Tulane University, and John Trimble, University of Tennessee

■

Between 1975 and 1988, the volume of U.S. corporate borrowing in the Eurodollar bond market grew at the astonishing rate of 63 percent annually. In 1975 U.S. firms borrowed approximately $30 million overseas, which accounted for less than one percent of total U.S. corporate borrowing. In 1987 they borrowed nearly $17 billion overseas, which represented roughly 17 percent of total U.S. corporate borrowing. This amount, moreover, was sharply down from the 1985 high of $42 billion, accounting for 42 percent of total corporate borrowing.

What is behind this huge increase in overseas borrowing? According to the chief financial officers of U.S. companies, it is extraordinarily favorable borrowing rates. Many CFOs, in fact, report interest cost savings between 25 and 100 basis points in the Eurodollar as compared with the domestic market.[1]

---

1. See W. Cooper, "Some Thoughts About Eurobonds," *Institutional Investor*, February 1985, pp. 157-158; S. Lohr, "The Eurobond Market Boom," *The New York Times*, December 31, 1985, p. 31; F. G. Fisher, *The Eurodollar Bond Market*, London, Euromoney Publications Limited, 1979; R. Karp, "How U.S. Companies are Catching the Eurobond Habit," *Institutional Investor* (August 1982), pp. 208-212; M. S. Mendelson, *Money on the Move*, New York, McGraw-Hill, 1980; Orion Royal Bank Limited, *The Orion Royal Guide to the International Capital Markets*, London, Euromoney Publications Limited, 1982; Securities Industry Association, *The Importance of Access to Capital Markets Outside the United States* (May 1983); and D. W. Starr, "Opportunities of U.S. Corporate Borrowers in the International Bond Markets," *Financial Executive* (June 1979), pp. 50-59.

Though intermittent, such savings have been available often enough to provide a significant advantage. And, harder to believe, the reported savings at times have been much larger than 100 basis points. On September 11, 1984, for example, Coca Cola issued $100 million of seven-year Eurodollar bonds priced at 80 basis points below comparable U.S. Treasury notes.[2] And, while interest cost savings as large as Coca Cola's are clearly an aberration, recent academic research provides support for claims in the financial press of substantial corporate savings in the Eurobond market.[3]

The existence of such a large and persistent borrowing advantage runs counter to the conventional wisdom of financial economists that international capital markets are becoming ever more "integrated." Expressed in simplest terms, the "integration" of two financial markets implies that the free flow of capital across boundaries should erase all but minor and momentary borrowing cost differences. Thus, if markets are truly integrated, the domestic and international yields in the primary market for domestic and Eurodollar bonds should be roughly equal.

How, therefore, does one explain the significant cant Eurobond savings that have recently been documented by academic studies? In this article we attempt to provide an "educated guess" about the real source of the savings—one which reflects fairly recent trends in international banking as well as other well-known features of the Eurobond market.

THE EURODOLLAR BOND MARKET

Historical Development

The recent availability of low-cost Eurobond financing has presented U.S. companies issuing debt with a new option: selling their bonds in international capital markets. A Eurobond is underwritten by an international syndicate of commercial banks or investment banks and sold principally, at times exclusively, in countries other than the country in whose currency the bond is denominated. Eurodollar bonds are dollar-denominated Eurobonds.

The first dollar-denominated Eurobond was sold in 1957 by Petrofina, a Belgian petroleum company. The dollar volume of Eurobonds began to grow in the early 1960s when the U.S. government enacted a series of measures designed to restrain the outflow of funds from the United States and to improve the country's balance of payments.[4] As a result, many American firms found it advantageous during this period (1963-74) to finance their international operations by selling securities overseas. By 1974, the government's capital control programs were dropped but the Eurodollar bond market still continued to grow.

Historically, most Eurobond issuers have been well-known financial institutions or industrial firms with extensive overseas holdings, such as American Express and Mobil Oil. Today, this is no longer true. Many lesser-known and smaller-sized firms have become Eurobond issuers. Between 1977 and 1984, more than 400 industrial firms sold straight debt in the Euromarket, totaling more than $41 billion.[5]

Eurobond Characteristics

Eurodollar bonds sold by domestic firms are similar in most respects to their domestic bonds. The majority of bonds are fixed-rate, unsecured, straight debt (i.e., no special features other than the call or sinking fund provisions) and are listed on a major exchange (U.S. or European). Most of the differences between domestic and Eurodollar bonds are attributable to the fact that they are designed for a different clientele of investors. In the U.S. market, corporate bonds are purchased primarily by life insurance companies and pension funds which, historically, have desired long-term debt instruments. The Eurobond market initially was dominated by individual investors who purchased securities through anonymous bank accounts and who preferred short-term maturities. In recent years, the market has become more institutional, with large participation by central banks and insurance companies. Such institutions, however, still prefer short-term maturities because of liquidity needs and foreign exchange risk. As a result, most Eurobonds issued by industrial companies have maturities of between three and ten years.

Other features that distinguish Eurodollar from

---

2. See W. Cooper, "Some Thoughts About Eurobonds," *Institutional Investor*, February 1985, pp. 157-158.

3. See M. W. Marr and J. L. Trimble "Domestic versus Euromarket Bond Sale: A Persistent Borrowing Cost Advantage," University of Tennessee Department of Finance Working Paper, 1988.

4. The federal government's capital control programs consisted of the Foreign Direct Investment Program, the Interest Equalization Tax, and the Voluntary Foreign Credit Restraint program.

5. See S. Lohr, "The Eurobond Market Boom," *The New York Times*, December 31, 1985, 31.

domestic bonds include annual (instead of semi-annual) coupon payments, no registration requirement, and smaller issue sizes. Annual coupon payments lower the yield for a Eurobond as compared with an identical bond issued in the United States. Also, most Eurobonds are in bearer form as compared with the registered form prevalent in the United States. Bearer bonds provide the holders with anonymity and the potential to avoid tax liabilities resulting from coupon income or capital gains. Such anonymity also allows investors to hide illicit or politically sensitive activities such as drug trafficking and covert arms sales. Finally, the typical Eurobond issue is smaller than the typical domestic bond issue. Whereas domestic issues have raised an average of a little over $100 million, the average Eurodollar bond issue has been around $85 million.

THE EURODOLLAR BOND BORROWING ADVANTAGE

Besides cost considerations, there could be other reasons why U.S. companies choose to issue Eurobonds. They may wish, for example, to broaden the market for their securities and attract investors who would not otherwise purchase securities registered in the United States. Or they may wish to avoid the disclosure requirements of regulations. But surely the predominant reason for the large volume of Eurodollar bonds is that U.S. companies perceive some cost advantage to borrowing overseas.[6]

In two recent studies we found that, in fact, Eurodollar bonds have offered issuers remarkable savings relative to comparable domestic bonds. Using a sample of 229 new debt issues sold by U.S. public utility firms between January 1979 and December 1983, we found that the average gross yield on 38 Eurodollar bond issues was approximately 58 basis points less than yields on 191 comparable domestic issues.[7] In a more recent study we found an even larger 104-basis-points saving for 118 industrial firms issuing Eurodollar bonds (relative to 198 domestic issues) during this same period. These are indeed significant savings. For a typical $100 million bond issue, for example, 104 basis points translates into a reduction in debt service cost of $1.04 million dollars a year.

WHY THE EUROBOND ADVANTAGE?

Why has a borrowing cost advantage in Eurodollar bonds persisted? The answer to this question surely lies in the forces that govern, and the linkages between, the primary and secondary markets for domestic and Eurodollar bonds. These forces appear to consist of temporary as well as more permanent elements. For while the Eurobond advantage has existed in long periods throughout the past 14 years, it does not appear to have been continuously present; at times domestic bonds have had a clear cost advantage. But, clearly, the trend on the whole has favored the Euromarket sale.

In this section, we suggest an explanation for the persistence of the savings that is rooted in these forces and is consistent with the facts concerning the domestic and Eurodollar bond markets. In the final analysis, however, much of the information that would answer our question is not available to the public (and thus to researchers like us). Our explanation, accordingly, should be viewed as at best an educated guess.

Privately, some observers have suggested that during the last decade money from investors in oil-producing states has gone principally to Eurobonds because such investors generally prefer anonymity. Because these investors are "segmented" from other investors in world financial markets, such an increase in demand could conceivably have caused a persistent differential in the *secondary-market* prices of Eurobonds relative to domestic bonds. But it does not explain how this differential in secondary-market prices would necessarily translate into a borrowing advantage for U.S. firms. Eurobond underwriters could price the Eurodollar issues only slightly below domestic bonds and then keep the balance of the secondary-market price differential for themselves. Which leads us to the following question: Why do only U.S. companies (and not, say, German or English firms) appear to be getting the lion's share of the cost savings from Eurobond offerings?

In addition, Ingo Walter has shown that the market for financial anonymity (of which the Eurobond market is a large part) is very complex.[8] Like most markets, the forces which govern price movements

---

6. Two empirical studies have documented the savings. They are D. S. Kidwell, M. W. Marr, and G. R. Thompson, "Eurodollar Bonds: Alternative Financing for U.S. Companies," *Financial Management* (Winter 1985), pp. 18-27, (a correction to the above study appears in *Financial Management* (Spring 1986), pp. 78-79); and, M. W. Marr and J. Trimble, "Domestic versus Euromarket Bond Sale: A Persistent

Borrowing Cost Advantage," University of Tennessee Working Paper, 1988.
7. *Ibid.*
8. Ingo Walter, *Secret Money*, Lexington, Mass.: Heath and Co., Lexington Books.

arise from both the demand and the supply sides. Consider the sources of demand. Half of the Euromarket's demand for bonds comes from institutional investors, many of which are likely to have legitimate preferences for anonymity. The other half is from retail investors, some of whom no doubt require anonymity for legitimate business and personal motives. Another part of the retail demand stems, however, from the desire to hide illicit activities. These investors include participants in international drug trafficking, fraud, insider trading, tax evasion, capital flight, and covert government operations such as arm sales and state-sponsored terrorism.

Thus, it is easy to see how, in the last decade, increases in the demand for financial secrecy could have come with equal force from sources other than investors in oil-producing states. But, without better information, we cannot determine with any confidence the extent to which retail demand for Eurodollar bonds is being driven by any particular source.

An explanation of the Eurobond puzzle must therefore provide answers to two fundamental questions: What might have caused a differential in secondary-market prices? And why would underwriters share a Eurobond price rise with U.S. borrowers? We will begin by addressing the second question first.

Why Would Underwriters Share A Price Differential?

Why Banks Might. Underwriting relationships with wealthy corporate clients generate large profits for underwriting institutions. Consequently, competitive banks are generally looking for opportunities to penetrate or increase their share of such underwriting markets. Of course, some banks will have stronger motives than others. For example, some U.S. commercial banks, apparently in anticipation of the repeal of the Glass Steagall Act, have sought entry into the Eurobond underwriting market by offering competitively low rates.[9]

Also, according to Walter, Swiss banks steadily lost international underwriting business to more competitive banks in London during the last decade.

In addition, he notes that the ability of the Swiss to compete in their traditional underwriting areas has been hampered by competition from a greater number of suppliers of financial secrecy and by unfavorable changes in Swiss tax laws.[10] To the extent Walter is right, it would be understandable if Swiss banks were to seek new markets in which to compete in international banking. And, in fact, the predominant lead manager of the syndicates underwriting Eurodollar bonds in the U.S. is Credit Suisse First Boston, a Swiss bank affiliate that is also typically involved in distributing these bonds.

Why the U.S. Market? There are six attractive features of the U.S. market. First, there is an abundance of wealthy corporations. Second, the dollar is an accepted international currency. Third, during much (1980-85) of the period we are considering, the dollar's value was rising against most other world currencies. Fourth, Euromarket investors prefer to invest in top credit quality U.S. corporations, and thus the bonds are relatively easy to distribute to retail investors in the Euromarket. Fifth, the U.S. capital market is the largest in the world and is relatively free of capital controls. Sixth, in the 1980s, U.S. interest rates (fueled by expansionary policies) were high relative to those in other developed countries.

How Would a Price Differential Be Shared? Historically, the relationship between underwriting fees in the Euromarket and the domestic market has been relatively stable, running at roughly 2.67 times.[11] A large portion of this difference in the underwriting fees arises because proportionately more Eurobonds are distributed to retail investors than in the U.S. The selling concession, a component of the underwriting fee which goes to the banks in the selling syndicate to compensate them for their retail effort, is thus much larger in the Euromarket than in the U.S. market.

Euromarket merchant banks are the only banks with established distribution networks to investors seeking anonymity. And, as such, they have the ability to exact gains from these investors which other banks do not. Therefore, when the demand from secrecy-seeking investors increases relative to the supply of bearer bonds, those merchant banks in the selling syndicate stand to profit from two sources.

---

9. But this is not the result of a price rise in the secondary market. Such competitive market pricing, moreover, is not the dominant reason for the Eurodollar bond borrowing advantage. There are too few banks pricing competitively for that to be true. See M. W. Marr, R. J. Rogowski, and J. L. Trimble, "The Competitive Effects of Commercial Bank Entry in Eurodollar Bond Underwriting," Working Paper, Tulane University School of Business Administration.

10. Walter, cited in note 8.

11. See Marr and Trimble, cited in note 3.

One is from selling more Eurobonds at higher prices to secrecy-seeking investors; the other is from the associated increase in volume of secrecy-related banking services, also a particularly high-margin business. Thus, when demand is strong, a lead manager of a Eurodollar bond issue will be offered the highest prices by affiliate banks offering financial anonymity to their clients. In this way, the lead manager can choose to distribute a greater share of the issue to investors seeking anonymity. Their profits will rise, as a result, and the proceeds could be used to help fund a desired long-range investment such as pricing bond underwritings to penetrate the U.S. market.

What Has Been Happening to the Eurobond Advantage?

During the 1977-83 period, the price of Eurodollar bonds was increasing relative to that of domestic bonds because demand was increasing faster than supply. Three causes contributed to this increase in relative demand.

High U.S. interest rates. Between 1977 and 1981, the demand for Eurodollar bonds by all foreign investors increased because U.S. interest rates were rising relative to other world interest rates. U.S. rates, fueled by an increasing money supply, rose in fact to extraordinarily high levels. By 1980 the prime rate had risen above 20 percent. As a result, foreign capital flowed into the U.S. market, causing domestic interest rates to rise.

Rising U.S. dollar. After 1980 the demand for Eurodollar bonds from all foreign investors continued to increase because the dollar rose in value against other world currencies. Under a tighter monetary policy, inflation subsided. As a result, domestic interest rates fell and the value of the U.S. dollar began a rise against most European currencies which lasted through 1985. Consequently, Eurodollar bonds were attractive to Euromarket investors during this period principally because of the gains in currency conversion.

Secrecy-seeking investors. It is likely that the demand for Eurodollar bonds also increased between 1977 and 1984 as a result of an increase in demand from investors seeking anonymity. A number of developments during this period could have spurred the demand for financial secrecy. State-sponsored terrorism emerged as a signficant political phenomenon; arms sales to revolutionary and counter-revolutionary groups were on the rise; increased social acceptance of cocaine by middle-class society increased cocaine demand and international drug trafficking; and increases in the number of countries and banks offering financial secrecy, aided by technological improvements and innovations in financial services, increased the possibilities for capital flight.

Regulation of the U.S. Market

Even given all the factors above, the development of the Eurodollar borrowing alternative could not have occurred if there were a largely unrestricted flow of capital flow between the U.S. and Eurodollar bond markets. From the point of view of Euromarket investors, the registration requirement on registered bonds, which is the norm in the U.S., are obstructions to the free flow of capital. But, from the point of view of the Internal Revenue Service (IRS), bearer bonds, which are the norm in Europe, are a threat to ensuring tax compliance by U.S. citizens.

Until 1984 the only instrument of U.S. policy bridging these markets was a 1948 treaty between the U.S. and the Netherlands Antilles. This treaty, which applies to affiliates of U.S. issuers, exempts foreign investors from the 30 percent withholding tax that U.S. citizens have to pay on the coupon income from bonds. In 1984 the exemption was extended to Eurobonds issued from within the U.S., but the treaty (though seemingly now ineffectual) remained in effect. Under either arrangement domestic corporations could, and may still, sell new-issue bearer bonds to Euromarket but not to U.S. investors. U.S. investors, however, may legally purchase these bonds after they have been "seasoned" in the secondary market.

THE FUTURE

Will the borrowing advantage in Eurodollar bonds continue? If our assessment of the situation is correct, that will depend on the rate at which the demand from anonymity-seeking investors grows and on the inclination of Eurobond underwriters to share a price gain with U.S. firms. Intuition tells us that secrecy demand will likely fluctuate with political and market conditions and that the incentive to penetrate the U.S. market will at some time reach a saturation point. Hence, a major borrowing advantage probably will not persist indefinitely. At the same time, however, Eurodollar bonds will likely remain a viable bor-

IN 1984 THE U.S. TREASURY, IN AN ATTEMPT TO CAPTURE SOME OF THE
LOW INTEREST RATES IN THE EUROMARKET, OFFERED A REGISTERED
ISSUE AT THE BEHEST OF THE IRS. THE ISSUE FAILED TO SELL,
HOWEVER, UNTIL IT WAS MODIFIED TO A "PARTIALLY" BEARER FORM
ACCEPTABLE TO EUROMARKET INVESTORS.

rowing source for U.S. firms.

Perhaps as important for the persistence of this borrowing advantage, however, is the possibility of change in government policy. The growth in the Eurodollar bond market is a symptom of changing times. Financial markets are becoming more international and this is likely to create pressures for change in government regulation of financial markets.

The Netherlands Antilles treaty (and its post-1984 counterpart, the repeal of withholding tax for foreign investors) is a critical link between secrecy-seeking investors in the Euromarket and corporate borrowers in the U.S. It gives U.S. borrowers a substitute financing source. This dampens pressures on domestic interest rates but at the expense of greater interdependency with Euromarket interest rates.

Because the capital movements promoted by the Antilles treaty and related U.S. policies have only recently become important, the corresponding policy issues are just beginning to surface. This seemed evident in June 1987 when the U.S. Treasury outraged major institutional investors and industry groups in the U.S. and in Europe by attempting to terminate the Antilles treaty. Apparently unaware that many Eurobond indentures carry special call provisions which trigger with any change in the market, including termination of the Antilles treaty, the Treasury moved to terminate the treaty on the grounds that it was unnecessary because the 30 percent withholding tax on Eurobonds had been terminated in 1984. After discovering that U.S. pension funds and insurance companies held Eurobonds in their portfolios and would lose millions of dollars if the treaty was terminated, the Treasury dropped their termination proposal.

An issue that likely will surface continually in the coming years concerns the trade-off between maintaining tax compliance of U.S. citizens on the one hand and promoting free capital movement on the other. Although this is not a new issue, the specific question is gaining renewed importance in policy implementation. And a recent conflict between the Treasury and the IRS indicates that there are important issues yet to be resolved (as well as suggesting the strength of investor demand for anonymity in the Euromarket). In 1984 the U.S. Treasury, in an attempt to capture some of the low interest rates in the Euromarket, offered a *registered* issue at the behest of the IRS. The issue failed to sell, however, until it was modified to a "partially" bearer form acceptable to Euromarket investors. And these so-called targeted Treasury bonds are still being offered in limited quantities.

There also are difficult welfare issues attending government policies that promote capital movements between these two markets. The issues arise because some segments of the domestic economy gain at the expense of others. For example, by bridging the domestic and Eurodollar bond markets, the Antilles Treaty promotes foreign investment in dollar bonds. Foreign investment causes the value of the dollar *vis-a-vis* other currencies to rise, which in turn causes our exports to become less competitive and our imports more competitive. But failing to bridge these markets generates even greater costs because the financial markets would be less integrated and thus less efficient worldwide. As a result, domestic interest rates would generally be higher than otherwise. Also, although U.S. citizens presently are prohibited from buying Eurodollar bonds until they are seasoned in the secondary market, the incentive to escape withholding taxes is strong and likely to increase as the technology of banking makes the Euromarket more accessible to U.S. residents.

PROJECT FINANCE: RAISING MONEY THE OLD-FASHIONED WAY

by John W. Kensinger and John D. Martin, University of Texas at Austin*

In the continual experimentation to discover more effective ways to organize economic ventures, a very old—one might even say ancient—form of financing is making a comeback. Non-recourse project financing, centuries older than stocks or bonds (or interest-bearing loans of any kind, for that matter), is now being used in the U.S. to fund oil and gas exploration, independent electric power generation, factory construction, and corporate research and development. Since the beginning of 1987, 83 project closings have been announced in the *Wall Street Journal*, representing almost $13 billion worth of new project financings.[1] (For a breakdown of such financings by category, see Tables 1 and 2.)[2]

Overseas commercial banks have been active investors and, for them, project finance is simply the extension of an older practice known as "merchant banking." But, with the progressive relaxation of Glass-Steagall, American banks such as Security Pacific are also becoming major sources of project finance. And, as this article was being prepared for print (August 1988), GE Capital announced that its project finance group has expanded into a new activity: the development of innovative financing packages to fund the construction and operation of industrial facilities.

Project financing has the power to be a catalyst for change in the governance of business activities. Generally, when a corporation chooses to undertake an investment project, cash flows from existing activities fund the newcomer; and management has the option to roll over the project's capital into still

---

1. Because many private placements are not announced, this is not necessarily a complete tabulation of all project financings.

2. The largest single category is electric power production, which accounts for $5.7 billion. These projects, which all together will provide over 5,000 megawatts of new generating capacity, represent twice the capacity of the giant double-reactor complex of the South Texas Nuclear Project (or the equivalent of about eight conventional coal-fired plants.)

TABLE 1 POWER PRODUCTION PROJECT FINANCINGS JANUARY 1, 1987 TO AUGUST 31, 1988			
TOTAL	$5,720.2 million	5,076.4 megawatts	57 projects
Cogeneration	$4,400.4 million	4,577.2 megawatts	38 projects
Geothermal	$709.2 million	284.8 megawatts	7 projects
Hydroelectric	$272.1 million	102.5 megawatts	7 projects
Wood-fired	$338.5 million	112.0 megawatts	5 projects

newer ventures within the company later on—without submitting them to the discipline of the capital market. This option gives corporate management considerable power, which has been a focal point in the debate over shareholder rights.[3] With project financing, by contrast, the assets and cash flows associated with each project are accounted for separately. Funding for the new project is negotiated from outside sources, and creditors have recourse only to the assets and cash flows of a specific project. As the project runs its course, furthermore, the capital is returned to the investors, and they decide how to reinvest it. By returning such decisions to the marketplace, project financing has the potential to accomplish a fundamental reform and, in the process, create considerable value for stockholders.

Viewed in this light, the resurgence of project finance is part of the current restructuring movement that is pushing companies toward greater specialization and decentralization. The success of such restructuring, of course, is far from implying that there are no longer benefits to corporate combinations, and that all merger and acquisition activity will suddenly come to a halt. But, when there are expected benefits from joining parts of the operations of two very different companies, project finance provides a means of carving out for investors only that part of the collaboration that is likely to be valuable, while avoiding the inefficiencies that tend to breed in conglomerate-type organizations.

For example, project financing is increasingly being used as the means of funding joint ventures and networking arrangements, both of which allow companies to pool their resources in large-scale efforts while retaining the benefits of specialization. A case in point is Catalyst Energy. Founded in 1982, in its first four years of existence this company established $1.5 billion worth of electric generation projects under its management, with fewer than two dozen employees. Catalyst contracted out most of the actual construction and design work, choosing instead to specialize in the process of finding sites, gaining the required licenses, negotiating contracts, and arranging financing. As this example is further meant to illustrate, project financing is giving smaller companies the means to compete vigorously with large, established corporations—which have enjoyed, perhaps for too long, a protected position through their privileged access to large pools of capital.

PROJECT FINANCING IS TIGHTLY BOUND BY RULES

To qualify as a project financing, a venture must be capable of standing alone as a completely independent entity, and its nature must be such that it has a clearly definable conclusion. The investors must receive cash flows from the project as they are generated. The legal entity set up to establish the project must have a finite life, so it cannot outlive its original purpose. Any creditors, furthermore, must have claims to the assets and cash flows of only the project itself, with no recourse to other assets of owners (except to the extent that any of the owners have other contractual obligations to the project).

When there is a single corporate sponsor, project financing can be arranged simply by negotiating non-recourse loans through special-purpose

---

3. For a comprehensive and insightful account of this controversy, see Michael Jensen, "The Takeover Controversy: Analysis and Evidence," *Midland Corporate Finance Journal* (Summer 1986).

TABLE 2
OTHER PROJECT
FINANCINGS
JANUARY 1, 1987 TO
AUGUST 31, 1988

TOTAL	$7,248.0 million	26 projects
Oil & Gas Development	$4,631.3 million	6 projects
Plant Construction	$1,344.9 million	5 projects
Resort Development	$593.3 million	5 projects
R&D Partnerships	$457.2 million	5 projects
Miscellaneous	$221.2 million	5 projects

subsidiaries or trusts. Other project financings are structured around non-recourse leveraged leases, in which the lease obligations are payable solely from the assets and cash flows of the project. In the case of joint ventures, the simplest form of a project financing is a general partnership among the parties in the venture. One example is a partnership formed to develop a specific oil field and then to dissolve when the properties are sold or depleted.

A limited partnership also provides a useful financing structure when some of the partners in a joint venture do not want to participate actively in the management of day-to-day operations (or in the special case where a single corporate sponsor wants to raise outside equity capital).[4] Because the debt is non-recourse, general partners enjoy limited liability with respect to the project's debt. But even with this protection, in order to contain potential liabilities arising from other types of claims, sponsoring companies often form separately incorporated subsidiaries to serve as general partner in their stead.[5]

For such ventures to gain non-recourse financing, however, the relationships among the participants must be spelled out in detailed contracts. To give up recourse to the sponsoring company, the creditors must be assured that they are protected against the failure of the sponsor (or other involved parties) to live up to their part of the bargain. If they do not, creditors can sue the project entity itself. In this way, the creditors' exposure is confined to a well-defined set of project-specific risks.

In short, the credit support provided by such contracts provides the foundation for project loans. Thus, project financing can work only in situations which allow such contracting to be accomplished (and enforced) at a supportable cost.[6]

An Example of Investors' Contractual Protection

In 1972, British Petroleum raised $945 million in project financing for the development of its North Sea oil field (the "Forties Field") from a syndicate of 66 banks. At the time, it was the largest industrial loan in history, and it offers a good illustration of how such a venture can be structured.[7] The basic terms of the arrangement dictated that the lenders had recourse only to the assets of the project (that is, oil) in the event of default, so that BP's other assets were protected from the consequences of project failure.

This segregation of assets was achieved by creating a new entity, Norex, which was controlled by the

4. For example, Catalyst Energy made effective use of this organizational form to structure its electric power generation project financings. The majority of the cost was raised through non-recourse debt, with most of the remainder provided by limited partnership equity. During the beginning years of a project, the cash flow left after debt support payments was committed to the limited partners. Only after retirement of the debt and return of the limited partner's capital (plus a prearranged minimum return on investment) would Catalyst Energy, as general partner, begin receiving a significant share of the cash flows. Thus, the limited partners' interest is similar to subordinated debt, while the general partner possesses the residual equity position. Catalyst chose projects well, and six years after its birth had established a level of cash flow that made it the object of a friendly acquisition, which promises to leave the founders very wealthy.

5. Innovators will undoubtedly find more ways to frame non-recourse project financings. The key, again, is to establish the project within a finite-lived organizational structure that separates it from its owners, yet preserves their control over the reinvestment of capital as it returns from the project.

6. The requirement that the project have independent substance has been addressed by another author in terms of sources of "credit support." These typically come in the form of contracts to purchase output from the project, or supply inputs at controlled cost. Thus, even though the project's sponsors do not provide an outright guarantee of the project's creditworthiness, they provide credit support in other, project-specific forms. See Jacob J. Worenklein, "Project Financing of Joint Ventures," *Public Utilities Fortnightly*, December 3, 1981, pp. 39-46.

7. This British Petroleum example is presented and analyzed at some length by Richard Brealey and Stewart Myers, *Principles of Corporate Finance*, 3rd Edition, McGraw-Hill, 1988, pp. 6 00-601.

banks. The loan was made to Norex, and Norex paid the proceeds to BP Development (a subsidiary of British Petroleum) in return for contracts for the future delivery of oil from the Forties Field.[8] Norex in turn contracted to sell the oil to BP Trading Company. With the funds from the sale of the oil, Norex would make debt service payments to the banks.[9]

The banks were willing to lend to the project without recourse because they were protected by contracts with BP Development setting out all of the development steps in detail; and compliance with the plan was guaranteed by British Petroleum. In short, a detailed set of contracts enabled BP to assure the participating banks that their sole risk was that the amount of oil available from the field would not be sufficient to repay the loans.

PROJECT FINANCING HAS A LONG HISTORY

Far from being a johnny-come-lately gimmick, non-recourse financing of finite-lived ventures has ancient roots. In fact, a financing arrangement that enabled medieval Italian bankers to undertake a mining venture in England offers a 700-year-old example with surprising parallels to the BP project. In 1299, the English Crown negotiated a loan from the Frescobaldi, a leading Florentine merchant-banking firm, for which payment was to be made in the form of output from the Devon silver mines. The arrangement was crystalized in the form of a one-year lease for the total output of the mines. The contract entitled the Italian venturers to control the operation of the mines for that year and to take as much unrefined ore as they could extract, while paying all costs of operation. No guarantees were made, however, concerning the total amount of ore that could be mined, or the value of refined metal extracted from the ore.[10]

In short, the risks faced by these bankers long ago were much like those faced by their modern-day counterparts in the North Sea venture.[11]

Project Financing Was the Rule until Trade Became a Continuous Process

Until the 17th century, moreover, the rule in commerce was to finance trading expeditions on a voyage-by-voyage basis. That is, cargoes and ships were liquidated, and the profits divided among investors, at the end of each voyage. New investors then had to be found to back the next one. Although many investors willingly "rolled over" their money, they did so at their own discretion. But, then overseas trade expanded rapidly, becoming the "growth industry" of its day. This rapid growth imposed mounting capital requirements that could be met only by expanding the base of investors beyond the traditional circle of merchant guilds.[12]

The means for raising capital directly from the public was found in the creation of "joint-stock" companies, the forerunners of the modern corporation, which could draw capital from anyone willing to risk it.[13] This ability was not entirely new, but rather represented an extension of the older practice of merchants taking deposits (hence "merchant-bankers"), either for interest or for a share of profits. But the formalization of the older merchant banking practices through the sale of stock allowed for the raising of capital on an unprecedented scale.

Unlike the modern corporation, though, the early companies were committed to allowing investors to withdraw their funds directly from the treasury upon demand (much like open-end mutual funds). The problem with this arrangement was that, to meet redemption demands, companies might be forced to liquidate inventories or other assets, which in the extreme could lead to ruin. When commerce with Asia became a continuous process, the trading companies found they needed permanent capital, and this led to a revolutionary change in business organization.

The Dutch East India Co., for example, began operations under a charter which authorized mem-

---

8. If the development were successful, BP Development would be obligated to deliver the oil on a specified schedule. Thus, this was in essence a reserved production agreement.

9. If British Petroleum produced more oil from the field in any given year than it was required to deliver to Norex, the funds from the sale of the extra oil would be placed in a special account upon which Norex could draw later if future oil deliveries were insufficient to meet debt service obligations.

10. Jean Gimpel, *The Medieval Machine: The Industrial Revolution of the Middle Ages*, Holt Rinehart Winston (New York: 1976) p. 73.

11. It may be worth noting that the taking of interest was strictly prohibited throughout the Christian world at the time. Since the bankers were at risk in this venture, however, the arrangement fell within the bounds allowed by canon law. Finding ways to cope with regulators, it turns out, is nothing new for innovative financiers.

12. It was not only growth, however, that displaced project financing. With the consolidation of political power at the end of the Middle Ages, sovereign states began to favor some of their large private enterprises, thereby creating "artificial," if you will, economies of scale. Companies of merchants were granted privileges in the form of preferential customs duties and outright monopolies—privileges that were not granted to individuals, but only to chartered trading companies. The governments, however, also levied a requirement. In return for their advantages and privileged position, the trading companies were expected to increase the national wealth. They were protected from domestic competition so they could compete more strongly against their foreign rivals.

13. The venerable British East India Company was chartered in 1600 and endured until 1858. The United Dutch East India Company arose through the 1602 consolidation of ten companies of merchant venturers. French, Spanish, and Portuguese companies were also formed at about the same time. A relative latecomer in 1670, the Hudson's Bay Company continues to this day.

bers to withdraw their capital at will, but suspended such repayments in 1612. Its rival, the British East India Co., also restricted such payments the same year. but this was apparently not an easy transition for the British company because, over the next half century, it vacillated between the traditional practice of settling accounts at each voyage's end and the newer practice of carrying forward the balances to later voyages.

The reasons both companies moved toward the "impounding" of permanent capital are fairly clear. Their funds were tied up in warehouse buildings and land (much of it half a world away from home), as well as great fleets; and the values of such assets could not be readily realized in the thin markets of the day. The situation also owed significantly to changes in ship-building, the "high technology" of the era, as well as to the voyages of discovery. Over the last half of the 16th century, the carrying power of merchant fleets increased dramatically, transforming inter-continental ocean commerce from a series of independent ventures into a process involving a steady flow of goods. An independent captain could not simply sail into an Asian port and expect to load a cargo from the dock-side markets at reasonable prices. Permanent representatives (called "factors") and warehouses ("factories") had to be stationed at the foreign ports, and treaties negotiated to protect them.

The large fixed costs for foreign warehouses required the companies to carry a burden of what was referred to at the time as "dead stock." Not only was it illiquid, it was also next to impossible to allocate fairly to the accounts of individual voyages. Liquidity for this dead stock came to be provided in the secondary markets in place of on-demand redemption.[14] Trading in the stock of the chartered companies joined the commodity-trading, foreign exchange, and insurance-brokering activities in the merchant's exchanges that then formed the hub of commerce in the major trading cities.[15]

PROJECT FINANCE AT PRESENT

What became, then, of the older tradition of pro-

ject financing? Project finance did not die out completely during this evolution toward the modern public corporation. It has continued to be employed down through the years in separately accountable ventures such as overseas mineral exploration projects. And, for reasons related to the current restructuring wave, it now appears to be experiencing a resurgence. Modern corporations continue, of course, to need permanent capital when value would be lost if the corporation were subject to precipitous liquidation. But, as the markets continue to reward companies for repurchasing their stock, spinning off and selling unrelated operations, and leveraging mature businesses, investors appear increasingly skeptical about granting companies the privilege of permanent capital. Just as changing technology and a changing political environment led to the innovation of permanent capital in the 17th century, new currents of change in the 20th century are eroding the need for it in certain key areas of business activity.

Project Financing Has Recently Expanded to Independent Power Production

Fertile ground for project financing was opened in the U.S. with the passage of the Public Utility Regulatory Policy Act (PURPA) in 1978. Under the terms of PURPA, local utilities are required to buy all the output of qualified independent power producers under long-term contracts, at a price equal to the utility's marginal cost of generating electricity. In so doing, PURPA provided the foundation of contractual obligations upon which non-recourse lending could take place.[16] And this in turn has brought about the development of a broad network composed of experienced project underwriters with access to large pools of institutional capital.

Fourteen hydroelectric and geothermal projects have been announced since January 1987, providing total capacity of nearly 400 megawatts at a total construction cost of just under $1 billion. Because these hydroelectric and geothermal plants are often located in remote areas, construction presents

---

14. E. L. J. Coornaert, The Cambridge Economic History of Europe, Vol. IV, Chapter IV, Cambridge University Press (1967), pp. 223-275.

15. In 17th-century Amsterdam, a market even developed in "nominal" shares which were not registered with the Dutch East India Company, and never could be. This nominal stock market allowed speculators to carry on their activities despite attempts by the Company to impose regulation on the trading in its stock. Source: Fernand Braudel, "The Wheels of Commerce," in *Civilization and Capitalism*, Vol.II', Harper & Row (New York: 1982) pp. 101-103.

16. In these electric power generation project financings, the creditors are protected by long-term contracts to sell electricity to the local utility company and

to buy fuel from a natural gas distributor or other supplier. In the case of hydro-power facilities, no fuel is necessary, but there can be uncertainty about river levels; and insurers have come forward who are willing to write policies against the risk of low water, enabling insured projects to maintain debt support payments. In addition, care for the facilities is provided under long-term, fixed-price operating contracts with engineering firms. Even the construction phase is accomplished under fixed-price, turnkey contracts protected by performance bonds. When lenders want variable interest rate loans, furthermore, underwriters arrange long-term interest rate swaps to protect a project against unfavorable changes in market interest rates.

significant challenges. Once deployed, however, these "robot" plants need no fuel and impose very little operating cost.

An interesting example is the $40 million project to refurbish a hydro-power dam on the Penobscot River in Maine and install automated generating equipment. Upon completion, the facility will have an expected useful life of about 50 years, and will sell its electricity to Central Maine Power Company under a long-term contract covering nearly half its expected life. Because it will require no fuel and only one full-time caretaker to operate, variable costs will be only a fraction of revenues.[17]

Such projects are thus quintessential cash cows. Holding a non-recourse loan in such a project, moreover, is a less risky investment than buying a long-term bond from the utility that has committed to buy the project's electricity. In the unlikely event the utility should go bankrupt, the project has the status of a supplier rather than a creditor, and thus can continue selling power to the reorganized utility company. With project financing, furthermore, the backers are assured that the capital will be returned to them as the project runs its course, rather than fall within the discretionary grasp of some corporate board.

Project Financing Is Also Beginning to Be Used to Build Factories

Project financing is now expanding into the realm of even larger machines—namely, manufacturing plants. In 1988 there have been five plant construction efforts undertaken through non-recourse project financings that have totalled some $1.3 billion. And just a few months ago, as mentioned at the outset of this article, GE Capital Corporation (which cut its teeth on independent electrical generation project financings) announced a significant expansion of its industrial project finance group, which will specialize in financing the construction and operation of industrial facilities.

Earlier in 1988, GE Capital arranged $72 million of non-recourse project loans to build the Bev-Pac beverage container plant, which provides a glimpse of the kind of projects it will be underwriting. This plant will make aluminum beverage cans, with a capacity of 1.2 billion cans annually. Unlike other such plants, however, the Bev-Pac plant will be owned and operated independently of any single beverage maker—that is, this plant represents a reversal of the process of vertical integration.

Why do project finance and independent ownership work well together? Much of the risk associated with financing such a large plant arises from uncertainty about whether it will be able to operate at full capacity. Independent ownership will enable it to enter into arms'-length agreements to supply competing beverage makers, giving it the flexibility to operate at a profitable level of output without depending on any single brand's success.[18] For a proprietary bottler, moreover, entering into long-term agreements for a portion of the output from such a plant is a cost-effective alternative to building a smaller one "in-house"; and such contracts in turn make it possible to gain the benefits of high leverage through non-recourse project financing.

The credit rating of the plant as an independent project, furthermore, is likely to be better than that of its customers. If one of its customers loses market share to another, for instance, the Bev-Pac plant can adjust. Like the robot power plants, moreover, it enjoys the status of a supplier rather than a creditor in the event a customer goes bankrupt.[19] Also, like the robot power plants, it is the sort of cash cow that investors like to keep on a short leash.

Another recent industrial project financing worth mention is the joint venture between Chrysler and Mitsubishi (called "Diamond-Star Motors") to build a new automobile plant in Illinois. This venture raised $500 million of the $700 million total cost through non-recourse loans from Japanese banks. With more than 470 robots, this futuristic plant is expected to have ten times the level of assembly automation found in most auto plants.[20]

Project finance, as suggested earlier, can also provide an attractive alternative to merger. Joint ventures such as the one by Chrysler with Mitsubishi offer the synergistic potential of a merger without the costs and other barriers that would confront a full-fledged corporate marriage.

---

17. Another example is the fully automated, unmanned hydro-power plant that went into operation June 5, 1987 on the Snoqualmie River near Seattle.

18. It would be more agreeable to Pepsi, for example, to contract for containers from an independent producer than to depend upon the excess capacity of a plant owned by Coke.

19. So-called "step-up" provisions are sometimes used in joint ventures to create a stronger financial entity than the individual sponsoring companies themselves. A step-up provision obligates the surviving companies to increase their participation, and take up the slack in the event of a default by another participant. In the jargon of financial theory, the members of the group provide each other with "co-insurance," thus gaining the advantage of merger without incurring the full costs. (See Worenklein, cited earlier in note 6.).

20. Estimate reported in *Business Week*, September 12, 1988, p. 73.

Shared Benefits in Cogeneration

Such joint venture project financing, although new to manufacturing, also has precedents in other areas of business. For example, the biggest single category of recent project financings involves the construction and operation of cogeneration facilities. Since the beginning of 1987, 38 such projects have been announced that, at a total cost of $4.6 billion, are expected to provide a total of 4,577 megawatts of new generating capacity. The list of participating corporations in such ventures includes familiar names like Boise Cascade, Union Carbide, Sun Oil, ARCO, and (through a subsidiary) Southern California Edison.

Cogeneration is the simultaneous production and commercial exploitation of electrical and thermal energy, from a single fuel source. Thermal energy, or heat, is a wasted by-product in the traditional process of producing electricity. Instead of dumping the left-over heat into the environment, cogeneration puts it to work, prompting one enthusiast to describe cogeneration as "exploring for oil in the cooling towers of America's utilities."[21] Whereas a stand-alone electrical generation plant is able to convert only about 33 percent of its fuel's available energy into usable output, a cogeneration facility is capable of 70 percent efficiency.

Commercial cogeneration thus requires the capability not only to sell electricity, but also to use the left-over heat for some commercial purpose. Such uses currently include the providing of process steam for a chemical plant or oil refinery, enhanced oil recovery, or heating a military installation or a college campus. A utility acting on its own cannot use the steam, however, because the scope of its activities is limited by regulators. Likewise, an industrial corporation acting on its own cannot sell electricity; nor are the two free to merge. In fact, Congress enacted PURPA because few, if any, discrete economic entities then in existence were capable of capturing within themselves the benefits of cogeneration along with the costs. PURPA was aimed at making it possible for ventures that incur the cost of cogeneration to be able to realize its benefits, thus enabling them to attract private capital.[22]

The decision to invest in cogeneration, then, is a decision by a non-utility to get into the power production business. As such, it typically represents a diversification of a firm's product line in order to exploit potential synergies with existing activities. By providing a cheaper source of power, cogeneration has been used to enhance the productivity of a variety of installations (including chemical plants, paper mills, oil fields, food processing plants, textile mills, and lumber mills), in some cases making the difference between closing a plant and keeping it open.[23] Although cogeneration plants represent competitors for utilities unaccustomed to having any, the utility companies are also likely to benefit from higher employment and commercial activity in its region.[24] They also benefit from greater planning flexibility due to shorter construction lead-times for cogeneration plants.[25]

Like most ventures funded by project finance, all the important relationships in a cogeneration project are detailed in contracts. For example, the local utility enters into a long-term contract (often at a fixed price) to purchase electricity from the project.

---

21. Comments by Thomas R. Casten in *Energy Utilities: The Next Ten Years*, proceedings of a symposium sponsored by the California Public Utilities Commission, at Stanford University, March 27-28, 1981, p.79.

22. Recognizing the bargaining advantage a utility could wield over cogenerators, PURPA requires regulated utilities not only to purchase cogenerated power at the utility's marginal cost, but also supply backup power at non-discriminatory rates. Small power producers (less than 80 megawatts) using renewable energy sources (i.e., hydro, geothermal, or biomass) were also included, as discussed earlier.

23. Union Carbide, for example, touted the cogeneration facility at its Seadrift plant in Texas as follows: "The improved economics provided by reduced energy costs improves the job security of all of our plant employees." Union Carbide News Release, 1/22/87.

24. To some people in the utility business, however, cogeneration is a dirty word because it has transformed major customers into suppliers blessed with the protection of federal regulators. Such transformations have, for example, coincided with efforts on the part of the rate-setting agency to force industrial customers to subsidize low rates for households. In other cases, the transformation has been made in the wake of frustrated efforts to get the utility to guarantee a minimum service level.

In some circles, cogeneration facilities are even derisively referred to as "PURPA machines," with the implication that they exist only because of favorable tax treatment. The 1986 tax reforms, however, wiped out the accelerated deprecia-

tion schedule, investment tax credits, and energy credits that were the basis of such criticism. The continued vitality of project financing for independent power production in the post-reform tax environment is testimony to the underlying economic viability of such ventures.

Furthermore, there need not be an adversarial relationship between the cogeneration plant's host and the local utility. Instead, project financing for cogeneration facilities can enable the utility company to share in the profit. For example, when Sun Energy and Exploration Company made plans in 1987 to build a 225 megawatt cogeneration project in conjunction with the steam generation plant at its Midway-Sunset Field in California (where the steam is used for enhanced oil recovery), it formed a 50-50 partnership with Mission Energy, an unregulated subsidiary of Southern California Edison.

Indeed, all utilities could share in the efficiencies of cogeneration even without direct participation, if they could negotiate contracts to buy electricity at prices below their own cost of generation. Currently, however, federal regulations require them to pay their own full long-term marginal cost (called "avoided cost"). This requirement, then, is the true bone of contention, and avoided cost issues are under vigorous debate in such industry forums as *The Public Utilities Fortnightly*, as well as in the corridors of power.

25. The lead time is two to three years for a cogeneration plant, compared with five to seven years for a conventional coal-fired plant—or up to ten years for a nuclear plant.

These contracts have become standardized, and frequently extend twenty or more years into the future. The assurances provided by such contracts in turn make it possible to reduce the cost of capital through the use of project financing.

If the host plant (that is, the refining or chemical plant where the cogeneration facility is located) were for some reason to shut down and default on its obligations to buy steam, project financing would again prove advantageous. The major expense for a normal cogeneration facility involves a few large pieces of machinery which can easily be shipped to a new site.[26] An independent cogeneration project has few employees who depend solely upon it for their livelihood (sometimes none) and few claims by other stakeholders. Thus, the courts can deal with the liquidation of an independent project much more expeditiously than would be the case if it were part of a corporate package. (Financial economists would describe this benefit of project finance as a reduction in "bankruptcy costs.")

Project financing therefore enhances the inherent flexibility of the equipment, making it cheaper and quicker to exercise the redeployment option. Without exercising too much poetic license, it might be said that the use of project financing puts "legal wheels" on assets that already possess a high degree of inherent mobility.

Joint Ventures in Mineral Exploration

Limited recourse lending arrangements have long been used to finance large natural resource projects involving several parties; and no discussion of project financing would be complete without mention of the Trans-Alaska Pipeline project, a joint venture among Standard Oil Company (Ohio), Atlantic Richfield, Exxon, British Petroleum, Mobil Oil, Phillips Petroleum, Union Oil, and Amerada Hess. The pipeline was financed through separately-incorporated subsidiaries, SOHIO Pipeline Corporation and BP Pipelines, Inc. SOHIO raised a billion dollars—most of its share in the cost of the pipeline and tanker fleet—by means of revenue bonds (issued by the Valdez Marine Terminal Authority), reserved production agreements, and tanker leases.[27]

A more recent joint venture was announced in mid-July to develop a major oil field off the coast of Newfoundland. Hibernia Oil Field Partners is a joint venture partnership with Mobil Oil of Canada slated to serve as managing general partner and project operator. Other partners include Gulf Canada Resources, Inc., Petro-Canada, and the Canadian units of Chevron Oil and Columbia Gas. The field, which will cost $4.1 billion to develop, is expected to produce 110,000 barrels of oil a day starting in 1995, with an expected productive life of 16 to 20 years.

Details of the financing have not yet been reported as we go to press, but the Canadian federal government, as well as the provincial government, have announced that they will support the project through direct grants, tax exemptions, and loan guarantees. Thus the makings are in place for a substantial amount of borrowing by the Hibernia Partnership, with limited recourse to the partners.

PROJECT FINANCING IS EVEN BEING USED FOR RESEARCH AND DEVELOPMENT

During the 1980s, the use of project financing has spread to industrial research and development, though in the form of limited partnership arrangements rather than the familiar non-recourse bank loans. In the early 1980s these were sometimes highly leveraged, but changes in the tax code in 1984 and 1986 have significantly reduced the leverage used in R&D Limited Partnership (RDLP) financings. In RDLPs since then, a group of equity participants takes the place of the syndicate of banks seen in project financings such as our North Sea example. Although they do not use non-recourse debt, such projects are nonetheless finite-lived ventures with clearly stated objectives and conclusions. Partnership cash flows, furthermore, are committed to be paid out to limited partners according to prearranged rules, thereby placing the reinvestment decision in the hands of investors.[28]

Such partnerships can be particularly valuable for joint ventures. For example, NaTec, Ltd, a 50-50 partnership between CRS Sirrine and Industrial Resources, Inc., was recently formed to develop a process that will use nahcolyte (a mineable, natural-

---

26. Few sites require more than general-purpose industrial buildings for protection from the elements. Exceptions are generally confined to high-density areas such as college campuses.

27. For details, see Paul D. Phillips, John C. Groth, and R. Malcolm Richards, "Financing the Alaskan Project: The Experience at Sohio," *Financial Management* 8 (Autumn 1979), pp. 7-16.

28. For detailed discussions of R&D Limited Partnerships and the impact of the Tax Reform Act of 1986, see John Kensinger and John Martin, "R&D Limited Partnerships and the New Tax Law," *Midland Corporate Finance Journal*, 4 (Winter 1987) pp. 44-54, and "An Economic Analysis of R&D Limited Partnerships," *Midland Corporate Finance Journal*, 3 (Winter 1986) pp. 33-45.

ly-occurring form of sodium bicarbonate) to clean up the emissions from coal-fired power plants.[29] The process promises to be cheaper and more efficient than current techniques. CRS Sirrine is a highly regarded, NYSE-listed construction and engineering company that builds and upgrades power plants, so the potential benefits to it are obvious. Industrial Resources (IR) is an over-the-counter company with practically no sales or operations—but it owns leases to large deposits of nahcolyte.

If Sirrine had gone ahead with the project alone, IR would have gotten a valuable free ride. But in order to make the project attractive to Sirrine, IR had to share in the costs as well as the benefits. One solution would have been to merge the two companies; but even if that were possible, it would have created complications beyond the scope of the nahcolyte project. A simple joint venture allowed both companies to create an entity which could capture enough benefits from the project to offset the cost.

Joint venturing is not the whole story for project financing in R&D, however. For instance, when Cummins Engine needed to fund its research effort on a new generation of hybrid diesel engines (combining ceramic turbines and pistons as sources of power in a single powerplant), it used R&D limited partnership financing to raise $20 million for the project. In another notable case, Genentech's clinical partnerships financed research into anti-cancer agents as well as human and animal growth hormones. Within the past few months, furthermore, Nova Pharmaceuticals and Amgen have announced their sponsorship of RDLPs totalling $120 million.

The use of RDLP financing has grown rapidly since the first one was formed in 1978. The U.S. Department of Commerce reported $1.7 billion of RDLP financing from 1978 to 1984. The *Wall Street Journal* reported another $1.7 billion for the period 1984-86.[30] Although the tax reforms of 1984 and 1986 eliminated some of the tax benefits associated with RDLPs, Robert A. Stanger Associates (the rating agency for limited partnerships) reports substantial recent growth in RDLP financing. Nor has the Revenue Enhancement Act of 1987 squelched investors' desire to own a "pure play" in high-tech research.

The RDLP field, moreover, has attracted the involvement of several major investment banking firms, which are structuring diversified pools of R&D projects for investors of moderate means. The first to enter this field was Merrill Lynch, which raised capital for its first ML Technology Ventures partnership in September 1985. In little more than two years, it had committed the entire $70 million raised to projects at fourteen different companies. Seven of them are expected to introduce new products in 1988.

Merrill Lynch is planning to close another $80 to $100 million RDLP in September 1988. Paine Webber closed its second $80 million RDLP in early 1988, and Prudential Bache has been regularly acquiring new funds each quarter for the last two years in its series of Pru-Tech partnerships.

These modern-day investment bankers are taking direct roles in high-tech venturing in much the same way as their merchant banking forebears engaged directly in commercial ventures. Merrill Lynch, for example, has formed a subsidiary, Merrill Lynch R&D Management, which serves as general partner in its RDLPs.[31] The R&D management company is responsible not only for managing the projects of the partnership, but also for selecting them. In finding projects, it focuses on smaller companies that have already developed base technologies and have reached the stage at which second-round financing is needed to develop patentable products. The partnership then pays a licensing fee for the use of the base technology and hires the technology's developer to conduct the remaining research. The resulting patents belong to the partnership. The partnership also frequently receives warrants to buy common stock in the companies it goes into business with, so it stands to gain from their other activities as well.

Merrill Lynch R&D Management Company is very much involved in the process of initiating and conducting research efforts, but it differs from an ordinary corporation in one very important sense. The RDLP it manages has a finite life. The partnership agreement states that it will terminate not later than January 31, 2005 (at which time it would be only 19 years old); and current plans are to terminate it sooner, as early as 1996. If new backers can be found for follow-on partnerships the process will continue, but there is no provision for automatic roll-over of proceeds from old ventures into new ones.

29. Reported in *Wall Street Journal*, 7/27/88, p. 4.
30. *Wall Street Journal*, March 10, 1986, p.12.

31. In-house expertise is provided by two vice-presidents with technical backgrounds. One is a Ph.D. chemist who was formerly director of corporate R&D at a major pharmaceuticals company, and the other is a Ph.D. in electrical engineering.

But Allocating Costs and Revenues to Individual Projects Can Present Problems

There is, however, a potential difficulty in carving RDLPs and other forms of project finance out of larger, complex organizations. First of all, project financing requires that the assets and cash flows must be allocated fairly to each project—a task which can be quite daunting. Second, even if such accounting *can* be done fairly, there may be no inexpensive way of ensuring that *will* be done so. For example, if a corporation owns pieces of independently-financed projects that are under its management, conflicts of interest can arise among its shareholders and owners of specific projects. The corporation, for example, may act as a contractor providing services for a fee to its partnerships, or one partnership may sell to another which is managed by the same general partner. Whenever goods or services flow through the network, problems can arise in setting fair transfer prices.

Management then has fiduciary obligations not only to the stockholders of the corporation (which owns a piece of the whole portfolio of projects) but also to the owners of each individual project. When the "good of the whole" is in conflict with the good of any of the parts, owners of individual projects can rationally expect that the management will tend to opt for the whole. That is, in the case of RDLPs or projects sponsored by a corporation, corporate management has an incentive to put the interests of the corporation ahead of those of limited partners. To compensate for their vulnerability, such investors accordingly charge for the expected cost in advance by offering a reduced price for a given project.

For this reason, premium prices are commanded by project financing arrangements which provide either contractual assurances limiting this conflict of interest or, alternatively, independent management. It is probably in large part for this reason (as suggested by the proliferation of lawsuits by limited partners against single corporate sponsors of RDLPs) that independent project management by investment banking subsidiaries seems to be overtaking the more conventional single-corporate-sponsored RDLPs in project financing for R&D. Since 1985, much of the money raised through RDLP financings has come from the pools formed by investment banking

firms. Managed by subsidiaries of the investment banker, these pools are independent of the corporations paid to conduct the research.

THE BENEFITS OF PROJECT FINANCE

Limited Management Discretion over Cash Flows from Caretaker Activities

But if the difficulties of assigning benefits and costs to individual projects may limit the growth of project financing, the advantages of rendering such an accounting, where possible, seem fairly clear. As suggested at the beginning of this article, the common advantage shared by all forms of project financing is that the entity created in a project financing has a finite life, and the "dividend policy" of the project can be spelled out in the contract. This means that investors rather than managers get to make the decisions about reinvesting the cash flows from the project. Conferring this power on investors is potentially valuable—at least in cases where companies face limited growth opportunities—because investors may have reason to doubt whether managers will be sufficiently demanding when comparing investment opportunities within the corporation to the alternatives available outside.[32]

Besides curbing unwise reinvestment, project finance holds out several other potential benefits.

Project Financing Can Reduce Taxes and Limit Other Liabilities

Project financing through limited partnership arrangements offers the not inconsiderable advantage of avoiding the double taxation to which U.S. corporations are exposed. Even those partnerships which are publicly traded are free of double taxation for a wide range of so-called passive activities. Under Section 7704 of the Internal Revenue Code (enacted in the Revenue Act of 1987), the list of allowable income sources includes the following activities involving natural resources: exploration, development, mining or production, processing, refining, transportation (including gas or oil pipelines) or the marketing of any mineral or natural resource (including fertilizer, timber, and geothermal energy).[33]

---

32. Michael Jensen has refined this argument into the "control function of debt" in his article, "Agency Costs of Free Cash Flow," *American Economic Review* (May 1986). See also the article cited in note 3.

33. In addition there are several other income sources that are commonly understood to be passive for income tax purposes: interest, dividends, real property rents or capital gains, and gains from commodities trading for a partnership specializing in such trading (including futures, forwards, and options).

The tax differential for partnerships continues to give them a significant potential edge in such "caretaker" activities. In the new tax environment, corporations will increasingly find it attractive to provide expertise under contract, while the ownership of high-dollar real estate and natural resource assets is transferred directly to investors.[34] Highly leveraged project financings with non-recourse loans likewise take advantage of the tax deductibility of interest, which effectively avoids double taxation of income from any source.

Besides reducing tax liabilities, project financing also insulates other activities of the corporation from the risks of the new project. Because investors forgo recourse to general corporate assets, project finance serves the function of shifting certain well-defined corporate risks away from stockholders and, perhaps more important, from management. Corporate managers may be considerably more willing to take on a large, risky project if the continued existence of their employer does not ride on its outcome.[35]

Taxes, however, are not the whole story. Nor is risk-shifting and limited liability, since the investors in a project financing know that their rewards depend exclusively upon the performance of the project, and charge appropriately for the risks they bear. Risks do not miraculously disappear simply because they are no longer recorded on the balance sheet, as some would have us believe.[36] Rather project finance simply transfers them from one set of investors to another. Admittedly, though, the greater ability or willingness of the latter group to bear such risks may indeed provide real benefits.

Project Financing Offers a Wider Array of Investment Choices and Reduces the Costs of Information Processing for Investors

A potentially significant non-tax benefit is that project financing makes the capital markets "more complete" by providing investors with a "pure play" that was not previously available. Without RDLPs, for example, an investor wishing to participate in a firm's research and development efforts would have to buy stock in the whole company. This is analogous to someone who wants a steak being forced to buy a whole steer. It can be argued that investors are willing to pay a premium in order to get the thing they want without being forced to take a package of other things along with it.[37]

In a project financing, furthermore, the investment is subjected to outside scrutiny before being undertaken. The investors, that is, have a direct say in the capital investment decision, thus enhancing the efficiency of resource allocation. Take the case of an oil and gas exploration project. The geophysical data necessary to estimate the value of oil reserves is difficult to obtain and expensive to analyze.[38] If the project were undertaken as part of a corporate whole, investors in all of the company's outstanding securities would need such information. By isolating the project, however, the need for such information is limited to the investors in the project financing, sparing others the cost of information acquisition. When bidding is concentrated upon a specific area rather than a pool of geographically dispersed holdings, furthermore, there are more potential bidders who can afford to become informed, thus enhancing the efficiency of valuation.

Project financing can reduce another kind of information cost as well. When managers have information that is not publicly available, raising funds for new investment opportunities may be difficult unless proprietary information of value to competitors is revealed to the public.[39] Financing a research and development project through a privately-placed project financing, for example, can solve the problem. By revealing the necessary information about the project to a small group of investors, a fair price for the financing can be obtained without revealing the proprietary information to the public. Since the investors in the project have a stake in maintaining confidentiality, the danger of an information leak is small.

34. The Marriott Corp., as just one example among many in a growing trend, created limited partnerships to own its hotels. The corporation itself manages those hotels through contracts with the LPs.

35. The problem of managerial aversion to risk was first discussed formally by Michael Jensen and William Meckling, "Theory of the Firm: Managerial Behavior, Agency Costs, and Ownership Structure," *Journal of Financial Economics* (1976).

36. Some have suggested that one of the principal benefits of project finance is that it provides "off-balance sheet financing." Financial economists, however, would argue that, in a reasonably efficient market—one in which investors and rating agencies are intelligent enough to see through paper transactions—the benefits derived from off-balance sheet financing are likely to be trivial or non-existent. At

least for the kinds of large companies that typically use project financing.

37. See Stewart Myers, "The Capital Structure Puzzle," *Journal of Finance* (1984).

38. For instance, when Tenneco announced its intention to put its domestic oil and gas properties up for sale, a potential bidder estimated that it would cost $20 million to analyze the data Tenneco made available to the public. Source: *Wall Street Journal*, 7/25/88, p.2.

39. This problem was first identified by Hayne Leland and David Pyle, in "Informational Asymmetries, Financial Structure, and Financial Intermediation," *Journal of Finance* 32 (1977), pp. 371-87.

Project Financing Can Enhance Flexibility and Thereby Further Reduce Risk

Project finance in the U.S., as we have seen, has been concentrated largely in independent power production and automated manufacturing plants. The common thread is that they are big, expensive machines which not only are capable of operating with relatively little direct labor input, but also are readily transferred to alternate uses. The bulk of their costs are incurred up-front, and their economic viability thus depends upon just two things: maintaining a market for the output and maintaining a positive spread between the cost of input and the price of output.

When the output is generic (as in the case of the Bev-Pac plant described earlier), maintaining a market is facilitated by remaining free from the fortunes of any particular brand name. Independent ownership makes it easier to find outlets to absorb the full capacity of the plant. When the viability of the equipment hinges upon geographic proximity to one large customer for a particular output, such as the steam from a cogeneration facility, it is often necessary to negotiate long-term contracts for purchase of inputs and sale of output. The existence of these contracts, as we have seen, makes project financing possible; and project financing, in turn, significantly reduces the frictions which would otherwise hinder asset redeployment.

Project Financing Can Provide Better Incentives for Key People

Project financing can improve incentives for key employees by enabling them to take a direct ownership stake in the operations under their control.[40] By establishing separate projects, companies can provide incentives for individuals that are much more directly based upon performance than those typically possible within a large corporate organization. The key players in Merrill Lynch R&D Management Company, for example, are among the general partners in the RDLP they manage. They are therefore strongly motivated to select the most promising projects and do all that is within their power to bring about successful outcomes.

THE FUTURE POTENTIAL OF PROJECT FINANCE

Old-fashioned investors had great difficulty seeing any value for themselves in turning over a large sum of capital to a company indefinitely, and had to be convinced by changes in the political and technological environment that it was in their best interests to grant companies "permanent capital." The transformation of commerce from a venture-by-venture sequence to a continuous process required a change in the way business was organized and financed. In the face of modern-day regulatory and technological changes, investors are once again finding considerable merit in that old-fashioned attitude, and the old-fashioned way of doing business that goes along with it. Whenever the nature of the activity is project-oriented rather than process-oriented, investors are likely to see themselves as better served by finite-lived contractual arrangements than by corporations with indefinite lives.

With modern information-processing technology, the set of activities for which we can accomplish individual project accounting at a reasonable cost is expanding rapidly. The exceptions are confined more and more to those cases in which there are undeniable synergies among the various parts of a company. The ability to write and enforce contracts at a reasonable cost is likewise improving. New technologies are also increasing the number of instances in which small-scale, stand-alone operations are competitive with their large-scale, integrated cousins. The number of opportunities to reap the benefits of project financing will therefore proliferate as we progress into the "Information Age."

New technologies also hold out important opportunities for project financing. The precedents set by the automated hydroelectric facilities and the independent beverage can factory have broad implications. For example, project finance would be ideally suited for financing flexible regional factories that make a variety of goods for the local market. Perhaps as early as the mid-1990s, such factories are expected to be able to produce a variety of products in small batches, with the cost per unit the same whether the production run is for one item, or several hundred.[41] Fabrication machines will accurately translate design

---

40. See J. Brickley, R. Lease, and C. Smith, "Ownership Structure and Firm Value," unpublished manuscript, Cornell University, September 1986.

41. For example, the flexible manufacturing cell at LTV's Voight Aerospace Division near Dallas regularly produces any of over 560 different aircraft parts in small batches, with retooling accomplished automatically by selecting different computer programs. The facility is capable of even greater flexibility, with robot machine-tools capable of making literally anything that can be shaped from a block of metal up to 32 inches on a side.

specifications from on-line data bases into finished products, with substantial latitude for customization.

Thus, the familiar proprietary factories of today will gradually give way to generalized factories that are the new-age analogue of the village blacksmith. They will produce many of our basic goods locally, and the local factory won't necessarily be owned by any particular product designer. With quality (that is, conformity to design specifications) assured within tight tolerances, competition will be on the basis of product design and delivered cost, where the edge belongs to organizations that stay flexible and provide an environment conducive to creativity.

Industry thus appears ready to make the transition from continuous process plants specializing in a narrow product line—and requiring an integrated marketing effort to sell a steady flow of goods—to batch process plants capable of producing a broad range of customized products at prices competitive with mass production. With their ability to operate profitably regardless of the fortunes of any particular product designer or brand name, flexible factories will be more responsive to market forces if they are owned independently.

Project financing will also be a likely means for financing remote solar collection sites as that technology is commercialized. It is likewise well-suited for the coming generation of large-scale, high-cost orbiting communications satellites and other space-based robot facilities. Like the earthbound renewable resource power plants, they will have high up-front costs, but low operating costs once they are in place and begin producing.

Like the corporate restructuring movement in general, continued expansion of project financing may even bring into question the long-standing concept of a corporation as simply a pool of projects— rather like a closed-end mutual fund— wherein portfolio management (which goes under the name "strategic planning") is the unchallenged prerogative of top management. It has the potential to open up these real-asset mutual funds, thus transferring much of the former top-management function to the marketplace. In this era, many corporations are likely to be smaller than they are now. And those corporate giants whose size continues to be justified, presumably by economies of scale and scope, can be expected to restrict their acquisitive activities to developing relationships based upon mutual interests—relationships which are too interdependent or too amorphous to be reduced to contracts or other formal statements.[42]

Carried to its ultimate bounds, project financing could conceivably lead to a progressive "whittling down" of corporations to the core of tightly-intertwined activities beyond which further splitting is not possible (the "atoms" of business organization). Joint ventures would allow them to form liaisons as necessary to exploit new opportunities. In such a future, it might become the norm for plants and equipment that form the infrastructure upon which commerce and industry are based. Who knows, but the post-industrial age may come to be characterized as the "post-continuous-process era"—one in which fewer and fewer companies will be able to justify impounding permanent capital, and financiers will quite naturally return to raising money the old-fashioned way.

---

42. The earliest proto-corporations, in fact, were loose-knit associations of individual merchants, bound together by the glue of mutual protection and benefit, and governed primarily by the forces of the marketplace. The Hanseatic League, perhaps the greatest commercial organization of all time, sold no stock to the public and had no formal central authority. But it thoroughly dominated Northern European commerce from the days of the Crusades until after the Protestant Reformation, even waging war against sovereign princes who abused its members (its activities covered the entire Baltic and North Sea area, from London to present-day Leningrad, including over 120 major trading cities). As the European states consolidated, however, the League's supranational status became intolerable, and national interests ultimately brought it down.

PART V

RISK MANAGEMENT

Wall-Street bashing is a time-honored practice, even among economists. In our lead article, "*Financial Innovation: Achievements and Prospects*," Merton Miller traces the popular skepticism about Wall Street and financial innovation to an 18th-century economic doctrine known as "Physiocracy." According to this theory, the ultimate source of national wealth lies in the production of physical commodities. All other forms of commercial activity were considered nonproductive, if not parasitic. "Modern-day Physiocrats," as Miller says, "automatically and enthusiastically consign to that nonproductive class all the many thousands on Wall Street and LaSalle Street now using the new instruments."

The subject of Miller's article is "the new instruments"—that is, the proliferation since the early 1970s of all variety of futures, swaps, and options. It is Miller's contention—and indeed the underlying thesis of this book—that the social benefits accruing from financial innovation far outweigh the costs.

What are these benefits? Perhaps the principal source of gain from the many securities innovations over the past 20 years has been an improvement in the allocation of risk within the financial system—which in turn has enabled the capital markets to do a better job of performing their basic task of channeling investor savings into productive corporate investment of all kinds. The foreign exchange futures market started in 1972, together with the host of "derivative" products that have risen up since then, have dramatically reduced the cost of transferring risks to those market participants with a comparative advantage in bearing them. "Efficient risk-sharing," as Miller says, "is what much of the futures and options revolution has been all about." By functioning much like "a gigantic insurance company," the options, futures, and other derivative markets also effectively raise the price investors pay for corporate securities, thus adding to corporate investment and general economic growth.

Consider, for example, the development of a national mortgage market made possible by investment bankers' pooling and repackaging of individual mortgages into securities. Such asset securitization, in turn made possible by the development of financial futures necessary to hedge the investment bankers' interest rate and prepayment exposures, has accomplished a massive transfer of interest rate risk away from financial institutions to well-diversified institutional investors. Besides lowering interest rates for homeowners, such risk-shifting should also help prevent a repeat of the S&L debacle.

Futures and options continue, of course, to have a big PR problem—one that stems mainly from the fact that they are used by "speculators" as well as hedgers. But economists know that speculators serve a purpose: Besides keeping markets "efficient" by channeling information rapidly into prices, they also help supply the liquidity essential to these markets. And, as Miller argues further, the widespread charges that index futures and options are the cause of growing stock price volatility (including the crash of 1987) are contradicted by a growing weight of academic evidence.

In short, popular indictments of the new instruments confound the messenger with the message: What price volatility shows up within the system (and today's volatility is by no means high by historical measures) is largely the reflection of fundamental events; index futures and options are simply methods allowing companies and investors to cope with it.

In "*The Evolution of Risk Management Products*," Waite Rawls and Charles Smithson provide a brief history of the derivative products devised by investment and commercial banks to help corporations and investors manage their exposures to interest rates, exchange rates, and commodity prices. The last 15 years have seen the introduction of the following:

- futures contracts on foreign exchange, interest rates, metals, and petroleum;
- currency, interest rate, and commodity swaps;
- options on foreign exchange, interest rates, and petroleum;
- options on futures and options; and
- hybrid securities conbining standard debt issues with option- or forward-like features.

Most of these products are not new, as the authors point out, but are simply variations of more basic instruments, some of which have around for centuries. What is new, though, is the formation of active market exchanges that dramatically reduce the costs to individuals of using such risk management tools.

In "*Strategic Risk Management*," Rawls and Smithson go on to provide a broad survey of the theory and current corporate practice of risk management. There is still a good deal of confusion in the corporate world about what constitutes, and thus about the extent of, real, economic corporate exposures to exchange rates, interest rates, and commodity prices. American corporations are accustomed to hedging accounting-based exposures that arise from contractual commitments to make future sales or purchases (known as "transaction exposures"). Many companies also attempt to smooth their earnings by hedging "contingent" exposures—that is, operating net cash flows that are relatively predictable, but not yet bound by contract and booked. Relatively new, however, are corporate efforts to quantify and manage "competitive" exposures—the longer-run effects of changes in financial variables on corporate revenues and net operating margins. Such competitive exposures are the most elusive, and potentially the most damaging, of all the corporate exposures the authors refer to collectively as "strategic risk."

The article then describes a variety of techniques for identifying and quantifying such exposures. Although gap and duration analysis are now widely used by financial institutions to measure interest rate exposures, the methods for evaluating industrial companies' exposures to interest rates and other financial variables are still in an early stage of development. Some companies such as Merck (see the last article in this section) are using sophisticated quantitative methods to simulate the effect of exchange rate changes on long-run currency earnings and cash flows. Others evaluate specific exposures by means of statistical regressions that measure the strength of correlation between stock price movements and changes in financial variables.

But, as Rawls and Smithson go on to argue, not all corporate exposures should be hedged. From the perspective of modern portfolio theory (MPT), foreign exchange risk, interest rate risk, and commodity price risk are all "diversifiable" risks. Stockholders, according to MPT, are able to manage such risks on their own simply by holding large, diversified portfolios. And thus active corporate management of these risks does not increase share values by reducing a company's cost of capital. (This would suggest, for example, that a multinational's success in reducing the volatility of its overseas earnings would not by itself cause investors to raise the P/E multiple on the stock.) There are, however, other important benefits from hedging that are likely to increase corporate market values: (1) a reduction in expected tax liabilities; (2) a lowering of the probability (and hence expected costs) of financial difficulty (or,

alternatively, an increase in the firm's debt capacity); and (3) an improvement of management's incentives to undertake valuable long-run investments.

Rawls and Smithson then step back to ask, To what extent does current corporate practice conform to the theory? Judging from recently published surveys of corporate risk managers, the authors argue that corporations are moving, however gradually, in the direction pointed by the theory. To explain the apparent reluctance of many companies to use risk management tools such as swaps, futures, and options, the authors point to corporate executives' unfamiliarity with such instruments and, perhaps more important, the failure of current accounting conventions to reflect the hedging role of these instruments.

But if there are good reasons in some cases for actively managing corporate exposures, there also seems little doubt that many corporations are needlessly hedging risks that are better borne by capital market investors. In "*The Corporate Insurance Decision*," Clifford Smith and David Mayers suggest that changes in the insurance industry beginning in the early 1980s were the result of management's increasing awareness of its ability to self-insure. Insurance companies, however, as the article points out, have long provided services other than risk transference; and, for many corporations, it is principally these non-risk functions that are now at the heart of the corporate demand for insurance.

In "*Managing Financial Risk*," Charles Smithson, Clifford Smith, and Sykes Wilford provide an introduction to the four basic instruments for managing financial risks: forwards, futures, swaps, and options. After demonstrating the close relationships among these four "financial building blocks," the article goes on to demonstrate the potential for combining these to achieve virtually any desired risk position. The framework also lends itself to the analysis and pricing of complex hybrid securities by breaking them down into the basic components.

In "*The Arithmetic of Financial Engineering*," Donald Smith extends the argument of the previous article by demonstrating how exotic financial instruments are constructed from more basic elements such as interest rate swaps, caps, and floors (which are themselves simple combinations of forwards and options). This synthesizing process, which Smith illustrates with a nice series of examples, is the means by which speculators seek out arbitrage profits and corporate treasury managers design low-cost hedging strategies.

In "*Pricing Financial Futures Contracts*," the University of Chicago's Ken French presents a remarkably simple model for valuing futures contracts—one that calculates futures prices as a function of three variables: (1) the current spot price; (2) current interest rates; and (3) the present value of any dividends or coupons forgone. The article also demonstrates how the model can be applied in each of the four cases of stock index futures, Treasury bill futures, Treasury bond futures, and foreign currency futures.

In "*How to Use the Holes in Black-Scholes*," Fischer Black, the co-originator of the Black-Scholes option pricing model, discusses each of the ten "unrealistic assumptions" underlying the model. The purpose of this exercise is twofold: first, to suggest how the model might be made to better reflect market prices by making the assumptions more "realistic"; second, to point out profitable trading strategies that depend on the user's having better knowledge than the market's in making specific assumptions. Such trading strategies typically focus on expectations about the volatility of the underlying asset (in part because volatility is the only variable in the Black-Scholes formula that cannot be directly observed, but also because option values are so sensitive to estimates of volatility). But, giving a somewhat new twist to the argument, Dr. Black shows how the presence of "mean reversion" in the stock market (the tendency, recently documented by at least two reputable studies, for the expected return on stocks to fall as the market rises) points to profitable trading strategies using options. This same "mean reversion" tendency, accentuated by the widespread use of portfolio insurance, also furnishes the author with an interesting theory about the stock market crash.

In "*The Evolving Market for Swaps*," Cliff Smith, Charles Smithson, and Lee Wakeman attempt to explain the rise and proliferation of currency and interest rate swaps. The popular account of the origination of swaps is that they provided corporate treasurers with substantial interest rate savings by drawing on other companies' "comparative advantage" in raising funds in certain segments of worldwide capital markets. By swapping, the advantaged company could effectively share its advantage with the less privileged company, and each would obtain funding at lower costs than otherwise.

The problem with this argument, at least as an explanation of the continuing expansion of the swaps market, is that the very process of "arbitraging" interest rate differences among world financial markets should soon eliminate further opportunities to do so; that is, the demand for loans in low-interest rate markets can be expected to raise rates until such opportunities disappear. A more plausible explanation for growth of swaps is that swaps provide companies with a low-cost means of (1) taking advantage of tax and regulatory differences in various markets to reduce funding costs and (2) managing interest rate and currency exposures. They also provide a way of creating securities that do not exist, such as long-dated currency forwards and options, long-dated interest rate futures, and Swiss T-bills.

In "*Forward Swaps, Swap Options, and the Management of Callable Debt*," Keith Brown and Donald Smith address a special problem in corporate debt management: Namely, if interest rates have fallen sharply after the issuance of callable debt, but the call protection has several years yet to run, how can management preserve the value of the company's in-the-money call option on interest rates? The swap market now appears to provide for more cost-effective alternatives to the large bond repurchases and futures-based hedging strategies sometimes used to accomplish the same end.

The last article presents a corporate attempt to deal with foreign currency exposures. In "*Identifying, Measuring, and Hedging Currency Risk at Merck*," Judy Lewent (Merck's CFO) and John Kearney (Assistant Treasurer) describe the company's effort to understand and manage the effect of exchange rate volatility on worldwide revenues and earnings. In a thought process that parallels the one laid out by Smith, Smithson et al, Merck's treasury arrived at the following conclusions: (1) the home currency value of cash flows regularly repatriated by its many overseas subsidiaries was vulnerable to a strengthening of the U.S. dollar; (2) although stock market analysts and investors do not appear much concerned about the exchange-related volatility of reported earnings, volatility in repatriated cash flows could interfere with the company's ability to make long-term investments in R&D and marketing (the principal sources of the company's future earnings); and (3) financial hedging through the purchase of currency options was the most cost-effective means of ensuring its ability to carry out its long-range strategic plan.

DHC

FINANCIAL INNOVATION: ACHIEVEMENTS AND PROSPECTS

*by Merton H. Miller, University of Chicago**

T he wonderment of Rip Van Winkle, awakening after his sleep of 20 years to a changed world, would pale in comparison to that felt by one of his descendants in the banking or financial services industry falling asleep (presumably at his desk) in 1970 and waking two decades later. So rapid has been the pace of innovation in financial instruments and institutions over the last 20 years that nothing could have prepared him to understand such now common-place notions as swaps and swaptions, index futures, program trading, butterfly spreads, puttable bonds, Eurobonds, collateralized-mortgage bonds, zero-coupon bonds, portfolio insurance, or synthetic cash—to name just a few of the more exotic ones. No 20-year period has witnessed such a burst of innovative activity.

What could have produced this explosive growth? Has all this innovation really been worthwhile from society's point of view? Have we seen the end of the wave of innovations, or must we brace for more to come? These are the issues I now address.

*This article will appear in *Japan and the World Economy*, Vol. 4 No. 2 (June, 1992).

WHY THE GREAT BURST OF FINANCIAL INNOVATIONS OVER THE LAST TWENTY YEARS?

Several explanations have been offered for the sudden burst of financial innovations starting some 20 years ago.[1]

The Move to Floating Exchange Rates

A popular one locates the initiating impulse in the collapse of the Bretton Woods, fixed-exchange rate regime. In the early 1970s, the U.S. government, with strong prodding from academic economists, notably Milton Friedman, finally abandoned the tie of gold to the dollar. The wide fluctuations in exchange rates following soon after added major new uncertainty to all international transactions. One response to that uncertainty was the development of exchange-traded foreign-exchange futures contracts by the Chicago Mercantile Exchange—an innovation that spawned in turn a host of subsequent products as the turbulence spread from exchange rates to interest rates.

But cutting the tie to gold cannot be the whole story because financial futures, influential as they proved to be, were not the only major breakthrough of the early 1970s. Another product introduced only a few months later, and almost equally important to subsequent developments, was not so directly traceable to the monetary events of that period. The reference, of course, is to the exchange-traded options on common stock of the CME's cross-town rival, the Chicago Board of Trade. That the CBOT's options did not precede the CME's financial futures was mainly luck of the bureaucratic draw. Both exchanges started the process of development at about the same time, impelled to diversify by the same stagnation in their traditional agricultural markets. Both needed the cooperation, or at least the toleration, of the appropriate regulators to break out in such novel directions.

The CME was the more fortunate in having to contend only with the U.S. Treasury and the Federal Reserve System—at a time, moreover, when both those agencies were strongly committed to the Nixon administration's push for floating exchange rates.[2] The CBOT, alas, faced the U.S. Securities and Exchange Commission, a New Deal reform agency always hypersensitive to anything smacking of speculative activity.[3] By the time the SEC had finished its detailed review of option trading, the CME had already won the race.

Computers and Information Technology

Another explanation for the sudden burst of financial innovation after 1970 finds the key in the information revolution and, especially, in the electronic computer. Computers in one form or another had been available since the 1950s. But only in the late 1960s, with the perfection of transistorized circuitry, did computers become cheap and reliable enough to design new products and strategies such as stock index arbitrage and collateralized mortgage obligations. And certainly the immense volume of transactions we now see regularly could not have been handled without the data-processing capacities of the computer.

But the basic and most influential innovations, financial futures and exchange-traded options, did not require computers to make them commercially feasible. Options on commodities in fact had been traded regularly on the CBOT until the U.S. Congress, in one of its periodic bouts of post-crash, anti-speculative zeal, ended the practice in 1934. That this long prior history of option trading is not better known may trace to the arcane CBOT terminology under which options were known as "privileges." But traded instruments designated with the modern terms puts and calls go back much further than that, to the Amsterdam Stock Exchange of the late 17th century.[4] Routine exchange trading of futures contracts has a history almost as long.

1. See, for example, my article, "Financial Innovation: The Last Twenty Years and the Next," *Journal of Financial and Quantitative Analysis* 21 (December 1986), 459-71; and James C. Van Horne, "Of Financial Innovations and Excesses," *Journal of Finance* 40 (July 1985), 621-36.

2. The then Secretary of the Treasury was George P. Shultz, a former colleague and long-time friend of Milton Friedman. The Chairman of the Federal Reserve Board was Arthur Burns, another old friend. With Milton Friedman's blessing, both gave a cordial audience to Leo Melamed of the CME and at least a *nihil obstat* to his proposal for an International Monetary Exchange. (See Leo Melamed, "The International Monetary Market," in *The Merits of Flexible Exchange Rates*, ed. Leo Melamed, George Mason University Press, Fairfax, Virginia, 1988, 417-29.)

3. Under the SEC's original dispensation, only calls could be traded because puts were regarded as potentially destabilizing. Word of the put-call parity theorem had apparently not yet reached the SEC staff.

4. Joseph de la Vega, *Confusion de Confusiones*, Amsterdam, 1688, translated by Hermann Kellenbenz, 1957, reprinted by Baker Library, Harvard Business School, 1988.

Innovation and World Economic Growth

Still another possibility, and the one I find most persuasive,[5] is that the seeming burst of innovation in the 1970s was merely a delayed return to the long-run growth path of financial improvement. The burst seems striking only in contrast to the dearth of major innovations during the long period of economic stagnation that began in the early 1930s and that for most of the world continued well into the 1950s.

The shrinkage in the world economy after 1929 was on a scale that few not actually experiencing it can readily imagine. The prolonged depression undermined any demand pull for developing new financial instruments and markets, and the increased regulatory role of the state throttled any impulses to innovate from the supply side. Much of this new regulation, particularly in the U.S., was in fact a reaction to the supposed evils—notably the Crash of 1929—flowing from the development of exchange-traded, and hence relatively liquid, common stock as a major investment and financing vehicle in the 1920s. Prior to the 1920s, U.S. companies had relied almost exclusively on bonds and preferred stock for raising outside capital.

Even in the depressed '30s, of course, financial innovation, though muted relative to the 1920s, did not come to a halt. But the major novelties tended to be government sponsored, rather than market induced. Examples are the special housing-related instruments such as the amortizing mortgage and the Federal Home Administration loan guarantees. Another government initiative of the '30s was the support direct and indirect of what later came to be called, rather unprophetically we now know, "thrift institutions." New U.S. Treasury instruments were developed, or at least used on a vastly expanded scale, notably Series E savings bonds for small savers and, at the other extreme, U.S. Treasury bills. Indeed, T-bills quickly became the leading short-term liquid asset for banks and corporate treasurers, displacing the commercial paper and call money instruments that had previously served that function.

Financial innovation by the private sector might perhaps have revived by the 1940s had not the War intervened. The War not only drained manpower and energy from normal market-oriented activity, but led to new regulatory restrictions on financial transactions, particularly international transactions.

Regulation and Deregulation as Stimuli to Financial Innovation

By a curious irony, the vast structure of financial regulation erected throughout the world during the 1930s and 1940s, though intended to and usually successful in throttling some kinds of financial innovation, actually served to stimulate the process along other dimensions. Substantial rewards were offered, in effect, to those successfully inventing around the government-erected obstacles. Many of these dodges, or "fiddles" as the British call them, turned out to have market potential far beyond anything dreamed of by their inventors; and the innovations thrived even after the regulation that gave rise to them was modified or abandoned.

The most striking example of such a regulation-propelled innovation may well be the swap in which one corporation exchanges its fixed-rate borrowing obligation for another's floating-rate obligation; or exchanges its yen-denominated obligations for another's mark-denominated obligations; and so on in an almost unimaginable number of permutations and combinations. Some swaps are arranged by brokers who bring the two counterparties directly together; others by banks who take the counterparty side to a customer order and then either hedge the position with forwards and futures or with an offsetting position with another customer.

The notional amount of such swaps, interest and currency, currently outstanding is in the trillions of dollars and rising rapidly. Yet, according to legend at least,[6] the arrangement arose modestly enough as vacation-home swapping by British overseas travelers, who were long severely limited in the amount of currency they could take abroad. Two weeks free occupancy of a London flat could compensate a French tourist for a corresponding stay in a Paris apartment or compensate an American for the use of a condominium at Aspen. If the ingenious British innovator happened to work for one of the merchant banks in the City, as is likely, the extension of the

---

5. See Miller (1986), cited in note 1.

6. The first currency swap appears to have been arranged by Continental Illinois' London merchant bank in 1976. The precise dates and places remain problematic because the originators sought secrecy in a vain attempt to maintain their competitive advantage. See Henry T. C. Hu, "Swaps, the Modern Process of Financial Innovation and the Vulnerability of a Regulatory Paradigm," *University of Pennsylvania Law Review* 128 (December 1989), pp. 333-435 (see especially note 73, p. 363).

The burst of innovations in the past 20 years seems striking only in contrast to the dearth of major innovations during the long period of economic stagnation that began in the early 1930s and that for most of the world continued well into the 1950s.

notion to corporate currency swaps was a natural one. The rest, as they say, is history.

The list of similar, regulation-induced or tax-induced innovations is long, and includes the Eurodollar market, the Eurobond market, and zero-coupon bonds, to name just some of the more far-reaching loopholes opened in the restrictive regulatory structure of the 1930s and 1940s.[7] Whether the private sector processes that produced the seemingly great wave of innovations after 1970 will continue to produce innovations if left unchecked is a topic to be taken up later. First let's consider some of the arguments currently being advanced for not leaving them unchecked.

HAS THE WAVE OF FINANCIAL INNOVATIONS MADE US BETTER OR WORSE OFF?

Free market economists have a simple standard for judging whether a new product has increased social welfare: are people willing to pay their hard-earned money for it? By this standard, of course, the new products of the 1970s and '80s have proved their worth many times over. But why have they been so successful? Whence comes their real "value added?" The answer, in large part, is that they have substantially lowered the cost of carrying out many kinds of financial transactions.

Consider, for example, a pension fund or an insurance company with, say, $200 million currently in a well-diversified portfolio of common stocks. Suppose that, for some good reason, the sponsors of the fund believe that the interests of their beneficiaries would be better served at the moment by shifting funds from common stocks to Treasury bills. The direct way would be first to sell the stock portfolio company by company, incurring commissions, fees, and "market impact" on each transaction. The cash proceeds, when collected, could then be put in Treasury bills, again incurring transaction costs. A second and much cheaper alternative, however, is simply to sell about 1,000 (at present price levels) S&P 500 index futures contracts. Thanks to the way the futures contracts must be priced to maintain intermarket equilibrium, that one transaction has the same consequences as the two transactions along the direct route. And at a fifth or even less of the cost in fees, commissions, and market impact!

Or, to take other kinds of financial costs, consider a bank maintaining an inventory of government bonds for resale. The availability of that inventory, like the goods on the shelf in a supermarket, means better and faster service for the bank's customers when they come to shop. But it also means considerable risk for the bank. Bond prices can fall, sometimes very substantially, even in the course of a single day.

To protect against such losses, the bank can hedge its inventory by selling Treasury bond futures. Should the price of the bonds fall during the life of the futures contract, the gain on that contract will offset the loss on the underlying inventory. Without this opportunity to shift the risk via futures, the bank must seek other and more costly ways of controlling its inventory exposure. Some banks might find no better solution than to shrink their inventory and, hence, the quality and immediacy of the services they offer. Others might well abandon the activity altogether.

Insurance and Risk Management

A bank's use of futures to hedge its own inventory does not, of course, eliminate the price risk of the underlying bonds. It merely transfers that risk to someone else who *does* want to bear the risk, either because he or she has stronger nerves, or more likely, because another firm or investor somewhere wants to hedge against a *rise* in bond prices. The futures and options exchanges have greatly reduced the time (and hence cost) that each risk-shifter might otherwise have spent searching for a counterparty with the opposite risk exposure.

The combined set of futures and options contracts and the markets, formal and informal, in which they are transferred has thus been likened to a gigantic insurance company—and rightly so. Efficient risk-sharing is what much of the futures and options revolution has been all about. And that is why the term "risk management" has come increasingly to be applied to the whole panoply of instruments and institutions that have followed in the wake of the introduction of foreign exchange futures in CME's International Money Market in 1972. Honesty requires one to acknowledge, however, that this essentially benign view of the recent great innova-

---

7. For a fuller account of tax- and regulation-induced innovations, see Miller (1986), cited in note 1.

tive wave is not universally shared by the general public or even by academic economists.

The Case Against the Innovations

Some of the complaints about the harmful social consequences of the financial innovations appear to be little more than updated versions of a once-popular 18th-century economic doctrine known as Physiocracy, which located the ultimate source of national wealth in the production of physical commodities, especially agricultural commodities. Occupations other than commodity production were nonproductive. Modern-day Physiocrats, disdaining consumer sovereignty, automatically and enthusiastically consign to that nonproductive class all the many thousands on Wall Street and LaSalle Street now using the new instruments.

A related complaint is that the new instruments, by lowering transactions costs, have led to too much short-term trading—trading that not only wastes resources, but which has unduly shortened the planning horizons of both firms and investors. That the volume of trading has in fact skyrocketed in recent years there can be no doubt. But the key stimulus to the surge in trading in the underlying stocks appears to have been less the introduction of index futures and options than the ending of the regime of high fixed commissions in 1974. For Treasury bonds, the spur was the huge expansion of Federal government debt beginning in 1981.

But the critics are surely right in believing that lower trading costs will induce more trading. More trading, however, need not mean more waste from society's point of view. Trading is part of the process by which economic information, scattered as it necessarily is in isolated bits and pieces throughout the whole economy, is brought together, aggregated, and ultimately revealed to all. The prospect of trading profits is the bribe, so to speak, that society uses to motivate the collection, and ultimately the revelation, of the dispersed information about supply and demand.

Index Futures and Stock Market Volatility. Although many of the complaints against the new financial investments are merely standard visceral reactions against middlemen and speculators, some are specific enough to be tested against the available data. Notable here is the widespread view, expressed almost daily in the financial press, that stock market volatility has been rising in recent years and that stock-index futures and options are responsible. The evidence, however, fails to support this widespread public perception of surging volatility.

Volatility, measured as the standard deviation of rates of return (whether computed over monthly, weekly or even daily intervals), is only modestly higher now than during the more placid 1950s and 1960s, and is substantially below levels reached in the 1930s and 1940s.[8] Even the 1950s and 1960s had brief, transitory bursts of unusually high volatility, with a somewhat longer-lasting major burst occurring in the mid-1970s. The number of large, one-day moves (that is, moves of 3% or more in either direction) has indeed been higher in the 1980s than in any decade since the 1930s, but almost entirely due to the several days of violent movements in the market during and immediately following the crash of October 1987. Such increased volatility seems to accompany every major crash (as the Japanese stock market showed through much of 1990).

In fact, the tendency of volatility to rise after crashes and fall during booms is one of the few, well-documented facts researchers have been able to establish about the time-series properties of the volatility series. These bursts of post-crash volatility typically die out within a few months, and that has been basically the case as well for the crash of 1987. Indeed, what makes the 1930s so different from more recent experience is that the high levels of post-1929-crash volatility persisted so long into the next decade.

Index Products and the Crash of 1987. The failure to find a rising trend in volatility in the statistical record suggests that the public may be using the word volatility in a different and less technical sense. They may simply be taking the fact of the crash of 1987 itself (and the later so-called mini-crash of October 13, 1989) as their definition of market volatility. And without doubt, the 20% decline during the crash of 1987 was the largest one-day shock ever recorded. (The mini-crash of October 13, 1989, at about 6%, was high, but far from record-breaking.) If the crash of 1987 is the source of the public perception of increased volatility, the task of checking for connections between the inno-

---

8. See G. William Schwert, "Why Does Stock Market Volatility Change over Time?", *Journal of Finance* 44 (December 1989), 1115-53.

The combined set of futures and options contracts and the markets, formal and informal, in which they are transferred has been likened to a gigantic insurance company—and rightly so. Efficient risk-sharing is what much of the futures and options revolution has been all about.

vative instruments and volatility becomes the relatively straightforward one of establishing whether index futures and options really were responsible either for the occurrence or the size of the crash. On this score, signs of a consensus are emerging, at least within academia, with respect to the role of two of the most frequently criticized strategies involving futures and options, portfolio insurance and index arbitrage.

For portfolio insurance, the academic verdict is essentially "not guilty of causing the crash," but possibly guilty of the lesser charge of "contributing to the delinquency of the market." Portfolio insurance, after all, was strictly a U.S. phenomenon in 1987, and the crash seems to have gotten under way in the Far East, well before trading opened in New York or Chicago. The extent of the fall in the various markets around the world, moreover, bore no relation to whether a country had index futures and options exchanges.[9] Even in the U.S., nonportfolio insurance sales on the 19th, including sales by mutual funds induced by the cash redemptions of retail investors, were four to five times those of the portfolio insurers.

Still, portfolio insurance using futures, like some older, positive-feedback strategies such as stop-loss orders or margin pyramiding, can be shown, as a matter of theory, to be potentially destabilizing.[10] The qualification "using futures" is important here, however, because the potentially destabilizing impact of portfolio insurance is much reduced when carried out with index options (that is, essentially, by buying traded puts rather than attempting to replicate the puts synthetically with futures via craftily-timed hedges). With exchange-traded puts, the bearishness in portfolio insurance would make its presence known immediately in the market prices and implicit volatility of the puts. With futures, by contrast, or with unhedged, over-the-counter puts, the bearishness may be lurking in the weeds, only to spring out on a less-than-perfectly forewarned public.[11]

Index Arbitrage: The New Villain. Whatever may or may not have been its role in the crash of 1987, portfolio insurance using futures rather than options has almost entirely vanished. Certainly it played no role in the mini-crash of October 13, 1989. Its place in the rogues' gallery of the financial press has been taken over by computerized "program trading" in general and by index arbitrage program trading in particular.

Why index arbitrage should have acquired such an unsavory public reputation is far from clear, however. Unlike portfolio insurance, which can be destabilizing when its presence as an information-less trade in the market is not fully understood, intermarket index arbitrage is essentially neutral in its market impact. The downward pressure of the selling leg in one market is always balanced by the equal and opposite buying pressure in the other. Only in rather special circumstances could these offsetting transactions affect either the level or the volatility of the combined market as a whole.

Index arbitrage might, possibly, increase market volatility if an initial breakout of the arbitrage bounds somehow triggered sales in the less-liquid cash market so massive that the computed index fell by more than needed to bring the two markets back into line. A new wave of arbitrage selling might then be set off in the other direction.

Despite the concerns about such "whipsawing" often expressed by the SEC, however, no documented cases of it have yet been found.[12] Careful studies find the market's behavior after program trades entirely consistent with the view that prices are being driven by "news," not mere speculative "noise" coming from the futures markets as the critics of index futures have so often charged.

Nor should these findings be considered in any way remarkable. The low cost of trading index futures makes the futures market the natural entry port for new information about the macro economy. The news, if important enough to push prices through the arbitrage bounds, is then carried from the futures market to the cash market by the program trades of the arbitragers. Thanks to the electronic order routing systems of the NYSE, the delivery is fast. But arbitrage is still merely the medium, not the message.

9. See Richard Roll, "The International Crash of October 1987," *Financial Analysts Journal* 22 (September 1988), 19-35.

10. See Michael J. Brennan and Eduardo S. Schwartz, "Portfolio Insurance and Financial Market Equilibrium," *Journal of Business* 62 (October 1989), pp. 455-72. Particularly interesting in their demonstration, however, is how small the destabilization potential really is, provided the rest of the investing public understands what is going on.

11. See Sanford J. Grossman, "An Analysis of the Implications for Stock and Futures Price Volatility of Program Trading and Dynamic Hedging Strategies," *Journal of Business* 61 (July 1988), 275-98.

12. See, for example, the very thorough searches described in Gregory Duffie, Paul Kupiec, and Patricia White, "A Primer on Program Trading and Stock Price Volatility: A Survey of the Issues and Evidence," Working Paper, Board of Governors, Federal Reserve System, Washington, D.C., 1990.

That so much recent criticism has been directed against the messenger rather than the message may reflect only the inevitably slow reaction by the public to the vast changes that have transformed our capital markets and financial services institutions over the last 20 years. Index futures, after all, came of age less than 10 years ago. The shift from a predominantly retail stock market to one dominated by institutional investors began, in a big way, less than 15 years ago. In time, with more experience, the public's understanding of the new environment will catch up. Unless, of course, new waves of innovation are about to sweep in and leave the public's perceptions even further behind.

FINANCIAL INNOVATIONS:
ANOTHER WAVE ON THE WAY?

Will the next 20 years see a continuation, or perhaps even an acceleration, in the flow of innovations that have so vastly altered the financial landscape over the last 20 years? I think not. Changes will still take place, of course. The new instruments and institutions will spread to every country in the developed world (and possibly even to the newly liberalized economies of Eastern Europe). Futures and options contracts will be written on an ever-widening set of underlying commodities and securities. But the process will be normal, slow, evolutionary change, rather than the "punctuated equilibrium" of the recent past.[13]

Long-range predictions of this kind are rightly greeted with derision. Who can forget the U.S. Patent Office Commissioner who recommended in the early 1900s that his agency be closed down because all patentable discoveries had by then been made? We know also that regulation and taxes, those two longstanding spurs to innovation, are still very much with us despite the substantial progress, at least until recently, in deregulation and in tax rate reduction. But something important has changed. In the *avant garde* academic literature of economics and finance today, few signs can be seen of new ideas and concepts like those that bubbled up in the '60s and '70s and came to fruition later in specific innovations.

The extent to which academic thinking and criticism prefigured the great wave of financial

innovations of the 1970s and 1980s is still too little appreciated. Calls for the creation of a foreign exchange futures market and analysis of the economic benefits that would flow from such an institution were common in the 1950s and 1960s, as noted earlier, in the writings of the academic supporters of floating exchange rates, especially Milton Friedman. On the common-stock front, major academic breakthroughs in the 1950s and 1960s were the Mean-Variance Portfolio selection model of Harry Markowitz and, building on it, the so-called Capital Asset Pricing Model of William Sharpe and John Lintner in which the concept of the "market portfolio" played a central role.

The notion of the market portfolio ultimately became a reality by the early 1970s when the first, passively-managed index funds were brought on line. That the world would move from there to the trading of broad market portfolios, either as baskets or as index futures and options, was widely anticipated. The fundamental Black-Scholes and Robert Merton papers on rational option pricing were published in the early 1970s, though manuscript versions of them had been circulating informally among academics well before then. These and other exciting prospects abounded in the academic literature 20 years ago. At the moment, however, that cupboard seems bare of new concepts and ideas waiting for the day of practical implementation.

Such hints of future developments as the current literature does have relate more to the structure of the exchanges themselves than to the products they trade. For academics, accustomed to spending their workdays staring at the screens of their PCs, the near-term transition of the markets from floor trading to electronic trading is taken for granted. Frequent references can be found in the many articles on the crash of 1987 to the presumed failings of the current exchange trading systems during that hectic period. Those systems are typically characterized pejoratively as "archaic" and "obsolete," in contrast to the screen-based trading systems in such non-exchange markets as government bonds or inter-bank foreign exchange.

That screen-based trading will someday supplant floor trading seems more than likely, but whether that transition will occur even by the end of

---

13. Evolution also involves "extinctions." Some of the recent innovations will inevitably fail in the competitive struggle. Others may be killed by heavy-handed regulation.

this century is far from clear. The case of the steamship is instructive. The new steam technology was clearly superior to sail-power in its ability to go up river and against winds and tides. Steam quickly took over inland river traffic but not, at first, ocean traffic. There steam was better, but vastly more expensive. Steam thus found its niche in military applications and in the high-unit-value fast passenger trade. Only as fuel costs dropped did steam take over more and more of the low-unit-value bulk trade in ocean freight. For some bulk commodities such as lumber, in fact, sail was often the lower-cost alternative up until the start of the first World War, more than 100 years after the first practical steamboat.

The same laws of comparative advantage apply to electronic trading systems. The open-outcry trading pits of the major futures exchanges may seem hopelessly chaotic and old-fashioned; but they are, for all that, a remarkably cheap way of handling transactions in large volume at great speed and frequency in a setting of high price volatility. Until recently, at least, electronic trading could not have come close to being cost-competitive in this arena. Screen trading found its niche elsewhere. And electronic computer systems found their niche in futures in tasks such as order routing, data processing and some kinds of surveillance rather than on the trading floor.

But screen-trading technology, like that of computing technology generally, continues to advance and a possibly crucial watershed for the trading systems in futures may soon be crossed. By mid-1992 the Chicago exchanges hope finally to bring on line the long-delayed Globex electronic network for after-hours trading of futures contracts. Unlike some past experiments with screen trading of futures, the test this time will be a valid one. The contracts to be traded, Eurodollars and foreign exchange rates, have long proven viable; the underlying spot markets are themselves screen traded; and substantial potential trading demand for the contracts might well exist outside the U.S. and after U.S. trading hours.

Even a successful Globex, however, need not doom the exchanges to disappear as functioning business entities. The transactions facilities the exchanges provide through their trading floors are currently the major and certainly the most glamorous, but by no means the only, services they offer. The exchanges also provide such humdrum but critical functions as clearing and settlement, guarantees of contract performance, record-keeping and audit trails, and the collection and dissemination of price information. The market for these services in supporting financial transactions not currently carried out via exchanges is potentially huge. The futures exchanges, by virtue of their expertise and their substantial existing capital investments, are well positioned to enter and to capture a significant share of these new markets, just as they were 20 years ago when the shrinkage in their agricultural business propelled them into financial futures and options.

THE EVOLUTION OF RISK MANAGEMENT PRODUCTS

by S. Waite Rawls III and Charles W. Smithson, Continental Bank*

T oday, financial price risk not only can affect quarterly profits but may determine a firm's very survival. Unpredictable movements in exchange rates, interest rates, and commodity prices present risks that cannot be ignored. It's no longer enough to be the firm with the most advanced production technology, the cheapest labor supply, or the best marketing team—because price volatility can put even well-run firms out of business.

Changes in exchange rates can create stiff competition where none previously existed. Similarly, commodity price fluctuations result in changes in input prices which can make substitute products—products made from different inputs—more affordable to end-consumers. Changes in interest rates can put pressure on the firm's costs; and, for those firms whose sales are hurt by higher interest rates, rising interest rates can lead directly to financial distress as sales dry up just when borrowing costs skyrocket.

Not surprisingly, the financial markets have responded to this increased price volatility. The past 15 years have witnessed the evolution of a range of financial instruments and strategies that can be used to manage the resulting exposures to financial price risk.

At one level, financial instruments now exist that permit the direct transfer of financial price risk to a third party more willing to accept that risk. For example, with the development of foreign exchange futures contracts, a U.S. exporter can transfer its foreign exchange risk to a firm with the opposite exposure or to a firm in the business of managing foreign exchange risk, leaving the exporter free to focus on its core business.

At another level, the financial markets have evolved to the point that financial instruments can be combined with debt issuance so as to unbundle financial price risk from the other risks inherent in the process of raising capital. For example, by coupling their bond issues with swaps, issuing firms are able to separate interest rate risk from traditional credit risk.[1]

* This paper is based on Chapter 1 of *Managing Financial Risk* by Clifford W. Smith, Jr., Charles W. Smithson, and D. Sykes Wilford (*Institutional Investor* Series, Ballinger, forthcoming).

1. This decoupling of interest rate risk and credit risk is stressed in Marcelle Arak, Arturo Estrella, Laurie Goodman, and Andrew Silver, "Interest Rate Swaps: An Alternative Explanation," *Financial Management*, Vol. 17 No. 2 (Summer 1988), pp. 12-18.

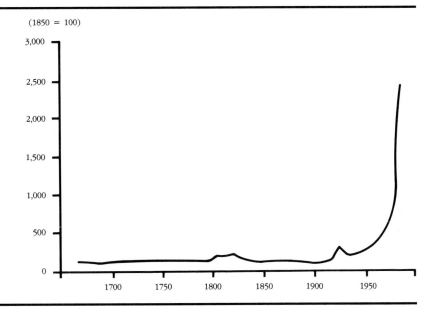

FIGURE 1
RETAIL PRICE INDEX
FOR ENGLAND

$(1850 = 100)$

THE WORLD BECAME A MORE RISKY PLACE...

There is general agreement that the financial environment is more risky today than it was in the past. Figure 1 provides some dramatic evidence of the change. Here we present what must be regarded as a long price series—namely the retail price index for England from 1666 to the mid-1980s. What jumps out at you from Figure 1 is that, from the seventeenth century until the late twentieth century, the price level in England was essentially stable. Prices did go up during wartime—the data series reflects conflicts like the one the British had with "that French person" in the early 19th century—but then fell to pre-war levels once the conflict ended.

In marked contrast, the price history for the last half of the twentieth century indicates that the financial environment changed. For the first time, prices have gone up—and stayed up. And this is not only a United Kingdom phenomenon; a similar pattern of price level behavior exists for the U.S. (albeit, as our British colleagues point out, with fewer data points). In fact, during this period of general uncertainty, the

developed economies generally began to experience unexpected price changes (primarily increases).

In short, the financial markets were confronted with increased price uncertainty. And this increased uncertainty about inflation was soon followed by uncertainty about foreign exchange rates, interest rates, and commodity prices.

Foreign Exchange Rates Became More Risky...

Panel A of Figure 2 shows monthly percentage changes in the U.S. Dollar/Japanese Yen exchange rate since 1957. This figure provides a very clear indication that the foreign exchange market has become more risky. And the reason for the increased volatility of foreign exchange rates in the early 1970s is evident: the breakdown of the Bretton Woods system of fixed exchange rates.[2]

Under the fixed exchange rate system of Bretton Woods, importers knew what they would pay for goods in their domestic currency and exporters knew how much they would receive in their local currency.

2. A description of the Bretton Woods system and its effect on prices is contained in Bluford Putman and D. Sykes Wilford, eds., *The Monetary Approach to International Adjustment* (New York: Praeger, 1986).

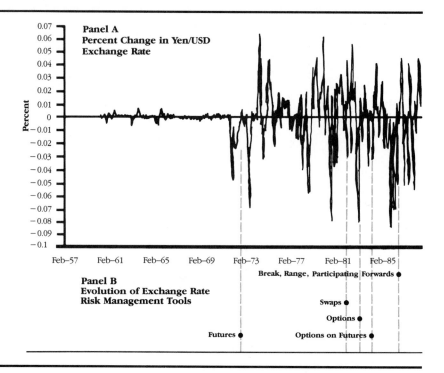

FIGURE 2
EXCHANGE RATES

If the importer could sell at a profit to the consumer, and the exporter's costs were below the export price, then gains from trade were had by all.

With the breakdown of Bretton Woods, the rules changed. Both sides to the transaction now faced exchange rate risk. Each party wanted to transact in his own currency to prevent being "whipsawed" by the market. The importer's profit margin could, and often did, evaporate if his currency weakened sharply and the imported goods were priced in the exporter's currency.

Exchange rate volatility also affects domestic producers. Exchange rate risk occurs whenever the value of future cash flows may change because of foreign exchange rate movements. With more volatile exchange rates, all market participants face greater exchange rate risk. The volatility of exchange rates also greatly affects the real return on domestic versus foreign financial assets. Adverse exchange rate movements can overshadow the interest payments or other income stream received on a foreign currency-deno-

minated asset. Consequently, exchange rate volatility influences the currency distributions of global portfolios, as both borrowers and lenders try to diversify their foreign exchange risk by holding assets or liabilities in different currencies.

Foreign exchange forward contracts had been available for decades. But, not surprisingly, it was only in the early 1970s that this market took on its own existence. But because a forward contract involves the extension of credit, the forward foreign exchange market had become primarily an interbank market.[3] For this reason, many firms confronted with foreign exchange risk were unable to take advantage of the forward market.

As illustrated in Panel B of Figure 2, the financial market responded to this need by creating a range of risk management instruments. The first to appear was futures contracts on foreign exchange. In May of 1972, the International Monetary Market of the Chicago Mercantile Exchange began trading futures contracts on the British Pound, Canadian Dollar,

---

3. For a description of the credit risk aspects of a forward contract, see *Managing Financial Risk*, chapters 3 and 4.

FIGURE 3
INTEREST RATES

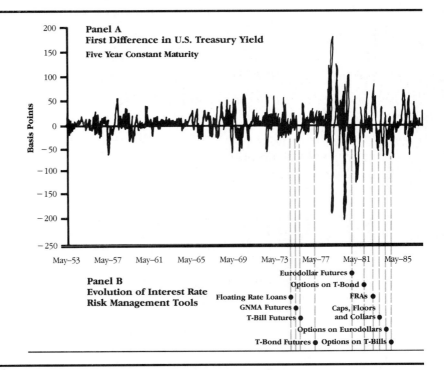

Panel A
First Difference in U.S. Treasury Yield
Five Year Constant Maturity

Panel B
**Evolution of Interest Rate
Risk Management Tools**

Deutsche Mark, Japanese Yen, and Swiss Franc.[4]

Currency swaps were next to appear. While precursors to swaps such as back-to-back and parallel loans had been used since the onset of volatility in foreign exchange rates,[5] the public introduction of currency swaps is normally marked by the World Bank-IBM swap of August 1981.

Option contracts on foreign exchange followed closely on the heels of swaps. In December 1982 the Philadelphia Stock Exchange introduced an options contract on the British Pound, which was followed by options on the Canadian Dollar, Deutsche Mark, Japanese Yen, and Swiss Franc in January-February 1983.[6]

The Chicago Mercantile Exchange followed with the introduction of options on foreign exchange futures in the following currencies: Deutsche Mark, January 1984; British Pound and Swiss Franc, February 1985; Japanese Yen, March 1986; and Canadian Dollars, June 1986.[7]

Commercial banks responded by offering their clients over-the-counter foreign exchange options. They also created forward foreign exchange contracts with option-like characteristics. "Break forwards," "range forwards," and "participating forwards" had all entered the market lexicon by 1987.[8]

In addition to the financial instruments themselves, the rise in foreign exchange rate volatility spawned a number of "hybrid securities."[9] For example, dual currency loans—loans where the bank

---

4. CME futures contracts on other currencies followed: French Franc, September 1974; European Currency Unit, January 1986; and Australian Dollar, January 1987.

5. For a description of the evolution of the currency swap from parallel loans, see Clifford W. Smith, Charles W. Smithson, and Lee Macdonald Wakeman, "The Evolving Market for Swaps," *Midland Corporate Finance Journal*, Vo. 3, No. 4, Winter 1986.

6. Option contracts on the French Franc began trading in 1984, followed by the ECU in 1986 and Australian Dollar in 1987.

7. Options on futures are not traded on the CME for French Francs, the ECU, or Australian Dollars.

8. In "Second-Generation Forwards: A Comparative Analysis," *Business International Money Report*, September 21, 1987, Sam Srivivasulu noted that "break forward" is the name used by Midland Bank. The same construction is known as a Boston Option (Bank of Boston), a FOX—Forward with Optional Exit (Hambros Bank), and a cancellable forward (Goldman Sachs). Likewise, "range forward" is the name used by Salomon Brothers. The same construction is known as a collar (Midland Montagu), a flexible forward (Manufacturers Hanover), a cylinder option (Citicorp), and option fence (Bank of America), and a mini-max (Goldman Sachs).

9. In general, a hybrid security is one that is made up of a combination of a credit extension instrument and one or more of the financial instruments.

can convert the debt to another currency at a future date at a specified exchange rate—were introduced by Privatbanken in 1985.[10]

Interest Rates Became More Risky...

Surprisingly, the increased volatility evident in the foreign exchange market did not spill over into the U.S. domestic money market at first. Indeed, compared to interest rates in the late 60s and early 70s, rates actually became more stable in 1977 through 1979. As shown in Panel A of Figure 3, interest rate volatility declined during this period,[11] even though interest rates were rising in response to the inflation rate.[12]

As illustrated in Panel A of Figure 3, however, uncertainty hit U.S. interest rates with a vengeance in 1979. On October 6, 1979 the newly-appointed Chairman of the Federal Reserve Board, Paul Volcker, abandoned the Fed practice of targeting interest rates and began to target money supply growth instead. As a consequence, interest rates became extremely volatile. For example, in the two years following October 1979, the volatility of 90-day Treasury bill interest rates was five times greater than that of the prior two years.

Perhaps the most widely cited example of the impact of the increased volatility of interest rates is the experience of the U.S. savings and loan (S&L) industry. In the 1970s, S&Ls looked like money machines. With an upward-sloping and *stable* yield curve, S&Ls profited by taking in short-term passbook deposits and making long-term, fixed-rate mortgage loans. In the 1980s, S&Ls changed from money machines to money pits. Those same long-term, low-rate loans to homeowners were now being financed with high-rate—and volatile—short-term funds. The increased interest rate risk changed the way the capital markets functioned. With the increased uncertainty about interest rates, financial institutions became less willing to make long-term rate commitments. They reacted by turning to floating-rate loans. Floating-rate loans first appeared following the increase in rates and vola-

tility in 1973 and 1974; by the 1980s, this structure was being used in earnest.

Floating-rate loans did help banks and S&Ls to manage their exposure to interest rate movements. But, it did so only by passing the interest rate risk to the borrower;[13] thus better tools for managing interest rate risk were required. And, as indicated in Panel B of Figure 3, they were not long in coming.

In contrast to the foreign exchange market, there was no historical forward market for interest rates. Consequently, financial futures were the first financial instrument designed to help firms manage their interest rate risk. The progression of futures contracts on U.S. dollar interest rates introduced on the Chicago Board of Trade (CBOT) and the Chicago Mercantile Exchange (CME) is presented below:

First Day Trading	Underlying Asset	Exchange
October 1975	GNMA	CBOT
January 1976	U.S. T-Bills	CME
August 1977	U.S. T-Bonds	CBOT
December 1981	Eurodollar	CME
May 1982	T-Notes	CBOT

Although the futures exchanges had established a large lead on interest rate management products, banks finally responded to the demand for these products. Banks first reacted by providing interest rate swaps in 1982. Then, in early 1983, they provided the missing forward market for interest rates with the introduction of forward rate agreements (FRAs).

As was the case with foreign exchange, the options contracts followed closely. Option contracts on the underlying asset itself appeared on the Chicago Board Options Exchange (CBOE); options on futures on the underlying asset were introduced on the CBOT and the CME.

First Day Trading	Underlying Asset	Exchange
October 1982	T-Bond Futures	CBOT
October 1982	T-Bond	CBOE
March 1985	Eurodollar Futures	CME
May 1985	T-Note Futures	CBOT
July 1985	T-Note	CBOE
April 1986	T-Bill Futures	CME

---

10. A dual currency loan is drawn in one currency, but the bank has the right to convert it to another currency at the spot rate on origination at a pre-arranged time, usually one year after drawing. Consequently, the dual currency loan is made up of a standard loan and a foreign exchange option. (See *International Financial Review* 742 (September 17, 1988) pg. 2989.) As noted in chapter 19 of *Managing Financial Risk*, a dual currency bond can be viewed as a combination of a standard bond and a long-dated foreign exchange forward contract.

11. For exposition, Figure 3 provides the monthly first difference in the rate rather than percentage change or some other measure more closely related to volatility.

12. Critics have argued that the then Chairman of the Federal Reserve Board, Bill Miller, paid for these stable domestic interest rates with higher inflation and a weaker dollar.

13. While floating-rate loans did deal with the immediate problem of interest rate risk, they did not turn out to be the panacea some expected. By passing the market risk to the borrower, floating rate loans increased the default risk of the borrower.

FIGURE 4
COMMODITY PRICES

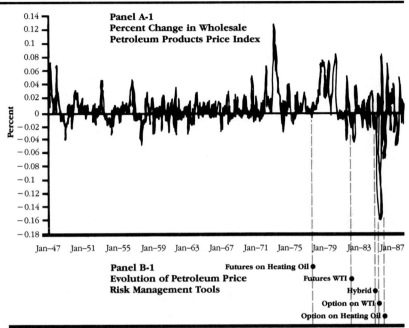

Panel A-1
Percent Change in Wholesale Petroleum Products Price Index

Panel B-1
Evolution of Petroleum Price Risk Management Tools

Futures on Heating Oil ●
Futures WTI ●
Hybrid ●
Option on WTI ●
Option on Heating Oil ●

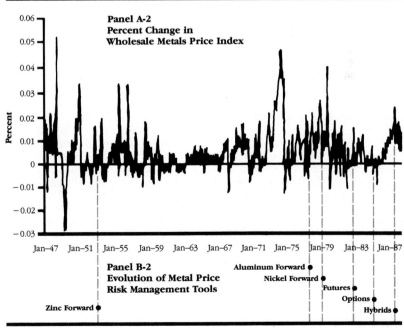

Panel A-2
Percent Change in Wholesale Metals Price Index

Panel B-2
Evolution of Metal Price Risk Management Tools

Zinc Forward ●
Aluminum Forward ●
Nickel Forward ●
Futures ●
Options ●
Hybrids ●

FIGURE 5
RELATIVE PRICE OF
COMMODITIES

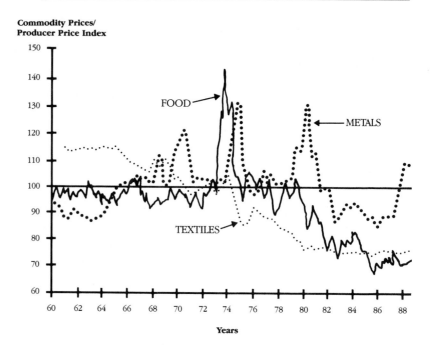

And, as in the case of foreign exchange, the banks responded to the exchanges by introducing over-the-counter options: caps, floors, and collars. These products first began to appear in late 1983.

Commodity Prices Became More Risky...

Volatility also increased in the commodity markets. The first commodity that comes to mind is oil. As Panel A-1 of Figure 4 indicates, the price of petroleum products became more volatile in the 1970s. But, so did the prices of most basic commodities. Panel A-2 of Figure 4, for example, presents data on monthly volatility for metals prices.

Figure 5 provides another way of looking at commodity prices by displaying data on the relative prices of commodities. Much of the increase in basic commodity prices in the 1970s was driven by inflation. The declining purchasing power of dollars increased the demand for commodities as assets, with the result that the prices of real goods were bid up relative to financial assets.

In the 1970s, commodity-exporting countries experienced a windfall. Wealth was transferred from the industrialized West to commodity producers, especially those producers of oil in the Middle East. Consequently, a commodity-exporting country could become wealthy by recycling "petro-dollars"—that is, by borrowing dollars, then subsequently repaying with dollars which had depreciated relative to its export prices. This simple process worked as long as the relative price of commodities was kept high by unanticipated inflation.

But when real interest rates rose sharply after the October 1979 shift in U.S. monetary policy, the opportunity cost of holding inventories of commodities also rose. So, the real value of commodities fell. Wealth was once again shifted, this time from the commodity producers to those holding floating-rate liens against those commodity assets. As Figure 5 indicates, the relative prices of commodities have fallen dramatically from their peaks in 1974 and 1979.

As with foreign exchange and interest rates, the financial markets responded to the increased commodity price risk with new instruments. The evolution of financial instruments to manage commodity price risk is traced in Panels B-1 and B-2 of Figure 4.

Metals. The behavior of the price of metals differs from that of foreign exchange, interest rates, and oil prices in that metals experienced a period of increased price volatility in the 1950s as well as the 1970s. Given what we have seen so far, then, it should come as no surprise that a forward contract on zinc was introduced on the London Metal Exchange (LME) in 1953. (Forward contracts on copper had been traded on the LME since 1883.) With the increase in volatility in the 1970s, forward contracts began trading on the LME on aluminum in 1978 and nickel in 1979.

Futures contracts appeared later on the COMEX—on copper in July 1983 and on aluminum in December 1983. An option on copper futures began trading on the COMEX in April 1986.

Petroleum. Because of the preponderance of long-term contracting in the oil industry, forward contracts have never been a significant feature of the petroleum market. But with the increased volatility of oil prices, futures contracts were not long in appearing. Heating oil futures appeared on the New York Mercantile Exchange (NYME) in November 1978, and futures on West Texas Intermediate (WTI) crude oil appeared in March 1983. And, as with all of the other instruments we have watched, options followed. Options on WTI crude oil futures were introduced in November 1986 and options on heating oil futures in June 1987.

Hybrids. Hybrid securities involving commodities have also appeared. With its June 1986 issue of Oil Interest-Indexed Notes, Standard Oil made the first inroad into oil warrants. At maturity, the holder of the note will receive not only the principal amount, but an additional payment tied to the value of crude oil. Specifically, holders of the 1990 notes will receive the excess of the crude price over $25 multiplied by 170.[14] In effect, investors in the 1990 notes have an embedded four-year option on 170 barrels of crude oil.

Hybrids have also begun to appear that modify the timing of the options embedded in the bond. Magma Copper Company's Copper Interest-Indexed Senior Subordinated Notes of November 1988 represent a case in point. This 10-year issue pays a quarterly interest payment that varies with the prevailing price of copper as follows:[15]

Average Copper Price	Indexed Interest Rate	Average Copper Price	Indexed Interest Rate
$2.00 or above	21%	$1.20	16%
1.80	20	1.10	15
1.60	19	1.00	14
1.40	18	0.90	13
1.30	17	0.80 or below	12

Hence, at each coupon date, the holder of the debenture has an option position on copper prices.[16] In effect, this 10-year debenture has embedded in it 40 option positions on the price of copper: one with maturity 3 months, one with maturity 6 months, ..., and one with maturity 10 years.

Commercial Bank Activities. In marked contrast to the markets for foreign exchange and interest rates, banks have not yet become active in providing risk management instruments for commodity prices. The Commodity Futures Trading Commission's December 1987 Release on Hybrid Instruments[17] has had, in the words of the Securities & Exchange Commission, a "chilling effect on new product development."[18] To date the activities of commercial banks in this area have been limited to a relatively small number of banks arranging commodity swaps offshore.

BUT HOW MUCH IS REALLY "NEW"?

In the preceding pages, we have traced the evolution in the 1970s and 1980s of financial structures that have come to be called "innovations" in the capital markets. Forward rate agreements; futures contracts on foreign exchange rates, interest rates, metals, and petroleum; currency, interest rate, and commodity swaps; options on foreign exchange rates, interest rates, and petroleum; and hybrid securities—all these represent innovations in the sense that they provide firms with the ability to deal with today's more risky financial environment.

But, it is misleading to think of these financial instruments as recent "discoveries." If anything, these risk management instruments have been "rediscovered" in the 1970s and 80s.

For example, while we in Chicago point with pride to the fact that futures contracts have been traded since 1865 on the Chicago Board of Trade, futures contracts are actually much older.[19] Historians sug-

---

14. For more details, see the Prospectus supplement of June 19, 1986. The holder of the 1992 note had the same payoff; but, for 200 barrels instead of 170.

15. From the November 23, 1988 Prospectus, page 5.

16. In effect the owner of the note is long a call option with an exercise price of $0.80 and is short a call with an exercise price of $2.00.

17. Commodity Futures Trading Commission, 17 CFR Part 34, Regulation of Hybrid and Related Instruments, Advance Notice of Proposed Rulemaking, December 11, 1987.

18. Response of the SEC to the CFTC, August 19, 1988, page 6.

19. The Board of Trade opened in 1842; but, in the early years of the board, it was forward rather than futures contracts which were traded. *Futures*, Chicago Board of Trade, 1988.

gest that futures contracts first appeared in Japan in the 1600s. The feudal lords of Japan used a market they called *cho-ai-mai*—"rice trade on book"—to manage the volatility in rice prices caused by weather, warfare, and other sources.[20] In Europe, formal futures markets also appeared in the Netherlands during the 1600s. Among the most notable of these early futures contracts were the tulip futures that developed during the height of the Dutch "tulipmania" in 1636.[21]

The forward contract is even older. Historians suggest that forward contracts were first used by Flemish traders who gathered for trade fairs on land held by the Counts of Champagne. At these medieval trade fairs, a document called a letter *de faire*—a forward contract specifying delivery at a later date—made its appearance in the twelfth century.[22]

Of the financial instruments, options were the last to appear and therefore seem to be the most innovative. But options are not new. As early as the seventeenth century, options on a number of commodities were being traded in Amsterdam.[23]

And, even the hybrid securities are not new. In other periods of uncertainty, similar securities have appeared. As both of us are Southerners, we would conclude by reminding you of the "cotton bonds" issued by the Confederate States of America.

In 1863, the Confederacy issued a 20-year bond denominated not in Confederate dollars but in French Francs and Pounds Sterling. The most interesting feature of this bond, however, is its convertibility (at the option of the bondholder) into cotton.[24] In the par-

lance of today's investment banker, the Confederate States of America issued a *dual-currency, cotton-indexed bond*.

CONCLUDING REMARKS

From the perspective of financial markets, the changes in the financial environment in the 1970s are important because they stimulated demand for new financial instruments. The financial environment is the key determinant of the kinds of instruments that will be successful in the marketplace. In short, financial innovation is a demand-driven phenomenon.

If the financial environment is stable, the market will use simple instruments. In the late 1800s, for example, the financial instrument of choice was the consol: a bond with a fixed interest rate but no maturity—it lasted forever. Investors were quite happy to hold infinite-lived British government bonds because British sovereign credit was good and expected inflation was nil. Confidence in price level stability led to a stable interest rate environment and therefore to long-lived bonds.

But when the financial environment is filled with uncertainty, then we can expect to see the proliferation of new risk management instruments and hybrid securities. Thus, such uncertainty, though causing many economic problems and disruptions, has also provided the impetus for much valuable financial innovation. Through this process of innovation, financial intermediaries can expand their activities by offering their customers products to manage risk, or even the ability to turn such risk to their own advantage. Through innovation, moreover, financial institutions can better evaluate and manage their own portfolios. Because price uncertainty cannot be eliminated, the clear trend now is to manage risk actively rather than to try to predict price movements.

20. Richard J. Teweles and Frank J. Jones, *The Futures Game*, Second Edition, McGraw-Hill, 1987.
21. Peter M. Garber, "The Tulipmania Legend, " Center for the Study of Futures Markets working Paper # CSFM-139, August 1986.

22. Teweles and Jones, cited earlier in note 20.
23. *Futures & Options Trading in Commodity Markets*, International Chamber of Commerce, Paris, 1986.
24. At a set rate of sixpence sterling per pound of cotton.

STRATEGIC RISK MANAGEMENT

by S. Waite Rawls, III and Charles W. Smithson, Continental Bank*

As we have listened to managers discuss their companies' exposures to financial price risk, we have heard them talk about several very different kinds of risk. Virtually every manager considers *accounting exposures*; and the accounting exposures that receive the most attention are transaction exposures—those that arise from direct expenses or sales to which the firm is contractually committed. In the foreign exchange environment, transaction exposures are defined very specifically by FAS 52. In the case of interest rates, the guidance is less formal, but most companies focus on managing their interest expense. In addition to transaction exposures, some companies, especially multinationals with large foreign holdings, are concerned about translation exposures—that is, possible changes in the value of the firm from converting the value of foreign assets into the home currency.

Beyond such accounting exposures, managers realize that while transaction exposures defined by FAS 52 deal only with "firm commitments," changes in exchange rates, interest rates, or commodity prices can affect the value of the firm through future transactions. Hence, some managers actively manage their *contingent exposures*—those resulting from the effects of financial price changes on transactions expected, but not yet booked.

Finally, some managers have begun to assess their firm's *competitive exposures*. Such an assessment attempts to evaluate the impact of changes in foreign exchange rates, interest rates, or commodity prices on the firm's sales, market share and, ultimately, net profits (or, more precisely, net cash flows).

In this article, we use the term *strategic exposure* to encompass the other three. A company has a strategic exposure to the extent that changes in foreign exchange rates, interest rates, or commodity prices affect its market value—that is, the present value of the expected future cash flows.[1] The increased volatility of exchange rates and interest rates in the 1970s has led more companies to recognize their strategic exposures. Unfortunately, many firms have been forced to recognize their exposures the hard way: Strategic exposures have put them out of business.

---

* This paper draws on *Managing Financial Risk*, a book Charles Smithson co-authored with Clifford W. Smith, Jr. and D. Sykes Wilford, Institutional Investor Series in Finance, New York: Harper & Row, (1990).

1. There are some accounting exposures that offset others. Moreover, some accounting exposures have no impact on the value of the firm. Hence, while the firm's strategic exposure does represent the firm's total economic exposure, this measure is *not* simply the sum of the other exposures.

FIGURE 1
THE IMPACT OF RISK
MANAGEMENT HEDGING IS
TO REDUCE THE VARIANCE
IN THE DISTRIBUTION OF
FIRM VALUE

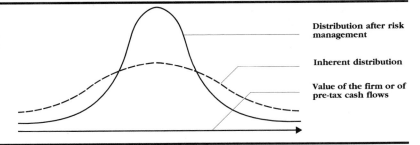

Distribution after risk
management

Inherent distribution

Value of the firm or of
pre-tax cash flows

In some cases, the exposure was a transaction exposure, arising from a mismatch in revenues and expenses . . .

HOW SIR FREDDIE SHOT HIMSELF DOWN

In the late 1970s, Laker Airlines was doing well—so well that their existing fleet of aircraft simply couldn't handle the volume of British vacationers. So, Freddie Laker bought five more DC10s, financing them in U.S. dollars. The problem was that, since the airline's revenues were primarily in pounds while the payments for the new DC10s were in dollars, Laker Airlines had a mismatch between revenues and expenses. When the dollar strengthened in 1981, revenues declined because British travelers could no longer afford the resulting higher cost of trans-Atlantic travel; and the increased liabilities sent Laker into bankruptcy.[2]

In other cases, the exposure was a competitive exposure, arising from the impact of a financial price on the firm's ability to compete . . .

CATERPILLAR'S FX WHAMMY

Throughout the early 1980s, Caterpillar cited the strong dollar as the primary cause of its difficulties. When the dollar strengthened relative to the yen, the price of Caterpillar equipment rose relative to the price of Komatsu equipment, giving Komatsu a competitive advantage on Caterpillar. And Caterpillar's sales, domestic as well as international, fell off sharply.[3]

As illustrated in Figure 1, the practice of risk management—that is, hedging exposures—reduces the volatility of the firm's pre-tax cash flows (and hence reduces the volatility of the value of the firm). Before a company decides to undertake a risk management program, however, two questions need to be answered:

1. **To what extent does my firm face strategic exposures to interest rates, foreign exchange rates, or commodity prices?**

2. **Would a risk management program increase the value of the firm? And, if so, how?**

In the pages that follow, we address these two questions. And, besides discussing how we think management ought to examine and deal with corporate exposures, we also summarize some empirical work that focuses on a third question:

3. **What are firms actually doing with respect to risk management?**

As we shall see, the available evidence indicates that a significant number of firms are using risk management tools. At the same time, however, there are a great many companies that still do not appear to be managing their exposures—which brings us to a fourth question:

4. **What are the stumbling blocks? What is keeping firms from using risk management tools?**

HOW TO MEASURE A FIRM'S STRATEGIC EXPOSURE

When confronted in the 1970s with the impact of volatile interest rates on their income, banks began using financial risk management techniques. A bank

---

2. This illustration is taken from a story by the same title which appeared in *Business Week*, (February 22, 1982) and from "How Smart Competitors Are Locking in the Cheap Dollar," Gregory J. Millman, *Corporate Finance*, (December 1988).

3. From "Caterpillar's Triple Whammy," Dexter Hutchins, *Fortune*, (October 27, 1986).

or a financial institution measures its exposure to interest rate changes using either a *maturity gap* approach or *duration* analysis. Maturity gap measures the sensitivity of an institution's *net interest income* to changes in the interest rate. Duration, by contrast, measures the sensitivity of the *value of assets* to changes in interest rates (as follows):[4]

$$D = \frac{\text{Percentage Change in V}}{\text{Percentage Change in } (1 + r)}$$

Moreover, because duration is "additive," the duration technique can be expanded to deal with the impact of changes in interest rates on the value of a portfolio or the value of the entire firm. The technique can also be used to calculate the duration of the firm's equity—that is, the sensitivity of the value of the firm to changes in interest rates.

Although gap and duration work well for financial institutions, they are not helpful if we want to examine the interest rate sensitivity of a nonfinancial institution. Neither gap nor duration, moreover, is useful in examining a firm's sensitivity to movements in other financial prices such as foreign exchange rates or commodity prices. We thus require a more general method for measuring financial price risk—one that can handle firms other than financial institutions and financial prices other than interest rates.

To get a measure of the sensitivity of the value of the firm to changes in the financial prices, we must first define the basis for the measure. It can be a "flow" (or single-period) measure like the maturity gap analysis above or a "stock" (or multi-period capitalized present value) measure such as duration.

Flow Measures. Within a specific company, the corporate treasury can evaluate the sensitivity of income flows to changes in financial prices as part of the budgeting/planning process. Some firms have begun using simulation models ("what-if" analyses) that allow them to evaluate the sensitivity of their pre-tax income to changes in interest rates, exchange rates, and commodity prices.

QUANTIFYING KODAK'S STRATEGIC RISK

Kodak is well aware that changes in the yen-dollar exchange rate affect its value. As the value of the dollar gets stronger, Kodak's competitive position deteriorates relative to Fuji's. Articles in the trade press suggest that Kodak begins with a base-case set of assumptions about the yen-dollar exchange rate and other financial prices to obtain a base-case forecast of revenues, costs, and pre-tax income. Then, using alternative values for interest rates, exchange rates, or commodity prices, alternate forecasts of revenues, costs, and pre-tax income are simulated. By observing how forecasts of sales, costs, and income move in response to changes in the financial prices, the risk managers at Kodak are able to quantify their exposures.

As David Fiedler, Kodak's Director of Foreign Exchange Planning, puts it, in managing "the real problem—the economic problem, I have to make an estimate of its magnitude." Mr. Fiedler recognizes that there is a large margin of error; but, by using simulations, they are "quite a bit closer to a real solution than saying we can't be precise about it; so, we'll ignore the problem. The latter response effectively estimates the problem at zero."[5]

In accomplishing such an evaluation, however, the analyst faces two major difficulties: (1) the approach requires substantial data and (2) it relies on the ability of the researcher to make accurate forecasts of sales and costs under alternative assumptions about the financial prices. Thus, such an approach is generally possible only for analysts inside a specific firm.

Stock Measures. Given the data requirements noted above, analysts outside the company generally rely on market valuations—typically, the value of the firm's equity. A good starting point for evaluating the risk of a given firm's equity is with the "market model," a statistical regression equation that reveals the sensitivity of a company's stock price movements

---

4. This equation holds only as an approximation. For the equation to be a true equality, we would be talking about "modified duration."

5. This illustration is based on "Daring to Hedge the Unhedgeable," Paul Dickins, *Corporate Finance*, (August 1988) and *Strategic Risk Management*, William Millar and Brad Asher, *Business International*, (January 1990).

to changes in the general market. Specifically, the market model regresses the rate of return on the firm's equity against the rate of return on the market portfolio; and the resulting correlation coefficient, known as "beta," is a measure of market (or "undiversifiable") risk.

The number of variables in the market model can then be expanded to measure "diversifiable" risks such as foreign exchange rate, interest rate, and commodity price exposures; and the resulting correlation coefficients can serve as estimates of the sensitivity of the firm's value to changes in each of these financial prices.

MEASURING WESTINGHOUSE'S STRATEGIC EXPOSURES

To estimate a firm's sensitivity to interest rates, exchange rates, and the price of oil, we would estimate an equation like the following:

$$R_t = \alpha + b_1(\Delta \text{ 3ML/3ML}) + b_2(\Delta \text{ 10YT/10YT})$$
$$+ b_3(\Delta \text{ } P_\pounds/P_\pounds) + b_4(\Delta \text{ } P_¥/P_¥) + b_5(\Delta \text{ } P_{OIL}/P_{OIL})$$

where

- R_t = rate of return for holding the firm's stock,
- $\Delta 3ML/3ML$ = percentage change in three month LIBOR;
- $\Delta 10YT/10YT$ = percentage change in the 10-year Treasury rate;
- $\Delta P_\pounds/P_\pounds$, $\Delta P_¥/P_¥$ = percentage changes in dollar prices of pounds and yen;
- $\Delta P_{OIL}/P_{OIL}$ = percentage change in crude oil price.

The coefficients b_1 and b_2 provide measures of the sensitivity of the value of the firm to changes in the three-month LIBOR rate and 10-year Treasury rate, while b_3 and b_4 estimate the sensitivity to the exchange rates and b_5 estimates the sensitivity to the oil price.

To estimate Westinghouse's price sensitivities, we calculate the rate of return on the firm's equity using daily data on share prices and dividends for the period October 1987 to October 1989. Likewise, we calculate the daily percentage changes in three-month LIBOR, the 10-year Treasury rate, the dollar prices of pounds and yen, and the price of West Texas Intermediate crude oil.

Sensitivity to	Parameter Estimate
3-Month LIBOR	−0.263*
10-Year T-Bond Yield	−0.681*
Price of Sterling	−0.517
Price of Yen	0.098*
Price of Oil	0.023

*Statistically significant at the 95% confidence level

The resulting estimates indicate that, over the two-year period, there is a statistically significant inverse relation between both 3-month LIBOR and the 10-year Treasury rate and the value of Westinghouse equity. That is, increases in (short or long) interest rates are associated with decreases in the value of Westinghouse shares. Conversely, there is a significant positive relation between the price of yen and the value of Westinghouse shares. Looking at each one-year period separately, we find that Westinghouse's exposure to LIBOR has decreased over time.[6]

WHY WOULD A FIRM WANT TO MANAGE STRATEGIC RISK?

If the value of a firm is sensitive to movements in interest rates, foreign exchange rates, or commodity prices, a tantalizing conclusion is that the value of the firm will necessarily rise if this exposure is managed. Albeit tantalizing, this conclusion does not follow directly. The fact that a firm is confronted with strategic risk is only a necessary condition for the firm to manage that risk. The sufficient condition is that the risk management strategy increase the expected value of the firm.

The value of a firm (V) can be thought of as the sum of all future expected net cash flows (E(NCF)), discounted by the company's cost of capital (r). Expressed in the form of an equation,

$$V = \sum_{t=0}^{T} \frac{E(NCF_t)}{(1 + r)^t}$$

---

6. This approach extends the analyses of Flannery/James (1984) ("The Effect of Interest Rate Changes on Common Stock Returns of Financial Institutions," *Journal of Finance*, (Vol. 39 No. 4) and Sweeney/Warga (1986) ("The Pricing of Interest Rate Risk: Evidence from the Stock Market," *Journal of Finance*, (Vol. 41 No. 2). The approach used here is described more completely in "Identifying and Quantifying Financial Risk," Charles W. Smithson and Leah Sonnenschein, working paper, Continental Bank, (1990).

IF RISK MANAGEMENT POLICIES ARE GOING TO INCREASE THE VALUE OF
THE FIRM, **THEN** SUCH POLICIES MUST EITHER REDUCE THE
FIRM'S TRANSACTION COSTS OR TAXES OR IMPROVE ITS
INVESTMENT DECISIONS.

FIGURE 2
THE IMPACT OF HEDGING
ON THE PROBABILITY OF
FINANCIAL DISTRESS

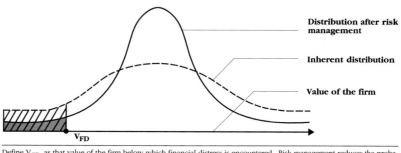

 P_{FD}
P'_{FD}

Define V_{FD} as that value of the firm below which financial distress is encountered. Risk management reduces the probability of V_{FD} from P_{FD} to P'_{FD}.

The insight provided by this equation is that, if the value of the firm is to increase, it must result from either an increase in expected net cash flows or a decrease in the discount rate.

Since we are talking about risk, the most obvious place to look for an effect is through a decrease in the discount rate. But, from the perspective of modern portfolio theory, foreign exchange rate risk, interest rate risk, and commodity price risk are all diversifiable risks; and shareholders can manage such risks effectively on their own simply by holding diversified portfolios. Therefore, actively managing these risks should have no effect on the company's cost of capital.[7] So, unless the firm is held by undiversified owners (as is the case, for example, in most private or closely held firms), risk management is not going to increase the expected value of the firm through a reduction in the discount rate.

Consequently, in the case of a company held by well-diversified investors, risk management can be expected to increase the value of the firm only by increasing expected net cash flows. But, this of course begs the question: How can hedging, or any other financial policy for that matter, have any impact on the real cash flows of the organization?

In 1958, Franco Modigliani and Merton Miller formally proposed that in a world with no taxes, no transaction costs, and fixed corporate investment policies, a company's value is unaffected by financial policies.[8]

That is, whether management decides to fund its operations with debt or equity, and what kinds of debt or equity securities it chooses to issue, should have no effect on the value of the company's shares. In such a world, financial decisions would be nothing more than ways of repackaging the company's operating cash flows for distribution to investors. The insight provided by M & M is that investors can efficiently repackage corporate earnings on their own. And just as investors can use "home-made" leverage to lever up debt-free companies, they can also create their own home-made risk management strategy by holding diversified portfolios.

The important message of the M & M proposition for corporate practitioners becomes evident only when the argument is turned upside down:

IF risk management policies are going to increase the value of the firm,

THEN such policies must either reduce the firm's transaction costs or taxes or improve its investment decisions.

Transaction Costs: Expected Costs of Financial Distress[9]

In Figure 1, we noted that risk management reduces the volatility of the cash flows of the firm. Figure 2 goes further to show that, by reducing cash

---

7. In the context of the market model, as long as interest rate, foreign exchange rate, and commodity price risks are diversifiable, managing these risk will have no impact on the firm's "beta." However, in actuality, interest rate, foreign exchange rate, and commodity price movements also influence the rate of return to the market portfolio; so managing financial price risk can change the firm's beta, albeit marginally.

8. The original M&M proposition was presented in, "The Cost of Capital, Corporation Finance and the Theory of Investment," *American Economic Review,* 48 (June 1958), pp. 261-97. The M&M proposition was extended to dividends in

1961, "Dividend Policy, Growth and the Valuation of Shares," *Journal of Business,* 34 (October 1961), pp. 411-33, arguing that "homemade" dividends can be created as the investor sells the firm's stock.

9. While we concentrate on the expected costs of financial distress, risk management could reduce other transaction costs as well. For instance, the cost of hedging by the management of the firm could be less than the cost of the shareholders' constructing a diversified portfolio, particularly in the case where the firm has access to information not disclosed to the shareholder.

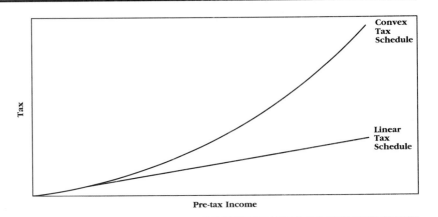

EXHIBIT 3
CONVEXITY IN THE
TAX FUNCTION

Convex
Tax
Schedule

Linear
Tax
Schedule

Tax

Pre-tax Income

flow volatility, risk management reduces the probability of the firm getting into financial difficulty and bearing the consequent costs.

How much risk management can reduce these costs depends on two obvious factors: (1) the probability of encountering financial distress if the firm does not hedge and (2) the costs imposed by such financial problems. The reduction in expected costs, and thus the expected benefit from risk management, will be larger the higher is the probability of distress and the greater are the associated costs.

Financial distress—the precursor of default—results when a firm's income is insufficient to cover its fixed claims. The probability of financial distress is thus determined by two factors: (1) fixed claims coverage (because the probability of default rises as the coverage of fixed claims declines); and (2) income volatility (the probability of default rises as the firm's income becomes more volatile).

If financial distress actually leads to bankruptcy and then to reorganization or liquidation, the firm would face substantial direct legal and accounting costs. But, even short of bankruptcy, financial distress can impose substantial indirect costs on the firm.[10] Such costs include higher contracting costs with customers, employees, and suppliers. For example, companies that provide service agreements or warranties have made a longer-term contract with

their customers. The value consumers place on the service agreements and warranties depends on their perception of the financial viability of the firm. If the future of the firm seems in doubt, consumers will place less value on the service agreements and warranties and are likely to turn to a competitor.

THE IMPACT OF FINANCIAL DISTRESS ON SALES[11]
The Case Of Wang

As reported in the Wall Street Journal, "the biggest challenge any marketer can face is selling the products of a company that is on the ropes." For Wang's customers, the guarantees and warranties (both explicit and implicit) are extremely important. As the *Journal* put it, "Wang's customers . . . want to be sure that their suppliers are stable, well-run companies that will be around to fix bugs and upgrade computers for years to come." Consequently, when Wang got into financial trouble, sales turned down. One of Wang's customers put it best when she noted that "before the really bad news, we were looking at Wang fairly seriously [but] their present financial condition means that I'd have a hard time convincing the vice president in charge of purchasing . . . At some point we'd have to ask 'How do we know that in three years you won't be in Chapter 11?'"

---

10. The work of Jerry Warner suggests that the direct costs of bankruptcy are small in relation to the value of the firm. See "Bankruptcy, Absolute Priority, and the Pricing of Risky Debt Claims," *Journal of Financial Economics*, 13 (May 1977), pp. 239-76. But the indirect costs are significant. See "Bankruptcy Costs: Some Evidence," *Journal of Finance*, 32 (May 1977), pp. 337-47.

11. This illustration is based on "Tough Pitch: Marketing on the Defense," William H. Bulkely, *Wall Street Journal*, October 18, 1989.

Taxes

Reducing the volatility of earnings through risk management can reduce corporate taxes if the firm's effective tax schedule is "convex." As shown in Figure 3, a convex tax schedule is one in which the firm's average effective tax rate is rising as pre-tax income rises.

REDUCING TAXES WITH RISK MANAGEMENT

Suppose that, without hedging, the distribution of the firm's pre-tax income is as shown below. For any given year, the firm could have a low pre-tax income (PTI_1) or a high pre-tax income (PTI_2), either with probability 50%.

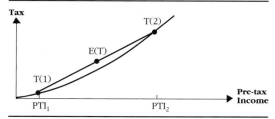

If the firm has pre-tax income PTI_1, it will pay tax $T(1)$; if its pre-tax income is PTI_2, the tax will be $T(2)$. Hence, if the firm does not hedge, expected tax will be $E(T) = [0.5 \times T(1)] + [0.5 \times T(2)]$.

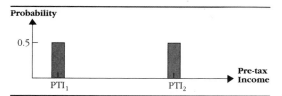

If this firm hedges, the volatility of its pre-tax income will decline; and both PTI_1 and PTI_2 will both move toward the mean income. For purposes of illustration, suppose that the firm hedges completely, such that the distribution of the firm's pre-tax income becomes a single point at the mean (PTI_{MEAN}).

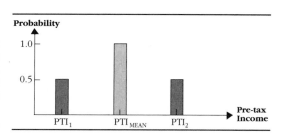

With income PTI_{MEAN}, the firm will pay a tax of $T(PTI_{MEAN})$.

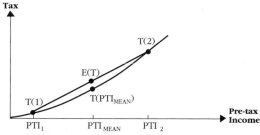

As is obvious, the tax on the hedged income is strictly less than the expected tax if the firm does not hedge.

As the preceding example illustrates, if the tax schedule is convex, risk management can lead to a reduction in the firm's expected taxes. The more convex is the tax schedule, and the more volatile the firm's pre-tax income stream, the greater are the tax benefits.

One obvious factor that would make a tax schedule convex is the degree of progressivity (a tax schedule in which the statutatory tax rate rises as income rises). Although the range of progressivity for corporation income taxes in the United States is relatively small, the Alternative Minimum Tax and tax shields like tax loss carryforwards and tax credits also make the tax schedule more convex.[12, 13]

Improving the Investment Decision and Increasing the Firm's Debt Capacity

As mentioned earlier, the MM "irrelevance" proposition rests on the assumption that corporate

12. There exists a substantial body of evidence on the convexity of the tax function and the factors which make it convex beginning with J.J. Siegfried "Effective Average U.S. Corporation Income Tax Rates" *National Tax Journal*, (June 1974), pp. 245-59 through papers like J.L. Zimmerman "Taxes and Firm Size" *Journal of Accounting and Economics*, (August 1983), pp. 119-49 to recent papers like P.J. Wilkie "Corporate Average Effective Tax Rates and Inferences about Relative Tax Preferences" *Journal of American Taxation Association*, (Fall 1988), pp. 75-88.

13. Moreover, since the Alternate Minimum Tax (AMT) gives tax authorities a claim which is similar to a call option on the pre-tax income of the firm, the AMT also makes the tax schedule more convex.

financial decisions do not affect investment and operating decisions. But, as we shall suggest here, reducing the volatility of cash flows by means of risk management can increase the value of the firm by improving management's incentives to undertake all profitable (positive NPV) projects while rejecting unprofitable ones. By so doing, risk management effectively expands the firm's "debt capacity" (or, put a little differently, reduces the firm's cost of borrowing).

How does risk management increase debt capacity? By reducing the volatility of cash flows, risk management also reduces the conflict of interest that can arise between stockholders and lenders in highly leveraged firms.[14] The conflict results from differences in the kind of claims each hold: bondholders hold fixed claims (and thus bear most of the downside risk) whereas shareholders hold claims that are equivalent to a call option on the value of the firm (and thus accrue the upside gains). Financial managers intent on maximizing stockholder value may have incentives to take actions that reduce the value of the fixed claims while increasing the value of the stock. Actions that increase the variability of the firm's cash flows such as undertaking riskier investments or further increasing financial leverage will "transfer" wealth from bondholders to stockholders. (Recall the effect of the KKR buyout proposal on RJR-Nabisco's bondholders.) The mere possibility of such action (popularly referred to as "event risk") should cause current lenders to limit the firm's future borrowings or to raise the coupon rate to compensate for bearing greater risk.

One determinant of the severity of the conflict between the shareholders and bondholders is the debt-equity ratio—the more debt in the capital structure, the sharper is the conflict.[15] The conflict between shareholders and bondholders is also determined by factors such as the range of investment opportunities available to the firm. Like the value of any other option, the value of shareholders' equity rises as the variance in the returns to the underlying asset increases. By switching from low-variance investment projects to high-variance projects, management can transfer wealth from bondholders to shareholders.[16]

At the end of the day, the bondholder (let's make that the potential bondholder) is concerned about the probability that he or she will be left holding the bag—i.e., the value of the assets of the firm will be insufficient to cover the face value of the debt. In addition to general concerns about future market conditions, the potential bondholder is concerned about opportunistic behavior on the part of the shareholder—the shareholders might declare a liquidating dividend, load the firm up with extra debt, or select risky investment projects. But, since potential bondholders realize that this opportunistic behavior could occur, they protect themselves by lowering the price they are willing to pay for the firm's bonds.

To get the bondholders to pay more for the bonds, the shareholders must assure the bondholders that the wealth transfers will not take place. Such assurances can be provided by attaching restrictive covenants to debt issues (restrictions on dividends and debt coverage ratios), issuing a mortgage bond (to preclude shifts into riskier projects), making the debt convertible (to align the interest of bondholders with those of the shareholders), or issuing preferred stock instead of debt (to reduce the probability that future market conditions will lead to default).

The shareholder-bondholder conflict can also be reduced by risk management. As illustrated in the following example, the combination of hedging instruments with a new bond issue reduced the probability of default and thereby increased the debt capacity of the firm.

14. This situation is one aspect of the agency problem which refers to the conflicts of interest which occur in virtually all cooperative activities among self-interested individuals. The agency problem was introduced by Michael C. Jensen and William H. Meckling in "Theory of the Firm: Managerial Behavior, Agency Costs and Ownership Structure," *Journal of Financial Economics*, 3 (1976), pp. 305-60.

15. While the optimal investment policy is to accept all positive NPV projects and reject all negative NPV projects, the *underinvestment problem* (introduced by S.C. Myers in "The Determinants of Corporate Borrowing," *Journal of Financial Economics*, 5 (November 1977), pp. 147-75) is proposed as an instance in which a firm will turn down a positive NPV project. If the firm has a large amount of debt in its capital structure and if the value of the firm's assets is low, shareholders may opt not to undertake a positive net present value project, because the gains accrue to the bondholders.

16. The problem referred to as *asset substitution* is a case in point. A firm can increase the wealth of its shareholders at the expense of its bondholders by (1) issuing debt with the promise of investing in low risk projects and (2) then investing the proceeds in high risk projects.

CUTTING RATE RISK ON BUYOUT DEBT
Reducing Shareholder-Debtholder Conflict in the RJR
Nabisco Deal

When Kohlberg, Kravis, Roberts and Co. got
ready to issue the senior bank debt for the RJR-Nabisco deal, they ran head-on into the shareholder-debtholder conflict. The use of risk management tools
enabled them to reduce the conflict and increase their
debt capacity.

The market was concerned about the interest rate
risk caused by such a large amount of debt. If the debt
was floating rate and if rates rose substantially, the
probability of default would rise dramatically. Therefore, to reduce the shareholder-debtholder conflict,
KKR was required to purchase interest rate insurance.
(In fact, the Vice Chairman of Chase Manhattan indicated that, before committing any money to finance a
corporate takeover, Chase routinely insists that steps be
taken to reduce the interest rate risk.)

Consequently, KKR agreed to keep interest rate
protection (in the form of swaps or caps) on half of the
outstanding balance of its bank debt. In this way, KKR
was able to borrow $13 billion. Without the rate in-
surance, the amount the banks would have been willing
to lend would almost certainly have been substantially
less.[17]

Why Firms Hedge: Summing Up

We have seen that companies are more likely to
manage financial risk under the following circumstances:

1. the firm faces a convex tax function, resulting
from the Alternative Minimum Tax and other tax
shields such as tax loss carryforwards and tax credits,
as well as progressivity in the tax code.

2. whether because of high leverage and/or a
volatile income stream, the firm faces a significantly
higher probability of a *costly* financial distress or
bankruptcy. Financial distress is likely to be costly if
the firm:

a. provides warranties or service agreements, or
produces a credence good (one whose intrinsic
worth cannot be verified prior to consumption, e.g.,
airline travel);

b. uses specialized labor or must provide specialized training for its workers;

c. requires customized service from its suppliers
or has few suppliers.

3. the characteristics of the firm are such that the
conflict between shareholders and bondholders is
likely to be severe (e.g., more debt in the capital
structure and a wider range of investment opportunities);

4. the firm is owned by ill-diversified investors
(e.g., private or closely held firms).

WHAT ARE FIRMS DOING?

Are Firms Practicing Risk Management?

A number of surveys have attempted to determine whether or not firms are using forwards, futures, swaps, or options. In 1982, banks and savings
and loan associations were surveyed by James
Booth, Richard Smith, and Richard Stolz about their
use of interest rate futures.[18] In 1985, the Fortune 500
firms were surveyed about their use of interest rate
futures and options by Stanley Block and Timothy
Gallagher.[19] In 1989, the members of the Financial
Executives Institute were surveyed by Henry Davis;[20]
and subscribers to Business International publications were surveyed by William Millar.[21] The results
of four studies are summarized in Table 1.

Risk Management as an Objective. The surveys by Davis and Millar asked the companies to
rank various financial policies according to their
relative importance to management. In both of these
surveys, risk management was regarded as important, ranking behind only the objectives of minimizing borrowing cost and maintaining/improving the
firm's credit. Despite the importance attributed to
risk management, both surveys also indicated that
formal statements of risk management policy were
rare.

---

17. Based on an article by the same title by Michael Quint in "Talking Deals,"
The New York Times, February 16, 1989.

18. J.R. Booth, R.L. Smith, and R.W. Stolz, "The Use of Interest Futures by
Financial Institutions," *Journal of Bank Research,* (Spring 1984), pp. 15-20.

19. S.B. Black and T.J. Gallagher, "The Use of Interest Rate Futures and
Options by Corporate Financial Managers," *Financial Management,* 15 (Autumn
1986), pp. 73-78.

20. "Financial Products for Medium-Sized Companies," a survey of the membership of the Financial Executives Institute by The Globecon Group, Ltd., 1989.

21. "New Directions in Financial Risk Management," the 1989 Treasury Survey
performed by Business International Corporation, as reported in *Strategic Risk
Management,* William Millar and Brad Asher, Business International, January 1990.

TABLE 1

	DAVIS (1989) 255 Members of FEI	MILLAR (1989) 173 Subscribers of Business International Pubs.	BOOTH/SMITH/STOLZ (1984) 238 Financial Institutions	BLOCK/GALLAGHER (1986) 193 of Fortune 500

1a. Rank Risk Management versus other financial objectives

	DAVIS	MILLAR		
Minimize Borrowing Cost	1 (100)			
Maintain/Improve Credits	2 (61)	1 (100)		
Maintain Financial Risk	3 (56)	2 (52)		
Broaden Funding Sources	4 (37)	3 (16)		

1b. How is the Risk Management function organized?

Percent of firms where treasury is profit center		7%	3%	16%
Percent of firms having risk management policy statement	15%	13%	20%	46%

2. Goals for Risk Management

Eliminate All Risk	2%	7%	58%	59%	
Eliminate Risk Selectively	31%	34%	52%	52%	67%
Allow Profits			8%	16%	
Actively Seek Profits			5%	7%	1%
Seek Competitive Advantage			29%	25%	32%
Tax/Reg./Acctg. Arbitrage			0%	4%	
Do Not Manage Risk	46%	22%	16%	1%	

3. What exposures does the firm manage?/How does the firm measure its exposure?

Gap	Translation	26%	39%
Duration	Transaction (Firm Com.)	14%	79%
Simulation	Transaction (Within 1 yr.)	52%	62%
	Transaction (Beyond 1 yr.)		16%
	Contingent Exposure		15%
	Competitive Exposure		15%

4. What Risk Management Instruments has the firm used?

Forwards		45%	35%	99%	
Futures	8%	14%	25%	20%	17%
Swaps	24%	9%	68%	64%	
Options	24%	9%	43%	48%	19%

▶ Combined ■ Interest Rates ▢ FX Rates

Goals of Risk Management. The Davis, Millar, and Booth/Smith/Stolz surveys all suggest that firms wish to reduce risks, although typically in a selective way—that is, they reduce some exposures while leaving others unhedged.

At the same time, however, both Millar and Booth/Smith/Stolz find a substantial number of firms using risk management products to secure a competitive advantage. Some companies use risk management to lock in advantageous market conditions. For example, if the dollar is weak, a U.S. producer can lock in a competitive advantage by hedging future sales. Moreover, the Booth/Smith/Stolz survey suggests that banks use interest rate risk management products to allow them to offer such products to their customers.

What Exposures are Managed? Only Millar asked questions about the measurement and management of specific exposures. Since most of the firms in Millar's sample were nonfinancials, it is not surprising that this survey found firms relying on the use of simulation rather than gap or duration when measuring their interest rate exposures. On the foreign exchange dimension, it is likewise not surprising that most emphasis is given to hedging transaction exposures. It is also important to note, however, the number of firms reporting their management of contingent and competitive exposures.

Instruments Used. The most widely used of these four instruments is the foreign exchange forward contract, a contract which has been used by many companies to hedge accounting exposures. Not surprisingly, the firms in these surveys report relatively little use of futures. Futures contracts tend to be used in companies where the treasury is run as a profit center and position-taking is the norm. Because so few of these firms run treasury as a profit center (see Part 1.b. in Table 1), it follows that one would expect the use of futures to be limited.

Are Firms Communicating With Their Shareholders?

So far, we have argued that there are several good reasons why risk management can increase a company's value. We have also provided evidence that more and more firms are examining their strategic exposures and using risk management instruments to reduce them.

From looking at the behavior of share prices (in analyses like the one we showed you for Westinghouse), we know that shareholders continually make judgments about the extent of companies' exposures to interest rate, foreign exchange rate, or commodity price risk in setting stock prices. If management has a different view of the magnitude of those risks—or if it has taken measures to reduce such risks—it seems self-evident that this information ought to be shared with the shareholders.

Our preliminary investigations suggest, however, that companies are typically not communicating this information to investors:

REPORTING ON RISK MANAGEMENT IN ANNUAL REPORTS

We selected a sample of 20 annual reports and searched for references to risk management. Of the 20 firms, only seven mentioned using some kind of risk management instrument. Of these seven companies,

■ Four indicated that they used currency swaps to convert foreign-denominated debt to dollar debt;

■ Three indicated that they had used interest rate swaps to convert fixed-rate debt to floating-rate debt;

■ Two indicated that they had used interest rate swaps to convert floating-rate debt to fixed-rate debt;

■ One had purchased a cap;

■ One had sold an interest rate option; and

■ One had hedged commodity price exposures.

In the argument made earlier about the benefits of shareholder diversification, the shareholders' ability to form an optimal portfolio is based in part on their having complete information about the firm's exposures. Our cursory examination of annual reports suggests that firms may not be disclosing the data necessary for shareholders to make disciplined portfolio decisions about corporate exposures and their consequences for future cash flows.

THE STUMBLING BLOCKS

Three of the four surveys noted in Table 1 also asked about difficulties encountered in using risk management products. The results of this inquiry, which are displayed in Table 2, correspond strongly with the impressions we have gained from conversations with a large number of corporate managers.

TABLE 2 RANK OF DIFFICULTIES WITH IMPLEMENTING RISK MANAGEMENT (RELATIVE RANKS)	DAVIS (1989) 255 members of F.E.I.	BOOTH / SMITH / STOLZ (1984) 238 Fin. Insts.	BLOCK / GAILAGHER (1986) 193 of Fortune 500
Resistance by Sr. Mgmt. or Board of Directors			
	4 (23)	2	2 (78)
Lack of Knowledge			
	2 (88)	1	3 (69)
Acctg/Legal Difficulties			
	5 (20)	2	5 (38)
Cost (Upfront fees or Foregone Gains)			
	3 (45)	—	1 (100)
No Suitable Instrument			
	1 (100)	—	4 (44)

The survey results indicate that the dominant reason for not managing financial risk is "Lack of Knowledge"—the perception that risk management is complex and difficult. Moreover, other common responses like "No Suitable Instrument" and "Resistance by Senior Management or the Board of Directors" also reflect a lack of understanding of or comfort with the risk management instruments and techniques.

Not surprisingly, the managers surveyed were concerned about the cost of the "insurance" protection. In the case of forwards, futures, and swaps, the cost is an opportunity cost. The transaction cost (bid-ask spread) of forwards, futures or swaps is small; the real cost of protecting against downside losses is that the firm must forgo upside gains. In the case of options, the cost is the upfront premium. However, we believe that the concern about the cost of these instruments can be linked directly to the "knowledge" issue mentioned above—managers are not yet comfortable with the way these instruments are priced—and the "accounting" issue. The latter concern is not so much about the cost itself but rather about how the cost will be reflected in the financial statements.

Although accounting and legal concerns ranked far behind lack of knowledge and cost as impediments to managing financial price risk, the accounting treatment for the risk management products has received a great deal of attention. Indeed, the November 1989 issue of the *Journal of Accountancy* focused largely on the subject of accounting for risk management products.

In one of the articles in that issue, James Parks created the following hypothetical dialogue between a CEO and his controller to demonstrate how current accounting rules and conventions can serve to increase rather than decrease the firm's riskiness.[22]

CEO: Let me see if I have this right. If we manage our investment portfolio in a prudent manner and minimize interest rate risk . . . we may have to . . . write down the portfolio to market. And, because we can't write the liabilities down to market, we risk running afoul of minimum capital requirements. On the other hand, if we blindly hold assets until their scheduled maturity, ignoring interest rate risk and sound portfolio management policies, we are allowed to continue carrying them at cost, even if our portfolio's future profitability is damaged in the process.

CONTROLLER: That's about the size of it.

In another article in the same issue, John Stewart focused on the two central problems the Financial Accounting Standards Board (FASB) faces as it attempts to address this problem: (1) the total absence of accounting guidance for many of the risk management instruments, including interest rate forwards, interest rate swaps, and almost all types of options; and (2) the inconsistency of current standards.[23]

22. "The Portfolio Accounting Controversy," *Journal of Accountancy*, Vol. 168 No. 5 (November 1989), pp. 81-86.

23. "The Challenge of Hedge Accounting," *Journal of Accountancy*, Vol. 168 No. 5 (November 1989), pp. 71-78.

A third article (by Halsey Bullen, Robert Wilkins, and Clifford Woods) proposes a solution to these problems that adopts the "building block" approach to evaluating risk management instruments that we introduced in our earlier work.[24] In effect, the proposed FASB approach breaks down complex financial instruments into their most basic parts to determine their underlying economic substance and thereby avoid inconsistency among accounting standards.[25] Such an approach, the authors note, will require that a number of current accounting standards be reviewed, and at least some of them changed.

At present, however, there remain major barriers to the accounting profession's coming to an understanding of, and then accommodating, the current practice of strategic risk management. For instance, at a recent meeting of FASB's Emerging Issues Task Force, the Securities and Exchange Commission's observer set off a firestorm by indicating that in the SEC's opinion, "Hedging net income is inappropriate" and that "hedge accounting would not be appropriate . . . [for] future revenues or costs . . . "[26] In short, there is great uncertainty about how and when such accounting issues will finally be resolved.

CONCLUDING REMARKS

In the face of unprecedented volatility in interest rates, foreign exchange rates, and commodity prices, corporate management has been forced to pay attention to the potential effect of such volatility on the value of the firm. As a consequence, companies are moving toward more sophisticated quantitative techniques to assess the extent of their exposures. They are also using relatively new—or at least unfamiliar—financial instruments like futures, swaps, and options to manage such exposures.

Since investors can manage many financial price risks on their own simply by holding well-diversified portfolios, reductions in the variability of corporate cash flows achieved by corporate risk management will increase firm value only by accomplishing one or more of the following ends:

1. reducing the expected costs of financial distress or bankruptcy (or, by so doing, expanding the firm's debt capacity);

2. reducing the company's expected tax liability (a role that has become more important with the passage of the Alternative Minimum Tax);

3. improving management's investment decision-making (which, again, could also have the effect of increasing the firm's debt capacity).

What evidence we have about current corporate hedging practices suggests that corporations are moving in the right direction. But what also seems clear is that the evolution of financial risk management is still in its relatively early stages. Besides corporate management's general lack of familiarity with the instruments themselves, there are also major accounting and organizational obstacles to more widespread use of the instruments—obstacles that are rooted in a general misunderstanding of their real economic function as a risk management tool. We are confident that, as the hedging role of such instruments comes to be recognized, these barriers to the further spread of risk management practices will fall.

---

24. "A Lego Approach to Financial Engineering: An Introduction to Forwards, Futures, Swaps, and Options," Charles W. Smithson, *Midland Corporate Finance Journal*, Vol. 4 No. 4 (Winter 1987), pp. 16-28.

25. "The Fundamental Financial Instrument Approach," *Journal of Accountancy*, Vol. 168 No. 5 (November 1989), pp. 71-78.

26. Minutes of the August 10, 1989 Open Meeting of the FASB Emerging Issues Task Force.

MANAGING FINANCIAL RISK

by Clifford W. Smith, Jr.,
University of Rochester,
Charles W. Smithson, Continental Bank,
and D. Sykes Wilford,
Chase Manhattan Bank*

T here is no doubt that the financial environment is a lot more risky today than it was in the 1950s and 1960s. With changes in some macroeconomic institutional structures—notably, the breakdown of the Bretton Woods agreement in 1972—have come dramatic increases in the volatility of interest rates, foreign exchange rates, and commodity prices.

Such increased volatility will not come as "news" to most corporate executives. Since the 1970s, many CEOs and CFOs have watched the profitability of their firms swing widely in response to large movements in exchange rates, interest rates, and commodity prices. What may be news, however, are the techniques and tools now available for measuring and managing such financial risks.

Recognition of the increased volatility of exchange rates, interest rates, and commodity prices should lead managers of the firm to ask three questions:

1. To what extent is my firm exposed to interest rates, foreign exchange rates, or commodity prices?

2. What financial tools are available for managing these exposures?

3. If my firm is significantly exposed, how do I use the financial tools to manage the exposure?

It is with these three questions that the following discussion deals.

---

*This article is an abbreviated version of Chapters 2, 3, and 19 of *Managing Financial Risk*, forthcoming Ballinger/ *Institutional Investor Series*. This material is used with the permission of the publisher.

IDENTIFYING AND MEASURING FINANCIAL RISK

The Risk Profile

U.S. savings and loans (S&Ls) are a widely cited example of firms subject to interest rate risk. Because S&Ls typically fund long-lived assets (e.g., 30-year fixed-rate mortgages) with liabilities that reprice frequently (passbook deposits), their value is negatively related to interest rates. When interest rates rise, the value of S&Ls' assets declines significantly, but the value of their liabilities changes little. So, the value of shareholders' equity falls.

The resulting relation between interest rates and the value of S&Ls is portrayed graphically in a *risk profile* in Figure 1.

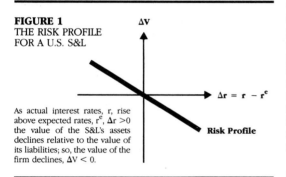

FIGURE 1
THE RISK PROFILE
FOR A U.S. S&L

As actual interest rates, r, rise above expected rates, r^e, $\Delta r > 0$ the value of the S&L's assets declines relative to the value of its liabilities; so, the value of the firm declines, $\Delta V < 0$.

The negative slope reflects the inverse relation between the financial price—i.e., interest rates—and the value of the S&L. The precise measure of the exposure is reflected by the slope of the line; and it is a measure of the slope that the techniques described below will provide.

But before considering the size of the exposure, the first question is: How do we go about identifying such exposures? In the case of S&Ls, the exposure to interest rates is apparent from the firm's balance sheet; the mismatch of maturities between assets and liabilities is obvious. Many companies, however, have economic or "operating" exposures that are not reflected on their balance sheets. Take, for example,

the vulnerability of building products firms to increases in interest rates. Increases in interest rates decrease the demand for building products. As sales and thus cash inflows decline—and to the extent that its costs and liabilities are fixed—the value of a building products firm declines.

We can make a similar observation about foreign exchange risk. In some instances, exposures are apparent. For example, a U.S. importer orders product from Germany and is expected to pay in Deutsche Marks (DM) for the products when they are delivered in 90 days. If, during those 90 days, the price of a DM rises—that is, the value of the dollar declines—the U.S. importer will have to pay more for the product. In this case, an increase in the price of the foreign currency leads to a decrease in the value of the importer.

Since 1972, firms have become adept at dealing with such transaction exposures.[1] However, a firm's exposure to foreign exchange rate risk can be more subtle; even firms that have no foreign receipts or payments may still be exposed to foreign exchange risk. If the dollar is strong, the dollar price of foreign products to U.S. consumers becomes cheaper and foreign firms make inroads into the U.S. market, thereby decreasing net cash flows to the U.S. producers and thus reducing their value. The reverse is true when the value of the dollar falls. Obvious for firms like automakers, this economic or competitive (or "strategic") risk is receiving more attention by the managers of other U.S. firms as well.[2]

Not surprisingly, the same relations appear with respect to commodity price risk. The exposures can be apparent: For example, as the price of oil rises, the costs for an airline rise; so rising oil prices are linked to falling firm values. Or, the exposures can be subtle. For example, a primary input in aluminum production is electric energy. Aluminum manufacturers in Iceland use electricity generated by that country's abundant geothermal energy. As the price of oil rises, the costs of competitors rise while the costs of Icelandic producers remain unchanged, thus improving the competitive position and increasing the value of Icelandic firms. It is when oil prices fall and competitors' costs decline that Icelandic producers worry.[3]

Financial price risk, then—whether caused by changes in interest rates, foreign exchange, or com-

1. A transaction exposure occurs when the firm has a payment or receipt in a currency other than its home currency. A translation exposure results when the value of foreign assets and liabilities must be converted into home currency values.
2. A case in point is Kodak, which has begun to manage "overall corporate performance in the long run." See Paul Dickens, "Daring to Hedge the Unhedgeable," *Euromoney Corporate Finance*, August 1988.
3. For this useful story about Icelandic aluminum producers, we are indebted to J. Nicholas Robinson of Chase Manhattan Bank.

TABLE 1
CALCULATION OF THE
VALUE & DURATION OF
THE BUSINESS LOAN

	(1)	(2)	(3)	(4)	(5)	(6)
	Time to Receipt (Years)	Cash Flow	Discount Rate	PV	Weight	Weight × Time
	0.5	90	7.75%	86.70	0.22	0.11
	1.0	90	8.00%	83.33	0.21	0.21
	1.5	90	8.25%	79.91	0.20	0.31
	2.0	90	8.35%	76.66	0.19	0.38
	2.5	90	8.50%	73.40	0.18	0.45
				400.00 Present Value		1.45 Duration

modity prices—consists of more subtle economic exposures as well as the obvious balance sheet mismatches and transactional exposures. And the *risk profile* mentioned earlier, in order to provide a useful measure of a firm's overall economic exposure, must reflect the total effect of both kinds of price risk.

The question that naturally arises, then, is: How do you determine the slope of the risk profile? That is, how do you estimate the change in firm value expected to accompany a given change in a financial price ($\Delta V/\Delta P$)?

Quantifying Financial Risk: A Special Case

Financial institutions, particularly banks, were the first to devote significant attention to quantifying financial exposures. Our S&L example is admittedly an extreme case of interest rate exposure, even for a financial institution. Nevertheless, because some mismatch between the maturities of assets and liabilities almost inevitably occurs in the normal course of their business, all financial institutions generally face some degree of interest rate risk. To measure this exposure to interest rates, financial institutions rely on two techniques: gap and duration.

GAP: The method most financial corporations use to measure their exposure to interest rate changes is called the "maturity gap" approach.[4] The approach gets its name from a procedure designed to quantify the "gap" between the market values of rate-sensitive assets (RSA) and rate-sensitive liabilities (RSL)—that is, GAP = RSA − RSL.[5] The financial institution determines the "gapping period"—the period over which it wants to measure its interest rate sensitivity—say, 6 months, one year, five years, and so forth. Then, for each of these periods, it measures its gap as defined above. In the context of a gap model, changes in interest rates affect a financial institution's market value by changing the institution's Net Interest Income (NII). Hence, once the GAP is known, the impact on the firm of changes in the interest rate can be calculated as follows:

$$\Delta NII = (GAP) \times (\Delta r)$$

Duration: Some financial institutions use an alternative to the GAP approach called "duration analysis" to measure their interest rate exposure.[6] In essence, the duration of a financial instrument provides a measure of when on average the present value of the instrument is received.

For example, let's look at the duration of a business loan with a maturity of 2.5 years and a sinking fund. Because part of the value is received prior to maturity, the duration of the instrument is clearly less than 2.5 years. To find out how much less, we need to ask the question "When on average is the present value received?"

4. For a discussion of the maturity gap model, see Alden L. Toevs, "Measuring and Managing Interest Rate Risk: A Guide to Asset/Liability Models Used in Banks and Thrifts," Morgan Stanley Fixed Income Analytical Research Paper, October 1984. (An earlier version of this paper appeared in *Economic Review*, The Federal Reserve Bank of San Francisco, Spring, 1983.)

5. The assets and liabilities that are "rate sensitive" are those that will reprice during the gapping period.

6. For a discussion of duration, see George G. Kaufman, "Measuring and Managing Interest Rate Risk: A Primer," *Economic Perspectives*, Federal Reserve Bank of Chicago. See also Stephen Schaefer, "Immunisation and Duration: A Review of the Theory, Performance, and Applications," *Midland Corporate Finance Journal*, Vol. 2 No. 3, Fall 1984.

Table 1 provides an illustration. Columns 1-4 provide the present value of the bond. To determine *when* the present value will be received, on average, we need to calculate the weighted average time of receipt. Column 5 provides the weights. Multiplying these weights (column 5) by the times the cash flows are received (column 1) and summing gives the duration of this business loan—1.45 years.

The use of duration effectively converts a security into its zero-coupon equivalent. In addition, duration relates changes in interest rates to changes in the value of the security.[7] Specifically, duration permits us to express the percentage change in the value of the security in terms of the percentage change in the discount rate $(1 + r)$ and the duration of the security, as follows:[8]

$$\frac{\Delta V}{V} = \frac{\Delta (1 + r)}{(1 + r)} \times D$$

For example, if the duration of a security is 1.45 years, and the discount rate increases by 1 percent (that is, if $\Delta (1 + r)/(1 + r) = 0.01$), the market value of the 2.5 year business loan will decrease by 1.45 percent. The concept of duration, moreover, can be extended to provide a measure of the interest rate exposure of an entire bank or S&L.

Quantifying Financial Price Risk: The General Case

While gap and duration work well for financial institutions, these techniques offer little guidance in evaluating the interest rate sensitivity of a nonfinancial institution; and, neither gap nor duration is useful in examining a firm's sensitivity to movements in foreign exchange rates or commodity prices. What is needed is a more general method for quantifying financial price risk—a method that can handle firms other than financial institutions and financial exposures other than interest rates.

To get a measure of the responsiveness of the value of the firm to changes in the financial prices, we must first define a measure of the value of the firm. As with interest rate risk for financial institutions, this value measure could be a "flow" measure (gap analysis uses net interest income) or a "stock" measure (duration uses the market value of the portfolio).

Flow Measures. Within a specific firm, estimation of the sensitivity of income flows is an analysis that can be performed as part of the planning and budgeting process. The trade press suggests that some firms have begun using simulation models to examine the responsiveness of their pre-tax income to changes in interest rates, exchange rates, and commodity prices.[9] Beginning with base case assumptions about the financial prices, the firm obtains a forecast for revenues, costs, and the resulting pre-tax income. Then, it considers alternative values for an interest rate or an exchange rate or a commodity price and obtains a new forecast for revenues, costs, and pre-tax income. By observing how the firm's projected sales, costs and income move in response to changes in these financial prices, management is able to trace out a risk profile similar to that in Figure 1.

In making such an estimation, two inherent problems confront the analyst: (1) this approach requires substantial data and (2) it relies on the ability of the researcher to make explicit, accurate forecasts of sales and costs under alternative scenarios for the financial prices. For both these reasons, such an approach is generally feasible only for analysts within a specific firm.

Stock Measures. Given the data requirements noted above, analysts outside the firm generally rely on market valuations, the most widely used of which is the current market value of the equity. Using a technique much like the one used to estimate a firm's "beta," an outside observer could measure the historical sensitivity of the company's equity value to changes in interest rates, foreign exchange rates, and commodity prices.

For example, suppose we wished to determine the sensitivity of a company's value to the following financial prices:
● the one-year T-bill interest rate;
● the Deutsche Mark / Dollar exchange rate;
● the Pound Sterling / Dollar exchange rate;
● the Yen / Dollar exchange rate; and
● the price of oil.

---

7. Note the contrast with the gap approach, which relates changes in the interest rate to changes in net interest income.

8. The calculations in Table 1 are based on the use of MacCauley's duration. If we continue to apply MacCauley's duration (D), this equation is only an approximation. To be exact, modified duration should be used. For a development of this relation, see George G. Kaufman, G.O. Bierwag, and Alden Toevs, eds. *Innovations in Bond Portfolio Management: Duration Analysis and Immunization* (Greenwich, Conn.: JAI Press, 1983).

9. See for instance, Paul Dickens, cited in note 2.

TABLE 2
MEASUREMENTS OF EXPOSURES TO INTEREST RATE, FOREIGN EXCHANGE RATES, AND OIL PRICES

Percentage Change In	Chase Manhattan		Caterpillar		Exxon	
	Parameter Estimate	T Value	Parameter Estimate	T Value	Parameter Estimate	T Value
Price of 1-Year T-Bill	2.598*	1.56	− 3.221**	1.76	1.354	1.24
Price of DM	− 0.276	0.95	0.344	1.07	− 0.066	0.35
Price of Sterling	0.281	1.16	− 0.010	0.38	0.237*	1.50
Price of Yen	− 0.241	0.96	0.045	0.16	− 0.278**	1.69
Price of WTI Crude	0.065	1.21	− 0.045	0.77	0.082***	2.33

* Significant at 90% single tailed
** Significant at 90%
*** Significant at 95%

We could estimate this relation by performing a simple linear regression as follows:[10]

$$R_t = a + b_1 \left(\frac{\Delta P_{TB}}{P_{TB}}\right)_t + b_2 \left(\frac{\Delta P_{DM}}{P_{DM}}\right)_t + b_3 \left(\frac{\Delta P_{\pounds}}{P_{\pounds}}\right)_t + b_4 \left(\frac{\Delta P_y}{P_y}\right)_t + b_5 \left(\frac{\Delta P_{OIL}}{P_{OIL}}\right)_t$$

where R is the rate of return on the firm's equity; $\Delta P_{TB} / P_{TB}$ is the percentage change in the price of a one-year T-bill; $\Delta P_{DM}/P_{DM}$, $\Delta P_{\pounds}/P_{\pounds}$, and $\Delta P_y/P_y$ are the percentage changes in the dollar prices of the three foreign currencies; and $\Delta P_{OIL} / P_{OIL}$ is the percentage change in the price of crude oil. The estimate of b_1 provides a measure of the sensitivity of the value of the firm to changes in the one-year T-bill rate; b_2, b_3, and b_4 estimate its sensitivity to the exchange rates; and b_5 estimates its sensitivity to the oil price.[11]

To illustrate the kind of results this technique would yield, we present three examples: a bank, Chase Manhattan, an industrial, Caterpillar, and an oil company, Exxon. For the period January 6, 1984 to December 2, 1988 we calculated weekly (Friday close to Friday close) share returns and the corresponding weekly percentage changes in the price of a one-year

T-bill rate, the dollar prices of a Deutsche Mark, a Pound Sterling, and a Yen, and the price of West Texas Intermediate crude. Using these data, we estimated our regression equation. The results of these estimations are displayed in Table 2.

Given the tendency of banks to accept short-dated deposits to fund longer-dated assets (loans), it is not surprising that our estimates for Chase Manhattan indicate an inverse exposure to interest rates. Although only marginally significant, the positive coefficient indicates that an increase in the one-year T-bill

TABLE 2.A

Bank	Estimated Sensitivity	T-Value
Bank of America	3.2	1.5
Bankers Trust	2.2	1.4
Chase	2.6	1.6
First Chicago	3.0	1.6
Manufacturers Hanover	3.2	1.9

---

10. In effect, this equation represents a variance decomposition. While it is a multifactor model, it is not related in any important way to the APT approach suggested by Ross and Roll. Instead, it is probably more accurate to view the approach we suggest as an extension of the market model. In its more complete form, as described in Chapter 2 of our book *Managing Financial Risk*, the regression equation would include the rate of return to the market ("beta") as well as the percentage changes in the financial prices, and would thus look as follows:

$$R_t = a + \beta R_{m,t} + b_1 PC(P_{TB}) + b_2 PC(P_{DM}) + b_3 PC(P_{\pounds}) + b_4 PC(P_y) + b_5 PC(P_{OIL})$$

This more complete model is based on a number of earlier studies: French/Ruback/Schwert (1983) ("Effects of Nominal Contracting on Stock Returns," *Journal of Political Economy*, Vol. 91 No. 1) on the impact of unexpected inflation on share returns, Flannery/James (1984) ("The Effect of Interest Rate Changes on Common Stock Returns of Financial Institutions," *Journal of Finance* Vol. 39 No. 4) and Scott/Peterson (1986) ("Interest Rate Risk and Equity Values of Hedged and Unhedged Financial Intermediaries," *Journal of Financing Research* Vol. 9 No. 6)

on the impact of interest rate changes on share prices for financial firms, and Sweeney/Warga (1986) ("The Pricing of Interest Rate Risk: Evidence from the Stock Market," *Journal of Finance* Vol. 41 No. 2) on the impact of interest rate risk on share prices for nonfinancial firms. This model does exhibit the problems of measuring the reaction of firm value to changes in exchange rates, which are described by Donald Lessard in "Finance and Global Competition: Exploiting Financial Scope and Coping with Volatile Exchange Rates," *Midland Corporate Finance Journal* (Fall 1986).

For expositional purposes, we use in this paper the shorter form of the equation. This abbreviated model is acceptable empirically given the small correlations which exist between the percentage changes in the financial prices and the market return.

11. These coefficients actually measure elasticities. Further, had we used the percentage change in the quantity, (1 + one-year T-bill rate), instead of the percentage change in the price of the one-year T-bill, the coefficient b_1 could be interpreted as a "duration" measure.

TABLE 2.B

	1984	1985	1986	1987	1988
Parameter Estimate for Percentage Change in Price of Yen	1.72	0.15	0.33	−1.08	−0.85
T-Value	1.59	0.31	0.65	1.08	1.53

TABLE 2.C

	1984	1985	1986	1987	1988
Parameter Estimate for Percentage Change in Price of Oil	0.80	0.15	0.09	0.05	−0.01
T-Value	3.94	0.85	2.79	0.37	0.17

rate (or a decrease in the price of the T-bill) is expected to lead to a decrease in the bank's value.

Additional information can be obtained by comparing the coefficient estimates among firms in the same industry. For example, we can compare the estimated sensitivity of Chase's value to the one-year T-bill rate to the sensitivities of other banks as shown in Table 2.A.

In contrast to the bank's inverse exposure, Caterpillar appears to have a positive exposure to the one-year T-bill rate. That is, the negative regression coefficient indicates that increases in the one-year T-bill rate (or decreases in the price of the T-bill) lead to increases in the value of the firm.

Even more surprising, though, given much that has been written about Caterpillar's exposure to foreign currency changes, is the lack of any significant exposure to the yen. This result is more understandable if we break up this 5-year span into shorter intervals and look at Caterpillar's sensitivity to the price of the yen on a year-by-year basis. (See Table 2.B.) The data reflect the fact that, as Caterpillar has moved its production facilities, the firm has changed from being positively exposed to the yen (such that an increase in the value of the dollar would harm Caterpillar) to being negatively exposed to the yen (an increase in the value of the dollar now helps Caterpillar).

Unlike the other two firms, the estimate for Exxon's exposure to interest rates is not statistically significant (not, at least, to the one-year T-bill rate). Exxon does exhibit the expected positive exposure to the price of oil. But our estimates also reflect the now common view, reported in the financial press and elsewhere, that Exxon's exposure to the price of oil has been declining over time—both in size and consistency (as measured by statistical significance). (See Table 2.C.) Given its international production and distribution, as well as its international portfolio of assets, Exxon also exhibits marginally significant exposures to foreign exchange rates. Our estimates suggest Exxon benefits from an increase in the value of the pound but is harmed by an increase in the value of the yen.

Measuring Corporate Exposure: Summing Up

The purpose of this first section, then, has been to outline a statistical technique (similar to that used to calculate a firm's "beta") that can be used to provide management with an estimate of the sensitivity of firm value to changes in a variety of financial variables. Such measures can be further refined by using information from other sources. For example, the same regression technique can be used, only substituting changes in the firm's periodic earnings and cash flows for the changes in stock prices in our model. There are, however, two principal advantages of our procedure over the use of such accounting numbers: (1) market reactions are likely to capture the entire capitalized value of changes in firm value in response to financial price changes; and (2) regression analysis using stock prices, besides being much faster and cheaper, can be done using publicly available information.

THE TOOLS FOR MANAGING FINANCIAL RISK: A BUILDING BLOCK APPROACH[12]

If it turns out that a firm is subject to significant financial price risk, management may choose to hedge that risk.[13] One way of doing so is by using an "on-balance-sheet" transaction. For example, a company could manage a foreign exchange exposure resulting from overseas competition by borrowing in the competitor's currency or by moving production abroad. But such on-balance sheet methods can be costly and, as firms like Caterpillar have discovered, inflexible.[14]

Alternatively, financial risks can be managed with the use of off-balance-sheet instruments. The four fundamental off-balance-sheet instruments are forwards, futures, swaps, and options.

When we first began to attempt to understand these financial instruments, we were confronted by what seemed an insurmountable barrier to entry. The participants in the various markets all seemed to possess a highly specialized expertise that was applicable in only one market to the exclusion of all others (and the associated trade publications served only to tighten the veil of mystery that "experts" have always used to deny entry to novices). Options were discussed as if they were completely unrelated to forwards or futures, which in turn seemed to have nothing to do with the latest innovation, swaps. Adding to the complexities of the individual markets was the welter of jargon that seems to have grown up around each, thus further obscuring any common ground that might exist. (Words such as "ticks," "collars," "strike prices," and "straddles" suddenly had acquired a remarkable currency.) In short, we seemed to find ourselves looking up into a Wall Street Tower of Babel, with each group of market specialists speaking in different languages.

But, after now having observed these instruments over the past several years, we have been struck by how little one has to dig before superficial differences give way to fundamental unity. And, in marked contrast to the specialized view of most Wall Street practitioners, we take a more "generalist" approach—one that treats forwards, futures, swaps, and options not as four unique instruments and markets, but rather as four interrelated instruments for dealing with a single problem: managing financial risk. In fact, we have come up with a little analogy that captures the spirit of our conclusion, one which goes as follows: The four basic off-balance-sheet instruments—forwards, futures, swaps, and options—are much like those plastic building blocks children snap together. You can either build the instruments from one another, or you can combine the instruments into larger creations that appear (but appearances deceive) altogether "new."

Forward Contracts

Of the four instruments, the forward contract is the oldest and, perhaps for this reason, the most straightforward. A forward contract obligates its owner to buy a specified asset on a specified date at a price (known as the "exercise price") specified at the origination of the contract. If, at maturity, the actual price is higher than the exercise price, the contract owner makes a profit equal to the difference; if the price is lower, he suffers a loss.

In Figure 2, the payoff from buying a forward contract is illustrated with a hypothetical risk profile. If the actual price at contract maturity is higher than the expected price, the inherent risk results in a decline in the value of the firm; but this decline is offset by the profit on the forward contract. Hence, for the risk profile illustrated, the forward contract provides an effective hedge. (If the risk profile were positively instead of negatively sloped, the risk would be managed by selling instead of buying a forward contract.)

Besides its payoff profile, a forward contract has two other features that should be noted. First, the default (or credit) risk of the contract is two-sided. The contract owner either receives or makes a payment, depending on the price movement of the underlying

12. This section of the article is adapted from Charles W. Smithson, "A LEGO Approach to Financial Engineering: An Introduction to Forwards, Futures, Swaps, and Options," *Midland Corporate Finance Journal* 4 (Winter 1987).

13. In this paper we do not address the question of why public corporations hedge. For a discussion of the corporate decision whether or not to hedge financial price exposures, see Alan Shapiro and Sheridan Titman, "An Integrated Approach to Corporate Risk Management," *Midland Corporate Finance Journal* 3 (Summer 1985). For other useful theoretical discussions of the corporate hedging decision, see David Mayers and Clifford Smith, "On the Corporate Demand for Insurance," *Journal of Business* 55 (April 1982) (a less technical version of which was published as "The Corporate Insurance Decision," *Chase Financial Quarterly* (Vol.

1 No. 3) Spring 1982); Rene Stulz, "Optimal Hedging Policies," *Journal of Financial and Quantitative Analysis* 19 (June 1984); Clifford Smith and Rene Stulz, "The Determinants of Firms' Hedging Policies," *Journal of Financial* and *Quantitative Analysis* 20 (December 1985).

For some empirical tests of the above theoretical work, see David Mayers and Clifford Smith, "On the Corporate Demand for Insurance: Some Empirical Evidence," working paper, 1988; and Deana Nance, Clifford Smith, and Charles Smithson, "The Determinants of Off-Balance-Sheet Hedging: An Empirical Analysis," working paper 1988.

14. See "Caterpillar's Triple Whammy," *Fortune*, October 27, 1986.

FIGURE 2
PAYOFF PROFILE
FOR FORWARD
CONTACT

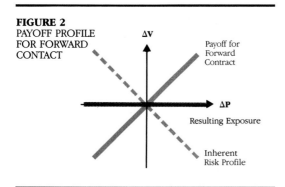

asset. Second, the value of the forward contract is conveyed only at the contract's maturity; no payment is made either at origination or during the term of the contract.

Futures Contracts

The basic form of the futures contract is identical to that of the forward contract; a futures contract also obligates its owner to purchase a specified asset at a specified exercise price on the contract maturity date. Thus, the payoff profile for the purchaser of a forward contract as presented in Figure 2 could also serve to illustrate the payoff to the holder of a futures contract.

But, unlike the case of forwards, credit or default risk can be virtually eliminated in a futures market. Futures markets use two devices to manage default risk. First, instead of conveying the value of a contract through a single payment at maturity, any change in the value of a futures contract is conveyed at the end of the day in which it is realized. Look again at Figure 2. Suppose that, on the day after origination, the financial price rises and, consequently, the financial instrument has a positive value. In the case of a forward contract, this value change would not be received until contract maturity. With a futures contract, this change in value is received at the end of the day. In the language of the futures

markets, the futures contract is "marked-to-market" and "cash settled" daily.

Because the performance period of a futures contract is reduced by marking to market, the risk of default declines accordingly. Indeed, because the value of the futures contract is paid or received at the end of each day, Fischer Black likened a futures contract to "a series of forward contracts [in which] each day, yesterday's contract is settled and today's contract is written."[15] That is, a futures contract is like a sequence of forwards in which the "forward" contract written on day 0 is settled on day 1 and is replaced, in effect, with a new "forward" contract reflecting the new day 1 expectations. This new contract is then itself settled on day 2 and replaced, and so on until the day the contract ends.

The second feature of futures contracts which reduces default risk is the requirement that all market participants—sellers and buyers alike—post a performance bond called the "margin."[16] If my futures contract increases in value during the trading day, this gain is added to my margin account at the day's end. Conversely, if my contract has lost value, this loss is deducted from my margin account. And, if my margin account balance falls below some agreed-upon minimum, I am required to post additional bond; that is, my margin account must be replenished or my position will be closed out.[17] Because the position will be closed before the margin account is depleted, performance risk is eliminated.[18]

Note that the exchange itself has not been proposed as a device to reduce default risk. Daily settlement and the requirement of a bond reduce default risk, but the existence of an exchange (or clearinghouse) merely serves to transform risk. More specifically, the exchange deals with the two-sided risk inherent in forwards and futures by serving as the counterparty to all transactions. If I wish to buy or sell a futures contract, I buy from or sell to the exchange. Hence, I need only evaluate the credit risk of the exchange, not of some specific counterparty.

The primary economic function of the exchange is to reduce the costs of transacting in futures

15. See Fischer Black "The Pricing to Commodity Contracts," *Journal of Financial Economics* 3 (1976), 167-179.

16. Keep in mind that if you buy a futures contract, you are taking a long position in the underlying asset. Conversely, selling a futures contract is equivalent to taking a short position.

17. When the contract is originated on the U.S. exchanges, an "initial margin" is required. Subsequently, the margin account balance must remain above the "maintenance margin." If the margin account balance falls below the maintenance level, the balance must be restored to the initial level.

18. Note that this discussion has ignored daily limits. If there are daily limits on the movement of futures prices, large changes in expectations about the underlying asset can effectively close the market. (The market opens, immediately moves the limit, and then is effectively closed until the next day.) Hence, there could exist an instance in which the broker desires to close out a customer's position but is not able to immediately because the market is experiencing limit moves. In such a case, the statement that performance risk is "eliminated" is too strong.

FIGURE 3

Panel A: An Interest Rate Swap

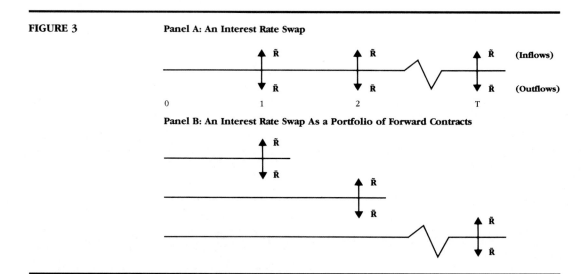

Panel B: An Interest Rate Swap As a Portfolio of Forward Contracts

contracts. The anonymous trades made possible by the exchange, together with the homogeneous nature of the futures contracts—standardized assets, exercise dates (four per year), and contract sizes—enables the futures markets to become relatively liquid. However, as was made clear by recent experience of the London Metal Exchange, the existence of the exchange does not in and of itself eliminate the possibility of default.[19]

In sum, a futures contract is much like a portfolio of forward contracts. At the close of business of each day, in effect, the existing forward-like contract is settled and a new one is written.[20] This daily settlement feature combined with the margin requirement allows futures contracts to eliminate the credit risk inherent in forwards.

Swap Contracts[21]

A swap contract is in essence nothing more complicated than a series of forward contracts strung together. As implied by its name, a swap contract obligates two parties to exchange, or "swap," some specified cash flows at specified intervals. The most common form is the interest rate swap, in which the cash flows are determined by two different interest rates.

Panel A of Figure 3 illustrates an interest rate swap from the perspective of a party who is paying out a series of cash flows determined by a fixed interest rate ($\bar{R}$) in return for a series of cash flows determined by a floating interest rate ($\tilde{R}$).[22]

Panel B of Figure 3 serves to illustrate that this swap contract can be decomposed into a portfolio of

19. In November of 1985, the "tin cartel" defaulted on contracts for tin delivery on the London Metal Exchange, thereby making the exchange liable for the loss. A description of this situation is contained in "Tin Crisis in London Roils Metal Exchange," *The Wall Street Journal*, November 13, 1985.

From the point of view of the market, the exchange does not reduce default risk. The expected default rate is not affected by the existence of the exchange. However, the existence of the exchange can alter the default risk faced by an individual market participant. If I buy a futures contract for a specific individual, the default risk I face is determined by the default rate of that specific counterparty. If I instead buy the same futures contract through an exchange, my default risk depends on the default rate of not just my counterparty, but on the default rate of he entire market. Moreover, to the extent that the exchange is capitalized by equity from its members, the default risk I perceive is further reduced because I have a claim not against some specific counterparty, but rather against the exchange. Therefore, when I trade through the exchange, I am in a sense purchasing an insurance policy from the exchange.

20. A futures contract is like a portfolio of forward contracts; however, a futures contract and a portfolio of forward contracts become identical only if interest rates are "deterministic"—that is, known with certainty in advance. See Robert A. Jarrow and George S. Oldfield, "Forward Contracts and Futures Contracts," *Journal of Financial Economics* 9 (1981), 373-382; and John A. Cox, Jonathan E. Ingersoll, and Stephen A. Ross, "The Relation between Forward Prices and Futures Prices," *Journal of Financial Economics* 9 (1981), 321-346.

21. This section is based on Clifford W. Smith, Charles W. Smithson, and Lee M. Wakeman, "The Evolving Market for Swaps," *Midland Corporate Finance Journal* Winter (1986), 20-32.

22. Specifically, the interest rate swap cash flows are determined as follows: The two parties agree to some notional principal, P. (The principal is notional in the sense that it is only used to determine the magnitude of cash flows; is is not paid or received by either party.) At each settlement date, 1, 2,..., T the party illustrated makes a payment $\bar{R} = \bar{r}P$, where $\bar{r}$ is the T-period fixed rate which existed at origination. At each settlement, the party illustrated receives $\tilde{R} = \tilde{r}P$, where $\tilde{r}$ is the floating rate for that period (e.g., at settlement date 2, the interest rate used is the one-period rate in effect at period 1).

forward contracts. At each settlement date, the party to this swap contract has an implicit forward contract on interest rates: the party illustrated is obligated to sell a fixed-rate cash flow for an amount specified at the origination of the contract. In this sense, a swap contract is also like a portfolio of forward contracts.

In terms of our earlier discussion, this means that the solid line in Figure 2 could also represent the payoff from a swap contract. Specifically, the solid line in Figure 3 would be consistent with a swap contract in which the party illustrated receives cash flows determined by one price (say, the U.S. Treasury bond rate) and makes payments determined by another price (say, LIBOR). Thus, in terms of their ability to manage risk, forwards, futures, and swaps all function in the same way.

But identical payoff *patterns* notwithstanding, the instruments all differ with respect to default risk. As we saw, the performance period of a forward is equal to its maturity; and because no performance bond is required, a forward contract is a pure credit instrument. Futures both reduce the performance period (to one day) and require a bond, thereby eliminating credit risk. Swap contracts use only one of these mechanisms to reduce credit risk; they reduce the performance period.[23] This point becomes evident in Figure 3. Although the maturity of the contract is T periods, the performance period is generally not T periods long but is instead a single period. Thus, given a swap and a forward contract of roughly the same maturity, the swap is likely to impose far less credit risk on the counterparties to the contract than the forward.

At each settlement date throughout a swap contract, the changes in value are transferred between the counterparties. To illustrate this in terms of Figure 3, suppose that interest rates rise on the day after origination. The value of the swap contract illustrated has risen. This value change will be conveyed to the contract owner not at maturity (as would be the case with a forward contract) nor at the end of that day (as would be the case with a futures contract). Instead, at the first settlement date, part of the value change is conveyed in the form of the "difference check" paid by one party to the other. To repeat,

then, the performance period is less than that of a forward, but not as short as that of a futures contract.[24] (Keep in mind that we are comparing instruments with the same maturities.)

Let us reinforce the two major points made thus far. First, a swap contract, like a futures contract, is like a portfolio of forward contracts. Therefore, the payoff profiles for each of these three instruments are identical. Second, the primary difference among forwards, futures, and swaps is the amount of default risk they impose on counterparties to the contract. Forwards and futures represent the extremes, and swaps are the intermediate case.

Option Contracts

As we have seen, the owner of a forward, futures, or swap contract has an *obligation* to perform. In contrast, an option gives its owner a *right*, not an obligation. An option giving its owner the right to buy an asset at a pre-determined price—a call option—is provided in Panel A of Figure 4. The owner of the contract has the right to purchase the asset at a specified future date at a price agreed-upon today. Thus, if the price rises, the value of the option also goes up. But because the option contract owner is not obligated to purchase the asset if the price moves against him, the value of the option remains unchanged (at zero) if the price declines.[25]

The payoff profile for the party who sold the call option (also known as the call "writer") is shown in Panel B. In contrast to the buyer of the option, the seller of the call option has the *obligation* to perform. For example, if the owner of the option elects to exercise his option to buy the asset, the seller of the option is obligated to sell the asset.

Besides the option to buy an asset, there is also the option to sell an asset at a specified price, known as a "put" option. The payoff to the buyer of a put is illustrated in Panel C of Figure 4, and the payoff to the seller of the put is shown in Panel D.

Pricing Options: Up to this point, we have considered only the payoffs to the option contracts. We have side-stepped the thorniest issue—the valuation of option contracts.

---

23. There are instances in which bond has been posted in the form of collateral. As should be evident, in this case the swap becomes very like a futures contract.

24. Unlike futures, for which all of any change in contract value is paid/received at the daily settlements, swap contracts convey only part of the total value change at the periodic settlements.

25. For continuity, we continue to use the $\Delta V, \Delta P$ convention in figures. To compare these figures with those found in most texts, treat ΔV as deviations from zero ($\Delta V = V - 0$) and remember that P measures deviations from expected price ($\Delta P = P - P_e$).

FIGURE 4
PAYOFF PROFILES OF
PUTS AND CALLS

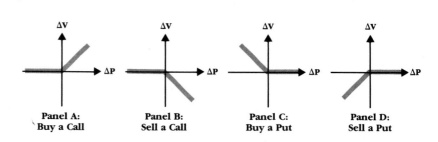

The breakthrough in option pricing theory came with the work of Fischer Black and Myron Scholes in 1973.[26] Conveniently for our purposes, Black and Scholes took what might be described as a "building block" approach to the valuation of options. Look again at the call option illustrated in Figure 4. For increases in the financial price, the payoff profile for the option is that of a forward contract. For decreases in the price, the value of the option is constant—like that of a "riskless" security such as a Treasury bill.

The work of Black and Scholes demonstrated that a call option could be replicated by a continuously adjusting ("dynamic") portfolio of two securities: (1) forward contracts on the underlying asset and (2) riskless securities. As the financial price rises, the "call option equivalent" portfolio contains an increasing proportion of forward contracts on the asset. Conversely, the replicating portfolio contains a decreasing proportion of forwards as the price of the asset falls.

Because this replicating portfolio is effectively a synthetic call option, arbitrage activity should ensure that its value closely approximates the market price of exchange-traded call options. In this sense, the value of a call option, and thus the premium that would be charged its buyer, is determined by the value of its option equivalent portfolio.

Panel A of Figures 5 illustrates the payoff profile for a call option which includes the premium. This figure (and all of the option figures thus far) illustrates an "at-the-money" option—that is, an option for which the exercise price is the prevailing ex-

pected price. As Panels A and B of Figure 5 illustrate, an at-the-money option is paid for by sacrificing a significant amount of the firm's potential gains. However, the price of a call option falls as the exercise price increases relative to the prevailing price of the asset. This means that if an option buyer is willing to accept larger potential losses in return for paying a lower option premium, he would then consider using an "out-of-the-money" option.

An out-of-the-money call option is illustrated in Panel C of Figure 5. As shown in Panel D, the out-of-the-money option provides less downside protection, but the option premium is significantly less. The lesson to be learned here is that the option buyer can alter his payoff profile simply by changing the exercise price.

For our purposes, however, the most important feature of options is that they are not as different from other financial instruments as they might first seem. Options do have a payoff profile that differs significantly from that of forward contracts (or futures or swaps). But, option payoff profiles can be duplicated by a combination of forwards and risk-free securities. Thus, we find that options have more in common with the other instruments than was first apparent. Futures and swaps, as we saw earlier, are in essence nothing more than portfolios of forward contracts; and options, as we have just seen, are very much akin to portfolios of forward contracts and risk-free securities.

This point is reinforced if we consider ways that options can be combined. Consider a portfolio constructed by buying a call and selling a put with the

26. See Fischer Black and Myron Scholes, "The Pricing of Options and Corporate Liabilities," *Journal of Political Economy* 1973. For a less technical discussion of the model, see "The Black-Scholes Option Pricing Model for Alterna-

tive Underlying Instruments," *Financial Analysts Journal*, November-December, 1984, 23-30.

FIGURE 5

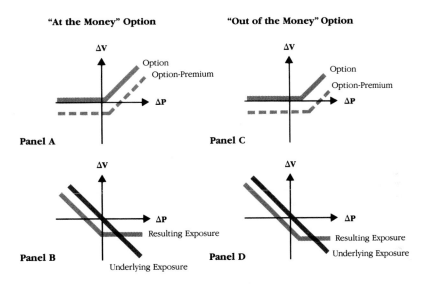

"At the Money" Option   "Out of the Money" Option

Panel A   Panel C

Panel B   Panel D

same exercise price. As the left side of Figure 6 illustrates, the resulting portfolio (long a call, short a put) has a payoff profile equivalent to that of buying a forward contract on the asset. Similarly, the right side of Figure 6 illustrates that a portfolio made up of selling a call and buying a put (short a call, long a put) is equivalent to selling a forward contract.

The relationship illustrated in Figure 6 is known more formally as "put-call parity." The special import of this relationship, at least in this context, is the "building block construction" it makes possible: two options can be "snapped together" to yield the payoff profile for a forward contract, which is identical to the payoff profile for futures and swaps.

At the beginning of this section, then, it seemed that options would be very different from forwards, futures, and swaps—and in some ways they are. But we discovered two building block relations between options and the other three instruments: (1) options can be replicated by "snapping together" a forward, futures, or swap contract together with a position in risk-free securities; and (2) calls and puts can be combined to become forwards.

The Financial Building Blocks

Forwards, futures, swaps, and options—they all look so different from one another. And if you read the trade publications or talk to the specialists that transact in the four markets, the apparent differences among the instruments are likely to seem even more pronounced.

But it turns out that forwards, futures, swaps, and options are not each unique constructions, but rather more like those plastic building blocks that children combine to make complex structures. To understand the off-balance-sheet instruments, you don't need a lot of market-specific knowledge. All you need to know is how the instruments can be linked to one another. As we have seen, (1) futures can be built by "snapping together" a package of forwards; (2) swaps can also be built by putting together a package of forwards; (3) synthetic options can be constructed by combining a forward with a riskless security; and (4) options can be combined to produce forward contracts—or, conversely, forwards can be pulled apart to replicate a package of options.

FIGURE 6

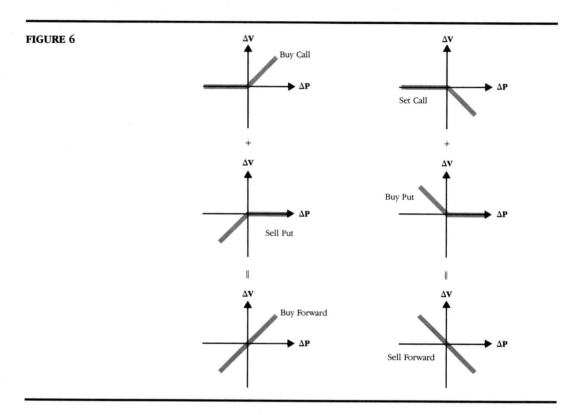

Having shown you all the building blocks and how they fit together in simple constructions, we now want to demonstrate how they can be used to create more complicated, customized financial instruments that in turn can be used to manage financial risks.

ASSEMBLING THE BUILDING BLOCKS

Using The Building Blocks to Manage an Exposure

Consider a company whose market value is directly related to unexpected changes in some financial price, P. The risk profile of this company is illustrated in Figure 7. How could we use the financial building blocks to modify this inherent exposure?

The simplest solution is to use a forward, a futures, or a swap to neutralize this exposure. This is shown in Panel A of Figure 8.

But, the use of a forward, a futures, or a swap

FIGURE 7

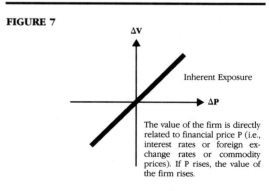

The value of the firm is directly related to financial price P (i.e., interest rates or foreign exchange rates or commodity prices). If P rises, the value of the firm rises.

eliminates possible losses by giving up the possibility of profiting from favorable outcomes. The company might want to minimize the effect of unfavorable outcomes while still allowing the possibility of gaining from favorable ones. This can be accom-

FIGURE 8

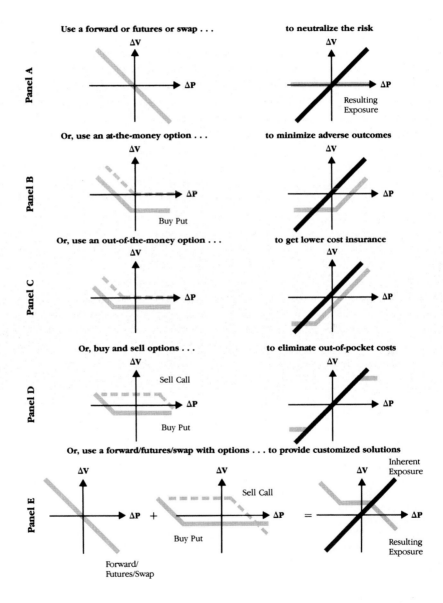

plished using options. The payoff profile of an at-the-money option (including the premium paid to buy the option) is shown on the left side of Panel B. Snapping this building block onto the inherent exposure profile gives the resulting exposure illustrated on the right side of panel B.

A common complaint about options—especially at-the-money options—is that they are "too expensive." To reduce the option premium, you can think about using an out-of-the-money option. As Panel C of Figure 8 illustrates, the firm has thereby given up some protection from adverse outcomes in return for paying a lower premium.

But, with an out-of-the-money option, some premium expense remains. Panel D illustrates how the out-of-pocket expense can be *eliminated*. The firm can sell a call option with an exercise price chosen so as to generate premium income equal to the premium due on the put option it wishes to purchase. In building block parlance, we snap the "buy-a-put" option onto the inherent risk profile to reduce downside outcomes; and we snap on the "sell-a-call" option to fund this insurance by giving up some of the favorable outcomes.

Panel E reminds us that forwards, futures, and swaps can be used in combination with options. Suppose the treasurer of the company we have been considering comes to you with the following request:

I think that this financial price, P, is going to fall dramatically. And, while I know enough about financial markets to know that P could actually rise a little, I am sure it will not rise by much. I want some kind of financial solution that will let me benefit when my predictions come to pass. But I don't want to pay any out-of-pocket premiums. Instead, I want this financial engineering product to pay me a premium.

If you look at the firm's inherent risk profile in Figure 7, this seems like a big request. The firm's inherent position is such that it would lose rather than gain from big decreases in P.

The resulting exposure profile shown on the right side of Panel E is the one the firm wants: it benefits from large decreases in P, is protected against small increases in P (though not against large increases) and receives a premium for the instrument.

How was this new profile achieved? As illustrated on the left side of Panel E, we first snapped a forward/futures/swap position onto the original risk profile to neutralize the firm's inherent exposure. We then sold a call option and bought a put option with exercise prices set such that the income from selling the call exceeded the premium required to buy the put.

No high level math was required. Indeed, we did this bit of financial engineering simply by looking through the box of financial building blocks until we found those that snapped together to give us the profile we wanted.

Using the Building Blocks to Redesign Financial Instruments

Now that you understand how forwards, futures, swaps, and options are all fundamentally related, it is a relatively short step to thinking about how the instruments can be combined with each other to give one financial instrument the characteristics of another. Rather than talk about this in the abstract, let's look at some examples of how this has been done in the marketplace.

Combining Forwards with Swaps: Suppose a firm's value is currently unaffected by interest rate movements. But, at a known date in the future, it expects to become exposed to interest rates: if rates rise, the value of the firm will decrease.[27] To manage this exposure, the firm could use a forward, futures, or swap commencing at that future date. Such a product is known as a *forward* or *delayed start* swap. The payoff from a forward swap is illustrated in Panel C of Figure 9, where the party illustrated pays a fixed rate and receives floating starting in period 5.

Although this instrument is in effect a forward contract on a swap, it also, not surprisingly, can be constructed as a package of swaps. As Figure 9 illustrates, a forward swap is equivalent to a package of two swaps:

Swap 1—From period 1 to period T, the party pays fixed and receives floating.

Swap 2—From period 1 to period 4, the party pays floating and receives fixed.

Forwards with Option-like Characteristics: The addition of option-like characteristics to forward

---

27. For example, the firm may know that, in one year, it will require funds which will be borrowed at a floating rate, thereby giving the firm the inverse exposure to interest rates. Or, the firm may be adding a new product line, the demand for which is extremely sensitive to interest rate movements—as rates rise, the demand for the product decreases and cash flows to the firm decrease.

FIGURE 9

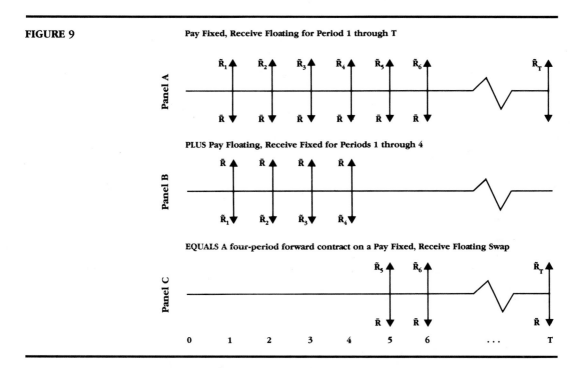

Pay Fixed, Receive Floating for Period 1 through T

PLUS Pay Floating, Receive Fixed for Periods 1 through 4

EQUALS A four-period forward contract on a Pay Fixed, Receive Floating Swap

contracts first appeared in the foreign exchange markets. To see how this was done, let's trace the evolution of these contracts.

Begin with a standard forward contract on foreign exchange. Panel A of Figure 10 illustrates a conventional forward contract on sterling with the forward sterling exchange rate (the "contract rate") set at $1.50 per pound sterling. If, at maturity, the spot price of sterling exceeds $1.50, the owner of this contract makes a profit (equal to the spot rate minus $1.50). Conversely, if at maturity the spot price of sterling is less than $1.50, the owner of this contract suffers a loss. The owner of the forward contract, however, might instead want a contract that allows him to profit if the price of sterling rises, but limits his losses if the price of sterling falls.[28] Such a contract would be a call option on sterling. Illustrated in Panel B of Figure 10 is a call option on sterling with an exercise price of $1.50. In this illustration we have assumed an

option premium of 5 cents (per pound sterling).

The payoff profile illustrated in Panel B of Figure 10 could also be achieved by altering the terms of the standard forward contract as follows:

1. Change the contract price so that the exercise price of the forward contract is no longer $1.50 but is instead $1.55. The owner of the forward contract agrees to purchase sterling at contract maturity at a price of $1.55 per unit; and

2. Permit the owner of the contract to break (i.e. "unwind") the agreement at a sterling price of $1.50.

This altered forward contract is referred to as a *break forward* contract.[29] In this break forward construction, the premium is effectively being paid by the owner of the break forward contract in the form of the above market contract exchange rate.

From our discussion of options, we also know that a call can be paid for with the proceeds from selling a put. The payoff profile for such a situation is

28. This discussion is adapted from Warren Edwardes and Edmond Levy, "Break Forwards: A Synthetic Option Hedging Instrument," *Midland Corporate Finance Journal* 5 (Summer 1987) 59-67.

29. According to Sam Srinivasulu in "Second-Generation Forwards: A Comparative Analysis," Business International Money Report, September 21, 1987, break forward is the name given to this construction by Midland Bank. It goes under other names: Boston Option (Bank of Boston), FOX—Forward with Optional Exit (Hambros Bank), and Cancelable Forward (Goldman Sachs)

FIGURE 10

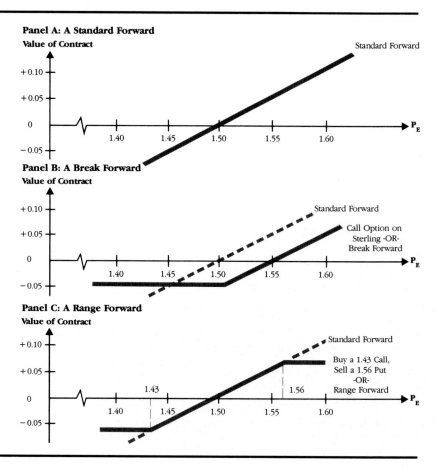

Panel A: A Standard Forward
Value of Contract

Panel B: A Break Forward
Value of Contract

Panel C: A Range Forward
Value of Contract

illustrated in Panel C of Figure 10. In this illustration, we have assumed that the proceeds of a put option on sterling with an exercise price of $1.56 would carry the same premium as a call option on sterling with an exercise price of $1.43.[30]

A payoff profile identical to this option payoff profile could also be generated, however, simply by changing the terms of a standard forward contract to the following:

• at maturity, the buyer of the forward contract agrees to purchase sterling at a price of $1.50 per pound sterling;

• the buyer of the forward contract has the right to break the contract at a price of $1.43 per pound sterling; and

• the seller of the forward contract has the right to break the contract at a price of $1.56 per pound sterling.

Such a forward contract is referred to as a *range forward*.[31]

Swaps with Option-like Characteristics: Given that swaps can be viewed as packages of forward contracts, it should not be surprising that swaps can also be constructed to have option-like

---

30. These numbers are only for purposes of illustration. To determine the exercise prices at which the values of the puts and calls are equal, one would have to use an option pricing model.

31. As Srinivasulu, cited note 29, pointed out, this construction also appears under a number of names: range forward (Salomon Brothers), collar (Midland Montagu), flexible forward (Manufacturers Hanover), cylinder option (Citicorp), option fence (Bank of America) and mini-max (Goldman Sachs).

FIGURE 11
PAY-OFF PROFILE FOR
FLOOR-CEILING SWAPS

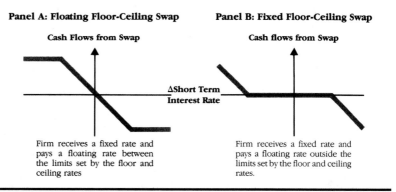

Panel A: Floating Floor-Ceiling Swap

Cash Flows from Swap

Panel B: Fixed Floor-Ceiling Swap

Cash flows from Swap

ΔShort Term
Interest Rate

Firm receives a fixed rate and pays a floating rate between the limits set by the floor and ceiling rates

Firm receives a fixed rate and pays a floating rate outside the limits set by the floor and ceiling rates.

characteristics like those illustrated for forwards. For example, suppose that a firm with a floating-rate liability wanted to limit its outflows should interest rates rise substantially; at the same time, it was willing to give up some potential gains should there instead be a dramatic decline in short-term rates. To achieve this end, the firm could modify the interest rate swap contract as follows:

As long as the interest rate neither rises by more than 200 basis points nor falls more than 100 basis points, the firm pays a floating rate and receives a fixed rate. But, if the interest is more than 200 basis points above or 100 basis points below the current rate, the firm receives and pays a fixed rate.
The resulting payoff profile for this floating floor ceiling swap is illustrated in Panel A of Figure 11.

Conversely, the interest rate swap contract could have been modified as follows:

As long as the interest rate is within 200 basis points of the current rate, the firm neither makes nor receives a payment; but if the interest rate rises or falls by more than 200 basis points, the firm pays a floating rate and receives a fixed rate.
The payoff profile for the resulting fixed floor-ceiling swap is illustrated in Panel B of Figure 11.

Redesigned Options: To "redesign" an option, what is normally done is to put two or more options together to change the payoff profile. Examples abound in the world of the option trader. Some of the more colorfully-named combinations are *straddles*, *strangles*, and *butterflies*.[32]

To see how and why these kinds of creations evolve, let's look at a hypothetical situation. Suppose a firm was confronted with the inherent exposure illustrated in Panel A of Figure 12. Suppose further that the firm wanted to establish a floor on losses caused by changes in a financial price.

As you already know, this could be done by purchasing an out-of-the-money call option on the financial price. A potential problem with this solution, as we have seen, is the premium the firm has to pay. Is there a way the premium can be eliminated?

We have already seen that buying an out-of-the-money call can be financed by selling an out-of-the-money put. However, suppose that this out-of-the-money call is financed by selling a put with precisely the same exercise price—in which case, the put would be in-the-money. As illustrated in Panel B of Figure 12, the proceeds from selling the in-the-money put would exceed the cost of the out-of-the-money call. Therefore, to finance one out-of-the-money call, one would need sell only a fraction of one in-the-money put.

In Panel B, we have assumed that the put value is twice the call value; so, to finance one call, you need sell only 1/2 put. Panel C simply combines the payoff profiles for selling 1/2 put and buying one call with an exercise price of X. Finally, Panel D of Figure 12 combines the option combination in Panel C with the inherent risk profile in Panel A.

Note what has happened. The firm has obtained the floor it wanted, but there is no up-front premium.

---

32. For a discussion of traditional option strategies like straddles, strangles, and butterflies, see for instance chapter 7 of Richard M. Bookstaber, *Option Pricing and Strategies in Investing* (Addison-Wesley, 1981).

OUR POSITION WITH RESPECT TO "FINANCIAL ENGINEERING" IS THAT
THERE IS LITTLE NEW UNDER THE SUN. THE "NEW" PRODUCTS TYPICALLY
INVOLVE NOTHING MORE THAN PUTTING THE BUILDING BLOCKS
TOGETHER IN A NEW WAY.

FIGURE 12

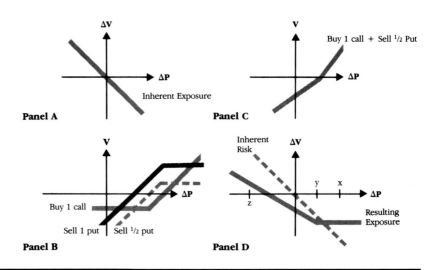

At the price at which the option is exercised, the value of the firm with the floor is the same as it would have been without the floor. The floor is paid for not with a fixed premium, but with a share of the firm's gains above the floor. If the financial price rises by X, the value of the firm falls to the floor and no premium is paid. If, however, the financial price rises by less, say Y, the value of the firm is higher and the firm pays a positive premium for the floor. And, if the financial price falls, say, by Z, the price it pays for the floor rises.

What we have here is a situation where the provider of the floor is paid with a share of potential gains, thereby leading to the name of this option combination—a *participation*. This construction has been most widely used in the foreign exchange market where they are referred to as *participating forwards*.[33]

Options on Other Financial Instruments

Options on futures contracts on bonds have been actively traded on the Chicago Board of Trade since 1982. The valuation of an option on a futures is a relatively straightforward extension of the tradi-tional option pricing models.[34] Despite the close relation between futures and forwards and futures and swaps, the options on forwards (*options on forward rate agreements*) and options on swaps (*swaptions*) are much more recent.

More complicated analytically is the valuation of an option on an option, also known as a *compound option*.[35] Despite their complexity and resistance to valuation formulae, some options on options have begun to be traded. These include options on foreign exchange options and, most notably, options on interest rate options (caps), referred to in the trade as *captions*.

Using the Building Blocks to Design "New" Products

It's rare that a day goes by in the financial markets without hearing of at least one "new" or "hybrid" product. But, as you should have come to expect from us by now, our position with respect to "financial engineering" is that there is little new under the sun. The "new" products typically involve nothing more than putting the building blocks together in a new way.

33. For more on this construction, see Srinivalsulu cited in note 29 and 31.

34. Options on futures were originally discussed by Fischer Black in "The Pricing of Commodity Options," *Journal of Financial Economics* 3 (January-March 1976). A concise discussion of the modifications required in the Black-Scholes formula is contained in James F. Meisner and John W. Labuszewski, "Modifying the Black-Scholes Option Pricing Model for Alternative Underlying Instruments," *Financial Analysts Journal* November/December 1984.

35. For a discussion of the problem of valuing compound options, see John C. Cox and Mark Rubinstein, *Options Markets* (Prentice-Hall, 1985) 412-415.

FIGURE 13
USING A SWAP TO
CREATE A REVERSE
FLOATING RATE LOAN

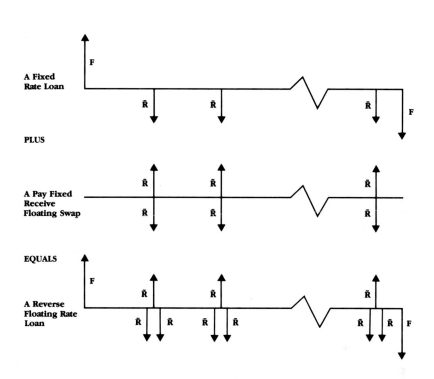

Reverse Floaters: One example of a hybrid security is provided in Figure 13. If we combine the issuance of a conventional fixed rate loan and an interest rate swap where the issuing party pays fixed and receives floating, the result is a reverse floating-rate loan. The net coupon payments on the hybrid loan are equal to twice the fixed rate ($\bar{r}$) minus the floating rate ($\tilde{r}$) times the principal (P), or

$$\textbf{Net Coupon} = (2\bar{r} - \tilde{r})P = 2\bar{R} - \tilde{R}$$

If the floating rate ($\tilde{r}$) rises, the net coupon payment falls.

Bonds with Embedded Options: Another form of hybrid securities has evolved from bonds with warrants. Bonds with warrants on the issuer's shares have become common. Bond issues have also recently appeared that feature warrants that can be exercised into foreign exchange and gold.

And, in 1986, Standard Oil issued a bond with an oil warrant. These notes stipulated that the principal payment at maturity would be a function of oil prices at maturity. As specified in the Prospectus, the holders of the 1990 notes will receive, in addition to a guaranteed minimum principal amount, "the excess...of the Crude Oil Price...over $25 multiplied by 170 barrels of Light Sweet Crude Oil." What this means is that the note has an embedded four-year option on 170 barrels of crude oil. If, at maturity, the value of Light Sweet Oklahoma Crude Oil exceeds $25, the holder of the note will receive (Oil Price − $25) x 170 plus the guaranteed minimum principal amount. If the value of Light Sweet Oklahoma Crude is less than $25 at maturity, the option expires worthless.[36]

The building block process has also been extended to changes in the timing of the options

---

36. Note that this issue did have a cap on the crude oil price at $40. Hence, the bondholder actually holds two options positions: long a call option at $25 per barrel and short a call option at $40 per barrel.

FIGURE 14

An Off-Market-Rate Bond

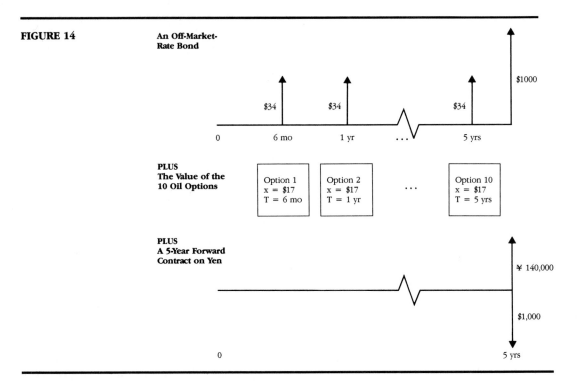

PLUS
The Value of the
10 Oil Options

PLUS
A 5-Year Forward
Contract on Yen

embedded in the bond. For a traditional bond with an attached warrant, there is only one option exerciseable at one point in time. More recent bonds have involved packages of options which can be exercised at different points in time.

The first time we saw this extension was in Forest Oil Corporation's proposed *Natural Gas Interest Indexed Debentures*. As set forth in the issue's red herring prospectus of July 1988, Forest Oil proposed to pay a stipulated base rate plus four basis points for each $0.01 by which the average gas spot price exceeds $1.76 per MMBTU (million British Thermal Units). In effect, then, this proposed 12-year "hybrid" debenture is a package consisting of one standard bond plus 24 options on the price of natural gas with maturities ranging from 6 months to 12 years.[37]

And, if we want to get a little fancier, we can consider the possibility of an *Oil Interest-Indexed, Dual-Currency Bond*.[38] Assume that the maturity of this issue is 5 years, with the semi-annual coupon pay-

ments indexed to the price of crude oil and the final principal repayment indexed to the value of yen. More specifically, assume that, for each $1000 of principal, the bondholder receives the following: (1) the greater of $34 or the value of two barrels of Sweet Light Crude Oil at each coupon date; and (2) 140,000 yen at maturity.

How would we value such a complicated package? The answer, again, is by breaking it down into the building blocks. As shown in Figure 14, this oil-indexed, dual currency bond consists of three basic components: (1) a straight bond paying $34 semi-annually; (2) 10 call options on the price of oil with an exercise price of $17 per barrel ($34/2) maturing sequentially every six months over a five-year period; and (3) a five-year forward contract on yen with an exercise price of 140 yen/dollar. As it turns out, then, this complicated-looking bond is nothing more than a combination of a standard bond, a series of options, and a forward contract.

37. As reported in the Wall Street Journal on September 21, 1988, Forest Oil withdrew its Natural Gas Indexed Bond in favor of a straight issue. However, in November of 1988, Magma Copper did issue senior subordinated notes on which the coupon payments were linked to the price of copper in much the same way as Forest's coupons would been linked to the price of natural gas.

38. Unlike the other structures discussed, this one has not yet been issued.

CONCLUDING REMARKS

The world is more volatile today than it was two decades ago. Today's corporate risk manager must deal with the potential impact on the firm of significant month-to-month (and sometimes day-to-day) changes in exchange rates, interest rates, and commodity prices. Volatility alone could put a well-run firm out of business, so financial price risk deserves careful attention. As this summary has demonstrated, there now exist techniques and tools for accomplishing this task.

This article makes three major points:

First, there are simple techniques that allow management (and outsiders as well) to identify and measure a firm's exposures. Besides managing "one-off" exposures (such as interest rate exposures from floating-rate borrowings or foreign exchange transaction and translation exposures), many firms are now recognizing their economic exposures. To measure such economic exposures, we have introduced the concept of the *risk profile*. Using this concept, we have proposed simple methods for quantifying the extent of an individual firm's exposures to interest rates, foreign exchange rates, and commodity prices. In the case of a financial firm's exposure to interest rate risk, the techniques of "gap" and "duration" analysis can be applied directly. For the more general case, we demonstrate how simple regression analysis (the same technique used in calculating a firm's "beta") can be used to measure a variety of exposures.

Second, the tools for managing financial risk are more simple than they appear. These financial instruments can be viewed as building blocks. The basic component is a forward contract. Both futures and swaps are like bundles of forward contracts; forwards, in fact, can be combined to yield futures and swaps. The primary differences between these two instruments are the way they deal with default risk and the degree of customization available.

Even options, moreover, can be related to forward contracts. An option on a given asset can be created by combining a position in a forward contract on the same asset with a riskless security; in short, forwards and T-bills can be combined to produce options.[39] Finally, options can be combined to create forward positions; for example, buying a call and shorting a put produces the same position as buying a forward contract.

Third, once you understand the four basic building blocks, it is a straightforward step to designing a customized strategy for managing your firm's exposure. Once the exposure is identified, it can be managed in a number of ways:

● by using one of the financial instruments—for example, by using an interest rate swap to hedge a building products firm's exposure to rising interest rates;

● by using combinations of the financial instruments—for example, buying a call and selling a put to minimize the out-of-pocket costs of the hedge; or

● by combining financial instruments with a debt instrument to create a hybrid security—for example, issuing an oil-indexed bond to hedge a firm's exposure to oil prices.

Our final point in all of this is very simple. Managing financial price risk with "financial engineering" sounds like something you need a degree from Caltech or M.I.T. to do. Designing effective solutions with the financial building blocks is easy.

---

39. This is most often referred to as a synthetic option or as dynamic option replication.

THE CORPORATE INSURANCE DECISION

by Clifford Smith, University of Rochester, and David Mayers, Ohio State University

Introduction

In 1980, American corporations paid more than $49 billion in property and liability insurance premiums. When set against the roughly $63 billion in corporate dividend payments during the same year, these insurance purchases seem particularly significant. Yet, in spite of the magnitude of these numbers, there has been little careful analysis of the decisions leading to such large expenditures. The finance and economics literature has devoted scant attention to the topic. There is, to be sure, a large separate body of academic insurance literature which purports to explain the corporate demand for insurance. But the approach of this insurance literature, we will argue, is fundamentally flawed.

We think there are useful answers to the question of why companies buy insurance, answers consistent with economic logic and the theory of modern finance. But these answers are less obvious than those that have been furnished by recognized authorities on insurance. Our approach also provides explanations of some fairly recent developments in corporate insurance: the appearance of retroactive liability coverage, in which companies purchase additional coverage *after* major disasters; the use of "claims only" insurance contracts, whereby insured companies pay for the services of an insurance company while bearing themselves the risk of losses through claims; and the growing trend toward self-insurance, reflected both in the use of higher deductibles and the establishment of captive insurance companies.

But, before examining the competing arguments for corporate insurance, let's take a careful look at what an insurance policy does.

The Economics of Insurance

Insurance does not eliminate risk; it is a contract which simply transfers risk from the policyholder to an insurance company. In return, the insurance company, of course, demands a premium. The real cost of insurance, called the "loading fee," is the difference between the premium and the expected payoff. As that difference increases, insurance becomes less attractive.

Let's begin by assuming that the decision to purchase insurance, whether by corporations or by individuals, is *solely* a decision to transfer risks from the policyholders to an insurance company. From the perspective of financial economics, this decision is justified only when the insurance company has a comparative advantage in bearing the risks in question. Such an advantage can derive from several sources: (1) from the reduction of risk achievable by pooling a large portfolio of risks, for which the expected loss is highly predictable; (2) from superior access to capital markets; and (3) from expertise acquired through specialization in evaluating and monitoring certain kinds of risks.

Now, we relax our initial assumption to allow that companies might be buying insurance for reasons other than to transfer risk. The expected payoff of the policy generally contains two components: (1) the monetary indemnity the insurer pays if a loss occurs, and (2) any services provided by the insurer

Companies might by buying insurance for reasons other than to transfer risk.

under the policy.[1] The distinction between monetary indemnity and service provision is important because, in types of insurance where relatively more services are provided, a larger difference exists between the premium and the expected indemnity. In other words, because a significant portion of the premium paid is used to provide the services rendered in conjunction with the policy, a relatively smaller portion will be used to satisfy claims. Thus, a fourth source of insurance companies' comparative advantage would be their specialization and economies of scale in providing services such as claims administration and settlement.

Only the last two are the exclusive province of insurance companies; and thus, only they are likely to constitute the principal comparative advantage of insurance companies over the large, widely-held corporations they insure. And the fact that some of the largest corporations have chosen to develop their own insurance expertise — or to form their own insurance captives — suggests that, in many cases, even these two advantages are not that significant.

The Important Difference between Individual and Corporate Insurance

Before proceeding further with the question of the corporate demand for insurance, we want to consider first the simplest case: the purchase of insurance by individuals. Why do individuals buy insurance? Most people are "risk averse."[2] Insurance contracts allow them to hedge risks, reducing uncertainty. And it is not hard to see that, relative to the risk-bearing capacity of insurance companies, the ability of most individuals to self-insure against large risks is severely limited. The private assets of individuals are not protected by the "limited liability" clause which shelters the other assets of corporate stockholders. Thus, decisions by individuals to pay premiums to insure their hard assets and human capital are economically "rational" choices based primarily on insurance companies' advantages in averaging,[3] and thus "diversifying away," such risks.

Private or closely-held corporations are likely to purchase insurance for the same reason — namely, their limited ability to bear certain risks relative to the risk-bearing capacity of insurance companies. The owners (who are also, of course, "risk-averse") of such companies often have a large proportion of their wealth invested in the firm; and, whether out of a desire to maintain control or some other motive, they do not fully diversify their own holdings. So, for many closely-held and private companies, logic and experience tell us that the companies' owners will self-insure only where they have specialized expertise and, thus, their own kind of comparative advantage.

The case of large, widely-held corporations, however, presents some important differences which the standard insurance literature has failed to acknowledge. The conventional wisdom says, in effect, that because the owners of corporations (their stockholders and bondholders) are risk averse, a prudent financial manager should attempt to minimize the corporate owners' exposure to risk. This prescription does not necessarily imply that all risks should be insured. For example, the standard theory rightly holds that a large national car rental agency, like Hertz, should not purchase collision insurance on its automobiles. With its large fleet of cars, Hertz can eliminate its collision risk, just as an insurance company does, by pooling its risks and averaging its losses. The purchase of collision insurance by Hertz would thus not only be needless duplication, but the payment of the "loading fees" built into the premiums would represent an outright loss to the company.[4]

But, in the case of a large corporation with a smaller fleet of more expensive vehicles, the conventional rationale for corporate insurance — which, again, holds that the underlying source of the corporate demand for insurance is risk-aversion — would argue *for* insuring those corporate assets. Because such a company does not have the ability to eliminate its collision risks by averaging, the owners are exposed to risk. Such risks, so the reasoning goes, are better borne by insurance companies; and

---

1. Insurance companies provide a range of administrative services associated with claims management. For example, for claims resulting from property losses, claims management is frequently accomplished through a nation-wide network of independent adjusters who are employed to negotiate certain types of settlements. The decisions are then reviewed by the claims department of the insurance company.

2. In the financial economics literature, risk aversion refers to an individual who prefers the average outcome, or the "expected value," of a gamble to taking a chance on the distribution of possible outcomes, some higher and some lower than the average outcome. Thus, a risk averse individual would pay to get out of a risky situation. There are, of course, different degrees of risk aversion; individuals displaying greater aversion to risk than the average stockholder might prefer holding government bonds to stocks. But, as a consequence of bearing less risk, they also have a lower expected return on their investment.

3. The essence of averaging is that by holding a portfolio of a large number of approximately equal-sized, but unrelated risks, the size of the loss on the portfolio of risks is virtually guaranteed. Thus there is no uncertainty with regard to the loss on the portfolio. Risks that can be eliminated by averaging are referred to as "insurable" risks.

4. In insurance jargon, the insurance premium would be actuarially unfair.

thus the corporation should purchase collision insurance.

The conventional explanation, however, is inadequate because it fails to recognize that the company's stockholders and bondholders have the incentive and the ability to diversify their own portfolios of corporate securities; and in so doing, they can and do eliminate precisely the kinds of risks that are insurable through an insurance company.

Stockholders and bondholders, on average, hold a lot of different securities because they are aware of the benefits of diversification. As the owners of corporate assets, they bear risks in many dimensions: some are insurable risks and some are not. By combining many securities in a portfolio, investors can effectively eliminate most insurable corporate risks by "averaging across" many securities—just as Hertz averages its automobile collision risk. The theory of finance tells us that because stockholders and bondholders can cheaply eliminate insurable risks by diversifying their own holdings, the corporate purchase of insurance for the sole purpose of reducing investors' exposure to risk is redundant; and, furthermore, it imposes needless costs on the company's stockholders.

One of the cardinal principles of modern finance is that, on average and over long periods of time, investors both expect and receive rewards commensurate with the risks they bear. As the bulk of the academic evidence also shows, however, average returns on investment correlate most strongly with what is known as "systematic" or "non-diversifiable" risk. The measure of this risk, known as "beta," is a measure of the sensitivity of individual stock prices to market-wide and general economic developments; and such risk cannot be reduced or eliminated by investors' diversification of their holdings. Nor, of course, is a company's "systematic" risk likely to be reduced by purchasing insurance—because insurable risks, to the extent they have no discernible correlation with broad economic cycles, are completely "diversifiable" for investors.

The capital markets, as logic would suggest, do not reward companies for eliminating "diversifiable" risks: Why should investors pay a premium for managements' reducing exposures to risk which rational investors have already eliminated through their own diversification? By reducing or eliminating diversifiable—and thus most insurable—risks, a company does not reduce the market's perception of its required rate of return or "cost of capital."

Thus, the prices of its stocks and bonds are not likely to be affected by the presence or absence of insurable risks. Consequently, just as in the Hertz case, the purchase of insurance by a corporation for the sole purpose of reducing insurable risks for the stockholders and bondholders would be redundant. It would also be a waste of stockholder funds because the premium charged for the insurance will not be actuarially fair.

For the widely-held corporation, then, where the owners have the incentive and the means to provide their own kind of self-insurance through diversification, the logic of modern finance says that corporations should not purchase insurance—not, at least, for the conventional reasons.

A Rationale for Corporate Insurance

At the same time, however, we believe there are important incentives that provide for a *rational* corporate demand for insurance, incentives which have nothing to do with investors' aversion to risk. In the remainder of this article, we will argue that this demand derives from the ability of insurance contracts to provide corporations with: (1) low-cost claims administration services; (2) assistance in assessing the value of safety and maintenance projects; (3) an improvement in their incentives to undertake investments in such projects; (4) a means of transferring risk away from those of the company's claimholders who are at a disadvantage in risk-bearing; and (5) a reduction of the company's expected tax liability. We also briefly analyze the special case of regulated companies, which have some additional incentives for buying insurance.

Efficiency in Claims Settlement.

Examining more closely the services provided under insurance contracts can provide a partial answer to the question of why corporations purchase insurance. Most obviously, insurance companies develop a comparative advantage in processing claims, an advantage which derives from specialization and from economies of scale. Accordingly, we would expect the corporate demand for insurance to be explained, at least in part, by insurance companies' relative expertise and efficiency in providing low-cost claims administration services.

The most striking confirmation of our argument is the existence of special "claims only" insurance contracts. Under the terms of a "claims only" contract, the insurance company provides only claims management services, while the firm pays all the claims.[5] There is no transfer of risk between the insured and the insuring company. We would expect such policies to be used by companies experiencing a large number of claims. In such cases, a "claims only" policy not only allows the insured company to pool and average its own risks; it also reduces the average cost of settling claims by enabling the insured company to pool and average its own risks; it also reduces the average cost of settling claims by enabling the insurance company to use its network of claims administrators more intensively.

One of the problems that could arise from a "claims only" arrangement is that the insurance company would lose its incentive to negotiate the best possible settlement, because it no longer has to pay the indemnity. But when claims are numerous, the insured company should be in a good position to review and evaluate the settlement record. This in turn should enable the insured to monitor the insurer's effectiveness in holding down the costs of claims. By contrast, in those cases where claims are relatively infrequent, it would be more difficult for the insured company to monitor the efficiency of the claims settlement procedure. In such cases, we expect to see standard policies where the insurer provides both claims administration and the indemnity.

Liability insurance provides another example of claims settlement services provided by the insurance companies. A liability insurance policy not only indemnifies the policyholder if a valid claim is presented, it also provides legal representation when the insured is faced with a suit. If the suit is for less than the policy limit—as is the case in most suits — the policyholder has little incentive to engage quality legal services. We suspect that it is largely because of these incentives, as well as insurance companies' greater familiarity with claims negotiations and settlements, that providing legal representation has become a standard part of liability insurance contracts.

In the unusual case where the suit greatly exceeds the limit on coverage, the roles—and thus the incentives — are reversed. Because the insurance company's liability is limited under the policy, it has less incentive to negotiate an efficient settlement.

Consider, for example, the following case reported in the *Wall Street Journal:*

When the fire hit the MGM Grand Hotel in Las Vegas last November 21, killing 85 persons, the hotel's owner had $30 million in liability insurance. Since then the hotel company has increased its liability coverage to nearly $200 million. Significantly, the new insurance is backdated to November 1, or 20 days before the catastrophic blaze.[6]

We believe that the incentives described above help to explain the purchase of retroactive liability coverage by MGM Grand. By retroactively increasing the coverage limit, MGM effectively restores the normal structure of incentives, so that the insurance company's lawyers have a stronger interest in negotiating an efficient settlement.

Efficiency in Project Evaluation.

Insurance companies also develop a comparative advantage in evaluating safety projects. As a simple illustration, insurance companies that sell boiler insurance also — as would be expected — provide inspection services. These inspections require a highly specialized engineer to inspect the boiler and its component parts. Although the company could obtain these services through an independent consultant, insurance companies are generally better suited for the task. And by agreeing to indemnify the firm for any losses, the insurance company, in effect, guarantees the quality of the inspection. This combining of insurance and inspection services provides the strongest incentive for the inspector to do a careful job.

To minimize property and casualty losses, insurance companies also generally prescribe safety projects. Such projects, of course, impose additional costs on the insured company. But a competitive market for insurance effectively restrains insurers from over-prescribing safety projects. At the same time, of course, those insurance companies which systematically under-prescribe such projects will not long survive the effects of continuing higher indemnity payments. In short, a competitive market provides insurance companies with the incentive to prescribe what should be the optimal level (based on expectations, of course, and not hindsight) of

5. "Claims only" policies represent only one extreme of a spectrum of insurance policies which allow the insured company to maintain a degree of self-insurance. More often employed are policies which provide retrospective rating. This type of policy continually adjusts the premium to reflect actual claims experience over the life of the policy. In a year with higher-than-expected claims, the company is required to pay higher premiums; while in a year with low claims, the company receives a rebate. So that the insured company is effectively bearing most of the risk of claims losses. Typically, however, the policy specifies a maximum on the additional premiums (and rebates), so that the insurance company continues to bear the risk of very large losses.

6. Tim Metz, "Why Insurers and Insured Like the Idea of Covering Disasters After They Happen," *Wall Street Journal,* May 12, 1981.

The combining of insurance and inspection services provides the strongest incentive for the inspector to do a careful job.

safety and maintenance investment for the insured and the insurer alike.

Besides maintaining a comparative advantage in prescribing the proper level of loss prevention measures, insurance contracts also simplify the insured company's project choice decisions by quoting a schedule of premiums associated with various levels of loss prevention. With insurance, the insured company simply asks if the cost of a safety project is less than the present value of the reduction in insurance premiums. If so, it should be undertaken.

Improvement of Investment Incentives.

Corporations often enter into contracts requiring the maintenance of insurance coverage. Bond covenants, for example, frequently require companies to purchase insurance. The conventional explanation of such requirements is that bondholders will not invest without such a provision.

We have a different explanation: namely, that in buying an insurance policy, the company provides a different kind of assurance to lenders — one which effectively guarantees or "bonds" a set of investment decisions by the corporation which gives the bondholders more protection. Such an assurance in turn lowers the borrowing costs to the company, while also providing the best possible incentives for the company's investment in maintenance and safety projects.

Before elaborating this point, let's take a closer look at the relationship between stockholder and bondholder interests. In the case of profitable companies with abundant cash flows, the interests of these two classes of the company's owners would appear to be fairly consonant. What's good for the one is, for the most part, good for the other.

However, in the case of financially distressed companies — or even those with relatively higher probabilities of someday facing financial distress — the interests of bondholders and stockholders can diverge sharply. In such cases, financial managers intent on maximizing stockholder wealth may have incentives to take actions which will reduce the value of the bonds while increasing the value of the stock. Actions that increase the variability of the firm's cash flows, e.g., undertaking riskier invest-

ments or taking on increased financial leverage, will tend to have this effect. By so increasing the variability of the company's future cash flows, management will have, of course, increased the probability of both large gains and large losses. The effect of the increase in the probability of large gains benefits only the stockholders (because the bondholder's is a fixed-income claim) and the effect of the increase in the probability of large losses falls mainly on the bondholders (because stockholders are protected by limited liability.)

Consider the case of a company with a large amount of debt outstanding. Assume also that the covenants on its existing debt have not required the purchase of insurance. How do these two conditions together influence the company's decision to invest in safety projects such as, say, a sprinkler system? Our theory says that a company carrying a large enough burden of debt would actually have a rational incentive to pass up good investments — like safety projects — which reduce the expected variability of cash flows. The company's failure to undertake such investments will decrease the value of its bonds by increasing the *expected* variability of cash flows. Our theory further tells us that, in reasonably sophisticated markets, potential bondholders will anticipate such actions by management; and without the stipulation of insurance by the covenants, they will place a lower value on the bonds when they are initially sold.[7]

By purchasing insurance, the company hedges any losses the bondholders would suffer if it did not invest in the sprinkler system, thus eliminating the bondholders' problem. But also, and perhaps more importantly, the stockholders' incentives are changed by the insurance contract. Having committed itself to carry insurance, the company now will choose to undertake any investment in safety and maintenance projects that is justified by the reduction in its insurance premiums. And lenders, provided with this assurance, will require a lower rate of interest from the company. By allowing mandatory insurance to be included in the indentures, companies are securing a reduction in their borrowing costs that is greater than the cost of the insurance "loading fees." For both of these reasons, then, it may be in the best interest of the company

---

7. If, at the time the bonds were offered, the company had another means of convincing potential bondholders that it would make the safety and maintenance investments (even in the absence of insurance), then the rate of interest on the bonds would also be lower.

and its stockholders to include some kinds of insurance coverage in its debt covenants.

Because the potential conflict of interest between bondholders and stockholders is also greater the riskier the bonds, the use of a debt covenant requiring insurance should be more valuable in riskier debt issues. For this reason, we would expect the covenants in private placements to contain more restrictive insurance provisions than those on public issues. Insurance provisions should also be employed more frequently in privately-placed than public issues because, with only a small number of parties involved, it is cheaper to administer and enforce more detailed insurance requirements.

Insurance covenants are also regularly included in other corporate contracts. For example, subcontracting agreements between corporations generally include provisions requiring the subcontractor to maintain an acceptable level of insurance coverage. In the event that an independent subcontractor were sued for a liability claim, the subcontractor might renege on the contract and declare bankruptcy. The subcontractor's failure to complete the project could impose large costs on the company, as well as increasing its own potential liability. The purchase of insurance by the subcontractor effectively bonds the promise that he makes not to default on the performance of his job.

In each of the aforementioned examples — claims administration, the evaluation of safety projects, and the improvement of investment incentives and guarantees — the insured company is paying primarily for a set of services which the insurance company offers at a lower cost than can be obtained elsewhere. The pure insurance aspect of the contract, the transference of risk, is secondary, if not completely irrelevant.

Riskshifting within the Corporation.

For large corporations with diffuse ownership, the risk aversion of the stockholders—as we argued earlier—does not provide a rational justification for the corporate purchase of insurance. Stockholders are equally capable of diversifying the kinds of risks that insurance companies are able to minimize by pooling. In the case of the closely-held company, as we also suggested, the owners' risk aversion and limited ability to achieve full diversification can provide an incentive for insurance purchases.

Up to this point, we have viewed the corporation only from the perspective of its investors and owners, the bondholders and stockholders. In reality, of course, the corporation is a vast network of contracts among various parties which have conflicting as well as common interests in the company. In addition to bondholders and stockholders, the managers, the employees, the suppliers, and even the customers all have a vested claim and interest— a form of investment (whether of physical or human capital)—in the company's continuation as a viable economic entity. Management and labor are likely to have a substantial investment of human capital in the company. The profitability of suppliers depends partly on the fortunes of the company buying its products. And even the buying decisions of customers, both actual and potential, can be influenced by their perceptions of the company's prospects.

Like the owners of private or closely-held companies, the corporation's managers, employees, suppliers, and customers may not be able to diversify away insurable risks; and such risks, if not insured against, can affect their future payoffs under their respective contracts. Because they are also "risk-averse," these individuals will require extra compensation to bear any risk not assumed by the owners or transferred to an insurance company. Employees, for example, will demand higher wages from a company where the probability of layoff is greater. Managers will demand higher salaries (or perhaps even an equity stake in the company) where the risks of failure, insolvency, and financial embarrassment are great. Suppliers will be more reluctant to enter into long-term contracts with companies whose prospects are uncertain, thus making the terms of those contracts more unfavorable. And customers, concerned about the company's ability to fulfil warranty obligations or service their products in the future, may be reluctant to buy those products.

Because of the limited liability clause, the amount of risk that can be allocated to the stockholders is limited by the capital stock of the company. Companies in service industries, for instance, are often thinly-capitalized. And for such companies, where the claims — and thus the risks — of managers and employees are likely to be very large relative to the claims of investors, there may be substantial benefits from shifting those risks to an insurance company. To the extent that the purchase of insurance reduces the possibility of layoffs, plant closings, or even bankruptcy, such corporations could — by transferring such risks to an insurance

There is no obvious reason to prefer the tax effects of insurance to those of self-insurance.

company — be providing themselves with significant reductions in required wages and salaries. To provide a simple illustration, the purchase of business interruption insurance covering the company's ordinary payroll would reduce the risk borne by employees that, say, a fire will cause a plant to shut down. The justification for the purchase of insurance, in this case, is that the cost of the insurance is more than covered by the reduction in employees' extra compensation required for otherwise bearing such risks themselves.

The Tax Advantage

One of the alleged benefits of corporate insurance is that insurance premiums are tax-deductible expenses, while reserves set aside for losses by self-insuring companies are not.[8] And though casualty losses sustained by companies which self-insure *are* tax-deductible, the conventional argument for a tax advantage from buying insurance rests on the premise that the guaranteed annual tax shield provided by premium payments is more valuable than the random tax shield provided by unforeseen future losses. This premise, in turn, seems to be based on the notion that the company can somehow exploit the time value of money by getting its tax deductions "up front" instead of in the uncertain future.

In some cases, such a strategy will result in a tax advantage; that is, the losses will take place far enough in the future that the tax savings to the insuring company — compounded at the interest rate reflecting the opportunity cost of those savings — will turn out to be significantly greater than the time-adjusted value of the tax shield created by uninsured losses. It is important to recognize, however, that decisions are made in the present, and on the basis of expected future probabilities. And on this basis, there is no obvious reason to prefer the tax effects of insurance to those of self-insurance. Remember that an insurance premium incorporates an insurance company's estimate of the expected level and timing of future losses. And thus, ignoring the effect of "loading fees" (and assuming that a company's marginal tax rate would not be reduced by a large casualty loss), the *expected* tax shields from buying insurance and self-insurance are identical.

As an example of the confusion which surrounds this tax issue, let's return to the case of MGM Grand's purchase of retroactive liability coverage. According to the *Wall Street Journal* article, cited earlier:

... MGM Grand, meanwhile, gets a tax break by insuring, rather than assembling a big cash reserve against losses. Premiums are tax deductible as a business expense right now while casualty reserves can't be written off until claims are paid. In MGM Grand's case, that could be years from now.

It is true that by buying the retroactive insurance, MGM did get a large tax deduction; and that the tax deduction is more valuable the earlier it is used. But what this argument fails to recognize is that if MGM had chosen to self-insure, it could have earned a normal rate of return on its capital prior to the date of any settlement. There will be no reason to prefer getting the tax savings up front to retaining and investing the so-called reserves. The income earned on those reserves, on an expected value basis, should exactly offset the value of getting the tax savings up front.

There are provisions in the tax code which, by reducing the expected tax shield from self-insurance, could favor the purchase of insurance. There is a three year carry-back and a seven year carry-forward provision. If an uninsured loss exceeds the sum of the most recent four years' earnings, the additional loss must be carried forward; and if the loss exceeds the earnings over the eleven-year period, the excess casualty loss is lost. Furthermore, when a company employs the carry-back provisions, the current year's tax must be totally offset before any of the previous year's taxes can be used.[9] Finally, if the uninsured loss forces the company into bankruptcy and liquidation, any loss carry-forward will be lost.

Thus, if MGM did not expect claims losses in any single year to be large enough to push the company into a lower marginal tax bracket (thus reducing the value of the random tax shield from deducting claims losses), then the *expected* values of the tax shields from insurance and self-insurance should be equal. If, however, the company did expect very large losses to fall within a given year, then there would have been a tax advantage from buying the insurance.

8. FASB #5 not only prohibits companies from deducting self-insurance reserves from taxable income, it also excludes them from published income statements. Thus, self-insurance reserves have no effect on reported earnings. The maximum required disclosure is a footnote to the accounting statement.

Moreover, neither Generally Accepted Accounting Procedures nor the IRS requires that "reserves" for uninsured losses actually be funded.

9. This is offset by the fact that the IRS pays interest on the tax refund.

To the extent, then, that the magnitude of potential losses is large relative to the company's expected annual taxable earnings, the expected value of the tax shield from insurance can be greater than the random tax shield provided by uninsured losses. This conclusion would suggest that the tax advantage of buying insurance is likely to be most significant for smaller companies with less diversified operations. For large companies with geographically dispersed operations, the tax benefits of insurance should not be important. (We would not expect Hertz to purchase collision insurance for tax purposes either). Finally, because uninsured losses do provide a (random) tax shield, companies which have other tax shields (e.g., investment tax credits, high interest expense) would be expected to buy more insurance because of the reduced value of the expected tax deductions from self-insurance.

Regulated Companies: A Special Case

The prices of the products or services of regulated companies are established by regulatory commissions with the intention of allowing those companies to earn a "fair" rate of return for their stockholders. At the risk of oversimplifying the rate regulation process, regulators set prices which are expected to generate revenues covering the sum of expected costs, taxes, depreciation, plus a normal rate of return on the rate base. Insurance premiums are allowed as part of expected costs. If a regulated company does not insure against a particular hazard, in order for it to earn a "fair" rate of return for its stockholders, the rate commission (or the company itself) must include an expected loss estimate in computing expected costs; and this expected cost figure used in establishing allowed revenues and prices must accurately reflect the probability and magnitude of potential uninsured losses. As the rate-setting is currently administered, however, such expected costs from uninsured losses are not allowed.

Also, because uninsured casualty or liability losses are insurable risks, the regulators — like the stock market itself — would not compensate an uninsured, regulated company for bearing such risks by allowing them a higher return on its equity base.[10]

This regulatory process provides incentives for regulated companies to buy insurance. First, because regulated companies are allowed revenues to cover the cost of expected losses *only* if they insure, they have a strong incentive to insure against all insurable risks. Second, the "loading fees" (the insurance company's expected profit after paying indemnities and providing associated ervices) reflected in the premiums are costs which are shifted by the regulatory process from the firm's owners to its customers. In an unregulated, competitive industry, where output prices and revenues are determined in the market — regardless of whether an individual company insures — insurance loading fees cannot be passed on to the consumer.[11] Third, because of its specialization, an insurance company is expected to have a comparative advantage in assessing the amount of expected losses. Regulators, in effect, "subcontract" this assessment by having the insurance company reflect its assessment of expected losses in the insurance premium. For all of the above reasons, we would expect a regulated company to buy significantly more insurance than a comparable, but unregulated company.

Compulsory Insurance Laws

Some forms of corporate insurance coverage are required by law. Workmen's compensation laws have been enacted in every state in the U.S. These laws essentially impose on employers the responsibility of providing no-fault insurance to their workers for job-related accidents. Although self-insurance is allowed in all but five states, to qualify for self-insurance under the law, the firm must demonstrate that it has sufficient size and diversification of risks. Some states (Massachusetts, New York and North Carolina) have adopted compulsory liability insurance statutes which require some companies to purchase insurance policies. Such regulation also has the effect of increasing the likelihood that other companies will buy insurance to protect themselves against the specific hazards addressed in those regulations.

Conclusion

Our purpose in this article has been to identify and analyze a set of incentives which justify the purchase of insurance by corporations. In so doing, we have provided a theory which attempts to explain, first, why large, widely-held companies should *not*

---

10. Recall from earlier the capital market compensates only for uninsurable ("non-diversifiable") risks, not insurable ("diversifiable") risks.

11. One exception to this rule is where insurance makes warranties or product guarantees more valuable. Recall our discussion of risk-shifting.

insure against some risks; and second, why they *should* insure against others.

We believe the majority of corporations are probably making the right insurance decisions; but perhaps, in many cases, for the wrong reasons. By asking the right questions, by focusing on the important issues, corporate managers can make fewer and less expensive mistakes.

The value of any theory lies, of course, in the strength of its correspondence with events we can observe in the "real world"; that is, in its ability to explain why things are being done as they are, and to predict how they will be done in the future. We think that our theory, besides being more consistent internally, does a better job of explaining recent developments in the insurance industry than the rationale for corporate insurance that has prevailed in the insurance literature.

Industry observers have noted a pronounced tendency toward corporate self-insurance. This trend has taken several forms: the increasing use of "claims only" policies, the creation of captive insurance companies, and the use of higher deductibles. In each of these developments, corporations are not using insurance to transfer risk from their investors to the insurer — as the conventional explanation holds — but for other reasons: for special insurance services like claims administration; for tax benefits (as in the formation of offshore insurance captives); and to provide assurances (in the case of "stop loss" contracts with higher deductibles) not so much to investors as to employees, managers, and suppliers — that very large property and casualty losses will not threaten the solvency of the company, or the continuity of its operations.

Part of this corporate trend toward self-insurance can be attributed to companies' increasing awareness of their ability to pool their own risks and average expected losses. And this, as we said earlier, is consistent with the conventional explanation of the corporate demand for insurance. We suspect, however, that another part of this movement reflects decisions, using an increasingly sophisticated framework for risk management, to allow companies' investors to bear insurable corporate risks themselves. In making such decisions on the correct basis (that is, except in special cases, from the point of view of well-diversified stockholders and bondholders), risk managers will be conserving corporate cash which can be put to better uses.

How can we summarize the implications of our theory for corporate risk management? All risks should not be insured, even though the owners of the company, the stockholders and bondholders, are individually risk averse. The fact that investors have access to capital markets and the ability and incentive to diversify their portfolio holdings can make the corporate purchase of insurance a waste of stockholder funds. Insurance companies, as we have seen, may have an advantage in providing certain kinds of claims services. There also may be tax benefits, though these may have been exaggerated because of a failure to focus on companies' *expected* tax liabilities.

In deciding whether to purchase insurance, it may also be important to focus on the set of contracts through which stockholders, bondholders, customers, suppliers, managers, employees and insurers interact. Some insurance contracts may help remedy a possible conflict of interest between bondholders and stockholders, especially in the case of companies with higher-risk investments and highly levered capital structures. Others may be valuable to the company by transferring risks away from managers, employees, and suppliers—groups which are at a relative disadvantage in bearing some insurable corporate risks. These solutions cannot, of course, be used indiscriminately, but must be applied carefully to specific corporate situations.

THE ARITHMETIC OF FINANCIAL ENGINEERING

by Donald J. Smith, Boston University

F inancial engineering is the construction of innovative asset and liability structures. The building blocks of financial engineering include traditional instruments, such as fixed-income bonds and floating-rate notes, as well as the new "off balance sheet" tools of the 1980s: interest rate swaps, caps, floors, collars, and many others. The role of the engineer is to combine such instruments to provide a risk-return configuration otherwise unavailable. Often the objective is simply to replicate an existing product or strategy at a lower transaction cost or with some gain in hedging efficiency. The ultimate prize is a "pure" (that is, riskless) arbitrage opportunity—the chance to buy and sell simultaneously an equivalent product at different prices. In reasonably efficient markets, however, such opportunities are likely to be scarce. More common is an opportunity for "risk arbitrage"—the chance for investors to earn higher expected rates of return, or for borrowers to reduce their expected cost of funds, while bearing a given level of risk.

The search for an arbitrage opportunity (or, alternatively, for a more efficient hedging vehicle) begins with the identification of a synthetic financial structure that mimics the characteristics of another, usually more obvious, type of asset or liability. The process is not as complex as it might seem. The logic of the combinations of the various securities is based on certain simple rules which can be viewed as the "arithmetic" of financial engineering. This arithmetic, the reader should be assured at the outset, involves only the most basic mathematical properties and operations.

THE ARITHMETIC RULES

The statement that a portfolio of security A and security B is equivalent to security C can be expressed as follows:

$$A + B = C \qquad (1)$$

The "equals" sign here means identical promised coupon and principal cash flows in terms of amount, currency, and timing. The maturity and coupon payment frequency are assumed to be the same on each side of the equation. Otherwise, the structures are not comparable and no meaningful statement can be made about an arbitrage opportunity.

Equation 1 refers to future *expected* cash flows. The yield to the investor, or cost of funds to the borrower, of A + B and C will be identical only if the current prices are the same. A yield-to-maturity is calculated as an internal rate of return—that is, the particular interest rate such that the present values of all future cash flows discounted by that rate exactly equal the current price. Prices, and therefore yields, can differ because the future cash flows are only promised; hence the notion of credit, or default, risk. If one stream of promised cash flows is viewed as more uncertain than another, the current price would be lower, and thus the calculated internal rate of return would be higher. The greater the credit risk, the higher the promised yield.

Suppose, then, that the credit risks are the same for A + B, the synthetic portfolio, as for C, the straight security. If the current prices differ, borrowers and investors would have clear preferences for one alternative over the other, all other things being equal. Obviously, investors would prefer a lower price and borrowers a higher price for the same promised future cash flows. When a synthetic financial structure obtains a preferential price, the relative gain is typically called "arbitrage."

The other-things-being-equal condition is important. Financial structures can differ along dimensions other than promised cash flows and current prices. Special covenants in the documentation, such as provisions for early termination (call or put options) as well as material adverse change, cross-default, and negative pledge clauses, can lead to a preference for one structure over another. We will therefore assume, for now at least, that the documentation and all accounting and taxation aspects on each side of the equation are the same to allow for direct comparison.

Financial engineering often involves taking long and/or short positions in different securities within a synthetic structure. In the arithmetic framework a " + " indicates a long position and a " − " indicates a short position. To "go long" means to buy, hold, or invest in a security. To "go short" means to issue, sell, or write a security. Being long represents a lending posture, being short a borrowing one.

Equation 1 can thus be rewritten as follows:

$$+ A + B = + C \qquad (2)$$

That is, a synthetic portfolio consisting of long positions in A and B is equivalent to a long position in C.

Multiplying through the above equation by -1 gives us the following:

$$- A - B = - C \qquad (3)$$

This means that issuing C directly entails making the same future cash payments as issuing both A and B.

Adding or subtracting from each side of the equation creates other configurations. For example, subtract B from each side of equation 2:

$$+ A = + C - B \qquad (4)$$

Buying security A is identical to a combination of buying C and writing B. An investor searching for arbitrage gains would ascertain if the net purchase price of buying C and issuing B is less than the price of buying A.

As another example, add A to each side of equation 3:

$$- B = - C + A \qquad (5)$$

Issuing security B is equivalent to a portfolio of a long position in A and a short position in C. A borrower would identify an arbitrage gain if the proceeds from selling B exceeded the net proceeds from issuing C and purchasing A.

INTEREST RATE SWAPS

Interest rate swaps are among the most important financial innovations of the 1980s.[1] In a typical "plain vanilla" rate swap, two counterparties exchange fixed for floating coupon payments based on some notional principal amount. The floating rate on the vast majority of swaps is three- or six-month LIBOR. In practice, settlement is often on a "net" basis: the fixed rate is compared to LIBOR and then only the difference times the notional principal, adjusted for the number of days elapsed, is paid by the owing counterparty at the end of the period.

For example, consider a $10 million notional principal swap with semi-annual settlements on March 15th and September 15th and having a fixed rate of 9%. Suppose that the six-month LIBOR index is determined to be 7.5% on March 15th. Assuming that both rates are quoted on a 360 day basis, the fixed-payer on the swap owes (9% − 7.5%) times (184/360) times $10 million, or $76,666.67, to the counterparty at the end of the period on September 15th. Note that there are 184 days between March 15th and September 15th. If LIBOR had instead been 10.5%, the fixed-payer would receive the same amount.

By market convention, the counterparty that agrees to pay the fixed rate and receive the floating rate is named the "buyer" of the swap. The fixed-payer has established a long position in the swap transaction and the fixed-receiver a short position. This terminology, however arbitrary, fits nicely into our arithmetic framework. A long position in a par value swap is equivalent to a synthetic portfolio of a long position in a par value unrestricted floating-rate note (FRN) and a short position in a par value fixed-rate note:

	Interest Rate Swap		Unrestricted FRN		Fixed Rate Note	(6)
+	Swap	=	+ FRN	−	Note	
	pay fixed, rec. LIBOR		**LIBOR**		**Swap-fixed rate**	

An unrestricted FRN has no constraint (other than a minimum of zero) on the floating rate. As indicated by equation 6, the fixed-payer on the swap is obligated to the same future cash flows as if an unrestricted FRN (at LIBOR flat) had been purchased from, and a fixed rate note (at the swap-fixed rate) sold to, the counterparty.

Now multiply both sides of equation 6 by −1.

	Interest Rate Swap		Unrestricted FRN		Fixed Rate Note	(7)
−	Swap	=	− FRN	+	Note	
	rec. fixed, pay LIBOR		**LIBOR**		**Swap-fixed rate**	

A short position in a par value swap—that is, receiving the fixed rate and paying floating—is equivalent to issuing an unrestricted FRN and buying a fixed-rate note.

The term "par value" swap means that there is no initial cash exchange between the two counterparties. This implies that the hypothetical unrestricted FRN and fixed rate note are both par value securities. Therefore, at the outset of the swap, the present values of the long and short positions are exactly offset and any exchange of principal would be redundant.

CAPS, COLLARS, AND FLOORS

Interest rate swaps belong to a general class of risk management tools known as forward contracts. In fact, a swap can be viewed as a series of interest rate forward transactions—one for each of the settlement dates over the life of the contract. The most important characteristic of a forward contract, for our purposes, is its "symmetric" payoff distribution. This means that interest rate changes can lead, in principle, to unlimited gains or losses on the contract. When the swap is used as a hedge, however, these value changes are designed to be offset by opposite changes in the underlying exposure.

The other broad class of risk management tools is option contracts. Options, unlike forwards, have an asymmetric or "truncated" payoff distribution. For example, a long position in an option has unlimited profit potential but losses are limited to just the purchase price of the option itself. Conversely, the short position, usually called the "writer" of the option, can have unlimited losses but gain only the sale price of the contract.

---

1. For more extensive discussion of interest rate swaps, see Jan Loeys, "Interest Rate Swaps: A New Tool for Managing Risk," *Federal Reserve Bank of Philadephia Business Review* (May/June 1985); James Bicksler and Andrew Chen, "An Economic Analysis of Interest Rate Swaps," *Journal of Finance* (July 1986); Clifford Smith, Charles Smithson, and Lee Wakeman, "The Evolving Market for Swaps," *Midland Corporate Finance Journal* (Winter 1986); and Steven D. Felgran, "Interest Rate Swaps: Use, Risk, and Prices," *New England Economic Review* (November/December 1987).

Interest rate caps, collars, and floors are all over-the-counter interest rate options.[2] A *cap* (or *ceiling*) agreement is analogous to a *put* option on a debt security. For an up-front fee known as the "premium," a buyer of a cap will receive from the cap writer the excess of some reference rate (almost always LIBOR) over the given cap rate (called the "strike rate"). The payment, if any, on each settlement date will be the annual rate difference, adjusted for the fraction of a year elapsed, times the specified notional principal. If LIBOR is less than the cap rate, no payment is made.

An interest rate *floor* agreement is analogous to a *call* option on debt. For an up-front premium, the buyer of the floor will receive from the floor writer the excess of the floor rate over LIBOR. Calculation of the settlement payment is the same as that on a cap. If LIBOR is above the floor rate, no payment is forthcoming.

Caps and floors are akin to interest rate insurance contracts. One can use them to insure against losses from LIBOR rising above or falling below certain levels. A rate *collar* is a combination of a cap and a floor. To buy a collar is to buy a cap and to write a floor. Note that a collar will always cost less than a cap for a given ceiling strike rate because the sale price of the floor serves to offset the purchase price of the cap. A long position in a 5-9% collar can be described in the arithmetic framework as follows:

$$+ \quad \underset{\text{5\%–9\%}}{\text{Collar}} \quad = \quad + \underset{\text{9\%}}{\text{Cap}} \quad - \quad \underset{\text{5\%}}{\text{Floor}} \quad (8)$$

As above, the plus signs mean long positions and the minus sign a short position. Multiplying both sides of this equation by -1 describes the short side of a collar:

$$- \quad \underset{\text{5\%–9\%}}{\text{Collar}} \quad = \quad - \underset{\text{9\%}}{\text{Cap}} \quad + \quad \underset{\text{5\%}}{\text{Floor}} \quad (9)$$

To write a collar, therefore, is to write a cap and to buy a floor. The cap and floor strike rates are usually set such that the writer of a collar receives a net premium payment. When the strike rates are structured so that the premiums exactly offset each other, the outcome is a *zero-cost collar*.

Premiums on option contracts depend on the particular strike rate, the current and expected future interest rate levels as embodied in the shape of the yield curve, the perceived volatility of future interest rates, and the maturity of the contract. For example, premiums on interest rate caps increase for lower strike rates and a steeper yield curve. Premiums on floors increase for higher strike rates and a flatter yield curve. Higher volatility and a longer maturity raise premiums on both caps and floors.

If the strike rates on the cap and the floor are identical, the resulting collar is equivalent to an interest rate swap. For example, buying a 9% cap on LIBOR and writing a 9% floor is the same as going long on a swap to pay 9% fixed and receive LIBOR.

$$+ \quad \underset{\text{9\%}}{\text{Cap}} \quad - \quad \underset{\text{9\%}}{\text{Floor}} \quad = \quad + \underset{\substack{\textbf{pay 9\% fixed,} \\ \textbf{rec. LIBOR}}}{\text{Interest Rate Swap}} \quad (10)$$

Intuitively, as the strike rates on the cap and floor get close, the collar "tightens" and eventually becomes a fixed- versus floating-rate swap. Notice that if 9% is the fixed rate on a "par value" swap (hence no exchange of principal), the premiums on the cap and floor at a 9% strike rate are equal.

SYNTHETIC STRUCTURES USING TYPICAL FRNs

Many innovative structures built by financial engineers in recent years have combined floating-rate notes with interest rate swaps, caps, and floors. A typical FRN has its coupon rate reset each period at a reference rate, often LIBOR, plus some fixed margin. This margin reflects the credit quality of the issuer and other characteristics of the security—for instance, maximum or minimum coupon rates and call or put options. The margin would be higher if there is more credit risk, if there is a maximum coupon rate, or if the issuer has a call option on the FRN. The margin would be lower if there is less credit risk, a minimum coupon rate, or if the investor has a put option. Although some unrestricted FRNs have been issued, most have a minimum coupon rate on the order of 5%.

In the context of the arithmetic framework, a typical FRN at LIBOR-plus-25 basis points with a 5% minimum coupon can be broken down into an unre-

---

2. See Ian Rowley and Henrik Neuhaus, "How Caps and Floors Can Influence Desired Cash Flows," *Euromoney Corporate Finance* (July 1986) and Donald J. Smith, "Putting the Cap on Options," *Euromoney Corporate Finance* (January 1987) for further discussion of interest rate cap and floor agreements.

stricted FRN at LIBOR flat plus a .25% annuity plus an interest rate floor agreement. The annuity, which represents the fixed margin on the typical FRN, is a series of level payments (if negative) or receipts (if positive).

$$
\underset{\substack{\textbf{LIBOR + 0.25\%,}\\ \textbf{min. 5\%}}}{\underset{\text{FRN}}{+\ \text{Typical}}} = \underset{\textbf{LIBOR}}{\underset{\text{FRN}}{+\ \text{Unrestricted}}} + \underset{\textbf{0.25\%}}{\text{Annuity}} + \underset{\textbf{4.75\%}}{\text{Floor}} \quad (11)
$$

A long position in the typical FRN thus offers the same promised future cash receipts as buying the unrestricted FRN and the annuity (which together provide LIBOR + 0.25%) combined with a floor on LIBOR at a 4.75% strike rate.[3]

SYNTHETIC FIXED-RATE DEBT

Equation 11 above can be rewritten to isolate the unrestricted FRN. Formulated in this way, a long position in the unrestricted FRN is equivalent to a long position in the typical FRN and short positions in the annuity and floor agreement. That portfolio can then be substituted into equation 6 to obtain the following relationship between a typical FRN, a fixed-rate note, and an interest rate swap.

$$
\underset{\substack{\textbf{pay}\\ \textbf{fixed,}\\ \textbf{rec.}\\ \textbf{LIBOR}}}{\underset{\substack{\text{Rate}\\ \text{Swap}}}{+\ \text{Interest}}} = \underset{\substack{\textbf{LIBOR}\\ \textbf{+0.25\%,}\\ \textbf{min. 5\%}}}{\underset{\text{FRN}}{+\ \text{Typical}}} - \underset{\textbf{0.25\%}}{\text{Annuity}} - \underset{\textbf{4.75\%}}{\text{Floor}} - \underset{\substack{\textbf{Swap-fixed}\\ \textbf{rate}}}{\underset{\substack{\text{Rate}\\ \text{Note}}}{\text{Fixed}}} \quad (12)
$$

Then, by rearranging the terms and combining the annuity and fixed-rate note, the following equivalence relationship is obtained:

$$
\underset{\substack{\textbf{Swap fixed}\\ \textbf{rate + 0.25\%}}}{\underset{\substack{\text{Rate}\\ \text{Note}}}{\text{Fixed}}} = \underset{\substack{\textbf{LIBOR + 0.25\%,}\\ \textbf{min. 5\%}}}{\underset{\text{FRN}}{-\ \text{Typical}}} + \underset{\substack{\textbf{pay fixed,}\\ \textbf{rec. LIBOR}}}{\underset{\substack{\text{Rate}\\ \text{Swap}}}{+\ \text{Interest}}} + \underset{\textbf{4.75\%}}{\text{Floor}} \quad (13)
$$

A synthetic fixed-rate issue equal to the swap rate plus the margin on the FRN can be constructed by issuing the typical FRN, buying the interest rate swap, and buying the interest rate floor.[4]

IDENTIFYING ARBITRAGE GAINS

Equation 13 represents one of the highly touted arbitrage opportunities that are claimed to have motivated the development of the swap market in the early 1980s. Companies having a natural preference for fixed-rate funding (for example, public utilities or thrift institutions) issued floating-rate debt and then "bought" fixed-interest rate swaps, thereby achieving a synthetic, fixed-rate debt instrument. The flip side to this arbitrage opportunity can be seen by moving the swap and floor agreements to the other side of the equation. Those companies having a natural preference for variable-rate debt (e.g., money-center banks) issued fixed-rate debt and "swapped into" a synthetic floating rate. When those synthetic rates achieved through swaps are less than the explicit fixed- and floating-rate alternatives, the firms have been able to "arbitrage" the swap market to lower their respective costs of funds.

The conventional explanation for this opportunity is the existence of differential credit risk premiums—that is, a higher credit premium (over the rate charged to a more creditworthy borrower) in the fixed-rate market than in the floating-rate market. The evidence supporting such an explanation, however, is largely anecdotal and thus unreliable. It is also suspect because of several problems in measuring arbitrage gains.[5] In measuring such gains, it is essential that a comparison is made between debt structures with the same covenants and provisions.

A common pitfall is to neglect the value of the call option included in most medium- to long-term corporate bonds. A callable bond must offer the investor a higher yield than otherwise comparable non-callable debt. The amount of this call premium depends on the length of the deferment period before the insurer can exercise the option, the specified call price, and the probability of exercise as indicated by the expected level and volatility of future rates.

For example, suppose that a corporate borrower undertakes the structure outlined in equation 13 to obtain a swap-driven fixed-rate cost of

---

3. The floor agreement corresponds to the minimum coupon on the typical FRN. Suppose that LIBOR is only 4% on a particular reset date. The minimum coupon on the typical FRN is binding at 5%. The unrestricted FRN and the annuity provide only 4.25% combined, but the long position in the in-the-money floor pays the additional 0.75%. In general, the required strike rate on the floor is the minimum coupon on the FRN less the fixed margin over LIBOR in the reset formula.

4. The yield-to-maturity will differ from that coupon rate as the net proceeds differ from the par value amount, as in any fixed income bond pricing problem. Also, the notional principal on the swap and floor are assumed to match the face value of the FRN.

5. This discussion is based in part on Donald J. Smith, "Measuring the Gains from 'Arbitraging' the Swap Market," *Financial Executive* (March/April 1988).

funds of, say, 9.75 percent. If the yardstick fixed-rate alternative is, say, 10 percent, the swap structure appears to deliver a 25 basis point arbitrage gain. But if this yardstick is the yield on a callable bond and the FRN and swap are noncallable, then the comparison is misleading. In this case, any arbitrage gain from the synthetic fixed-rate debt instrument must be measured relative to a noncallable debt issue. As a practical matter, call options on corporate debt are very common while similar exit options on interest rate swaps, caps, and floors are rare.

As another example, suppose that the FRN in equation 13 had a put option attached which granted the right of the holder to sell the FRN back to the issuer at par value. Then, the fixed margin of 0.25% would be lower than for an FRN without such an option. That put option could even be implicit, such as a material adverse change clause whereby the lender can advance the maturity date if the issuer's credit standing deteriorates. (Such clauses are quite common on bank revolving credit agreements.) In this case, the synthetic fixed rate structure would have to be compared to an explicit fixed-rate security offering investors the same put option.

If measured against a fixed-rate note with no such provision (or, worse yet, against one with a call option), the synthetic structure might only appear to be advantageous. The lower cost of funds could merely represent the fair value of the options contained in the documentation.

In comparing the costs of synthetic with conventional fixed-rate debt, one must also recognize the role of the floor agreement in the synthetic structure in offsetting the minimum coupon constraint contained in most FRNs on the market. Suppose that the floor on LIBOR is omitted in a structure such as that presented in equation 13. The all-in synthetic fixed-rate cost of funds would be reduced by the amount of the amortized cost of the premium on the floor.

In fact, market rates were quite high in the early 1980s and a floor on LIBOR at 4.75%, even if available, would have been a very inexpensive, deep out-of-the-money option. Nevertheless, if a "quasi-fixed" cost of funds is favorably compared to a truly fixed rate rate, one can only conclude that the *expected* cost of funds is lowered by the financial engineering.

Still another requirement for comparing synthetic with conventional debt instruments is to account for the degree of credit risk the issuer accepts by entering into the interest rate swap. If the counterparty to the swap defaults, the firm would have to replace the swap to maintain a synthetic fixed rate. If market rates have risen at the time of the default, the firm would pay a higher fixed rate on the replacement swap, raising its all-in cost of funds.[6] Therefore, the synthetic fixed-rate structure always has an element of credit risk. Any gain in the cost of funds over a straight fixed rate alternative should be measured net of the cost of bearing the estimated default risk.

ASSET SWAPS

Asset swaps are another synthetic structure that have emerged in the last few years.[7] These can be illustrated by multiplying both sides of equation 13 by -1:

Fixed Rate + Note		Typical + FRN		Interest Rate - Swap	- Floor	(14)
Swap fixed rate + 0.25%	**=**	**LIBOR + 0.25%, min. 5%**		**rec. fixed, pay LIBOR**	**4.75%**	

A synthetic fixed-rate asset is constructed by buying the FRN, selling the swap to receive the fixed rate, and writing the floor agreement. Notice that a synthetic floating-rate asset is obtained simply by moving the swap and floor agreements to the other side of the equation.

The motivation for asset swaps is to change the cash flow characteristics of the underlying asset—in the case of equation 14, the FRN. Consider an institutional investor that would like to carry a certain issuer's name on its books but does not like the coupon characteristics of the debt that is available on the market. For example, a pension fund might want to invest in fixed-income securities and prefer, or be constrained, to hold only high-quality debt of top-tier corporate and sovereign names. An investment banker can package an available FRN with a swap—perhaps even mixing in the floor agreement—and deliver the desired asset to the investor. Even in the event of default on the swap, the investor retains own-

---

6. In fact, the counterparty would never default if rates have fallen since the swap would have positive economic value. Also, if the floor writer defaults when LIBOR is below 4.75%, the firm's cost of funds would rise. Note that the credit risks on the swap and the floor are somewhat offsetting since it is most unlikely that both counterparties would default in the same interest rate environment.

7. See Daniel Stillet, "Unravelling the Asset Swap," *Euromoney Corporate Finance* (April 1987) for a description and applications of this innovation.

ership of the underlying high-quality asset.

One final observation should be made before proceeding to the more exotic structures. The synthetic fixed coupon rates and yields-to-maturity implied by equations 13 and 14 will not be equal because of the market-maker's bid-ask spreads on the interest rate swap and floor agreements. The market-maker will set a lower fixed rate on a swap when it pays fixed than when it receives fixed in order to make a profit and cover its own operational costs. Likewise, a market-maker will buy a floor at a lower up-front premium than when it writes the option.

Therefore, from a firm's perspective, the fixed rate on the swap and the premium on the floor are both higher in equation 13 than in equation 14. As would be expected, the synthetic fixed-rate cost of funds for a firm is somewhat higher than the synthetic fixed return on an asset when each is constructed from the same typical FRN.

SYNTHETIC STRUCTURES USING INNOVATIVE FRNs

Mini-Max Floaters

A security that became popular in 1985 was the "mini-max," or "collared," FRN. This is in essence a typical FRN with the addition of a maximum coupon rate. The investor in a mini-max FRN trades off a ceiling on potential coupon receipts for a higher fixed margin over the variable reference rate. This higher margin can be viewed as the amortized cost of a cap written by the investor and sold back to the issuer.

The structure of a 5-9% mini-max FRN with a coupon reset formula of LIBOR + 0.50% can be broken down using the arithmetic framework as follows:

$$
\begin{array}{lllll}
\text{Mini-Max} & \text{Unrestricted} & & & (15) \\
+ \text{ FRN} & = + \text{ FRN} & + \text{ Annuity} & - \text{ Cap} & + \text{ Floor} \\
\textbf{LIBOR} & \textbf{LIBOR} & \textbf{0.50\%} & \textbf{8.50\%} & \textbf{4.50\%} \\
\textbf{+0.50\%} & & & & \\
\textbf{min. 5\%,} & & & & \\
\textbf{max. 9\%} & & & &
\end{array}
$$

A long position in the mini-max FRN is equivalent in terms of future cash flows to buying a hypothetical unrestricted FRN at LIBOR flat, buying an annuity which pays 0.50%, writing a cap on LIBOR with a strike rate of 8.50%, and buying a floor on LIBOR with a strike rate of 4.50%. The last two transactions are the same as selling a 4.50%-8.50% interest rate collar, similar to equation 9 above. Multiplying through

equation 15 by −1 would show that issuing a mini-wax FRN is identical to issuing the unrestricted FRN and the annuity, buying the cap, and writing the floor. In sum, the issuer buys an interest rate collar from the investor.

The introduction of FRNs containing an embedded interest rate cap is noteworthy because it led to an arbitrage opportunity in "stripping" the cap and selling it at a profit. To see how this was done, first note that the combination of long positions in the unrestricted FRN, the annuity, and the floor agreement in equation 15 is equivalent to buying a typical FRN with a reset formula of LIBOR + 0.50% and minimum coupon rate of 5% (as in equation 11). Therefore, buying a mini-max FRN is the same as buying a typical FRN with no ceiling rate and writing an interest rate cap:

$$
\begin{array}{lllll}
\text{Mini-Max} & & \text{Typical} & & (16) \\
+ \text{ FRN} & = & + \text{ FRN} & - \text{ Cap} & \\
\textbf{LIBOR} + \textbf{0.50\%,} & & \textbf{LIBOR} + \textbf{0.50\%,} & \textbf{8.50\%} & \\
\textbf{min. 5\%, max. 9\%} & & \textbf{min. 5\%} & &
\end{array}
$$

Multiplying both sides of equation 16 by −1 and rearranging terms shows that issuing the mini-max FRN and writing the cap agreement is equivalent to issuing a typical FRN.

$$
\begin{array}{lllll}
\text{Mini-Max} & & & \text{Typical} & (17) \\
- \text{ FRN} & - \text{ Cap} & = & - \text{ FRN} & \\
\textbf{LIBOR} + \textbf{0.50\%,} & \textbf{8.50\%} & & \textbf{LIBOR} + \textbf{0.50\%,} & \\
\textbf{min. 5\%, max. 9\%} & & & \textbf{min. 5\%} &
\end{array}
$$

Suppose that the firm could issue a typical FRN directly in the capital market at par value, i.e., a price of 100, assuming that it had a reset formula of LIBOR + 0.50% and a minimum coupon rate of 5%. Also, suppose that the mini-max FRN could be sold only at discount—say, at a price of 98—to reflect the ceiling rate constraint. Then, if the issuing firm can write a cap agreement and sell it for an up-front premium of more than 200 basis points (times the notional principal equaling the face value of the FRN), a pure arbitrage gain is made. The desired type of variable rate funding is obtained at a lower cost of funds since the net proceeds exceed that of the direct alternative. Moreover, there is no credit risk since the firm is the writer of the option.

This structure was apparently executed a number of times in 1985, initially by Shearson Lehman Brothers and subsequently by other investment and commercial banks.[8] Interest rate cap market-makers were willing to buy the "stripped" caps at a price which gave the issuing firms a lower cost of funds because they in turn could sell the caps at a still higher price. Prior to this innovation, the cap market was fairly thin for maturities beyond a few years because hedging exposed positions was difficult due to the absence of exchange-traded futures and options contracts. "Cap stripping" created a supply of options which deepened and extended the maturity range of the market.

Inverse Floaters

An important innovation in the FRN market came in 1986 with the introduction of the inverse floater, also known as a "bull floater" or yield curve note. These have a fundamentally different coupon reset formula, one that commonly takes the form of a fixed percentage rate *minus* LIBOR. As LIBOR increases, the coupon payment on an inverse floater decreases. Inverse floaters have been issued by SallieMae, GMAC, and Citicorp, among others. By design, this type of security would be attractive to investors who are bullish on bond prices and expect market rates to fall. The attraction of the inverse floater is that its price increase in percentage terms will be greater than—indeed typically about double—that of a fixed rate note of the same maturity.[9] Also, the initial coupon rate is typically higher than those on traditional FRNs. In this way, inverse FRNs are similar to capped or collared FRNs. There is a pick-up in yield if market rates remain steady or decline but at the risk of larger price declines if rates rise.

One motive for issuers of inverse floaters is to hedge an exposure to floating interest rates. For instance, thrift institutions, which often are exposed to higher deposit rates, could issue inverse floaters to smooth out their cost of funds. The combination of an inverse floater and a traditional floater is in essence a fixed-rate note because the variable reference rate cancels out.

Another motive for issuing inverse floaters is arbitrage gains. Issuers commonly use interest rate swaps and caps to transform the inverse floater to the

desired type of fixed rate or traditional floating-rate debt. The claim is that such financial engineering lowers the cost of funds.

To see one way in which this innovative structure is put together, first note that issuing an inverse floater with a coupon reset formula of 16% − LIBOR is equivalent to issuing two fixed rate notes at 8%, buying an unrestricted FRN at LIBOR flat, and writing a cap on LIBOR with a strike rate of 16%.

$$
\begin{array}{ccccccc}
 & & \text{Two} & & & & (18) \\
 & \text{Inverse} & \text{Fixed Rate} & & \text{Unrestricted} & & \\
- & \text{Floater} & = - & \text{Notes} & + & \text{FRN} & - & \text{Cap} \\
 & \text{16\% − LIBOR} & & \text{8\%} & & \text{LIBOR} & & \text{16\%}
\end{array}
$$

The cap is needed in the structure because the inverse floater would pay a zero coupon rate if LIBOR rises above 16%.

As shown earlier (in equation 6), a long position in an unrestricted FRN can be isolated and set equal to a long position in a fixed-rate note at the swap rate and a long position in an interest rate swap. Substituting that relationship into equation 18 gives the following:

$$
\begin{array}{cccccc}
 & \text{Two} & \text{Fixed} & \text{Interest} & (19) \\
 \text{Inverse} & \text{Fixed Rate} & \text{Rate} & \text{Rate} & \\
- \text{Floater} = - & \text{Notes} & + \text{Note} & + \text{Swap} & - \text{Cap} \\
 \text{16\% −} & \text{8\%} & \text{Swap-fixed} & \text{pay fixed,} & \text{16\%} \\
 \text{LIBOR} & & \text{rate} & \text{rec. LIBOR} &
\end{array}
$$

Then, after combining the fixed-rate notes and rearranging terms, we see how an inverse floater can be converted with a swap into a synthetic fixed-rate note.

$$
\begin{array}{ccccc}
 & & \text{Interest} & & (20) \\
 \text{Fixed Rate} & \text{Inverse} & \text{Rate} & & \\
- \text{Note} & = - \text{Floater} & \text{Swap} & + & \text{Cap} \\
 \text{16\% − Swap} & \text{16\% − LIBOR} & \text{rec. fixed,} & & \text{16\%} \\
 \text{fixed rate} & & \text{pay LIBOR} & &
\end{array}
$$

Issuing the inverse floater, receiving the fixed rate on an interest rate swap, and buying a cap on LIBOR with a 16% strike rate creates a synthetic fixed coupon rate of 16% minus the swap rate.

A firm would claim (or its investment banker

---

8. The background to this innovation and strategy is described in David Shirreff, "Caps and Options: The Dangerous New Protection Racket," *Euromoney* (March 1986).

9. Jess Yawitz, in "Pricing and Duration of Inverse Floating Rate Notes," Goldman Sachs (March 1986), shows that the duration of an inverse floater is typically about double that of a fixed rate note with the same maturity. Twice the duration means

twice the price volatility. This result is also obtained by Joseph Ogden, "An Analysis of Yield Curve Notes," *Journal of Finance* (March 1987), by means of a simulation study. See also Donald J. Smith, "The Pricing of Bull and Bear Floating Rate Notes: An Application of Financial Engineering," *Financial Management* (Winter 1988) for further discussion.

would claim on its behalf) to have engineered a lower cost of funds if the all-in yield-to-maturity given the net proceeds is less than on a straight fixed rate note issue.[10] However, as with any structure that includes swaps or long positions in options, the inevitable credit risk should be evaluated and subtracted from any claimed arbitrage gain. (And, as emphasized earlier, one cannot directly compare the cost of a noncallable swap-driven structure to the yield on a callable bond.)

INNOVATIONS IN INTEREST RATE RISK MANAGEMENT

Besides structuring synthetic funding alternatives and seeking arbitrage opportunities, financial engineers have developed innovative products for managing interest rate risk. The motivation here is typically to provide interest rate protection without major balance sheet restructuring. For instance, suppose that a firm would like to set a ceiling on its floating-rate cost of funds but views the up-front premium on an interest rate cap to be prohibitively expensive. One alternative is a collar agreement whereby the firm sells an interest rate floor back to the cap writer, reducing the net premium. In fact, a floor strike rate can be found for any given cap rate so that the collar has no initial cost.

Another alternative, recently developed by financial engineers, can be generically called a "participation agreement." This is a variation of the zero-cost collar described above; but instead of setting the floor strike rate so that the premiums offset, the notional principal of the floor is adjusted. The outcome is that the buyer of a participation agreement has the benefit of a ceiling on LIBOR but makes settlement payments at a constant fraction of the rate differential when LIBOR is below the ceiling.[11]

An example is useful to illustrate this structure. Suppose that in the current interest rate environment a three-year 10% cap on LIBOR costs 150 basis points times the notional principal (NP). For instance, if NP = $10 million, the up-front premium would be $150,000. Also, suppose that a 6.50% floor costs 150 basis points while a 10% floor costs 400 basis points. A firm with $10 million in floating-rate debt could get interest rate protection with a 6.50%-10% zero-cost collar. Alternatively, it could buy a 10% cap for NP = $10 million and write a 10% floor for NP = $3.75 million. That would represent a zero-cost participation agreement because the sale price of the floor also would be $150,000, equalling the cost of the cap. When LIBOR is below the 10% ceiling, the firm, as writer of the floor, would make payments equal to 37.5% of that on a 10% floor if the notional principal had been $10 million. Hence, the firm shares, or "participates" in, 62.5% of the difference between the 10% ceiling rate and LIBOR. The participation rate (PR) is said to be 62.5%.

Using the arithmetic framework, a long position in a 10% ceiling zero-cost participation agreement for any given amount of interest rate protection, NP* (e.g., the amount of underlying debt) and a 62.5% PR is equivalent to buying a 10% cap for NP = NP* and writing a 10% floor for NP = $(1 - PR)NP*$ = .375NP*.

$$
\begin{array}{lcll}
& & & \text{(21)} \\
+ \ \begin{array}{c} \text{Participation} \\ \text{Agreement} \end{array} = & + \text{ Cap} & - \text{ Floor} \\
\textbf{10\% ceiling} & \textbf{10\%} & \textbf{10\%} \\
\textbf{NP = NP*} & \textbf{NP = NP*} & \textbf{NP = .375NP*}
\end{array}
$$

In general, the zero-cost participation rate will be one minus the ratio of the premiums on the cap and the floor for a given strike rate.

Notice that a cap and a floor at the same strike rate is equivalent to an interest rate swap, as shown earlier (in equation 10).

$$
\begin{array}{lcll}
& & & \text{(22)} \\
+ \ \begin{array}{c} \text{Interest Rate} \\ \text{Swap} \end{array} = & + \text{ Cap} & - \text{ Floor} \\
\textbf{pay 10\% fixed,} & \textbf{10\%} & \textbf{10\%} \\
\textbf{rec. LIBOR} & &
\end{array}
$$

This would be a non-par value (or "off-market") swap if the premiums on the cap and the floor are not equal. For instance, if the fixed rate on a par value swap is only 8.50%, the fixed-payer at 10% would require an up-front receipt for the present value of the stream of differences between 10% and 8.5% times the notional principal. That payment would also

---

10. For example, Albert Lord, the CFO of SallieMae, in describing their first yield curve note issue which had a reset formula of 17.2% minus LIBOR, is quoted in *Euromoney Corporate Finance* (April 1986, page 26) saying, "The formula worked out that the bull floater, or yield curve note, plus the swap resulted in us paying 17.2% and receiving fixed rate funds pegged to Treasuries....The end cost of funds, including the cost of the cap, was very competitive—below the five year Treasury rate."

11. See Keith C. Brown and Donald J. Smith, "Recent Innovations in Interest Rate Risk Management and the Reintermediation of Commercial Banking," *Financial Management* (Winter 1988) for an extended analysis of the trade-offs between interest rate collars and participation agreements.

equal the difference between the premiums on the cap and the floor at a 10% strike rate.

Since a 10% cap on LIBOR for NP = NP* in equation 21 can be separated into two 10% caps, one at NP = .375 NP* and another at NP = .625 NP*, the long position in a zero-cost position in a zero-cost participation agreement can also be written as follows:

$$
\begin{array}{ccccc}
\text{Participation} & & & & \text{Interest Rate} \quad (23) \\
+ \quad \text{Agreement} & = & + \text{ Cap} & + & \text{Swap} \\
\textbf{10\% ceiling} & & \textbf{10\%} & & \textbf{pay 10\% fixed,} \\
\textbf{NP} = \textbf{NP*} & & \textbf{NP} = \textbf{.625NP*} & & \textbf{rec. LIBOR} \\
\textbf{62.5\% PR} & & & & \textbf{NP} = \textbf{.375NP*}
\end{array}
$$

Therefore, a participation agreement can be viewed as a weighted average of an interest rate cap and an interest rate swap, using the participation rate to determine the respective notional principals. Full 100% participation in rates below the ceiling is a pure cap; zero participation is a pure swap.

SUMMARY AND CONCLUSIONS

Financial engineering is fundamentally the art and science of designing financial structures that create an otherwise unavailable risk-return trade-off. Much of this involves combining the new off-balance sheet products such as interest rate swaps, caps, and floors with traditional on-balance sheet securities like fixed- and floating-rate notes. Fortunately, simple arithmetic and the technique of describing long and short positions in a portfolio by pluses and minuses can illustrate the process of creating synthetic securities. Also, although all of the products and structures discussed in this article have been designed for interest rates within a given currency, the same framework can be applied to the foreign exchange market and to currency swaps and options. In fact, many innovations are first seen in the cross-currency Euromarkets and subsequently introduced to the domestic market.

The key to applying the arithmetic approach to financial engineering is to identify structures which provide the same promised future cash flows. Comparisons between synthetic and conventional fixed-rate debt, for example, are grossly misleading if the values of the embedded call and put options are not accounted for properly. But, if the cash flows are indeed equivalent, then any difference in the present values of the portfolios represents a genuine arbitrage opportunity. This opportunity ranges from "pure" arbitrage to "risk" arbitrage, depending on the degree of uncertainty about the promised cash receipts. In particular, structures which involve interest rate swaps and long positions in caps and floors always have some degree of credit risk. Given credit enhancements and the quality of the counterparty, these risks might be deemed to be negligible. In that case, financial engineers can confidently claim a higher *expected* return to investors (or lower cost of funds to borrowers). Nevertheless, the outcome should not be mistaken for pure arbitrage which entails no risk.

PRICING FINANCIAL FUTURES CONTRACTS: AN INTRODUCTION

by Kenneth R. French,
University of Chicago*

INTRODUCTION

Financial futures contracts are among the most actively traded securities. The volume of financial futures traded each day, measured in dollars, exceeds the daily volume of trading in stocks. Contracts representing more than 1.5 trillion dollars in stocks were traded in the Chicago Mercantile Exchange's S&P 500 futures pit during 1988. The annual volume in the Treasury bond futures pit at the Chicago Board of Trade for 1988 was more than 7.0 trillion dollars. In contrast, the total volume for all stocks on the New York Stock Exchange was only 1.4 trillion dollars in 1988.

A futures contract is a commitment made today to purchase an asset in the future. All terms of the trade are agreed on when the contract is initiated. For example, in March two investors might initiate a September Swiss franc futures contract with a price of $0.50 per franc. One trader (called the short) agrees to deliver 125,000 Swiss francs in September and the other trader (called the long) agrees to pay $62,500 (125,000 × $0.50) in September. No money changes hands when the contract is initiated; payment occurs on delivery.

The current (spot) price and the futures price for an asset differ for two reasons. First, in the spot market, the buyer must pay for his purchase today. In the futures market, the buyer pays for the asset when the contract matures. This delayed futures payment allows the buyer to earn interest on his money over the life of the contract, and it tends to increase the futures price relative to the spot price.

Second, purchases in the spot market entitle the buyer to all future dividend or coupon payments. With a delayed purchase in the futures market, the buyer does not receive any dividend or coupon payments that are made before the contract matures. This reduces the benefits of a delayed purchase and lowers the futures price.

In the next section, I illustrate the basic ideas by examining the delayed sale of a painting. In the sections that follow thereafter, I use these concepts to price futures contracts on stock indexes, Treasury bills, Treasury bonds, and foreign currencies. I ignore several complications, including taxes, transactions costs, and daily settling up in the futures market. Although these factors do affect futures prices, the simple relations summarized below provide a good description of the prices observed in the trading pits

THE BASIC IDEA

The owner of a valuable art collection is about to sell a painting by van Gogh for $1,000,000 when the buyer asks to delay the sale. The buyer wants to sign a contract today to buy the painting in six months. Although the contract would specify the purchase price and the delivery date, neither payment nor delivery would take place for six months. What is the minimum price the owner of the painting should accept for this delayed sale?

*This article was originally published in *Financial Markets and Portfolio Management* Vol. 2 1988. The research is supported by the University of Chicago's Center for Research in Security Prices.

BY DELAYING THE PURCHASE, THE BUYER CAN EARN INTEREST ON THE SPOT PRICE, BUT HE FORFEITS THE BENEFITS OF OWNERSHIP. THUS, THE DELAYED PRICE EQUALS THE ACCUMULATED VALUE OF THE SPOT PRICE MINUS THE ACCUMULATED VALUE OF THE BENEFITS.

No Costs or Benefits of Holding the Painting

The minimum acceptable price depends on the interest rate and the costs (or benefits) of holding the painting for six months. Suppose the interest rate is 8% per year or 4% over six months. Also, suppose the costs and benefits of holding the painting are small enough that they can be ignored. Finally, suppose the seller is confident that the buyer will fulfil his commitment in six months.

Since the owner could sell the painting today for $1,000,000, put the money in the bank, and receive $1,040,000 ($1,000,000 × 1.04) in six months, he should not accept the delayed sale unless the fixed future price is at least $1,040,000. If the owner agrees to the delayed sale, he loses the interest on the money he could have received today. Thus, the price on the delayed sale must be at least the current price, $1,000,000, plus interest, $40,000.

FIGURE 1

Immediate Sale for $1000000

$1000000 ——————— Earn 4% in the bank ——————▶ $1040000

today   6 months

Delayed Sale for $1040000

                                                     $1040000

today   6 months

What is the highest price the buyer should be willing to pay in the delayed sale? If the buyer accepts the delayed sale, he keeps his $1,000,000 for an extra six months. The six-month interest rate is 4%, so his money will grow to $1,040,000 ($1,000,000 × 1.04). The buyer should accept a delayed price up to $1,040,000. If the delayed price is higher, he is better off buying the painting today.

The seller will not accept a delayed price below $1,040,000, and the buyer will not accept a delayed price above $1,040,000. If the current (spot) price S is $1,000,000 and the six-month interest rate R is 4%, the delayed (futures) price F must be $1,040,000:

$$F = S \times (1 + R).$$

The buyer pays nothing until delivery, so the delayed price equals the future value of the current price.

Dividends from Owning the Painting

The appropriate price in the delayed sale is different if the costs or benefits of holding the painting are substantial. For example, suppose the current owner is planning to exhibit his collection in six months. If the sale of the van Gogh is delayed, the owner can include the painting in the exhibit and increase his ticket sales by $10,000. How does this affect the price he is willing to accept in the delayed sale?

If the owner sells the painting today for $1,000,000, he can put the money in the bank and earn 4% over the next six months; he will have $1,040,000 ($1,000,000 × 1.04) in six months. If the sale is delayed, the owner will receive the delayed price and an additional $10,000 in ticket sales in six months. The owner should not accept a delayed price below $1,030,000 ($1,040,000 − 10,000). Suppose the owner will exhibit his collection in three, rather than six, months. In this case the owner will accept an even lower delayed price. If the annual interest rate is 8%, the additional $10,000 ticket revenues will grow by 2%, to $10,200, over the three months before the delayed sale. Thus, the owner should be willing to accept a delayed sale price of $1,029,800 ($1,040,000 − 10,200).

FIGURE 2

Immediate Sale for $1000000

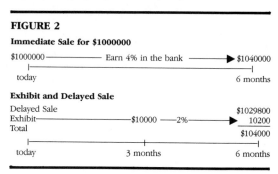

Exhibit and Delayed Sale

Delayed Sale		$1029800
Exhibit ——————— $10000 ——2%—— ▶		10200
Total		$104000

today   3 months   6 months

If the owner receives benefits (dividends) from holding the asset, the delayed price is reduced by the future value of the benefits D, such that

$$\begin{aligned} F &= S \times (1 + R) - D \\ &= \$1000000 \times 1.04 - \$10200 \\ &= \$1029800. \end{aligned}$$

By delaying the purchase, the buyer can earn interest on the spot price, but he forfeits the benefits of ownership. Thus, the delayed price equals the accumulated value of the spot price minus the accumulated value of the benefits.

PRICING STOCK INDEX FUTURES

A stock index futures contract is similar to the delayed sale of a painting. In essence, one trader, like the seller in the example above, agrees to deliver the stock index when the contract matures. The other trader, analogous to the buyer, agrees to pay the futures price at that time.[1]

Non-Dividend-Paying Stocks

Like the delayed price of a painting, the futures price for a stock index contract depends on the interest rate and the dividends that accrue to the owner of the underlying portfolio. If none of the stocks in the portfolio pays dividends, the futures price is just the future value of the current level of the index.

Consider an investor comparing an immediate sale of his stocks in March with a delayed sale in September. Suppose the current value of his portfolio is $210.00, and the six-month interest rate (from March to September) is 5%.[2] What is the minimum price the investor should accept to sell his portfolio using a September futures contract?

If the investor sells his portfolio today, he can invest the revenue for six months at 5% and receive $220.50 ($210.00 × 1.05) in September. Thus, he should not accept the delayed sale (futures contract) unless the futures price is at least $220.50.

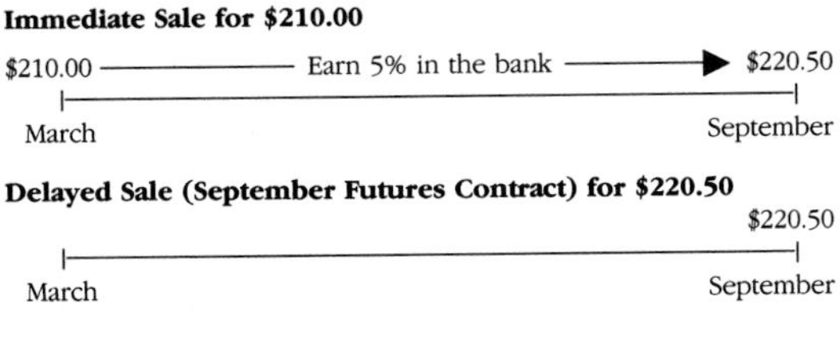

What about an investor who wants to buy the stocks? He can buy them today for $210.00. Or he can put his money in the bank and take a long September futures position, agreeing to buy the portfolio in September. The six-month interest rate is 5%, so a deposit of $210.00 today will grow to $220.50 in September. The investor is better off with a delayed purchase if the futures price is less than $220.50. If the futures price is above $220.50, the investor should buy the portfolio in the spot market.

Since sellers are unwilling to accept a delayed price below $220.50, and buyers are unwilling to accept a delayed price above $220.50, the September futures price must be $220.50.

More generally, define $F(t,T)$ as the futures price now (time t) for a contract that matures later (at time T), define $S(t)$ as the current portfolio or index value, and define $R(t,T)$ as the interest rate over the life of the futures contract. The futures price for an index on non-dividend-paying stocks must be the current index value times one plus the interest rate:

$$F(t, T) = S(t) \times [1 + R(t, T)]$$
$$= 210.00 \times 1.05$$
$$= 220.50.$$

The Effect of Dividends

If an investor sells his stocks in the spot market, he is not entitled to any dividends that are paid in the future. If he makes a delayed sale in the futures market, he receives all of the dividends paid before his futures contract matures. Thus, dividends are like the additional ticket revenue in the example above. They increase the benefits of a delayed sale and reduce the futures price the seller is willing to accept.

Suppose the stocks in the investor's portfolio will pay $5.00 in September, just before the futures contract matures. He can sell his portfolio today for $210.00, invest the money at 5% for six months, and receive $220.50 in September. Alternatively, he can take a short futures position, promising to deliver the portfolio in six months. In September he receives not only the futures price, but also $5.00 in dividends. The investor is better off with a delayed sale if the futures price is above $215.50 ($220.50 − 5.00).

FIGURE 3

Immediate Sale for $210.00

$210.00 ——————— Earn 5% in the bank ——————▶ $220.50

March   September

Delayed Sale (September Futures Contract) for $220.50

$220.50

March   September

1. Because of the large transactions costs involved in delivering all of the stocks in the index in exactly the right proportions, stock index futures actually use cash settlement rather than physical delivery. If the index is above the futures price at maturity, the buyer receives the difference from the seller. If the index is below the futures price, the seller receives the difference. Cash settlement is equivalent to having the seller "deliver" the maturity value of the index, and having the buyer pay the futures price.

2. Note that 5% is not an annualized interest rate. An investor who deposits $1.00 in the bank in March receives $1.05 in September.

FIGURE 4

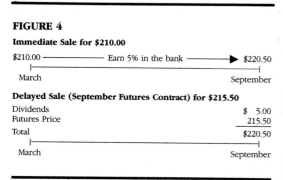

Immediate Sale for $210.00

$210.00 ——————— Earn 5% in the bank ——————→ $220.50

March   September

Delayed Sale (September Futures Contract) for $215.50

Dividends	$ 5.00
Futures Price	215.50
Total	$220.50

March   September

An investor purchasing the portfolio makes the same comparison. If he buys the portfolio in the spot market, he pays $210.00 today. In September, he has the portfolio plus a dividend of $5.00. If he buys the portfolio in the futures market, he can keep his money in the bank until September, but he does not receive the dividend. By September, his money will have grown to $220.50 ($210.00 × 1.05). After completing the delayed purchase, he will have the portfolio plus the difference between $220.50 and the futures price. The investor should buy in the spot market if this difference is less than $5.00 or, equivalently, if the futures price is above $215.50 ($220.50 − 5.00).

FIGURE 5

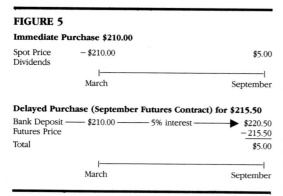

Immediate Purchase $210.00

Spot Price	− $210.00	
Dividends		$5.00

March   September

Delayed Purchase (September Futures Contract) for $215.50

Bank Deposit —— $210.00 —— 5% interest ——→ $220.50
Futures Price   − 215.50
Total $5.00

March   September

In general, the futures price is reduced by the maturity value of the dividends paid over the life of the

contract. Suppose the portfolio of stocks will pay a $10.00 dividend tomorrow and a $5.00 dividend in six months. Again, the owner can sell the portfolio today for $210.00, put the money in the bank, and receive $220.50 in September. Or he can make a delayed sale in the futures market. In this case, he receives $10.00 in dividends tomorrow, plus $5.00 in dividends and the futures price in September. Tomorrow's dividends grow to $10.50 ($10.00 × 1.05) in six months, so his total revenue in September is $15.50 ($10.50 + 5.00) plus the futures price. If the futures price is $205.00 ($220.50 − 15.50), the seller is indifferent between an immediate sale in the spot market and a delayed sale in the futures market.

More generally, define $D(t,T)$ as the maturity value of the dividends paid over the life of the futures contract, from time t to T. The price for a stock index futures contract is the accumulated value of the index minus the maturity value of the dividends:

$$
\begin{aligned}
F(t, T) &= S(t) \times [1 + R(t, T)] - D(t, T) \\
&= 210.00 \times 1.05 - 10.00 \times 1.05 - 5.00 \\
&= 205.00.
\end{aligned}
$$

PRICING TREASURY BILL FUTURES

As the name suggests, a Treasury bill futures contract is a delayed sale of a United States Treasury bill. One trader agrees to deliver a Treasury bill when the contract matures, and the other agrees to pay the futures price. The standard contract requires delivery of bills that will mature three months after delivery. For example, a futures contract that matures in September requires delivery of bills that mature in December.

Since the owner of a Treasury bill receives no payments before the bill matures, a Treasury bill futures contract is similar to a stock index futures contract on non-dividend-paying stocks. The spot and futures prices differ only because of the delayed payment in the futures contract.

Consider an investor comparing an immediate and a delayed sale of a nine-month Treasury bill. Suppose the six-month interest rate (from March to September) is 5% and the nine-month interest rate (from March to December) is 7%.[3] The investor can

---

3. Again, 7% is not an annualized interest rate. An investor who puts $1.00 in nine month bills in March receives $1.07 in December. Treasury bill spot and futures prices are quoted on an annualized discount basis. For example, suppose the actual price on a 90 day bill is $98.00 (per $100.00 face value). The annualized discount is ($100.00 − 98.00) × 360/90 = $8.00, and the quoted price is $100.00 − 8.00 = $92.00. The annualized discount complicates the relation between quoted spot and futures prices, so I concentrate on actual, rather than quoted, prices.

sell his nine-month (December) bills today for $93.46 ($100/1.07) per $100 face value, deposit the revenue in the bank, and receive $98.13 ($93.46 × 1.05) in September. Alternatively, the investor might take a short September Treasury bill futures position, promising to sell his December bills in September. Since an immediate sale will generate $98.13 in September, the investor should not accept a delayed sale unless the futures price is at least $98.13.

FIGURE 6

Immediate Sale for $93.46

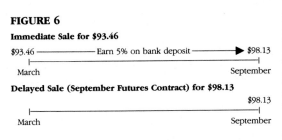

Delayed Sale (September Futures Contract) for $98.13

Similarly, a buyer who purchases December bills in the futures markets retains the use of his funds until the contract matures. He can buy the bills today for $93.46 ($100.00/1.07). Or he can deposit this money in the bank and take a long futures position, agreeing to buy December bills in September. The bank deposit will grow to $98.13 ($93.46 × 1.05) in September, so he should be willing to accept any futures price up to $98.13.

The seller will not accept a delayed price below $98.13, and the buyer will not accept a price above $98.13, so the futures price must be $98.13.

More generally, define F(t,T) as the futures price at time t for a contract that matures at T, define S(t) as the spot price at t for the deliverable Treasury bill, and define R(t,T) as the interest rate over the life of the futures contract. Because of the delayed payment in the futures market, the futures price is the future value of the current spot price:

$$F(t, T) = S(t) \times [1 + R(t, T)]$$
$$= \$93.26 \times 1.05$$
$$= \$98.13.$$

This is identical to the relation between the spot and futures prices for a contract on non-dividend-paying stocks.

TREASURY BOND FUTURES

Treasury bond futures contracts are a very popular tool for managing interest rate risk. More than one quarter of all futures contracts traded in 1988 were traded in the Chicago Board of Trade Treasury bond futures pit. Nominally, all Treasury bond futures contracts call for delivery of bonds with 8% annual coupon payments, $100,000 face value, and 20 years to maturity when the contract matures.

The relation between spot and futures prices for Treasury bond futures is similar to the relation for stock index futures on dividend-paying stocks. Delayed payment in the futures market increases the futures price, while coupon payments in the spot market reduce the futures price. However, the pricing of Treasury bond futures contracts is complicated slightly by accrued interest; although the buyer must pay accrued interest, it is not included in the quoted spot and futures prices.

Treasury bond coupons are paid semi-annually. After a coupon is paid, interest accrues until the next coupon payment. For example, an 8% bond with a face value of $100,000 pays a coupon of $4000 ($100,000 × 4%) every six months. If there are 182 days between coupons, the accrued interest grows by $21.98 ($4000/182) each day. An investor buying the bond on the day after a coupon must pay the quoted price plus $21.98. An investor buying the bond 100 days after a coupon payment must pay the quoted price plus $2198.00.

If one includes accrued interest, the relation between the actual payments in the Treasury bond spot and futures markets is identical to the one between the spot and futures prices for stock index futures. The futures payment FP(t,T) is the accumulated value of the spot payment SP(t) minus the maturity value of the coupons over the life of the contract C(t,T):

$$FP(t, T) = SP(t) \times [1 + R(t, T)] - C(t, T).$$

The spot payment SP(t) is the quoted spot price S(t), plus the current accrued interest on the deliverable bond i(t). The futures payment FP(t,T) is the futures price F(t,T) plus the accrued interest on the deliverable bond at delivery i(T). Using the relation between the spot and futures payments,

$$F(t, T) + i(T) = [S(t) + i(t)] \times$$
$$[1 + R(t, T)] - C(t, T),$$

the Treasury bond futures price is as follows:[4]

$$F(t, T) = [S(t) + i(t)] \times [1 + R(t, T)] - C(t, T) - i(T).$$

For example, consider an investor who is trying to decide whether to buy an 8% Treasury bond in the spot or futures market. The bond pays coupons on May 15 and November 15. If the quoted spot price on May 20 is $103.00 per $100.00 face value, he can buy the bond for $103,000.00 plus accrued interest of $109.90 ($21.98 × 5). Alternatively, he can deposit this money in the bank and make a delayed purchase using a September futures contract. What is the highest price he should accept in the futures market?

Since there is no coupon payment on the bond before the contract matures, the only issue is whether the bank deposit will pay both the futures price and the accrued interest when the contract matures. Suppose the interest rate from May to September is 2%, so the deposit will grow to $105,172.10 ($103,109.90 × 1.02) in September. If the contract matures on September 1, the accrued interest is $2395.82 ($21.98/day × 109 days between May 15 and September 1). Thus, the investor should be willing to accept any futures price less than or equal to $102,776.28 ($105,172.10 − 2395.82).

Using the relation above,

$$
\begin{aligned}
F(t, T) &= [S(t) + i(t)] \times [1 + R(t, T)] \\
&\quad - C(t, T) - i(T) \\
&= [\$103000.00 + 109.90] \times 1.02 - 0.00 \\
&\quad - 2395.82 \\
&= \$102776.28.
\end{aligned}
$$

FOREIGN CURRENCY FUTURES

A foreign currency futures contract is a commitment to exchange a specific quantity of some currency for U.S. dollars at a specific time in the future. For example, a September Swiss franc futures contract commits the short to deliver 125,000 Swiss francs in September and it commits the long to pay the futures price for each franc.

Foreign currency traders price futures contracts using the concept of interest rate parity. This implies that, after adjusting for exchange rate differences, interest rates must be equal across countries.

Consider an investor planning to invest dollars in March to obtain dollars in September. The simple approach is to deposit his money in a U.S. bank in March and then to withdraw the money in September. Alternatively, he can exchange his dollars for Swiss francs today, deposit the francs in a Swiss bank, and take a short futures position, promising to exchange francs for dollars in September. The return from these two riskless strategies must be identical.

Suppose the current exchange rate is $0.80 per Swiss franc, the dollar interest rate from March to September is 5% and the Swiss franc interest rate is 3%. If he chooses, the investor can (a) exchange $1,000,000 for 1,250,000 ($1,000,000/$0.80) Swiss francs today, (b) deposit this money in a Swiss bank, (c) withdraw 1,287,500 (1,250,000 × 1.03) francs in September, and (d) sell these francs in the futures market for 1,287,500 times the futures price. Since he can get $1,050,000 ($1,000,000 × 1.05) by depositing his money in a U.S. bank, the Swiss franc approach is preferable if the futures price is above $0.8155 ($1,050,000/1,287,500).

FIGURE 7

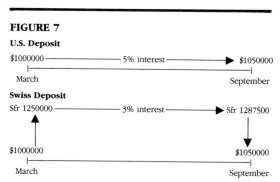

For example, suppose the September futures price is $0.90. By committing to a delayed sale of francs in the futures market, the investor can lock in a payment of $1,158,750 ($0.90 × 1,287,500) in September for $1,000,000 today. This risk-free return of almost 16% dominates the domestic interest rate, so anyone planning to lend money in the U.S. would prefer to combine a short futures position with lending in Switzerland. This would put pressure on the futures price until it fell to $0.8155.

---

4. This discussion ignores the delivery options available to the seller in the Treasury bond futures contract. See Gerald D. Gay and Steven Manaster, "Implicit Delivery Options and Optimal Delivery Strategies for Financial Futures Contracts," *Journal of Financial Economics* 16 (May, 1986), 41-72.

Alternatively, suppose the futures price is below $0.8155. Then anyone planning to lend money in Switzerland would be better off (a) converting their francs to dollars, (b) depositing them in a U.S. bank, and (c) taking a long futures position to convert the dollars to francs in September. The demand for long futures positions would drive the futures price back up to $0.8155.

More generally, define S(t) as the current price in dollars of the foreign currency (the exchange rate), define R(t,T) as the domestic (U.S.) interest rate from t to T, and define R*(t,T) as the foreign interest rate from t to T. Then the futures price at t for a contract that matures at T is

$$F(t, T) = S(t) \times [1 + R(t, T)] / [1 + R^*(t, T)]$$
$$= \$0.80 \times 1.05/1.03$$
$$= \$0.8155.$$

The futures price for foreign currency contracts is determined by the same two factors that determine the prices for other financial futures contracts. An investor can buy Swiss francs today at the current exchange rate. Alternatively, he can make a delayed purchase in the futures market, promising to pay the futures price when the contract matures. Because of the delayed payment in the futures market, the futures price is increased by the U.S. interest rate. However, with the delayed purchase, the investor forfeits the interest he could earn on the Swiss francs if he bought them today. This interest is similar to dividends or coupon payments forfeited by traders in the stock index and Treasury bond futures markets. It reduces the price the investor is willing to pay in the delayed purchase.

For example, suppose the U.S. interest rate is 30% and the Swiss interest rate is 1%. By making a delayed purchase, the investor invests his dollars at a high interest rate before the contract matures, and he gives up little by not having francs to invest. The difference in interest rates makes the delayed purchase attractive and raises the futures price. On the other hand, suppose the U.S. interest rate is 1% and the Swiss interest rate is 30%. There is little return from investing dollars before the delayed payment and the cost of not having francs to invest is high. This difference makes the delayed purchase unattractive and lowers the futures price.

INSTITUTIONAL ENVIRONMENT AND EMPIRICAL ACCURACY

In developing the relation between spot and futures prices, I have assumed that the only cash payments occur when the contract matures. In fact, there is a daily transfer, or settling up, between the traders. After each day's trading, the futures price is compared with the closing price from the previous day. If the price has fallen, the investor who is long (committing himself to purchase the asset) must pay the short the amount of the decrease. If the futures price has risen, the long receives the increase from the short. After this transfer, the contract is "marked to market," or rewritten at the current price.

Daily settling up reduces the likelihood that either trader will default and it reduces the costs if a trader does default. Without it, a trader's losses can accumulate over the life of the contract. Daily settling up limits this exposure to one day's price change.

But this protection is not free. The daily transfer of profits and losses increases bookkeeping costs and forces traders to hold liquid assets. Apparently, the benefits usually outweigh the costs.

There are a few forward markets that do not settle up daily. The most prominent is the interbank foreign currency market. This market is only available to banks and large corporations. Presumably, the creditworthiness of these firms is sufficient to guarantee their financial performance; there is little reason to bear the transactions costs of daily settling up. On the other hand, individuals and small corporations wishing to trade foreign currencies must transact on futures exchanges, such as the International Monetary Market at the Chicago Mercantile Exchange. Because of the higher default risk of these traders, the futures contracts are settled daily.

Daily settling up appears to have little impact on the relation between spot and futures prices. A 1981 study by Brad Cornell and Marc Reinganum compares the prices for foreign exchange forward contracts (without daily settling up) and futures contracts (which are settled daily). They find small random differences between the forward and futures prices.[5] Similarly, a study I published in 1983 reports small differences between forward and futures prices for copper and silver.[6]

---

5. See Bradford Cornell and Marc Reinganum, "Forward and Futures Prices: Evidence from the Foreign Exchange Market," *Journal of Finance* 36 (December, 1981), 1035-1045.

6. See Kenneth R. French, "A Comparison of Futures and Forward Prices," *Journal of Financial Economics* 12 (November, 1983), 311-342.

Transactions costs have a larger impact on the accuracy of the pricing relations described above. In general, arbitragers insure that the actual futures price will be close to the theoretical price described by the relations above. For example, suppose the actual Swiss franc futures price is high relative to the theoretical price. Then an arbitrager can lock in a profit by shorting the futures contract and buying Swiss francs. This will drive the futures price up relative to the spot price and bring the actual futures price closer to the theoretical price. When the futures price is too low, buying pressure drives the price up. Arbitrage will continue until any potential profits are eliminated by transactions costs.

In general, transactions costs are relatively low and the actual futures price is close to the theoretical futures price. For example, foreign currency futures prices are almost always within one percent of their theoretical value. Typical transactions costs for arbitrage in the stock index market are about 0.5 percent; under normal circumstances, index arbitrage will force the futures price to remain within 0.5 percent of the value described above.

These tight arbitrage bounds were removed on Black Monday, October 19, 1987. Because of enormous trading pressures at the stock and futures exchanges, the effective transaction costs for index arbitrage became substantially higher on both October 19 and 20. The transactions costs, in turn, precluded arbitragers from exploiting differences as large as 10 or 15 percent between the actual and theoretical futures prices. Fortunately, pricing errors of this size are as rare as the price changes that precipitated them.

SUMMARY

The relation between spot and futures prices for financial futures contracts is determined by two factors. With a delayed purchase in the futures market, a buyer retains the use of his funds before the contract matures. This increases the futures price he is willing to accept. However, the buyer forfeits any dividends or coupons that are paid to the owner of the asset before the contract matures. This reduces the futures price he is willing to accept.

In the special case of foreign currency futures, interest payments on the foreign currency increase the quantity of the deliverable asset. Therefore, the adjustment for these "dividends" is multiplicative. That is,

$$F(t, T) = S(t) \times [1 + R(t, T)] / [1 + R^*(t, T)].$$

For all other financial futures contracts, the futures price equals the maturity value of the current spot price, minus the maturity value of any dividends or coupons that are paid over the life of the contract. Thus, $F(t,T)$

$$F(t, T) = S(t) + [1 + R(t, T)] - D(t, T).$$

HOW TO USE THE HOLES IN BLACK-SCHOLES

by Fischer Black, Goldman, Sachs & Co.*

T he Black-Scholes formula is still around, even though it depends on at least 10 unrealistic assumptions. Making the assumptions more realistic hasn't produced a formula that works better across a wide range of circumstances.

In special cases, though, we can improve the formula. If you think investors are making an unrealistic assumption like one of those we used in deriving the formula, there is a strategy you may want to follow that focuses on that assumption.

The same unrealistic assumptions that led to the Black-Scholes formula are behind some versions of "portfolio insurance." As people have shifted to more realistic assumptions, they have changed the way they use portfolio insurance. Some people have dropped it entirely, or have switched to the opposite strategy.

People using incorrect assumptions about market conditions may even have caused the rise and sudden fall in stocks during 1987. One theory of the crash relies on incorrect beliefs, held before the crash, about the extent to which investors were using portfolio insurance, and about how changes in stock prices cause changes in expected returns.

* This article is a revised version of an earlier article, "The Holes in Black-Scholes," which appeared in Vol. 1 No. 4 of *Risk* in March of 1988.

THE FORMULA

The Black-Scholes formula looks like this:

$$w\,(x,t) = xN(d_1) - ce^{-r(t^* - t)}N(d_2)$$

where

$$d_1 = \frac{\ln(x/c) + (r + 1/2v^2)\,(t^* - t)}{v\sqrt{t^* - t}}$$

and

$$d_2 = \frac{\ln(x/c) + (r - 1/2v^2)\,(t^* - t)}{v\sqrt{t^* - t}}$$

In this expression, w is the value of a call option or warrant on the stock, t is today's date, x is the stock price, c is the strike price, r is the interest rate, t^* is the maturity date, v is the standard deviation of the stock's return, and N is something called the "cumulative normal density function." (You can approximate N using a simple algebraic expression.)

The value of the option increases with increases in the stock's price, the interest rate, the time remaining until the option expires, and the stock's volatility. Except for volatility, which can be estimated several ways, we can observe all of the factors the Black-Scholes formula requires for valuing options.

Note that the stock's expected return doesn't appear in the formula. If you are bullish on the stock, you may buy shares or call options, but you won't change your estimate of the option's value. A higher expected return on the stock means a higher expected return on the option, but it doesn't affect the option's value for a given stock price.

This feature of the formula is very general. I don't know of any variation of the formula where the stock's expected return affects the option's value for a given stock price.

HOW TO IMPROVE THE ASSUMPTIONS

In our original derivation of the formula, Myron Scholes and I made the following unrealistic assumptions:
- The stock's volatility is known, and doesn't change over the life of the option.
- The stock price changes smoothly: it never jumps up or down a large amount in a short time.
- The short-term interest rate never changes.
- Anyone can borrow or lend as much as he wants at a single rate.
- An investor who sells the stock or the option short will have the use of all the proceeds of the sale and receive any returns from investing these proceeds.

- There are no trading costs for either the stock or the option.
- An investor's trades do not affect the taxes he pays.
- The stock pays no dividends.
- An investor can exercise the option only at expiration.
- There are no takeovers or other events that can end the option's life early.

Since these assumptions are mostly false, we know the formula must be wrong. But we may not be able to find any other formula that gives better results in a wide range of circumstances. Here we look at each of these 10 assumptions and describe how we might change them to improve the formula. We also look at strategies that make sense if investors continue to make unrealistic assumptions.

Volatility Changes

The volatility of a stock is not constant. Changes in the volatility of a stock may have a major impact on the values of certain options, especially far-out-of-the-money options. For example, if we use a volatility estimate of 0.20 for the annual standard deviation of the stock, and if we take the interest rate to be zero, we get a value of $0.00884 for a six-month call option with a $40 strike price written on a $28 stock. Keeping everything else the same, but doubling the volatility to 0.40, we get a value of $0.465.

For this out-of-the-money option, doubling the volatility estimate multiplies the value by a factor of 53.

Since the volatility can change, we should really include the ways it can change in the formula. The option value will depend on the entire future path that we expect the volatility to take, and on the uncertainty about what the volatility will be at each point in the future. One measure of that uncertainty is the "volatility of the volatility."

A formula that takes account of changes in volatility will include both current and expected future levels of volatility. Though the expected return on the stock will not affect option values, expected changes in volatility will affect them. And the volatility of volatility will affect them too.

Another measure of the uncertainty about the future volatility is the relation between the future stock price and its volatility. A decline in the stock price implies a substantial increase in volatility, while an increase in the stock price implies a substantial decrease in volatility. The effect is so strong that it is even

TO BUY PURE VOLATILITY, BUY BOTH PUTS AND CALLS IN A RATIO THAT
GIVES YOU NO ADDED EXPOSURE TO THE STOCK; TO SELL PURE
VOLATILITY, SELL BOTH PUTS AND CALLS IN THE SAME RATIO.

possible that a stock with a price of $20 and a typical daily move of $0.50 will start having a typical daily move of only $0.375 if the stock price doubles to $40.

John Cox and Stephen Ross have come up with two formulas that take account of the relation between the future stock price and its volatility.[1] To see the effects of using one of their formulas on the pattern of option values for at-the-money and out-of-the money options, let's look at the values using both Black-Scholes and Cox-Ross formulas for a six-month call option on a $40 stock, taking the interest rate as zero and the volatility as 0.20 per year. For three exercise prices, the value are as follows:

Exercise Price	Black Scholes	Cox-Ross
40.00	2.2600	2.2600
50.00	0.1550	0.0880
57.10	0.0126	0.0020

The Cox-Ross formula implies lower values for out-of-the-money call options than the Black-Scholes formula. But putting in uncertainty about the future volatility will often imply higher values for these same options. We can't tell how the option values will change when we put in both effects.

What should you do if you think a stock's volatility will change in ways that other people do not yet understand? Also suppose that you feel the market values options correctly in all other respects.

You should "buy volatility" if you think volatility will rise, and "sell volatility" if you think it will fall. To buy volatility, buy options; to sell volatility, sell options. Instead of buying stock, you can buy calls or buy stock and sell calls. Or you can take the strongest position on volatility by adding a long or short position in straddles to your existing position. To buy pure volatility, buy both puts and calls in a ratio that gives you no added exposure to the stock; to sell pure volatility, sell both puts and calls in the same ratio.

Jumps

In addition to showing changes in volatility in general and changes in volatility related to changes in stock price, a stock may have jumps. A major news development may cause a sudden large change in the stock price, often accompanied by a temporary suspension of trading in the stock.

When the big news is just as likely to be good as

bad, a jump will look a lot like a temporary large increase in volatility. When the big news, if it comes, is sure to be good, or is sure to be bad, the resulting jump is not like a change in volatility. Up jumps and down jumps have different effects on option values than symmetric jumps, where there is an equal chance of an up jump or a down jump.

Robert Merton has a formula that reflects possible symmetric jumps.[2] Compared to the Black-Scholes formula, his formula gives higher values for both in-the-money and out-of-the-money options and lower values for at-the-money options. The differences are especially large for short-term options.

Short-term options also show strikingly different effects for up jumps and down jumps. An increase in the probability of an up jump will cause out-of-the-money calls to go way up in value relative to out-of-the-money puts. An increase in the probability of a down jump will do the reverse. After the crash, people were afraid of another down jump, and out-of-the-money puts were priced very high relative to their Black-Scholes values, while out-of-the-money calls were priced very low.

More than a year after the crash, this fear continues to affect option values.

What should you do if you think jumps are more likely to occur than the market thinks? If you expect a symmetric jump, buy short-term out-of-the-money options. Instead of stock, you can hold call options or more stock plus put options. Or you can sell at-the-money options. Instead of stock, you can hold more stock and sell call options. For a pure play on symmetric jumps, buy out-of-the-money calls and puts, and sell at-the-money calls and puts.

For up jumps, use similar strategies that involve buying short-term out-of-the-money calls, or selling short-term out-of-the-money puts, or both. For down jumps, do the opposite.

Interest Rate Changes

The Black-Scholes formula assumes a constant interest rate, but the yields on bonds with different maturities tell us that the market expects the rate to change. If future changes in the interest rate are known, we can just replace the short-term rate with the yield on a zero-coupon bond that matures when the option expires.

---

1. See John Cox and Stephen Ross, *Journal of Financial Economics* (January/March 1976).

2. See John Cox, Robert Merton, and Stephen Ross, *Journal of Financial Economics* (January/March 1976).

But, of course, future changes in the interest rate are uncertain. When the stock's volatility is known, Robert Merton has shown that the zero-coupon bond yield will still work, even when both short-term and long-term interest rates are shifting.[3] At a given point in time, we can find the option value by using the zero-coupon bond yield at that moment for the short-tern rate. When both the volatility and the interest rate are shifting, we will need a more complex adjustment.

In general, the effects of interest rate changes on option values do not seem nearly as great as the effects of volatility changes. If you have an opinion on which way interest rates are going, you may be better off with direct positions in fixed-income securities rather than in options.

But your opinion may affect your decisions to buy or sell options. Higher interest rates mean higher call values and lower put values. If you think interest rates will rise more than the market thinks, you should be more inclined to buy calls, and more inclined to buy more stocks and sell puts, as a substitute for a straight stock position. If you think interest rates will fall more than the market thinks, these preferences should be reversed.

Borrowing Penalties

The rate at which an individual can borrow, even with securities as collateral, is higher than the rate at which he can lend. Sometimes his borrowing rate is substantially higher than his lending rate. Also, margin requirements or restrictions put on by lenders may limit the amount he can borrow.

High rates and limits on borrowing may cause a general increase in call option values, since calls provide leverage that can substitute for borrowing. The interest rates implied by option values may be higher than lending rates. If this happens and you have borrowing limits but no limits on option investments, you may still want to buy calls. But if you can borrow freely at a rate close to the lending rate, you may want to get leverage by borrowing rather than by buying calls.

When implied interest rates are high, conservative investors might buy puts or sell calls to protect a portfolio instead of selling stock. Fixed-income investors might even choose to buy stocks and puts, and sell calls, to create a synthetic fixed-income position with a yield higher than market yields.

Short-Selling Penalties

Short-selling penalties are generally even worse than borrowing penalties. On U.S. exchanges, an investor can sell a stock short only on or after an uptick. He must go to the expense of borrowing stock if he wants to sell it short. Part of his expense involves putting up cash collateral with the person who lends the stock; he generally gets no interest, or interest well below market rates, on this collateral. Also, he may have to put up margin with his broker in cash, and may not receive interest on cash balances with his broker.

For options, the penalties tend to be much less severe. An investor need not borrow an option to sell it short. There is no uptick rule for options. And an investor loses much less interest income in selling an option short than in selling a stock short.

Penalties on short selling that apply to all investors will affect option values. When even professional investors have trouble selling a stock short, we will want to include an element in the option formula to reflect the strength of these penalties. Sometimes we approximate this by assuming an extra dividend yield on the stock, in an amount up to the cost of maintaining a short position as part of a hedge.

Suppose you want to short a stock but you face penalties if you sell the stock short directly. Perhaps you're not even allowed to short the stock directly. You can short it indirectly by holding put options, or by taking a naked short position in call options. (Though most investors who can't short stock directly also can't take naked short positions.)

When you face penalties in selling short, you often face rewards for lending stock to those who want to short it. In this situation, strategies that involve holding the stock and lending it out may dominate other strategies. For example, you might create a position with a limited downside by holding a stock and a put on the stock, and by lending the stock to those who want to short it.

Trading Costs

Trading costs can make it hard for an investor to create an option-like payoff by trading in the underlying stock. They can also make it hard to create a stock-like payoff by trading in the option. Sometimes they

---

3. Robert Merton, *Bell Journal of Economics and Management Science* (1977).

can increase an option's value, and sometimes they can decrease it.

We can't tell how trading costs will affect an option's value, so we can think of them as creating a "band" of possible values. Within this band, it will be impractical for most investors to take advantage of mispricing by selling the option and buying the stock, or by selling the stock and buying the option.

The bigger the stock's trading costs are, the more important it is for you to choose a strategy that creates the payoffs you want with little trading. Trading costs can make options especially useful if you want to shift exposure to the stock after it goes up or down.

If you want to shift your exposure to the market as a whole, rather than to a stock, you will find options even more useful. It is often more costly to trade in a basket of stocks than in a single stock. But you can use index options to reduce your trading in the underlying stocks or futures.

Taxes

Some investors pay no taxes; some are taxed as individuals, paying taxes on dividends, interest, and capital gains; and some are taxed as corporations, also paying taxes on dividends, interest, and capital gains, but at different rates.

The very existence of taxes will affect option values. A hedged position that should give the same return as lending may have a tax that differs from the tax on interest. So if all investors faced the same tax rate, we would use a modified interest rate in the option formula.

The fact that investor tax rates differ will affect values too. Without rules to restrict tax arbitrage, investors could use large hedged positions involving options to cut their taxes sharply or to alter them indefinitely. Thus tax authorities adopt a variety of rules to restrict tax arbitrage. There may be rules to limit interest deductions or capital loss deductions, or rules to tax gains and losses before a position is closed out. For example, most U.S. index option positions are now taxed each year—partly as short-term capital gains and partly as long-term capital gains— whether or not the taxpayer has closed out his positions.

If you can use capital losses to offset gains, you may act roughly the same way whether your tax rate is high or low. If your tax rate stays the same from year to year, you may act about the same whether you are forced to realize gains and losses or are able to choose the year you realize them.

But if you pay taxes on gains and cannot deduct losses, you may want to limit the volatility of your positions and have the freedom to control the timing of gains and losses. This will affect how you use options, and may affect option values as well. I find it hard to predict, though, whether it will increase or decrease option values.

Investors who buy a put option will have a capital gain or loss at the end of the year, or when the option expires. Investors who simulate the put option by trading in the underlying stock will sell after a decline, and buy after a rise. By choosing which lots of stock to buy and which lots to sell, they will be able to generate a series of realized capital losses and unrealized gains. The tax advantages of this strategy may reduce put values for many taxable investors. By a similar argument, the tax advantages of a simulated call option may reduce call values for most taxable investors.

Dividends and Early Exercise

The original Black-Scholes formula does not take account of dividends. But dividends reduce call option values and increase put option values, at least when there are no offsetting adjustments in the terms of the options. Dividends make early exercise of a call option more likely, and early exercise of a put option less likely.

We now have several ways to change the formula to account for dividends. One way assumes that the dividend yield is constant for all possible stock price levels and at all future times. Another assumes that the issuer has money set aside to pay the dollar dividends due before the option expires. Yet another assumes that the dividend depends in a known way on the stock price at each ex-dividend date.

John Cox, Stephen Ross, and Mark Rubinstein have shown how to figure option values using a "tree" of possible future stock prices.[4] The tree gives the same values as the formula when we use the same assumptions. But the tree is more flexible, and lets us relax some of the assumptions. For example, we can put on the tree the dividend that the firm will pay for each possible future stock price at each future time. We can also test, at each node of the tree,

---

4. John Cox, Mark Rubinstein, and Stephen Ross, "Option Pricing: A Simplified Approach," *Journal of Financial Economics* Vol. 7 (1979), 229-263.

whether an investor will exercise the option early for that stock price at that time.

Option values reflect the market's belief about the stock's future dividends and the likelihood of early exercise. When you think that dividends will be higher than the market thinks, you will want to buy puts or sell calls, other things equal. When you think that option holders will exercise too early or too late, you will want to sell options to take advantage of the opportunities the holders create.

Takeovers

The original formula assumes the underlying stock will continue trading for the life of the option. Takeovers can make this assumption false.

If firm A takes over firm B through an exchange of stock, options on firm B's stock will normally become options on firm A's stock. We will use A's volatility rather than B's in valuing the option.

If firm A takes over firm B through a cash tender offer, there are two effects. First, outstanding options on B will expire early. This will tend to reduce values for both puts and calls. Second, B's stock price will rise through the tender offer premium. This will increase call values and decrease put values.

But when the market knows of a possible tender offer from firm A, B's stock price will be higher than it might otherwise be. It will be between its normal level and its normal level increased by the tender offer. Then if A fails to make an offer, the price will fall, or will show a smaller-than-normal rise.

All these factors work together to influence option values. The chance of a takeover will make an option's value sometimes higher and sometimes lower. For a short-term out-of-the-money call option, the chance of a takeover will generally increase the option value. For a short-term out-of-the-money put option, the chance of a takeover will generally reduce the option value.

The effects of takeover probability on values can be dramatic for these short-term out-of-the-money options. If you think your opinion of the chance of a takeover is more accurate than the market's, you can express your views clearly with options like these.

The October 19 crash is the opposite of a takeover as far as option values go. Option values then, and since then, have reflected the fear of another crash. Out-of-the-money puts have been selling for high values, and out-of-the-money calls have been selling for low values. If you think another crash is unlikely, you may want to buy out-of-the-money calls, or sell out-of-the-money puts, or do both.

Now that we've looked at the 10 assumptions in the Black-Scholes formula, let's see what role, if any, they play in portfolio insurance strategies.

PORTFOLIO INSURANCE

In the months before the crash, people in the U.S. and elsewhere became more and more interested in portfolio insurance. As I define it, portfolio insurance is any strategy where you reduce your stock positions when prices fall, and increase them when prices rise.

Some investors use option formulas to figure how much to increase or reduce their positions as prices change. They trade in stocks or futures or short-term options to create the effect of having a long-term put against stock, or a long-term call plus T-bills.

You don't need synthetic options or option formulas for portfolio insurance. You can do the same thing with a variety of systems for changing your positions as prices change. However, the assumptions behind the Black-Scholes formula also affect portfolio insurance strategies that don't use the formula.

The higher your trading costs, the less likely you are to create synthetic options or any other adjustment strategy that involves a lot of trading. On October 19, the costs of trading in futures and stocks became much higher than they had been earlier, partly because the futures were priced against the portfolio insurers. The futures were at a discount when portfolio insurers wanted to sell. This made all portfolio insurance strategies less attractive.

Portfolio insurance using synthetic strategies wins when the market makes big jumps, but without much volatility. It loses when market volatility is high, because an investor will sell after a fall, and buy after a rise. He loses money on each cycle.

But the true cost of portfolio insurance, in my view, is a factor that doesn't even affect option values. It is the mean reversion in the market: the rate at which the expected return on the market falls as the market rises.[5]

5. For evidence of mean reversion, see Eugene Fama and Kenneth French, "Permanent and Temporary Components of Stock Prices," *Journal of Political Economy* Vol. 96 No. 2 (April 1988), 246-273; and James Poterba and Lawrence Summers, "Mean Reversion in Stock Prices: Evidence and Implications," *Journal of Financial Economics* Vol. 22 No. 1 (October 1988), 27-60.

Mean reversion is what balances supply and demand for portfolio insurance. High mean reversion will discourage portfolio insurers because it will mean they are selling when expected return is higher and buying when expected return is lower. For the same reason, high mean reversion will attract "value investors" or "tactical asset allocators," who buy after a decline and sell after a rise. Value investors use indicators like price-earnings ratios and dividend yields to decide when to buy and sell. They act as sellers of portfolio insurance.

If mean reversion were zero, I think that more investors would want to buy portfolio insurance than to sell it. People have a natural desire to try to limit their losses. But, on balance, there must be as many sellers as buyers of insurance. What makes this happen is a positive normal level of mean reversion.

THE CRASH

During 1987, investors shifted toward wanting more portfolio insurance. This increased the market's mean reversion. But mean reversion is hard to see; it takes years to detect a change in it. So investors did not understand that mean reversion was rising. Since rising mean reversion should restrain an increase in portfolio insurance demand, this misunderstanding caused a further increase in demand.

Because of mean reversion, the market rise during 1987 caused a sharper-than-usual fall in expected return. But investors didn't see this at first. They continued to buy, as their portfolio insurance strategies suggested. Eventually, though, they came to understand the effects of portfolio insurance on mean reversion, partly by observing the large orders that price changes brought into the market.

Around October 19, the full truth of what was happening hit investors. They saw that at existing levels of the market, the expected return was much lower than they had assumed. They sold at those levels. The market fell, and expected return rose, until equilibrium was restored.

MEAN REVERSION AND STOCK VOLATILITY

Now that we've explained mean reversion, how can you use your view of it in your investments?

If you have a good estimate of a stock's volatility, the stock's expected return won't affect option values. Since the expected return won't affect values, neither will mean reversion.

But mean reversion may influence your estimate of the stock's volatility. With mean reversion, day-to-day volatility will be higher than month-to-month volatility, which will be higher than year-to-year volatility. Your volatility estimates for options with several years of life should be generally lower than your volatility estimates for options with several days or several months of life.

If your view of mean reversion is higher than the market's, you can buy short-term options and sell long-term options. If you think mean reversion is lower, you can do the reverse. If you are a buyer of options, you will favor short-term options when you think mean reversion is high, and long-term options when you think it is low. If you are a seller of options, you will favor long-term options when you think mean reversion is high, and short-term options when you think it's low.

These effects will be most striking in stock index options. But they will also show up in individual stock options, through the effects of market moves on individual stocks and through the influence of "trend followers." Trend followers act like portfolio insurers, but they trade individual stocks rather than portfolios. When the stock rises, they buy; and when it falls, they sell. They act as if the past trend in a stock's price is likely to continue.

In individual stocks, as in portfolios, mean reversion should normally make implied volatilities higher for short-term options than for long-term options. (An option's implied volatility is the volatility that makes its Black-Scholes value equal to its price.) If your views differ from the market's, you may have a chance for a profitable trade.

425

THE EVOLVING MARKET FOR SWAPS

by Clifford Smith, University of Rochester, Charles Smithson, Chase Manhattan Bank, and L. Macdonald Wakeman, MTK Global

A recent advertisement extols swaps as "a tool no financial manager can ignore."[1] While this statement has the hyperbolic ring of Madison Avenue prose, it is nevertheless quite clear that the swaps market — a relatively new and rapidly developing market — has become increasingly important. As with other evolving markets in the past, there exists confusion about certain economic implications of this market, especially among some corporate treasurers to whom these instruments are being marketed. Questions that deserve consideration include: (1) How does the swaps market relate to other financial markets? (2) How (and why) did the swaps market evolve? (3) What goes into the pricing of a swap, particularly the evaluation of credit risk? (4) What direction might the swaps market be expected to take in the future? Our paper focuses on these questions; and, in so doing, it proposes a general analytical framework that should prove helpful in evaluating both the broad variety of swaps now available, and those that are yet to be devised.

Analysis of Swap Transactions

As its name implies, a swap is normally defined as an exchange. More specifically, it is an exchange of cash flows over time between two parties (generally referred to as the "counterparties"). The first swaps developed from parallel loans arranged between two companies in different countries, a form popular in the 1970s. To illustrate a parallel loan, suppose a British company makes a loan denominated in pounds to a US company, which in turn makes a loan of equal value denominated in dollars to the British company. As illustrated in Figure 1, these loans have parallel interest and principal repayment schedules. By entering into this parallel loan agreement, the British company is able to transform a debt incurred in pounds into a fully-hedged US dollar liability. There are, however, two potentially important problems with parallel loans: (1) default by one party does not release the other from making its contractually obligated payments; (2) although the loans effectively cancel one another, they remain on-balance-sheet items for accounting and regulatory purposes. Early in the 1980s a new transaction known as a "currency swap" was devised to overcome these problems; and because of its success, it effectively displaced the use of parallel loans.

The Currency Swap. A currency swap involves the same pattern of cash flows as a parallel loan. Indeed, without any modification, Figure 1 could be used to illustrate the cash flows for a fixed currency swap where firm A pays a fixed interest rate in dollars and receives a fixed rate in pounds, while the counterparty, firm B, pays fixed-rate pounds and receives fixed-rate dollars. (In this context, the short arrows in Figure 1 denote the cashflows exchanged during the term of the agreement, while the long arrows denote the initial exchange of principals at time 0 and the reexchange at maturity, time T.) Alternatively, a swap transaction could be illustrated by looking at the cash flows paid and received over time by one of the counterparties. Figure 2 illustrates the position of the British firm A in this fixed currency swap.

Although a swap is defined as an "exchange" of cash flows, there need not be an actual exchange of payments. Instead, at specified intervals, only the net

1. Bankers Trust Company, "The International Swap Market," Advertising Supplement to *Euromoney Corporate Finance*, September 1985.

FIGURE 1
Cash Flows in a Parallel Loan Agreement

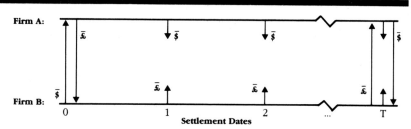

The British firm A simultaneously borrows dollars from American firm B and loans an equivalent amount denominated in pounds to firm B at time 0. During the term of the loan, firm A makes interest payments in dollars to firm B, while firm B makes interest payments in pounds to firm A. At maturity (time T) the two firms make their final interest payments and return the principals. Firm A returns dollars and firm B returns pounds.

FIGURE 2
Cash Flows from a Fixed Currency Swap

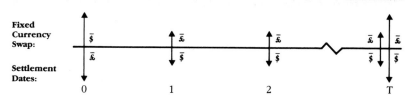

The British firm A pays interest at a fixed dollar rate ($\overline{\$}$) and receives interest at a fixed pound rate ($\overline{\pounds}$). The long arrows denote the initial exchange of principal and the reexchange at maturity; the short arrows denote the cash flows exchanged over the course of the agreement.*

cash flows could be exchanged, and the party that would have received the lower of the cash flows could simply pay the other the difference in the two cash flows. In the case of currency swaps, the counterparties do exchange interest payments; however, the exchange is conditional in the sense that if one party defaults, the other is released from its obligation. In currency swaps, moreover, the counterparties generally exchange the principals at an agreed-upon rate of exchange and then reexchange at the end of the agreement; but this exchange also need not occur. The principal could instead be "notional," as is generally the case in interest rate swaps (which we take up later).

By thus converting the older parallel loan transaction into a conditional exchange of the cash flows, the currency swap reduces the probability and magnitude of default. Furthermore, as implied above, current regulatory and accounting practice treats swap contracts as off-balance-sheet items. Thus, as stated earlier, the currency swap accomplishes the goals of its predecessor, the parallel loan agreement, while eliminating the major remaining problems with that transaction.

Swaps as Packages of Forward Contracts. One of the major themes of this paper, to which we shall return throughout, is the fundamental similarity between swaps and forward contracts. In fact, it is our contention that any swap can be decomposed into a series of forward contracts.

Again consider Figure 2, which illustrates the cash flows in a fixed currency swap — one in which the firm pays fixed-rate interest in one currency and receives fixed-rate interest in another. The cash flows for the counterparty receiving pounds and paying dollars at time 1 are equivalent to those from holding

---

*In this figure and in similar figures to follow, we adopt the convention of showing inflows above the line and outflows below the line.

a long position in pounds in a pound-dollar forward contract. This also applies to each settlement date between 2 and T; hence this currency swap for firm A is equivalent to a package of T long forward contracts in pounds. The positions are reversed for the counterparty.

We believe this decomposition of swaps into forward contracts is the most productive way of evaluating swaps, particularly the pricing of swaps. Simple swaps have been standardized and are now quoted virtually as commodities; and for such swaps this method of analysis will seem roundabout. But, as we will demonstrate, for more complicated swaps, where the timing of cash-flow exchanges differ or where the principal changes, decomposition of cash flows into forward contracts is the simplest, most effective analytical approach.

Currency Coupon Swaps. In a currency swap, as we have seen, the counterparties agree on the timing of the exchanges, the principal amounts of the currencies that will be exchanged, the interest rates (which reflect credit market forward prices) that will determine the future cash flows, and the exchange rates used to calculate the net cash flows. The earliest currency swaps were fixed currency swaps, which specified fixed interest rates in both currencies. Soon after came a variant of the fixed currency swap called the currency coupon swap. In such an arrangement, the interest rate in one currency is fixed and the other is floating.

Interest Rate Swaps. The interest rate swap, which was introduced shortly after currency swaps, is a special case of the currency coupon swap — one in which all the cash flows are denominated in a single currency. Figure 3 illustrates a simple interest rate swap. The primary difference between Figures 2 and 3 is that the exchanges of principal flows at time 0 and T net to zero because they are of the same amount and denominated in the same currency.

Basis Rate Swaps. To this point, we have described swaps in which both interest rates are fixed (fixed currency swaps) and swaps in which one interest rate is fixed and one is floating (simple interest rate swaps and currency coupon swaps). In a basis rate swap, both interest rates are floating. The primary effect of such swaps is to allow floating-rate cash flows calculated on one basis to be exchanged for floating rate cash flows calculated on another. For example, it permits firms to make conversions from one-month LIBOR to six-month LIBOR, or from LIBOR to US commercial paper rates. A basis rate swap is equivalent to

pairing two simple interest rate swaps such that the flows are converted from floating to fixed, and then converted from fixed to floating (but on a different basis).

Commodity Swaps. A swap is, in effect, an exchange of net cash flows calculated to reflect changes in designated prices. So far, we have considered only two prices, interest rates and exchange rates. However, swaps defined in prices other than interest rates and foreign exchange rates are also possible. Once a principal amount is determined and that principal contractually converted to a flow, any set of forward prices can be used to calculate the cash flows (and thus the difference checks).

Consider, for example, the possibility of swaps denoted in commodities such as oil and wheat. The counterparties could agree to some notional principal and to the conversion of this principal to flows using a fixed dollar interest rate and the US price of wheat. Such a swap is analytically no different from a currency swap where forward prices of wheat replace the forward currency prices. In addition, neither firm need be in the wheat business; the difference checks are paid in dollars, not wheat. Moreover, in a swap in which the firm elects to pay with wheat, it can receive either fixed or floating rates in any currency or commodity.

Swaps with Timing Mismatches. In addition to differences resulting from the price used to calculate the cash flows (i.e., interest rates, foreign exchange rates, and commodity prices), swaps can differ in the timing of the cash flows. At the simplest level, it could be that one party is paying on a monthly basis while the other is on a quarterly schedule. More significant differences in the timing of the cash flows include so-called "zero" swaps — swaps in which one party makes no payment until maturity — and customized swaps in which the payments from one party vary, either in terms of timing or amount.

Swaps with Option-Like Payoffs. We have stressed the similarity of swaps to forward contracts. Indeed, the payoff profile for a simple swap contract is identical to that of a forward contract. Fig. 4 presents a simple case in which the firm pays a floating interest rate and receives a fixed rate. This firm has positive net cash flows when the short-term interest rate is below that existing at the contract origination date.

Swaps can also be constructed so as to have option-like provisions which limit the range of outcomes. For example, suppose that a firm with a

Swaps defined in prices other than interest rates and foreign exchange rates are clearly possible. Once a principal amount is determined and that principal converted to a flow, any set of forward prices can be used to calculate the net cash flows.

**FIGURE 3
Cash Flows in an
Interest Rate Swap**

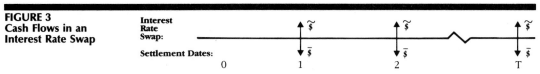

The firm illustrated pays a fixed dollar interest rate ($\bar{\$}$) and receives interest computed on a floating dollar rate ($\tilde{\$}$). The counterparty pays floating and receives fixed.

**FIGURE 4
Payoff Profile of an
Interest Rate Swap
for Firm Paying Floating
Rate and Receiving
Fixed Rate**

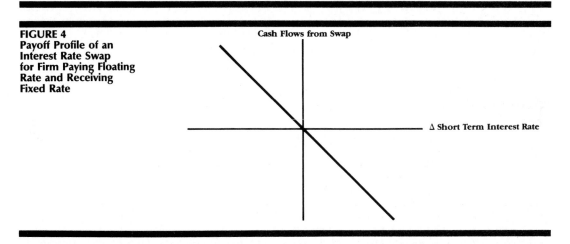

**FIGURE 5
Pay-off Profile for
Floor-Ceiling Swaps**

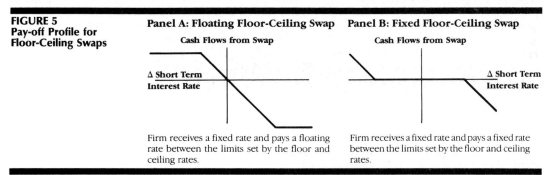

Firm receives a fixed rate and pays a floating rate between the limits set by the floor and ceiling rates.

Firm receives a fixed rate and pays a fixed rate between the limits set by the floor and ceiling rates.

floating-rate liability wanted to limit its outflows should interest rates rise substantially and was willing to give up some potential gains should there instead be a dramatic decline in short-term rates. To achieve this end the firm could modify a simple interest rate swap contract to read as follows: As long as the interest rate neither rises by 200 basis points nor falls more than 100 basis points, the firm pays a floating rate and receives a fixed rate; but, if the interest is more than 200 basis points above or 100 basis points below the current rate, the firm receives and pays a fixed rate. The resulting payoff profile for this floating floor-ceiling swap is illustrated in Panel A of Figure 5. (It is also the payoff profile for a "spread.")[2]

2. Note also that if the floor and ceiling rates are equal, this side of the contract is equivalent to a fixed rate obligation since a long call plus a short put with the same terms equals a long forward contract.

The popular argument seems to be that the cost savings is based on some kind of financial arbitrage across different capital markets....The problem with this argument, however, is that the very process of exploiting this kind of opportunity should soon eliminate it.

Conversely, the contract could have been modified as follows: As long as the interest rate is within 200 basis points of the current rate, the firm receives and pays a fixed rate; but if the interest rate rises or falls by more than 200 basis points, the firm pays a floating rate and receives a fixed rate. The payoff profile for the resulting fixed floor-ceiling swap is illustrated in panel B of Figure 5.

Given the range of swaps described above, we agree with the market participant who noted that "the future potential structures....are limited only by the imagination and ingenuity of those participating in the market."[3]

Development of the Swaps Market

The swaps market is still relatively new. As we noted, its origins can be traced to the parallel loan products of the 1970s. However, a market for swaps did not exist in any meaningful sense until the 1980s. Currency swaps are slightly older than interest rate swaps; their public introduction was the World Bank-IBM transaction in August 1981. US dollar-denominated interest rate swaps started in 1982. While not as old as the currency swaps market, the US interest rate swaps market is now the largest of the swaps markets.

Given the growth in swaps that has occurred, there are two questions we want to consider in this section: (1) Since swaps are so similar to forward contracts, WHY did this market evolve? (2) In order to provide a framework for looking at the future of this market, what path has the evolution of this market followed so far — HOW did this market evolve?

Why Did the Swaps Market Evolve?

Trade journals and market participants agree that the growth of the swaps market has resulted from the ability to receive "significant cost savings" by combining a bond issue with a swap.[4] Using swaps, the firm ends up with lower borrowing costs than it could have obtained with a single transaction. For example, with the use of swaps, companies have obtained funding at LIBOR minus 75-100 basis

points. Obviously, a satisfying explanation of why the swaps market evolved must identify the source of this cost saving.

Financial Arbitrage. The popular argument seems to be that the cost savings is based on some kind of financial arbitrage across different capital markets. That is, prices in various world capital markets are not mutually consistent; and firms can lower their borrowing costs by going to foreign capital markets with lower rates, borrowing there, and then swapping their exposure back into their domestic currency, thereby ending with cheaper funding than that obtainable from simply borrowing at home.

The problem with this argument, however, is that the very process of exploiting this kind of opportunity should soon eliminate it. The opening and expansion of a swap market effectively increases the demand for loans in low-rate markets and reduces the demand in higher-rate markets, thereby eliminating the supposed rate differences. Moreover, if this were the only economic basis for swaps, the benefits to one party would come at the expense of the other. Thus, in reasonably efficient and integrated world capital markets, it seems difficult to attribute the continuing growth of the swaps market simply to interest rate differences, and thus financial arbitrage, among world capital markets.

Tax and Regulatory Arbitrage. Swaps allow companies to engage in what might be termed tax and regulatory arbitrage. Prior to the existence of a well-functioning swap market, a firm issuing dollar-denominated, fixed-rate bonds generally did so in US capital markets and thus had to comply with US securities regulation. Moreover, the issuing firm, as well as the security purchasers, were generally faced with the provisions of the US tax code. The introduction of the swap market allows an "unbundling," in effect, of currency and interest rate exposure from the regulation and tax rules in some very creative ways. For example, with the introduction of swaps, a US firm could issue a yen-denominated issue in the Eurobond market, structure the issue so as to receive favorable tax treatment under the Japanese tax code, avoid much of the US securities regulation, and yet still manage its currency exposure by swapping the transaction back into dollars. Unlike the classic financial arbitrage de-

---

3. Bankers Trust Company, "The International Swap Market," cited earlier.
4. As an example of the popular literature on swaps, see Tanya S. Arnold,

"How to Do Interest Rate Swaps," *Harvard Business Review*, September-October 1984, pp.96-101.

*Unlike classic financial arbitrage, there is no reason for opportunities
for tax or regulatory arbitrage to disappear (barring changes, of course,
in the various tax and regulatory codes).*

scribed above, there is no reason for opportunities for tax or regulatory arbitrage to disappear (barring changes, of course, in the various tax and regulatory codes).

To illustrate the manner in which tax and regulatory arbitrage induces swaps, consider the way one US firm used swaps to take advantage of special tax and regulatory conditions in Japan:

(1) Until recently, zero coupon bonds received extremely favorable treatment under the Japanese tax code: taxes were not due until maturity, and at maturity the difference between the purchase price and the face value of the bond was taxed at the capital gains rate.

(2) The Ministry of Finance limited the amount a pension fund could invest in non-yen-denominated bonds issued by foreign corporations to at most 10%

of their portfolio.

In response to these conditions, a US firm issued a zero coupon yen bond plus a dual currency bond with interest payments in yen and principal repayment in dollars. The zero coupon yen bond permitted the firm to take advantage of the tax treatment of yen zeros. The Ministry of Finance ruled that the dual currency bonds qualified as a yen issue for purposes of the 10% rule, even though the dual currency bond has embedded within it a dollar-denominated zero. Hence, by issuing the dual currency bond, the US firm was able to capitalize on the desire of Japanese pension funds to diversify their portfolios internationally, while at the same time adhering to the regulation imposed by the Ministry of Finance.

The same US firm also, however, wanted to transform its resulting yen exposure to a US dollar expo-

**FIGURE 6
Cash Flows in a Dual Currency Bond Issue Plus a Zero Coupon Yen Issue Combined with a Fixed Currency Swap and Spot Currency Transaction**

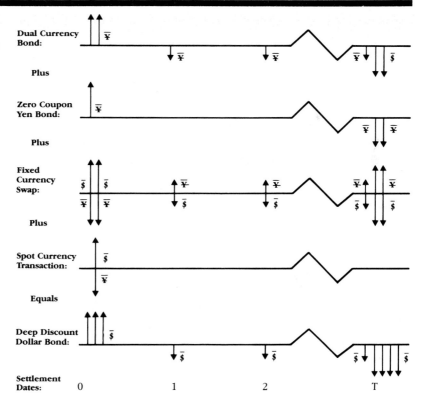

The final cash flows are equivalent to those of a deep discount dollar bond.

The swap market can be used as a way of synthetically "completing" the financial markets.

FIGURE 7
Payoff Profile of a Currency Swap Used to Hedge the Financial Risk Exposure from its Underlying Business

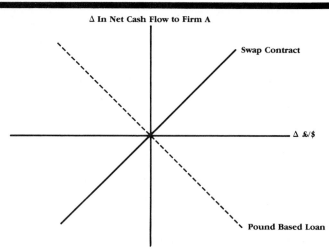

The dashed line represents the exposure of the firm's net cash flow to changes in the £/$ exchange rate without hedging. The payoff profile for the swap is the solid line. Thus, after the swap, the firm is completely hedged against changes in this exchange rate.

sure. To transform the bond issues, the firm used a currency swap together with a spot $/¥ transaction. (There is less liquidity in non-standard, annuity-type swaps. By combining the principal repayment of the yen zero with the coupon payments of the dual currency bond, a standard, bond-type swap could be used to hedge.) The resulting cash flows are solely in dollars (see Figure 6). Indeed, the swap transaction has created a synthetic deep discount dollar bond, and the rates were such that the firm lowered its total borrowing costs. By using the swap transaction, the firm capitalized on both the favorable regulatory ruling concerning dual currency bonds and the favorable tax treatment of zero coupon bonds, while retaining a fixed dollar interest rate exposure.

Exposure Management. Swaps also allow firms to lower the transactions costs of managing their exposure to interest rates, currency prices, or commodity prices. As we noted, a fixed currency swap can be used by a firm to transform a debt incurred in pounds into a dollar liability. This transformation is illustrated in Figure 7. The payoff profile for a loan incurred in pounds relative to changes in the £/$ exchange rate is shown as the dashed line. The payoff profile for the swap is shown as the solid line. Viewed in this context, the swap contract behaves like a conventional long-dated foreign exchange forward contract; losses on the dollar-based loan resulting from exchange rate changes will be offset by gains on the swap contract.

For example, consider the case of a firm just entering a foreign market. Although well-known at home, the company might have difficulty placing debt in the foreign credit market where access to information about the firm is more expensive. In this case, it might be less expensive to issue debt in domestic capital markets and swap into the foreign currency exposure.

Conversely, suppose a firm's cash flow exposure in Deutschemarks declines, reducing the amount of DM-denominated debt desired in the firm's balance sheet. Without swaps, the firm would have to call outstanding DM bonds to manage its exposure, an expensive alternative if German interest rates have risen. With access to a liquid swap market, the firm may have a lower-cost means of reducing its DM-denominated liabilities.[5]

Completing Markets. Finally, the swaps

5. For discussions of corporate motives for hedging, see David Mayers and Clifford Smith, "The Corporate Insurance Decision," *Chase Financial Quarterly* (Spring 1982), and "Corporate Insurance and the Underinvestment Problem," Working Paper, The University of Rochester Managerial Economics Research Center, 1985. See also Clifford Smith and Rene Stulz, "The Determinants of Firms' Hedging Policies," *Journal of Financial and Qualitative Analysis*, December 1985; and Alan Shapiro and Sheridan Titman, "An Integrated Approach to Corporate Risk Management," *Midland Corporate Finance Journal* (Summer 1985).

As the product became more standardized, the intermediaries began to accept swap contracts without a counterparty, taking the risk into their own books.

market contributes to the integration of financial markets by allowing market participants to fill gaps left by missing markets. An obvious gap filled by the swaps market is the forward market in interest rates. Until recently, there were no forward interest rate contracts available. But, because an interest rate swap behaves like a series of forward contracts, a swap could be used in place of the missing forward contract. Hence, the swap market can be used as a way of synthetically "completing" the financial markets.

Less obvious is the manner in which currency and interest rates swaps have been used to fill gaps in the international financial markets. For example, there is no Swiss Treasury Bill market. Currency and interest rate swaps, however, can be used to create this market synthetically.

In sum, there are four primary reasons WHY the swaps market evolved: (1) classic financial arbitrage opportunities; (2) profit opportunities from regulatory and tax arbitrage; (3) lower transaction costs for some types of financial risk exposure management; and (4) financial market integration. It appears that the first of these is significantly less important today than when swaps markets first opened. Spreads which were initially available have been substantially reduced by the very process of financial arbitrage which produced the original cost savings. As one market observer has commented, *"...at the outset of the market, a 'AAA' issuer could reasonably expect to achieve 75-100 basis points below LIBOR on a bond/swap; under current conditions, this same issuer might expect only 25-30 basis points below...Many issuers now find it more cost-effective to approach the floating rate note market than the bond/swap market."*[6] But if the opportunities for classic financial arbitrage have been eroded by competition, the other three factors remain important and can be expected to stimulate further activity in swaps.

How Did the Swaps Market Evolve?

A picture of the historical development of the swaps market can be obtained by looking either at the evolution of the products or at changes in the market's participants. Both tell the same story. We first look at the products.

As we noted, currency swaps were the first to appear. The earliest swaps were done on a one-off basis, which involved a search for matching counterparties — matching not only in the currencies, but also in the principal amounts desired. These early swaps were custom-tailored products. Because the deals were all one-off, they involved a great deal of work by the financial institution arranging the swap; but — and this is a crucial point — they involved virtually no direct exposure for the intermediary. In the language of the market participants, the early swaps required "creative problem solving" rather than capital commitment from the intermediary.

As interest rate swaps began to appear, the movement toward a more standardized product began. With the US dollar interest rate swaps, there were fewer areas in which counterparties might not match than had been the case for currency swaps. The product had become more homogeneous; and because the product had become more homogeneous, there was less demand for one-off deals. Instead of requiring an exactly matching counterparty, the intermediary could bundle counterparties.

With the move toward homogeneity and the reduced reliance on an identifiable counterparty, markets for swaps — in particular, interest rate swaps — began to look more and more like markets for commodities. Increased competition forced down the spreads. And, with the increased competition, an extensive search for a counterparty or group of counterparties was unprofitable for the intermediary. Instead, the intermediaries began to accept swap contracts without a counterparty, taking the risk into their own books and either matching it internally with an offsetting position or hedging it with government securities or instruments in the financial futures market.

Hence, the evolution of the products offered in the swaps market paralleled that of most markets; swaps evolved from a customized, client-specific product to a standardized product. With the customized product, the role of the intermediary had been one of problem solving. As the product became more standardized, the role of the intermediary changed considerably, with less emphasis on arranging the deal and more on transactional efficiency and capital commitment.

Looking at the participants in the swaps market, the dominant intermediaries in the early stage of development were investment banks. As the market

---

6. Bankers Trust Company, "The International Swap Market," cited earlier.

Standardization has been more pronounced for interest rate swaps, which may go a long way in explaining why this market has grown more rapidly than that for currency swaps.

evolved, the entrants into this market were more highly capitalized firms, in particular commercial banks. This evolution fits precisely with that of the products. In the early stages the emphasis was on the intermediary arranging the transaction rather than accepting risk from the transaction; thus investment banks were the natural intermediaries. But, as the swaps became more standardized, it became essential for the intermediary to be willing and able to accept part or all of a potential transaction into its books. Hence commercial banks, with their greater capitalization, became a more significant factor.

As we noted, the path the swaps market followed in its evolution is similar to that of other markets have taken — most notably, the development of the options market. Prior to 1973, the market for put and call options in the U.S. was an over-the-counter market. Members of the Put and Call Dealer's Association would write options, but only on a one-off basis. Each option was virtually unique because (1) the maturity date was set 181 days from the date the contract was written and (2) the exercise price was set as a function of the prevailing stock price (usually at the stock price). The result was that, for options, there was little volume, little liquidity, and virtually no secondary market. The growth of the options market occurred after the Chicago Board Options Exchange standardized the contracts (maturity dates and exercise prices) and developed an active secondary market. Dealing with a homogeneous product rather than individual customized deals, market makers were able to manage their risks by managing bid-ask spreads to maintain a neutral exposure rather than hedging each transaction on a one-off basis. While over-the-counter options are still offered, the real liquidity in the options market is in exchange-listed options. The options market evolved by moving from an individualized, custom-made product to one resembling a commodity.

While swaps have not evolved to the point of becoming exchange-traded instruments (a point to which we will return in our final section), the paths of evolution — particularly the major factors —have been similar. As was the case with options, contract standardization has played a major role. One market observer put it well by noting that "swaps have become a high volume, lower margin business, rather than the personalized, corporate financial deal of the

past."[7] As we have pointed out, the standardization has been more pronounced for interest rate swaps, which may go a long way in explaining why this market has grown more rapidly than that for currency swaps.

Also paralleling the development of options markets, the growth of the swap market corresponded to the liquidity available through the secondary market. While positions can be traded, the secondary market in swaps normally involves the reversing(unwinding) of a position. The simplest method to unwind a swap would involve a cancellation of the agreement, with a final difference check determined on the basis of the remaining value of the contract. However, since this simple "unwind" could result in taxable income, the more common method of unwinding a swap is by writing a "mirror" swap to cancel out the original. Most market observers indicate that this market is sufficiently deep to decrease risks in the primary market, particularly for short-term swaps. Indeed, a 24-hour market now exists for dollar interest rate swaps of up to 12-year maturities and amounts to $500 million.

Pricing Swaps

The pricing of a swap transaction is the aspect of the swap market that has received the most attention, especially that part of pricing which concerns credit risk. The pricing of a swap involves more, however, than just that single dimension. In fact swap pricing can be viewed as having three major components: forward prices, transaction costs, and the credit risk inherent in the transaction.

Forward Prices. Central to any swap agreement is the forward price — whether it be the forward interest rate, the forward exchange rate, or the forward price of a commodity — embodied in the exchange. Earlier we demonstrated that a swap contract is fundamentally a series of forward contracts.[8] In this view, the forward rate embodied in a swap contract must be the same as the forward rates employed in other corresponding financial contracts such as bonds and futures. And the empirical evidence bears this out: the difference between the two-year swap rate and the forward rate implied by Euro-dollar futures declined from over 50 basis points in

---

7. K. Henderson Schuyler, "The Constraints on Trading Swaps," *Euromoney,* May 1985, pp.63-64

8. Floor-ceiling swaps also involve options.

*Because a swap is a package of forward contracts, the forward rates
reflected in the swap must conform to the market's view of the future
as reflected in the prevailing term structure.*

1982 and 1983 to less than 20 basis points in 1984; the remaining 20 basis points essentially reflect the difference in transaction costs and credit risk. This development also confirms our expectation that once the initial financial arbitrage opportunities discussed earlier are exhausted, the forward rates for swaps must conform to the market's view of the future as reflected in the prevailing term structure.

The forward rate component of the pricing of a swap, then, is determined neither by the intermediary nor by the swap market. It is determined by competition from other credit market instruments. Because a swap is a package of forward contracts, the forward rates reflected in the swap must conform to the market's view of the forward rate, or financial arbitrage will be profitable.

Transaction Costs. This component would be reflected in the bid/ask spread for a risk-free transaction plus any origination fees that are charged.[9] The primary determinant of the bid/ask spread is the demand for liquidity. Put another way, the bid/ask spread is determined not by the market maker but, like the forward rate component, by competition in the market. The bid-ask spread, in short, is a market-determined price which reflects the costs of market-making activities.[10]

Credit Risk. In contrast to the preceding components, both of which are independent of the counterparties, the credit risk premium is determined by the specific credit risk of the intermediary and/or the counterparties. The premium added to the bid/ask spread to reflect nonperformance risk depends on characteristics of the counterparty and of the intermediary arranging the swap; it must therefore reflect an appropriate compensation for the probability of default.

It has been argued by some observers that credit risk in a swap contract is priced "too low" relative to the pricing of credit risk in the loan market. To attempt to evaluate such a statement, we examine the determinants of the credit risk premium.

In a loan, the lender has at risk not only the obligated interest payments, but also the loan principal. In a swap the intermediary has at risk only the net cash flow difference at each settlement date. The difference in exposure implies that, for equal levels of nonperformance risk, the credit-risk premium associated with a swap would be far smaller than for a loan of comparable size.

As with a loan, the exposure of the intermediary issuing the swap contract to this firm — or, more precisely, its portfolio exposure to similar firms — is a determinant of the credit-risk premium. However, one element is significantly more important in the case of a swap contract. If the counterparty is arranging the swap as a hedge and if the counterparty has outstanding lines of credit with the intermediary, the swap decreases expected nonperformance losses of the loan. A counterparty which uses a swap to hedge its financial exposure is reducing its overall probability of financial distress.[11] The probability of default for a swap, and therefore the risk premium, depend critically on whether or not the swap has been arranged as a hedge.

Consider the situation in which the swap is a hedge. During periods when the firm would be in financial distress, the swap contract would be in the firm's favor; the firm would be receiving difference checks. For example, consider a firm that experiences some financial difficulty if short-term interest rates rise. Suppose that this firm has entered into an interest rate swap to hedge its interest rate exposure. When short-term interest rates rise, the firm does indeed experience a decline in operating cash flow from its core business; but, at the same time, the firm is receiving inflows from the swap contract. In such a situation, even a firm in financial distress would have no incentive to default on the swap contract.

Therefore, if the swap is a hedge, the probability of default on the swap contract, as well as the probability of default on other liabilities such as loan contracts, are both reduced by this active financial risk exposure management; and the credit risk premiums attached to swap contracts should reflect this difference.

By contrast, if the swap had been used *not* to create a hedge, but rather to speculate on

---

9. In this paper, we do not differentiate between transaction costs reflected in the bid/ask spread and those reflected in up-front origination fees. In essence, we assume that the firm is indifferent about the manner in which it receives its fee for transaction costs.

10. See Harold Demsetz, "The Cost of Transacting," *Quarterly Journal of Economics*, 1968, pp.33-53; and Jack Treynor, "The Only Game In Town," *Financial Analysts Journal*, March-April 1971, pp.12-22.

11. Another way of looking at this is that a hedge can make the cost of credit endogenous. It may be advantageous to negotiate swaps and lines of credit simultaneously, since a swap used as a hedge could reduce the cost of the credit line.

If the US decided to place burdensome regulations on swaps, the principal effect on swap activity would be to change the location of swap transactions.

FIGURE 8
A Currency Coupon Swap from Fixed-Rate Pounds to Floating-Rate Dollars Viewed as a Combination of a Fixed Currency Swap from Pounds to Dollars Plus an Interest Rate Swap from Fixed-Rate Dollars to Floating-Rate Dollars

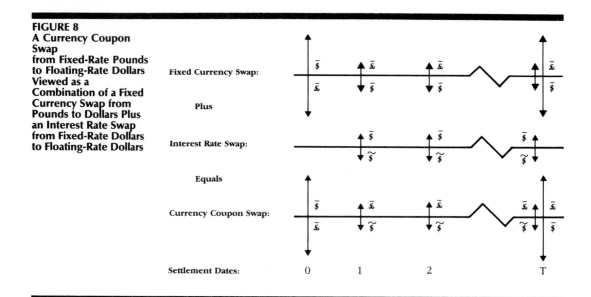

movements in financial markets, the probability of default on the swap is higher and the risk premium should be correspondingly greater. In the same way, if the swap is acting as a reverse hedge, the swap would increase the intermediary's exposure.

The above argument suggests that the credit risk assigned to a swap contract should not be based solely on a credit review of the counterparty. The credit risk associated with a swap contract depends on the exposure of the intermediary to firms similar to the one seeking a swap contract and on whether or not the swap acts as a hedge.

We have purposely not dealt with more technical aspects of credit risk, such as the degree to which risks change if a swap is unwound, the credit risk implications of trading swap positions, and the legal standing of swap contracts in a bankruptcy. (Some of these will be considered in the next section.) Instead, our objective has been to point out what we think are the special features in evaluating the credit risk of a swap: (1) there is no principal at risk so we have "settlement risk" rather than "credit risk" per se; and (2) whether the swap is used as a hedge is an important factor. On the basis of what we have seen, we tend to be more optimistic than many observers about the probability of defaults. One piece of evidence consistent with our view is the fact that in June of 1985, Citicorp determined that it had been

overcautious, and thus reduced its assessment of credit risk, in its pricing of swaps.

Pricing Restrictions from Arbitrage. Our major emphasis has been on viewing swaps as packages of forward contracts. We believe that the approach of pricing swaps by breaking them down into a set of fundamental cash flows is by far the most general, and thus the least restrictive, framework for evaluating new products; it is also likely to be the most flexible in solving pricing problems for very tailored swaps. At the same time, however, we have suggested that complicated swaps can also be decomposed into more simple swaps. For example, as Figure 8 demonstrates, a currency coupon swap is equivalent to a fixed currency swap plus a simple interest rate swap. The idea of unbundling swaps into other swaps can be important in identifying arbitrage opportunities within the market. For example, the cost of a currency coupon swap should be compared to the cost of a simple interest rate swap plus a fixed currency swap. Because they are equivalent transactions, the sum of the prices of the least costly alternative for each component is the best guide to pricing the complex swap.

Moreover, from the perspective of the intermediary, swap decomposition is important for exposure management by the intermediary. Again considering a currency swap, it may be easier to find

If swaps move further toward exchange trading, investment banks will be the major beneficiary. On the other hand, if the intermediary continues to bear risk (or if the liability for the intermediary is increased), commercial banks will be the beneficiary.

counterparties for a currency coupon swap by looking for separate counterparties for the interest rate and the currency swap components.

The Future of the Swap Market

We do not purport to be able to predict the future for this market. Indeed, we subscribe to the adage that "he who lives by the crystal ball ends up eating ground glass." Certain factors, however, are likely to have the largest impact on the future evolution of this market. In this section, we will point out those factors we think are most important and suggest possible outcomes.

Liability of the Intermediary. Much of what we have read in the trade journals and heard from the market participants involves conjecture about the swap market "after the first major default." This reflects uncertainty about the legal standing of swap contracts and, more significant, a good deal of controversy over the liability borne by the intermediary (both the current level and the appropriate level).

At one extreme, there are those who argue that the intermediary should assume no liability. Proponents of this view recommend making swaps more like exchange-traded instruments. Suggestions include marking swaps to market with callable margins (or with variable fees) and collateralization (with or without a clearing house).

At the other extreme are those who argue that the intermediary should always retain part of the risk. Arguing against the move toward exchange trading, proponents of this position note that, because swaps are like bundles of forward contracts, credit risk of the counterparties is an important element; and the intermediary (who has a comparative advantage in assessing the credit risk) is effectively a counterparty to each side of the contract.

Secondary Market. As we noted, the growth of the secondary market has made possible much of the growth of the swaps market, and future growth depends on the existence of an active secondary market. Whether a still broader secondary market should be encouraged inevitably throws us back on the earlier question of the liability of the intermediary. Proponents of making swaps exchange-traded instruments point out that marking to market or collateralizing permit contract standardization as well as providing effective guarantees against contractual default. Furthermore, if contracts are effectively bonded, as would be the case with marking to market or collateralizing, the secondary markets can be more anonymous.

Opponents of the move toward exchange trading for swaps point out that secondary markets can be active even if the assets are not homogeneous. For example, there exists an active secondary market for mortgaged-backed securities. In this market, performance is guaranteed by mortgage insurance and the reputation of the originating institution. And it is argued that similar mechanisms are also possible in the swaps market.

Regulation. As might be expected, the divisions evident in the preceding issues are also evident when it comes to questions concerning appropriate regulation of this market. One group argues that additional contractual guarantees are necessary if abuses in this market are to be avoided. Hence, in this view, regulation should take the form of codifying the contractual guarantees — for example, requiring that the contracts be marked to market or collateralized. Those taking the opposite position argue that this market is an simply an extension of credit markets and that imposing liability on the financial intermediary is the best way to limit potential abuses.

Besides this controversy over how to regulate, there is also the issue of who should regulate swaps. There are differences in regulatory bodies across countries, and also multiple regulatory bodies within the same country, that need to be considered. (For example, in the United States, the interested regulatory authorities include the Federal Reserve, the SEC, and the Financial Accounting Standards Board.) Under such circumstances, effective regulation will be difficult if not impossible because it requires coordination both within and among countries. If the US, for example, decided to place burdensome regulations on swaps, the principal effect on swap activity would be to change the location of swap transactions. Even if a group of the major countries acted in concert, the economic incentives for swaps discussed earlier suggest that there would be strong motive for some country to supply a favorable legal environment.

The future of the swaps market, then, appears to turn on whether that market moves further in the direction of becoming a widely-traded exchange. While we are not comfortable in predicting the direction the market will actually take, we are confident that the future composition of this market, both the users and the intermediaries, will depend

While the market will continue to develop a more homogeneous set of products with greater liquidity, there will continue to exist a subset of swaps which are custom-tailored.

strongly on the resolution of the above uncertainty. If swaps move further toward exchange trading, investment banks will be the major beneficiary. Removing the liability for the intermediary by marking to market or collateralizing would diminish the emphasis on capital commitment; and if so, investment banks might well regain the dominance they enjoyed in the earliest stages in the evolution of this market. On the other hand, if the intermediary continues to bear risk (or if the liability for the intermediary is increased), commercial banks will be the beneficiary.

The degree to which the swap market moves toward exchange trading will also determine the users of this market. With credit risk borne by the intermediaries, entry to the swaps market may well be denied to lesser credits. Hence, the predominant users of swaps will be the best credit risks. If the swaps market moves toward exchange trading, however, this composition will change. Lesser credit risks will

be able to enter the swap market. Furthermore, to the extent that collateralization or some other form of bonding raises the cost of a swap transaction, the best credits will be expected to exit the market, refusing to pay the implicit insurance premium.

Because of the considerable dispute about the appropriateness of moving further toward exchange trading, there is no consensus about the future form of the swaps market. But there are issues where a consensus is possible. Most observers agree, for example, that while the market will continue to develop a more homogeneous set of products with greater liquidity, there will continue to exist a subset of swaps which are custom-tailored. The commercial banks should dominate in the homogeneous swaps market, which will be characterized by high volume, low spreads, and a significant capital commitment. Investment banks should continue to have a comparative advantage in the customized end of the market.

FORWARD SWAPS, SWAP OPTIONS, AND THE MANAGEMENT OF CALLABLE DEBT

by Keith C. Brown,
University of Texas at Austin and
Donald J. Smith, Boston University

C ompanies issuing intermediate- to long-term fixed-rate bonds generally choose to attach call provisions to those issues. Such a call provision gives management the *option* to buy back the bonds (usually at a slight premium over par) after a specified period of "call protection." After the call protection period, if interest rates have fallen below the rate on the outstanding issue, management can reduce its cost of funds by calling and refunding the issue with lower-cost debt.[1]

A good deal of academic work has been devoted to the problem of when a corporation should call its outstanding bond issues. The consensus to date is that it is optimal to exercise the refinancing option as soon as the bond trades in the market at a price sufficiently greater than its contractual call price to cover the transactions costs of refunding.[2] This decision rule and the supporting analysis are based, of course, on the assumption that it is possible to call the bond whenever it is advantageous to the issuer—that is, the bond is no longer "call-protected."

The problem this paper addresses is somewhat different: What if interest rates have fallen significantly since the bond was originally placed, but the call provision cannot be exercised for several more years?

A callable bond that is still in its deferment, or protection, period contains what amounts to a European-style, but unmarketable option. It is like a European option, which cannot be exercised until maturity, in the sense that its exercise must be deferred to a future "call" date. Further, since it is attached to the underlying bond, it cannot be sold directly as a separate instrument.

The option's current value to the issuer—that is, the value of the option if exercised today—is roughly equivalent to the difference between the price of the callable bond and the price of the same issue if it were noncallable. Alternatively, the intrinsic value of the option can be thought of as the present value of the cost savings that management could achieve by retiring the issue at the date of first call and then issuing a (noncallable) fixed-rate issue at today's lower interest rates.[3]

As the holder of this surrogate call option on interest rates, management has three choices: (1) it can wait until the protection period ends, thus risking future increases in rates (which would reduce the current value of the call option) while benefiting from further declines; (2) it can take steps to preserve the value of the option until it can be exercised by hedging against future increases in rates; or (3) it can attempt to find a way to effectively "sell" the option to a third party.

Taking the first approach, management can capture part of the value of the call feature immediately by refunding the entire outstanding debt

---

1. Financial theorists have argued that, in a capital market free from "imperfections," the inclusion of such covenants would be a matter of indifference to issuers. That is, in a world without taxes, transaction costs, and informational "asymmetries," the cost of the call to issuers in the form of higher interest rates required by bond market investors should equal the expected benefits.

However, several recent studies have presented cogent explanations for the pervasiveness of callable bonds based on the tax and informational asymmetries that exist between the firm's various agents and investors. See, for instance, Z. Bodie and B. Taggart, "Future Investment Opportunities and the Value of the Call Provision on a Bond," *Journal of Finance* 33 (September 1978), pp. 1187-1200, A. Barnea, R. Haugen and L. Senbet, "A Rationale for Debt Maturity Structure and Call Provisions in the Agency Theory Framework," *Journal of Finance* 35 (December 1980), pp. 1223-1234 and I. Brick and B. Wallingford, "The Relative Tax Benefits of Alternative Call Features in Corporate Debt," *Journal of Financial and Quantitative Analysis* 20 (March 1985), pp. 95-105.

2. On this point, see A. Kraus, "The Bond Refunding Decision in an Efficient Market," *Journal of Financial and Quantitative Analysis* 8 (December 1973), pp. 793-806. For a less technical version of the same, see "The Corporate Refunding Decision," *Midland Corporate Finance Journal* (Stern Stewart & Co., publisher), Vol. 1 No. 1 (Spring 1983).

3. Assuming a common coupon rate and maturity date.

through a tender offer or open market repurchase program while issuing new noncallable bonds as replacements. There are, however, major uncertainties in implementing such a bond repurchase program. In the case of a tender offer, management fixes the repurchase price (typically at a significant premium over market), but has no direct control over the quantity of bonds that are actually tendered.[4] With a direct market repurchase, by contrast, management faces considerable uncertainty about the average price necessary to buy back the outstanding bonds, especially in the case of large debt issues. Moreover, to the extent management is forced to pay a price above the call premium, such buyback strategies effectively give away much of the current option value—which derives from the firm's right to retire the debt at a fixed price over par.[5]

Over the last few years, investment and commercial banks have promoted the use of interest rate swaps with delayed starting dates (or "forward swaps") and options on swaps ("swaptions") as ways of reducing the uncertainty attending the above refunding strategies. As a number of scholars have pointed out, an interest rate swap is essentially a series of over-the-counter forward contracts, wherein two counterparties agree to exchange fixed for floating payments based on a notional principal amount.[6] Because of their forward-like structure, swaps are ideal vehicles for hedging "symmetric" interest rate risks—for example, situations in which an increase in rates leads to a proportionate decrease in the value of the asset and vice versa. Companies seeking to realize the current value of their embedded call options, presumably to protect against rises in market rates between now and the call date, can use either a forward swap or a swap option in a hedging scheme similar to those using exchange-traded futures and options on futures.

The key difference between the use of swaps and exchange-traded instruments in call management is that swaps are flexible, negotiated contracts that can be tailored by a market-maker to match the dates and amount of the targeted call provision. That flexibility can be used to improve the hedge by reducing its basis risk. Further, it allows callable debt

management strategies for deferment periods extending beyond the relatively short delivery dates of available futures contracts. In sum, the swap-based hedging techniques described in this paper represent advances over both traditional capital market refunding strategies and the use of exchange-traded financial futures and options.

FORWARD SWAPS AND CALLABLE DEBT

Forward swaps can be used to manage callable debt in two different ways. First, management can preserve the value of an (in-the-money) option to call its own debt by entering into an "on-market" forward swap—that is, a delayed-start swap agreement at the prevailing market (forward) swap rate set to begin at the date of first call. This would effectively "lock in" the current level of interest rates until the call exercise date. Alternatively, it can choose a forward swap rate different from the current rate (thus creating an "off-market" forward swap) and thereby capture immediately (or "monetize") the present value of the bond's call option.

Preserving the Value of the Call With an On-Market Forward Swap

Let us start by assuming that if rates have fallen significantly since a callable bond was originally issued, management would choose to sell the call option (thereby locking in current rates) if it could indeed be separated from the host bond. The problem arises from the fact that the embedded call cannot be separated and sold as such.

This is a classic hedging problem: rates could rise or fall by more than is generally expected during the time until the call date. If rates rise, the call option loses value; if rates fall, the call gains value. Management's concern is that interest rates might rise prior to the call date, reducing or even wiping out the value of the option. If management is uncomfortable with the uncertainty of these outcomes, a negatively correlated position in another instrument can be acquired to serve as a hedge. The objective

4. Bond tender offers are, on average, only 76% successful at obtaining the desired number of outstanding instruments. See J. Finnerty, A. Kalotay and F. Farrell, *Evaluating Bond Refunding Opportunities*, Hagerstown: Ballinger Publishing (1988).

5. Note that exercising an option that could be sold on the market captures only the "intrinsic value" and forgoes the remaining "time value." This approach can lead to a deadweight loss in the option's value due to the extinguishment of

the benefits associated with potential exercise features. See M. Livingston, "Measuring the Benefit of a Bond Refunding: The Problem of Non Marketable Call Options," *Financial Management* 16 (Spring 1987), pp. 38-40.

6. For a background discussion on the swap market, see C. Smith, C. Smithson and L. Wakeman, "The Evolving Market for Swaps," *Midland Corporate Finance Journal* Vol. 3 No. 4 (Winter 1985).

THE DESIGN FLEXIBILITY AND EASE OF OPERATIONAL MANAGEMENT OF
INTEREST RATE SWAP CONTRACTS CAN ALSO BE USED TO REDUCE THE
BASIS RISK IN THE HEDGING STRATEGY THAT OFTEN ATTENDS THE USE OF
FINANCIAL FUTURES.

EXHIBIT 1
MARKER EVENTS IN THE
CALL MANAGEMENT
PROBLEM

Years			
0	2	4	7
Original Issue Date	Current Date	Call Date	Maturity Date

of the hedge is to smooth the range of future payoffs, if not indeed to "lock in" the future value of the asset. (It should be noted, however, that one can only hedge against unexpected changes because the forward rates used in hedging already reflect market expectations.)

The most obvious means of hedging the interest rate risk is to take a short position in a financial futures contract. The short position would gain when interest rates rise and thus futures prices fall. An alternative would be to buy a put option on the futures contract. The put option, which upon exercise allows the holder to acquire a short position in the futures contract at the strike price, would also appreciate in value as rates rise.

The problem with exchange-traded futures and futures options, however, is often the absence of a suitable contract. The call date on the bond can be several years away, but liquidity in the futures market (and indeed the availability of the futures option) usually is limited to the nearest delivery months. Also, futures contracts require frequent managerial attention to deal with the margin account and daily mark-to-market valuation and settlement.

Forward interest rate swaps, by contrast, are over-the-counter, directly negotiated instruments that represent the hedging equivalent of financial futures contracts. In particular, as we shall demonstrate later, a "pay-fixed" forward swap is functionally equivalent to a short position in futures in terms of reducing the interest rate risk in the future value of the call option. Moreover, the design flexibility and ease of operational management of interest rate swap contracts can also be used to reduce the basis risk in the hedging strategy that often attends the use of financial futures.

A Simple Case. A numerical example will be useful to illustrate the use of forward swaps to preserve the call rate. Suppose that two years ago a corporation issued $100 million in seven-year 12% coupon bonds at par value. Assume also that the bonds pay coupons semi-annually, the issue was originally callable at par in four years, and two years remain in the call protection period. (See Exhibit 1.)

Now suppose that an on-market, $100 million notional principal forward swap is available such that the corporation could pay 10.25% and receive six-month LIBOR for three years, starting two years from now. This forward swap is simply a deferred-start transaction. The deferral period corresponds to (and is set to equal) the time remaining in the call protection period; and the maturity (or "tenor") of the swap corresponds to the remaining maturity on the underlying bonds as of the call date. There is no initial cash settlement on the transaction, hence the term "on-market" swap. (As we will discuss later, an "off-market" swap would require an initial payment from one counterparty to another.)

This on-market forward swap agreement will appreciate in value if interest rates rise over the next two years by more than had been generally expected (as reflected in the forward swap rate). The gain on the swap, like that on a comparable short position in interest rate futures, would offset the decline in the value of the call option. Unlike the use of futures, however, the timing of the forward swap can be set to match exactly the call and maturity dates—an outcome that would only occur by coincidence with standardized, exchange-traded futures.

Pricing Forward Swaps. The fixed rates on forward swaps are determined by the rates available in the current swap spot market—that is, for swaps that begin at once. Suppose that a company could simultaneously enter a five-year, pay-fixed swap at 9.75% and a two-year, receive-fixed swap at 9.00%, both versus six-month LIBOR. As illustrated in Exhibit 2, that combination of swaps effectively constructs a three-year, pay-fixed (since the initial LIBOR flows cancel) swap that is deferred for two years. Unless the two-year and five-year fixed rates are identical (which is highly unlikely), there will be a remaining fixed rate payment or receipt during the initial "stub" period.

Pricing the forward swap, then, is basically an exercise in the time value of money. The problem is to transfer the first four cash payments forward in time and spread them evenly amongst the latter six. In practice this is done using implied forward rates

EXHIBIT 2
PRICING AN ON-MARKET
FORWARD SWAP

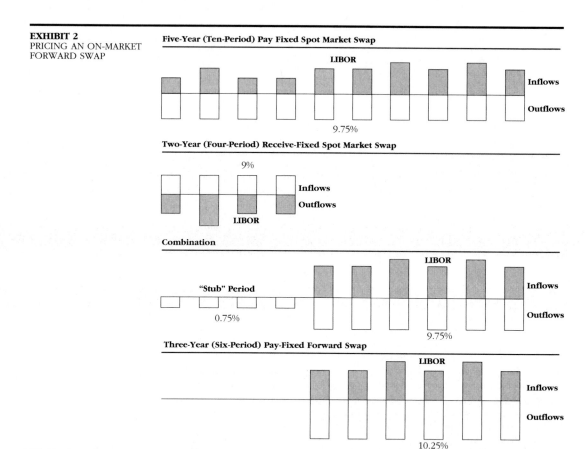

Five-Year (Ten-Period) Pay Fixed Spot Market Swap

LIBOR

Inflows

Outflows

9.75%

Two-Year (Four-Period) Receive-Fixed Spot Market Swap

9%

Inflows

Outflows

LIBOR

Combination

"Stub" Period

LIBOR

Inflows

Outflows

0.75%

9.75%

Three-Year (Six-Period) Pay-Fixed Forward Swap

LIBOR

Inflows

Outflows

10.25%

derived from a zero-coupon swap yield curve. Here, and in the continuation of this example that follows, we simply assume that the result of that exercise is a forward swap fixed rate of 10.25%.

The effectiveness, and inherent risks, of this forward swap hedging strategy can be demonstrated by considering the various decisions that must be made at the call date in two years. First, management must decide whether to call the underlying debt. It is reasonable to assume that it will do so only if the fixed-rate cost of funds for the remaining three years turns out to be lower than 12%. Second, if the debt is called, management must decide if it will refinance with fixed- or floating-rate debt. Third, it must decide if it will retain the swap or close it out by entering into an offsetting, receive-fixed swap. If management wants to continue with fixed-rate funding, then

the second and third decisions are not independent: If the swap is closed out, the firm can just issue fixed-rate notes; but if the swap is retained, management will have to issue LIBOR-based floating-rate debt to obtain a net fixed-rate cost of funds.

A Digression on The Relationship between Swap and Bond Spreads. At this point it is necessary to introduce some notation to describe the relevant market rates prevailing at the call date in two years. Following market conventions, we decompose all fixed rates into the Treasury yield (T) for a comparable maturity (in this case, three years) and a spread over that Treasury yield. For example, the three-year fixed-rate cost of funds is denoted T + BS, where BS stands for "bond (market) spread." In a similar fashion, the fixed rate on a three-year swap (versus six-month LIBOR) is denoted T + SS, where

EXHIBIT 3
CALL VALUE PRESERVATION
USING AN ON-MARKET
FORWARD SWAP

	Treasury Yield (T)			
	9%	10%	11%	12%
Refunding Fixed Rate (T + BS)	9.75%	10.75%	11.75%	12.75%
Decision	Call	Call	Call	Not Call
Value of the Call Option	$1,125,000	$625,000	$125,000	0
Swap Fixed Rate (T + SS)	9.50%	10.50%	11.50%	12.50%
Gain on the Forward Swap	− $375,000	$125,000	$625,000	$1,125,000
Total Gain	$750,000	$750,000	$750,000	$1,125,000
Present Value	$3,822,034	$3,761,539	$3,702,522	$5,467,406

Numerical Example Assuming BS = 0.75%, CS = 0.25%, and SS = 0.50%
Value of the Call Option (as an Annuity) = (12% − Refunding Fixed Rate) × (1/2) × $100 Million,
Gain on the Forward Swap (as an Annuity) = (Swap Fixed Rate − 10.25%) × (1/2) × $100 Million
Total Gain = Value of the Call Option plus the Gain on the Forward Swap
Present Value (as of the Call Date) of the Total Gain per Semi-Annual Period for Six Remaining Semi-Annual Periods, Discounted at the Refunding Fixed Rate

SS means "swap (market) spread." The reset rate for a three-year floating rate note is LIBOR + CS, where CS stands for "credit (market) spread."[7]

When the swap market is "in equilibrium," the general relationship between these three spreads is that SS = BS − CS—that is, the swap spread equals the bond spread minus the credit spread. We assume that the corporation at the call date in two years can either issue fixed-rate debt at T + BS or floating-rate debt at LIBOR + CS. Then suppose that it issues fixed-rate debt and also enters a swap agreement to receive a fixed rate of T + SS and to pay LIBOR. Its net "synthetic" floating-rate cost of funds would be LIBOR + (BS − SS) since the fixed Treasury yield (T) cancels out. In equilibrium, that floating rate should equal the explicit floating rate of LIBOR + CS; and simple algebra tells us that BS − SS = CS.[8]

The Effectiveness of Forward Swaps as a Hedge. Exhibit 3 shows the results of the forward swap hedge assuming four different interest rate outcomes. On the call date, Treasury yields are allowed to range from 9% to 12% (while bond credit and swap spreads are assumed to remain fixed, and in equilibrium, at BS = 0.75%, CS = 0.25%, and SS = 0.50%).

For example, if the three-year Treasury yield turns out to be 10% at the time of the call date, the corporation is assumed (1) to call and refund its 12% debt with a three-year fixed-rate note at 10.75% and (2) to close out its pay-fixed 10.25% forward swap by entering into a three-year receive-fixed swap at 10.50%. As shown in Exhibit 3 (third row, second column), the value of exercising the call option expressed as a six-period (three-year) annuity turns

---

7. BS and CS represent the issuing corporation's marginal risk relative to the Treasury yield and LIBOR in the fixed- and floating-rate markets, respectively. Those spreads depend largely on default risk, but also reflect any differing degrees of marketability, taxation, and so forth. Note that there is no particular reason for BS to equal CS since the former is expressed relative to risk-free Treasuries and the latter to "bank-risk," or LIBOR.

8. This discussion abstracts from the bid-ask spread on swaps in practice. Since the swap market-maker, typically a commercial or investment bank, will need to cover the credit risk inherent in the transaction as well as other hedging and regulatory (e.g., capital adequacy) costs, it will always quote a higher receive-fixed rate than its pay-fixed rate. The bid-ask spread has narrowed markedly in recent years as testimony to the competitiveness of the swap market and now ranges between 4-10 basis points.

out to be $625,000 per period (or [12.00% − 10.75%] × 1/2 × $100 million). The value of the forward swap hedge is also positive because management is able to close out the 10.25% pay-fixed forward swap with a 10.50% receive-fixed swap; and the per period savings are $125,000 per period ([10.50% − 10.25%] × 1/2 × $100 million) for the six remaining semi-annual periods. The sum of the two sources of gain, the call and the hedge, is an annuity of $750,000. The present value of that annuity, as of the call date, is $3,761,539, calculated using the 10.75% fixed rate cost of funds as the discounting factor.

The salient features of the call rate preservation strategy are apparent in this simulation exercise. As shown in Exhibit 3, the payoffs on closing out the pay-fixed forward swap are negatively correlated with the value of the call option. For the given values of BS, CS, and SS, the strategy "locks in" the future gain for varying levels of market rates. (Actually, the "locked in" value is a nominal annuity, the present value of which depends on the level of the rate used for discounting.) Notice, however, that although the net gain is constant when it is optimal to call the existing debt (that is, when the refunding rate is less than the existing rate), the gains rise when it is not optimal to call (i.e., when rates rise above 12%). This means that the forward swap strategy, in effect, "overhedges" the risk.

This "overhedging" arises from the use of a symmetric-payoff instrument like a futures contract or swap agreement to hedge an "asymmetric" or one-sided risk exposure. This asymmetric exposure in turn arises from the fact that management's option to call its bond has a minimum value of zero. (Remember that the issuer effectively paid for the call right in the form of a higher interest rate when it issued the bonds.) If the refunding rate exceeds 12%, the call option value falls to zero but is never negative; but the value of the forward swap hedge continues to rise proportionately with increases in rates above 12%.

If management wanted to eliminate (or at least minimize) this overhedging effect, then it would have to substitute the use of an asymmetric (or option-like) hedging instrument to offset its one-sided exposure. As we will show later in this paper, call monetization strategies using swap options instead of swaps can be used to accomplish this end.

The Problem of Basis Risk. The forward swap hedge, as illustrated in Exhibit 3, immunizes the corporation against changes in future Treasury yields. But, it is important to recognize that the amount of the future gain—and thus the effectiveness of the hedge—depends on the corporation's future refunding rates. Specifically, it depends on the firm-specific risk spreads represented by BS and CS, as well as on the swap spread SS.

Suppose that the credit standing of the corporation deteriorates at the time of the call date, such that BS rises to 0.95% while SS remains at 0.50%. The value of the call option falls for any level of T, while the payoff on closing out the swap hedge is unchanged. This shift in the bond spread relative to the swap spread lowers the net gain either as a future annuity or as a present value.

This type of basis risk is common in hedging programs. In effect, such hedging programs reduce general market interest rate risk while continuing to bear some spread risk. The assumption underlying these strategies is that the variance in the spread over Treasuries will be much less than the variance in the Treasury yield itself. Nevertheless it should be clear that the hedge does entail risk. As a worst-case scenario, suppose that the combined Treasury yield and swap spread remain less than 10.25%, and thus the forward swap can only be closed out at a loss, while the bond spread rises such that the call option value falls to zero. The corporation would be worse off for having hedged than not.

To assess the level of basis risk, it is instructive to break the annuity gain of $750,000 per period in our example into two components: a non-random part that depends on the existing coupon rate vis-a-vis the forward swap rate, and a random part that depends on the bond and swap spreads at the future call date. The first part is $875,000 per period, calculated as (12% − 10.25%) × 1/2 × $100 million. That amount is known with certainty at the current date when the hedging strategy is undertaken since both rates are observable. The second part, in general, is (SS − BS) × 1/2 × $100 million. In Exhibit 3, where it is assumed that SS = 0.50% and BS = 0.75%, this second amount is −$125,000 per period. Adding the two gives the annuity gain of $750,000. The key point here is that (SS − BS), the difference between the swap and bond market spreads over Treasuries, is the source of basis risk in the hedging program. (In a later section, we will examine some empirical evidence attesting to the size and variance of these spreads.)

Basis Risk Also Affects The Call Decision. Up to this point, we have assumed that when the call

EXHIBIT 4
PRICING AN OFF-MARKET
FORWARD SWAP

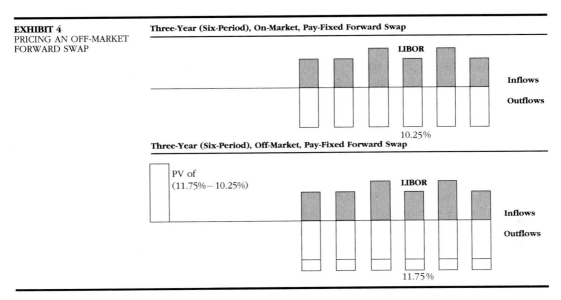

Three-Year (Six-Period), On-Market, Pay-Fixed Forward Swap

LIBOR

Inflows

Outflows

10.25%

Three-Year (Six-Period), Off-Market, Pay-Fixed Forward Swap

PV of
(11.75% − 10.25%)

LIBOR

Inflows

Outflows

11.75%

date arrives, the decision whether to call or not is made simply by comparing the current three-year fixed rate to the existing coupon rate; that is, if T + BS is less than 12%, management calls the bonds. Management also, however, has two other alternatives. It can call the debt and refund in the floating-rate market at LIBOR + CS and retain the swap to pay 10.25% and receive LIBOR. That alternative yields a net fixed-rate cost of funds of 10.25% + CS (since the LIBOR-based cash flows cancel). Or, it can choose not to call, maintain the 12% debt and close out the swap. That entails receiving T + SS while paying 10.25%; and the net cost of funds would be 12% + [10.25% − (T + SS)].

Given this analysis, the decision to call or not depends on a comparison of 10.25% + CS to 12% + [10.25% − (T + SS)]. Simplifying that comparison, the decision rule becomes to call if T + SS + CS is less than 12%. If swap markets are in equilibrium (and thus BS = SS + CS), then the two decision rules—one based on the fixed spread and one on the floating-plus-swap spread—will yield identical call decisions. If swap markets are not in equilibrium, then the two rules could produce conflicting decisions.

The importance of this last result is that there can be circumstances when a corporation appears to be making a sub-optimal call decision if only the fixed-rate cost of funds is observable. For instance, suppose that T = 11.30%, BS = 0.75%, CS = 0.20%,

and SS = 0.40% on the call date. The fixed-rate refunding alternative of 12.05% would indicate that the call option has a value of zero and that calling the debt would be irrational. At the same time, however, the (likely short-lived) disequilibrium in the swap market would allow the firm to call the debt, refund at LIBOR + 0.20%, and pay 10.25% on the forward swap, obtaining a net fixed rate of 10.45%. That strategy generates a six-period annuity gain of $775,000 per period, whereas not calling the debt and simply closing out the swap by agreeing to receive the current swap fixed rate of 11.70% against the payments of 10.25% generates an annuity gain of only $725,000. Naturally, in an efficient capital market one would not expect disequilibrium conditions like this to persist.

In summary, the future value of the firm's embedded call option depends on future interest rates. That risk exposure can be hedged in principle by short positions in financial futures contracts or by the use of pay-fixed forward swaps. While the forward swap can lock in some of the current value of the call option—although only the amount that reflects the generally expected level of future rates—there is still basis risk. In this context, the basis risk is represented by the relationship between the (fixed-rate) bond spread, the (floating-rate) credit spread, and the swap market spread. Unexpected changes in those spreads can reduce the effectiveness of the hedge.

EXHIBIT 5
CALL MONETIZATION USING
AN OFF-MARKET FORWARD
SWAP

	Treasury Yield (T)			
	9%	**10%**	**11%**	**12%**
Refunding Fixed Rate (T + BS)	9.75%	10.75%	11.75%	12.75%
Decision	Call	Call	Call	Not Call
Value of the Call Option	$1,125,000	$625,000	$125,000	0
Swap Fixed Rate (T + SS)	9.50%	10.50%	11.50%	12.50%
Gain on the Forward Swap	− $1,125,000	− $625,000	− $125,000	$375,000
Total Gain	0	0	0	$375,000
Present Value	0	0	0	$1,822,469

Numerical Example Assuming BS = 0.75%, CS = 0.25%, and SS = 0.50%
Value of the Call Option (as an Annuity) = (12% − Refunding Fixed Rate) × ($1/2$) × $100 Million,
Gain on the Forward Swap (as an Annuity) = (Swap Fixed Rate − 11.75%) × ($1/2$) × $100 Million
Total Gain = Value of the Call Option plus the Gain on the Forward Swap
Present Value (as of the Call Date) of the Total Gain per Semi-Annual Period for Six Remaining Semi-Annual Periods, Discounted at the Refunding Fixed Rate

Monetizing the Call Value with an Off-Market Forward Swap

The use of an on-market, pay-fixed forward swap effectively locks in the future value of the call option, subject to the basis risk mentioned above. That future value, as we have seen, is an annuity that reflects the difference between the existing coupon rate and the forward swap rate multiplied by the principal. For instance, in Exhibit 3, the annuity (or semi-annuity) is a cost savings of $750,000 per period for six remaining semi-annual periods.

Call monetization, by contrast, refers to strategies that transform this deferred annuity into a single current cash payment that is equal to the present value of the series of payments. To return to our earlier example, management could monetize the value of the call by entering into a pay-fixed forward swap at 11.75% for three years instead of using the on-market

forward swap with a fixed rate of 10.25%. Of course, the corporation would be willing to pay the higher fixed rate only if it receives something in return—in fact, an immediate payment for the present value of the annuity represented by the difference between the rates. That annuity is $750,000 ([11.75% − 10.25%] × 1/2 × $100 million) for six semi-annual periods.

The actual amount of cash that the corporation will receive upon agreeing to the off-market forward swap will depend on the discount factors used to calculate the present value. Typically, a commercial bank is the counterparty to these swaps. The bank should view this off-market transaction as a combination of an on-market forward swap and a loan agreement. The on-market swap calls for no immediate exchange of cash; however, the bank is effectively lending the corporation a specific amount now and later expects to be repaid in six installments of $750,000. Based on this reasoning, the appropriate

---

9. Notice that if the corporation enters an off-market forward swap to pay fixed at less than 10.25%, it would effectively be making a deposit to the bank. Then, the bank's lower deposit rates would be used for discounting, thereby raising the amount of the requisite immediate payment.

discount factors are the bank's lending rate for zero-coupon transactions ("bullet" loans) maturing in 2 1/2 to 5 years (See Exhibit 4).[9]

The Effectiveness of an Off-Market Forward Hedge. The implications of hedging the call value with an off-market, forward swap are apparent in Exhibit 5 (which, like Exhibit 3, also assumes BS = 0.75%, CS = 0.25%, and SS = 0.50%, and T ranging from 9% to 12%). The structure by design has transferred the future gain of $750,000 per period to the current date. In cases when it would be optimal to call the debt (for example, when Treasury yields turn out to be 9, 10, or 11%), the value of the call option is completely offset by the loss on the forward swap. If rates rise to 12% or higher (and thus the call option's value falls to zero), there is a gain on the forward swap, thus leading to the same asymmetric outcome associated with the use of on-market swaps. As explained earlier, this overhedging phenomenon arises from the use of forward-based instruments with symmetric payoffs to hedge one-sided risks.

This strategy also contains the same basis risk that attends the use of on-market forward swaps: namely, that which results from possible changes in the relationship between the swap spread and the bond spread (SS − BS). The future annuity gain would be reduced for any level of T, and even could be negative, if BS turns out to be higher than 0.75% or SS lower than 0.50%.

For example, assume that on the current date the expected future values for BS, CS, and SS are 0.75%, 0.25%, and 0.50%, as in Exhibits 3 and 5. These expectations would likely be based on current spreads and the assumption of swap market equilibrium. In this case, the off-market forward swap rate of 11.75% is simply the one that makes the expected annuity gain zero (at least, over that range of interest rates when the call would be exercised). The corporation could have chosen any number of other forward rates—12%, for instance, to match the existing coupon rate.

In short, the choice of a different forward rate merely transfers the certain portion of the annuity gain from a future value to a present value, but it does not remove the basis risk.

SWAP OPTIONS AND CALLABLE DEBT[10]

Another way of monetizing the current value of the bond's embedded call option is through the use of swap options (also known as "swaptions"). In contrast to hedges with off-market forward swaps, the use of swaptions has the advantage of reducing the overhedging problem that affects forward swap-based hedging schemes. But these benefits are also accompanied by one new drawback: because the strategy requires the callable debt issuer to sell a swap option, the swaption holder must decide when to exercise the option, thereby introducing—as we shall see—another dimension of risk into the problem.

Because the market for options on swaps is not as well developed as the swap market itself, it might be helpful to begin this section with a brief description of the product. Broadly speaking, in exchange for a front-end premium, the holder of a swap option has the right, but not the obligation, to enter into a swap on or before a specific exercise date. The agreement also specifies which counterparty pays the fixed rate. By convention, the holder of the right to enter into a pay-fixed swap is said to own a call option; and the holder of the right to enter a receive-fixed swap is said to have a put. Finally, the swaption contract also designates the amount of notional principal, the level of the fixed rate (i.e., strike rate) and the particular index used to represent the floating rate (e.g., six-month LIBOR).

To extend the example of the previous section, assume once again that the firm holds an option to call its original $100 million of 12% debt and that it would like to convert this asset into cash today. But, because the call feature is attached to the bond, it cannot be sold separately nor can it be exercised for another two years. What can be sold today is an option on a swap market transaction.

Monetizing the bond option in this context involves selling a swap option having terms set as closely as possible to those of the original debt issue. Specifically, the firm would sell a put option (i.e., the right to receive the fixed rate) on a three-year swap, exercisable in two years with a strike rate of 12% and notional principal of $100 million. In this case, the two-year expiration date on the swaption matches that on the bond option while the three-year swap tenor matches the difference between the bond's call date and its maturity.

Like the off-market forward swap strategy discussed earlier, the sale of a swap option converts the benefits of the call into an immediate receipt of cash.

---

10. The discussion in this section is an expanded version of a portion of our article "The Swap-Driven Deal," *Intermarket* 6 (March 1989), pp. 15-19.

EXHIBIT 6
SEMI-ANNUAL FUNDING
COST WITH THE SWAP
OPTION-BASED CALL
MONETIZATION STRATEGY

Treasury Yield (T)	Bond Spread (BS)	Swap Spread (SS)		
		0.25%	0.50%	0.75%
10.5%	0.50%	$6,125,000	$6,000,000	$5,875,000
	0.75%	6,250,000	6,125,000	6,000,000
	1.00%	6,375,000	6,250,000	6,125,000
11.0%	0.50%	$6,125,000	$6,000,000	$5,875,000
	0.75%	6,250,000	6,125,000	6,000,000
	1.00%	6,375,000	6,250,000	6,125,000
11.5%	0.50%	$6,125,000	$6,000,000	$6,000,000
	0.75%	6,125,000	6,000,000	6,000,000
	1.00%	6,125,000	6,000,000	6,000,000
12.%	0.50%	$6,000,000	$6,000,000	$6,000,000
	0.75%	6,000,000	6,000,000	6,000,000
	1.00%	6,000,000	6,000,000	6,000,000

In this display, the funding cost is calculated as: **(Funding Rate)** $\times$ **(1/2)** $\times$ **($100 million)** where Funding Rate = Min[12%, (T + BS)] + Max[0, 12% − (T + SS)].
Decisions: (i) Call option on bond is exercised if (T + BS) < 12%, (ii) Swap option is exercised if (T + SS) < 12%.

The swap option strategy, however, is complicated by an unknown that does not present itself with the forward swap hedge. In the case of the swaption hedge, when the call date arrives two years later, there are two decisions to be made (or two options that can be exercised) by two different parties: (1) management may decide to call and refinance its original debt; and (2) the swap option holder must decide at that point whether to enter into a receive-fixed swap on the designated terms.

The complicating factor is not the presence of two separate parties in the decision process, but rather the fact that their decisions will be based on movements in two different interest rates. As in the case of forward swaps, the firm's decision to refund at the call date will be determined by the prevailing level for three-year fixed-rate debt in relation to the 12% coupon it is currently paying. On the same call date, the swaption holder will evaluate the economic merits of entering into a three-year swap to receive the fixed rate of 12% based on the prevailing three-year swap rate.

Generally speaking (that is, if interest rates are the only factor), a firm that has chosen to monetize its debt option through the sale of a swaption faces four different possible outcomes:

1. The bond is called if (T + BS) < 12%
   The swap option is exercised if (T + SS) < 12%,
2. The bond is called if (T + BS) < 12%
   The swap option is not exercised if (T + SS) ≥ 12%,
3. The bond is not called if (T + BS) ≥ 12%
   The swap option is exercised if (T + SS) < 12%,
4. The bond is not called if (T + BS) ≥ 12%
   The swap option is not exercised if (T + SS) ≥ 12%.

Whether the options are exercised either independently or simultaneously depends once again on the relationship between BS and SS. Thus, as with the forward swap-based alternative, the basis risk between the bond and swap market yields becomes an important factor.

The Effectiveness of the Hedge Using Swaptions. In Exhibit 6, we have calculated the semi-annual funding cost to the firm employing this swap option-based monetization strategy under several representative interest rate outcomes. For purposes of this analysis, we also assume that if management chooses to call its original debt, it will issue new three-year fixed-rate debt having a coupon rate of (T + BS). Also, if the swap option holder chooses to exercise its contract, the firm—which would then be forced into paying a 12% fixed swap rate in exchange for LIBOR—will counterbalance its position with an offsetting receive-fixed swap at (T + SS).[11]

11. Under these assumptions, the post-call date funding cost can be expressed in an annual percentage rate as follows: Min[12%, (T + BS)] + Max[0, 12% − (T + SS)].

EXHIBIT 7
PAYOFF DIAGRAMS
ILLUSTRATING THE
RELATIONSHIP BETWEEN
FORWARD SWAPS AND
SWAP OPTIONS

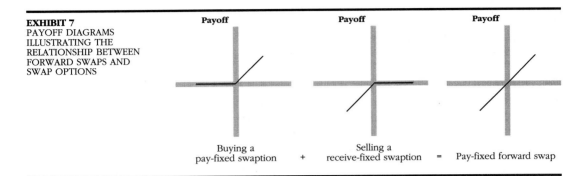

The most intriguing thing about the display is that it indicates that the firm's funding cost could be either higher, lower, or the same as its present expense depending on the relationship between the credit spreads in the swap and bond markets. More precisely, notice that the semi-annual funding cost will remain at its current level of $6 million if the prevailing rates in both markets exceed 12% at the call date. In this case, neither option will be exercised and so the firm simply will continue to repay its original debt issue. Alternatively, notice that even when (T + BS) and (T + SS) are both below 12%—implying that both options will be exercised—the funding cost will still be $6 million *as long as the swap and bond spreads are equal.*

On the other hand, whenever SS < BS, the funding cost to the firm will increase any time it is optimal to exercise the swap option (i.e., when (T + SS < 12%). And, as we have suggested, it can be profitable to exercise the swap option even when it doesn't make sense to refund the bond. Conversely, if BS < SS, the funding cost may be reduced below the $6 million level. The important point here, once again, is that while the sale of the swaption can provide a hedge against general movements in Treasury yields, it does not protect the firm against changes in the relationship between BS and SS.

Management may be justified in having some confidence in the stability of the spread differential, in which case its assessment of the amount of basis risk would be relatively low. For instance, in the preceding examples we assumed that the initial spreads were SS = 0.50% and BS = 0.75%. Without

reason to believe otherwise, the company might expect this differential of −0.25% to continue through the call date. In such a case, a conservative firm might actually set the strike rate on the swaption it sells 25 basis points lower (i.e., at 11.75%). This decision would result in a lower premium received, but reduce the firm's exposure to future changes in the spread differential.

Before leaving the subject of swaptions, it is instructive to compare the front-end premiums generated by the sale of swaptions to the cash payments accompanying the use of off-market forward swaps. By extending the well-known "put-call-futures" parity relationship, we can show that entering into the pay-fixed side of a three-year off-market swap two years forward at the rate of 11.75% is equivalent to the following transactions: (1) buying a pay-fixed option that can be exercised in two years on an 11.75% three-year swap; and (2) selling a receive-fixed option on the same swap.[12] (The pay-off diagrams illustrating put-call parity are shown in Exhibit 7.) Because both of these options carry the same strike rate, which is greater than the assumed on-market forward swap rate of 10.25%, only the latter option will be in-the-money upon issue.

What this exercise reveals is that the forward swap monetization strategy effectively requires the firm to purchase an out-of-the-money pay-fixed swap option that it does not really need to hedge changes in the value of its call provision. As demonstrated earlier, the off-market forward swap overhedges the firm's call option relative to the sale of a swaption. And, because the forward swap strategy involves the purchase of this

---

12. For a detailed discussion of the theoretical foundations for this result, see H. Stoll, "The Relationship Between Put and Call Option Prices," *Journal of Finance* 24 (December 1969), pp. 801-824 and E. Moriarty, S. Phillips and P. Tosini, "A Comparison of Options and Futures in the Management of Portfolio Risk," *Financial Analysts Journal* 37 (January/February 1981), pp. 61-67.

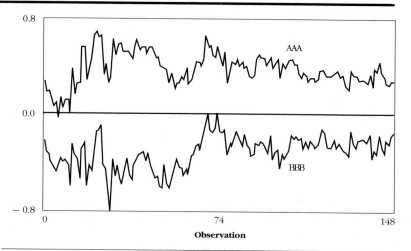

EXHIBIT 8
DIFFERENCES BETWEEN
SWAP AND BOND CREDIT
SPREADS (I.E., SS − BS)
FOR SEVEN-YEAR UTILITY
BONDS RATED AAA
AND BBB

In this display, Observations 1, 74 and 148 refer to the calendar dates January 10, 1986, June 5, 1987 and November 4, 1988, respectively.

unnecessary option, the premium the firm receives from the use of forward swaps must always be less than that generated by the sale of swaptions.

THE BASIS RISK IN SWAP-BASED STRATEGIES

In the previous sections, we have demonstrated that all of the swap-based approaches to callable debt management provide an explicit hedge against unanticipated movements in Treasury rates during the protection period. What we have also emphasized, however, is that the general level of interest rates is not the only factor determining the effectiveness of the hedging strategy. The difference between swap and bond credit spreads (i.e., SS − BS) at the call date—which, of course, is not known at the time the initial decision is made—will also play a significant role. This source of uncertainty, which we call basis risk, arises from the issuing firm's attempt to "sell" its debt option through a parallel transaction in the swap market.

To get a better sense of the extent to which this credit spread differential changes over time, we analyzed several different series of weekly swap and bond yields from Salomon Brothers' *Bond Market*

Roundup during the period spanning January 10, 1986 to November 4, 1988.[13] To calculate bond market spreads, we used the average yield-to-maturity (i.e., T + BS) on seven-year utility bond indices in two different Standard & Poor's credit rating classes: AAA and BBB. These data were then adjusted by subtracting the yield on seven-year Treasury bonds in order to isolate the bond credit spread component. Each of these adjusted series was then compared to weekly quotes of the fixed-rate credit spread (SS) for seven-year U.S. dollar interest rate swaps using three-month LIBOR as the floating rate. Exhibit 8 shows the resulting spread differential series for the 148 observations in the data set.

As the graph rather strikingly illustrates, the relationship between the swap and bond markets, as measured by (SS − BS), has not been stable over time. For the AAA and BBB rating classes, the range between the maximum and minimum values was 72 and 84 basis points, respectively. This represents a considerable degree of volatility considering that the historical bond yield differential between the two credit grades is typically only about 150 basis points.[14] Consequently, even if it is assumed that the credit rating of the firm doesn't change during the

---

13. We are indebted to Dave Hartzell for furnishing us with this data.
14. See J. Bicksler and A. Chen. "An Economic Analysis of Interest Rate Swaps." *Journal of Finance* 41 (July 1986), pp. 645-655.

call protection period, movements in this basis risk component can generate considerable uncertainty about the ultimate effectiveness of the hedge.

There is also another potential complication in that changes in the spread differential documented in Exhibit 8 appear to vary considerably across the two credit grades. (In fact, the correlation between the spread differentials for AAA-rated and for BBB-rated debt in this sample was only 0.258.) This means that if the credit quality of the firm should deteriorate after any of the swap-based management strategies are initiated, the degree of basis risk volatility at the beginning of the hedge will be an unreliable indication of what it can expect on the call date.

CONCLUDING COMMENTS

The events of the last several years have created a tremendous demand for new tools and strategies designed to manage a corporation's exposure to interest rate movements. Interest rate swaps are among the most prominent of the new products introduced by investment and commercial banks during the past decade. Although the ability of swaps to transform current cash flows has received a great deal of recent attention, little has been written about some of their more creative uses.

In this paper, we explain how interest rate swaps with delayed starting dates can be used to preserve the value of the call option built into a seasoned callable debt issue. We also demonstrate how such instruments offer protection against movements in the underlying term structure of Treasury rates. In so doing, however, they leave the firm exposed to potentially volatile movements in the risk premium differential between swap and credit markets. Finally, we also show how the basic hedge, as well as one involving options on swaps, can be modified to allow the company, in effect, to detach the call feature from the original bond and sell an otherwise unmarketable asset.

Perhaps the most critical advantage of the swap-based hedging strategies—at least, relative to the exchange-traded financial futures and options that can be used to accomplish the same end—is that swaps and swaptions can be tailored to meet the exact requirements of the end user. This kind of flexibility is one of the primary by-products of the ongoing search in our capital markets for innovative solutions to traditional problems. On the downside, however, it must also be recognized that the more specialized the structure, the less liquid it is likely to be. The lack of liquidity, in turn, makes the default potential of the financial intermediary a concern that must be carefully evaluated. Further, our evidence on bond and swap spread volatility indicates that, over the past three years, the basis risk inherent in these strategies would have been large and unpredictable.

IDENTIFYING, MEASURING, AND HEDGING CURRENCY RISK AT MERCK

by Judy C. Lewent and A. John Kearney, Merck & Co., Inc.

The authors would like to thank Francis H. Spiegel, Jr., Senior Vice President and CFO of Merck & Co., Inc., and Professors Donald Lessard of M.I.T. and Darrell Duffie of Stanford for their guidance throughout.

The impact of exchange rate volatility on a company depends mainly on the company's business structure, both legal and operational, its industry profile, and the nature of its competitive environment. This article recounts how Merck assessed its currency exposures and reached a decision to hedge those exposures. After a brief introduction to the company and the industry, we discuss our methods of identifying and measuring our exchange exposures, the factors considered in deciding whether to hedge such risks, and the financial hedging program we put in place.

AN INTRODUCTION TO THE COMPANY

Merck & Co., Inc. primarily discovers, develops, produces, and distributes human and animal health pharmaceuticals. It is part of a global industry that makes its products available for the prevention, relief, and cure of disease throughout the world. Merck itself is a multinational company, doing business in over 100 countries.

Total worldwide sales in 1989 for all domestic and foreign research-intensive pharmaceutical companies are projected to be $103.7 billion. Worldwide sales for those companies based in the U.S. are projected at $36.4 billion—an estimated 35% of the world pharmaceutical market; and worldwide sales for Merck in 1989 were $6.6 billion. The industry is highly competitive, with no company holding over 5% of the worldwide market. Merck ranks first in pharmaceutical sales in the U.S. and the world, yet has only a 4.7% market share worldwide. The major foreign competitors for the domestic industry are European firms and emerging Japanese companies.

Driven by the need to fund high-risk and growing research expenditures, the U.S. pharmaceutical industry has expanded significantly more into foreign markets than has U.S. industry as a whole. In 1987, the leading U.S. pharmaceutical companies generated 38% of their sales revenues overseas; and 37% of their total assets were located outside the U.S. In contrast, most U.S. industry groups report foreign sales revenues in the range of 20% to 30%. Merck, with overseas assets equal to 40% of total and with roughly half of its sales overseas, is among the most internationally-oriented of U.S. pharmaceutical companies.

The U.S. pharmaceutical industry also differs in its method of doing business overseas. In contrast to U.S. exporters, who often bill their customers in U.S. dollars, the pharmaceutical industry typically bills its customers in their local currencies. Thus, the effect of foreign currency fluctuations on the pharmaceutical industry tends to be more immediate and direct.

The typical structure is the establishment of subsidiaries in many overseas markets. These subsidiaries, of which Merck has approximately 70, are typically importers of product at some stage of manufacture, and are responsible for finishing, marketing, and distribution within the country of incorporation. Sales are denominated in local currency, and costs in a combination of local currency for finishing, marketing, distribution, administration, and taxes, and in the currency of basic manufacture and research—typically, the U.S. dollar for U.S.-based companies.

EXHIBIT 1
MERCK SALES INDEX

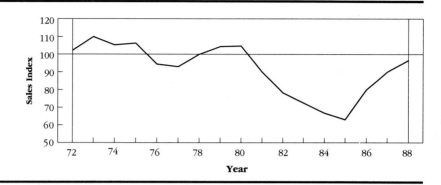

IDENTIFICATION AND MEASUREMENT OF EXPOSURE

It is generally agreed that foreign exchange fluctuations can affect a U.S. company's economic and financial results in three ways:

1. By changing the dollar value of net assets held overseas in foreign currencies (known as "translation" exposures) or by changing the expected results of transactions in non-local currencies ("transaction" exposures).

2. By changing the dollar value of future revenues expected to be earned overseas in foreign currencies ("future revenue" exposures).

3. By changing a company's competitive position—for example, a competitor whose costs are denominated in a depreciating currency will have greater pricing flexibility and thus a potential competitive advantage ("competitive" exposures).

Competitive exposures have been the subject of much of the recent academic work done on exchange risk management. Such exposures are best exemplified by the adverse effect of the strong dollar on the competitive position of much of U.S. industry in the early 1980s. This was true not only in export markets but also in the U.S. domestic market, where the strengthening U.S. dollar gave Japanese and European-based manufacturers a large competitive advantage in dollar terms over domestic U.S. producers.

For the pharmaceutical industry, however, the pricing environment is such that competitive exposure to exchange fluctuations is generally not significant. The existence of price controls through-

out most of the world generally reduces flexibility to react to economic changes.

Hence, Merck's exposure to exchange tends to be limited primarily to net asset and revenue exposures. The potential loss in dollar value of net revenues earned overseas represents the company's most significant economic and financial exposure. Such revenues are continuously converted into dollars through interaffiliate merchandise payments, dividends, and royalties, and are an important source of cash flow for the company. To the extent the dollar value of these earnings is diminished, the company suffers a loss of cash flow—at least over the short term. And, as discussed in more detail later, the resulting volatility in earnings and cash flow could impair the company's ability to execute its strategic plan for growth.

With its significant presence worldwide, Merck has exposures in approximately 40 currencies. As a first step in assessing the effect of exchange rate movements on revenues and net income, we constructed a sales index that measures the relative strength of the dollar against a basket of currencies weighted by the size of sales in those countries.[1] When the index is above 100%, foreign currencies have strengthened versus the dollar, indicating a positive exchange effect on dollar revenues. When the index is below 100%, as was the case through most of the 1980s, the dollar has strengthened versus the foreign currencies, resulting in income statement losses due to exchange.

As Exhibit 1 illustrates, the index was relatively stable from 1972 to 1980. But, as the dollar strengthened in the early 1980s, the index declined to the

---

1. The index uses 1978 as its base year. The currency basket excludes hyperinflationary markets where exchange devaluation is measured net of price increases.

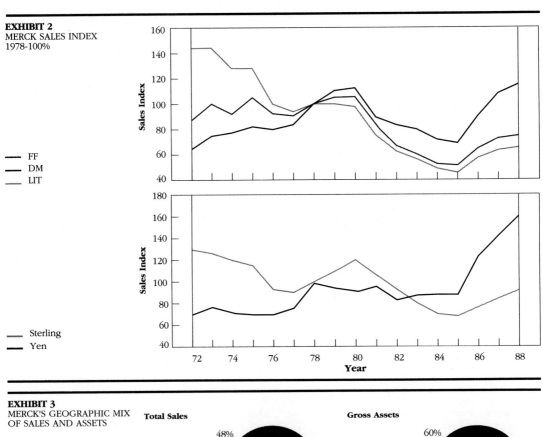

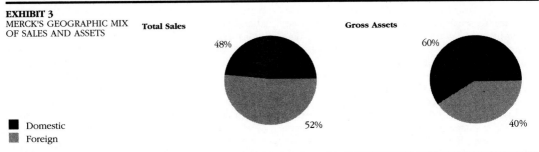

60% level, resulting in a cumulative exchange reduction in sales of approximately $900 million. But, then, as the dollar weakened in the later 1980s, the index increased to roughly 97%, returning to its 1972-1980 range.

But, as Exhibit 2 also shows, although the overall index returned as of 1988 to the earlier range, not all currencies have moved together against the dollar. The strengthening in the yen and the deutschemark has offset the decline of historically weaker currencies such as the Italian lira and French franc, while the British pound is very near 1978 levels.

RESOURCE ALLOCATION

Given the significant exchange exposure of our net overseas revenues, as reflected by our experience in early 1980s, we next decided to review the company's global allocation of resources across currencies and, in the process, to determine the extent to which revenues and costs were matched in individual currencies. Our analysis (the main findings of which are illustrated in Exhibit 3) revealed that the distribution of Merck's assets differs somewhat from the sales mix, primarily because of the concentration of research, manufacturing, and headquarters operations in the U.S.

On the basis of this analysis, it was clear that Merck has an exchange rate mismatch. To reduce this mismatch, we first considered the possibility of redeploying resources in order to shift dollar costs to a different currency. This process would have involved relocating manufacturing sites, research sites, and employees such as headquarters and support staff. We soon reached the conclusion, however, that because so few support functions seemed appropriate candidates for relocation, a move would have had only a negligible effect on our global income exposure. In short, we decided that shifting people and resources overseas was not a cost-effective way of dealing with our exchange exposure.

HEDGING MERCK'S EXPOSURES WITH FINANCIAL INSTRUMENTS

Having concluded that resource deployment was not an appropriate way for Merck to address exchange risk, we considered the alternative of financial hedging. Thinking through this alternative involved the following five steps:

1. Exchange Forecasts. Review of the likelihood of adverse exchange movements.

2. Strategic Plan Impact. Quantification of the potential impact of adverse exchange movements over the period of the plan.

3. Hedging Rationale. Critical examination of the reasons for hedging (perhaps the most important part of the process).

4. Financial Instruments. Selection of which instruments to use and how to execute the hedge.

5. Hedging Program. Simulation of alternative strategies to choose the most cost-effective hedging strategy to accommodate our risk tolerance profile (an ongoing process supported by a mathematical model we have recently developed to supplement our earlier analysis).

STEP 1: Projecting Exchange Rate Volatility

Our review of the probability of future exchange rate movements was guided by four main considerations:

(1) The major factors expected to affect exchange rates over the strategic plan period—for example, the U.S. trade deficit, capital flows, the U.S. budget deficit—all viewed in the context of the concept of an "equilibrium" exchange rate.

(2) Target zones or government policies designed to manage exchange rates. To what extent will government policies be implemented to dampen exchange rate volatility, particularly "overshooting," in the future?

(3) Development of possible ranges for dollar strength or weakness over the planning period.

(4) Summary of outside forecasters—a number of forecasters were polled on the outlook for the dollar over the plan period.

Our review of outside forecasters showed they were almost evenly split on the dollar's outlook. Although almost no one predicted a return to the extremes of the early 1980s, we nonetheless concluded that there was a potential for a relatively large move in either direction.

We developed a simple method for quantifying the potential ranges that reflects the following thought process:

■ Except for 1986, the upper limit of the year-to-year move in average exchange rates for the deutschemark and the yen has been about 20%. We used this as the measure of potential volatility in developing the probabilistic ranges in the forecast. (The deutschemark, incidentally, was used as a proxy for all European currencies.)

■ The widest ranges would likely result from one-directional movements—that is, 5 years of continued strengthening or weakening.

■ However, as the effect of each year's movement is felt in the economy and financial markets, the probability of exchange rates' continuing in the same direction is lessened. For example, if the dollar were to weaken, the favorable effects on the trade balance and on relative asset values would likely induce increased capital flows and cause a turnaround.

Based in part on this concept of exchange rate movements as a "mean-reverting" process, we developed ranges of expected rate movements (as shown in Exhibit 4) by assigning probabilities to the dollar continuing to move along a line of consecu-

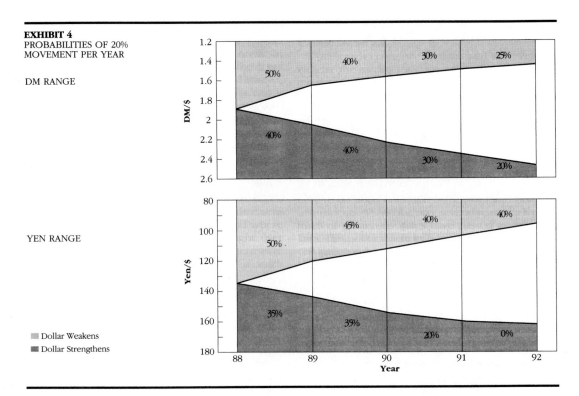

EXHIBIT 4
PROBABILITIES OF 20%
MOVEMENT PER YEAR

DM RANGE

YEN RANGE

■ Dollar Weakens
■ Dollar Strengthens

tive years' strengthening or weakening. For example, the dollar was considered to have a 40% probability of strengthening by 20% versus the DM in 1989. If the dollar does appreciate by 20% in 1989, then we also assume that the probability of its strengthening by a further 20% in 1990 is also 40%, but that the chance of this pattern continuing in 1991 is only 30% and falls to 20% in 1992.

Such ranges represent our best guess about the likely boundaries of dollar strength or weakness. The actual probability of exchange rate movements reaching or exceeding these boundaries is small, but the use of such extreme rates allows us to estimate the extent of our exposure. These exchange boundaries were also used in quantifying the potential impact of unfavorable exchange rate movements on our Strategic Plan.

STEP 2: Assessing the Impact on the 5-Year Strategic Plan

To assess the potential effect of unfavorable exchange rates, we converted our Strategic Plan into U.S. dollars on an exchange neutral basis (that is, at the current exchange rate) and compared these cash flow and earnings projections to those we expected to materialize under both our strong dollar and weak dollar scenarios. (See Exhibit 5.)

Further, we measured the potential impact of exchange rate movements on a cumulative basis as well as according to the year-to-year convention that is standard in external reporting. Exhibit 6 shows the effect of translating the year-to-year data from Exhibit 5 on a cumulative basis. (The total bar represents the cumulative variance, while the top portion represents the variance as determined by the change in rates from one period to the next.) Because it looks beyond a one-year period, the cumulative exchange variance provides a more useful estimate of the size of the exchange risk associated with Merck's long-range plan. Use of a cumulative measure also provides the basis for the kind of multi-year financial hedging program that, as we eventually determined, is appropriate for hedging multi-year income flows.

EXHIBIT 5
UNHEDGED NET INCOME
1989-1992

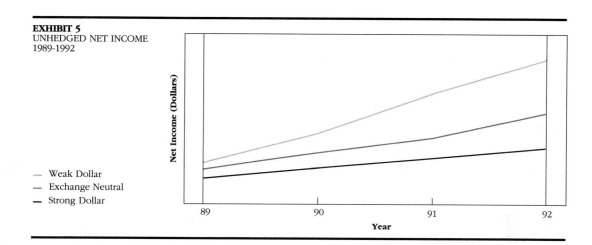

— Weak Dollar
— Exchange Neutral
— Strong Dollar

EXHIBIT 6
EXCHANGE IMPACT
STRONG DOLLAR
SCENARIO

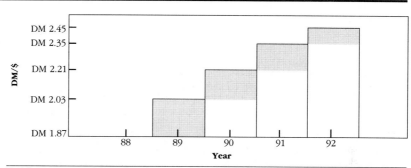

Total Bar represents cumulative exchange impact. Shaded area represents year-on-year impact.

STEP 3: Deciding Whether to Hedge the Exposure

Over the long term, foreign exchange rate movements have been—and are likely to continue to be—a problem of volatility in year-to-year earnings rather than one of irreversible losses. For example, most of the income statement losses of the early 1980s were recouped in the following three years. The question of whether or not to hedge exchange risk thus becomes a question of the company's own risk profile with respect to interim volatility in earnings and cash flows.

The desirability of reducing earnings volatility due to exchange can be examined from both external and internal perspectives.

External Concerns. These center on the perspective of capital markets, and accordingly in-volve matters such as share price, investor clientele effects, and maintenance of dividend policy. Although exchange fluctuations clearly can have material effects on reported accounting earnings, it is not clear that exchange-related fluctuations in earnings have significant effects on stock price. Our own analysis (as illustrated in Exhibit 7) suggests only a modest correlation in recent years between exchange gains and losses and share price movements, and a slight relationship in the strong dollar period—the scenario of greatest concern to us.

Industry analysts' reports, moreover, tend to support our analysis by arguing that exchange gains and losses are at most a second-order factor in determining the share prices of pharmaceutical companies. While invariably stressing the importance of new products as perhaps the most critical share price variable, analysts

EXHIBIT 7
TRADE WEIGHTED
DOLLAR VERSUS
DRUG INDEX

— Trade Weighted $
— Drug Index

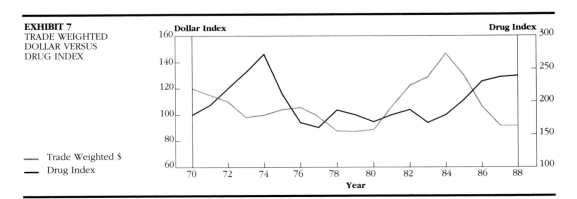

also often comment on the regulated price environment overseas (which, as we pointed out earlier, limits competitive exposure by reducing the effect of exchange changes on sales volume).[2]

With respect to investor clientele, exchange would seem to have mixed effects. To the extent that some investors—especially overseas investors—see Merck's stock as an opportunity for speculating on a weak dollar, hedging would be contrary to investors' interests. But, for investors seeking a "pure play" on the stocks of ethical drug companies, significant exchange risk could be undesirable. Thus, given this potential conflict of motives among investors, and recognizing our inability to ascertain the preferences of all of Merck's investor clienteles (potential as well as current), we concluded that it would be inappropriate to give too much weight to any specific type of investor.

On the issue of dividend policy, we came to a somewhat different conclusion. Maintaining Merck's dividend, while probably not the most important determinant of our share price, is nevertheless viewed by management as an important means of expressing our confidence in the company's prospective earnings growth. It is our way of reassuring investors that we expect our large investment in future research (funded primarily by retained earnings) to provide requisite returns. And, although both Merck and the industry in general were able to maintain dividend rates during the strong dollar period, we were concerned about the company's ability to maintain a policy of dividend *growth*

during a future dollar strengthening. Because Merck's (and other pharmaceutical companies') dividend growth rates did indeed decline during the strong dollar 1981-1985 period, the effect of future dollar strengthening on company cash flows could well constrain future dividend growth. So, in considering whether to hedge our income against future exchange movements, we chose to give some weight to the desirability of maintaining growth in the dividend.

In general, then, we concluded that although our exchange hedging policy should consider capital market perspectives (especially dividend policy), it should not be dictated by them. The direct effect of exchange fluctuations on shareholder value, if any, is unclear; and it thus seemed a better course to concentrate on the objective of maximizing long-term cash flows and to focus on the potential effect of exchange rate movements on our ability to meet our internal objectives. Such actions, needless to say, are ultimately intended to maximize returns for our stockholders.

Internal Concerns. From the perspective of management, the key factors that would support hedging against exchange volatility are the following two: (1) the large proportion of the company's overseas earnings and cash flows; and (2) the potential effect of cash flow volatility on our ability to execute our strategic plan—particularly, to make the investments in R & D that furnish the basis for future growth. The pharmaceutical industry has a very long planning horizon, one which reflects the complexity

2. Some analysts have also claimed to detect an inverse relationship between drug stock prices and inflation that also acts to reduce currency exposure. Drug stocks, as this reasoning goes, are growth stocks and generally benefit from low inflation because the discount factor used to price growth stocks declines under low inflation which increases shareholder value. Likewise a high inflation environment will depress share prices for growth stocks. Since generally high inflation leads to a weaker dollar, the negative impact of high inflation would over time limit the positive effect of a weaker dollar and the reverse would also be true.

EXHIBIT 8
ALTERNATIVE HEDGING
INSTRUMENTS

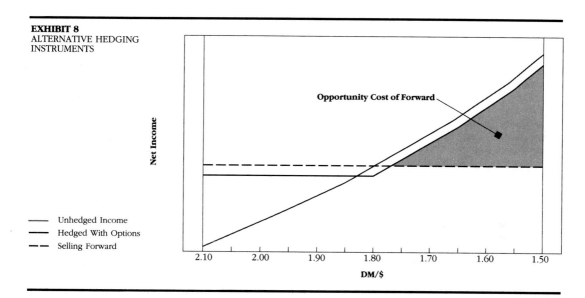

of the research involved as well as the lengthy process of product registration. It often takes more than 10 years between the discovery of a product and its market launch. In the current competitive environment, success in the industry requires a continuous, long-term commitment to a *steadily increasing* level of research funding.

Given the cost of research and the subsequent challenges of achieving positive returns, companies such as Merck require foreign sales in addition to U.S. sales to generate a level of income that supports continued research and business operations. The U.S. market alone is not large enough to support the level of our research effort. Because foreign sales are subject to exchange volatility, the dollar equivalent of worldwide sales can be very unstable. Uncertainty can make it very difficult to justify high levels of U.S. based-research when the firm cannot effectively estimate the pay-offs from its research. Our experience, and that of the industry in general, has been that the cash flow and earnings uncertainty caused by exchange rate volatility leads to a reduction of growth in research spending.

Such volatility can also result in periodic reductions of corporate spending necessary to expand markets and maintain supportive capital expenditures. In the early 1980s, for example, capital expenditures by Merck and other leading U.S. pharmaceutical companies experienced a reduction in rate of growth similar to that in R & D.

Our conclusion, then, was that we should take action to reduce the potential impact of exchange volatility on future cash flows. Reduction of such volatility removes an important element of uncertainty confronting the strategic management of the company.

STEP 4: Selecting the Appropriate Financial Instruments

While we will not discuss the various hedging techniques in detail, we do wish to share the thought processes that led us to choose currency options as our risk management tool. Our objective was to select the most cost-effective hedging instrument that accommodated the company's risk preferences.

Forward foreign exchange contracts, foreign currency debt, and currency swaps all effectively fix the value of the amount hedged regardless of currency movements. With the use of options, by contrast, the hedging firm retains the opportunity to benefit from natural positions—albeit at a cost equal to the premium paid for the option. As illustrated in Exhibit 8, under a strong dollar scenario (based on 1988 spot rates and forward points), Merck would prefer a forward sale because the contract would produce the same gains as the option but without incurring the cost of the option premium. But, under the weak dollar scenario, both the unhedged and the option positions would be preferred to hedging with the forward contract.

Given the possibility of exchange rate movements in either direction, we were unwilling to forgo the potential gains if the dollar weakened; so options were strictly preferred. We also concluded, moreover, that a certain level of option premiums could be justified as the cost of an insurance policy designed to preserve our ability to carry through with our strategic plan.[3]

STEP 5: Constructing a Hedging Program

Having selected currency options as our hedging vehicle and designated the 5-year period of our strategic plan as our hedging horizon, we then considered several implementation strategies, including:

Varying the term of the hedge. That is, using year-by-year rather than multi-year hedging.

Varying the strike price of the foreign exchange options. For example, out-of-the-money options were considered as a means of reducing costs.

Varying the amount. That is, different percentages of income could be covered, again, to control costs.

After simulating the outcome of alternative strategies under various exchange rate scenarios, we came to the following decisions: (1) we would hedge for a multi-year period, using long-term options to protect our strategic cash flow; (2) we would not use far-out-of-the-money options to reduce costs; and (3) we would hedge only on a partial basis and, in effect, self-insure for the remainder.

We continue to refine this decision through our use of increasingly more sophisticated modeling. Recognizing this as a quantitative process whereby decisions can be improved by application of better techniques, Merck has been developing (with the guidance of Professor Darrell Duffie of Stanford University) a state-of-the-art computer model that simulates the effectiveness of a variety of strategies for hedging. The model is a Monte Carlo simulation package that presents probability distributions of unhedged and hedged foreign income for future periods (the shortest of which are quarters). By so doing, it allows us to visualize the effect of any given hedging policy on our periodic cash flows, thus permitting better-informed hedging decisions.

The model has six basic components:

1. Security Pricing Models: State-of-the-art financial analytics are used to calculate theoretical prices for various securities such as bonds, futures, forwards, and options.[4]

2. Hedging Policy: We can specify a variety of hedging policies, with each representing a portfolio of securities to buy or sell in each quarter. The number of hedging policies is essentially unlimited, reflecting a variety of hedge ratios, proxy currencies, accounting constraints, security combinations, etc. For example, the model permits us to compare a hedging program of purchasing options that cover the exposures of the 5-year planning period and holding them until maturity with the alternative of a dynamic portfolio revision strategy. A dynamic hedge would involve not only the initial purchase of options, but a continuous process of buying and selling additional options based on interim changes in exchange rates.

3. Foreign Income Generator: Before simulating changes in hedging policy, however, we start by building our strategic plan forecast of local currency earnings into the model. The model then generates random earnings by quarter according to a specified model of forecast projections and random forecast errors. This process provides us with an estimate of the variability of local currency earnings and thereby allows us to reflect possible variations versus plan forecasts with greater accuracy.

4. Exchange Rate Dynamics: The model uses a Monte Carlo simulator to generate random exchange rates by quarter. The simulator allows us to adjust currency volatilities, rates of reversion, long-term exchange rates, and coefficients of correlation among currencies. We can test the sensitivity of the simulator to stronger or weaker dollar exchange rates by modifying the inputs. We can also use the Monte Carlo simulation package to re-examine the development of exchange scenarios and ranges described earlier.[5]

3. It was also recognized that to the extent hedge accounting could be applied to purchased options, this represents an advantage over other foreign currency instruments. The accounting ramifications of mark-to-market versus hedge accounting were, and remain, an important issue and we have continued to monitor developments with respect to the ongoing controversy over accounting for currency options.

4. In pricing options, we have the choice of using the Black-Scholes model or an alternative highly advanced valuation model. These models provide reasonably reliable estimates of the expected true cost, including transaction fees, of the option program. Although Black Scholes is the predominant pricing model in pricing many kinds of options, alternative models appear to have an advantage in the pricing of long-dated currency options. Black Scholes implicitly assumes that the volatility of exchange rates grows exponentially with time to maturity. General-

ly speaking, the further out the expiry date, the higher the price. The alternative model has a sophisticated approach in its assumption of a dampened exponential relationship between time to maturity, expected volatility, and price. For this reason, in the case of long-dated options, the Black Scholes model generally overstates option prices relative to the alternative model.

5. The model will also have the ability to simulate historic exchange trends. The model will have access to a large database of historic exchange rates. We will be able to analyze the impact of hedging on a selected time period, for example, the strong dollar period of the 1980's. Or, we can have the model randomly select exchange rate movements from a historical period, resulting in a Monte Carlo simulation of that period.

EXHIBIT 9
MERCK FOREIGN
CASH FLOW
UNHEDGED VS. HEDGED*

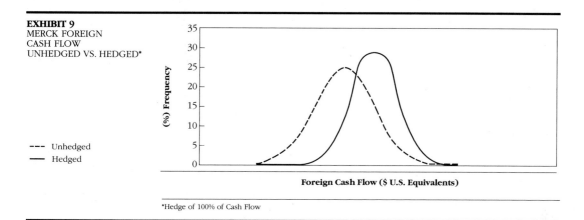

--- Unhedged
—— Hedged

*Hedge of 100% of Cash Flow

5. Cash Flow Generator: The model collects information from each of the above four components so as to calculate total cash flow in U.S. dollars by quarter for each random scenario.

6. Statistical and Graphical Output: The quarterly cash flow information for each of a large number of scenarios is collected and displayed graphically in frequency plots, and in terms of statistics such as means, standard deviations, and confidence levels. Exhibit 9 provides an example of the graphical output from our simulator, comparing distributions of unhedged and hedged cash flows. In this case, the hedged curve assumes 100% of Merck's exposure has been covered through the purchase of foreign currency options. Given the pattern of exchange rate movements simulated, the hedging strategy has shifted the hedged cash flow distribution to the right, cutting off a portion of unfavorable outcomes. In addition, the hedged cash flow distribution has a higher mean value as well as a lower standard deviation. Therefore, in this scenario, hedging would be preferable to not hedging, resulting in higher returns as well as lower risk. (Again, of course, the trade-off is the initial cost of the option premiums that would have to be balanced against the improved risk/return pattern.) Other scenarios may indicate that a lower hedge ratio or not hedging is the preferred strategy.

In sum, the model provides Merck with a powerful tool to determine the optimal strategy for reducing our exposure to foreign currency risk. The simulator allows us to analyze a wide range (in fact, an infinite number) of exchange scenarios, hedging policies, and security combinations. This in turn gives us the ability to select the hedging policy that is both cost-effective and consistent with our desired risk profile.

CONCLUSION

Identifying a company's exchange risk and reaching a decision with respect to what action, if any, should be taken requires extensive analysis. We believe that, as a result of this kind of analysis of Merck's currency exposures, we have developed an appropriate financial hedging plan—one that provides management with what amounts to an insurance policy against the potentially damaging effect of currency volatility on the company's ability to carry out its strategic plan. We continue to refine the actual implementation process as we move forward.

PART VI

CORPORATE RESTRUCTURING

The 1980s saw an unprecedented wave of corporate acquisitions, divestitures, spin-offs, split-ups, buybacks, ESOPs, partial public offerings, limited partnerships, and leveraged buyouts—all of which have been yoked together under the name of "corporate restructuring." In *The Takeover Controversy: Analysis and Evidence*," Jensen uses his "free cash flow" theory of takeovers to provide a remarkably ambitious and coherent explanation of the 1980s' restructuring wave. His argument leads to conclusions like the following:

- mergers in a wide range of mature or shrinking industries (most notably oil and gas, but also forest products, minerals, tobacco, broadcasting, food processing, and financial services) reduced waste and curbed unprofitable reinvestment, thereby creating value for shareholders and promoting the national interest;
- the use of large amounts of debt to finance acquisitions, leveraged buyouts, and large stock buybacks increased corporate efficiency;
- junk bonds played a major role in the restructuring process by reducing the effectiveness of sheer size as a deterrent to takeover;
- the stock market, contrary to the frequent claims of management and the press, is quite capable of taking the long view in assessing corporate performance (even though management often does not);
- the capital markets brought about the dismemberment of inefficient conglomerates through takeovers, divestitures, spinoffs, and LBOs;
- golden parachutes, when properly structured, can be used to unify management and stockholder interests;
- the practice of greenmail should, and could have been quite easily, prevented by corporate boards; and
- court decisions to uphold poison pills and otherwise ban takeovers undermined the contractual agreement between management and stockholders that is at the heart of the corporate form of organization.

In *The Quiet Restructuring*," John Kensinger and John Martin reinforce Jensen's argument that much corporate restructuring activity represents the return by management of corporate reinvestment decisions to the marketplace. The once popular model of the large corporation as a self-financing, self-perpetuating entity (promoted by the Boston Consulting Group and other strategists) has gone into eclipse. Drawing on Jensen's "debt control" hypothesis, the authors argue that the pressures exerted by heavy debt financing, combined with greater concentrations of equity ownership by management, has led to widespread corporate downsizing along with dramatic improvements in managerial accountability and incentives.

But even as this general pressure to return capital to investors is causing many Fortune 500 companies to shrink, much of this released capital is finding its way into small, start-up ventures and growing middle market companies. This massive recycling of capital from the moribund to the vital is seen by the authors as part of a "downsizing" process in which business functions are increasingly being performed as parts of smaller, independent firms and tax-advantaged partnerships. Corporate America, they suggest, has become the site of an ongoing market test weighing the benefits of scale economies and access to public capital against what increasingly appear to be the inefficiencies of large, especially conglomerate organizations.

In *The Causes and Consequences of Hostile Takeovers*," Amar Bhide shows why "hostile" takeovers tend to produce significantly better results for stockholders than do "friendly" transactions. Specifically, Bhide's study attempts the following: (1) to determine the acquirers' motives in all 47 hostile takeovers over $100 million attempted in 1985 and 1986; (2) to examine the economic consequences (including effects on employment, capital investment, and R&D) of the 28 of those 47 takeovers that were either successful (20 cases) or led to restructurings (8); and (3) to compare the motives and consequences of the hostile transactions to those of a control group of friendly takeovers in the same period.

The differences in apparent motive are striking. Whereas most friendly deals appear designed to take advantage of "synergies" or to diversify the corporate "strategic portfolio," the large majority of hostile takeovers are clearly motivated by anticipated profits from "restructuring"—that is, from changing the target's capital structure, cutting overhead, improving focus by selling unrelated businesses, or ending unprofitable reinvestment. The targets of hostile and friendly deals are accordingly different: Whereas the targets of friendly mergers tend to be single-industry firms that have performed quite well (as measured by earnings growth, ROE, and stockholder returns) and have higher insider ownership, the targets of hostile deals are typically low-growth, poorly performing, and often highly diversified companies in which management has a low equity stake.

The differences in effects between friendly and hostile deals are also pointed, although some are not as dramatic as they have been made out to be. Contrary to the claims of takeover critics, hostile deals do not typically cause large cutbacks in investment or employment. And, in the cases where they do (usually in consolidating industries with excess capacity), the cutbacks are roughly proportional to those undertaken by industry competitors that have not been subjected to takeover. Layoffs, to be sure, are much more strongly associated with hostile takeovers; but, again, those layoffs tend to be concentrated in corporate headquarters and not on the factory floor. As for the R&D issue, the targets of hostile takeovers tend not to spend much on R&D to begin with.

Given, then, that these economic "side-effects" of takeovers seem so mild, why all the controversy? And, if they are not laying off rank-and-file workers and gutting investment and research programs in the drive to make a quick buck, then how are corporate raiders—after paying large premiums over market and hefty fees to investment bankers and lawyers—paying the rent? The answer Bhide offers is that raiders are playing a "limited, but significant arbitrage role" in buying uneconomic conglomerates, dismantling them, and then selling the parts for a sum greater than the value of the conglomerate whole. As Bhide points out, of the 81 businesses divested by the 28 targets in his sample, as many as 78 had been previously acquired rather than developed from within. And roughly 75% of those divested operations were eventually sold off either to singly-industry firms or to private investment groups in combination with operating management. This, as Bhide argues, is persuasive evidence that capital market pressures are forcing corporate America toward greater focus.

In "*Reversing Corporate Diversification*," Amar Bhide extends the argument of the previous article by providing a detailed comparison of diversified and single-business companies that points toward the obsolescence of the conglomerate structure (at least in its current form with dispersed public ownership). Unlike most proponents of the restructuring movement, Bhide

attempts to explain not only why the market judged conglomerates so harshly in the 1980s, but also why it encouraged their formation in the 1960s.

In "*Lessons From A Middle Market LBO*, " Professors George Baker and Karen Wruck tell the story of the O.M Scott Company, a $200 million lawn gardening firm purchased by Clayton & Dubilier in a leveraged buyout from ITT in 1986. According to the authors, the combination of financial leverage (91% debt to capital), concentrated equity ownership (Clayton & Dubilier owned over 60% and Scott management 17.5%), and an active and financially interested board of directors led to a fundamental change" in "both organizational structure and the management decision-making process." The details of the transformation of Scott under Clayton & Dubilier also speak volumes about what went wrong at U.S. conglomerates like ITT.

In "*Equity Carve-Outs*," Katherine Schipper and Abbie Smith describe a transaction that was popular throughout much of the 1980s, and which has continued to be widely used in the 1990s. Such equity carve-outs, which amount to sales to the public of minority interests in subsidiaries, are the only kind of equity offering that elicits a positive response from the market. Whereas announcements of conventional corporate equity offerings depress stock prices by about 3% on average, companies offering partial interests interests have experienced an almost 5% increase in the value of the shares in the month surrounding announcement of the offering.

The popular explanation for the positive market reaction to equity carve-outs is that they allow investors to evaluate exceptional growth opportunities on a stand-alone basis, which in turn increases the value of the parent (which typically retains a majority interest). Such an argument appears, at least at first glance, to be premised on an exploitable inefficiency in stock market pricing. While the authors concede that providing investors with more extensive financial disclosure on an involuntary, periodic basis may affect the market's assessment of a subsidiary's value, and while such securities in some cases may even have scarcity value to investors unable to find "pure plays," they also offer other suggestions. For one thing, by separating an unambiguously profitable project from the parent, a carve-out may help overcome the information problem that attends conventional equity offerings.

If such is the case, the subsidiary might obtain funding on better terms alone than as part of a large organization. Perhaps equally important, the fact that carve-outs are parts of large, diversified conglomerates suggests that one of the motives for carve-outs may be expected improvements in operating efficiency. Carve-outs, as the authors point out, are often accompanied by major changes in the responsibilities and incentives of subsidiary management; for example, stock options in the newly-trading subsidiary's shares are almost always provided the top managers.

In "*Financing Dynamic Networks,*" Professors John Kensinger and John Martin argue that advances in information technology and economic pressures for specialization are giving rise to a somewhat new organizational form. The rise of "networks"—"tightly coordinated liaisons" of independent companies that specialize in functions like product design, production, marketing, and distribution—can be viewed as the extreme development of the corporate "downsizing" trend of the 80s. Because networks are typically designed for a specific project with a well-defined time horizon, network financing generally takes unconventional forms like limited partnerships (equity as well as debt), project finance, and other forms of asset-backed debt.

Networks may also provide the answer to the corporate dilemma described by Robert Reich in a recent Atlantic cover story: to wit, the inability of large, high-tech corporations to restrict the flight of "human capital." As Kensinger and Martin point out,

The combination of flexibility and equity ownership provided by network organizations provides an ideal solution to the problem of containing fluid "human capital." Networks are perfectly designed to harness the talents of entrepreneurs—and then, when the appointed task is completed, to release them back into the marketplace.

In "*Rethinking Corporate Real Estate,*" two real estate academics, William Brueggeman and Jeffrey Fisher, collaborate with Goldman Sachs's David Porter to describe the profound effect the corporate restructuring movement has had on the way corporations evaluate their real estate holdings. Prior to the 1980s, corporate real estate assets acquired decades before were simply handed down unexamined from one generation of management to the next. And even if the current market value of such assets clearly far exceeded historic costs, real estate tended to be viewed as more or less "dead stock"—that is, an illiquid, non-income-producing store of

capital committed by investors long ago. It was a potential source of value, to be sure. But it was not the kind of value that could be readily converted into increases in reported earnings and balance sheet equity—effects that were not only thought to impress stockholders, but also governed the size of management bonuses. Consequently, guided by the certainty that what was not recorded in earnings would not affect their paycheck and, to a lesser extent, by the presumption that what did not affect earnings would not influence stock prices, corporate management felt little need to "manage" its real estate.

But with the escalation of corporate takeovers in the early 80s and the rise of junk-bond-financed raiders a few years later, attention to corporate real estate was, in many cases, forced upon reluctant managements. Indeed, the availability of "undervalued (or, perhaps more likely, mismanaged) real estate has been described as an important source of "hidden value" in as many as half the LBOs, other recapitalizations, and leveraged acquisitions in the 1980s. As the authors show, corporate management of real estate increasingly included large asset sales, spin-offs of real estate subsidiaries, sale-leasebacks of real estate facilities, and a variety of real-estate-backed financings.

In Part I of "*The Methods and Motives of Corporate Restructuring,*" Bennett Stewart and David Glassman show how current methods of restructuring—especially ESOPs, LBOs, and leveraged "cashouts"—increase corporate values by strengthening management incentives to serve stockholders. Part II of "*The Methods and Motives*" extends the earlier arguments about the role of debt financing in improving managerial focus, incentives, and accountability. But it also dwells at length on the potential efficiency gains from separating businesses with different operating characteristics and financing requirements in order to eliminate "destructive cross-subsidies." Besides describing the importance of adapting financial structure to operations, Stewart and Glassman also speculate about the potential value of separating "entrepreneurial, value-creating activities from the commodity end of the business, proven low-risk earnings streams from unproven speculative investment opportunities, and creative development activities from the ownership and operation of the resulting assets." "If you really want to create value," the authors say, "Don't split your stock, split your company."

DHC

THE TAKEOVER CONTROVERSY: ANALYSIS AND EVIDENCE*

*by Michael Jensen,
Harvard Business School[1]*

Introduction

The market for corporate control is fundamentally changing the corporate landscape. Transactions in this market in 1985 were at a record level of $180 billion, 47 percent above the $122 billion in 1984. The purchase prices in 36 of the 3,000 deals exceeded a billion dollars in 1985, compared with 18 in 1984.[2] These transactions involve takeovers, mergers, and leveraged buyouts. Closely associated are corporate restructurings involving divestitures, spinoffs, and large stock repurchases for cash and debt.

The changes associated with these control transactions are causing considerable controversy. Some argue that takeovers are damaging to the morale and productivity of organizations and therefore damaging to the economy. Others argue that takeovers represent productive entrepreneurial activity that improves the control and management of assets and helps move assets to more productive uses.

The controversy has been accompanied by strong pressure on regulators and legislatures to enact restrictions that would curb activity in the market for corporate control. In the spring of 1985 there were over 20 bills under consideration in Congress that proposed new restrictions on takeovers. Within the past several years the legislatures of New York, New Jersey, Maryland, Pennsylvania, Connecticut, Illinois, Kentucky, and Michigan have passed antitake-over laws. The Federal Reserve Board entered the fray early in 1986 when it issued its controversial new interpretation of margin rules that restricts the use of debt in takeovers.

Through dozens of studies, leading financial economists have accumulated considerable evidence and knowledge about the effects of the takeover market. Since most of the results of the work completed prior to 1984 are well summarized elsewhere,[4] I focus here on current aspects of the controversy and on new results. In a nutshell, the previous work tells us the following:

- Takeovers benefit target shareholders—premiums in hostile offers historically exceed 30 percent on average, and in recent times have averaged about 50 percent.
- Acquiring-firm shareholders on average earn about 4 percent in hostile takeovers and roughly zero in mergers.
- Takeovers do not waste credit or resources; they generate substantial gains—historically 8.4 percent of the total value of both companies. Recently the gains seem to have been even larger.
- Actions by managers that eliminate or prevent offers or mergers are most suspect as harmful to shareholders.
- Golden parachutes for top-level managers do not, on average, harm shareholders.
- The activities of takeover specialists such as Icahn,

* This article is a somewhat shortened version of Michael C. Jensen's "The Takeover Controversy: Analysis and Evidence," which will appear in the forthcoming volume, *Takeovers and Contests for Corporate Control* (Oxford University Press, 1987), edited by John Coffee, Louis Lowenstein, and Susan Rose-Ackerman. It is printed here with permission of the publisher.

1. Michael Jensen holds a joint appointment as Professor of Business Administration, Harvard Business School, and LaClare Professor of Finance and Business Administration and Director of the Managerial Economics Research Center at the University of Rochester's Graduate School of Management. This research is supported by the Division of Research, Harvard Business School, and the Managerial Economics Research Center, University of Rochester.

2. W. T. Grimm, *Mergerstat Review* (1985).

4. A detailed summary of this evidence is available in Michael C. Jensen and Richard S. Ruback, "The Market for Corporate Control: The Scientific Evidence," *Journal of Financial Economics* 11 (April, 1983); and in Michael C. Jensen, "Takeovers: Folklore and Science", *Harvard Business Review* (November/December, 1984). See also Paul J. Halpern,, "Empirical Estimates of the Amount and Distribution of Gains to Companies in Mergers," *Journal of Business*, V. 46, No. 4 (October, 1973) pp. 554-575.

Posner, Steinberg, and Pickens, on average, benefit shareholders.[5]

• Takeover gains do not come from the creation of monopoly power.

This paper analyzes the controversy surrounding takeovers and provides both theory and evidence to explain the central phenomena at issue. The paper is organized as follows. Section 2 contains basic background analysis of the forces operating in the market for corporate control—analysis which provides an understanding of the conflicts and issues surrounding takeovers and the effects of activities in this market. Section 3 discusses the conflict between managers and shareholders over the payout of free cash flow and how takeovers represent both a symptom and a resolution of the conflict. Sections 4, 5, and 6 discuss the relatively new phenomena of, respectively, junk-bond financing, the use of golden parachutes, and the practice of greenmail. Section 7 analyzes the problems the Delaware court is having in dealing with the conflicts that arise over control issues and its confused application of the business judgment rule to these cases.

The following topics are discussed:

• The reasons for takeovers and mergers in the petroleum industry and why they increase efficiency and thereby promote the national interest.

• The role of debt in bonding management's promises to pay out future cash flows, to reduce costs, and to reduce investments in low-return projects.

• The role of high-yield debt (junk bonds) in helping to eliminate mere size as a takeover deterrent.

• The effects of takeovers on the equity markets and claims that managers are pressured to behave myopically.

• The effects of antitakeover measures such as poison pills.

• The misunderstandings of the important role that "golden parachutes" play in reducing the conflicts of interests associated with takeovers and the valuable function they serve in alleviating some of the costs and uncertainty facing managers.

• The damaging effects of the Delaware court decision in Unocal vs. Mesa that allowed Unocal to make a self-tender offer that excluded its largest shareholder (reverse greenmail).

• The problems the courts are facing in applying the model of the corporation subsumed under the traditional business judgment rule to the conflicts of interest involved in corporate control controversies.

The Market for Corporate Control — Background

The Benefits of Takeovers

The market for corporate control is creating large benefits for shareholders and for the economy as a whole. The corporate control market generates these gains by loosening control over vast amounts of resources and enabling them to move more quickly to their highest-valued use. This is a healthy market in operation, on both the takeover side and the divestiture side.

Gains to target firms. Total benefits created by the control market have been huge, as reflected in gains of $40 billion to stockholders of acquired firms in 260 tender offers alone in the period from January 1981 through May 1985.[6] This figure does not include the gains from other control transactions such as mergers, leveraged buyouts, or divestitures. Nor does it include the gains from reorganizations such as those of Phillips, Unocal and others that have been motivated by takeover attempts. (The Phillips, Unocal and ARCO reorganizations created gains of an additional $6.6 billion.) One study estimates the total premiums received by shareholders of target firms to have been approximately $75 billion in $239 billion of merger and acquisition deals in 1984 and 1985.[6a]

Gains to bidding firms. The evidence on the returns to bidding firms is mixed. The data indicate that prior to 1980 shareholders of bidding firms earned on average about zero in mergers (which tend to be voluntary) and about 4 percent of their equity value in tender offers (which tend to be hostile).[7] These differences in returns are associated with the form of payment rather than the form of the

---

5. Clifford G. Holdnerness and Dennis P. Sheehan, "Raiders or Saviors? The Evidence on Six Controversial Investors," *Journal of Financial Economics* 14 (December, 1985); and Wayne H. Mikkelson and Richard S. Ruback, "An Empirical Analysis of the Interfirm Equity Investment Process," *Journal of Financial Economics* 14 (December, 1985).

6. As estimated by the Office of the Chief Economist of the SEC and provided to the author in private communication.

6a. John D. Paulus, "Corporate Restructuring, 'Junk,' and Leverage: Too Much or Too Little?" (Morgan Stanley, February 1986).

7. See Jensen and Ruback [1983, Tables 1 and 2], cited earlier in note 4.

Major changes in energy markets have required a radical restructuring of and retrenchment in that industry; and takeovers have played an important role in accomplishing these changes.

offer (tender offers tend to be for cash and mergers tend to be for stock).[8]

Although there are measurement problems that make it difficult to estimate the returns to bidders as precisely as the returns to targets,[12] it appears the bargaining power of target managers, coupled with competition among potential acquirers, grants much of the acquisition benefits to selling shareholders. In addition, federal and state regulation of tender offers appears to have strengthened the hand of target firms; premiums received by target-firm shareholders increased substantially after introduction of such regulation.[13]

Causes of Current Takeover Activity

The current high level of takeover activity seems to be caused by a number of factors:
- the relaxation of restrictions on mergers imposed by the antitrust laws;
- the withdrawal of resources from industries that are growing more slowly or that must shrink;
- deregulation in the financial services, oil and gas, transportation, and broadcasting markets that is bringing about a major restructuring of those industries;
- and improvements in takeover technology, including a larger supply of increasingly sophisticated legal and financial advisers, and improvements in financing technology (for example, the strip financing commonly used in leveraged buyouts and the original issuance of high-yield non-investment-grade bonds).

Each of these factors has contributed to the increase in total takeover and reorganization activity in recent times. Moreover, the first three factors (antitrust relaxation, exit, and deregulation) are generally consistent with data showing the intensity of takeover activity by industry. For example, the value of merger and acquisition transactions by industry in the period 1981-84 (see Table 1) indicates that acquisition activity was highest in oil and gas, followed by banking and finance, insurance, food processing,

and mining and minerals. For comparison purposes, the last column of the table presents data on industry size measured as a fraction of the total value of all firms. All but two of the industries, retail and transportation, represent a larger fraction of total takeover activity than their representation in the economy as a whole.

Many areas of the U.S. economy have been experiencing slowing growth and, in some cases, even retrenchment—a phenomenon that has many causes, including substantially increased competition from foreign firms. This has increased takeover activity because takeovers play an important role in facilitating exit from an industry or activity. Major changes in energy markets have required a radical restructuring of and retrenchment in that industry; and, as discussed in detail below, takeovers have played an important role in accomplishing these changes. Deregulation of the financial service market is consistent with the high ranking in Table 1 of banking and finance and insurance. Deregulation has also been important in the transportation and broadcasting industries. Mining and minerals has been subject to many of the same forces affecting the energy industry, including the changes in the value of the dollar.

Takeovers Provide Competition for Top-level Management Jobs

The market for corporate control is best viewed as a major component of the managerial labor market. It is the arena in which different management teams compete for the rights to manage corporate resources.[14] Understanding this is crucial to understanding much of the rhetoric about the effects of hostile takeovers.

Managers formerly protected from competition for their jobs by antitrust constraints that prevented takeover of the nation's largest corporations are now facing a more demanding environment and a more uncertain future.

The development of innovative financing

8. See Yen-Sheng Huang and Ralph A. Walkling, "Differences in Residuals Associated with Acquisition Announcements: Payment, Acquisition Form, and Resistance Effects" (Manuscript, Georgia Institute of Technology and Ohio State University, November, 1985).

12. See B. Espen Eckbo, "Do Acquiring Firms Gain From Merger?" (unpublished manuscript, University of British Columbia, June, 1985). Eckbo concludes that the zero returns to U.S. bidding firms is due to difficulties in measuring the gains to bidding firms when the bidder is substantially larger than the

target firm. In his sample the average Canadian bidder was approximately the same size as the average target while the average U.S. bidder is approximately 8 times the size of the average Canadian target. See also Jensen and Ruback [1983, pp 18ff.], cited earlier in note 4.

13. See Gregg Jarrell and Michael Bradley, "The Economic Effects of Federal and State Regulation of Cash Tender Offers," *Journal of Law and Economics* 23 (1980), pp. 371-407.

14. See Jensen and Ruback [1983], cited earlier in note 4.

When the internal processes for change in large corporations are too slow, costly, and clumsy to bring about the required restructuring or management change, the capital markets are doing so through the operation of the market for corporate control.

TABLE 1
Intensity of Industry Takeover Activity: 1981–1984

Intensity of industry takeover activity as measured by the value of merger and acquisition transactions in the period 1981–84 (as a percent of total takeover transactions for which valuation data are publicly reported) compared to industry size (as measured by the fraction of overall corporate market value).

Industry classification of seller	Percent of total takeover activity*	Percent of total corporate market value**
Oil and gas	26.3%	13.5%
Banking and finance	8.8	6.4
Insurance	5.9	2.9
Food processing	4.6	4.4
Mining and minerals	4.4	1.5
Conglomerate	4.4	3.2
Retail	3.6	5.2
Transportation	2.4	2.7
Leisure and entertainment	2.3	.9
Broadcasting	2.3	.7
Other	39.4	58.5

*Source: W. T. Grimm, *Mergerstat Review* (1984), p. 41.
**As of 12/31/84. Total value is measured as the sum of the market value of common equity for 4,305 companies, including 1,501 companies on the NYSE, 724 companies on the ASE plus 2,080 companies in the Over-The-Counter market. Source: *The Media General Financial Weekly,* (December 31, 1984), p. 17.

vehicles, such as high-yield, non-investment-grade bonds ("junk" bonds), has removed size as a significant impediment to competition in this market. Although they have not been widely used in takeovers yet, these new financing techniques permit small firms to obtain resources for acquisition of much larger firms by issuing claims on the value of the venture (that is, the target firm's assets) just as in any other corporate investment activity. It is not surprising that many executives of large corporations would like relief from this new competition for their jobs, but restricting the corporate control market is not the efficient way to handle the problems caused by the increased uncertainty in their contracting environment.

Takeovers Provide External Control

The internal control mechanisms of corporations, which operate through the board of directors, generally work well. On occasion, however, they break down. One important source of protection for investors in these situations is the takeover market. Other management teams that recognize an opportunity to reorganize or redeploy an organization's assets and thereby create new value can bid for the control rights in the takeover market. To be successful, such bids must be at a premium over current market value. This gives investors an opportunity to realize part of the gains from reorganization and redeployment of the assets.

The Market for Corporate Control Is an Agent for Change

Takeovers generally occur because changing technology or market conditions require a major restructuring of corporate assets. In some cases takeovers occur because incumbent managers are incompetent. When the internal processes for change in large corporations are too slow, costly and clumsy to bring about the required restructuring or management change in an efficient way, the capital markets are doing so through the operation of the market for corporate control. In this sense, the capital markets have been responsible for bringing about substantial changes in corporate strategy in recent times.

Managers often have difficulty abandoning strategies they have spent years devising and im-

Some firms in the oil industry have to go out of business. This is cheaper to accomplish through merger and the orderly liquidation of marginal assets of the combined firms than by a slow, agonizing death in a competitive struggle in an industry with overcapacity.

plementing, even when those strategies no longer contribute to the organization's survival. Such changes often require abandonment of major projects, relocation of facilities, changes in managerial assignments, and closure or sale of facilities or divisions. It is easier for new top-level managers with no ties with current employees or communities to make such changes. Moreover, normal organizational resistance to change commonly lessens significantly early in the reign of new top-level managers. For example, the premium Carl Icahn was able to offer for TWA, and his victory over Texas Air in the battle for control of TWA, were made possible in part by the willingness of the TWA unions to negotiate favorable contract concessions with Icahn—concessions that TWA itself was unable to attain prior to the takeover conflict. Such organizational factors that make change easier for newcomers, coupled with a fresh view of the business, can be a major advantage to new managers after a takeover. On the other hand, lack of detailed knowledge about the firm also poses risks for new managers and increases the likelihood of mistakes.

Takeovers are particularly important in bringing about efficiencies when exit from an activity is required. The oil industry is a good example. Changing market conditions mandate a major restructuring of the petroleum industry, and none of this is the fault of management. Management, however, must adjust to the new energy environment and recognize that many old practices and strategies are no longer viable. It is particularly hard for many managers to deal with the fact that some firms in the oil industry have to go out of business. This is cheaper to accomplish through merger and the orderly liquidation of marginal assets of the combined firms than by a slow, agonizing death in a competitive struggle in an industry with overcapacity. The end of the latter process often comes in the bankruptcy courts, with high losses and unnecessary destruction of valuable parts of organizations that could be used productively by others.

In short, the external takeover market serves as a court of last resort that plays an important role in (1) creating organizational change, (2) motivating the efficient use of resources, and (3) protecting shareholders when the corporation's internal controls and board-level control mechanisms are slow, clumsy, or defunct.

Divestitures Are the Subject of Much Erroneous Criticism

If assets are to move to their most highly valued use, acquirers must be able to sell off assets to those who can use them more productively. Therefore, divestitures are a critical element in the functioning of the corporate control market, and it is thus important to avoid inhibiting them. Indeed, over 1200 divestitures occurred in 1985, a record level.[15] Labeling divestitures with emotional terms such as "bustups" is not a substitute for analysis or evidence.

Moreover, it is important to recognize that divested plants and assets do not disappear; they are reallocated. Sometimes they continue to be used in similar ways in the same industry, and in other cases they are used in very different ways and in different industries. But in all cases they are moving to uses that their new owners believe are more productive. This process is beneficial to society.

Finally, it is useful to recognize that the takeover and divestiture market provides a private market constraint against bigness for its own sake. The potential gains available to those who correctly perceive that a firm can be purchased for less than the value realizable from the sale of its components provide incentives for entrepreneurs to search out these opportunities and to capitalize on them by reorganizing such firms into smaller entities.

The mere possibility of such takeovers also motivates managers to avoid putting together uneconomic conglomerates and to break up existing ones. This is now happening. Recently it has appeared that many firms' defenses against takeovers have led to actions similar to those proposed by potential acquirers. Examples are the reorganizations occurring in the oil industry, the sale of "crown jewels," and divestitures brought on by the desire to liquidate large debts incurred to buy back stock or to make other payments to stockholders. Unfortunately, the basic economic sense of these transactions is often lost in a blur of emotional rhetoric and controversy.

The sale of a firm's crown jewels, for example, benefits shareholders when the price obtained for the division is greater than the present value of the future cash flows to the current owner. A takeover bid motivated by the desire to obtain such an underused division can stimulate current managers to re-

---

15. W. T. Grimm, *Mergerstat Review* (1985).

It is important to recognize that divested plants and assets do not disappear; they are reallocated...to uses that their new owners believe are more productive. This process is beneficial to society.

examine the economics of the firm's current structure and to sell one or more of its divisions to a third party who is willing to pay even more than the initial offerer. Brunswick's sale of its Sherwood Medical Division to American Home Products after a takeover bid by Whittaker (apparently motivated by a desire to acquire Sherwood) is an example of such a transaction. The total value to Brunswick shareholders of the price received for selling Sherwood to American Home Products plus the remaining value of Brunswick without Sherwood (the proceeds from the sale of Sherwood were distributed directly to Brunswick's shareholders) was greater than Whittaker's offer for the entire company.[16]

Managers May Behave Myopically But Markets Do Not

It has been been argued that growing institutional equity holdings and the fear of takeover cause managers to behave myopically and therefore to sacrifice long-term benefits to increase short-term profits. The arguments tend to confuse two separate issues: 1) whether *managers* are shortsighted and make decisions that undervalue future cash flows while overvaluing current cash flows (myopic managers); and 2) whether *security markets* are shortsighted and undervalue future cash flows while overvaluing near-term cash flows (myopic markets).

There is little formal evidence on the myopic managers issue, but I believe this phenomenon does occur. Sometimes it occurs when managers hold little stock in their companies and are compensated in ways that motivate them to take actions that increase accounting earnings rather than the value of the firm. It also occurs when managers make mistakes because they do not understand the forces that determine stock values.

There is much evidence inconsistent with the myopic markets view and none that supports it:

• Even casual observation of the equity markets reveals that the market values more than current earnings. It values growth as well. The mere fact that

price/earnings ratios differ widely among securities indicates the market is valuing something other than current earnings. Indeed, the essence of a growth stock is one that has large investment projects yielding few short-term cash flows but high future earnings and cash flows.

• The continuing marketability of new issues for start-up companies with little record of current earnings—the Genentechs of the world—is also inconsistent with the notion that the market does not value future earnings.

• A recent study provides evidence that (except in the oil industry) stock prices respond positively to announcements of increased investment expenditures, and negatively to reduced expenditures.[17] This evidence is inconsistent with the notion that the equity market is myopic.

• The vast evidence on efficient markets indicating that current stock prices appropriately incorporate all currently available public information is also inconsistent with the myopic markets hypothesis. Although the evidence is not literally 100 percent in support of the efficient market hypothesis, there is no better documented proposition in any of the social sciences.[18]

The evidence indicates, for example, that the market appropriately interprets the implications of corporate accounting changes that increase reported profits but cause no change in corporate cash flows.[19]

Additional evidence is provided by the 30 percent increase in ARCO's stock price that occurred when it announced its major restructuring in 1985. This price increase is inconsistent with the notion that the market values only short-term earnings. Even though ARCO simultaneously revealed that it would have to take a $1.2 billion write-off as a result of the restructuring, the market still responded positively.

• Recent versions of the myopic markets hypothesis emphasize increasing institutional holdings and the pressures institutional investors face to show high returns on a quarter-to-quarter basis. It is argued that these pressures on institutions are a major cause of pressures on corporations to generate high current

16. See the analysis in Jensen [1984, p. 119], cited in note 4.

17. John J. McConnell and Chris J. Muscarella, "Corporate Capital Expenditure Decisions and the Market Value of the Firm," *Journal of Financial Economics* 14, No. 3 (1985).

18. For an introduction to the literature and empirical evidence on the theory of efficient markets, see E. Elton and M. Gruber, *Modern Portfolio Theory and Investment Analysis*, (New York: Wiley, 1984), Chapter 15, p. 375ff. and the 167 studies referenced in the bibliography.

19. Examples are switches from accelerated to straight-line depreciation techniques and adoption of the flow-through method for reporting investment tax credits. Here the evidence indicates that "security prices increase around the date when a firm first announces earnings inflated by an accounting change. The effect appears to be temporary, and, certainly by the subsequent quarterly report, the price has resumed a level appropriate to the true economic status of the firm." See R. Kaplan and R. Roll, "Investor Evaluation of Accounting Information: Some Empirical Evidence," *Journal of Business*, (April, 1972), 225-257.

I believe this phenomenon [myopic managerial behavior] does occur. Sometimes it occurs when managers hold little stock in their companies and are compensated in ways that motivate them to take actions that increase accounting earnings rather than the value of the firm.

earnings on a quarter-to-quarter basis. The institutional pressures are said to lead to increased takeovers of firms (because institutions are not loyal shareholders) and to decreased research and development expenditures. It is argued that because R&D expenditures reduce current earnings, firms making them are therefore more likely to be taken over, and that reductions in R&D are leading to a fundamental weakening of the corporate sector of the economy.

A recent study of 324 firms by the Office of the Chief Economist of the SEC finds substantial evidence that is inconsistent with this version of the myopic markets argument.[20] The evidence indicates the following:

• increased institutional stock holdings are not associated with increased takeovers of firms;

• increased institutional holdings are not associated with decreases in research and development expenditures;

• firms with high research and development expenditures are not more vulnerable to takeovers;

• stock prices respond positively to announcements of increases in research and development expenditures.

Those who make the argument that takeovers are reducing R&D spending also have to come to grips with the aggregate data on such spending, which is inconsistent with the argument. Total spending on R&D in 1984, a year of record acquisition activity, increased by 14 percent according to *Business Week's* annual survey of 820 companies. (The sample companies account for 95 percent of total private-sector R&D expenditures.) This represented "the biggest gain since R&D spending began a steady climb in the late 1970s."[21] All industries in the survey increased R&D spending with the exception of steel. Moreover, R&D spending increased from 2 percent of sales, where it had been for five years, to 2.9 percent.

An Alternative Hypothesis

There is an alternative hypothesis that explains the current situation, including the criticisms of management, quite well.

Suppose that some managers are simply mistaken—that is, their strategies are wrong—and that the financial markets are telling them they are wrong. If they don't change, their stock prices will remain low. If the managers are indeed wrong, it is desirable for the stockholders and for the economy to remove them to make way for a change in strategy and more efficient use of the resources.

Free Cash Flow Theory of Takeovers[22]

More than a dozen separate forces drive takeover activity, including such factors as deregulation, synergies, economies of scale and scope, taxes, managerial incompetence, and increasing globalization of U.S. markets.[23] One major cause of takeover activity are the agency costs associated with conflicts between managers and shareholders over the payout of corporate free cash flow. Though this has received relatively little attention, it has played an important role in acquisitions over the last decade.

Managers are the agent of shareholders, and because both parties are self-interested, there are serious conflicts between them over the choice of the best corporate strategy. Agency costs are the total costs that arise in such cooperative arrangements. They consist of the costs of monitoring managerial behavior (such as the costs of producing audited financial statements and devising and implementing compensation plans that reward managers for actions that increase investors' wealth) and the inevitable costs that are incurred because the conflicts of interest can never be resolved perfectly. Sometimes these costs can be large and, when they are, takeovers can reduce them.

Free Cash Flow and the Conflict Between Managers and Shareholders

Free cash flow is cash flow in excess of that required to fund all projects that have positive net values when discounted at the relevant cost of capital. Such free cash flow must be paid out to share-

20. Office of the Chief Economist, Securities and Exchange Commission, "Institutional Ownership, Tender Offers, and Long-Term Investments," April 19, 1985.

21. "R&D Scoreboard: Reagan & Foreign Rivalry Light a Fire Under Spending", *Business Week*, July 8, 1985), p. 86 ff.

22. This discussion is based on my article, "Agency Costs of Free Cash Flow,

Corporate Finance and Takeovers," forthcoming in *American Economic Review*, (May, 1986).

23. Richard Roll discusses a number of these forces in "Empirical Evidence on Takeover Activity and Shareholder Wealth," (presented at the Conference on Takeovers and Contests for Corporate Control, Columbia University, November, 1985).

Free cash flow [that which cannot be profitably reinvested by management inside the firm] must be paid out to shareholders if the firm is to be efficient and to maximize value for shareholders.

holders if the firm is to be efficient and to maximize value for shareholders.

Payment of cash to shareholders reduces the resources under managers' control, thereby reducing managers' power, and potentially subjecting them to the monitoring by the capital markets that occurs when a firm must obtain new capital. Financing projects internally avoids this monitoring and the possibility that funds will be unavailable or available only at high explicit prices.

Managers have incentives to expand their firms beyond the size that maximizes shareholder wealth.[24] Growth increases managers' power by increasing the resources under their control. In addition, changes in management compensation are positively related to growth.[25] The tendency of firms to reward middle managers through promotion rather than year-to-year bonuses also creates an organizational bias toward growth to supply the new positions that such promotion-based reward systems require.[25a]

The tendency for managers to overinvest resources is limited by competition in the product and factor markets, which tends to drive prices toward minimum average cost in an activity. Managers must therefore motivate their organizations to be more efficient to improve the probability of survival. Product and factor market disciplinary forces are often weaker in new activities, however, and in activities that involve substantial economic rents or quasi-rents.[26] In these cases, monitoring by the firm's internal control system and the market for corporate control are more important. Activities yielding substantial economic rents or quasi-rents are the types of activities that generate large amounts of free cash flow.

Conflicts of interest between shareholders and managers over payout policies are especially severe when the organization generates substantial free cash flow. The problem is how to motivate managers to disgorge the cash rather than invest it at below the cost of capital or waste it through organizational inefficiencies.

Some finance scholars have argued that financial flexibility (unused debt capacity and internally generated funds) is desirable when a firm's managers have better information about the firm than outside investors.[26a] Their arguments assume that managers act in the best interest of shareholders. The arguments offered here imply that such flexibility has costs: financial flexibility in the form of free cash flow, large cash balances, and unused borrowing power provides managers with greater discretion over resources that is often not used in the shareholders' interests.

The theory developed here explains (1) how debt-for-stock exchanges reduce the organizational inefficiencies fostered by substantial free cash flow, (2) how debt can substitute for dividends, (3) why "diversification" programs are more likely to be associated with losses than are expansion programs in the same line of business, (4) why mergers within an industry and liquidation-motivated takeovers will generally create larger gains than cross-industry mergers, (5) why the factors stimulating takeovers in such diverse businesses as broadcasting, tobacco, cable systems and oil are essentially identical, and (5) why bidders and some targets tend to show abnormally good performance prior to takeover.

The Role of Debt in Motivating Organizational Efficiency

The agency costs of debt have been widely discussed,[27] but the benefits of debt in motivating managers and their organizations to be efficient have largely been ignored. I call these effects the "control hypothesis" for debt creation.

24. See Gordon Donaldson, *Managing Corporate Wealth*, (Praeger: 1984). Donaldson, in a detailed study of 12 large Fortune 500 firms, concludes that managers of these firms were not driven by maximization of the value of the firm, but rather by the maximization of "corporate wealth." He defines corporate wealth as *"the aggregate purchasing power available to management for strategic purposes during any given planning period. ...* this wealth consists of the stocks and flows of cash and cash equivalents (primarily credit) that management can use at its discretion to implement decisions involving the control of goods and services." (p. 3, emphasis in original) "In practical terms it is cash, credit, and other corporate purchasing power by which management commands goods and services." (p.22).

25. Where growth is measured by increases in sales. See Kevin J. Murphy, "Corporate Performance and Managerial Remuneration: An Empirical Analysis," *Journal of Accounting and Economics* 7, Nos. 1-3 (April, 1985), pp. 11-42. This positive relationship between compensation and sales growth does not imply, although it is consistent with, causality.

25a. See George Baker, "Compensation and Hierarchies" (unpublished, Harvard Business School, January, 1986).

26. Rents are returns in excess of the opportunity cost of the resources committed to the activity. Quasi-rents are returns in excess of the short-run opportunity cost of the resources to the activity.

26a. See Stewart C. Myers and Nicholas S. Majluf, "Corporate Financing and Investment Decisions When Firms Have Information That Investors Do Not Have," *Journal of Financial Economcics* 13 (1984), pp. 187-221.

27. See Michael C. Jensen and William H. Meckling, "Theory of the Firm: Managerial Behavior, Agency Costs and Ownership Structure," *Journal of Financial Economics*, V. 3 (1976), pp. 305-360; Stewart C. Myers, "Determinants of Corporate Borrowing," *Journal of Financial Economics*, V. 5, No. 2 (1977), pp. 147-175; and Clifford W. Smith, Jr. and Jerold B. Warner, "On Financial Contracting: An Analysis of Bond Covenants," *Journal of Financial Economics*, V. 7 (1979), pp. 117-161.

The control function of debt is more important in organizations that generate large cash flows but have low growth prospects, and it is even more important in organizations that must shrink.

Managers with substantial free cash flow can increase dividends or repurchase stock and thereby pay out current cash that would otherwise be invested in low-return projects or otherwise wasted. This payout leaves managers with control over the use of future free cash flows, but they can also promise to pay out future cash flows by announcing a "permanent" increase in the dividend.[28] Because there is no contractual obligation to make the promised dividend payments, such promises are weak. Dividends can be reduced by managers in the future with little effective recourse to shareholders. The fact that capital markets punish dividend cuts with large stock price reductions is an interesting equilibrium market response to the agency costs of free cash flow.[29]

Debt creation, without retention of the proceeds of the issue, enables managers effectively to bond their promise to pay out future cash flows. Thus, debt can be an effective substitute for dividends, something that is not generally recognized in the corporate finance literature.[30] By issuing debt in exchange for stock, managers bond their promise to pay out future cash flows in a way that simple dividend increases do not. In doing so, they give shareholder-recipients of the debt the right to take the firm into bankruptcy court if they do not keep their promise to make the interest and principal payments.[31] Thus, debt reduces the agency costs of free cash flow by reducing the cash flow available for spending at the discretion of managers.

Issuing large amounts of debt to buy back stock sets up organizational incentives to motivate managers to pay out free cash flow. In addition, the exchange of debt for stock also helps managers overcome the normal organizational resistance to retrenchment that the payout of free cash flow often requires. The threat of failure to make debt-service payments serves as a strong motivating force to make

such organizations more efficient. Stock repurchase for debt or cash also has tax advantages. Interest payments are tax-deductible to the corporation; the part of the repurchase proceeds equal to the seller's tax basis in the stock is not taxed at all, and that which is taxed is subject to capital-gains rates.

The control hypothesis does not imply that debt issues will always have positive control effects. For example, these effects will not be as important for rapidly growing organizations with large and highly profitable investment projects but no free cash flow. Such organizations will have to go regularly to the financial markets to obtain capital. At these times the markets will have an opportunity to evaluate the company, its management, and its proposed projects. Investment bankers and analysts play an important role in this monitoring, and the market's assessment is made evident by the price investors pay for the financial claims.

The control function of debt is more important in organizations that generate large cash flows but have low growth prospects, and it is even more important in organizations that must shrink. In these organizations the pressures to waste cash flows by investing them in uneconomic projects are most serious.

[The original paper contains a section here entitled "Evidence from Financial Transactions in Support of the Free Cash Flow Theory of Mergers," which appears in the "Appendix" to this article.]

The Evidence from Leveraged Buyout and Going-Private Transactions

Many of the benefits of going-private and leveraged buyout transactions seem to be due to the control function of debt. These transactions are creating a new organizational form that competes

---

28. Interestingly, Graham and Dodd, in their treatise, *Security Analysis*, placed great importance on the dividend payout in their famous valuation formula: V = M (D + .33E),(p.454). V is value, M is the earnings multiplier when the dividend payout rate is a "normal two-thirds of earnings," D is the expected dividend, and E is expected earnings. In their formula, dividends are valued at three times the rate of retained earnings, a proposition that has puzzled many students of modern finance (at least of my vintage). The agency cost of free cash flow that leads to overretention and waste of shareholder resources is consistent with the deep suspicion with which Graham and Dodd viewed the lack of payout. Their discussion (chapter 34) reflects a belief in the tenuous nature of the future benefits of such retention. Although they do not couch the issues in terms of the conflict between managers and shareholders, the free cash flow theory explicated here implies that their beliefs, sometimes characterized as "a bird in the hand is worth two in the bush," were perhaps well founded. See Chapters 32, 34, and 36 in Benjamin Graham and David L. Dodd, *Security Analysis: Principles and Technique* (New York, McGraw-Hill, 1951).

29. See Guy Charest, "Dividend Information, Stock Returns, and Market Efficiency-II, *Journal of Financial Economics* 6, (1978), pp. 297-330; and Joseph Aharony and Itzhak Swary, "Quarterly Dividend and Earnings Announcements and Stockholder's Returns: An Empirical Analysis," *Journal of Finance* 35 (1980), pp. 1-12.

30. Literally, principal and interest payments are substitutes for dividends. However, because interest is tax-deductible at the corporate level and dividends are not, dividends and debt are not perfect substitutes.

31. Two studies argue that regular dividend payments can be effective in reducing agency costs with managers by assuring that managers are forced more frequently to subject themselves and their policies to the discipline of the capital markets when they acquire capital. See Frank H. Easterbrook, "Managers' Discretion and Investors' Welfare: Theories and Evidence," *Delaware Journal of Corporate Law*, V. 9, No. 3 (1984b), pp. 540-571; and Michael Rozeff, "Growth, Beta and Agency Costs as Determinants of Dividend Payout Ratios", *Journal of Financial Research*, V.5 (1982), pp. 249-59.

If managers [of companies with strip financing] withhold dividends to invest in value-reducing projects or if they are simply incompetent, strip holders have recourse to remedial powers not available to the equity holders [in firms without strip financing].

successfully with the open corporate form because of advantages in controlling the agency costs of free cash flow. In 1984, going-private transactions totaled $10.8 billion and represented 27 percent of all public acquisitions.[36] The evidence indicates premiums paid averaged over 50 percent.[37]

Desirable leveraged buyout candidates are frequently firms or divisions of larger firms that have stable business histories and substantial free cash flow (that is, low growth prospects and high potential for generating cash flows)—situations where agency costs of free cash flow are likely to be high. Leveraged buyout transactions are frequently financed with high debt; ten-to-one ratios of debt to equity are not uncommon. Moreover, the use of strip financing and the allocation of equity in the deals reveal a sensitivity to incentives, conflicts of interest, and bankruptcy costs.

Strip financing, the practice in which risky non-equity securities are held in approximately equal proportions, limits the conflict of interest among such security holders and therefore limits bankruptcy costs. A somewhat oversimplified example illustrates the point. Consider two firms identical in every respect except financing. Firm A is entirely financed with equity, and Firm B is highly leveraged with senior subordinated debt, convertible debt, and preferred as well as equity. Suppose Firm B securities are sold only in strips—that is, a buyer purchasing X percent of any security must purchase X percent of all securities, and the securities are "stapled" together so they cannot be separated later. Security holders of both firms have identical unlevered claims on the cash flow distribution, but organizationally the two firms are very different. If Firm B managers withhold dividends to invest in value-reducing projects or if they are simply incompetent, strip holders have recourse to remedial powers not available to the equity holders of Firm A. Each Firm B security specifies the rights its holder has in the event of default on its dividend or coupon payment—for example, the right to take the firm into bankruptcy or to have board representation. As each security above equity goes into default the strip holder receives new rights to intercede in the organization. As a result, it is quicker and less expensive to replace managers in Firm B.

Moreover, because every security holder in the highly levered Firm B has the same claim on the firm, there are no conflicts between senior and junior claimants over reorganization of the claims in the event of default; to the strip holder it is a matter of moving funds from one pocket to another. Thus, Firm B need never go into bankruptcy. The reorganization can be accomplished voluntarily, quickly, and with less expense and disruption than through bankruptcy proceedings.

Securities commonly subject to strip practices are often called "mezzanine" financing and include securities with priority superior to common stock yet subordinate to senior debt. This seems to be a sensible arrangement. Because of several other factors ignored in our simplified example, IRS restrictions deny tax deductibility of debt interest in such situations and bank holdings of equity are restricted by regulation. Riskless senior debt need not be in the strip because there are no conflicts with other claimants in the event of reorganization when there is no probability of default on its payments.

It is advantageous to have top-level managers and venture capitalists who promote the transactions hold a larger share of the equity. Top-level managers frequently receive 15 to 20 percent of the equity, and venture capitalists and the funds they represent generally retain the major share of the remainder. The venture capitalists control the board of directors and monitor managers. Managers and venture capitalists have a strong interest in making the venture successful because their equity interests are subordinate to other claims. Success requires, among other things, implementation of changes to avoid investment in low-return projects in order to generate the cash for debt service and to increase the value of equity. Finally, when the equity is held primarily by managers or generally by a small number of people, greater efficiencies in risk bearing are made possible by placing more of the risk in the hands of debt holders when the debt is held in well-diversified institutional portfolios.

Less than a handful of these leveraged buyout ventures have ended in bankruptcy, although more have gone through private reorganizations. A thorough test of this organizational form requires the passage of time and another recession.

Some have asserted that managers engaging in a

---

36. By number. See W. T. Grimm, Mergerstat Review (1985), Figs. 36 and 37.

37. See H. DeAngelo, L. DeAngelo and E. Rice, "Going Private: Minority Freezeouts and Stockholder Wealth," *Journal of Law and Economics*, V. 27, No. 2 (October, 1984), pp. 367-401; and Louis Lowenstein, "Management Buyouts," *Columbia Law Review*, V. 85 (May, 1985), pp. 730-784. Lowenstein also mentions incentive effects of debt but argues tax effects play a major role in explaining the value increase.

Because the venture capitalists are generally the largest shareholder and control the board of directors, they have both greater ability and stronger incentives to monitor managers than directors representing diffuse public shareholders in the typical public corporation.

buyout of their firm are insulating themselves from monitoring. The opposite is true in the typical leveraged buyout. Because the venture capitalists are generally the largest shareholder and control the board of directors, they have both greater ability and incentives to monitor managers effectively than directors representing diffuse public shareholders in the typical public corporation.

Evidence from the Oil Industry

The oil industry is large and visible. It is also an industry in which the importance of takeovers in motivating change and efficiency is particularly clear. Therefore, detailed analysis of it provides an understanding of how the market for corporate control helps motivate more efficient use of resources in the corporate sector.

Reorganization of the industry is mandatory. Radical changes in the energy market from 1973 through the late 1970s imply that a major restructuring of the petroleum industry had to occur. These changes are as follows:
- a ten-fold increase in the price of crude oil from 1973 to 1979;
- reduced annual consumption of oil in the U.S.;
- reduced expectations of future increases in the price of oil;
- increased exploration and development costs;
- and increased real interest rates.

As a result of these changes the optimal level of refining and distribution capacity and crude reserves fell over this period, and since the late 1970s the industry has been plagued with excess capacity. Reserves are reduced by reducing the level of exploration and development, and it pays to concentrate these reductions in high-cost areas such as the United States.

Substantial reductions in exploration and development and in refining and distribution capacity meant that some firms had to leave the industry. This is especially true because holding reserves is subject to economies of scale, whereas exploration and development are subject to diseconomies of scale.

Price increases created large cash flows in the industry. For example, 1984 cash flows of the ten largest oil companies were $48.5 billion, 28 percent of the total cash flows of the top 200 firms in Dun's Business Month [1985] survey. Consistent with the agency costs of free cash flow, management did not pay out the excess resources to shareholders. Instead, the industry continued to spend heavily on exploration and development even though average returns on these expenditures were below the cost of capital.

Paradoxically, the profitability of oil exploration and drilling activity can decrease even though the price of oil increases if the value of reserves in the ground falls. This can happen when the price increase is associated with reductions in consumption that make it difficult to market newly discovered oil. In the late 1970s the increased holding costs associated with higher real interest rates, reductions in expected future oil price increases, increased exploration and development costs, and reductions in the consumption of oil combined to make many exploration and development projects uneconomic. The industry, however, continued to spend heavily on such projects.

The hypothesis that oil-industry exploration and development expenditures were too high during this period is consistent with the findings of the earlier-mentioned study by McConnell and Muscarella.[38] Their evidence indicates that announcements of increases in exploration and development expenditures by oil companies in the period 1975-1981 were associated with systematic decreases in the announcing firms' stock prices. Moreover, announcements of decreases in exploration and development expenditures were associated with increases in stock prices. These results are striking in comparison with their evidence that exactly the opposite market reaction occurs with increases and decreases in investment expenditures by industrial firms, and with SEC evidence that increases in research and development expenditures are associated with increased stock prices.[38a]

Additional evidence of the uneconomic nature of the oil industry's exploration and development expenditures is contained in a study by Bernard

---

38. John J. McConnell and Chris J. Muscarella, "Corporate Capital Expenditure Decisions and the Market Value of the Firm," *Journal of Financial Economics*, V. 14, No. 3 (1985).

38a. Office of the Chief Economist, Securities and Exchange Commission, "Institutional Ownership, Tender Offers, and Long-Term Investments," April 19, 1985.

Wall Street was not undervaluing the oil; it was valuing it correctly, but it was also correctly valuing the wasted expenditures on exploration and development that oil companies were making.

Picchi of Salomon Brothers. His study of rates of return on exploration and development expenditures for 30 large oil firms indicated that on average the industry did not earn "even a 10% return on its pretax outlays" in the period 1982-84. Estimates of the average ratio of the present value of future net cash flows of discoveries, extensions and enhanced recovery to expenditures for exploration and development for the industry ranged from less than .6 to slightly more than .9, depending on the method used and the year. In other words, even taking the cost of capital to be only 10 percent on a pretax basis, the industry was realizing on average only 60 to 90 cents on every dollar invested in these activities. Picchi concludes:

For 23 of the [30] companies in our survey, we would recommend immediate *cuts of perhaps 25%-30% in exploration and production spending. It is clear that much of the money that these firms spent last year on petroleum exploration and development yielded subpar financial returns—even at $30 per barrel, let alone today's $26-$27 per barrel price structure."*[39]

The waste associated with excessive exploration and development expenditures explains why buying oil on Wall Street was considerably cheaper than obtaining it by drilling holes in the ground, even after adjustment for differential taxes and regulations on prices of old oil. Wall Street was not undervaluing the oil; it was valuing it correctly, but it was also correctly valuing the wasted expenditures on exploration and development that oil companies were making. When these managerially imposed "taxes" on the reserves were taken into account, the net price of oil on Wall Street was very low. This provided incentives for firms to obtain reserves by purchasing other oil companies and reducing expenditures on non-cost-effective exploration.

High profits are not usually associated with retrenchment. Adjustment by the energy industry to the new environment has been slow for several reasons. First, it is difficult for organizations to change operating rules and practices like those in the oil industry that have worked well for long periods in the past, even though they do not fit the new situation. Nevertheless, survival requires that organizations adapt to major changes in their environment.

Second, the past decade has been a particularly puzzling period in the oil business because at the same time that changes in the environment have required a reduction of capacity, cash flows and profits have been high. This is a somewhat unusual condition in which the average productivity of resources in the industry increased while the marginal productivity decreased. The point is illustrated graphically in Figure 1.

As the figure illustrates, profits plus payments to factors of production other than capital were larger in 1985 than in 1973. Moreover, because of the upward shift and simultaneous twist of the marginal productivity of capital schedule from 1973 to 1985, the optimal level of capital devoted to the industry fell from Q_1 to Q_2. Thus, the adjustment signals were confused because the period of necessary retrenchment coincided with substantial increases in value brought about by the tenfold increase in the price of the industry's major asset, its inventory of crude oil reserves.

The large cash flows and profits generated by the increases in oil prices both masked the losses imposed on marginal facilities and enabled oil companies to finance major expenditures internally. Thus, the normal disciplinary forces of the product market have been weak, and those of the capital markets have been inoperative, during the past decade.

Third, the oil companies' large and highly visible profits subjected them to strong political pressures to reinvest the cash flows in exploration and development to respond to the incorrect, but popular, perception that reserves were too low. Furthermore, while reserves were on average too high, those firms which were substantially short of reserves were spending to replenish them to avoid the organizational consequences associated with reserve deficiencies. The resulting excessive exploration and development expenditures by the industry and the considerable delays in retrenchment of refining and distribution facilities wasted resources.

In sum, the stage was set for retrenchment in the oil industry in the early 1980s. Yet the product and capital markets could not force management to change its strategy because the industry's high internal cash flows insulated it from these pressures.

The fact that oil industry managers tried to invest funds outside the industry is also evidence that they could not find enough profitable projects within the industry to use the huge inflow of resources

---

39. Bernard J. Picchi, "The Structure of the U.S. Oil Industry: Past and Future" (Salomon Brothers Inc.) July, 1985, emphasis in original.

Partly as a result of Mesa's efforts, firms in the [oil] industry were led to merge, and in the merging process they paid out large amounts of capital to shareholders, reduced excess expenditures on exploration and development, and reduced excess capacity in refining and distribution.

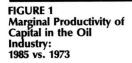

**FIGURE 1
Marginal Productivity of
Capital in the Oil
Industry:
1985 vs. 1973**

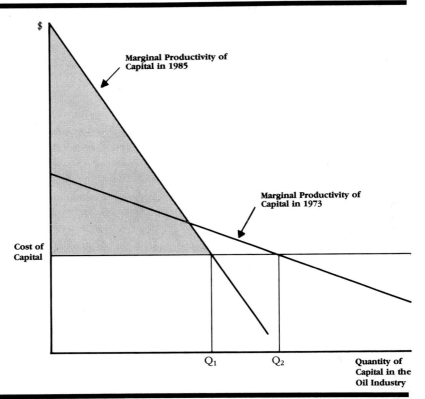

Marginal Productivity of
Capital in 1985

Marginal Productivity of
Capital in 1973

Cost of
Capital

Q_1 Q_2 **Quantity of
Capital in the
Oil Industry**

efficiently. Unfortunately these efforts failed. The diversification programs involved purchases of companies in retailing (Marcor by Mobil), manufacturing (Reliance Electric by Exxon), office equipment (Vydec by Exxon), and mining (by Sohio, Anaconda Minerals by ARCO, Cyprus Mines by Amoco). These acquisitions turned out to be among the least successful of the last decade, partly because of bad luck (e.g., the collapse of the minerals industry) and partly because of a lack of managerial expertise outside the oil industry.

The effects of takeovers. Ultimately the capital markets, through the takeover market, have begun to force managers to respond to the new market conditions. Unfortunately, there is widespread confusion about the important role of takeovers in

bringing about the difficult but necessary organizational changes required in the retrenchment.

Managers, quite naturally, want large amounts of resources under their control to insulate them from the uncertainties of markets.[40] Retrenchment requires cancellation or delay of many ongoing and planned projects. This affects the careers of the people involved, and the resulting resistance means that such changes frequently do not get made without the major pressures associated with a crisis. A takeover attempt can create the crisis that brings about action where none would otherwise occur.

T. Boone Pickens of Mesa Petroleum perceived early that the oil industry must be restructured. Partly as a result of Mesa's efforts, firms in the industry were led to merge, and in the merging process they

40. See Gordon Donaldson, *Managing Corporate Wealth* (Praeger: 1984).

Horizontal mergers for cash or debt in declining industries generate gains by encouraging exit of resources (through payout to shareholders) and by substituting existing capacity for investment in new facilities by firms that are short of capacity.

paid out large amounts of capital to shareholders, reduced excess expenditures on exploration and development, and reduced excess capacity in refining and distribution.

The result has been large gains in efficiency. Total gains to the shareholders in the Gulf-Chevron, Getty-Texaco and Dupont-Conoco mergers, for example, were over $17 billion. Much more is possible. A study by Allen Jacobs estimates that, as of December 1984, the total potential gains from eliminating the inefficiencies in 98 petroleum companies amounted to roughly $200 billion.[41]

Recent events indicate that actual takeover is not necessary to bring about the required adjustments:

• The Phillips restructuring plan, in response to the threat of takeover, has involved substantial retrenchment and return of resources to shareholders; and the result was a $1.2 billion (20%) gain in Phillips' market value. It repurchased 53 percent of its stock for $4.5 billion in debt, raised its dividend 25 per-cent, cut capital spending and initiated a program to sell $2 billion of assets.

• Unocal's defense in the Mesa tender offer battle resulted in a $2.2 billion (35%) gain to shareholders from retrenchment and return of resources to shareholders. It paid out 52 percent of its equity by repurchasing stock with a $4.2 billion debt issue and will reduce costs and capital expenditures.

• The voluntary restructuring announced by ARCO resulted in a $3.2 billion (30%) gain in market value. ARCO's restructuring involves a 35 to 40 percent cut in exploration and development expenditures, repurchase of 25 percent of its stock for $4 billion, a 33 percent increase in its dividend, withdrawal from gasoline marketing and refining east of the Mississippi, and a 13 percent reduction in its work force.

• The announcement of the Diamond-Shamrock reorganization in July 1985 provides an interesting contrast to the others and further support for the theory because the company's market value *fell* 2 percent on the announcement day. Because the plan results in an effective increase in exploration and capital expenditures and a reduction in cash payouts to investors, the restructuring does not increase the value of the firm. The plan involved reducing cash

dividends by $.76/share (−43%), creating a master limited partnership to hold properties accounting for 35 percent of its North American oil and gas production, paying an annual $.90/share dividend in partnership shares, repurchasing 6 percent of its shares for $200 million, selling 12 percent of its master limited partnership to the public, and *increasing* its expenditures on oil and gas exploration by $100 million per year.

Free Cash Flow Theory of Takeovers

Free cash flow is only one of approximately a dozen theories to explain takeovers, all of which are of some relevance in explaining the numerous forces motivating merger and acquisition activity.[41a] The agency cost of free cash flow is consistent with a wide range of data for which there has been no consistent explanation. Here I sketch some empirical predictions of the free cash flow theory for takeovers and mergers, and what I believe are the facts that lend it credence.

The positive market response to debt creation in oil and other takeovers is consistent with the agency costs of free cash flow and the control hypothesis of debt.[41b] The data is consistent with the notion that additional debt has increased efficiency by forcing organizations with large cash flows but few high-return investment projects to pay out cash to investors. The debt helps prevent such firms from wasting resources on low-return projects.

Acquisitions are one way managers spend cash instead of paying it out to shareholders. Therefore, free cash flow theory predicts which kinds of mergers and takeovers are more likely to destroy rather than to create value. It shows how takeovers are both evidence of the conflicts of interest between the shareholders and managers and a response to the problem. The theory implies that managers of firms with unused borrowing power and large free cash flows are more likely to undertake low-benefit or even value-destroying mergers. Diversification programs generally fit this category, and the theory predicts they will generate lower total gains. The major benefit of such diversifying transactions may be that they involve less waste of resources than if the funds had been invested

41. Allen Jacobs, "The Agency Cost of Corporate Control: The Petroleum Industry," (MIT, unpublished paper, March, 1986).

41a. See Roll, 1986, cited earlier.
41b. See Robert Bruner, "The Use of Excess Cash and Debt Capacity as a Motive for Merger," (unpublished, Colgated Darden Graduate School of Business, December, 1985).

Firms with a mismatch between growth and resources—firms with high growth, low liquidity, and high leverage, and firms with low growth, high liquidity, and lower leverage—are more likely to be taken over.

internally in unprofitable projects.[41c]

Low-return mergers are more likely to occur in industries with large cash flows where the economics dictate retrenchment. Horizontal mergers (where cash or debt is the form of payment) within declining industries will tend to create value because they facilitate exit; the cash or debt payments to shareholders of the target firm cause resources to leave the industry directly. Mergers outside the industry are more likely to have low or even negative returns because managers are likely to know less about managing such firms.

Oil fits this description and so does tobacco. Tobacco firms face declining demand as a result of changing smoking habits, but they generate large free cash flow and have been involved in major diversifying acquisitions recently—for example, the $5.6 billion purchase of General Foods by Philip Morris. The theory predicts that these acquisitions in non-related industries are more likely to create negative productivity effects—though these negative effects appear to be outweighed by the reductions in waste from internal expansion.

Forest products is another industry with excess capacity and acquisition activity, including the acquisition of St. Regis by Champion International and Crown Zellerbach by Sir James Goldsmith. Horizontal mergers for cash or debt in such an industry generate gains by encouraging exit of resources (through payout) and by substituting existing capacity for investment in new facilities by firms that are short of capacity.

Food-industry mergers also appear to reflect the expenditure of free cash flow. The industry apparently generates large cash flows with few growth opportunities. It is therefore a good candidate for leveraged buyouts, and these are now occurring; the $6.3 billion Beatrice LBO is the largest ever.

The broadcasting industry generates rents in the form of large cash flows on its licenses and also fits the theory. Regulation limits the overall supply of licenses and the number owned by a single entity. Thus profitable internal investments are limited and the industry's free cash flow has been spent on organizational inefficiencies and diversification programs, making these firms takeover targets. The CBS debt-for-stock exchange and restructuring as a defense against the hostile bid by Turner fits the theory, as does the $3.5 billion purchase of American Broadcasting Company by Capital Cities Communications. Completed cable systems also create agency problems from free cash flows in the form of rents on their franchises and quasi-rents on their investment, and are thus likely targets for acquisition and leveraged buyouts.

Large cash flows earned by motion picture companies on their film libraries also represent quasi-rents and are likely to generate free cash flow problems. Similarly, the attempted takeover of Disney and its subsequent reorganization is consistent with the theory. Drug companies with large cash flows from previous successful discoveries and few potential future prospects are also likely candidates for large agency costs of free cash flow.

The theory predicts that value-increasing takeovers occur in response to breakdowns of internal control processes in firms with substantial free cash flow and organizational policies (including diversification programs) that are wasting resources. It predicts hostile takeovers, large increases in leverage, the dismantling of empires with few economies of scale or scope to give them economic purpose (e.g. conglomerates), and much controversy as current managers object to loss of their jobs or changes in organizational policies forced on them by threat of takeover.

The debt created in a hostile takeover (or takeover defense) of a firm suffering severe agency costs of free cash flow need not be permanent. Indeed, sometimes it is desirable to "over-leverage" such a firm. In these situations, levering the firm so highly it cannot continue to exist in its old form yields

---

41c. Acquisitions made with cash or securities other than stock involve payout of resources to (target) shareholders, and this can create net benefits even if the merger creates operating inefficiencies. To illustrate the point, consider an acquiring firm, A, with substantial free cash flow that the market expects will be invested in low-return projects with a negative net present value of $100 million. If Firm A makes an acquisition of Firm B that generates zero synergies but uses up all of Firm A's free cash flow (and thereby prevents its waste) the combined market value of the two firms will *rise* by $100 million. The market value increases because the acquisition eliminates the expenditures on internal investments with negative market value of $100 million. Extending the argument, we see that acquisitions that have *negative* synergies of up to $100 million in current value will still increase the combined market value of the two firms. Such negative-synergy mergers will also increase social welfare and aggregate productivity whenever the market value of the negative productivity effects on the two merging firms is less than the market value of the waste that would have occurred with the firms' investment programs in the absence of the merger. The division of the gains between the target and bidding firms depends, of course, on the bargaining power of the two parties. Because the bidding firms are using funds that would otherwise been spent on low- or negative-return projects, however, the opportunity cost of the funds is lower than their cost of capital. As a result, they will tend to overpay for the acquisition and thereby transfer most, if not all, of the gains to the target firm's shareholders. In extreme cases they may pay so much that the bidding-firm share price falls, in effect giving the target-shareholders more than 100 percent of the gains. These predictions are consistent with the evidence.

The abolition of mere size as a deterrent to takeover...has made possible the realization of large gains from reallocating larger collections of assets to more productive uses.

benefits. It creates the crisis to motivate cuts in expansion programs and the sale of those divisions that are more valuable outside the firm. The proceeds are used to reduce debt to a more normal or permanent level. This process results in a complete rethinking of the organization's strategy and structure. When it is successful, a much leaner, more efficient, and competitive organization results.

Some Evidence from Merger Studies

Consistent with the data, free cash flow theory predicts that many acquirers will tend to perform exceptionally well prior to acquisition. That exceptional stock price performance will often be associated with increased free cash flow which is then used for acquisition programs. The oil industry fits this description. Increased oil prices caused large gains in profits and stock prices in the mid-to-late 1970s. Empirical evidence from studies of both stock prices and accounting data also indicates exceptionally good performance for acquirers prior to acquisition.[42]

Targets will tend to be of two kinds: firms with poor management that have done poorly before the merger, and firms that have done exceptionally well and have large free cash flow that they refuse to pay out to shareholders....In the best study to date of the determinants of takeover, Palepu [1986] finds strong evidence consistent with the free cash flow theory of mergers. He studied a sample of 163 firms that were acquired in the period 1971-1979 and a random sample of 256 firms that were not acquired. Both samples were in mining and manufacturing and were listed on either the New York or American Stock Exchange. He finds that target firms were characterized by significantly lower growth and lower leverage than the nontarget firms, although there was no significant difference in their holdings of liquid assets. He also finds that poor prior performance (measured by the net-of-market returns in the four years before the acquisition) is significantly related to the probability of takeover, and, interestingly, that accounting measures of past performance such as

return on equity are unrelated to the probability of takeover. He also finds that firms with a mismatch between growth and resources are more likely to be taken over. These are firms with high growth (measured by average sales growth), low liquidity (measured by the ratio of liquid assets to total assets) and high leverage, and firms with low growth, high liquidity, and low leverage. Finally, Palepu's evidence rejects the hypothesis that takeovers are due to the undervaluation of a firm's assets as measured by the market-to-book ratio.[42a]

High-Yield ("Junk") Bonds

The last several years have witnessed a major innovation in the financial markets with the establishment of active markets in high-yield bonds. These bonds are rated below investment grade by the bond rating agencies and are frequently referred to as junk bonds, a disparaging term that bears no relation to their pedigree. They carry interest rates that are 3 to 5 percentage points higher than the yields on government bonds of comparable maturity. High-yield bonds are best thought of as commercial loans that can be resold in secondary markets. By traditional standards they are more risky than investment-grade bonds and therefore carry higher interest rates. An early study finds the default rates on these bonds have been low and the realized returns have been disproportionately higher than their risk.[43a]

High-yield bonds have been attacked by those who wish to inhibit their use, particularly in the financing of takeover bids. The invention of high-yield bonds has provided methods to finance takeover ventures like those companies use to finance more traditional ventures. Companies commonly raise funds to finance ventures by selling claims to be paid from the proceeds of the venture; this is the essence of debt or stock issues used to finance new ventures. High-yield bonds used in takeovers work similarly. The bonds provide a claim on the proceeds of the venture, using the assets and cash flows of the target

42. See the following two papers which were presented at the Conference on Takeovers and Contests for Corporate Control, Columbia University, November, 1985: Ellen B. Magenheim and Dennis Mueller, "On Measuring the Effect of Acquisitions on Acquiring Firm Shareholders, or Are Acquiring Firm Shareholders Better Off After an Acquisition Than They Were Before?"; and Michael Bradley and Gregg Jarrell, "Evidence on Gains from Mergers and Takeovers." See also Paul R. Asquith and E. Han Kim, "The Impact of Merger Bids on the Participating Firms' Security Holders," *Journal of Finance*, 37, 1209-1228; Gershon Mandelker, "Risk and Return: The Case of Merging Firms," *Journal of Financial Economics*, V. 1, No. 4 (December, 1974), pp. 303-336; and T.C. Langetieg, "An Application of A Three-Factor Performance Index to Measure Stockholder Gains from Merger," *Journal of Financial Economics*, V. 6 (December, 1978), pp. 365-384.

42a. Palepu (1986), presented at the Conference on Takeovers and Contests for Corporate Control, Columbia University, November, 1985.

43a. Marshall E. Blume and Donald B. Keim, "Risk and Return Characteristics of Lower-Grade Bonds" (unpublished paper, The Wharton School, December, 1984).

The Federal Reserve System's own data are inconsistent with the reasons given for its restrictions on the use of debt.

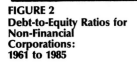

FIGURE 2
Debt-to-Equity Ratios for Non-Financial Corporations: 1961 to 1985

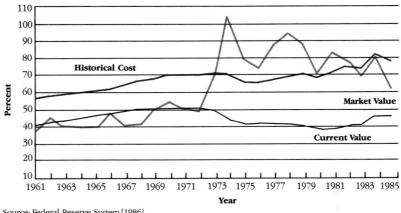

Source: Federal Reserve System [1986]

plus the equity contributed by the acquirer as collateral. This basic structure is the common way that individuals purchase homes; they use the home plus their down payment as collateral for the mortgage. There is nothing inherently unusual in the structure of this contract, although those who would bar the use of high-yield bonds in takeover ventures would have us believe otherwise.

Some might argue that the risk of high-yield bonds used in takeover attempts is "too high." But high-yield bonds are by definition less risky than common stock claims on the same venture. Would these same critics argue that stock claims are too risky and thus should be barred? The risk argument makes logical sense only as an argument that the transactions costs associated with bankruptcy are too high in these ventures or that the promised yields on the bonds are too low and that investors who purchase them will not earn returns high enough to compensate for the risk they are incurring. This argument makes little sense because there is vast evidence that investors are capable of pricing risks in all sorts of other markets. It is inconceivable they are peculiarly unable to do so in the high-yield bond market.

In January 1986 the Federal Reserve Board issued a new interpretation of the margin rules that restricts the use of debt in takeovers to 50 percent or less of the purchase price. This rule reintroduces size as an effective deterrent to takeover. It was apparently motivated by the belief that the use of corporate debt had become abnormally and dangerously high and was threatening the economy.

This assessment is not consistent with the facts. Figure 2 plots three measures of debt use by nonfinancial corporations in the U.S. The debt/equity ratio is measured relative to three bases: market value of equity, estimated current asset value of equity, and accounting book value of equity measured at historical cost.

Although debt/equity ratios were higher in 1985 than in 1961, they were not at record levels. The book value debt/equity ratio reached a high of 81.4 percent in 1984, but declined to 78 percent in 1985. The fact that debt/equity ratios measured on an historical cost basis are relatively high is to be expected, given the previous decade of inflation. Maintenance of the same inflation-adjusted debt/equity ratio in times of inflation implies that the book value ratio must rise because the current value of assets in the denominator of the inflation-adjusted ratio is rising. The current value ratio, which takes account of inflation, fell from 50.7 percent in 1970 to 46.5 percent in 1985. The market-value ratio rose from 54.7 percent in 1970 to 80.5 percent in 1984 and plummeted to 60.8 percent in 1985. The 1985 market-value ratio was 45 percentage points below its 1974 peak of 105.2 percent. In short, the Federal Reserve System's own data are inconsistent with the reasons given for its restrictions on the use of debt.

High-yield bonds were first used in a takeover bid in early 1984 and have been involved in relatively few bids in total. In 1984, only about 12 percent of the $14.3 billion of new high-yield debt was associated with mergers and acquisitions. In 1985, 26 per-

When correctly implemented they [golden parachutes] help reduce the conflicts of interest between shareholders and managers at times of takeover and therefore make it more likely that the productive gains stemming from changes in control will be realized.

cent of the $14.7 billion of new high-yield debt was used in acquisitions.[44] Some of the acquisitions, however, such as the Unocal and CBS offers (both unsuccessful), have received intense attention from the media; and this publicity has fostered the belief that high-yield bonds are widely used in takeovers. Nevertheless, high-yield bonds are an important innovation in the takeover field because they help eliminate mere size as a deterrent to takeover. They have been particularly influential in helping to bring about reorganizations in the oil industry.

Historical default rates on high-yield bonds have been low, but many of these bonds are so new that the experience could prove to be different in the next downturn. Various opponents have proposed regulations or legislation to restrict the issuance of such securities, to penalize their tax status, and to restrict their holding by thrifts, which can now buy them as substitutes for the issuance of nonmarketable commercial loans. These proposals are premature. Policymakers should be wary of responding to the clamor for restrictions by executives who desire protection from the discipline of the takeover market and by members of the financial community who want to restrict competition from this new financing vehicle.

The holding of high-yield bonds by thrifts is an interesting issue that warrants further analyis. The recent deregulation of the banking and thrift industries presents many opportunities and challenges to the thrifts. Elimination of restrictions on interest paid to depositors has raised the cost of funds to these institutions. Thrifts have also received the right to engage in new activities such as commercial lending. Survival requires these institutions to take advantage of some of these new business opportunities.

The organizational costs of developing commerical lending departments in the 3,500 thrifts in the country is substantial. Thousands of new loan officers will have to be hired and trained. The additional wage and training costs and the bad-debt losses that will be incurred in the learning phase will be substantial. High-yield bonds provide a promising solution to this problem. If part of the commercial lending function can be centralized in the hands of investment bankers who provide commerical loans in the form of marketable high-yield debt, the thrifts can substitute the purchase of this high-yield debt for their commercial lending and thereby avoid the huge investment in such loan departments.

The Legitimate Concerns of Managers

Conflicts of Interest and Increased Costs to Managers

The interests of corporate managers are not the same as the interests of corporations as organizations, and conflicts of interest can become intense when major changes in the organization's strategy are required. Competition causes change, and change creates winners and losers, especially in that branch of the managerial labor market called the takeover market.

Managers' private incentives sometimes run counter to overall efficiency. The costs of takeovers have fallen as the legal and financial skills of participants in the takeover market have become more sophisticated, as the restrictions on takeovers imposed by antitrust laws have been relaxed, and as financing techniques have improved. Except for new regulatory constraints on the use of debt, this means that the largest of the Fortune 500 companies are now potentially subject to takeover. The abolition of mere size as a deterrent to takeover is desirable because it has made possible the realization of large gains from reallocating larger collections of assets to more productive uses.

This new susceptibility to takeover has created a new contracting environment for top-level managers. Many managers are legitimately anxious, and it will take time for the system to work out an appropriate set of practices and contracts reflecting the risks and rewards of the new environment. Some of the uncertainty of top-level managers formerly insulated from pressures from the financial markets will fade as they learn how their policies affect the market value of their companies.

The Desirability of Golden Parachutes

Unfortunately, a major component of the solution to the conflict of interest between shareholders and managers has been vastly misunderstood. I am referring to severance contracts that compensate managers for the loss of their jobs in the event of a

---

44. Source: Drexel Burnham Lambert, private correspondence.

change in control—what have been popularly labeled "golden parachutes."

These contracts are clearly desirable, even when judged solely from the viewpoint of the interests of shareholders; but they are also efficient from a social viewpoint. When correctly implemented they help reduce the conflicts of interest between shareholders and managers at times of takeover and therefore make it more likely that the productive gains stemming from changes in control will be realized. The evidence indicates that stock prices of firms that adopt severance-related compensation contracts for managers on average rise about 3 percent when adoption of the contracts is announced.[45] There is no easy way to tell how much of this could be due to the market interpreting the announcement as a signal that a takeover bid is more likely and how much is due to the reduction in conflict between managers and shareholders over takovers.

At times of takeover, shareholders are implicitly asking the top-level managers of their firm to negotiate a deal for them that frequently involves the imposition of large personal costs on the managers and their families. These involve substantial moving costs, the loss of position, power and prestige, and even the loss of their jobs. Shareholders are asking the very people who are most likely to have invested considerable time and energy (in some cases a life's work) in building a successful organization to negotiate its sale and the possible redirection of its resources.

It is important to face these conflicts and to structure contracts with managers to reduce them. It makes no sense to hire a realtor to sell your house and then penalize him for doing so. Yet that is the implication of many of the emotional reactions to control-related severance contracts. The restrictions and tax penalties imposed on these severance payments by the Deficit Reduction Act of 1984 are unwise interferences in the contracting freedoms of shareholders and managers; and they should be eliminated. Moreover, it is important to eliminate the misunderstanding about the purpose and effects of these contracts that has been fostered by past rhetoric on the topic so that boards of directors can get on with the job of structuring these contracts.

Golden parachutes can also be used to restrict

takeovers and to entrench managers at the expense of shareholders. How does one tell whether a particular set of contracts crosses this line?

The key is whether the contracts help solve the conflict-of-interest problem between shareholders and managers that arises over changes in control. Solving this problem requires extending control-related severance contracts beyond the chief executive to those members of the top-level management team who must play an important role in negotiating and implementing any transfer of control. Contracts that award severance contracts to substantial number of managers beyond this group are unlikely to be in the shareholders' interests. The contracts awarded by Beneficial Corp. to 234 of its managers are unlikely to be justified as in the shareholders' interests.[46]

It is particularly important to institute severance-related compensation contracts in situations where it is optimal for managers to invest in organization-specific human capital—that is, in skills and knowledge that have little or no value in other organizations. Managers will not so invest where the likelihood is high that their investment will be eliminated by an unexpected transfer of control and the loss of their jobs. In such situations the firm will have to pay for all costs associated with the creation of such organization-specific human capital, and it will be difficult to attract and retain highly talented managers when they have better opportunities elsewhere. In addition, contracts that award excessive severance compensation to the appropriate group of managers will tend to motivate managers to sell the firm at too low a price.

No simple rules can be specified that will easily prevent the misuse of golden parachutes because the appropriate solution will depend on many factors that are specific to each situation (for example, the amount of stock held by managers, and the optimal amount of investment in organization-specific human capital). In general, contracts that award inappropriately high payments to a group that is excessively large will reduce efficiency and harm shareholders by raising the cost of acquisition and by transferring wealth from shareholders to managers. The generally appropriate solution is to make the control-related severance contracts pay off in a way that is tied to the premium earned by the stockholders. Stock op-

---

45. See R. Lambert and D. Larcker, "Golden Parachutes, Executive Decision-Making, and Shareholder Wealth", *Journal of Accounting and Economics*, V. 7 (April, 1985), pp. 179-204.

46. Ann Morrison, "Those Executive Bailout Deals," *Fortune*, (December 13, 1982).

Greenmail is the Trojan horse of the takeover battle in the legal and political arenas...Management can easily prohibit greenmail without legislation: it need only announce a policy that, like Ulysses tying himself to the mast, prohibits it from making such payments.

tions or restricted stock appreciation rights that pay off only in the event of a change in control are two options that have some of the appropriate properties. In general, policies that encourage increased stock ownership by managers and the board of directors will provide incentives that will tend to reduce the conflicts of interests with managers.

Targeted Repurchases

The evidence indicates takeovers generate large benefits for shareholders. Yet virtually all proposals to protect shareholders from asserted difficulties in the control market will harm them by either eliminating or reducing the probability of successful hostile tender offers. These proposals will also block the productivity increases that are the source of the gains.

Most proposals to restrict or prohibit targeted repurchases (transactions pejoratively labeled "greenmail") are nothing more than antitakeover proposals in disguise. Greenmail is an appellation that suggests blackmail; yet the only effective weapon possessed by a greenmailer is the right to offer to purchase stock from other shareholders at a substantial premium. The "damage" to shareholders caused by this action is difficult to find. Those who propose to "protect" shareholders hide this fact behind emotional language designed to mislead. Greenmail is actually a targeted repurchase, an offer by *management* to repurchase the shares of a subset of shareholders at a premium, an offer not made to other shareholders.

Greenmail is the Trojan horse of the takeover battle in the legal and political arenas. Antitakeover proposals are commonly disguised as anti-greenmail provisions. Management can easily prohibit greenmail without legislation: it need only announce a policy that, like Ulysses tying himself to the mast, prohibits management or the board from making such payments.[47]

Problems in the Delaware Court

Delaware courts have created over the years a highly productive fabric of corporate law that has benefited the nation. The court is having difficulty, however, in sorting out the complex issues it faces in the takeover area. The court's problems in settling conflicts between shareholders and management over control issues reflect a fundamental weakness in its model of the corporation, a model that has heretofore worked quite well. The result has been a confusing set of decisions that, in contrast to much of the court's previous history, appears to make little economic sense.[49]

Altruism and the Business Judgment Rule

The Delaware court's model of the corporation is founded in the business judgment rule—the legal doctrine that holds that unless explicit evidence of fraud or self-dealing exists the board of directors is presumed to be acting solely in the interests of shareholders....The courts must not apply the business judgment rule to conflicts over control rights between principals and agents. If the business judgement rule is applied to such conflicts, the courts are effectively giving the *agent* (management) the right unilaterally to change the control rights. In the long run, this interpretation of the contract will destroy the possibility of such cooperative arrangements because it will leave principals (stockholders) with few effective rights.

Recently the courts have applied the business judgment rule to the conflicts over the issuance of poison pill preferred stock, poison pill rights, and discriminatory targeted repurchases, and have given managers and boards the rights to use these

47. Three excellent studies of these transactions indicate that when measured from the initial toehold purchase to the final repurchase of the shares, the stock price of target firms rises. Therefore, shareholders are benefited, not harmed, by the whole sequence of events. (See Clifford Holderness and Dennis Sheehan, "Raiders or Saviors: The Evidence on Six Controversial Investors," *Journal of Financial Economics* (December, 1985), Wayne H. Mikkelson, and Richard S. Ruback, "An Empirical Analysis of the Interfirm Equity Investment Process," *Journal of Financial Economics*, V. 14 (December, 1985), and Wayne H. Mikkelson and Richard S. Ruback, "Targeted Repurchases and Common Stock Returns", (unpublished manuscript, June, 1986).) There is some indication, however, that the stock price increases might represent the expectation of future takeover premiums in firms in which the targeted repurchase was not sufficient to prevent ultimate takeover of the firm. If so, it may well be that, much as in the final defeat of tender offers found by Bradley, Desai and Kim (Michael Bradley,

Michael, Anand Desai and E. Han Kim, "The Rationale Behind Interfirm Tender Offers: Information or Synergy?" *Journal of Financial Economics*, V. 11 (April, 1983), pp. 183-206), all premiums are lost to those shareholders in firms for which the repurchase and associated standstill agreements successfully lock up the firm. The evidence on these issues is not yet sufficient to issue a final judgement either way.

49. See, for example, Moran v. Household Intl, Inc., 490 A.2d 1059 (Del.Ch.1985) aff'd. 500 A.2d 1346 (Del.1985) (upholding poison pill rights issue), Smith v Van Gorkom, 488 A.2d 858, (holding board liable for damages in sale of firm at substantial premium over market price), Unocal v Mesa, 493 A.2d 946, 954 (Del. 1985) (allowing discriminatory targeted repurchase that confiscates wealth of largest shareholder), Revlon Inc. v MacAndrews & Forbes Holdings Inc., 506 A.2nd 173, 180 (Del. 1986), (invalidation of Revlon's lockup sale of a prime division to Forstmann Little at a below-market price).

Rights issues like Household's and Crown Zellerbach's harm shareholders. They will fundamentally impair the efficiency of corporations that adopt them, and for this reason they will reduce productivity in the economy if widely adopted.

devices.[52] In so doing the courts are essentially giving the agents (managers and the board) the right unilaterally to change critical control aspects of the contract—in particular the right to fire the agent. This has major implications for economic activity, productivity, and the health of the corporation. If the trend goes far enough, the corporation as an organizational form will be serioiusly handicapped.

Poison Pills

Poison pill securities change fundamental aspects of the corporate rules of the game that govern the relationship between shareholders, managers, and the board of directors. They do so when a control-related event occurs, such as a takeover offer or the acquisition of a substantial block of stock or voting rights by an individual or group. The Household International version of the poison pill rights issue is particularly interesting because it was a major test case in the area.

When the Household International board of directors issued its complicated right to shareholders, it unilaterally changed the nature of the contractual relationship with Household's shareholders in a fundamental way. The right effectively restricts the alienability of the common stock by prohibiting shareholders from selling their shares, without permission of the board, into a control transaction leading to merger at a price that involves a premium over market value of less than $6 billion. Since Household had a market value of less than $2 billion at the time, this was a premium of over 300 percent—more than 6 times the average takeover premium of 50 percent common in recent times—a premium that is difficult to justify as in the shareholders' interests.

The November 1985 Delaware court decision upholding the Household International rights issue will significantly restrict hostile takeovers of firms that adopt similar provisions. Before that decision, 37 pills of various forms had been adopted. Over 150 corporations adopted pills in the seven months following that decision.[53] Unlike most other antitakeover

devices, this defense is very difficult for a prospective acquirer to overcome without meeting the board's terms (at least one who desires to complete the second-step closeout merger). An SEC study analyzed the 37 companies introducing pills between June 1983, when Lenox introduced the first one, and December 1985. Eleven of these 37 firms experienced control changes: five experienced a negotiated change in control while the pill was in effect (Revlon, Cluett Peabody, Great Lakes, Int., Lenox, and Enstar), two were taken over by creeping acquisitions (Crown Zellerbach and William Wright), two were taken over after their pills were declared illegal (AMF and Richardson Vicks), one (Superior Oil) was acquired after the pill was withdrawn in the face of a lawsuit and proxy fight by its largest holder, and one (Amsted) has proposed a leveraged buyout. The SEC study finds that "Announcements of [twenty] poison pill plans in the midst of takeover speculations have resulted in an average 2.4 percent net of market price declines for firms adopting the plans." The effects of another twelve plans adopted by firms that were not the subject of takeover speculation were essentially nil.[53a]

Sir James Goldsmith recently gained control of Crown Zellerbach, which had implemented a rights issue similar to Household International's. Goldsmith purchased a controlling interest in the open market after Crown's board opposed his tender offer and refused to recall its rights issue. In this situation the acquirer must either tolerate the costs associated with leaving the minority interest outstanding and forsake the benefits of merging the assets of the two organizations, or incur the costs of the premium required by the rights on execution of the second-step closeout merger. The Crown case revealed a loophole in the Household/Crown version of the pill (which has been closed in newly implemented versions). Although Goldsmith could not complete a second-step merger without paying the high-premium required by the rights, he could avoid it by simply liquidating Crown.

Rights issues like Household's and Crown Zellerbach's harm shareholders. They will fundamentally impair the efficiency of corporations that adopt them, and for this reason they will reduce

52. Moran v Household Intl., and Unocal v Mesa.
53. See Office of the Chief Economist of the SEC, "The Economics of Poison Pills," (March 5, 1986), and Corporate Control Alert, (February, March and April, May and June, 1986).

53a. Ibid.

The Unocal victory over Mesa cost the Unocal shareholders $1.1 billion ($9.48 per post-offer share). This is the amount by which the $9.4 billion Mesa offer exceeded the $8.3 billion value of Unocal's "victory."

productivity in the economy if widely adopted.[53b]

A broad interpretation of the business judgment rule is important to the effectiveness of the corporation because a system that puts the courts into the business of making managerial decisions will generate great inefficiencies. The court has erred, however, in allowing the Household board, under the business judgement rule, to make the fundamental change in the structure of the organization implied by the rights issue without votes of its shareholders. It is unlikely the court would allow the board to decide unilaterally to make the organization a closed corporation by denying shareholders the right to sell their shares to anyone at a mutually agreeable price without the permission of the board. The Household International rights issue places just such a restriction on the alienability of shares, but only in the case of a subset of transactions—the control-related transactions so critical for protecting shareholders when the normal internal board-level control mechanisms break down. Several other poison pill cases have been heard by the courts with similar outcomes, but a New Jersey and two New York courts have recently ruled against poison pills that substantially interfere with the voting rights of large-block shareholders.[54] An Illinois District Court recently voided a poison pill (affirmed by the Seventh Circuit Court of Appeals) and two weeks later approved a new pill issued by the same company.[55]

The problem with these special securities and the provision they contain is not with their appropriateness (some might well be desirable), but with the manner in which they are being adopted—that is, without approval by shareholders. Boards of directors show little inclination to refer such issues to shareholders.

One solution to the problems caused by the Household decision is for shareholders to approve amendments to the certificate of incorporation to restrict the board's power to take such actions without shareholder approval. This is not an easy task, however, given the pressure corporate managers are bringing to bear on the managers of their pension funds to vote with management.[56] Even more problematic is the provision in Delaware law that requires certificate amendments to be recommended to shareholders by the board of directors.[57]

Exclusionary Self Tenders: The Unocal v. Mesa Decision[58]

The Delaware Supreme Court surprised the legal, financial, and corporate communities in the spring of 1985 by giving Unocal the right to make a tender offer for 29 percent of its shares while excluding its largest shareholder, Mesa Partners II, from the offer. This decision enabled the Unocal management and board to avoid loss of control to Mesa. The decision imposed large costs on Unocal shareholders and, if not reversed, threatens major damage to shareholders of all Delaware corporations.

The Unocal victory over Mesa cost the Unocal shareholders $1.1 billion ($9.48 per post-offer share). This is the amount by which the $9.4 billion Mesa offer exceeded the $8.3 billion value of Unocal's "victory."[59] This loss represents 18 percent of Unocal's pre-takeover value of $6.2 billion. The $2.1 billion net increase in value to $8.3 billion resulted from Unocal's $4.2 billion debt issue which, contrary to assertions, benefits its shareholders. It does so by effectively bonding Unocal to pay out a substantial fraction of its huge cash flows to shareholders rather than to reinvest them in low-return projects, and by reducing taxes on Unocal and its shareholders.

For his services in generating this $2.1 billion gain for Unocal shareholders, T. Boone Pickens has

53b. Another study of the effects of poison pills (Paul H. Malatesta and Ralph A. Walkling, "The Impact of Poison Pill Securities on Stockholder Wealth," (unpublished, University of Washington, 1985) also indicates they have a negative effect on stock prices. On average, stock prices fell by a statistically significant 2 percent in the 2 days around the announcement in the *Wall Street Journal* of adoption of a poison pill for a sample of 14 firms that adopted these securities between December 1982 and February 1985. This price decline, however, was smaller than the average 7.5 percent increase in price that occurred in the 10 days prior to the adoption of the pill. Firms adopting pills appear to be those in which managers and directors bear a substantially smaller fraction of the wealth consequences of their actions. In all but three of the firms the percentage of common shares owned by officers and directors was substantially below the industry average ownership of shares. The average ownership of firms in the same industry was 16.5 percent and for the firms adopting pills it was 7.5 percent.

54. Ministar Acquiring Corp. v AMF Inc., 621 Fed Sup 1252. So Dis NY, 1985, Unilever Acquisition Corp. v Richardson-Vicks, Inc., 618 Fed Supp 407. So Dist. NY 1985, Asarco Inc. v M.R.H. Holmes a Court, 611 Fed Sup 468. Dist Ct of NJ,

1985, and Dynamics Corp. of America v CTS Corporation.

55. Dynamics Corp. of America v. CTS Corp., *et al.* U.S. District Court, Northern District of Illinois, Eastern Division, No. 86 C 1624, (April 17, 1986), affirmed Seventh Circuit Court of Appeals Nos. 86-16-1, 86-1608, and Dynamics Corp. of America v. CTS Corp., *et al.* (May 3, 1986).

56. See Joe, Koleman, "The Proxy Pressure on Pension Fund Managers", Institutional Investor, (July, 1985), pp. 145-147, and Investor Responsibility Research Center, Inc., Corporate Governance Service: Voting by Institutional Investors on Corporate Governance Questions, 1985 Proxy Season, pp. 19-25.

57. 8 *Del. C.* 242(c)(1).

58. This discussion is based on my article, "When Unocal Won over Pickens, Shareholders and Society Lost," *Financier,* V. IX, No. 11 (Nov., 1985), pp. 50-53.

59. The $8.3 billion value of Unocal securities held by its shareholders is calculated as $4.1 billion in stock (116 million shares at $34 7/8 on May 24, the first trading day after close of the offer), and $4.2 billion in Unocal debt trading at $73.50.

In addition to Mesa's losses, shareholders of all Delaware corporations lose because the court's decision gives management a weapon so powerful it essentially guarantees that no Delaware corporation that uses it will be taken over by a tender offer.

been vilified in the press, and Mesa Partners II has incurred net losses before taxes—obviously a perversion of incentives.

In addition to Mesa's losses, shareholders of all Delaware corporations lose because the court's decision gives management a weapon so powerful it essentially guarantees that no Delaware corporation that uses it will be taken over by a tender offer. A determined board could, in the extreme, pay out all the corporation's assets and leave the acquirer holding a worthless shell. Because of this new power, shareholders are denied the benefits of future actions by Pickens and others to discipline managers whose strategies are wasting resources.

Society also loses. The decision will have a chilling effect on takeovers, blocking the productivity increases that are the source of the takeover gains and thereby handicapping Delaware corporations in the competition for survival.

Unocal's self-tender for 29 percent of its shares at $72 per share ($26 over the market price) was designed to defeat Mesa's $54 per share cash offer for 50.4 percent of Unocal's shares plus $54 per share in debt securities for the remaining 49.6 percent. The Unocal offer would have paid 59 percent of Unocal's pretakeover equity to other shareholders while denying participation to the 13.6 percent minority holding of Mesa Partners II. This would transfer about $248 million from Mesa's holdings to other Unocal stockholders—a classic case of corporate raiding that contrasts with the beneficial effects of the actions of takeover specialists like Pickens, Carl Icahn and Irwin Jacobs on other shareholders.

Faced with the threat of legalized expropriation of $248 million, Mesa accepted a settlement in which Unocal backed off from the Mesa exclusion. The settlement involved repurchase of part of Mesa's shares at the terms of the tender offer, a 25-year standstill agreement, a promise to vote its shares in the same proportion as other shares are voted, and constraints on Mesa's rights to sell its remaining shares.

The essential characteristics of Unocal's exclusionary repurchase defense are now incorporated in newly popular poison pill plans called back-end plans.[60] These plans give shareholders a right to tender their shares for securities worth more than the

market value of their stock when a shareholder exceeds a certain maximum limit of stock ownership that ranges from 30 to 50 percent. As with Unocal's exclusion of Mesa, the large shareholder is denied the same right to tender his shares. This threatens a shareholder who violates the holding limit with potentially large dilution of his holdings. It thereby limits the existence of large stock holdings.

"Protection" From Two-Tier Tender Offers. The court ruled that the objective of Unocal's offer was to protect its shareholders against "a grossly inadequate and coercive two-tier, front-end-loaded tender offer" and against greenmail. This assessment of the situation was upside down. Paradoxically, the court's ruling imposed on Unocal shareholders exactly the evil it purported to prevent. Unocal defeated Mesa's $1.1 billion higher offer precisely because Mesa's offer was a level $54 offer and Unocal's offer was an extreme front-end loaded two-tier offer—$72 for 29 percent of its shares in the front-end with a back-end price of $35 for the remaining 71 percent of the shares. (The back-end price was implicit, but easy to calculate and reported in the press at the time of the offer.) The effective price of the Unocal offer was therefore only $45.73 per pre-offer share (the weighted average of the front- and back-end prices).

Comparing the Unocal offer with SEC estimates of average minimums in two-tier tender offers indicates the extreme nature of the Unocal two-tier offer. Historically the average back-end premium on outside two-tier offers is 45 percent higher than the stock price measured 20 trading days prior to the offer.[61] This contrasts sharply with the *negative* back-end premium on Unocal's self tender of -25 percent. That is, the $35 back-end price was 25 percent below the Unocal market price of $46 3/8 twenty days before the offer.

The negative back-end premium on Unocal's offer means the holders of 20 million Unocal shares who failed to tender to the first tier of the Unocal offer were particularly hurt. As of the close of the offer they suffered total losses of $382 million, $215 million from the loss of $37.12/share on 29 percent of their shares,[62] plus a loss of $167 million from being denied the $54 in debt securities they would have received in

---

60. See Office of the Chief Economist of the SEC, "The Economics of Poison Pills" (March 5, 1986).

61. See Comment, Robert, and Gregg A. Jarrell, "Two-Tier Tender Offers: The Imprisonment of the Free-Riding Shareholder," (unpublished manuscript, March 1, 1986); an earlier version appeared as Office of the Chief Economist,

Securities and Exchange Commission, "The Economics of Any-or-All, Partial, and Two-Tier Tender Offers," *Federal Register*, June 29, 1984, pp. 26,751-26,761.

62. Calculated as the $72 value of the Unocal debt offered in exchange for 29% of their shares less the $34.875 post-offer closing price of the shares.

Responsible boards of directors interested in the welfare of shareholders and the survival of the corporation as an organizational form will implement procedures to ban all targeted repurchases that carry premiums over market value.

the back end of the Mesa offer.[63]

Protection From Targeted Repurchases. The court also erred in its concern over greenmail. In ruling to eliminate the threat of greenmail, the court in fact authorized Unocal to make a greenmail transaction that differs from the usual variety only in that it penalized, rather than benefited, the large-block holder (i.e., reverse greenmail). In authorizing this form of targeted repurchase, the court granted large benefits to managers who desire protection from competition but harmed shareholders.

One of the great strengths of the corporation is the long-held principle that holders of a given class of securities are treated identically in transactions with the corporation. The Unocal decision threatens to turn the corporation into a battleground where special-interest groups of shareholders fight over the division of the pie much as special interests in the public sector do. The result will be a much smaller pie.

Responsible boards of directors interested in the welfare of shareholders and the survival of the corporation as an organizational form will implement procedures to ban all targeted repurchases that carry premiums over market value.

Conclusion

Although economic analysis and the evidence indicate the market for corporate control is benefiting shareholders, society, and the corporation as an organizational form, it is also making life more uncomfortable for top-level executives. This discomfort is creating strong pressures at both the state and federal levels for restrictions that will seriously cripple the workings of this market. In 1985 there were 21 bills on this topic in the Congressional hopper, all of which proposed various restrictions on the market for corporate control. Some proposed major new restrictions on share ownership and financial instruments. Within the past several years the legislatures of numerous states have passed antitakeover laws. This political activity is another example of special interests using the democratic political system to change the rules of the game to benefit themselves at the expense of society as a whole. In this case the special interests are top-level corporate managers and other groups who stand to lose from competition in the market for corporate control. The result will be a significant weakening of the corporation as an organizational form and a reduction in efficiency.

---

63. See Michael Bradley and Michael Rosensweig, "The Law and Economics of Defensive Stock Repurchases and Defensive Self-Tender Offers, (Unpublished manuscript, University of Michigan, 1985) for a thorough discussion of the issues involved in self tender offers.

APPENDIX: Evidence From Financial Transactions in Support of the Free Cash Flow Theory of Mergers

Free cash flow theory helps explain previously puzzling results on the effects of various financial transactions. Smith [1986]* summarizes more than twenty studies of stock price changes at announcements of transactions that change capital structure as well as various other dividend transactions. These results are summarized in Table 2.

For firms with positive free cash flow, the theory predicts that stock prices will increase with unexpected increases in payouts to shareholders and decrease with unexpected decreases in payouts. It also predicts that unexpected increases in demand for funds from shareholders via new issues will cause stock prices to fall. In addition, the theory predicts stock prices will increase with increasing tightness of the constraints binding the payout of future cash flow to shareholders and decrease with reductions in the tightness of these

constraints. These predictions do not apply, however, to those firms with more profitable projects than free cash flow to fund them.

The predictions of the agency cost of free cash flow are consistent with all but three of the 32 estimated abnormal stock price changes summarized in Table 2. Moreover, one of the inconsistencies is explainable by another phenomenon.

Panel A of Table 2 shows that stock prices rise by a statistically significant amount with announcements of the initiation of cash dividend payments, increases in dividends, and payments of specially designated dividends; they fall by a statistically significant amount with decreases in dividend payments. (All coefficients in the table are significantly different from zero unless noted with an asterisk.)

Panel B of Table 2 shows that security sales and

---

* See Cliff Smith, "Investment Banking and the Capital Acquisition Process," *Journal of Financial Economics* 15 (1986) for references to all studies cited in this Appendix.

TABLE 2
The Stock Market Response to Various Dividend and Capital Structure Transactions

Summary of two-day average abnormal stock returns associated with the announcement of various dividend and capital structure transactions.

Returns are weighted averages, by sample size, of the returns reported by the respective studies. All returns are significantly different from zero unless noted otherwise by .*

Type of Transaction	Security Issued	Security Retired
PANEL A: Dividend changes that change the cash paid to shareholders		
Dividend initiation[1]		
Dividend increase[2]		
Specially designated dividend[3]		
Dividend decrease[2]		
PANEL B: Security sales (that raise cash) and retirements (that pay out cash) and simultaneously		
Security sale (industrial)[4]	debt	none
Security sale (utility)[5]	debt	none
Security sale (industrial)[6]	preferred	none
Security sale (utility)[7]	preferred	none
Call[8]	none	debt
PANEL C: Security sales which raise cash and bond future cash flow payments only minimally		
Security sale (industrial)[4]	conv. debt.	none
Security sale (industrial)[7]	conv. preferred	none
Security sale (utility)[7]	conv. preferred	none
PANEL D: Security retirements that pay out cash to shareholders		
Self tender offer[9]	none	common
Open market purchase[10]	none	common
Targeted small holdings[11]	none	common
Targeted large block repurchase[12]	none	common
PANEL E: Security sales or calls that raise cash and do not bond future cash flow payments		
Security sale (industrial)[13]	common	none
Security sale (utility)[14]	common	none
Conversion-forcing call[20]	common	conv. preferred
Conversion-forcing call[20]	common	conv. debt
PANEL F: Exchange offers, or designated use security sales that increase the bonding of payout of		
Designated use security sale[15]	debt	common
Exchange offer[16]	debt	common
Exchange offer[16]	preferred	common
Exchange offer[16]	debt	preferred
Exchange offer[17]	income bonds	preferred
PANEL G: Transaction with no change in bonding of payout of future cash flows		
Exchange offer[18]	debt	debt
Designated use security sale[19]	debt	debt
PANEL H: Exchange offers, or designated use security sales that decrease the bonding of payout		
Security sale[19]	conv. debt	debt
Exchange offer[16]	common	preferred
Exchange offer[16]	preferred	debt
Security sale[19]	common	debt
Exchange offer[21]	common	debt

[1] Asquith and Mullins (1983).
[2] Calculated by Smith (1986, Table 1) from Charest (1978), and Aharony and Swary (1980).
[3] From Brickley (1983).
[4] Calculated by Smith (1986, Table 1) from Dann and Mikkelson (1984), Eckbo (1986), Mikkelson and Partch (1986).
[5] Eckbo (1986).
[6] Calculated by Smith (1986, Table 1) from Linn and Pinegar (1985), Mikkelson and Partch (1986).
[7] Linn and Pinegar (1985).
[8] Vu (1986).
[9] Calculated by Smith (1986, Table 1) from Dann (1981), Masulis (1980), Vermaelen (1981), Rosenfeld (1982).
[10] Dann (1980), Vermaelen (1981).
[11] Bradley and Wakeman (1983).
[12] Calculated by Smith (1986, Table 4) from Dann and DeAngelo (1983), Bradley and Wakeman (1983).
[13] Calculated by Smith (1986, Table 1) from Asquith and Mullins (1986), Kolodny and Suhler (1985), Masulis and Korwar (1986) Mikkelson and Partch (1986), Schipper and Smith (1986).

retirements that raise cash or pay out cash and simultaneously provide offsetting changes in the constraints bonding the payout of future cash flow are all associated with returns insignificantly different from zero. The insignificant return on retirement debt fits the theory because the payout of cash is offset by an equal reduction in the present value of promised future cash payouts. If the debt sales are associated with no changes in the expected investment program, the insignificant return on announcements of the sale of debt and preferred also fits the theory. The acquisition of new funds with debt or preferred

Average Sample Size	Average Abnormal Two-Day Announcement Period Return	Sign Predicted by Free Cash Flow Theory	Agreement with Free Cash Flow Theory?	Agreement with Tax Theory
160	3.7%	+	yes	no
281	0.9	+	yes	no
164	2.1	+	yes	no
48	−3.6	−	yes	no

provide off-setting changes in the constraints bonding future payment of cash flows.

248	−0.2*	0	yes	no
140	−0.1*	0	yes	no
28	−0.1*	0	yes	yes
249	−0.1*	0	yes	yes
133	−0.1*	0	yes	no
74	−2.1	—	yes	no
54	−1.4	—	yes	no
9	−1.6	—	yes	no
147	15.2	+	yes	yes
182	3.3	+	yes	yes
15	1.1	+	yes	yes
68	−4.8	+	no**	no**
215	−3.0	—	yes	yes
405	−0.6	—	yes	yes
57	−0.4*	—	no	yes
113	−2.1	—	yes	yes

future cash flows

45	21.9	+	yes	yes
52	14.0	+	yes	yes
9	8.3	+	yes	no
24	3.5	+	yes	yes
18	1.6	+	yes	yes
36	0.6	0	no	no
96	0.2*	0	yes	yes

of future cash flows

15	−2.4	—	yes	yes
23	−2.6	—	yes	no
9	−7.7	—	yes	yes
12	−4.2	—	yes	yes
81	−1.1	—	yes	yes

[14] Calculated by Smith (1986, Table 1) from Asquith and Mullins (1986), Masulis and Korwar (1986), Pettway and Radcliffe (1985).
[15] Masulis (1980).
[16] Masulis (1983). These returns include announcement days of both the original offer and, for about 40 percent of the sample, a second announcement of specific terms of the exchange.
[17] McConnell and Schlarbaum (1981).
[18] Dietrich (1984).
[19] As calculated by Smith (1986, Table 3) from Eckbo (1986), Mikkelson and Partch (1986).
[20] Mikkelson (1981).
[21] Rogers and Owers (1985, Peavy and Scott 1985, Finnerty 1985).
* Not statistically different from zero.
** Explained by the fact that these transactions are frequently associated with the termination of an actual or expected control bid. The price decline appears to reflect the loss of an expected control premium.

is offset exactly by a commitment bonding the future payout of cash flows of equal present value.

Panel C shows that sales of convertible debt and convertible preferred are associated with significantly negative stock price changes. These security sales raise cash and provide little effective bonding of future cash flow payments for the following reason: when the stock into which the debt is convertible is worth more than the face value of the debt, management has incentives to call them and force conversion to common.

Panel D shows that, with one exception, security

retirements that pay out cash to shareholders increase stock prices. The price decline associated with targeted large block repurchases (often called "greenmail") is highly likely to be due to the reduced probability that a takeover premium will be realized. These transactions are often associated with standstill agreements in which the seller of the stock agrees to refrain from acquiring more stock and from making a takeover offer for some period into the future.

Panel E summarizes the effects of security sales and retirements that raise cash and do not bond future cash flow payments. Consistent with the theory, negative abnormal returns are associated with all such changes. However, the negative returns associated with the sale of common through a conversion-forcing call are statistically insignificant.

Panel F shows that all exchange offers or designated-use security sales that increase the bonding of payout of future cash flows result in significantly positive increases in common stock prices. These include stock repurchases and exchange of debt or preferred for common, debt for preferred, and income bonds for preferred. The two-day gains range from 21.9 percent (debt for common) to 2.2 percent (debt or income bonds for preferred).

Panel G of Table 2 shows that the evidence on transactions with no cash flow and no change in the bonding of payout of future cash flows is mixed. The returns associated with exchange offers of debt for debt are significantly positive, and those for designated-use security sales are insignificantly different from zero.

Panel H of Table 2 shows that all exchanges, or designated-use security sales that have no cash effects but reduce the bonding of payout of future cash flows result, on average, in significant decreases in stock prices. These transactions include the exchange of common for debt or preferred or preferred for debt, or the replacement of debt with convertible debt. The two-day losses range from −9.9% (common for debt) to −2.4% (for designated-use security sale replacing debt with convertible debt).

In summary, the results in Table 2 are remarkably consistent with free cash flow theory, which predicts that, except for firms with profitable unfunded investment projects, prices will rise with unexpected increases in payouts to shareholders (or promises to do so) and will fall with reductions in

payments or new requests for funds from shareholders (or reductions in promises to make future payments). Moreover, the size of the value changes is positively related to the change in the tightness of the commitment bonding the payment of future cash flows. For example, the effects of debt-for-preferred exchanges are smaller than the effects of debt-for-common exchanges.

Tax effects can explain some of these results, but not all—for example, the price changes associated with exchanges of preferred for common or replacements of debt with convertible debt, neither of which which have any tax effects. The last column of Table 2 denotes whether the individual coefficients are explainable by these pure corporate tax effects. The tax theory hypothesizes that all unexpected changes in capital structure which decrease corporate taxes increase stock prices and vice versa.[34] Therefore, increases in dividend and reductions of debt interest should cause stock price to fall and vice versa.[35] Thirteen of the 32 coefficients are inconsistent with the corporate tax hypothesis. Simple signaling effects, where the payout of cash signals the lack of present and future investments that promise returns in excess of the cost of capital, are also inconsistent with the results—for example, the positive stock price changes associated with dividend increases and stock repurchases.

If anything, the results in Table 2 seem too good. The returns summarized in the table do not distinguish firms that have free cash flow from those that do not have free cash flow. Yet the theory tells us the returns to firms with no free cash flow will behave differently from those which do. In addition, only unexpected changes in cash payout or the tightness of the commitments bonding the payout of future free cash flows should affect stock prices. The studies summarized in Table 2 do not, in general, control for the effects of expectations. If the free cash flow effects are large and if firms on average are in a positive free cash flow position, the predictions of the theory will hold for the simple sample averages. If the effects are this pervasive, the waste due to agency problems in the corporate sector is greater than most scholars have thought. This helps explain the high level of activity in the corporate control market over the last decade. More detailed tests of the propositions that control for growth prospects and expectations will be interesting.

THE QUIET
RESTRUCTURING

*by John W. Kensinger and John D. Martin,
University of Texas at Austin*

E *very individual, therefore, endeavors as much as he can both to*

employ his capital in the support of domestic industry, and so to

direct that industry that its produce may be of the greatest value

... and he is in this, as in many other cases, led by an invisible

hand to promote an end which was no part of his intention.

— Adam Smith, 1776[1] —

While the spotlight of the financial press has been turned squarely on "corporate raiders," other less dramatic manifestations of the same market forces are accomplishing a "quiet restructuring" of corporate America—without fanfare and largely unnoticed by politicians and the press. Even if the raiders were suddenly to oblige their critics and disappear, the "invisible hand" would continue subtly but relentlessly prodding management to seek out more efficient forms of organization and better uses for corporate assets.[2]

For, even as troubled sectors of American industry are being made to shrink, the abundance and variety of investment opportunities offered in today's economy have never been greater. For an entrepreneur just setting out, there are venture capitalists and business incubators to help in the birthing process. For a promising technology start-up company, there are billions of dollars available through mezzanine loans, joint ventures, project financing, and public stock offerings. For an established corporate giant, there are not only concerns about hostile takeovers and flak from militant stockholders, but also attractive opportunities—such as converting the treasury function into a profit center through securities trading and international financial arbitrage, or securitizing assets (or even entire subsidiaries) and turning them into ready cash. Then, too, there is the prospect of dramatically enlarging management's own risk-reward profile by means of a leveraged buyout.

The good news is that the financial markets have evolved to the point where capital can flow quickly to start-up companies to develop new products and technologies. The unfortunate part is that some of this money must come from the process of cutting big companies apart and wringing cash from uneconomic operations. When the capital released by these often difficult decisions reaches investors, it is *they* who decide where to reinvest in new businesses.

This widespread return of the corporate reinvestment decision to the marketplace is a relatively new development. Established tradition is that investors, in contributing capital to public corporations, voluntarily relinquish control of their funds to the managements of those corporations. In ceding such control to management—which can be reclaimed by unhappy stockholders only through the extremes of proxy contest or hostile takeover—the market effectively agrees to the substitution of management fiat for the "invisible hand" in directing the flow of capital from old to new enterprises.[3]

Not long ago, in fact, it was widely accepted that the ideal corporation consisted of a portfolio of projects at various stages of development which was balanced so that the cash flows from the mature activities were used to nourish fledgling projects. In the parlance of the Boston Consulting Group, "cash cows" were milked to feed the "rising stars." As they grew old, "stars" and "cows" became "dogs," which were harvested to feed more "rising stars" for the company.

Over this menagerie stood the corporate managers, who performed "strategic planning," deciding which new projects to finance. If their own organization was not generating enough cash to support its rising stars, they would even go out into the market to buy someone else's cash cow. If, on the other hand, they had lots of cash cows but too few deserving new projects, they might buy another company's rising star.

This approach has not stood the test of time, however, because today's investors have a much broader spectrum of opportunities than do corporate managers investing internally. Stockholder discontent with this old model has in fact played a major role in stimulating takeovers in the 1980s (which, unlike those of the 60s and 70s, represent a movement away from conglomerate structures and toward horizontal consolidations). Simply put, investors have declared their preference to milk the cash cows themselves.

If an organization runs out of natural growth opportunities when its industry matures, it no longer has such a need for cash. At this point investors legitimately demand a return of control to their own hands. And when control over resource allocation is returned to the marketplace, investors get to make all of the reinvestment decisions because *they* have first claim to the cash flows. With cash in hand, investors can choose among venture capital funds, initial public offerings (IPOs), real estate, energy explora-

---

1. Vol.1, *The Wealth of Nations* (edited by Edwin Cannan), The University of Chicago Press, reprinted 1976, p.477.

2. A play on Adam Smith's words, the "visible foot," has been used to describe the tactics and consequences of raiders. See William A. Brock and Stephen P. Magee, "The Invisible Foot and the Waste of Nations: Redistribution and Economic Growth," in *Neoclassical Political Economy* (David C. Colander, ed.), Ballinger, 1984.

3. See A. M. Spence, "The Economics of Internal Organization: An Introduction," *Bell Journal of Economics* (Spring 1975), pp. 163-72. Spence views the firm as a "mini capital market" with internal investment selection which parallels the activities of external capital markets.

tion partnerships, R&D project pools, or any other investment vehicle. Investors regain direct control over their money, and managers of corporations thereby give way to investment bankers in the role of guiding funds from the cash cows into the rising stars.

Corporate managements, needless to say, are not happy about this trend and often try to perpetuate the growth (or just the independence) of their firm—often at large costs to their own stockholders. But why would managers try to keep the firm going beyond its useful life, past the point where it has an economic advantage that justifies its control over resources? Management understandably feels commitments to many other corporate stakeholders than just the investors who contributed capital.[4] It often has far stronger ties to the corporation's employees, for example, and to the community which houses the corporation than to a faceless and widely dispersed group of public investors.

It can be very difficult, therefore, for professional managers to envision a future in which their corporation does not exist in some form. After the purpose for which it was conceived has been served, there are still strong pressures, both emotional and political, to extend the firm's life by redirecting its resources into some new set of activities, even though they may not be the most highly-valued use for the resources. Managers who are trying their best to be good citizens and to do what they perceive to be right for their employees and local communities may have interests which are very much at odds with those of investors and the economy at large. This sort of conflict can present some very tough decisions. But it ultimately demands resolution of the question of whether to let the marketplace achieve the highest-valued uses for the world's resources—or try to slow down economic progress and avoid making difficult decisions.

While this debate proceeds in Congress and the courts, however, the "invisible hand" remains at work, nudging management into voluntarily releasing control over resource allocation decisions in a variety of ways. Now, through various means that limit management control over the reinvestment of corporate cash flows, the give and take of the marketplace is creating a new kind of cash cow.[5] The cash flow from mature operations is being channeled back into the marketplace for reinvestment—often into unknown start-up ventures. And even though it may not be part of management's conscious intention, this process is leading to better resource allocation and an improvement in corporate America's competitive position.

THE URGE TO USE LEVERAGE

Whoever has discretionary power over the reinvestment of a firm's operating cash flows has fundamental power over its future. The extreme use of debt—in leveraged share repurchases, leveraged buyouts (LBOs) and, most recently, leveraged recapitalizations—substantially reduces management's control over the deployment of cash flows generated by a firm's mature operations.

Consider the effect of leveraged share repurchases such as those Boone Pickens forced on Phillips Petroleum and Unocal. (Something like it also happened with Gulf, in that Chevron was forced to borrow heavily in order to buy out the Gulf stockholders.) These events all had something very basic in common: stockholders came away with a substantial wealth increase—in cash. (Also, it came in the form of capital gains for most of them, so the maximum tax rate anyone had to pay was 20 percent—these things happened, of course, before the Tax Reform Act of 1986.) These shareholders were then free to choose how to reinvest their wealth, selecting from the full array of opportunities in the marketplace.

Where did this wealth increase for the stockholders come from? Part of it came from the tax benefits of leverage, but that is not the whole story. Besides any possible tax effect, the leverage fundamentally constricted the scope of managerial discretion.

Michael Jensen recently formulated his "debt control hypothesis" to explain this constructive effect of leverage, and has applied this explanation to the oil industry as follows: When highly leveraged, an oil company's operating cash flows become committed to interest and debt retirement for a significant period into the future. New projects thus have to compete for external funding rather be sustained by the

---

4. For a discussion of these other corporate constituencies, see Bradford Cornell and Alan Shapiro, "Corporate Stakeholders and Corporate Finance," *Financial Management* 16, (Spring 1987), pp. 5-14.

5. For a longer discussion of this development than appears here, see our earlier article, "Royalty Trusts, Master Partnerships, and other Organizational Means of 'unfirming' the Firm," *Midland Corporate Finance Journal*, Vol.4 No.2 (Summer 1986), pp. 72-80.

cash flows from the oil fields. Besides the tax effect, then, the leverage brings with it a change in the processes by which management actions are monitored, and thus a change in managerial incentives. The mountain of debt forces the cash to flow out of the firm, rather than circulate within it.[6]

If there is any danger that management might not be as demanding as the marketplace in scrutinizing internal investments, then this change increases the probability that the cash flows will find their way to the highest-valued uses. After the leveraged share repurchases, there was much less of a chance that Phillips or Unocal might buy a Reliance Electric or a Montgomery Ward or a Kennecott Copper. Nor would their managements be able to follow up on any temptation to get into the office products business, as did Exxon with such poor success. With cash flows committed to debt service, management had their wings clipped and stockholders had their money. As one would expect, managers were less happy about it than were the stockholders.

Some people raise the concern that diverting cash flows from oil and gas production into the marketplace might be detrimental in the long run. That is, the oil may eventually be depleted without replacement of reserves. Phillips' management, for example, lamented the impact of the "crushing mountain of debt" upon their exploration efforts, claiming that pleasing the financial marketplace requires short-run maximization of cash flows at the expense of long-run economic viability.

The marketplace, however, is the ultimate source of resources for commitment to any venture. When investors put a high enough value on oil and gas exploration, new drilling partnerships can be formed quickly. Meanwhile, there are opportunities in electronics, robotics, artificial intelligence, and bioengineering that hold more promise for investors. And the fact, incidentally, that investors are willing to commit themselves to ventures years in advance of their producing a penny in revenues should be sufficient answer to those protesting the market's short-term focus.

Also relevant to this issue, a recent study of the effect of new internal investments upon corporate stock values found strong evidence contradicting the claims of Phillips' management. The study found that, on average, the announcements of new capital expenditures by corporations resulted in increased stock values across a variety of different industries. The only exception was the petroleum industry, where announcements of increased expenditures on oil drilling and exploration have been greeted with systematic stock price declines since the beginning of the 1980s.[7]

LEVERAGED BUYOUTS

What was accomplished through leveraged share repurchases at Phillips Petroleum and Unocal has been done in other industries through LBOs. There have been many explanations offered for the LBO phenomenon, each of which may have some element of truth. Without claiming to offer the definitive explanation, however, it is possible to make some general observations.

First of all, stockholders are able to sell their stock for cash, at a premium over the market value, and are immediately free to reinvest the cash in the most attractive opportunities available anywhere in the marketplace.

Second, managers gain a shot at ownership and, without changing jobs, go to work for new bosses—themselves. They are free of the burden of reporting to a large group of public shareholders.

In place of the shareholders, however, management must answer to the LBO specialist, whose group generally takes a strong position on the board of directors. Also, in place of a host of public shareholders demanding ever-increasing earnings and dividends, the managers have to placate a small group of creditors who demand that every stray penny be applied to a speedy repayment of the debt used to finance the buyout.

In a buyout, then, managers do not escape monitoring; they merely exchange one form of monitoring for another. Nor do they escape pressure. In fact, it might seem that the pressure on them increases as a result of the leverage. They have the advantage, to be sure, that the bite taken from cash flows by income tax is reduced, giving them more to work with. But they are not "their own men" until the debt is taken care of. With cash flows committed to debt support, new projects will not have access to the

6. Michael C. Jensen, "Agency Costs of Free Cash Flow, Corporate Finance and Takeovers," *American Economic Review* (May 1986).

7. John J. McConnell and Chris J. Muscarella, "Corporate Capital Expenditure Decisions and the Market Value of the Firm," *Journal of Financial Economics*, (Sept 1985), pp. 399-422.

milk from the old cash cow, and any growth plans must face the test of the marketplace.

Critics of LBOs protest that the pressure of all this leverage stifles the economy, but it must not be forgotten that the stockholders got an infusion of cash at the very beginning. They will be reinvesting in growth opportunities elsewhere. In addition, the creditors of the newly-private company will be receiving regular installments of milk from the cash cow, which they will be able to reinvest in the best available opportunities. Only when the debt is repaid will the managers, at that point certainly older and perhaps wiser, once again have access to the cash spigot to finance internal expansion projects. Then it will be their own money they are spending and they may be more demanding in evaluating potential projects than when they were employees of a public corporation.

ESOPS

Besides the garden-variety LBO, there is another new player on the scene. Leveraged Employee Stock Ownership Plans (ESOPs) have been the vehicle for several buyouts in recent years. Through such an arrangement it is possible for the corporation to eliminate income tax completely, and make the entire pretax cash flow of the corporation available for debt retirement. Only if the corporation retains earnings for new investment is there be any need to pay income tax—which represents a significant turning of the tax tables. Not long ago, income tax laws had the effect of keeping cash inside a company since paying dividends resulted in double taxation. In the case of a buyout by a leveraged ESOP under current tax rules, the tax penalty is instead levied against retention of earnings for reinvestment. Instead of retaining earnings, then, the best way for an ESOP-owned corporation to raise expansion capital is by selling new stock to the ESOP; and when this requires the ESOP to go to the market for loans, the growth plans must meet outside scrutiny.

Besides giving employees a chance to own their companies, then, the new ESOPs do two other important things. First, they put cash into the hands of stockholders, who then make the reinvestment decisions themselves. Second, leveraged ESOPs commit the firm's cash flows to debt retirement, thereby returning capital to the marketplace where it can be used to fund the highest-valued new ventures.[8]

THE URGE TO SELL PIECES OF THE COMPANY

There are several means available to "securitize" a specialized pool of assets. It is now commonplace for financial institutions to sell insured mortgages in the form of securities. Credit card receivables and auto and truck loans are likewise packaged into high-denomination securities for resale. Receivables can also be held by a corporation's financial subsidiary, and a portion of the subsidiary sold to the public. Whole divisions may also be set up as parent-controlled subsidiaries, with a portion of stock offered to the public.

In addition, there are now more than ninety publicly-traded master limited partnerships (MLPs). Originated in the oil and gas industry, they have spread to timberland properties, cable television systems, real estate, mortgages, restaurant services, and mortgage loan servicing. Non-listed partnerships also own large scale hydro and geothermal power-generating plants, cogeneration facilities, and even oil refineries. All sorts of income-producing operations which require little more than caretaker management have been separated from corporations, organized as partnerships, and sold. Management-intensive operations such as R&D projects have also been financed as separate projects.[9]

The choice of organizational form used for securitizing assets is sensitive to the tax environment. Because the 1987 tax act ended favored tax treatment for some publicly-traded partnerships, a corporate subsidiary or a nontraded partnership may be the organizational form chosen as the reposi-

---

8. In these arrangements a special trust is formed to purchase stock and credit it to the accounts of individual employees. The Tax Reform Act of 1984 added two very attractive new sweeteners for leveraged ESOPs. Since January 1985, dividends paid to stock owned by an ESOP have been tax deductible. In addition, lenders need pay income tax on only half of the interest paid to them by an ESOP. Thus ESOPs are able to borrow at low interest rates, in order to buy stock in the employer corporation. Finally, employer corporations are allowed to make tax-deductible contributions of cash or stock to ESOPs, and through 1987 may even earn tax credits in addition. With these incentives, an ESOP can borrow the money to finance a buyout of an employer's stock, with the employer's guarantee on the loan.

Debt support payments would come from dividends and employer cash contributions, so the entire amount—both principal and interest—can be tax-deductible.

9. For a review of project financing for R&D and a discussion of its contribution to the set of organizational possibilities, see our article, "An Economic Analysis of R&D Limited Partnerships," *Midland Corporate Finance Journal* Vol.3 No.4 (Winter 1986), pp. 33-45. We also updated our analysis in a subsequent article, "R&D Limited Partnership Financing and the New Tax Law," *Midland Corporate Finance Journal* Vol.4 No.4 (Winter 1987), pp. 44-54.

tory for the assets to be sold. One certainly should not underestimate, however, the ability of innovative financial professionals to cope with changes in the tax environment. On the real estate front, for example, they are turning once again to trusts. This continual give-and-take between innovative financial engineers and the taxing authorities reflects the "regulatory dialectic" at work; that is, as fast as the authorities close one avenue, innovators find new ways to carry on.[10]

Managements of many large corporations have welcomed the infusion of capital that comes from securitizing assets, perhaps without noticing an important effect on managerial incentives. The sale of a corporation's real estate holdings to a trust or limited partnership, for example, has the side-effect of returning resource allocation decisions to the marketplace.

Consider the following example. When a company owns its operating space, it serves as its own landlord—and thus part of its profit really represents rent. If the property is sold to a specialized subsidiary, there is the obvious tax benefit: when the corporation's reported profit drops because it begins paying explicit rent, the corporation's income tax drops accordingly. (When the subsidiary is carefully constructed, its income can escape taxation at the corporate level altogether.)

At the same time, however, something else happens that may not have been intended: the corporation becomes subject to eviction. When it owned the property, the corporation could weather a bad year or two without having to confess that it was losing money. Without the necessity of writing rent checks, the management could ignore the fact that the company was not earning enough to justify the space it occupied. After the sale of the company's real estate, however, the management would have to give an accounting if the company could not pay its rent.

In the traditional model of the corporation, as we have seen, managers are expected not only to run existing operations efficiently, but also to take primary responsibility for deciding how to reinvest the cash flows. They may decide to pay cash dividends, which the stockholders are then free to reinvest as they see fit, yet managers have first crack at the money. But when assets are sold to special-purpose subsidiaries, things often work on a different basis. These subsidiaries frequently involve high financial leverage and often take the organizational form of the limited partnership. Management is charged with the efficient operation of existing enterprises but, once again, the need to make debt service payments restricts management's role in the reinvestment decision. In the case of limited partnerships, moreover, the managing partner's discretion in dividend and reinvestment matters is further restricted because revenues and expenses are credited directly to the partners' individual accounts according to a fixed contractual formula. Once the accounting decisions are made, the individual partners receive their pro rata share of the cash produced by the partnership assets, and the reinvestment decisions are their own.[11]

In some cases, however, the general partner may enjoy considerable discretion in the early years of the partnership. Boone Pickens has even parlayed this kind of discretion into takeover attempts.[12] As time passes, however, that discretion is progressively returned to the limited partners.

CHANGING TREASURY ROLES

As a recent study noted, "The decisions made by corporate treasurers have a potential impact on corporate profits which is often as large as the earnings from operations."[13] At first this statement might conjure up images of bond refunding or treasury stock transactions, but there is much more involved. In a growing number of companies, the corporate

10. For more on the regulatory dialectic, see Andrew Chen and John Kensinger, "Innovations in Corporate Financing: Tax-Deductible Equity," *Financial Management* 15 (Winter 1985) pp. 44-51. See also, Kane, "Good Intentions and Unintended Evil: The Case Against Selective Credit Allocation," *Journal of Money, Credit, and Banking* (February 1977) pp. 55-69.

11. Limited partnerships are very flexible organizational forms which convey to investors the corporate advantage of limited liability, but without double taxation (except when they are publicly traded). There is wide latitude possible in the terms that can be stated in the partnership agreement. After the agreement is entered into, however, the general partners' discretion over the use of partnership assets is bound by its terms. These partnerships are finite-lived, with a well defined set of conditions for their demise. Although limited partners give up day-to-day control of the enterprise in exchange for limited liability, they still have access to the partnership ledgers to monitor compliance with the agreement and can vote in extraordinary circumstances (e.g., the removal of a general partner). Furthermore, the partnership agreement spells out explicitly how the partnership profits are to be paid out to the partners.

12. For example, Mesa Partners II was the major stockholder in Unocal during the recent takeover attempt. Then in January 1986, Mesa Limited Partnership made a run at KN Energy, the Colorado-based natural gas concern. Typically such partnerships are structured to take maximum advantage of the tax situation. By recomputing the tax basis of depletable properties, for example, the partnership may generate large losses in the early years. These losses are credited to the individual partners' accounts according to the partnership agreement. Subsequent profits must be credited up to a predefined point before cash payments begin to flow to limited partners.

13. Ian Cooper and Julian Franks, "Treasury Performance Measurement," *Midland Corporate Finance Journal*, Vol.4 No.4 (Winter 1987), pp. 29-43.

treasury no longer serves simply as a means to raise funds in support of operations; and many financial executives are discovering the possibilities for transforming the treasury into a profit center for securities trading. In October 1984, for example, Exxon Capital Corporation (a wholly owned subsidiary of Exxon Corporation), issued twenty-year Eurobonds with principal of $1.8 billion, and invested the proceeds in U.S. Treasury securities. The transaction was arranged in such a way that Exxon realized a substantial riskless profit after taxes, by taking advantage of tax differentials and international restrictions on capital flows.[14]

On the surface this may seem like an aberration, an occasional incursion by an oil company onto the turf of bankers. But it has an important implication. When the treasury itself becomes a profit center, alternative internal investments must compete with *it* for funding. As it grows, the trading function offers employment for more and more of the corporation's internal cash flow. Thus, potential investments in operations must compete with the array of opportunities in the full external capital market. If for example the rate of return on an investment in new plant or capital equipment, taking risk into account, is not competitive with outside investments, such internal projects will languish.

This, of course, is how things are *supposed* to have been done all along, at least according to our theory of capital budgeting. But there often needs to be a practical incentive to get management to adopt the perspective of its stockholders. Aggressive outside investment by the treasury, with the potential of investing in the full range of opportunities available in the marketplace, is likely to provide such an incentive for change. With an outward-looking treasury channeling funds into external markets, a corporation is less likely to view itself as an isolated, self-funding portfolio of businesses.

OPPORTUNITIES IN NEW TECHNOLOGIES

Major industrial research traditionally has been conducted within the confines of large integrated corporations, financed by the cash flows from established operations. The idea of the product life cycle, which came into vogue some sixty years ago, provides the foundation for the traditional concept of an integrated corporation that exploits products through all phases of their life cycles. *The heart of such a traditional integrated corporation is R&D.* As old products decline so that reinvesting cash flows in the associated production processes no longer pays, the excess cash flow is channeled to research and development of new products; and this process ensures continual renewal of the corporation.

Entrepreneurship, however, can be very attractive to today's scientists, who are likely to work harder (or at least in a more focused manner) when they have a chance to get rich as a result. In the not too distant past, though, entrepreneurship was the exception among researchers. Scientists generally remained content to enjoy the safety of a "good job" in a solid corporation. Patents added to one's prestige and job security, but the employer kept the lion's share of their value. Today, however, due to better access to venture capital, it is a quantum leap easier for a bright researcher to convert an idea into the seed of a new company. Lured by the prospect of riches, and prodded by the prospect of failure, the modern entrepreneur is exposed to far stronger incentives than was his "company-man" father.

Large corporations which cannot keep their brightest researchers happy within the salary structures of hierarchical organizations must find ways to cooperate with start-ups.[14] Dupont and Monsanto, for example, have learned the advantages of letting small, young organizations conduct research and then stepping on stage themselves when products are ready for manufacturing and marketing. DuPont has recently been buying up new companies which have developed biotechnology products in agrichemicals and pharmaceuticals, areas in which its own research efforts have come up short. The company is also trying joint ventures, which it traditionally shunned in order to keep its research efforts confidential.[15]

Monsanto, too, is sampling the benefits of cooperation with new ventures. In a recent interview CEO Richard J. Mahoney stated, "Monsanto decided it wanted to be in the biotechnology and pharmaceutical business many years ago...In fact, we were helping start up a number of these companies with venture capital. We bought Continental Pharmaceutical last year because we had a number of leads that had to be developed, and we didn't have anybody to develop

---

14. For a detailed analysis of the Exxon transaction, see John D. Finnerty, "Zero Coupon Bond Arbitrage: an Illustration of the Regulatory Dialectic at Work," *Financial Management* 14, (Winter 1985) pp. 13-17.

15. See C.S. Eklund and A.L. Cowan, "What's Causing the Scratches in DuPont's Teflon," *Business Week*, December 8, 1986, pp. 60f.

them."[16] Lacking the necessary in-house capability, Chrysler also turned to a joint venture—in this case with a Silicon Valley artificial intelligence start-up firm to bring expert systems into Chrysler cars in the 1990s.

DuPont, Monsanto, and Chrysler are not alone in seeking outside help for new product development. Indeed, one of Silicon Valley's latest contributions to the vocabulary of business is the "wizard shop." For example, Schlage Lock Company, the leading maker of mechanical locks, turned to San Franscisco's Theta Resources for the design work on an electronic lock system for hotels. Schlage's own internal R&D efforts had come up dry after a five-year effort. Theta Resources completed the job in just 18 months, and Schlage now has two patents plus a backlog of orders for its system.[17]

SRI International, a contract-research laboratory headquartered in Menlo Park, California, may be on its way to becoming the granddaddy of all wizard shops. General Electric recently *gave* its Sarnoff Laboratory to SRI. The Sarnoff Lab, which developed color television, the liquid crystal display and the VCR, to name a few of its achievements, came to GE in its merger with RCA. Sarnoff's New Jersey facilities give SRI a strong presence on both coasts, and make it a formidable factor in research circles.[18]

In sum, then, increasing opportunities in the financial markets for young, vigorous technology start-up companies spell an erosion of competitive advantage in R&D for large, integrated corporations—while stimulating the development of new technologies. Very simple changes in financing "technology" are stimulating changes in the way businesses organize themselves to do business. "Smaller," it seems, is now not only prettier but, in a growing number of cases, more efficient.

DYNAMIC NETWORK ORGANIZATIONS

We have painted a picture of a process which is grinding firms down to ever-finer, smaller, more fo-cused entities. Old, mature corporations are returning resources to the marketplace, which in turn nurture young start-ups. This development is leading to temporary, project-specific liaisons known as "dynamic networks."[19] Dynamic networks thrive in fast-changing environments such as consumer electronics and apparel. One of them, the sports shoe marketer, Nike, has become quite well-known. Nike contracts its manufacturing to offshore factories, itself serving as developer and marketer of products.[20]

As product life cycles contract in response to continuing advances in computer-assisted design (CAD) and computer integrated manufacturing (CIM), more of the business world is being transformed into the natural habitat of the dynamic networks. Even in auto manufacturing, the bastion of traditional industrial organization, product life cycles are shrinking. It used to take five years or more to bring a new automobile to market. Ford Motor Company has cut that to two years, and it will keep getting shorter.

In networks of the future, the work might be done by professional firms specializing in research, product design, or marketing. Manufacturing is likely to be contracted out to offshore factories, or to flexible automated factories near the final market. Finally, the key role of putting all the pieces together would go to specialized brokers, perhaps a new breed of merchant bankers.

Recent experiments with partnership forms of organization may be laying the foundations of a new way of financing dynamic networks. Only time, of course, will tell the extent to which it will displace integrated corporations. But in this alternative form, investors still retain their limited liability while relinquishing much less power to managers. Investors are the direct recipients of cash flows from mature operations. They are then free to choose whether or not they wish to provide funding for the development of new products by participating directly in R&D project financing. If development

16. "Richard J. Mahoney Reshapes Monsanto for the Future," *DH&S Review*, Deloitte Haskins & Sells, December 9, 1985, pp. 1-3.

17. Theta Resources is not alone, and the list of customers contains some surprises. David Kelley Design of Palo Alto, for example, designed the mouse that is so familiar to users of the Macintosh computer. Stephen Beck and Edward Goldfarb of BeckTech designed the innards of an electronic hand puppet, Talking Wrinkles, for Coleco Industries' 1986 Christmas toy line. Burt Rutan, himself a "wizard" in aviation circles (his Mojave, California firm builds exotic flying prototypes for aerospace firms such as Raytheon's Beech Aircraft Division) turned to Robert Conn's Connsult Inc. to design a microelectronic monitor to record continuously

the airspeed and altitude of the Voyager on its historic round-the-world flight. (See Michael Rogers, "Silicon Valley's Newest Wizards," *Newsweek*, January 5, 1987, pp. 36-7.)

18. See Otis Port, Evert Clark, and James Norman, "GE Gift-Wraps a Landmark Lab," *Business Week*, February 16, 1987, p.35.

19. For a detailed description of dynamic network organizations and predictions for their future role, see Raymond E. Miles and Charles C. Snow, "Network Organizations: New Concepts for New Forms," *California Management Review* (Spring 1986), pp. 62f.

20. See *Business Week* (March 3, 1986).

efforts are successful, the rights may be sold or licensed to a manufacturer/marketer. Alternatively, investors may choose to participate in manufacturing and marketing by means of still other partnerships.

Recently, with strong encouragement and support from the U.S. Department of Commerce, a few firms have experimented with limited partnerships formed for the purpose of promoting and marketing a specific product. Energy Sciences Corporation offers an example. It developed a data networking system which sends data via low-frequency radio signals over existing phone or power lines, while leaving normal utility services undisturbed. The development was funded through project financing.

Now the company is preparing a marketing campaign financed by what it calls "technology marketing partnerships."[21] These marketing partnerships are in essence very simple. They are business organizations formed for the purpose of bringing a specific product or group of products to market. The general partner may manufacture the product itself, or contract the manufacturing to a third party. The general partner also contracts with third parties for advertising and promotion. The partnership owns the trademark and brandname supported by its advertising, and has an exclusive distributorship for the product. It earns revenues from royalties or commissions paid out of sales by the manufacturer. In some cases they are set up with an option for the manufacturer to buy out the distributorship for a lump sum.

There can be tax advantages from such arrangements, but they also provide a project-specific organizational alternative to the corporation. It is possible for a product to be developed by a partnership and brought to market by another partnership, with heavy reliance upon capital raised in the public market. In such a complex of small, specialized organizations, the primary role of managers would be to run existing operations efficiently. In order to increase the assets under their

management, however, they would have to compete by continually creating attractive new opportunities to be offered in the marketplace for capital.

OPPORTUNITIES FOR LARGE CORPORATIONS

All is not lost, however, for big established companies. Whenever they have strong competitive advantages from economies of scale in production or marketing, they have much to gain by cooperating with start-ups or design consultants which have new technologies to offer. It seems that large corporations have the opportunity to benefit from letting small, nimble, low-cost organizations develop new products and technologies, so long as they themselves have strengths to offer in manufacturing or marketing.

No less than the giant IBM has recently undertaken a massive shift in focus, redeploying its resources from design and manufacturing to marketing and customer service.[22] When the large organizations have an edge in manufacturing or marketing, they may continue to prosper despite declining in-house R&D. The integrating core, however, will no longer be a common technological base, but instead a common manufacturing, distribution, or marketing base.

Yet the long term may bring continuing pressure upon large corporations because these advantages, too, will melt away for some companies as automated manufacturing spreads and as mass markets fragment. For example, the advent of practical computer integrated manufacturing (CIM) systems in widespread use, on the horizon perhaps as early as the mid-90s, will erode the advantages of large size in many areas of manufacturing, since such systems erase economies of scale and in their place bring tremendous economies of scope.[23] Even one of today's somewhat primitive CIM cells can produce any one of several hundred different parts, at the same cost per unit whether the production run is for a hundred units or only one unit.[24] As such CIM cells

---

21. For more details, see *Financial Planning* (October 1985), pp. 181-188.

22. See Dennis Kneale, "Tough Choices—Cutting Output, IBM Tells Some Workers: Move, Retire, or Quit," *Wall Street Journal*, April 8, 1987, p.1. See also Geoff Lewis, "Big Changes at Big Blue," *Business Week*, February 15, 1988, pp. 92f.

23. Economies of scope derive from cost reduction as a result of applying assets to the production of a variety of different products. Economies of scale, in contrast, derive from cost reduction as a result of applying assets intensely to the high-volume production of a small range of products. For the earliest development of ideas about economies of scope, see J. Panzar and R. Willig, "Economies of Scale and Economies of Scope in Multi-Output Production," and "Economies of Scope," Bell Laboratories Economic Discussion Papers No.33 (1975) and No.197 (1981), respectively.

24. The CIM cell at General Dynamics in Fort Worth, for example, can produce any of over 500 different aircraft parts, with "retooling" accomplished merely by selecting a different computer program. The automated assembly operation at the IBM plant in Austin, Texas offers another mind-stretching example. There, the PC Converible production is done entirely by robots. Machines sort the components, assemble them into finished computers, perform all systems tests, and pack the new computers in their boxes. Human workers don't enter the scene until it is time to load the finished computers onto trucks for shipment. The assembly system could be readily reprogrammed for a variety of new products.

become widespread and the bugs are smoothed out, the cost advantage will no longer be with large centrally-located factories, but instead with networks of small geographically-dispersed flexible factories that are close to final markets.[25] These flexible factories, moreover, will be capable of producing a broad range of goods under license to different designers.

Thus, the familiar specialized product-specific factories of today will give way to generalized factories that are the new-age analogue of the village blacksmith. Such factories will produce many of our basic goods locally, and in fact the local factory may well not be owned by any particular product designer. Such factories will really be more like utilities. With quality (that is, conformity to design specifications) assured within tight tolerances, competition will be on the basis of product design, where the edge seems to belong to organizations that are small enough to be flexible and provide an environment that is conducive to creativity.

The advantages of mass marketing are also eroding, with the fragmentation of the media. Cable and satellite television, VCR technology, and specialization within the print media have reduced the value of a blanket advertising appeal to the mass market, and enhanced the value of focusing on a particular audience. To take one prominent example, Campbell's Soup, a pioneer in mass marketing during the early days of radio, has recently begun shifting to a regional and ethnic focus in its product line.

CONCLUDING REMARKS

The financial marketplace is maturing rapidly, well on its way to attaining a truly world-wide scope, and the array of opportunities offered to investors is proliferating at a breakneck pace. The optimist sees opportunity in this and, indeed, the opportunities for people with good ideas have never been more abundant. Nor have the opportunities for those with cash ever seemed more promising.

To make way for these new opportunities, however, mature corporations in shrinking industries are now facing pressure to return their capital to the marketplace; and this contraction (in extreme cases, disappearance) of large firms will have unfortunate consequences for many. But, so long as vigorous new enterprises step in to replace declining operations, the net result is a stronger economy overall. Thus, where critics see only the lifeblood draining from venerable institutions, economists perceive the workings of the "invisible hand," leading to a more creative and competitive American industry with no formal central planning.

Perhaps the hardest realization for many to accept is that decisions which once fell indisputably within the province of an elite corps of corporate and regulatory minds are increasingly being made in the faceless, apparently chaotic marketplace. But in the end, of course, this is a major step toward greater democracy in economic affairs.

---

25. Recent research leads to the disquieting conclusion that many of the "bugs" now troubling some of the American pioneers in CIM are the fault of management rather than the systems themselves. It seems that American managers often try to force CIM into working the "old fashioned way," with large production runs and little variety. Their Japanese competitors, in contrast, play to the strengths of CIM by utilizing the inherent flexibility in short production runs for a variety of products. In time, U.S. management will either learn to use the flexible systems effectively, or fall by the wayside. (See Ramachanran Jaikumar, "Postindustrial Manufacturing,"

Harvard Business Review, Vol.64 No.6 (November-December 1986) pp. 69-76.)

Besides flexibility and low cost, furthermore, the new systems offer superior quality. Because of this Robert Kaplan recently warned that companies which choose not to invest in the new manufacturing technologies may find themselves in the unenviable position of being high-cost producers of inferior products. (See Robert Kaplan, "Must CIM Be Justified by Faith Alone?" *Harvard Business Review*, Vol.64 No.2 (March-April 1986), pp. 87-97.)

THE CAUSES AND CONSEQUENCES OF HOSTILE TAKEOVERS

by Amar Bhide, Harvard Business School

INTRODUCTION

"There can be absolutely no doubt," says Peter Drucker, "that hostile takeovers are exceedingly bad for the economy." Acquired companies are burdened with "heavy debt," which is said to "severely impair the company's potential for economic performance." And the sell-offs of "the most valuable parts of the acquired businesses" that often follow takeovers "impair both their own productivity and that of the remaining assets."[1]

Drucker's views resonate throughout corporate America. The Business Roundtable, comprising the chief executives of America's 200 largest companies, complains that hostile takeovers "create no new wealth but merely shift ownership and replace equity with large amounts of debt."[2] Shortsighted institutional investors, the argument runs, undervalue companies whose current earnings are temporarily depressed by long-term investment. And this underpricing leaves well-run companies vulnerable to rapacious raiders who devour the corporate future in their drive for quick profits.

The Reagan administration, many financial economists, and—not surprisingly—corporate "raiders" like Boone Pickens and Sir James Goldsmith have taken a very different view of the causes and consequences of hostile takeovers. Contests for corporate control arise, they say, when outsiders believe they can derive greater value from a corporation's assets than the incumbent management team. As stated in the President's Economic Report of 1985, "the external market for corporate control disciplines managers who believe they have maximized the value of their corporation's shares when, in fact, they have not." The Report goes on to confirm the existence of persuasive evidence demonstrating that takeovers "improve efficiency, transfer scarce resources to higher-valued uses, and stimulate effective corporate management."[3]

---

1. Peter F. Drucker, "The Problem of Corporate Takeovers—What is to Be Done?", *The Public Interest* (Winter 1986), pp. 3-24.
2. As reported in *The Economist* (June 1, 1985), p. 73
3. 1985 President's Economic Report.

Inconclusive Evidence

Neither advocates nor critics of hostile takeovers, however, can muster evidence that seems wholly convincing.

Advocates base their case on increases in stock market values. Michael Jensen, for example, estimates that gains from mergers and acquisitions in the period 1977-1986 amounted to some $400 billion—roughly $350 billion in the form of takeover premia paid to target shareholders and about $50 billion through the higher valuations the market placed on the stocks of bidders.[4] These gains, it is argued, are an accurate reflection of the substantial contribution of takeovers because the stock market is an unbiased and efficient arbiter of long-term economic value.

It is now a commonplace that target shareholders are paid a premium price—at least relative to the market if not to their expectations—when acquirers purchase the stock. Evidence of gains to bidders, however, is far from clear-cut.

For one thing, "event studies" of gains to bidders (measured by estimating the "excess" stock returns around the time a takeover is announced) show mixed results. Some show positive excess returns, while others show below-normal returns. Jensen's claim of small positive returns to bidders is based on "averaging" the results of several of these studies.[5]

Second, the period from which the data is drawn raises questions about the reliability of the results. Every study cited by Jensen that shows positive bidder returns uses pre-1980 data. Such studies thus include the results of takeovers from the days of the "go-go conglomerates" of the 1960s—a period during which, many reasonable people now argue, the stock market may not have been a particularly reliable barometer of value creation.

Third, as Richard Roll has argued, "The interpretation of bidding firm returns is complicated by several potential measurement problems. The bid can convey contaminating information, that is, information about the bidder rather than about the takeover itself. The bid can be partially anticipated and thus result in an announcement effect smaller in absolute value than the true economic effect."[6]

The results of studies that have sought to measure the "aggregate net changes" in the *sum* of the values of bidders' and targets' stocks are also inconclusive. As Roll comments, "The available empirical evidence indicates that the measured combined value has increased in some studies and decreased in others. It has been statistically significant in none."[7] Therefore we cannot rule out the possibility that gains to target shareholders have come out of the pockets of the bidders' shareholders.

In short, the claim that takeovers lead to net positive changes in stock market values is at best an informed guess.

On the other hand, the claims of takeover critics that the myopia of institutional investors creates opportunities for hostile takeovers are not based on any evidence whatsoever. It may be true that institutional investors are pressured by their sponsors to adopt a quarter-to-quarter perspective. But, there is no reason why even short-term traders should discriminate against companies with "good" managers following "long-term strategies." The evidence, in fact, suggests that the stock market pays a premium for long-term growth and investment opportunities.[8]

Critics may be on somewhat firmer ground in their claims about the consequences of takeovers. Most studies show that performance declines after a takeover. Returns on capital and market share drop and a high proportion of acquisitions are eventually divested.[9] There are virtually no studies which show that takeovers are followed by an improvement in performance.

One problem with the post-takeover profitability studies is that they rely on accounting measures, which may not accurately reflect economic reality. A more serious problem, though, is that the studies focus on mergers in general, and thus make no attempt to distinguish between the effects of hostile and friendly acquisitions.

Studies of the long-term consequences of hostile transactions are scarce because such deals are of recent vintage and still relatively uncommon. W. T. Grimm

4. See Michael Jensen, "The Takeover Controversy: Analysis and Evidence," *Midland Corporate Finance Journal* (Summer 1986), pp. 6-32.

5. See Michael Jensen and Richard Ruback, "The Market for Corporate Control: The Scientific Evidence," *Journal of Financial Economics* 11 (1983), pp. 5-50.

6. Richard Roll, "The Hubris Theory of Corporate Takeovers," *Journal of Business* 59 no. 2 (1986), pp. 197-216.

7. Ibid.

8. For a review of the evidence supporting this position, see Jensen (1986), cited earlier in note 4, pp. 11-12.

9. For studies demonstrating poor post-merger and -acquisition performance, see David J. Ravencraft and Frank M. Scherer, "Mergers and Managerial Performance," in John C. Coffee, Jr., Louis Lowenstein, and Susan Rose-Ackerman, eds., *Knights, Raiders, and Targets: The Impact of the Hostile Takeover* (Oxford University Press, 1988); and Michael Porter, "From Competitive Advantage to Corporate Strategy," *Harvard Business Review*, (May-June 1987).

identifies 1974, when Morgan Stanley represented International Nickel Company of Canada in its unsuccessful hostile offer for ESB Inc., as the year in which hostile raids became "an established acquisition strategy."[10] The most controversial deals, launched not by corporations but by individuals such as Goldsmith and Carl Icahn, have come into vogue only since 1983. And the total number of successful transactions is small: from 1974 through 1986, there were only 155 successful contested tender offers (out of 283 attempts). In contrast, there were thousands of successful friendly mergers every year during the same period.

The absence of data and accumulated knowledge on hostile transactions wouldn't matter if, as some economists claim, the only difference between friendly and unfriendly transactions is the attractiveness of the price offered and the incentives of incumbent managers to go along with the takeover. But, as I will show, there are significant differences between hostile and friendly transactions. Hence, the record of the more common friendly transactions ought not to be used to evaluate the relatively new and infrequent unfriendly deals.

Approach of the Study

My doctoral thesis at the Harvard Business School examined the motives and consequences of all 47 hostile takeovers over $100 million that were attempted in 1985 and 1986, and then compared them to the motives and effects of a randomly selected control group of friendly takeovers during the same period.

Unlike most studies undertaken by financial economists, I did not try to measure the "value created" in these transactions. Although determining the economic value added is certainly a useful exercise, it is not a feasible one in the case of hostile deals. A significant proportion of hostile acquirers are private individuals or partnerships. Consequently, they do not have the stock trading history needed to measure "value" using the event study approach; nor are they required to make public the data necessary for a post-merger study of profitability.

Rather than estimate the value created according to some absolute economic standard, I instead sought to determine the source of the *expected* benefits of the acquisition. What value or benefit, I tried to determine, do acquirers expect that makes them willing to go to the expense and trouble of attempting a takeover? This more modest issue, I found, could be explored with the available data even on private acquirers.

The second set of questions addressed by my research concerns the near-term consequences of hostile takeovers. We may not be able to determine the long-term consequences of the post-1983 hostile takeovers for another decade or so. But, in the meantime, it would be useful to bring evidence to bear on popular claims about their immediate effects: Do they lead to "dangerous" increases in financial risk? Are they followed by shortsighted cutbacks in long-term investment? How common are "bust-up" takeovers? And do they lead to a loss of useful synergies? Are gains to stockholders created at the expense of the target's employees? And, do takeovers lead to an improvement in the quality of management in the target organizations?

The methods I employed were also significantly different from those of most previous studies of takeovers. The typical econometric study uses a model of value creation that has one dependent variable (usually changes in stockholder wealth, sometimes profitability) and a handful of independent variables. In my study, instead of relying on any one model, I used scores of different analyses to investigate the issues raised above. Standing alone, no single analysis was conclusive; but, taken together, the results fall into what I believe is a clear and coherent pattern.

A second difference concerns the nature and sources of my data. Traditional studies of takeovers by financial economists make use of masses of quantitative data, often drawn from large public data bases such as CRSP or COMPUSTAT. My study relied instead on "soft variables" derived from data bases I constructed myself. The data consisted of information taken from such public sources as SEC filings, analyst reports, news reports, and stock research.

Findings: Criticisms Unfounded

By way of a brief preview, let me say here at the outset that the findings of my research are not consistent with most of the charges that have been levelled against hostile takeovers.

---

10. W.T. Grimm, *Mergerstat Review* (1986).

Stock market shortsightedness or irrationality does not appear to play a major role in motivating acquirers. A majority of hostile takeovers in 1985 and 1986 were motivated rather by acquirers' beliefs that value could be created by "restructuring" the target—that is, by substantially changing its financial policies, cost structures, or diversification strategies.

Nor do the consequences of hostile deals appear to be as dire as they have been painted by the press and the Business Roundtable. My research suggests that hostile takeovers in 1985 and 1986:

■ *Did not lead to dangerous permanent increases in financial risk.* Although several takeovers were financed by speculative-grade debt, in virtually all such cases debt levels were quickly reduced by asset sales, new equity issues, or innovative refinancings.

■ *Did not sacrifice long-term investments.* Except in two cases, the reported cuts in investment that followed the takeovers would, in all likelihood, have been made without a change in management control since extensive industry-wide cuts were taking place at the same time. And, in any event, few of the targets were making substantial long-term investments before they were taken over, since most belonged to mature, low-tech industries.

■ *Were usually followed by divestitures,* especially if they had been motivated by expectations of restructuring profits. These divestitures, however, do not appear to have led to the loss of synergies; rather they appear to be reversals of the targets' past policies of diversification into unrelated businesses.

■ *Did not lead to substantial job losses.* Takeovers were often followed by layoffs and plant closings. In over half of such cases, however, the layoffs would probably have occurred without changes in control because of severe industry-wide competitive pressures. As noted above, targets were often found in mature or declining industries. The number of jobs lost that can be reasonably attributed to hostile takeovers is, therefore, a small fraction of the job losses in corporate America that have been caused by competitive pressures since the 1982 recession.

■ *Do not appear to have displaced "good managers."* An overwhelming percentage of the targets had poor, or at best mediocre, performance records.

In rather dramatic contrast to my findings about hostile takeovers, I found that in friendly transactions, perceived synergies or the advancement of some corporate "portfolio" strategy were the most common benefits expected by acquirers. Targets of friendly mergers were much more likely to be well-managed companies with attractive growth prospects. Cutbacks in investment and employment, whether induced by product-market competition or otherwise, were consequently rare. And, the top management teams of the targets were much more likely to be left undisturbed.

As mentioned earlier, the findings of most studies of post-merger profitability, which focus perforce mainly on friendly transactions, suggest uninspiring performance. And, combining these results with my findings about merger motives in friendly deals, it is not difficult to see why friendly acquisitions of "good" growth companies often prove to be disappointments and are subsequently divested. The target may well be performing at its peak at the time of its acquisition, well-intentioned efforts to realize synergies may prove to be disruptive, and the target's management team may lose interest along with its independence. In contrast, the poorly performing targets of hostile takeovers often have no place to go but up.

EXPECTED BENEFITS: WHAT'S IN IT FOR THE RAIDERS?

Understanding the benefits sought by acquirers is an important step in sorting out the rival claims about hostile takeovers. For example, if we find that a large proportion of takeovers are launched because acquirers believe that the targets' stocks are undervalued, then Drucker's claims that the stock market's irrationality leads to hostile acquisitions would be buttressed. Likewise, if it can be demonstrated that acquirers believe they can profit handsomely by changing the way target companies are managed, then we would have a stronger case for the theory that management inefficiencies are behind hostile takeovers. Or, if it turns out that most acquirers proceed with the expectation of creating synergies, we would tend to reject both the stock market inefficiency and managerial incompetence hypotheses.

Knowing where the raiders are headed will also enable us to speculate more intelligently about where they will eventually end up. If hostile acquisitions are made in order to bet on "undervalued" stocks or to build empires, we would then be more skeptical about their long-term economic contribution. If instead we find that raiders usually pounce on what they perceive to be incompetent managers, we can then ask: Were the incumbent managers really "incompetent" by the yardsticks of long-term performance, or did they merely fail to deliver short-term e.p.s. growth? And what is the nature and desirability of the changes that the raiders implement after the incumbents are purged?

Approach

I began by grouping the most likely motives for acquisitions into the following six categories:[11]

1. *Create Operating Synergies:* My definition of synergies included only those benefits expected from combining or coordinating non-financial functions such as production or marketing. I intentionally removed those cases where acquirers expected to create value by coordinating only the financial or resource allocation functions of the target with their existing businesses.

2. *Build or Redeploy Corporate Portfolio:* This category was intended to include all cases in which the principal expected benefit of acquisition was the advancement of the acquirers' diversification strategy.[12]

3. *Acquire Undervalued Asset:* This was meant to include all cases in which acquirers believed the target was worth more than the purchase price, either because of stock market undervaluation or because of some anticipated change in demand, price, or costs affecting the firm's value.

4. *Improve Efficiency by Restructuring:* This category was intended to hold all cases in which the acquirer expected to profit from changing the target's strategy—for example, by increasing leverage, divesting certain business units, implementing cost reductions, or discontinuing unprofitable reinvestment.[13]

5. *Maintain Independence:* This category covers only those cases in which the acquirers themselves were under imminent threat of being taken over and were seeking an acquisition to neutralize this threat.

6. *Tax Motives:* All takeovers have tax implications and acquirers naturally seek to maximize their tax benefits. But, in most cases, it is difficult to determine how important these tax benefits were in the decision to proceed with a takeover. I therefore restricted this category to those cases in which the search for an acquisition was motivated by the acquirer's desire to take advantage of existing tax credits or tax loss carry forwards.

Having set out this classification scheme, I then attempted to determine which motive (or, in a few cases, motives) was likely to have been the most important in each of the transactions I examined.

It is, of course, impossible to observe directly the underlying motives for corporate acquisitions. Acquirers, to be sure, often make public statements about the expected benefits. But such statements, which range from the forthright to the utterly misleading, do not provide a reliable guide to the real motives. Expected benefits must therefore be inferred from a broader set of circumstantial evidence.

Fortunately, there is no dearth of qualitative and quantitative data on acquirers, targets, and transactions. The real challenge I faced was to devise reasonable rules of inference that would take advantage of the available information while minimizing the need to make subjective judgments about each case. Through a process of trial and error, I arrived at the following tests to provide "first pass" judgements about acquirers' expected benefits.

What was the acquirer's form?
■ Synergistic or portfolio benefits were ruled out if the acquirer was a private partnership organized for the transaction or a private investment shell.
■ If the acquirer was an on-going operating company, synergistic benefits were inferred, especially if the company operated in a single industry.
■ If the acquirer was a diversified company, portfolio benefits were assumed.

What was the acquirer's diversification strategy and track record in previous takeovers?
■ Synergistic benefits were inferred if the acquirer exhibited a pattern of making acquisitions in the same (or related) industry and integrating

---

11. My categories are adapted from a classification scheme devised by Richard Roll (1986), cited earlier in note 6.

12. My use of the category closely corresponds to Michael Porter's description (source cited in note 9) of a portfolio strategy wherein:

The corporation acquires sound attractive companies with competent managers who agree to stay on... The acquired units are autonomous and the teams that run them are compensated according to unit results. The corporation supplies capital and works with each to infuse it with professional management techniques. At the same time, top management provides objective and dispassionate review of business unit results...

13. My use of the term restructuring closely parallels Porter's description of a firm following a restructuring strategy:

Unlike its passive role as a portfolio manager, when it serves as banker and reviewer, a company that bases its strategy on restructuring becomes an active restructurer of business units. The new businesses are not necessarily related to existing units. All that is necessary is unrealized potential... The parent intervenes, frequently changing the unit management team, shifting strategy, or infusing the company with new technology.

TABLE 1		1985	1986	Total
CONTESTED TENDER OFFERS IN 1985 AND 1986	■ Number of Contested Offers	32	40	62
	■ Contested Offers > $100m of which:	24	23	47
	Successful Offers	12	8	20
	Unsuccessful—target rescued by White Knight	8	11	19
	Unsuccessful—target remained independent	4	4	8

acquired businesses into existing operations. Dun and Bradstreet, with its strategy of acquiring small database companies, is an example.

■ Portfolio benefits were inferred if the acquirer exhibited a pattern of making acquisitions in a variety of businesses and industries; treating acquired companies as stand-alone businesses and making few efforts to coordinate non-financial functions across businesses; and rarely divesting acquisitions unless they were perceived to be "failures." Conglomerates like ITT, RCA, and Allied Corp. fit this pattern.

■ Investment benefits were assumed if the acquirer exhibited the pattern of making opportunistic acquisitions in one or more industries; treating acquired companies as stand-alone businesses and making few efforts to coordinate non-financial functions across businesses; being willing to take non-controlling positions in companies; and frequently selling its holdings at a profit. The most prominent example is Warren Buffet's Berkshire Hathaway.

■ Restructuring benefits were indicated if the acquirer exhibited a pattern of making substantial changes in the strategy or operations of the acquired companies, for example, by increasing leverage, divesting assets or renegotiating wage contracts. Examples of such acquirers are Hanson Trust, Sir James Goldsmith, and Asher Edelman.

Was the acquirer under attack before it initiated its takeover?

■ Defensive benefits were inferred if a raider had accumulated a substantial and unwelcome stake in the acquirer (or had actually made an overture).

Was the acquirer's takeover search motivated by the need to utilize substantial tax-credits or loss carry forwards?

■ If so, then financial synergies were assumed.

The most critical of these tests is obviously the one relating to the bidder's prior acquisition "strategy." Recurring patterns of acquisition behavior provide more reliable insights into an acquirer's motives than a "snapshot picture" of an individual transaction. But, in cases where it was difficult to get information about an acquirer's past strategy, I also used supplementary tests to refine (or confirm) inferences arising from the primary tests. Such supplementary tests examined public statements of motives, statements about post-merger changes, analysts reports, and stock price and balance sheet data.

Sample Selection

Core Sample: The core of my sample comprised all contested tender offers over $100 million made in 1985 and 1986—a total of 47 takeover attempts. The years 1985 and 1986 were chosen because of the high level of hostile takeover activity as well as the relatively easy availability of the data. Because I was interested in investigating expected benefits, I included both successful as well as unsuccessful contested tender offers. As Table 1 shows, a majority of attempts were in fact foiled, and thus my sample would have been considerably smaller if I had excluded the failed attempts.

Control Group: I also picked a control group consisting of 30 randomly selected "friendly" (or, at any rate, not contested) takeovers in 1985. The purpose of selecting this group was to determine whether the distribution of apparent motives in friendly transactions was appreciably different from those in hostile transactions.[14]

Using the classification procedure described in the previous section, I then assigned each of the 47

---

14. In my doctoral dissertation, on which this article is based, I also constructed a second control group consisting of hostile transactions attempted in 1981. The purpose behind selecting this group was to test the hypothesis that the benefits expected by acquirers in hostile transactions in the 1981, "pre-junk bond" era were different from those of the more recent raiders. Specifically, I expected to find that the incidence of "restructuring" motives would be lower in the 1981 takeovers while synergy and portfolio motives would be higher. Although the finding provided some support for this supposition, the sample was so small (13 acquirers greater than $75 million) that the results must be viewed as extremely tentative.

TABLE 2
DISTRIBUTION OF
EXPECTED BENEFITS
IN HOSTILE TAKEOVERS

Nature and Source of Expected Benefit	Percentage of Targets (n = 47)
Restructuring	68%
Portfolio	17%
Synergy	28%
Investment	4%
Financial (Tax)	4%

hostile bidders, as well as the 30 friendly acquirers, to one (or more) of the six categories listed above. (A listing of these transactions and the ascribed motives is provided in Appendix A.)

Findings on Expected Benefits

As presented in Table 2, the pursuit of "restructuring" profit appeared to be the primary motive in over two-thirds (32 of 47) of the hostile attempts, while evidence of expected "portfolio," "synergistic," and "investment" benefits was found in a considerably smaller portion.

This distribution of motives is clearly not consistent with claims that undervaluation by the stock market leads to hostile takeovers. In only 3 of the hostile takeover attempts studied is there any evidence that acquirers expected to benefit from undervaluation of the target. And in two of these three cases, the acquirer's bet appeared to be more on the undervaluation of some underlying resource market than on the stock market: Sir James Goldsmith seemed to believe that the market for timberland was depressed when he bid for Crown Zellerbach; likewise, the chief executive of Burlington Northern (who had once been the CFO of a large oil company) appeared to have been betting on rising oil prices "through" the acquisition of Southland Royalty.[15]

Other evidence, drawn from Value Line's stock reports on the targets, also suggests it is unlikely that market misvaluation was an important factor in the 1985 takeovers:

■ *Acquirers did not bid bargain prices relative to the book values or historic price earnings (p/e) ratios of their targets. On average, acquisition p/e ratios were roughly three times the median 10-year p/e ratios of the target, and there were no cases of acquisition p/e's being less than the long-run p/e.*

■ *Occasionally (as in Maxwell's attempted takeover of Harcourt Brace Jovanovich) it is claimed that raiders seek to snap up companies after their prices have fallen steeply. This does not appear to be the case with most of the takeover attempts in our sample. On average, acquisition prices were 40% greater than the highest price reached in the prior year.*

■ *Value Line, one of the rare stock-picking services that appears consistently to outperform the market, deemed only one target stock to be an attractive purchase shortly before takeover bids were made.*

In short, stock market irrationality, real or perceived, seems unlikely to have played a major role in inducing hostile takeovers in 1985 and 1986.[16]

The second important point I would make about these findings is that they are strongly consistent with financial economists' concept of a "market for corporate control" that disciplines poor management and thereby improves efficiency. In about two thirds of the cases, acquirers apparently believed they could profit from a takeover by "doing something different" with the target, and were willing to put their theory to the financial test. In fact, in over half the cases, restructuring was the only expected

---

15. In the other "restructuring"-motivated takeover attempts of oil companies (for example, Pickens' tender offer for Unocal), the implicit bet about oil prices merely was that they would not *fall* to a level that would jeopardize interest payments on the debt raised to finance the acquisition.

16. As previously mentioned, takeover critics like Drucker have implied that a short-sighted, volatile stock market creates opportunities for raiders. The link between such myopia and opportunities for raiders is not always clearly drawn, but a simple mechanism may be posited as follows: Short-term traders generate sharp swings in the market, thus causing prices sometimes to be too high relative to a firm's true value and sometimes too low. Sharp-eyed raiders who have a

better feel for values could step in and acquire a company on the cheap when the herd has irrationally bid down its stock.

Although such views are at odds with the prevailing financial economists' paradigm, I do not believe that the possibility of occasional lapses in stock market rationality can be ruled out. Evidence attesting to the random nature of stock price movements and the stock market's ability to see through certain accounting changes does not rule out the possibility that, on occasion, the stock market may be too volatile, and even heavily traded securities may be undervalued. What is possible with the universe of stocks, however, is not necessarily what is probable with respect to the particular takeover targets studied.

TABLE 3
DISTRIBUTION OF
EXPECTED BENEFITS:
HOSTILE VERSUS FRIENDLY
TAKEOVERS

Primary Expected Benefit(s)	Attempts in which observed	
	Hostile Attempts (N = 45)	Friendly transactions (N = 29)
Restructuring	25	3
Portfolio	6	13
Synergistic	4	6
Investment	0	1
Defensive	0	2
Portfolio + Synergistic	4	2
Restructuring + Synergistic	6	2

benefit; in these cases acquirers appeared to be looking exclusively at what could be done with the target, without any reference to how it fit with their existing businesses.

If all the attempts involving a "restructuring" motive had succeeded, the main outcome would probably have been the redrawing of corporate boundaries. In 27 of the 32 attempts I identified as motivated primarily by restructuring aims, the "doing something different with the target" apparently included the intent to sell subsidiaries. Changing financial structure was probably anticipated in about 15 of the 32 attempts, while cutting costs seemed to be a major factor in only 6 cases.

The Contrast with Friendly Takeovers

As shown in Table 3, the distribution of expected benefits in friendly takeovers is markedly different from the distribution of benefits in hostile takeovers.

One major difference between the friendly and hostile distributions is the relatively low level of "restructuring" cases. Where two thirds of the acquirers in hostile attempts expected restructuring profits to be a major benefit of their takeovers, only 5 of the 30 (17%) acquirers harbored such expectations in friendly transactions.[17] This finding is consistent with the hypothesis that the directors and senior executives of a target are more apt to resist acquirers who are expected to make wholesale changes in their companies.

It is also instructive to look at the few cases where "restructuring" benefits were involved, and to speculate as to why the transaction was nevertheless friendly. In three out of the five cases, special factors seem to have been involved.

■ In the case of the Uniroyal and Alamito acquisitions, incumbent managers were key players in the acquiring group. It was also apparent that if the management-led group didn't acquire and restructure the target in an ostensibly friendly transaction, raiders would do the job after a hostile takeover.

■ Analysts suggested that ABC voluntarily merged with Capital Cities, in spite of the latter's reputation as a tough cost cutter, because ABC's chairman, who was on the verge of retirement, and its board believed that (1) there was no natural successor to the chairman within the company; (2) Capital Cities' executives were exceptional managers and would be good for the institution in the long term and (3) ABC needed protection against "undesirable" raiders like Saul Steinberg and Turner Broadcasting who had reputedly been accumulating ABC's stock.[18]

Balancing out the low proportion of "restructuring" benefits in friendly takeovers is a high proportion of "portfolio" and "synergistic" benefits. Advancement of some "portfolio" objective was a major benefit expected by acquirers in nearly half, and "realization of synergies" in just under a quarter, of friendly announcements.

17. The evidence is also consistent with the findings of Morck, Vishny and Schleifer (1988), who found that "targets of hostile and friendly bids have asset and ownership characteristics that one would expect of the targets of disciplinary and synergistic mergers, respectively." See Randall Morck, Andrei Schleifer, and Robert Vishny, "Characteristics of Hostile and Friendly Takeover Targets," National Bureau of Economic Research, working paper.

18. See, for example, Value Line's Report of April 5, 1985. Also potentially important to understanding why the deal was friendly is the fact that it made ABC's chairman, Harvey Goldstein, $20 million richer.

A benign reading of these proportions is that the hand of "strategy" and "portfolio management" theories is writ large over friendly takeovers and is largely missing in hostile takeovers. A less charitable interpretation may also be offered. Because a diversified portfolio strategy is often designed to achieve financial self-sufficiency (as in the once popular BCG model in which "cash cows" were used to fund "stars") and thereby reduce management's dependence on capital markets, it is hard to observe the difference between the advancement of managerial self-interest and the pursuit of financial synergies. If one ungenerously believes that portfolio-building takeovers are really motivated by managerial self-interest, one may infer that friendly takeovers are more likely than hostile deals to be motivated by executives' desires to build empires and thus preserve their independence from shareholders. And, thus, if results track intentions, the skeptic may expect worse consequences for shareholders from friendly takeovers than from the much maligned hostile deals.

These differences in expectations between hostile and friendly acquirers, it might be observed in passing, are likely to arise in part from the dissimilar backgrounds of the key players. In over 70% of the cases in my sample of friendly takeovers, the key players in the acquiring organizations could be described as "professional managers." They had spent their careers rising through the ranks of large organizations and been extensively exposed to beliefs about the value of synergy and diversification and the continuity of institutions. Lacking significant personal equity stakes in the enterprises they managed, these executives may have been more prone to regard stockholders as a potentially hostile pressure group. Such men were also more likely to inspire confidence in the targets' decision makers that they were "the right kind" of acquirers, and thus less likely to arouse resistance to their merger overtures.

In contrast, over two thirds of the key individuals involved in making hostile raids were what might be called "entrepreneurs." They had not risen through the ranks of large companies. They were instead, like Boone Pickens of Mesa Petroleum, founders of their own companies, or financial dealmakers like Carl Icahn. As "outsiders," they might be expected to be

more questioning of the *status quo* and more willing to make radical changes after their acquisitions.

I also discovered that insider equity ownership of hostile acquirers exceeded 20% in almost two thirds of the bids, whereas the majority of friendly acquirers had insider ownership of less than 5%. Because they own significant stakes in their enterprises, hostile acquirers are much less likely to make acquisitions that are not in the best interests of their principals. Nor is it surprising that target board members and executives appear to offer far more resistance to offers by takeover "entrepreneurs" than to those made by "one of their own."

THE CONSEQUENCES OF HOSTILE TAKEOVERS

The long-term record of takeovers in general, which is quite dismal, is not a reliable predictor of how the current crop of hostile takeovers will eventually turn out.[19] Pending the unfolding of history, the next best thing we can do is to evaluate the shorter-term consequences of the raiders' handiwork. There are, however, few facts to guide us in this appraisal. The lively controversy about whether raiders dangerously leverage up companies, slash long-term investment, and consign good managers and legions of rank-and-file workers to unemployment is based almost entirely on anecdote and speculation. The research I describe below represents an attempt to bring some evidence to bear on a number of these claims.

Financial Leverage. Critics of takeovers claim that corporations are severely hobbled by the excessive debt that is assumed to finance their acquisitions. High interest payments have to be made at the expense of long-term investments and can turn what would otherwise be a moderate downturn into a Chapter 11 bankruptcy filing.

Advocates like Michael Jensen reply that targets are likely to be underleveraged before they are acquired. Quite apart from their tax shield effects, higher debt levels can create real economic value, especially in mature companies that generate high free cash flow and thus have excess capital. High interest payments force managers of such companies to operate their assets as efficiently as they can and to pay out the cash they cannot profitably reinvest,

19. See Ravenscraft and Scherer (1988), and Porter (1987), both cited earlier in note 9. See also Dennis C. Mueller, "A Theory of Conglomerate Mergers," *Quarterly Journal of Economics*, vol. 83 (November 1969), pp. 643-59.

instead of frittering away potential profits in organizational inefficiencies or making frivolous acquisitions at inflated prices.[20]

Investment. Critics claim that in order to recoup the premia they have paid, and because so much of their cash flow is committed to servicing debt, acquirers stop investing for the future. Spending on capital equipment, R&D and the development of new products or markets is cut back and acquisitions are "harvested" for cash or short-term profits.

Advocates counter that a rational acquirer has no incentive to forgo promising investment opportunities. Profit-maximizing acquirers cut only those investment projects that have negative net present values, usually in companies operating in mature industries that need to reduce capacity.

Redistribution Issues: Efficiency versus Equity. If stockholders gain through a takeover, critics argue, it is often at the expense of other parties who also have a legitimate stake in the corporation.[21] Acquirers pilfer pension plans. Implicit and sometimes even explicit promises that have been made to employees about job security are broken. Suppliers and sometimes whole communities may be devastated.

Advocates would regard some of the actions that follow a takeover as a redress of injustices previously suffered by shareholders. Workers in the past enforced illegitimate property rights over jobs and claimed wages that were considerably in excess of market rates. These rights and wages were ceded by managers who were breaching their fiduciary duties towards shareholders. Besides, an efficiently functioning market system requires periodic redeployment of resources, which in turn leads to unavoidable social disruption. Takeovers are, if anything, a relatively humane and efficient mechanism by which the redeployment of resources takes place. Without takeovers, many targets would slowly and painfully end in bankruptcy and much more social value would be destroyed.

Divestitures. Acquirers make a quick killing, complain critics, by dismembering companies. When the most valuable assets and businesses are sold off in a so-called "bust-up," critical synergies are destroyed. Organizational morale plummets in the units that are sold off, as well as in the businesses that remain.

Unless the new owners of the pieces that are spun off are irrational, advocates of takeovers respond, value cannot be destroyed in a profitable break-up. In fact, acquirers create value when they unbundle conglomerates; the disparate pieces are transferred to new owners who can either realize synergies by combining the divested units with their existing businesses or can give the units their undivided attention. Splitting up conglomerates may also expose the chronic losses of certain businesses and induce greater efficiency in their operation.

Quality of Management. Experienced senior executives, it is claimed, who have managed their companies with the long term in view are replaced by "carpet-bagging" speculators or empire builders who have no knowledge of the businesses they gain control of. Consequently, long-term performance deteriorates after a hostile takeover.

"New brooms sweep clean" is the counter argument. Executives conditioned by a certain environment (for example, of continuous growth or strict regulation) and who have developed close personal ties to their organizations may not be effective when environmental changes (such as slower growth or deregulation) require radical breaks with the past. Besides, it is not always clear that the experienced executives who are replaced have a real record of having delivered long-term results.

Another benefit claimed for takeovers is that they can lead to a better alignment of owner-manager interests. Senior managers of many large corporations, who own only a small percentage of the outstanding stock, may not be sufficiently motivated to act in the shareholder interest. After a takeover, the senior executives often have a significant equity stake in the company they are responsible for managing.

Findings on the Consequences of Hostile Takeovers

The Sample. In studying the consequences of hostile takeovers, I used a somewhat smaller sample of the 1985 and 1986 transactions described earlier. Here I included the 20 successful transactions along with eight other cases in which the target managers repelled raiders and retained control. I excluded the other 19 contests that culminated in "white knight"

---

20. This argument was made formally as part of Michael Jensen's "free cash flow" theory of takeovers. See Jensen (1986), as cited in note 4.

21. See Andrei Schleifer and Lawrence H. Summers, "Hostile Takeovers as Breaches of Trust," unpublished paper (1987).

rescues. The eight successful resisters were included because the evidence indicates they maintained their independence by committing to undertake the sort of "restructuring" that was urged upon them by their hostile suitors. The white knight cases were excluded because control passed into the hands of "acceptable" suitors whose commitments and post-takeover actions are more typical of friendly acquirers.

The Effect on Leverage. There is little doubt that hostile takeovers, particularly those financed by junk bonds, lead to significant increases in financial risk. In fact, I found that 56% of the hostile takeovers in my sample resulted in downgradings of the target's bonds into speculative grades (and the number rises to 68% if we exclude those firms that remained independent). But this finding doesn't tell the real story about the role of leverage in these transactions.

In fact, if one looks beyond the immediate consequences of the transactions, quite a different conclusion emerges. For most hostile acquirers, junk bond financing was intended not as permanent financing but rather as a stop-gap measure. As shown in Table 4, asset sales, stock issues, or innovative financing arrangements soon raised substantial funds for acquirers and put them on a more stable financial footing. In fact, only three out of the 12 hostile takeovers that used junk bond financing were not quickly followed by major reductions in leverage. The use of leverage, I concluded, was not an end in itself, but rather the means for gaining control of the target while often achieving another important benefit of these transactions: concentration of ownership.

Investment. Long-term investment can be sacrificed to increase short-term earnings or cash flow in many ways other than merely cutting outlays on what accountants classify as capital expenditures. Long-term "investment" in a business may consist of advertising, new product development, R&D and several other items that are not recorded as part of a firm's capital stock, and a raider may "harvest" an acquired company by cutting back on any of these expenses.

A large amount of publicly available data was scanned in order to determine whether investment, broadly defined, was cut after an acquisition attempt. No effort was made to quantify the extent of these cuts (which would have been an impossible task). Rather my objective was merely to determine whether there was any evidence at all of harvesting by the acquirer.

Evidence of cutbacks was found after only seven (25%) of the 28 hostile takeover attempts in 1985 and 1986. In 17 (65%) of these takeovers, no reports of cutbacks were found; while in the rest, the evidence indicates that investment may actually have been stepped up after the takeover.

Not only is the proportion of takeovers followed by investment cutbacks small, it is not even clear that these cuts were due to takeovers. Of the seven takeovers in which investment cuts were either planned or executed, four were in oil or oil-related industries. As is well known, there were extensive cutbacks in investment in exploration and development after the precipitous fall in crude prices in the winter of 1985. The cuts in the capital spending budgets of the four oil-related targets were not significantly different from those by other companies in the industry. Thus, in only three of the 28 hostile takeovers in my sample does there appear to have been a deliberate strategy of cutting back on long-term investment that would not have occurred without a change in control.[22]

There may of course be slippage between the public record and investment cuts actually made. But, as my research also confirms, most of the targets of hostile takeovers were not in high-growth businesses that demanded much new investment. (See Appendix B for a list of these firms and their capital and R&D spending.) Cash flow generally well exceeded annual investment needs, and most targets reported little or no R&D expenses. So even the opportunities for raiders to boost short-term cash flow at the expense of long-term investment were limited.

Redistribution Issues. In order to examine the proposition that gains to targets' stockholders or acquirers are achieved at the expense of the targets'

---

22. The three cases were as follows:

Pacific Lumber, facing a high debt burden, scrapped the "continuous yield" cutting process which had previously been followed and doubled harvesting of its redwood properties. This "dis-investment" in redwood was not dictated by changes in demand or competition.

Informatics General, according to *Business Week,* "had popular products and a stable revenue stream of annual maintenance and support fees. So [the acquirer]

scaled back development; cut employment by 40% and found new markets for existing products".

Owens-Corning Fiberglass. "In order to increase cash flow to service its debt," claimed *Forbes* in 1987, "the company has let go 480 of its 970 employees [and] slashed its research budget in half... Projects Owens Corning has discarded include an attempt to develop combination materials of fiberglass and carbon for sales to the aerospace and strategic materials industry."

THANKS TO A SEVERE RECESSION IN 1982 AND A RISING DOLLAR, EMPLOYMENT IN FORTUNE 500 COMPANIES FELL BY 6% FROM 1981 TO 1986. COMPANIES LIKE AT&T, EXXON, AND GENERAL ELECTRIC SHED TENS OF THOUSANDS OF JOBS IN THE ABSENCE OF ANY TAKEOVER THREAT.

TABLE 4
FINANCIAL RISK
REDUCTION AFTER
TAKEOVERS

▶ Target ■ Acquirer	Funds raised after acquisition/Financial risk reduced by
▶ Crown Zellerbach ■ Goldsmith	Sales of paper operations and other assets. After sales Moodys restored debt rating to pre-takeover level.
▶ Am. Natl. Res. ■ Coastal Corp.	Coastal greenmailed Sonat Corp. into buying its 8.5% 10 year debentures to retire the 15.2% debt incurred while buying ANR.
▶ AMF ■ Minstar	Sales of 50% of assets. Yielded virtually entire purchase price paid.
▶ Revlon ■ Pantry Pride	Sales of most non-beauty care businesses.
▶ Gt. Lakes Intl. ■ Itel	Itel (new parent of Gt. Lakes) persuaded lenders to accept 1/3 of interest payments in common stock.
▶ Informatics Genl. ■ Sterling Software	Common stock issue (1986). Sales of division. Retirement of debt through cash flow.
▶ Uniroyal Inc. ■ Mgmt. LBO	Liquidation of company.
▶ Frigitronics ■ Revlon	Sales of division to J&J. Yielded virtually entire purchase price paid.
▶ Allied Stores ■ Campeau	Sales of 16 of 24 stores. $400m of equity issues.

employees, I examined the public record for evidence of any economic harm that may have been visited on employees after a takeover. Evidence of "redistribution" effects—layoffs, plant closings, withdrawal of pension plans—was found in about two thirds of hostile takeovers in 1985 and 1986. Thus, the redistribution issue, like the leverage issue, appears to be significant.

A different picture emerges, however, when the circumstances and extent of the apparent penalties imposed on target employees is examined. First we should note that large companies in the U.S. began reducing jobs about two to three years before raiders became a serious threat. Thanks to a severe recession in 1982 and a rising dollar, employment in Fortune 500 companies fell by 6% from 1981 to 1986. Companies like AT&T, Exxon, and General Electric shed tens of thousands of jobs in the absence of any takeover threat.

Consistent with this overall pattern, employment had been shrinking in most targets of hostile takeovers before they came under attack. As Table 5 shows, employment had fallen 7%, on average, between 1981 and 1985. And many of the targets that did report employment growth over the period appear to have achieved the increase by acquiring other businesses.

Second, in about half of the cases where redistribu-

tion effects were observed after a hostile takeover attempt, the evidence suggests that employment would have continued to decline without a change in control, because the targets and the industries they belonged to were facing severe profitability problems.

CBS, for example, was being squeezed (along with ABC and NBC) between rising costs on the one hand and declining viewership and revenues resulting from competition from the cable industry on the other. Uniroyal was suffering, along with other U.S. manufacturers, from excess capacity and foreign competition. The breakdown of pricing discipline within OPEC was hurting Unocal and Phillips and everybody else in the industry.

Targets and non-targets alike in these industries were cutting employment and capacity in 1986 and 1987. Exxon, for example, which has never faced the hint of a takeover threat, instituted a sweeping early retirement program, while many private wildcatters shut down operations altogether. The link between hostile takeover attempts and job losses in companies like Unocal, Phillips Petroleum, Crown Zellerbach, and Uniroyal therefore seems tenuous.

In the cases of nine targets, an argument could be made that redistribution issues arose because of (rather than simply followed) takeovers. Here it may

| TABLE 5 | | Employment change 1981-85 | |
CHANGES IN EMPLOYMENT OF TARGETS BEFORE TAKEOVER ATTEMPTS	Target	Percent of '81 work force	Total number of employees
	NL Industries	−51.3	−11910
	White Consolidated	−45.3	−11600
	Amer. Nat'l Res.	−33.9	−5600
	Crown Zellerbach	−32.9	−9332
	CBS Inc.	−27.5	−9789
	SCM Corp.	−24.3	−6700
	Uniroyal	−23.5	−5793
	Great Lakes Int'l.	−20.0	−300
	McGraw Edison	−16.5	−5600
	Phillips Petroleum	−15.1	−5200
	Revlon	−15.1	−5300
	AMF Inc.	−12.4	−2636
	Union Carbide	−10.8	−11889
	Gillette Co.*	−2.8	−900
	Pacific Lumber	0.0	0
	Allied Stores	0.0	0
	Ponderosa Inc.	0.0	0
	Carter Hawley Hale	1.8	1000
	Informatics General	3.8	100
	Southland Royalty	5.7	30
	Frigitronics*	8.3	175
	Easco Corp.	9.1	460
	Unocal Corp.	20.1	3464
	Owens Corning Fiberglass*	21.4	5100
	Ryan Homes	28.0	385
	Saga Corp.*	52.5	21000
	AVERAGE	−7	−2239
	T-STAT FOR HYPOTHESIS OF NO CHANGE	−1.5	−1.8

*Significant acquisition activity reported in the period.

be reasonably claimed that the target (or its industry) faced no imminent financial difficulties that would have forced the plant closings and job losses that were reported in 1986 and 1987.

The size of these effects, however, borders on the trivial. Compared to the average 7% job cuts that had already been made in the targets after 1981, the "avoidable" job losses in almost every case involved layoffs of a relatively small number of corporate and administrative staffs rather than the much more numerous line or production employees (see Table 6). Although accurate estimates are difficult to come by, the administrative job losses were on the order of a few hundred jobs per target company. And the total employment loss "caused" by all significant hostile takeover activity in 1985 and 1986 was probably under ten thousand jobs.

Divestitures. Significant divestitures were made or attempted after about 60% of hostile takeovers in my sample. By "significant" I mean those cases in which half or more of the target's businesses in terms of total sales were sold, or those in which asset sales covered most of the acquisition price.

The question I wanted to investigate here is whether value was created or destroyed in these divestitures. Value could be destroyed when a firm

OUT OF THE 81 BUSINESSES THAT WERE PUT ON THE BLOCK AFTER HOSTILE TAKEOVERS, THE RECORD CLEARLY INDICATES THAT 66 HAD PREVIOUSLY BEEN ACQUIRED BY THE TARGET; 12 HAD PROBABLY BEEN PREVIOUSLY ACQUIRED; AND ONLY 3 HAD PROBABLY BEEN DEVELOPED INTERNALLY . . . IN SHORT, THE TARGETS OF "BUST-UP" TAKEOVERS CLEARLY APPEAR TO BE COMPANIES THAT HAD DIVERSIFIED THROUGH ACQUISITION.

TABLE 6
REDISTRIBUTIVE ACTIONS "INDUCED" BY HOSTILE TAKEOVERS

Target	Pre-Takeover Employment	Reported Layoffs, Plant Closings, Etc.
McGraw Edison	28,000	Some administrative employees laid off. Campbell chain production moved overseas.
AMF	36,000	Most (approx. 400) corporate staff laid off.
SCM	20,900	Corporate level staff probably laid off, but no record available.
Revlon	29,900	Took $105m from excess pension funds. Some corp. level staff prob. laid off, but no public record available.
Informatics General	2,600	Approx. 100 staff laid off at headquarters, and, possibly another 100 programmers.
White Consolidated	14,000	900 laid off in 3 plant closings; however planned to add 500 in Webster City plant expansion.
Ponderosa	20,000	Approx. 120 laid off at headquarters.
Saga Corp.	64,000	Approx. 245 laid off at headquarters.
Gillete	34,100	2400 layoffs announced; 1200 reported implemented by 5/88.
O.C.F.	26,900	Up to 5000 terminations planned.
Total employees	276,400	

is split up if there were synergies between the separated businesses. Such synergies may, broadly speaking, be classified into "operating" synergies—economies realized by exploiting interrelationships between businesses—and administrative or financial synergies—the advantages that may be gained from managing even totally unrelated businesses under a single corporate umbrella. While we cannot make inferences from the available evidence about the latter kind of synergies, the record does suggest that the divestitures that followed hostile takeovers probably did not lead to the loss of significant "operating" synergies.

First, in the overwhelming majority of divestitures that followed the hostile takeovers of 1985-1986, the units separated served distinct markets with distinct products, making the loss of material economies of scope or scale highly unlikely.[23]

Second, the speed with which most divestitures were accomplished—usually within eighteen months of the takeover—also suggests that the linkages between the businesses separated in the process were probably not great. It seems unlikely that the businesses could have been acceptably parceled off to buyers if there was extensive sharing of facilities or coordination of sales.

Third, out of the 81 businesses that were put on the block after hostile takeovers, the record clearly indicates that 66 had previously been acquired by the target; 12 had probably been previously acquired (although because of name changes, etc., it is difficult to absolutely sure); and only 3 had probably been developed internally.

In short, the targets of "bust-up" takeovers clearly appear to be companies that had diversified through acquisition. To the extent this appearance corresponds

23. Only in two cases of hostile takeovers (Informatics General and Allied Stores) does any claim of lost synergies seem remotely tenable. The units sold from Informatics Legal Systems and Information systems served distinct customer groups but it is conceivable that they could have shared technologies and programmers. Likewise it is possible that the stores spun out of Allied might have enjoyed economies in joint purchasing.

FINANCING AN ACQUISITION WITH DEBT REDUCES MANAGEMENT'S
PROTECTION FROM CAPITAL MARKETS SINCE SOME OF THE CASH GENERATED
BY THE ACQUIRED BUSINESS HAS TO BE APPLIED TO INTEREST PAYMENTS.
STOCK FINANCING, BY CONTRAST, INCREASES FINANCIAL SUFFICIENCY BECAUSE
NO CASH HAS TO BE PAID OUT BY THE ACQUIRER EITHER AT THE TIME OF THE
TRANSACTION OR AFTERWARDS.

with the reality, so-called "bust-up" takeovers do not destroy valuable synergies. Instead they telescope into a short period the divestitures that would have taken place in the normal course of events.

It is also worth investigating whether the divestitures resulted in a "net" increase in focus or whether the divested units simply fell into the hands of other diversified corporations. Although the data is not complete, my findings suggest that, on balance, the activity of raiders results in greater focus in the enterprises they split up.

■ *In 20 (or 30%) of the 64 divestitures that followed hostile takeovers in 1985-1986, the buyers were investment groups or the units' managers who intended to operate the business as a stand-alone entity.*

■ *In 26 (or 40%) of the 64 cases, the buyers were single-business companies who were in the same (or closely related) industry as the divested unit.*

■ *In the remaining 18 cases, the buyers were companies who were following diversification strategies similar to those undertaken by the targets being split up. And, it is interesting to note, within the next year and a half, a third of these buyers—including Goodyear, Bell and Howell, and Harcourt, Brace, and Jovanovich—were themselves being courted by unwelcome suitors.*

Hostile takeovers, it is also important to note, had the effect of transferring ownership of several businesses from publicly held targets to privately-owned organizations. In 36 of the 64 divestitures, the buyers were private companies or partnerships.

Quality of Management. There were significant management changes after 17 of the 19 successful hostile takeovers in 1985. An entire corporate level of managers seems to have been wiped out, or at least drastically pared back, in the takeovers of seven companies in my sample. And significant changes in key personnel took place in almost all of the other targets.

The question, then, is: Did these managers "deserve" to go, or did "good" managers lose their jobs? The evidence shows that the track record of the targets of hostile takeovers is at best mediocre when judged by the following standards:

■ *The targets' four-year average return on equity (ROE) relative to the industry.* Seventy percent of the (41) targets of hostile takeovers had lower average ROEs than those of their industry. (The average difference was −2.2%).

■ *The targets' five-year (risk-adjusted) total stock return compared to that of the market as a whole.* Fifteen of the 20 targets of hostile takeovers in 1985 provided risk-adjusted total returns to their stockholders that were lower than would have been earned by investing in a diversified pool of equities. (The average difference between target and market returns was −4.0%.)

■ *The opinion of their peers.* The results of a *Fortune* poll on the "quality of management" applied to 15 of the targets in my sample. In this poll the respondents (including executives, directors, and analysts) associated with 32 industries were asked to rate the quality of management of 10 companies in their industry. Each company was then ranked within its industry on a scale ranging from "1" (the highest quality of management) to "10." Only three of the 15 targets' managements were rated above a "6"; three of the companies received a "10" rating; and the median rank was "7."

Whether hostile takeovers resulted in a transfer of control of these low-performing targets into the hands of "better" managers is difficult to answer, especially since two-thirds of the acquirers had no reliable public record of profitability or stock price history. What such takeovers clearly did accomplish, however, was to transfer control from groups who had a low equity stake in their organizations to groups that had a high equity stake. In the sample of takeovers I examined, only 12% of hostile takeover targets, as compared to 68% of their hostile acquirers, had insider ownership exceeding 20% of their total stock.

Contrast with Friendly Takeovers

Leverage. Unlike hostile takeovers, a majority of which were financed with high risk debt, 64% of friendly takeovers resulted in the addition of little to no financial risk. Payment to target shareholders was typically made with the acquirer's stock or excess cash rather than by raising much new debt.

This mode of financing lends further credence to the possibility that managers' pursuit of "financial self-sufficiency" was behind many friendly takeovers. As discussed earlier, acquisitions can insulate managers from potential interference by the capital markets by diversifying the acquiring corporation's profit and cash flow base. Financing an acquisition with debt reduces this protection since some of the cash generated by the acquired business has to be applied to interest payments. Stock financing, by contrast, increases financial sufficiency because no cash has to be paid out by the acquirer either at the time of the transaction or afterwards.

TABLE 7
PERFORMANCE AND OWNERSHIP CHARACTERISTICS OF TAKEOVER TARGETS

Characteristic	Mean of sample		t-test for diff. of means (degrees of freedom)
	Hostile Targets	Friendly Targets	
Target R.O.E. − Industry R.O.E.	−2.2	3.4	−3.2 (52)
Target 5 yr. Stock Returns − Market Returns	−4.0	18.3	−4.39 (29)
Percent of Stock Held by Insiders	6.5	15.6	−1.6 (61)

*Includes only 1985 hostile targets

Investment. Far fewer investment cutbacks followed friendly takeovers, and a higher proportion were followed by increases in investment. It should be pointed out, however, that the greater propensity of friendly acquirers to increase investment reflects in large part the significantly more attractive growth prospects of their targets. A comparison of Value Line's projections of five-year sales growth rates of friendly and hostile targets before the acquisitions were announced shows that over 60% of friendly targets had expected sales growth rates in excess of 10%, while fewer than 13 percent of hostile targets were expected to grow at that rate. The difference of average expected growth rates between friendly and hostile targets was 4.6% (10.6% − 6%).

This difference in the growth prospects of hostile and friendly targets is almost certainly no accident. High-growth companies may not be subject to hostile takeover attempts for several reasons. First, growth companies may be perceived to be more dependent on the talents of their existing personnel and raiders may see no point in acquiring such companies after alienating their managers. The value of low-growth companies may not be perceived to be in as much jeopardy if the incumbent managers leave.

Second, founder-managers of high-growth companies often own a large enough block of stock to defeat a hostile takeover attempt. Mature low-growth companies are more likely to have passed the phase of being managed by founders who own a controlling interest.

Third, high-growth companies are difficult to value. They sell at high multiples to current earnings and book value, indicating that most of the value is based on profits that are expected to be earned in the distant future. The great uncertainties inherent in valuing these future profits are unlikely to attract the typical entrepreneurial raider. Furthermore, the low ratio of hard assets to market price of the target makes it difficult for the raider to finance a takeover with borrowed funds. In contrast, the typical friendly acquirers are likely to be less concerned about "overpaying" for growth; and, being able to make

acquisitions for stock, they don't have to worry about the lack of target "collateral."

Redistribution Issues. Redistribution was even less of an issue in friendly than in hostile takeovers. We have seen previously that the high incidence of layoffs and plant closings that follow hostile takeovers reflects the ongoing decline in the fortunes of the target firms. Similarly, we may infer that the lower job losses in friendly takeovers reflect the same factors that were probably behind the higher occurrence of investment increases: the hostile raiders have a natural tendency to go after mature businesses with low growth prospects and declining employment, whereas friendly acquirers are more likely to seek targets that present high-growth opportunities.

Divestitures. Significant divestitures (or attempted divestitures) were made after only 11% of friendly takeovers, as compared to 60% of hostile takeovers. This difference also reflects differences between the companies sought by friendly and hostile acquirers. 75% of friendly targets were single-business companies, as compared to only 25% of hostile targets. Focused targets probably "fit" the corporate strategies of "portfolio"- and "synergy"-motivated acquirers since they were less likely to contain incompatible businesses than diversified targets. In contrast, hostile acquirers in the business of buying and dismantling companies have less opportunity to profit from the restructuring of already focused, single-business companies. Therefore, while the activities of hostile acquirers appear to have brought greater focus to companies, the activities of friendly acquirers, especially of the "portfolio" variety, have diffused it.

Quality of Management. Far fewer "significant" management changes were made after friendly takeovers than after hostile takeovers. Managers of the targets of friendly takeovers, moreover, were more likely to have better performance records than managers of hostile targets. As shown in Table 7, the 5-year average ROEs of friendly targets were some 3 percent higher than their industry average (as compared to 2 percent lower for hostile targets); and their 5-year average stock returns outperformed the industry average by a whopping 18 percent (as compared to −4 percent for hostile targets). Not surprisingly, the average percentage of insider ownership of the targets was almost twice as high in friendly deals as in hostile transactions.

SUMMARY AND IMPLICATIONS

We now have a clearer picture of corporate raiders and their activities. The typical raider, we saw, is a self-made entrepreneur or dealmaker rather than a manager who has worked his way through and to the top of a large corporation. His acquisition vehicle is usually just a shell organization. Consequently, we found, most hostile deals stand on their own economic merits. Unlike many friendly mergers, they are rarely, if ever, designed to realize the portfolio benefits from acquiring unrelated businesses.

In addition, as an independent operator, the typical raider does not have access to discretionary corporate funds. Instead he must raise financing, usually through junk bonds, on a deal-by-deal basis. Consequently, the raider has to convince investors in the junk bonds of the economic soundness of each deal. And the need to produce a credible business plan usually precludes takeovers that expect to profit by:

■ *Acquiring companies at bargain prices.* The raider has to be more than a stock picker. Financiers do not need him merely to buy undervalued stocks for them. Besides, it would be unreasonable to expect that an entire firm could be bought at a throwaway price after paying an acquisition premium and incurring considerable legal expenses. And, in fact, our data did show that by most conventional valuation standards, acquisition prices are not cheap.

■ *Cutting back on long-term investment.* Raiders would have a hard time making a credible case for acquiring high-growth, high investment targets. Such companies are difficult to value since their stock prices are heavily weighted by the profits that current investments are expected to produce in the distant future. Not only do such growth companies fail to provide collateral for lenders, but their value is often tied to the motivation of employees, which may be at risk in a hostile proceeding. Therefore, as we have seen, typical targets are companies in mature businesses that are not doing much investment to start with, and significant investment cuts do not usually follow.

■ *Turning around troubled companies by cutting costs or wages.* Assessing the probability of success of rescuing distressed firms is a risky proposition under any circumstances; and rescuers usually find problems they had not initially anticipated. Attempting a turnaround through a hostile transaction, where the raider does not have access to the target's books, would be an extraordinary gamble. Furthermore, the average raider does not have the operating experience necessary to convince investors of his ability to pull off a rescue. The targets of hostile takeovers are typically firms with mediocre performance rather than those that are bleeding to death. And, the record indicates, the extensive job and wage cuts that are typical of a turnaround project do not follow most hostile takeovers.

■ *Assuming permanently high levels of debt.* Junk bonds used in hostile takeovers are intended only as "bridge financing." Investors in takeovers are interested in being repaid quickly, not in holding the paper of firms permanently on the edge of bankruptcy. And, again, the record indicates that the junk debt used in hostile takeovers is quickly paid down.

The True Significance of Hostile Takeovers

The seemingly innocuous consequences of hostile takeovers ought to make us wonder about whether they produce the benefits claimed for them. If they are not shutting down plants, laying off workers, or sacrificing the corporate future to make high interest payments, then how—after paying substantial premiums to target shareholders and hefty fees to lawyers and investment bankers—do corporate raiders pay the rent? And what positive contribution do they make to the public weal?

My research suggests that the real source of gains in hostile takeovers lies in splitting up diversified companies. Raiders play a limited but significant role in this process. They seek "arbitrage" profits by selling the constituent businesses of target companies, often in the "private" market, for more than they pay for the entire company.[24]

---

24. What raiders are engaged in today has been called "balance sheet arbitrage." "In today's takeovers," comments Goodson and Gogel, "the opportunity for arbitrage arises because there is an identifiable difference between the price of a company's securities and the value of its assets. The critical element is the investor's ability to identify that discrepancy."

IN SHORT, MY RESEARCH SUGGESTS THAT IF IT WEREN'T FOR FRIENDLY
ACQUISITIONS, THERE WOULDN'T BE VERY MANY HOSTILE TAKEOVER ATTEMPTS.
COMPANIES APPEAR TO BECOME TARGETS FOR "SPLIT-UP ARBITRAGE" PRECISELY
BY VIRTUE OF THEIR PREVIOUS ACQUISITION ACTIVITY, NOT BECAUSE OF THE
BUSINESSES THEY DEVELOPED WITHIN.

This "discrepancy" between break-up and market value is apparently most easily identified, in the absence of insider operating information, in the case of diversified corporations. The raider assesses whether the sum of the prices the individual businesses will command, on an as-is basis, is higher than the cost of the company as a whole. If it is, the takeover can proceed at relatively low risk with "bridge financing" provided by lenders who are confident they will be quickly repaid. Sometimes, as in the cases of Revlon and Frigitronics, the risk can be further reduced by pre-selling some of the businesses.

The enterprise leverages the raiders' dealmaking skills but does not require operating expertise. With some notable exceptions (for example, Icahn's takeover of TWA), their deals are not contingent upon achieving operational efficiencies. Free-lance raiders, unlike their corporate counterparts who may seek intangible strategic advantages, are in the game for tangible dollars. To determine whether a profit can be made in a takeover by instituting operational efficiencies requires a detailed knowledge of the target's revenues and costs. And, of course, in an unfriendly deal the incumbent managers do not volunteer such information. Besides, many raiders are not steeped in operations and "running businesses better" is not their business. The payback to raiders and their financiers is quick, and the economics of a bust-up can be estimated without recourse to the target's internal data.

Adding value to individual businesses by instituting operational improvements, making strategic changes, or adopting the right capital structure is then the responsibility not of the raider, but of the ultimate buyer who has the skills and the inclination to run the business. And, in fact, it is probably the potential for adding value that attracts buyers and enables raiders to divest individual businesses so quickly.

Friendly takeovers, we found, represent a study in contrast. They are engineered by the managers of established companies. Since friendly acquirers usually have the standing to issue equity or investment grade debt, they rarely use junk bond financing. Consequently, the economics do not have to be immediately compelling; and the acquisition of over-priced growth companies can be justified by invoking a long-term strategic goal. And, most frequently, the goal in question is the advancement of some portfolio strategy—the addition of high-technology, growth, energy or some other type of business to the confederation that constitutes a modern diversified firm.

So where hostile takeovers reduce diversification, friendly takeovers increase it. Where hostile takeovers dismantle the corporate staffs that manage unit managers, friendly takeovers expand their powers. And whereas hostile takeovers often transfer ownership of businesses from public to private hands, in friendly takeovers public firms often absorb private ones. In short, my research suggests that if it weren't for friendly acquisitions, there wouldn't be very many hostile takeover attempts. Companies appear to become targets for "split-up arbitrage" precisely by virtue of their previous acquisition activity, not because of the businesses they developed within.[25]

Refocusing American Industry

This seemingly limited "arbitrage" function performed by raiders of buying businesses wholesale and selling them retail is, in fact, quite significant. It challenges a fundamental, long-term trend in the evolution of American industry: the growth of the diversified, multi-business corporation. As observed by Alfred Chandler, the single- or dominant-business firm began to disappear from the ranks of the Fortune 500 after the second World War, giving way to the diversified corporation.[26] The percentage of diversified companies in the Fortune 500 more than doubled from 1949 to 1974, rising from under 30% to over 60%.[27] Most merger activity during this period—and indeed throughout the remainder of the 1970s and early 1980s as well—was geared to diversification rather than expansion within existing businesses. Over 70% of the assets acquired by industrial companies between 1961 to 1978 resulted from acquisitions that the FTC has classified as "diversifying" acquisitions.[28]

The principal effect of hostile takeovers seems to have been to bring about greater "focus" in American

25. This conclusion is reinforced by the findings of a recent study by SEC economists Kenneth Lehn and Mark Mitchell entitled, "Do Bad Bidders Make Good Targets?," which demonstrates that firms which "overpay" for acquisitions increase the probability that they will in turn be taken over.

26. Alfred D. Chandler, *Strategy and Structure: Chapters in the History of the American Industrial Enterprise* (Cambridge: MIT Press, 1962).

27. As documented by Richard P. Rumelt, "Strategy, Structure, and Economic Performance," Division of Research, Graduate School of Business Administration, Harvard University.

28. See Malcolm Salter and Wolf Weinhold, *Diversification through Acquisition: Strategies for Creating Economic Value* (New York, The Free Press, 1979), p. 14. This category includes all acquisitions extending operations beyond present production or geopgraphical markets.

industry by transferring assets from diversified corporations to single-business entities (including many owned by private companies and investment groups). Therefore, the principal question we need to address regarding hostile takeovers concerns their impact on corporate diversification—not whether they lead to too much debt or to cuts in investment. We need to know whether the multi-business corporate form is still a valuable one; or, if it has outlived its utility, whether hostile takeovers are the least costly means (taking into account all social costs of dislocation) of doing away with it.

The stock market apparently doesn't believe diversification is useful, judging from the substantial discount to the value of their component businesses at which the shares of diversified corporations usually trade. But it should be recalled that, in the 1960s, the stock market seemed to favor diversification and valued conglomerates at premiums to their component businesses. Was the market in error then or now? Or, has the utility of diversification declined?

I believe that the market is probably more sophisticated in valuing companies today and that the value of diversification has declined over time. The multi-business corporation may once have been a more efficient allocator of resources than the external capital markets, and there may still be a few executives that can manage a portfolio of businesses exceptionally well. But, whatever the merits of diversification may once have been, with the increasing sophistication of U.S. capital markets, the single business firm now represents a more efficient form of organization.

The raiders' attack on diversification rather than on inefficiencies in individual businesses may also explain the animosity of the Business Roundtable towards hostile takeovers. The executives who are under attack do not manage businesses; they manage managers who manage businesses. Takeovers often create opportunities for the latter to get very rich. For example, after Jacobs's takeover of AMF, his first priority was to sell the individual businesses to their managers. Hanson Trust, as another example, is reputed to establish very attractive incentives for the operating managers of the businesses it acquires. On the other hand, hostile takeovers threaten the managers' managers very function; the question of how they do their jobs is secondary to the question of whether their jobs ought to exist at all. Do we really need executives to allocate resources among businesses if the capital markets can do the job better?

If the profit opportunity for raiders was provided merely by operating inefficiencies or unused debt capacity, incumbent executives could preempt raiders by working harder, surrendering some of their value-destroying perquisites, or swallowing their distaste for high leverage. But, to the extent that the opportunity arises from the inappropriateness of the multi-business form, the managers' managers cannot fully preempt raiders without working themselves out of a job.

Hence, the extreme antipathy to raiders; and hence also the difficulty of reversing diversification without a change in control. Hostile takeovers may be clumsy and messy and the reputations of some of the raiders may leave something to be desired, but we don't yet have a better way of effecting the "creative destruction" of obsolete organizations.

Implications for Managers

Different types of managers are affected differently by hostile takeovers. The findings of this research should comfort operating managers while giving pause to corporate executives.

Operating Managers: Raiders usually do not pose a threat to "hands on" operating managers of individual businesses since most raiders have little ability or incentive to intervene in operational matters. In fact, the raider who buys a diversified company with the intention of selling off its units needs the cooperation of the managers of the units. This is because many potential buyers of divested units (for example, the LBO funds) do not have hands-on management capability, and would be reluctant to purchase businesses without competent managers in place. Often these buyers will give operating managers a significant equity stake to encourage them to stay and to do a good job. So operating managers could even look upon raiders as benefactors who liberate them from corporate bureaucracies and help set them up as partners in the business they manage.

Corporate Executives: The positions of corporate level executives, on the other hand, appear to be in some jeopardy. The function they serve—that of monitoring performance and allocating resources—now appears to be better performed by external capital markets. This is not necessarily a reflection on the lack of competence of the executives, but rather on the growing competence of external markets—a development over which managers have no control. And short of voluntarily splitting up their companies and thus extinguishing their own jobs, it is not apparent, at least to me, how corporate executives can reliably protect themselves against raiders.

At the margin, however, corporate executives may be able to reduce the vulnerability of their corporations to arbitrage-type hostile takeovers by adopting a toned-down version of the raiders' strategy. Such a program might include:

Reducing the number of corporate employees. The costs and inefficiencies associated with the corporate headquarters office may cause the diversified corporation to be valued by the stock market at less than the sum of its parts. This "conglomerate discount" may be reduced by cutting the number of corporate employees to an absolute minimum.

Narrowing the scope of the corporation. The conglomerate discount may also be reduced by restricting a diversified corporation's activities to a group of related industries, for two reasons. First, security analysts are specialized by industry, and diversified firms which do not fall into any clear industry category tend to get ignored or only superficially analyzed. And, all other things being equal, poorly followed (or misunderstood) firms are more likely to be out of favor with institutional investors and therefore to be cheaply priced with respect to their component businesses.

Second, focusing on a narrow range of industries may allow the internal capital markets to allocate resources and monitor performance more effectively. A corporate staff that focuses on, say, just the "leisure time" industry is more likely to achieve parity of expertise and information with "outside" industry analysts than a corporate staff that oversees entirely unrelated businesses.

It may also be claimed that focusing on related businesses opens opportunities to realize synergies by "exploiting interrelationships among businesses." But I am not at all convinced by this argument. However valuable the interrelationships may look on paper, in practice corporate attempts to mandate cooperation between units can create a stifling bureaucracy in which coordination becomes an obsessive goal rather than a means to an end. And where cooperation is truly useful, there is little evidence that independent firms are any worse at pooling resources than the units of diversified firms. The different businesses within IBM, for example, have not been shown to cooperate to better effect in setting standards than, say, Sun Microsystems and Xerox.[29]

Leasing instead of owning assets. Hard assets such as real estate can also be a source of a version of the conglomerate discount. Stockholders do not need firms to invest in real estate on their behalf any more than they need firms to create a diversified stock portfolio. Consequently the stock prices of companies like Allied and Federated Stores may not fully reflect the value of their real estate holdings. Therefore managers should minimize their firms' ownership of hard assets and lease what they need instead.

Using at least moderate levels of debt. Maintaining high levels of unused debt capacity is as wasteful as holding high levels of raw material inventory, and an additional attraction to raiders seeking arbitrage profits. If a diversified firm has very little debt, it becomes especially easy to raise takeover financing against the value of its assets. Therefore, as a defensive measure, managers in low to moderately risky businesses should use at least moderate amounts of debt. As a general rule, the less risky the business, the more leverage that should be employed.

Instituting controls and incentives for unit managers to run their businesses at peak efficiency. The break-up price of a firm reflects estimates of value based on aggressive (and perhaps even unrealistic) plans for extracting value from the component businesses. Therefore if corporate executives tolerate "satisficing" performance in the businesses they oversee, the gap between market value and break-up value is likely to be wide. In order to narrow this gap, executives need to ensure that all their businesses are operated at maximum efficiency all the time. This goal may in turn require incentive schemes for the unit managers that provide exceptional rewards for exceptional performance in their individual businesses. In other words, corporate executives may need to provide the same financial packages for operating managers that LBO firms do.

Managers should recognize that the actions necessary to avoid takeovers today are at odds with past strategies for managerial independence. For example, as Gordon Donaldson has shown, managers have traditionally sought to protect their independence by pursuing policies of financial self-sufficiency.[30] These policies have included maintaining operating slack which could be squeezed in times of

---

29. Salter and Weinhold (1979), cited in the preceding note.

30. Gordon Donaldson, *Managing Corporate Wealth* (New York: Praeger, 1984).

need, following conservative debt policies and diversifying into many industries so that the corporation would not be hostage to the fortunes of any one business. The traditional strategies may no longer be appropriate because the nature of the threats to managerial independence has changed. In the past, constraints imposed by lenders and competitors were visible and real; disaffected equity holders posed only an amorphous threat. Now, thanks to the existence of raiders, the constituency of stockholders has to be taken more seriously. Financial self-sufficiency, achieved by a cash-balanced portfolio of businesses or low interest payments, may not promote managerial goals if it leads to break-up opportunities for raiders.

Implications for Investors

Investors have reason to be both pleased and disturbed by hostile takeovers. On the one hand, they can thank raiders for handsome takeover premia that are paid for the companies that are taken over as well as for forcing all managers to pay greater attention to shareholder interests. On the other hand, raiders expose investors' impotence. The very fact that raiders can pay a 30% to 50% takeover premium and still make significant gains demonstrates the degree to which investors have failed to discipline managers. If investors were capable of enforcing their claims, they would be the sole beneficiaries of the value represented by takeover premia and raiders' profits. By relying on raiders to bring about corporate restructuring, investors realize only a part of the potential value of the firms they own.

Although investors are constrained by laws and regulations, much of their impotence is of their own making. As the raiders have shown, owners of many large firms do not need great operating or industry skills to create value; a few critical decisions can have great leverage. And stockholders, particularly the large institutional investors, could begin to influence these decisions.

They could start by putting up candidates for boards of directors. Today, most independent or external directors have little reason to vigorously advance the interests of the stockholders they supposedly represent. External directors, many of whom are executives in other large companies, are invited to join boards by management, not stockholders. And, since they rarely hold significant ownership positions, directors are not overly concerned with stock prices. They serve on boards because of the prestige and contacts it brings or because they want to do their CEO friends a favor.

Directors therefore have much to lose and little to gain by opposing management decisions, for example, to undertake diversifying acquisitions. Directors don't suffer the adverse financial consequences of a bad acquisition, but could find themselves with fewer directorships if they got the reputation for being troublemakers.

Institutional investors could break this cozy arrangement by claiming (as J. P. Morgan used to) representation on the boards of the companies they own. Or, if institutions are unwilling to take on directorships themselves, they might consider collaborating to elect directors to represent them. The same academics and retired cabinet officers might have a different attitude about looking after the shareholder interest if investors rather than managers controlled entry into the Directors Register.

Implications for Public Policy

The single most important contribution of hostile takeovers is that they cut down on corporate sprawl, and bring more focus to U.S. industry. The problem of value-destroying friendly mergers documented by my research would be much less serious if we had an effective system of firm governance in place. If shareholders were properly represented by boards of directors, fewer uneconomic friendly transactions would take place and past acquisition mistakes would be quickly rectified. In fact, as the still very high level of friendly takeovers indicates, managers continue to enjoy considerable freedom from pliable boards. And the most important challenge for public policy is *not* the design of new laws to ensure a fair bidding process in hostile takeovers, but rather the establishment of boards of directors who truly represent shareholder interests.

Reform of the election process would be a major step. Today, an official slate of directors is proposed by incumbent managers and is almost always elected unopposed. In the rare circumstance that someone actually challenges the official slate of candidates, incumbent managers inevitably retain a law firm, a PR firm, and an investment bank to fight the upstart; and while the challenger has to pay his own expenses, the tab run up by the incumbent managers is picked up by the shareholders. Finally, if the matter does come to a vote, there is rarely a secret ballot. Institutional investors who manage pension funds for large corporations may therefore be reluctant to vote against the official slate for fear of being labelled "anti-management" by their other clients.

A similar process in the political arena, most people would agree, would not produce a very representative form of government. If the existing Congress and Executive offered an official slate of candidates, incumbents routinely sued opponents and used public funds to pay their legal fees, and voting were not by secret ballot, we probably wouldn't have a government for the people. Likewise, it is fair to assume that the current election process does not ensure a board of directors dedicated to protecting the shareholder interest.

Three changes could bring about greater shareholder democracy: (1) the abolition of official slates of candidates (although incumbent directors and managers would of course be free to nominate candidates, but only in their capacity as shareholders); (2) a prohibition on the expendi-

ture of firm funds to protect the seats of incumbent directors in proxy fights; and (3) the institution of a secret ballot on all shareholder votes. These changes would still leave existing managers and boards with several advantages of incumbency, but the playing field would be more level and the threat of retribution for anti-shareholder policies would be greater.

In the long run, both owners and managers could benefit from boards that truly represented owners. Current owners could realize the entire difference between the current and potential value of a company instead of sharing it with a raider. And directors who really enjoyed the confidence of shareholders could also structure more compelling incentives for managers. Today, because directors can't be seen to be too obviously feathering the nests of their friends, the rewards for superior performance in public companies are often modest compared to those available to managers of LBOs and start-up ventures. Boards who were more independent could structure compensation schemes that provided extraordinary reward for extraordinary performance.

APPENDIX A
BENEFITS EXPECTED IN CONTESTED TENDER OFFERS

Target	Suitor	Primary Expected Benefit		Secondary Expected Benefit	
Crown Zellerbach	James Goldsmith	R/I	Divestitures/Bet on timber		
Am. Natl. Resources	**Coastal Corp.**	**R**	**Leverage**	**I**	**Depressed industry, cheap stock**
AMF Inc.	Minstar	R	Divestitures		
SCM Corp.	**Hanson Trust**	**R**	**Divestitures**		
Revlon	Pantry Pride	R	Divestitures + Lev.	F	Tax considerations
Pacific Lumber	**Maxxam Grp. Inc.**	**R**	**Lev. + divestiture + acc. harvest**	**F**	**Need op. co. for tax reasons**
Easco Corp.	Equity Group	R	Divestitures		
Gt. Lakes Intl.	**Itel Corp**	**R/I**	**Leverage/bet on bus. upturn**	**F**	**Tax considerations**
Southland Royalty	Burlington Northern	P	Add energy cos.	I	Bet on energy
McGraw Edison	**Cooper Industries**	**P/R**	**Add elect. bus/cut costs**		
Informatics Genl.	Sterling Software	S/R	Consol. mktg., adm. & pdt. lines		
Uniroyal Inc	**Carl Icahn**	**R**	**Divestitures**		
Cluett Peabody	Paul Bilzerian	R	Divest + Lev.		
Midcon Corp	**Freeport/W&B**	**R**	**Divest. + Lev.**		
J.M. Tull Ind	Inland Steel	P	Diversity out of steel	S	Fit with metals bus.
Frontier Holdings	**Texas Air**	**R/S**	**Integrate routes/cut costs**		
Richardson Vicks	Unilever	S/P	Lev. channels/Exp. U.S. pres.		
Hook Drugs	**Rite Aid**	**S**	**Skills/Scale con.**		
Unidynamics	Nortek	P	Growth thru acq.	R	Divestitures
Times Fiber	**LBO**	**R**	**Divest. + cut costs**		
Unocal	Mesa Pete.	R	Lev. + Harvest resv. + div.		

APPENDIX A CONT. NEXT PAGE

Target	Suitor	Primary Expected Benefit		Secondary Expected Benefit
Phillips Pete.	**Carl Icahn**	**R**	**Lev. + Div.**	
Union Carbide	GAF Corp.	R	Lev. + Div.	R Rationalize some chem. bus.
CBS Inc.	**Turner Broad.**	**P/S**	**Build ent. empire/common skills**	
White Consolidated	A.B. Electrolux	R/S	Cut Costs/Broaden prod. line	
Saga Corp.	**Marriot Corp.**	**S**	**Scale econ. + supplier power**	
Ryan Homes	N.V. Homes	S	Broaden prod. line	
Ponderosa	**A. Edelman**	**R**	**Lev. + Div.**	
C.H. Masland	Burlington Ind.	P/S	Enter automotive carpeting	
N.L. Industries	**Harold Simmons**	**R**	**Spin off chem. unit**	
Frigitronics	Revlon Group	R	Divestitures	
Allied Stores	**Campeau Corp.**	**R/S**	**Lev. + Div/Real estate synergies**	
Safeway	Dart Group	R	Ops. improvements + Lev. + Div.	
Chesebrough Ponds	**American Brands**	**P**	**Diversity out of cigarettes**	
National Gypsum	Wickes Cos.	F	Use tax credits	R Lev.
Sanders Assoc.	**Loral Corp.**	**S/P**	**Techn. fit + expand def. elec.**	
Hammermill Paper	P. Bilzerian	R	Div. + Lev.	
Fruehauf Corp.	**A. Edelman**	**R**	**Div. + Lev. + cost cuts**	
Anderson Clayton	Bear Stearns	R	Div. + reduce excess cash	
Joy Mfg.	**Pullman Peabody**	**P/R**	**Reduce earnings cyclicality**	
John Blair	MacFadden Hldgs.	R	Divestitures	
Mayflower Grp.	**Laidlaw Transp.**	**S/R**	**Div. + Shared skills**	
Avondale Mills	Dominion Text	S	Op'nal Synergies	
Gillette Co.	**Revlon**	**R/S**	**Div. + Lev. + shared channels**	
Owens Corn. F'glass	Wickes Cos	F/S	Tax credits + fit with roofn'g bus.	
Carter Hawley Hale	**E.J. Debartolo**	**R/S**	**Divest. + real est. syn.**	
Strawbridge & Cloth.	Berry Acq.	R	Div. + Lev.	

APPENDIX B
BENEFITS EXPECTED IN
FRIENDLY MERGER
ANNOUNCEMENTS IN 1985

Target	Suitor	Primary Expected Benefit		Secondary Expected Benefit
R.C.A.	General Electric	P	Acq. cash generator	S Mktg. & tech. econ.
Amer. Broad. Co.	**Capital Cities**	**S/R**	**Shared skills/cut costs**	
Jack Eckerd Corp.	Mgmt. + Merrill	D	Escape Dart takeover	R Cut costs + lev.
Gulf Broadcast Co.	**Taft Broadcast. Co.**	**P**	**Emphasize b'cast + geog. expn.**	**I Bet on sunbelt**
Gulfstream Aerospace	Chrysler Corp.	P	Diversify out of autos	S Tech. transfer
SCOA Ind. Inc.	**T.H. Lee + Drexel**	**R**	**Divest. + lev.**	**I Cheap stock**
Hoover Universal	Johnson Controls	D	Excape Posner takeover	S Common techn.
Lorimar Inc.	**Telepictures Corp.**	**S**	**Access to network mkts.**	
Conwood Corp.	Dalfort Corp.	F/R	Tax benefits/Lev. + div.	
Commun. Ind.	**Pacific Telesis**	**P**	**Acq. Unregulated bus.**	
Union Trust Banccorp	Bank of Virginia Co.	S	Shared skills	
Alamito Co.	**Mgmt. LBO**	**R**	**Lev.**	
Scott Fetzer Co.	Berkshire Hathway	I	Undervalued stock	
Chilton Corp.	**Borg Warner Corp.**	**P**	**Add to svs. holdings**	
Farm & Home Svgs.	Pacific Realty	P	Div. out of real estate	S Backward integ.
G.C. Murphy Co.	**Ames Dept. Stores**	**S/R**	**Shared skills/cost cuts**	**I Buy cheap co.**
1st Bnkrs. Corp of Fla.	1st Union Corp	S/P	Shared skills/Geog. xpn.	
Shop & Go Inc.	**Circle K Corp.**	**S**	**Mktg. & dist. econ.**	**R Lev.**
International Bank	USLICO	P	Growth thru' acq.	R Divestitures
Dyco Petro Corp.	**Diversified Ener.**	**P**	**Acq. unreg. sub. invest excess FCF**	
Franklin Bancorp	United Jersey Banks	S	Shared skills	D NJ banks attractive targets
Mite Corp.	**Emhart Corp.**	**P**	**Inv. excess cash**	
Cluett Peabody	West Pt. Pepperel	P	Diversify out of textiles	S Fit with text. mfg.
Hook Drugs	**Kroger Co.**	**P**	**Add drugstores**	**S Acquire skills**
J.M. Tull	Bethlehem Steel	P	Vert. diversification	F Profitable co. to offset losses.
Unidynamics	**Crane Co.**	**P**	**New mkt. entry**	
Midcon	Occidental Pete.	P/S	Add energy/vert. Mntg.	I Buy undervalued cos.
Uniroyal	**Mgmt. LBO**	**R**	**Divestiture**	
Frontier Hldg.	People Exp.	S	Acq. routes/gates	
Richardson Vicks	**P & G**	**S**	**Broaden prod. line.**	**P Exp. OTC drugs bus.**

APPENDIX C
CAPITAL SPENDING AND R&D EXPENDITURES OF TAKEOVER TARGETS IN 1985 AND 1986

Target	Cash Flow ($ per Share)	Cap. Spd. ($ per Share)	Excess C.F ($ per Share)	R&D/ Sales	Target	Cash Flow ($ per Share)	Cap. Spd. ($ per Share)	Excess C.F ($ per Share)	R&D/ Sales
CBS Inc.	12.4	3.85	8.55		Uniroyal	4.15	3	1.15	
Safeway stores	**8.6**	**1**	**7.6**		**Frigitronics**	**2.28**	**1.15**	**1.13**	
Great Lakes Int'l	12.35	7	5.35		Joy Mfg. Co.	2.7	1.75	0.95	
Carter Hawley Hale	**6.2**	**1**	**5.2**		**Unidynamics Corp.**	**3.95**	**3.05**	**0.9**	
National Gypsum	8.1	3.1	5		Tull (J.M.) Inds.	1.6	0.8	0.8	
Revlon	**6.55**	**2.1**	**4.45**		**Midcon Corp.**	**11.9**	**11.33**	**0.57**	
Allied Stores	5.2	1	4.2		NL Industries	1.97	1.5	0.47	2.6
McGraw Edison	**9.65**	**6**	**3.65**	1.5	**Fruehauf Corp.**	**6.25**	**5.8**	**0.45**	
SCM Corp.	11.95	8.66	3.29	1.5	AMF Inc.	2.7	2.3	0.4	4.3
Union Carbide	**12.4**	**9.5**	**2.9**	2.8	**Anderson Clayton**	**4.3**	**4**	**0.3**	
Amer. Nat'l Res.	12.15	9.25	2.9		Easco Corp.	3.05	2.8	0.25	
Ponderosa Inc.	**4.7**	**2**	**2.7**		**Sanders Associates**	**2.55**	**2.5**	**0.05**	4.5
Gillette Co.	4.45	1.9	2.55		Southland Royalty	1.95	2.55	−0.6	
Phillips Petroleum	**13.8**	**11.5**	**2.3**	0.7	**Mayflower Group Inc.**	**3.15**	**4**	**−0.85**	
Cheesebrough Ponds	5.95	3.75	2.2		White Consolidated	5	6	−1	
Richardson-Vicks	**3.34**	**1.16**	**2.18**	3.1	**Saga Corp.**	**4.3**	**6**	**−1.7**	
Owens Corn. F'glass	8.61	6.51	2.1		Unocal Corp.	9.65	12	−2.35	0.6
Informatics Gen'l	**3.15**	**1.25**	**1.9**	2.4	**Crown Zellerbach**	**6.45**	**9**	**−2.55**	
Cluett. Peabody	3.4	1.85	1.55		Hammermill Paper	7.4	15	−7.6	
Pacific Lumber	**2.3**	**0.85**	**1.45**						

APPENDIX D
DIVESTITURES FOLLOWING HOSTILE TAKEOVERS

Seller
- **Unit Sold**

Crown Zellerbach
- Headquarters Bldg.
- Gaylord Cont. div.
- Zellerbach dist.
- Zellerbach Paper
- Virginia Paper
- Southern Paper
- Office products

AMF Inc.
- Bowling Prods.
- Specialty Matls.
- Control Syst.
- Long Mile Rubber
- Tire Eqpt.
- Potter & Brumfield
- Paragon Elect.
- Belkins Records

SCM Corp.
- Sylvachem
- Durkee Famous Foods
- Glidden Paint

Revlon
- Technicon Group
- Adams Drug.
- Norcliff Thayer
- Drug and Pharm. Bus.
- Devon Stores

Pacific Lumber
- Welding Divn.

Easco Corp.
- Hand Tool Divn.
- Indust. Grat. Div.

McGraw Edison
- 63% Int. in Onan

Informatics Genl.
- Inf. Legal Syst.
- Insurance Syst.

Times Fiber
- Comm. Syst. Divn.
- CATV switch mfg.
- HQ and mfg. bldg.

Unocal
- Stake in Magma

Phillips Petroleum
- Coal & Geochem. assets
- O & G Int. in Calif.

Union Carbide
- Packaging Divn.
- Polymers and Comp.
- Battery Unit
- Home & Auto Prods.

CBS Inc.
- Musical Inst. Ops.
- 25% stake in Tristar
- Book Publishing
- SBK Ent. World

Uniroyal Inc.
- Tire bus.
- Chem. Businesses
- Plastics Co.
- Rubber plantation

White Consolidated
- 7 steel & Food eqpt. divs.
- 140 acres + w'house

Saga Corp.
- Rest. Businesses
- 100 Straw Hut Pizza outlets
- Headquarters Bldg.

Ponderosa
- Casa Lupita Rest.
- ESI Meats Inc.
- HQ Bldg. + jet + art collectn.

N.L. Industries
- Treating Chems. Divn.
- Hycalog (drill bit mfg.)
- Acme Tool Divn.
- Schaffer Divn.
- Chemicals Divn.

Frigitronics
- Intraocular Lens Business

Allied Stores
- Bonwit Teller
- Jerry Leonard divn.
- Miller & Rhoads Divn.
- Pomeroy's Divn.
- Joske's & Cain Sloan Divn.
- Block's Inc.
- 5 Shopping Centers
- Garfinkel's
- Donaldson Dept. stores
- Catherines
- Plymouth shops

Gillette
- Jafra Cosmetics
- Elizabeth Grady sub.
- Misco. cataloger
- S.T. DuPont

Owens Corn. Fiberglass
- Hitco
- F.R.P.
- F.R.P. Components
- Mineral Prods. plant
- Ladish Co. Inc.
- Closed Plant, eqpt.
- Foam Prods Plants
- Performance Contracting
- Ormet Stake

Carter Hawley Hale
- 2 stores in Denver
- Neiman-Marcus
- John Wanamaker

REVERSING CORPORATE DIVERSIFICATION

by Amar Bhide,
Harvard Business School

uring the 1980s a number of corporate raiders enriched stockholders (and presumably themselves) by paying large premiums over market to acquire and then break up large conglomerates. The instinctive pronouncement of classical economists on such "bust-up" takeovers has been that if splitting up diversified companies is profitable, then it must be adding value. That is, unless buyers are systematically overpaying or target shareholders selling out at too low a price, the diversified form must be less efficient than the undiversified—at least for those companies taken over.[1]

Although its logic is compelling, the argument raises several questions. How do we know buyers and sellers are being "rational"? Why were the diversified corporations put together in the first place, and why did they survive for so long? What has changed in the meantime to make them less efficient? And, finally, is the public diversified form "wrong" only for the relatively small number of companies that are taken over, or are the divestitures by the raiders symptomatic of a more fundamental shift?

Although the possibility of irrational buyers and sellers cannot be ruled out, I shall argue that the breaking up of diversified corporations by raiders very likely has a sound economic basis. As such, it represents a significant development that all large companies will have to come to terms with. In this article, I will explore the following propositions:

■ The diversified conglomerate has significant economic advantages and disadvantages relative to the undiversified firm. Over time, however, the disadvantages have come to outweigh the advantages; and thus the reported shareholder gains from "bust-ups" are not simply "paper" gains, as critics of takeovers claim, but are likely to reflect real changes in operating efficiency.

■ It is primarily the increasing sophistication of capital markets that has eroded the advantages of the conglomerate form, making the diversified corporation a much less valuable institution than it once may have been.

■ Investor power, which has grown along with capital market sophistication, has reduced the ability of managers to preserve an inefficient organizational form. Therefore attacks on diversified corporations, rather than isolated instances of uneconomic behavior (or attempts to profit in the short run at the expense of the future), are likely to prove an important step in the evolution of U.S. industrial structure.

ADVANTAGES AND DISADVANTAGES OF DIVERSIFIED COMPANIES

The Two Key Differences

Although a diversified corporation typically contains units that are capable of existing as independent companies, it is more (or less!) than the sum of its parts. A $10 billion diversified corporation is different from ten $1 billion independent companies in two important respects.

One set of differences derives from the mere fact of common ownership. The dealings of stockholders, lenders, the IRS, employees, suppliers, and customers with a diversified firm are affected by the aggregated fortunes of its constituent businesses. This means, for example, that the tax liability of a diversified corporation may be more or less than the sum of the liabilities of an equivalent set of independent companies. Likewise, the risks faced by suppliers in collecting their receivables or by employees in keeping their jobs may be different for a diversified corporation than for a single business entity.

---

1. Provided there are no negative externalities.

Differences also arise because of the additional administrative layer (or layers) that exists in a diversified corporation. Whereas the managers of an independent business are directly answerable to their owners, managers of the business units of a diversified corporation report to a corporate or general office. Executives and their staffs in the corporate office perform functions that would otherwise be performed by the external capital markets. Like stock analysts, they evaluate and monitor the performance of units. Like stock or bond underwriters, they evaluate funding proposals and make resource allocation decisions. Like a commercial bank, they offer cash management services. And, like the venture capitalists who sit on the boards of companies in which they invest, they offer strategic advice. As Oliver Williamson has argued, the corporate office constitutes in effect an "internal capital market."[2]

In theory, the corporate office may also try to coordinate the functional or "operating" resources of the units in order to achieve economies of scale or scope. This role, however, will not be given much consideration here for two reasons. First, as my own research has clearly demonstrated,[3] the typical targets of hostile takeovers are composed of a group of unrelated business units, most of which were previously acquired rather than developed internally. Thus, the potential for realizing operating synergies is very limited. Second, it is not clear that even companies with the potential for operating synergies among business units are very effective in realizing them. As Malcolm Salter and Wolf Weinhold have observed, while operating synergies are "widely trumpeted" as a benefit of diversification, they are rarely achieved because they require "significant changes in the company's organizational format and administrative behavior" that are difficult to come by.[4]

In fact, most large corporations have come to insist upon an arms'-length relationship between their units. They have learned that whatever benefits might be gained by coordinating the activities of multiple units (such as economies of scale in production or purchasing) are more than offset by internal bickering, delays, and the difficulty of allocating costs and revenues.

Consequently, over 80 percent of large and medium-sized companies are organized into independent strategic business units or profit centers that have limited dealings with one another. And those transactions that do take place between units are often conducted as if they were between independent firms, using market-based transfer pricing methods.[5]

Thus, when I talk about diversification and diversified companies throughout this article, I am referring only to "unrelated" diversification with little or no potential for operating synergies.

Advantages of Common Ownership

The most obvious advantage of a diversified firm is the potential for reducing corporate taxes. Owning multiple businesses allows a diversified company to transfer cash from units with excess funds to units facing cash deficits without the tax payment that might result if the transfer were to be made between two independent companies.

Diversification may also provide "insurance" benefits by pooling the fortunes of unrelated businesses and thus reducing the consolidated entity's "unsystematic risk" (or the variability of its year-to-year operating cash flow). Lower unsystematic risk may in turn lead to lower capital costs. If investors cannot easily diversify away such risks on their own, they might look to conglomerate firms for such insurance and, in return, provide equity or debt financing at a lower cost than they would for a single business firm.

Lower unsystematic risk may also help the diversified firm reduce its cost of "human capital." The assets of corporations include the skills and experience its employees develop through their continued association with the company. Some skills, moreover, are "firm-specific"—that is, they cannot be transferred readily from one employer to another. For example, IBMers knowledge of "how things get done around here" is of great value to IBM but may be of limited use to other employers.

All companies must invest, in one way or another, in their employees' acquisition of firm-specific skills.[6] Making a complete, up-front cash payment is risky

2. Oliver E. Williamson, *Markets and Hierarchies* (New York, The Free Press, 1979).

3. See Amar Bhide, "The Causes and Consequences of Hostile Takeovers," *Journal of Applied Corporate Finance*, Vol. 2 No. 2 (Summer 1989).

4. Malcolm Salter and Wolf Weinhold, *Diversification Through Acquisition: Strategies for Creating Economic Value* (New York, The Free Press, 1979).

5. These rules of engagement are apparently taken seriously. Business folklore includes many tales of entrepreneurs profiting by "buying oil from the 18th floor of Exxon and selling it to the 33rd floor" or by "establishing a swap with Citibank New York on one side and Citibank Tokyo on the other".

6. Amar Bhide and Howard Stevenson, "Promissory and Convenience Relationships: Application to Employment Issues," Working Paper, Division of Research, Harvard Business School (1978).

because, unlike physical capital, human capital cannot be alienated; and it is difficult for corporations to ensure that employees paid to develop skills today will use those skills for the benefit of the firm in the future. Instead of such up-front payments, companies typically make a number of "implicit" commitments to reward employees as they deliver on their skills in the future.

These rewards, which might include favored promotion opportunities and job security, are vulnerable to the same accidents that can jeopardize dividend checks. Therefore, all other things being equal, employees will put greater store by the promises of firms whose fortunes are not dependent on a single business; and a diversified firm will enjoy a comparable advantage in contracting for its specific human skills.

The argument is easily extended to relationships with suppliers and customers, who may also have to make "firm-specific investments" that put them at risk. G.M.'s suppliers, for example, may have to invest in molds for stamping out parts that only G.M. will buy. Likewise Lotus's customers may invest in developing applications for its 1-2-3 software. These investments may be more readily made by the customers and suppliers of diversified firms that are perceived to be less exposed to unsystematic risk.[7]

Disadvantages of Common Ownership

One disadvantage of common ownership, however, is the "moral hazard" that attends any pooling of risks. All insurance schemes tempt individuals to take advantage of others in the group: If I buy health insurance, and if the insurance company cannot effectively discourage unnecessary visits, I have an incentive to see a doctor more often than I otherwise would. Since most other participants are faced with the same temptation, total benefits paid for doctors visits are likely to increase. And high benefits may in turn lead to higher premiums, thus inducing the healthiest participants to drop out of the scheme.

Similar problems may undermine the risk pooling arrangement provided by the diversified corporation. Consider, for example, a company whose chronic losses in the steel business are offset by the profits of its energy division. As long as the corporation as a whole is in the black, workers and managers of the steel subsidiary may be less willing to accept the pain-ful adjustments necessary to restore profitability than if they belonged to a stand-alone enterprise.

Managers of the healthy energy division, on the other hand, will have an incentive to withhold contributions to the parent corporation—say, by hiding potential profits in organizational slack or by making investments with low expected pay-offs. Or, if they have better opportunities, managers of the profit-making entity may simply quit. To cite a much publicized case, in early 1988 Wasserstein, Perella, and others in First Boston's mergers and acquisitions department left the firm to start their own operation because they believed the profits generated by their department were being unfairly used to subsidize the trading operation.

Risk pooling also may create a conflict of interest for management. Top managers, like other stakeholders who invest in firm-specific skills, have an interest in reducing the unsystematic risks faced by their companies. They can legitimately claim that *corporate* diversification is a necessary part of their compensation package.

This self-dealing problem arises because top managers have considerable latitude in setting their own level of "diversification compensation" and because their principals, the shareholders, cannot determine whether this compensation is excessive. Whereas out-of-line cash compensation can be flagged by salary surveys, there are no external or market guidelines to indicate how much diversification represents fair compensation for a given level of firm-specific investment. In fact, such investment cannot even be objectively measured. Only corporate management can make the subjective judgments about the amount of insurance against unsystematic risk necessary for their companies to develop long-term relationships with suppliers, customers, and their employees. Under these circumstances, the temptation to exaggerate the value of diversification is great, especially since diversification may further other managerial goals such as corporate growth (often simply for growth's sake) and independence from shareholder interference.

Advantages of Internal Capital Markets

According to Oliver Williamson, the "internal capital markets" supplied by the corporate staff of

---

7. We should note that the advantage the diversified firm potentially enjoys in contracting with it stakeholders may not be realized if it has previously been unwilling to draw upon the resources of healthy units to meet commitments made by units in trouble. If a diversified corporation is perceived to be a loose federation of businesses committed to a policy of "each tub on its own bottom," then stakeholders are likely to deal with each business as if it were a stand-alone entity.

diversified firms have an information advantage over external capital markets. Unit managers cannot hide embarrassing facts from their bosses in the corporate office as easily as they can from outside shareholders. They are required to prepare voluminous monthly or quarterly reports, which they cannot easily doctor because unit controllers often report to the corporate offices rather than to unit managers. And if corporate executives are dissatisfied with the information they routinely receive, they have the right to demand more. By contrast, outside investors may have to file suit to force the managers to produce something as innocuous as a list of shareholders.

Internal capital markets may also be better suited to handle sensitive data. Whereas a firm cannot easily prevent information provided to outside investors from falling into the wrong hands, data provided to the corporate office can be expected to stay within the firm.

The hierarchical structure of internal capital markets may also allow management to act more effectively than outside investors on the information they possess. The executives of diversified corporations, at least in theory, possess great power: the CEO has the right to add or withhold resources from units, change their policies, or even fire their mangers. External investors are rarely organized to wield such authority. As a consequence, although they may individually know what needs to be done, outside investors may find it difficult to act collectively to bring about the necessary changes.

Superior knowledge and the power to act may also give internal capital markets an advantage in performing the following functions:

Evaluating Investments Designed to Yield "First Mover Advantages." Suppose a firm invents a widget that promises to be very profitable as long as competitors don't quickly imitate the product, allowing the inventor time to build market share. If the firm wants to raise funds from outside investors to develop the widget, such investors may demand information which, if leaked, would destroy the value of the project. But if the firm is a subsidiary of a diversified corporation, the project can be evaluated by the internal capital market without compromising its confidentiality.

On the other hand, it should be remembered that some companies are able to raise funds quite regularly for "general corporate purposes" and thus without disclosing their intended uses. This ability

suggests that, if the company has established a reputation for using capital effectively, then full disclosure may not be necessary.

Preventing a Business that Throws Off Surplus Cash from Reinvesting its Profits in Marginal Projects. Managers often have a strong preference for reinvesting cash instead of returning it to investors, even in cases where shareholders might have more attractive opportunities outside the firm. The superior monitoring and disciplinary capabilities of the top officers of a diversified corporation may give them an advantage relative to outside investors in extracting cash from constituent businesses that do not face attractive investment opportunities and thus preventing value-destroying investments.

Problem Solving. Outside investors face great handicaps in identifying and correcting problems in the companies they own. In the best of times, many managers view stockholders with suspicion and are reluctant to divulge more information than is strictly necessary. If things are going badly, they may clam up entirely. In contrast, the detailed reports that corporate executives receive may be expected to flag signs of trouble more quickly. And, as has been mentioned, the CEO of a diversified corporation can (at least in theory) intervene quickly to change personnel or policies, whereas shareholders may not be able to force change unless the problems really come to a head.

Providing Managerial Assistance. The internal capital markets may have an edge not just in times of crisis, but in providing ongoing managerial assistance as well. Take the case of an exceptionally gifted manager—say, a Harold Geneen—one whose ability in cost control or consumer marketing or making astute technological bets cannot be fully used by any one firm or industry. Such an individual could be retained by investors to sit on several boards of directors, but his effectiveness as an outsider might be limited. As a CEO of a diversified corporation, however, such an individual might be better positioned to put his ideas into practice. The same argument can be extended, of course, to include a management team or function whose skills cannot be fully used by a single firm.

Advancing Short-Term Credit. It has been argued that large companies, particularly those that have diversified across unrelated businesses, can achieve significant savings from centralized cash management. To the extent its various operations represent different levels of production or different stages of the business cycle, the diversified corporation can perform the role of banker, channeling cash from units with excess cash to those requiring funds. In fact, such a system could conceivably eliminate the company's need to access capital from outside sources.[8]

But why should a corporate office playing banker be more efficient than the real thing? Again, the assumption must be that the corporate office has informational and disciplinary advantages over "outside" financial institutions. It can do better "credit analysis," monitor "loans" more carefully and has greater power to recover funds.

Disadvantages of Internal Markets

The advantages of internal capital markets arise, then, from the power that is concentrated in the corporate office. The underlying assumption is that the CEO's demands, whether for information or action, are more readily obeyed than similar demands made by outside shareholders.

This concentration of power comes, however, at a cost. The corporate office may suffer from several disadvantages, including:

Slow Reaction Time. The value added by corporate staffs has to be weighed against the direct and indirect costs imposed by the additional layer of management. Decisions made by unit managers that might otherwise be quickly approved by an independent firm's board (or which might not go before a board at all) may be scrutinized by several corporate employees. For example, in a diversified company, investment proposals typically have to be approved by seven levels of management.[9] The additional scrutiny may weed out poorly conceived initiatives, but may also delay projects whose success depends on quick execution.

High Overhead. Corporate second guessing can be expensive as well as slow. In 1986, for example, the average fully loaded cost of a corporate employee was estimated to be between $75,000 and $100,000 per year; and thus the total costs of a typical 400 person staff could run as high as $40 million a year.

Limited Range of Investments. Whereas the diversified company may be better than the external capital market at extracting excess cash from individual businesses, it may be at a disadvantage in reinvesting this cash. The bias towards reinvesting in existing businesses applies to diversified corporations as much as it does to focused companies—that is, corporate officers are more likely to fund investments in existing units (or make an acquisition) than to return excess funds to stockholders. And regardless of how diversified a corporation becomes, the investment opportunities available within the firm are narrower than those available in the capital markets at large. Where the resource allocators within a diversified firm may have at most several dozen business opportunities they can fund, independent investors have their pick among thousands of stocks.

Politicized Decision-Making. Since corporate officers belong to the same organization as the unit managers, they may be able to get better information than outside investors from an independent company. On the other hand, membership in the same organization may lead to less objectivity and more "politics" in resource allocation and other decisions.

Misaligned Incentives. Problems of high overhead, bureaucratic decision-making, and the like, while commonly observed in diversified corporations, are not necessarily insurmountable. Consider for example, Berkshire Hathaway, a multi-billion dollar corporation whose businesses include insurance, newspapers, confectionery, discount furniture, and children's encyclopedias. Corporate management consists of Chairman Warren Buffet, Vice Chairman Charlie Munger and five other employees (including support staff). World Headquarters (in Kiewit Plaza, Omaha) occupies less than 1500 square feet. The success of this "lean machine" is legendary.

But the average CEO of a diversified corporation usually does not have the incentives to manage like a Buffet. Rewards and punishments in the job are rarely an effective prod for superior performance. Managers of diversified corporations cannot be easily disciplined if they deliver poor performance. Size protects incumbents. The CEO of a $1 billion conglomerate is more firmly entrenched than the CEO of a $100 million dollar business—and for two reasons. First, the raiders who might be attracted

8. See Salter and Weinhold (1979), cited in note 4.

9. Joseph L. Bower, "Planning within the Firm," *The American Economic Review* (May 1970), pp. 186-94.

by the turnaround opportunity that a poorly managed corporation represents will find it more difficult to raise $1 billion of takeover financing than $100 million. Second, the larger corporation is likely to have more widely dispersed shareholders, which raises the odds against a successful tender offer or proxy fight against incumbent management. And the smaller the threat of being displaced, of course, the weaker the incentives for managers to act in the best interest of shareholders.

The size of diversified companies is also an impediment to establishing appropriate financial incentives. Common sense, theoretical models, and empirical research all tell us that managers who own a lot of equity are more likely to think and behave like shareholders; whereas managers with small equity stakes are more likely to pursue private interests at the expense of their shareholders. High managerial ownership in a small single business firm is easily achieved. Quite commonly, managers are founders who retain a significant ownership stake. And if they are not, they can easily be allowed to "earn in" a reasonable share of the equity over a period of time. For example, as is common in professional partnerships, managers may be given a loan (to be repaid out of future income) to buy equity.

There are, however, a few managers of diversified corporations who do own significant stakes. To cite my earlier example, Warren Buffet and his wife own 45% of Berkshire Hathaway's stock. But Buffet is an exception. He built Berkshire Hathaway out of a small textile company; and, in contrast to the development of most conglomerates, he didn't dilute away his stake by issuing stock to acquire companies. He paid cash. Over the 25-year period (through 1989) since Buffet took control, corporate net worth has increased well over 100 times while shares outstanding have increased by less than 1%.

More generally, though, high equity ownership by managers of a diversified corporation is rare. Founding managers are less likely to be around. Diversification is typically undertaken only at an advanced stage in a corporation's "life"—that is, after growth opportunities in the original businesses have been exhausted. And even if the founders are still managing the firm, chances are that the substantial amounts of stock that are usually issued to effect diversifying acquisitions will have diluted their equity stake to an insignificant proportion.

Nor is it easy to conceive of a mechanism by which a non-founding CEO of a diversified company can be allowed to "earn in" a significant share of equity. Consider two hypothetical firms—a $100 million market value single business firm and a $1 billion conglomerate consisting of ten $100 million units—both of which have newly appointed CEOs. The small firm lends its new CEO $5 million, which allows her to purchase 5% of its outstanding stock. The CEO is expected to pay back the $5 million loan, at the rate of $500,000 a year for ten years, out of savings from an expected annual salary of $1 million. Suppose we wanted to set up a similar deal for the CEO of the diversified firm. To purchase the same 5% stake, the CEO would have to be loaned $50 million and, assuming similar tax and saving rates, be paid $10 million a year to service that debt.

But, on what grounds can we justify paying the CEO of the $1 billion firm ten times the salary of the CEO of the $100 million firm? It is not at all clear that the CEO who allocates resources and monitors the performance of ten businesses "adds more value" than the CEO who has full operational and strategic responsibility for a single business. Indeed it may be argued that the former plays a more passive, distant role and is less likely to produce bottom-line improvements than the latter.

Nor is there any evidence that higher salaries are justified by an extreme shortage of the skills required to be the CEO of a diversified corporation. Most diversified corporations have many experienced executives in their ranks. The problem in selecting a new CEO is typically one of choosing among several equally qualified candidates.

Perhaps the only serious argument for paying the CEOs of diversified corporations a premium is that they are capable of doing more harm to shareholders. And indeed, we do see in practice that CEO compensation is correlated with firm size. On average, the studies suggest, the CEO of the $1 billion corporation is likely to earn three times as much as the CEO of a $100 million firm.[10]

The Problem with Stock Options. Unable to provide their top managers with significant equity stakes, diversified firms often give them stock op-

10. Kevin J. Murphy, "Corporate Performance and Managerial Remuneration: An Empirical Analysis," *Journal of Accounting and Economics* 7 (1985), pp. 11-42.

tions instead. Stock options, however, are an imperfect substitute for significant equity ownership. First, stock options create an incentive for managers to maximize stock price rather than total returns. For example, because dividend payments cause share prices to be lower than they would otherwise be, managers may choose to retain cash in the firm rather than paying it out as dividends—even when attractive investment opportunities are not available.

Second, options give managers an incentive to make risky investments. Consider, for example, the CEO of a railroad who expects to retire in five years and whose stock is not expected to do much of anything during that period. Suppose it is early 1986, oil prices have fallen to $15 a barrel, and an investment banker recommends the acquisition of an oil company that will look terrific if oil prices rise above $30 a barrel (but not otherwise). While shareholders might balk, the CEO's stock options will give him a strong incentive to go through with the acquisition. If oil prices do rise, so will the value of his options; if they don't, the CEO has little to lose—at worst his options will expire unexercised. In other words, incentives may get misaligned because, although shareholders can gain or lose real money, managers who own options enjoy only the upside of changes in the price of their stock.

The difficulty of setting the right incentives for the CEO of a diversified firm is similar to the problem of compensating a money manager with substantial funds under management. If a money manager has several billion dollars under management, a "performance-based" fee may induce him to invest in the riskiest stocks. This way, if the investments pay off, the manager makes a huge fortune; whereas if the value of the portfolio declines even by a small percentage, there is no way clients can make the manager share in the losses. Largely for this reason, managers of large funds are usually given an annual fee equal to about 0.6% of assets, which is paid regardless of performance. The downside, however, is that although managers are thus discouraged from excessive risk-taking, they also have little incentive to add much value. (Under this arrangement, however, clients can at least withdraw their funds when they become dissatisfied; shareholders of conglomerates are effectively denied this option.)

In small investment partnerships, by contrast, it is more common to find managers being paid an incentive fee (similar to the earn-in arrangement previously described) to motivate them to maximize returns for their investors.

THE INCREASING SOPHISTICATION OF CAPITAL MARKETS

In the previous section we established that corporate diversification amounts to much more than a simple "financial" or cosmetic rearrangement of individual enterprises. For this reason, bust-up takeovers are likely to have significant consequences for corporate operating efficiency. And the question we now turn to is whether these consequences are likely to be positive on the whole.

The answer to this question could, of course, vary from firm to firm. That is, whether any particular organization can take advantage of the benefits of diversification while minimizing its liabilities will depend, to some extent, upon the talents of the individuals who manage it and upon the history and culture of the institution. My interest here, however, is in the general case: We would like to examine why the diversified firm, which was so popular throughout the 1960s and 1970s, came under pressure during the 1980s. Is it merely a temporary shift in fashion, or has something fundamental changed that would undermine the advantages offered by the diversified firm?

Such a change, I will argue in this section, has in fact occurred. The increased sophistication and efficiency of the external capital markets have largely eliminated the advantages of the internal markets of diversified firms. Wall Street, which was once a cozy club, has been transformed. Business once conducted on the basis of connections has become much more competitive and today requires strong analytical and market-making skills. The development of these skills has in turn greatly improved the external capital market's ability to monitor corporate performance, allocate resources, and help investors diversify away unsystematic risk—all functions that were performed primarily by the managements of diversified firms in the 60s and 70s.

The Evolution of External Markets

In the heyday of the conglomerate, the internal capital markets described by Williamson may well have possessed a significant edge because the external markets were not highly developed. In those days, one's success on Wall Street reportedly depended far more heavily on personal connections than analytical prowess. But, the end of fixed stock commissions and other deregulatory changes such as the institution of shelf registration have dramatically altered the basis of Wall Street competition over the last decade or so. Investment banks and other participants in the capital markets were forced to search for the best analytical talent and to build market-making capabilities. This competitive process has resulted in a significant increase in the ability of our external capital markets to monitor corporate performance and allocate resources.

The Old Days. Two decades ago Wall Street was a sedate club. Robert Baldwin, a former chairman of Morgan Stanley, describes the work environment of the 60s as follows: "When I first came to work, every senior person left their office a little before 12:00 and came back a little after 2:00, and they all went to the Bond Club luncheons. Everybody on Wall Street did the same thing. It was a different time schedule than you have today."

Competition was less than intense. "What you got paid for in Wall Street in those days," recounts another Morgan Stanley director, "was your origination. And your origination was a relationship business. It was unconscionable for someone to buy business."

As Leon Levy of Odyssey Partners has remarked, "It was the only aristocratic business in the U.S. By that I mean the only business where a father, if he were a senior partner, could count on passing the business on to his son." Fixed commissions and issuer loyalty meant that "you didn't have to be a genius to earn a living." Investment banking fathers could therefore "pass on a franchise that was protected by 'The Club'. All the qualities for inheritance were there."[11]

By today's standards, Wall Street firms were small and thinly capitalized. In 1970, for example, Morgan Stanley, then the premier institution of the industry, had 265 employees, $7.5 million in capital, and no research department. The total capital of NYSE member firms was about $4 billion.

Deregulation. Then came "Mayday" 1975 and the end of fixed commissions. This meant that institutional customers could negotiate the fees they paid for trading and individuals could use discount brokers. The average commission paid by institutions fell from 26 cents per share in April 1975 to 7.5 cents per share in 1986. Where individuals paid 30 cents per share in commissions before Mayday, discount brokers were offering trades at 10 cents per share in 1976.[12]

Competition was further intensified with the SEC's adoption of Rule 415 in 1982, which allowed qualified companies to file a statement listing the amount of stock or bonds they expected to issue over the next two years. Whenever they believed market conditions were appropriate, these companies could quickly sell all or some portion of these securities to investors without having to prepare a new prospectus. And just as Mayday put an end to fat trading commissions, Rule 415 cut sharply into lucrative underwriting fees.

As one observer has put it, these changes "dragged the whole industry kicking and screaming into the twentieth century." Prices fell and several hundred securities firms went under. And because old established firms could no longer rely on relationships to provide underwriting or commission income, the ability to market securities became critical for survival.

The Rise of the Professional Researcher. Wall Street firms thus had to develop professional research departments to analyze the prospects of the companies whose stocks they were competing to distribute. In the mid-1970s, investment banks accordingly began to hire legions of analysts. Research methods became more sophisticated and quantitative. As one veteran analyst commented, "There used to be analysts whose spreadsheets were on the back of envelopes. But the perception was they knew what they were talking about. No one wanted to see their numbers. They moved stocks. Now I think you see a more fully rounded job. You see a demand that the analyst conduct a pretty rigorous research."[13]

Analysts also began to specialize in order to cover few companies in greater depth. "Today you have one guy doing domestic oil, another doing international oil, a third doing exploration companies, a fourth guy doing oil service," comments another experienced analyst who used to cover all these sectors *as well as* electronics companies.[14] In short, to survive in the new environment, securities firms had to develop strong analytical and monitoring skills.

Attracting customers also required firms to develop their market-making capabilities. The leading investment banks committed capital and personnel to build "block trading" desks that provided liquidity to clients who wanted to trade large blocks of stock. The stock exchanges also instituted technological changes

11. *Institutional Investor* (June 1987), p. 291.
12. Report of the Presidential Task Force on Market Mechanisms, pp. 11-15.

13. Bennett Kaplan, *Institutional Investor* (June 1987), p. 183.
14. Barry Good, *Institutional Investor* (June 1987), pp. 313-318.

that, by 1986, could easily handle 200-million-share trading days. Large and small investors alike thus gained access to the liquidity that would enable them to diversify away unsystematic risk on their own at little cost.

The Consequences of Deregulation. As with many other industries that have been deregulated, total demand and revenues rose as prices and margins fell. Increased competition, and one of the greatest bull markets in history, created a stronger and more prosperous securities industry that was able to pay for the new capabilities it had to develop.

Here are a few facts attesting to this growth:[15]
- From 1975 through 1986, annual trading volume rose from 4.7 to 35.7 billion shares, and commissions earned on stock trading increased from $2.9 to $13.4 billion.
- Between 1980 and 1986, total revenues for the securities industry rose from $16 billion to $50.1 billion, and total profits increased from $2.3 billion to $5 billion.
- From 1975 through 1986, the total capital of NYSE member firms rose from $3.6 billion to $30.1 billion. Morgan Stanley's capital, for example, increased from under $10 million to $786 million over the same period.

Increased revenues allowed securities firms to pay the higher salaries necessary to build professional research and trading staffs. In 1978, for example, there were only 41 analysts who made more than $100,000. In 1987 there were about 20 who earned more than $1 million; and compensation of between $250,000 and $400,000 was commonplace. Total employment in the securities industry grew 9.5% per year from 1980 to 1986, as compared to 1.9% in the rest of the economy. Incomes grew at an even faster rate of 21.3% as compared to 7.3% generally.[16]

With merit thus replacing birth as the primary qualification for entry and advancement, ambitious young men and women who might have previously taken up positions in large diversified companies flocked to Wall Street. In 1986, one third of Yale's graduating class reportedly applied for jobs at a single securities firm. In the same year investment banks attracted three times as many MBAs from Harvard as did industrial companies—which represents a complete reversal of the ratios that prevailed in 1979.

This shift did not mean, as some critics have claimed, that Wall Street was stealing talent away from the "real" economy. Few of the MBAs of the 1960s and 1970s were wholly devoted to getting their hands dirty on the production line. More fre-

quently, they filled positions in the internal capital market, preparing budgets and capital appropriation requests (in-house "prospectuses") or evaluating them (in-house "buy-side" research). Financial roles had been central to their careers, regardless of what their job titles implied. The principal difference in the 1980s was that they were now performing the same functions on Wall Street that they earlier would have been assigned by public conglomerates.

Furthermore, the blossoming of the external capital market was not confined to the public stock markets. Increased competition encouraged companies to seek opportunities in untraditional fields. The venture capital industry, which could fund new businesses with speed and secrecy, was one beneficiary of this process. Net new funds committed to venture capital rose from $10 million in 1975 to $4.5 billion in 1986.[17]

Entrepreneurs could approach venture capitalists with some confidence that proprietary ideas would be protected and that the venture capitalists would not behave as bureaucratically as the resource allocators of diversified companies. The venture capital industry was young; firms in the business were small and freewheeling. In 1986, the average $30 million independent fund employed only two professionals. Whereas investments made by a diversified firm might require the "due diligence" of seven layers of management, venture capital funds could act expeditiously. And, unlike the functionaries of internal capital markets, they were prepared to bet on the visionary ideas of long-haired ex-TM instructors and to cut deals which had the potential to make the entrepreneurs whose projects they funded very rich. Thus, the external capital markets could now claim an edge even in funding information-sensitive investments—formerly a distinctive advantage of the internal market.

Rising Disclosure Requirements

Accompanying and reinforcing the financial industry's growing analytical abilities was a quiet but substantial improvement in the extent and reliability of information about companies' performance and prospects. Increasing disclosure requirements narrowed the information advantage that internal capital markets may have previously enjoyed.

As one commentator has written, accounting standards, both before and through the go-go '60s

---

15. NYSE Factbooks.
16. *BusinessWeek* (10/16/87), p. 31.

17. Venture Economics, *Venture Capital Yearbook* (1987), p. 17.

market, were "whatever you wanted them to be."
Companies would "shop around for opinions"—that
is, try to find pliable accounting firms that would
endorse their creative book keeping. "Instant earnings" were created by the "front ending" of revenue
and "rear ending of expenses."[18]

Accounting illusions, however, were exposed in
the bear market and the economic contraction of the
early 1970s, as several high fliers went bankrupt. The
large national CPA firms became defendants "in
literally hundreds of class-action and other civil-
damage suits, which took a heavy toll in the diversion of partner time, legal fees, and rapid escalation
in premiums and deductibles for liability insurance."[19] Partners of big eight accounting firms were
convicted of criminal fraud in the Commercial Vend-
ing and National Student Marketing cases.

In addition to shareholder suits, the accounting
profession came under pressure from Congressional
investigations. A Senate sub-committee produced a
highly critical report called *The Accounting Establishment*. Legislation was introduced in the House proposing the creation of a federal statutory organization
to regulate accountants who audited public companies.

To protect itself against lawsuits and to head off
demands for more federal regulation, the profession
moved for an improvement and stricter enforcement of
accounting standards. Following the recommendations
of the Wheat committee, the Financial Accounting
Standards Board (FASB) was established in 1972. At the
same time, the American Institute of Certified Public
Accounts (AICPA) adopted a rule which mandated that
AICPA members comply with FASB standards.

Self-regulation was further tightened in 1977,
when accounting firms (rather than just individuals)
first became subject to regulation. Such firms were
required to have their system of quality control reviewed by a group of peers every three years. In
addition firms that audited public corporations became subject to the oversight of a board composed
of five prominent public members.

These changes greatly expanded the scope and
reliability of the information available to the external
capital markets. By the end of 1986, FASB had issued
more than 80 opinions requiring public firms to
disclose, among other things, information by line of
business, unfunded pension liabilities, foreign currency exposures, and replacement cost accounts.

And because standards were now less flexible, outside analysts could place greater confidence in the
data and more accurately compare the performance
of different investment opportunities.

Increasing disclosure and the growth of the securities industry's analytical capability reinforced one
another. As securities firms developed strong analytical
skills, their appetite for information grew and they began
to set standards for disclosure that exceeded regulatory
requirements. Conversely, higher regulatory standards
provided more grist for the analytical mill and enabled
brokerage firms to expand their monitoring capability.

INCREASING INVESTOR POWER

The greater sophistication of external capital
markets not only undermined the economic utility of
diversified firms, it also eroded managers' ability to
maintain a form that did not provide economic
value. A sub-industry developed to take advantage
of opportunities to profit from breaking up diversified firms. It included analysts who analyzed "break-
up" values of diversified firms, investment bankers
and lawyers with the deal-making skills needed to
complete bust-up takeovers, and junk-bond financiers who provided raiders with bridge financing.

Another important trend which undermined the
diversified form was a resurgence of shareholder
power. Absent strong shareholders, many managers
would likely have chosen to maintain a conglomerate
structure—at the expense of their stockholders—in
order to increase their employees' (not to mention their
own) job security and to reduce their reliance on
external markets for funding. But the rising power and
sophistication of shareholder activists, which grew up
alongside of the securities industry, made preservation
of the status quo difficult and aided raiders' efforts to
break up companies.

***The Conglomeration of the 1960s: A Break with
the Past.*** At the height of the conglomerate boom in
the '60s, control of the large American corporation
seemed to have passed permanently into the hands of
managers. This was quite a switch from the early days
of the modern American enterprise, when financiers
wielded great influence. Although they played no part
in the day-to-day management, such financiers sat on
the boards of companies, had veto power over major
decisions and, when the occasion demanded, changed

---

18. Wallace E. Olson, *The Accounting Profession*, (New York, American
Institute of Certified Public Accountants, 1982).

19. Ibid.

senior executives. Bankers, for example, were instrumental in replacing Durant with Sloan at the helm of General Motors.[20]

The key to the financiers' power was that wealth was highly concentrated. In 1919, the wealthiest 1 percent of the population earned 74 percent of all dividend income; and the ownership of companies, although separated from their management, was nonetheless heavily concentrated among wealthy individuals. Such concentration conferred on the financiers the ability to bring about change.

Over time, however, the importance of the financiers has declined. Ownership by a few large shareholders has given way to ownership by many small shareholders. Why this dispersion took place is not well understood, but probable causes include the booming retail demand for stocks in the bull market of the 1920s, redistributive taxes, and the Malthusian dilution of family fortunes. (By 1948, the wealthiest 1 percent's share of dividend income had fallen to 53 percent from its 1919 level of 74 percent.) Another likely cause of this dilution of ownership were legislative acts in the 1930s and 1940s—most notably, the Glass-Steagall Act—which prevented financial institutions from taking large equity ownership positions in corporations.

Yet another reason for the eclipse of the financiers, as Alfred Chandler has suggested, was that as the rapid growth of large corporations slowed, they had less need for external capital and therefore did not have to accommodate investment bankers on their boards. "Financial" capitalism, as Chandler calls it, thus gave way to "managerial" capitalism.[21]

Managers had great power under the new order. They were relatively free of the discipline of the market because the firms they managed faced a limited number of competitors, and they didn't have sharp-eyed shareholders peering over their shoulders. Consequently, managers had considerable discretion in pursuing their own goals, including growth through diversifying acquisitions.

Managerial capitalism, it may be claimed in retrospect, peaked in the late 1960s. When John Kenneth Galbraith's *New Industrial State* was published in 1967, economists of Keynesian persuasion and managers of Fortune 500 companies were in charge, and all was

right with the world. The economy was growing, almost without interruption: "In the two decades since World War II," noted Galbraith, "serious recessions have been avoided." Large firms enjoyed reliable profits and thus independence from meddlesome stockholders. "The big corporations," continued Galbraith, "do not lose money. In 1957, a year of mild recession in the U.S., not one of the 100 largest U.S. Corporations failed to turn a profit. Only one of the largest 200 finished the year in the red."[22]

But just when the technocracy of large corporations seemed invincible, the pendulum began to swing back in favor of stockholders. Managerial control was threatened by three trends that increased the power of the "suppliers" of capital.

First, the financial self-sufficiency of the large corporations was imperiled by changes in the general economic climate. In 1970, the U.S. faced its first recession after nearly a decade. In 1973, oil prices tripled, precipitating a severe world-wide recession in 1975. A relatively mild recession in 1980 was followed by a business downturn in 1982, which produced Depression-level unemployment in some geographic and industry sectors. In addition, U.S. firms began to face aggressive new entrants from overseas, most notably from Japan.

Large firms no longer enjoyed immunity from losses. Penn Central filed for bankruptcy; Lockheed and Chrysler were spared this fate only by federal bailouts. In the 1982 recession, eight of the top 100 industrial companies and 21 of the largest 200 ended the year with a deficit. As profits declined and some firms suffered real losses, many companies lost their cherished independence from capital markets and the need for external funds became unavoidable. Corporate equity issues rose exponentially, from $16.6 billion in 1980 to $57 billion in 1986.[23] Managers could therefore no longer thumb their noses, so to speak, at investors.

Second, particularly after 1981, the federal government became an attractive alternative "customer" for capital. Large budget deficits forced the U.S. government to raise substantial funds from the capital markets, in competition with private corporations. With 14 percent annual yields and the full faith and credit of the Treasury, government bonds provided investors ("for

---

20. Alfred Chandler, *Strategy and Structure: Chapters in the History of American Industrial Enterprise* (Cambridge, MIT Press, 1962).

21. Alfred Chandler, *The Visible Hand: The Managerial Revolution in American Business* (Cambridge, Harvard University Press, 1977).

22. John Kenneth Galbraith, *The New Industrial State*, (Boston, Houghton Mifflin, 1967).

23. *Securities Industry Trends* (March 30, 1987), p. 9.

the first time in our lives," in the words of one money manager) with a compelling alternative to stocks.

Third, and most important, stockholders became more concentrated. As managers advanced their own interests at the expense of their shareholders', they reduced the value of their company's stock. In only seven of the 40 years between 1945 and 1985 did the stocks of the 500 largest U.S. companies trade above the replacement value of their assets. With greater competition, slower economic growth, and higher bond yields, stocks took a particularly fierce drubbing after 1973. In fact, inflation-adjusted returns to stockholders were substantially negative over the 1970s. And, even after the bull market following 1982, the Dow Jones average at the end of 1987 was fully one third below its real value at the end of 1966.

Individual investors, therefore, withdrew from the stock market and put their money into housing or small entrepreneurial ventures where they could exercise more control over their investments. By 1986, stocks accounted for only 21% of individuals' financial assets compared to 43% in 1968. Individuals had been net sellers of stocks in every year since 1972. And as individual investors fled, the stockholders who remained were a relatively small number of large institutions who were potentially a more equal match for management.

Institutional ownership of stocks, which grew from 31% to 39% between 1970 and 1986, was especially pronounced in the large firms. Institutions were attracted to large companies because they could invest substantial sums in such stocks; and individuals were ready sellers as they had learned to shun companies where management did not hold a significant ownership stake. Consequently, in 1986, institutional ownership of the top 100 industrial firms was about 53%, and was roughly 50% of the next 100 firms. Institutions accounted for a majority of the ownership in nearly two thirds of the top 200 companies.

The resulting increase in shareholder power has facilitated raiders' efforts to break up diversified companies that might have been held together for purely managerial reasons. Investors, for example, are more likely to sell their shares to a raider when they have attractive investment alternatives, such as government bonds with high real yields or stock issued reluctantly at depressed prices. Similarly, raiders stand a better chance of winning the support of a small number of professional institutional investors, who have the resources to analyze and respond to proxy solicitations, rather than of many dispersed individuals.

CONCLUDING COMMENTS

On average, the unraveling of diversified companies probably makes economic sense. External capital markets have come of age, while there has been no evidence of a corresponding improvement in the functioning of internal corporate hierarchies. The diversified firm is therefore a less valuable institution than it might once have been. And, as a practical matter, because investors today are more concentrated and enjoy broader investment opportunities, they are less tolerant of an organizational form that reflects managerial desires to perpetuate growth (often for growth's sake) and achieve financial self-sufficiency.

This is not to claim that all diversified firms destroy value or that every bust-up is guaranteed to be a financial success in the long term. Some buyers have overpaid for divested units while following the new conventional wisdom that free-standing businesses become significantly more valuable when parted from conglomerates. Nor are all external capital markets the epitome of rationality and foresight. (In fact, I have argued elsewhere that there are serious deficiencies in our public stock market, as compared to the external markets for *private* capital.)

But it is reasonable to claim that even if *some* bust-ups prove to be mistaken (that is, end up reducing long-run value), as they almost certainly will, the general economic basis for such transactions is nonetheless sound. And although some sectors of the external capital markets have flaws, they almost certainly have an edge today over the "internal markets" of diversified companies in monitoring corporate performance and allocating capital resources.

LESSONS FROM A MIDDLE MARKET LBO: THE CASE OF O.M. SCOTT

by George P. Baker and Karen H. Wruck, Harvard Business School*

I n 1986 The O.M. Scott & Sons Company, the largest producer of lawn care products in the U.S., was sold by the ITT Corporation in a divisional leveraged buyout. The company was founded in Marysville, Ohio in 1870 by Orlando McLean Scott to sell farm crop seed. In 1900, the company began to sell weed-free lawn seed through the mail. In the 1920s, the company introduced the first home lawn fertilizer, the first lawn spreader, and the first patented bluegrass seed. Today, Scott is the acknowledged leader in the "do-it-yourself" lawn care market, with sales of over $300 million and over 1500 employees.

Scott remained closely held until 1971, when it was purchased by ITT. The company then became a part of the consumer products division of the huge conglomerate, and operated as a wholly-owned subsidiary for 14 years. In 1984, prompted by a decline in financial performance and rumors of takeover and liquidation, ITT began a series of divestitures. Over the next two years, total divestitures exceeded $2 billion and, after years of substandard performance, ITT's stock price significantly outperformed the market.

On November 26, 1986, in the midst of this divestiture activity, ITT announced that the management of Scott, along with Clayton & Dubilier (C & D), a private firm specializing in leveraged buyouts, had agreed to purchase the stock of Scott and another ITT subsidiary, the W. Atlee Burpee Company. The deal closed on December 30.

Clayton & Dubilier raised roughly $211 million to finance the purchase of the two companies. Of that $211 million, almost $191 milion, or 91% of the total, was debt: bank loans, subordinated notes, and subordinated debentures. The $20 million of new equity was distributed as follows: roughly 62% of the shares were held by a C & D partnership, 21% by Scott's new subordinated debtholders, and 17.5% by Scott management and employees.

After this radical change in financial structure and concentration of equity ownership, Scott's operating performance improved dramatically. Between the end of December 1986 and the end of September 1988, sales were up 25% and earnings before interest and taxes (EBIT) increased by 56%. As shown in Table 1, this increase in operating earnings was not achieved by cutting back on marketing and distribution or R & D. In fact, spending on marketing and distribution increased by 21% and R & D spending went up by 7%. Capital spending also increased by 23%.

*This is a shorter, less technical version of "Organizational Changes and Value Creation in Leveraged Buyouts: The Case of The O.M. Scott Company," *Journal of Financial Economics*, 25 (1989).

We would like to thank everyone at The O.M. Scott & Sons Company and Clayton & Dubilier who gave generously of their time and so made this study possible: Lorel Au, Martin Dubilier, Richard Dresdale, Rich Martinez, Larry McCartney, Tadd Seitz, John Smith, Bob Stern, Homer Stewart, Hank Timnick, Ken Tossey, John Wall, Craig Walley, and Paul Yeager. In addition, we would like to thank Ken French, Robin Cooper, Bob Eccles, Leo Herzel, Mike Jensen, Steve Kaplan, Ken Merchant, Krishna Palepu, Bill Schwert, Eric Wruck, and the participants of the Financial Decisions and Control Workshop at Harvard Business School and of the Conference on the Structure and Governance of Enterprise sponsored by the JFE for their helpful comments and suggestions. Support from the Division of Research, Harvard Business School, is gratefully acknowledged.

C & D did not sell shares to managers reluctantly; in fact, it insisted that managers buy equity and that they do so with their own, not the company's, money.

TABLE 1		Pre-buyout: Year ended 12/30/86	Post-buyout: Year ended 9/30/88	Percent change
FINANCIAL AND OPERATING DATA FOR O.M. SCOTT & SONS CO. ($ in millions)	INCOME STATEMENT			
	EBIT	$18.1	$28.2	55.8%
	Sales	158.1	197.1	24.7
	Research & development	4.1	4.4	7.3
	Marketing & distribution	58.4	70.7	21.1
	BALANCE SHEET*			
	Average working capital	59.3	36.2	-39.0
	Total assets	243.6	162.0	-33.5
	Long-term debt	191.0	125.8	34.1
	Adjusted net worth	20.0	38.3	91.5
	OTHER			
	Capital expenditures	$3.0	$3.7	23.3
	Employment	868	792	-8.9

*Balance sheet figures are reported at the close of the buyout transaction. Adjusted net worth is GAAP net worth adjusted for accounting effects of the buyout under APB no. 16. In Scott's case the bulk of the adjustment is adding back the effects of an inventory write-down of $24.7 million taken immediately after the buyout.

In terms of its capital structure, managerial equity ownership, and improvement in operating performance, Scott is a highly representative LBO. Three major academic studies of LBOs have collectively concluded that following an LBO:

- the average debt-to-capital ratio is roughly 90%;
- managerial equity ownership stakes are typically around 17-20%;
- operating income increases by about 40%, on average, over a period ranging from two to four years after a buyout.[1]

Such findings raise major questions about the effects of changes in organizational and financial structure on management decision-making. For example, does the combination of significant equity ownership and high debt provide management with stronger incentives to maximize value than those facing managers of public companies with broadly dispersed stockholders? Are the decentralized management systems with pay-for-performance plans that typically accompany LBOs likely to produce greater operating efficiencies than centralized structures relying largely on financial controls? Are LBO boards, characterized by controlling equity ownership, an improvement over the standard governance of public companies where directors have "fiduciary duty," but little or no equity ownership?

Although the broad evidence cited above suggests that the answer to all these questions is yes, little academic research to date has examined the changes in organizational structure and managerial decision-making that actually take place after LBOs. In 1989, we were given the opportunity to examine confidential data on the Scott buyout and to conduct extensive interviews with C & D partners and managers at all levels of the Scott organization. We found that both organizational structure and the management decision-making process changed fundamentally as a consequence of the buyout.

In the pages that follow, we attempt to explain the role of high leverage, concentrated equity ownership, and strong governance by an active board in bringing about specific operating changes within Scott. Critics of LBOs will doubtless continue to object that highly leveraged capital structures lead to an unhealthy emphasis on "short-term" results. But the changes we witnessed at Scott lend no support to this view. These changes ranged from sharply increased attention to working capital management, vendor relations, and an innovative approach to production to a much greater willingness to entertain long-range opportunities presented by new markets and strategic acquisitions. Especially in light of Scott's post-LBO performance and spending patterns, it

1. The studies are as follows: Steven Kaplan, "Management Buyouts: Evidence on Post-buyout Operating Changes," *Journal of Financial Economics*, 1991; Abbie Smith, "Corporate Ownership Structure and Performance: The Case of Manage-ment Buyouts," *Journal of Financial Economics*, 1991; and Chris Muscarella and Michael Vetsuypens, "Efficiency and Organizational Structure: A Study of Reverse LBOs," Southern Methodist University working paper, 1988.

TABLE 2
OWNERS OF COMMON
STOCK OF O.M. SCOTT &
SONS CO. AFTER THE LBO
(As of 9/30/88)

	Number of Shares	Percent of Shares
Clayton & Dubilier private limited partnership	14,900	61.4%
Subordinated debtholders	5,000	20.6
Mr. Tadd Seitz, President, CEO	1,063	4.4
Seven other top managers (250,000 shares each)	1,750	7.2
Scott profit sharing plan	750	3.1
Twenty-two other employees	687	2.8
Mr. Joseph P. Flannery, Board Member	100	0.4
Total	24,250	100.0%

All shares were purchased by owners at $1 per share. Percentages don't foot due to rounding error.

would be difficult to argue that any of these initiatives sacrificed long-term value for short-run cash flow.

CHANGES IN INCENTIVES AND COMPENSATION

Management Equity Ownership

The final distribution of equity in the post-buyout Scott organization was the product of negotiations between C & D and Scott's management—negotiations in which ITT took no part. ITT sold its entire equity interest in Scott through a sealed bid auction. Eight firms bid for Scott; although bidding was open to all types of buyers, seven bidders were buyout firms. ITT was interested primarily in obtaining the highest price for the division.

Scott managers did not participate in the buyout negotiations and thus had no opportunity to extract promises or make deals with potential purchasers prior to the sale. Scott managers had approached ITT several years earlier to discuss the possibility of a management buyout at $125 million; but at that time ITT had a no-buyout policy. The stated reason for this policy was that a management buyout posed a conflict of interest.

Each of the bidders spent about one day in Marysville and received information about the performance of the unit directly from ITT. Prior to Martin Dubilier's visit, Scott managers felt that they preferred C & D to the other potential buyers because of its reputation for working well with operating managers. The day did not go well, however, and C & D fell to the bottom of the managers' list. According to Tadd Seitz, president of Scott:

To be candid, they weren't our first choice. It wasn't a question of their acumen, we just didn't think we had the chemistry. But as we went through the controlled bid process, it was C & D that saw the greatest value in Scott.

There is no evidence that ITT deviated from its objective of obtaining the highest value for the division, or that it negotiated in any way on behalf of Scott managers during the buyout process. C & D put in the highest bid. ITT did not consider management's preferences and accepted this bid even though managers were left to work with one of their less favored buyers. Nor did ITT concern itself with the distribution of common stock after the sale.

Immediately following the closing, C & D controlled 79.4% of Scott's common stock. The remaining shares were packaged and sold with the subordinated debt. C & D was under no obligation to offer managers equity participation in Scott, and the deal clearly could be funded without any contribution by managers. But, on the basis of their experience, the C & D partners viewed management equity ownership as a way to provide managers with strong incentives to maximize firm value. Therefore, after C & D purchased Scott, it began to negotiate with managers over the amount of equity they would be given the opportunity to purchase. C & D did not sell shares to managers reluctantly; in fact, it insisted that managers buy equity and that they do so with their own, not the company's, money.

The ownership structure that resulted from the negotiations between C & D and Scott management is presented in Table 2. There are 24,250,000 shares outstanding, each of which was purchased for $1.00. As the general partner of the private limited partnership that invested $14.9 million in the Scott buyout, C & D controlled 61.4% of the common stock. The individual C & D partners responsible for overseeing Scott operations carried an ownership interest through their substantial investment in the C & D limited partnership. Subordinated debtholders owned 20.6%.

The remaining 17.5% of the equity was distributed among Scott's employees. Eight of the firm's top managers contributed a total of $2,812,500 to the buyout and so hold as many shares, representing 12% of the shares outstanding. Tadd Seitz, president of Scott, held the largest number of these shares (1,062,500, or 4.4% of the shares outstanding). Seven other managers purchased 250,000 shares apiece (1% each of the shares outstanding). As a group, managers borrowed $2,531,250 to finance the purchase of shares. Though the money was not borrowed from Scott, these loans were guaranteed by the company.

The purchase of equity by Scott managers represented a substantial increase in their personal risk. For example, Bob Stern, vice-president of Associate Relations,[2] recalled that his spouse sold her interest in a small catering business at the time of the buyout; they felt that the leverage associated with the purchase of Scott shares was all the risk they could afford.

Top management had some discretion over how their allotment of common shares was further distributed. Without encouragement from C & D, they chose to issue a portion of their own shares to Scott's employee profit-sharing plan and other employees of the firm. Although they allowed managers to distribute the stock more widely, C & D partners felt that the shares would have stronger incentive effects if they were held only by top managers. Craig Walley, general counsel for Scott, described the thinking behind management's decision to extend equity to additional managers and employees as follows:

We [the managers] used to get together on Saturdays during this period when we were thinking about the buyout to talk about why we wanted to do this. What was the purpose? What did we want to make Scott? One of our aims was to try to keep it independent. Another was to try to spread the ownership widely. One of the things we did was to take 3% of the common stock out of our allocation and put it into the profit-sharing plan. That took some doing and we had some legal complications, but we did it. There are now 56 people in the company who own some stock,
and that number is increasing. Compared to most LBOs that is really a lot, and Dubilier has not encouraged us in this.

A group of 11 lower-level managers bought an additional 687,500 shares (2.8% of the total) and the profit-sharing plan bought 750,000 shares (3.1%). These managers were selected not by their rank in the organization, but because they were employees who would be making decisions considered crucial to the success of the company.

The substantial equity holdings of the top management team, along with their personal liability for the debts incurred to finance their equity stakes, led them to focus on two distinct aspects of running Scott: (1) preserving their fractional equity stake by avoiding default (including technical default) on the firm's debt; and (2) increasing the value of that stake by making decisions that increased the long-run value of the firm.

If the company failed to make a payment of interest or principal, or if it violated a debt covenant, it would be "in default" and lenders would have the option to renegotiate the terms of the debt contract. If no agreement could be reached, the company could be forced to seek protection from creditors under Chapter 11. Because both private reorganizations and Chapter 11 generally involve the replacement of debt with equity claims, one likely consequence of default is a substantial dilution of the existing equity; and to the extent managers are also equityholders, such dilution reduces their wealth. But managers face other costs of default that are potentially large: they may end up surrendering control of the company to a bankruptcy court, and they could even lose their jobs.[3] In this sense, equity ownership bonds managers against taking actions that lead to a violation of the covenants.

We examined Scott's debt covenants in detail to determine what managerial actions lenders encouraged and prohibited (see Table 3 for a summary). The overall effect of these covenants is to restrict both the source of funds for scheduled interest and principal repayments and the use of funds in excess of this amount. Cash to pay debt obligations must come primarily from operations or the issuance of common

---

2. Scott refers to all of its employees as "associates." Stern's position, therefore, is equivalent to vice-president of human resources or personnel.

3. Stuart Gilson provides evidence that the managers of firms in financial distress are quite likely to lose their jobs as a part of the recovery process. See "Management Turnover and Financial Distress," *Journal of Financial Economics*, 25 (1989), pp. 241-262.

TABLE 3
SUMMARY OF DEBT COVENANTS OF SCOTT BORROWINGS TO FINANCE THE BUYOUT

	Bank Debt Restrictions	**Subordinated Debt Restrictions**
ECONOMIC ACTIVITIES RESTRICTED		
Sale of Assets	Only worn-out or obsolete assets with value less than $500,000 can be sold	75% of proceeds must be used to repay debt in order of priority
Capital Expenditures	Restricted to specific $ amount each year debt is outstanding	None
Changes in corporate structure	Prohibited	Mandatory redemption if change in control No acquisition if in default Must acquire 100% equity of target Must be able to issue $1 more debt without covenant violation after acquisition
FINANCING ACTIVITIES RESTRICTED		
Issuance of additional debt	Capitalized leases: max = $3,000,000 Unsecured credit: max = $1,000,000 Commercial paper: max = amount available under revolving credit agreement	Additonal senior debt: max = $15,000,000 For employee stock purchases: max = $4,250,000 Pre-tax cash flow/interest expense: min = 1.0 for four quarters preceding issuance
Payment of cash dividends	Prohibited	Prohibited if in default Prohibited if adjusted net worth < $50,000,000
ACCOUNTING-BASED RESTRICTIONS		
Adjusted net worth*	Specific min at all times, min increases from $20.5 million in 1986 to $43.0 million after 1992	If adjusted net worth falls below $12.0 million then must redeem $17.0 million notes and $5.0 million debentures at 103
Interest coverage	Min 1.0 at end of each fiscal quarter	None
Current ratio	Min at end of each fiscal quarter	None
Adjusted operating profit	Min at end of each fiscal quarter, min increases from $22.0 million in 1987 to $31.0 million after 1990	None

*Adjusted net worth and adjusted operating profit are the GAAP numbers adjusted for accounting effects of the buyout under APB no. 16. In Scott's case the bulk of the adjustment is adding back the effects of an inventory write-down of $24.7 million taken immediately after the buyout.

stock. It cannot come from asset liquidation, stock acquisition of another firm with substantial cash, or the issuance of additional debt of any kind. Excess funds can be used for capital expenditures only within prescribed limits, and cannot be used to finance acquisitions or be paid out as dividends to shareholders. Thus, once the capital expenditure limit has been reached, excess cash must be either held, spent in the course of normal operations, or used to pay down debt ahead of schedule.

A second important effect of equity ownership was to encourage managers to make decisions that increased the long-run value of the company. Because managers owned a capital value claim on the firm, they had strong incentives to meet debt obligations and avoid default in a way that increased the long-term value of the company. That is, managers

had strong incentives to resist cutbacks in brand-name advertising and plant maintenance that would increase short-run cash flow at the expense of long-run value.

As mentioned earlier, there were no cutbacks in productive capital spending at Scott. In fact, as shown in Table 1 earlier, capital spending, R&D, and marketing and promotion expenditures all increased significantly over the first two years after the buyout. Thus, in Scott's case, high leverage combined with equity ownership provided managers with the incentive to generate the cash required to meet the debt payments without bleeding the company.

The increase in capital expenditures following Scott's LBO is one way in which Scott differs from the average LBO. The large-sample studies cited earlier find that capital spending falls on average following an LBO. Whether this average reduction in capital expenditures creates or destroys value is difficult to determine, because not all corporate spending cutbacks are short-sighted. To make that determination, one has to know whether LBO companies were spending too much or too little on capital expenditure prior to their LBOs. The large stockholder gains from the leveraged restructuring movement of the 1980s suggest that much prior corporate "long-term" investment was little more than a waste of stockholder funds in the name of preserving growth.

High leverage combined with leveraged equity ownership provides strong incentives for managers to evaluate long-term investments more critically, to undertake only value-increasing projects, and to return any "free cash flow"—that is, cash in excess of that required to fund all positive-NPV investments—to investors.[4] Leverage will cause managers to cut back on productive expenditures only if such cutbacks are the only way to avoid default *and* the cost to managers of default is greater than the loss in equity value from myopic decisions.

The LBO sponsor—in this case C & D—also plays an important role in guiding such investment decisions and preventing short-sighted cutbacks. Indeed, the experience and competence of the sponsor in valuing the company, evaluating the strengths of operating management, and arranging the financial structure is critical to an LBO's success.[5]

Changes in Incentive Compensation

Among the first things C & D did after the buyout was to increase salaries selectively and begin to develop a new management compensation plan. A number of managers who were not participants in the ITT bonus plan became participants under the C & D plan. The new plan substantially changed the way managers were evaluated, and increased the fraction of salary that a manager could earn as an annual bonus. While some of these data are confidential, we are able to describe many of the features of C & D's incentive compensation plan and compare it with the ITT compensation system.

Salaries. Almost immediately after the close of the sale, the base salaries of some top managers were increased. The president's salary increased by 42%, and the salaries of other top managers increased as well. Henry Timnick, a C & D partner who works closely with Scott, explains the decision to raise salaries as follows:

We increased management salaries because divisional vice presidents are not compensated at a level comparable to the CEO of a free-standing company with the same characteristics. Divisional VPs don't have all the responsibilities. In addition, the pay raise is a shot-in-the-arm psychologically for the managers. It makes them feel they will be dealt with fairly and encourages them to deal fairly with their people.

In conversations with managers and C & D partners, it became clear that C & D set higher standards for management performance than ITT. Increasing the minimum level of acceptable performance forces managers to work harder after the buyout or risk losing their jobs. Indeed, there was general agreement that the management team was putting in longer hours at the office. Several managers used the term "more focused" to described how their work habits had changed after the buyout.

The increase in compensation also served as the reward for bearing greater risk. As stated earlier, Scott managers undertook substantial borrowings to purchase the equity. Requiring managers to borrow to buy equity and adopting an aggressive incentive compensation plan greatly increases managers' exposure to Scott's fortunes. Because managers cannot diversify away this "firm-specific" risk in the same way passive investors can, they require an increase in the expected *level* of their pay to remain equally well-off.

Finally, C & D may have increased salaries because Scott managers are more valuable to C & D than they were to ITT. Consistent with this argument, managers at Scott felt ITT depended on them much less than did C & D. One Scott manager reported:

4. See Michael C. Jensen, "Agency Costs of Free Cash Flow, Corporate Finance, and Takeovers," *American Economic Review,* 76 (1986), pp. 323-329.

5. For examples of poorly structured LBOs, consider the cases of Revco, D.S. and Campeau's acquisition of Federated, both of which have been held up as representative of the problems with LBOs. A case study (by one of the present authors) reveals clearly that top management problems coupled with an inexperienced (and distracted) LBO sponsor contributed greatly to Revco's poor performance (see Karen Wruck and Michael Jensen with Adam M. Berman and Mark Wolsey-Paige, "Revco D.S., Incorporated," Harvard Business School Case 9-190-202 [1991]). In the case of Campeau's acquisition of Federated, a study by Steve Kaplan has shown that overpayment financed by leverage led to the company's default and subsequent Chapter 11 filing (see Steven Kaplan, "Campeau's Acquisition of Federated: Value Destroyed or Value Added," *Journal of Financial Economics,* 25 (1989), pp. 191-212.

"When ITT comes in and buys a company, the entire management team could quit and they wouldn't blink." As we will discuss later, ITT created a control system that allowed headquarters to manage a vast number of businesses, but did not give divisional managers the flexibility or incentives to use their specialized knowledge of the business to maximize its value.

Because C & D relied much more heavily on managers' operating knowledge, it was presumably willing to pay them more to reduce the risk of the managers quitting. At the same time, C & D was not completely dependent on incumbent managers to run Scott. Several C & D partners had extensive experience as operating managers. These partners had on several occasions stepped in to run C & D buyout firms, and they were available to run Scott if necessary. But, they clearly lacked specific knowledge of the Scott organization and were thus willing to provide financial incentives to incumbent managers to secure their participation.

Bonus. Scott's bonus plan was completely redesigned after its buyout. The number of managers who participated in the plan increased, and the factors that determined the level of bonus were changed to reflect the post-buyout objectives of the firm. In addition, both the maximum bonus allowed by the plan and the actual realizations of bonus as a percentage of salary increased by a factor of two to three.

After the buyout 21 managers were covered by the bonus plan. Only ten were eligible for bonuses under ITT. The maximum payoff under the new plan ranged from 33.5% to 100% of base salary, increasing with the manager's rank in the company. For each manager, the amount of the payoff was based on the achievement of corporate, divisional, and individual performance goals. The weights applied to corporate, divisional, and individual performance in calculating the bonus varied across managers. For division managers, bonus payoff was based 35% on overall company performance, 40% on divisional performance, and 25% on individual performance. Bonuses for corporate managers weighted corporate performance 50% and personal goals 50%.

At the beginning of each fiscal year performance targets (or goals) were set, and differences between actual and targeted performance entered directly into the computation of the bonus plan payoffs. All corporate and divisional performance measures were quantitative measures of cash generation and utiliza-

tion and were scaled from 80 to 125, with 100 representing the attainment of target. For example, corporate performance was evaluated by dividing actual EBIT by budgeted EBIT, and dividing actual average working capital (AWC) by budgeted AWC; the EBIT ratio was weighted more heavily, at 75% as compared to a 25% weight assigned the AWC ratio. The resulting number, expressed as a percentage attainment of budget, was used as a part of the bonus calculation for all managers in the bonus plan.

Thus, the bonus plan was designed such that the payoff was highly sensitive to changes in performance. This represented a significant change from the ITT bonus plan. As Bob Stern, vice-president of Associate Relations, commented:

I worked in human resources with ITT for a number of years. When I was manager of staffing of ITT Europe we evaluated the ITT bonus plan. Our conclusion was that the ITT bonus plan was viewed as nothing more than a deferred compensation arrangement: all it did was defer income from one year to the next. Bonuses varied very, very little. If you had an average year, you might get a bonus of $10,000. If you had a terrible year you might get a bonus of $8,000, and if you had a terrific year you might go all the way to $12,500. On a base salary of $70,000, that's not a lot of variation.

The following table presents actual bonus payouts for the top ten managers as a percent of salary for two years before and two years after the buyout.

Rank	Before the Buyout		After the Buyout	
	1985	**1986**	**1987**	**1988**
1	18.3%	26.6%	93.8%	57.7%
2	14.0	23.4	81.2	46.8
3	12.8	18.8	79.5	46.0
4	13.3	20.6	81.2	48.5
5	11.2	19.4	80.7	46.8
6	10.5	17.1	76.5	46.0
7	7.1	10.8	29.6	16.6
8	6.1	22.9	78.0	46.7
9	4.6	6.3	28.7	16.8
10	5.1	6.6	28.4	16.4
Mean	10.3%	17.3%	65.8%	38.8%

The new bonus plan gives larger payouts and appears to generate significantly more variation in bonuses than occurred under ITT. Average bonuses

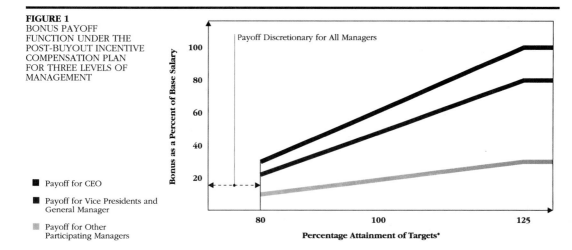

FIGURE 1
BONUS PAYOFF
FUNCTION UNDER THE
POST-BUYOUT INCENTIVE
COMPENSATION PLAN
FOR THREE LEVELS OF
MANAGEMENT

■ Payoff for CEO

■ Payoff for Vice Presidents and
General Manager

■ Payoff for Other
Participating Managers

*Based on a weighted average of corporate, divisional, and individual performance.

as a percent of salary for the top ten managers increased from 10% and 17% in the two years before the buyout to 66% and 39% in the two years after, a period during which operating income increased by 42%. There also appears to be much greater variation in bonus payout across managers within a given year. In the two years prior to the buyout, bonus payout ranged from 5% to 27% of base salary, whereas over the two years following the buyout, it ranged from 16% to 94% of base salary.

In addition to measures that evaluated management performance against quantitative targets, each manager had a set of personal objectives that were tied into the bonus plan. These objectives were set by the manager and his or her superior, and their achievement was monitored by the superior. Personal objectives were generally measurable and verifiable. For instance, one objective for a personnel manager was to integrate the benefits package of a newly acquired company with that of Scott within a given period. An objective for the president of the company was to spend a fixed amount of time outside of Marysville talking to retailers and salespeople. At the end of the year, the superior evaluated whether the manager had achieved these objectives, and quantified the achievement along the same 80-

125 point range. This rating was then combined with the quantitative measures to come up with a total performance measure.

The weighted average of corporate, divisional, and personal target achievements was then used to determine total bonus payoffs. Figure 1 shows how payoffs were varied with rank and performance. If a manager achieved an 80% weighted average attainment of target goals, the payoff varied from about 30% of salary for the CEO to about 10% for lower-level managers.[6] At 125% attainment, bonuses varied from about 100% to about 30%. Between 80% and 125%, bonus payouts as a percentage of salary varied linearly with target attainment. Below 80%, payments were at the discretion of the president and the board.

The combination of equity ownership by eight top managers with a more "highly leveraged" bonus plan for thirteen others substantially changed the incentives of the managers at Scott. For those managers who held equity, the bonus plan, with its emphasis on EBIT and working capital management, served to reinforce the importance of cash generation. Those managers who were not offered equity were nevertheless provided financial incentives to make the generation of cash a primary concern.

---

6. For confidentiality, these numbers have been left intentionally vague.

THE MONITORING OF TOP MANAGERS

Purpose and Composition of the Board

The purpose of Scott's board of directors was to monitor, advise, and evaluate the CEO. As Henry Timnick describes it:

The purpose of the board is to make sure the company has a good strategy and to monitor the CEO. The CEO cannot be evaluated by his management staff, so we do not put the CEO's people on the board. Scott's CFO and the corporate secretary attend the meetings, but they have no vote. The outside directors are to be picked by the CEO. We will not put anyone on the board that the CEO doesn't want, but we [C & D] have to approve them. We do not view board members as extensions of ourselves, but they are not to be cronies or local friends of the CEO. We want people with expertise that the CEO doesn't have. The CEO should choose outside directors who are strong in areas in which he is weak.

At the close of the buyout Scott's board had five members. Only one, Tadd Seitz, was a manager of the firm. Of the remaining four, three were C & D partners: Martin Dubilier was the chairman of the board and voted the stock of the limited partnership, Henry Timnick was the C & D partner who worked most closely with Scott management, and Alberto Cribiore was a financing specialist. The outside director was Joe Flannery, then CEO of Uniroyal, which had been taken private by C & D in 1985. Later, Flannery left Uniroyal and became a C & D partner. He stayed on the Scott board, becoming an inside, rather than outside, director.

Over the next few years three new directors were added. One was an academic, one was a consumer products expert, and one, Don Sherman, was the president of Hyponex, a company acquired by Scott after its buyout. The academic, Jim Beard, was one of the country's leading turf researchers. Henry Timnick described the process of putting him on the board as follows:

Our objective was to find the best turf specialist and researcher in the country. We wanted someone to keep us up with the latest developments and to scrutinize the technical aspects of our product line. We found Jim Beard at Texas A&M. It took Jim a while to be enthusiastic about being on the board, and it

took Tadd a while to figure out how to get the most out of Jim. After Jim was appointed to the board, we encouraged Tadd to have Jim out on a consulting basis for a couple of days. Now Tadd is making good use of Jim.

Seitz and Timnick wanted an individual with extensive experience in consumer products businesses to be the second outside director. They chose Jack Chamberlain, who had run GE's Consumer Electronics Division as well as Lenox China and Avon Products. All board members were stockholders; upon joining the board they were each given the opportunity to purchase 50,000 shares at adjusted book value. All the directors chose to own stock.

This board structure was typical for a C & D buyout. Martin Dubilier explains:

We have tried a number of board compositions and we found this to be the most effective. If you have too many insiders the board becomes an operating committee. Outsiders fortify the growth opportunities of the firm.

The board of directors met quarterly. A subset of the board, the executive committee, met monthly. The executive committee was made up of Martin Dubilier, Tadd Seitz, and Henry Timnick. In their meetings they determined policy, discussed personnel matters, and tested Seitz's thinking on major issues facing the firm. The board meetings were more formal, usually consisting of presentations by members of the management team other than Seitz.

The Operating Partner

In each of C & D's buyouts, a partner with extensive operating experience serves as "liaison" between the firm's managers and C & D. The operating partner functions as an advisor and consultant to the CEO, not a decision maker. Henry Timnick was Scott's liaison partner. He had been CEO of a division of Mead that was purchased through a leveraged buyout, and had since worked with several of C & D's other buyout firms. Timnick spent several weeks in Marysville after the buyout closed. Following that period, he was in touch with Seitz daily by telephone and continued to visit regularly.

Timnick would advise Seitz, but felt it was important that Seitz make the decisions. When he

and Seitz disagreed, Timnick told him, "If you don't
believe me, go hire a consultant, then make your own
decision." Initially, Seitz continued to check with
Timnick, looking for an authorization for his decisions. Henry Timnick explains:

> Tadd kept asking me "Can I do this? Can I do
> that?" I told him, "You can do whatever you want so
> long as it is consistent with Scott's over-all strategy."

This consultative approach to working with
Scott managers was quite different from ITT's approach. Martin Dubilier explains:

> ITT challenges managers not to rock the boat, to
> make budget. We challenge managers to improve the
> business. Every company takes on the personality of
> its CEO. Our main contribution is to improve his
> performance. All the rest is secondary.

Scott managers confirmed Dubilier's assessment. Meetings between ITT managers and Scott
managers were large and quite formal, with as many
as 40 members of ITT's staff present. Scott managers
found the meetings antagonistic, with the ITT people
working to find faults and problems with the operating units' reported performances. By meeting the
formal goals set by ITT, Scott could largely avoid
interference from headquarters. Avoiding such interference was an important objective. As Paul Yeager,
CFO, describes it:

> Geneen [then CEO of ITT] said in his book that the
> units would ask for help from headquarters; that the
> units came to look at headquarters staff as outside
> consultants who could be relied upon to help when
> needed. I have worked in many ITT units, and if he
> really thought that, then he was misled. If a division
> vice president went to headquarters for help, in effect
> he was saying, 'I can't handle it.' He wouldn't be a
> vice president for very long.

ORGANIZATIONAL CHANGES AND CHANGES IN DECISION MAKING

The changes in organizational structure and
decision making that took place at Scott after the
buyout fall broadly into two categories: improved
working capital management and a new approach to
product markets. These changes were not forced on
managers by C & D. The buyout firm made some

suggestions, but the specific plans and their implementation were the responsibility of Scott managers.
Few of the changes represent keenly innovative or
fundamentally new insights into management problems. As one observer noted, "It ain't rocket science."
These changes, however, led to dramatic improvements in Scott's operating performance.

Management's ability and talents did not change
after the buyout, nor did the market or the assets they
were managing. The only changes were those in the
incentive structure described earlier and in the
management control system. According to Scott
managers, the biggest difference between working
at Scott before and after the buyout was an increase
in the extent to which they could make and implement decisions without approval from superiors.

ITT, by contrast, maintained control over its
divisions through an inflexible formal planning and
reporting structure. Changing a plan required approval at a number of levels from ITT headquarters,
and a request for a change was likely to be denied.
In addition, because ITT was shedding its consumer
businesses, Scott managers found their requests for
capital funds routinely denied. After the buyout, Seitz
could pick up the phone and propose changes in the
operating plan to Timnick. This, of course, improved
the company's ability to respond quickly to changes
in the marketplace.

The Working Capital Task Force

Shortly after the buyout, a task force was
established to coordinate the management of working capital throughout the company. The members
of the task force were drawn from every functional
area. The group was charged with reducing working
capital requirements by 42%, or $25 million dollars,
in two years. They exceeded this goal, reducing
average working capital by $37 million. The task
force helped Scott managers learn to manage cash
balances, production, inventories, receivables, payables, and employment levels more effectively.

Cash Management. Before the buyout, Scott's
managers never had to manage cash balances. John
Wall, chairman of the working capital task force,
describes how cash was controlled under ITT:

> Under the ITT system, we needed virtually no
> cash management. The ITT lock box system swept our
> lock boxes into Citibank of New York. Our disburse-
> ment bank would contact ITT's bank and say we need

$2 million today and it automatically went into our disbursement account.

To control cash flow in its numerous businesses, ITT established a cash control system that separated the collection of cash from cash disbursements. Receipts went into one account and were collected regularly by ITT's bank. Once deposited, these funds were not available to divisional managers. Cash to fund operations came from a different source, and through a different bank account. This system allowed ITT to centrally manage cash and control divisional spending.

When Scott was a division of ITT, cash coming into Scott bore little relation to the cash Scott was allowed to spend. After the LBO, all of Scott's cash was available to managers. They needed to establish a system to control cash so that operations were properly funded, and to meet debt service requirements. Wall describes the process as follows:

In the first six months after the LBO we had to bring in a state-of-the-art cash management system for a business of this size. We shopped a lot of treasury management systems and had almost given up on finding a system that would simply let us manage our cash. We didn't need a system that would keep track of our investment portfolios because we had $200 million borrowed. Finally, we found a product we could use. Under the LBO cash forecasting has become critical. I mean cash forecasting in the intermediate and long range. I don't mean forecasting what is going to hit the banks in the next two or three days. We could always do that, but now we track our cash flows on a weekly basis and we do modeling on balance sheets, which allows us to do cash forecasting a year out.

Production and Inventories. Between 1986 and 1988, the efforts of the task force increased the frequency with which Scott turned over its inventory from 2.08 to 3.20 times per year, or by 54%. During this period both sales and production increased. Because Scott's business is highly seasonal, inventory control had always been a management problem. Large inventories were required to meet the spring rush of orders; however, financing these inventories was a cash drain. Scott's production strategy under ITT exacerbated the inventory problem. Before the buyout, Scott produced each product once a year. Slow-moving products were produced

during the slow season so that long runs of fast-moving products could be produced during the busy season. Before the spring buying began, almost an entire year's worth of sales were in inventory.

The old production strategy took advantage of the cost savings of long production runs. But, under ITT, managers did not consider the trade-off between these cost savings and the opportunity cost of funds tied up in inventory. The cash requirements of servicing a large debt burden, the working capital-based restrictions in the debt agreements, and the inclusion of working capital objectives in the compensation system gave managers a strong incentive to consider this opportunity cost. As Wall explained,

What the plant managers had to do was to figure out how they could move the production of the slow-moving items six months forward. That way the products we used to make in May or early June would be made in November or December. Now [instead of producing long runs of a few products] production managers have to deal with setups and changeovers during the high-production period. It requires a lot more of their attention.

Managing inventories more effectively required that products be produced closer to the time of shipment. Because more setups and changeovers were necessary, the production manager's job became more complicated. Instead of producing a year's supply of one product, inventorying it, and then producing another product, managers had to produce smaller amounts of a variety of products repeatedly throughout the year.

Inventories were also reduced by changing purchasing practices and inventory management. Raw material suppliers agreed to deliver small quantities more often, reducing the levels of raw materials and finished goods inventories. By closely tracking inventory, Scott managed to reduce these levels without increasing the frequency of stock-outs of either raw materials or finished goods.

Receivables and Payables. Receivables were an important competitive factor and retailers expected generous payment terms from Scott. After the buyout, however, the timing of rebate and selling programs was carefully planned, allowing Scott to conserve working capital. Scott also negotiated with suppliers to obtain more favorable terms on prices, payment schedules, and delivery. Lorel Au, manager of Contract Operations stated,

Within two months of the LBO, the director of manufacturing and I went out to every one of our contract suppliers and went through what a leveraged buyout is, and what that means. We explained how we were going to have to manage our business. We explained our new goals and objectives. We talked about things like just-in-time inventory, talked terms, talked about scheduling. Some suppliers were more ready to work with us than others. Some said, 'OK, what can we do to help?' In some cases, a vendor said, 'I can't help you on price, I can't help you on terms, I can't help you on scheduling.' We said: 'Fine. Good-bye.' We were very serious about it. In some cases we didn't have options, but usually we did.

The company succeeded in getting suppliers to agree to extended terms of payment, and was also able to negotiate some substantial price cuts from major suppliers in return for giving the supplier a larger fraction of Scott's business.

Scott managers felt that the buyout put them in a stronger bargaining position vis-a-vis their suppliers. Wall states:

One reason we were able to convince our suppliers to give us concessions is that we no longer had the cornucopia of ITT behind us. We no longer had unlimited cash.

The suppliers understood that if they did not capitulate on terms, Scott would have to take its business elsewhere or face default.[7]

Employment. Scott had a tradition of being very paternalistic toward its employees and was a major employer and corporate citizen in the town of Marysville. Some have argued that an important source of cash and increasing equity value in buyouts is the severing of such relationships.[8] There is no evidence of this at Scott. Scott's traditional employee relations policies were maintained, and neither wages nor benefits were cut after the buyout. Scott continues to maintain a large park with swimming pool, tennis courts, playground, and other recreational facilities for the enjoyment of employees and their families. The company also continues to make its auditorium, the largest in Marysville, available for community use at no charge.

Scott did begin a program of hiring part-time employees during the busy season rather than bringing on full-time employees. This allowed the company to maintain a core of full-time, year-round employees who enjoyed the complete benefits plan of the company, while still having enough people to staff the factory during busy season. As a consequence, average annual full-time employment has dropped by about 9%, entirely through attrition, over the first two years after the buyout.

New Approaches to the Product Markets

Scott is the major brand name in the do-it-yourself lawn care market and has a reputation for high-quality products. Ed Wandtke, a lawn industry analyst, says of the company:

O.M. Scott is ultra high price, ultra high quality. They absolutely are the market leader. They have been for some time. No one else has the retail market recognition. Through its promotions, Scott has gotten its name so entrenched that the name and everything associated with it—quality, consistency, reliability—supersede the expensive price of the product.

In 1987, Scott had a 34% share of the $350 million do-it-yourself market. Industry experts report, however, that the market had been undergoing major changes since the early 1980s. Indeed, Scott's revenue fell by 23% between 1981 (the historical high at that time) and 1985. The buyout allowed Scott managers the flexibility to adapt to the changing marketplace, assuring a future for the company.

The do-it-yourself market was shrinking because an increasing number of consumers were contracting with firms to have their lawns chemically treated. Seitz had proposed that Scott enter this segment of the professional lawn-care market for years, but ITT continually vetoed this initiative. Among the first actions taken after the buyout was the creation of a group within the professional division whose focus was to sell to the commercial

---

7. Schelling supports the potential for an increase in bargaining power to occur as the result of a precarious financial situation. He states: "The power to constrain an adversary may depend on the power to bind oneself.... In bargaining, weakness is often strength, freedom may be freedom to capitulate, and to burn bridges behind one may suffice to undo an opponent. ... [M]ore financial resources, more physical strength, more military potency, or more ability to withstand losses...are by no means universal advantages in bargaining situations; they often have a contrary value." T. Schelling, *The Strategy of Conflict*, (Cambridge, Mass: Harvard University Press, 1960).

8. See A. Shleifer and L. Summers, "Breach of Trust in Hostile Takeovers," in A. Auerbach, ed., *Corporate Takeovers: Causes and Consequences* (University of Chicago Press, 1988).

turf maintenance market. Within two years, the segment comprised 10% of the sales of the professional division and was growing at a rate of almost 40% per year.

In response to major changes in Scott's product markets, the company also made a major acquisition less than two years after the buyout. At the time, Scott's position in the do-it yourself market was being challenged by the growth of private label brands sold at lower prices, and by a shift in volume away from Scott's traditional retailers—hardware and specialty stores—to mass merchandisers. Under ITT Scott managers did not try to develop new channels of distribution. Timnick described it as too "risky" an experiment for ITT. The acquisition of Hyponex gave Scott access to the private label market. Says Wandtke,

With Hyponex, Scott will capture a greater percentage of the home consumer market. Hyponex is a much lower priced product line. It gives them [Scott] access to private labeling, where they can produce product under another label for a lesser price. ...This will improve their hold on the retail market.

Hyponex was a company virtually the same size as Scott, with $125 million in sales and 700 employees, yet the acquisition was financed completely with bank debt. The successful renegotiation of virtually all of Scott's existing debt agreements was required to consummate the transaction. Because the new debt was senior to the existing notes and debentures, a consent payment of $887,500 was required to persuade bondholders to waive restrictive covenants. That such a large acquisition was possible so soon after the buyout demonstrates the potential flexibility of the LBO organizational form. It also demonstrates the ability of contracting parties to respond to a valuable investment opportunity in the face of restrictions that appear to forbid such action.

CONCLUSIONS

This study documents the organizational changes that took place at The O.M. Scott & Sons Company in response to its leveraged buyout. In so doing, it lends support to the findings of large-sample studies of leveraged buyouts that suggest the pressure of servicing a heavy debt load combined with management equity ownership leads to improved operating performance.

Such improvements were not the result of financial sleight of hand, but of important changes in operating strategy and management decision-making. These organizational changes came about not only because of Scott's new financial structure and equity ownership, but also as a consequence of other factors that have been largely overlooked:

■ debt covenants that restrict how the cash required for debt payments can be generated;

■ the adoption of a strong incentive compensation plan;

■ a reorganization and decentralization of decision making; and

■ the close relationship between Scott managers, the partners of C & D, and the board of directors.

We attribute the improvements in operating performance after Scott's leveraged buyout to changes in the incentive, monitoring, and governance structure of the firm. Managers were given strong incentives to generate cash and greater decision-making authority, but checks were established to guard against behavior that would be damaging to firm value. In the Scott organization, high leverage was effective in forcing managers to generate cash flow in a productive way largely because debt covenants and equity ownership countered short-sighted behavior. Value was created by decentralizing decision making largely because managers were monitored and supported by an expert board of directors who were also the controlling equityholders.

We view this study as a first step toward understanding how radical changes in financial structure, equity ownership, and compensation systems can be used as tools to improve managerial incentives and corporate performance. For companies in mature industries, the combination of high leverage and management equity ownership can provide an organizational discipline that adds value.

EQUITY CARVE-OUTS

by Katherine Schipper and Abbie Smith, University of Chicago

Late in 1981 Condec Corporation filed a prospectus describing a plan to sell to the public slightly over 20 percent of the equity in its wholly-owned subsidiary, Unimation, Inc. In this "equity carve-out" (also known as a "partial public offering"), Condec sold 1.05 million common shares of Unimation at $23 each, thereby raising $22.5 million in new equity capital (after fees and expenses). The purpose of the offering, as stated in the prospectus, was to use "$19.4 million to repay all [of Unimation's] outstanding long-term indebtedness to Condec, and the remainder to provide working capital." The market's response to Condec's announcement resulted in a 19 percent stock price increase (after taking account of market movements).

Why did Condec choose this relatively unusual method of raising capital instead of, say, selling more of its own common equity? Why, furthermore, did the market respond so favorably to the announcement of the offering—especially since announcements of common stock offerings generally signal bad news to investors?

In this article, we attempt to provide answers to these questions based on our own recently published study of 76 equity carve-out announcements by New York and American Stock Exchange companies over the period 1965-1983.[1] Our study finds, in brief, that the stockholders of parent companies earn on average almost 2 percent positive market-adjusted returns during the five-day period surrounding announcements of the carve-outs—and almost 5 percent if an additional two weeks preceding the announcement are included. In contrast, the stock prices of companies announcing seasoned equity offerings fall some 3 percent or more, on average, around the time of announcement; and announcements of convertible debt offerings provoke an average negative reaction of 1 or 2 percent. Thus, according to the findings of recent research, equity carve-outs represent the only form of new equity financing by public companies which results, on average, in an increase in shareholder wealth.

The Popular Argument

One popular explanation for the positive market reaction to equity carve-out announcements is that carve-outs allow investors to evaluate exceptional corporate growth opportunities on a stand-alone basis. This explanation would imply that Condec, a large, defense-oriented conglomerate, decided to carve out 20 percent of Unimation, a robot manufacturer, to reinforce the market's perception of the value of that subsidiary and thus, presumably, to increase the market's valuation of Condec as a whole. As another example, MGM/UA's 1982 carve-out of its Home Entertainment Group has been described as a means of "cash[ing] in on the craving of investors for a share in what may become an enormous market for pay television and home videos."[2] Commenting on this same transaction, an analyst at Bear Stearns stated that such a partial public offering provided "a way for studios to enhance their own valuations and for investors to get a piece of the fast-growing market [for home video]."[3]

The assumption underlying this explanation seems to be that investors are attracted to subsidiary growth opportunities when these are isolated from the consolidated entity (that is, available for separate purchase). By creating a separate public market for Unimation's common stock, the popular argument seems to run, the carve-out allowed Condec to benefit by allowing direct investment in the growth opportunities of the robot subsidiary.

A variant of this popular argument holds that investors might value a specific investment opportu-

---

1. See Katherine Schipper and Abbie Smith, "A Comparison of Equity Carve-outs and Seasoned Equity Offerings: Share Price Effects and Corporate Restructuring," *Journal of Financial Economics* 15 (1986), pp. 153-186.

2. From "The Old Razzle-Dazzle," *Forbes*, February 14, 1985, pp. 43-44.
3. From "MGM/UA Movie-distributing Unit's Rise Has Other Studios Studying Its Strategy," *Wall Street Journal*, October 21, 1983.

nity more highly when set apart from a conglomerate if and when it offers them a scarce commodity: that is, a so-called "pure play." It might be difficult for investors to invest in, say, stand-alone public robotics manufacturers. (Such an advantage is likely to last only as long as there are few "pure plays" around.) This variant is illustrated, in the case of Unimation, by the following analysis:

The Unimation offering is among the first opportunities for substantial investment in the growing robot industry and it attracted considerable interest when it was announced last month. Most robotics companies that are publicly traded over the counter are too small to attract major investors. (Wall Street Journal, *November 27, 1981*)

In this article, we argue that although equity carve-outs may indeed create securities which have scarcity value, there are also other explanations for the market's positive response to partial public offerings. First of all, equity carve-outs may overcome the problem of the information gap between insiders and investors that attends all seasoned equity offerings (for a discussion of this problem, see Clifford Smith's article, "Raising Capital," immediately preceding). They may also provide more information to the market about the subsidiary, thereby stimulating new investor demand (not to mention the interest of potential corporate acquirers). Perhaps more important, however, is that although the parent company generally retains a majority interest in the "carved-out" subsidiary, equity carve-outs are often accompanied by important changes in management responsibilities and incentive contracts. Expected improvements in performance from changes in managerial accountability and incentives may partially explain the market's positive reaction.

In the pages that follow we shall explain more precisely what an equity carve-out is, and how it

differs from and resembles both spin-offs and seasoned equity offerings. We then review our own recent research on carve-outs, and discuss differences between equity carve-outs and conventional parent equity offerings that might account for the systematically negative response to the latter and the generally positive response to the former. Last, we take a look at what happens to subsidiaries after they have had partial public offerings. Seldom do carved-out subsidiaries remain unchanged for very long, with the public simply maintaining its minority interest in the firm. Instead they are generally either reacquired by the parent, completely spunoff, acquired by management through an LBO, or acquired by some other firm. We attempt to make sense of these developments.

The Market Reaction to Related Events: Seasoned Equity Offerings and Spin-Offs

An equity carve-out resembles a primary offering of seasoned stock in that cash is received from the investing public. Several recent studies of the market's response to seasoned equity offerings have confirmed average negative returns to stockholders of 2 to 3 percent over the two-day period surrounding the announcement of the issue.[4] In addition, our own study of carve-outs found that for those companies which had a seasoned common stock offering within five years of a carveout, the average price reaction to the parent stock offering was −3.5 percent over the five-day period ending with the announcement.

Many of the features which distinguish a subsidiary equity offering from a seasoned equity offering represent similarities with a voluntary spin-off.[5] In a spin-off, distinct equity claims of a wholly-owned subsidiary are distributed as a dividend to the consolidat-

4. The share price reaction of NYSE and ASE listed firms to an announcement of a public offering of seasoned common stock is the subject of the following published studies, all of which appeared in Volume 15 (1986) of the *Journal of Financial Economics*: Ronald Masulis and Ashok Korwar, "Seasoned Equity Offerings: An Empirical Investigation"; Paul Asquith and David Mullins, "Equity Issues and Offering Dilution"; and Wayne Mikkelson and Megan Partch, "Valuation Effects of Security Offerings and the Issuance Process." The share price reactions to public offerings of convertible debt claims on NYSE and ASE listed firms were examined by Larry Dann and Wayne Mikkelson in "Convertible Debt Issuance, Capital Structure Change and Financing-Related Information: Some New Evidence," *Journal of Financial Economics* 13 (1984). The results of these studies are as follows: For offerings by industrial firms, a statistically significant negative average abnormal stock return of 2 or 3 percent is documented in the two-day period ending with the *Wall Street Journal* announcement date. In the case of equity offerings by public utilities, the return is smaller (less than one per cent), but still negative and statistically significant. Furthermore, a negative average share price effect of an increase in outstanding common equity through exchange offers

and conversions of debt to common stock is documented by the following studies: Ron Masulis, "The Effects of Capital Structure Changes on Security Prices," Unpublished doctoral dissertation, University of Chicago, 1978; and Wayne Mikkelson, "Convertible Calls and Security Returns," *Journal of Financial Economics* 9 (1981).

Conversely, evidence exists that an increase in share price is associated with a *reduction* in outstanding common equity through repurchases of shares and exchange offers: Larry Dann, "Common Stock Repurchases: An Analysis of Returns to Bondholders and Stockholders," *Journal of Financial Economics* 9 (1981); Ron Masulis, "Stock Repurchase by Tender Offer: An Analysis of the Causes of Common Stock Price Changes *Journal of Finance* 35 (1980), 305-319, (as well as the Ph.D. dissertation cited above); and Theo Vermaelen, "Common Stock Repurchases and Market Signalling: An Empirical Study," *Journal of Financial Economics* 9 (1981). Thus, the evidence suggests that an increase in outstanding equity is associated on average with a decrease in stock price, and a decrease in equity is associated with an increase in stock price.

In an equity carve-out, the parent company typically does not relinquish control over the subsidiary; instead a public minority interest is created.

ed entity's shareholders and begin to trade in public equity markets. Thus, in both spin-offs and equity carve-outs, a subsidiary's equity claims begin to trade separately from equity claims on the consolidated entity. Studies of the market reaction to announcements of corporate spin-offs all document positive abnormal returns of about 3 percent in the two-day period ending with the *Wall Street Journal* announcement date.[6]

A subsidiary equity offering differs in two respects from a corporate spin-off. First, as mentioned, whereas in a spin-off the subsidiary stock is distributed to the existing shareholders of the consolidated entity, the equity carve-out is a sale of subsidiary stock which raises new capital. Second, in a spin-off the parent company typically relinquishes control over the subsidiary by distributing all of the subsidiary stock. In an equity carve-out, the parent company typically does not relinquish control over the subsidiary; instead a public minority interest is created. Because a subsidiary equity offering partly resembles both a seasoned equity offering (associated with a negative share price reaction) and a corporate spin-off (associated with a positive reaction), it was not obvious ex ante what the market's reaction to carve-outs would be.

The Market Reaction to Equity Carve-Outs

Our study examined the stock market's response to 76 announcements of equity carve-outs by 63 NYSE and ASE firms over the period 1965 to 1983.[7] These announcements were clustered in the late 1960s through 1972 and in the early 1980s; there were no announcements in the five years 1973-1977.[8] This pattern differs from the pattern of seasoned common

stock offerings reported in three recent studies; in these samples about one-fourth to one-third of common stock offerings over the same 19-year period occurred in the five-year period 1973-77.[9] The pattern of equity carve-outs does, however, conform roughly to that of initial public offerings.[10]

In our sample of 76 carve-out announcements, 37 of the announcements state that the firm "has proposed" or "is considering" offering a portion of a subsidiary to the public. The remaining 39 report that an offering has been filed with the SEC. Some of these provide no details, while others describe what is being offered, when and why. Regardless of the nature of the announcement, our share price reaction tests are based on the date the earliest announcement about the subsidiary equity offering appears in the *Wall Street Journal*. To increase the likelihood that the test period captures the first public disclosure of information about the subsidiary equity offering, the test period is defined as the five trading days ending with the day of the *Wall Street Journal* announcement.

Seventy-three percent of the carve-out offerings were underwritten. The percentage of the subsidiary's equity offered ranged from 4 percent to 75 percent, with 81 per cent of the sample with available data falling between 10 percent and 50 percent. The proceeds of the offerings ranged from $300,000 to $112,200,000. Carve-out proceeds as a percentage of the parent's common equity value ranged from .3 per cent to 69 per cent, with a median of about 8 per cent.[11]

A subset of 26 sample firms also made a total of 39 public offerings of their own common stock or convertible debt (hereafter called "parent equity") within five years of their subsidiary equity offerings. Parent equity issues of sample firms were identified by searching the *Wall Street Journal* Index for each of the five years prior to, the year of, and, where possible, the

5. A subsidiary equity offering also resembles a divestiture in that cash is received. However, a divestiture does not in general initiate the trading of subsidiary stock. Two studies (G. Alexander, P. Benson and J. Kampmeyer, "Investigating the Valuation Effects of Announcements of Voluntary Corporate Selloffs," *Journal of Finance* 29 (1984); and April Klein, "Voluntary Corporate Divestitures: Motives and Consequences," Unpublished doctoral dissertation, University of Chicago, 1983) both report positive abnormal returns of about 1 per cent or less in a three-day period (Klein) and a two-day period (Alexander et al.) ending with the announcement of the divestiture in the *Wall Street Journal*.

6. See Katherine Schipper and Abbie Smith, "Effects of Recontracting on Shareholder Wealth: The Case of Voluntary Spin-offs," *Journal of Financial Economics* 12 (1983); Gailen Hite and James Owers, "Security Price Reactions around Corporate Spin-off Announcements," *Journal of Financial Economics* 12 (1983); and J. Miles and J. Rosenfeld, "An Empirical Analysis of the Effects of Spin-off Announcements on Shareholder Wealth," *Journal of Finance* 38 (1983).

7. Although there are 76 carve-out announcements, there are actually 81 subsidiaries in the sample because four announcement dates account for nine subsidiaries. That is, three announcement dates involve two subsidiaries each and one date involves three subsidiaries. The number of parents (63) is also less than

the number of announcements because of multiple carve-outs by the same firm. The largest number of carve-out announcements by a single firm is three (by W.R. Grace); ten firms announced at least two carve-outs. Of the 81 subsidiaries in the announcement sample, eight were not carved-out during the sample period, which ends in December 1983. Thus, carve-outs of eight subsidiaries were announced and later cancelled. Details of the sample selection procedures can be found in Schipper and Smith [1986], cited in footnote 1.

8. While it is possible that a number of carve-outs occurred during 1973-1977 that we were not able to find, we do not think this is likely. Every initial public offering on the SEC's *Registrations and Offerings Statistics* tape for the years 1973-77 was checked and none was a carve-out by an NYSE or ASE listed firm.

9. See footnote 4 for full citations of the three studies of the market's response to announcements of seasoned equity offerings.

10. See Jay Ritter, "The 'Hot Issue' Market of 1980," *Journal of Business* 57 (1984).

11. The market value of parent common equity is measured by share price multiplied by the number of outstanding common shares at the end of the month preceding the carve-out announcement.

five years following that firm's announcement of a subsidiary equity offering. The share price reactions to these 39 announcements are measured by the abnormal stock returns (percentage price changes adjusted for general market movements) over the five-day period ending with the date of the *Wall Street Journal* announcement.

The market reactions to the 76 equity carve-out announcements in our sample were estimated by calculating abnormal stock returns over the five-day period leading up to the *Wall Street Journal* announcement.[12] In addition to measuring five-day returns, we also measured cumulative average abnormal stock returns for the 76 carve-out announcements over an 85-day period beginning 44 days before the *Wall Street Journal* announcement and ending 40 days after. (These returns are shown in Figure 1.) During the period starting 13 days before the announcement, the cumulative abnormal return drifts upward at an increasing rate from + 0.8 percent to + 4.95 percent at the announcement day. The cumulative abnormal return is nearly level in the subsequent eight weeks, ending with a value of + 4.45 percent 40 trading days after the announcement.

In the case of the 39 sample firms which issued either seasoned equity or convertible debt within five years of the carve-outs, the cumulative return drops from + 0.2 percent four days before the announcement of the offering of parent equity to −3.3 percent on the announcement day (see Figure 1). In the eight weeks following the announcement of the parent equity offering, the return drifts downward to −4.7 percent by 40 trading days after the announcement.[13]

The variation in the market reaction to both the sample of carve-out announcements and the sample of parent equity offering announcements is considerable. Abnormal returns at carve-out announcements range from −12.1 percent to +19.5 percent, with a median of +1.6 percent. About two-thirds of these returns (50 of 76) are positive. In contrast, about 69 percent of abnormal returns (27 of 39) at the announcement of parent equity offerings are negative. The median abnormal return for this sample is −2 percent, and the range is from −16 percent to +17.5 percent.[14]

Why, Then, The Different Market Response to Equity Carve-outs?

There are three differences between equity carve-outs and parent equity offerings which might account for the market's positive response to the former: (1) the separation of subsidiary investment projects from those of the parent firm for external financing; (2) the creation of a public market for subsidiary common stock; and (3) the restructuring of asset management and incentive contracts.

Separate Financing for Subsidiary Investments

An offering of seasoned parent equity simply increases the number of outstanding equity claims on the consolidated assets. In contrast, an initial subsidiary equity offering "carves out" the assets of the subsidiary from the assets of the original entity. Thus, an equity carve-out allows a subsidiary to obtain separate funding for subsidiary growth opportunities.[15] The equity securities publicly offered represent claims on the cash flows of the subsidiary projects only.

12. For details of the procedures used to compute abnormal returns and to perform statistical tests, see the appendix to Schipper and Smith [1986], cited in footnote 1.

13. t-tests for the significance of abnormal returns do not imply rejection at the .05 level (two-tailed) of the null hypothesis that the abnormal return is zero within the periods before or after the carve-out announcement. However, the t-statistic of + 2.55 in the five-day announcement period leads to rejection of the null hypothesis of zero abnormal returns at better than the .02 level (two-tailed). Similarly, the abnormal returns before and after the announcement of the parent equity offerings are not significantly different from zero at the .05 level (two-tailed). However, the abnormal return of − 3.5 percent in the five-day event period period is significantly different from zero at better than the .01 level (two-tailed).

The difference in the cumulative abnormal returns over the event period for the announcement of 76 subsidiary equity offerings versus 39 parent equity offerings is + 5.3 percent, significant at better than the .005 level (one-tailed). The average difference in the cumulative abnormal returns in the five-day event period for 26 matched pairs of subsidiary and parent equity offerings by the same firm is + 5.5 percent, also significant at better than the .005 level (one-tailed). For these pairwise comparisons, each subsidiary equity offering announcement is matched, if possible, with a parent equity offering announcement by the same company. If more than one parent equity offering was available for matching, priority was given to common stock over convertible debt offerings, and to proximity to the subsidi-

ary equity offering announcement date.

14. Previous tests of share price reactions to announcements of offerings of seasoned equity have used a two-day event period (e.g., Asquith and Mullins [1986], Dann and Mikkelson [1984], Masulis and Korwar [1986], and Mikkelson and Partch [1986], all cited earlier in footnote 4. Because many of our announcements refer to SEC filings, we use a five-day event period. A two-day period, however, is reasonable for the 37 *Wall Street Journal* announcements of intentions to undertake an equity carve-out. For this subsample, the average two-day abnormal return is + 1.2 per cent (t = 1.91) and the median two-day abnormal return is + 1.7 per cent. A binomial test of the null hypotheses of an equal portion of positive versus negative two-day event period abnormal returns results in a z-statistic of + 2.48, which is significant at the .007 level. In the entire sample, however, the two-day event period does not appear to capture the initial information release. For the entire sample of 37 intention announcements and 39 announcements that a registration statement has been filed, the two-day abnormal return is + .7 per cent (t = 1.59). These significance tests should be interpreted with caution, as they are not independent.

15. Other mechanisms for separate financing of investment projects include spin-offs and sales of limited partnership interests to finance research and development. In some cases, the tax code provides special incentives for the latter financing mechanism.

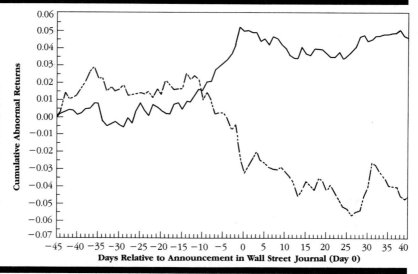

FIGURE 1
The Stock Market Response to Announcements of Equity Carve-Outs and Parent Equity Offerings

Cumulative abnormal returns for 76 equity carve-out announcements made during the period 1965-1983 are shown by the solid line. Cumulative abnormal returns for 39 seasoned equity offering announcements made by the same firms are shown by the broken line. Market model parameters are estimated for each sample firm over trading days -280 to -161 relative to the announcement in the *Wall Street Journal*.

If parent equity had instead been offered to finance the subsidiary's investment projects, the offered securities would represent a joint claim on both the parent and subsidiary projects. By separating the subsidiary projects from those of the parent, a carve-out may reduce the asymmetry of information between managers and investors about the asset base underlying the securities offered.[16]

The separate financing of subsidiary projects by an equity carve-out is expected to have a positive share price effect under either of two circumstances: (1) information is publicly revealed about the subsidiary's planned investment in a positive net present value project without negative implications about the value of the other assets of the consolidated firm; (2) separate financing implies that management will not forgo *future* positive net present value projects.

Support for viewing some carve-outs as a means of financing growth opportunities of the subsidiary apart from the parent company is found in the stated motives for our sample carve-outs. In the case of 59 of the 81 subsidiaries whose carve-outs were announced, we were able to find stated motives by reading annual reports, 10-Ks, registration statements, prospectuses and articles in the financial press. For 19 of these 59, at least part of the declared motivation was

to enable the subsidiary to obtain its own financing for expected growth.

Additional support for viewing some carve-outs as a means of financing growth opportunities of the subsidiary is found in the nature of some of the carve-outs. In six cases, registration statements or prospectuses described a specific growth opportunity to be funded with the proceeds of the subsidiary equity offering. For example, Interferon Sciences was formed by National Patent Development in 1981 to develop its interferon program. The parent contributed basic technology and patents, which were reported as having a book value of about $600,000 or $.20 per share. Shortly thereafter, 25 percent of Interferon Sciences was offered to the public at $10 a share; the proceeds were $10 million. The stated purpose of the offering was to finance the development of the interferon technology transferred by the parent to its subsidiary. Thus, Interferon Sciences represented primarily a growth opportunity, with virtually no assets-in-place. Other projects included investments in Atlantic City casinos, Hawaiian condominiums, oil drilling, and bioengineering products. In each case, the parent firm apparently rejected the option of funding the project by issuing parent equity and chose to offer separate equity claims on the growth

---

16. For a discussion of the information asymmetry financing problem, and why it may pay to fund growth opportunities separately from assets-in-place, see Stewart Myers and Nicholas Majluf, "Corporate Financing and Investment

Decisions When Firms Have Information That Investors Do Not Have," *Journal of Financial Economics* 9 (1984).

By making possible an equity investment in the subsidiary alone, the carve-out also increases the incentives of both individual investors and potential acquiring firms to gather and analyze information about subsidiary activities.

opportunity by means of a carve-out.

Assuming that one purpose of a carve-out is to finance investment projects, a measure of the relative size of those projects is the proceeds of the carve-out offering as a percentage of the market value of parent equity. This size measure, it turns out, is positively correlated with the share price reactions of parent firms; that is, the larger the carve-out as a percentage of the total equity of the consolidated company, the larger in general was the positive market reaction.[17]

To provide evidence of the anticipated growth of carved-out subsidiaries, we computed the P/E ratios of 70 subsidiaries with available data at the time of or immediately after the carve-out. Relative to their parent firms, the carved-out subsidiaries had high P/E ratios. The median subsidiary P/E ratio was 21.7 (after excluding negative values caused by losses). In contrast, the median contemporaneous P/E ratio of the parent firms was 15. For the 58 parent-subsidiary pairs with available P/E ratios, the subsidiary had the higher P/E ratio in 43 cases (74 per cent).[18]

Creation of a Public Market for Subsidiary Stock

An equity carve-out initiates public trading of the common stock of the previously wholly-owned subsidiary. The subsidiary is thus subject to all financial and other reporting requirements of public companies (for example, 10-Q and 10-K reports and proxy statements filed with the SEC, and annual reports issued to stockholders). These requirements can impose considerable costs on the parent company's stockholders. These costs consist of the direct costs of preparing audited financial statements and other required reports for the subsidiary, as well as any indirect costs of disclosing proprietary information to subsidiary competitors.

Such costs, however, may be more than offset by the benefits to parent stockholders of the increased supply of and demand for information about the

subsidiary's growth opportunities. The carve-out of subsidiary stock *commits* the subsidiary to supply audited periodic financial reports prepared in accordance with prescribed measurement and disclosure rules, as well as other nonfinancial information about firm activities (such as the information in proxy statements). By making possible an equity investment in the subsidiary alone, the carve-out also increases the incentives of both individual investors and potential acquiring firms to gather and analyze information about subsidiary activities. The increase in both the supply of and demand for information about the subsidiary may increase the perceived value of subsidiary stock to individual and corporate investors.

Such an improvement in investor understanding is cited as a motive for 14 equity carve-outs in our sample. It is also cited in a recent announcement by Perkin-Elmer Corporation of its plan to carve out and sell to the public up to 19 percent of its minicomputer business, which was named Concurrent Computer Corporation. According to a *Wall Street Journal* report, the chairman of Perkin-Elmer said the carve-out plan "is intended to improve the visibility of Perkin-Elmer computers and thus improve sales and help attract investors."[19]

Perkin-Elmer completed the equity carve-out in January 1986 and described its advantages to parent company shareholders in a full-page *Wall Street Journal* advertisement with the following copy:

Higher visibility and a sharp, singular focus will help Concurrent Computer Corporation attract and retain a strong, motivated management team. And lead to increased recognition in the financial community where shareholders will be able to benefit from its full potential.

As the Perkin-Elmer Data Systems Group, our computer business was not accorded its true value. Yet, in just one week after its initial offering, the market has placed Concurrent Computer Corporation's worth at nearly a quarter of a billion dollars— enriching Perkin-Elmer's ownership as the major shareholder.[20]

---

17. The Spearman rank correlation between our size measure and the five-day abnormal returns associated with carve-out announcements is .27, which is significant at better than the .05 level (two-tailed).

18. A Wilcoxon test of the null hypothesis that the two samples are drawn from populations with the same median generates a t-statistic of 3.83, leading to rejection of the null hypothesis at better than .01 probability level. Hence, subsidiary P/E ratios tend to exceed the P/E ratios of the corresponding parent firms. Furthermore, these high subsidiary P/E ratios cannot be explained by low levels of risk. Of the 23 sample subsidiaries with returns on the CRSP Daily Excess Returns Tape within two years after the equity carve-out, 14 (61 per cent) belong to the three highest of ten beta portfolios (6,5,3 respectively). It also is unlikely that the high P/E ratios can be attributed to the use of highly conservative accounting methods

to measure subsidiary earnings. Through 1982, earnings figure reported in subsidiary registration statements were not required to include such corporate costs as interest, taxes, amortization of purchased goodwill, and certain administrative costs. It was not until 1983 that the SEC issued "carve-out accounting" rules that require proportionate allocation of these corporate costs to the subsidiary's earnings statement. Hence it is likely that the high subsidiary P/E ratios in our sample are indicative of high anticipated growth in subsidiary earnings. However, the high P/E ratios may also reflect the low earnings figures of young firms due to high research and development expenses and depreciation charges.

19. From "Perkin-Elmer Organizes New Computer Firm," *Wall Street Journal*, November 14, 1985.

20. *Wall Street Journal*, February 19, 1986.

Of the 63 sample carve-out subsidiaries for which data are available, 59 (that is, 94 per cent) adopted incentive compensation plans based on the subsidiary's stock—generally stock option plans.

The Restructuring of Asset Management and Incentive Contracts

Many carve-outs are associated with a major restructuring of managerial responsibilities and incentives. Divisions are often regrouped into a new subsidiary for the public offering with a consequent realignment in the responsibilities of various managers. Furthermore, the incentive contracts of subsidiary managers are usually revised to incorporate subsidiary share prices and profits as measures of performance. Such internal structural shifts are seldom associated with seasoned equity offerings.

Stated motives for 11 of 59 sample subsidiaries mentioned a change in corporate focus through a restructuring program or a reduction by the parent of investment in the line of business of the carved-out subsidiary. Also worth noting is that 38 of the 73 carved-out subsidiaries (52 per cent) had been formed as little as one year before the carve-out.[21] The formation of the new subsidiaries typically involved combining the operations of existing units, divisions or subsidiaries under a single management. Finally, management responsibilities in 12 cases were changed to the extent that one or more persons resigned a top management position with the parent to become president or CEO of the subsidiary.

Two pieces of qualitative evidence suggest that changes in the incentives of subsidiary managers are important considerations in carve-outs. The first is 10 statements of motive which focus on the improvements in managerial incentives associated with a public market for subsidiary shares. For example, in W.R. Grace's explanation of its decision to carve out a

27 per cent interest in its El Torito restaurant chain, Charles Erhart, vice-chairman of Grace, said the environment at Grace inhibited the entrepreneurial style of El Torito's management. "These are people-sensitive businesses. They [El Torito management] are independent cats who need a piece of the action to motivate them."[22]

The second piece of evidence concerns the use of subsidiary share prices and profit figures in contracts with subsidiary managers. Of the 63 sample carve-out subsidiaries for which data are available, 59 (that is, 94 per cent) adopted incentive compensation plans based on the subsidiary's stock—generally stock option plans. Most of these adoptions occurred within one year of the carve-out. In addition, at least 23 subsidiaries adopted incentive plans based on subsidiary net income.

This evidence suggests that restructuring of managerial responsibilities and incentives is frequently associated with equity carve-outs. To the extent the market expects such restructuring to lead to improvements in management's efficiency in using corporate assets, we would expect a favorable share price reaction.[23]

After the Carve-Out

Carved-out subsidiaries often experience some form of change in ownership following the carve-out. For our entire sample of 73 carve-outs, all but 14 of the subsidiaries as of February 1986 had undergone further changes since the initial public offering.[24]

One common fate of carved-out subsidiaries is complete separation from the parent by one of the

---

21. Of the 32 subsidiaries in existence at least 1 year before the equity carve-out announcement, 17 had been previously acquired, 4 had been formed as part of a joint venture, and 11 were formed from existing divisions.

22. *Business Week*, December 19, 1983, contains additional information.

23. The principle of "informativeness," as developed by Shavell and by Holmstrom (See S. Shavell, "Risk Sharing and Incentives in the Principal and Agent Relationship" and B. Holmstrom, "Moral Hazard and Observability," both in the *Bell Journal of Economics* 10 (1979)), maintains that any (costless) variable which is marginally informative about an agent's actions can be used to increase the efficiency of the contract with the principal. Hence, if the subsidiary share price contains additional information about subsidiary managers' actions, agency theory suggests that the efficiency of managers' contracts can be improved by linking compensation to the subsidiary stock price performance.

This requirement does not appear to be overly restrictive. The aggregation of the parent company with the subsidiary company for purposes of equity market valuation and financial reporting (i.e., presentation of consolidated financial statements) is likely to result in loss of information about the subsidiary's management's production, investment, and financing decisions. The contracting gains which may result from disaggregating agent performance measures for unrelated operations is discussed in the context of responsibility accounting in the following study: S. Baiman and J. Demski, Economically Optimal Performance Evaluation and Control Systems," *Journal of Accounting Research* 18 (1980)

Supplement, 184-220. Although the performance of the subsidiary and the parent company may be measured separately with internal (managerial) accounting procedures even before the equity carve-outs, in general such "divisional" accounting measures are unlikely to contain all the information contained in the subsidiary share price with respect to subsidiary management's actions. On this last point, see D. Diamond and R. Verrecchia, "Optimal Managerial Contracts and Equilibrium Security Prices," *Journal of Finance* 37 (1982), 275-287.

24. At the time of the original carve-out announcement, the market does not appear to respond differently to those carve-outs which later undergo some kind of restructuring. For carve-outs announced before 1983, a Mann-Whitney test for differences in abnormal returns at announcements of carve-outs that were later restructured versus those that remain unchanged results in a z-statistic of .82, which is not significant at conventional levels. Thus, there is not an ex ante perceived difference, in terms of impact on shareholder wealth, between carve-outs that were later reacquired, divested, spun-off or liquidated and those that have not undergone some further ownership or structural change.

Parent firm share price reactions to announcements that subsidiaries are being divested or reacquired are small and positive. For a sample of eight divestiture announcements, the two-day average abnormal return is 2.8 percent (t = 1.88). For a sample of 13 reacquisition announcements, the two-day average abnormal return is 0.6 percent (t = .55). These results are consistent with little or no revision in market expectations associated with restructuring announcements.

The parent may have expected that the disclosure associated with a public market for subsidiary shares would eventually lead to a greater understanding (and thus willingness to pay a higher price) on the part of the potential acquirers.

following means: spin-off, purchase by the subsidiary of its stock held by the parent, leveraged buyout, sale to another firm, and bankruptcy/liquidation. Of the 73 carve-outs in our sample, 30 had separated from their parents by one of the above means as of February 1986 (see Table 1). Fifteen of these 30 separations involved the outright sale of the subsidiary to another firm. Four were acquired by management in leveraged buyouts (though all of these occurred after November 1984, reflecting the newness of the LBO phenomenon).

The length of the period between the carve-out and the separation varies considerably within our sample. Some separations occurred almost immediately (that is, within one or two years), while one divestiture occurred 19 years after the carve-out. The average period, however, is approximately four or five years for most of these changes.

The fact that so many carve-outs are followed by complete separation suggests that management may have originally intended the carve-out as a way of advertising the subsidiary—that is, as an intermediary stage in a process whose final goal was divestiture. The parent may have expected that the disclosure associated with a public market for subsidiary shares would eventually lead to a greater understanding (and thus willingness to pay a higher price) on the part of the potential acquirers.[25] For example, some insurance executives speculated that the 1985 carve-out of 49 per cent of Fireman's Fund by American Express was "a way to attract higher bids for a sale of its entire interest in Fireman's Fund."[26]

Only slightly less common than complete separation, however, is the reacquisition of carved-out subsidiaries by the parent. In our sample, 26 subsidiaries were reacquired and another reacquisition is pending. Why do companies reacquire carved-out subsidiaries? One possible explanation is that the original carve-out decision was a mistake. An alternative explanation, however, is that reacquisition is attractive if the objectives of the carve-out can be accomplished with only a temporary public market for sub-

sidiary shares. For example, the need for external equity financing of subsidiary growth will decline if the subsidiary's investment projects mature to the point where they generate sufficient profits for internal equity financing. The objective of informing individual investors and potential acquirers about a subsidiary's growth potential through audited subsidiary financial statements and other reports, as well as the increased incentives for private information collection, may be achieved by a temporary public market for subsidiary stock. Even the contracting gains associated with incorporating subsidiary stock price in the incentive contracts of subsidiary managers may be temporary.

One example of a carve-out followed quickly by a reacquisition proposal is the case of First Data Resources. American Express sold 25 per cent of First Data for $14 a share in September 1983, and announced a plan to reacquire the shares for $36 a share (27 times earnings) in August 1985. The reacquisition was announced as part of a plan to narrow the corporate focus on consumer financial services. While some analysts speculated that the reacquisition might imply that the original carve-out was a mistake, the president of American Express, Louis Gerstner, Jr. disputed this point by saying that the equity ownership taken by First Data management as part of the 1983 carve-out offering helped stimulate the subsidiary's rapid growth. (In the first six months of 1985, First Data's income was nearly 50 per cent higher than in 1984.)[27]

The MGM/UA carve-out of its Home Entertainment Group mentioned earlier in this article was also followed by a reacquisition. Late in 1984 MGM/UA proposed a reacquisition at $28 in notes or MGM/UA stock; the carve-out offering price was $12. It might be concluded from this proposal that the original purpose of the carve-out had been served and there was no longer a need for a public market for HEG stock.[28]

Subsequent ownership changes are easier to accomplish if the parent retains control of its carved-out subsidiary. In our sample, parent firms typically offered only a minority interest to the public, while

---

25. As stated in footnote 24 earlier, parent firm share price reactions to announcements that subsidiaries are being divested are small and positive. For a sample of eight divestiture announcements, the two-day average abnormal return is 2.8 percent (t = 1.88).

26. See "Fireman's Fund Stock Offer Set by Parent Firm," *Wall Street Journal*, June 26, 1985. The carve-out offering was completed in October 1985 at $27.75 a share. By February 25, 1986, Fireman's Fund stock was selling at about $37.75 a share; to capitalize on this gain, American Express announced a plan to offer as many as 10 million shares plus warrants for another 10 million shares. (See "American Express Plans to Reduce Stake in Fireman's Fund by Second Offering," *Wall Street Journal*, February 26, 1986).

27. See "American Express Seeks Rest of Concern," *Wall Street Journal*, August 22, 1985.

28. These reacquisitions often involve premia over the current market price of subsidiary shares or lawsuits by minority stockholders to increase the reacquisition price, or both. In the case of the Home Entertainment Group, settlement of a shareholder suit resulted in a reacquisition for $28 in cash (*Wall Street Journal*, April 24, 1985).

As mentioned in footnote 24, parent firm share price reactions to announcements that subsidiaries are being reacquired are small and positive. For a sample of 13 reacquisition announcements, the two-day average abnormal return is 0.6 percent (t = .55).

TABLE 1
Ownership Changes for 73 Subsidiaries Carved-Out During 1965–1983[1]

Reacquisition by parent	Number	Number of Years Between Carve-out and Event	
		Average	Range
Transaction complete	26	5.1	2–12
Proposal pending	2	5.5	5–6
Transaction proposed but failed	1	3	NA
Separation from parent			
Spin-off or purchase by subsidiary of its shares held by parent	7	5	1–12
Leveraged buyout complete or pending	4	3.5	1–5
Sale to another firm	15	6.7	1–19
Bankruptcy or liquidation	4	3.75	1–7
	59[2]		

[1] These data cover the period from the carve-out announcement through February 1986.
[2] We found no information for five subsidiaries. Nine subsidiaries (of which eight were carved-out in 1983) have had no ownership changes.

retaining a majority or supermajority interest. Some of the parent companies in our sample also maintain control over the carved-out subsidiary by creating a special class of stock which increases the parent's voting power. For example, the parent might create and hold 100 per cent of class B common stock carrying four votes while issuing common stock with one vote in a carve-out. These kinds of special stock arrangements were found in 15 of the 73 subsidiaries in our sample.

Besides facilitating ownership changes, there are two other advantages to the parent of maintaining a majority or supermajority voting interest in a carved-out subsidiary. First, effective control allows any existing operating and/or financial synergies to be maintained (although it is possible that the absence of operating synergies, in many cases, is an important motive for the carve-out in the first place). Second, 80 per cent voting control of the subsidiary is required if the subsidiary is to be consolidated for tax purposes. Tax consolidation is beneficial if operating losses or tax credits which would otherwise go unused by either the parent or subsidiary can be used to offset taxable income of the more profitable firm, thereby reducing taxes to the consolidated entity.

The benefits of tax consolidation were cited in the case of Trans World Corporation's 1983 carve-out of its airline subsidiary. After the carve-out, public ownership was 19 per cent of the common stock and 5 per cent of the voting control (the parent retained preference shares with 10 votes apiece). Because the airline subsidiary generated both tax losses and investment tax credits that could be used to shield earnings of other units from taxation (as long as a consolidated tax return was filed), this arrangement was described as "having cake and eating it too."[29] Presumably, the "cake" came from the $78 million cash generated by the offering, which permitted the subsidiary to purchase new equipment, especially Boeing 767's.

Summary and Conclusions

We recently completed a study of 76 equity carve-out announcements by public companies traded on the New York and American Stock Exchanges. Our results indicate that in the five-day period culminating with the announcement of such carve-outs, the stock prices of parent companies announcing the carve-outs outperformed the market by almost 2 percent on average; the size of the average reaction is a positive 4 to 5 percent if an additional two weeks preceding the announcement are included.

In contrast, announcements of public offerings of parent common stock and convertible debt by a subset of the same companies have been associated

---

29. See "Let Them Eat Stock," *Forbes*, April 25, 1983.

with average shareholder losses of over 3 percent. Such a negative reaction to announcements of *parent* equity offerings is consistent, furthermore, with prior research on the stock price effects of changes in outstanding equity through public sale or repurchase of common stock and convertible debt, debt conversion, and exchange offers to current security holders.[30] Initial public offerings of subsidiary stock are thus the only means of raising outside equity capital (of which we are aware) which appear to communicate a positive signal to the stock market.

How do we account for this difference in the market's response to announcements of carve-outs and seasoned equity offerings?

An equity carve-out, first of all, allows public investment in subsidiary growth opportunities apart from an investment in the parent's assets. Such a security, by offering investors a "pure play," may have scarcity value if such opportunities are typically buried within a conglomerate structure.

A partial public offering also appears to offer an effective means of overcoming the financing problem caused by the potential information gap between insiders and public investors which appears to make conventional equity offerings quite expensive. Still another possibility is that the equity carve-out may improve public understanding of the subsidiary's growth opportunities. By making the subsidiary a public company, the carve-out may increase the supply of and demand for information about the subsidiary. Periodic, audited financial statements prepared by the subsidiary in accordance with regulations are issued to the public. Investors accordingly may have added incentives to analyze publicly available data and to search for private information about the subsidiary because of the new opportunity to trade subsidiary stock. Also, the readily observable market price of subsidiary stock may attract an acquiring firm and facilitate negotiations concerning the purchase price. If such an increased flow of information increases the perceived value of subsidiary stock to individual or corporate investors, it may partially explain the more favorable share price response to equity carve-outs than to parent equity offerings.

Alternatively, the market may be saying that the conglomerate is an inefficient organizational structure for capitalizing on such growth opportunities, and for providing the entrepreneurial climate necessary to do so. Equity carve-outs often are associated with a major restructuring of managers' responsibilities and incentive contracts, and the market may associate such restructuring with improvements in management's efficiency in putting corporate assets to their most valuable uses.

---

30. See footnote 4 earlier for a review of this research, or see Clifford Smith's "Raising Capital," which appears at the beginning of this issue.

FINANCING NETWORK ORGANIZATIONS

by John W. Kensinger,
University of North Texas,
and John D. Martin,
University of Texas at Austin

Most large firms are not large, single station facilities... Large size is the result of joining a series of stations within a single administrative entity...The interfaces between stations could instead be mediated by market exchanges.

—Oliver Williamson[1]—

I n the above statement, Oliver Williamson points squarely at a question that has fueled a long and spirited debate among practitioners as well as theorists of corporate organization. Namely, are markets more efficient than management hierarchies in organizing business activities? If a collection of independent companies operates far more efficiently than the same group under a large bureaucracy, then management hierarchies must eventually give way—if not to completely separate firms, then at least to looser decentralized structures.

But why have large integrated corporations at all? Economist Ronald Coase offered the classic explanation more than 50 years ago, arguing that large, integrated companies are justified by the "transactions costs" savings that result from combining smaller operations into larger ones.[2] Such savings come in a variety of obvious ways, such as reductions in legal and administrative fees as well as any "excess profits" accruing to "middlemen" along the value-added chain. But the savings can also take a more subtle form, such as the gains from specialization afforded by bringing together wealthy investors with professional managers (although, as we will see later, the resulting separation of ownership from control can have significant costs as well as benefits). Professional managers, as Williamson himself ar-

gued, are also likely to have some information advantages over outside investors (although this, too, may be a mixed blessing).

But, when the information gap between management and investors narrows, and when new technologies tip the balance toward smaller, more flexible organizations, once cost-effective management hierarchies become an unnecessary burden. And new technologies in manufacturing, information handling, and communications are indeed shifting the balance between hierarchies and markets. In the days of mass production of uniform products, manufacturers were driven by scale economies to integrate marketing and distribution functions to ensure a steady flow of goods. Yet, with new developments in computer-aided design and factory automation, the primary need is for a quick response to the changing demands of customers, and for custom-designed products designed to accommodate a growing range of individual tastes.

Today, of course, anti-takeover laws, HLT restrictions, and other regulatory measures designed to curb financial market "excesses" are slowing the pace of change. Yet such artificial barriers cannot stop, but can only delay, the fundamental technological and economic forces that have shaped the restructurings of the past decade.

1. Oliver Williamson, "The Organization of Work: A Comparative Institutional Assessment," *Journal of Economic Behavior and Organization* 1 (1980) pp. 5-38 (quote from p. 11).

2. Ronald H. Coase, "The Nature of the Firm," *Economica N.S.* 4 (1937), 386-405. Reprinted in G.J. Stigler and K.E. Boulding (eds.) *Readings in Price Theory* (Homewood, IL: Richard D. Irwin, 1952).

As competitive pressures have led to greater specialization, independent companies have drawn together in tightly coordinated liaisons that provide resources in such distinct activities as product design, production, marketing, and distribution.

In an article titled "The Incredible Shrinking Company," *The Economist* recently put the case as follows: "One way or another, information technology may force the successful big firm of tomorrow to look more and more like a confederacy of small ones."[3] Such a "confederacy" has come to be known as a *network organization*, a hybrid organizational form that combines some of the coordinating functions of integrated hierarchies with a decentralized structure of independent firms spread all along the value-added chain. Although the participants are independent companies, they form relationships for mutual benefit—typically coordinated by a "strategic" broker[4]—that make the individual firms cohere into something more than a loose assembly of arm's-length traders. For example, as competitive pressures have led to greater specialization, independent companies have drawn together in tightly coordinated liaisons that provide resources in such distinct activities as product design, production, marketing, and distribution. Some network organizations are relatively stable relationships known as "strategic partnerships" or "value-adding partnerships" (VAPs). Others, called "dynamic networks," are temporary, finite-lived associations that grow up in fast-changing environments such as consumer electronics and apparel.[5]

Changing organizational forms present new financing requirements, and the methods for financing network activities are very different from those commonly used to fund corporate hierarchies. Whereas corporations have indefinite lifespans supported in part by a strong base of permanent equity capital, network organizations are finite-lived, can thrive upon temporary capital, and often use debt extensively. Where integrated corporations accumulate extensive asset holdings, small business units within network organizations avoid asset ownership and instead simply contract for the use of equipment or other assets as needed.[6] Moreover, these business units also take advantage of a financing trend called asset "securitization": They rent space in investor-owned buildings, are willing clients for equipment leasing partnerships, and are likely to use their trade receivables as collateral for financing.

THE HOW AND WHY OF NETWORK ORGANIZATIONS

There are strong competitive pressures propelling a continued evolution toward increasingly smaller, specialized firms—firms that in turn form cooperative relationships with other independent specialists.[7] Network organizations combine the scale economies of large organizations with the adaptability of small ones in a seemingly limitless variety of ways. Moreover, they can often be more flexible and responsive than in-house operations. For example, Lewis Galoob Toys, makers of Micro Machines and other popular toys, can tap independent inventors for new designs, contract for production by "partner" factories in Hong Kong, and then hit the shelves in cities across the nation—all in a matter of weeks from start to finish. To achieve this global capability, Galoob relies on only about a hundred employees of its own.[8]

In one sense, of course, networking is nothing new. It has long been the norm in the construction industry, where general contractors routinely serve as brokers for networks of specialized subcontractors. It also represents the further development of an already pronounced corporate trend toward "outsourcing." Ford Motor Company, once so thoroughly integrated it made its own steel, now outsources over half of the components for its cars; and the Japanese-run auto plants in the U.S. outsource half again as much. Not only Ford, but also corporations such as Motorola, Northrop, Apple Computer, and Schlage Lock, to name a few, are taking advantage of the inherent flexibility and responsiveness of such liaisons to enhance their competitiveness in the global economy.

The inherent operational flexibility of network organizations makes them attractive to line manage-

---

3. "The Incredible Shrinking Company," *The Economist*, December 15, 1990, p. 66.

4. In an article entitled "The Coming of the New Organization," Peter Drucker recently compared the role of the generalist in one of today's professional organizations with the conductor of a symphony orchestra, who does not know how to play all of the individual instruments, but who coaxes exquisite order out of the efforts of the individual players. See Peter F. Drucker, "The Coming of the New Organization," *Harvard Business Review* (January-February 1988).

5. For a detailed description of network organizations and predictions for their future role, see Raymond E. Miles and Charles C. Snow, "Network Organizations: New Concepts for New Forms," *California Management Review* (Spring 1986), pp. 62f.

6. Peter Bison, "Ownership Isn't Always the Best Strategy," *Wall Street Journal*, December 5, 1988.

7. Russell Johnston and Paul Lawrence, "Beyond Vertical Integration-the Rise of the Value-Adding Partnership," *Harvard Business Review* (July-August 1988).

8. For more information on Galoob and other networks, see "And Now, the Post-Industrial Corporation," *Business Week*, March 3, 1986, pp. 64-71.

ment, but another kind of flexibility makes them especially valuable to investors. Networks not only possess the capability to expand rapidly by adding new partners; but perhaps even more important, they can disband quickly and easily when the job is done. At that point, the individual firms simply go their separate ways and enter new relationships in pursuit of further opportunities. As suggested earlier, when the group effort is focused upon an ongoing process, the network can be stable for many years. But when efforts are focused on specific projects, networks can be dissolved when the project ends.

Network organizations, moreover, don't suffer from the separation of ownership from control that troubles many large corporations. The top managers in network member firms typically have large equity stakes that provide them with the right incentives—both to invest capital when the returns are promising, but also to return that capital to investors when the expected returns fall below competitive levels.

By contrast, a large integrated corporation may be able to grow quickly, but shrinks only with great difficulty, impounding its resources and delaying their redeployment to higher-valued uses. Management's reluctance to shrink the size of their companies is all too clear in Harvard Professor Gordon Donaldson's detailed study of twelve large Fortune 500 firms. The managers he observed did not try to maximize shareholders' wealth, but instead sought to maximize "corporate wealth," defined as "the aggregate purchasing power available to management for strategic purposes during any given planning period." "This wealth," Donaldson continues,

consists of the stocks and flows of cash and cash equivalents (primarily credit) that management can use at its discretion to implement decisions...In practical terms it is cash, credit, and other corporate purchasing power by which management commands goods and services. [9]

This management proclivity for growth often comes at the expense of stockholders, who would often prefer to have excess capital returned to them.[10]

Yet, however costly to stockholders, this management orientation does not necessarily constitute crass self-interest on the part of managers, who understandably feel commitments to many other corporate stakeholders besides the investors who contributed capital.[11] Managers are typically far closer to the corporation's employees, for example, than to investors. Likewise, they feel closer ties to their host community than to a faceless and widely dispersed group of stockholders. Moreover, many corporate executives are undoubtedly sincere in their conviction that building long-lived corporate institutions is best for the stockholders in the long run, even in the absence of confirmation from the stock market in the short run.[12]

Nevertheless, as we learned from the 1980s, there are limits to investors' willingness to provide capital for companies that consistently fail to maximize value. Network organizations correct this problem facing many large, especially diversified, companies by concentrating equity ownership in the hands of a few key players.

In so doing, networks also address another problem confronting our largest companies. In a recent cover story in *The Atlantic*, Harvard Professor Robert Reich argues that big U.S. companies are today threatened by their inability to hold onto what is increasingly becoming their most valuable asset: "human capital." The combination of flexibility and equity ownership provided by network organizations provides an ideal solution to the problem of containing fluid "human capital." Networks are perfectly designed to harness the talents of entrepreneurs—and then, when the appointed task is completed, to release them back into the marketplace. For example, an investor need not set up an integrated corporation to fabricate and market a new product. Instead, a network of independent specialists can be formed to accomplish this task.

The current legal environment is also playing a role in the decline of hierarchies. As the years pass, a traditional corporation assumes a growing burden of potential liabilities stemming from the actions of employees long-since retired or moved on.[13] In the

9. Gordon Donaldson, *Managing Corporate Wealth* (New York: Praeger, 1984) pp. 3 and 22.

10. Michael C. Jensen, "Agency Cost of Free Cash Flow, Corporate Finance, and Takeovers," *American Economic Review* (May 1986).

11. Bradford Cornell and Alan Shapiro, "Corporate Stakeholders and Corporate Finance," *Financial Management* 16, (Spring 1987), pp. 5-14.

12. John G. Smale, "What About Shareowner's Responsibility?" *Wall Street Journal*, October 16, 1987.

13. For example, Dow Chemical Company now faces substantial potential liabilities stemming from Sarabond, a bonding agent used in mortar. Whole building facades and tunnel interiors built with Sarabond in the 'Sixties are crumbling as a result of an apparent flaw in the product. Even though Dow sold its rights to Sarabond in 1976, it is still potentially liable. *Wall Street Journal*, March 21, 1989, p. A1.

Whereas corporations have indefinite lifespans supported in part by a strong base of permanent equity capital, network organizations are finite-lived, can thrive upon temporary capital, and often use debt extensively.

face of such large and indeterminate liabilities, it is rational for business organizations to have lifespans that more closely parallel those of the people whose energy and drive give them life.[14] In short, as the trend toward substantial employee ownership progresses, more enterprises will continue to operate as small independent firms—companies with finite lives (and thus somewhat definable liabilities) along with an identity tied to the people who give them substance.

IN FINANCING NETWORK ORGANIZATIONS, FORM FOLLOWS FUNCTION

The Putting-Out System

Modern network brokers have rediscovered a cooperative system well-known to historians, the "putting out" system. In this simplest of all network financing arrangements, the network broker provides financial assistance to fabricators by providing raw materials to be paid for when the finished goods are delivered. Historians refer to such arrangements as the *Verlagsystem*, which fueled the rapid growth of the cottage textile industry in rural Europe beginning in the 13th century.[15] In this system, a merchant (*Verleger*) "puts out" work by providing an artisan with raw materials and a partial wage, followed by full settling-up upon delivery of the finished goods.

Modern high-tech network brokers have rediscovered the putting-out system. For example Novella Systems Inc., a semiconductor equipment company, booked $51 million of sales in 1989 with only seven employees in its own production facilities. This productivity was achieved by outsourcing component production to several strategic partners. According to Novellus president, Robert Graham, if a supplier needs financial help in order to provide just-in-time delivery, "We'll buy the inventory and sell it back to them. They don't pay until it's delivered as finished product."[16]

Credit Support by Purchase Orders

Another straightforward alternative is available when the broker has well-established credit. In that case, the broker provides credit support by means of contracts to purchase components or services from other members of the network. Network members who possess relatively little borrowing power on their own can tap substantial debt financing when it is underwritten by purchase orders from a government agency or major corporation that serves as the network hub. But if no such deep-pocketed sponsor is involved directly within the network, credit for the members can instead be supported by a financial institution that becomes part of the network.

In Eli Whitney's time, for example, financing the War Department's network of musket-building contractors was simplicity itself. The government issued a purchase order, which served as solid collateral for the loans needed to buy materials and pay wages while the work was in progress. The government did not have to pay, however, until the goods were delivered and accepted. Thus the lenders' risk arose only from the possibility that the contractor would not be able to complete the order and pay its bills. So the task of credit analysis came down to assessing the contractor's capacity to accomplish the job on schedule without cost overruns.

The lenders had no recourse to the government. Furthermore, the financing arrangements supported just the activities necessary to fulfill a particular order, and were settled in full upon completion of the job. The capital provided by the financiers was not automatically rolled over into new activities of the contractor (as is the case, of course, with corporate equity financings). Instead, financing for further orders had to be negotiated anew.

Today Motorola uses the same basic procedure in its acquisition of micro-chip manufacturing equipment. Needing radically new equipment for producing and testing semiconductors to stay competitive in the fiercely-contested global market, Motorola has developed strategic partnerships with several small but well-established makers of specialty equipment. Rather than trying to develop an in-house capability to produce such machines, Motorola continues to focus on its own distinctive areas of expertise. At the same time, however, it does not wait passively until the equipment it needs is developed by other companies. Instead, Motorola engineers meet regularly with partner companies to generate concepts for innovative equipment. The partners in turn

---

14. John Kensinger and John Martin, "Assets as Hostage: Optimal Bonding of Corporate Activities," Department of Finance Working Paper, University of Texas at Austin, 1990.

15. Fernand Braudel, *The Wheels of Commerce* (New York: Harper & Row, 1979) p. 316.

16. Quoted in "Factory of the Future," *INC.*, August 1990, p. 72.

develop the concepts into working machines, and Motorola serves as the testbed.

Motorola contracts to buy the "first fruits" of these efforts, which generally amount to at least the first year's production capabilities of its partners. Afterwards, the partners are free to sell equipment in the open market. As long as the cycle of innovation continues, however, Motorola maintains a crucial lead on its competitors. Also important, its partners have an incentive to protect Motorola's confidential information to maintain the special relationship. At the same time, the partners have a large potential market for their products. Thus all members benefit from the partnership.

In such arrangements, the network broker's risks are contained. Once specifications are agreed upon, Motorola issues a purchase order and the strategic partners arrange their own financing. Armed with their purchase orders, the contractors (most of whom are not publicly held) have the ability to obtain large-scale financing without expanding their permanent equity base. Lenders, however, have no recourse to Motorola should a contractor not be able to deliver. Thus, the risks associated with progressing from concept to factory floor are transferred away from the network hub—in this case, Motorola—making it easier for the company's engineers to gain consent from corporate headquarters to get involved in such projects. Motorola, moreover, need not arrange financing until the working machinery is ready; and its obligation does not affect its balance sheet until the goods are delivered.

Project Financing

When all obligations within the network are spelled out clearly in the form of binding purchase orders, it may even be possible to arrange a project financing. Project finance is a special case of network financing—one in which it is possible to organize the enterprise as a separate legal entity such as a general partnership, limited partnership, or limited-purpose corporation. Since the beginning of 1987, over $36 billion worth of project financings have been announced by underwriters.

Such arrangements differ fundamentally from traditional corporate financing in two significant ways: (1) the legal entity that houses the project is finite-lived, with its identity defined by a specific project; and (2) the cash flows generated by the project are paid out directly to the investors, who make the reinvestment decisions themselves. That is, unlike the traditional integrated corporation, management does not have the "first option" in deciding how to reinvest the project's cash flows.

When the project entity borrows, the creditors have recourse only to the assets and cash flows of the project itself, and not to the sponsors. The use of debt in a project financing is thus comparable to the issuance of revenue bonds by a municipality, with payments restricted to the proceeds from a particular set of user fees or tax revenues; and a project's viability as an independent financial entity likewise depends upon the reliability of the projected revenue stream. Therefore, project financings are possible only when there are enough contractual commitments from the members of the network to provide credit support for the project entity.

In electric power generation project financings, for example, lenders generally require that a project meet certain key criteria. The project should not require the use of any new or untested technology. Construction contracts should be available from reliable contractors on a fixed-price, turnkey basis, with performance bonding provided. Once up and running, the facilities should have low operational manpower requirements, and adherence to performance criteria should be enforceable. Fuel supplies must be available under long-term contracts. Finally, output must typically be "pre-sold" in the form of long-term, fixed-price purchase contracts.

Such extensive contracting provides hedges against most risks, except for the credit risks of the counterparties. The major banks and institutional investors that finance such projects are equipped to evaluate the risks, however, and have demonstrated their willingness to make substantial loans on a limited recourse basis.

General Electric Capital Corporation offers an example of the possibilities for innovative applications of project financing. It recently announced formation of a new group specializing in project financing for the construction and operation of independent industrial facilities. In one of its first projects, GE Capital arranged $105 million of limited-recourse project financing to build the BevPak beverage container plant. BevPak was founded in January 1988 by a former USX executive. The Monticello, Indiana plant makes beverage cans, but is independent of any beverage producer. BevPak now has three state-of-the-art production lines running with capacity of 1,600 steel beverage cans per minute each, giving it an annual capacity of 2 billion cans (about 40% of the total steel beverage can output in the U.S.). It has contracts with Coca-Cola and Pepsi for as much as 20% of their canning needs. It also has a contract with Miller Brewing Company, and Anheuser-Busch is considering a switch to its steel cans. BevPak's competitive edge comes not only from the economies of automation, but also from its ability to take advantage of the lower cost of tin-plated steel cans as compared to aluminum. It also has the flexibility to switch to aluminum should the relative price of aluminum drop.[17]

Much of the risk associated with financing such a large and highly-automated plant arises from uncertainty about whether it will be able to operate at full capacity. Independent ownership enables BevPak to enter into contracts to supply competing beverage makers, giving it the flexibility to operate at a profitable level of output without depending on any single brand's success. For a proprietary bottler, moreover, entering into long-term agreements for a portion of the output from such a large-scale plant is a cost-effective alternative to building a smaller one in-house.

Minority Equity Stakes

When credit support is not forthcoming, there is yet another alternative to internal expansion. Several companies have filled the void by taking minority equity positions in start-up companies.

For example, Hewlett-Packard holds an equity stake in Conductus Inc., a closely-held Silicon Valley start-up that produces superconducting chips. Conductus has invented new equipment for forming brittle superconducting ceramics into the thin films needed to make micro-chips. A Hewlett-Packard official was quoted as saying, "Research in superconductors is better done by small companies such as Conductus. It's a very valuable relationship for us."[18]

Conductus was founded in September 1987 by venture capitalists, soon after break-throughs were announced in high-temperature super-conductivity. Hewlett-Packard took a minority stake in 1988. Conductus quickly wooed top researchers from around the U.S., including scientists and lab managers from IBM and Rockwell. Its advisory board

includes top scientists from universities such as Stanford and Berkeley.

In July 1990 Conductus announced the opening of its new factory in Sunnyvale, California to produce custom chips at the rate of 25,000 per year, for which it has orders from seven companies. By that time, total investment in the company stood at $11.5 million. Japanese companies, by comparison, remain well behind in this race toward commercialization after pouring hundreds of millions of dollars into similar efforts.

Several other large corporations that cannot keep the brightest researchers happy within the confines of their own hierarchical organizations are also providing seed capital for new ventures. For example, in a recent interview Monsanto's CEO Richard J. Mahoney stated, "Monsanto decided it wanted to be in the biotechnology and pharmaceutical business many years ago. In fact, we were helping start up a number of these companies with venture capital."[19]

IBM also holds equity stakes in small research firms, such as Plessey-Corning Optical, based in Thousand Oaks, California. Started a decade ago as a joint venture between a British electronics firm and Corning Glass Company to develop applications for fiber-optic cable, the company is now owned by employees, Corning, and IBM. It remains small and independent, but its engineers maintain close relationships with its bigger partners.

Such links have even been forged among publicly-traded corporations seeking world-class competitiveness through specialization. In July 1990, NYSE-listed Cummins Engine announced the sale of a 27% equity stake to three of its strategic partners: Ford Motor Company, Tenneco, and Japan's Kubota Ltd.[20] Ford and Tenneco each received a seat on Cummins' board, and all three got special voting, standstill, and other provisions extending for six years. With 10.2 million shares of Cummins stock outstanding at a market price of $50.75 per share, Ford paid $100 million for 1.6 million newly-issued shares (at a price of $62.50 per share), with an option to buy more—enough to increase its stake to as much as 20% of Cummins stock. Ford, which already buys heavy-duty truck engines from Cummins, also signed a long-term agreement to purchase medium-range

17. *Wall Street Journal*, June 8, 1989, p.B1.
18. Stephen Yoder, "Chip Maker Gets a Jump on Japanese," *Wall Street Journal*, July 12, 1990, p. B1.

19. "Richard J. Mahoney Reshapes Monsanto for the Future," *DH&S Review*, Deloitte Haskins & Sells, December 9, 1985, pp. 1-3.
20. *Wall Street Journal*, July 16, 1990, p. A3.

diesel engines for its light trucks. Since Ford sells about 48,000 such trucks annually, the agreement represents several hundred million dollars of new business for Cummins. Ford, which previously made its own engines, was attracted by Cummins' improved technologies.

Tenneco, whose J.I. Case farm equipment unit already is engaged in a 50-50 joint venture with Cummins, also is paying $100 million for 1.6 million new shares. Although it did not purchase an option to buy more shares, Tenneco reportedly anticipates additional opportunities to expand its partnership with Cummins.

Kubota invested $50 million in return for 800,000 shares. Cummins currently manufactures Kubota-designed generators for the U.S. market under a licensing agreement, and the companies are discussing a joint venture to manufacture Kubota engines in Europe.

The board seats, options, and other provisions partially explain the partners' willingness to pay a premium over market value. More important, however, the new capital has strengthened a strategic partner expected to contribute significantly to their future success. The $250 million capital infusion has bolstered Cummins' financial position significantly, and the substantial equity stake in the hands of the three partners provides a defense against unwanted suitors who might divert Cummins' expertise to the benefit of their competitors.[21]

R&D Partnerships

A special case of project financing arises when a research and development objective can be defined as a finite project rather than an ongoing sequence of effort. In that case, R&D limited partnership (RDLP) financing may be attractive. For example, Genentech's clinical partnerships financed the company's research into anti-cancer agents as well as human and animal growth hormones. Also, in 1984, Cummins Engine used RDLP financing to raise $20 million to fund research on a new genera-

tion of hybrid diesel engine—one that would combine ceramic turbines and pistons as sources of power in a single powerplant. Indeed, some of its investors were corporate customers who would benefit from the new technology in ways far beyond their share of partnership income. Thus R&D limited partnership financing offers another means of equity infusion.

Indeed, RDLPs lend themselves readily to financing joint ventures. For example, NaTec Ltd, a 50-50 partnership between CRS Sirrine and Industrial Resources, Inc. was recently formed to develop a process that will use nahcolyte (a mineable, naturally-occurring form of sodium bicarbonate) to clean up the emissions from coal-fired power plants.[22] The process promises to be cheaper and more efficient than current techniques. Industrial Resources (IR) owns leases to large deposits of nahcolyte, but is an over-the-counter company with practically no sales or operations. It has limited sources of financing, and no presence in the power generation industry. CRS Sirrine, however, is a NYSE-listed construction and engineering company that builds and upgrades power plants. The potential benefits to both parties are obvious.

RDLP financing has grown rapidly since the first one was formed in 1978. We can account for $3.7 billion worth of RDLP financings since then, involving 239 separate projects.[23] Although the tax reforms of 1984 and 1986 ended some abuses involving RDLPs, Robert A. Stanger Associates (the rating agency for limited partnerships) reports continued use of RDLP financing. Nor has the Revenue Enhancement Act of 1987 squelched investors' desire to own a "pure play" in high-tech research.[24] Since January 1987, we know of more than $700 million worth of RDLPs. For example, Amgen announced an $84 million RDLP in 1987, Nova Pharmaceuticals sponsored a $42 million RDLP in 1988, Genentech backed a $72 million RDLP in 1989, and Synergen announced a $52.5 million RDLP in February of this year. Since the tax reforms, most R&D limited partnerships have been all-equity private place-

21. Moreover, the stock market endorsed this strategic alliance by raising Cummins' stock price by about 7% on the announcement, while Ford's and Tenneco's stock remained little changed. In NYSE trading Friday, July 13 (the date of the press release) Cummins rose 50¢ from $50.75, Ford rose 25¢ from $44, and Tenneco rose 12.5¢ from $69.50. On Monday, July 16 Cummins rose another $3.125 to $54.375, Ford dropped 62.5¢ to $43.625, and Tenneco rose another 12.5¢ to $60.75. The S&P 500 rose 0.51% on Friday, and 0.45% on Monday.

22. *Wall Street Journal*, July 27, 1988, p. 4.

23. Andrew H. Chen, John W. Kensinger, and John D. Martin, "Integration Without Merging: Project Financing," Department of Finance Working Paper, University of Texas at Austin, 1991.

24. For more complete discussion of RDLP financing, see John D. Martin and John W. Kensinger, "An Economic Analysis of R&D Limited Partnerships," in Stern, Stewart, and Chew (eds.), *Corporate Restructuring and Executive Compensation* (Cambridge, Mass: Ballinger Publishing Company, 1989) pp. 265-284. See also John W. Kensinger and John D. Martin, "Project Financing for Research and Development," *Research in Finance* Vol.8, JAI Press, 1990, pp. 119-148.

The combination of flexibility and equity ownership provided by network organizations provides an ideal solution to the problem of containing fluid "human capital." Networks are perfectly designed to harness the talents of entrepreneurs.

ments; but they are nonetheless project-oriented entities with finite lives.

Technology Marketing Partnerships

Investment bankers who underwrite RDLPs often serve as network brokers, finding manufacturing and marketing partners for corporations sponsoring the research. Recent experiments with partnership forms of organization may be laying the foundations for a new way of financing the marketing and distribution efforts of network organizations. Starting in the early 1980s, with strong encouragement and support from the U.S. Department of Commerce, some firms have been experimenting with limited partnerships formed for the purpose of promoting and marketing a specific product. Energy Sciences Corporation offers an example. It developed a data networking system that sends data via low-frequency radio signals over existing phone or power lines while leaving normal utility services undisturbed. The development was funded through an R&D limited partnership, with the marketing campaign financed by what it calls a "technology marketing partnership."[25]

These marketing partnerships are formed for the purpose of bringing a specific product or group of products to market. The partnership owns the trademark and brandname supported by its advertising, and has an exclusive distributorship for the product. The general partner may manufacture the product, or contract the manufacturing to a third party. The general partner also contracts with third parties for advertising and promotion. The partnership earns revenues from royalties or commissions paid out of sales by the manufacturer. It may also be set up such that the manufacturer has an option to buy out the distributorship for a lump sum.

In addition to the tax advantages generated by these arrangements, they also afford a finite-lived organizational alternative to the integrated corporation, allowing investors to enjoy limited liability without relinquishing long-term control over their capital to managers. Through a combination of RDLPs and technology marketing partnerships, a network broker serving as general partner can coordinate product development, manufacturing, distribution, and marketing.

MERCHANT BANKERS AS NETWORK BROKERS

Trading securities is perhaps the most competitive game in the world, and it is generally considered a matter of luck if an investor "beats the market" consistently. Investors seeking superior performance are therefore turning over more of their capital to "merchant bankers"—that is, people who raise funds to invest directly in real markets for products and services. Unlike passive investment in relatively efficient financial markets, direct investment in real products and services markets allows merchant bankers to exploit much greater inefficiencies—and hence promise considerably higher expected returns to the investors they represent. Bankers and financiers who know the capabilities of a variety of specialized business units, and who can recognize common interests and effectively coordinate aspects of their activities, can use their capital far more profitably than in either normal passive investment or active securities trading. These financiers are actively engaged in choosing which fields offer the greatest potential, as well as selecting the business units with the best skills for the chosen tasks. At the same time, though, they remain passive for tax purposes because they are not directly involved in producing or distributing goods.

Merchant bankers have comparative advantages as network brokers. They combine access to capital with proprietary data bases on individual companies that enable them to evaluate not only creditworthiness, but also operational capabilities. In addition, financial experts who have gained experience in analyzing specialized types of projects enjoy economies of scale in evaluating other similar projects. For example, the single largest category of project financings in the past decade is for electric power generation plants, which are virtually "cookie cutter" projects. They involve proven technologies and, because one plant is very similar to another, a little study goes a long way.

If financing by purchase orders or project financing is not feasible, significant financing can still be arranged with the backing of a letter of credit from a solid financial institution. Thus, a merchant banker has a comparative advantage in the brokering role for a network that depends upon implicit rather than explicit contracting among a group of small inde-

---

25. For more details, see *Financial Planning* (October 1985), pp. 181-188.

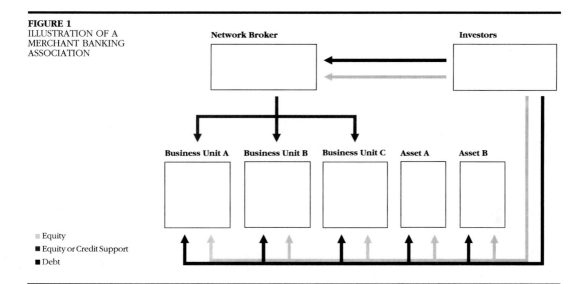

FIGURE 1
ILLUSTRATION OF A
MERCHANT BANKING
ASSOCIATION

Network Broker

Investors

Business Unit A   Business Unit B   Business Unit C   Asset A   Asset B

■ Equity
■ Equity or Credit Support
■ Debt

pendent business units. For example, when explicit contracts among the network participants are not possible or economically justified, the merchant banking network broker can provide credit support through irrevocable letters of credit.

The basic structure of a merchant banking association is explained in Figure 1.[26] Investors place debt and equity in the generalist network broker, as well as directly in the independent business units that come together in the network organization. In addition, investors have direct ownership of the assets used by the network organization. Investors are free to choose the specific business units and assets that best fit their overal portfolios. And because of the extended web of relationships, none of the members of the network need to grow big themselves in order to do big things.

Catalyst Energy Corporation: An Example of a Financial Entrepreneur as Network Broker

Catalyst Energy Corporation is an excellent example of not only a modern network broker, but also of a sophisticated network financier. Founded by a team of former Salomon Brothers investment bankers to develop independent electric power production facilities, Catalyst was incorporated January 1982 and went public December 1984 at $6 per share. Three more public offerings followed in quick succession, and by December 1986 the company had raised over $117 million from public equity markets. Its stock was then selling above $20 per share. On the eve of its fifth birthday, this fledgling company had completed or commenced work on $1.5 billion worth of projects, and soon achieved listing on the New York Stock Exchange. In 1988 the stockholders cashed out in a friendly acquisition.

Its projects were set up as independently-financed entities, and creditors had recourse only to the cash flows of a specific project (with recourse to Catalyst or the site owner strictly limited). These arrangements usually took the form of either joint venture partnerships with the site owner or limited partnerships with Catalyst as managing general partner; but sale and lease-back arrangements were also used in some cases to achieve similar effect. Although favorable tax treatment was taken advantage of whenever possible, these arrangements were not set up with tax sheltering as their *primary* function.

---

26. This is an extension of the concept of LBO associations discussed in Michael C. Jensen, "Eclipse of the Public Corporation," *Harvard Business Review* (September-October 1989).

The growth of network organizations brings into question the longstanding concept of a corporation as simply a pool of projects—rather like a closed-end mutual fund. Networking has been working to open up these real-asset mutual funds, and will continue to do so. In the process, they will transfer much of top management's function and control back to the marketplace.

Catalyst's role as developer of independent power generation facilities included the following primary activities: (1) locate physically favorable sites, (2) obtain licensing from the Federal Energy Regulatory Commission and other appropriate authorities, (3) negotiate construction contracts, (4) negotiate contracts for purchase of fuel, (5) negotiate contracts for sale of electric power to the local utility and thermal energy to the site owner, (6) negotiate contracts for operation and maintenance of the facility, and (7) arrange project financing.

Despite the sophisticated legal arrangements, however, there was something very simple at the heart of these transactions. Most of the required services were provided by outside sources. Catalyst's role was simply to bring together the players and "conduct the symphony." Although the majority of its projects were located in California or New England, its corporate offices were positioned at the true focal point of its activities—the New York financial district. Through most of the company's life, its president split his time evenly between Catalyst and the private merchant bank he founded. The real surprise, though, is that it was able to develop so many projects with a permanent staff of less than two dozen people.

TECHNOLOGICAL TRENDS FOSTER NETWORK ORGANIZATIONS

Industry is making the transition from continuous process plants specializing in narrow product lines (and requiring an integrated marketing effort to sell a steady flow of goods) to batch- or job-process plants capable of producing a broad range of customized products at prices competitive with mass production. As these trends progress, the familiar specialized factories of today (such as "car factories" or "radio factories") will give way to generalized factories that are the new-age analogue of the village blacksmith. And like the blacksmith, they will produce many of our goods locally. Fabrication machines will accurately translate design specifications from on-line data bases into finished products, with substantial latitude for customization.

Much of the risk associated with financing such plants arises from uncertainty about whether they will be able to operate at full capacity. As suggested earlier, independent ownership enables them to enter into relationships with several product designers. With their ability to operate profitably regardless of the fortunes of any particular product designer or brand name, flexible factories can be more responsive to market forces if they are independent from specific product designers.

These developments point to a future in which the work will be done by professional firms, much like law firms or accounting firms, that specialize in research, product design, or marketing. Manufacturing will be contracted out to the lowest-cost fabricator, likely a flexible automated factory near the final market. With quality—that is, conformity to design specifications—assured within tight tolerances, competition will be on the basis of product design and delivered cost, where the edge belongs to flexible organizations that provide an environment conducive to creativity. Finally, the key role of putting all the pieces together will go to specialized brokers, a new breed of investment bankers.

The growth of network organizations brings into question the longstanding concept of a corporation as simply a pool of projects—rather like a closed-end mutual fund in which top management functions as the portfolio managers, choosing new businesses to replace or complement old ones. Networking has been working to open up these real-asset mutual funds, and will continue to do so. In the process, they will transfer much of top management's function and control back to the marketplace.

CONCLUDING REMARKS

Large, diversified corporations were dismantled throughout the 1980s, in large part as a consequence of hostile takeovers and leveraged management buyouts. As a result of leveraged restructurings, the excess capital that made such conglomerations possible was returned to the marketplace, adding substantially to the pool of funds available to small firms, including young start-ups. The further consequence was that the playing field for large and small companies in the 80s was levelled as never before. Before the onset of the current "credit crunch," small companies with innovative ideas were routinely tapping into big-league financing by means of venture capital funds, high-yield "mezzanine" loans accompanied by stock-purchase warrants, and private equity placements with institutional investors. Today's management-owned versions of once-large, old-line companies (or at least divisions of them) are leaner and more disciplined. Like the startups they resemble, they must depend upon outside sources of capital to finance new activities.

Many entrepreneurs, as well as solidly-established small businesses, are shunning the venture capitalists and public offerings. They quite simply believe that the financiers want too much—too much control and too big a share of the pie. They reject the notion that a company must become big in order to do big things. The financial arrangements found in network organizations allow small businesses to work on relatively large-scale projects without giving up their independence, while at the same time offering financiers a chance to participate in ways that benefit all concerned.

In many respects, moreover, the trend toward networking represents a return to "old-fashioned" ways of doing business. If this trend continues toward its logical conclusion, we could see business organization return to strong, yet highly flexible, associations in the tradition of the old merchant venturers or the Hanseatic League. The earliest proto-corporations, in fact, were loose-knit associations of individual merchants, bound together by the glue of mutual protection and benefit, with no board of directors or other central governing body.[27] In such organizations individuals band together for mutual benefit, yet hold no common capital in perpetuity. Land, buildings, and equipment are held by owner-managers or leased from investors; and the active participants work for a share in the profits. Their common actions are governed by informal liaisons rather than formal hierarchies.

---

27. The Hanseatic League, perhaps the greatest commercial organization of all time, sold no stock to the public and had no formal central authority, but thoroughly dominated Northern European commerce from the days of the Crusades until after the Protestant Reformation. Its activities covered the entire Baltic and North Sea area, from London to present-day Leningrad, including over 120 major trading cities, and it even waged war against sovereign princes who abused its members. As the European states consolidated, however, the League's supranational status became intolerable, and national interests ultimately brought it down.

RETHINKING CORPORATE REAL ESTATE

by William B. Brueggeman,
Southern Methodist University,
Jeffrey D. Fisher, Indiana University, and
David M. Porter, Goldman, Sachs & Co.*

C orporations are by far the largest owners of commercial real estate in the United States. It is estimated that as much as 75% of all commercial real estate is in corporate hands. On a book value basis, moreover, roughly one third of the total assets of the Fortune 500 is estimated to be real estate. With such a large concentration of corporate wealth in commercial property, it is worth taking a closer look at the rapidly changing attitudes of corporate managers and investors toward corporate real estate ownership.

The business environment of the 1980s, which featured widespread deregulation, heightened international competition, and increased shareholder activism, forced American corporations to re-examine many aspects of their operations in the attempt to increase shareholder value (and, in some cases, to defend against raiders). By stepping up the urgency of management's search for efficiencies, these competitive forces produced an unprecedented number of mergers and acquisitions, divestitures, spin-offs, leveraged buyouts, and other major recapitalizations. Real estate assets were often a focal point in these restructurings.

As a consequence of this restructuring activity, corporate managements today are far more likely to question the traditional notion that corporations have a comparative advantage in owning real estate. It is important to remember that corporate real assets, while functioning as facilities in corporate operations, are part of local and regional property markets. And unless the company is a dominant force in a small local economy, the market value of those assets will typically be governed by factors very different from those that drive the value of the firm's operating business. Developers and real estate investors are likely to be more alert to changes in property values, and to opportunities to take advantage of such changes, than a corporate management focused on operations.

This lesson of comparative advantage also applies, perhaps with far greater force, to those industrial companies that have chosen to create their own real estate development subsidiaries. The two most common rationales for such decisions have been the arguments that real estate development "complements" the core business activities and that it provides an opportunity to diversify away from the basic business. But today, as the market appears increasingly unwilling to reward corporate diversification, the sphere of activities once considered "complementary" is contracting sharply. Corporate managements are being made to take a hard look at the question: Do we have a comparative advantage over other developers and investors in this business? Companies like Marriott and Holiday Corp. are choosing not to own their hotels, but instead to focus on managing them. And companies like McCormick and Canadian Pacific with real estate development subsidiaries are choosing to sell or spin off those subsidiaries and concentrate on their core businesses. As evidence of this trend away from corporate real estate ownership, a recent study shows corporate ownership of commercial real estate in the U.S. declining from 84% in 1982 to 74% in 1988.[1]

Much of this transfer of real estate assets from corporations to other investors was driven, to be sure, by changes in the tax code brought about by the

*The authors gratefully acknowledge the assistance of A. Richard Moore of Goldman Sachs and Michael Holmberg of the Continental Bank, as well as the editorial work of Don Chew.

1. See *Real Estate Capital Flows*, Equitable Real Estate Management, Inc., 1988.

Economic Recovery Tax Act of 1981.[2] And subsequent changes in the code, under the Tax Reform Act
of 1986, have substantially reduced the corporate tax
disadvantage to owning real estate. But this does not
mean that market pressures for companies to
"manage" their real estate have disappeared.

A relatively new source of pressure is the
emerging reality that many major corporate assets
are now priced in a worldwide market. Regardless
who owns them, major properties are increasingly
valued as part of an international market that includes overseas institutional investors as well as U.S.
pension funds and insurance companies. Such international investors, in their quest for diversification
across geographic as well as asset boundaries, are
reportedly pricing properties based on location and
other criteria that have allowed them to pay considerably more for certain properties than their value as
a real estate investment to U.S. corporations.

*Capturing "Hidden Value": The Challenge to
Real Estate Management.* The appreciation in value
of some corporate real estate poses a critical problem for management. Many observers claim that,
because accounting conventions require companies
to carry real estate assets on a "lower of cost or
market" basis and many properties contribute little
to reported earnings, the value of corporate real
estate is "hidden" from investors and therefore not
fully reflected in stock prices.[3] To the extent that real
estate values are not reflected in share prices, corporate management is vulnerable to the predations
of raiders who are able to buy companies at bargain
prices and then sell off the undervalued assets.

There is an alternative explanation for such
"hidden" values—one that is reasonably consistent
with the economist's idea of an efficient market in
which investors compete vigorously for information.
Although we explore this issue in more detail (see
inset), we will simply mention here that this other
explanation of the real estate "discount" in share
prices relies on factors such as high "information

costs" in discovering the values of corporate real
assets as well as investor uncertainty about corporate efficiencies in managing real estate. Also potentially important, as mentioned above, are tax and
diversification benefits to some real estate investors
that would make corporations less-advantaged
owners of real estate.

But whether caused by market failure, management inefficiency, or external factors, the perceived
"undervaluation" of corporate real estate is leading
corporate managers to take careful inventory of real
assets and to evaluate their alternative uses. In some
cases, this process has led to outright property sales
accompanied by major relocations, in others to sale-
leasebacks, and in still others to a variety of asset-backed refinancings designed to capture "hidden" values.
At the same time, some companies are attempting to
reduce occupancy costs as well as the potential for
future "hidden value" problems through the use of
"equity leases" and joint ventures. Such methods allow
corporations to participate in the appreciation of real
estate projects in which they are major tenants, while
avoiding the costs associated with a major capital
commitment to real estate.

In this article, we begin by reviewing the role of
real estate in the restructuring of the 1980s and attempt
to explain further why stock market investors might
"rationally" value companies with large real estate
holdings at prices well below "break-up" value. Then,
after commenting briefly on some relatively recent
changes in the real estate investment market, we discuss various steps that some companies have taken to
eliminate the real estate discount in their share values.
Finally, we review the key issues facing companies in
their decisions to acquire new real estate.

CORPORATE RESTRUCTURING AND
REAL ESTATE ASSETS

The volume of mergers and acquisitions increased dramatically in the 1980s, rising from $44

---

2. In 1981, the Economic Recovery Tax Act [ERTA] reduced depreciable lives of
real estate improvements to 15 years. This encouraged the purchase of assets and
allowed the acquiring firm to depreciate the stepped up depreciable basis over a
relatively short depreciable life. The Deficit Reduction Act of 1984 moderately extended the depreciable life of such assets and in 1986 the Tax Reform Act extended
useful lives to 31.5 years. It also increased the effective capital gains rate at both the
corporate and personal levels and eliminated the General Utilities doctrine, which had
previously allowed selling corporations to avoid capital gains tax at the corporate level
in planned corporate liquidations.

For a discussion of how such tax changes affected corporate restructuring
activity, see Myron S. Scholes and Mark A. Wolfson, "The Effects of Changes in
Tax Laws on Corporate Reorganization Activity", *Journal of Business*, Vol. 63

No. 1, pt. 2, pp. s141-s164. Scholes and Wolfson argue that favorable tax
treatment in ERTA accounted for much of the merger activity from 1981 to 1986 and
that the Tax Reform Act of 1986 has accounted for much of the decline in merger
activity since 1987.

3. Michael Brennan, in his 1989 Presidential Address to the American Finance
Association, used the term "latent assets" to describe situations in which the value
of assets owned by a corporation may not be accurately reflected in its stock price.
Indeed, he cites real estate holdings as one class of assets for which this term
applies. According to Brennan, the existence of latent assets may justify a
corporation's "signaling" to the market the value of these assets in order to
encourage shareholders to capitalize potential future value into stock prices.

billion in 1980 to a peak of over $200 billion in 1986.[4] What these numbers obscure, however, is the fact many of these corporate restructurings led to more focused, if not indeed smaller, corporations. Some 35 to 40 percent of the mergers and acquisitions reported by W.T. Grimm in the 1980s were divestitures of divisions or subsidiaries by other companies.[5] The consequence of such transactions was often to transfer unrelated business units from large conglomerates to single-business companies and private investment groups in combination with operating management.[6] At the same time, there was a proliferation of corporate "spin-offs," or pro-rata distributions to existing stockholders of new shares in subsidiaries. Such spin-offs, which were sometimes followed by divestiture, provided another means for companies to split off operations that did not contribute to their basic business mission.

Real estate often played a central role in such sales and spin-offs. For example, in 1988 McCormick & Company, a leading spice manufacturer, sold its real estate subsidiary for over $500 million to TIAA and the Rouse Company, a real estate development company. (Between the announcement and the closing of the transaction, moreover, the company saw its stock price increase by some 45% relative to 8% for the S & P 500.)

Another prominent case is that of Union Pacific, whose real estate development subsidiary has land and improved properties estimated to be worth over $500 million. After an aborted attempt to sell the entire sub earlier this year, the company has now put up for sale thousands of acres of its holdings in the Western U.S. Such asset sales are being being held up by management as a sign of its renewed commitment to its core transportation activities.

With similar intent, Canadian Pacific recently announced its intention to spin off its real estate subsidiary, Marathon Realty Co., into a separate publicly held company. The parent company, a railroad and hotel conglomerate, plans to distribute 80% of Marathon's shares to its current shareholders while retaining a 20% interest. Unlike the announcement of an asset sale or divestiture, such a strategy does not immediately establish a value for the real estate assets. But because the realty unit will have its own stock price, the market will be forced to view

WHY THE REAL ESTATE "DISCOUNT"?

The belief that corporate real estate is undervalued—at least until a company is "put into play"—seems almost universally held by corporate executives and investment bankers. The existence of apparent real estate bargains clearly raises doubts about the pricing "efficiency" of the stock market. But whether such undervaluation really contradicts the principle of market efficiency needs to be examined more carefully.

The efficient markets hypothesis holds, in brief, that competition among investors for information should cause *current* stock prices to reflect all available public (as well as much private) information about a company's *future* profitability. Current values accordingly should be *unbiased* estimates of the present value of future cash flows. By "unbiased" we mean that today's value should, when adjusted for risk and future market levels, turn out to have been neither too low nor too high on average. Translated into the vernacular, stock prices should not leave a lot of money on the table for corporate raiders.

The case of real estate, however, could present special problems. For one thing, the costs for outside investors to ascertain the values of such real estate may be large enough to warrant a large discount, especially if management (1) does not know the value of its own real estate or (2) does know it but fails to communicate it to investors.

Second, investors may discount too heavily (if they consider at all) the expected future value of real estate that produces no current operating cash flow—especially if they believe that management has no intention of selling or developing the real estate. For example, if prices of undeveloped land have risen dramatically but management does not inspire confidence that it has a plan to "harvest" such value, then investors may be justified in assigning low values to such growth options. Investors, after all, do not have the control necessary to realize hidden values.

the real estate operations independently of the conglomerate. Moreover, to the extent a separately trading entity furnishes the market with better information, and provides operating management with stronger incentives, the market may place a

---

4. See Scholes and Wolfson, cited earlier.

5. See Fred Weston, "Divestitures: Mistakes or Learning?," *Journal of Applied Corporate Finance*, Volume 2 No. 2, Summer 1989.

6. See Amar Bhide, "The Causes and Consequences of Hostile Takeovers, *Journal of Applied Corporate Finance*, Volume 2 No. 2, Summer 1989.

7. For a summary of this literature on divestitures, see Fred Weston, cited in note 5. See also Michael Rozeff and Scott Linn, "The Corporate Sell-Off," *Midland*

Third, in the case of operating real estate, the fact that management persists in using assets with much higher-valued alternative uses in marginally profitable operations would also warrant a large discount in the stock—again, provided management does not signal to the market its intent to sell or convert the asset.

Still another potential problem in valuing real estate arises even in the case of income-producing properties. Because accounting depreciation charges generally exceed true economic depreciation, the reported earnings of real estate companies typically understate the level of operating cash flow. And if the market responds mechanically to reported earnings, then it could systematically undervalue real estate assets, thus leaving companies prey to raiders concerned only about cash flow. But if markets do look through earnings to cash flow, as much academic research suggests, then accounting conventions should not lead to the undervaluation of real estate.

On the other hand, as mentioned earlier, the ability of acquirers to take over "asset-rich" companies, write up the value of acquired real assets to market, and then depreciate their values over shorter lives (provided by the Economic Recovery Tax Act of 1981) clearly provided an artificial stimulus to takeover activity in the early 1980s. Such a stimulus was removed, however, with the Tax Reform Act of 1986.

To summarize, then, besides the possibility of market inefficiency, there are information and control problems that could be responsible for large disparities between stock prices and perceived real estate values. First, in the case of large industrial companies with dispersed real estate assets, the costs to investors of ascertaining such values may be very large. Second, even if the market knows the value of such assets, the remaining uncertainty about *whether* management will take steps to realize the value of such real estate options, and *when* such steps will be taken, could lead investors to heavily discount real assets in setting stock prices.

generally been well received by the stock market.[7] For example, a study by Gailen Hite, James Owers, and Ronald Rogers showed that, during the period from 1962 to 1982, the share prices of 33 companies announcing spin-offs of real estate assets increased by 5.7%, on average, around the announcement date. Perhaps more striking, the positive reaction to spin-offs by the *non-real estate* companies in the sample was considerably larger (9.1%) than the average price change of the real estate companies (which was not significantly different from zero).[8] From this evidence, one could draw two conclusions: (1) given adequate information, the stock market may indeed be capable of evaluating real estate assets; and (2) market investors place higher values on real estate development operations when conducted by real estate companies rather than diversified conglomerates.

MOVING CORPORATE REAL ESTATE TO ITS "HIGHEST AND BEST USE"

Besides serving as production, retail, and administrative facilities, corporate real estate assets, as we observed earlier, are rooted in local and regional property markets. Prices in these markets are set by the competition among businesses firms for land and buildings that provide the desired facilities and access to transportation routes and labor markets. This process of competition should ensure that, regardless of whether the assets are leased or owned, corporate real estate is put to its "highest and best use."[9] And, to the extent corporations indeed commit their real estate to its highest and best use, then those assets are being managed so as to minimize costs and/or maximize earnings. The outcome is that shareholder value should be maximized in the process.

The need for active corporate real estate management arises from the fact that real estate values, and hence best alternative uses, change over time. For example, deregulation and the globalization of business have resulted in a pronounced shift from manufacturing to services across the U.S. economy. This shift has in turn brought about a change in the demand for CBD and suburban office space, and in the location of manufacturing facilities as well.

higher value on the self-standing operation.

There is considerable academic evidence to support these propositions. Like corporate divestitures and spin-offs in general, announcements of corporate real estate sales and spin-offs have

Corporate Finance Journal, Volume 2 No. 2, Summer 1984. For a good review of the literature on spin-offs, see "The Corporate Spin-off Phenomenon," *Midland Corporate Finance Journal*, Volume 2 No. 2, Summer 1984.

8. Gailen L. Hite, James E. Owers and Ronald C. Rogers, "The Separation of Real Estate Operations by Spinoff," *AREUEA Journal*, Vol. 12 No. 3, pp. 318-332.
9. This term is widely used in real estate valuation theory to determine which type of improvement (office, retail, etc.) will maximize land value.

Changing demographics and the location of public infrastructure such as mass transit and highways have also greatly affected prices in property markets.

As a consequence of this change, corporate real estate assets that may once have been optimally employed often turn out to have higher-valued uses. To illustrate, demographic changes affecting retail demand made warehouses along Baltimore's waterfront suitable for redevelopment by the Rouse Corporation into a very successful mixed-use, retail-based project. In New York, Chicago and other major cities, increased demand for downtown office space over the years has resulted in dramatic increases in rent. For companies such as Citicorp and Sears, the higher rents eventually outweighed the benefits from use of prime real estate for administrative support activities. Consequently, they have chosen to vacate that space (which may then be rented to many smaller corporate office users willing to pay higher rents) and relocate such "back-office" activities to a lower-rent suburban setting.

It is possible, of course, to argue that the appreciation of the Citicorp and Sears properties should be reflected in their respective share values. But to the extent companies persist in using prime real estate for activities that could housed elsewhere for a fraction of the current rent, the reluctance of management to act on such opportunities is likely to be reflected in lower share prices.

As evidence of this proposition, consider the following cases:

- In 1984, the Bass brothers offered $125 million to acquire Alexander's, a marginally profitable New York retailer. At the time, analysts estimated the value of the midtown Manhattan site of the company's flagship store to be as much as $100 million—the rough equivalent of the pre-offer stock market value of the entire 15-store chain.
- In 1989, a subsidiary of the British WPP Group paid about $540 million to acquire J. Walter Thompson. After the purchase, it sold Thompson's 100,000 square foot Tokyo office building (with a book value of approximately $30 million) to a Japanese life insurance company for $200 million.

As such cases are meant to suggest, managements intent on increasing share values may find it important to monitor the values of their real estate assets in their "highest and best uses." At the extreme, the potential cost of neglecting this principle of real estate management is loss of control of the company.

REAL ESTATE ASSETS AS AN "INSTITUTIONAL-GRADE" INVESTMENT

Another reason why corporate real estate assets may appear undervalued is the emergence of new investor groups, both domestic and overseas, that seem willing to pay more (or, alternatively, accept lower yields on investment) in return for the diversification benefits provided by U.S. real estate. Further, pension funds have tax-exempt status, while overseas investors may enjoy favorable tax treatment on their U. S. real estate investments.

U.S. Pension Funds

The 1980s saw a significant increase in pension fund investment in large-scale urban properties as part of a portfolio diversification strategy. Surveys of pension fund managers continue to indicate that real estate has been targeted eventually to represent 10 percent of total plan assets. Although billions of dollars in properties have been acquired to date, such acquisitions are currently estimated to represent only about 4% of total U.S. pension plan assets. Well-located urban properties, occupied by multiple corporate tenants with good credit ratings, now constitute an investment-grade asset for most pension investors. In some cases, pension funds' desire to diversify combined with their tax-exempt status are likely to make real estate investments attractive to them at yields that are well below expected (risk-adjusted) returns on corporate investment. In such cases, corporations would clearly benefit from selling (or selling and leasing back) their real estate and then using the proceeds to reinvest in their core business or buy back their stock.

Overseas Investors

The significant increase in foreign investment in some U.S. real estate markets has also affected many corporate real estate values. Together with pension funds, this relatively new source of demand has probably increased the real estate "discount" faced by corporations owning investment-grade properties. The current values of many office properties and hotels in Hawaii, California, and large Eastern cities now reflect prices that have been paid for comparable properties by foreign investors. Sales of the Exxon building and Time Inc.'s interest in Rockefeller Center to Japanese investors—and, much more recently, the sale of Sak's Fifth Avenue for $1.5 billion to a Middle Eastern financial group—are good illustrations of a global market for top-quality real estate. Based on the prices paid in these transactions, we can infer both a scarcity of investment opportunities abroad, as well as perhaps a strong desire to diversify.[10]

The presence of these new investors, needless to say, has clearly had an important effect on urban property markets. Moreover, the willingness of such investors to place higher values on U.S. real estate represents an opportunity for American companies. On the other hand, failure to exploit such opportunities is an invitation to outside investors who will pay for the right to arbitrage appreciated real estate between the corporate user/investor market and the broader international real estate investment market.

STRATEGIES FOR CAPTURING HIDDEN REAL ESTATE VALUES

Given the possibility that certain corporate real estate values may not be reflected in share prices, there are a number of strategies that should be considered by management to achieve market recognition of those values. Most of these strategies can also be used, and indeed have been used, as takeover defenses.

Asset Sales and Divestitures

In cases where real estate assets have market value greater than their value in their current corporate use, the most obvious step would be to sell the assets and relocate corporate facilities. The after-tax cash proceeds can then either be returned to shareholders or reinvested in the basic business.

Besides the asset sales by Union Pacific and the McCormick & Co. divestiture cited earlier, some other recent examples are as follows:

■ In 1987, Citicorp sold one third of its headquarters building on Park Avenue and two thirds of Citicorp Center on Lexington Avenue to a Japanese insurance company. Although Citicorp continues to maintain a corporate "presence" and equity interest in both buildings, much of its administrative staff has been moved to a new office tower in Queens.

■ Manufacturer's Hanover sold the Adelphi, its 306,000 square foot office building in London, to Middle Eastern investors for approximately $200 million.

■ Imasco, a Canadian conglomerate, raised $185 million by selling the land and buildings (but not the franchises) of 279 Hardee's restaurants to a U.S. real estate partnership.

■ In 1987, Tenneco sold over $250 million of property as part of a general leveraged restructuring designed to narrow its range of businesses.

■ In 1988, Alcoa sold $200 million in real estate to JMB Realty with the declared aim of concentrating its focus on the aluminum business.

■ In the same year, J.C. Penney's sold its Manhattan office tower to real estate partnerships for $353 million and moved both headquarters and production facilities to Plano, Texas.

■ Also in 1988, the May Co. sold 25 shopping centers to a joint venture owned in three equal parts by the company, Prudential Insurance, and a real estate developer. May's proceeds from the sale (which was structured so as to avoid gains tax at the corporate level), were then used to buy back its stock.

Sales and Leasebacks

In cases where an immediate sale and relocation is not practicable, companies can also sell properties and then lease them back from their new owners. In 1988, for example, Time, Inc. sold its 45-percent interest in its Rockefeller Center headquarters to the building's former co-owner, the Rockefeller group, and then arranged a long-term lease.

What is accomplished by such a strategy? A sale-leaseback, like any asset sale, removes an option of potential raiders to use real estate as a means of financing. And provided management can profitably reinvest the sale proceeds in its basic business or returns the cash to shareholders, then the opportunity for outside investors to profit from takeover by selling or refinancing real estate is foreclosed. Furthermore, if the company leases with a short-term lease, it retains its option to relocate. But, if a company simply sells and then commits itself to a long-term lease, there may be no economic gain from such an ownership transfer. The capital inflow from

---

10. Moreover, the fact that Japanese real estate investors in the U.S. include firms like Sumitomo Life, Dai-Ichi Mutual, and Mitsui Fudosan—all of which hold large portfolios of office buildings and other real estate in Japan—suggests that such investors are seeking higher-yielding U.S. assets with investment characteristics that are very familiar to the acquiring entities.

the sale may simply be offset over time by the higher rent charged by the new owner. Moreover, if the sale triggers a large tax liability payment, then the transaction could actually reduce shareholder value.

Assuming, however, that companies can shelter capital gains,[11] corporate shareholders could benefit from sale-leasebacks to the extent U.S. institutional or foreign investors were willing to accept lower yields than the returns required by corporate investors (again, adjusted for risk and leverage). In such cases, the sale proceeds to the company could exceed the present value of the new lease stream as well as any forgone tax savings from ownership.

Another potential benefit of sale-leasebacks is its role as a "signaling" device.[12] To the extent investors have been unable or unwilling to recognize real estate values, a sale-leaseback clearly demonstrates those values to the marketplace. Perhaps equally important, sale-leasebacks, especially when combined with stock repurchases, may also persuade investors that management has become more serious about its commitment to increasing shareholder value. For companies in mature industries with limited investment opportunities, a sale-leaseback together with a large distribution to shareholders may add value by returning excess capital to investors.[13]

Still another possible benefit from sale-leasebacks is to provide a source of capital that can be used to fund growth opportunities or to refinance existing high-priced debt. Fred Meyer, Inc., for example, recently sold and leased back thirty-five stores and a distribution center, thereby raising $400 million. Each store was leased for 20 years with a fixed-payment, net-lease rate and an operating lease structure that allowed off-balance sheet treatment.[14] This transaction effectively enabled the company to capture the full market value of real estate assets, use the sale proceeds to retire some of its higher-yielding debt, and retain control the assets by means of long-term leases.

Refinancing as a "Signaling" Strategy

Another way of alerting the market to hidden value in corporate real estate is to refinance the assets or, if they are completely unleveraged, to borrow against them. Because the loan proceeds are based on appraisals of value by lenders, refinancing provides a third-party "certification" of current asset value similar to that provided by sales and sale-leasebacks. Such a strategy also deters takeover by making use of excess corporate debt capacity, thereby eliminating one tool at the raider's disposal.

This approach was used by Transamerica Corp. when it obtained $85 million by refinancing its landmark Transamerica Pyramid in San Francisco. As in the case of sale-leasebacks, refinancings provide information to the investing public about real estate values without relinquishing control over the asset. As may also be the case in sale-leasebacks, refinancing per se does not benefit shareholders by reducing occupancy costs. Management, however, does retain the option eventually to sell the real estate in question *and* then move most or all operations to lower-rent facilities. Increased market recognition of the value of this option could lead to a gain in the current share price.

Refinancing with Secured Debt

There are cases where lower credit quality firms with a portfolio of less visible properties may want to consider a mortgage-based financing instead of traditional, unsecured debt. Among the major benefits of this approach are longer maturities and reduced amortization requirements. Real estate lenders are accustomed to making 15-30 year non-recourse loans that require "interest only" payments over the first two to five years. For relatively small, non-investment grade borrowers, real estate financings are also likely to be available at lower interest rates than those on

11. Of course, there will always be cases where sale/leasebacks may be used to recognize gains from the sale of assets to offset any loss carryforwards that a corportion may want to utilize.

12. However, as Michael Brennan points out (cited in note 3), firms whose stock prices do not fully reflect the value of their real estate may choose to sell assets and lease them back even if it is costly to do so. He argues further that a positive stock price reaction to the sale-leaseback announcement might even be expected even when the sale-leaseback transaction itself has a negative net present value.

13. This is the substance of Michael Jensen's argument known as the "agency costs of free cash flow." For a non-technical explanation of this concept and its

reflection in corporate restructuring activity, see Michael Jensen, "The Takeover Controversy: Analysis and Evidence, *Midland Corporate Finance Journal*, Volume 4 No. 2, Summer 1986.

14. Under FASB guidelines, off-balance sheet treatment of lease obligations now require that the lessee may not have an explicit repurchase option in the lease agreement and have no residual interest in future asset values. FASB guidelines have also been revised severely restricting the use of unconsolidated subsidiaries. In the past, unconsolidated subs provided a way for corporations to own real estate assets but report only equity ownership interests and earnings on consolidated financial statements.

unsecured bank loans—and without the strict operating covenants that such loans typically require.[15]

In 1989, for example, Payless Cashways, Inc. raised $230 million through a non-recourse loan secured by 143 retail stores and two large distribution centers. The company then used the proceeds to refinance 40% of the higher-cost and shorter-maturity bank debt that it used to fund its $1.1 billion LBO in 1988. The loan structure provided for three years of interest-only payments followed by a 15-year amortization schedule.

Structured Mortgage Financings. Within the past year, the Kroger Company used a "two-tiered" variation of this structure with a subordinated as well as a senior layer to refinance over $600 million of outstanding bank debt. In this refinancing, AAA-guaranteed bonds financed the first 66% of appraised property value and the subordinate lender provided funding secured by the next 22%. Because lenders underwrote almost 90% of the appraised value of its real estate, Kroger largely eliminated any real estate "discount" that may have reduced its share price. Use of the mortgage structure also allowed the company to lengthen its debt maturity while lowering its financing costs and retaining control over its retail operations.

Convertible Mortgages. Sears recently announced a transaction designed to raise $850 million through a convertible mortgage financing backed by the Sears Tower in Chicago. Such mortgages are much like convertible bonds.[16] In return for accepting a below-market coupon on the debt, Sears would give the lender the option to convert its mortgage interest to an equity interest after 15 years. Such a refinancing strategy, when weighed against an outright sale or sale-leaseback of the building, would allow Sears both to defer payment of federal income taxes and to effect a gradual transfer of certain operations from the CBD to a suburban location.

Participating Mortgages. Like a convertible mortgage, a participating mortgage allows the lender to share in the profits of the real estate venture. As part of its $5.1 billion LBO in 1986, Macy's raised $800 million by means of a non-recourse, participating mortgage secured by 70 department stores. Mortgage lenders receive a combination of below-market base interest and contingent interest payments based on a percentage of future cash flows generated by the real estate project. Unlike a convertible mortgage, though, there is no option to convert the debt interest to equity. Instead, the participating lender receives a final participation in the appraised appreciation of the property at maturity.

Marking Assets to Market (Internally as Well as Externally)

To the extent management feels that its real estate values are "hidden" from the market, it also might consider disclosing the results of third-party appraisals of its real estate values to shareholders. In a strategy pioneered by the Rouse Company, and since adopted by Hilton and others with large real estate holdings, some corporations now regularly include estimates of current asset values in their financial statements. In many countries, such as Britain, real estate is appraised annually for balance sheet purposes, thus giving investors information about current real estate values.

There are some major obstacles, to be sure, to the widespread adoption of this practice in the U.S. Most important are lack of agreement on appropriate appraisal methods and uncertainty about the sharing of liability between auditors and appraisers. But in cases of corporations with significant, widely dispersed real estate holdings, the benefits of providing potential investors with more information about current asset values may well exceed the costs.

Another barrier to fuller corporate disclosure may in fact be the failure of corporate compensation committees to provide stronger incentives to increase shareholder value. For example, management might

15. On the cost side, however, secured, real estate based financings generally involve higher transaction costs in the form of fees for property appraisals, legal services, surveys, title insurance, and recording taxes. To such out-of-pocket costs one must add the additional time required to complete due diligence in comparisons with other financing alternatives.

For a good comparison of real estate financing in corporate restructuring and excellent examples, see Thomas J. Healey, Richard N. Papert and Scott P. Shepard, "Real Estate Finance Alternatives in Corporate Restructuring," *The Real Estate Finance Journal*, Spring 1990, pp. 9-16.

16. There are many differences between convertible mortgages and convertible bonds. Some of the more important ones are these: (1) convertible mortgages

usually provide investors with a European option allowing conversion to equity only at a specified time in the future (in contrast to the American option provided in most convertible bond offerings, which usually allows conversion to stock at any time between the date of issuance and expiration date); (2) convertible mortgages generally do not allow the borrower to call the mortgage in exchange for call premiums in order to refund the debt prior to the expiration date; (3) convertible mortgages may also contain a participation feature, whereby the lender receives a below-market interest coupon and shares in income produced by the property; and (4) the convertible mortgage lender may retain the right to subordinate its interest to a subsequent first lien holder in the event property values rise during the option period, or interest rates decline.

be more inclined to provide shareholders with better current information on corporate real estate values if its incentive compensation were based on share prices rather than reported earnings.

Real estate appraisals, whether performed by outsiders or corporate staff, would also be useful for internal management purposes. When the market value of corporate real estate far exceeds acquisition costs, the GAAP-based practice of allocating historic depreciation costs significantly understates the cost of running a business, thus overstating profitability and encouraging inefficient use. Marking corporate real estate to market, besides helping management decide when to sell facilities and/or relocate, also provides a sounder basis for allocating market-based lease costs for facilities used by different operating divisions and profit centers.

CAPTURING REAL ESTATE VALUES WITHOUT GETTING INTO THE DEVELOPMENT BUSINESS

As suggested earlier, to the extent a company's property values are determined by local markets and independently of its operating success, local developers and investors are likely to have a comparative advantage in exploiting opportunities in real estate. That advantage, combined with the market's skepticism about corporate diversification, reinforces the now popular prescription that companies should specialize in doing "what they do best." According to this rule, if a company's core operations are generating excess cash, management is best advised to buy back its stock rather than diversify into the real estate development business.

Avoiding the pitfalls of corporate diversification, however, does not necessarily mean shunning all real estate opportunities. There are in fact circumstances in which management might be faulted for not taking advantage of development opportunities: namely, those real estate projects whose value depends critically on the company's continuing presence and, perhaps, its credit rating. Corporations can participate in the success of such projects through a variety of alternatives—including the purchase of options on land, joint ventures, lease concessions, and equity leases—without making a

major capital or management commitment to the development business.

For example, companies like Walt Disney that own and operate recreational parks and resorts have found that their operating success causes adjacent land values to rise. To capture such "spill-over" benefits, such companies now routinely consider buying or purchasing options to buy the surrounding land. And if the operating business has the expected effect on adjacent property values, the companies will then either sell the sites or enter into a joint venture with a developer to realize the potential returns.

Corporate retail operations have also sought for some time to capture real estate spill-overs. In such cases, developers routinely give major concessions to "anchor" retail tenants as an inducement to lease space in shopping malls.

In the case of office buildings, large corporate tenants are often able to extract not only major lease concessions, but also an equity interest in the building itself. Known as "equity leases," such leases are generally long term and provide the tenant with a share in project cash flows as well as a participation in project appreciation upon sale or refinancing.

IBM has very successfully used a joint venture, or partnership, approach with real estate developers to share in potential development profits from office projects in which it is a major tenant. IBM is able to secure a good portion of the profits from such ventures not only because its participation helps in securing other tenants, but also because its presence makes otherwise speculative developments highly financeable. In 1987, for example, IBM and its developer partner were able to secure a AAA LOC to back financing of $279 million of non-recourse, 12-year, 7.75 percent notes for an IBM corporate office complex in Southbury, Connecticut.[17]

LEASE VS. OWN REVISITED

If the market does not reflect real estate values in stock prices—whether owing to investor myopia, information costs, or management inefficiency—the question then arises: Should corporations ever own their real estate? In other words, why don't companies lease all their real estate assets?

---

17. A public-offering of AAA-rated notes was issued by the partnership and was secured by the project and a letter of credit issued by Mitsubishi Trust. The result was a financing cost far less than the cost the developer could have obtained, and a limitation of the project risk to partnership assets and the LOC.

The traditional approach to analyzing whether a company should lease or own discounts the incremental cash flows associated with leasing versus owning the asset, and then compares that number to the purchase price.[18] In effect, the analysis says, "Add the present value of all the after-tax lease costs to the sum of the depreciation tax savings from ownership and the expected resale value of the asset when the lease expires. If that number exceeds the purchase price, then buy the asset."[19]

In theory, if we ignore taxes, transactions costs, and other market "imperfections," purchase and lease prices should be set such that companies are indifferent between owning and leasing. In practice, of course, taxes and control issues often make the own vs. lease decision far from a matter of indifference.

An area of some confusion among corporate practitioners is the estimation of resale or "residual" value—that is, the reversion value of land and improvements at the end of the lease term. Some analysts effectively assume this value is zero; such values, they argue, are realized so far in the future that, when discounted, they have at best a minor effect on NPV. Analysts at the other extreme assume such high rates of appreciation (or use such low discount rates) that the analysis is systematically biased toward ownership. Still others take an intermediate position between these extremes, discounting residual values at rates higher than those used to discount the contractual lease payments and tax savings in order to reflect the greater uncertainty about future property values.

Which method is correct? The answer may depend on who is asking the question, whether it be a small local company, a large multinational corporation, or a well-diversified institutional investor. Remember that real estate is different from other corporate assets in that, at the end of the lease term, the range of possible residual values runs from well below to well above the initial cost of the property. As discussed earlier, over the life of a medium- to long-term lease, local, regional, and even international economic factors can cause the market values of corporate real estate to depart significantly from its value to the corporation. By deciding to own, a corporation chooses in effect to bear residual real estate risk that may be completely unrelated to its operating success. For example, most companies that chose to own office buildings in the Southwest before the "energy bust" now wish they had leased. (And, in fact, oil companies that did buy real estate in the Southwest effectively leveraged their bets on oil prices. If such companies insist on participating in residual real estate values, then a far less costly policy would have been to arrange equity leases that would have provided them with a one-sided exposure to real estate prices.)

When viewed in this light, a thorough lease vs. own analysis should carefully consider any relationship between the factors that influence the company's operating value and those driving local property markets. The aim of such consideration should be to determine whether other real estate investors have a comparative advantage in bearing the risk associated with local real estate markets. Pension funds, for example, generally hold unlevered portfolios of real estate diversified both by property type (offices, warehouses, etc.) and by geographic region. Such institutions, as well as REITs, are likely to be able to diversify risks in property markets much more efficiently than all but the largest corporations. When a given real estate investment represents a large proportion of the company's total capital, the comparative advantage of other investors in bearing such risks may create a strong preference for leasing.

Conditions Favoring Leasing. Leasing is also likely to be favored under the following conditions:
- The company's space requirements are far less than what is optimal to develop on a given site.
- The length of time that a company expects to use the space is less than the economic life of the building.
- The company does not have a comparative advantage relative to developers and other investors in managing property and eventually selling it.

Like relative risk-bearing capacity, the above considerations may be difficult to incorporate within the framework of a standard lease vs. buy NPV analysis, but they nevertheless explain why some companies choose to own, why others choose to lease, and why still others choose to do both. For example, in cases where the amount of space desired by a corporate user is less than the optimal building scale that should be developed on a site, we expect

---

18. For a discussion of the Standard NPV approach, see Brealey and Meyers, *Principles of Corporate Finance*, McGraw Hill Book Co., 1988.

19. It is also argued that these net cash flows should be discounted at the after-tax borrowing rate under the assumption that the lease liability displaced debt on the balance sheet. That is, leasing creates a liability equal to the present value of the lease payments. This reduces corporate debt capacity by an equal amount; therefore leasing is considered to be equivalent to owning with 100 percent financing.

(and typically find) corporate users leasing and developers (and their investment partners) assuming real estate market risks. Even in cases where a corporate lessee will be the dominant tenant, it may be preferable for the corporate user to lease. As illustrated in our IBM example, management may be able to negotiate lease concessions (or a share of the developer's profits) that reflect the developer's use of the corporate credit when obtaining development financing.

In cases where the expected life of an asset far exceeds the company's projected period of use, companies will also generally choose to lease rather than bear the costs associated with selling an illiquid asset. This tendency can be explained, in part, by the comparative advantage of lessors in creating or locating alternative uses for such assets.

Conditions Favoring Ownership.[20] There are a number of asset characteristics that, holding all else equal, are likely to make ownership preferable to leasing. Three major ones come to mind:

1. For reasons of relative risk-bearing capacity described above, larger companies with broadly dispersed operations are more likely to own than smaller companies with geographically concentrated operations.

2. Companies are more likely to own assets whose values are highly sensitive to the level of maintenance.

3. Companies are more likely to own buildings that have been "customized" for its operations, especially when those operations are unusual and the company has few competitors.

Lessors that own maintenance-sensitive building, unless protected by enforceable maintenance provisions,[21] are likely to charge higher lease rates to compensate for lower expected levels of maintenance undertaken by (particularly short-term) tenants. Therefore, unless corporate users find some means of reassuring lessors that maintenance is in the user's as well as the owner's best interest (perhaps through a very long-term lease), corporate users are likely to find it more economical to own.

To illustrate the case of "customized" corporate real estate, we typically observe corporations owning rather than leasing buildings outfitted for hi-tech, R&D operations.[22] (Bulk distribution warehouses, by contrast, are far more likely to be leased than owned.) The high costs of relocating specialized corporate fixtures and machinery is one obvious incentive to own rather than lease. In the case of many single-tenant, special-purpose buildings, the value of the real estate may well be far higher in its current corporate use than in any conceivable alternative use. To the extent this is the case, a lessor would effectively be holding a corporate security whose value depended almost entirely on the company's operating success. In such cases, corporate users would likely have a considerable advantage over real estate investors in bearing such firm-specific risk.

Tax Considerations

Tax considerations have always played a major role in the standard lease vs. buy analysis.[23] We have largely deferred discussion of taxes until this point—not because taxes have become unimportant, but principally because it is less clear today than it was prior to 1986 whether corporations or individuals (whether through the medium of partnerships or institutions) are the tax-favored owners of real estate.

The simple rule-of-thumb on taxes in lease vs. buy is as follows: If the lessor is in a higher tax bracket than the lessee, then leasing puts "ownership" of the asset in the hands of the party that can most benefit from the tax shelter provided by depreciation.[24] From 1981 to 1986, there were two elements of the tax code that together encouraged the ownership of real estate by high-tax-paying individuals: (1) depreciation lives were considerably shorter for real estate assets, thus increasing the depreciation tax shield; and (2) the marginal tax rate for wealthy individuals (50%) was higher than the highest marginal tax rate for corporations (46%) and many companies had other tax shields that effectively lowered their marginal rate well below the statutory 46% rate. These two conditions, combined

20. See Clifford W. Smith, Jr. and L. MacDonald Wakeman, "Determinants of Corporate Leasing Policy," *Journal of Finance*, Vol. XL No. 3, July 1985, pp. 895-910.

21. Effective contracting may be very difficult to achieve even if a net lease is negotiated with the lessor because of time losses in monitoring, assessing blame, and resolving disputes over excessive equipment failures or other problems caused by poor building design or other flaws believed to be the responsibility of the lessor.

22. The maintenance and specialization issues may in fact be closely related. For example, in an R&D facility requiring specific hardware in its design, technicians employed by the corporate entity may be better able to diagnose and

respond to maintenance problems. In such cases, ownership would be preferable to constructing intricate provisions in lease contracts for the lessor to maintain such assets.

23. For a review of the tax issues, see Brealey and Myers, op.cit.

24. This tax shelter benefit occurs when tax depreciation exceeds actual economic depreciation in the value of the asset. For a discussion see William B. Brueggeman, Jeffrey D. Fisher, and Leo D. Stone, *Real Estate Finance*, Eighth Edition, Richard D. Irwin, Inc., 1989, Appendix to Chapter 11, "Depreciation and Effective Tax Rates."

with the ability of partnerships to "pass through" operating losses directly to investors and avoid the double taxation of corporate dividends, created strong incentives for partnerships of high-tax individuals to own real estate and lease it to corporations. And, as we argued earlier, these tax incentives for corporations to sell real estate to individuals coupled with the market's perceived reluctance to reflect real estate values in stock prices explain much of the real estate sales and sale-leasebacks that occurred during this time period.

The Tax Reform Act of 1986 has now reduced the incentive for individuals to lease to corporations in several ways. First, tax depreciation lives have been lengthened (from 15 to 31.5 years), thus lowering the tax shield. Second, the highest marginal tax rate for corporations (34%) is now slightly higher than that of wealthy individuals (28%). Third, individuals are subject to limitations on "passive" losses that restrict their ability to use accounting losses from real estate to offset other income. These tax law changes have leveled the playing field among partnerships, corporations, and tax-exempt entities such as pension funds as owners of real estate.[25] For this reason, taxes are far less likely today to be the deciding factor in corporate lease-versus-own decisions.

CONCLUSION

Corporate real estate is increasingly being given a high level of focus by corporate CFOs, who realize the importance of property to their bottom line and share price. Facilities managers today must justify ownership of real estate against a variety of alterna-tives that combine the operating control provided by ownership with reduced investment and greater flexibility. Such alternatives, which include a variety of leasing forms as well as joint venture ownership, are likely to become more widely accepted by corporations as ownership is seen as unnecessary to maintaining operating control of real estate.

In the 1980s the stock market consistently rewarded public corporations for selling, spinning off, or refinancing their real estate assets. Large price jumps in response to the announcements of such transactions have raised doubts about the ability of stock market investors to value non-income producing assets. But whether such investor response is a sign of market inefficiency or management's failure to put corporate real estate to its "highest and best use" remains an unresolved issue.

What is clear, however, is that the relatively recent emergence of U.S. pension funds and overseas institutions as major players in the U.S. real estate market is adding to market pressures for more active management of corporate real estate. To the extent such investors are willing to accept lower yields on corporate real estate—whether because of diversification benefits or favorable tax treatment—their expanded presence will only increase the gap between corporate stock prices and "break-up" values.

Besides real estate sales, divestitures, and spin-offs, corporations are also responding to perceived undervaluation of their real estate with a variety of asset-backed refinancings. Such refinancings, in addition to providing the market an indicator of underlying asset value, also serve shareholders by eliminating unused debt capacity, thus shielding operating earnings from taxes and preempting would-be raiders.

---

25. In fact, some researchers now claim that, for tax purposes under certain conditions, corporations rather than partnerships may be the optimal organizational form for holding real estate. See Jeffrey D. Fisher and George Lentz, "Tax Reform and Organizational Forms for Holding Investment Real Estate: Corporation vs. Partnership," *The American Real Estate and Urban Economics Association Journal*, Vol. 17 No. 3, 1989.

THE MOTIVES AND METHODS OF CORPORATE RESTRUCTURING*

*by G. Bennett Stewart III and
David M. Glassman, Stern Stewart & Co.*

■

There can be no doubt that the restructuring boom has richly rewarded the dealmakers. But, just as many investors rightly ask their stockbrokers — "but where are our yachts?" — you may be wondering whether the restructurings of the past decade have benefited our economy, shareholders, management and employees.

Do corporate "raiders," as the label suggests, pillage companies for their personal enrichment, leaving a weakened economy in their wake? Or do they instead promote improvements in corporate performance and increases in market values for all to share? If raiders are a force for good, can we learn from them any lessons about how to structure your company more effectively? You may be concerned, for example, that your company's "breakup" value exceeds its current stock price. If so, you may ask why does the discount exist, and could you do anything to close this worrisome gap?

These and other questions prompted us to undertake a review of some 300 financial restructuring transactions completed in the past decade. Our single most important discovery was that, in the vast majority of cases, corporate restructurings have led to sustained increases in both market values and operating performance.

While initially skeptical of such financial alchemy, and even more reluctant to embrace the explanations proffered by most investment bankers, we eventually became convinced that there were "real" economic explanations for the impressive increases in value and performance accompanying restructurings. Among the most important restructuring "motives" are these:

*This article was previously published by, and is reprinted with the permission of, *Cash Flow* magazine.

- Strengthening incentives;
- Achieving a better business fit;
- Sharpening management focus;
- Creating pure-plays that have unique investment appeal;
- Curtailing an unproductive reinvestment of cash flow;
- Eliminating subsidies for underperforming businesses;
- Achieving a higher-valued use for assets;
- Increasing debt capacity; and
- Saving taxes;

Our explanations are fundamentally different from those of most investment bankers, who seem to think that restructurings lift stock prices merely by raising the market's *awareness* of the intrinsic value of a company, without any fundamental change in operating efficiency. In view of the strong evidence of market sophistication, and based upon our own evaluations of restructuring transactions, we are convinced that restructuring does indeed change the way corporations are run.

Our research has uncovered some 20 or so recurring methods of restructuring. For convenience, we divide the restructuring methods into three categories:

(1) *Asset restructurings* are techniques that change the ownership of the assets that support a business. These methods include the use of partnerships or trusts to save taxes, discharge surplus cash flow, and split companies into more productive business units.

(2) *Business unit restructurings* can increase value in three ways: (a) by promoting growth through acquisitions, joint ventures, or offering a subsidiary's shares to the public; (b) by separating a business unit from the firm through a sale, spin-off, split-off or partial liquidation; and (c) by undertaking an internal leveraged recapitalization (a transaction which we will describe later).

(3) *Corporate restructurings* change the ownership structure of the parent company through (1) issues of a new form of debt, preferred stock, or common stock; (2) share repurchases; (3) leveraged ESOPs; (4) leveraged cash-outs or leveraged buyouts; or, most radically, (5) complete sales, liquidations or split-ups of the firm.

To introduce our restructuring framework, let's start with what is perhaps the most controversial method of restructuring: increasing leverage.

WHY LEVERAGE MATTERS

The leverage ratios of many American companies have increased dramatically over the past decade, as the result of leveraged buyouts, share repurchases, recapitalizations, debt-financed acquisitions, and the proliferation of junk bonds. Has this leveraging strengthened or sapped the competitiveness of American

companies? Felix Rohatyn, senior partner at Lazard Frères, articulates the naysayers' viewpoint:

This [the high degree of leverage in LBOs] has two consequences, both highly speculative. First, it bets the company on a combination of continued growth and lower interest rates, with no margin for error. Second, it substitutes debt for permanent capital, which is exactly the opposite of what our national investment objectives ought to be.[1]

While increased leverage has probably raised the level of expected corporate bankruptcies, we also believe that there are three reasons why the aggressive use of debt has been a positive force for the economy as a whole, a catalyst for many American companies to increase their productivity and value:

- Debt is cheaper than equity because interest payments are tax-deductible.
- A debt-financed recapitalization, by concentrating the ownership of equity, can strengthen incentives for investors to monitor their investment, and for management and employees to perform.
- To retire debt, a company may be forced to forgo unprofitable investment and to sell underperforming or unrelated assets or businesses to more productive owners; in general, the need to repay debt creates a compulsion to improve efficiency.

TAX BENEFITS

First of all, debt is a less expensive form of financing than equity because interest expense is tax-deductible while dividend payments are not. Start with the notion that all capital has a cost—if nothing else, an opportunity cost—equal to the rate of return investors would expect to earn by owning other securities of similar risk.

By substituting debt for equity, you will not change the overall amount of capital used in a business, nor the total rate of return needed to compensate investors for bearing business risk. But the implicit cost of equity has been replaced, at least partially, by the explicit tax-deductible cash cost of debt. Substituting debt for equity within prudent limits increases a company's intrinsic market value because debt shelters operating profits from being fully taxed.

This can be true even when the interest rate rises that must be paid on the debt. However high the rate on debt may be, the implied interest rate on the equity it replaces must be higher still because equity is riskier to own, and its cost is not subsidized by a corporate tax savings. Junk bonds, in other words, should not be thought of as expensive debt financing. Junk bonds are rather an inexpensive,

---

1. "On a Buyout Binge and a Takeover Tear," *The Wall Street Journal* (May 18, 1984).

because tax-deductible, form of equity.

Corporate raiders know well debt's value as a tax shelter. By highly leveraging their targets, they are able to capitalize the value of pre-tax instead of after-tax profits: *"Accountants just assume taxes have to be paid," says Mario J. Gabelli, a money manager, buyout specialist, and aficionado of cash flow analysis long before it was fashionable. "But you don't have to pay taxes... Remember you're an owner-investor, not a passive shareholder, and you have control of the cash. You don't care about profit. So you take on a bundle of debt and devote the cash flow more towards servicing the debt than to producing taxable profits. And as you pay down the debt, your equity in the company automatically grows.*[2]

We frequently encounter chief financial officers who, though they acknowledge the tax advantage of debt, argue against its use because they do not "need" to borrow money. They point out that their companies already generate more cash than they can productively invest; so, for them, borrowing money is unnecessary. We think this view is mistaken. In order to take full advantage of the tax benefit of debt, a company should borrow if it is able to, not because it needs to. In fact, *the less a company needs to raise capital to finance expansion, the more money it should borrow.*

Instead, it is those companies that need to raise new capital that should shun debt, preferring equity to preserve financing flexibility. For Apple Computer, for example, the need to fund technological innovation and market expansion is so much more important than saving taxes that the company quite rightly borrows no money whatsoever: equity supports Apple's growth. It is ironic but true that the more a company needs money to finance a wealth of attractive new investment opportunities, the less money it should borrow.

But when a company has surplus cash flow, making it easy to service debt, new debt should be raised to take advantage of the tax shelter it provides. Raising debt is advisable in these circumstances even if the proceeds are used just to retire common shares.

A leveraged buyout carries this premise to its logical extreme. The classic LBO candidate is eminently bankable precisely because it generates a steady stream of cash to repay debt. Will Rogers apparently was right in observing that "bankers lend money to their friends, and to those who don't need it." Our recommendation, then, is to borrow money if you can, not because you must. Neglecting debt's tax benefit is one sure way for a strong cash generator to attract the attention of the raiders.

But while we are on the subject of saving taxes, why not convert to a partnership to avoid paying corporate income taxes entirely? As a flow-through vehicle, a partnership incurs no tax liability. Instead, the investors in a partnership are taxed as individuals on their share of partnership income. With the personal tax rate now beneath the corporate tax rate for the first time in memory, the logic of housing income-producing assets in a partnership is compelling. Why put assets in a corporation where earnings are taxed once at 34 percent and twice if distributed, when the same assets put in a partnership would have their earnings taxed just once at 28 percent?

There is a problem, however. Moving assets already housed in a corporation into a partnership triggers a corporate tax on the difference between the current value of the assets and their tax basis. Depending on how the conversion is accomplished, it may require shareholders to pay a tax. A decision to convert an existing corporation to a partnership thus becomes a straightforward capital budgeting exercise, weighing the up-front tax costs against an ongoing tax savings.

Unfortunately, the tax code may be revised to tax certain limited partnerships as corporations, thereby subjecting them to double taxation. The value of the on-going tax benefit must be discounted for this uncertainty, further tipping the present value calculation against conversion. But help is on its way. We can dress up a corporation and make it behave like a partnership. Here's how. What two essential economic attributes distinguish a partnership from a corporation? Partnerships are not taxed and generally distribute all cash flow to investors. The answer, then, is to lever up a corporation and use the proceeds to retire equity. The corporation is thereby effectively converted into a partnership while avoiding any up-front corporate tax! Interest expense now largely shelters the company's operating profits from corporate income tax. The operating profits instead mostly flow through as interest income to be taxed to the holders of the company's bonds.

Moreover, paying interest and principal on the debt raised causes the company's cash flow to be discharged, again much as it would be in a partnership. The equity investors that survive the recapitalization, like the general partners in a partnership, still have control of the firm. And yet, unlike general partners, the liability of these shareholders is limited.

In short, a highly-leveraged corporation can match the desirable tax and cash flow attributes of a partnership, while retaining the corporate advantages of limited liability and trading liquidity—truly the best of both worlds.

But, however important taxes are in making debt more attractive than equity, the tax benefit alone cannot account for the great increase in leverage in recent years. If anything, the reduction in the corporate tax rate would reduce the incentive to use debt as a tax shelter. The raiders have taught us that there are at least four more reasons to use debt aggressively.

---

2. "The Savviest Investors Are Going With The (Cash) Flow," *Business Week* (September 7, 1987).

CASH DISGORGEMENT

A good reason to borrow money is to repay it! When a company incurs debt, the obligation to pay it back it removes from management the temptation to reinvest surplus cash in substandard projects or overpriced acquisitions. Like Ulysses lashed to the mast, management's hands are tied by its debts. Then, though the siren calls of investment opportunities may beckon, the company ship rows assuredly onward, avoiding the fate of the failed projects that litter the shore. Repaying debt need not entirely preclude growth, but with the cash flow that a company internally generates dedicated to retiring debt, expansion must be financed with new capital, subjecting management's investment plans to the discipline of a market test.

The Standard Oil Company of Ohio ("SOHIO") provides a good example of the "reinvestment risk" that corporations impose on their stockholders. SOHIO for many years was a sleepy regional refiner and marketer of oil. After finding extensive oil reserves on the Alaskan north slope, it became an enormously profitable cash cow. Curiously, SOHIO sold for a depressed price-to-earnings ratio, even though it earned a very high return on equity and sold for the highest price-to-book ratio of any of the major oil companies.

How do we account for that? The high return on equity and price-to-book ratio resulted from SOHIO's successful investments. Value had unquestionably been added to the capital that SOHIO had invested in Alaska. The low price-to-earnings ratio signalled the market's lack of confidence in SOHIO's future profitability. In fact, it resulted from a downright fear that the flood of cash from the North Slope would be wasted in SOHIO's basic businesses or in unjustifiable premiums for acquisitions.

SOHIO justified investors' fears by choosing both downhill paths. Management splurged on costly oil forays (of which the dry-as-a-prune Mukluk well is but one prominent example), bought extensive mining reserves at inflated prices, and made the exceedingly expensive ($1.77 billion) and highly suspect acquisition of Kennecott, the copper company. The results of SOHIO's capital investments were so bad that British Petroleum, SOHIO's part owner, let go SOHIO's chairman and brought in a new team to reverse the company's misfortunes.

But why single out SOHIO when almost all the major oil companies have made similar blunders (Exxon with its office systems venture and Reliance Electric acquisition, Mobil with Montgomery Ward, ARCO with Anaconda, and so on)? It's just human nature to spend money when you get your hands on it.

Nevertheless, it is a fundamental tenet of corporate finance that the wisdom of making an investment does *not* depend on whether funding comes from inside or outside the company. Even if internal cash flow finances growth, those funds could just as well have been repatriated to investors and then explicitly raised. Internalizing the cost of capital does not avoid it. In practice, however, the inclination to invest is more highly related to the availability of cash than to the presence of attractive uses.

Why is this textbook lesson so widely ignored? The answer lies in reasons of great importance to senior management and of grave concern to investors. A large and growing company is more powerful and prestigious (and, in the past, was less vulnerable to takeover before junk bond financing became available) than a small, contracting one. Moreover, a diversified company is more stable than one reliant on a single business, and can justify a corporate bureaucracy with no direct operating responsibility or accountability. And, as Professor Michael Jensen has observed, middle level managers also are inclined to root for expansion if it creates new senior management positions to be filled.[3] For all these reasons, most companies prefer to reinvest cash flow rather than to pay it out.

Consider the case of Ford, which [at the time of this writing], after two years of record profits, now sits on top of over $9 billion in cash and securities.

Where will Ford pounce? The stock markets buzz almost daily with rumors about takeover plays by Ford, which openly says it wants to buy companies to offset the auto industry's cyclical swings. In recent months, Boeing, Lockheed, and Singer have been rumored targets.[4]

While it is easy to see the benefits diversification may bring to Ford's senior managers and employees (to say nothing of its investment bankers), is diversification in the best interest of its shareholders and our economy? Was it not the company's dependence upon the auto market that forced management to streamline production and to innovate in order to survive—and that is thus the cause of their present success?

By making survival less dependent on Ford's ability to compete in the auto industry, diversification will dampen the company's drive to make painful, necessary adjustments should hard times come again. Perhaps Ford can justify buying an electronics or aerospace company to obtain technology. But would it not be more efficient to license the technology, or form a joint venture, if that is the motivation? Most fundamentally, would an acquisition be made if Ford had to raise the cash, or is the mere availability of cash prompting its use?

Warren Buffet, Chairman of Berkshire Hathaway,

---

3. "How to Detect a Prime Takeover Target," *The New York Times* (March 9, 1986).

4. "Can Ford Stay on Top?," *Business Week* (September 28, 1987).

states the problem in typically eloquent and witty style in his 1984 Annual Report:

Many corporations that show consistently good returns have, indeed, employed a large portion of their retained earnings on an economically unattractive, even disastrous, basis. Their marvelous core businesses camouflage repeated failures in capital allocation elsewhere (usually involving high-priced acquisitions). The managers at fault periodically report on the lessons they have learned from the latest disappointment. They then usually seek out future lessons. (Failure seems to go to their heads.)

In such cases, shareholders would be far better off if the earnings were retained to expand only the high-return business, with the balance paid in dividends or used to repurchase stock (an action that increases the owner's interest in the exceptional business while sparing them participation in the sub-par businesses). Managers of high-return businesses who consistently employ much of the cash thrown off by those businesses in other ventures with low returns should be held to account for those allocation decisions, regardless of how profitable the overall enterprise is.

Are we suggesting, then, that senior managers are tempted by self-interest to sometimes make decisions contrary to their shareholders' welfare? Yes, we are. Reinvesting cash flow without shareholder approval is the corporate equivalent of taxation without representation. Just as our founding fathers understood that no single body of men could be entrusted to serve the public interest and created a system of checks and balances, so do many financial restructurings take away from management the power to reinvest a company's cash flow and restore that power to the shareholders. Management, in such cases, is then forced to appeal to investors to vote for its investment plans by contributing new capital.

Are we also saying that the market is more astute than management in making investment decisions? Yes, again. How, for example, can Fred Hartley, Chairman of the Union Oil Company, know that drilling for more oil is the most productive present use of society's scarce resources? Impossible, obviously. The resources freed up by not drilling for oil would be invested in activities where Mr. Hartley has no relevant experience—for example, developing the next generation of supercomputer, or in biotechnology. Yet such resource allocation tradeoffs are decided by portfolio managers everyday when they choose which companies' shares to buy and which to sell. Moreover, the advent of powerful microcomputers, extensive financial databases and a growing body of business school graduates well-versed in powerful analytical methods has enhanced the market's ability to make accurate and rapid-fire evaluations.

Corporate managements, on the other hand, labor under an inflated sense of the importance of their products or industry relative to competing alternatives. They maintain a dogmatic optimism in the face of justifiable market skepticism and, perhaps most important, persist in ignoring the strong evidence showing that stock prices tend to be an accurate barometer of a company's intrinsic value (meaning that the upside potential is offset by an honest assessment of the downside risk).

For all these reasons, we are convinced that *the current wave of restructurings has much to do with the increasing sophistication of capital markets worldwide, and not the alleged lack of it.*

There are five ways that responsible management—or, failing that, a corporate raider—can return control of discretionary cash flow to the market and eliminate the discount on value caused by the market's perception of reinvestment risk. All five can be illustrated with examples drawn from the oil industry.

Repurchase Shares

The most flexible method is to discharge surplus cash voluntarily by repurchasing common shares in the open market over time. Exxon did this. Responding aggressively to overcapacity in the oil industry, Exxon cut its employment, refinery capacity, and service stations by a third from 1980 to 1986. It then used the cash generated by this move to buy back common stock on the open market, over $7 billion worth from June, 1983, earning it the following accolades from *Business Week*:

In effect, Exxon has sent a message to its stockholders and the public: "Our industry is shrinking, at least for the present, and we think we should shrink a bit along with it. So we are returning some capital to our shareholders. They, not Exxon management, will decide how this money should be reinvested in the U.S. economy." That is good for the economy.[5]

Exxon's share return (dividend and price appreciation) since the buyback plan was first announced has bettered the share return produced by both Unocal and Phillips, where restructuring was forced upon management by a raider. Both of those companies had announced aggressive expansion plans despite declining fundamentals in the oil business, a "damn the facts, full speed ahead" approach guaranteed to put them directly "in harm's way."

Leveraged Share Repurchases

The second way to cure reinvestment risk, then, is to buy back stock aggressively and finance the purchase with

---

5. *Business Week* (August 19, 1985)

states the problem in typically eloquent and witty style in his 1984 Annual Report:

Many corporations that show consistently good returns have, indeed, employed a large portion of their retained earnings on an economically unattractive, even disastrous, basis. Their marvelous core businesses camouflage repeated failures in capital allocation elsewhere (usually involving high-priced acquisitions). The managers at fault periodically report on the lessons they have learned from the latest disappointment. They then usually seek out future lessons. (Failure seems to go to their heads.)

In such cases, shareholders would be far better off if the earnings were retained to expand only the high-return business, with the balance paid in dividends or used to repurchase stock (an action that increases the owner's interest in the exceptional business while sparing them participation in the sub-par businesses). Managers of high-return businesses who consistently employ much of the cash thrown off by those businesses in other ventures with low returns should be held to account for those allocation decisions, regardless of how profitable the overall enterprise is.

Are we suggesting, then, that senior managers are tempted by self-interest to sometimes make decisions contrary to their shareholders' welfare? Yes, we are. Reinvesting cash flow without shareholder approval is the corporate equivalent of taxation without representation. Just as our founding fathers understood that no single body of men could be entrusted to serve the public interest and created a system of checks and balances, so do many financial restructurings take away from management the power to reinvest a company's cash flow and restore that power to the shareholders. Management, in such cases, is then forced to appeal to investors to vote for its investment plans by contributing new capital.

Are we also saying that the market is more astute than management in making investment decisions? Yes, again. How, for example, can executives of oil companies know that drilling for more oil is the most productive present use of society's scarce resources? Impossible, obviously. The resources freed up by not drilling for oil would be invested in activities where oil company executives have no relevant experience—for example, developing the next generation of supercomputer, or in biotechnology. Yet such resource allocation tradeoffs are decided by portfolio managers every day when they choose which companies' shares to buy and which to sell. Moreover, the advent of powerful microcomputers, extensive financial databases and a growing body of business school graduates well-versed in powerful analytical methods has enhanced the market's ability to make accurate and rapid-fire evaluations.

Corporate managements, on the other hand, labor under an inflated sense of the importance of their products or industry relative to competing alternatives. They maintain a dogmatic optimism in the face of justifiable market skepticism and, perhaps most important, persist in ignoring the strong evidence showing that stock prices tend to be an accurate barometer of a company's intrinsic value (meaning that the upside potential is offset by an honest assessment of the downside risk).

For all these reasons, we are convinced that *the current wave of restructurings has much to do with the increasing sophistication of capital markets worldwide, and not the alleged lack of it.*

There are five ways that responsible management—or, failing that, a corporate raider—can return control of discretionary cash flow to the market and eliminate the discount on value caused by the market's perception of reinvestment risk. All five can be illustrated with examples drawn from the oil industry.

Repurchase Shares

The most flexible method is to discharge surplus cash voluntarily by repurchasing common shares in the open market over time. Exxon did this. Responding aggressively to overcapacity in the oil industry, Exxon cut its employment, refinery capacity, and service stations by a third from 1980 to 1986. It then used the cash generated by this move to buy back common stock on the open market, over $7 billion worth from June, 1983, earning it the following accolades from *Business Week*:

In effect, Exxon has sent a message to its stockholders and the public: "Our industry is shrinking, at least for the present, and we think we should shrink a bit along with it. So we are returning some capital to our shareholders. They, not Exxon management, will decide how this money should be reinvested in the U.S. economy." That is good for the economy.[5]

Exxon's share return (dividend and price appreciation) since the buyback plan was first announced has bettered the share return produced by both Unocal and Phillips, where restructuring was forced upon management by a raider. Both of those companies had announced aggressive expansion plans despite declining fundamentals in the oil business, an approach guaranteed to put them directly "in harm's way."

Leveraged Share Repurchases

The second way to cure reinvestment risk, then, is to buy back stock aggressively and finance the purchase with

---

5. *Business Week*, (August 19, 1985).

debt. In such cases, the retirement of stock that may have taken place voluntarily over time is forcefully discounted to the present. Boone Pickens' threats prodded Unocal and Phillips to use corporate debt and leveraged ESOPs to finance a wholesale stock buyback, thus forcing recalcitrant management to discharge cash they otherwise would have used for unrewarding drilling projects or costly diversification.

Such leverage admittedly leaves Unocal and Phillips less able to withstand or capitalize on changing fortunes in the oil industry—one reason why companies that voluntarily restructure almost always outperform those forced to give in to a raider. *Business Week* concurs:

Exxon's program of stock buyback makes a lot more sense than scrambling around to buy new properties. If the oil business comes back, Exxon, tighter and richer, will be in far better shape to benefit than many oil companies now overloaded with debt.[6]

Partnerships

The third means to give investors control over the reinvestment of cash flow is to house assets in a partnership. We previously noted that a partnership can benefit investors by avoiding double taxation of earnings. Partnerships can cure reinvestment risk as well. By law, the investors in a partnership must include in taxable income their share of the partnership's earnings, whether distributed or not. Because there is no additional tax liability, investors usually insist that partnerships distribute all available cash flow.

On August 25, 1985, the board of Mesa Petroleum announced a plan to convert the corporation to a partnership, explaining the rationale for this move in a shareholders' prospectus:

Historically, the Company has paid out little of its cash flow as dividends and has been committed to a policy of replacing its annual production of oil and gas reserves through exploration and development and through acquisitions. The Company has paid relatively low amounts of federal income taxes because of deductions resulting from its expenditures. In recent years, however, the Company has significantly reduced its exploration and development expenditures in response to industry conditions, which will result in the Company's paying substantial federal income taxes if it continues its business as presently conducted.

In view of the limited reinvestment opportunities available to the Company, the Board of Directors believes that the

interests of stockholders will be better served if a substantial portion of its available cash flow is distributed directly to its owners. To distribute substantially greater cash flow more efficiently, the Board of Directors believes that the partnership form is preferable to the corporate form.

Mesa's stock price soared from $14 to $18 over the period surrounding the announcement. Although the voice of the market is all that really matters, analysts also saw the wisdom of the change and applauded it. A DLJ research bulletin responded as follows:

Properties appear to be worth full value in partnership form because the owners have control of the reinvestment as the partnership pays out most of its cash flow. Avoidance of the corporate tax and a higher basis for cost depletion add to the appeal of newly formed partnerships.[7]

Or, as an L.F. Rothschild analysis put it,

We anticipate that future capital expenditures, while rather limited, will have a relatively high rate of return because of the selectivity available to management.[8]

Although partnerhips normally pay out all available cash flow, this does not preclude them from expanding. Indeed, since becoming a partnerhip, Mesa has aggressively sought acquisitions, starting with Diamond Shamrock, usually by offering to swap new partnership units for a target's outstanding shares. Such expansion is not precluded, therefore, but must pass a market test.

Leveraged Acquisitions

Michael Jensen, cited earlier, has noted that debt-financed mergers also can assure investors that future cash flow will not be wasted. After a highly-leveraged acquisition is completed, the consolidated entity must dedicate the cash flows of both companies to repay debt. The result is much the same as if both firms independently had borrowed to buy back their own stock and then agreed to merge through a stock-for-stock swap.[9] A highly-leveraged merger milks two cash cows with one stroke.

SOCAL's acquisition of Gulf provides a good example, with Boone Pickens again playing the protagonist. Mr. Pickens' threats to acquire Gulf and convert it to a royalty trust prompted management to seek out a white knight. SOCAL answered their plea, paying $13.2 billion, all financed with debt, to acquire Gulf. Before the merger, SOCAL's leverage ratio (total debt-to-total debt and equity capital) was 10 percent and Gulf's was 20 percent. Afterwards, SOCAL and Gulf emerged with a consolidated leverage ratio of 40 percent, a debt burden still being paid off.

---

6. Ibid.

7. Donaldson Lufkin & Jenrette, *Securities Corporation Research Bulletin* (September 30, 1985).

8. L. F. Rothschild, Underberg, Towbin, Company Research (September 25, 1985).

9. "The Takeover Controversy: Analysis and Evidence," *Midland Corporate Finance Journal*, Vol. 4 No. 2 (Summer 1986), pp. 6-31.

Our calculations show that in the period surrounding the takeover, the combined market value of SOCAL and Gulf rose over $5 billion, compared to a portfolio of oil stocks. This remarkable increase in value is attributable to three things:

● first, the value of operating synergies—the textbook benefits derived from consolidation, rationalization, economies of scale, etc;

● second, the tax benefit of the new debt; and

● third, the elimination of a discount for reinvestment risk that had been placed on the value of both companies. Investors would be more inclined to fully value the future cash generated by both companies knowing it would be used to retire debt.

Dividends

The last method that commits a company to disgorge cash is to pay or increase dividends. Because most companies' boards are reluctant to cut dividends once they have been raised, an increase in dividends usually is interpreted by the market as a lasting commitment to pay out future cash flows to shareholders.

Arco, for example, increased dividends as part of an overall restructuring announced in May, 1985. Capital spending was cut 25 percent, annual operating expenses were reduced $500 million, and refining and marketing operations east of the Mississipi were put up for sale, freeing up cash for Arco to buy back 25 percent of its stock for $4 billion and to increase the dividend by 33 percent. Although Arco also took a $1.3 billion writedown of its eastern assets, investors reacted favorably, sending Arco's stock price rocketing from about $50 to $62.50, a gain in market value of $2.8 billion.

Although we have just demonstrated how increasing dividends increased market value as part of an overall restructuring, increasing dividends is usually a less desirable method for distributing cash. For one thing, it is not tax effective. From the company's viewpoint, dividends are less attractive than interest payments because they are not tax deductible. Investors also generally prefer a share repurchase program to receiving dividends for the following reasons: receiving dividends is compulsory but selling shares is voluntary; a capital gain from a stock sale can be offset by capital losses; and while dividends are taxed entirely, the gain to be taxed on repurchased shares is reduced by the investor's tax basis. Perhaps most important, though, the obligation a company incurs to pay dividends is not as compelling as servicing debt with its threat of bankruptcy (a topic we return to later).

Partial Public Offerings

Offering the public stock of a subsidiary unit stands in contrast to the methods that force the disgorgement of cash. A partial public offering binds the *use* of cash. Investors know that the cash raised from such a public sale will be used by the unit they have chosen to invest in, unlike an offering by the parent, where the funds raised must flow through a pachinko machine of competing internal uses with no assurance they will ever reach the most promising ventures.

Consider the case of McKesson Corporation, a $6 billion distributor of drugs, beverages, and chemicals that last year sold to the public a 16.7 percent stake in its Armor All subsidiary. Although Armor All accounted for only $90 million in sales (less than 2 percent of total revenues), McKesson's stock increased by 10 percent (from $60 to $66 a share) upon the announcement of the intended offering.

Armour All, however, is a rapidly growing (20% annually, compared to 10% for McKesson), highly profitable unit that McKesson could use to launch an expansion into consumer products. Able now to access capital directly, Armour All is more likely to reach its full growth. A public market for Armor All stock also helps establish a separate identity and sense of autonomy for employees, and enables the unit to attract and retain key executives through stock options, an important consideration in a heavily marketing-oriented and entrepreneurially-driven businesses.

Goodbye, Boston Consulting

These restructuring examples refute a planning paradigm popularized many years ago by The Boston Consulting Group wherein a company's mature "cash cows" were supposed to fund the growth of promising businesses ("question marks") into highly-performing "stars." By making a company self-funding and self-perpetuating, the BCG approach appealed to corporate managers because it circumvented the monitoring processes of the capital markets. In reality, the poorly-performing "dogs" ate the cash, while the "question marks" either were starved, overmanaged, or were acquired for obscene premiums.

Our analysis of stock prices has demonstrated that severing the link between mature cash cows and promising growth opportunites creates value. Let the "cows" pass their cash directly to investors. And let the "question marks" depend directly on the markets. Such a roundabout route is the most direct way to assure that value is created.

INCENTIVES

A debt-financed recapitalization can dramatically strengthen incentives. Raising debt to retire equity concentrates the remaining common shares in fewer hands. This increases the incentive for shareholders to monitor their investment closely and for management and employees, if they are given equity or an equity-like stake, to perform well.

Investor Incentives

The reason why concentrating equity benefits investors is first cousin to the theory that won James Buchanan the Nobel prize in economics. Mr. Buchanan wanted to understand why Congress passed laws that did not meet with general approval. The reason, he speculated, was that special interest groups successfully lobbied legislators to pass laws to benefit them at the expense of all taxpayers. When benefits are concentrated and costs are diffused, he believed, our democratic system of government lacks a safeguard to stop a minority from exploiting the majority.

A similar conflict exists in large, broadly-capitalized firms, this time between management and shareholders. Suppose that in an understandable search for job security, prestige, stability, and so forth, management made decisions that failed to maximize shareholders' wealth. While all shareholders would benefit from better management, the costs of waging a proxy fight or otherwise rallying investors would be borne selectively. Given the uneven distribution of costs and benefits, it may not make sense for an investor or small group of investors to shoulder the costs of opposing management.

But if debt were raised to retire shares, the equity of the firm would be concentrated in fewer investors' hands. With the cost of the value lost through mismanagement now more forcefully registered on each share, shareholders have greater motive to monitor the company's performance, giving management a greater incentive to perform.

To illustrate, suppose that a company starts with 10 million common shares selling at $10 each for a total market value of $100 million, and no debt. Assume that misguided management reduces value by $20 million, or $2 a share, so that the shares would trade for $12 if the company were properly managed.

Even this 20 percent discount might not lead shareholders to rebel. But if management could be induced, for example, to borrow $50 million to retire 5 million common shares in the open market, the $20 million of lost value would be spread over only 5 million remaining shares. The result—a $4 a share discount—would now be a full 40 percent of value, a gap which might indeed incite a shareholder revolt. Management, alert to the greater incentive that investors have to monitor their performance, would have to be more attentive to creating value for shareholders and less preoccupied with pursuing their own agenda.

For example, shortly after Sir James Goldsmith prompted Goodyear to buy back 48 percent of its stock, Robert E. Mercer, chairman and chief executive officer, said that Goodyear "will be more attuned to the stock price than before."[10] Goodyear reversed its wasteful diversification program, selling its aerospace unit to Loral and its oil reserves to Exxon for hefty premiums. Goodyear now concentrates on improving the value of its core tire and rubber operations.

A leveraged buyout carries even further the benefit of investor concentration. In these transactions, a broad herd of equity investors is replaced by a small group of "lead steers"—sophisticated debt and equity players—who act quickly and surely to restructure liabilities or replace management if such action is warranted. An LBO realigns management's interests with those of investors.

Incentives for Management and Employees

If, in the process of recapitalizing the company, management and employees receive an equity stake, the motivational benefits of equity concentration are further amplified. The accompanying "Compensation Risk Map" shows how restructuring incentives—moving left to right, from low risk to high risk—can create value.

No Guts-No Glory

The most secure, debt-like approach to compensation (on the far left of the chart) would be to pay a wage and provide a defined-benefit pension, a "no guts and no glory" scheme that clearly separates compensation from the success of the business. Employees are treated as bondholders and naturally they adopt the risk-averse mentality of creditors as they go about their appointed tasks. Worse yet, employees effectively become senior creditors because wages and pension payments are paid even before debt is serviced and, in the event of a bankruptcy, are senior to unsecured creditors. Such a compensation scheme robs a company of its capacity to raise debt.

Profit-Sharing

Let's move one notch to the right on the risk map and reduce wages (if not immediately, then over time), eliminate the defined-benefit pension, and introduce a very special sort of profit-sharing plan. This sort of compensation mix works more like a convertible security; one part provides the employee with the fixed return of a bond, while the other, like equity, is tied to the success of the firm.

Restructuring compensation this way accomplishes two things in one fell swoop:
● Incentives for employees are created for the first time and
● Debt capacity is augmented.

---

10. "Goodyear Tire and Rubber Sees Proceeds From Asset Sales Exceeding $3 Billion," *Wall Street Journal* (January 19, 1987).

FIGURE 1
COMPENSATION RISK MAP

Debt-like					Equity-like
Wage	Lower Wage	Lower Wage	Lower Wage	Lower Wage	X
Defined Benefit Pension	X	X	X	X	X
Interest Expense (Creditors)					
	Profit Sharing	Profit Sharing	Profit Sharing	Profit Sharing	X
		ESOP	ESOP	ESOP	X
			Leveraged Equity Purchase Plan	Leveraged Equity Purchase Plan	Leveraged Equity Purchase Plan
				Leveraged Cash-Out	

What should concern lenders is where they stand in line for payout on a company's income statement (or, to be more precise, on the cash flow statement), not their alleged priority on the balance sheet. Conventional accounting statements mistakenly show profit-sharing distributions as an expense that is senior to the payment of interest when, in fact, profits are shared only after interest expense has been covered. Because lenders are in line for payout before profits are shared, but after wages are paid, introducing a profit-sharing plan in lieu of wages increases debt capacity. It is unfortunate that most widely-followed leverage statistics fail to capture the substitution of income statement equity for balance sheet leverage that takes place as many companies restructure compensation.

To the greatest extent possible, bonuses should be based on the profits earned at a decentralized level—activity-by-activity, plant-by-plant, business unit-by-business unit—and not according to the results achieved by the company overall. Only that will forge a direct link between performance and compensation. If bonuses are based on general corporate profits, the link between pay and performance is so weak that profit-sharing has little value as an incentive.

Worthington Industries is one of a handful of large American companies that use profit-sharing to account for a major portion of employee compensation—at least 25 percent and in some cases as high as 50 percent. Management insists that its profit-sharing arrangement provides strong productivity incentives to workers. Moreover, by substituting variable for fixed costs, it virtually eliminates the need for layoffs and stabilizes profits in economic downturns.

ESOPs

Let's turn the compensation amplifier up another notch by introducing an Employee Stock Ownership Plan ("ESOP"), possibly in exchange for an even further reduction in wages. Providing employees with common stock in the firm through an ESOP accomplishes four things beyond sharing profits.

First, common stock represents a share in current and *future* profits. Employees are given the incentive to consider the long-term consequences of their actions.

Second, ESOP incentives accumulate: the number of shares an employee owns increases with each year's allocation, making their monetary and emotional stake in the firm grow over time. Profit-sharing incentives are unchanging. Nothing carries over from one year to the next.

Third, an ESOP can build up a company's debt capacity more effectively than can a profit-sharing plan because it is self-financing. By law, the cash a company contributes to an ESOP must be applied to purchase common shares in the sponsoring corporation (even if a company chooses to contribute common shares directly to the ESOP, the result is the same as if cash first was contributed to the ESOP and then used to buy company stock). An ESOP makes cash boomerang, carrying it out the front door as compensation and returning with it through the back door as new equity.

With profit-sharing, what goes out, stays out. Profit-sharing distributions, though calculated after interest expense is paid, need to be financed and may not necessarily be financed with company equity. Such financing risks are of concern to lenders and may limit a company from attaining its full debt capacity. ESOP contributions, however, are automatically equity-financed, a distinctive benefit that expands a company's debt capacity in a way that most conventional leverage ratios fail to acknowledge.

Fourth, Congress has granted ESOPs a number of special tax breaks that are not applicable to profit-sharing plans. For example, a commercial bank may exclude from its taxable income one-half of the interest received on a loan made to an ESOP. Because of this, ESOPs can borrow at favorable rates (usually less than 85% of prime) to pre-purchase shares in the sponsoring corporation (a "leveraged ESOP"). The ESOP trustee applies subsequent cash contributions from the company to pay down the ESOP loan and allocates inventoried shares of equivalent value to the employees (with vesting over a three-to-seven year period of plan participation). Even with such a leveraged ESOP, it still is true that contributions to the ESOP are equity financed. The equity financing simply takes place in advance.

Accounting for the formation of a leveraged ESOP is identical to a share repurchase: the company's debt goes up (by the amount of the ESOP loan) and its equity goes down (by the cost of the shares the ESOP purchases). The ESOP loan is considered a company liability because the company guarantees the loan and the loan must be repaid with cash contributed from the company. It is what happens afterwards that makes a leveraged ESOP different from a share repurchase.

As the company makes future cash contributions to the ESOP, its debt goes down and its equity goes up, a double-barreled reduction in leverage that is unique to ESOP's. Company debt declines as the ESOP loan is repaid. Equity is written up by the value of the common shares allocated to employees—a value that matches the debt retired. A share repurchase, by contrast, is followed by just a single-barreled blast at leverage: debt goes down as it is repaid, but equity does not automatically accrue. The two-fisted unleveraging of a leveraged ESOP is perhaps its greatest advantage as a tool of corporate finance: a company's ability to recover quickly from a debt-financed share repurchase dramatically increases with its use.

Having just sung the praises of leveraged ESOPs, we hasten to add that their benefits often are exaggerated by overzealous proponents. For example, much has been made of the fact that, whereas corporate debt must be amortized from a company's after-tax cash flow, ESOP debt is repaid from cash contributions that are tax-deductible. The alleged benefit arises from confusing an operating expense and a financing flow. . . . (See the Appendix for a more detailed account, and qualification, of the tax benefits of ESOP financing.)

The bottom line on ESOPs is that incentive, debt capacity and tax benefits team up to make them an attractive compensation restructuring device for many companies. A careful evaluation of an ESOP's real advantages is advisable, however, before taking action.

Leveraged Equity Purchase Plans

Now, let's turn the heat up yet several more degrees and make management sweat. While there are many ways to provide key managers with incentives to create value, one of the most exciting new concepts is the "leveraged equity purchase plan," a method popularized by the Henley Group.

Henley was formed in early 1986 as the spinoff of 35 poorly performing units from Allied-Signal. It floated to an initial market value of $1.2 billion, a remarkably lofty value considering that the businesses comprising Henley collectively lost $27 million the year before. To what can we attribute this impressive market value placed upon Henley? To Chairman Michael Dingman, his management team, and the expectation of very strong incentives for management to create value.

Henley unveiled an incentive scheme so powerful that we expect it to be widely imitated. On October 10, 1986, twenty of Henley's top executives bought, at a slight premium to market value, freshly issued shares in Henley amounting to about 5 percent of the company's common equity capitalization. The executive team financed the $108 million price tag for the 5.1 million with (1) a $97 million non-recourse loan from Henley that was secured by the shares and (2) with $11 million of their own capital. Not only is this a boon for management, it also benefits the company's investors. Here's why.

Should Henley's share value fall after the plan is initiated, the executives may tender their shares to Henley in satisfaction of the loan and without recourse to their personal assets. Granted, management can lose *only* their $11 million investment. But are the other shareholders hurt because the loan is non-recourse? Not in our opinion. An additional $11 million will be in the corporate coffers and no additional shares will be outstanding.

Should Henley perform well, it is true shareholders face a 5 percent dilution in upside value. But remember two things. First, Henley executives fully paid for the *initial* market value of the shares by incurring debt (which must be repaid before the shares could be sold) and by contributing capital. Shareholders are diluted only on the *increase* in value.

And second, management now has a dramatically heightened incentive to create value. Does it not make sense to offer the baker a piece of the pie if, as a result, he is apt to bake a much larger one for all to share?

Some may ask what separates the Henley incentive plan from ones where management simply is paid to increase value or proxies for value. In theory, nothing; in practice, everything.

First, no matter how good are the measures used to determine cash bonuses, there is no substitute for a traded stock price as an indicator of value. Most performance measures, for example, capture the results of a single period, while stock prices capitalize the value of good management decisions over the life of the business.

To illustrate this crucial difference, suppose that sound management leads to a competitive advantage, one improving operating profits after taxes by $20 million a year. If management is awarded a 5% share of the profits, the bonus pool would rise $1 million.

The share value of the company, however, is apt to capitalize the value of the annual profit improvement. If,

BESIDES PROVIDING A POWERFUL INCENTIVE TO MANAGEMENT, THE
HENLEY SCHEME ALSO IS AN EFFECTIVE FORM OF FINANCIAL
COMMUNICATION. JUST BY ANNOUNCING THEIR PARTICIPATION IN SUCH
A PLAN, MANAGEMENT ISSUES A STRONG STATEMENT ABOUT THEIR
CONFIDENCE IN AND COMMITMENT TO THE VALUE OF THE COMPANY.

for example, the cost of capital is 10 percent for our hypothetical company, value would rise $200 million ($20 million/.10). If management had obtained 5% of the shares through a leveraged equity purchase plan, the value of their stake would increase $10 million, or 10 times what they might expect from a profit-sharing plan. Owning equity amplifies the reward for good management decisions—and the penalties for poor ones.

There is, in addition, a crucial accounting difference between a cash bonus payment and a share ownership scheme. Cash bonus payments are recorded as an expense; an appreciation in the value of shares held by management is not. This remarkable inconsistency in accounting treatment is one reason, we believe, why many boards of directors feel uncomfortable about providing unlimited cash bonuses even in circumstances where management clearly deserves them. The preoccupation with maximizing reported earnings stands in the way of paying people what they are worth.

Another reason cash bonus payments often are limited is that they must be financed by the company whereas share appreciation is financed by the market. Though either selling shares or borrowing against them can compensate the manager who owns stock, neither drains financial resources directly from the firm. So, much like an ESOP, the compensation managers receive by participating in a leveraged equity purchase plan is automatically equity financed. This augments debt capacity, while cash compensation payments use it up.

Besides providing a powerful incentive to management, the Henley scheme also is an effective form of financial communication. Just by announcing their participation in such a plan, management issues a strong statement about their confidence in and commitment to the value of the company. When we encounter senior management groups who claim that their company is undervalued, we suggest it would be an opportune time to introduce a leveraged equity purchase plan. "Well, we are not *that* undervalued," they say.

The Henley plan assures more than just equity investors of management's commitment to creating value. It provides important safeguards for creditors as well. Lender's know that there is no surer way to guarantee the value of their debt than to provide management with an incentive to increase the value of the equity that stands beneath it. And, in a downturn, creditors must be comforted knowing of management's desire to recoup the $11 million of equity they contributed to the business. Again, published statistics on leverage fail to account for the crucial distinction between equity provided by management and equity provided by the market.

Chairman Michael Dingman explains his intentions: *"We believe that substantial borrowing and equity risk tak-*

ing by key executives will create the entrepreneurial conditions that are critical to Henley's success."[11]
Dingman also commented that the leveraged equity purchase program was modelled on the way executives participate in a leveraged buyout and was better than a stock option plan because executives make an up-front investment and can watch the value of that investment fluctuate with the stock price.

Henley is so pleased with the plan that it is making the same offer to key executives of its subsidiary business units. For example, after a stake in Fischer Scientific, a medical products subsidiary, was distributed to shareholders and began to trade, top executives there were able to purchase stock in the unit under a similar leveraged purchase plan. Henley's restructuring suggests that decentralized, pay-for-performance compensation schemes are coming into vogue for management as well as for the rank and file.

Where does corporate leverage fit into a leveraged equity purchase plan? Corporate leverage can make it easier for management to acquire a significant stake in the assets underlying the equity, an important consideration because managers really manage assets, not equity.

To illustrate, suppose that senior management was willing to invest $1 million to purchase equity in a company that had $100 million of assets. If the company were financed entirely with equity, management could acquire a mere 1% interest. If, however, the company borrowed $80 million to retire common shares, management could obtain a full 5% stake in the remaining $20 million of equity.

Such a recapitalization makes it possible for management to invest an amount equal to just 1% of the assets and to reap 5% of the payoff from improved asset management. Corporate leverage, by amplifying the benefit derived from a more productive use of resources, will multiply management's incentive to perform. This suggests that combining corporate leverage with a leveraged equity stake for management may be an extremely potent formula for creating value. The next step forward along our compensation risk path does just that.

The Empire Strikes Back: Leveraged Cash-Outs

The next step out, actually something of a great leap, takes us to the "leveraged cash-out," a powerful financial restructuring method that uses corporate leverage to amplify the incentive that owning equity provides to management and employees. Leveraged cash-outs have promoted such dramatic increases in market values that they have proven very effective in warding off hostile takeover bids.

With the value generated by the recapitalization as an ace up its sleeve, management can up the ante to the point where raiders usually decide to fold their cards or not

---

11. "Henley Group Says 20 Officials to Buy 5.1 Million Shares in Unusual Program," *Wall Street Journal* (October 10, 1986).

BY VOLUNTARILY TAKING ON A LEVERAGED EQUITY STAKE, [FMC'S]
MANAGEMENT IS EXPRESSING ITS COMMITMENT TO AND CONFIDENCE
IN CREATING AT LEAST $85 WORTH OF SHARE VALUE OUT OF A
COMPANY THAT WAS SELLING FOR JUST $70 A SHARE AT THE TIME OF
RECAPITALIZATION.

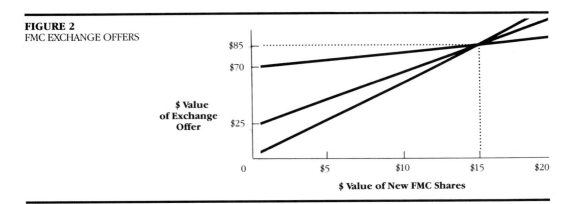

FIGURE 2
FMC EXCHANGE OFFERS

enter the bidding at all. Then, instead of a raider, a company's own stakeholders—its management, employees, customers and shareholders—walk away with a pot of added value.

The management of FMC Corporation, for example, sensing the company's vulnerability to an unsolicited offer, initiated a leveraged cash-out. As a pre-emptive strike to deter a raider, their restructuring followed the masochist's creed: be the first to do unto yourself as others would do unto you. No competing offer was forthcoming, and today FMC operates very successfully as an independent, publicly-traded entity. Let's see why.

On February 20, 1986, FMC proposed to exchange a package of cash and new shares for each common share held. At that time, FMC's shares were selling for about $70. There were three parties to the transaction, and three exchange offers:

● the "public" received $70 and 1 new share
● the thrift plan received $25 and 4 new shares
● management and PAYSOP received no cash and 5 2/3 new shares.

By accepting less cash but more new shares than the public, insiders increased their ownership in FMC from 14% to 41%. The recapitalization thus served to concentrate equity in the hands of management and employees, dramatically strengthening their incentive to perform (and to sell the company, should an attractive offer be made). The heightened incentives may be illustrated by plotting the exchange offers.

The horizontal axis represents the value of the new FMC shares, and the vertical axis is the corresponding value of the proposed exchange offer to the three parties. The points of intersection on the vertical axis are the cash portions of the offers: $70 for the public, to fully cash out the current market value of their shares, $25 for the thrift, and nothing for the management. The slope of the lines drawn from those points simply adds the value of the new

shares on top of the cash portion (1 share for the public, 4 for the thrift, and 5 2/3 for management).

All three intersect at a common point reflecting the "intrinsic" value of the transaction. Note that, should the new shares sell for $15, all three parties would hold $85 of value. The public, at one extreme, has $70 of cash and one new share worth $15. Management, at the other end, holds 5 2/3 shares also worth $85.

Should the new shares sell for more than $15 each, management (and the PAYSOP) would be the greatest beneficiary. For example, if the new shares sold for $20, management's 5 2/3 new shares would be worth $113.33, while the public's combination of $70 plus 1 new share would sum to a value of just $90. Should the new shares sell for less than $15 each, management would be the greatest loser. This aggressive payoff schedule indicated that, after the recapitalization, management would hold a Henley-like leveraged equity stake in FMC. FMC's message to investors sounds a lot like Henley's, too. By voluntarily taking on a leveraged equity stake, management is expressing its commitment to and confidence in creating at least $85 worth of share value out of a company that was selling for just $70 a share at the time of recapitalization.

The message was heeded by the market: FMC's shares rose from a price of $70 to just over $85 as the recapitalization was first announced. Before the deal was sealed, however, FMC's shares nearly touched $100. Apparently Ivan Boesky, as a result of sound financial analysis (and some inside information), was buying FMC shares. To mollify the public and turn back Boesky's threat, management subsequently had to increase the public's cash portion to $80.

With nearly 25 million shares outstanding, the recapitalization increased FMC's total market value by $750 million ($30 price increase x 25 million shares), an increase in value that is net of $60 million in costs incurred and fees paid to professional advisors.

This remarkable appreciation in value can be attribut-

TABLE 1
SUMMARY OF FMC'S
PERFORMANCE
($ MILLIONS)

	Before Recap	After Recap	
	1981-1985*	1986	1987 (6 mo.)
Revenue Growth	(1)%	(8)%	3%
EBIT/Capital	13%	18%	23%
EBIT/Sales	7%	10%	12%
Working Capital/Sales	13%	3%	5%
Free Cash Flow**	$250	$320	$500
Total Debt/Total Capital	20%	100%	90%
EBIT/Interest	6.6×	2.2×	1.5×
Stock Price Appreciation	17%	62%	35%

* Average over 5-year period
** Cash flow from operations, after taxes but before financing charges, net of new investment in working capital and fixed
assets.

ed largely to the benefits of debt financing:
• Operating profits for the foreseeable future will be sheltered almost entirely from corporate taxation;
• With discretionary cash flow dedicated to debt service the risk of an unproductive reinvestment has been eliminated;
• Management and employees have greater incentives to perform, and more obvious penalties for failure.

Just how much debt financing was used? Gulp!! To finance the cash payments, FMC became *very* highly leveraged. In fact, debt initially increased from 25 percent to over 125 percent of combined debt and equity capital. Because the cash paid to investors handily exceeded the book value of FMC's common shares, the company emerged from the recapitalization with a negative accounting net worth. (Not to worry, however, because market capitalization exceeded $700 million.) How is it possible that such astounding leverage could be serviced?

First, FMC announced that the new shares would not pay dividends. By conserving cash that otherwise would flow to its shareholders, FMC augmented its ability to retire debt. Non-tax-deductible dividends were converted to fully-deductible interest payments. But far more important than dividend retention is the fact that every important measure of corporate health, except growth, improved after the recapitalization.

The carrot of incentives and the stick of potential bankruptcy spurred FMC's management and employees to exceptional performances. Widening profit margins and a more efficient management of working capital improved profitability. Free Cash Flow, the single best indicator of ability to service debt, exploded. The combination of slower growth and improved profitability opened the floodgates on the discretionary cash generated to pay down debt. The money that FMC disgorged will pour back into our economy to be investment in promising ventures.

An additional appeal of leveraged cash-outs is that they avoid many of the ethical complications of LBO's. In a leveraged buyout, management benefits richly if the value of the company can be increased beyond the price offered to buy out the public shareholders. This creates a conflict between management's responsibility to shareholders and its self-interest. There is no way to get around the suspicion that management steals the company from the public shareholders in an LBO that subsequently performs well.

With a leveraged cash-out, however, investors participate in the value created after the recapitalization because they retain shares in the sponsoring company. Moreover, a shareholder could, if he wished, duplicate management's stake. In the FMC transaction, for example, the $70 of cash that a public shareholder received could be used to purchase 4 and 2/3 new shares (at the intrinsic share price of $15). When those new shares are added to the one new share issued in the exchange, the public shareholder, like the insiders, would hold 5 and 2/3 new shares.

A public shareholder also could reverse the recapitalization. By using the cash received from the exchange offer to buy a representative slice of the debt issued by FMC to finance the exchange offer, a shareholder could restore the claim that shareholders held on FMC's earnings before the recapitalization. Now, however, FMC's original common equity is divided into a lower risk-for-lower expected reward, interest-earning claim (the junk debt) and a higher risk-for-higher expected reward, non-dividend-paying claim (the new FMC shares). Such a financial restructuring cannot change the risk in the underlying assets, nor can it force a shareholder, or society at large, to bear more risk.

The benefit of hindsight indicates that joining management, and thus maximizing one's equity stake in FMC, would have been a wise decision. Since the recapitalization, the new FMC shares have sold for as much as $60, giving the 5 2/3 new shares a peak value of $340, certainly not a bad return for a stock that sold for $70 before the recapitalization was announced.

FMC did not escape the October, 1987 market meltdown, however. FMC's common shares by late 1987 were selling for approximately $30 each, at roughly half their $60 peak. The S&P 500 had dropped a mere 30% during that interval. Does this disparity challenge the wisdom of FMC's leveraged cash-out? Not at all.

FMC's shares fell further in value than the S&P 500 because of their greater financial risk, making the comparison grossly unfair. Investment risk must be the same in order to meaningfully compare return outcomes. To properly compare how well FMC's public shareholders would have done with and without the leveraged cash-out, we must assume that the cash proceeds received in the exchange offer were used to purchase FMC's junk debt. Comparing the return on $70 worth of FMC junk debt (actually $80 worth with the revised offer) and one new FMC share with the S&P 500 is a fair measure of the wisdom of the leveraged cash-out. Because FMC's debt declined in value only modestly after the market crash, the risk-adjusted performance of FMC actually was better than the S&P 500—an endorsement of the leveraged cash-out.

That is all well and good for the fortunate public shareholders. But what about management who, by design of the exchange offer, were forced to hold just new shares in FMC? Of course the crash hurt them more than shareholders who could place the cash proceeds from the exchange offer into lower risk investments. But do not weep for management. Even the marked-down $30 value for the new shares they hold is 50% more than their initial $20 value. Moreover, the 5 2/3 shares given to management in the recapitalization are still worth nearly $170, a 140 percent gain over the original $70 share value.

The Ultimate Incentive

The most equity-like compensation on the risk map provides no wage, pension, profit sharing or ESOP. Indeed, the last step is the Lee Iaccoca plan: a $1 salary combined with a load of stock options. Terrific incentive, Lee. How one eats before your ship comes in we can only surmise.

[The two final sections of this article, "Forced Sales" and "Organizational Imperatives," will appear in the next issue of this journal.]

APPENDIX: QUALIFYING THE TAX BENEFITS OF ESOPS

An ESOP is much the same as compensating employees with cash and then requiring them to purchase an equivalent value of company common shares (all without imposing a current tax on the employee, a benefit common to all qualified retirement plans). A company's contributions to an ESOP are tax-deductible because they are a real compensation expense of the firm. The fact that the compensation is converted into company stock does not diminish its cost, nor does the fact that the company's liability to repurchase those shares may be deferred until the distant future. The expected present value cost to repurchase shares allocated to employees, no matter how far off, is, by definition, the current value of those shares.

A leveraged ESOP is just an ordinary ESOP coupled with an up-front, debt-financed share repurchase. A leveraged ESOP entails much the same thing as:
- first, compensating employees with cash (a tax-deductible expense);
- next, requiring them to use the cash to buy company common shares of an equivalent value from the ESOP; and
- lastly, making the ESOP apply the proceeds from the stock sale to pay down its debt (a non-tax-deductible financial event).

By sleight of hand, many ESOP peddlers would have their clients erroneously associate the benefit of deducting the ESOP contribution with the repayment of the debt when in fact, the tax-deduction arises from incurring a compensation expense—the granting of shares to employees. Despite appearances, it simply is not cheaper to amortize debt through an ESOP than it is through the company itself.

In truth, the benefits of a leveraged ESOP over an ordinary one are that money can be borrowed at a lower interest rate (but not that principal can be serviced more cheaply), it permits the company to contribute to the ESOP each year up to $60,000 per employee instead of $30,000, and maybe one more thing.

In the Tax Reform Act of 1986, Congress enacted a change in the treatment of dividends that many leveraged ESOP boosters claim is a sure-fire benefit. In fact, it may or may not be helpful, depending upon the circumstances.

A company can now deduct from its taxable income dividends that it pays on common shares held by an ESOP, but only if the ESOP trustee uses those dividends to repay an ESOP loan, an action that frees-up additional shares to be allocated to employees.

If the dividends used to repay the ESOP loan come from shares that the ESOP already had allocated to employees, there is a real benefit. In such a case, the company gets a tax-deduction without incurring an additional expense and without harm to the plan participants. The cash dividends that would have credited to the participants' accounts are simply transformed into company common shares of equivalent value. No harm done, but the company gets a tax-deduction merely for effecting this bit of financial alchemy.

If, however, the dividends used to repay the ESOP loan come from shares held in escrow—that is, not yet allocated by the ESOP to plan participants—there is an offsetting cost. In such a case, the shares allocated to employees represent additional compensation. The tax deduction the company receives on the dividend is only consistent with the expense incurred in granting employees new shares to which they would not otherwise be entitled. Unless the added expense is offset by the benefits arising from improved employee incentive, or from reductions in other forms of compensation, using such dividends to repay the ESOP loan may turn out to be an expensive way for a company to amortize debt.

Another problem many ESOP afficiondos gloss over is that, no matter which of the preceding cases applies, tax-deductible dividends can lead to one of life's most unpleasant experiences—a minimum tax liability. By law, one-half of the difference between taxable income (after certain adjustments) and reported income is a tax preference item subject to a minimum tax of 20%. Deductible for tax but not book purposes, ESOP dividend payments give rise to just such a tax preference, and a potential minimum tax assessment. The Lord giveth and the Lord taketh away.

The IRS reserves one of the most generous of an ESOP's tax benefits for the owners of private companies. They are entitled to sell shares to an ESOP and to defer paying a tax on any gain (provided that the proceeds are reinvested in domestic companies and the ESOP owns at least 30% of the company stock after the sale). This tax code provision enables the owners of private corporations to cash-out and diversify their accumulated wealth without incurring a current tax, while providing for the eventual transfer of the shares to company employees, a nifty benefit to be sure.

In addition, private companies can establish ESOP's for employees of individual business units within the overall company, a benefit that generally is denied to public firms. Under such a plan, the ESOP trustee uses cash contributed by a subsidiary to acquire the subsidiary's shares (either existing shares held by the parent or new shares issued by the sub) and allocates those shares to the plan participants, giving them an incentive to improve the performance and value of the particular business unit that they directly influence.

A public company can establish an ESOP for a subsidiary unit only if the unit is taken public through an offering of a partial interest. In the absence of such a partial public offering, a public company is required to use parent company stock in an ESOP, a restriction that makes it difficult for a public company to forge a link between pay and performance as strong as that available to employees of private firms.

THE MOTIVES AND METHODS OF CORPORATE RESTRUCTURING: PART II

by G. Bennett Stewart III and David M. Glassman, Stern Stewart & Co.*

FORCED SALES

When a company undergoes a dramatic leveraging, one often will hear it said that its debt load is "intolerable." But our answer to this, in the majority of cases, is "Quite right and deliberately so!" Management's response to a staggering debt load must be to sell unrelated and underperforming assets and businesses, thereby reaping the dual benefits of "fit" and "focus."

Fit

When a business or asset is worth more to another company or under a different management team, it can be sold for a value greater than it contributes to the seller, a tangible reward for finding a better "fit."

A shrewd seller will look at a divestiture first from the buyer's perspective. When scrutinizing an acquisition candidate, a buyer will figure into the potential purchase price the value of all the synergies he expects to derive, and then will try to pay something less than that. In practice, however, buyers often tend to overpay, letting their natural enthusiasm for expansion overrule pure economic logic.

For the seller, the buyer's logic and emotion are reversed. The seller receives, up-front and in cash, much (if not all or even more than all) of the value that the buyer expects to create, while the buyer is left with hopeful expectations and risk. Is it any wonder that the break-up values of many companies exceed their current trading prices?

Take Beatrice, for example. After its LBO, Beatrice was saddled with $7.5 billion of debt, and just over $400 million of equity. Don Kelley, recalled from semi-retirement to run the company, had to sell assets quickly. Two of his most prominent divestitures were the sale of the Coca-Cola Bottling Company of Los Angeles to the Coca Cola Company, and the sale of the dairy business to Borden.

Coca-Cola subsequently packaged the LA franchise with other bottling properties and sold a 51 percent stake to the public. Some of the benefits that Coca-Cola obtained by this restructuring were passed back to Beatrice in the price paid to acquire Coke of LA. Borden likewise rewarded Beatrice with part of the value created by combining Beatrice's dairy operation with its own. It becomes clear, with the benefit of hindsight, that the banks which financed Beatrice's LBO were lending not against Beatrice's cash flow or its assets, but against the value of its businesses in the hands of other, more productive owners.

In a divestiture what counts is the question of relative, not absolute value—that is, whether the asset or business is worth more in someone else's hands than it is in ours. Such logic is not widely practiced. If a broad cross-section of corporate management were asked to identify candidates for divestiture, many would ignore considerations of relative worth, and would instead simply rank their business units from the best to worst performing, and offer to dispose of the ones at the bottom of the heap. This kind of mistaken thinking has been derided by Warren Buffet as "gin-rummy divestitures": simply discard your worst card at each turn.

Union Carbide provides a good illustration of the importance of weighing relative instead of absolute values. To defeat GAF's all-cash bid, Union Carbide had to go deeply into debt to retire shares at a premium price. If you had asked management, before the debt gun was pointed to their head, which of their businesses they would have liked to sell, they might well have offered up the company's traditional chemicals business.

Instead, they sold Eveready battery and their home and automotive consumer businesses, widely regarded as the company's crown jewels. Did this move make sense? Robert D. Kennedy, Chairman

---

*This article was previously published by, and is reprinted with the permission of, *Cash Flow* magazine.

and Chief Executive Officer of Union Carbide, seems to think so:

Did we like parting with a billion-dollar battery products business that was a leader in its field? I'd be lying if I said it was something we would have done without a gun to our heads. But if your mission is getting value to your shareholders, a good case can be made that it was the right thing to do even before the gun was drawn. In fact, I'm inclined to think that all strategic planning should be done as if somebody had a gun to your head. It forces you to make the tough choices.

Now, after the fact, I can tell you that it might have been time to sell battery products precisely because it was a good business, and there wasn't much we could do to make it better. . . . As for the purchaser, Ralston Purina—a total consumer products company with broad consumer distribution, with wholesaler leverage, with consumer-marketing smarts, and the ability to look at a mega-buck consumer advertising budget without feeling faint—the battery business is in a much more congenial environment than it ever was at Carbide. That's a fact. And a lesson learned.[1]

Just as in international trade, divestitures ought to follow comparative advantage. The question to consider is not whether a business has bright or deteriorating prospects (it will have those same prospects for the buyer), but whether the buyer possesses a distinct advantage the seller cannot duplicate.

From this perspective, a divestiture need not imply a failure on the part of the seller. Rather, it can be the result of good management, a harvesting of the fruits of past successful investments, with a transfer to those most able to further increase value.

Buy, Build, Harvest

One firm that considers divestitures to be a sign of success is Bairnco, a name recalling the Scottish expression for children. Bairnco's philosophy is to acquire a family of separate companies with focused product lines, nurture them to the point where they may stand on their own, and then harvest their value through a distribution of shares to Bairnco shareholders (a "spinoff"). Managers who know they may eventually share in the value they help to create

while they are with Bairnco have a special motivation to perform, one that is usually not offered to managers of most companies.

The first such company to be spun-off, Kaydon Corporation, a Michigan-based maker of specialty bearings, left the Bairnco fold in April, 1984 through a one-for-one stock dividend to Bairnco stockholders. The officers of Kaydon owned 20 percent of the stock of the company at the time of the spinoff.

As a further incentive (as if owning a significant equity stake were not enough), a staggering $60 million of debt was loaded onto the shoulders of Kaydon's $10 million of equity. By spinning off Kaydon in this form, Bairnco realized for its investors the benefits of a leveraged cash-out structure: the tax savings of debt financing, the forced disgorgement of cash, and the exceptional incentives to perform and penalties for failure.

Not surprisingly, Kaydon, like FMC, has performed exceptionally well. From an initial stock price of $2.50, Kaydon's shares rose to over $25 a share, a 1,000 percent increase, directly benefiting those Bairnco shareholders who held onto the Kaydon shares they received.

Indeed, an investor who owned Bairnco shares from 1975 to 1985, and who held onto the Kaydon shares distributed, would have achieved a better than 40% compound average annual return. Bairnco is but one of many examples we could cite to demonstrate that buying, building and harvesting is a powerful new formula for creating value, one apparently superior to the more traditional buy-and-hold or buy-and-sell strategies.

Focus

Focus is the benefit that comes when unrelated activities have been divested and management can concentrate on solving problems and finding attractive investment opportunities in the remaining businesses. With the simplification of the company, moreover, superfluous bureaucratic layers often can be slashed, speeding decision-making and promoting initiative.

One of the theories supporting conglomerates was that good managers can manage anything. Maybe. But even if true, good managers cannot effectively

---

1. Robert D. Kennedy, Chairman and CEO of Union Carbide, "The New Union Carbide: Some Assembly Required, Batteries Not Included," *Planning Review* May/June 1987, p. 10.

manage everything at the same time.

Several years ago, at a roundtable discussion our firm sponsored covering effective financial communication with investors, an investment banker suggested that conglomerates sold at a discount because securities analysts found them difficult to follow. Michael Sherman, head of investment strategy for Shearson Lehman Brothers, bristled. "It's not that conglomerates are difficult for analysts to understand. We worry that conglomerates are difficult for management to understand," he countered.

Perhaps investment bankers are just being politic when they blame the market for management's shortcomings. But in so doing, they obscure the real motives underlying the need to restructure.

To conclude, divestitures can create value in two ways:

● The seller receives, in cash and in advance, a part if not more than all of the value that a buyer expects to create; and

● Management can devote its undivided attention to creating value with the assets left behind.

The Case of Trinova

One of the clearest illustrations of the dual benefits of fit and focus comes from Libby Owens Ford (now called "Trinova"). LOF's original flat glass business carried the company's lowest profit margin and required substantial capital investment to remain competitive. The company's other businesses, fluid power and plastics, offered far brighter growth prospects and higher profitability. Meanwhile, Pilkington Brothers, a British glass company, had acquired a 30 percent stake in LOF.

The restructuring, first announced on February 27 and then confirmed on March 10, 1986, saw LOF swap the flat glass business for the shares Pilkington held. Upon the announcement, LOF's shares increased in value from approximately $60 a share to just over $75, a 25 percent gain, representing more than $200 million in total gains for its shareholders.

The impressive value created by this financial restructuring can be attributed to improvements in fit and focus. Start with the fact that, due to operating economies, the glass business was more valuable in Pilkington's hands than in LOF's. As a consequence, Pilkington Brothers could afford to pay, through the value of the shares surrendered, a price that more

than adequately compensated LOF and still come out ahead. That is the hallmark of a "win-win" transaction: the value created by a more efficient use of assets transferred is shared by the two parties.

But in our desire to extol the benefits of a better "fit," let us not forget to cite "focus." After the spinoff of glass, LOF could more reliably and aggressively realize the full value of its other businesses. As a *Value Line* analyst commented, "We like the deal...By divesting itself of the unit, LOF will be able to concentrate its efforts on the fluid power and plastics businesses (which) offer far better growth potential than does the glass industry."

The growth of the new Trinova has been so rapid that, even with the divestiture, the new company has already become larger than its predecessor. Management has admitted that growth in fluid power and plastics would have been stunted by the diversion of time and capital resources to glass.

Debt admittedly was not a part of LOF's restructuring. All the better, really. Parting with businesses worth more to others, and concentrating on your opportunities, is a maxim that should not need debt to prove it. Of necessity, however, we do need debt to instill a vital organizational drive for excellence (if not survival), our next and final topic.

ORGANIZATIONAL IMPERATIVE

Equity is soft, debt hard. Equity is forgiving, debt insistent. Equity is a pillow, debt a sword. Equity and debt are the yin and yang of corporate finance.

Equity lulls management to sleep, forgiving their sins more readily than a death-bed priest. A surplus of stock muffles the alarms that should be heard when earnings decline. Forgive and forget is equity's creed.

Debt's edge jabs management awake, demanding attention. A staggering debt load is a credible threat, compelling necessary changes and exceptional performance.

"With leverage," say Nelson Peltz and Peter May, "managements get tougher, they go out and make sales, and they do all the things that built America."[2] Peltz and May relied almost exclusively on debt to finance their acquisitions of National Can and American Can, building their flagship company, Triangle Industries, from a pipsqueak juke box concern to a powerful industrial empire in just three years. They

---

2. *Business Week*, September 15, 1986.

tell us there is a potent psychological difference between living on the edge with debt and slumbering upon an equity pillow.

The Japanese know this, too. In fact, they may have learned it first. By now the benefits of the Japanese "just-in-time" production system are widely acknowledged. Adopting a precise, seemingly impossible, schedule forces workers to iron out problems as they arise and at their source. By purposely taking flexibility out of the system, the system must be fine-tuned to work better.

Can the corollary benefit of Japanese financial structures built upon towering leverage ratios go unnoticed? Debt is the "just-in-time" financial system. The precise obligation to repay it is another mechanism to squeeze out operating inefficiencies. Leaving no margin for error guarantees that fewer errors are committed. Enlarging the consequences of making a mistake ensures that fewer mistakes are made. The result is a more valuable enterprise.

Incentives are the carrot. The threat of bankruptcy is the stick. Both are important motivators.

Earnings or Cash Flow

Besides supplying the impetus to perform well, debt also compels managers to reckon with one of the most fundamental questions of corporate value: Is it earnings or cash flow that really matters?

Many senior managers of publicly-traded companies, captivated by the cant of the popular press, securities analysts, and investment bankers, believe in the myth that the market wants earnings. To satisfy their shareholders' supposedly irrational longing for reported profits, they feel compelled to capitalize outlays that should be expensed to save taxes, to give short shrift to sensible R&D and market-building expenditures, to stay the execution of dying businesses and, perhaps worst of all, to fuel earnings growth by over-investing in mature ones.

Put a lot of debt on their books and sight is restored to the blind. With the earnings myth vanquished, management's attention is directed to the wellspring of all corporate values—the generation of cash.

It was many years ago that we first witnessed this magical transformation, and our faith has been reinforced many times since. It happened when we questioned the CFO of a midwestern company that had recently gone private about his management's attitude towards the LBO:

"Fantastic," he said. " At one time we thought there was an income statement and a balance sheet to manage. Now we see that there is only one statement that matters—sources and uses of cash. Can we pay back the banks?"

"And," he said, "we are now looking three to five years out, to a time when we can take the company public or sell it. It's value creation that concerns us. Before the LBO we were preoccupied with quarterly E.P.S. growth."

"One last thing. We are increasing our research and development in selected areas. Before we were reluctant to do so because it would have reduced our earnings. But now we can see the real benefit."

It seems a shame that only by going private can management be brought to see the light. It is a pity, indeed, because there is strong evidence to show that, even for public companies, share values are determined by expected cash generation over the life of the business. Our suggestion: run your public company as if it were privately held—that is, with the attitude that cash is king—and you will be making the right decisions for your public shareholders.

Hospital Corporation of America: A Case Study in Value Creation

The formation of HealthTrust, Inc. (HT), a spinoff of Hospital Corporation of America (HCA), provides a good case study—one that clearly demonstrates a change in management's motivation brought about by debt.

Through a long chain of acquisitions, HCA had become the largest investor-owned hospital company in the United States. Its rapid growth made the company a darling of Wall Street. But then HCA's earnings fell under intense pressure, battered by forces that had laid low the entire industry. The use of hospitals had declined because of more stringent rules on insurance reimbursements and increased competition from such health care alternatives as HMOs.

One sign of overcapacity was HCA's proposal to combine with American Hospital Supply (AHS) in mid-1985. By offering to join one of the industry's primary suppliers of medical equipment, HCA sought to maintain its growth through vertical integration. Investors, however, sensing that other hospitals would refuse to purchase medical supplies from a competitor, attached a negative value to the merger. In the wake of HCA's announcement of the intended takeover, the market value of HCA and AHS, both buyer and seller, fell, a phenomenon almost unique in the annals of corporate acquisitions.

To the relief of HCA's shareholders, Baxter Travenol eventually acquired AHS. But scar tissue remained. Once burned, investors would be twice shy about paying a premium to own HCA's shares. HCA's share value was penalized thereafter by a discount for reinvestment risk, an enticement to a raider.

On April 10, 1987 HCA received the inevitable takeover bid which, while later withdrawn, did reveal the company's vulnerability. To their credit, management responded with an effective restructuring plan.

On June 1, 1987, HCA's board approved a plan to sell 104 of its least profitable general hospitals to a newly-formed employee-owned company, Health-Trust, Inc. HCA would retain 78 of the larger, more profitable general hospitals, mostly concentrated in the Southeast, and all 50 of the company's lucrative psychiatric hospitals.

HealthTrust financed the $1.6 billion price tag for the hospitals by selling 99.5 percent of its shares to an ESOP formed for the benefit of its employees. The ESOP, in turn, funded the share purchase by raising $1.6 billion though Drexel Burnham and a consortium of banks, a staggering debt burden indeed.

Interestingly, HealthTrust's new chairman and chief executive officer, R. Clayton McWhorter, was formerly the president and chief operating officer of the old HCA. He and other members of management agreed to purchase the one-half percent common stock interest in HT not held by the ESOP, and to have an incentive plan that could eventually award them as much as 10 percent of the stock. That's the carrot. McWhorter describes the stick: "It's amazing what you'll do when your back is to the wall and you're highly leveraged. When I get up in the morning, I don't have to worry about the board or the founder. I just think about the lenders."[3]

For most of his tenure at HCA, McWhorter says, the priority was growth. That did not leave much time to improve operating efficiencies or to focus on any one small hospital. McWhorter and his management team now march to a different drummer. To fend off lenders, they must now concentrate on harvesting cash from the small hospitals, a change in emphasis brought about by the financial restructuring—and fear.

Besides improving management's motivation, HCA's restructuring also cured an organizational deficiency. It is generally accepted that smaller hospitals have to look for profitable niches and avoid loss-leaders that big hospitals may sustain in order to attract patient volume. The problem at HCA was that management was playing in both the major and the minor leagues—two businesses inside one company. "It was hard to think small in the morning and big in the afternoon," notes McWhorter of his tenure at HCA.

BIFURCATION

This points to a powerful restructuring theme: "bifurcation," or the splitting of a business into two or more units which sum to a value greater than that of the original whole. Bifurcations create value by improving management focus, sharpening incentives, creating pure-plays that have a unique investment appeal, increasing debt capacity, and establishing market-driven transfer prices.

HCA's bifurcation involved separating the small from the large, the unprofitable from the profitable, the mature from the growing.

One resulting benefit is improved focus for management on both sides of the transaction. With the sale of the small hospitals to HealthTrust, HCA will withdraw completely from many states, leaving its management free to emphasize markets where it has clusters of hospitals, such as Houston and Nashville.

A second advantage is that incentives for management are made more precise. Without the small hospitals, HCA's stock price will become more responsive to management's success in overseeing the large hospitals and in growing from a concentrated geographic base, making stock options and other equity-linked compensation plans more effective as incentives to perform.

The Case of Minnetonka

A similar, though perhaps more extensive, bifurcation was carried out last year at Minnetonka, a company driven by the creative genius of its founder, Mr. Robert Taylor.

Minnetonka's first big hit was Softsoap, the original pump-dispensed liquid soap. After enjoying several years of skyrocketing growth in the early 1980's,

3. "Big Debt Burden Forces Head of Former Units to Set Priorities," *The Wall Street Journal*, November 17, 1987.

Minnetonka almost went bankrupt when Proctor & Gamble and Colgate-Palmolive launched competing products backed by overwhelming advertising campaigns. Near desperation, Minnetonka introduced Check-Up, the first pump-dispensed toothpaste to emphasize tartar control. That success, and the stabilization of Softsoap's market share, saved the company.

In recent years, Minnetonka has grown by emphasizing upscale beauty products less suspectible to being dethroned by the mass-marketing giants, a strategy that began with the acquisition of Calvin Klein cosmetics. Surely not even the most hardened couch potato could have missed Minnetonka's bizarre but effective television advertisements for the newly-formulated Obsession line of perfumes and colognes, another big winner ringing up over $100 million in sales and unconscionable profits within two years of its introduction.

Encouraged by this success, Minnetonka made a conscious decision to "bifurcate." It moved from "mass" to "class," divesting its established mass-market product lines. In early 1987, Soaftsoap was sold to Colgate Palmolive and Check-Up toothpaste to S. C. Johnson, leaving behind Calvin Klein, new product ventures, and a focus on upscale cosmetics.

What are the benefits of Minnetonka's bifurcation? Both Softsoap and Check-Up had settled into a stable market share, where generating incremental profitability depended upon manufacturing efficiencies and international expansion—areas in which other firms held a comparative advantage. Departing from these businesses left Minnetonka free to concentrate on growth opportunities in the upscale market.

So far, these sound like the standard divestiture benefits of a better business fit and an improved focus for management. True. But there are additional benefits to the bifurcation. Minnetonka's stock, absent the steady annuity streams from its mature product lines, will be far more responsive to management's success in bringing new products to market, making equity ownership a stronger incentive for management to perform.

Without the restructuring, moreover, Minnetonka might have adopted a consolidated capital structure that had both too little and too much debt—too little to take full advantage of the debt capacity of its mature product lines, but too much debt to provide Minnetonka with the flexibility needed to carry out its aggressive plans for growth. Take away its leveragable businesses, and Minnetonka can adopt a conservative financial posture—one relying heavily on equity to finance risky new product development and acquisitions—without attracting the attention of the raiders. The bifurcation, in other words, made it possible for appropriate financial structures to be set for businesses in different stages of their life cycles, an important benefit.

Lastly, the sale of the two mature product lines informs investors that Minnetonka has made an important strategic decision: it will concentrate on developing new, upscale products, leaving on-going product management to others. The bifurcation separates the value that Minnetonka creates in product development from the mere ownership and maintenance of assets. If Minnetonka can establish a track record by bringing still more successful consumer products to market and selling the resulting businesses for premium values, the recurring gains on such sales would enter the company's stock price with a manufacturing multiple.

In this respect Minnetonka is much like a real estate developer. To be successful, a developer must select the right property to develop at the right time for the right purpose and with the right market appeal, all at a cost that is affordable. Once a new property is completed and fully leased, the developmental process ends, and is succeeded by the mere ownership and maintenance of an annuity stream.

The Case of Koger Properties

One company that uses financial restructuring to highlight the value created by developing real estate is Koger Properties of Jacksonville, Florida. A measure of the value that they create in developing new commercial properties is the difference between the value of the property appraised at the moment it is first fully leased, and the capitalized cost of all investment made to that point. To isolate and highlight this measure of performance, Koger in 1976 formed a separate entity, the Koger Partnership, for the special purpose of acquiring fully-developed properties from Koger Properties, and then owning and managing them.

The Koger Partnership purchases properties from Koger Properties at a price established by independent appraisal and at a time when the new properties are first over 95 percent leased. In other words, the transfer takes place when the developmental process has been completed and when it is first possible to make an accurate appraisal of value.

Because Koger sells newly-developed properties to the Koger Partnership on a regular basis, the sales Koger Properties records are analogous to the revenues of a manufacturing company. With Koger Properties' investment basis in the transferred-properties serving as a cost of goods sold, the gain on sale is the net operating profit for the developmental machinery.

With this separate but integrated structure, Koger isolates the profitability of the creative developmental process—its "value added"—from the ownership and maintenance of an annuity stream, making the true performance of the company easier for shareholders and lenders to appraise.

The bifurcation brings additional benefits to Koger:
• it allows the company to obtain equity financing for its projects without carving in new investors to the flagship company, Koger Properties;
• it enhances debt capacity by separating the proven, predictable cash flow streams from the unproven ventures;
• it creates two relatively unique pure plays for investors—one, in the low risk seasoned properties and the other, in risky new property development;
• it fine-tunes incentives for management by making Koger Properties stock price reflect solely the entrepreneurial value-added;
• and it saves taxes (although we won't go into that here).

Commercial Banks, Coca-Cola, and Others

Other recent commercial bank restructurings are reminiscent of HCA's, whose bifurcation separated problems from opportunities. A growing number of banks are similarly shedding their problem loans by putting them into a separate unit and spinning the unit off to shareholders, enabling management to concentrate on the bank's opportunities without the distractions of the problems:

Believing that its troubled loans are unfairly depressing its stock price, First Interstate plans to spin off some $400 million of its own troubled loans to its shareholders later this year. 'We think we're worth more as two parts than as a whole,' said Frederick J. Elsea, a senior vice president of First Interstate.[4]

Probably the original and classic bifurcator is the Coca-Cola Company. Ever since 1886, the company has concentrated on advertising and promotion and new product development, creating intangible values while leaving the brutish business of production and distribution to its independently-owned and operated bottler franchisees. Coke's de-integration strategy maintains a clarity of purpose, separates risks and responsibilities, enhances debt capacity, improves incentives, and establishes a meaningful transfer price. Faithful to this long-standing policy, Coca-Cola was quick to sell to the public a majority interest in Coca-Cola Enterprises shortly after it had been formed with the bottling assets Coke acquired from Beatrice and J. T. Lupton.

Taking a step in Coke's direction, Chrysler Corporation last year deposited its components manufacturing operation into a separate subsidiary, Acustar, with intimations of a possible future spinoff. If carried out, a structure similar to Coca-Cola's will emerge: the commodity manufacturing activity will be separated from product design and development and advertising and promotion.

Permit us one final example. On April 28th, 1987, Apple Computer announced plans to create an independent software company, Claris Corporation, whose aim was to develop, acquire and market software applications under its own brand name, eliminating the Apple logo. To separate mind from matter, software from hardware, Apple intends that Claris will become an independent company as soon as possible, although it will retain a minority interest.

The dimensions of meaningful bifurcation are limited only to one's imagination. In our consulting practice we have found a broad range of restructurings to yield increases in corporate performance and value:
• separating the entrepreneurial, value-creating activities from the commodity end of the business;
• separating proven, low-risk earnings streams from unproven, speculative investment opportunities;
• segmenting creative development activities from the ownership and operation of the resulting assets;
• isolating activities with different success factors and cultural requirements;
• vertically de-integrating;
• compartmentalizing different stages of the product/business life cycle;

---

4. "A New Way To Shed Bad Loans," *The New York Times.*

BECAUSE COMMON SHAREHOLDERS ENJOY LIMITED LIABILITY, IT
OBVIOUSLY IS IMPOSSIBLE FOR THE SHARES OF A PUBLICLY TRADED
COMPANY TO HAVE A NEGATIVE VALUE. . .BUT WHEN THE STRONG
SUBSIDIZE THE WEAK WITHIN A COMPANY, AN UNPROFITABLE BUSINESS
UNIT ACTUALLY CAN HAVE A NEGATIVE VALUE.

- cutting off cash generators from cash users; and
- separating leverageable assets and businesses from those requiring equity.

Bifurcation is a consequence of the power of specialization and an irreversible trend toward increasing market sophistication. The more efficient are our markets, the more able they are to process information and impound it quickly and accurately into a multitude of prices. A more decentralized, disaggregated, atomistic economy generates more prices—both stock prices and transfer prices—to guide resource allocation, improve operating efficiency, and sharpen incentives.

We conclude if you really want to create value, don't split your stock. Next time, split your company.

ELIMINATE CROSS SUBSIDIES

The impetus debt provides to perform well often leads management to ferret out previously overlooked opportunities to create value. One important form of damage control is the elimination of cross-subsidies, inefficiencies that sap companies of their vitality.

- An *operating* cross-subsidy is manifest on the income statement when a unit within a consolidated company, by incurring losses that are subsidized by other profitable activities, creates a negative value.
- A *strategic* cross-subsidy appears on the balance sheet when internal cash flow is reinvested in business units unlikely to earn sufficient rates of return over time.
- An *economic* cross-subsidy occurs when assets that support a business have a more highly valued alternative use.

Operating Cross-Subsidies: The Case of TWA

Trans World Airlines (TWA) offers a good example of the value that can be created through the elimination of an operating cross-subsidy. Its parent, Trans World Corporation (TWC), composed of Hilton International, Century 21, Canteen and Spartan Food Systems, was consistently profitable. TWA, by contrast, had lost money each year since the deregulation of airlines in 1978, in large measure due to uneconomic wage levels for employees. With a strong parent for support, there was no incentive for them to make necessary wage concessions. In effect, TWC's shareholders were being forced to subsidize TWC's employees, an obvious inequity.

The curtain started to rise when Odyssey Partners, a New York investment group, acquired a stake in TWA, asserting that TWC's "breakup" value exceeded its actual market value by a wide margin. The case can be made not only that TWC's businesses might benefit from a better fit with other owners but, more to the point, that the apparent perpetual subsidization of TWA's losses caused value to be subtracted from the overall company.

Because common shareholders enjoy limited liability, it obviously is impossible for the shares of a publicly traded company to have a negative value. Common shares, by law, are fully paid-up and non-assessable. But when the strong subsidize the weak within a company, an unprofitable business unit actually can have a negative value.

The first restructuring step was the sale of a 19 percent stake in TWA to the public in February of 1983. In April of that year, Odyssey Partners waged an unsuccessful proxy fight to press TWA to separate its various units, claiming that the sum would be greater than the whole. Finally, on September 23, the remaining shares of TWA were spun off to shareholders, creating a separate, publicly-trading entity. Upon the announcement, TWA's stock fell nearly 4 percent, while that of its parent, TWC, rose more than 11 percent. These share price reactions reflect the elimination of the cross-subsidy, and value creation overall.

TWA's president, C. B. Meyer, Jr., cited competitive industry conditions as the reasons that TWA employees "must reduce labor costs and make permanent changes to gain greater productivity. TWA's employees for too long have felt they could rely on a rich and fat parent. They may currently see that their fate remains in their own hands."

TWA's problem was attributable in large part to employees' unwillingness to reconcile themselves to the competitive forces unleashed by deregulation. Operating cross-subsidies are more frequently caused, however, by management's insistence on "turning around" businesses better left face down.

GTE's commitment to support Sprint, a perennial big money loser, is one egregious example. Since acquiring Sprint in 1983 for $1 billion, GTE has pumped in $2.5 billion in operating losses and capital and written off $1.7 billion in assets. Worse, the losses are unlikely to be recovered as long-distance phone rates continue to plummet, wearing away Sprint's price advantage over AT&T. Not to worry. GTE makes more than enough money in its local telephone and telecommunications operations to subsidize Sprint's losses almost indefinitely, no doubt a pleasing prospect for shareholders.

It did not take long for the raiders to spot this black hole. The Belzbergs, after acquiring a 5 percent stake in GTE in the fall of 1987, pressed for a partial breakup, claiming that the continued support of Sprint was depressing GTE's value by a full $10 a share. Though GTE fended off the Belzbergs by legal legal maneuvering and some half-hearted financial measures, stay tuned for further developments. Merge Sprint with MCI, anyone?

Strategic Cross-Subsidies

Strategic cross-subsidies occur when management invests in business units unlikely to earn attractive returns, or denies others the access to capital they desperately need and deserve. When investors learn, through repetitive example, to expect such capital misappropriations to continue, a vast discount gets subtracted from a company's current market value. This is the only way that new investors can be enticed to buy shares without fearing the harmful consequences of management's future investment decisions. Eliminating this depressing discount is a prime objective of any raider worth his salt.

In past years, every time Mr. Peter Grace announced his intention to split up his company, W. R. Grace's stock price would leap on the order of 20 to 25 percent. Capital misallocation within the firm had been so rife over the years, all excused with the wave of the conglomerate wand (invest in your businesses even in their bad times because you never know when you may need their support), that the prospect of subjecting the business units to the discipline of a market test for new capital made the shareholders salivate. The increase in the company's market value following these announcements was only a conservative measure of the cost of internal capital misallocations suffered by the company's investors.

The event that finally tipped Grace's hand was the sale of the Flick Group of West Germany, a friendly holder of a 26 percent block of W. R. Grace stock. To prevent it from falling into unfriendly hands, the company purchased the block for nearly $600 million, incurring an onerous load of debt that forced an acceleration of a restructuring program to the applause of investors. The company completely divested all retail and restaurant operations and, most significantly, its fertilizer business into which

mounds of cash had been shoveled over the years for a very unsatisfactory rate of return.

Strategic cross-subsidies need not be so blatant to be important. Often they arise from a decision to invest capital unwisely because of a preoccupation with uncertain, long-term payoffs.

One of the accusations hurled at raiders is that they force management to focus on shorter-term payoffs to the detriment of longer-term values. The raiders are guilty as charged. But they are also to be applauded for righting a wrong that arises from a common confusion between gross future values and net present values.

If less money is invested in a business, its future value is reduced. The inevitable consequence of trimming investment spending is a smaller size, fewer products, a less impressive market position and, indeed, a lower long-run value for any business. And yet, even though all these consequences are real, none provides a sufficient justification for investing capital.

All these statements focus myopically on gross future values—that is, in practice, the value of a business at some future point as envisioned in the mind of an empire builder. By that time, all of the outlays required to achieve the enviable position management foresees will be sunk costs, irrelevant to computing its value in the mind's eye. The way to maximize the "long-run" value of any business, to build an empire, is to spend as much money as possible—hardly a meaningful capital budgeting prescription.

The stock market, raiders, and indeed all value-builders focus on net present values—the anticipated value of the future position, discounted to the present and net of all outlays required to fuel growth. Net present value calculations ought to drive corporate decisions because they implicitly consider the benefit that may be derived from deploying resources to grow other businesses, and seek the highest ratio between gross future values and the outlays required to produce them. By undertaking those projects holding the prospect of generating the greatest net present values, management ensures the greatest future value for society at large from investing our limited capital resources.

Capital budgeting is the question of deciding which businesses ought *not* to grow, so that other, more promising ones, can grow even more rapidly. A failure to heed this basic corporate finance principle when making internal capital budgeting decisions will attract raiders like bees to honey.

Economic Cross-Subsidies

An economic cross-subsidy arises when the assets that support a business are worth more than the business itself—a reliable sign that there is a more highly-valued alternative use for the assets. For example, when we met with the CFO of one of the largest grocery store chains in the nation, he said that the value of the real estate beneath his stores exceeded the company's current market value: "Where does the value of our real estate appear in the market value of this company?," he asked. "Why, we could liquidate our real estate and realize far more than our current stock price."

In view of the facts, we suggested that liquidation sounded like the appropriate strategy. "Well," he said, "I was just speaking hypothetically."

But that was the point. So long as their real estate served as sites of grocery stores, its value would be limited to the cash flow the grocery stores would generate. Because management had conditioned the market to expect a continuation of the grocery operations, the company sold for less than its "break-up value."

Part of the CFO's confusion arose from his belief that, in figuring the worth of his company, the market should add the value of the real estate to the value of the grocery business when, in fact, any company's value is an either/or proposition. You can either have the value of a company's assets, or the value of its business, but not both. That our client's stock price reflected the lower of the two values was due to management's decision to use fortuitous gains from asset appreciation to subsidize unrecorded, but nevertheless real operating losses.

How so? Imagine, first, that the assets of the company are held in a separate financing subsidiary. This financial subsidiary leases the assets to internal operating subsidiaries at fair market rental rates. These operating units, in turn, use the assets in the grocery business, receiving all revenues, paying all operating expenses (including rents), without owning any assets.

This "bifurcation" of the company into operating and ownership units, and the introduction of a market-driven transfer price between them, permits the company's overall profits to be divided in two components. The income of the financing subsidiary—namely, the rents—is set so as to provide just a fair return on a current appraised value of the assets. By design, the financing subsidiary just breaks even in economic terms. The income recorded by the operating subsidiary, by contrast, is a residual that reflects management's ability to add value to the assets employed in their business.

Consider, for example, a company that records $75 million of income on $500 million of book assets, giving the appearance of a respectable 15 percent return ($75/$500), quality management, and no vulnerability to a hostile takeover. If, however, the assets supporting the business have a current appraised value of $1 billion, and the prevailing cost of capital is 10 percent, the internal lease rate from owner to operator is $100 million (10% applied to $1 billion), leaving a deficit of $25 million from the operations ($75-$100). The $75 million of consolidated reported profits divides into $100 million attributable to the ownership of appreciated assets, and a true operating loss of $25 million, a cross-subsidy that any raider would be pleased to eliminate by selling the assets to a more highly-valued alternative use.

That our hypothetical company can earn an attractive return on the original cost, but not the current value of its assets, simply indicates that the optimal use of its assets has changed over time. What may have started as an isolated grocery store built on top of a paved-over cornfield may today be in the midst of a burgeoning office park. The value of that location has appreciated as its preferred use has changed, an important development that the company's accounting books have failed to record, and its management to act on.

The elimination of economic cross-subsidies is yet another manifestation of Joseph Schumpeter's "creative destruction," a process in which capitalism improves the productivity of people and assets through constant change. Being attuned to the changing value of assets, and their most productive current use, is an important management responsibility—one that is too frequently delegated to a raider.

PART VII

WORKOUTS AND BANKRUPTCY

While producing large gains for stockholders (and thus, likely significant increases in corporate operating efficiency), the leveraged restructuring movement has also regrettably been accompanied by a sharp rise in cases of corporate financial distress. Given the widespread use of high leverage, this is not surprising. What *has* surprised some economists, however, is the size of the costs of dealing with financial distress. The costs of reorganizing troubled companies have, in many cases, turned out to be far greater than economists like Michael Jensen predicted—in large part because new obstacles to out-of-court workouts have driven many companies into the much more costly and inefficient Chapter 11 process.

Workout veteran David Schulte, adviser to Revco, sums up the current state of corporate reorganization as follows:

I've always hated bankruptcy. The problem I have with Chapter 11 is that it takes a business problem and turns it...into a legal case. I don't know what a guy who wears a black robe has to offer that the parties in interest can't do privately themselves...If we could devise a simple way for exchange offers to work outside of Chapter 11... investors would be well served and we'd all be a lot better off. In short, I'd like to have a non-bankruptcy bankruptcy. It's virtually impossible to do an out-of-court deal right now. All in all, 1990 was a very bad year for exchange offers.

Leonard Rosen, noted bankruptcy counsel, finds current trends in reorganization equally disturbing:

I always thought that the purpose of a workout was first to create the biggest possible pot, and then to fight about the division of the pot afterwards. That was the spirit in which workouts used to be done in the old days.... What worries me today is that, if creditor fights about the division of the pot start at the beginning of the process, then nobody's paying attention to more fundamental questions like: Have we got the right management running the business? And are they making the right strategic and operating decisions?... We're strarting the fights so early , spending so much energy on the intercreditor struggle, and creating such divisiveness in the process that we're making it much less likely that companies will be restructured quickly and economically.

"*Leverage,*" Merton Miller's 1990 Nobel Prize Lecture, is a deft display of economic reasoning aimed at ridding the popular mind of what Miller calls its "virulent strain of anti-leverage hysteria." After noting that the large gains from LBOs and other leveraged restructurings reflected "substantialreal efficiency gains by reconcentrating corporate control and redeploying assets," Miller devotes the remainder of the piece to explaining why current fears about the consequences of the "supposed financial excesses" of the 1980s are greatly exaggerated.

In brief, Miller's arguments are these: (1) our private capital markets have self-correcting mechanisms that prevent corporate overleveraging; (2) even if such "overleveraging"did take place (and Miller is clearly skeptical), *corporate* leveraging is not likely to increase risk for the economy as a whole; (3) the financial difficulties of some highly-leveraged companies involve "mainly private not social" costs; and (4) regulations designed to reinforce our capital markets' built-in controls against overleveraging are generally not only unnecessary, but positively harmful to the economy. As Miller warns,

Recent efforts by our regulators to override these built-in market mechanisms by destroying the junk bond market and by imposing additional direct controls over leveraged lending by banks will thus have all the unintended consequences normally associated with such regulatory interventions. They will lower efficiency and raise costs (in this case, the cost of capital) to important sectors of our economy.

In "*Corporate Control and the Politics of Finance,*" Harvard professor Michael Jensen fleshes out and extends part of Miller's argument, maintaining that the concerted "re-regulation" of our financial markets beginning in 1989 has contributed greatly the current weakness of the economy. In looking back at the 1980s, Jensen comes to the following conclusions:

(1) New evidence of major improvements in the productivity of American manufacturing throughout the 1980s is "dramatically inconsistent with" the popular argument that leveraged restructuring was sacrificing the future of the U.S. industrial economy for short-term gain.

(2) The restructuring movement of the 1980s reflected the re-emergence of active investors—a group essentially dormant since the 1930s—whose principal economic accomplishment was to squeeze

excess capital ("free cash flow") out of mature industries with excess capacity.

(3) "LBO associations" like KKR and Forstmann Little represent "new organizational forms" designed to overcome the deficiencies of large public conglomerates by substituting concentrated equity ownership and other financial incentives for the direct monitoring and financial controls of the typical corporate headquarters.

(4) The highly leveraged transactions of the '80s, though more likely to get into financial trouble, created far stronger incentives to reorganize troubled companies outside of court. Such a shift in incentives was leading to a (Japanese-like) "privatization of bankruptcy" in which active investors (like the main banks in Japanese *keiretsu*) were using low-cost means (typically involving exchange offers) of avoiding our costly and chronically efficient Chapter 11 process. This process, however, came to an abrupt halt in 1989 as a result of regulatory interference with the bond and credit markets, a change in the tax code, and a misguided bankruptcy court ruling.

(5) Our private capital markets were not, of course, wholly blameless in provoking this regulatory reaction. A gross misalignment of incentives (which Jensen calls a "contracting failure") between dealmakers and suppliers of capital in LBOs and other HLTs led to a concentration of overpriced deals in the latter years of the 1980s But capital market adjustments to this problem—including larger equity commitments, lower upfront fees, and more conservative deal prices—were already well underway when the set of regulatory initiatives launched in 1989 overrode them, thereby adding significantly to HLT defaults and bankruptcies.

(6) Much of the chronic inefficiency, including the intensity of intercreditor conflicts, of our current Chapter 11 process could be eliminated by auctioning the control of bankrupt companies to the highest bidder at the outset of the Chapter 11 process.

In "*Tax Obstacles to Voluntary Financial Restructuring*," Merton Miller exposes the logical absurdity of the provision in the U.S. tax code that penalizes distressed companies with a *positive* corporate income tax liability when they receive concessions from their lenders outside of Chapter 11. Miller concludes with a proposal for tax reform "so simple, so obvious (but also so seemingly radical) that it has been largely overlooked."

In "*Managing Default*," Stuart Gilson summarizes recent academic evidence (much of it his own) on the motives for and consequences of corporate choices between private workouts or Chapter 11. Among Gilson's findings are these: (1) almost half of the 192 NYSE and ASE companies defaulting between 1980 and 1986 were reorganized out of court; (2) the direct costs of exchange offers are roughly one tenth of those in formal bankruptcy; (3) companies successful in reorganizing privately experienced a 40% increase in stock price between the announcement of default and announcement of a reorganization plan (whereas firms filing Chapter 11 see a further 40% decline); and (4) top corporate management is about equally likely to lose their jobs in private reorganizations (in 60% of the cases) and bankruptcy (70%).

In "*What Really Went Wrong at Revco?*" Karen Wruck supplies the following answer:

Stating that too much leverage was the fundamental cause of Revco's problems does not offer much insight into what went wrong. Management disarray, a weak and inexperienced LBO sponsor, a fee structure almost guaranteed to produce overpayment, and a disastrous midstream shift in strategy all conspired with the use of debt financing to put Revco into Chapter 11.

This explanation fails to mention one factor, the intractability of Revco's intercreditor conflicts *after* entering Chapter 11, that appears to have generated significant costs.

In "*The Bankruptcy Code and Violations of Absolute Priority*," Larry Weiss reports finding deviations from absolute priority in 80% of 37 bankruptcy reorganizations he examined. Besides encouraging equity holders and junior creditors to hold out longer, thus diminishing the prospects for successful reorganization, such large and frequent violations of priority have the even more destructive consequence of raising the corporate cost of capital for smaller and otherwise risky companies.

But amidst the general pessimism about the state of corporate reorganization, there is at least one promising sign. In "*The Economics of Pre-Packaged Bankruptcy*," John McConnell and Henri Servaes describe a relatively new hybrid form that attempts to combine the advantages of Chapter 11—particularly its ability to bind minority holdouts—with the celerity and lower costs of workouts.

DHC

LEVERAGE

by Merton H. Miller,
University of Chicago

NOBEL MEMORIAL PRIZE LECTURE
THE ROYAL SWEDISH ACADEMY OF SCIENCES
STOCKHOLM ■ DECEMBER 7, 1990*

Under the terms of Alfred Nobel's will, the Prizes were to be awarded for an "important discovery or invention." Let it be clear from the outset, therefore, that my case must be one of the former, not the latter. Contrary to what you may have read in some press accounts following the announcement of the 1990 Nobel Prizes in Economic Sciences, I am not the co-inventor of the leveraged buyout—the transaction that perhaps more than any other has come to symbolize the supposed financial excesses of the 1980s.

Leveraged buyouts, in which the younger, active managers of a firm borrowed the funds to buy the controlling shares from a firm's retired founder (or from his estate), were an established feature of the corporate landscape long before Franco Modigliani, the 1985 laureate, and I published our first joint paper on leverage and the cost of capital in 1958.[1] The LBOs of the 1980s differed only in scale, in that they involved publicly-held rather than privately-held corporations and in that the takeovers were often hostile.

---

*© The Nobel Foundation 1990. It is reprinted here with permission of the Nobel Foundation. Helpful comments on an earlier draft were made by my colleagues Steven Kaplan and Robert Vishny.

1. Franco Modigliani and Merton H. Miller, "The Cost of Capital, Corporation Finance and the Theory of Investment," *American Economic Review* 48 (June 1958): 261-297.

Mikhail Gorbachev, the 1990 Peace Prize Winner, may have popularized the term *perestroika*, but the LBO entrepreneurs of the 1980s actually did it...and on a scale not seen since the early years of this century... LBO entrepreneurs have achieved substantial real efficiency gains by reconcentrating corporate control and redeploying assets.

That Franco Modigliani and I should be credited with inventing these takeovers is doubly ironic since the central message of our M&M Propositions was that the value of the firm was independent of its capital structure. Subject to one important qualification to be duly noted below, you couldn't hope to enhance shareholder value merely by leveraging up. Investors would not pay a premium for corporate leverage because they could always leverage up their own holdings by borrowing on personal account. Despite this seemingly clear prediction of the M&M analysis, the LBOs of the 1980s were routinely reporting premiums to the shareholders of more than 40 percent, in some cases as high as 100 percent—and all this, mind you, even after the huge fees the deal-making investment bankers were extracting.

The qualification to the M&M value-invariance proposition mentioned earlier concerns the deductibility of interest payments under the unintegrated U.S. corporate income tax. That deductibility can lead, as we showed in our 1963 article,[2] to substantial gains from leveraging under some conditions; and gains of this tax-driven kind have undoubtedly figured both in the rise of corporate debt ratios generally in the 1980s and in some recent LBOs and voluntary restructurings in particular. But after netting out the offsetting tax costs of leveraged capital structures (such as those discussed in my 1977 paper, "Debt and Taxes,"[3] and its follow-up literature), tax savings alone cannot plausibly account for the observed LBO premiums.

LEVERAGED BUYOUTS: WHERE THE GAINS CAME FROM

The source of the major gains in value achieved in the LBOs of the 1980s lies, in fact, not in our newly-recognized field of finance at all, but in that older and long-established field of economics, industrial organization. Perhaps industrial *re*organization might be an apter term. Mikhail Gorbachev, the 1990 Peace Prize Winner, may have popularized the term *perestroika*, but the LBO entrepreneurs of the 1980s actually did it—and on a scale not seen since the

early years of this century when so much of what we think of as big business was being put together by the entrepreneurs of consolidation like J. P. Morgan and John D. Rockefeller.

That the LBO entrepreneurs have achieved substantial real efficiency gains by reconcentrating corporate control and redeploying assets has been amply documented in a multitude of academic research studies.[4] But this basically positive view of LBOs and takeovers is still far from universally accepted among the wider public. Some are reacting to the layoffs and factory closings that have sometimes followed hostile takeovers—although far more of both have occurred in our automobile industry, which has so far been immune from takeovers. Others worry that these short-run gains may represent merely the improvident sacrifice of opportunities for high, but long deferred future profits—an argument presuming, among other things, that the market cannot properly compute discounted present values. Even more fear that the real efficiency gains, if any, will be more than offset by the collateral damage from the financial leveraging used to bring about the restructuring.

THE PROBLEMS OF CORPORATE LEVERAGING: REAL OR IMAGINED?

These fears will be the main focus of this lecture. The statutes of the Nobel Foundation stipulate that the subject of the Nobel lecture "should be on or associated with the work for which the prize was awarded," which in my case means the M&M propositions. Rather than simply reviewing them, however, or discussing the subsequent research they have inspired,[5] I propose here instead to show how those propositions bear on current concerns about overleveraging—concerns that in some quarters actually border on hysteria. In particular I will argue, first, that the highly visible losses and defaults on junk bonds do not mean that overleveraging did in fact occur; second, paradoxical as it may sound, that increased leveraging by corporations does not imply increased risk for the economy as a whole; third, that

---

2. Franco Modigliani and Merton H. Miller, "Corporate Income Taxes and the Cost of Capital: A Correction," *American Economic Review* 53 (June 1963): 433-443.

3. Merton H. Miller, "Debt and Taxes," *Journal of Finance* 32 (May, 1977): 261-275.

4. See, for example, Steven N. Kaplan, "The Effects of Management Buyouts on Operations and Value," *Journal of Financial Economics* 24 (June, 1989): 217-254.

5. I undertook this project earlier. See, for example, my earlier article in this journal, "The Modigliani-Miller Propositions after Thirty Years," *Journal of Applied Corporate Finance*, Vol. 2 No. 1 (Spring 1989). A longer, more technical version of the same piece appeared earlier in the *Journal of Economic Perspectives* 2 (Fall 1988): 99-120.

the financial distress being suffered by some highly leveraged firms involves mainly private, not social costs; and, finally, that the capital markets have built-in controls against overleveraging—controls, more-over, that are very much in evidence at the moment. Recent efforts by our regulators to override these built-in market mechanisms by destroying the junk bond market and by imposing additional direct controls over leveraged lending by banks will thus have all the unintended consequences normally associated with such regulatory interventions. They will lower efficiency and raise costs (in this case, the cost of capital) to important sectors of our economy.

That the current emphasis on the evils of overleveraging may be misplaced does not mean, of course, that all is well. My message is not: "Relax. Be happy. And, don't worry." Worry we should, but about the serious problems confronting us, such as our seeming inability to bring government spending under rational control or to halt the steady deterioration of our once-vaunted system of public education. Let us not waste our limited worrying capacity on second-order and largely self-correcting problems like financial leveraging.

I hope I will be pardoned for dwelling in what follows almost exclusively on U.S. examples. It's just that a particularly virulent strain of the anti-leverage hysteria seems to have struck us first. Perhaps others can learn from our mistakes.

THE PRIVATE AND SOCIAL COSTS OF CORPORATE LEVERAGING

The charge that the U.S. became overleveraged in the 1980s will strike some as perhaps too obvious to require any extensive documentation. What could offer more compelling evidence of the overissuance of debt than the defaults of so many junk-bond issuers in late 1989, with news of additional or pending defaults now almost a daily occurrence?

Junk Bonds As Just Another Risky Security

To argue in this all too natural way, however, is to put too much emphasis on the word "bond" and not enough on the word "junk." Bonds are, indeed, promises to pay. And certainly the issuers of the bonds hoped to keep those promises. But if the firm's cash flow, for reasons competitive or cyclical, fails to cover the commitments, then the promises cannot be kept, or at least not kept in full.

The buyers of the junk bonds, of course, also *hoped* that the promises would be kept. But they clearly weren't counting on it! For all save the most hopelessly gullible, the yields *expected* (in the Markowitz sense of yield outcomes weighed by probability of occurrence) on junk bonds were below the nominal or promised yields. The high promised yields that might be earned during the good years were understood as compensation for the possible bad years in time and bad bonds in the total junk bond portfolio. The high nominal yields, in short, were essentially risk premiums. And in 1989, for many of the junk bonds issued earlier, the risk happened.

Although the presumption in finance is that defaults represent bad outcomes *ex post*, rather than systematic misperception of the true *ex ante* odds (which seems to be the conventional view), that presumption cannot yet be established conclusively. The time series of rates of return on junk bonds is still too short for judging whether those returns are indeed anomalously low—or perhaps even anomalously high—relative to accepted asset-pricing models like those of my co-laureate William Sharpe and his successors. Few such anomalous asset classes have so far been identified; and nothing in the nature of high-yield bonds strongly suggests they will wind up on that short list.

Some may question the fairness of my treating these realized risks on junk bonds as essentially exogenous shocks, like earthquakes or droughts. Surely, they would contend, the very rise of corporate leverage that the junk bonds represent must itself have increased the total risk in the economy. On that point, however, modern finance in general and the M&M propositions in particular offer a different and, in many respects, a counter-intuitive perspective.

Does Increased Corporate Leverage Add to Society's Risk?

Imagine that you, as a venerable academic professor of finance, are in a dialogue with an equally grizzled corporate treasurer who believes, as most of them probably do, that leveraging *does* increase total risk. "You will surely concede, Professor," he is likely to begin, "that leveraging up the corporate capital structure will make the remaining equity riskier. Right?" "Right," you say. A company with a debt/equity ratio of 1, for example, earning a

20 percent rate of return on its underlying assets and paying 10 percent on its bonds, which, of course, have the first claim on the firm's earnings, will generate an enhanced 30 percent rate of return for its equity holders. Should the earning rate on the underlying assets decline by 25 percent, however, to 15 percent, the rate of return on equity will fall by an even greater extent (33 1/3 percent in this case). That, after all, is why we use the graphic term leverage (or the equally descriptive term "gearing" that the British seem to prefer). And this greater variability of prospective rates of return to leveraged shareholders means greater risk, in precisely the sense used by my colleagues here, Harry Markowitz and William Sharpe.

That conceded, the corporate treasurer goes on to ask rhetorically: "And, Professor, any debt added to the capital structure must, necessarily, be riskier debt, carrying a lower rating and bearing a higher interest rate than any debt outstanding before the higher leveraging. Right?" "Right," you again agree, and for exactly the same reason as before. The further a claimant stands from the head of the line at payoff time, the riskier the claim.

Now the treasurer moves in for the kill. "Leveraging raises the risk of the equity and also raises the risk of the debt. It must, therefore, raise the total risk. Right?" "Wrong," you say, preparing to play the M&M card. The M&M propositions are the finance equivalents of conservation laws. What gets conserved in this case is the risk of the earning stream generated by the firm's operating assets. Leveraging or deleveraging the firm's capital structure serves merely to partition that risk among all of the firm's security holders.[6]

To see where the risk goes, consider the following illustrative example. Suppose a firm has 10 security holders, of whom 5 hold the firm's bonds and the remaining 5 hold equal shares in the firm's leveraged equity. Suppose further that the interest due on the 5 bonds is covered sufficiently for those bonds to be considered essentially riskless. The entire risk of the firm must thus be borne by the 5 shareholders who will, of course, expect a rate of return on their investment substantially higher than on the assumed riskless bonds.

Let 2 of the common stockholders now come to feel that their share of the risks is higher than they want to bear. They ask to exchange their stockholdings for bonds, but they learn that the interest payments on the 2 additional bonds they will get in exchange could not be covered in all possible states of the world. To avoid diluting the claims of the old bondholders, the new bonds must be made junior to the old bonds. Because the new bonds are riskier, the 2 new bondholders will expect a rate of return higher than on the old riskless bonds, but a rate still less, of course, than on their original, and now even higher-risk, holdings of common stock.

The *average* risk and the average expected interest rate of the 7 bondholders taken together has thus risen. At the same time, the risk assumed by the remaining 3 equity holders is also higher (since the 2 shifting stockholders now have taken a prior claim on the firm's earnings) and their expected return must rise as well. Both classes of securities are thus riskier on average, but the *total* risk stays exactly the same as before the 2 stockholders shifted over. The increased risk to the 3 remaining stockholders is exactly offset by the decreased risk to the 2 former stockholders, who have moved down the priority ladder to become junk bondholders.[7]

Leverage and The Deadweight Costs of Financial Distress

That aggregate risk might be unaffected by modest changes of leverage some might willingly concede, but not when leverage is pushed to the point that bankruptcy becomes a real possibility. The higher the leverage, the greater the likelihood, of course, that just such an unfortunate event will occur.

Actually, however, the M&M conservation of risk continues to hold, subject to some qualifications to be duly noted below, even in the extreme case of default. That result seems paradoxical only because the emotional and psychological overtones of the word "bankruptcy" give that particular outcome

---

6. In the original M&M paper, that underlying real earning stream was taken as a given, and assumed to be independent of the financing decisions. Subsequent research has identified many possible interactions between the real and the financial sides of the firm; but their effects on risk are not always in the same direction and, for present purposes, they can be regarded as of only second-order importance.

7. Note, incidentally, that this story would have exactly the same conclusion if the 2 defecting common stockholders had opted for preferred stock rather than junior bonds. Even though accountants classify preferred stocks as equity, preferreds are functionally equivalent to junior debt. Preferred stocks, in fact, were effectively the "junk bonds" of finance (often with the same bad press) prior to the 1930s when the steep rise in corporate tax rates made them less attractive than tax-deductible, interest-bearing securities of equivalent priority.

more prominence than it merits on strictly economic grounds. From a bloodless finance perspective, a default signifies merely that the stockholders have now lost their entire stake in the firm. Their option, so to speak, has expired worthless. The creditors now become the new stockholders and the return on their original debt claims becomes whatever of value is left in the firm.

The qualification to the principle of risk conservation noted earlier is that the very process of transferring claims from the debtors to the creditors can itself create risks and deadweight costs over and beyond those involved when the firm was a going concern. Some of these "costs of financial distress," as they have come to be called, may be incurred even before a default occurs. Debtors, like some poets, do not "go gentle into that good night." They struggle to keep their firms alive, even if sometimes the firm would be better off dead by any rational calculation. They are often assisted in those efforts at life-support by a bankruptcy code that materially strengthens their hands in negotiations with the creditors. Sometimes, of course, the reverse can happen and over-rapacious creditors can force liquidation of firms that might otherwise have survived. About all we can safely conclude is that, once the case is in bankruptcy court, all sides in these often-protracted negotiations will be assisted by armies of lawyers whose fees further eat away at the pool of assets available to satisfy the claims of the creditors. For small firms, the direct costs of the bankruptcy proceedings can easily consume the entire corpus (an apt term), but they are essentially fixed costs and hence represent only a small portion of the recoveries in the larger cases. In the aggregate, of course, direct bankruptcy costs, even if regarded as complete social waste, are miniscule relative to the size of the economy.[8]

The Costs of Financial Distress: Private or Social?

Small as the aggregate deadweight costs of financial distress may be, bankruptcies can certainly be painful personal tragedies. Even so generally unadmired a public figure as Donald Trump has almost become an object of public sympathy as he struggles with his creditors for control over his garish Taj Mahal Casino. But even if he does lose, as seemed probable at the time of this writing, the loss will be his, not society's. The Trump casino and associated buildings will still be there (perhaps one should add, alas). The only difference will be the sign on the door: "Under New Management."[9]

The social consequences of the isolated bankruptcy can be dismissed perhaps, but not, some would argue, bankruptcies that come in clusters. The fear is that the bankruptcy of each overindebted firm will send a shock wave to the firm's equally overindebted suppliers, leading in turn to more bankruptcies until eventually the whole economy collapses in a heap. Neither economics generally nor finance in particular, however, offers much support for this notion of a leverage-induced "bankruptcy multiplier" or a contagion effect. Bankrupt firms, as noted earlier, do not vanish from the earth. They often continue operating pretty much as before, though with different ownership and possibly on a reduced scale. Even when they do liquidate and close down, their inventory, furniture and fixtures, employees and customers flow to other firms elsewhere in the economy. Profitable investment opportunities that one failing firm passes up will be assumed by others—if not always immediately, then later when the economic climate becomes more favorable. Recent research in macro-economics suggests that much of what we once considered output irretrievably lost in business cycles is really only output postponed, particularly in the durable goods industries.

To say that the human and capital resources of bankrupt firms will eventually be reemployed is not to deny, of course, that the personal costs of disemployment merit consideration, particularly when they become widespread. All modern economies take steps to ease the pains of transferring human resources to other and better uses; and perhaps they should do even more. But, as the economies of Eastern Europe are discovering, delaying or preventing the needed movements of resources will also

---

8. The deadweight costs of bankruptcy, and of financial distress more generally, may be small in the aggregate, but they do exist. A case can be made, therefore, on standard welfare-economic grounds for eliminating the current tax subsidy to debt implicit in our current unintegrated corporate income tax. Achieving complete neutrality between debt and equity, however, would require elimination of the corporate tax—a step not likely to be undertaken in the foreseeable future.

9. Actually, according to recent press reports, Trump's creditors have allowed him to keep control, at least temporarily. Should he fail to meet stipulated cash-flow targets, however, the creditors can take over his remaining interests in a so-called "pre-packaged" bankruptcy, that is, one without formal bankruptcy proceedings (and expenses). Further use of this ingenious and efficient method for transferring control can be confidently predicted.

> **Bankrupt firms...do not vanish from the earth. They often continue operating pretty much as before, though with different ownership and possibly on a reduced scale. Even when they do liquidate and close down, their inventory, furniture and fixtures, employees, and customers flow to other firms elsewhere in the economy.**

have social costs that can be even higher over the long run.

The successive waves of bankruptcies in the early 1930s may seem to belie this relatively benign view of bankruptcy as a matter essentially of private costs with no serious externalities, but not really.[10] Contrary to widely-held folk belief, bankruptcies did not bring on the Great Depression. The direction of causation runs from depressions to bankruptcies, not the other way around. The collapse of the stock market in 1928, and of the U.S. banking system during 1931-2, may well have created the appearance of a finance-driven disaster. But that disaster was not just the inevitable bursting of another overleveraged tulip bubble, as some have suggested. (Recent research has even cast doubt on the existence of the *original* tulip bubble.[11]) Responsibility for turning an ordinary downturn into a depression of unprecedented severity lies primarily with the managers of the Federal Reserve System. They failed to carry out their duties as the residual supplier of liquidity to the public and to the banking system. The U.S. money supply imploded by 30 percent between 1930 and 1932, dragging the economy and the price level down with it. When that happens, even AAA credits get to look like junk bonds.

That such a nightmare scenario might be repeated under present day conditions is always possible, of course. But, until recently at least, most economists would have dismissed it as extremely unlikely. The current chairman of the Federal Reserve Board himself, as well as his staff, are known to have studied the dismal episode of the early 1930s in great depth and to be thoroughly aware of how and why their ill-fated predecessors had blundered. The prompt action by the Federal Reserve Board to support the liquidity of the banking system after the stock market crash of October 19, 1987—and again after the mini-crash of October 13, 1989—is testimony to the lessons learned.

The fear of some at the moment, however, is that both the willingness and the ability of the Federal Reserve to maintain the economy's liquidity and its credit system are being undermined by regulatory overreaction to the S&L crisis—an overreaction that stems in part from underestimating the market's internal controls on overleveraging.

THE SELF-CORRECTING TENDENCIES IN CORPORATE LEVERAGING

Just what combination of demand shifts and supply shifts triggered the big expansion in leveraged securities in the 1980s will eventually have to be sorted out by future economic historians. The main point to be emphasized here is that, whether we are talking about automobiles or leveraged equity or high-yield bonds, the market's response to changes in tastes (or to changes in production technology) is limited and self-regulating. If the producers of any commodity expand its supply faster than the buyers want, the price will fall and output eventually will shrink. And the same holds for the financial marketplace: if the public's demand for junk bonds is overestimated by takeover entrepreneurs, the higher interest rates they must offer to junk-bond buyers will eat into the gains from the deals. The process of further leveraging will slow and perhaps even be reversed.

Something very much like this endogenous slowing of leveraging could be discerned in early 1989 even before a sequence of government initiatives—including the criminal indictments of the leading investment bankers and market makers in junk bonds, the forced dumping of junk bond inventories by beleaguered S&Ls, and the stricter regulations on leveraged lending by commercial banks—combined to undermine the liquidity of the high-yield bond market. The issuance of high-yield bonds not only ground to a halt, but many highly-leveraged firms moved to replace their now high-cost debts with equity.[12]

Junk Bonds and the S&L Crisis

To point out that the market has powerful inbuilt controls against overleveraging does not mean that who holds the highly leveraged securities is

---

10. True externalities arise, as in the case of air pollution, only when actions by one firm increase the costs of others. A possible analog to pollution for corporate debt might be the shifting to the government, and hence to the taxpayers, of the pension costs of failed firms. Once again, however, the aggregate impact is of only second-order significance.

11. See Peter Garber, "Tulipmania," *Journal of Political Economy* 97 (June 1989): 535-560.

12. The process of swapping equity for debt (essentially the reverse of the parable set forth above) would have gone even further by now for an unfortunate feature of U.S. tax law. Swapping equity for debt selling at less than face value creates taxable income from "cancellation of indebtedness." An exception is made for firms in bankruptcy, making that option more attractive than it otherwise might be for firms whose debts are at a sizeable discount.

never a matter of concern. Certainly the U.S. Savings and Loan Institutions should not have been using government-guaranteed savings deposits to buy high-risk junk bonds. But to focus so much attention on the junk bonds losses of a handful of these S&Ls is to miss the main point of the whole sorry episode. The current hue and cry over S&L junk bonds serves merely to divert attention from those who expanded the government deposit guarantees and encouraged the S&Ls to make investments with higher expected returns—but also, alas, with higher risk than their traditional long-term home mortgages.

Some, at the time, defended the enlargement of the government's deposit guarantees as compensation for the otherwise disabling interest rate risks assumed by those undertaking the socially-desirable task of providing fixed-rate, long-term mortgages. Quite apart, however, from the presence even then of alternative and less vulnerable ways of supplying mortgage money, the deposit guarantees proved to be—as most finance specialists predicted at the time—a particularly unfortunate form of subsidy to home ownership. Because the deposit guarantees gave the owners of the S&Ls what amounted to *put options* against the government, they actually encouraged the undertaking of uneconomic long-odds projects, some of which made junk bonds look safe by comparison. The successes went to the owners, the failures to the insurance fund.

More is at stake, however, than merely assigning proper blame for these failed attempts to overrule the market's judgment that this politically powerful industry was not economically viable. Drawing the wrong moral from the S&L affair can have consequences that extend far beyond the boundaries of this ill-fated industry. The American humorist, Mark Twain, once remarked that a cat, having jumped on a hot stove, will never jump on a stove again, even a cold one. Our commercial bank examiners seem to be following precisely this pat-tern. Commercial banking may not quite be a cold stove at the moment, but it is at least a viable industry. Unlike the S&Ls, moreover, it plays a critical role in financing businesses—particularly, but not only, those too small or too little known to support direct access to the public security markets. Heavy-handed restrictions on bank loans by examiners misreading the S&L experience will thus raise the cost of capital to—and hence decrease the use of capital by—this important business sector.[13]

Whether regulatory restrictions of these and related kinds have already gone so far as to produce a "credit crunch" of the kind associated in the past with monetary contraction is a subject much being argued at the moment, but one I prefer to leave to the specialists in money and banking. My concerns as a finance specialist are with the longer-run and less directly visible consequences of the current anti-leverage hysteria. This hysteria has already destroyed the liquidity of the market for high-yield bonds. The financial futures markets, currently under heavy attack for their supposed overleveraging, are the next possible candidates for extinction, at least in their U.S. habitats.

Many in academic finance have viewed these ill-founded attacks on our financial markets, particularly the newer markets, with some dismay. But they have, for the most part, stood aside from the controversies. Unlike some of the older fields of economics, the focus in finance has not been on issues of public policy. We have emphasized positive economics rather than normative economics, striving for solid empirical research built on foundations of simple, but powerful organizing theories. Now that our field has officially come of age, as it were, perhaps my colleagues in finance can be persuaded to take their noses out of their data bases from time to time and to bring insights of our field, and especially the public policy insights, to the attention of a wider audience.

---

13. Examples of such restrictions are the guidelines—recently promulgated jointly by the Federal Deposit Insurance Corporation, the Comptroller of the Currency, and the Federal Reserve Board—governing so-called Highly Leveraged Transactions (HLTs). These guidelines have effectively shut off lending for corporate restructuring, whether friendly or hostile. But the rules are so vaguely drawn and so uncertain in their application as to be inhibiting other kinds of loans as well. Bank loans these days often carry provisions calling for automatic interest rate increases of 100 basis points or more if the loans are later classified by the bank examiners as HLTs.

CORPORATE CONTROL AND THE POLITICS OF FINANCE

by Michael C. Jensen,
Harvard Business School*

T he U.S. market for corporate control reached the height of its activity and influence in the last years of the 1980s. Among their many accomplishments, mergers and acquisitions, LBOs, and other leveraged restructurings of the past decade sharply reduced the effectiveness of size as a deterrent to takeover. The steady increase in the size of the deals throughout the 80s culminated in the $25 billion buyout of RJR-Nabisco in 1989 by KKR, a partnership with fewer than 30 professionals.

The effect of such transactions was to transfer control over vast corporate resources—often trapped in mature industries or uneconomic conglomerates—to those prepared to pay large premiums to use those resources more efficiently. In some cases, the acquirers functioned as agents rather than principals, selling part or all of the assets they acquired to others. In many cases, the acquirers were unaffiliated individual investors (labelled "raiders" by those opposed to the transfer of control) rather than other large public corporations. The increased asset sales, enlarged payouts, and heavy use of debt to finance such takeovers led to a large-scale return of equity capital to shareholders.

The consequence of this control activity has been a pronounced trend toward smaller, more focused, more efficient—and in many cases private—corporations.[1] And while capital and resources were being forced out of our largest companies throughout the 80s, the small- to medium-sized U.S. corporate sector was experiencing vigorous growth in employment and capital spending. At the same time our capital markets were bringing about this massive transfer of corporate resources, the U.S. economy was experiencing a 92-month expansion and record-high percentages of people employed.

The resulting transfer of control from corporate managers to increasingly active investors has aroused enormous controversy. The strongest opposition has come from groups whose power and influence have been challenged by corporate restructuring: notably, the Business Roundtable (the voice of managers of large corporations), organized labor, and politicians whose ties to wealth and power were being weakened. The media, always responsive to popular opinion even as they help shape it, have succeeded in reinvigorating the American populist tradition of hostility to Wall Street "financiers." The current controversy pitting Main Street against Wall Street has been wrought to a pitch that recalls the intensity of the 1930s. Newspapers, books, and magazines have obliged the public's desire for villains by furnishing unflattering detailed accounts of the private doings of those branded "corporate raiders."

*I appreciate the research assistance of Brian Barry, Susan Brumfield, and Steve-Anna Stephens, editorial and substantive comments and help from Don Chew and Karen Wruck, and research support provided by the Division of Research of the Harvard Business School. I bear all responsibilities for errors.

1. For supporting evidence, see Sanjai Bhagat, Andre Shleifer, and Robert W. Vishny, "Hostile Takeovers in the 1980s: The Return to Corporate Specialization," *Brookings Papers: Microeconomics 1990*, pp. 1-84; Steven N. Kaplan, "The Effects of Management Buyouts on Operating Performance and Value," *Journal of Financial Economics*, Vol. 24, No. 2 (October 1989), pp. 217-254; and Robert Comment and Gregg Jarrell, "Corporate Focus and Stock Returns," (Bradley Policy Research Center, Working Paper MR 91-01, May 1991).

Barbarians at the Gate, for example, the best-selling account of the RJR-Nabisco transaction, is perhaps best described as an attempt to expose the greed and chicanery that goes into the making of some Wall Street deals. And, on that score, the book is effective (though it's worth noting that, amidst the general destruction of reputations, the principals of KKR and most of the Drexel team come across as professional and principled). But what also emerges from the 500 plus pages—though the authors seem to fail to grasp its import—is clear evidence of corporate-wide inefficiencies at RJR-Nabisco, including massive waste of corporate "free cash flow," that would allow KKR to pay existing stockholders $12 billion over the previous market value for the right to bring about change.

And now that over two years have passed since that control change, KKR has defied skeptics not only by managing the company's huge debt load, but by creating another $5 billion in value (providing the original LBO warrant and equity holders with a compound annual rate of return of 59%), extracting almost $6 billion in capital through asset sales, and bringing the company public again.[2] In the process, it has also paid off almost $13 billion of the original $29 billion in debt (without, according to KKR, any losses to note or bondholders). Thus, the consequences to date of the RJR buyout for all investors, buying as well as selling, appear to be a remarkable $17 billion in added value.[3]

For economists and management scientists concerned about corporate efficiency, the RJR story is deeply disturbing. What troubles us is not so much the millions of dollars spent on sports celebrities and airplanes—or the greed and unprofessional behavior of several leading investment bankers—but rather the waste of billions in unproductive capital expenditures and organizational inefficiencies.[4] Viewed in this light—although, here again, the authors don't seem aware of what they have discovered—*Bar-*

barians is testimony to the massive failure of the internal control system led by RJR's board of directors. As former SEC Commissioner Joseph Grundfest has put it, the real "barbarians" in this book were *inside* the gates.[5]

Moreover, the fact that Ross Johnson, RJR's CEO, could be held up by *Fortune* as a model corporate leader only months before the buyout[6] attests to the difficulty of detecting even such gross inefficiencies and thus suggests that organizational inefficiencies of this magnitude may extend well beyond RJR. Although parts of corporate America may be guilty of underinvesting—as the media continually assert—there is little doubt that many of our largest U.S. companies have grossly *over*invested, whether in desperate attempts to maintain sales and earnings in mature or declining businesses or by diversifying outside of their core businesses. Many of our best-known companies—GM, IBM, Xerox, and Kodak come to mind most readily—have wasted vast amounts of resources over the last decade or so. The chronic overinvestment and overstaffing of such companies reflects the widespread failure of our corporate internal control systems. And it is this fundamental control problem that gave rise to the corporate restructuring movement of the 80s.

The Media and the Academy. But the role of takeovers and LBOs in curbing corporate inefficiency is not the story told by our mass media. When media accounts manage to raise their focus above the "morality play" craved by the public to consider broader issues of economic efficiency and competitiveness, the message is invariably the same: Leveraged restructurings are eroding the competitive strength of U.S. corporations by forcing cutbacks in employment, R&D, and capital investment. The journalistic method of inquiry is the investigation of selected cases, a process potentially subject to "selection bias." And the typical journalistic product

2. The equity gains are based on RJR-Nabisco's July 15, 1991 stock and warrant prices of $11.50 each. The original LBO investors contributed about $3.2 billion in equity ($1.5 billion initially on 2/9/89 and $1.7 billion in the restructuring on 7/16/90); as of 7/15/91, the total value of this equity had grown to $7.3 billion. The new public equity purchased for cash or exchanged for debt in March and April of 1991 totaled $2.0 billion; and the total value of this equity had increased to $2.8 billion as of 7/15/91.

3. Given these conclusive indications of success, it seems ironic that one of the most recent journalist attempts to capitalize on the antagonism to corporate restructuring, Sarah Bartlett's *The Money Machine* (New York: Warner Books, 1991), should describe the RJR deal as "the deal...people regard as most symptomatic of the excesses on Wall Street." "RJR Nabisco was not a departure," she goes on to say, "it was the culmination of a process that had gone badly out of control." *The Money Machine*, p. 237.

4. As revealed in the book, John Greeniaus, head of Johnson's baking unit, told KKR that if "the earnings of this group go up 15 or 20%...I'd be in trouble." His charter was to spend the excess cash in his Nabisco division to limit earnings in order to produce moderate, but smoothly rising profits—a strategy that would mask the potential profitability of the business. (See Bryan Burrough and John Helyar, *Barbarians at the Gate*, [Harper & Row, 1990], pp. 370-371.)

The Wall Street Journal reported that Greeniaus told them that the company was "looking frantically for ways to spend its tobacco cash," including a $2.8 billion plant modernization program that was expected to produce pre-tax returns of only 5%. (Peter Waldman, "New RJR Chief Faces a Daunting Challenge at Debt-Heavy Firm, *Wall Street Journal*, March 14, 1989, p. A1:6.

5. Joseph Grundfest, "Just Vote No or Just Don't Vote," Stanford Law School working paper (1990).

6. Bill Saporito, "The Tough Cookie at RJR Nabisco," *Fortune* (July 18, 1988).

*Although parts of corporate America may be guilty of underinvesting—as the media continually assert—there is little doubt that many of our largest U.S. companies have grossly **over**invested, whether in desperate attempts to maintain sales and earnings in mature or declining businesses or by diversifying outside of their core businesses.*

is a series of anecdotes—stories that almost invariably carry with them a strong emotive appeal for the "victims" of control changes, with little or no attention paid to long-run efficiency effects.[7]

Using very different methods and language, academic economists have subjected corporate control activity to intensive study. And the research contradicts the popular rhetoric. Indeed, I know of no area in economics today where the divergence between popular belief and the evidence from scholarly research is so great.

The most careful academic research strongly suggests that takeovers—along with leveraged restructurings prompted by the threat of takeover—have generated large gains for shareholders and for the economy as a whole. My estimates indicate that over the 14-year period from 1976 to 1990, the $1.8 trillion of corporate control transactions—that is, mergers, tender offers, divestitures, and LBOs—created over $650 billion in value for selling-firm shareholders.[8] And this estimate includes neither the gains to the buyers in such transactions nor the value of efficiency improvements by companies pressured by control market activity into reforming without a visible control transaction.

Some of the shareholder gains in highly leveraged transactions (HLTs) have come at the expense of bondholders, banks, and other creditors who financed the deals. But the amount of such losses is not likely to exceed $50 billion; a current best estimate would probably run around $25 billion.[9] (To put this number into perspective, IBM alone has seen its equity value fall by $25 billion in the past six

months.)[10] And thus far, there is no reliable evidence that any appreciable part of the remaining $600 billion or so of net gains to stockholders has come at the expense of other corporate "stakeholders" such as employees, suppliers, and the IRS.[11]

The well-documented increases in shareholder value have been largely dismissed by journalists and other critics of restructuring as "paper gains" having little bearing on the long-term vitality and competitiveness of American business. Some even point to such gains as evidence of a "short-term" orientation that is said to be destroying American business.

For financial economists, however, theory and evidence suggest that as long as such value increases are not arising from pure transfers from other parties to the corporate "contract," they are reliable predictors of increases in corporate operating efficiency. And, as I discuss later in this paper, research on LBOs has indeed produced direct evidence of such efficiencies; moreover, macro-economic data now reveal a dramatic improvement in the health and productivity of American industry during the 1980s.

The Present. In the past two years, restructuring transactions have come to a virtual standstill, and there are few signs today of a well-functioning corporate control market. Total M&A transactions fell 56% from a peak of $247 billion in 1988 to $108 billion in 1990; and this decline has accelerated through the first six months of 1991.

Widespread S&L failures (along with some failures of commercial banks and insurance companies) and a number of highly-publicized cases of troubled HLTs have combined with the criminaliza-

---

7. To compound the problem of selection bias, such journalistic accounts often contain inaccurate, or at best misleading, reporting of the facts. Jude Wanniski, Editor of the *MediaGuide* (and a former *Wall Street Journal* reporter), calls attention to such reporting in his comments on a *Wall Street Journal* article on the 1986 Safeway LBO that, ironically, was awarded a Pulitzer Prize for "explanatory journalism" (Susan Faludi, "The Reckoning: Safeway LBO Yields Vast Profits but Extracts a Heavy Human Toll," *Wall Street Journal*, May 16, 1990). As Wanniski comments, "This was not business reporting, nor was it a human interest story. This was pure and simple propaganda, the work of an ideologue using the *Journal's* front page to propagate a specific opinion about how corporate America should conduct its affairs." Jude Wanniski, *Financial World*, Dec. 11, 1990, p. 13.

8. Measured in 1990 dollars. Measured in nominal dollars, the total value of transactions and total gains were $1,239 billion and $443 billion, respectively.

9. As reported by the Salomon Brothers High Yield Research Group (*Original Issue High-Yield Default Study—1990 Summary*, January 28, 1991), as of the end of 1990, the face value of defaulted publicly placed or registered privately placed high-yield bonds in the period 1978-1990 was roughly $35 billion (about $20 billion of which entered bankruptcy). Given that recovery rates historically average about 40%, actual losses may well be below $20 billion. Not all of these bonds were used to finance control transactions, but I use the total to obtain an upper-bound estimate of losses.

Although the authorities have not released the totals of HLT loans and losses, bankers have told me privately that such losses are likely to be well below $10 billion.

10. More precisely, between February 19, 1991 (before announcing two consecutive declines in quarterly earnings) and July 17, 1991 (the time of this writing).

11. A 1989 study by Laura Stiglin, Steven Kaplan, and myself demonstrates that, contrary to popular assertions, LBO transactions result in increased tax revenues to the U.S. Treasury—increases that average about 60% per annum on a permanent basis under the 1986 IRS code. (Michael C. Jensen, Steven Kaplan, and Laura Stiglin, "Effects of LBOs on Tax Revenues of the U.S. Treasury," *Tax Notes*, Vol. 42, No. 6 (February 6, 1989), pp. 727-733.).

The data presented by a study of pension fund reversions reveal that only about 1% of the premiums paid in all takeovers can be explained by reversions of pension plans in the target firms (although the authors of the study do not present this calculation themselves). (Jeffrey Pontiff, Andrei Shleifer, and Michael S. Weisbach, "Reversions of Excess Pension Assets after Takeovers," *Rand Journal of Economics*, Vol. 21, No. 4 (Winter 1990), pp. 600-613.).

Joshua Rosett, analyzing over 5,000 union contracts in over 1,000 listed companies in the period 1973 to 1987, shows that less than 2% of the takeover premiums can be explained by reductions in union wages in the first six years after the change in control. Pushing the estimation period out to 18 years after the change in control increases the percentage to only 5.4% of the premium. For hostile takeovers only, union wages *increase* by 3% and 6% for the two time intervals, respectively. (Joshua G. Rosett, "Do Union Wealth Concessions Explain Takeover Premiums? The Evidence on Contract Wages," *Journal of Financial Economics*, Vol. 27, No. 1 (September 1990), pp. 263-282.

tion of securities law disclosure violations and the high-profile RICO and insider trading prosecutions to create a highly charged political climate.[12] Such political forces have produced a major re-regulation of our financial markets. The political origin of such regulatory initiatives is revealed by the fact that bad real estate loans dwarf junk bond losses and bad HLT loans as contributors to the current weakness of our financial institutions.[13]

With the eclipse of the new issue market for junk bonds, the application of HLT rules to commercial bank lending,[14] and new restrictions on insurance companies,[15] funding for large highly-leveraged transactions has all but disappeared. Even if financing were available, court decisions (including those authorizing the use of poison pills and defensive ESOP plans) and state antitakeover and control shareholder amendments have significantly increased the difficulty of making a successful hostile offer.

As a result, takeovers today are likely to revert to the pattern of the 60s and the 70s, when large companies used takeovers of other companies to build corporate "empires." The recent AT&T acquisition of NCR is an example. And if the past is a reliable guide, many such acquisitions are likely to end up destroying value and reducing corporate efficiency.

Contracting Problems Compounded by Politics. As prices were bid up to more competitive levels in the second half of the 1980s, the markets "overshot." Contracting problems between the promoters of HLTs and the suppliers of capital, as I will argue later, led to too many overpriced deals. In this sense, the financial press is right in attributing *part* of the current conditions in our debt and takeover markets to too many unsound transactions. Such transactions, especially those completed after 1985, were overpriced by their promoters and, as a consequence, overleveraged (and it is important to keep this order of causality in mind).

But it is also clear that intense political pressures to curb the corporate control market have greatly compounded the problems caused by this "contracting failure." However genuine and justified their concern about our deposit insurance funds, the reactions of Congress, the courts, and regulators to losses (which, again, are predominantly the result of real estate, not HLT loans) have had several unfortunate side-effects. They have sharply restricted the availability of capital to non-investment grade companies, thereby significantly increasing the rate of corporate defaults. They have also limited the ability of financially troubled companies to reorganize outside of court, thus ensuring that most defaulted companies wind up in bankruptcy. All of this, in my view, has contributed significantly to the current weakness of the economy.[16]

In this article, I have seven major aims.

First, I review new macroeconomic evidence on changes in productivity in American manufacturing that is dramatically inconsistent with popular claims that corporate control transactions were crippling the industrial economy in the 80s.

Second, I show how the restructuring movement of the 1980s reflected the re-emergence of active investors in the U.S.—a group that had been essentially dormant since the 1930s. In so doing, I argue that much of this leveraged restructuring activity addressed a fundamental problem facing many large, mature public companies: the conflict between management and shareholders over control of corporate "free cash flow."

Third, I summarize my conception of "LBO associations" as new organizational forms—structures that overcome the deficiencies of large public conglomerates. I also discuss the similarity between LBO associations and Japanese business financing networks known as "keiretsu."

Fourth, I extend this overseas comparison by summarizing my argument that the highly-leveraged financial structures of the 1980s should lead to the "privatization" of bankruptcy (i.e., out-of-court reorganization) that characterizes Japanese practice in reorganizing troubled companies.

12. Many of the most visible of these prosecutions by U.S. Attorney Giuliani have now either been dropped for lack of a case or reversed. The only RICO conviction, Princeton/Newport, has been reversed (although other securities law violations have been upheld), and so too the GAF, Mulheren, and Chestman cases. Only one major conviction of that era remains (Paul Bilzerian) and it is under appeal. The guilty pleas often obtained under threat of RICO prosecution, of course, remain.

For a brief discussion of pressures from Congress on the SEC to bring down investment bankers, arbs and junk bonds, see Glenn Yago, "The Credit Crunch: A Regulatory Squeeze on Growth Capital," (pp. 99-100) in the Spring 1991 issue of this journal.

13. The more fundamental cause of problems among banks is excess capacity caused by regulation and restrictions on takeovers of financial institutions. For elaboration of this point, see note 61.

14. See Creighton Meland, "Clarifying the New Guidelines for Highly-Leveraged Transactions," (Unpublished manuscript, Latham and Watkins, 1990).

15. See "NAIC (National Association of Insurance Companies) Policy Regarding Insurance Companies," Merrill Lynch Fixed-Income Research, June 12, 1990.

16. See the "Middle Market Roundtable" as well as the five articles on the "credit crunch" in the Spring 1991 issue of this journal.

The political origin of such regulatory initiatives is revealed by the fact that bad real estate loans dwarf junk bond losses and bad HLT loans as contributors to the current weakness of our financial institutions.

Fifth, I present a theory of "boom-bust" cycles in venture markets that explains how private contracting problems combined with the political interference mentioned above to bring about financial distress in many of the leveraged transactions put together in the latter half of the 80s.

Sixth, I argue that misguided changes in the tax and regulatory codes and in bankruptcy court decisions have blocked the normal economic incentives for creditors to come to agreement outside of Chapter 11, thus almost putting an end to out-of-court reorganizations. The consequence has been an increase in the costs of financial distress, and a sharp rise in the number of Chapter 11 filings.

Seventh and last, I propose a set of changes in the Chapter 11 process designed to correct the gross inefficiencies built into the current process. Rather than attempting to preserve the control of current management and extend the life of organizations (in some cases, without economic justification), my proposals reflect the thinking of academic economists and lawyers about how to reduce the costs of financial distress and thus maximize the total value of the firm to all investors.

NEW INSIGHTS FROM MACRO-ECONOMIC DATA

In addition to the continuing stream of scholarly work documenting efficiency gains by LBO companies, productivity gains are also visible in the aggregate data. As summarized in the top two panels of Figure 1, the pattern of productivity and unit labor costs in the U.S. manufacturing sector over the period 1950-1989 is inconsistent with popular characterizations of the 80s as the decade of the dismantling of American industry. Beginning in 1982, there was a dramatic increase in the productivity of the manufacturing sector (see panel A)—a turnaround unmatched in the last 40 years. In panel B, we see

a sharp acceleration of the steady decline in real unit labor costs since about 1960—a decline that stalled in the 1970s.[17]

Such cost reductions and efficiency gains have not come at the expense of labor generally (although *organized* labor has certainly seen its influence wane). As shown in Panels C, D, and E, there has been a rise in total employment and hours worked since the end of the 81-82 recession; hourly compensation has continued to rise since 1982 (although at a somewhat slower rate than before); and percentage unemployment has fallen dramatically since 1982.

The Effect on Capital Investment. Critics of leveraged restructuring also claim that corporate capital investment was a casualty of the M&A activity of the 80s. But, as shown in Panel F, after a pause in 1982, capital growth in the manufacturing sector has continued to rise—although, again, at a slower rate than previously. This pattern is consistent with my "free cash flow" argument that corporate restructuring was a response to excessive capital in many sectors of American industry. The pattern also suggests that, although capital was being squeezed out of the low-growth manufacturing sector by the payouts of cash and substitution of debt for equity, it was being recycled back into the economy. Some of that capital was transferred to smaller companies, including large inflows to the venture capital market. At the same time, the resulting organizational changes and efficiency gains at larger companies have provided the basis for renewed capital spending.[18]

The Effect on R&D. Another persistent objection to the control market is that it reduces valuable R&D expenditures. But, as shown in Figure 2, while M&A activity was rising sharply after the 82 recession (until plummeting in 1990), real R&D expenditures were reaching new highs in each year of the period from 1975 to 1990. R&D also rose from 1.8% to 3.4% of sales during this period.[19]

17. Interestingly, the Japanese economy experienced a similar turnaround in the growth of per unit labor costs almost a decade earlier than the United States.

18. Safeway, for example, went through an LBO in 1986 and sold half its stores. It has since come back public and has also launched a record five-year $3.2 billion capital program focused on store remodeling and new store construction.

19. The discrepancy between the data and the impression left by critics turns on a confusion between the level and the rate of increase of R&D spending. While achieving record levels, R&D spending grew more slowly in the late 1980s.

In a study of 600 acquisitions of U.S. manufacturing firms during 1976-1985, Bronwyn Hall found that acquired firms did not have higher R&D expenditures (as a fraction of sales) than firms in the same industry that were not acquired. Also, she found that "firms involved in mergers showed no difference in their pre- and post-merger R&D performance over those not so involved." See "The Effect of Takeover Activity on Corporate Research and Development," Chapter 3 in

Corporate Takeovers: Cause and Consequences, ed. Alan Auerbach, University of Chicago Press, 1988. In two recent papers, "The Impact of Corporate Restructuring on Industrial Research and Development," *Brookings Papers on Economic Activity*, Microeconomics 1990, pp. 85-124, and "Corporate Restructuring and Investment Horizons," University of California, Berkeley, unpublished manuscript, December 1990, Hall finds little relation between mergers, control changes, and LBOs and R&D expenditures, but finds a negative effect of leveraged restructurings on R&D.

A study by the Office of the Chief Economist at the SEC ("Institutional Ownership, Tender Offers, and Long-Term Investments," 4/19/85) also concludes: (1) increased institutional stock holdings are not associated with increased takeovers of firms; (2) increased institutional holdings are not associated with decreases in R&D expenditures; (3) firms with high research and development expenditures are not more vulnerable to takeovers; and (4) stock prices respond positively to announcements of increases in R&D expenditures.

FIGURE 1
TRENDS IN MANUFACTURING, 1950-1989:
PRODUCTIVITY, UNIT LABOR COSTS, EMPLOYMENT, COMPENSATION, AND CAPITAL

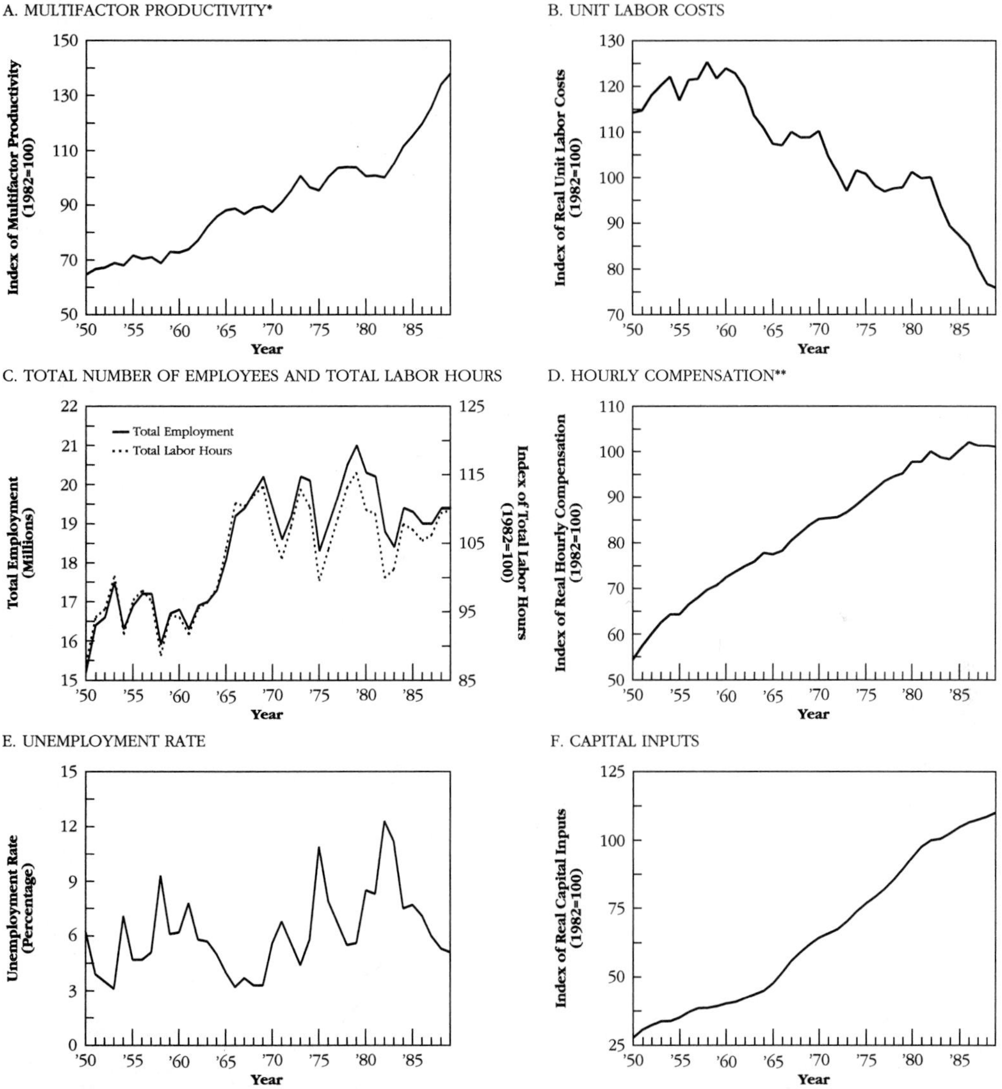

A. MULTIFACTOR PRODUCTIVITY*

B. UNIT LABOR COSTS

C. TOTAL NUMBER OF EMPLOYEES AND TOTAL LABOR HOURS

D. HOURLY COMPENSATION**

E. UNEMPLOYMENT RATE

F. CAPITAL INPUTS

Sources: **Panels A and F**—Bureau of Labor Statistics, "Multifactor Productivity, 1988 and 1989," Table 3. **Panels B and D**—Bureau of Labor Statistics, "International Comparisons of Manufacturing Productivity and Labor Cost Trends, 1989," (July 1990) USDL #90-383, Table 2. **Panel C**—Bureau of Labor Statistics, "Employment and Earnings," supplement obtained from Office of Employment and Unemployment; Bureau of Labor Statistics, "International Comparisons of Manufacturing Productivity and Labor Cost Trends, 1989" (July 1990) USDL #90-383, Table 2. **Panel E**—Bureau of Labor Statistics, "Labor Force Statistics Derived from the Population Survey, 1948-1987," (August 1988) Bulletin 2307, Table A-35; Bureau of Labor Statistics, "Employment and Earnings, January 1990," Table 11. *Multifactor Productivity is real output per unit of combined capital and labor. **Hourly Compensation includes wages and salaries, supplements, employer payments for social security, and other employer-financed benefit plans.

> [A]lthough capital was being squeezed out of the low-growth manufacturing sector by the payouts of cash and substitution of debt for equity... the resulting organizational changes and efficiency gains at larger companies have provided the basis for renewed capital spending.

FIGURE 2
M&A ACTIVITY VS. INDUSTRY R&D EXPENDITURES
(1975-1990)

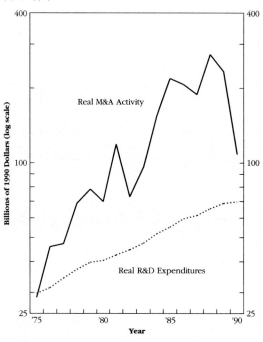

Source: *Business Week*, "R&D Scoreboard," annual; and Merrill Lynch, *Mergerstat Review, 1990*, Figure 5.

In short, although the macro data do not establish control market activity as a *cause* of the dramatic productivity improvements, they provide no support for the popular outcry against the workings of the corporate control market.[20]

The Costs of Restructuring (and the Alternative to Takeovers)

There is no doubt that the corporate restructuring movement resulted in changes painful to many individuals. With the shrinkage of some companies, there has been loss of jobs among top management and corporate staff, though not among blue collar workers as a group.[21] Much of the contraction resulting from takeovers is fundamentally a reflection of larger economic forces—forces that dictate that changes be made if resources are to be used efficiently and industrial decline is to be halted. Hostile takeovers typically achieve quickly—and thus, I would argue, with considerably lower social costs—the same end brought about in more protracted fashion by intense competition in product markets.[22]

Consider the current plight of our auto industry. Few industries have experienced as severe a retrenchment as the one this industry went through in the 1977-1982 period—and will surely have to experience in the future.[23] It is precisely the auto industry's past immunity to takeover and major restructuring, along with government protection from foreign competitors, that is responsible for the extent of its present requirement to downsize. Had normal economic forces like competition, failure, and takeover been allowed to operate, the massive contraction still required to restore competitiveness to our automobile industry would have been largely behind us today, and the social costs and dislocations would have been far smaller. The devastated economies of Eastern and Central Europe today are vivid examples of what happens when state protection prevents normal economic forces, including failure, from moving resources from lower- to higher-valued uses.

---

20. I have been unable to find references to the sources of data that have formed the bases for the critics' conclusions. Other sectors show somewhat lower rates of growth of productivity than does manufacturing, but I have been unable to find any significant evidence of declines in the aggregate data to support the claims of critics.

21. In their study of 20,000 plants involving control changes, Frank Lichtenberg and Donald Siegel found that changes in control reduce white collar employment in non-production facilities, but do not reduce blue collar or R&D employees. They also found significant increases in total factor productivity after both acquisitions and LBOs. For a summary of this work, see Frank Lichtenberg and Donald Siegel, "The Effect of Control Changes on the Productivity of U.S. Manufacturing Plants," *Journal of Applied Corporate Finance* (Summer 1989), pp. 60-67.

22. On rare occasions, the internal control systems manage to accomplish significant change without the threat of product or capital markets. General Mills is an example. In a case study of General Mills, Gordon Donaldson describes the

company's decade-long restructuring—a very gradual adjustment process that was finally successful in reversing a disastrous diversification strategy. (See Gordon Donaldson, "Voluntary Restructuring: The Case of General Mills," *Journal of Financial Economics*, Vol. 27, No. 1 (September 1990).)

Donaldson raises the possibility that such a gradual adjustment process has lower social costs than the abrupt change enforced by dramatic restructurings or takeovers. I believe a careful estimate of the social waste associated with keeping people unemployed or underemployed (while still on the payroll) and the wasteful utilization of assets over a decade-long period makes the year-long adjustment following a takeover or LBO a far lower-cost social strategy.

23. From 1977-1982, total employment fell by 336,000 from its high of over 1,000,000 in 1977. From 1982 to 1989, when the industry succeeded in gaining protection by means of import quotas, industry profits increased and employment in the industry rose to almost 840,000 even as U.S. automakers were losing significant market share.

While change imposes costs on some individuals, such costs are outweighed by the benefits to the general economy. At the end of the 1970s, when the Dow Jones average was around 900, Lester Thurow complained that one of the principal shortcomings of a "mixed" economy like ours was its inability to "disinvest"—that is, to move capital out of declining industries and into vital ones.[24] But this forced "disinvestment," I would argue, is the primary accomplishment of the wave of restructurings we saw in the 1980s. Such restructuring, as I argue in the next section, reflected the efforts of a new breed of "active" investors to prevent management from wasting resources by reinvesting cash flow in mature, low-return businesses with excess capacity. This is why restructuring activity was concentrated in industries such as oil, tobacco, tires, food processing, retailing, publishing, broadcasting, forest products, commodity chemicals, and financial services.

THE RETURN OF ACTIVE INVESTORS

Over the last 50 years, institutional investors and financial institutions have been driven out of their former role as active investors. By "active investor" I mean one who holds large equity and/or debt positions and actually monitors management, sits on boards, is sometimes involved in dismissing management, is often closely involved in the strategic direction of the company and, on occasion, even manages. That description fits people like Warren Buffet, Carl Icahn, Sir James Goldsmith, the Pritzkers, and Kohlberg, Kravis, and Roberts (KKR).

Before the mid-1930s, investment banks and commercial banks played a much more important role on boards of directors, monitoring management and occasionally engineering changes in management. At the peak of their activities, J.P. Morgan and several of his partners served on boards of directors and played a major role in the strategic direction of many firms.[25]

The diminished role of banks in corporate governance and strategy over the past 50 years is the result of a number of factors. Among the most important are laws passed in the 30s that increased the costs of being actively involved in the strategic direction of a company while also holding large amounts of its debt or equity.[26] Such regulations, together with today's strongly pro-management and chronically inefficient proxy mechanism,[27] do much to explain why money managers do not serve on boards today and seldom think of getting involved in the strategy of their portfolio companies.

The restrictive laws of the l930s were passed after an outbreak of populist attacks on the investment banking and financial community. During the formative years of the SEC, then chairman William O. Douglas shocked Wall Street investment bankers with the statement:

> [T]he banker [should and will be] restricted to...underwriting or selling. Insofar as management [and] formulation of industrial policies [are concerned]...the banker will be superseded. The financial power which he has exercised in the past over such processes will pass into other hands.[28]

As Mark Roe interprets Douglas's statement, "Main Street America did not want to be controlled by Wall Street. Congress responded to Main Street, not Wall Street; laws discouraging and prohibiting control resulted."[29]

The consequence of these political forces over the past 50 years has been to leave managers increasingly unmonitored. At present, when the U.S. institutions that own more than 40 percent of all U.S.

24. Lester Thurow, *The Zero-Sum Society* (Basic Books, 1980), p. 81.

25. See Vincent Carosso, *Investment Banking in America: A History* (Harvard University Press, 1970).

26. For example, the Glass-Steagall Act significantly restricted commercial bank equity holdings as well as bank involvement in investment banking activities. The Chandler Act restricted banks' involvement in the reorganization of companies in which they have substantial debt holdings. In addition, the l940 Investment Company Act put restrictions on the maximum holdings of investment funds. (See Mark Roe, "Political and Legal Restraints on Ownership and Control of Public Companies," *Journal of Financial Economics*, Vol. 27, No. 1 (September 1990), pp. 7-42; and Joseph Grundfest, "Subordination of American Capital," *Journal of Financial Economics*, Vol. 27, No. 1 (September 1990), pp. 89-117.)

27. For an historical account of the evolution of our proxy system into its current form, see John Pound, "Proxy Voting and the SEC: Investor Protection Versus Market Efficiency," *Journal of Financial Economics* (forthcoming).

Bernard Black, formerly on the legal staff of the SEC, concludes his analysis of proxy regulation as follows: "In fact, institutional shareholders are hobbled by a complex web of legal rules that make it difficult, expensive, and legally risky to own large percentage stakes or undertake joint efforts. Legal obstacles are especially great for shareholder efforts to nominate and elect directors, even to a minority of board seats. The proxy rules, in particular, help shareholders in some ways, but mostly hinder shareholder efforts to nominate and elect directors."

See Bernard Black, "Shareholder Passivity Reexamined," *Michigan Law Review*, (December 1990) p. 523.

28. As cited in Roe (1990) p. 8, cited in note 26.

29. Extending Roe's analysis of the influence of politics on finance, former SEC Commissioner Joseph Grundfest analyzes the process through which politicians take advantage of the agency problems between managers and shareholders to transfer wealth to favored constituencies (particularly managers, who are one of the most powerful constituencies in the process) through the securities regulation process. See Grundfest (1990), cited in note 26.

corporate equity become dissatisfied with management, they have few options other than to sell their shares. Moreover, managers' complaints about the churning of financial institutions' portfolios ring hollow: most prefer churning to a system in which those institutions would actually have direct power to correct a management problem. Few CEOs today like the idea of having institutions with substantial stock ownership sitting on their corporate board. That would bring about the monitoring of managerial activities by people who bear part of the wealth consequences of managerial mistakes and who are not beholden to the CEO for their directorships.

After financial institution monitors left the scene in the post-1940 period, many managers came to believe that their companies belonged to them and that stockholders were merely one of many "stakeholders" the firm had to serve.[30] The growth of this "managerialist" attitude also coincided with a 10-fold reduction in the percentage equity ownership of the CEOs of our largest companies—from roughly 3 percent in 1937 to less than .03 percent today.[31] U.S. companies, to be sure, also became much larger (even in inflation-adjusted dollars) over this period; but while management equity ownership was falling by a factor of 10, average company size increased by only about three to four times. The consequence, as Adolph Berle warned us back in the 30s, is that for almost 50 years we experienced a widening of the divide between ownership and control in our largest public companies.

Why Corporations Should Maximize Value. Financial economists have long understood that the fundamental aim of our corporations ought to be the maximization of their "long-run" value.[32] The critical role of the value-maximizing rule is to provide guidance to decision-makers evaluating trade-offs of resources at different points in time. (Extended to

incorporate the effects of uncertainty, this rule is the essence of modern capital theory.) When Congress and the courts begin to interfere with this primary mandate, they lose sight of what creates value and raises the standard of living in our society. It is precisely by allowing corporations to concentrate on that aim that the long-run interests of all other stakeholders—employees, creditors, suppliers, taxpayers, and so forth—are ultimately best served.[33] Again, the poverty of Eastern and Central Europe today is largely the consequence of eliminating all pressure, or incentive, to maximize the value of business enterprise.

Value-maximizing does not mean that stockholders are an especially deserving group, or that corporate stakeholders other than stockholders should be ignored in management's decision-making. Even the most aggressive maximizer of stockholder wealth must care about other constituencies such as employees, customers, suppliers, and local communities. Maximizing value, in fact, means allocating corporate resources (to the point where marginal costs equal marginal benefits) among all groups or interests that affect firm value. Value-maximizing decision-making devotes resources to members of each important corporate constituency to improve the terms on which they contract with the company, to maintain the firm's reputation, and to reduce the threat of restrictive regulation. In this sense, there is no conflict between management's service to its stockholders and to other corporate stakeholders.

The Increase in Agency Costs. The banning of financial institutions from fulfilling their critically important monitoring role has resulted in major corporate inefficiencies. The increase in "agency costs"[34] after the 30s—loosely speaking, the loss in value resulting from the separation between ownership and control in widely held public corpora-

30. This view is expressed in the Business Roundtable's March 1990 report, *Corporate Governance and American Competitiveness*. That statement, moreover, is significantly different from a statement it issued 12 years earlier, which emphasized accountability to shareholders alone. For a discussion of this "retreat" from shareholder accountability, see Robert Monks and Nell Minow, *Power and Accountability* (Harper Collins, 1991), pp. 81-84.

31. Michael C. Jensen and Kevin J. Murphy, "CEO Incentives: It's Not How Much You Pay, But How," *Harvard Business Review*, Vol. 90, No. 3 (May/June, 1990), pp. 138-153.

32. I put "long-run" in quotes because financial economists do not distinguish between current and "long-run" values. Virtually all credible evidence that we have suggests the market is willing to and capable of taking the long view of a corporation's prospects. It does of course make errors, but the evidence indicates that, without inside information, it is almost impossible for investors to tell whether those errors are positive or negative at any given time.

33. Value maximizing is socially optimal assuming there are no externalities or monopoly power. Externalities are the impositions of costs (or conferring of

benefits) by one party on others in which the acting party does not bear the costs (or have the opportunity to charge for the benefits). The pollution of air and water, without tax penalties or compensation to those affected, are examples.

34. Agency costs, more generally, reflect management's natural predisposition to growth rather than profitability and the incentives they face to expand their firms beyond the size that maximizes shareholder wealth. (See Gordon Donaldson, *Managing Corporate Wealth* (Praeger, 1984).)

Corporate growth is also associated with increases in the level of management compensation. One of the better-documented propositions in compensation theory is that, for every 10 percent increase in the size of the company, the CEO's compensation goes up by 3 percent. (G. Baker, M. Jensen, and K. Murphy, "Compensation and Incentives," *Journal of Finance* (July 1988). Also, the tendency of companies to reward middle managers through promotion rather than year-to-year bonuses also creates an organizational bias toward growth. Only growth can supply the new positions that such promotion-based reward systems require. (See George Baker, "Pay-for-Performance for Middle Managers: Causes and Consequences," *Journal of Applied Corporate Finance* (Fall 1990), pp. 50-61.)

tions—appears to have taken a sharp rise in the mid to late l960s when a substantial part of corporate America launched diversification programs that led to the assembly of conglomerates. We now know this course was unproductive, and it has been in large part reversed over the past 10 years.[35]

It is ironic, moreover, that while most attacks on takeovers have been directed at unaffiliated entrepreneurs such as Icahn and Goldsmith, it is the diversifying acquisitions by our largest corporations such as DuPont, Exxon, R.J. Reynolds, Goodyear, and U.S. Steel that have proven to be the least productive. Given the evidence attesting to the waste caused by corporate diversification, the criticism directed at the KKR buyout of RJR-Nabisco (a transaction that has led to renewed focus) seems misplaced, especially given the lack of controversy surrounding the recent AT&T takeover of NCR. This misdirected criticism of takeover entrepreneurs ("raiders"), while sparing corporate conglomerators, lays bare the political origins of the opposition.

The fact that takeover and restructuring premiums regularly average about 50 percent indicates that managers have been able to destroy up to a third of the value of the organizations they lead before facing serious threat of displacement.[36] This destruction of value generates large profit opportunities. In response to such opportunities, we have seen the rise of new kinds of institutions whose principal purpose has been to recapture that lost value. Along with the takeover specialists have come others such as the family funds (owned by the Bass Brothers, the Pritzkers, and the Bronfmans), Warren Buffet's Berkshire Hathaway, and Lazard Frères' Corporate Partners Fund—institutions that have discovered ways to bear the costs associated with insider status while being active in the strategic direction of the firm. These new institutions purchase substantial interests in (or entire) companies and play an active role in them. They often *are* the boards of directors. Because of their significant ownership interest, such institutional directors have far stronger incentives to monitor management than the typical outside directors of our public companies.

THE LBO ASSOCIATION: A NEW ORGANIZATIONAL FORM

LBO associations such as KKR, Clayton & Dubilier, and Forstmann-Little represent new organizational forms—in effect, a new model of general management. The diversity of the businesses owned by these LBO partnerships makes such organizations look like conventional corporate conglomerates. But such conglomerates, the result of the rush to diversify in the 60s and 70s, have generally been overcome by their own internal organizational failures. During the height of the restructuring activity in the 80s, they were routinely broken up and indirectly replaced by LBO associations that have solved the internal problems of the typical conglomerate.

LBO associations generate large increases in efficiency. They are generally run by partnerships instead of the headquarters office in the typical large, multi-business diversified corporation. These partnerships perform the monitoring and peak coordination function with a staff numbering in the tens of people, and replace the typical corporate headquarters staff of hundreds or thousands.

But while the new LBO associations may look like conventional conglomerates, they have a fundamental affinity with Japanese groups of firms called "keiretsu." LBO partnerships play a dual funding and oversight role that is similar in many ways to that of the main banks in the Japanese keiretsu. Like the main banks, which typically hold significant equity stakes in their corporate borrowers, the leaders of the LBO partnerships hold substantial amounts of equity in their companies and control access to the rest of the capital. Further like the Japanese banks, the LBO partners are actively involved in the monitoring and strategic direction of these firms.

Unlike the typical conglomerate (or the keiretsu, for that matter), the operating heads of the individual business units comprising the typical LBO association also have substantial equity ownership—ownership that gives them a pay-to-performance sensitivity that, on average, is 20 times greater than that experienced by the average corporate CEO.[37] More-

35. See Comment and Jarrell (1991), cited in note 1. See also Michael Porter, "From Competitive Advantage to Corporate Strategy," *Harvard Business Review* (May-June 1987).

36. A 50% premium that recovers the previous value of the firm means that 33% of the previous value was destroyed (50/150=.33).

37. Kaplan (1989), cited in note 1, documents that the median CEO receives $64 per $1,000 change in shareholder wealth from his 6.4 percent equity interest alone. By contrast, Kevin Murphy and I find that the average CEO in the Forbes 1000 receives total pay (including salary, bonus, deferred compensation, stock options and equity) that changes by only about $3.25 for every $1,000 change in stockholder value. (See Jensen and Murphy (1990), cited in note 31.)

In their clinical study of the 1986 OM Scott LBO from ITT, George Baker and Karen Wruck show that after the buyout, in addition to a substantial equity stake, Scott's managers were subject to an annual cash bonus plan that increased the average payouts from 3 to 6 times. (See "Organizational Changes and Value Creation in Leveraged Buyouts," *Journal of Financial Economics*, 25 (1989).)

During the 1980s, conglomerates were routinely being broken up and indirectly replaced by LBO associations that have solved the internal problems of the typical conglomerate... In effect, the LBO association substitutes incentives provided by compensation and ownership plans for the direct monitoring and often centralized decision-making in the typical corporate bureaucracy.

over, the managing partners in the LBO associations—which is really the proper comparison with the CEOs of conglomerates—have an even larger pay-for-performance as a result of their 20% override on the value created in the company.

LBO business unit heads also have far less bureaucracy to deal with, and far more decision-making freedom, in running their businesses. In effect, the LBO association substitutes incentives provided by compensation and ownership plans for the direct monitoring and often centralized decision-making in the typical corporate bureaucracy. The compensation and ownership plans make the rewards to managers highly sensitive to the performance of their business units, something that rarely occurs in major corporations.

Also important, the contractual relationship between the partnership headquarters and the suppliers of capital to the buyout funds is very different from that between the corporate headquarters and stockholders in the diversified firm. The buyout funds are organized as limited partnerships in which the managers of the partnership headquarters are the general partners. Unlike the diversified firm, the contract with the limited partners denies partnership headquarters the right to transfer cash or other resources from one LBO business unit to another. Instead, cash payouts from each LBO business unit must be paid out directly to the limited partners of the buyout funds. This reduces the waste of free cash flow that is so prevalent in diversified corporations.[38]

The Evidence on LBOs

Financial economists studying LBOs have produced substantial evidence documenting gains in operating efficiency as well as increases in stockholder value.

Stockholder Gains. As would be expected in a competitive corporate control market, the gains to selling stockholders in LBOs have been roughly comparable to shareholder gains from takeovers. Estimates of the average premium over market two months prior to the buyout range from 40 percent to

50 percent.[39] For buyouts that came back public or were otherwise sold or valued, the total value (adjusted for market movements) increased 96 percent from two months before the buyout to the final sale about three years after the buyout. These gains were divided roughly equally between the pre- and post-buyout investors.[40] The median net-of-market return on the post-buyout equity alone was approximately 785 percent.[41]

Increases in Operating Efficiency. In addition to the studies of value changes, studies examining the operating performance of large samples of LBOs after the buyout have found real increases in productivity. The Kaplan study cited above finds average increases in annual operating earnings of 42 percent from the year prior to the buyout to the third year after the buyout, and increases of 25 percent when adjusted for industry and business cycle trends. He also finds 96 percent increases in cash flow in the same period (80 percent increases after adjustment for industry and business cycle trends).

The Bottom Line. In a review paper published in 1990, my Harvard colleague Krishna Palepu summarized the findings of more than two dozen studies of LBOs and their effects as follows:

- *Stockholders of firms undergoing LBOs earn substantial returns from the transactions.*
- *Company productivity and operating performance improve substantially in the years immediately following a buyout. The improvements are a result of the changes in financial and management structure associated with the buyout. There is little evidence of a decline in employment levels or average wage rates of blue-collar workers after a buyout, suggesting that the post-buyout cash-flow improvements are not the result of widespread wealth transfers from workers.*
- *Although some pre-buyout bondholders suffer losses at the buyout, these losses account for a very small fraction of the total gains to pre-buyout shareholders.*
- *Buyouts give companies increased depreciation and interest tax shields which account for some of the equity gains from these transactions. Buyouts also increase tax revenues to the U.S. Treasury in several*

---

38. See Michael C. Jensen, "The Agency Costs of Free Cash Flow: Corporate Finance and Takeovers," *American Economic Review*, Vol. 76, No. 2 (May, 1986). For additional evidence, see also Larry Lang, Rene Stulz, and Ralph Walkling, "A Test of the Free Cash Flow Hypothesis: The Case of Bidder Returns," *Journal of Financial Economics* (forthcoming).

39. For a survey of research on the economic effects of LBOs, see Krishna Palepu, "Consequences of Leveraged Buyouts," *Journal of Financial Economics* 27 (1990) and the references therein.

40. Kaplan (1989), cited in note 1.

41. Average total buyout fees amounted to 5.5% of the equity two months prior to the buyout proposal.

ways, however, and the net effect of LBOs on aggregate tax revenues is likely to be positive.

■ *LBOs appear to have two opposing effects on firm risk. Although the leverage increase associated with the buyout increases financial risk, the changes in the organizational structure and strategy appear to reduce business risk. The net result is that LBO investors bear significantly lower risk than comparable levered investments in public corporations.*[42]

THE PRIVATIZATION OF BANKRUPTCY

The high leverage associated with LBOs and other HLTs—notwithstanding its benefits as a monitoring and incentive device,[43] and the related reductions in business risk just cited—was bound to increase the probability of companies getting into financial trouble. Indeed, when testifying before the House on LBOs in February 1989, I expressed surprise at how few mistakes we had witnessed in a revolution in business practice as great as that occurring over the last decade.[44] At that time, fewer than 30 of some 1500 going-private transactions completed since 1979 had gone into formal bankruptcy. Since then, of course, the number of HLTs in default or bankruptcy has risen sharply.

As I also pointed out in my testimony, the costs of dealing with corporate insolvency could be expected—barring unforeseen changes in capital market regulations and the bankruptcy courts—to be much smaller in the new world of high leverage ratios than they have been historically. The reason for my prediction has much to do with the fact that the HLTs that get into trouble today are likely to be fundamentally different from the traditional corporate bankrupts of the past. In contrast to the traditionally low-levered firms that end up eating through their large equity bases and becoming candidates for liquidation, today's troubled HLTs are likely to be fundamentally profitable companies generating large positive (pre-interest) cash flows. And, given our costly and cumbersome court-supervised bankruptcy process (a subject I return to later), it seems clear that far more of this operating value can be preserved by privately resolving conflicts among the firm's claimants rather than filing under Chapter 11.[45]

Because of these stronger incentives to preserve value in the new leverage model, I argued that a different set of institutional arrangements were arising to substitute for the usual bankruptcy process. In short, I predicted that the reorganization process would be "privatized."[46]

Extending The Japanese Parallel. As mentioned above, the funding and governance of companies by LBO associations are strikingly similar to many of the practices of Japanese keiretsu. And this similarity also extends to their practice in reorganizing troubled companies. Japanese companies make intensive use of leverage, far more so than their American counterparts; and Japanese banks appear to allow companies to go into bankruptcy only when it is economic to liquidate them—that is, only when the firm is more valuable dead than alive. As leader of the consortium of banks lending to any firm, the Japanese main bank takes responsibility for evaluating the economic viability of an insolvent firm, and for planning its recovery—including the infusion of new capital and top-level managerial manpower (often drawn from the bank itself). Other members of the lending consortium commonly follow the lead of the main bank and contribute additional funding, if required, to the reorganization effort. The main bank bonds its role by making the largest commitment of funds to the effort.[47]

42. Krishna Palepu (1990), pp. 260-261, cited in note 39.

43. See Jensen (1986), cited in note 38. See also Karen Wruck, "Financial Distress, Reorganization, and Organizational Efficiency," *Journal of Financial Economics* 27 (1990).

44. Michael C. Jensen, "The Effects of LBOs and Corporate Debt on the Economy," Remarks before the Subcommittee on Telecommunications and Finance, U.S. House of Representatives Hearings on Leveraged Buyouts (Washington, D.C., February 22, 1989).

45. Bankruptcy, however, does have special advantages in some cases; for example, in retailing, trade credit is crucial to continuation of the business and it is difficult to negotiate privately with hundreds or thousands of trade suppliers.

46. See my article, "Active Investors, LBOs, and the Privatization of Bankruptcy," *Journal of Applied Corporate Finance* (Spring, 1989). My argument was anticipated in part by Robert Haugen and Lemma Senbet in their article, "The Insignificance of Bankruptcy Costs to the Theory of Optimal Capital Structure," *Journal of Finance*, 33 (1978), pp. 383-393.

47. For a more detailed discussion, see Carl Kester later in this issue, "Japanese Corporate Governance and The Conservation of Value in Financial Distress."

As I have argued earlier, however, even as our system has begun to look more like the Japanese, the Japanese economy is undergoing changes that are reducing the role of large active investors and thus making their system resemble ours. With the progressive development of U.S.-like capital markets, Japanese managers have been able to loosen the controls once exercised by the banks. So successful have they been in bypassing banks that the top third of Japanese companies are no longer net bank borrowers. As a result of their past success in product market competition, Japanese companies are now "flooded" with free cash flow. Their competitive position today reminds me of the position of American companies in the late 1960s. And, like their U.S. counterparts in the 60s, Japanese companies today appear to be in the process of creating conglomerates.

My prediction is that, unless unmonitored Japanese managers prove to be much more capable than American executives of managing large, sprawling organizations, the Japanese economy is likely to produce large numbers of those conglomerates that U.S. capital markets have spent the last 10 years trying to pull apart. And if I am right, then Japan is likely to experience its own leveraged restructuring movement. (See Michael C. Jensen, "Eclipse of the Public Corporation," *Harvard Business Review*, Vol. 89, No. 5 (September-October, 1989), pp. 61-74.)

We now know that LBOs frequently got into trouble in the early 80s. But instead of entering formal bankruptcy, they were typically reorganized in a short period of time (several months was common), often under new management, and at apparently lower cost than would occur in the courts.

Reorganization in the 80s. Similar practices appear to be the norm in the American LBO community. (In fact, the recent restructuring of RJR's balance sheet together with a new equity infusion is a nice illustration of this process.) The combination of debt and equity claims held by Japanese banks had an American analogue in the "strip financing" techniques commonly observed in the early LBOs. The practice of strip financing—wherein roughly proportional "strips" of all securities in the capital structure were held by most of the claimants—reduces the conflicts of interest among classes of claimants that inevitably arise in troubled companies.[48] The intensity of such conflicts—which, as I will argue later, are aggravated by our system—are contributing to the current costs of workouts and bankruptcies.

The stronger incentives created by high leverage to manage the insolvency process more efficiently were also reflected in the extremely low frequency with which LBOs actually entered bankruptcy in the first half of the 1980s, as well as the general experience of troubled companies at that time. For example, 91, or 47%, of the 192 NYSE and ASE companies that defaulted during the period 1980-1986 were reorganized privately.[49] Some assert that the early success of LBOs was ensured by the bull market of the middle 80s. The story was not that simple, however, because during the late 70s and the first half of the 80s, major sectors of the economy experienced bad times, and buyouts occurred in many of these sectors.

We now know that LBOs frequently got into trouble in the early 80s. But instead of entering formal bankruptcy, they were typically reorganized in a short period of time (several months was common), often under new management, and at apparently lower cost than would occur in the courts. Drexel Burnham Lambert, which underwrote much of the high-yield bond offerings throughout the 80s, also transformed the 3(a)9 exchange offer into a valuable innovation in the workout and reorganization process. The available evidence indicates, moreover, that the direct costs of exchange offers are only about 10% of those in the average Chapter 11 of comparable size.[50] Such innovation is to be expected when there are such large efficiency gains to be realized from new reorganization and recontracting procedures.

Moreover, I warned in my House testimony (in February 1989) that serious problems would result among Drexel's clients if regulators hampered its ability to handle reorganizations and workouts. Drexel's position in the high-yield bond market gave it a unique ability to perform this function and no substitute was likely to emerge soon.

Today, of course, Drexel is gone. And, though I seem to have been right about the consequences of Drexel's demise, my predictions about the continuing privatization of bankruptcy could not have been more wrong. What I failed to anticipate were major new regulatory initiatives, a critical change in the tax code, and a misguided bankruptcy court decision that together are forcing many troubled companies into Chapter 11.

CONTRACT FAILURE IN VENTURE MARKETS

Judging from press reports, academic case studies of failed transactions,[51] and a recent study of 119 large LBOs by Steven Kaplan and Jeremy Stein, it now seems clear that more of the transactions completed in recent years have been overpriced and, as a result of the overpricing, overleveraged. According to Kaplan and Stein, of the 66 large LBOs (greater than $100 million in value) completed during the period 1986 to 1988, 18 have defaulted and 7 have filed for bankruptcy. In contrast, only 4 of the 53 large LBOs completed during 1980-1985 have defaulted, and 3 filed for bankruptcy.[52] The question troubling economists is this: Are there *systematic* factors that would account for the high concentration of defaults among deals transacted in the latter stages of the leveraged restructuring movement?

---

48. For a discussion of strip financing, see Michael C. Jensen, "Takeovers: Their Causes and Consequences," *Journal of Economic Perspectives*, Vol. 2, No. 1 (Winter 1988).

49. See Stuart Gilson's article in this issue. Wruck (1990, p. 425-426, cited in note 43), using data obtained privately from Stuart Gilson, reports that only 51% of all 381 firms performing in the lowest 5% of the NYSE and ASE defaulted in the period 1978-1987. It seems likely that many of these companies avoided default by means of private reorganizations.

50. See Stuart Gilson's article in this issue. See also Stuart Gilson, Kose John, and Larry Lang, "Troubled Debt Restructurings: An Empirical Study of Private

Reorganization of Companies in Default," *Journal of Financial Economics*, Vol. 27, No. 2 (September 1990).

51. See Wruck's study of Revco in this issue. See also Steven N. Kaplan, "Campeau's Acquisition of Federated: Value Destroyed or Value Added," *Journal of Financial Economics*, Vol. 25, No.2 (December 1989), pp. 191-212.

52. See Steven N. Kaplan and Jeremy Stein, "The Evolution of Buyout Pricing and Financial Structure in the 1980s," (unpublished manuscript, University of Chicago, April 1991).

I believe there have been two major factors contributing to problems in the market for highly leveraged transactions. First, the HLT market experienced a "contracting failure"—one that gives rise to the boom-and-bust cycles common in venture markets such as real estate development, oil and gas drilling, and the venture capital market. Second, major changes in the regulatory and legal environment have greatly compounded the problems arising from this contract failure by reducing the ability of companies to refinance their existing debt and, when necessary, to reorganize claims efficiently. Such flexibility is essential to the privatization of bankruptcy I described earlier. By increasing the cost of high leverage, significantly restricting companies' ability to adjust their capital structures, and interfering with the private workout process, regulatory intervention has substantially increased both the frequency and the costs of financial distress and bankruptcy. (In this sense, as I argue later, the regulatory attack on high leverage has become a self-fulfilling prophecy.)

Boom and Bust

My explanation for the boom-and-bust cycles in venture markets—one which applies in particular to the LBO market—centers on a misalignment of incentives between dealmakers and the creditors and investors they bring together. I call this misalignment a *contracting* failure because it can be corrected (without government intervention) by the private parties entering into the arrangements. I call it a *failure* because corrections seem to take too long to appear and the mistakes repeat themselves too often to be consistent with our theory of rational investors.

As explained above, *after* the deal has been completed, the general structure of LBOs provides strong incentives to the relevant parties to maximize value. I refer in particular to the governance structure of the LBO partnership, the 20% override received by the LBO general partners as well as their cash investment in the LBO equity, management incentive contracts with high pay-for-performance sensitivity, the control effect of high leverage, constraints

on the cross-subsidization of one LBO by another, and the large percentage equity holdings of managers made possible by high leverage.

The contracting failure that concerns me is the tendency for venture markets to evolve in a way that fails to provide incentives for the dealmakers to select and promote *only* deals that are worth more than they cost. Such a misalignment of incentives goes far in explaining not only why LBOs and other HLTs became overpriced, but also why other activities like real estate, venture capital, and oil and gas well drilling go through boom-and-bust cycles.

The Case of LBOs. In the earlier years of the LBO movement, the partnerships that promoted the LBOs put up significantly more equity capital than they did in the latter part of the 80s. They were forced to do so by the novelty of the transactions and investors' understandable resistance to the unknown. But, as the initial deals succeeded and equity returns were reported to be in excess of 100% per year, investment capital began to flow into the industry.

In the next stage of this process, both limited partners and suppliers of debt capital demanded and received more of the equity, thus reducing both the dealmaker's commitment of capital and back-end stake in the success of the transaction. Further distorting the incentives of dealmakers, the flood of capital into LBO funds allowed the dealmakers to command "front-end-loaded" fees simply for closing the transactions.[53] Such fees, which often substituted for the actual commitment of equity capital, combined with the convention of the 20-percent override (which amounts in practice to a free warrant on the outcome of the venture), enabled dealmakers both to profit upfront and to hold a residual interest while shifting virtually all downside risk to the creditors and limited partners.[54]

Such an arrangement, whereby dealmakers are effectively being paid for "doing" deals, ensures that too many deals will be done. In such situations, it pays dealmakers who do not value their reputations (or have no reputation to protect) to do deals that they know (or should know) cost more than the value they are expected to produce. Although this arrangement cannot be sustained indefinitely be-

53. Kaplan and Stein (1991), cited in note 52, find that, in the 53 large LBOs done prior to 1986, total fees amounted to 2.7% of the purchase price of the equity. By contrast, in the 66 large LBOs completed between 1986 and 1988, total fees rose to 4.9% of the purchase price of the equity.

54. Venture capital organizations are structured similarly. See William Sahlman, "The Structure and Governance of Venture Capital Organizations,"

Journal of Financial Economics, Vol. 27, No. 2 (September 1990). Some contracts with limited partners help reduce these incentives by making the sharing rule cumulative on all deals funded by the partnership. Under these contracts the dealmaker can't avoid the losses as easily.

cause of the losses it's bound to generate, the several-year information lag revealing the profitability of the deals allows it to continue for some time. During this time, dealmakers can earn fees on bad deals.

As the information on high returns continues to make itself known, and the market continues to mature, the probability of failure also rises because new and inexperienced dealmakers (who thus have less reputational capital at stake) enter the market; the supply of attractive deals thus begins to shrink and prices are bid up to competitive levels. Under these circumstances, the market is likely to over-shoot and bidders are more likely to overpay. As a direct consequence, limited partners and creditors—both of whom must rely to some extent on the reputation and assurances of the dealmaker—are more likely to experience losses. In this situation, the "go/no-go" decision effectively falls back on the suppliers of credit, who are generally not able to obtain the necessary information at reasonable cost to make good decisions.[55]

What, then, corrects this contracting failure and restores the market to equilibrium? As losses begin to appear, investors pull back, yields rise sharply—and with them the cost of high leverage. The reputations of many dealmakers are tarnished, and the whole activity becomes tainted. In the meantime, however, some LBO specialist firms—especially well-established dealmakers such as KKR, Clayton & Dubilier, Forstmann Little, and others—continue to have a strong interest in maintaining their reputational capital. Such firms, even if they have fallen to the temptation of front-end-loaded structures, will work hard to salvage troubled deals and to minimize losses to their investment partners.

In contrast, many of the newer players entering the market have considerably less to lose from walking away from a bad deal. The perceived potential reward to breaking into the market with a big success often far outweighs the risk of loss—provided you don't have to commit the firm's capital.

The Revco and Fruehauf failures provide good examples of this problem (see Karen Wruck's analysis of Revco in this issue); and so do the bankruptcies following Interco's leveraged restructuring and Campeau's acquisitions of Allied and Federated.[56] It is interesting that none of these deals was sponsored (or promoted, in the Interco and Campeau cases) by established LBO partnerships; rather they were all either sponsored or promoted by non-partnership newcomers eager to enter the business.

Incentives to overpay in highly levered transactions were also exaggerated by another set of conflicts of interest. In some of these transactions, the substantial amounts paid to the current managers for their old stock far exceeded their investment in the equity of the newly levered company. Such large upfront distributions almost surely encouraged them—especially if their jobs were also being threatened by a hostile offer—to go along with deals whose expected returns were not commensurate with the risks.

In effect, if not by conscious intent, the investment bankers structured deals that *paid* the managers to abandon their normal caution so that the deals could get done and the fees collected. Again, Revco, Interco, and Campeau provide illustrative examples. In each of these cases, there was no LBO partnership with a long-run reputation to protect. The investment bankers that promoted the deals invested no net money of their own and took out substantial fees. And, in the cases of Revco and Interco, the managers were paid substantial sums to do the deals.[57]

COMPOUNDING THE PROBLEMS BY REGULATION AND NEW BARRIERS TO WORKOUTS

After almost a decade of progressive deregulation across many sectors of American industry, we are now experiencing "re-regulation" of our financial markets. Much of the S&L industry has effectively

---

55. The decision-making by suppliers of credit may also be distorted by their own "agency problems." Commercial lenders, for example, were often rewarded principally for loan and fee generation, which in turn arose from the efforts of banks to retain market share by underpricing loans in an industry troubled by chronic excess capacity. High-yield bond mutual fund managers, to the extent they are paid on the basis of funds under management, also have some incentive to gamble on uneconomic deals rather than return funds to subscribers. For an exposition of such "agency problems," see Martin S. Fridson, "Agency Costs: Past and Future," see Martin S. Fridson, "Agency Costs: Past and Future," Merrill Lynch *Extra Credit*, (June 1991). For a related theory of cycles founded on information lags, not incentives, see DeLong, Shleifer, Summers, and Waldmore, "Positive Feedback Investment Strategies and Destabilizing Rational Speculations," *Journal of Finance* (June, 1990).

56. Interestingly, the Campeau acquisitions of Allied and Federated and the leveraged restructuring of Interco were all promoted by the same non-LBO partnership investment bank. See Kaplan (1989), cited in note 51.

57. See Wruck's discussion of Revco in this issue. In the case of the Interco restructuring, Interco's managers owned $12.3 million in equity prior to the deal (1.15%). They were paid $15.8 million in cash, $13.3 million in debt in the restructured company, and ended up with 4.14% of the equity (a trivial amount relative to normal standards) with only a $7.9 million total value. (Source: Interco May 1989 proxy statement.) For a critical review of the price-setting process, see George Anders and Francine Schwadel, "Costly Advice: Wall Streeters Helped Interco Defeat Raiders But at a Heavy Price," *Wall Street Journal*, July 11, 1990.

been nationalized. Drexel Burnham Lambert, one of the prime movers in the leveraged restructuring movement, has been destroyed. And, with the proliferation of poison pills, state anti-takeover laws, and growing legal support for the "just say no" defense, the once vigorous market for corporate control is now largely dormant.

As suggested earlier, the regulatory measures designed to purge our credit markets of "speculative excesses" have greatly added to the current difficulties in our HLT markets. When regulators began to step in during the summer of 1989, there were already signs of a normal correction as participants began to realize that the LBO market had overshot the "efficient margin." There was already underway a return to larger equity commitments, less debt, lower prices, lower projected growth rates, and lower bank fees.[58] In the absence of most regulatory intervention, these fundamentally self-correcting processes would have disciplined participants in the venture and credit markets, thereby providing the basis for renewed activity at sustainable prices.

Unfortunately, however, the flurry of legislative and regulatory initiatives provoked by real estate losses overrode such normal market correctives and created a "downward spiral" in prices (and business activity generally). The S&L legislation (FIRREA),[59] HLT regulations, and much tightened oversight by banking regulators depressed high-yield bond prices further, raised the cost of high leverage, and made adjustments to overleveraged capital structures all the more difficult. In so doing, such regulations have caused non-price rationing of credit, along with a sharp constriction of its availability to middle market and small firms.[60] They have also reduced the flexibility of lenders to work with highly leveraged companies who cannot meet lending covenants or current debt service payments. These changes, coming on top of the departure of Drexel, the principal market maker, have caused a sharp increase

in defaults. Indeed, 19 defaults among the Kaplan and Stein sample of 119 large LBOs have occurred since the beginning of 1989; only three in that sample defaulted prior to that time.

Problems with Workouts. Compounding the problem with losses and defaults is surely not what most Congressmen and regulators intended when they enacted such policy shifts. In addition to the "political" objections to the control market I've cited earlier, much of the impetus for the new rules and regulations undoubtedly came from legitimate concern about the protection of deposit insurance funds and the soundness of our financial institutions.[61] But, I can think of no such charitable explanation to account for the barriers to private workouts recently thrown up by bankruptcy judges and tax authorities.

As stated earlier, a major means of reorganizing distressed companies in the 1980s was the 3(a)9 exchange offer employed by Drexel during the early 1980s. Such a technique, even in the absence of Drexel, should have been useful for accomplishing out-of-court settlements under current conditions. In January 1990, however, Judge Burton Lifland ruled in the LTV case that bondholders who participate in exchange offers thereby reduce the value of their claim in bankruptcy to the market value of the claim accepted. Because such market values are typically well below face value, bondholders today are not likely to tender their bonds into an offer if there is any serious chance the firm will later file Chapter 11. This ruling, together with tax penalties imposed in 1990 by Congress on reorganizations outside the bankruptcy court,[62] has caused exchange offers to slow to a trickle, and bankruptcies to rise sharply. For example, only two of the 119 LBOs in the Kaplan and Stein study entered bankruptcy prior to 1989. Since then, eight more have followed.

In sum, our political, regulatory, and legal system has produced a set of policy changes that are frustrating instead of encouraging the normal market

58. See Kaplan and Stein (1991), cited in note 52.

59. The Financial Institutions Reform, Recovery and Enforcement Act, passed in the summer of 1989, which banned the purchase and effectively banned the holding of high-yield bonds by thrifts.

60. See the "Middle Market Roundtable" as well as the five articles on the "credit crunch" in the Spring 1991 issue of this journal.

61. There are admittedly complex economic and political forces at work today that make it difficult for regulators to formulate policy. But, in their obsession with protecting the deposit insurance funds, regulators are responding to symptoms while ignoring the fundamental cause of the problems in our S&L and banking systems. With over 12,000 commercial banks, the banking system has substantial excess capacity and is inefficiently organized. It seems unlikely that the new bank reforms now being entertained by Congress will allow for the orderly exit and radical restructuring of the industry that is needed to restore profitability. An active

market for corporate control has not been allowed to function in this industry; and it seems doubtful it will be allowed to do so in the future. In the absence of takeovers, the most likely exit route will be through bankruptcies, forced mergers, and liquidations in response to losses caused by the intense competition in the financial products markets. Without the capital markets to aid in the exit of resources, we can expect individual banks to struggle to add to their capital base to ensure that, when the music stops, they will be one of the survivors. This process, by increasing capacity in an industry that already has to shrink, has led and will continue to lead to substantial waste of scarce resources.

62. Under the Revenue Reconciliation Act of 1990, when new bonds issued in an exchange offer have lower interest rates, the firm must realize taxable income on the exchange. Such exchanges, tax-exempt prior to the Act, are now tax-exempt only if issued in bankruptcy.

adjustment process that was underway in 1989. Indeed, from an economist's perspective, such changes seem virtually the opposite of what is necessary to promote the efficient reorganization of troubled companies, an expansion in the availability of debt capital, and a general return to growth. By drying up traditional credit sources, regulation has sharply increased the cost of debt and thus increased the number of defaults. At the same time, other changes have interfered with the private workout process, thus ensuring that many of those defaults will turn into bankruptcies. All this might not be so troubling, except that the rulings and practices of our bankruptcy courts are making the Chapter 11 process seemingly ever more costly, adding to the waste of resources.

A PROPOSAL FOR REFORMING THE BANKRUPTCY PROCESS

The function of the bankruptcy courts is to enforce contracts between the firm and its creditors, and to provide a formal process for breaking such contracts when they cannot be fulfilled, and when private parties cannot resolve their conflicts outside of court. In addition, bankruptcy courts resolve ambiguities about the size, legitimacy, and priority of claims. Unfortunately, the U.S. bankruptcy system seems to be fundamentally flawed. It is expensive,[63] it exacerbates conflicts among different classes of creditors, and it often takes years to resolve individual cases. As a result of such delays, much of the operating value of businesses can be destroyed.[64]

Much of the problem stems from the following two fundamental premises underlying the revised (1978) U.S. Bankruptcy Code: (1) reorganization is strongly preferred to liquidation (and current management should be given ample opportunity to lead that reorganization); and (2) the restructuring of the firm's contractual claims should, whenever possible,

be *completely* voluntary. In practice, a majority in number (representing at least two thirds of the value) of any class of claimants deemed to be impaired[65] must approve a reorganization. Judges have the power to "cram down" a settlement on a class of creditors without their approval, but they seldom do it. Reflecting the pro-debtor bias in the code, the managers of the firm are effectively given the sole right to propose a plan for 120 days after the filing. Bankruptcy judges also regularly approve multiple extensions of this exclusivity period.[66] As I will argue later, these features of the code give rise to chronic inefficiencies.

Absolute Priority: Theory vs. Practice

In thinking about what we want the bankruptcy system to accomplish and how it might be improved, it is important to distinguish between the different conditions of firms filing for Chapter 11. I find it useful to classify these companies into the following four categories:

(1) Companies with profitable operations but the "wrong" capital structures—that is, cases in which the promised time path of payments to claimants does not match the availability of cash flow to make those payments, and a rearrangement of the timing will allow all payments to be made.

(2) Companies with profitable operations whose value is being maximized under the current management team, but whose total firm value for reasons now beyond management's control is below the value of total liabilities. In such cases, regardless how payments on those liabilities are reordered through time, their total face value cannot be covered.

(3) Companies with potentially profitable, but poorly managed, operations that could meet their total obligations provided the firm's operating strategy (or the management team) were changed (and perhaps the timing of payments reordered as well).

---

63. Frank Easterbrook, however, has pointed out that the direct costs of bankruptcy are lower than the direct costs of taking a company public. See "Is Corporate Bankruptcy Efficient," *Journal of Financial Economics*, Vol. 27, No. 2 (September 1990). No one has as yet obtained a good estimate of the indirect costs of bankruptcy; but, as illustrated in the Eastern Airlines case, they can be substantial.

64. Judge Lifland of the New York bankruptcy court wasted at least hundreds of millions of dollars of creditors' and society's resources by allowing Eastern Airlines to continue to operate in an industry flooded with excess capacity in which exit had to occur and in the face of extremely hostile unions (who prevented a potential sale of the airline and were rumored to want to destroy it). According to Eastern's 10K filed in April 1989 (p. 3), the company had sufficient assets ($4.8 billion) to repay fully its $3.8 billion in liabilities at the time of its bankruptcy filing in 1989. In March of 1990, a year later, management proposed a plan to pay

creditors 48 cents on the dollar (or about $1.7 billion), but then backed out of it. It appears $1.2 billion in secured claims has been paid and that little will be paid on the remaining pre-bankruptcy liabilities. Thus, projected losses appear to be in the billions of dollars. Much of the reduction in the value of Eastern's assets while in Chapter 11 illustrates the cost of our current bankruptcy process.

65. In the sense that the plan doesn't promise to pay them what they would get in a straight liquidation under Chapter 7 of the code.

66. This is what Judge Lifland did in the Eastern case. Consistent with these policies, he just approved (in June 1991) the *eighth* extension of Lomas Financial Corporation's manager's sole right to propose a plan for reorganization. Such extensions are especially problematical in cases where the managers' strategy has been responsible for the firm's financial difficulties. But it is very difficult, of course, for a judge to make this judgment when he or she has little or no prior knowledge of, or experience with, the company or the industry.

(4) Companies that cannot meet their contractual obligations and whose liquidation value exceeds their going concern value.

In principle (and setting aside for now the problem of investor uncertainty about which of these categories fits a given company), the broad outlines of the bankruptcy process should be very simple.

For companies falling into case 1—fundamentally profitable firms with the wrong capital structure—the solution is simply to rearrange the timing of the payments through a voluntary financial restructuring in the capital markets. And if such private restructurings are not practicable—because of regulatory constraints on lenders, tax problems, or holdouts—then a simple, low-cost reorganization of the claims in bankruptcy court (using, if possible, the new "pre-packaged bankruptcy" format)[67] should be able to provide complete value to all claimholders.

In case 2—the well-managed firm in which the maximum total firm value is less than the total claims held by creditors—the company can be reorganized by creating a new capital structure and distributing those claims to each of the claimants, giving value equal to 100% of each of the claims until total firm value is exhausted. The last class of claimants to be paid would not in general receive full payment, but would receive mostly equity claims on the new entity. This solution follows what is called *absolute priority*.

Case 3—the case in which the firm's operating strategy is wrong—would involve a change in the operating strategy (and/or management) of the firm together with a new capital structure and a distribution in accordance with absolute priority.

Case 4—in which the firm is worth more dead than alive—calls for the liquidation of the firm's assets, and distribution of the proceeds according to the absolute priority rule.

In practice, court-supervised solutions to financial distress seldom bear any relation to these conceptual solutions. A study by Larry Weiss of 37 bankruptcies administered under the 1978 code finds that actual solutions violate the contractually agreed-upon priority rules in almost 80% of the cases.[68] Equityholders and lower priority claimants routinely receive partial payment on their claims even though more senior claimants are not fully paid. In two particularly flagrant cases, equityholders retained 100% of the equity while unsecured creditors received only 37% and 60% of their claims.

As suggested earlier, such priority violations are virtually guaranteed when the courts (1) routinely allow the current management team to remain in place, and (2) require reorganization plans to receive the approval of all impaired creditor classes. Through these practices, the courts give management and junior creditors a major lever—in practice, the threat of dragging out the proceedings and thereby adding substantially to the legal and opportunity costs—which they use to expropriate value from more senior claimants.

The Consequences of Failing to Enforce Strict Priority

Current court practices—especially the failure to enforce absolute priority and to limit the period of management's monopoly rights to propose a restructuring to 120 days—are very difficult to justify on efficiency grounds.[69] I can see no argument for violating the contractually agreed-upon priority of valid claims.[70,71] Consistent and widespread violations of absolute priority will generate large inefficiencies in the economy. And they will do it in two principal ways.

First, the larger the deviations from strict priority the system tolerates, the harder the junior creditors will push to expropriate value from the senior claimants. This means more intractable, longer, and more costly conflicts among claimholders. Such

---

67. For a discussion of this technique—which amounts to a hybrid between private workout and bankruptcy—see the article in this issue by John McConnell and Henri Servaes, "The Economics of Pre-packaged Bankruptcy."

68. Assuming the courts determine impairment correctly. See the article by Weiss that appears in this issue, which is based in turn on Lawrence A. Weiss, "Bankruptcy Resolution: Direct Costs and Violation of Priority of Claims," *Journal of Financial Economics*, Vol. 27, No. 2 (September 1990).

69. For a sophisticated attempt to justify the efficiency of the current system, see Easterbrook (1990), cited in note 63.

70. As Leonard Rosen (noted bankruptcy counsel and senior partner of Wachtell, Lipton, Rosen & Katz) comments in the Roundtable in this issue, subordinated claimants have shown considerable ingenuity in devising new theories to justify the violation of the priority of the contracts they signed. One that is now popular, and is apparently used frequently as a bargaining threat, is "fraudulent

conveyance." Under this theory, which has yet to be widely accepted by the courts, the argument goes that the banks' secured claims should be subordinated to all others because they loaned money to an LBO or other levered transaction in which they earned fees—all the while knowing that the new entity was insolvent.

This argument makes little economic sense, and for two reasons: (1) the banks are putting large amounts of their own capital at risk in the deal (unlike the investment bankers who receive large fees and frequently play a large role in promoting the deal); and (2) the subordinated debt holders are put in the position of denying that they had information in the prospectus revealing that the transaction was highly levered and risky, and that they were being paid a risk premium for accepting this risk.

While there can be legitimate cases of fraud in which assets are bled from a firm in a leveraged transaction and the new owners end up owning only a shell, conflicts prolong the length and increase the costs of bankruptcy; in so doing, they reduce the value of debtor firms.

But the effect of such violations is not limited to troubled companies in reorganization. Of greater consequence, large and frequent deviations from strict priority will interfere with voluntary contracting and specialization in bearing default risk. This will raise the corporate cost of capital (especially for those smaller and riskier firms that generated much of the economic gains of the 80s). Senior creditors accustomed to seeing their claims violated will increasingly refuse to allow junior claimants into the capital structure. And when junior claimants are allowed, senior creditors will refuse to lend to all but the highest-rated credits. In the extreme, such a development would reduce all claimants to the same status, which in turn would dictate that the capital structures of all companies with significant default risk would become the equivalent of 100% equity.

Given the risk-bearing and control benefits of debt financing, the costs to the economy in the form of increased inefficiencies from thus restricting debt would likely be enormous. As suggested, it would also substantially raise the cost of capital to American firms, especially smaller ones. A significant increase in the "cost of capital" may not sound consequential; but, as demonstrated by the plight of non-investment grade companies during the current "credit crunch," a higher cost of capital means not only fewer leveraged control transactions, but less corporate capital investment, fewer jobs, and reduced growth for the economy as a whole.

The Information Problem (and the Role of Auctions in Solving It)

One of the major, and heretofore unrecognized, reasons for the intractability of intercreditor conflicts is the "information problem" aggravated—if not actually *created*—by our current bankruptcy system.[72] In outlining solutions for the four different classes of bankruptcies listed above, I made the assumption that all claimants have reliable information about the firm's prospects, and that their assessments of the value of the reorganized and restructured firm are identical. In practice, of course, there is tremendous uncertainty about the value of the reorganized company. Adding to this uncertainty, there are few, if any, incentives in the current process for interested parties to provide unbiased estimates of the true value of the firm.

To see the issue clearly, let us ignore the optimal capital structure problem and assume the firm's claimants will be paid entirely in common stock in the unlevered reorganized firm.[73] Senior claimants have incentives to underestimate the value of the firm so they will be awarded a larger fraction of the equity. Equityholders have incentives to overestimate the value so they will retain a larger fraction. Junior claimants have more complicated incentives, depending on whether their claim is clearly "in the money" (in which case their incentives are identical to senior creditors') or "out of the money" (in which their position is much like the equityholders'). Current managers want to retain control, which means they are likely to resist valuable changes in firm strategy (especially if they have no significant equity stake) that would also reduce the probability of their retaining their jobs. The bankruptcy judges—those effectively charged with solving this "information problem"—have neither the information nor the expertise to assess the firm's value.

One way to solve the information and incentive problem would be to allow any party—outsiders as well as current claimants—to make an all-cash bid for the control rights to the company. At the close of the auction, the highest bidder would *immediately* assume control of the company and its operations. The current managers could themselves bid, or they

---

the beneficiaries of such fraud are those old shareholders and bondholders who collected the proceeds, not the banks or others who put large amounts of money into the new entity. The theory seems designed to transfer wealth from the banks simply because they are on the scene at the time of the bankruptcy litigation.

Widespread acceptance of the theory of fraudulent conveyance would be another important and unwise step in forbidding banks, bondholders, insurance companies and individuals from engaging in the specialization of bearing default risk in transactions that had any positive probability of ending up in bankruptcy court.

71. Another argument used to justify deviations from strict priority is based on "equitable subordination." The principle of equitable subordination in American law seriously hinders the efficient resolution of financial distress. It does so by prohibiting banks from working closely with financially distressed companies to whom they have loaned money.

The Japanese system works exactly the opposite. Indeed it is considered a moral obligation of the company's main bank to play a major role in working with the managers of a financially distressed client to resolve the problem. And this historically has frequently involved placing bank personnel in positions of major responsibility in the client firm. Nissan, for example, was run for years by an alumnus of the Industrial Bank of Japan after IBJ helped it get out of its financial difficulties.

72. Karen Wruck analyzes this generally unrecognized problem in her recent *Journal of Financial Economics* paper (see Wruck (1990), cited in note 43) and in her clinical study of the Revco LBO later in this issue.

73. Or that the claimants will all receive a proportionate strip of all claims in the new capital structure.

could bid as part of an investor group (including creditors). The investor groups themselves, by bidding for the services of, or deliberately excluding, the current management team, would thus be forced to ascertain whether the managers were valuable to the reorganization of the business, or were instead a continuing part of the problem. The firm's new capital structure, moreover, would be in the hands of the bidding groups; and, in determining how they raised the funds, they would be subjected to the market test.

Such an auction process would also do much to reduce the problem of biased information produced by our current system. It would do so by forcing current equityholders attempting to preserve control to back *with their own money* their (otherwise biased) estimates of firm value—or at least to find outside investors willing to back those estimates. The same requirement would apply to creditors, who frequently claim to be able to create more value than the settlement being worked out in the voluntary process.

In such an auction system, the role of the bankruptcy court would be sharply narrowed. After investing the proceeds from the auction of the firm in riskless securities, the court would then proceed with the allocation of that value among claimholders. All claims would accrue interest at the riskless rate, thereby limiting the bias for junior claimants to drag out the proceedings. After determining the legitimacy and priority of claims, the court would then distribute the auction proceeds in *strict accordance with absolute priority*. In contrast to the reality of our Chapter 11 process, the court allocation process (with funds held in a riskless portfolio) could proceed at its own pace without concern that firm value was being eroded by management distractions or uncertainty among employees, customers, or suppliers about the future of the firm.

The auction process would thus have two major advantages over the current system. First, it would separate the task of assessing the firm's value from that of dividing that value among creditors and equityholders, effectively assigning the first to capital markets and the second to the courts. Second, it would shelter the value of the firm's operations from the destructive conflicts among creditors and equityholders over the division of firm value—conflicts that make the current formal bankruptcy process so inefficient.

The auction process would also effectively take the control rights to the firm out of the hands of the court (which effectively delegates them to managers in most bankruptcies) and transfer them to the highest bidder in the market. In so doing, it would also take the court out of the awkward position of having to decide whether current management should be replaced, and having to "second guess" the business judgment of professional managers.[74]

CONCLUSIONS: WHERE WE ARE HEADED

Given the current political climate, we are almost certain to see further regulation of our capital markets in the attempt to prevent active investors from playing a major role in corporate governance. Bank and insurance company financing for highly leveraged transactions is now almost unavailable; and even when it is, it is expensive and available in much smaller amounts than previously.

In emasculating the market for corporate control, regulators will continue to remove the discipline imposed by the new institutional monitors on corporate management. The consequence is likely to be a sharp decline in the productivity and competitiveness of our corporations in the 1990s and beyond. It could well mean a return to the economic stagnation of the 1970s, a period in which corporate returns on capital fell well below investors' cost of capital—and in which inflation-adjusted stockholder returns were thus substantially negative.

In the short run, we are also facing capital shortages for small- to medium-sized companies—those that created most of the growth in the 1980s. Denying credit to such companies has two serious consequences. First, it has contributed significantly to the recent recession and is now slowing our recovery from it. Second, and perhaps even more

---

74. In fact, the beneficial effects of an auction are sometimes obtained even in our current system. Some companies—Fruehauf, for example—have resolved financial distress privately by sale of all or a major part of the assets to others. And some firms have been purchased out of bankruptcy: A.H. Robins was purchased by American Home Products. But current procedures give managers significant veto power over such offers. The $925 million bid by the Bass Group for Revco in bankruptcy was reportedly blocked, in part, by resistance from management.

For additional analysis of an auction system, see Douglas G. Baird, "The Uneasy Case for Corporate Reorganizations," *Journal of Legal Studies* (January, 1986), pp. 127-147.

For a useful discussion of the current legal maze facing acquirers of bankrupt companies, see Mark D. Brodsky and Joel B. Zwiebel, "Chapter 11 Acquisitions: Payoffs for Patience," *Mergers & Acquisitions* (September-October, 1990), pp. 47-53.

> **The auction process would have two major advantages... First, it would separate the task of assessing the firm's value from that of dividing that value among creditors and equityholders, effectively assigning the first to capital markets and the second to the courts. Second, it would shelter the value of the firm's operations from the destructive conflicts among creditors and equityholders.**

important, by removing a major source of competition for large firms, a "credit crunch" will remove another important discipline that acts to limit inefficiencies in our largest companies.

In the absence of a well-functioning control market and vigorous competition from small U.S. firms, the major remaining source of discipline on corporate management is the pressure exerted by international product markets. Provided we can resist the appeals to shield our companies from global competition by means of quotas and restrictive tariffs—regulations that continue to allow our largest steel and auto companies to remain high-cost producers—the pressure now exerted on corporate management by the globalization of product markets is likely to be the most powerful force for productivity increases. Barring overseas competition, the only other disciplines on corporate management are our current system of internal monitoring by corporate boards of directors and, as a last resort—and the worst of all possible choices—government intervention.

The evidence of the last 40 years indicates, to me at least, that the conventional model of internal management control supervised by outside directors has generally failed as an effective control mechanism in our public corporations. As stated earlier, it is not likely to work well in the case of mature companies with large cash flow and few good investment opportunities. There are certainly companies that have reformed without any tangible threat of takeover, or without a crisis in the product markets. For example, the case of General Mills is one that has been well-documented by my colleague, Gordon Donaldson;[75] and General Electric's restructuring and reorganization under Jack Welch has been spectacular. But, in the vast majority of cases, unless management and the board has a large ownership stake, major *voluntary* reversals in corporate strategy (such as selling or shutting down a major business) are highly unlikely to come about without pressure from capital or product markets.

In the absence of capital market pressure, international competition is most likely to bring about necessary change. But, given the incentives and ability of U.S. companies to use the political process to insulate themselves from overseas competitors as well as from the control market, I predict that finding new ways to improve existing internal corporate controls will become an issue of great urgency in the decade ahead of us—one that will attract the attention of politicians, regulators, institutional investors, and management scientists. Coming to a resolution of this issue will be difficult and contentious, but the consequences of failing to restore effective corporate control mean that we must not fail.

TAX OBSTACLES TO VOLUNTARY CORPORATE RESTRUCTURING

by Merton H. Miller,
University of Chicago*

W riters often turn to Lewis Carroll for neat examples of how reasoning, correct in every step, can still lead to nonsensical conclusions when starting from a false premise. Our tax laws and regulations have their share and more of such logically consistent absurdities. But perhaps none are more unfortunate at the moment than those flowing from IRC Section 61(a)(12), which defines taxable gross income to include gains from the discharge or cancellation of indebtedness (hereafter "COD"). The general rule embodied in that section—combined with some of the specific "exceptions" introduced by the tax laws over the years, and modified recently by the Revenue Reconciliation Act of 1990—makes it uneconomic for many of today's distressed corporations to seek *voluntary*, mutually satisfactory agreements with creditors to restructure existing debt contracts.

*This is an expanded version of comments presented during the session on "Strategies of Corporate Restructuring and Turnarounds" at the *Conference on Leverage, Workouts and Bankruptcy*, Graduate School of Management, Rutgers University, June 27-8, 1991. I have benefited from discussing the issues with my colleagues Steven Kaplan, Henri Servaes and especially Walter Blum. The usual disclaimers apply, with even more that the usual force.

To savor the full Alice-In-Wonderland flavor of current tax law, consider the following tale:

XYZ Corporation began life with a sale of stock worth $50x and of bonds worth $50x. The combined cash proceeds of $100x were invested in operating assets. XYZ Corporation later encountered times so hard that the market value of its assets fell by half to $50x. The bondholders and the stockholders recognized the new reality and agreed voluntarily to restructure the firm as follows: the bondholders received new bonds worth $26x; and the stockholders retained the entire equity, now worth $24x.

What should be the income-tax consequences of this entirely voluntary retailoring of the old claims to fit the new total market value of $50x? Economists would actually call for *negative* taxes (in the sense of allowable tax deductions) for the security holders in this case. Both the bondholders and the stockholders have suffered real combined losses of $50x on their original investments. Under present tax laws, the bondholders could indeed receive immediate redress in the form of bad debt deductions for their losses on the exchange of bonds. The stockholders must wait, however, until they ultimately sell their shares; and even then, their losses would be capital losses that cannot always be fully offset against other income.

But, for the stockholders, that is the *good* news. The bad news is that under the current U.S. tax code, the mere act of voluntary restructuring gives rise to a *positive* corporate income tax liability. XYZ Corporation would be deemed to have earned $24x from writing down the original $50x of debt to $26x. That the market value of the whole firm had to fall by $50x ($26x of which loss was suffered by the stockholders) for XYZ Corporation and its stockholders to reap this supposed benefit of $24x cuts no ice under 61(a)(12). The taxable income of XYZ would, in principle, include the full amount of the $24x gain from the discharge or cancellation of indebtedness.

If you think that's weird, consider the tax treatment of a *stock*-for-debt exchange. Suppose the old bondholders had settled for a 52 percent (i.e., controlling) interest in the stock of XYZ Corporation. The market value of their 52 percent stake, under the assumptions, would again be $26x. The XYZ Corporation, as before, would still have taxable COD of $24x. But now the old bondholders (who are the new controlling shareholders) would be bearing 52

percent of the tax—52 percent of the tax on a supposed gain that was really their loss!

Clearly, literal enforcement of the COD rules in these circumstances makes no sense, as Congress itself has long since conceded. Under the "insolvency exception," the tax on COD gains has always been waived to the extent that the firm's pre-insolvency liabilities exceeded the current recoverable value of its assets. (Big deal! Ever tried getting blood from a turnip?) But a more meaningful way out has also been left for firms like XYZ that are distressed but not technically insolvent: just file for bankruptcy (currently under Chapter 11 of the Bankruptcy Code) and any COD income occasioned by the reorganization can be excluded from taxable gross income.

Although Congress chooses not to exact its full pound of flesh from the bankrupt corporation, it does manage, however, to cut off a few ounces. IRC Section 108(b) makes the bankrupt corporation pay for the presumed privilege of COD forgiveness by reducing other tax benefits the firm may have coming, such as its future depreciation deductions or its accumulated net operating loss carryovers (NOLs). Sometimes, ironically enough, this hard-nosed approach by Congress can actually backfire, leaving a firm ahead of the game on net tax account by electing to take the COD hit on its NOLs. The NOLs seemingly lost under Section 108(b) can be brought back from the dead by invoking IRC Section 1273(a)(1) governing so-called original issue discount (OID). An artful exchange of zero-coupon or low-coupon debt for the old debt may permit a stream of future (non-cash) interest deductions extending beyond the time the lost NOLs would have expired. (Shades of Br'er Rabbit and the Briar Patch.)

Common sense clearly mandates some escape routes from the COD rules for solvent firms in distress. But the question remains: Why has Congress directed these exits through the bankruptcy courts? Mercy for unfortunate bankrupts surely cannot account for it. Firms and individuals in bankruptcy, after all, must still pay full tax on their other income when they have it, as they often do. Nor has the Service hesitated to assert its place at the head of the queue in bankruptcy proceedings, as the non-government creditors of Drexel Burnham recently learned to their sorrow. Perhaps nothing more than ordinary bureaucratic buck-passing is involved. The Chapter 11 requirement relieves the IRS of the burden of determining precisely when and under what conditions the exceptions to taxing COD gains are to apply. The tax code and its associated regulations can then dispense with complex sections on "qualified workouts" of the kind originally contemplated in the Tax Reform Act of 1984, but killed subsequently in 1986 before they actually became effective. Thanks to the Chapter 11 requirements, moreover, the bankruptcy court not only decides what qualifies for tax relief, but does so off the IRS's budget.

Any cost savings to the IRS from this "privatization," of course, are merely transferred to the bankruptcy courts and ultimately to the estates of the debtor firms that support the whole process. They must also be offset against the additional delays and costs of restructuring for those firms now forced to seek bankruptcy that might otherwise have negotiated settlements. Clearly not all workouts will achieve consensus. Sometimes, perhaps even most of the time, hold-outs can be overcome only by resorting to the formal court proceedings and class-by-class voting rules of Chapter 11. But if the parties *can* reach a voluntary agreement (achieving thereby what economists dub a "pareto-improving solution"), surely wise social policy should smile, not frown, on their efforts. And especially so when our bankruptcy court system is already buckling under its load.

Calls for reducing the tax-induced bias toward bankruptcy and against voluntary restructuring have been heard with increasing frequency since passage of the Revenue Reconciliation Act of 1990 last October. Most of the suggested remedies merely add complications to an already almost incomprehensible tax code. But there is one way so simple, so obvious (but also so seemingly radical) that it has largely been overlooked: repeal Section 61(a)12 for corporations transacting in their own securities! That won't eliminate all current tax obstacles to efficient restructuring. Stock-for-debt exchanges, for example, would still be discouraged to the extent that a change in control leads to forfeiting the firm's NOLs. But getting 61(a)12 out of the way would at least expunge the false premise from which flow so many of the absurdities in the current sections on corporate reorganizations.

The mere thought of dumping 61(a)12 will surely send shivers of horror down the backs of much of the legal profession. The principle that income arises from buying back one's debts for less than face value has been enshrined in our tax law almost from its very beginnings. And it has been sanctified by the Supreme Court itself in the much-cited *U.S. v. Kirby Lumber Company* (284 U.S. 1 (1931)). By the standards of economics, however, the Court's reasoning in *Kirby* is suspect.

Consider the following stripped-down version of the essential points in *Kirby* and assume initially, to simplify the present-value computations, that all the bonds in question are perpetuities. Suppose Kirby had issued $10x of bonds last year when interest rates were 5 percent, committing thereby to a stream of $.5x in interest payments in perpetuity. This year, rates have suddenly risen to 10 percent. Suppose further that the managers of Kirby, undismayed by this rise in their firm's future borrowing costs, actually see it as a fantastic investment opportunity. Just buy back the bonds issued last year, now selling for only 50 cents on the dollar, and earn an immediate rate of return of 100 percent on the transaction!

What the managers of Kirby, and the Supreme Court as well, have overlooked, of course, is that the money to buy back the old bonds has to come from somewhere. Suppose it came from floating $5x of bonds at the now current rate of 10 percent. Is Kirby as a firm, or are its original owners, better off in any way by having "discharged" the original debt at half its face value? The firm's annual interest bill is exactly the same as before, as is the market value (that is, the true economic value) of its liabilities. The market value of the *equity* may well be higher now; but any such rise would trace to the fall in the market value of the firm's liabilities when interest rates rose—a testimonial to the firm's skill or luck in having floated its $10x *before* rates went up. The addition to the stockholders' real net worth on that account is theirs to keep, whether management retires the debt or not, and regardless of what specific source of funds the firm taps to implement any buy-back.

The essentials of the argument change in no way if the firm's original and replacement debt issues had been of finite term rather than perpetuities. Floating a replacement issue with a present (and market) value equal to that of the issue being retired would no longer produce an exactly matching stream of interest payments year by year. And the market value of a finite-lived replacement issue would not return precisely to the original level, as would the be the case for perpetuities, if interest rates should happen to return to 10 percent. But any gains that did arise from debt replacement under those conditions would be of second order at best; and such gains certainly seem far removed from the Court's concerns in *Kirby*.

The Internal Revenue Service (or Bureau as it was known in those days) and the Supreme Court both seem to have been mesmerized in *Kirby* by the rise in book net worth that must occur under the conventions of double-entry bookkeeping whenever securities are retired at prices less than those at which they originally entered the company's books. Those gains must get to the net worth account somehow; otherwise the books won't balance. Unhappily, the only route to net worth the Bureau and the Court could seem to find at that time led through the income account. Nowadays accountants just treat the net worth write-ups following debt retirements as "extraordinary items," which is to say, they just post them to net worth directly.

Curiously, the Court did have at hand a precedent for such direct net-worth adjustments after security repurchases, had it only chosen to follow it. The nonrecognition of gain or loss when a company

buys back its own *stock* was a thoroughly settled principle of corporate tax law well before *Kirby* came to final judgment.

The Court blew it because our corporate law then, as now, regards debt and equity as fundamentally distinct species (in contrast to modern finance theory, which treats them as basically equivalent sources of "capital" for most, though certainly not all, purposes). The overly strict legal separation of the two sources is the root cause of many more anomalies in our corporate income tax than just those of corporate restructuring that have been of concern here. Getting rid of them all would require eliminating the corporate income tax altogether, not a prospect likely soon to be realized. Repeal of the corporate income tax, after all, has no obvious constituency. Economics assures us only that the burden of the corporate income tax falls ultimately on an economy's workers, consumers, and savers; it cannot yet tell us precisely on which ones. And, even better from a politician's point of view, neither can the voters who are really paying it.

MANAGING DEFAULT: SOME EVIDENCE ON HOW FIRMS CHOOSE BETWEEN WORKOUTS AND CHAPTER 11

*by Stuart C. Gilson,
Harvard Business School**

A s more and more U.S. companies default on their debt and file for bankruptcy, financial economists have become increasingly interested in understanding how companies deal with financial distress. In particular, academic concern has focused on whether the costs of resolving default are excessive, and whether the process by which firms recontract with their creditors can be made more efficient.

Companies have good reason to be concerned with these issues as well. In 1990, almost $25 billion worth of junk bonds went into default, and 749,956 U.S. firms filed for bankruptcy.[1] The costs of restructuring the balance sheets of troubled companies can be daunting. LTV Corporation, for example, has spent over $150 million on legal and other professional fees since it filed for Chapter 11 in 1986. And this figure ignores other, potentially greater, costs of financial distress such as any loss of business occasioned by the bankruptcy.

There are two basic methods for reorganizing troubled companies: private workouts and formal bankruptcy. In either case, new financial claims are exchanged for the firm's outstanding debt contracts on terms the firm finds more affordable. The net effect of the exchange is either to reduce the level of interest and principal payments, to extend the payment dates, or to substitute equity for debt. The main difference between the two approaches is that, in bankruptcy, this exchange is supervised by the court.

Viewed in this light, the workout-bankruptcy choice has an obvious parallel with the decision faced by plaintiffs and defendants over whether to settle out of court or go to trial. If settling privately is appreciably less expensive, then both sides have an incentive to avoid going to court. But if the affected parties are unable to agree on how to split the cost savings, then a trial may still be necessary even though the combined wealth of both parties is ultimately lower.

*I am grateful for the helpful comments of Max Holmes, the valuable research assistance of Joe Basset, and the research support provided by the Division of Research of the Harvard Business School.
1. Source: *Turnarounds and Workouts*, Washington, D.C.

To the alarm of many, however, a recent bankruptcy court ruling ("the LTV decision") and changes in the tax law have made such private restructuring much more difficult.

Recently, Professor Michael Jensen has suggested that today's highly leveraged companies that get into trouble have far stronger incentives to reorganize privately than their low-leveraged counterparts of the early 1980s. When a highly leveraged company misses an interest payment, management is forced to take corrective action much sooner than otherwise, thus leaving more of the company's operating value intact. In the absence of such an "early warning system," operating performance could be allowed to deteriorate much longer—in the extreme, making liquidation the only sensible alternative. To the extent private workouts are less costly than the formal Chapter 11 process, the "privatization of bankruptcy" envisioned by Jensen should ensure that more of the firm's value survives the recontracting process, thus benefiting creditors as well as shareholders.[2]

Workouts in the 80s. In a recently published study, Kose John, Larry Lang, and I examined a sample of 169 New York and American Stock Exchange-listed companies that defaulted on their debt during the 1980s.[3] Eighty, or almost half, of these companies successfully restructured their debt in workouts while the rest filed for Chapter 11. And for 62 of the 89 companies (or almost 70%) that ended up in bankruptcy, we found reports in the *Wall Street Journal* of attempts to restructure privately. (Because a good number of other attempts at restructuring almost certainly were unreported, this 70% figure should be construed as a "lower bound.")

Thus, during the 1980s, private restructuring was generally the preferred method for dealing with default. The fact that attempts at private restructuring have been so frequent would seem to confirm that workouts are indeed less costly on average than Chapter 11.

To the alarm of many, however, a recent bankruptcy court ruling ("the LTV decision") and changes in the tax law have made such private restructuring much more difficult. To understand the import of these developments, it is necessary to know more about the relative costs of workouts vs. Chapter 11. In the pages that follow, I begin by reviewing recent academic research on the costs of financial restructuring. I then go on to present the findings of my own work that attempts to determine what factors distressed companies consider in choosing between private workouts and bankruptcy.

COSTS OF WORKOUTS VS. CHAPTER 11

Legal and Professional Fees

For several reasons, payments for legal and other professional services are likely to be higher if a company restructures its debt in bankruptcy court. Lawyer and investment banker fees effectively accrue on an hourly basis, and therefore increase with the length of time spent in creditor negotiations. In the Gilson-John-Lang study cited earlier, the average length of time spent by 89 companies in Chapter 11 was over 20 months; the average length of the 80 workouts was about 15 months.

This difference was significantly greater in the 30 cases in our sample that involved the private restructuring of publicly-traded debt. Such debt was always restructured through exchange offers in which bondholders were free to tender, or not tender, their bonds in exchange for a package of new securities. (In 87% of these exchanges, moreover, this package included new common stock or securities that could be converted into common stock.) The average length of exchange offers in our sample was just under seven months.

Workouts may be less time-consuming in part because firms need deal only with creditors whose claims are in default. Of the workouts we examined, 30% of the firms with publicly-traded debt, as well as 10% of the firms with debt owed to banks and insurance companies, avoided having to restructure such debt. By contrast, cross-default provisions included in most debt contracts virtually guarantee that, when a company files for Chapter 11, it will have to negotiate with all its creditors.

In addition, total legal fees in Chapter 11 are based on the number of billable hours.[4] Because legal and other professional fees have priority over

---

2. See Michael Jensen, "Active Investors, LBOs, and the Privatization of Bankruptcy," *Journal of Applied Corporate Finance* (Spring, 1989).

3. Stuart Gilson, Kose John, and Larry Lang, "Troubled Debt Restructurings: An Empirical Study of Private Reorganization of Firms in Default," *Journal of Financial Economics* 26 (1990). We constructed our sample by first ranking all New York and American Stock Exchange-listed companies by their common stock returns (measured over three consecutive years), and then identifying all firms in the bottom five percent of these returns that were either in default on their debt,

bankrupt, or restructuring their debt to avoid bankruptcy, based on coverage of these firms in the *Wall Street Journal*. This selection process was repeated for various years, resulting in a sample of firms that first experienced financial difficulty throughout the period 1978-1987.

4. A darkly humorous account of how the Bankruptcy Code sometimes creates perverse incentives for lawyers to prolong the firm's stay in Chapter 11 (for example, by filing excessive motions with the court) can be found in Sol Stein, *A Feast for Lawyers* (M. Evans and Company, Inc.,1989).

TABLE 1
DIRECT COSTS OF
EXCHANGE OFFERS FOR
TROUBLED JUNK BONDS*

	Mean	Median	Range
■ Exchange offer costs ($1,000s)	799	424	200-2,500
■ Offer costs as a percentage of the book value of assets	0.65	0.32	0.01-3.40
■ Offer costs as a percentage of the face value of bonds restructured under offer	2.16	2.29	0.27-6.84

*Sample consists of eighteen exchange offers undertaken during 1981-1988 for which data were available. Costs consist of cash compensation paid to the exchange and information agent, legal, accounting, brokerage, and investment banking fees, and the value of any common stock warrants issued to the firm's investment bank advisor (as estimated in the exchange offer prospectus).

all the firm's other claims in Chapter 11, the professional advisers involved in the case have no obvious financial incentive to minimize the amount of time the firm spends in Chapter 11. Although bankruptcy judges will often scale back requested fees or partially withhold payment of fees until the end of the case ("witholding rates" of 25% are common), lawyers can easily anticipate the adjustments and charge accordingly.

A potential solution to this problem would be to pay lawyers and investment bankers using the same securities distributed to shareholders and creditors as currency, thus giving them an interest in preserving the value of the *surviving* firm and an incentive to get out of Chapter 11 quickly.[5] An interesting alternative approach was recently taken by Ames Department Stores, which filed for Chapter 11 in April 1990. Ames has established a special bonus plan for its CEO, Stephen Pistner, which will pay him $3.5 million if Ames is successfully reorganized within 18 months of its Chapter 11 filing, and successively smaller amounts if the reorganization takes longer; no bonus will be paid if Ames is still in Chapter 11 after 39 months. Such innovative compensation schemes, however, are all too rare.[6]

A direct comparison of legal and professional fees for Chapter 11 and private restructuring is difficult because firms are not required to report these costs outside of Chapter 11. Nevertheless, firms that privately restructure their bonds through exchange offers are required to disclose an estimate of all offer-related costs in the exchange offer circular distributed to bondholders. As a result, I was able to obtain reliable cost data for a sample of 18 exchange offers undertaken by New York and American Stock Exchange-listed companies.[7]

As summarized in Table 1, these costs amounted on average to only 0.65 percent of the book value of assets (measured just prior to the exchange offer); the corresponding median percentage was only 0.32 percent. By contrast, academic studies have found that average legal and professional fees reported by Chapter 11 companies range from 2.8 percent to 7.5 percent of total assets (generally measured within one year of the filing).[8] Although comparisons across studies are made difficult by differences in the samples and the definitions of costs, these results clearly suggest that private restructuring through exchange offers is much less costly than formal reorganization in Chapter 11, perhaps by as much as a factor of ten.

Management by Bankruptcy Judges

Greater waste of corporate assets is also possible in Chapter 11 because the Bankruptcy Code effectively requires judges to set corporate operating policies. Of course, judges also have the potential to

5. See proposals by Michael Price and Wilbur Ross in the Roundtable discussion in this issue.

6. For evidence on how distressed firms pay their senior managers, see Stuart Gilson and Michael Vetsuypens, "CEO Compensation in Financially Distressed Firms," unpublished Harvard University and Southern Methodist University working paper (1991).

7. This table is taken from Gilson, John, and Lang, cited in note 3. Exchange offer costs include cash compensation paid to the exchange and information agent, legal, accounting, brokerage and investment banking fees, and the value of any common stock warrants issued to the firm's investment bank (as estimated in the offer circular).

8. See Jerold Warner, "Bankruptcy Costs: Some Evidence," *Journal of Finance* 32 (1977); James Ang, Jess Chua, and John McConnell, "The Administrative Costs of Corporate Bankruptcy: A Note," *Journal of Finance* 37 (1982); and Lawrence A. Weiss, "Bankruptcy Resolution: Direct Costs and Violation of Priority of Claims," *Journal of Financial Economics* 26 (1990). These studies calculate average costs using different definitions of the firm's assets, including the assets' market value (Warner, Weiss), liquidation value (Ang et al) and book value (Weiss).

> A potential solution to this problem [of high fees] would be to pay lawyers and investment bankers using the same securities distributed to shareholders and creditors as currency, thus giving them an interest in preserving the value of the *surviving* firm and an incentive to get out of Chapter 11 quickly.

add value by arbitrating disputes among the firm's claimholders, thus reducing the length of time required to restructure the debt.

In their traditional role, judges are supposed to interpret and administer the law. In Chapter 11, however, because they must approve all major business decisions, bankruptcy judges have broad powers to influence how the firm's assets are managed. A company's future profitability may depend critically on how the bankruptcy judge rules on proposed corporate actions such as major asset divestitures and capital expenditures.

Moreover, the Bankruptcy Code does not require judges to base their decisions on whether corporate assets will be put to uses that produce the highest rate of return to all investors. For a company's plan of reorganization to be "confirmed" in bankruptcy court (the last legal hurdle to be crossed before exiting from Chapter 11), the judge is required by law to ensure only that two conditions are met: (1) each claimholder must receive at least what he or she would have been paid if the firm were liquidated;[9] and (2) the company must not appear to be in danger of going bankrupt again in the near future. However honorable their intentions, judges have no financial interest in the outcome of reorganizations, and generally lack relevant management experience. It is thus hardly surprising that corporate assets end up being worth less when judges set corporate policies.

Lost Investment Opportunities

To the extent dealing with creditors (and, in bankruptcy, the judge) diverts management's attention from operating the business, then the firm may forgo profitable investment opportunities. Value lost by not capitalizing on such opportunities is no less real a cost of financial distress than lawyers' fees, and should also be considered in the context of the workout-bankruptcy decision. Although these costs cannot be directly measured, it is reasonable to assume that the extent of any damage will be greater

the longer it takes to renegotiate the firm's debts. Hence the "opportunity costs" of financial trouble are likely to be greater in Chapter 11 than in private workouts.

Chapter 11 creates additional delays and distractions due to various procedural demands placed on managers. Before making any decision not in the ordinary course of the firm's business (such as hiring an investment bank to provide advice on asset sales), management must file an application with the court. They may file such an application, moreover, only after first notifying creditors in writing and allowing them sufficient time to file objections. Because the firm can act only after the judge approves the application, otherwise routine decisions can take months to complete. After Public Service Company of New Hampshire filed for bankruptcy in 1988, D.P.G. Cameron, the firm's vice president and general counsel, commented that "the proceedings...left us breathless."[10]

One proxy, admittedly crude, for the extent of a company's investment opportunities is the difference between its value as an ongoing concern and its liquidation value—what I refer to as "excess going concern value."[11] To the extent investment opportunities are more likely to be lost in Chapter 11 than in private workouts, troubled companies have incentives to avoid bankruptcy and restructure their debt privately. In the extreme, if Chapter 11 leads to liquidation, creditors and shareholders effectively forfeit all of the firm's excess going concern value by not settling privately.[12]

The importance of preserving going concern value in these situations is well demonstrated by the case of Tiger International, a cargo shipper and lessor of transportation equipment. In early 1983, the company initiated what turned out to be a successful workout. As reported at the time in *The Wall Street Journal* (February 16, 1983),

Wayne M. Hoffman, Tiger chairman, said the company was getting "excellent cooperation" in the early meetings with lenders. He said that he expects

---

9. This is referred to as the "best interests of creditors" test in Section 1129(a)(7) of the Bankruptcy Code. Strictly speaking, this standard only applies if all impaired classes of claimholders assent to the proposed plan (which generally happens). If one or more classes votes against the plan, then the relevant standard is the "fair and equitable" test (Section 1129(b)(2)), which basically requires that each impaired class receives the present value of its allowed claims under the plan (or whatever is available after all senior classes have been paid in full, provided more junior classes receive nothing). If a plan is fair and equitable, then dissenting classes can be forced to accept its terms under a court-imposed "cramdown."

10. See Stein, cited in note 4.

11. Of course, excess going concern value will also reflect other sources of value such as monopoly power and goodwill.

12. Of the Chapter 11 companies I examined (all of them New York and American Stock Exchange companies), only 5% were completely liquidated through a conversion to Chapter 7. For smaller, private companies, the rate is generally higher.

sessions to continue "for some weeks," but that he was confident a rescheduling of debt would be the result. "It's in the lender's interests to do this. All of them agree that the going concern is the important thing."

Consistent with the outcome of this case, the Gilson-John-Lang study found that troubled companies are more likely to reorganize privately when they have greater excess going concern value. For companies that successfully restructured their debt out of court, the average ratio of excess going concern value to liquidation value prior to restructuring was 0.83; for firms that filed for Chapter 11 that average ratio was only 0.61.

HOW DO SHAREHOLDERS FARE?

To the extent private workouts are less costly than Chapter 11, both shareholders and creditors should be made better off when attempts to restructure debt privately succeed.[13] My own research suggests shareholders have generally done better in workouts than in Chapter 11.[14] The Gilson-John-Lang study found that shareholders of companies that successfully restructured their debt out of court realized an average 41% increase in the value of their common stockholdings over the period of restructuring (beginning with announcement of the default and net of general market movements). By contrast, for companies that tried to restructure privately but failed, average cumulative returns to shareholders were *negative* 40% over the period of restructuring that ended with a Chapter 11 filing. At least part of the 80% difference in these returns can be viewed as the market's estimate of the shareholder portion of the total cost savings from avoiding Chapter 11 and restructuring privately. (Some part of this 80%, of course, may also reflect the possibility that firms ultimately filing Chapter 11 were systematically less profitable *after* negotiations with creditors began— or that operating problems were far worse than

investors initially suspected at the time of default— than firms that did not end up filing.)

Shareholders are also typically allowed to retain a significantly higher percentage of the equity in workouts than in bankruptcy. As I found in a recent study, creditors on average receive 20% of the common stock in workouts, as compared to 67% of the outstanding stock in Chapter 11.[15] Shareholders will be harmed by dilution of their equity to the extent creditors effectively purchase the new shares at a below-market price, or if the value of control conferred by large blocks is dissipated by the issuance of new shares. In some Chapter 11s, of course, shareholders are completely wiped out, as happened recently in the bankruptcy of Sharon Steel (which emerged from Chapter 11 late last year). In workouts, obviously, shareholders never voluntarily consent to such a plan.

ADVANTAGES OF CHAPTER 11

Although evidence from the 1980s suggests that Chapter 11 is more costly than private restructuring *in the average case*, bankruptcy also provides certain benefits that offset at least part of this cost difference and cause some companies to file for Chapter 11 directly. There are four principal advantages to filing.

First, the Bankruptcy Code allows firms to issue new debt that ranks senior to all debt incurred prior to filing ("prepetition debt"). Such "debtor-in-possession (DIP)" financing is valuable because the firm can borrow on cheaper terms and thus conserve on scarce cash.[16] Over the last few years, increasing sophistication of DIP lenders and growth of the market for tradable bank debt have resulted in more firms entering Chapter 11 with a DIP facility already in place (two recent examples are Ames Department Stores and Pan Am).

Second, interest on prepetition unsecured debt stops accruing while the firm is in bankruptcy, again freeing up cash.[17]

---

13. If only a subset of the firm's debt is restructured, a private restructuring plan could in principle harm nonparticipating creditors (for example, participating creditors' claims could be given more security or made more senior). However, such harm will be limited by the right of nonparticipating creditors to sue the firm (and other creditors), by covenants that restrict the issuance of more senior debt, and by cross-default covenants that restrict the firm's ability to exclude certain creditors from participating in the restructuring.

14. Assessing the relative returns to creditors is more difficult because their claims trade much less frequently and market price data are either unreliable or nonexistent. There is nonetheless some evidence that creditors take bigger writedowns of their claims in Chapter 11 that in workouts. See Julian Franks and Walter Torous, "How Firms Fare in Workouts and Chapter 11 Reorganizations,"

London Business School and University of California at Los Angeles working paper (1991).

15. See Stuart Gilson, "Bankruptcy, Boards, Banks, and Blockholders," *Journal of Financial Economics* 26 (1990). Such percentages assume that none of the warrants or convertible debt and preferred stock received by creditors are eventually converted. Assuming such securities are fully converted, the average creditor holdings increase to approximately 40% and 80%, respectively.

16. For an excellent description of current DIP lending practices see Mark Rohman and Michael Policiano, "Financing Chapter 11 Companies in the 1990s," *Journal of Applied Corporate Finance* (Summer, 1990).

17. Interest on secured debt continues to accrue up to the excess, if any, of the security's assessed value over the debt's face value.

Third, the Bankruptcy Code's automatic stay provision protects the firm from creditor harassment while it reorganizes, thus allowing the business to function with fewer disruptions.

Fourth, it is easier to get a reorganization plan accepted in Chapter 11 because the voting rules are less restrictive. Acceptance of the plan requires an affirmative vote by only a majority (one-half in number, but representing two-thirds in value) of the claimholders in each class whose claims are impaired. By contrast, a workout cannot pass without the consent of all who participate, thus increasing the incidence of creditor holdouts.

THE HOLDOUT PROBLEM

Whether the cost savings from private restructuring are realized will depend on whether creditors unanimously agree to the terms of the restructuring. Any factors that increase the likelihood of creditor holdouts thus make attempts at private workouts less likely to succeed. Of course, many of these factors are either difficult or impossible to quantify, such as creditors' relative bargaining strength or the amount of antipathy that creditors feel towards shareholders and management. Nonetheless, some academic work has succeeded in identifying factors that can be used to predict the likelihood of holdouts.

The extent of the holdout problem depends partly on what type of debt is restructured. As noted previously, publicly traded bonds have traditionally been restructured through voluntary exchange offers. The holdout problem in these offers can be quite severe. Provided enough bonds are tendered that the firm stays out of bankruptcy, the bondholders who do not tender (and thus, typically, do not agree to a reduction in the value of their claims) benefit at the expense of those who do. The alternative to an exchange offer—namely, modifying the interest rate, principal amount, or maturity of the outstanding bonds by a vote of bondholders—is made virtually impossible by the Trust Indenture Act of 1939, which requires *every* bondholder to agree to such changes. (Modification of all other, "non-core" covenants of the bond indenture usually requires only a simple or two-thirds majority.)

To address this problem, exchange offers are structured to penalize holdouts. New bonds offered in these exchanges, in addition to having a lower coupon rate or principal amount, are also typically more senior, and of shorter maturity, than the outstanding bonds they will replace.[18] Holders are also sometimes asked jointly to tender their bonds and vote for the elimination of non-core protective covenants in the old bonds (called an "exit consent solicitation"). By so doing, bondholders who tendered will be in a better position than those who don't if the firm later files for bankruptcy.

This situation changed dramatically, however, in January 1990 when Judge Burton Lifland ruled in LTV's bankruptcy that bondholders who tendered in a previous exchange offer were entitled to a claim in bankruptcy equal only to the *market* value of the bonds accepted under the offer; bondholders who held onto their original bonds were allowed a claim equal to the bonds' full face value. Since bonds of distressed companies usually sell at big discounts, the effect of this ruling was to reward LTV's holdouts. Although the LTV decision is currently under appeal, the effect of the ruling has been a dramatic fall-off in attempted exchange offers.[19]

With regard to private debt, my research suggests that holdouts are less common, and private restructurings thus more likely to succeed, when more of the firm's debt is owed to commercial banks—and, to a lesser extent, to insurance companies. The Gilson-John-Lang study found that, on average, bank debt amounted to 40% of total liabilities in firms that successfully restructured, but only 25% in firms that filed for Chapter 11 (median debt ratios were 36% and 20%, respectively).

As one would expect, bank lenders tend to be more sophisticated and fewer in number than other kinds of creditors, and are more likely to recognize the potential benefits of private restructuring. Trade creditors, by contrast, are generally less predisposed to settle. Bankruptcy professionals frequently characterize trade creditors as "unsophisticated" and "acrimonious." Consistent with this characterization, so-called vulture investors often buy out a firm's trade debt at the very start of their involvement with the company.

---

18. As pointed out to me by an investment banker acquaintance, the effect of the exchange is similar to offering passengers on the Titanic the chance to move up from steerage to first class.

19. In the preceding Roundtable, David Schulte calls 1990 a "very bad year for exchange offers." And according to investment bankers with whom I have

spoken privately, an additional consequence of the ruling has been that companies give up more easily (and file for Chapter 11) when an exchange offer generates a low initial tender rate. During the 1980s, by contrast, it was not uncommon for companies to revise the terms of exchange offers up to half a dozen times until some desired tender rate was attained.

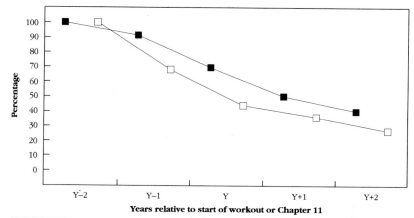

FIGURE 1
PERCENTAGE OF ORIGINAL SENIOR MANAGERS (CEO, CHAIRMAN, AND PRESIDENT) WHO REMAIN WITH THEIR FIRMS THROUGHOUT PERIOD OF FINANCIAL DISTRESS

■ Workouts
□ Chapter 11

Years relative to start of workout or Chapter 11

*Sample consists of 196 managers initially employed by 126 New York and American Stock Exchange listed companies (sixty-nine firms in Chapter 11 and fifty-seven private workouts) that first defaulted on their debt during 1979-1984.

Our results also indicate that private restructuring succeeds more often when there are fewer distinct classes of long-term debt outstanding.[20] The simplest way to interpret this evidence is that having more creditors increases the likelihood that any one creditor will hold out, and thus make disputes among creditors more likely. The number of debt classes also serves as a measure of the complexity of a firm's capital structure. Complex capital structures will be more difficult to restructure privately, especially if the claims are more difficult to value and there is greater disagreement among creditors over whether they are being treated "fairly" relative to other creditors or shareholders.

INCENTIVES OF MANAGERS AND DIRECTORS

Although the workout-bankruptcy decision has a significant impact on a company's stock price, surprisingly few workout proposals are formally put to a shareholder vote. In only one out of every five workouts that I studied did firms first solicit shareholders' approval, either to increase the number of authorized shares or to sell off assets. This raises the interesting question whether managers can personally gain by settling with creditors on overly generous terms, and thus at shareholders' expense. One obvious reason why managers might strike a deal with creditors is to protect their jobs.

To investigate this possibility, I analyzed turnover among the senior managers (the CEO, chairman, and president) of 126 New York and American Stock Exchange-listed firms that defaulted on their debt during the early 1980s.[21] As shown in Figure 1, management turnover was substantial regardless of which restructuring method was chosen. At the end of a four-year period starting two years prior to the start of a workout or Chapter 11 filing, only 40% of the original senior managers remained in firms that privately restructured, and only 30% were left in firms that filed for Chapter 11. Turnover among directors of these firms was also high; approximately half the board was replaced during a typical workout or bankruptcy.[22]

Executives' professional reputations also appear to suffer when they are replaced. Although the average age of departing managers in my study was only 52 years, not one of these managers later found

---

20. As identified in the notes to the firm's balance sheet in its annual 10-K report. More precisely, we deflate this variable by the book value of long-term debt, to provide a measure of the number of creditors *per dollar of debt owed.* The rationale for this adjustment is that smaller creditors have less of their wealth at risk if a private restructuring attempt fails, and therefore are more likely to hold out, everything else unchanged.

21. See Stuart Gilson, "Management Turnover and Financial Distress," *Journal of Financial Economics* 25 (1989).

22. See Gilson, cited in note 15.

work with another exchange-listed firm for at least three years after leaving. Similarly, departing directors subsequently sat on a third fewer boards of other companies three years after leaving, suggesting that their services as directors were valued less highly by other firms. (Of course, these individuals may also have been generally less inclined to serve with large public corporations as managers or directors after their experience with financial distress.)

In short, my own research suggests that managers and other corporate insiders do not gain from systematically choosing a particular restructuring method. Moreover, it lends no support to the popular view, so often aired in the financial press, that Chapter 11 offers a "safe harbor" for the firm's managers.[23] To be sure, Chapter 11 does give the filing firm the exclusive right to file the first reorganization plan for at least 120 days; and it's also true that bankruptcy judges usually grant extensions—sometimes for several years. But such extensions, however potentially costly for investors, represent at most a temporary reprieve for senior managers.

Indeed, in the ten largest bankruptcies in 1990, seven firms replaced their CEOs, generally within one month of filing. In the bankruptcy of Circle K, for example, Karl Eller resigned as chairman and CEO approximately one week before his firm filed (despite his ownership of over seven percent of Circle K's common stock). Peter Hollis resigned as president and CEO of Ames Department Stores two days after it filed for Chapter 11.

In addition to my finding that managers are routinely displaced when their firms file, I also found that one of every five top-level management changes was initiated at the behest of creditors—in particular, bank lenders. Creditors are thus far from powerless in these situations. In short, Chapter 11's automatic stay protects the *firm* from creditor harassment, but not its managers.

POLICY IMPLICATIONS

Distressed firms can preserve more of their value by restructuring their debt privately, when possible, and thus avoiding Chapter 11. My own research suggests that the professional fees incurred in exchange offers are about one-tenth those incurred in a typical Chapter 11 case.

Unfortunately, two recent developments threaten to turn more troubled companies towards the bankruptcy courts. First, as discussed above, the LTV decision has undermined bondholders' incentives to tender in exchange offers for publicly traded junk debt. The second development has been a shift in the tax law toward less favorable treatment of firms that restructure their debt outside of Chapter 11.

Following the Tax Reform Act of 1986, distressed firms have found it more difficult to preserve their net operating loss carryforwards, and to avoid paying taxes on forgiveness-of-debt income, when they operate outside of bankruptcy. Since late last year, firms have been subject to a new tax on private exchange offers. Under the Revenue Reconciliation Act of 1990, whenever new bonds issued in an exchange offer sell at a discount below their stated face value (as is most often the case), the firm must book the difference as taxable income. Prior to the Act, such original issue discounts were tax exempt.[24]

Although it is still too early to assess the full impact of these developments on corporate reorganizations, some preliminary evidence suggests that troubled firms are more often choosing to deal with default in Chapter 11. I examined press reports for all firms that were identified in *The Wall Street Journal* as having filed for Chapter 11 between January 1990 and February 1991.[25] Almost 70% of these companies apparently made no attempt to restructure their debt privately before filing. During the 1980s, by contrast, only 30% of financially distressed firms sought Chapter 11 protection as a first resort. Also, for those companies that did attempt to restructure privately in 1990, only three months elapsed, on average, before a Chapter 11 filing. In the 80s, companies spent an average of eight months attempting to find a private solution before filing Chapter 11.

Society loses when firms are forced to use the more expensive method for dealing with financial

---

23. For example, see Roger Lowenstein and George Anders, "Firms that default find their troubles may have just begun," *The Wall Street Journal* (April 17, 1991), p.A1.

24. The tax on OIDs could be avoided in two ways. First, any OID was nontaxable if the new bonds had the same face value as the old bonds retired under the exchange offer, and both old and new bonds were considered "securities" for tax purposes (among other things, this effectively required both issues to have a term to maturity of at least five years). Second, firms could qualify for the "stock-

for-debt" exception, under which the OID would be nontaxable if stock was also issued under the exchange (in sufficient amount to satisfy the IRS that the firm's principal motive for issuing stock was not simply to avoid paying taxes).

However, the 1990 Act reduces the effectiveness of the stock-for-debt exception by also imposing tougher standards with respect to the type and amount of stock that must be issued for an exchange to receive favorable tax treatment.

25. I excluded firms that were already attempting to privately restructure their debt at the beginning of 1990.

distress. The LTV decision has made it less likely that bondholders will consent to private exchanges, even though the other cost benefits of private workouts relative to Chapter 11 remain unaltered. Although entering Chapter 11 to preserve tax benefits helps the firm's securityholders, these gains are essentially financed by other taxpayers; as such, they represent wealth transferred rather than wealth created.

Public policy should be directed toward breaking down these and other barriers to private contracting (or recontracting). For example, a strong case can be made for repealing the Trust Indenture Act to facilitate private restructuring of publicly held debt.[26] Corporate default could also be made less costly by relaxing current regulatory constraints on commercial banks' ability to hold equity in distressed firms; banks are currently required to divest any stock received under a bankruptcy or restructuring in approximately two years. Allowing creditors to hold equity and debt jointly, which is the norm in Japan and Germany, would also streamline the reorganization process by reducing costly, time-consuming conflicts between creditors and shareholders.

One recent development that offers hope is the increasing use of "prepackaged" Chapter 11, in which a firm jointly files its bankruptcy petition and reorganization plan (after having first secured creditors' informal consent to the plan). Prepackaged bankruptcy is a hybrid of private restructuring and Chapter 11—one that potentially incorporates the best features of both methods. Provided the firm has adequately disclosed details of its financial condition to creditors before filing, it is possible for the plan to be confirmed almost immediately. Republic Health recently completed a prepackaged bankruptcy in only four months. Such innovations in financial contracting deserve the full support of lawmakers and economists alike.

---

26. See Mark Roe, "The Voting Prohibition in Bond Workouts," *The Yale Law Review* 97 (1987), and Robert Gertner and David Scharfstein, "A Theory of Workouts and the Effects of Reorganization Law," *The Journal of Finance* (forthcoming).

WHAT REALLY WENT WRONG AT REVCO?

by Karen H. Wruck,
*Harvard Business School**

REVCO D.S. ANNOUNCES PRIVATE INVESTOR GROUP ACQUISITION

(*PR Newswire*, December 29, 1986)

REVCO D.S., SUBSIDIARIES, AND PARENT FILE CHAPTER 11

(*Daily News Record*, July 29, 1988)

REVCO'S LBO ENDS WITH A WHIMPER

(*Business Week*, August 15, 1988)

REVCO SAGA: OR HOW BUY-OUT BONANZA
BECAME A FRENZY OF FEES IN CHAPTER 11

(*Wall Street Journal*, May 16, 1991)

O n December 29, 1986, Revco D.S., Inc. went private. It was one of the nation's largest retail drug chains, operating over 2,000 stores in 30 states. Approximately $1.55 billion was raised to finance the purchase of the company. (The securities issued and the investors purchasing them are listed in Table 1.) The deal raised management's equity stake from 3% to 31%, and increased the company's debt from $309 million to $1.3 billion.

In July 1988, less than two years after the buyout, Revco filed for protection from its creditors under Chapter 11 of the U.S. Bankruptcy Code. Given the company's heavy debt burden, many observers viewed this outcome as inevitable. For example, Theodore J. Forstmann, senior partner of the buyout firm Forstmann Little & Co., commented: "Revco is a case study of what happens when companies take on too much debt. Where junk bonds are concerned, there will be many more Revcos."[1]

At the time, Revco was the largest highly-leveraged transaction (HLT) to fail. Since Revco's Chapter 11, defaults and Chapter 11 filings by HLT companies such as Allied, Federated, Carter Hawley Hale, Harcourt Brace Jovanovich, and U.S. Gypsum have been highly publicized. Indeed, from reading press accounts of HLT failures, one could easily be left with the impression that *all* highly leveraged companies have been victims of the "excesses of the 80s."

---

*The author would like to thank Brian Barry for providing research assistance, Adam Berman and Mark Wolsey-Paige for work on a case study of Revco on which this paper draws, and George Baker, Donald Chew, and Michael Jensen for helpful comments and suggestions.

1. Stephen Phillips, "The LBO Where Everything Went Wrong," *Business Week*, May 9, 1988, p. 47.

The overall junk bond statistics, however, tell a different story. Between 1977 and the end of 1990, over $219 billion in funds were raised through the issuance of high-yield debt. As of December 31, 1990, issues representing $36.2 billion, or roughly 16%, of the total value of these securities had defaulted—implying an average weighted annual default rate of 4.64%;[2] $20.9 billion of the defaulted securities wound up in Chapter 11. Put another way, of the several thousand companies that have issued junk bonds since 1977, only about 200 had defaulted by the end of 1990—and of these less than 100 had filed Chapter 11. And, today, of course, the junk bond market appears to be recovering smartly, with investor oversubscriptions of several recent new issues.

But if the past record and likely future of junk bonds are much more encouraging than the financial press would have led us to believe, the fate of many highly leveraged firms in default or Chapter 11 nevertheless remains uncertain. Initially, many observers of the high-yield market were optimistic about the prospects for reorganizing defaulted companies quickly and cheaply. For example, Michael Jensen argued that high leverage had considerable control as well as tax benefits for mature companies, and that such benefits would likely far outweigh the costs of financial distress—in large part because the bankruptcy process itself would be "privatized," with few firms resorting to Chapter 11.[3] Unfortunately, a number of factors, including recent bankruptcy court decisions and the eclipse of the high-yield market, have combined to make private reorganizations increasingly unlikely. Also, the emergence of active creditors has compounded the creditor holdout problem that complicates formal Chapter 11 as well as out-of-court reorganizations. In short, the costs of financial distress today appear considerably higher than economists like Jensen once predicted.

Why do some highly leveraged companies fail? Is it really "too much debt," or do HLT failures often arise from fundamental operating and governance problems? What are the prospects today for highly leveraged firms in financial distress? How do the legal rules of the game for reorganization and bankruptcy affect a firm's ability to cope with financial distress? What legal and regulatory reforms would help preserve the value of these companies? This article analyzes Revco's LBO in an attempt to shed some light on these issues.

WAS REVCO A GOOD LEVERAGED BUYOUT CANDIDATE?

It has long been recognized that the most likely LBO candidates are companies in mature industries producing—or at least capable of producing—a strong and predictable cash flow stream. Put a little differently, prime LBO candidates are businesses in which the requirement to pay out large amounts of cash on a regular basis does not destroy value.

What has not been widely acknowledged—though LBO practitioners understand this quite well—is the extent to which the success of an LBO depends on a strong management team and an effective sponsor organization. Managers clearly have to know their business and be capable of adapting to a different, generally more demanding, operating environment. The sponsor's role is to provide effective oversight and to help management in making the transition to managing for cash flow.

As will become clear in the following pages, Revco's management team was in disarray at the time of the LBO. And its LBO sponsors—Transcontinental Services, Golenberg & Company, and Salomon Brothers—were at best distracted.

REVCO'S MANAGEMENT TEAM

Sidney Dworkin, CEO of Revco at the time of its buyout, had held that title for almost 20 years. Under his leadership, the company had grown rapidly by acquiring and opening new stores. An important factor in Revco's success was its "everyday low price" strategy using discount prices to attract customers and profiting from high volume and low overhead. The company also diversified into businesses outside its retail core; acquisitions included a liquid generic drug manufacturer, an alarm maker, a computer software company, an insurance company, and a vitamin manufacturer. From 1971 to 1984, Revco's sales grew at a compound annual rate

2. The average annual default rate is calculated by first computing total dollar defaults as a percentage of total dollar issuances (16.5%) and then dividing this percentage by the weighted average number of years the bonds were outstanding prior to default (3.57 years). See the Salomon Brothers High Yield Research Group, *Original Issue High-Yield Default Study—1990 Summary*, January 28, 1991.

3. See Michael Jensen, "Active Investors, LBOs, and the Privatization of Bankruptcy," *Journal of Applied Corporate Finance*, Vol. 2, No. 1 (Spring 1989).

Arranging the leveraged buyout of a firm with an unstable management team is
something experienced buyout sponsors avoid. In highly leveraged transactions,
there usually isn't enough slack to allow severe operating problems to work
themselves out.

TABLE 1
REVCO'S CAPITAL AND
OWNERSHIP STRUCTURE,
DECEMBER 1986
($ IN MILLIONS)

Investor	Amount	Security
NEW DEBT SECURITIES:	$1267	
■ Wells Fargo Bank and Marine Midland Bank	$567	■ Bank Term loan and working capital loan at prime + 1 3/4%, or LIBOR[1] + 2 3/4% at Revco's option
■ Public Investors	$700	■ 13 1/8% Senior Subordinated Notes ■ 13.3% Subordinated Notes ■ 13.3% Junior Subordinated Notes
NEW PREFERRED STOCK:	$245	
■ New York Life and Morgan Guaranty	$85	■ Convertible preferred stock
■ Public Investors	$130	■ Exchangeable preferred stock
■ Transcontinental (a publicly traded investment firm) and Salomon Brothers	$30	■ Junior preferred stock
NEW COMMON STOCK:	$35	
■ Transcontinental	$19.0	■ 51.0% or 2,715,000 common shares
■ Revco Management	$10.7	■ 28.9% or 1,537,000 common shares
■ Salomon Brothers	$4.8	■ 13.1% or 697,500 common shares
■ Golenberg & Co. (a small Cleveland-based investment bank)	$0.5	■ 1.4% or 75,000 common shares[2]
PRE-EXISTING DEBT ASSUMED IN LBO:	$175	
TOTAL CAPITAL	$1,722	

Source: Revco D.S., Inc.: November 14, 1986 Proxy Statement.
1. LIBOR is the London Interbank Offered Rate.
2. Percentage ownership adds to 94.4% because 300,000 common shares (5.6% of the total) were offered with the notes to the public.

of 21.1%, and gross profit margins averaged 6.8%. In January of 1984, Revco was operating more drugstores than any other retail drug chain in the nation, and its stock price reached an historical high of $37.50 per share.

Then Revco's troubles began. On April 12, E-Ferol, a vitamin product manufactured by the company's Carter-Glogau subsidiary, was blamed for the death of 38 infants. Revco's stock price fell from from $31 1/4 to $24, losing almost 25% of its value, over the next two days. As Revco's stock continued to perform poorly over the following months (see Figure 1), takeover rumors began to surface.

Dworkin "solved" the takeover problem by arranging a deal between Revco and Odd Lot Trading, Inc., a chain of 66 discount stores selling merchandise purchased at distressed prices from troubled retailers. In May 1984, Revco purchased 100% of Odd Lot for $113 million worth of Revco common stock. The deal gave Bernard Marden and Isaac Perlmutter, founders and sole owners of Odd Lot, a 12% equity stake in Revco.

But Dworkin's solution backfired. By placing 12% of Revco's stock with Marden and Perlmutter, Dworkin thought he had brought on board a strong set of allies. What he got instead was a pair of active investors who had many ideas for improving Revco's operations. In June 1984, about ten days after the Odd Lot acquisition was finalized, Marden and Perlmutter sent Dworkin the first of a series of critical memos about Revco operations. The memos contained charges of nepotism and centered on allega-

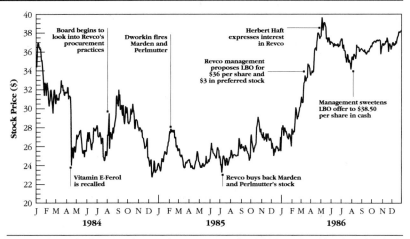

FIGURE 1
STOCK PRICE
PERFORMANCE OF
REVCO D.S., INC.
1984-1986

Board begins to
look into Revco's
procurement
practices

Dworkin fires
Marden and
Perlmutter

Herbert Haft
expresses interest
in Revco

Revco management
proposes LBO for
$36 per share and
$3 in preferred stock

Management sweetens
LBO offer to $38.50
per share in cash

Vitamin E-Ferol
is recalled

Revco buys back Marden
and Perlmutter's stock

Stock Price ($)

J F M A M J J A S O N D J F M A M J J A S O N D J F M A M J J A S O N D
1984   1985   1986

Source: Stock price data from Center for Research in Security Prices (CRSP) database, adjusted for splits and dividends.
Information on the company from the *Wall Street Journal Index* and other news sources.

tions of questionable procurement practices by Dworkin's son, then in charge of the purchasing department. Another son was executive vice-president of marketing and a member of the board of directors.

Marden and Perlmutter then led a group of dissident shareholders in threatening to make a tender offer for the company. A special committee of outside directors and auditors was appointed to investigate Revco's purchasing procedures, and Dworkin's son was temporarily relieved from his purchasing responsibilities. Later the dissident group demanded not only six seats on Revco's 13-member board of directors, but Sidney Dworkin's ouster. The board, however, supported Dworkin and, in February 1985, Marden and Perlmutter were fired.

Additionally, around this time Revco competitors such as Eckerd and Rite Aid adopted more aggressive pricing tactics. Revco's earnings and cash flows fell sharply. Earnings before interest, taxes, and depreciation (EBITD) dropped 44% from $204 million in 1984 to $113 million in 1985.

In response to the company's operating and financial problems, the board hired a new president. In June 1985, William B. Edwards, the CEO of a 30-

store chain of discount drugstores in Detroit, joined Revco as President and Chief Operating Officer (COO). In July, after much litigation and public recrimination, Revco rid itself of Marden and Perlmutter by repurchasing their stock for $98 million, or $22.50 per share.

The company was in essentially the same shape when, two months later, Dworkin was approached by Glenn Golenberg, managing director of Golenberg & Company, a small Cleveland-based investment banking firm, to discuss the possibility of a leveraged buyout. Golenberg also approached Salomon Brothers and Transcontinental Services (a publicly traded investment firm) to explore their interest in participating in the LBO.

REVCO'S LBO SPONSORS
AND BOARD OF DIRECTORS

Buyout sponsors typically play a critical role in LBOs, monitoring operating performance, advising and motivating senior management, and, in some cases, guiding the strategic direction of the company.[4] Arranging the leveraged buyout of a firm with an unstable management team is something experi-

4. For a discussion of the role of the buyout sponsor in the context of the O.M. Scott LBO, see George P. Baker and Karen H. Wruck, "Organizational Changes and Value Creation in Leveraged Buyouts: The Case of The O.M. Scott & Sons Company," *Journal of Financial Economics* 24 (1989), pp. 163-190. See also the shorter, less technical version of that article, "Lessons from a Middle Market LBO," which appeared in the Spring 1991 issue of this journal.

enced buyout sponsors avoid. In highly leveraged transactions, there usually isn't enough slack to allow severe operating problems to work themselves out. Salomon Brothers, however, had never done a major LBO before Revco.

The board of directors of the LBO company was elected by equity blockholders as specified in a Stockholders' Agreement. Three directors—Sidney Dworkin, Edwards, and Dworkin's son—were appointed by the unanimous vote of Dworkin and Edwards; they were the only pre-LBO directors on the new board. Two directors were appointed by Transcontinental, one by Salomon, one by Transcontinental and Salomon jointly, one by the holders of the convertible preferred stock, and one was specified to be Glenn Golenberg. With the single exception of the director appointed by Salomon, all non-management directors had financial service rather than retailing backgrounds.

Shortly after the buyout, Revco's new board committed what proved with hindsight to be a major strategic blunder: they allowed a new CEO to make a fundamental change in Revco's strategy. In March 1987, just three months after the close of the LBO, Edwards became the new CEO. Dworkin retained the chairmanship. A banker who worked on the deal explained: "With Edwards, we were going for youth. Sid had seen his best days."[5]

In place of "everyday low prices," Edwards introduced weekly sales and promotions on selected merchandise. He also expanded Revco's product offerings to include televisions, furniture, and videocassette recorders. Stocking these more expensive products required significant cash outlays, thus putting added strain on an organization already pressured to increase cash flow.

Under Edwards' "mini-department-store" strategy, Revco's operating cash flow quickly plunged. Edwards then attempted to reverse Revco's deteriorating performance by halving the number of district managers and reorganizing stores to move pharmacies from the side to the back. These moves succeeded in confusing customers, but failed to increase operating margins. EBITD for the first full fiscal year

after the buyout (ending May 1987) was $167.8 million—about $40 million short of management's pre-buyout projections.

In September 1987, when the buyout was not yet a year old, the board made its second set of management changes. Boake Sells, formerly president of the large retailer Dayton Hudson, joined Revco as Chairman and CEO. Edwards became COO. Dworkin stepped down as chairman, selling the family stock back to the company in return for $4 million in cash and ownership of four stores.[6] Edwards resigned in March 1988 and received $1.6 million in severance compensation.

Approval from bank lenders was necessary to facilitate these management changes because they involved cash payments and share repurchases prohibited by lending agreements. As a condition for approval, the banks required that board members and remaining management contribute additional capital by purchasing $3.8 million of common stock. Sells purchased $520,000 of the $3.8 million.[7]

After his arrival, Sells had little time to make significant changes before the crucial 1987 Christmas season. (He later said he felt unprepared for Revco's extraordinarily difficult operating environment: "I didn't understand the cash flow problems of Revco during the recruiting process."[8]) It turned out to be a disaster. Stores experienced shortages of basic items, such as toothpaste, while expensive inventory items, such as television sets, sat on the shelves. Reflecting its disappointing Christmas, Revco took substantial inventory markdowns in the third and fourth quarters of fiscal 1988. And, in May 1988, the second full year of post-LBO operations, the company reported an EBITD of just $96 million—as compared to a pre-buyout management forecast of $260 million for fiscal 1988.

To add to the disarray created by management turnover, Revco's directors from Transcontinental were distracted by problems at their own company. Transcontinental was the target of a successful takeover attempt by Banner Industries and two new directors representing that company were appointed to Revco's board.[9]

---

5. Stephen Phillips, "Revco, Anatomy of an LBO That Failed," *Business Week*, October 3, 1988, pp. 59-61.

6. Dworkin and his son also received a total of $4.8 million in severance and other compensation. In addition, their severance agreement included health benefits, life insurance, and allowed for the purchase from Revco of cars, a condominium, and shares in another company. *Source:* Final Report of Examiner Professor Barry Lewis Zaretsky, Northern District of Ohio Bankruptcy Court, pp. 142-148.

7. Barry Zaretsky, examiner

8. Phillips, cited in note 5.

9. According to an account in *The American Lawyer*, following Banner's acquisition of Transcontinental, most of that company's investments, with the exception of its equity holdings in Revco, were sold. See "Revco in Ruins," by Susan Beck, *The American Lawyer*, June, 1990, pp. 56-64.

TABLE 2
AN EVALUATION OF
REVCO'S CASH FLOW
POSITION FOLLOWING ITS
LEVERAGED BUYOUT
($ IN MILLIONS)

ESTIMATED INTEREST AND PRINCIPAL:

Security	Principal Amount	Interest Rate	Estimated Interest Outlay	Required Principal Repayment
■Bank Term and working capital loans	$567 [1]	11.500%	$65.2	$45.00
■13 1/8% Senior Subordinated Notes	$400	13.125%	$52.5	
■13.3% Subordinated Notes, and				
13.3% Junior Subordinated Notes	$300	13.300%	$39.9	
■Pre-Existing Debt Assumed in LBO	$175 [1]	11.000%	$19.3	
Total			$176.9 + $45.00 = $221.9	

CASH SHORTFALL RELATIVE TO PROJECTED ASSET SALES FOR 1987:

Based on Management Forecasts:

■Sum of Estimated Interest & Principal	$221.9
■Forecast EBITD (as per LBO prospectus)	(207.6)
■Estimated Shortfall	(14.3)
■Estimated Shortfall/Projected Asset Sales ($225)	6%

Based on Actual Results:

■Sum of Estimated Interest & Principal	$221.9
■Actual EBITD	(167.8)
■Estimated Shortfall	(54.1)
■Estimated Shortfall/Projected Asset Sales ($225)	24%

Sources: Revco D.S., Inc.: November 14, 1986 Proxy Statement, COMPUSTAT Financial Database, Final Report of Examiner Professor Barry Lewis Zaretsky, Northern District of Ohio Bankruptcy Court.
1. Estimated interest rates.

On April 15, 1988, Revco announced it could not make a $46 million interest payment on $700 million in subordinated notes. In a press release issued that day, Sells said: "Revco believes that its business is strong and its operations solid; however, our current capitalization is not the appropriate one for the company. After evaluation, Revco's board has determined that a financial restructuring is appropriate."[10] Sells also reported that major asset sales would be completed by November 1988.

WAS REVCO'S CAPITALIZATION WRONG FROM THE START?

One way to examine the soundness of Revco's LBO and the factors leading to its financial problems is to compare Revco's required cash interest and principal payments to forecast and actual operating cash flow (or EBITD). According to management forecasts (see Table 2), operating cash flow was expected to fall about $14 million short of cash requirements in the first year. Management forecast

an improvement in EBITD of 45% over two years following the buyout, and 56% over three years following the buyout.

In fact, Revco underperformed management's projections by 19% in the first year. By the end of the second year after the buyout, actual EBITD was 63% lower than pre-LBO projections. Based on actual results, the 1987 cash shortfall was about $54 million, and in 1988 the deficit was over $160 million. By the end of fiscal 1988—a year in which the company's cash and equivalents fell from $49 million to $3.3 million—cash on hand was not sufficient to cover a continuing shortfall.

Deteriorating operating performance thus clearly played an important role in Revco's cash flow problems. Also important, however, was the failure to execute an integral part of the LBO plan: namely, the sale of seven non-drugstore subsidiaries. In September 1986 Duff & Phelps appraised these assets at $225 million, and the successful completion of less than 25% of the planned asset sales would have been enough to cover Revco's cash shortfall

---

10. "Revco to Develop Financial Restructuring Plan," *PR Newswire* (4/15/88).

during its first year of operations. In fact, the bank term loan agreement signed three months later *required* the sale of assets yielding proceeds of $255 million by November 1988.

After the close of the LBO, Revco retained Salomon to sell these assets. By April 1988, however, Salomon had only succeeded in selling assets appraised at $45 million, and for total proceeds of only $32.7 million.[11] Because the period following Revco's LBO was not one in which other companies generally had trouble selling assets, it is not clear why Salomon was unsuccessful in completing the required sales. What is clear, however, is that assuming the successful completion of planned asset sales— an assumption quite reasonable at the time of the buyout—Revco's LBO capital structure does not seem inappropriate.

WHAT WAS THE EFFECT OF THE "FEE FRENZY?"

The financial press has made much of the fees paid to advisers in arranging Revco's LBO. The primary criticism of the fees was that they were "too high." The real problem with the fees in Revco's LBO was not the *level* of fees, but rather a *fee structure* that encouraged the company's financial advisers and managers to overpay for Revco.

In a leveraged buyout, every additional dollar the investor group pays to buy the company is a benefit to the selling shareholders and a cost to the new investors. Thus, the higher the price offered by the investor group, the greater the probability that shareholders will tender their shares and the transaction be accomplished.

The incentives faced by managers and their financial advisers in pricing LBOs are more complicated. To the extent managers own shares and do not "roll over" the value of their holdings into shares in the new LBO, they also clearly benefit from a higher price for their shares. Financial advisers—especially those that function primarily as "agents" and don't put significant capital into their deals—also benefit from higher prices that increase the odds of deals going through. Not only do advisers generally receive higher fees for larger deals, but many times a

substantial portion of those fees are paid *only* if the transaction is completed.

To the extent managers and advisers are also investing in the common stock of the LBO company, they also have incentives to *under*pay.[12] In this sense, both management and advisers who invest significant capital face a trade-off between receiving a higher cash payout from doing the deal and preserving a higher value for their stock in the LBO company.

The important point here is this: While *in the process* of negotiating the terms of an LBO, share-owning managers and financial advisers have incentives *not* to maximize the value of the new LBO firm, but rather to maximize *the sum* of their cash payout and the value of their LBO equity.[13] To the extent managers and intermediaries gain more from today's cash payout than they lose in tomorrow's LBO equity value, they have clear incentives to overpay in order to close the deal. It is only *after* the transaction closes, and upfront cash payouts are no longer an issue, that LBO equity ownership provides incentives to maximize firm value.

Even if Revco's LBO equity were worthless at the close of the deal, managers and LBO sponsors together would have received a net cash inflow of $21.4 million (see Table 3). This inflow, however, was not equally distributed across managers or sponsors. Sidney Dworkin, age 65 at the time, was the primary management beneficiary. Proceeds from the sale of his old stock and options were over $29 million, and he put approximately $1.6 million into the LBO company. Other managers made a net investment in Revco's LBO. So did Transcontinental, contributing approximately $34 million and taking a fee of $600,000. Salomon Brothers, by contrast, received roughly $19 million more in fees than it invested; and Golenberg took out $5.5 million more than he put in.

Compared to other LBO transactions in the 1980s, Revco's management team invested less in the LBO and paid more in fees to advisers. In a recent study of 124 LBOs completed between 1980 and 1989, Steven Kaplan and Jeremy Stein find that the median dollar value of management's investment in the LBO amounted to 46% of the value of their old

---

11. Final report of examiner Barry Zaretsky

12. Thus giving rise to the "self-dealing" problem that also, paradoxically, troubles LBO critics. LBO critics are thus put into the uncomfortable position of claiming that managements both systematically overpay and underpay for companies they take private.

13. To the extent overpayment in an LBO jeopardizes the firm's future, some managers will also likely include the value of continued employment with the firm in this calculus. For managers near the end of their careers like Dworkin, this factor is less important. LBO sponsors will also consider the likely effect of overpayment on their reputation and, hence, on their future ability to do deals.

TABLE 3
LBO COMMON
STOCKHOLDERS'
INVESTMENTS AND FEES
($ IN MILLIONS)

Investor	Common and Preferred Investment	Fees Received	Cash Received for Old Revco Equity	Net Cash Received in Revco's LBO
▪Revco Management	($10.7)	$0.0	$41.0[1]	$30.3
▪Transcontinental	($34.0)[2]	$0.6	-NA-	($33.4)
▪Salomon Brothers	($19.8)[2]	$38.8	$19.0	$19.0
▪Golenberg & Co.	($0.5)	$6.0	-NA-	$5.5
Total[3]	($65.0)	$45.4	$41.0	$21.4

Sources: Revco D.S., Inc.: November 14, 1986 Proxy Statement, Final Report of Examiner Professor Barry Lewis Zaretsky, Northern District of Ohio Bankruptcy Court.
1. Equals total management shares times $38.50 per share.
2. Assumes Salomon and Transcontinental put $15 million each in their joint $30 million preferred investment.
3. Additional fees totalling $34.4 million were paid to bank lenders, other preferred investors and other advisors—implying total fees of $79.9 million.

equity. In the case of Revco, management invested only about 26% of that value, with Dworkin investing only 5.5%. Kaplan and Stein also find that, in the median case, total fees amounted to 3.8%; Revco paid 5.1%.[14] The relatively high fees and low investment in Revco's LBO are consistent with strong incentives on the part of Dworkin, Golenberg, and Salomon to pay too much for Revco.

DID THE LBO INVESTOR GROUP OVERPAY?

To attempt to assess whether the LBO investors overpaid, I calculated five simple estimates of Revco's value at the time of the LBO (see Table 4). One estimate is based on American Appraisal's September 1986 appraisal of Revco's assets. The other four are based on prices paid in transactions similar to Revco's LBO. (A list of comparables and their transaction prices is presented in the Appendix.) Because Eckerd's LBO is probably the closest comparable, a valuation based on it is presented separately; the other estimates are based on average multiples across all four comparable transactions.

By four of these five estimates, the investor group paid too much for Revco. Estimates of the amount of overpayment range from -$57 million (underpayment) to over $400 million. Assuming the data from Eckerd's LBO provide the best value estimate, it appears the investor group paid somewhere between $200 and $350 million too much for Revco.

Overpayment financed with debt is thus one explanation of how Revco wound up in financial distress. This assumes, however, that Revco was not worth a higher EBITD multiple than Eckerd. There is the possibility that, properly managed, Revco could have been more valuable per dollar of EBITD than Eckerd. To the extent this was the case, the failure of Revco is more aptly described as a failure of its management and LBO sponsors—a failure that led to a post-LBO cash flow crisis.

THE EFFECTS OF OVERPAYMENT

Overpayment simply means investors' claims are worth less than they paid for them. For example, if Revco's LBO investors overpaid by $350 million, they paid $1.55 billion for a company worth only $1.2 billion. Theoretically, this loss would be absorbed by claimholders according to the priority of their claims; shareholders would lose their value first, followed by junior subordinated lenders, and so on until the amount of the overpayment was covered.

Overpayment, then, does not lead to financial distress provided there is enough equity to absorb it. When companies with large equity bases such as ITT or GTE overpay for acquisitions, such overpayments destroy stockholder value; bondholders and creditors remain relatively unaffected.

When overpayment is "financed" by debt, the company may be put in a situation where it is contractually required to pay out more cash flow

14. Steven N. Kaplan and Jeremy C. Stein, "The Pricing and Financial Structure of Management Buyouts in the 1980s," University of Chicago working paper, January 25, 1991.

TABLE 4
ESTIMATES OF REVCO'S
VALUE BASED ON
APPRAISALS AND
EARNINGS MULTIPLES
($ IN MILLIONS)

Price Paid for Revco by Investor Group	Basis for Value Estimate	Value Estimate	Implied over (+) or under(-) payment[1]
$1,545.9	Asset Appraisal	$1,132.4[2]	+$413.5
	Eckerd's one year EBITD multiple	$1,349.5	+$196.4
	Eckerd's average 5-year EBITD multiple	$1,198.6	+$347.3
	Mean one year EBITD multiple[3]	$1,511.9	+$34.0
	Mean five year EBITD multiple[4]	$1,603.1	-$57.2

1. For each value estimate the implied over- or under-payment is calculated by subtracting the value estimate from the price paid by the Investor Group.
2. Equals American Asset Appraisal's net asset value of $823 plus Revco's 1986 total debt of $309.4.
3. From appendix excluding Revco=9.075.
4. From appendix excluding Revco=10.7.

than it is capable of generating. Of the funds raised for Revco's LBO, $280 million, or 17% of total capitalization, were preferred and common equity funds. This percentage is, in fact, considerably *higher* than the 10% equity typical of LBO transactions in the 80s. But, if the investor group overpaid by more than $280 million, Revco's equity alone would not have absorbed the economic loss.

REVCO FILES CHAPTER 11

Faced, then, with a cash flow shortage in April 1988, Revco required a financial restructuring. Salomon presented a proposal to the company. But Sells, unhappy with the way Salomon handled Revco's asset sales, decided to get proposals from other investment banks. Drexel Burnham Lambert was chosen to replace Salomon, and Salomon's director resigned from Revco's board.

Drexel attempted to restructure the company's debt through a private workout, but was unsuccessful. For example, in mid-May it was proposed that public bondholders exchange their subordinated notes for new classes of equity. LBO common stockholders would retain only 5% of the company's common stock. (That this proposal would have left the original equityholders with only 5% of the equity is consistent with both overpayment by the investor group and the destruction of any equity value remaining after overpayment through poor operating performance.) The proposal was not approved by the company's equityholders.

As Drexel attempted a debt restructuring, bondholders formed a steering committee advised by Goldman Sachs and composed of Magten Asset Management, Fidelity Investments, and Keystone Custodian Funds. As Revco had gotten into trouble, Magten—a firm that invests in distressed securities—had begun purchasing its 13 1/8% senior subordinated notes, which were then trading at about 50 cents on the dollar. By late June, it had accumulated 25% of the class ($100 million in face value). Magten's block of subordinated notes gave it the power to veto any reorganization plan, whether court-supervised or private. Such power effectively gave Magten the ability to "hold out" for higher returns before consenting to a plan.

On July 7, 1988, bondholders granted a one-month "standstill," thus precluding any action against Revco for missing its June interest payment. Cash flow was not improving, however, and the company wanted still more time. Drexel then proposed a six-month extension of the standstill agreement. On July 19, the extension was denied. Three days later, bondholders led by Magten demanded full and immediate payment of their principal and interest. This triggered cross-default provisions that put Revco in default on all its borrowings.[15] Revco filed for protection under Chapter 11 on July 28, 1988.

At the filing, Sells commented, "it became abundantly clear to us that the bondholders' decision to accelerate would create even more uncertainty about Revco. In our view, we had no choice other than to seek the protection of the courts. We

15. Cross-default provisions are debt covenants in which default on one debt security is a condition for technical default on another. Such provisions result in much more complicated negotiations to resolve distress.

protected the integrity of our company and we believe that we have acted in the best long-term interests of our employees, vendors and customers."[16] Magten's head, Talton Embry, however, had little faith in Revco's ability to solve its problems, describing the company as "the equivalent of an Olds 98 competing in the Indianapolis 500."[17]

WHAT HAPPENED TO THE "PRIVATIZATION OF BANKRUPTCY"?

In Revco's case, high leverage accomplished part of what Jensen argued it would. It performed a control function by forcing a firm with a failing strategy, a management team in disarray, and weak governance to renegotiate—or at least attempt to renegotiate—its contracts with creditors. And this very process should force management to address the problems that led to distress in the first place.

What failed to happen, however, was the quick, efficient private reorganization Jensen argued was likely to follow (or even precede) defaults by highly leveraged companies.[18] Revco has been in Chapter 11 for almost three years and has spent $40.5 million (or 2.7% of the buyout price) in bankruptcy fees.[19] As David Schulte, the financial adviser to Revco's noteholders since its Chapter 11, remarked recently, "The deal was a failure, the attempted workout was a failure, and now the Chapter 11's proving to be a failure; and we can't get out of our own way yet."[20]

Why, then, were Revco's attempts at private reorganization unsuccessful? Two factors likely played important roles: (1) the special advantages of Chapter 11 for retailers; and (2) the information problems and conflicts of interest that beset attempts at reorganization under our current bankruptcy system.

CHAPTER 11'S BENEFITS FOR RETAILERS

Chapter 11 has benefits that are particularly advantageous to retailers. First, retailers have numerous trade creditors who are likely to have claims with different characteristics. Reaching a private agreement with each of them is very difficult. Under Chapter 11, such diffuse creditors can be dealt with as a single class, making negotiation manageable and settling protracted disputes once and for all.

Second, Chapter 11 allows the issue of new senior credit (debtor-in-possession, or DIP, financing), which may be crucial to the firm's survival. Pre-Chapter 11 trade creditors and other unsecured creditors have low priority, coming just before equityholders. Claims of creditors lending to the firm after it files under Chapter 11 are second in priority only to legal and administrative expenses. Distressed firms requiring new credit thus have incentives to file Chapter 11, and would-be creditors have incentives to withhold credit until after the filing.

Almost all highly-leveraged retail firms that defaulted went on to file Chapter 11 shortly afterward. In total, the retail industry issued $14.7 billion in high-yield debt between 1977 and 1990. At the end of 1990, $5 billion of that debt had defaulted.[21] Allied, Ames, Circle K, Dart Drugs, Federated, Revco and Southland accounted for $4.8 of that $5.0 billion; and all of these retailers ended up filing under Chapter 11. After Revco filed, it secured $145 million in DIP financing from Marine Midland and Wells Fargo, and convinced many vendors to extend new credit.

CONFLICTS OF INTEREST LEAD TO BAD INFORMATION

The conflicts among management, creditors, and other securityholders in distressed firms—conflicts that are exacerbated by our laws and court system—can greatly complicate the reorganization process.

Consider that creditors and securityholders in troubled companies have two basic ways of maximizing the value of their claims. One is by uniting with other claimholders to ensure that firm value is

16. "Revco Voluntarily Seeks Chapter 11 Reorganization," *PR Newswire* (7/28/88).

17. Phillips, Stephen, "Revco, Anatomy of an LBO That Failed," *Business Week* (10/3/88), pp. 59-61.

18. See Michael C. Jensen, "Active Investors, LBOs, and the Privatization of Bankruptcy," *Journal of Applied Corporate Finance* (Spring, 1989). In support of his argument, Jensen cited the fact that, in the 1980s many debt restructurings in highly leveraged firms were completed even before the firm defaulted. Most of these were done by Drexel under section 3(a)9 of the Securities Act.

19. Bankruptcy fees were reported in Anders, George, "Revco Saga: Or How Buy-Out Bonanza Became a Frenzy of Fees in Chapter 11," *The Wall Street Journal*, 5/16/91. A large body of scientific evidence has established that bankruptcy fees

are about 3% of the firm's pre-distress market value; so Revco's fees thus far are not out of line. See for example, Jerold B. Warner, "Bankruptcy Costs: Some Evidence," *Journal of Finance* 32 (1977), pp. 337-347, and Lawrence A. Weiss, "Priority of Claims and Ex-post Re-contracting in Bankruptcy," *Journal of Financial Economics*, volume 27 (1990), pp. 285-314.

20. From "Bankruptcies, Workouts and Turnarounds: A Roundtable Discussion," *Journal of Applied Corporate Finance*, this issue.

21. The high percentage of defaults in retailing—34% of total dollar issuance as opposed to an overall default rate of 16.5%—reflects the recent massive downsizing and restructuring of an industry with chronic excess capacity. For confirmation of this argument, see Francine Schwadel, "Shop Talk: What's in Store for Retailers," *Wall Street Journal*, April 9, 1991.

Stating that too much leverage was the *fundamental cause* of Revco's problems does not offer much insight into what went wrong. Management disarray, a weak and inexperienced LBO sponsor, a fee structure almost guaranteed to produce overpayment, and a disastrous midstream shift in strategy all conspired with the use of debt financing to put Revco into Chapter 11.

as large as possible, thereby increasing the value of all claims. The other is by trying to transfer value from other classes of securityholders. The mere possibility for such transfers leads to intense, and costly, conflicts among creditors and securityholders. As bankruptcy attorney Leonard Rosen warns about the current state of corporate reorganizations,

If creditor fights about the division of the pot start at the beginning of the process, then nobody's probably paying attention to more fundamental questions like: Have we got the right management running the business? And are they making the right strategic and operating decisions?... We're starting to litigate so early, spending so much energy on the intercreditor struggle, and creating such divisiveness in the process that we're making it much less likely that companies will be restructured quickly and economically.[22]

Even without such conflicts, the job of determining the value of a distressed firm and the actions necessary to preserve and expand that value is a difficult one. It requires making projections of future cash flows, and there is room for legitimate disagreement about the firm's prospects.

Conflicts between management and securityholders, and among securityholders themselves, preclude the sharing of accurate information and make it difficult to trust information received from other parties. In pursuing their own interests, all claimants have incentives to present biased and inaccurate information. Shareholders have incentives to claim the firm's problems are only temporary because it increases the likelihood they will retain a larger fraction of the equity. Creditors have incentives to claim that the equityholders' investment has been wiped out because it increases the likelihood that, in addition to restructured debt, they will wind up with the firm's equity. And managers have an incentive to propose plans designed to preserve their jobs. In short, no single party to the negotiation has all the relevant information and sufficient incentive to reveal that information to others.

One potential solution to this information problem is to hire a workout specialist—a firm or group

of professionals within a firm whose reputation depends on providing accurate and unbiased information to claimholders. It now appears that Drexel played such a role in reorganizing financially troubled companies during the 80s. The fact that Drexel executed hundreds of exchange offers in the high-yield market—and, in many cases, for companies that were not Drexel clients to begin with—suggests that its reputation played a role in resolving conflicts. In this light, it seems clear why Revco chose Drexel to replace Salomon Brothers as its investment banker.

Ultimately, however, Drexel was unsuccessful in resolving conflicts between Revco's equity and debtholders. A look at proposed reorganization plans reflects the conflicts at Revco that likely contributed to the failure of Drexel's workout attempts. A plan proposed by the LBO equityholders, which was presented to creditors in September 1989, called for equityholders to invest an additional $150 million and retain 55% of the common stock. Trade creditors, which had $200 million in claims, would get $55 million in cash and 5% of the common stock; and the noteholders, with over $700 million in claims, would get new bonds and 45% of the common stock. The proposals offered to noteholders and trade creditors were valued alike at 25¢ on the dollar.

The noteholders rejected this plan and then proposed a counterplan in which they would invest an additional $75 million and get 94% of the common stock; LBO equity investors would retain 5-6% of the equity. As a Revco insider assessed the situation, "The fight is between the noteholders and the equity people; we're just the prize being fought over."[23]

In November of 1989, Acadia Partners and the Robert Bass Group approached Revco with an offer valued at $925 million. In return for raising $410 million to put into Revco ($150 million cash and $260 million through a new debt issue), Acadia/Bass would own a majority of the common stock. Noteholders were to receive claims valued at about 34¢ on the dollar. Neither management nor the creditors expressed much enthusiasm for the deal. There were rumors that the Acadia/Bass plan did not include Revco's management team.[24] And Schulte indicated that noteholders were disappointed both with the

---

22. Comment from "Bankruptcies, Workouts and Turnarounds: A Roundtable Discussion," *Journal of Applied Corporate Finance*, this issue.

23. See Frederick, James, "The future for Revco hinges on creditors," *Drugstore News*, August 28. 1989; Vaczek, David, "Revco's bondholders battle for control," *Drugstore News*, September 25, 1989; and Frederick, James, "Revco

reorganization battle heats up: Court rules bondholders can query chain's board," *Drugstore News*, October 23, 1989.

24. Acadia owns Reliable Drugs whose CEO, Roger Grass, formerly an executive of Rite Aid, has years of industry experience. Observers speculated that he would run Revco.

664

price and the minority equity stake they would receive, although he felt the offer should be "recognized." In the face of such resistance, this plan did not progress farther.[25]

On June 12, 1990, Revco's bankruptcy took a long and expensive detour when the court appointed an examiner, law professor Barry Zaretsky, to assess the validity of fraudulent conveyance claims against Revco's pre-LBO shareholders and advisors. Zaretsky determined that there were grounds for these claims, and the resolution of this issue is progressing slowly.[26] As Schulte commented, "We wound up in the Revco case with an examiner even though no party of interest wanted it, and the examiner added a year to the case."[27]

From Revco's filing date, July 28, 1988, until October 31, 1990, management was granted the exclusive right to file a reorganization plan. Finally, the court refused to grant management an extension. Creditors petitioned the court for the right to propose their own plan, but still progress is slow. As Schulte remarked, "We ended exclusivity in the Revco case last November. And here it is April, and the world doesn't feel any better to me. We are the creditors and we have a plan on the table, but we're still in the swamp."[28]

WHAT REALLY WENT WRONG AT REVCO?

As the analysis above suggests, stating that too much leverage was the *fundamental* cause of Revco's problems does not offer much insight into what went wrong. Management disarray, a weak and inexperienced LBO sponsor, a fee structure almost guaranteed to produce overpayment, and a disastrous midstream shift in strategy all conspired with the use of debt financing to put Revco into Chapter 11.

What was the role of debt in all this? Consider what would have happened if the firm had remained publicly traded and successfully defended itself from a takeover *without using leverage*. Although it probably would not have filed Chapter 11 so soon, its stock price performance would undoubtedly have been abysmal. Much of the losses borne by bondholders

and creditors would simply have been imposed on the old shareholders instead. On the other hand, the failure to reorganize Revco quickly and efficiently has undoubtedly compounded the company's operating problems; and, in this sense, part of the direct and indirect costs of the ongoing reorganization represent a cost of debt financing.

Revco's main problem at present—and the company's survival depends on its ability to solve this problem—is to disentangle itself from Chapter 11 claimants still battling over who gets what piece of the pie. And conflicts among claimholders appear to be diminishing its size. The Acadia/Bass offer suggests that in November of 1989 Revco was still worth at least $925 million. In January 1990, Revco announced it would sell 712, or 38%, of its 1,873 drugstores, and use the expected proceeds of $250 million to help it reorganize, narrowing its focus to operations in 10 eastern states. The Acadia/Bass offer effectively expired in April when Reliable Drugs, owned by Acadia Partners, bought 220 Revco stores. In total, Revco has sold over 700 stores since the Chapter 11 filing (though proceeds have not been disclosed), and the company currently owns 1,100 stores.

In May 1991, Schulte estimated Revco's current market value capitalization (debt and equity) at $340 million—that is, about 37% of the Acadia/Bass offer.[29] In June, Eckerd expressed an interest in buying Revco. The offer, however, was deemed to provide "insufficient value to warrant further discussion" by Revco's board and creditors. A Revco lawyer recently estimated the value of the firm at $835 million.[30] The almost $500 million difference between creditor and shareholder estimates of firm value are consistent with the information problem discussed earlier.

WHAT WILL HELP PRESERVE THE VALUE OF COMPANIES LIKE REVCO?

The legal "rules of the game" in bankruptcy—notably, unanimity provisions of the Trust Indenture Act, exclusivity and routine extensions thereof, and

25. Alfaro, Charles, "Revco receives $925 million bid from Bass Group," *Chain Drug Review*, November 11, 1989, and Frederick, James, "Revco draws takeover interest," *Drug Store Review*, November 20, 1989.

26. In April 1991, pre-LBO shareholders owning less than 1000 shares were excluded from the case. Larger shareholders and advisors are still under scrutiny.

27. Comment from "Bankruptcies, Workouts and Turnarounds: A Roundtable Discussion," *Journal of Applied Corporate Finance*, this issue.

28. Ibid.

29. Anders, George, "Revco Saga: Or How Buy-Out Bonanza Became a Frenzy of Fees in Chapter 11," *Wall Street Journal*, May 16, 1991.

30. "Eckerd May Add to Revco Offer," *New York Times*, June 16, 1991.

The conflicts of interest and information problems that complicate the process of reorganizing troubled companies... could be reduced by encouraging the development of a liquid market for distressed companies' assets and allowing bankrupt firms or divisions of bankrupt firms to be acquired more easily.

failures to enforce strict priority of claims—have exacerbated the conflicts of interest and information problems that complicate the process of reorganizing troubled companies. Such problems could be reduced by encouraging the development of a liquid market for distressed companies' assets and allowing bankrupt firms or divisions of bankrupt firms to be acquired more easily. Other countries, notably Germany, have successfully developed such systems. This kind of process effectively separates the valuation of the assets—while also shielding the management of those assets—from destructive squabbles over how that value is to be divided among claimholders.

In the absence of the legal system's willingness to rely on or encourage the development of such markets, the problems associated with Chapter 11 can be reduced only by encouraging private workouts. Creating an environment friendly to workouts helps firms avoid Chapter 11 and allows investors in financial markets to play a role in resolving distress. Unfortunately, the demise of Drexel and recent court decisions suggest the U.S. is moving away from, rather than toward, this solution. Judge Lifland's 1990 ruling in the LTV case discourages out-of-court exchange offers by reducing the value of voluntarily exchanged claims in bankruptcy.[31] And the 1990 tax act imposes new taxes on troubled companies by making it more difficult to structure nontaxable exchange offers and making debt forgiveness taxable to the firm. Unless these changes are reversed, the result will be more bankruptcy filings.

IF YOUR FIRM ISN'T IN FINANCIAL DISTRESS... (OR, PLANNING FOR TROUBLE)

In making financing decisions, managers should consider how the company's financial structure will affect management's ability to recontract should the firm get into trouble. The experience of Chrysler over the past 10 years offers a good illustration. Steve Miller, Vice Chairman, explained Chrysler's shift in financial policy as follows:

Companies should plan for the possibility of financial trouble by reducing the complexity of their credit agreements. The more complex the credit structure, the more difficult and costly the workout process. ...We just renegotiated our corporate revolving credit agreement with our 38 participating institutions. And that group of 38 is down from over 450 ten years ago.[32]

A simpler financial structure that aligns the interests of various claimholders reduces incentives for claimants to jockey for advantage in the event of distress.

One solution to the problem, of course, is to avoid the use of debt financing altogether. But, given the tax and organizational incentive benefits of leverage, there are likely to be few cases where maximizing firm value can be achieved by minimizing the likelihood of getting into financial trouble. The solution lies instead in improving the alignment of management's interests with those of shareholders, and in uniting the interests of creditors and shareholders as well. Financial structures in which creditors hold equity are common in Japan and Germany, and in both of these countries financial distress is generally resolved through private workouts.[33] And, in this country, many of the HLTs of the early 80s made use of "strip financing" techniques designed, among other things, to minimize potential workout conflicts. Perhaps we can expect to see a return to such financing methods in the future.

In sum, a company's financing policy, governance structure, and compensation policy can all be used to increase the probability of a quicker, more efficient workout process.

---

31. Judge Lifland ruled that LTV's bondholders who participated in out-of-court exchange offers before the firm's Chapter 11 filing were not entitled to a claim equal to the face value of their old bonds. Instead their claims were limited to the market value of their new bonds. See "U.S. Bankruptcy Judge Rules in Favor of LTV," January 31, 1990, *Reuters Newswire*.

32. See the Roundtable discussion in this issue.
33. See the article on Japanese reorganizatons by Carl Kester later in this issue.

APPENDIX: VALUATION STATISTICS FOR SELECTED DRUGSTORE MERGERS AND ACQUISITIONS, 1985-1986

Date of Announcement	■ Acquired/Acquired by □ Business Description of Acquired	Firm Value[2]		Firm Value as a Multiple of:[1]		
				Sales	EBIT	EBITD
05/28/86	■ Thrifty Corp./Pacific Enterprises	$1052.7	One Year Prior:	.75x	14.3x	11.4x
			Five Year Avg:	.81x	18.0x	14.3x
	□ The Company primarily operated 555 retail drug and discount stores in California and eight other western states. The company also operated 89 Big 5 sporting goods stores, and owned a 34% interest in Crown books and a 50% interest in Trak Auto Parts stores.					
03/10/86	■ Revco D.S., Inc./Private Investors including Management	1545.9	One Year Prior:	.56x	11.6x	9.3x
			Five Year Avg:	.72x	12.3x	10.3x
	□ The Company operated the largest domestic drugstore chain (in units). There were nearly 2,000 stores in 24 states. The stores operated on a self-service, cash and carry basis, emphasizing high volume, low overhead and everyday low prices.					
10/10/85	■ Jack Eckerd Corporation/Private Investors including Management, Employees, and Merrill Lynch	1391.9	One Year Prior:	.55x	10.6x	8.1x
			Five Year Avg:	.62x	9.6x	8.0x
	□ The Company operated drugstores, optical centers, department stores and casual wear clothing stores. It also operated a photo-finishing laboratory.					
02/14/85	■ Hook Drugs Inc./Kroger Co.	176.4	One Year Prior:	.50x	10.4x	8.4x
			Five Year Avg:	.61x	11.6x	9.5x
	□ The Company's primary business was the operation of more than 300 retail drugstores in Indiana, Illinois, Kentucky, and Ohio, including the largest chain in Indiana.					
01/14/85	■ Payless Drug Stores/ K-Mart Corp.	593.1	One Year Prior:	.70x	10.1x	8.4x
			Five Year Avg:	.84x	13.4x	11.0x
	□ The Company operated 144 stores under the name "Payless Drug Stores." These stores sold a complete line of prescription and over-the-counter drug items, appliances, household consumer products, and durable products.					

1. Sales, EBIT, and EBITD ratios are based first on data from the most recent fiscal year ending before the transaction announcement, and second on an average of these values for the five years before the transaction.
2. Firm value is the sum of amount paid for the common stock of the company, the amount used to repay pre-existing debt, and the book value of debt assumed in the transaction.

THE BANKRUPTCY CODE AND VIOLATIONS OF ABSOLUTE PRIORITY

by Lawrence A. Weiss, Tulane University

T he costs of bankruptcy are typically classified into two categories: direct and indirect. Direct costs encompass the legal and administrative fees, including the costs of lawyers, accountants, and other professionals involved in the bankruptcy filing. Indirect costs include a wide range of unobservable opportunity costs, such as lost sales, increased operating costs, and reduced competitiveness.

Another cost of bankruptcy—one that affects not just bankrupt companies, but all firms that raise debt capital—arises from the failure of the bankruptcy courts to enforce contracts between lenders and corporate debtors. In particular, the courts routinely fail to enforce the rule of *absolute priority*. For absolute priority to be upheld, senior creditors must be paid in full before junior claimholders (including shareholders) receive any payments whatsoever.

Economists have long argued that bankruptcy courts mistakenly fail to enforce priority of claims. In 1977, William Meckling observed, "The courts, the Congress, and the Securities and Exchange Commission refuse to relegate stockholders to the status of purely residual claimants."[1] And as Merton Miller noted in the same year, "Permitting stockholders to claim court protection and thereby retain control of a corporation in default amounts to giving them a call option at the expense of the creditors."[2] The failure of the courts to enforce strict priority imposes significant losses on creditors. To the extent priority violations are widespread and anticipated by lenders, they end up raising the cost of debt financing for all but the most creditworthy companies.

---

1. William Meckling, "Financial Markets, Default, and Bankruptcy: The Role of the State," *Law and Contemporary Problems*, 41 (1977), pp. 13-38.
2. Merton Miller, "The Wealth Transfers of Bankruptcy: Some Illustrative Examples," *Law and Contemporary Problems*, 41 (1977), pp. 39-46.

In this article, I summarize the findings of my recently completed study of 37 companies that filed for bankruptcy between 1979 and 1986. Besides providing clear evidence of the courts' failure to enforce priority of claims, I also take note of a variety of other related bankruptcy practices that appear to be generating unnecessary social costs.

A Word on the Sample. I first compiled a list of all NYSE and Amex firms declaring bankruptcy from November 1979 (shortly after the new bankruptcy code went into effect) to December 1986, and found 99 companies that filed for bankruptcy in 32 jurisdictions. The court documents required for my study are available only at the federal courts where the bankruptcy petitions were filed. Constraints of time and budget forced me to confine my data collection efforts to the following seven districts: Central District of California; Southern District of Florida; Northern District of Illinois; District of Massachusetts; Northern District of Michigan; Southern District of New York; and Northern District of Ohio. These locations were the sites of 51 filings, or just over half of the 99 filings I started with.

I then eliminated an additional 14 cases either because their bankruptcies were not resolved by May 31, 1989, or because the data from the cases had been removed from the court to an archive. This process left me with 37 cases. For these 37 companies, the average time from filing of the bankruptcy petition to resolution was 2.5 years (with a standard deviation of 1.4 years). The shortest bankruptcy took just under 8 months, the longest more than 8 years.

For 31 of the 37 cases, I was able to find complete data on fees. This in turn allowed me to determine that the direct costs—again, the professional and administrative fees associated with the bankruptcy filing—averaged 20% of the market value of the equity (one year prior to the filing) or 3% of the book value of debt plus the market value of equity.

THE NEW BANKRUPTCY CODE AND PRIORITY OF CLAIMS

Two types of bankruptcy filings are available to corporations: Chapter 7 and Chapter 11. Chapter 7 provides for the orderly liquidation of a firm's assets by a court-appointed trustee, and payment to claimants in order of priority is always maintained. Chapter 11 provides for reorganization of a firm. Participants in a Chapter 11 filing must approve a plan of reorganization, leaving room for substantial negotiations among the various parties and for violation of priority of claims. In a Chapter 11 bankruptcy, the debtor's management operates the firm and works out the reorganization unless an interested party can prove management is either incompetent or has committed fraud, in which case the court appoints a trustee.

Of the 37 firms in my sample, only two filed under Chapter 7. The law also provides for conversion from Chapter 11 to Chapter 7. Thirty of the 35 firms in my sample that filed under Chapter 11 were eventually reorganized; the other five were liquidated under Chapter 11.

Bankruptcy law alters creditors' contracts by giving management, junior creditors, and residual claimants the ability to delay the final resolution and to force the firm to incur additional costs. The first restriction on creditors is the difficulty they face in presenting their own plan for reorganization. The debtor-in-possession or trustee is automatically given a 120-day period to formulate a plan, and during that period no one else can propose a plan.

The bankruptcy judge can extend the initial exclusive period, and often does. In the LTV bankruptcy case, the judge has extended the exclusive period for five years. A creditor can propose a reorganization plan only if the exclusive period is over and a debtor's plan has not been accepted within 180 days of the bankruptcy filing. Creditors, unlike debtors, must support their evaluation of the firm's asset values by means of appraisals, a costly process. All this has made creditor plans for reorganization rare. In fact, there was only one instance among the 35 Chapter 11 filings in my sample in which a creditor plan was confirmed.

The voting procedure further restricts creditors. Unimpaired creditors—those who receive payment in full with interest or who have had their claims reinstated in full with any defaults cured—do not vote on the reorganization plan. The reorganization plan must be approved by a majority in number and at least two-thirds in amount of each class of impaired creditors before the plan can be confirmed by the bankruptcy court. Equityholders must also approve the plan by a two-thirds majority, giving them leverage over creditors.

If the bankruptcy judge does not believe agreement will be reached, he or she can force acceptance of a plan by using a procedure known as a "cram-down." Before applying a cram-down, the judge must order costly valuation hearings to ensure that any dissenting class of impaired creditors receives at least as much under the plan as it would in a liquidation. The prospect of such hearings is often enough to make creditors approve a plan in which their priority is violated.

Creditors may also be willing to allow a violation of priority to obtain their proceeds sooner than otherwise. Initially, the trustee, management, or an outside consultant ascertains whether a class of claimants is impaired or unimpaired, and whether each class will receive more from the plan than it would if the firm were liquidated. Any claimant who disagrees with any part of the plan is allowed to argue that position in court, further delaying the resolution. If the bankruptcy judge, after hearing arguments from dissenting claimants, determines that the estimated values and status of claimants contained in the plan are "unfair," a vote cannot be taken, and a new plan must be prepared.

Secured creditors whose collateral is worth less than the principal plus accrued interest may give up part of their claims to avoid losing additional interest.[3] Secured creditors may also be willing to violate priority to reduce the risk of decay in the value of their collateral. Bankruptcy law instructs the trustee or debtor-in-possession to protect the interests of the secured creditors so they will receive, at a minimum, what they would have received if the bankruptcy had not been filed. But, providing such protection is not an exact science. Numerous cases have tried to determine what constitutes adequate protection for secured creditors, but the answer is still vague.

Tax laws also influence bankruptcy resolutions. Under current tax law, cooperation of the equityholders is essential to maintain the corporate shell and preserve tax loss carryforwards. Equityholders may receive a distribution of funds from an insolvent firm in return for their cooperation.

Finally, pro-debtor bankruptcy judges go outside their legal jurisdiction and interfere with the right of private parties to contract. Creditor contracts are violated when pro-debtor judges award resources to equityholders, management, and labor that rightfully belong to creditors. Among the most egregious of such cases was Eastern Airlines. In presiding over that case, Judge Lifland, a bankruptcy judge in the Southern District of New York, expressed "strong feeling that, given the nature of Eastern's business, [the court] shouldn't just look to the preference of the creditors but also to the public interest."[4] The general public, however, is not a claimant in bankruptcy court. Nor is Judge Lifland likely to be the best candidate for determining what constitutes the public interest in such matters. (See the insert in which Eastern's bankruptcy counsel Harvey Miller and I argue this point.)

MEASURING DEVIATIONS FROM ABSOLUTE PRIORITY

To determine the extent to which priority of claims is violated in practice, I examined the reorganization plans confirmed by the bankruptcy court in 35 cases along with other court documents. The reorganization plan offers the best guide as to whether priority of claims was violated *at the time agreement among the parties was reached*. Most of the reorganized firm's securities do not trade publicly, thus the only evidence of their value is the value provided in the reorganization plan. Whenever possible, I also spoke with lawyers involved in the negotiation process of each of the plans.

Use of these values has several limitations. First, the amount of a creditor's claim is the amount allowed by the court, and the courts accept management valuations unless a creditor establishes a different value through costly hearings. Second, the court may understate the amount of the claim by failing to provide appropriate interest. Finally, the court will accept management's view of whether creditors are impaired, and creditors may decide it is not worth the effort and expense to prove otherwise. Despite such limitations, the plan of reorganization remains the most timely and objective source of information about what each claimant expects to receive from the bankruptcy process.

VIOLATIONS OF STRICT PRIORITY

Strict priority of claims was violated in 29 (or almost 80%) of the 37 cases I examined. As shown

---

3. Bankruptcy law has traditionally been vague about whether secured creditors receive interest on their claims over the bankruptcy period. The Supreme Court has recently clarified this issue in *United Savings Association of Texas v. Timbers of Inwood Forest Associates, Ltd.* According to an opinion written by Justice Scalia, secured creditors receive interest on their loans only as long the value of the loan plus accrued interest does not exceed the value of the collateral.

4. *Wall Street Journal*, Dec. 6, 1990.

■

SHOULD JUDICIAL DISCRETION IN BANKRUPTCY BE LIMITED?
THE CASE OF EASTERN AIRLINES*

"BEWARE THE BANKRUPTCY JUDGES"
by Lawrence A. Weiss
(*New York Times Forum* ■ Sunday, April 28, 1991)

Pro-debtor bankruptcy judges are violating creditor contracts and the spirit of the bankruptcy code as they award to shareholders, management and labor the resources that rightfully belong to creditors.

Bankruptcy law was not designed to redistribute wealth nor was it designed to restrict the operation of a free market. Bankruptcy law is meant to prevent premature liquidation after the company has defaulted on its debt and to provide an orderly environment to enforce creditors' claims. Bankruptcy judges are given broad powers to prevent creditors from racing to grab assets, but issues must be decided on the terms of the contracts—not on a judge's sense of public policy.

In the 1989 bankruptcy case of Eastern Airlines, the judge, Burton Lifland, decided to keep Eastern alive for the benefit of consumers. But the general public was not a claimant in the case. Nor is it likely that the judge knew what was in the public's best interests. His decision to artificially support a weak company may ultimately lead other airlines, which had to lower prices to compete with Eastern's desperation fares, to fail....

By straying from the spirit of the law, pro-debtor judges act like bureaucrats, accrue power unto themselves, raise costs to society and harm the economy they claim they are trying to help. Judges are experts on law and should make decisions based on legal, not economic, aspects. They should leave their biases at home, stick to legal issues, and stop creating inefficiencies by destroying the right to private contract.

"THE DELICATE BANKRUPTCY BALANCING ACT"
(*New York Times Forum* ■ Sunday, May 19, 1991)

To the Editor:

In "Beware the Bankruptcy Judges" (April 28), Lawrence A. Weiss, without any understanding of the underlying philosophy of the American bankruptcy reorganization law, argues that pro-debtor bankruptcy judges violate creditor contracts. He ignores that the immediate impact of a bankruptcy case is the suspension of contractual rights and remedial rights of creditors.

He fails to recognize that the rehabilitation and reorganization of business entities, under bankruptcy law, requires balancing creditors' rights and debtors' protections in the perspective of prevailing economic circumstances and the national interest. To assert that public policy plays no role in a socio-economic statute is to be oblivious to the obvious.

In the bankruptcy reorganization of the Penn Central Railroad, a United States District Court judge determined that the public policy underlying the railroad reorganization provisions of the then Bankruptcy Act mandated that the railroad keep operating, notwithstanding huge losses. The remedial rights of creditors under contracts were suspended.

In a similar fashion, Bankruptcy Judge Burton R. Lifland conceived that the maintenance, preservation and operation of an airline served the same public interest. He followed the long-established principle that a debtor should be given a reasonable opportunity to rehabilitate and reorganize itself within the precepts and philosophy of the bankruptcy law. Whether he erred in allowing too long a period is not subject to scientific certainty.

The spirit of the bankruptcy law has always been the protection of the interests of all parties, equality of distribution within legal classes and a fresh start for the debtor, including the rehabilitation of businesses when consistent with the Bankruptcy Code. Professor Weiss has not yet discovered that spirit.

Harvey R. Miller
New York, April 29

The author is a senior partner in Weil, Gotshal & Manges, attorneys of Eastern Airlines and Revere Copper and Brass; the firm also represents creditors in reorganization cases.

The Author Responds:

"DID EASTERN DESERVE SPECIAL TREATMENT?"
(*New York Times Forum* ■ Sunday, June 16, 1991)

To the Editor:

In "The Delicate Bankruptcy Balancing Act" (May 19), Harvey Miller, Eastern Airline's lawyer, argues that Judge Lifland's actions in Eastern's bankruptcy were justified by precedents set in the Penn Central Railroad bankruptcy. Mr. Miller conveniently forgets that Congress wrote special rules for the heavily regulated railroads. No such special provisions were ever made for airlines. Furthermore, there was never a legitimate economic reason to argue, as Judge Lifland did, that Eastern was a national asset that must be saved. The public welfare was never threatened since other airlines had excess capacity and could easily take over Eastern's assets.

I recognize the need to suspend creditors' rights and try to balance competing claims in bankruptcy. However, Congress did not mandate that companies should be saved at any cost. Judge Lifland did not suspend creditors' rights, and then try to balance competing claims. Judge Lifland first ignored creditors' rights and then destroyed them. This is obviously bad law and clearly violates the spirit of the Code.

Because he is a leading practitioner and someone who appears before Judge Lifland and on the side of the debtor quite often, it is understandable that Mr. Miller would want to argue on the judge's behalf. My view is based on an academic assessment, with no financial incentives to argue one side or the other.

Lawrence A. Weiss
May 23, 1991

Strict priority of claims was violated in 29 of the 37 (or almost 80%) cases I examined... [Moreover, it] was violated in all 20 cases of companies in my sample with total assets over $100 million—14 of which filed in New York.

TABLE 1
SUMMARY OF CLAIMS RESOLUTION FOR 37 EXCHANGE-LISTED FIRMS FILING FOR BANKRUPTCY BETWEEN 1980 AND 1986

Firm Name	Percentage or Description of Claims Paid		
	Secured Creditors	Unsecured Creditors	Equity Holders
PRIORITY HELD*			
Bobbie Brooks	100%	100%	100%
Branch Inds	100%	100%	100%
Brody (B) St	100%	51%	0
Flanigan's	100%	100%	0
Garland Corp	100%	100%	>0
Ronco Telepd	100%	Balance	0
Tenna Corp	74%	0	0
U.N.A. Corp	100%	1 CS[1] per $1 claim	0
PRIORITY VIOLATED FOR UNSECURED CREDITORS ONLY			
AM Intl	100%	94%	47%
Anglo Energy	100%	58%	25%
Beker Inds	100%	<20%	38%
Berry Inds	100%	Cash & PS[2]	60%
Combustion	100%	From 49% to 82%	$316,000
Cook United	100%	93% of CS	7%
Goldblatt	100%	24%	53%
HRT Inds	100%	75%	25%
Imperial Inds	100%	37%	100%
KDT Inds	100%	36%	$1,500,000
Lionel Corp	100%	Up to 100%	100%
Manville	100%	Up to 100%	5%
McLouth Stl	100%	90% of CS	10%
Morton Cos	100%	33%	$233,000
Penn-Dixie	100%	45% of claim+50% CS	50%
Revere Copper	100%	65%	77%
Richton Intl	100%	60%	100%
Salant Corp	100%	97%	99%
Saxon Inds	100%	From 33% to 49%	PS
Seatrain Ln	100%	CS	Warrants
Shelter Res	100%	5% of CS	5%
Spencer Cos	100%	30% of claim+60% CS	17%
Tacoma Boat	100%	96% of CS	4%
Towle Mfg	100%	60%	7%
White Motor	100%	51%	10%
Wickes Cos	100%	From 59% to 92%	19%
PRIORITY VIOLATED FOR SECURED CREDITORS			
Crompton Co	85%	20%	0
Evans Pds	76%	87%	0
Stevcoknit	From 37-77%	33%	12%

*Priority of claims holds when secured creditors are satisfied first, then holders of various grades of subordinated debt, and equity holders last.
1. CS = Common stock
2. PS = Preferred stock

in Table 1 (which reports the percentages of claims actually paid in each case), shareholders received nothing in only seven cases (about 20%). In three cases, they received small, all-cash settlements rang- ing from $233,000 to $1,500,000. In 15 cases (41%), shareholders received 25% or less of the equity of the reorganized company. And in 12 cases (32%), they ended up with more than 25% of the equity.

In six cases, shareholders retained virtually all of the reorganized firm's equity. In two of these cases (Bobbie Brooks and Branch Industries), the companies recovered sufficiently to repay the creditors fully. In two other such cases (Lionel Corporation and Salant Corporation), the secured creditors were paid in full and the unsecured creditors received over 90% of their claims. In the remaining two cases (Imperial Industries and Richton International), however, although the secured creditors were paid in full, the unsecured creditors received only 37% and 60% of their claims respectively. The resolutions of these last two cases represent, of course, a clear breach of the debt contracts. One lawyer explained it by saying, "Shareholders were tossed a bone, crumbs off the table, to get the deal done and save any tax-loss carryforwards."

Within the various classes of unsecured creditors (e.g., senior and subordinated debentures), strict priority of claims almost never holds. For example, in the White Motor reorganization plan, the senior unsecured bondholders received 61% of their claims; the senior unsecured creditors 55%; the general unsecured creditors 51%; and the subordinated unsecured bondholders 14%. The lawyers interviewed either claimed not to know or were unwilling to say why the senior unsecured creditors were not fully repaid before the junior unsecured creditors received anything. The lawyers agreed that priority was largely ignored within the group of unsecured creditors but insisted the consensual settlements made everyone better off.

By contrast, the priority of claims of secured creditors was maintained in most (34 of 37, or over 90%) of the cases in my sample. The three cases of violation were Crompton, Evans Products, and Stevcoknit. In the case of Crompton, a textile company, priority broke down because of litigation by the unsecured creditors against the secured creditors.[5] After nearly four years of prolonged negotiations, a settlement was reached whereby the secured creditors received 85% of their claims, the unsecured creditors received 20% of their claims, and the equity holders received nothing.

Evans Products, a supplier of building materials and home mortgages, was the first major case in which a creditor-initiated reorganization plan was confirmed by the court. Secured creditors decided to go forward with the effort and expense of a creditor plan when they were unable to reach a settlement with reclusive buyout specialist Victor Posner, who held a controlling interest in the company's stock. Although the plan did freeze out the equity holders, unsecured creditors actually received a higher percentage of their claims (87%) than secured creditors (76%). The total claims of the unsecured holders, however, amounted to less than one-fourth of the secured creditors' claims. According to lawyers involved in this case, the secured creditors offered the unsecured creditors a sweetened deal to ensure approval—a deal that, with the benefit of hindsight, was probably more generous to the unsecured creditors than was necessary.

In the case of Stevcoknit, a producer of knitted fabrics for sportswear, the secured creditors accepted only 57% of their claims because, according to lawyers involved in the case, the market value of their collateral had fallen far below the value of their claims. Unsecured creditors received 33% of their claims, and equity holders were given an 11% share of the reorganized firm.

HOW PRIORITY OF CLAIMS IS VIOLATED

My discussions with lawyers indicate that two factors are important in predicting whether there will be significant deviations from strict priority: firm size and location of bankruptcy. According to the lawyers, the larger, more complicated bankruptcies present more opportunities for equity holders and small groups of unsecured creditors to extract concessions from other creditors. The lawyers also noted, however, that different jurisdictions treat debtors differently, and debtors respond by filing in the district they think will be most favorable to them.

Theoretically, of course, such differences are not supposed to exist within the system. Bankruptcy falls under federal law and, except for certain state-law issues, the administration and enforcement of the bankruptcy code is supposed to be uniform across the United States. The practical reality, however, appears to be that different jurisdictions have notable biases. For example, a 1989 *Miami Review* article describes how the Southern District of Florida's chief

---

5. The unsecured creditors argued that the secured creditors were not entitled to payment from the surplus in Crompton's pension plan and Crompton's holdings of export-related commercial paper.

> [T]o find the primary cause [why so many cases are filed in New York], I strongly doubt we need look much beyond the fact that equityholders are routinely awarded a much more valuable call option on the firm's assets in the Southern District of New York than elsewhere.

bankruptcy judge is much tougher on debtors than judges in some other districts. By contrast, the Southern District of New York has been widely cited as an egregiously pro-debtor court.

To receive bankruptcy protection, a firm must file in the United States court district either where the firm had its principal place of business for the preceding 180 days, or where most of the firm's assets are located, or in a district that facilitates negotiations with creditors. This provides corporations with assets and operations in several jurisdictions considerable latitude in deciding where to file.

For example, Eastern Airlines resorted to an interesting technical maneuver in order to file in the Southern District of New York. Ionosphere Inc., the travel club subsidiary of Eastern Airlines located in New York City, filed for bankruptcy in the Southern District of New York. Eastern Airlines filed for bankruptcy six minutes later, asking to be attached to the Ionosphere case. Ionosphere Inc., incidentally, had assets of $2 million and liabilities of less than $1 million, and may not really have needed bankruptcy protection. Had Eastern been denied the right to file in New York, it could have been forced to file in Miami, the site of corporate headquarters.

In my own study, both the larger firms and firms filing in New York were more likely to violate strict priority of claims. Strict priority was violated in all 20 cases of companies in my sample with total assets over $100 million—14 of which filed in New York. For firms with less than $100 million in assets, strict priority held in eight of 17 cases.

Because New York is the headquarters for a majority of the larger companies in my sample, it is not immediately clear that large firms were seeking to take advantage of a pro-debtor bias in New York. Nevertheless, the lawyers I spoke with in both Florida and Illinois insisted that judges and lawyers in their jurisdictions are significantly more willing to freeze out equity holders than judges and lawyers in New York.[6] Moreover, my study revealed that priority of claims was upheld in only one of the 18 cases filed in New York—and in that case the firm's fortunes turned around during the bankruptcy so there were sufficient funds to repay all creditors in full. By contrast, priority of claims held for seven of the 19 cases filed outside of New York.

New York lawyers acknowledged both the high number of filings there and the generous treatment of debtors. Their favored explanation was that there is less fighting among parties in New York owing to the greater sophistication of the creditors, the professional actions of the bankruptcy lawyers, and a willingness by creditors to compromise priority in order to settle the case quickly.

There is no evidence, however, to support the assertion that cases are resolved more quickly in New York than in other parts of the country. The average time needed to resolve the New York cases in my sample was 974 days, as compared with 850 days for the cases outside New York. And it was not just the large size of the New York cases at work here. Even when comparing only large cases (total assets of more than $100 million), filing in New York appears to add significantly to a company's stay in Chapter 11.

Another piece of telling evidence: All the cases filed outside of New York were filed in the jurisdiction where the firm's headquarters or principal place of business was located. By contrast, six of the 18 firms filing in New York (Beker, HRT, KDT, Manville, Tacoma Boatbuilding, and Towle) did not have their headquarters or principal place of business there.

Why does New York attract such a disproportionate share of the bankruptcy filings? New York may indeed have more lawyers and judges with the expertise to work on large cases; it may happen to be the location of the firm's headquarters or its principal place of business; and it may be a convenient location for the firm and its creditors. But, to find the primary cause, I strongly doubt we need look much beyond the fact that equityholders are routinely awarded a much more valuable call option on the firm's assets in the Southern District of New York than elsewhere.

CONCLUSION

Bankruptcy judges have been given broad powers to prevent premature liquidation of companies that have defaulted on their debt and to provide an orderly environment to enforce creditors' claims. Some judges, however, in an apparent desire to perpetuate corporate enterprises, have repeatedly

---

6. One lawyer interviewed about the Evans Products case stressed that only the New York lawyers involved in the case were willing to give the equityholders a sizeable piece of the reorganized company. Only after the New York lawyers became frustrated by Victor Posner's demands were the Florida lawyers able to persuade their New York colleagues to propose a creditor plan and freeze out the shareholders.

shown themselves willing to ignore what most of us would take to be their primary responsibility: namely, to enforce private contracts between debtors and lenders. The professional and administrative costs of bankruptcy, combined with the loss of creditor confidence in the enforcement of strict priority, raises the corporate cost of capital for all companies with risky debt.

Priority of claims was violated in 29 of 37 cases I examined. Unsecured creditors were frequently denied priority over both equityholders and lower-ranked unsecured creditors. Secured creditors, however, received their full claim in all but three of the 37 cases.

Equityholders of larger firms appear to fare better than their smaller-firm counterparts, probably because junior claimants are better able to delay the resolution in the larger, more complex cases, and to threaten the loss of tax loss carryforwards. The disproportionate number of cases in which equity-holders in New York received some compensation in violation of priority of claims, combined with the disproportionate number of cases filed there, seems to indicate that debtors shop around for the best place to file—and correctly choose New York.

The following are a few simple changes to the bankruptcy code which, I believe, would go a long way toward restoring creditors' rights:

The initial exclusive period during which only a debtor can file a plan of reorganization should be limited to the 120-day period immediately following the bankruptcy filing without the possibility of any extensions. Debtors have the ability to begin preparing a plan prior to the bankruptcy filing, and cannot justify requests for extensions by arguing the allotted 120 day exclusive period provides insufficient time. Once the 120 day period has expired, creditors should be free to present their own plans of reorganization without interference from the bankruptcy judge.

A 1990 ruling of Judge Lifland in the LTV case should be reversed or changed by Congress. Claims exchanged prior to a bankruptcy filing with the intent of reorganizing a distressed firm should be valued in bankruptcy as if the exchange had never gone through. This would promote less costly private reorganizations without court interference, and reduce the current strain on the system.

Finally, management should not be allowed to shop for judges. Whenever a firm files in a district where it does not have a principal place of business, or when a company asks to be attached to the case of a related company that is substantially smaller in size (by a predetermined fixed percentage), the creditors committee should be given the right to change the location of the filing.

These changes represent a start at giving back to creditors the rights they lose when they face pro-debtor bankruptcy judges. These changes will also send a message to bankruptcy judges that they should rule on legal issues alone and stop interfering with the right to contract.

THE ECONOMICS OF PRE-PACKAGED BANKRUPTCY

*by John J. McConnell,
Purdue University, and
Henri Servaes,
University of Chicago*

A new kind of bankruptcy has emerged in the last few years. It can be thought of as a "hybrid" form—one that attempts to combine the advantages (and exclude the disadvantages) of the two customary methods of reorganizing troubled companies: workouts and bankruptcy.

In a workout, a debtor that has already violated its debt covenants (or is about to do so) negotiates a relaxation or restructuring of those covenants with its creditors. In many cases, the restructuring includes an exchange of old debt securities for a package of new claims that can include debt, equity, or cash. Informal reorganizations take place outside the court system, but typically involve corporate officers, lenders, lawyers, and investment bankers. And though such negotiations are often contentious and protracted, informal workouts are widely held to be less damaging, less expensive and, perhaps, less stressful than reorganizations under Chapter 11.[1]

Recently, however, a number of firms that have had most or all of the ingredients in place for a successful workout outside the courtroom have filed for bankruptcy anyway. In such cases, the distressed firms file a plan of reorganization along with their filing for bankruptcy. And largely because most creditors have agreed to the terms of the reorganization plan prior to the Chapter 11 filing, the time (and presumably the money) actually spent in Chapter 11 has been significantly reduced.[2]

---

1. Arguments along these lines have been made by Robert Haugen and Lemma Senbet, 1978, "The insignificance of bankruptcy costs to the theory of optimal capital structure," *Journal of Finance* 33, 383-393 and Michael C. Jensen, 1989, "Active Investors, LBOs and the Privatization of Bankruptcy", *Journal of Applied Corporate Finance* 2, 35-44. Stuart C. Gilson, Kose John and Larry H.P. Lang, 1990, "Troubled debt restructurings: An empirical study of private reorganizations of firms in default", *Journal of Financial Economics* 27, 315-353, provide evidence that stockholders are better off when debt is restructured privately.

2. Section 1126 of the bankruptcy code allows a debtor to negotiate with its creditors for a restructuring of its debt obligations before filing for Chapter 11 protection.

Kroy, Inc., an Arizona-based maker of low-tech office labelling equipment, is a good example. After undergoing a leveraged buyout in 1986, the company suffered a slump in sales and profit margins that left it unable to meet its debt obligations. The company's primary lenders were the Minneapolis First Bank and Quest Equities Corporation. Both were receptive to a pre-negotiated bankruptcy reorganization. With a pre-negotiated plan in place, the company filed its plan of reorganization along with its bankruptcy petition on May 15, 1990. The company emerged from bankruptcy proceedings 89 days later. Such an untraditional reorganization has been dubbed "prepackaged bankruptcy."[3]

The appearance of this new mechanism for corporate reorganization gives rise to a number of questions: How are they structured? Are they motivated by real economic gains and, if so, what are the sources of such gain? What are the particular circumstances in which a prepackaged bankruptcy is more sensible than an informal reorganization outside the courts? What does the future hold for prepackaged bankruptcy reorganizations?

In this article, we explore prepackaged bankruptcies and arrive at the following conclusions:
■ A prepackaged bankruptcy should be viewed as an administrative extension of an informal reorganization. It is not likely to be useful in resolving complex, litigious disputes among hundreds of creditor groups with sharply divergent interests—the kind we often see in a traditional, highly contentious Chapter 11 reorganization. (For example, cases involving extensive claims held by trade creditors are not likely to lend themselves to this new method.)
■ The benefits of a prepackaged bankruptcy are essentially these:

1. Prepackaged bankruptcies can alleviate problems with creditor holdouts who interfere with informal reorganizations.

2. A prepackaged bankruptcy can preserve the integrity of creditor claims that could be invalidated (in large part because of the recent Lifland ruling in the LTV case) following an informal reorganization in which not all creditors participate.

3. In some cases, tax benefits can be secured under a prepackaged plan that are not available under an informal reorganization.

AN EXAMPLE

The first major corporation to undergo a prepackaged bankruptcy reorganization was Crystal Oil Company, an independent crude oil and natural gas exploration and production company headquartered in Louisiana. The company filed for bankruptcy on October 1, 1986 and emerged less than three months later, its capital structure completely reorganized. The total indebtedness of the firm was reduced from $277 million to $129 million. In exchange for giving up their debt claims, debtholders received a combination of common stock, convertible notes, convertible preferred stock, and warrants to purchase a common stock. Little time was spent in Chapter 11 because most major creditors had already agreed to the plan of reorganization.

The original reorganization proposal had been presented to creditors three months before the Chapter 11 filing. It was accepted by all classes of public debtholders. Within each class, more than half of the debtholders, representing more than two thirds in value of the outstanding debt, accepted the proposal. The initial plan was not accepted, however, by Crystal Oil's most senior creditors: Bankers Trust and Halliburton Company. Both of these creditors' claims were securitized by a lien on the company's oil and gas properties. Bankers Trust accepted a revised plan, but Halliburton never gave in.[4] Eventually, the bankruptcy court "crammed down" the revised plan on Halliburton.

Since its reorganization, Crystal Oil has returned to profitability and it has been able to further reduce its debt burden and continue its operations on a smaller scale.

THE BENEFITS OF PREPACKAGING

Solving the Holdout Problem

Why does a firm that has most of the ingredients in place for a successful informal reorganization file under Chapter 11? First, it should be recognized that Chapter 11 is an administrative procedure designed to facilitate the successful reorganization of temporarily distressed, but otherwise economically viable, businesses. As such, the code provides certain

---

3. Strategic aspects of prepackaged bankruptcy are discussed by Thomas J. Salerno and Craig D. Hansen, 1991, "A Prepackaged Bankruptcy Strategy," *The Journal of Business Strategy*, 36-41.

4. The revised plan did not alter the exchange offer to the public debtholders. It simply altered the distribution of cash flows allocated to service the private debtholders.

advantages to the distressed firm that are not available under an informal reorganization.

Perhaps chief among these advantages is the smaller fraction of creditors required to approve the reorganization plan. Under most bond indenture agreements, a significant majority of the holders—typically 90 percent or more—must approve any change in the terms of the agreement in order for the change to become effective. This means, for example, that if one investor owns 11% of a bond issue, that investor can effectively block any relaxation of the terms of the agreement.

Alternatively, the firm can propose an exchange of some of its old debt obligations for new debt or a combination of new debt and other securities. The problem with such an exchange offer is that it may strengthen the position of bondholders that do not participate relative to those who do participate. This leads to the well known "holdout" problem. In brief, each individual bondholder has an incentive to reject any restructuring of his claim even though the restructuring collectively benefits all bondholders.

The same phenomenon is at work among other creditors who own an entire loan rather than a fraction of a single bond issue. Suppose that a firm has loans with four different banks, all of which have claims of equal priority, and that three of the four banks agree to a restructuring of their loans that reduces the principal owed by 25%. If the fourth bank does not agree to the plan, its claim to the assets of the firm remains intact and that lender gains at the expense of the other banks. Thus, each bank has the incentive to hold out, even if the reorganization would benefit all banks acting in unison.

This holdout problem can be mitigated by choosing a prepackaged Chapter 11 filing. Under Chapter 11, a plan of reorganization can become effective if it is approved by 50% of the creditors by number in each class and two thirds by dollar amount. Thus, a plan of reorganization can be forced upon a set of recalcitrant creditors who could have effectively blocked an informal reorganization.

For example, Republic Health Corp. filed a prepackaged reorganization plan under Chapter 11 on December 15, 1989 after the firm had been unable to persuade a sufficient fraction of its debtholders to reorganize out of court. The prepackaged plan was approved by 86% of Republic Health's debtholders. The firm entered bankruptcy with total debt of $645 million and came out of Chapter 11 on May 1, 1990 with this amount pared to $379 million.

Similar circumstances prevailed in the case of JPS Textile Group. JPS was formed in November 1988 when a group of investors led by Odyssey Partners acquired the assets of J. P. Stevens and Co., a leading textile maker, in a leveraged transaction arranged by Drexel Burnham. In mid-1990 it became apparent that JPS could not meet the interest payments on the $579 million of debt outstanding. Management attempted to reduce the company's debt burden through a voluntary exchange offer in which equity and low coupon debt would be exchanged for the then outstanding high yield bonds. The offer was conditional on 95% of the bondholders agreeing to changes in certain debt covenants. After sweetening and extending the offer seven times, management withdrew the offer because an insufficient number of bondholders had tendered their securities.

JPS continued to negotiate with bondholders and, in February 1991, the company filed a prepackaged plan of bankruptcy reorganization. Prior to the filing, the company announced that nearly all creditors had approved the plan. News accounts indicate that the bankruptcy petition was filed to ensure that all creditors participated in the reorganization.

Preserving the Integrity of Creditors' Claims

In much the same fashion as it resolves holdout complications, a prepackaged Chapter 11 reorganization can be used to preserve the integrity of creditors' claims that might be diluted in an informal reorganization. Assume, as often happens in an informal reorganization, a subset of creditors agrees to reduce the principal amount due under their loan agreements, but not all creditors participate. In such a case, those creditors who participate have reduced their claim to the firm's assets.

This problem has become more troublesome as a result of a January 1990 court ruling in the LTV bankruptcy case. Prior to filing for bankruptcy in 1986, LTV had negotiated a swap with some of its creditors. In the swap, bondholders received bonds with market value substantially below face value. The courts ruled that the bondholders who participated in the swap could value the bonds for purposes of a bankruptcy claim only at their discounted value, not their face value. Had LTV undergone a prepackaged bankruptcy in 1986 instead of an informal reorganization, and had all creditors been forced to participate on a *pro rata* basis, the relative market value of each claimant would have been preserved.

The LTV ruling is likely to cause more debtholders to hold out in informal reorganizations because, if they participate, their claim in any further bankruptcy proceedings will be substantially diluted. Thus, to the extent the holdout problem is exacerbated by this ruling, prepackaged bankruptcies are likely to become an even more attractive tool for corporations considering informal reorganization.

Tax Benefits

Taxes can also play a role in encouraging firms that would otherwise have undergone an informal workout to file a prepackaged Chapter 11 reorganization. Two aspects of the tax law require particular attention.[5]

First, net operating losses are treated differently in bankruptcy than in a workout. In an informal reorganization, if debtholders exchange their debt for equity claims such that the old equityholders hold less than 50% of their original ownership, the company forfeits its net operating losses. For companies that have accumulated losses over a large number of years, the loss of these carryforwards can have a significant effect on future cash flows of the firm. In bankruptcy, by contrast, firms do not lose their carryforwards and thus could conceivably file for bankruptcy simply to keep the net operating losses intact.[6]

On the other hand, carryforwards are not lost in an informal workout if the firm is deemed by the courts to be "insolvent." A firm is considered legally insolvent if the market value of its assets is less than the face value of its liabilities.

The second aspect of the tax law favoring use of Chapter 11 is the treatment of cancellation of indebtedness (COD). For example, in an informal workout, if debt with a face value of $1000 is exchanged for debt with a value of $500, the reduction of $500 in the firm's debt is considered to be income for tax purposes. If, however, a similar exchange is executed through a formal bankruptcy filing, it does not lead to an income tax liability.[7]

Thus, the elimination of COD income taxes that occurs in Chapter 11 appears to provide a powerful incentive for firms to file for Chapter 11 after a reorganization plan has already been approved by creditors.

By eliminating some of the ambiguity surrounding the exact method of computing COD income, recent tax changes have made prepackaged filings even more compelling. Prior to the 1990 Tax Act, COD income was determined as the difference between the face value of the old and the new debt. Before the 1990 Tax Act, companies could exchange $1000 face value debt with an interest rate of 5% for $1000 face value debt with an interest rate of 15% without creating COD income. The 1990 Tax Act provided that the market value of the new debt should be used in this computation. Thus, if the new debt is valued at $700, the firm will be taxed on $300. To avoid income taxes on the $300, the firm must either claim insolvency or undergo a prepackaged bankruptcy.

A GLITCH IN THE SOUTHLAND CASE

One potential problem that can arise when a firm initiates a prepackaged bankruptcy can be illustrated with the case of Southland Corporation. In 1987, Southland, the firm that operates the 7-Eleven convenience stores, underwent a leveraged buyout to thwart a hostile takeover attempt by Samuel Belzberg. By 1989, the company could not service its $4 billion of debt and sought to restructure these claims. After 9 months of unsuccessful negotiations with creditors, Southland management concluded that the company would have to reorganize through the bankruptcy process.

A prepackaged bankruptcy was proposed to resolve the impasse and Southland sent solicitations to its debtholders in early October. The bankruptcy petition was filed on October 24. Southland claimed that a sufficient number of debtholders had accepted the plan for confirmation by the court. The voting procedure, however, was challenged by a number of debtholders who were not satisfied with the outcome. Three basic objections to the voting process

5. For greater detail, see Fred T. Witt and William H. Lyons, 1990, "An Examination of the Tax Consequences of Discharge of Indebtedness," *Virginia Law Review*, 10, 1-112 and Timothy C. Sherck, 1990, "Restructuring Today's Financially Troubled Corporation Taxes," 881-905.

6. But if this motive appears compelling on the surface, we have been unable to identify firms that have undergone a pre-packaged bankruptcy simply for the

purpose of retaining tax loss carryforwards. The primary reason for lack of such evidence is that the companies that have undergone prepackaged bankruptcies to date have not had large loss carryforwards.

7. Once again, though, if the firm is legally insolvent, COD income taxes can be avoided even in an informal workout. However, the firm has the responsibility to argue for insolvency.

**Although economists did not foresee the new obstacles to workouts, the rise of
prepackaged bankruptcies can be viewed as evidence in support of the
"privatization" [of bankrupcy] argument.**

were raised: (1) the debtholders did not have sufficient time to cast their votes; (2) brokers often voted for their customers; (3) votes were not counted properly. The judge ruled in favor of the dissidents and the voting process was invalidated.

The Southland case illustrates that a prepackaged bankruptcy always entails the risk that dissident creditors will challenge the legitimacy of the voting process. But such challenges are not necessarily a major obstacle to prepackaged bankruptcies. Southland later sweetened its offer, which was then accepted by the majority of the debtholders. The company ended up emerging from bankruptcy in March of 1991 after a stay of only four months.

THE FUTURE

Prepackaged bankruptcy can facilitate a successful, and relatively low-cost, reorganization by forcing holdouts to accept the plan of reorganization. It also provides a means of circumventing two relatively new obstacles that have substantially dampened out-of-court exchange offers: the LTV ruling and the change in the tax code penalizing debt forgiveness.

To make use of this new "hybrid" form of bankruptcy, however, a significant fraction of creditors must be able to reach agreement outside of the court. A prepackaged bankruptcy cannot be forced on a significant number of reluctant creditors. Nevertheless, given the possibility of a pre-negotiated bankruptcy reorganization, a greater fraction of creditors may be willing to agree to the plan precisely because holdouts can be forced to participate by filing Chapter 11.

This new development has in some sense been anticipated by financial economists. Reviving and expanding upon an argument presented by Robert Haugen and Lemma Senbet in the late 70s, Michael Jensen recently suggested that the bankruptcy process can be expected to undergo a "privatization." According to this line of thought, because private reorganizations are likely to be much less expensive than formal bankruptcy, workouts can be expected to replace bankruptcies—that is, barring major tax and legal obstacles.

Although economists did not foresee the new obstacles to workouts, the rise of prepackaged bankruptcies can be viewed as evidence in support of this privatization argument. As we suggested earlier, firms that have succeeded in prepackaging their bankruptcies have most of the elements in place necessary to reorganize successfully outside of court. Indeed, several of the prepackaged bankruptcies, including those of Republic Health and JPS, were filed after first achieving considerable progress toward an out-of-court settlement. Based on these and a growing number of other "success stories," it seems likely that prepackaged bankruptcies will significantly speed up the process of reorganization—but, again, provided that a reasonable degree of creditor consensus can be reached informally.